UNABRIDGED

MATTHEW HENRY'S

COMMENTARY ON THE WHOLE BIBLE

MATTHEW HENRY

Published by
GRAPEVINE BOOKS

www.grapevinebooks.com
email: contact@grapevinebooks.com

Ordering Information:
Quantity sales: Special discounts are available on quantity purchases
by corporations, associations, and others.
For details, reach out to the publisher.

First published by Grapevine Books, 2025

Contents

Genesis

Genesis is a name taken from the Greek, and signifies "the book of generation or production;" it is properly so called, as containing an account of the origin of all things. There is no other history so old. There is nothing in the most ancient book which exists that contradicts it; while many things recorded by the oldest heathen writers, or to be traced in the customs of different nations, confirm what is related in the book of Genesis.

Chapter 1

Verses 1, 2

The first **verse** of the Bible gives us a satisfying and useful account of the origin of the earth and the heavens. The faith of humble Christians understands this better than the fancy of the most learned men. From what we see of heaven and earth, we learn the power of the great Creator. And let our make and place as men, remind us of our duty as Christians, always to keep heaven in our eye, and the earth under our feet. The Son of God, one with the Father, was with him when he made the world; nay, we are often told that the world was made by him, and nothing was made without him. Oh, what high thoughts should there be in our minds, of that great God whom we worship, and of that great Mediator in whose name we pray! And here, at the beginning of the sacred volume, we read of that Divine Spirit, whose work upon the heart of man is so often mentioned in other parts of the Bible. Observe, that at first there was nothing desirable to be seen, for the world was without form, and void; it was confusion, and emptiness. In like manner the work of grace in the soul is a new creation: and in a graceless soul, one that is not born again, there is disorder, confusion, and every evil work: it is empty of all good, for it is without God; it is dark, it is darkness itself: this is our condition by nature, till Almighty grace works a change in us.

Verses 3–5

God said, Let there be light; he willed it, and at once there was light. Oh, the power of the word of God! And in the new creation, the first thing that is wrought in the soul is light: the blessed Spirit works upon the will and affections by enlightening the understanding. Those who by sin were darkness, by grace become light in the Lord. Darkness would have been always upon fallen man, if the Son of God had not come and given us understanding, **1Jo 5:20**. The light which God willed, he approved of. God divided the light from the darkness; for what fellowship has light with darkness? In heaven there is perfect light, and no darkness at all; in hell, utter darkness, and no gleam of light. The day and the night are the Lord's; let us use both to his honour, by working for him every day, and resting in him every night, meditating in his law both day and night.

Verses 6–13

The earth was emptiness, but by a word spoken, it became full of God's riches, and his they are still. Though the use of them is allowed to man, they are from God, and to his service and honour they must be used. The earth, at his command, brings forth grass, herbs, and fruits. God must have the glory of all the benefit we receive from the produce of the earth. If we have, through grace, an interest in Him who is the Fountain, we may rejoice in him when the streams of temporal mercies are dried up.

Verses 14–19

In the fourth day's work, the creation of the sun, moon, and stars is accounted for. All these are the works of God. The stars are spoken of as they appear to our eyes, without telling their number, nature, place, size, or motions; for the Scriptures were written, not to gratify curiosity, or make us astronomers, but to lead us to God, and make us saints. The lights of heaven are made to serve him; they do it faithfully, and shine in their season without fail. We are set as lights in this world to serve God; but do we in like manner answer the end of our creation? We do not: our light does not shine before God, as his lights shine before us. We burn our Master's candles, but do not mind our Master's work.

Verses 20–25

God commanded the fish and fowl to be produced. This command he himself executed. Insects, which are more numerous than the birds and beasts, and as curious, seem to have been part of this day's work. The Creator's wisdom and power are to be admired as much in an ant as in an elephant. The power of God's providence preserves all things, and fruitfulness is the effect of his blessing.

Verses 26–28

Man was made last of all the creatures: this was both an honour and a favour to him. Yet man was made the same day that the beasts were; his body was made of the same earth with theirs; and while he is in the body, he inhabits the same earth with them. God forbid that by indulging the body, and the desires of it, we should make ourselves like the beasts that perish! Man was to be a creature different from all that had been hitherto made. Flesh and spirit, heaven and earth, must be put together in him. God said, "Let us make man." Man, when he was made, was to glorify the Father, Son, and Holy Ghost. Into that great name we are baptized, for to that great name we owe our being. It is the soul of man that especially bears God's image. Man was made upright, Ec **7:29**. His understanding saw Divine things clearly and truly; there were no errors or mistakes in his knowledge; his will consented at once, and in all things, to the will of God. His affections were all regular, and he had no bad appetites or passions. His thoughts were easily brought and fixed to the best subjects. Thus holy, thus happy, were our first parents in having the image of God upon them. But how is this image of God upon man defaced! May the Lord renew it upon our souls by his grace!

Verses 29, 30

Herbs and fruits must be man's food, including corn, and all the products of the earth. Let God's people cast their care upon him, and not be troubled about what they shall eat, and what they shall drink. He that feeds his birds will not starve his babes.

Verse 31

When we come to think about our works, we find, to our shame, that much has been very bad; but when God saw his work, all was very good. Good, for it was all just as the Creator would have it to be. All his works, in all places of his dominion, bless him; and therefore, bless thou the Lord, O my soul. Let us bless God for the gospel of Christ, and when we consider his almighty power, let us sinners flee from the wrath to come. If new—created unto the image of God in holiness, we shall at length enter the "new heavens and new earth, wherein dwelleth righteousness."

Chapter 2

Verses 1–3

After six days, God ceased from all works of creation. In miracles, he has overruled nature, but never changed its settled course, or added to it. God did not rest as one weary, but as one well pleased. Notice the beginning of the kingdom of grace, in the sanctification, or keeping holy, of the sabbath day. The solemn observing of one day in seven as a day of holy rest and holy work, to God's honour, is the duty of all to whom God has made known his holy sabbaths. At this time none of the human race were in being but our first parents. For them the sabbath was appointed; and clearly for all succeeding generations also. The Christian sabbath, which we observe, is a seventh day, and in it we celebrate the rest of God the Son, and the finishing the work of our redemption.

Verses 4–7

Here is a name given to the Creator, "Jehovah." Where the word "LORD" is printed in capital letters in our English Bibles, in the original it is "Jehovah." Jehovah is that name of God, which denotes that he alone has his being of himself, and that he gives being to all creatures and things. Further notice is taken of plants and herbs, because they were made and appointed to be food for man. The earth did not bring forth its fruits of itself: this was done by Almighty power. Thus grace in the soul grows not of itself in nature's soil, but is the work of God. Rain also is the gift of God; it came not till the Lord God caused it. Though God works by means, yet when he pleases he can do his own work without them; and though we must not tempt God in the neglect of means, we must trust God, both in the use and in the want of means. Some way or other, God will water the plants of his own planting. Divine grace comes down like the dew, and waters the church without noise. Man was made of the small dust, such as is on the surface of the earth. The soul was not made of the earth, as the body: pity then that it should cleave to the earth, and mind earthly things. To God we must shortly give an account, how we have employed these souls; and if it be found that we have lost them, though it were to gain the world, we are undone for ever! Fools despise their own souls, by caring for their bodies before their souls.

Verses 8–14

The place fixed upon for Adam to dwell in, was not a palace, but a garden. The better we take up with plain things, and the less we seek things to gratify pride and luxury, the nearer we approach to innocency. Nature is content with a little, and that which is most natural; grace with less; but lust craves every thing, and is content with nothing. No delights can be satisfying to the soul, but those which God himself has provided and appointed for it. Eden signifies delight and pleasure. Wherever it was, it had all desirable conveniences, without any inconvenience, though no other house or garden on earth ever was so. It was adorned with every tree pleasant to the sight, and enriched with every tree that yielded fruit grateful to the taste and good for food. God, as a tender Father, desired not only Adam's profit, but his pleasure; for there is pleasure with innocency, nay there is true pleasure only in innocency. When Providence puts us in a place of plenty and pleasure, we ought to serve God with gladness of heart in the good things he gives us. Eden had two trees peculiar to itself. **1**. There was the tree of life in the midst of the garden. Of this man might eat and live. Christ is now to us the Tree of life, Re **2**:7; **22**:**2**; and the Bread of life, Joh **6**:**48**, **51**. **2**. There was the tree of the knowledge of good and evil, so called because there was a positive revelation of the will of God about this tree, so that by it man might know moral good and evil. What is good? It is good not to eat of this tree. What is evil? It is evil to eat of this tree. In these two trees God set before Adam good and evil, the blessing and the curse.

Verse 15

After God had formed Adam, he put him in the garden. All boasting was thereby shut out. Only he that made us can make us happy; he that is the Former of our bodies, and the Father of our spirits, and none but he, can fully provide for the happiness of both. Even in paradise itself man had to work. None of us were sent into the world to be idle. He that made our souls and bodies, has given us something to work with; and he that gave us this earth for our habitation, has made us something to work upon. The sons and heirs of heaven, while in this world, have something to do about this earth, which must have its share of their time and thoughts; and if they do it with an eye to God, they as truly serve him in it, as when they are upon their knees. Observe that the husbandman's calling is an ancient and honourable calling; it was needful even in paradise. Also, there is true pleasure in the business God calls us to, and employs us in. Adam could not have been happy if he had been idle: it is still God's law, He that will not work has no right to eat, **2**Th **3**:**10**.

Verses 16, 17

Let us never set up our own will against the holy will of God. There was not only liberty allowed to man, in taking the fruits of paradise, but everlasting life made sure to him upon his obedience. There was a trial appointed of his obedience. By transgression he would forfeit his Maker's favour, and deserve his displeasure, with all its awful effects; so that he would become liable to pain, disease, and death. Worse than that, he would lose the holy image of God, and all the comfort of his favour; and feel the torment of sinful passions, and the terror of his Maker's vengeance, which must endure for ever with his never dying soul. The forbidding to eat of the fruit of a particular tree was wisely suited to the state of our first parents. In their state of innocence, and separated from any others, what opportunity or what temptation had they to break any of the ten commandments? The event proves that the whole human race were concerned in the trial and fall of our first parents. To argue against these things is to strive against stubborn facts, as well as Divine revelation; for man is sinful, and shows by his first actions, and his conduct ever afterwards, that he is ready to do evil. He is under the Divine displeasure, exposed to sufferings and death. The Scriptures always speak of man as of this sinful character, and in this miserable state; and these things are true of men in all ages, and of all nations.

Verses 18–25

Power over the creatures was given to man, and as a proof of this he named them all. It also shows his insight into the works of God. But though he was lord of the creatures, yet nothing in this world was a help meet for man. From God are all our helpers. If we rest in God, he will work all for good. God caused deep sleep to fall on Adam; while he knows no sin, God will take care that he shall feel no pain. God, as her Father, brought the woman to the man, as his second self, and a help meet for him. That wife, who is of God's making by special grace, and of God's bringing by special providence, is likely to prove a help meet for a man. See what need there is, both of prudence and prayer in the choice of this relation, which is so near and so lasting. That had need to be well done, which is to be done for life. Our first parents needed no clothes for covering against cold or heat, for neither could hurt them: they needed none for ornament. Thus easy, thus happy, was man in his state of innocency. How good was God to him! How many favours did he load him with! How easy were the laws given to him! Yet man, being in honour, understood not his own interest, but soon became as the beasts that perish.

Chapter 3

Verses 1–5

Satan assaulted our first parents, to draw them to sin, and the temptation proved fatal to them. The tempter was the devil, in the shape and likeness of a serpent. Satan's plan was to draw our first parents to sin, and so to separate between them and their God. Thus the devil was from the beginning a murderer, and the great mischief maker. The person tempted was the woman: it was Satan's policy to enter into talk with her when she was alone. There are many temptations to which being alone gives great advantage; but the communion of saints tends very much to their strength and safety. Satan took advantage by finding her near the forbidden tree. They that would not eat the forbidden fruit, must not come near the forbidden tree. Satan tempted Eve, that by her he might tempt Adam. It is his policy to send temptations by hands we do not suspect, and by those that have most influence upon us. Satan questioned whether it were a sin or not, to eat of this tree. He did not disclose his design at first, but he put a question which seemed innocent. Those who would be safe, need to be shy of talking with the tempter. He quoted the command wrong. He spoke in a taunting way. The devil, as he is a liar, so he is a scoffer from the beginning; and scoffers are his children. It is the craft of Satan to speak of the Divine law as uncertain or unreasonable, and so to draw people to sin; it is our wisdom to keep up a firm belief of God's command, and a high respect for it. Has God said, Ye shall not lie, nor take his name in vain, nor be drunk, &c.? Yes, I am sure he has, and it is well said; and by his grace I will abide by it. It was Eve's weakness to enter into this talk with the serpent: she might have perceived by his question, that he had no good design, and should therefore have started back. Satan teaches men first to doubt, and then to deny. He promises advantage from their eating this fruit. He aims to make them discontented with their present state, as if it were not so good as it might be, and should be. No condition will of itself bring content, unless the mind be brought to it. He tempts them to seek preferment, as if they were fit to be gods. Satan ruined himself by desiring to be like the Most High, therefore he sought to infect our first parents with the same desire, that he might ruin them too. And still the devil draws people into his interest, by suggesting to them hard thoughts of God, and false hopes of advantage by sin. Let us, therefore, always think well of God as the best good, and think ill of sin as the worst evil: thus let us resist the devil, and he will flee from us.

Verses 6–8

Observe the steps of the transgression: not steps upward, but downward toward the pit. **1**. She saw. A great deal of sin comes in at the eye. Let us not look on that which we are in danger of lusting after, Mt **5**:**28**. **2**. She took. It was her own act and deed. Satan may tempt, but he cannot force; may persuade us to cast ourselves down, but he cannot cast us down, Mt **4**:**6**. **3**. She did eat. When she looked perhaps she did not intend to take; or when she took, not to eat: but it ended in that. It is wisdom to stop the first motions of sin, and to leave it off before it be meddled with. **4**. She gave it also to her husband with her. Those that have done ill, are willing to draw in others to do the same. **5**. He did eat. In neglecting the tree of life, of which he was allowed to eat, and eating of the tree of knowledge, which was forbidden, Adam plainly showed a contempt of what God had bestowed on him, and a desire for what God did not see fit to give him. He would have what he pleased, and do what he pleased. His sin was, in one word, disobedience, Ro **5**:**19**; disobedience to a plain, easy, and express command. He had no corrupt nature within, to betray him; but had a freedom of will, in full strength, not weakened or impaired. He turned aside quickly. He drew all his posterity into sin and ruin. Who then can say that Adam's sin had but little harm in it? When too late, Adam and Eve saw the folly of eating forbidden fruit. They saw the happiness they fell from, and the misery they were fallen into. They saw a loving God provoked, his grace and favour forfeited. See her what dishonour and trouble sin is; it makes mischief wherever it gets in, and destroys all comfort. Sooner or later it will bring shame; either the shame of true repentance, which ends in glory, or that shame and everlasting contempt, to which the wicked shall rise at the great day. See here what is commonly the folly of those that have sinned. They have more care to save their credit before men, than to obtain their pardon from God. The excuses men make to cover and lessen their sins, are vain and frivolous; like the aprons of fig-leaves, they make the matter never the better: yet we are all apt to cover our transgressions as Adam. Before they sinned, they would have welcomed God's gracious visits with humble joy; but now he was become a terror to them. No marvel that they became a terror to themselves, and full of confusion. This shows the falsehood of the tempter, and the frauds of his temptations. Satan promised they should be safe, but they cannot so much as think themselves so! Adam and Eve were now miserable comforters to each other!

Verses 9–13

Observe the startling question, Adam, where art thou? Those who by sin go astray from God, should seriously consider where they are; they are afar off from all good, in the midst of their enemies, in bondage to Satan, and in the high road to utter ruin. This lost sheep had wandered without end, if the good Shepherd had not sought after him, and told him, that where he was straying he could not be either happy or easy. If sinners will but consider where they are, they will not rest till they return to God. It is the common fault and folly of those that have done ill, when questioned about it, to acknowledge only that which is so manifest that they cannot deny it. Like Adam, we have reason to be afraid of approaching to God, if we are not covered and clothed with the righteousness of Christ. Sin appears most plainly in the glass of the commandment, therefore God set it before Adam; and in it we should see our faces. But instead of acknowledging the sin in its full extent, and taking shame to themselves, Adam and Eve excuse the sin, and lay the shame and blame on others. There is a strange proneness in those that are tempted, to say, they are tempted of God; as if our abuse of God's gifts would excuse our breaking God's laws. Those who are willing to take the pleasure and profit of sin, are backward to take the blame and shame of it. Learn hence, that Satan's temptations are all beguilings; his arguments are all deceits; his allurements are all cheats; when he speaks fair, believe him not. It is by the deceitfulness of sin the heart is hardened. See Ro **7**:**11**; Heb **3**:**13**. But though Satan's subtlety may draw us into sin, yet it will not justify us in sin. Though he is the tempter, we are the sinners. Let it not lessen our sorrow for sin, that we were beguiled into it; but let it increase our self-indignation, that we should suffer ourselves to be deceived by a known cheat, and a sworn enemy, who would destroy our souls.

Verses 14, 15

God passes sentence; and he begins where the sin began, with the serpent. The devil's instruments must share in the devil's punishments. Under the cover of the serpent, the devil is sentenced to be degraded and accursed of God; detested and abhorred of all mankind: also to be destroyed and ruined at last by the great Redeemer, signified by the breaking of his head. War is proclaimed between the Seed of the woman and the seed of the serpent. It is the fruit of this enmity, that there is a continual warfare between grace and corruption, in the hearts of God's people. Satan, by their corruptions, buffets them, sifts them, and seeks to devour them. Heaven and hell can never be reconciled, nor light and darkness; no more can Satan and a sanctified soul. Also, there is a continual struggle between the wicked and the godly in this world. A gracious promise is here made of Christ, as the Deliverer of fallen man from the power of Satan. Here was the drawn of the gospel day: no sooner was the wound given, than the remedy was provided and revealed. This gracious revelation of a Saviour came unasked, and unlooked for. Without a revelation of mercy, giving some hope of forgiveness, the convinced sinner would sink into despair, and be hardened. By faith in this promise, our first parents, and the patriarchs before the flood, were justified and saved. Notice is given concerning Christ. **1**. His incarnation, or coming in the flesh. It speaks great encouragement to sinners, that their Saviour is the Seed of the woman, bone of our bone, Heb **2**:**11**, **14**. **2**. His sufferings and death; pointed at in Satan's bruising his heel, that is, his human nature. And Christ's sufferings are continued in the sufferings of the saints for his name. The devil tempts them, persecutes and slays them; and so bruises the heel of Christ, who is afflicted in their afflictions. But while the heel is bruised on earth, the Head is in heaven. **3**. His victory over Satan thereby. Christ baffled Satan's temptations, rescued souls out of his hands. By his death he gave a fatal blow to the devil's kingdom, a wound to the head of this serpent that cannot be healed. As the gospel gains ground, Satan falls.

Verses 16–19

The woman, for her sin, is condemned to a state of sorrow, and of subjection; proper punishments of that sin, in which she had sought to gratify the desire of her eye, and of the flesh, and her pride. Sin brought sorrow into the world; that made the world a vale of tears. No wonder our sorrows are multiplied, when our sins are so. He shall rule over thee, is but God's command, Wives, be subject to your own husbands. If man had not sinned, he would always have ruled with wisdom and love; if the woman had not sinned, she would always have obeyed with humility and meekness. Adam laid the blame on his wife; but though it was her fault to persuade him to eat the forbidden fruit, it was his fault to hearken to her. Thus men's frivolous pleas will, in the day of God's judgment, be turned against them. God put marks of displeasure on Adam. **1**. His habitation is cursed. God gave the earth to the children of men, to be a comfortable dwelling; but it is now cursed for man's sin. Yet Adam is not himself cursed, as the serpent was, but only the ground for his sake. **2**. His employments and enjoyments are imbittered to him. Labour is our duty, which we must faithfully perform; it is part of man's sentence, which idleness daringly defies. Uneasiness and weariness with labour are our just punishment, which we must patiently submit to, since they are less than our iniquity deserves. Man's food shall become unpleasant to him. Yet man is not sentenced to eat dust as the serpent, only to eat the herb of the field. **3**. His life also is but short; considering how full of trouble his days are, it is in favour to him that they are few. Yet death being dreadful to nature, even when life is unpleasant, that concludes the punishment. Sin brought death into the world: if Adam had not sinned, he had not died. He gave way to temptation, but the Saviour withstood it. And how admirably the satisfaction of our Lord Jesus, by his death and sufferings, answered the sentence passed on our first parents! Did travailing pains come with sin? We read of the travail of Christ's soul, Isa **53**:**11**; and the pains of death he was held by, are so called, Ac **2**:**24**. Did subjection came in with sin? Christ was made under the law, Ga **4**:**4**. Did the curse come in with sin? Christ was made a curse for us, he died a cursed death, Ga **3**:**13**. Did thorns come in with sin? He was crowned with thorns for us. Did sweat come in with sin? He sweat for us, as it had been great drops of blood. Did sorrow come in with sin? He was a man of sorrows; his soul was, in his agony, exceeding sorrowful. Did death come in with sin? He became obedient unto death. Thus is the plaster as wide as the wound. Blessed be God for his Son our Lord Jesus Christ.

Verses 20, 21

God named the man, and called him Adam, which signifies red earth; Adam named the woman, and called her Eve, that is, life. Adam bears the name of the dying body, Eve of the living soul. Adam probably had regard to the blessing of a Redeemer, the promised Seed, in calling his wife Eve, or life; for He should be the life of all believers, and in Him all the families of the earth should be blessed. See also God's care for our first parents, notwithstanding their sin. Clothes came in with sin. Little reason have we to be proud of our clothes, which are but the badges of our shame. When God made clothes for our first parents, he made them warm and strong, but coarse and very plain; not robes of scarlet, but coats of skin. Let those that are meanly clad, learn from hence not to complain. Having food and a covering, let them be content; they are as well off as Adam and Eve. And let those that are finely clad, learn not to make the putting on of apparel their adorning. The beasts, from whose skins they were clothed, it is supposed were slain, not for man's food, but for sacrifice, to typify Christ, the great Sacrifice. Adam and Eve made for themselves aprons of fig-leaves, a covering too narrow for them to wrap themselves in, Isa **28**:**20**. Such are all the rags of our own righteousness. But God made them coats of skin, large, strong, durable, and fit for them: such is the righteousness of Christ; therefore put ye on the Lord Jesus Christ.

Verses 22–24

God bid man go out; told him he should no longer occupy and enjoy that garden: but man liked the place, and was unwilling to leave it, therefore God made him go out. This signified the shutting out of him, and all his guilty race, from that communion with God, which was the bliss and glory of paradise. But man was only sent to till the ground out of which he was taken. He was sent to a place of toil, not to a place of torment. Our first parents were shut out from the privileges of their state of innocency, yet they were not left to despair. The way to the tree of life was shut. It was henceforward in vain for him and his to expect righteousness, life, and happiness, by the covenant of works; for the command of that covenant being broken, the curse of it is in full force: we are all undone, if we are judged by that covenant. God revealed this to Adam, not to drive him to despair, but to quicken him to look for life and happiness in the promised Seed, by whom a new and living way into the holiest is laid open for us.

Chapter 4

Verses 1–7

When Cain was born, Eve said, I have gotten a man from the Lord. Perhaps she thought that this was the promised seed. If so, she was wofully disappointed. Abel signifies vanity: when she thought she had the promised seed in Cain, whose name signifies possession, she was so taken up with him that another son was as vanity to her. Observe, each son had a calling. It is the will of God for every one to have something to do in this world. Parents ought to bring up their children to work. Give them a Bible and a calling, said good Mr. Dod, and God be with them. We may believe that God commanded Adam, after the fall, to shed the blood of innocent animals, and after their death to burn part or the whole of their bodies by fire. Thus that punishment which sinners deserve, even the death of the body, and the wrath of God, of which fire is a well-known emblem, and also the sufferings of Christ, were prefigured. Observe that the religious worship of God is no new invention. It was from the beginning; it is the good old way, Jer **6**:**16**. The offerings of Cain and Abel were different. Cain showed a proud, unbelieving heart. Therefore he and his offering were rejected. Abel came as a sinner, and according to God's appointment, by his sacrifice expressing humility, sincerity, and believing obedience. Thus, seeking the benefit of the new covenant of mercy, through the promised Seed, his sacrifice had a token that God accepted it. Abel offered in faith, and Cain did not, Heb **11**:**4**. In all ages there have been two sorts of worshippers, such as Cain and Abel; namely, proud, hardened despisers of the gospel method of salvation, who attempt to please God in ways of their own devising; and humble believers, who draw near to him in the way he has revealed. Cain indulged malignant anger against Abel. He harboured an evil spirit of discontent and rebellion against God. God notices all our sinful passions and discontents. There is not an angry, envious, or fretful look, that escapes his observing eye. The Lord reasoned with this rebellious man; if he came in the right way, he should be accepted. Some understand this as an intimation of mercy. "If thou doest not well, sin, that is, the sin-offering, lies at the door, and thou mayest take the benefit of it." The same word signifies sin, and a sacrifice for sin. "Though thou hast not done well, yet do not despair, the remedy is at hand." Christ, the great sin-offering, is said to stand at the door, Re **3**:**20**. And those well deserve to perish in their sins, that will not go to the door to ask for the benefit of this sin-offering. God's acceptance of Abel's offering did not change the birthright, and make it his; why then should Cain be so angry? Sinful heats and disquiets vanish before a strict and fair inquiry into the cause.

Verses 8–15

Malice in the heart ends in murder by the hands. Cain slew Abel, his own brother, his own mother's son, whom he ought to have loved; his younger brother, whom he ought to have protected; a good brother, who had never done him any wrong. What fatal effects were these of our first parents' sin, and how must their hearts have been filled with anguish! Observe the pride, unbelief, and impenitence of Cain. He denies the crime, as if he could conceal it from God. He tries to cover a deliberate murder with a deliberate lie. Murder is a crying sin. Blood calls for blood, the blood of the murdered for the blood of the murderer. Who knows the extent and weight of a Divine curse, how far it reaches, how deep it pierces? Only in Christ are believers saved from it, and inherit the blessing. Cain was cursed from the earth. He found his punishment there where he chose his portion, and set his heart. Every creature is to us what God makes it, a comfort or a cross, a blessing or a curse. The wickedness of the wicked brings a curse upon all they do, and all they have. Cain complains not of his sin, but of his punishment. It shows great hardness of heart to be more concerned about our sufferings than our sins. God has wise and holy ends in prolonging the lives even of very wicked men. It is in vain to inquire what was the mark set upon Cain. It was doubtless known, both as a brand of infamy on Cain, and a token from God that they should not kill him. Abel, being dead, yet speaketh. He tells the heinous guilt of murder, and warns us to stifle the first risings of wrath, and teaches us that persecution must be expected by the righteous. Also, that there is a future state, and an eternal recompence to be enjoyed, through faith in Christ and his atoning sacrifice. And he tells us the excellency of faith in the atoning sacrifice and blood of the Lamb of God. Cain slew his brother, because his own works were evil, and his brother's righteous, **1**Jo **3**:**12**. In consequence of the enmity put between the Seed of the woman and the seed of the serpent, the war broke out, which has been waged ever since. In this war we are all concerned, none are neuter; our Captain has declared, He that is not with me is against me. Let us decidedly, yet in meekness, support the cause of truth and righteousness against Satan.

Verses 16–18

Cain cast off all fear of God, and attended no more on God's ordinances. Hypocritical professors, who dissemble and trifle with God, are justly left to themselves to do something grossly scandalous. So they throw off that form of godliness to which they have been a reproach, and of which they deny the power. Cain went out from the presence of the Lord, and we never find that he came into it again, to his comfort. The land Cain dwelt in was called the land of Nod, which means, 'shaking,' or 'trembling,' and so shows the restlessness and uneasiness of his own spirit, or 'the land of a vagabond:' they that depart from God cannot find rest any where else. Those on earth who looked for the heavenly city, chose to dwell in tabernacles or tents; but Cain, as not minding that city, built one on earth. Thus all who are cursed of God seek their settlement and satisfaction here below.

Verses 19–24

One of Cain's wicked race is the first recorded, as having broken the law of marriage. Hitherto, one man had but one wife at a time; but Lamech took two. Wordly things, are the only things that carnal, wicked people set their hearts upon, and are most clever and industrious about. So it was with this race of Cain. Here was a father of shepherds, and a father of musicians, but not a father of the faithful. Here is one to teach about brass and iron, but none to teach the good knowledge of the Lord: here are devices how to be rich, and how to be mighty, and how to be merry; but nothing of God, of his fear and service. Present things fill the heads of most. Lamech had enemies, whom he had provoked. He draws a comparison betwixt himself and his ancestor Cain; and flatters himself that he is much less criminal. He seems to abuse the patience of God in sparing Cain, into an encouragement to expect that he may sin unpunished.

Verses 25, 26

Our first parents were comforted in their affliction by the birth of a son, whom they called Seth, that is, 'set,' 'settled,' or 'placed;' in his seed mankind should continue to the end of time, and from him the Messiah should descend. While Cain, the head of the apostacy, is made a wanderer, Seth, from whom the true church was to come, is one fixed. In Christ and his church is the only true settlement. Seth walked in the steps of his martyred brother Abel; he was a partaker of like precious faith in the righteousness of our God and Saviour Jesus Christ, and so became a fresh witness of the grace and influence of God the Holy Spirit. God gave Adam and Eve to see the revival of religion in their family. The worshippers of God began to do more in religion; some, by an open profession of true religion, protested against the wickedness of the world around. The worse others are, the better we should be, and the more zealous. Then began the distinction between professors and profane, which has been kept up ever since, and will be, while the world stands.

Chapter 5

Verses 1–5

Adam was made in the image of God; but when fallen he begat a son in his own image, sinful and defiled, frail, wretched, and mortal, like himself. Not only a man like himself, consisting of body and soul, but a sinner like himself. This was the **reverse** of that Divine likeness in which Adam was made; having lost it, he could not convey it to his seed. Adam lived, in all, **930** years; and then died, according to the sentence passed upon him, "To dust thou shalt return." Though he did not die in the day he ate forbidden fruit, yet in that very day he became mortal. Then he began to die; his whole life after was but a reprieve, a forfeited, condemned life; it was a wasting, dying life. Man's life is but dying by degrees.

Verses 6–20

Concerning each of these, except Enoch, it is said, "and he died." It is well to observe the deaths of others. They all lived very long; not one of them died till he had seen almost eight hundred years, and some of them lived much longer; a great while for an immortal soul to be prisoned in a house of clay. The present life surely was not to them such a burden as it commonly is now, else they would have been weary of it. Nor was the future life so clearly revealed then, as it now under the gospel, else they would have been urgent to remove to it. All the patriarchs that lived before the flood, except Noah, were born before Adam died. From him they might receive a full account of the creation, the fall, the promise, and the Divine precepts about religious worship and a religious life. Thus God kept up in his church the knowledge of his will.

Verses 21–24

Enoch was the seventh from Adam. Godliness is walking with God: which shows reconciliation to God, for two cannot walk together except they be agreed, Am **3**:**3**. It includes all the parts of a godly, righteous, and sober life. To walk with God, is to set God always before us, to act as always under his eye. It is constantly to care, in all things to please God, and in nothing to offend him. It is to be followers of him as dear children. The Holy Spirit, instead of saying, Enoch lived, says, Enoch walked with God. This was his constant care and work; while others lived to themselves and the world, he lived to God. It was the joy of his life. Enoch was removed to a better world. As he did not live like the rest of mankind, so he did not leave the world by death as they did. He was not found, because God had translated him, Heb **11**:**5**. He had lived but **365** years, which, as men's ages were then, was but the midst of a man's days. God often takes those soonest whom he loves best; the time they lose on earth, is gained in heaven, to their unspeakable advantage. See how Enoch's removal is expressed: he was not, for God took him. He was not any longer in this world; he was changed, as the saints shall be, who are alive at Christ's second coming. Those who begin to walk with God when young, may expect to walk with him long, comfortably, and usefully. The true christian's steady walk in holiness, through many a year, till God takes him, will best recommend that religion which many oppose and many abuse. And walking with God well agrees with the cares, comforts, and duties of life.

Verses 25–32

Methuselah signifies, 'he dies, there is a dart,' 'a sending forth,' namely, of the deluge, which came the year that Methuselah died. He lived **969** years, the longest that any man ever lived on earth; but the longest liver must die at last. Noah signifies rest; his parents gave him that name, with a prospect of his being a great blessing to his generation. Observe his father's complaint of the calamitous state of human life, by the entrance of sin, and the curse of sin. Our whole life is spent in labour, and our time filled up with continual toil. God having cursed the ground, it is as much as some can do, with the utmost care and pains, to get a hard livelihood out comfort us." It signifies not only that desire and expectation which parents generally have about their children, that they will be comforts to them and helpers, though they often prove otherwise; but it signifies also a prospect of something more. Is Christ ours? Is heaven ours? We need better comforters under our toil and sorrow, than the dearest relations and the most promising offspring; may we seek and find comforts in Christ.

Chapter 6

Verses 1–7

The most remarkable thing concerning the old world, is the destroying of it by the deluge, or flood. We are told of the abounding iniquity of that wicked world: God's just wrath, and his holy resolution to punish it. In all ages there has been a peculiar curse of God upon marriages between professors of true religion and its avowed enemies. The evil example of the ungodly party corrupts or greatly hurts the other. Family religion is put an end to, and the children are trained up according to the worldly maxims of that parent who is without the fear of God. If we profess to be the sons and daughters of the Lord Almighty, we must not marry without his consent. He will never give his blessing, if we prefer beauty, wit, wealth, or worldly honours, to faith and holiness. The Spirit of God strove with men, by sending Enoch, Noah, and perhaps others, to preach to them; by waiting to be gracious, notwithstanding their rebellions; and by exciting alarm and convictions in their consciences. But the Lord declared that his Spirit should not thus strive with men always; he would leave them to be hardened in sin, and ripened for destruction. This he determined on, because man was flesh: not only frail and feeble, but carnal and depraved; having misused the noble powers of his soul to gratify his corrupt inclinations. God sees all the wickedness that is among the children of men; it cannot be hid from him now; and if it be not repented of, it shall be made known by him shortly. The wickedness of a people is great indeed, when noted sinners are men renowned among them. Very much sin was committed in all places, by all sorts of people. Any one might see that the wickedness of man was great: but God saw that every imagination, or purpose, of the thoughts of man's heart, was only evil continually. This was the bitter root, the corrupt spring. The heart was deceitful and desperately wicked; the principles were corrupt; the habits and dispositions evil. Their designs and devices were wicked. They did evil deliberately, contriving how to do mischief. There was no good among them. God saw man's wickedness as one injured and wronged by it. He saw it as a tender father sees the folly and stubbornness of a rebellious and disobedient child, which grieves him, and makes him wish he had been childless. The words here used are remarkable; they are used after the manner of men, and do not mean that God can change, or be unhappy. Does God thus hate our sin? And shall not we be grieved to the heart for it? Oh that we may look on Him whom we have grieved, and mourn! God repented that he had made man; but we never find him repent that he redeemed man. God resolves to destroy man: the original word is very striking, 'I will wipe off man from the earth,' as dirt or filth is wiped off from a place which should be clean, and is thrown to the dunghill, the proper place for it. God speaks of man as his own creature, when he resolves upon his punishment. Those forfeit their lives who do not answer the end of their living. God speaks of resolution concerning men, after his Spirit had been long striving with them in vain. None are punished by the justice of God, but those who hate to be reformed by the grace of God.

Verses 8–11

Noah did not find favour in the eyes of men; they hated and persecuted him, because both by his life and preaching he condemned the world: but he found grace in the eyes of the Lord, and this made him more truly honourable than the men of renown. Let this be our chief desire, let us labour that we may be accepted of him. When the rest of the world was wicked, Noah kept his integrity. God's good-will towards Noah produced this good work in him. He was a just man, that is, justified before God, by faith in the promised Seed. As such he was made holy, and had right principles; and was righteous in his conversation. He was not only honest, but devout; it was his constant care to do the will of God. God looks down upon those with an eye of favour, who sincerely look up to him with an eye of faith. It is easy to be religious when religion is in fashion; but it shows strong faith and resolution, to swim against the stream, and to appear for God when no one else appears for him; Noah did so. All kinds of sin were found among men. They corrupted God's worship. Sin fills the earth with violence, and this fully justified God's resolution to destroy the world. The contagion spread. When wickedness is become general, ruin is not far off; while there is a remnant of praying people in a nation, to empty the measure as it fills, judgments may be long kept off; but when all hands are at work to pull down the fences, by sin, and none stand in the gap to make up the breach, what can be expected but a flood of wrath?

Verses 12–21

God told Noah his purpose to destroy the wicked world by water. The secret of the Lord is with them that fear him, Ps **25**:**14**. It is with all believers, enabling them to understand and apply the declarations and warnings of the written word. God chose to do it by a flood of waters, which should drown the world. As he chooses the rod with which he corrects his children, so he chooses the sword with which he cuts off his enemies. God established his covenant with Noah. This is the first place in the Bible where the word 'covenant' is found; it seems to mean, **1**. The covenant of providence; that the course of nature shall be continued to the end of time. **2**. The covenant of grace; that God would be a God to Noah, and that out of his seed God would take to himself a people. God directed Noah to make an ark. This ark was like the hulk of a ship, fitted to float upon the waters. It was very large, half the size of St. Paul's cathedral, and would hold more than eighteen of the largest ships now used. God could have secured Noah without putting him to any care, or pains, or trouble; but employed him in making that which was to be the means to preserve him, for the trial of his faith and obedience. Both the providence of God, and the grace of God, own and crown the obedient and diligent. God gave Noah particular orders how to make the ark, which could not therefore but be well fitted for the purpose. God promised Noah that he and his family should be kept alive in the ark. What we do in obedience to God, we and our families are likely to have the benefit of. The piety of parents gets their children good in this life, and furthers them in the way to eternal life, if they improve it.

Verse 22

Noah's faith triumphed over all corrupt reasonings. To rear so large a building, such a one as he never saw, and to provide food for the living creatures, would require from him a great deal of care, and labour, and expense. His neighbours would laugh at him. But all such objections, Noah, by faith, got over; his obedience was ready and resolute. Having begun to build, he did not leave off till he had finished: so did he, and so must we do. He feared the deluge, and therefore prepared the ark. And in the warning given to Noah, there is a more solemn warning given to us, to flee from the wrath to come, which will sweep the world of unbelievers into the pit of destruction. Christ, the true Noah, which same shall comfort us, hath by His sufferings already prepared the ark, and kindly invites us by faith to enter in. While the day of his patience continues, let us hear and obey his voice.

Chapter 7

Verses 1–12

The call to Noah is very kind, like that of a tender father to his children to come in-doors when he sees night or a storm coming. Noah did not go into the ark till God bade him, though he knew it was to be his place of refuge. It is very comfortable to see God going before us in every step we take. Noah had taken a great deal of pains to build the ark, and now he was himself kept alive in it. What we do in obedience to the command of God, and in faith, we ourselves shall certainly have the comfort of, first or last. This call to Noah reminds us of the call the gospel gives to poor sinners. Christ is an ark, in whom alone we can be safe, when death and judgment approach. The word says, "Come;" ministers say, "Come;" the Spirit says, "Come, come into the Ark." Noah was accounted righteous, not for his own righteousness, but as an heir of the righteousness which is by faith, Heb **11**:**7**. He believed the revelation of a saviour, and sought and expected salvation through Him alone. Thus was he justified by faith, and received that Spirit whose fruit is in all goodness; but if any man have not the Spirit of Christ, he is none of his. After the hundred and twenty years, God granted seven days' longer space for repentance. But these seven days were trifled away, like all the rest. It shall be but seven days. They had only one week more, one sabbath more to improve, and to consider the things that belonged to their peace But it is common for those who have been careless of their souls during the years of their health, when they have looked upon death at a distance, to be as careless during the days, the few days of their sickness, when they see death approaching; their hearts being hardened by the deceitfulness of sin. As Noah prepared the ark by faith in the warning given that the flood would come, so he went into it, by faith in this warning that it would come quickly. And on the day Noah was securely fixed in the ark, the fountains of the great deep were broken up. The earth had within it those waters, which, at God's command, sprang up and flooded it; and thus our bodies have in themselves those humours, which, when God pleases, become the seeds and springs of mortal diseases. The windows of heaven were opened, and the waters which were above the firmament, that is, in the air, were poured out upon the earth. The rain comes down in drops; but such rains fell then, as were never known before or since. It rained without stop or abatement, forty days and forty nights, upon the whole earth at once. As there was a peculiar exercise of the almighty power of God in causing the flood, it is vain and presumptuous to attempt explaining the method of it, by human wisdom.

Verses 13–16

The ravenous creatures were made mild and manageable; yet, when this occasion was over, they were of the same kind as before; for the ark did not alter their natures. Hypocrites in the church, who outwardly conform to the laws of that ark, are yet unchanged; and it will appear, one time or other, what kind they are after. God continued his care of Noah. God shut the door, to secure him and keep him safe in the ark; also to keep all others for ever out. In what manner this was done, God has not been pleased to make known. There is much of our gospel duty and privilege to be seen in Noah's safety in the ark. The apostle makes it a type of christian baptism, **1**Pe **3**:**20**, **21**. Observe then, it is our great duty, in obedience to the gospel call, by a lively faith in Christ, to come into that way of salvation which God has provided for poor sinners. Those that come into the ark, should bring as many as they can with them, by good instructions, by persuasions, and by good examples. There is room enough in Christ for all comers. God put Adam into paradise, but did not shut him in, so he threw himself out; but when God put Noah into the ark, and so when he brings a soul to Christ, the salvation is sure: it is not in our own keeping, but in the Mediator's hand. But the door of mercy will shortly be shut against those that now make light of it. Knock now, and it shall be opened, Lu **13**:**25**.

Verses 17–20

The flood was increasing forty days. The waters rose so high, that the tops of the highest mountains were overflowed more than twenty feet. There is no place on earth so high as to set men out of the reach of God's judgments. God's hand will find out all his enemies, Ps **21**:**8**. When the flood thus increased, Noah's ark was lifted up, and the waters which broke down every thing else, bore up the ark. That which to unbelievers betokens death unto death, to the faithful betokens life unto life.

Verses 21–24

All the men, women, and children, that were in the world, excepting those in the ark, died. We may easily imagine what terror seized them. Our Saviour tells us, that till the very day that the flood came, they were eating and drinking, Lu **17**:**26**, **27**; they were deaf and blind to all Divine warnings. In this posture death surprised them. They were convinced of their folly when it was too late. We may suppose they tried all ways and means possible to save themselves, but all in vain. And those that are not found in Christ, the Ark, are certainly undone, undone for ever. Let us pause, and consider this tremendous judgment! Who can stand before the Lord when he is angry? The sin of sinners will be their ruin, first or last, if not repented of. The righteous God knows how to bring ruin upon the world of the ungodly, 2Pe **2**:**5**. How tremendous will be the day of judgment and perdition of ungodly men! Happy they who are part of Christ's family, and safe with him as such; they may look forward without dismay, and rejoice that they shall triumph, when fire shall burn up the earth, and all that therein is. We are apt to suppose some favourable distinctions in our own case or character; but if we neglect, refuse, or abuse the salvation of Christ, we shall, notwithstanding such fancied advantages, be destroyed in the common ruin of an unbelieving world.

Chapter 8

Verses 1–3

The whole race of mankind, except Noah and his family, were now dead, so that God's remembering Noah, was the return of his mercy to mankind, of whom he would not make a full end. The demands of Divine justice had been answered by the ruin of sinners. God sent his wind to dry the earth, and seal up his waters. The same hand that brings the desolation, must bring the deliverance; to that hand, therefore, we must ever look. When afflictions have done the work for which they are sent, whether killing work or curing work, they will be taken away. As the earth was not drowned in a day, so it was not dried in a day. God usually works deliverance for his people gradually, that the day of small things may not be despised, nor the day of great things despaired of.

Verses 4–12

The ark rested upon a mountain, whither it was directed by the wise and gracious providence of God, that might rest the sooner. God has times and places of rest for his people after their tossing; and many times he provides for their seasonable and comfortable settlement, without their own contrivance, and quite beyond their own foresight. God had told Noah when the flood would come, yet he did not give him an account by revelation, at what times and by what steps it should go away. The knowledge of the former was necessary to his preparing the ark; but the knowledge of the latter would serve only to gratify curiosity; and concealing it from him would exercise his faith and patience. Noah sent forth a raven from the ark, which went flying about, and feeding on the carcasses that floated. Noah then sent forth a dove, which returned the first time without good news; but the second time, she brought an olive leaf in her bill, plucked off, plainly showing that trees, fruit trees, began to appear above water. Noah sent forth the dove the second time, seven days after the first, and the third time was after seven days also; probably on the sabbath day. Having kept the sabbath with his little church, he expected especial blessings from Heaven, and inquired concerning them. The dove is an emblem of a gracious soul, that, finding no solid peace of satisfaction in this deluged, defiling world, returns to Christ as to its ark, as to its Noah, its rest. The defiling world, returns to Christ as to its ark, as to its Noah, its rest. The carnal heart, like the raven, takes up with the world, and feeds on the carrion it finds there; but return thou to my rest, O my soul; to thy Noah, so the word is, Ps **116**:**7**. And as Noah put forth his hand, and took the dove, and pulled her to him, into the ark, so Christ will save, and help, and welcome those that flee to him for rest. (Ge **8**:**13-19**)

Verses 13–19

God consults our benefit, rather than our desires; he knows what is good for us better than we do for ourselves, and how long it is fit our restraints should continue, and desired mercies should be delayed. We would go out of the ark before the ground is dried; and perhaps, if the door, is shut, are ready to thrust off the covering, and to climb up some other way; but God's time of showing mercy is the best time. As Noah had a command to go into the ark, so, how tedious soever his confinement there was, he would wait for a command to go out of it again. We must in all our ways acknowledge God, and set him before us in all our removals. Those only go under God's protection, who follow God's direction, and submit to him.

Verses 20–22

Noah was now gone out into a desolate world, where, one might have thought, his first care would have been to build a house for himself, but he begins with an alter for God. He begins well, that begins with God. Though Noah's stock of cattle was small, and that saved at great care and pains, yet he did not grudge to serve God out of it. Serving God with our little is the way to make it more; we must never think that is wasted with which God is honoured. The first thing done in the new world was an act of worship. We are now to express our thankfulness, not by burnt-offerings, but by praise, and pious devotions and conversation. God was well pleased with what was done. But the burning flesh could no more please God, than the blood of bulls and goats, except as typical of the sacrifice of Christ, and expressing Noah's humble faith and devotedness to God. The flood washed away the race of wicked men, but it did not remove sin from man's nature, who being conceived and born in sin, thinks, devises, and loves wickedness, even from his youth, and that as much since the flood as before. But God graciously declared he never would drown the world again. While the earth remains, and man upon it, there shall be summer and winter. It is plain that this earth is not to remain always. It, and all the works in it, must shortly be burned up; and we look for new heavens and a new earth, when all these things shall be dissolved. But as long as it does remain, God's providence will cause the course of times and seasons to go on, and makes each to know its place. And on this word we depend, that thus it shall be. We see God's promises to the creatures made good, and may infer that his promises to all believers shall be so.

Chapter 9

Verses 1–3

The blessing of God is the cause of our doing well. On him we depend, to him we should be thankful. Let us not forget the advantage and pleasure we have from the labour of beasts, and which their flesh affords. Nor ought we to be less thankful for the security we enjoy from the savage and hurtful beasts, through the fear of man which God has fixed deep in them. We see the fulfilment of this promise every day, and on every side. This grant of the animals for food fully warrants the use of them, but not the abuse of them by gluttony, still less by cruelty. We ought not to pain them needlessly whilst they live, nor when we take away their lives.

Verses 4–7

The main reason of forbidding the eating of blood, doubtless was because the shedding of blood in sacrifices was to keep the worshippers in mind of the great atonement; yet it seems intended also to check cruelty, lest men, being used to shed and feed upon the blood of animals, should grow unfeeling to them, and be less shocked at the idea of shedding human blood. Man must not take away his own life. Our lives are God's, and we must only give them up when he pleases. If we in any way hasten our own death, we are accountable to God for it. When God requires the life of a man from him that took it away unjustly, the murderer cannot render that, and therefore must render his own instead. One time or other, in this world or in the next, God will discover murders, and punish those murders which are beyond man's power to punish. But there are those who are ministers of God to protect the innocent, by being a terror to evil-doers, and they must not bear the sword in vain, Ro **13**:**4**. Wilful murder ought always to be punished with death. To this law there is a reason added. Such remains of God's image are still upon fallen man, that he who unjustly kills a man, defaces the image of God, and does dishonour to him.

Verses 8–17

As the old world was ruined, to be a monument of justice, so this world remains to this day a monument of mercy. But sin, that drowned the old world, will burn this. Articles of agreement among men are sealed, that what is promised may be the more solemn, and the doing of what is covenanted the more sure to mutual satisfaction. The seal of this covenant was the rainbow, which, it is likely, was seen in the clouds before, but was never a seal of the covenant till now it was made so. The rainbow appears when we have most reason to fear the rain prevailing; God then shows this seal of the promise, that it shall not prevail. The thicker the cloud, the brighter the bow in the cloud. Thus, as threatening afflictions abound, encouraging consolations much more abound. The rainbow is the reflection of the beams of the sun shining upon or through the drops of rain: all the glory of the seals of the covenant are derived from Christ, the Sun of righteousness. And he will shed a glory on the tears of his saints. A bow speaks terror, but this has neither string nor arrow; and a bow alone will do little hurt. It is a bow, but it is directed upward, not toward the earth; for the seals of the covenant were intended to comfort, not to terrify. As God looks upon the bow, that he may remember the covenant, so should we, that we may be mindful of the covenant with faith and thankfulness. Without revelation this gracious assurance could not be known; and without faith it can be of no use to us; and thus it is as to the still greater dangers to which all are exposed, and as to the new covenant with its blessings.

Verses 18–23

The drunkenness of Noah is recorded in the Bible, with that fairness which is found only in the Scripture, as a case and proof of human weakness and imperfection, even though he may have been surprised into the sin; and to show that the best of men cannot stand upright, unless they depend upon Divine grace, and are upheld thereby. Ham appears to have been a bad man, and probably rejoiced to find his father in an unbecoming situation. It was said of Noah, that he was perfect in his generations, ch. **6**:**9**; but this is meant of sincerity, not of a sinless perfection. Noah, who had kept sober in drunken company, is now drunk in sober company. Let him that thinks he stands, take heed lest he fall. We have need to be very careful when we use God's good creatures plentifully, lest we use them to excess, Lu **21**:**34**. The consequence of Noah's sin was shame. Observe here the great evil of the sin of drunkenness. It discovers men; what infirmities they have, they betray when they are drunk; and secrets are then easily got out of them. Drunken porters keep open gates. It disgraces men, and exposes them to contempt. As it shows them, so it shames them. Men say and do that when drunken, which, when sober, they would blush to think of. Notice the care of Shem and Japheth to cover their father's shame. There is a mantle of love to be thrown over the faults of all, **1**Pe **4**:**8**. Beside that, there is a robe of reverence to be thrown over the faults of parents and other superiors. The blessing of God attends on those who honour their parents, and his curse lights especially on those who dishonour them.

Verses 24–29

Noah declares a curse on Canaan, the son of Ham; perhaps this grandson of his was more guilty than the rest. A servant of servants, that is, The meanest and most despicable servant, shall he be, even to his brethren. This certainly points at the victories in after-times obtained by Israel over the Canaanites, by which they were put to the sword, or brought to pay tribute. The whole continent of Africa was peopled mostly by the descendants of Ham; and for how many ages have the better parts of that country lain under the dominion of the Romans, then of the Saracens, and now of the Turks! In what wickedness, ignorance, barbarity, slavery, and misery most of the inhabitants live! And of the poor negroes, how many every year are sold and bought, like beasts in the market, and conveyed from one quarter of the world to do the work of beasts in another! But this in no way excuses the covetousness and barbarity of those who enrich themselves with the product of their sweat and blood. God has not commanded us to enslave negroes; and, without doubt, he will severely punish all such cruel wrongs. The fulfilment of this prophecy, which contains almost a history of the world, frees Noah from the suspicion of having uttered it from personal anger. It fully proves that the Holy Spirit took occasion from Ham's offence to reveal his secret purposes. "Blessed be the Lord God of Shem." The church should be built up and continued in the posterity of Shem; of him came the Jews, who were, for a great while, the only professing people God had in the world. Christ, who was the Lord God, in his human nature should descend from Shem; for of him, as concerning the flesh, Christ came. Noah also blesses Japheth, and, in him, the isles of the gentiles that were peopled by his seed. It speaks of the conversion of the gentiles, and the bringing of them into the church. We may read it, "God shall persuade Japheth, and being persuaded, he shall dwell in the tents of Shem " Jews and gentiles shall be united together in the gospel fold; both shall be one in Christ. Noah lived to see two worlds; but being an heir of the righteousness which is by faith, he now rests in hope, waiting to see a better than either.

Chapter 10

Verses 1–7

This chapter shows concerning the three sons of Noah, that of them was the whole earth overspread. No nation but that of the Jews can be sure from which of these seventy it has come. The lists of names of fathers and sons were preserved of the Jews alone, for the sake of the Messiah. Many learned men, however, have, with some probability, shown which of the nations of the earth descended from each of the sons of Noah To the posterity of Japheth were allotted the isles of the gentiles; probably, the island of Britain among the rest. All places beyond the sea from Judea are called isles, Jer **25**:**22**. That promise, Isa **42**:**4**, The isles shall wait for his law, speaks of the conversion of the gentiles to the faith of Christ.

Verses 8–14

Nimrod was a great man in his day; he began to be mighty in the earth, Those before him were content to be upon the same level with their neighbours, and though every man bare rule in his own house, yet no man pretended any further. Nimrod was resolved to lord it over his neighbours. The spirit of the giants before the flood, who became mighty men, and men of renown, Ge **6**:**4**, revived in him. Nimrod was a great hunter. Hunting then was the method of preventing the hurtful increase of wild beasts. This required great courage and address, and thus gave an opportunity for Nimrod to command others, and gradually attached a number of men to one leader. From such a beginning, it is likely, that Nimrod began to rule, and to force others to submit. He invaded his neighbours' rights and properties, and persecuted innocent men; endeavouring to make all his own by force and violence. He carried on his oppressions and violence in defiance of God himself. Nimrod was a great ruler. Some way or other, by arts or arms, he got into power, and so founded a monarchy, which was the terror of the mighty, and bid fair to rule all the world. Nimrod was a great builder. Observe in Nimrod the nature of ambition. It is boundless; much would have more, and still cries, Give, give. It is restless; Nimrod, when he had four cities under his command, could not be content till he had four more. It is expensive; Nimrod will rather be at the charge of rearing cities, than not have the honour of ruling them. It is daring, and will stick at nothing. Nimrod's name signifies rebellion; tyrants to men are rebels to God. The days are coming, when conquerors will no longer be spoken of with praise, as in man's partial histories, but be branded with infamy, as in the impartial records of the Bible.

Verses 15–32

The posterity of Canaan were numerous, rich, and pleasantly seated; yet Canaan was under a Divine curse, and not a curse causeless. Those that are under the curse of God, may, perhaps, thrive and prosper in this world; for we cannot know love or hatred, the blessing or the curse, by what is before us, but by what is within us. The curse of God always works really, and always terribly. Perhaps it is a secret curse, a curse to the soul, and does not work so that others can see it; or a slow curse, and does not work soon; but sinners are reserved by it for a day of wrath Canaan here has a better land than either Shem or Japheth, and yet they have a better lot, for they inherit the blessing. Abram and his seed, God's covenant people, descended from Eber, and from him were called Hebrews. How much better it is to be like Eber, the father of a family of saints and honest men, than the father of a family of hunters after power, worldly wealth, or vanities. Goodness is true greatness.

Chapter 11

Verses 1–4

How soon men forget the most tremendous judgments, and go back to their former crimes! Though the desolations of the deluge were before their eyes, though they sprang from the stock of righteous Noah, yet even during his life-time, wickedness increases exceedingly. Nothing but the sanctifying grace of the Holy Spirit can remove the sinful lusts of the human will, and the depravity of the human heart. God's purpose was, that mankind should form many nations, and people all lands. In contempt of the Divine will, and against the counsel of Noah, the bulk of mankind united to build a city and a tower to prevent their separating. Idolatry was begun, and Babel became one of its chief seats. They made one another more daring and resolute. Let us learn to provoke one another to love and to good works, as sinners stir up and encourage one another to wicked works.

Verses 5–9

Here is an expression after the manner of men; The Lord came down to see the city. God is just and fair in all he does against sin and sinners, and condemns none unheard. Pious Eber is not found among this ungodly crew; for he and his are called the children of God; their souls joined not themselves to the assembly of these children of men. God suffered them to go on some way, that the works of their hands, from which they promised themselves lasting honour, might turn to their lasting reproach. God has wise and holy ends, in allowing the enemies of his glory to carry on their wicked projects a great way, and to prosper long. Observe the wisdom and mercy of God, in the methods taken for defeating this undertaking. And the mercy of God in not making the penalty equal to the offence; for he deals not with us according to our sins. The wisdom of God, in fixing upon a sure way to stop these proceedings. If they could not understand one another, they could not help one another; this would take them off from their building. God has various means, and effectual ones, to baffle and defeat the projects of proud men that set themselves against him, and particularly he divides them among themselves. Notwithstanding their union and obstinacy God was above them; for who ever hardened his heart against him, and prospered? Their language was confounded. We all suffer by it to this day: in all the pains and trouble used to learn the languages we have occasion for, we suffer for the rebellion of our ancestors at Babel. Nay, and those unhappy disputes, which are strifes of words, and arise from misunderstanding one another's words, for aught we know, are owing to this confusion of tongues. They left off to build the city. The confusion of their tongues not only unfitted them for helping one another, but they saw the hand of the Lord gone out against them. It is wisdom to leave off that which we see God fights against. God is able to blast and bring to nought all the devices and designs of Babel-builders: there is no wisdom nor counsel against the Lord. The builders departed according to their families, and the tongue they spake, to the countries and places allotted to them. The children of men never did, nor ever will, come all together again, till the great day, when the Son of man shall sit upon the throne of his glory, and all nations shall be gathered before him.

Verses 10–26

Here is a genealogy, or list of names, ending in Abram, the friend of God, and thus leading towards Christ, the promised Seed, who was the son of Abram. Nothing is left upon record but their names and ages; the Holy Ghost seeming to hasten through them to the history of Abram. How little do we know of those that are gone before us in this world, even of those that lived in the same places where we live, as we likewise know little of those who now live in distant places! We have enough to do to mind our own work. When the earth began to be peopled, men's lives began to shorten; this was the wise disposal of Providence.

Verses 27–32

Here begins the story of Abram, whose name is famous in both Testaments. Even the children of Eber had become worshippers of false gods. Those who are through grace, heirs of the land of promise, ought to remember what was the land of their birth; what was their corrupt and sinful state by nature. Abram's brethren were, Nahor, out of whose family both Isaac and Jacob had their wives; and Haran, the father of Lot, who died before his father. Children cannot be sure that they shall outlive their parents. Haran died in Ur, before the happy removal of the family out of that idolatrous country. It concerns us to hasten out of our natural state, lest death surprise us in it. We here read of Abram's departure out of Ur of the Chaldees, with his father Terah, his nephew Lot, and the rest of his family, in obedience to the call of God. This chapter leaves them about mid-way between Ur and Canaan, where they dwelt till Terah's death. Many reach to Charran, and yet fall short of Canaan; they are not far from the kingdom of God, and yet never come thither.

Chapter 12

Verses 1–3

God made choice of Abram, and singled him out from among his fellow-idolaters, that he might reserve a people for himself, among whom his true worship might be maintained till the coming of Christ. From henceforward Abram and his seed are almost the only subject of the history in the Bible. Abram was tried whether he loved God better than all, and whether he could willingly leave all to go with God. His kindred and his father's house were a constant temptation to him, he could not continue among them without danger of being infected by them. Those who leave their sins, and turn to God, will be unspeakable gainers by the change. The command God gave to Abram, is much the same with the gospel call, for natural affection must give way to Divine grace. Sin, and all the occasions of it, must be forsaken; particularly bad company. Here are many great and precious promises. All God's precepts are attended with promises to the obedient. **1.** I will make of thee a great nation. When God took Abram from his own people, he promised to make him the head of another people. **2.** I will bless thee. Obedient believers shall be sure to inherit the blessing. **3.** I will make thy name great. The name of obedient believers shall certainly be made great. **4.** Thou shalt be a blessing. Good men are the blessings of their country. **5.** I will bless them that bless thee, and curse him that curseth thee. God will take care that none are losers, by any service done for his people. **6.** In thee shall all the families of the earth be blessed. Jesus Christ is the great blessing of the world, the greatest that ever the world possessed. All the true blessedness the world is now, or ever shall be possessed of, is owing to Abram and his posterity. Through them we have a Bible, a Saviour, and a gospel. They are the stock on which the Christian church is grafted.

Verses 4, 5

Abram believed that the blessing of the Almighty would make up for all he could lose or leave behind, supply all his wants, and answer and exceed all his desires; and he knew that nothing but misery would follow disobedience. Such believers, being justified by faith in Christ, have peace with God. They hold on their way to Canaan. They are not discouraged by the difficulties in their way, nor drawn aside by the delights they meet with. Those who set out for heaven must persevere to the end. What we undertake, in obedience to God's command, and in humble attendance on his providence, will certainly succeed, and end with comfort at last. Canaan was not, as other lands, a mere outward possession, but a type of heaven, and in this respect the patriarchs so earnestly prized it.

Verses 6–9

Abram found the country peopled by Canaanites, who were bad neighbours. He journeyed, going on still. Sometimes it is the lot of good men to be unsettled, and often to remove into various states. Believers must look on themselves as strangers and sojourners in this world, Heb **11:8**, **13**, **14**. But observe how much comfort Abram had in God. When he could have little satisfaction in converse with the Canaanites whom he found there, he had abundance of pleasure in communion with that God, who brought him thither, and did not leave him. Communion with God is kept up by the word and by prayer. God reveals himself and his favours to his people by degrees; before, he had promised to show Abram this land, now, to give it to him: as grace is growing, so is comfort. It should seem, Abram understood it also as a grant of a better land, of which this was a type; for he looked for a heavenly country, Heb **11:16**. As soon as Abram was got to Canaan, though he was but a stranger and sojourner there, yet he set up, and kept up, the worship of God in his family. He not only minded the ceremonial part of religion, the offering of sacrifice; but he made conscience of seeking his God, and calling on his name; that spiritual sacrifice with which God is well pleased. He preached concerning the name of the Lord; he taught his family and neighbours the knowledge of the true God, and his holy religion. The way of family worship is a good old way, no new thing, but the ancient usage of the saints. Abram was rich, and had a numerous family, was now unsettled, and in the midst of enemies; yet, wherever he pitched his tent, he built an altar: wherever we go, let us not fail to take our religion along with us.

Verses 10–20

There is no state on earth free from trials, nor any character free from blemishes. There was famine in Canaan, the glory of all lands, and unbelief, with the evils it ever brings, in Abram the father of the faithful. Perfect happiness and perfect purity dwell only in heaven. Abram, when he must for a time quit Canaan, goes to Egypt, that he might not seem to look back, and meaning to tarry there no longer than needful. There Abram dissembled his relation to Sarai, equivocated, and taught his wife and his attendants to do so too. He concealed a truth, so as in effect to deny it, and exposed thereby both his wife and the Egyptians to sin. The grace Abram was most noted for, was faith; yet he thus fell through unbelief and distrust of the Divine providence, even after God had appeared to him twice. Alas, what will become of weak faith, when strong faith is thus shaken! If God did not deliver us, many a time, out of straits and distresses which we bring ourselves into, by our own sin and folly, we should be ruined. He deals not with us according to our deserts. Those are happy chastisements that hinder us in a sinful way, and bring us to our duty, particularly to the duty of restoring what we have wrongfully taken or kept. Pharaoh's reproof of Abram was very just: What is this that thou hast done? How unbecoming a wise and good man! If those who profess religion, do that which is unfair and deceptive, especially if they say that which borders upon a lie, they must expect to hear of it; and they have reason to thank those who will tell them of it. The sending away was kind. Pharaoh was so far from any design to kill Abram, as he feared, that he took particular care of him. We often perplex ourselves with fears which are altogether groundless. Many a time we fear where no fear is. Pharaoh charged his men not to hurt Abram in any thing. It is not enough for those in authority, that they do not hurt themselves; they must keep their servants and those about them from doing hurt.

Chapter 13

Verses 1–4

Abram was very rich: he was very heavy, so the Hebrew word is; for riches are a burden; and they that will be rich, do but load themselves with thick clay, Hab **2:6**. There is a burden of care in getting riches, fear in keeping them, temptation in using them, guilt in abusing them, sorrow in losing them, and a burden of account at last to be given up about them. Yet God in his providence sometimes makes good men rich men, and thus God's blessing made Abram rich without sorrow, Pr **10:22**. Though it is hard for a rich man to get to heaven, yet in some cases it may be, Mr **10:23**, **24**. Nay, outward prosperity, if well managed, is an ornament to piety, and an opportunity for doing more good. Abram removed to Bethel. His altar was gone, so that he could not offer sacrifice; but he called on the name of the Lord. You may as soon find a living man without breath as one of God's people without prayer.

Verses 5–9

Riches not only afford matter for strife, and are the things most commonly striven about; but they also stir up a spirit of contention, by making people proud and covetous. Mine and thine are the great make-bates of the world. Poverty and labour, wants and wanderings, could not separate Abram and Lot; but riches did so. Bad servants often make a great deal of mischief in families and among neighbours, by their pride and passion, lying, slandering, and talebearing. What made the quarrel worse was, that the Canaanite and the Perizzite dwelt then in the land. The quarrels of professors are the reproach of religion, and give occasion to the enemies of the Lord to blaspheme.

It is best to keep the peace, that it be not broken; but the next best is, if differences do happen, with all speed to quench the fire that is broken out. The attempt to stay this strife was made by Abram, although he was the elder and the greater man. Abram shows himself to be a man of cool spirit, that had the command of his passion, and knew how to turn away wrath by a soft answer. Those that would keep the peace, must never render railing for railing. And of a condescending spirit; he was willing to beseech even his inferior to be at peace. Whatever others are for, the people of God must be for peace. Abram's plea for peace was very powerful. Let the people of the land contend about trifles; but let not us fall out, who know better things, and look for a better country. Professors of religion should be most careful to avoid contention. Many profess to be for peace who will do nothing towards it: not so Abram. When God condescends to beseech us to be reconciled, we may well beseech one another. Though God had promised Abram to give this land to his seed, yet he offered an equal or better share to Lot, who had not an equal right; and he will not, under the protection of God's promise, act hardly to his kinsman. It is noble to be willing to yield for peace' sake.

Verses 10–13

Abram having offered Lot the choice, he at once accepted it. Passion and selfishness make men rude. Lot looked to the goodness of the land; therefore he doubted not that in such a fruitful soil he should certainly thrive. But what came of it? Those who, in choosing relations, callings, dwellings, or settlements, are guided and governed by the lust of the flesh, the lust of the eye, or the pride of life, cannot expect God's presence or blessing. They are commonly disappointed even in that which they principally aim at. In all our choices this principle should rule, That is best for us, which is best for our souls. Lot little considered the badness of the inhabitants. The men of Sodom were impudent, daring sinners. This was the iniquity of Sodom, pride, fulness of bread, and abundance of idleness, Eze **16**:**49**. God often gives great plenty to great sinners. It has often been the vexatious lot of good men to live among wicked neighbours; and it must be the more grievous, if, as Lot here, they have brought it upon themselves by a wrong choice.

Verses 14–18

Those are best prepared for the visits of Divine grace, whose spirits are calm, and not ruffled with passion. God will abundantly make up in spiritual peace, what we lose for preserving neighbourly peace. When our relations are separated from us, yet God is not. Observe also the promises with which God now comforted and enriched Abram. Of two things he assures him; a good land, and a numerous issue to enjoy it. The prospects seen by faith are more rich and beautiful than those we see around us. God bade him walk through the land, not to think of fixing in it, but expect to be always unsettled, and walking through it to a better Canaan. He built an altar, in token of his thankfulness to God. When God meets us with gracious promises, he expects that we should attend him with humble praises. In outward difficulties, it is very profitable for the true believer to mediate on the glorious inheritance which the Lord has for him at the last.

Chapter 14

Verses 1–12

The wars of nations make great figure in history, but we should not have had the record of this war if Abram and Lot had not been concerned. Out of covetousness, Lot had settled in fruitful, but wicked Sodom. Its inhabitants were the most ripe for vengeance of all the descendants of Canaan. The invaders were from Chaldea and Persia, then only small kingdoms. They took Lot among the rest, and his goods. Though he was righteous, and Abram's brother's son, yet he was with the rest in this trouble. Neither our own piety, nor our relation to the favourites of Heaven, will be our security when God's judgments are abroad. Many an honest man fares the worse for his wicked neighbours: it is our wisdom to separate, or at least to distinguish ourselves from them, **2**Co **6**:**17**. So near a relation of Abram should have been a companion and a disciple of Abram. If he chose to dwell in Sodom, he must thank himself if he share in Sodom's losses. When we go out of the way of our duty, we put ourselves from under God's protection, and cannot expect that the choice made by our lusts, should end to our comfort. They took Lot's goods; it is just with God to deprive us of enjoyments, by which we suffer ourselves to be deprived of the enjoyment of him.

Verses 13–16

Abram takes this opportunity to give a real proof of his being truly friendly to Lot. We ought to be ready to succour those in distress, especially relations and friends. And though others may have been wanting in their duty to us, yet we must not neglect our duty to them. Abram rescued the captives. As we have opportunity, we must do good to all.

Verses 17–20

Melchizedek is spoken of as a king of Salem, supposed to be the place afterwards called Jerusalem, and it is generally thought that he was only a man. The words of the apostle, Heb **7**:**3**, state only, that the sacred history has said nothing of his ancestors. The silence of the Scriptures on this, is to raise our thoughts to Him, whose generation cannot be declared. Bread and wine were suitable refreshment for the weary followers of Abram; and it is remarkable that Christ appointed the same as the memorials of his body and blood, which are meat and drink indeed to the soul. Melchizedek blessed Abram from God. He blessed God from Abram. We ought to give thanks for other's mercies as for our own. Jesus Christ, our great High Priest, is the Mediator both of our prayers and praises, and not only offers up ours, but his own for us. Abram gave him the tenth of the spoils, Heb **7**:**4**. When we have received some great mercy from God, it is very fit we should express our thankfulness by some special act of pious charity. Jesus Christ, our great Melchisedek, is to have homage done him, and to be humbly acknowledged as our King and Priest; not only the tithe of all, but all we have, must be given up to him.

Verses 21–24

Observe the king of Sodom's grateful offer to Abram, Give me the souls, and take thou the substance. Gratitude teaches us to recompense to the utmost of our power, those that have undergone fatigues, run hazards, and been at expense for our service and benefit. Abram generously refused this offer. He accompanies his refusal with a good reason, Lest thou shouldest say, I have made Abram rich: which would reflect upon the promise promise and covenant of God, as if He would not have enriched Abraham without the spoils of Sodom. The people of God must, for their credit's sake, take heed of doing any thing that looks mean or mercenary, or that savors of covetousness and self-seeking. Abraham can trust the Possessor of Heaven and earth to provide for him.

Chapter 15

Verse 1

God assured Abram of safety and happiness; that he should for ever be safe. I am thy shield; or, I am a shield to thee, present with thee, actually caring for thee. The consideration that God himself is, and will be a shield to his people, to secure them from all evils, a shield ready to them, and a shield round about them, should silence all perplexing, tormenting fears.

Verses 2–6

Though we must never complain of God, yet we have leave to complain to him; and to state all our grievances. It is ease to a burdened spirit, to open its case to a faithful and compassionate friend. Abram's complaint is, that he had no child; that he was never likely to have any; that the want of a son was so great a trouble to him, that it took away all his comfort. If we suppose that Abram looked no further than outward comfort, this complaint was to be blamed. But if we suppose that Abram herein had reference to the promised Seed, his desire was very commendable. Till we have evidence of our interest in Christ, we should not rest satisfied; what will all avail me, if I go Christless? If we continue instant in prayer, yet pray with humble submission to the Divine will, we shall not seek in vain. God gave Abram an express promise of a son. Christians may believe in God with respect to the common concerns of this life; but the faith by which they are justified, always has respect to the person and work of Christ. Abram believed in God as promising Christ; they believe in him as having raised him from the dead, Ro **4**:**24**. Through faith in his blood they obtain forgiveness of sins.

Verses 7–11

Assurance was given to Abram of the land of Canaan for an inheritance. God never promises more than he is able to perform, as men often do. Abram did as God commanded him. He divided the beasts in the midst, according to the ceremony used in confirming covenants, Jer **34**:**18**, **19**. Having prepared according to God's appointment, he set himself to wait for the sign God might give him. A watch must be kept upon our spiritual sacrifices. When vain thoughts, like these fowls, come down upon our sacrifices, we must drive them away, and seek to attend on God without distraction.

Verses 12–16

A deep sleep fell upon Abram; with this sleep a horror of great darkness fell upon him: a sudden change. The children of light do not always walk in the light. Several things were then foretold. **1**. The suffering state of Abram's seed for a long time. They shall be strangers. The heirs of heaven are strangers on earth. They shall be servants; but Canaanites serve under a curse, the Hebrews under a blessing. They shall be suffers. Those that are blessed and beloved of God, are often sorely afflicted by wicked men. **2**. The judgment of the enemies of Abram's seed. Though God may allow persecutors and oppressors to trample upon his people a great while, he will certainly reckon with them at last. **3**. That great event, the deliverance of Abram's seed out of Egypt, is here foretold. **4**. Their happy settlement in Canaan. They shall come hither again. The measure of sin fills gradually. Some people's measure of sin fills slowly. The knowledge of future events would seldom add to our comfort. In the most favoured families, and most happy lives, there are so many afflictions, that it is merciful in God to conceal what will befall us and ours.

Verses 17–21

The smoking furnace and the burning lamp, probably represented the Israelites' severe trials and joyful deliverance, with their gracious supports in the mean time. It is probable that this furnace and lamp, which passed between the pieces, burned and consumed them, and so completed the sacrifice, and testified God's acceptance of it. So it intimates that God's covenants with man are made by sacrifice, Ps **50**:**5**. And we may know that he accepts our sacrifices, if he kindles in our souls pious and devout affections. The bounds of the land granted are stated. Several nations, or tribes, are spoken of, that must be cast out to make room for the seed of Abram. In this chapter we perceive in Abram faith struggling against, and triumphing over, unbelief. Wonder not, believers, if you meet with seasons of darkness and distress. But it is not the will of God that you should be cast down: fear not; for all that he was to Abram he will be to you.

Chapter 16

Verses 1–3

Sarai, no longer expecting to have children herself, proposed to Abram to take another wife, whose children she might; her slave, whose children would be her property. This was done without asking counsel of the Lord. Unbelief worked, God's almighty power was forgotten. It was a bad example, and a source of manifold uneasiness. In every relation and situation in life there is some cross for us to bear: much of the exercise of faith consists in patiently submitting, in waiting the Lord's time, and using only those means which he appoints for the removal of the cross. Foul temptations may have very fair pretences, and be coloured with that which is very plausible. Fleshly wisdom puts us out of God's way. This would not be the case, if we would ask counsel of God by his word and by prayer, before we attempt that which is doubtful.

Verses 4–6

Abram's unhappy marriage to Hagar very soon made a great deal of mischief. We may thank ourselves for the guilt and grief that follow us, when we go out of the way of our duty. See it in this case, Passionate people often quarrel with others, for things of which they themselves must bear the blame. Sarai had given her maid to Abram, yet she cries out, My wrong be upon thee. That is never said wisely, which pride and anger put into our mouths. Those are not always in the right, who are most loud and forward in appealing to God: such rash and bold imprecations commonly speak guilt and a bad cause. Hagar forgot that she herself had first given the provocation, by despising her mistress. Those that suffer for their faults, ought to bear it patiently, **1**Pe **2**:**20**.

Verses 7–16

Hagar was out of her place, and out of the way of her duty, and going further astray, when the Angel found her. It is a great mercy to be stopped in a sinful way, either by conscience or by providence. Whence comest thou? Consider that thou art running from duty, and the privileges thou wast blest with in Abram's tent. It is good to live in a religious family, which those ought to consider who have this advantage. Whither wilt thou go? Thou art running into sin; if Hagar return to Egypt, she will return to idol gods, and into danger in the wilderness through which she must travel. Recollecting who we are, would often teach us our duty. Inquiring whence we came, would show us our sin and folly. Considering whither we shall go, discovers our danger and misery. And those who leave their space and duty, must hasten their return, how mortifying soever it be. The declaration of the Angel, "I will," shows this Angel was the eternal Word and Son of God. Hagar could not but admire the Lord's mercy, and feel, Have I, who am so unworthy, been favoured with a gracious visit from the Lord? She was brought to a better temper, returned, and by her behaviour softened Sarai, and received more gentle treatment. Would that we were always suitably impressed with this thought, Thou God seest me!

Chapter 17

Verses 1–6

The covenant was to be accomplished in due time. The promised Seed was Christ, and Christians in him. And all who are of faith are blessed with faithful Abram, being partakers of the same covenant blessings. In token of this covenant his name was changed from Abram, "a high father," to Abraham, "the father of a multitude." All that the Christian world enjoys, it is indebted for to Abraham and his Seed.

Verses 7–14

The covenant of grace is from everlasting in the counsels of it, and to everlasting in the consequences of it. The token of the covenant was circumcision. It is here said to be the covenant which Abraham and his seed must keep. Those who will have the Lord to be to them a God, must resolve to be to him a people. Not only Abraham and Isaac, and his posterity by Isaac, were to be circumcised, but also Ishmael and the bond-servants. It sealed not only the covenant of the land of Canaan to Isaac's posterity, but of heaven, through Christ, to the whole church of God. The outward sign is for the visible church; the inward seal of the Spirit is peculiar to those whom God knows to be believers, and he alone can know them. The religious observance of this institution was required, under a very severe penalty. It is dangerous to make light of Divine institutions, and to live in the neglect of them. The covenant in question was one that involved great blessings for the world in all future ages. Even the blessedness of Abraham himself, and all the rewards conferred upon him, were for Christ's sake. Abraham was justified, as we have seen, not by his own righteousness, but by faith in the promised Messiah.

Verses 15–22

Here is the promise made to Abraham of a son by Sarai, in whom the promise made to him should be fulfilled. The assurance of this promise was the change of Sarai's name into Sarah. Sarai signifies my princess, as if her honour were confined to one family only; Sarah signifies a princess. The more favours God confers upon us, the more low we should be in our own eyes. Abraham showed great joy; he laughed, it was a laughter of delight, not of distrust. Now it was that Abraham rejoiced to see Christ's day; now he saw it and was glad, Joh **8**:**56**. Abraham, dreading lest Ishmael should be abandoned and forsaken of God, put up a petition on his behalf. God gives us leave in prayer to be particular in making known our requests. Whatever is our care and fear, should be spread before God in prayer. It is the duty of parents to pray for their children, and the great thing we should desire is, that they may be kept in covenant with Him, and may have grace to walk before him in uprightness. Common blessings are secured to Ishmael. Outward good things are often given to those children of godly parents who are born after the flesh, for their parents' sake. Covenant blessings are reserved for Isaac, and appropriated to him.

Verses 23–27

Abraham and all his family were circumcised; so receiving the token of the covenant, and distinguishing themselves from other families that had no part nor lot in the matter. It was an implicit obedience; he did as God said unto him, and did not ask why or wherefore. He did it because God bade him. It was a speedy obedience; in the self-same day. Sincere obedience makes no delay. Not only the doctrines of revelation, but the seals of God's covenant, remind us that we are guilty, polluted sinners. They show us our need of the blood of atonement; they point to the promised Saviour, and teach us to exercise faith in him. They show us that without regeneration, and sanctification by his Spirit, and the mortification of our corrupt and carnal inclinations, we cannot be in covenant with God. But let us remember that the true circumcision is that of the heart, by the Spirit, Ro **2**:**28**, **29**. Both under the old and new dispensation, many have had the outward profession, and the outward seal, who were never sealed by the Holy Spirit of promise.

Chapter 18

Verses 1–8

Abraham was waiting to entertain any weary traveller, for inns were not to be met with as among us. While Abraham was thus sitting, he saw three men coming. These were three heavenly beings in human bodies. Some think they were all created angels; others, that one of them was the Son of God, the Angel of the covenant. Washing the feet is customary in those hot climates, where only sandals are worn. We should not be forgetful to entertain strangers, for thereby some have entertained angels unawares, Heb **13**:**2**; nay, the Lord of angels himself; as we always do, when for his sake we entertain the least of his brethren. Cheerful and obliging manners in showing kindness, are great ornaments to piety. Though our condescending Lord vouchsafes not personal visits to us, yet still by his Spirit he stands at the door and knocks; when we are inclined to open, he deigns to enter; and by his gracious consolations he provides a rich feast, of which we partake with him, Re **3**:**20**.

Verses 9–15

Where is Sarah thy wife? was asked. Note the answer, In the tent. Just at hand, in her proper place, occupied in her household concerns. There is nothing got by gadding. Those are most likely to receive comfort from God and his promises, who are in their proper place, and in the way of their duty, Lu **2**:**8**. We are slow of heart to believe, and need line upon line to the same purport. The blessings others have from common providence, believers have from the Divine promise, which makes them very sweet, and very sure. The spiritual seed of Abraham owe their life, and joy, and hope, and all, to the promise. Sarah thinks this too good news to be true; she laughed, and therefore cannot as yet find in her heart to believe it. Sarah laughed. We might not have thought there was a difference between Sarah's laughter and Abraham's, ch. **17**:**17**; but He who searches the heart, saw that the one sprung from unbelief, and the other from faith. She denied that she had laughed. One sin commonly brings in another, and it is not likely we shall strictly keep to truth, when we question the Divine truth. But whom the Lord loves he will rebuke, convict, silence, and bring to repentance, and if they sin before him.

Verses 16–22

The two who are supposed to have been created angels went toward Sodom. The one who is called Jehovah throughout the chapter, continued with Abraham, and would not hide from him the thing he intended to do. Though God long forbears with sinners, from which they fancy that the Lord does not see, and does not regard; yet when the day of his wrath comes, he will look toward them. The Lord will give Abraham an opportunity to intercede with him, and shows him the reason of his conduct. Consider, as a very bright part of

Abraham's character and example, that he not only prayed with his family, but he was very careful to teach and rule them well. Those who expect family blessings must make conscience of family duty. Abraham did not fill their heads with matters of doubtful dispute; but he taught them to be serious and devout in the worship of God, and to be honest in their dealings with all men. Of how few may such a character be given in our days! How little care is taken by masters of families to ground those under them in the principles of religion! Do we watch from sabbath to sabbath whether they go forward or backward?

Verses 23–33

Here is the first solemn prayer upon record in the Bible; and it is a prayer for the sparing of Sodom. Abraham prayed earnestly that Sodom might be spared, if but a few righteous persons should be found in it. Come and learn from Abraham what compassion we should feel for sinners, and how earnestly we should pray for them. We see here that the effectual, fervent prayer of a righteous man avails much. Abraham, indeed, failed in his request for the whole place, but Lot was miraculously delivered. Be encouraged then to expect, by earnest prayer, the blessing of God upon your families, your friends, your neighbourhood. To this end you must not only pray, but you must live like Abraham. He knew the Judge of all the earth would do right. He does not plead that the wicked may be spared for their own sake, or because it would be severe to destroy them, but for the sake of the righteous who might be found among them. And righteousness only can be made a plea before God. How then did Christ make intercession for transgressors? Not by blaming the Divine law, nor by alleging aught in extenuation or excuse of human guilt; but by pleading HIS OWN obedience unto death.

Chapter 19

Verses 1–29

Lot was good, but there was not one more of the same character in the city. All the people of Sodom were very wicked and vile. Care was therefore taken for saving Lot and his family. Lot lingered; he trifled. Thus many who are under convictions about their spiritual state, and the necessity of a change, defer that needful work. The salvation of the most righteous men is of God's mercy, not by their own merit. We are saved by grace. God's power also must be acknowledged in bringing souls out of a sinful state If God had not been merciful to us, our lingering had been our ruin. Lot must flee for his life. He must not hanker after Sodom. Such commands as these are given to those who, through grace, are delivered out of a sinful state and condition. Return not to sin and Satan. Rest not in self and the world. Reach toward Christ and heaven, for that is escaping to the mountain, short of which we must not stop. Concerning this destruction, observe that it is a revelation of the wrath of God against sin and sinners of all ages. Let us learn from hence the evil of sin, and its hurtful nature; it leads to ruin.

Verses 30–38

See the peril of security. Lot, who kept chaste in Sodom, and was a mourner for the wickedness of the place, and a witness against it, when in the mountain, alone, and, as he thought, out of the way of temptation, is shamefully overtaken. Let him that thinks he stands high, and stands firm, take heed lest he fall. See the peril of drunkenness; it is not only a great sin itself, but lets in many sins, which bring a lasting wound and dishonour. Many a man does that, when he is drunk, which, when he is sober, he could not think of without horror. See also the peril of temptation, even from relations and friends, whom we love and esteem, and expect kindness from. We must dread a snare, wherever we are, and be always upon our guard. No excuse can be made for the daughters, nor for Lot. Scarcely any account can be given of the affair but this, The heart is deceitful above all things, and desperately wicked: who can know it? From the silence of the Scripture concerning Lot henceforward, learn that drunkenness, as it makes men forgetful, so it makes them to be forgotten.

Chapter 20

Verses 1–8

Crooked policy will not prosper: it brings ourselves and others into danger. God gives Abimelech notice of his danger of sin, and his danger of death for his sin. Every wilful sinner is a dead man, but Abimelech pleads ignorance. If our consciences witness, that, however we may have been cheated into a snare, we have not knowingly sinned against God, it will be our rejoicing in the day of evil. It is matter of comfort to those who are honest, that God knows their honesty, and will acknowledge it. It is a great mercy to be hindered from committing sin; of this God must have the glory. But if we have ignorantly done wrong, that will not excuse us, if we knowingly persist in it. He that does wrong, whoever he is, prince or peasant, shall certainly receive for the wrong which he has done, unless he repent, and, if possible, make restitution.

Verses 9–13

See here much to blame, even in the father of the faithful. Mark his distrust of God, his undue care about life, his intent to deceive. He also threw temptation in the way of others, caused affliction to them, exposed himself and Sarah to just rebukes, and yet attempted an excuse. These things are written for our warning, not for us to imitate. Even Abraham hath not whereof to glory. He cannot be justified by his works, but must be indebted for justification, to that righteousness which is upon all and unto all them that believe. We must not condemn all as hypocrites who fall into sin, if they do not continue in it. But let the unhumbled and impenitent take heed that they do not sin on, thinking that grace may abound. Abimelech, being warned of God, takes the warning; and being truly afraid of sin and its consequences, he rose early to pursue the directions given him.

Verses 14–18

We often trouble ourselves, and even are led into temptation and sin, by groundless suspicions; and find the fear of God where we expected it not. Agreements to deceive generally end in shame and sorrow; and restraints from sin, though by suffering, should be thankfully acknowledged. Though the Lord rebuke, yet he will pardon and deliver his people, and he will give them favour in the sight of those with whom they sojourn; and overrule their infirmities, when they are humbled for them, so that they shall prove useful to themselves and others.

Chapter 21

Verses 1–8

Few under the Old Testament were brought into the world with such expectations as Isaac. He was in this a type of Christ, that Seed which the holy God so long promised, and holy men so long expected. He was born according to the promise, at the set time of which God had spoken. God's promised mercies will certainly come at the time which He sets, and that is the best time. Isaac means "laughter," and there was good reason for the name, ch. **17**:**17**; **18**:**13**. When the Sun of comfort is risen upon the soul, it is good to remember how welcome the dawning of the day was. When Sarah received the promise, she laughed with distrust and doubt. When God gives us the mercies we began to despair of, we ought to remember with sorrow and shame our sinful distrust of his power and promise, when we were in pursuit of them. This mercy filled Sarah with joy and wonder. God's favours to his covenant people are such as surpass their own and others' thoughts and expectations: who could imagine that he should do so much for those that deserve so little, nay, for those that deserve so ill? Who would have said that God should send his Son to die for us, his Spirit to make us holy, his angels to attend us? Who would have said that such great sins should be pardoned, such mean services accepted, and such worthless worms taken into covenant? A short account of Isaac's infancy is given. God's blessing upon the nursing of children, and the preservation of them through the perils of the infant age, are to be acknowledged as signal instances of the care and tenderness of the Divine providence. See Ps **22**:**9**, **10**; Ho **11**:**1**, **2**.

Verses 9–13

Let us not overlook the manner in which this family matter instructs us not to rest in outward privileges, or in our own doings. And let us seek the blessings of the new covenant by faith in its Divine Surety. Ishmael's conduct was persecution, being done in profane contempt of the covenant and promise, and with malice against Isaac. God takes notice of what children say and do in their play; and will reckon with them, if they say or do amiss, though their parents do not. Mocking is a great sin, and very provoking to God. And the children of promise must expect to be mocked. Abraham was grieved that Ishmael should misbehave, and Sarah demand so severe a punishment. But God showed him that Isaac must be the father of the promised Seed; therefore, send Ishmael away, lest he corrupt the manners, or try to take the rights of Isaac. The covenant seed of Abraham must be a people by themselves, not mingled with those who were out of covenant: Sarah little thought of this; but God turned aright what she said.

Verses 14–21

If Hagar and Ishmael had behaved well in Abraham's family, they might have continued there; but they were justly punished. By abusing privileges, we forfeit them. Those who know not when they are well off, will be made to know the worth of mercies by the want of them. They were brought to distress in the wilderness. It is not said that the provisions were spent, or that Abraham sent them away without money. But the water was spent; and having lost their way, in that hot climate Ishmael was soon overcome with fatigue and thirst. God's readiness to help us when we are in trouble, must not slacken, but quicken our endeavours to help ourselves. The promise concerning her son is repeated, as a reason why Hagar should bestir herself to help him. It should engage our care and pains about children and young people, to consider that we know not what great use God has designed them for, and may make of them. The angel directs her to a present supply. Many who have reason to be comforted, go mourning from day to day, because they do not see the reason they have for comfort. There is a well of water near them in the covenant of grace, but they are not aware of it, till the same God that opened their eyes to see their wound, opens them to see their remedy. Paran was a wild place, fit for a wild man; such as Ishmael. Those who are born after the flesh, take up with the wilderness of this world, while the children of the promise aim at the heavenly Canaan, and cannot be at rest till they are there. Yet God was with the lad; his outward welfare was owing to this.

Verses 22–34

Abimelech felt sure that the promises of God would be fulfilled to Abraham. It is wise to connect ourselves with those who are blessed of God; and we ought to requite kindness to those who have been kind to us. Wells of water are scarce and valuable in eastern countries. Abraham took care to have his title to the well allowed, to prevent disputes in future. No more can be expected from an honest man than that he be ready to do right, as soon as he knows he has done wrong. Abraham, being now in a good neighbourhood, stayed a great while there. There he made, not only a constant practice, but an open profession of his religion. There he called on the name of the Lord, as the everlasting God; probably in the grove he planted, which was his place of prayer. Abraham kept up public worship, in which his neighbours might join. Good men should do all they can to make others so. Wherever we sojourn, we must neither neglect nor be ashamed of the worship of Jehovah.

Chapter 22

Verses 1, 2

We never are secure from trials In Hebrew, to tempt, and to try, or to prove, are expressed by the same word. Every trial is indeed a temptation, and tends to show the dispositions of the heart, whether holy or unholy. But God proved Abraham, not to draw him to sin, as Satan tempts. Strong faith is often exercised with strong trials, and put upon hard services. The command to offer up his son, is given in such language as makes the trial more grievous; every word here is a sword. Observe, **1**. The person to be offered: Take thy son; not thy bullocks and thy lambs. How willingly would Abraham have parted with them all to redeem Isaac! Thy son; not thy servant. Thine only son; thine only son by Sarah. Take Isaac, that son whom thou lovest. **2**. The place: three days' journey off; so that Abraham might have time to consider, and might deliberately obey. **3**. The manner: Offer him fro a burnt-offering; not only kill his son, his Isaac, but kill him as a sacrifice; kill him with all that solemn pomp and ceremony, with which he used to offer his burnt-offerings.

Verses 3–10

Never was any gold tried in so hot a fire. Who but Abraham would not have argued with God? Such would have been the thought of a weak heart; but Abraham knew that he had to do with a God, even Jehovah. Faith had taught him not to argue, but to obey. He is sure that what God commands is good; that what he promises cannot be broken. In matters of God, whoever consults with flesh and blood, will never offer up his Isaac to God. The good patriarch rises early, and begins his sad journey. And now he travels three days, and Isaac still is in his sight! Misery is made worse when long continued. The expression, We will come again to you, shows that Abraham expected that Isaac, being raised from the dead, would return with him. It was a very affecting question that Isaac asked him, as they were going together: "My father," said Isaac; it was a melting word, which, one would think, should strike deeper in the heart of Abraham, than his knife could in the heart of Isaac. Yet he waits for his son's question. Then Abraham, where he meant not, prophesies: "My son, God will provide a lamb for a burnt-offering." The Holy Spirit, by his mouth, seems to predict the Lamb of God, which he has provided, and which taketh away the sin of the world. Abraham lays the wood in order for his Isaac's funeral pile, and now tells him the amazing news: Isaac, thou art the lamb which God has provided! Abraham, no doubt, comforting him with the same hopes with which he himself by faith was comforted. Yet it is necessary that the sacrifice be bound. The great Sacrifice, which, in the fulness of time, was to be offered up, must be bound, and so must Isaac. This being done, Abraham takes the knife, and stretches out his hand to give the fatal blow. Here is an act of faith and obedience, which deserves to be a spectacle to God, angels, and men. God, by his providence, calls us to part with an Isaac sometimes, and we must do it with cheerful submission to his holy will, **1**Sa **3**:**18**.

Verses 11–14

It was not God's intention that Isaac should actually be sacrificed, yet nobler blood than that of animals, in due time, was to be shed for sin, even the blood of the only begotten Son of God. But in the mean while God would not in any case have human sacrifices used. Another sacrifice is provided. Reference must be had to the promised Messiah, the blessed Seed. Christ was sacrificed in our stead, as this ram instead of Isaac, and his death was our discharge. And observe, that the temple, the place of sacrifice, was afterwards built upon this same mount Moriah; and Calvary, where Christ was crucified, was near. A new name was given to that place, for the encouragement of all believers, to the end of the world, cheerfully to trust in God, and obey him. Jehovah-jireh, the Lord will provide; probably alluding to what Abraham had said, God will provide himself a lamb. The Lord will always have his eye upon his people, in their straits and distresses, that he may give them seasonable help.

Verses 15–19

There are high declarations of God's favour to Abraham in this confirmation of the covenant with him, exceeding any he had yet been blessed with. Those that are willing to part with any thing for God, shall have it made up to them with unspeakable advantage. The promise, ver. #(**18**), doubtless points at the Messiah, and the grace of the gospel. Hereby we know the loving-kindness of God our Saviour towards sinful man, in that he hath not withheld his Son, his only Son, from us. Hereby we perceive the love of Christ, in that he gave himself a sacrifice for our sins. Yet he lives, and calls to sinners to come to him, and partake of his blood-bought salvation. He calls to his redeemed people to rejoice in him, and to glorify him. What then shall we render for all his benefits? Let his love constrain us to live not to ourselves, but to Him who died for us, and rose again. Admiring and adoring His grace, let us devote our all to his service, who laid down his life for our salvation. Whatever is dearest to us upon earth is our Isaac. And the only way for us to find comfort in an earthly thing, is to give it by faith into the hands of God. Yet remember that Abraham was not justified by his readiness to obey, but by the infinitely more noble obedience of Jesus Christ; his faith receiving this, relying on this, rejoicing in this, disposed and made him able for such wonderful self-denial and duty. (Ge **22**:**20-24**)

Verses 20–24

This chapter ends with some account of Nahor's family, who had settled at Haran. This seems to be given for the connexion which it had with the church of God. From thence Isaac and Jacob took wives; and before the account of those events this list is recorded. It shows that though Abraham saw his own family highly honoured with privileges, admitted into covenant, and blessed with the assurance of the promise, yet he did not look with disdain upon his relations, but was glad to hear of the increase and welfare of their families.

Chapter 23

Verses 1–13

The longest life must shortly come to a close. Blessed be God that there is a world where sin, death, vanity, and vexation cannot enter. Blessed be his name, that even death cannot part believers from union with Christ. Those whom we most love, yea, even our own bodies, which we so care for, must soon become loathsome lumps of clays, and be buried out of sight. How loose then should we be to all earthly attachments and adornments! Let us seek rather that our souls be adorned with heavenly graces. Abraham rendered honour and respect to the princes of Heth, although of the ungodly Canaanites. The religion of the Bible enjoins to pay due respect to all in authority, without flattering their persons, or countenancing their crimes if they are unworthy characters. And the noble generosity of these Canaanites shames and condemns the closeness, selfishness, and ill-humour of many that call themselves Israelites. It was not in pride that Abraham refused the gift, because he scorned to be beholden to Ephron; but in justice and in prudence. Abraham was able to pay for the field, and therefore would not take advantage of Ephron's generosity. Honesty, as well as honour, forbids us to take advantage of our neighbour's liberality, and to impose, upon those who give freely.

Verses 14–20

Prudence, as well as justice, directs us to be fair and open in our dealings; cheating bargains will not bear the light. Abraham, without fraud or delay, pays the money. He pays it at once in full, without keeping any part back; and by weight, current money with the merchant, without deceit. See how anciently money was used for the help of trade, and how honestly it should be paid when it is due. Though all the land of Canaan was Abraham by promise, yet the time of his possessing it not being come, what he had occasion for he bought and paid for. Dominion is not founded in grace. The saints' title to an eternal inheritance does not entitle them to the possessions of this world, nor justify them in doing wrong. Ephron honestly and fairly makes a good title to the land. As that which is bought, must be honestly paid for, so that which is sold, must be honestly delivered and secured. Let us manage our concerns with punctuality and exactness, in order to avoid contention. Abraham buried Sarah in cave. or vault, which was in the purchased field. It would tend to endear the land to his posterity. And it is worth noting, that a burying-place was the only piece of the land which Abraham possessed in Canaan. Those who have least of this earth, find a grave in it. This sepulchre was at the end of the field; whatever our possessions are, there is a burial-place at the end of them. It was a token of his belief and expectation of the resurrection. Abraham is contented to be still a pilgrim while he lives, but secures a place where, when he dies, his flesh may rest in hope. After all, the chief concern is, with whom we shall rise.

Chapter 24

Verses 1–9

The effect of good example, good teaching, and the worship of God in a family, will generally appear in the piety, faithfulness, prudence, and affection of the servants. To live in such families, or to have such servants, both are blessings from God which should be highly valued, and thankfully acknowledged. But no concern in life is of greater importance to ourselves, to others, or to the church of God, than marriage. It therefore ought always to be undertaken with much care and prudence, especially with reference to the will of God, and with prayer for his direction and blessing. Where good parents are not consulted and regarded, the blessing of God cannot be expected. Parents, in disposing of their children, should carefully consult the welfare of their souls, and their furtherance in the way to heaven. Observe the charge Abraham gave to a good servant, one whose conduct, faithfulness, and affection, to him and his family, he had long known. Observe also, that Abraham remembers that God had wonderfully brought him out of the land of his birth, by the call of his grace; and therefore doubts not but He will prosper his care, not to bring his son thither again. God will cause that to end in our comfort, in which we sincerely aim at his glory.

Verses 10–28

Abraham's servant devoutly acknowledged God. We have leave to be particular in recommending our affairs to the care of Divine providence. He proposes a sign, not that he intended to proceed no further, if not gratified in it; but it is a prayer that God would provide a good wife for his young master; and that was a good prayer. She should be simple, industrious, humble, cheerful, serviceable, and hospitable. Whatever may be the fashion, common sense, as well as piety, tells us, these are the proper qualifications for a wife and mother; for one who is to be a companion to her husband, the manager of domestic concerns, and trusted to form the minds of children. When the steward came to seek a wife for his master, he did not go to places of amusement and sinful pleasure, and pray that he might meet one there, but to the well of water, expecting to find one there employed aright. He prayed that God would please to make his way in this matter plain and clear before him. Our times are in God's hand; not only events themselves, but the times of them. We must take heed of being over-bold in urging what God should do, lest the event should weaken our faith, rather than strengthen it. But God owned him by making his way clear. Rebekah, in all respects, answered the characters he sought for in the woman that was to be his master's wife. When she came to the well, she went down and filled her pitcher, and came up to go home with it. She did not stand to gaze upon the strange man his camels, but minded her business, and would not have been diverted from it but by an opportunity of doing good. She did not curiously or confidently enter into discourse with him, but answered him modestly. Being satisfied that the Lord had heard his prayer, he gave the damsel some ornaments worn in eastern countries; asking at the same time respecting her kindred. On learning that she was of his master's relations, he bowed down his head and worshipped, blessing God. His words were addressed to the Lord, but being spoken in the hearing of Rebekah, she could perceive who he was, and whence he came.

Verses 29–53

The making up of the marriage between Isaac and Rebekah is told very particularly. We are to notice God's providence in the common events of human life, and in them to exercise prudence and other graces. Laban went to ask Abraham's servant in, but not till he saw the ear-ring, and bracelet upon his sister's hands. We know Laban's character, by his conduct afterwards, and may think that he would not have been so free to entertain him, if he had not hoped to be well rewarded for it. The servant was intent upon his business. Though he was come off a journey, and come to a good house, he would not eat till he had told his errand. The doing our work, and the fulfilling our trusts, either for God or man, should be preferred by us before our food: it was our Saviour's meat and drink, Joh **4**:**34**. He tells them the charge his master had given him, with the reason of it. He relates what had happened at the well, to further the proposal, plainly showing the finger of God in it. Those events which to us seem the effect of choice, contrivance, or chance, are "appointed out" of God. This hinders not, but rather encourages the use of all proper means. They freely and cheerfully close with the proposal; and any matter is likely to be comfortable, when it proceeds from the Lord. Abraham's servant thankfully acknowledges the good success he had met with. He was a humble man, and humble men are not ashamed to own their situation in life, whatever it may be. All our temporal concerns are sweet if intermixed with godliness.

Verses 54–67

Abraham's servant, as one that chose his work before his pleasure, was for hastening home. Lingering and loitering no way become a wise and good man who is faithful to his duty. As children ought not to marry without their parents' consent, so parents ought not to marry them without their own. Rebekah consented, not only to go, but to go at once. The goodness of Rebekah's character shows there was nothing wrong in her answer, though it be not agreeable to modern customs among us. We may hope that she had such an idea of the religion and godliness in the family she was to go to, as made her willing to forget her own people and her father's house. Her friends dismiss her with suitable attendants, and with hearty good wishes. They blessed Rebekah. When our relations are entering into a new condition, we ought by prayer to commend them to the blessing and grace of God. Isaac was well employed when he met Rebekah. He went out to take the advantage of a silent evening, and a solitary place, for meditation and prayer; those divine exercises by which we con**verse** with God and our own hearts. Holy souls love retirement; it will do us good to be often alone, if rightly employed; and we are never less alone than when alone. Observe what an affectionate son Isaac was: it was about three years since his mother died, and yet he was not, till now, comforted. See also what an affectionate husband he was to his wife. Dutiful sons promise fair to be affectionate husbands; he that fills up his first station in life with honour, is likely to do the same in those that follow.

Chapter 25

Verses 1–10

All the days, even of the best and greatest saints, are not remarkable days; some slide on silently; such were these last days of Abraham. Here is an account of Abraham's children by Keturah, and the disposition which he made of his estate. After the birth of these sons, he set his house in order, with prudence and justice. He did this while he yet lived. It is wisdom for men to do what they find to do while they live, as far as they can. Abraham lived **175** years; just one hundred years after he came to Canaan; so long he was a sojourner in a strange country. Whether our stay in this life be long or short, it matters but little, provided we leave behind us a testimony to the faithfulness and goodness of the Lord, and a good example to our families. We are told that his sons Isaac and Ishmael buried him. It seems that Abraham had himself brought them together while he lived. Let us not close the history of the life of Abraham without blessing God for such a testimony of the triumph of faith.

Verses 11–18

Ishmael had twelve sons, whose families became distinct tribes. They peopled a very large country that lay between Egypt and Assyria, called Arabia. The number and strength of this family were the fruit of the promise, made to Hagar and to Abraham, concerning Ishmael.

Verses 19–26

Isaac seems not to have been much tried, but to have spent his days in quietness. Jacob and Esau were prayed for; their parents, after being long childless, obtained them by prayer. The fulfilment of God's promise is always sure, yet it is often slow. The faith of believers is tried, their patience exercised, and mercies long waited for are more welcome when they come. Isaac and Rebekah kept in view the promise of all nations being blessed in their posterity, therefore were not only desirous of children, but anxious concerning every thing which seemed to mark their future character. In all our doubts we should inquire of the Lord by prayer. In many of our conflicts with sin and temptation, we may adopt Rebekah's words, "If it be so, why am I thus?" If a child of God, why so careless or carnal? If not a child of God, why so afraid of, or so burdened with sin?

Verses 27, 28

Esau hunted the beasts of the field with dexterity and success, till he became a conqueror, ruling over his neighbours. Jacob was a plain man, one that liked the true delights of retirement, better than all pretended pleasures. He was a stranger and a pilgrim in his spirit, and a shepherd all his days. Isaac and Rebekah had but these two children, one was the father's darling, and the other the mother's. And though godly parents must feel their affections most drawn over towards a godly child, yet they will not show partiality. Let their affections lead them to do what is just and equal to every child, or evils will arise.

Verses 29–34

We have here the bargain made between Jacob and Esau about the right, which was Esau's by birth, but Jacob's by promise. It was for a spiritual privilege; and we see Jacob's desire of the birth-right, but he sought to obtain it by crooked courses, not like his character as a plain man. He was right, that he coveted earnestly the best gifts; he was wrong, that he took advantage of his brother's need. The inheritance of their father's worldly goods did not descend to Jacob, and was not meant in this proposal. But it includeth the future possession of the land of Canaan by his children's children, and the covenant made with Abraham as to Christ the promised Seed. Believing Jacob valued these above all things; unbelieving Esau despised them. Yet although we must be of Jacob's judgment in seeking the birth-right, we ought carefully to avoid all guile, in seeking to obtain even the greatest advantages. Jacob's pottage pleased Esau's eye. "Give me some of that red;" for this he was called Edom, or Red. Gratifying the sensual appetite ruins thousands of precious souls. When men's hearts walk after their own eyes, Job **31**:**7**, and when they serve their own bellies, they are sure to be punished. If we use ourselves to deny ourselves, we break the force of most temptations. It cannot be supposed that Esau was dying of hunger in Isaac's house. The words signify, I am going towards death; he seems to mean, I shall never live to inherit Canaan, or any of those future supposed blessings; and what signifies it who has them when I am dead and gone. This would be the language of profaneness, with which the apostle brands him, Heb **12**:**16**; and this contempt of the birth-right is blamed, ver. #(**34**). It is the greatest folly to part with our interest in God, and Christ, and heaven, for the riches, honours, and pleasures of this world; it is as bad a bargain as his who sold a birth-right for a dish of pottage. Esau ate and drank, pleased his palate, satisfied his appetite, and then carelessly rose up and went his way, without any serious thought, or any regret, about the bad bargain he had made. Thus Esau despised his birth-right. By his neglect and contempt afterwards, and by justifying himself in what he had done, he put the bargain past recall. People are ruined, not so much by doing what is amiss, as by doing it and not repenting of it.

Chapter 26

Verses 1–5

Isaac had been trained up in a believing dependence upon the Divine grant of the land of Canaan to him and his heirs; and now that there is a famine in the land, Isaac still cleaves to the covenant. The real worth of God's promises cannot be lessened to a believer by any cross providences that may befall him. If God engage to be with us, and we are where he would have us to be, nothing but our own unbelief and distrust can prevent our comfort. The obedience of Abraham to the Divine command, was evidence of that faith, whereby, as a sinner, he was justified before God, and the effect of that love whereby true faith works. God testifies that he approved this obedience, to encourage others, especially Isaac.

Verses 6–11

There is nothing in Isaac's denial of his wife to be imitated, nor even excused. The temptation of Isaac is the same as that which overcame his father, and that in two instances. This rendered his conduct the greater sin. The falls of those who are gone before us are so many rocks on which others have split; and the recording of them is like placing buoys to save future mariners. This Abimelech was not the same that lived in Abraham's days, but both acted rightly. The sins of professors shame them before those that are not themselves religious.

Verses 12–17

God blessed Isaac. Be it observed, for the encouragement of poor tenants who occupy other people's lands, and are honest and industrious, that God blessed him with a great increase. The Philistines envied Isaac. It is an instance of the vanity of the world; for the more men have of it, the more they are envied, and exposed to censure and injury. Also of the corruption of nature; for that is an ill principle indeed, which makes men grieve at the good of others. They made Isaac go out of their country. That wisdom which is from above, will teach us to give up our right, and to draw back from contentions. If we are wrongfully driven from one place, the Lord will make room for us in another.

Verses 18–25

Isaac met with much opposition in digging wells. Two were called Contention and Hatred. See the nature of worldly things; they make quarrels, and are occasions of strife; and what is often the lot of the most quiet and peaceable; those who avoid striving, yet cannot avoid being striven with. And what a mercy it is to have plenty of water; to have it without striving for it! The more common this mercy is, the more reason to be thankful for it. At length Isaac digged a well, for which they strove not. Those that study to be quiet, seldom fail of being so. When men are false and unkind, still God is faithful and gracious; and his time to show himself so is, when we are most disappointed by men. The same night that Isaac came weary and uneasy to Beer-sheba, God brought comforts to his soul. Those may remove with comfort who are sure of God's presence.

Verses 26–33

When a man's ways please the Lord, he maketh even his enemies to be at peace with him, Pr **16**:**7**. Kings' hearts are in his hands, and when he pleases, he can turn them to favour his people. It is not wrong to stand upon our guard in dealing with those who have acted unfairly. But Isaac did not insist on the unkindnesses they had done him; he freely entered into friendship with them. Religion teaches us to be neighbourly, and, as much as in us lies, to live peaceable with all men. Providence smiled upon what Isaac did; God blessed his labours.

Verses 34, 35

Esau was foolish in marrying two wives together, and still more in marrying Canaanites, strangers to the blessing of Abraham, and subject to the curse of Noah. It grieved his parents that he married without their advice and consent. It grieved them that he married among those who had no religion. Children have little reason to expect God's blessing who do that which is a grief of mind to good parents.

Chapter 27

Verses 1–5

The promises of the Messiah, and of the land of Canaan, had come down to Isaac. Isaac being now about **135** years of age, and his sons about **75**, and not duly considering the Divine word concerning his two sons, that the elder should serve the younger, resolved to put all the honour and power that were in the promise, upon Esau his eldest son. We are very apt to take measures rather from our own reason than from Divine revelation, and thereby often miss our way.

Verses 6–17

Rebekah knew that the blessing was intended for Jacob, and expected he would have it. But she wronged Isaac by putting a cheat on him; she wronged Jacob by tempting him to wickedness. She put a stumbling-block in Esau's way, and gave him a pretext for hatred to Jacob and to religion. All were to be blamed. It was one of those crooked measures often adopted to further the Divine promises; as if the end would justify, or excuse wrong means. Thus many have acted wrong, under the idea of being useful in promoting the cause of Christ. The answer to all such things is that which God addressed to Abraham, I am God Almighty; walk before me and be thou perfect. And it was a very rash speech of Rebekah, "Upon me be thy curse, my son." Christ has borne the curse of the law for all who take upon them the yoke of the command, the command of the gospel. But it is too daring for any creature to say, Upon me be thy curse.

Verses 18–29

Jacob, with some difficulty, gained his point, and got the blessing. This blessing is in very general terms. No mention is made of the distinguishing mercies in the covenant with Abraham. This might be owing to Isaac having Esau in his mind, though it was Jacob who was before him. He could not be ignorant how Esau had despised the best things. Moreover, his attachment to Esau, so as to disregard the mind of God, must have greatly weakened his own faith in these things. It might therefore be expected, that leanness would attend his blessing, agreeing with the state of his mind.

Verses 30–40

When Esau understood that Jacob had got the blessing, he cried with a great and exceeding bitter cry. The day is coming, when those that now make light of the blessings of the covenant, and sell their title to spiritual blessings for that which is of no value, will, in vain, ask urgently for them. Isaac, when made sensible of the deceit practised on him, trembled exceedingly. Those who follow the choice of their own affections, rather than the Divine will, get themselves into perplexity. But he soon recovers, and confirms the blessing he had given to Jacob, saying, I have blessed him, and he shall be blessed. Those who part with their wisdom and grace, their faith and a good conscience, for the honours, wealth, or pleasures of this world, however they feign a zeal for the blessing, have judged themselves unworthy of it, and their doom shall be accordingly. A common blessing was bestowed upon Esau. This he desired. Faint desires of happiness, without right choice of the end, and right use of the means, deceive many unto their own ruin. Multitudes go to hell with their mouths full of good wishes. The great difference is, that there is nothing in Esau's blessing which points at Christ; and without that, the fatness of the earth, and the plunder of the field, will stand in little stead. Thus Isaac, by faith, blessed both his sons, according as their lot should be.

Verses 41–46

Esau bore malice to Jacob on account of the blessing he had obtained. Thus he went in the way of Cain, who slew his brother, because he gained that acceptance with God of which he had rendered himself unworthy. Esau aimed to prevent Jacob or his seed from having the dominion, by taking away his life. Men may fret at God's counsels, but cannot change them. To prevent mischief, Rebekah warned Jacob of his danger, and advised him to withdraw for his safety. We must not presume too far upon the wisdom and resolution, even of the most hopeful and promising children; but care must be taken to keep them out of the way of evil. When reading this chapter, we should not fail to observe, that we must not follow even the best of men further than they act according to the law of God. We must not do evil that good may come. And though God overruled the bad actions recorded in this chapter, to fulfil his purposes, yet we see his judgment of them, in the painful consequences to all the parties concerned. It was the peculiar privilege and advantage of Jacob to convey these spiritual blessings to all nations. The Christ, the Saviour of the world, was to be born of some one family; and Jacob's was preferred to Esau's, out of the good pleasure of Almighty God, who is certainly the best judge of what is fit, and has an undoubted right to dispense his favours as he sees proper, Ro **9**:**12**–**15**.

Chapter 28

Verses 1–5

Jacob had blessings promised both as to this world and that which is to come; yet goes out to a hard service. This corrected him for the fraud on his father. The blessing shall be conferred on him, yet he shall smart for the indirect course taken to obtain it. Jacob is dismissed by his father with a solemn charge. He must not take a wife of the daughters of Canaan: those who profess religion, should not marry with those that care not for religion. Also with a solemn blessing. Isaac had before blessed him unwittingly; now he does it designedly. This blessing is more full than the former; it is a gospel blessing. This promise looks as high as heaven, of which Canaan was a type. That was the better country which Jacob and the other patriarchs had in view.

Verses 6–9

Good examples impress even the profane and malicious. But Esau thought, by pleasing his parents in one thing, to atone for other wrong doings. Carnal hearts are apt to think themselves as good as they should be, because in some one matter they are not so bad as they have been.

Verses 10–15

Jacob's conduct hitherto, as recorded, was not that of one who simply feared and trusted in God. But now in trouble, obliged to flee, he looked only to God to make him to dwell in safety, and he could lie down and sleep in the open air with his head upon a stone. Any true believer would be willing to take up with Jacob's pillow, provided he might have Jacob's vision. God's time to visit his people with his comforts, is, when they are most destitute of other comforts, and other comforters. Jacob saw a ladder which reached from earth to heaven, the angels going up and coming down, and God himself at the head of it. This represents, **1**. The providence of God, by which there is a constant intercourse kept up between heaven and earth. This let Jacob know that he had both a good guide and a good guard. **2**. The mediation of Christ. He is this ladder; the foot on earth in his human nature, the top in heaven in his Divine nature. Christ is the Way; all God's favours come to us, and all our services go to him, by Christ, Joh **1**:**51**. By this way, sinners draw near to the throne of grace with acceptance. By faith we perceive this way, and in prayer we approach by it. In answer to prayer we receive all needful blessings of providence and grace. We have no way of getting to heaven but by Christ. And when the soul, by faith, can see these things, then every place will become pleasant, and every prospect joyful. He will never leave us, until his last promise is accomplished in our everlasting happiness. God now spake comfortably to Jacob. He spake from the head of the ladder. All the glad tidings we receive from heaven come through Jesus Christ. The Messiah should come from Jacob. Christ is the great blessing of the world. All that are blessed, are blessed in him, and none of any family are shut out from blessedness in him, but those that shut out themselves. Jacob had to fear danger from his brother Esau; but God promises to keep him. He had a long journey before him; to an unknown country; but, Behold, I am with thee, and God promises to bring him back again to this land. He seemed to be forsaken of all his friends; but God gives him this assurance, I will not leave thee. Whom God loves, he never leaves.

Verses 16–19

God manifested himself and his favour, to Jacob, when he was asleep. The Spirit, like the wind, blows when and where it listeth, and God's grace, like the dew, tarrieth not for the sons of men. Jacob sought to improve the visit God had made him. Wherever we are, in the city or in the desert, in the house or in the field, in the shop or in the street, we may keep up our intercourse with Heaven, if it is not our own fault. But the more we see of God, the more cause we see for holy trembling before him.

Verses 20–22

Jacob made a solemn vow on this occasion. In this observe, **1**. Jacob's faith. He trusts that God will be with him, and will keep him; he depends upon it. **2**. Jacob's moderation in his desires. He asks not for soft clothing and dainty meat. If God give us much, we are bound to be thankful, and to use it for him; if he gives us but little, we are bound to be content, and cheerfully to enjoy him in it. **3**. Jacob's piety, and his regard to God, appear in what he desired, that God would be with him, and keep him. We need desire no more to make us easy and happy. Also his resolution is, to cleave to the Lord, as his God in covenant. When we receive more than common mercy from God, we should abound in gratitude to him. The tenth is a fit proportion to be devoted to God, and employed for him; though it may be more or less, as God prospers us, **1**Co **16**:**2**. Let us then remember our Bethels, how we stand engaged by solemn vows to yield ourselves to the Lord, to take him for our God, and to devote all we have and are to his glory!

Chapter 29

Verses 1–8

Jacob proceeded cheerfully in his journey, after the sweet communion he had with God at Beth-el. Providence brought him to the field where his uncle's flocks were to be watered. What is said of the care of the shepherds for their sheep, may remind us of the tender concern which our Lord Jesus, the great Shepherd of the sheep, has for his flock the church; for he is the good Shepherd, that knows his sheep, and is known of them. The stone at the well's mouth was to secure it; water was scarce, it was not there for every one's use: but separate interests should not take us from helping one another. When all the shepherds came together with their flocks, then, like loving neighbours, they watered their flocks together. The law of kindness in the tongue has a commanding power, Pr **31**:**26**. Jacob was civil to these strangers, and he found them civil to him.

Verses 9–14

See Rachel's humility and industry. Nobody needs to be ashamed of honest, useful labour, nor ought it to hinder any one's preferment. When Jacob understood that this was his kinswoman, he was very ready to serve her. Laban, though not the best humoured, bade him welcome, and was satisfied with the account Jacob gave of himself. While we avoid being foolishly ready to believe every thing which is told us, we must take heed of being uncharitably suspicious.

Verses 15–30

During the month that Jacob spent as a guest, he was not idle. Wherever we are, it is good to employ ourselves in some useful business. Laban was desirous that Jacob should continue with him. Inferior relations must not be imposed upon; it is our duty to reward them. Jacob made known to Laban the affection he had for his daughter Rachel. And having no wordly goods with which to endow her, he promises seven years' service Love makes long and hard services short and easy; hence we read of the labour of love, Heb **6**:**10**. If we know how to value the happiness of heaven, the sufferings of this present time will be as nothing to us. An age of work will be but as a few days to those that love God, and long for Christ's appearing. Jacob, who had imposed upon his father, is imposed upon by Laban, his father-in-law, by a like deception. Herein, how unrighteous soever Laban was, the Lord was righteous: see Jud **1**:**7**. Even the righteous, if they take a false step, are sometimes thus recompensed in the earth. And many who are not, like Jacob, in their marriage, disappointed in person, soon find themselves, as much to their grief, disappointed in the character. The choice of that relation ought to be made with good advice and thought on both sides. There is reason to believe that Laban's excuse was not true. His way of settling the matter made bad worse. Jacob was drawn into the disquiet of multiplying wives. He could not refuse Rachel, for he had espoused her; still less could he refuse Leah. As yet there was no express command against marrying more than one wife. It was in the patriarchs a sin of ignorance; but it will not justify the like practice now, when God's will is plainly made known by the Divine law, Le **18**:**18**, and more fully since, by our Saviour, that one man and woman only must be joined together, **1**Co **7**:**2**.

Verses 31–35

The names Leah gave her children, expressed her respect and regard, both to God and to her husband. Reuben, or See a son, with this thought, Now will my husband love me; Levi, or joined, expecting, Now will my husband be joined unto me. Mutual affection is both the duty and comfort of the married relation; and yoke-fellows should study to recommend themselves to each other, **1**Co **7**:**33**, **34**. She thankfully acknowledges the kind providence of God in hearing her. Whatever supports and comforts us under afflictions, or tends to our deliverance from them, God must be owned in it. Her fourth son she called Judah, or praise, saying, Now will I praise the Lord. This was he, of whom, as concerning the flesh, Christ came. Whatever is the matter of our rejoicing, ought to be the matter of our thanksgiving. Fresh favours should quicken us to praise God for former favours; Now will I praise the Lord more and better than I have done. All our praises must centre in Christ, both as the matter of them, and as the Mediator of them. He descended after the flesh from him whose name was "Praise," and He is our praise. Is Christ formed in my heart? Now will I praise the Lord.

Chapter 30

Verses 1–13

Rachel envied her sister: envy is grieving at the good of another, than which no sin is more hateful to God, or more hurtful to our neighbours and ourselves. She considered not that God made the difference, and that in other things she had the advantage. Let us carefully watch against all the risings and workings of this passion in our minds. Let not our eye be evil towards any of our fellow-servants, because our Master's is good. Jacob loved Rachel, and therefore reproved her for what she said amiss. Faithful reproofs show true affection. God may be to us instead of any creature; but it is sin and folly to place any creature in God's stead, and to place that confidence in any creature, which should be placed in God only. At the persuasion of Rachel, Jacob took Bilhah her handmaid to wife, that, according to the usage of those times, her children might be owned as her mistress's children. Had not Rachel's heart been influenced by evil passions, she would have thought her sister's children nearer to her, and more entitled to her care than Bilhah's. But children whom she had a right to rule, were more desirable to her than children she had more reason to love. As an early instance of her power over these children, she takes pleasure in giving them names that carry in them marks of rivalry with her sister. See what roots of bitterness envy and strife are, and what mischief they make among relations. At the persuasion of Leah, Jacob took Zilpah her handmaid to wife also. See the power of jealousy and rivalship, and admire the wisdom of the Divine appointment, which joins together one man and one woman only; for God hath called us to peace and purity.

Verses 14–24

The desire, good in itself, but often too great and irregular, of being the mother of the promised Seed, with the honour of having many children, and the reproach of being barren, were causes of this unbecoming contest between the sisters. The truth appears to be, that they were influenced by the promises of God to Abraham; whose posterity were promised the richest blessings, and from whom the Messiah was to descend.

Verses 25–43

The fourteen years being gone, Jacob was willing to depart without any provision, except God's promise. But he had in many ways a just claim on Laban's substance, and it was the will of God that he should be provided for from it. He referred his cause to God, rather than agree for stated wages with Laban, whose selfishness was very great. And it would appear that he acted honestly, when none but those of the colours fixed upon should be found among his cattle. Laban selfishly thought that his cattle would produce few different in colour from their own. Jacob's course after this agreement has been considered an instance of his policy and management. But it was done by intimation from God, and as a token of his power. The Lord will one way or another plead the cause of the oppressed, and honour those who simply trust his providence. Neither could Laban complain of Jacob, for he had nothing more than was freely agreed that he should have; nor was he injured, but greatly benefitted by Jacob's services. May all our mercies be received with thanksgiving and prayer, that coming from his bounty, they may lead to his praise.

Chapter 31

Verses 1–21

The affairs of these families are related very minutely, while (what are called) the great events of states and kingdoms at that period, are not mentioned. The Bible teaches people the common duties of life, how to serve God, how to enjoy the blessings he bestows, and to do good in the various stations and duties of life. Selfish men consider themselves robbed of all that goes past them, and covetousness will even swallow up natural affection. Men's overvaluing worldly wealth is that error which is the root of covetousness, envy, and all evil. The men of the world stand in each other's way, and every one seems to be taking away from the rest; hence discontent, envy, and discord. But there are possessions that will suffice for all; happy they who seek them in the first place. In all our removals we should have respect to the command and promise of God. If He be with us, we need not fear. The perils which surround us are so many, that nothing else can really encourage our hearts. To remember favoured seasons of communion with God, is very refreshing when in difficulties; and we should often recollect our vows, that we fail not to fulfil them.

Verses 22–35

God can put a bridle in the mouth of wicked men, to restrain their malice, though he do not change their hearts. Though they have no love to God's people, they will pretend to it, and try to make a merit of necessity. Foolish Laban! to call those things his gods which could be stolen! Enemies may steal our goods, but not our God. Here Laban lays to Jacob's charge things that he knew not. Those who commit their cause to God, are not forbidden to plead it themselves with meekness and fear. When we read of Rachel's stealing her father's images, what a scene of iniquity opens! The family of Nahor, who left the idolatrous Chaldees; is this family itself become idolatrous? It is even so. The truth seems to be, that they were like some in after-times, who sware by the Lord and by Malcham, Zep **1**:**5**; and like others in our times, who wish to serve both God and mammon. Great numbers will acknowledge the true God in words, but their hearts and houses are the abodes of spiritual idolatry. When a man gives himself up to covetousness, like Laban, the world is his god; and he has only to reside among gross idolaters in order to become one, or at least a favourer of their abominations.

Verses 36–42

If Jacob were willingly consumed with heat in the day, and frost by night, to become the son-in-law of Laban, what should we refuse to endure, to become the sons of God? Jacob speaks of God as the God of his father; he thought himself unworthy to be regarded, but was beloved for his father's sake. He calls him the God of Abraham, and the fear of Isaac; for Abraham was dead, and gone to that world where perfect love casts out fear; but Isaac was yet alive, sanctifying the Lord in his heart, as his fear and his dread.

Verses 43–55

Laban could neither justify himself nor condemn Jacob, therefore desires to hear no more of that matter. He is not willing to own himself in fault, as he ought to have done. But he proposes a covenant of friendship between them, to which Jacob readily agrees. A heap of stones was raised, to keep up the memory of the event, writing being then not known or little used. A sacrifice of peace offerings was offered. Peace with God puts true comfort into our peace with our friends. They did eat bread together, partaking of the feast upon the sacrifice. In ancient times covenants of friendship were ratified by the parties eating and drinking together. God is judge between contending parties, and he will judge righteously; whoever do wrong, it is at their peril. They gave a new name to the place, The heap of witness. After this angry parley, they part friends. God is often better to us than our fears, and overrules the spirits of men in our favour, beyond what we could have expected; for it is not in vain to trust in him.

Chapter 32

Verses 1–8

The angels of God appeared to Jacob, to encourage him with the assurance of the Divine protection. When God designs his people for great trials, he prepares them by great comforts. While Jacob, to whom the promise belonged, had been in hard service, Esau was become a prince. Jacob sent a message, showing that he did not insist upon the birth-right. Yielding pacifies great offences, Ec **10**:**4**. We must not refuse to speak respectfully, even to those unjustly angry with us. Jacob received an account of Esau's warlike preparations against him, and was greatly afraid. A lively sense of danger, and quickening fear arising from it, may be found united with humble confidence in God's power and promise.

Verses 9–23

Times of fear should be times of prayer: whatever causes fear, should drive us to our knees, to our God. Jacob had lately seen his guards of angels, but in this distress he applied to God, not to them; he knew they were his fellow-servants, Re **22**:**9**. There cannot be a better pattern for true prayer than this. Here is a thankful acknowledgement of former undeserved favours; a humble confession of unworthiness; a plain statement of his fears and distress; a full reference of the whole affair to the Lord, and resting all his hopes on him. The best we can say to God in prayer, is what he has said to us. Thus he made the name of the Lord his strong tower, and could not but be safe. Jacob's fear did not make him sink into despair, nor did his prayer make him presume upon God's mercy, without the use of means. God answers prayers by teaching us to order our affairs aright. To pacify Esau, Jacob sent him a present. We must not despair of reconciling ourselves to those most angry against us.

Verses 24–32

A great while before day, Jacob being alone, more fully spread his fears before God in prayer. While thus employed, One in the likeness of a man wrestled with him. When the spirit helpeth our infirmities, and our earnest and vast desires can scarcely find words to utter them, and we still mean more than we can express, then prayer is indeed wrestling with God. However tried or discouraged, we shall prevail; and prevailing with Him in prayer, we shall prevail against all enemies that strive with us. Nothing requires more vigour and unceasing exertion than wrestling. It is an emblem of the true spirit of faith and prayer. Jacob kept his ground; though the struggle continued long, this did not shake his faith, nor silence his prayer. He will have a blessing, and had rather have all his bone put out of joint than go away without one. Those who would have the blessing of Christ, must resolve to take no denial. The fervent prayer is the effectual prayer. The Angel puts a lasting mark of honour upon him, by changing his name. Jacob signifies a supplanter. From henceforth he shall be celebrated, not for craft and artful management, but for true valour. Thou shalt be called Israel, a prince with God, a name greater than those of the great men of the earth. He is a prince indeed that is a prince with God; those are truly honourable that are mighty in prayer. Having power with God, he shall have power with men too; he shall prevail, and gain Esau's favour. Jacob gives a new name to the place. He calls it Peniel, the face of God, because there he had seen the appearance of God, and obtained the favour of God. It becomes those whom God honours, to admire his grace towards them. The Angel who wrestled with Jacob was the second Person in the sacred Trinity, who was afterwards God manifest in the flesh, and who, dwelling in human nature, is called Immanuel, Ho **12**:**4**, **5**. Jacob halted on his thigh. It might serve to keep him from being lifted up with the abundance of the revelations. The sun rose on Jacob: it is sun-rise with that soul, which has had communion with God.

Chapter 33

Verses 1–16

Jacob, having by prayer committed his case to God, went on his way. Come what will, nothing can come amiss to him whose heart is fixed, trusting in God. Jacob bowed to Esau. A humble, submissive behaviour goes far towards turning away wrath. Esau embraced Jacob. God has the hearts of all men in his hands, and can turn them when and how he pleases. It is not in vain to trust in God, and to call upon him in the day of trouble. And when a man's ways please the Lord he maketh even his enemies to be at peace with him. Esau receives Jacob as a brother, and much tenderness passes between them. Esau asks, Who are those with thee? To this common question, Jacob spoke like himself, like a man whose eyes are ever directed towards the Lord. Jacob urged Esau, though his fear was over, and he took his present. It is well when men's religion makes them generous, free-hearted, and open-handed. But Jacob declined Esau's offer to accompany him. It is not desirable to be too intimate with superior ungodly relations, who will expect us to join in their vanities, or at least to wink at them, though they blame, and perhaps mock at, our religion. Such will either be a snare to us, or offended with us. We shall venture the loss of all things, rather than endanger our souls, if we know their value; rather than renounce Christ, if we truly love him. And let Jacob's care and tender attention to his family and flocks remind us of the good Shepherd of our souls, who gathers the lambs with his arm, and carries them in his bosom, and gently leads those that are with young, Isa **40**:**11**. As parents, teachers or pastors, we should all follow his example.

Verses 17–20

Jacob did not content himself with words of thanks for God's favour to him, but gave real thanks. Also he kept up religion, and the worship of God in his family. Where we have a tent, God must have an altar. Jacob dedicated this altar to the honour of El-elohe-Israel, God, the God of Israel; to the honour of God, the only living and true God; and to the honour of the God of Israel, as a God in covenant with him. Israel's God is Israel's glory. Blessed be his name, he is still the mighty God, the God of Israel. May we praise his name, and rejoice in his love, through our pilgrimage here on earth, and for ever in the heavenly Canaan.

Chapter 34

Verses 1–19

Young persons, especially females, are never so safe and well off as under the care of pious parents. Their own ignorance, and the flattery and artifices of designing, wicked people, who are ever laying snares for them, expose them to great danger. They are their own enemies if they desire to go abroad, especially alone, among strangers to true religion. Those parents are very wrong who do not hinder their children from needlessly exposing themselves to danger. Indulged children, like Dinah, often become a grief and shame to their families. Her pretence was, to see the daughters of the land, to see how they dressed, and how they danced, and what was fashionable among them; she went to see, yet that was not all, she went to be seen too. She went to get acquaintance with the Canaanites, and to learn their ways. See what came of Dinah's gadding. The beginning of sin is as the letting forth of water. How great a matter does a little fire kindle! We should carefully avoid all occasions of sin and approaches to it.

Verses 20–31

The Shechemites submitted to the sacred rite, only to serve a turn, to please their prince, and to enrich themselves, and it was just with God to bring punishment upon them. As nothing secures us better than true religion, so nothing exposes us more than religion only pretended to. But Simeon and Levi were most unrighteous. Those who act wickedly, under the pretext of religion, are the worst enemies of the truth, and harden the hearts of many to destruction. The crimes of others form no excuse for us. Alas! how one sin leads on to another, and, like flames of fire, spread desolation in every direction! Foolish pleasures lead to seduction; seduction produces wrath; wrath thirsts for revenge; the thirst of revenge has recourse to treachery; treachery issues in murder; and murder is followed by other lawless actions. Were we to trace the history of unlawful commerce between the sexes, we should find it, more than any other sin, ending in blood.

Chapter 35

Verses 1–5

Beth-el was forgotten. But as many as God loves, he will remind of neglected duties, one way or other, by conscience or by providences. When we have vowed a vow to God, it is best not to defer the payment of it; yet better late than never. Jacob commanded his household to prepare, not only for the journey and removal, but for religious services. Masters of families should use their authority to keep up religion in their families, Jos **24**:**15**. They must put away strange gods. In families where there is a face of religion, and an altar to God, yet many times there is much amiss, and more strange gods than one would suppose. They must be clean, and change their garments. These were but outward ceremonies, signifying the purifying and change of the heart. What are clean clothes, and new clothes, without a clean heart, and a new heart? If Jacob had called for these idols sooner, they had parted with them sooner. Sometimes attempts for reformation succeed better than we could have thought. Jacob buried their images. We must be wholly separated from our sins, as we are from those that are dead and buried out of sight. He removed from Shechem to Beth-el. Though the Canaanites were very angry against the sons of Jacob for their barbarous usage of the Shechemites, yet they were so kept back by Divine power, that they could not take the opportunity now offered to avenge them. The way of duty is the way of safety. When we are about God's work, we are under special protection; God is with us, while we are with him; and if He be for us, who can be against us? God governs the world more by secret terrors on men's minds than we are aware of.

Verses 6–15

The comfort the saints have in holy ordinances, is not so much from Beth-el, the house of God, as from El-beth-el, the God of the house. The ordinances are empty things, if we do not meet with God in them. There Jacob buried Deborah, Rebekah's nurse. She died much lamented. Old servants in a family, that have in their time been faithful and useful, ought to be respected. God appeared to Jacob. He renewed the covenant with him. I am God Almighty, God all-sufficient, able to make good the promise in due time, and to support thee and provide for thee in the mean time. Two things are promised; that he should be the father of a great nation, and that he should be the master of a good land. These two promises had a spiritual signification, which Jacob had some notion of, though not so clear and distinct as we now have. Christ is the promised Seed, and heaven is the promised land; the former is the foundation, and the latter the top-stone, of all God's favours.

Verses 16–20

Rachel had passionately said, Give me children, or else I die; and now that she had children, she died! The death of the body is but the departure of the soul to the world of spirits. When shall we learn that it is God alone who really knows what is best for his people, and that in all worldly affairs the safest path for the Christian is to say from the heart, It is the Lord, let him do what seemeth him good. Here alone is our safety and our comfort, to know no will but his. Her dying lips called her newborn son Ben-oni, the son of my sorrow; and many a son proves to be the heaviness of her that bare him. Children are enough the sorrow of their mothers; they should, therefore, when they grow up, study to be their joy, and so, if possible, to make them some amends. But Jacob, because he would not renew the sorrowful remembrance of the mother's death every time he called his son, changed his name to Benjamin, the son of my right hand: that is, very dear to me; the support of my age, like the staff in my right hand.

Verses 21–29

What a sore affliction Reuben's sin was, is shown, "and Israel heard it." No more is said, but that is enough. Reuben thought that his father would never hear of it; but those that promise themselves secrecy in sin, are generally disappointed. The age and death of Isaac are recorded, though he died not till after Joseph was sold into Egypt. Isaac lived about forty years after he had made his will, chap. **27**:**2**. We shall not die an hour the sooner, but much the better, for timely setting our hearts and houses in order. Particular notice is taken of the agreement of Esau and Jacob at their father's funeral, to show how God had wonderfully changed Esau's mind. It is awful to behold relations, sometimes for a little of this world's goods, disputing over the graves of their friends, while they are near going to the grave themselves.

Chapter 36

Esau and his descendants.

—The registers in this chapter show the faithfulness of God to his promise to Abraham. Esau is here called Edom, that name which kept up the remembrance of his selling his birth-right for a mess of pottage. Esau continued the same profane despiser of heavenly things. In outward prosperity and honour, the children of the covenant are often behind, and those that are out of the covenant get the start. We may suppose it a trial to the faith of God's Israel, to hear of the pomp and power of the kings of Edom, while they were bond-slaves in Egypt; but those that look for great things from God, must be content to wait for them; God's time is the best time. Mount Seir is called the land of their possession. Canaan was at this time only the land of promise. Seir was in the possession of the Edomites. The children of this world have their all in hand, and nothing in hope, Lu **16**:**25**; while the children of God have their all in hope, and next to nothing in hand. But, all things considered, it is beyond compare better to have Canaan in promise, than mount Seir in possession.

Chapter 37

Verses 1–4

In Joseph's history we see something of Christ, who was first humbled and then exalted. It also shows the lot of Christians, who must through many tribulations enter into the kingdom. It is a history that has none like it, for displaying the various workings of the human mind, both good and bad, and the singular providence of God in making use of them for fulfilling his purposes. Though Joseph was his father's darling, yet he was not bred up in idleness. Those do not truly love their children, who do not use them to business, and labour, and hardships. The fondling of children is with good reason called the spoiling of them. Those who are trained up to do nothing, are likely to be good for nothing. But Jacob made known his love, by dressing Joseph finer than the rest of his children. It is wrong for parents to make a difference between one child and another, unless there is great cause for it, by the children's dutifulness, or undutifulness. When parents make a difference, children soon notice it, and it leads to quarrels in families. Jacob's sons did that, when they were from under his eye, which they durst not have done at home with him; but Joseph gave his father an account of their ill conduct, that he might restrain them. Not as a tale-bearer, to sow discord, but as a faithful brother.

Verses 5–11

God gave Joseph betimes the prospect of his advancement, to support and comfort him under his long and grievous troubles. Observe, Joseph dreamed of his preferment, but he did not dream of his imprisonment. Thus many young people, when setting out in the world, think of nothing but prosperity and pleasure, and never dream of trouble. His brethren rightly interpreted the dream, though they abhorred the interpretation of it. While they committed crimes in order to defeat it, they were themselves the instruments of accomplishing it. Thus the Jews understood what Christ said of his kingdom. Determined that he should not reign over them, they consulted to put him to death; and by his crucifixion, made way for the exaltation they designed to prevent.

Verses 12–22

How readily does Joseph wait his father's orders! Those children who are best beloved by their parents, should be the most ready to obey them. See how deliberate Joseph's brethren were against him. They thought to slay him from malice aforethought, and in cold blood. Whosoever hateth his brother is a murderer, **1**Jo **3**:**15**. The sons of Jacob hated their brother because their father loved him. New occasions, as his dreams and the like, drew them on further; but this laid rankling in their hearts, till they resolved on his death. God has all hearts in his hands. Reuben had most reason to be jealous of Joseph, for he was the first-born; yet he proves his best friend. God overruled all to serve his own purpose, of making Joseph an instrument to save much people alive. Joseph was a type of Christ; for though he was the beloved Son of his Father, and hated by a wicked world, yet the Father sent him out of his bosom to visit us in great humility and love. He came from heaven to earth to seek and save us; yet then malicious plots were laid against him. His own not only received him not, but crucified him. This he submitted to, as a part of his design to redeem and save us.

Verses 23–30

They threw Joseph into a pit, to perish there with hunger and cold; so cruel were their tender mercies. They slighted him when he was in distress, and were not grieved for the affliction of Joseph, see Am **6**:**6**; for when he was pining in the pit, they sat down to eat bread. They felt no remorse of conscience for the sin. But the wrath of man shall praise God, and the remainder of wrath he will restrain, Ps **76**:**10**. Joseph's brethren were wonderfully restrained from murdering him, and their selling him as wonderfully turned to God's praise.

Verses 31–36

When Satan has taught men to commit one sin, he teaches them to try to conceal it with another; to hide theft and murder, with lying and false oaths: but he that covers his sin shall not prosper long. Joseph's brethren kept their own and one another's counsel for some time; but their villany came to light at last, and it is here published to the world. To grieve their father, they sent him Joseph's coat of colours; and he hastily thought, on seeing the bloody coat, that Joseph was rent in pieces. Let those that know the heart of a parent, suppose the agony of poor Jacob. His sons basely pretended to comfort him, but miserable, hypocritical comforters were they all. Had they really desired to comfort him, they might at once have done it, by telling the truth. The heart is strangely hardened by the deceitfulness of sin. Jacob refused to be comforted. Great affection to any creature prepares for so much the greater affliction, when it is taken from us, or made bitter to us: undue love commonly ends in undue grief. It is the wisdom of parents not to bring up children delicately, they know not to what hardships they may be brought before they die. From the whole of this chapter we see with wonder the ways of Providence. The malignant brothers seem to have gotten their ends; the merchants, who care not what they deal in so that they gain, have also obtained theirs; and Potiphar, having got a fine young slave, has obtained his! But God's designs are, by these means, in train for execution. This event shall end in Israel's going down to Egypt; that ends in their deliverance by Moses; that in setting up the true religion in the world; and that in the spread of it among all nations by the gospel. Thus the wrath of man shall praise the Lord, and the remainder thereof will he restrain.

Chapter 38

The profligate conduct of Judah and his family.

—This chapter gives an account of Judah and his family, and such an account it is, that it seems a wonder that of all Jacob's sons, our Lord should spring out of Judah, Heb **7**:**14**. But God will show that his choice is of grace and not of merit, and that Christ came into the world to save sinners, even the chief. Also, that the worthiness of Christ is of himself, and not from his ancestors. How little reason had the Jews, who were so called from this Judah, to boast as they did, Joh **8**:**41**. What awful examples the Lord proclaims in his punishments, of his utter displeasure at sin! Let us seek grace from God to avoid every appearance of sin. And let that state of humbleness to which Jesus submitted, when he came to put away sin by the sacrifice of himself, in appointing such characters as those here recorded, to be his ancestors, endear the Redeemer to our hearts.

Chapter 39

Verses 1–6

Our enemies may strip us of outward distinctions and ornaments; but wisdom and grace cannot be taken from us. They may separate us from friends, relatives, and country; but they cannot take from us the presence of the Lord. They may shut us from outward blessings, rob us of liberty, and confine us in dungeons; but they cannot shut us out from communion with God, from the throne of grace, or take from us the blessings of salvation. Joseph was blessed, wonderfully blessed, even in the house where he was a slave. God's presence with us, makes all we do prosperous. Good men are the blessings of the place where they live; good servants may be so, though mean and lightly esteemed. The prosperity of the wicked is, one way or other, for the sake of the godly. Here was a wicked family blessed for the sake of one good servant in it.

Verses 7–12

Beauty either in men or women, often proves a snare both to themselves and others. This forbids pride in it, and requires constant watchfulness against the temptation that attends it. We have great need to make a covenant with our eyes, lest the eyes infect the heart. When lust has got power, decency, and reputation, and conscience, are all sacrificed. Potiphar's wife showed that her heart was fully set to do evil. Satan, when he found he could not overcome Joseph with the troubles and the frowns of the world, for in them he still held fast his principle, assaulted him with pleasures, which have ruined more than the former. But Joseph, by the grace of God, was enabled to resist and overcome this temptation; and his escape was as great an instance of the Divine power, as the deliverance of the three children out of the fiery furnace. This sin was one which might most easily beset him. The tempter was his mistress, one whose favour would help him forward; and it was at his utmost peril if he slighted her, and made her his enemy. The time and place favoured the temptation. To all this was added frequent, constant urging. The almighty grace of God enabled Joseph to overcome this assault of the enemy. He urges what he owed both to God and his master. We are bound in honour, as well as justice and gratitude, not in any thing to wrong those who place trust in us, how secretly soever it may be done. He would not offend his God. Three arguments Joseph urges upon himself. **1**. He considers who he was that was tempted. One in covenant with God, who professed religion and relation to him. **2**. What the sin was to which he was tempted. Others might look upon it as a small matter; but Joseph did not so think of it. Call sin by its own name, and never lessen it. Let sins of this nature always be looked upon as great wickedness, as exceedingly sinful. **3**. Against whom he was tempted to sin, against God. Sin is against God, against his nature and his dominion, against his love and his design. Those that love God, for this reason hate sin. The grace of God enabled Joseph to overcome the temptation, by avoiding the temper. He would not stay to parley with the temptation, but fled from it, as escaping for his life. If we mean not to do iniquity, let us flee as a bird from the snare, and as a roe from the hunter.

Verses 13–18

Joseph's mistress, having tried in vain to make him a guilty man, endeavoured to be avenged on him. Those that have broken the bonds of modesty, will never be held by the bonds of truth. It is no new thing for the best of men to be falsely accused of the worst of crimes, by those who themselves are the worst of criminals. It is well there is a day of discovery coming, in which all shall appear in their true characters.

Verses 19–23

Joseph's master believed the accusation. Potiphar, it is likely, chose that prison, because it was the worst; but God designed to open the way to Joseph's honour. Joseph was owned and righted by his God. He was away from all his friends and relations; he had none to help or comfort him; but the Lord was with Joseph, and showed him mercy. Those that have a good conscience in a prison, have a good God there. God gave him favour in the sight of the keeper of the prison; he trusted him to manage the affairs of the prison. A good man will do good wherever he is, and will be a blessing even in bonds and banishment. Let us not forget, through Joseph, to look unto Jesus, who suffered being tempted, yet without sin; who was slandered, and persecuted, and imprisoned, but without cause; who by the cross ascended to the throne. May we be enabled to follow the same path in submitting and in suffering, to the same place of glory.

Chapter 40

Verses 1–19

It was not so much the prison that made the butler and baker sad, as their dreams. God has more ways than one to sadden the spirits. Joseph had compassion towards them. Let us be concerned for the sadness of our brethren's countenances. It is often a relief to those that are in trouble to be noticed. Also learn to look into the causes of our own sorrow. Is there a good reason? Is there not comfort sufficient to balance it, whatever it is? Why art thou cast down, O my soul? Joseph was careful to ascribe the glory to God. The chief butler's dream foretold his advancement. The chief baker's dream his death. It was not Joseph's fault that he brought the baker no better tidings. And thus ministers are but interpreters; they cannot make the thing otherwise than it is: if they deal faithfully, and their message prove unpleasing, it is not their fault. Joseph does not reflect upon his brethren that sold him; nor does he reflect on the wrong done him by his mistress and his master, but mildly states his own innocence. When we are called on to clear ourselves, we should carefully avoid, as much as may be, speaking ill of others. Let us be content to prove ourselves innocent, and not upbraid others with their guilt.

Verses 20–23

Joseph's interpretation of the dreams came to pass on the very day fixed. On Pharaoh's birth-day, all his servants attended him, and then the cases of these two came to be looked into. We may all profitably take notice of our birth-days, with thankfulness for the mercies of our birth, sorrow for the sinfulness of our lives, and expectation of the day of our death, as better than the day of our birth. But it seems strange that worldly people, who are so fond of living here, should rejoice at the end of one year after another of their short span of life. A Christian has cause to rejoice that he was born, also that he comes nearer to the end of his sin and sorrow, and nearer to his everlasting happiness. The chief butler remembered not Joseph, but forgot him. Joseph had deserved well at his hands, yet he forgot him. We must not think it strange, if in this world we have hatred shown us for our love, and slights for our kindness. See how apt those who are themselves at ease are to forget others in distress. Joseph learned by his disappointment to trust in God only. We cannot expect too little from man, nor too much from God. Let us not forget the sufferings, promises, and love of our Redeemer. We blame the chief butler's ingratitude to Joseph, yet we ourselves act much more ungratefully to the Lord Jesus. Joseph had but foretold the chief butler's enlargement, but Christ wrought out ours; he mediated with the King of Kings for us; yet we forget him, though often reminded of him, and though we have promised never to forget him. Thus ill do we requite Him, like foolish people and unwise.

Chapter 41

Verses 1–8

The means of Joseph's being freed from prison were Pharaoh's dreams, as here related. Now that God no longer speaks to us in that way, it is no matter how little we either heed dreams, or tell them. The telling of foolish dreams can make no better than foolish talk. But these dreams showed that they were sent of God; when he awoke, Pharaoh's spirit was troubled.

Verses 9–32

God's time for the enlargement of his people is the fittest time. If the chief butler had got Joseph to be released from prison, it is probable he would have gone back to the land of the Hebrews. Then he had neither been so blessed himself, nor such a blessing to his family, as afterwards he proved. Joseph, when introduced to Pharaoh, gives honour to God. Pharaoh had dreamed that he stood upon the bank of the river Nile, and saw the kine, both the fat ones, and the lean ones, come out of the river. Egypt has no rain, but the plenty of the year depends upon the overflowing of the river Nile. See how many ways Providence has of dispensing its gifts; yet our dependence is still the same upon the First Cause, who makes every creature what it is to us, be it rain or river. See to what changes the comforts of this life are subject. We cannot be sure that to-morrow shall be as this day, or next year as this. We must learn how to want, as well as how to abound. Mark the goodness of God in sending the seven years of plenty before those of famine, that provision might be made. The produce of the earth is sometimes more, and sometimes less; yet, take one with another, he that gathers much, has nothing over; and he that gathers little, has no lack, Ex **16**:**18**. And see the perishing nature of our worldly enjoyments. The great harvests of the years of plenty were quite lost, and swallowed up in the years of famine; and that which seemed very much, yet did but just serve to keep the people alive. There is bread which lasts to eternal life, which it is worth while to labour for. They that make the things of this world their good things, will find little pleasure in remembering that they have received them.

Verses 33–45

Joseph gave good advice to Pharaoh. Fair warning should always be followed by good counsel. God has in his word told us of a day of trial before us, when we shall need all the grace we can have. Now, therefore, provide accordingly. Pharaoh gave Joseph an honourable testimony. He is a man in whom the spirit of God is; and such men ought to be valued. Pharaoh puts upon Joseph marks of honour. He gave him such a name as spoke the value he had for him, Zaphnath-paaneah, "a revealer of secrets." This preferment of Joseph encourages all to trust in God. Some translate Joseph's new name, "the saviour of the world." The brightest glories, even of the upper world, are put upon Christ, the highest trust lodged in his hand, and all power given him, both in heaven and earth.

Verses 46–57

In the names of his two sons, Manasseh and Ephraim, Joseph owned the Divine providence. **1**. He was made to forget his misery. **2**. He was made fruitful in the land of his affliction. The seven plenteous years came, and were ended. We ought to look forward to the end of the days, both of our prosperity and of our opportunity. We must not be secure in prosperity, nor slothful in making good use of opportunity. Years of plenty will end; what thy hand finds to do, do it; and gather in gathering time. The dearth came, and the famine was not only in Egypt, but in other lands. Joseph was diligent in laying up, while the plenty lasted. He was prudent and careful in giving out, when the famine came. Joseph was engaged in useful and important labours. Yet it was in the midst of this his activity that his father Jacob said, Joseph is not! What a large portion of our troubles would be done away if we knew the whole truth! Let these events lead us to Jesus. There is a famine of the bread of life throughout the whole earth. Go to Jesus, and what he bids you, do. Attend to His voice, apply to him; he will open his treasures, and satisfy with goodness the hungry soul of every age and nation, without money and without price. But those who slight this provision must starve, and his enemies will be destroyed.

Chapter 42

Verses 1–6

Jacob saw the corn his neighbours had bought in Egypt, and brought home. It is a spur to exertion to see others supplied. Shall others get food for their souls, and shall we starve while it is to be had? Having discovered where help is to be had, we should apply for it without delay, without shrinking from labour, or grudging expense, especially as regards our never-dying souls. There is provision in Christ; but we must come to him, and seek it from him.

Verses 7–20

Joseph was hard upon his brethren, not from a spirit of revenge, but to bring them to repentance. Not seeing his brother Benjamin, he suspected that they had made away with him, and he gave them occasion to speak of their father and brother. God, in his providence, sometimes seems harsh with those he loves, and speaks roughly to those for whom yet he has great mercy in store. Joseph settled at last, that one of them should be left, and the rest go home and fetch Benjamin. It was a very encouraging word he said to them, "I fear God;" as if he had said, You may be assured I will do you no wrong; I dare not, for I know there is one higher than I. With those that fear God, we may expect fair dealing.

Verses 21–24

The office of conscience is to bring to mind things long since said and done. When the guilt of this sin of Joseph's brethren was fresh, they made light of it, and sat down to eat bread; but now, long afterward, their consciences accused them of it. See the good of afflictions; they often prove the happy means of awakening conscience, and bringing sin to our remembrance. Also, the evil of guilt as to our brethren. Conscience now reproached them for it. Whenever we think we have wrong done us, we ought to remember the wrong we have done to others. Reuben alone remembered with comfort, that he had done what he could to prevent the mischief. When we share with others in their sufferings, it will be a comfort if we have the testimony of our consciences for us, that we did not share in their evil deeds, but in our places witnessed against them. Joseph retired to weep. Though his reason directed that he should still carry himself as a stranger, because they were not as yet humbled enough, yet natural affection could not but work.

Verses 25–28

The brethren came for corn, and corn they had: not only so, but every man had his money given back. Thus Christ, like Joseph, gives out supplies without money and without price. The poorest are invited to buy. But guilty consciences are apt to take good providences in a bad sense; to put wrong meanings even upon things that make for them.

Verses 29–38

Here is the report Jacob's sons made to their father. It troubled the good man. Even the bundles of money Joseph returned, in kindness, to his father, frightened him. He laid the fault upon his sons; knowing them, he feared they had provoked the Egyptians, and wrongfully brought home their money. Jacob plainly distrusted his sons, remembering that he never saw Joseph since he had been with them. It is bad with a family, when children behave so ill that their parents know not how to trust them. Jacob gives up Joseph for gone, and Simeon and Benjamin as in danger; and concludes, All these things are against me. It proved otherwise, that all these things were for him, were working together for his good, and the good of his family. We often think that to be against us, which is really for us. We are afflicted in body, estate, name, and in our relations; and think all these things are against us, whereas they are really working for us a weight of glory. Thus does the Lord Jesus conceal himself and his favour, thus he rebukes and chastens those for whom he has purposes of love. By sharp corrections and humbling convictions he will break the stoutness and mar the pride of the heart, and bring to true repentance. Yet before sinners fully know him, or taste that he is gracious, he consults their good, and sustains their souls, to wait for him. May we do thus, never yielding to discouragement, determining to seek no other refuge, and humbling ourselves more and more under his mighty hand. In due time he will answer our petitions, and do for us more than we can expect.

Chapter 43

Verses 1–14

Jacob urges his sons to go and buy a little food; now, in time of dearth, a little must suffice. Judah urges that Benjamin should go with them. It is not against the honour and duty children owe their parents, humbly to advise them, and when needful, to reason with them. Jacob saw the necessity of the case, and yielded. His prudence and justice appeared in three things. **1**. He sent back the money they had found in the sack. Honesty obliges us to restore not only that which comes to us by our own fault, but that which comes to us by the mistakes of others. Though we get it by oversight, if we keep it when the oversight is discovered, it is kept by deceit. **2**. He sent as much again as they took the time before; the price of corn might be risen, or they might have to pay a ransom for Simeon. **3**. He sent a present of such things as the land afforded, and as were scarce in Egypt, balm, and honey, &c. Providence dispenses not its gifts to all alike. But honey and spice will never make up the want of bread-corn. The famine was sore in Canaan, yet they had balm and myrrh, &c. We may live well enough upon plain food, without dainties; but we cannot live upon dainties without plain food. Let us thank God that what is most needful and useful, generally is most cheap and common. Though men value very highly their gold and silver, and the luxuries which are counted the best fruits of every land, yet in a time of famine they willingly barter them for bread. And how little will earthly good things stand us in stead in the day of wrath! How ready should we be to renounce them all, as loss, for the excellency of the knowledge of Jesus Christ! Our way to prevail with man is by first prevailing with the Lord in fervent prayer. But, Thy will be done, should close every petition for the mercies of this life, or against the afflictions of this life.

Verses 15–25

Jacob's sons went down the second time into Egypt to buy corn. If we should ever know what a famine of the word means, let us not think it much to travel as far for spiritual food, as they did for bodily food. Joseph's steward had orders from his master to take them to his house. Even this frightened them. Those that are guilty make the worst of every thing. But the steward encouraged them. It appears, from what he said, that by his good master he was brought to the knowledge of the true God, the God of the Hebrews. Religious servants should take all fit occasions to speak of God and his providence, with reverence and seriousness.

Verses 26–34

Observe the great respect Joseph's brethren paid to him. Thus were Joseph's dreams more and more fulfilled. Joseph showed great kindness to them. He treated them nobly; but see here the early distance between Jews and gentiles. In a day of famine, it is enough to be fed; but they were feasted. Their cares and fears were now over, and they ate their bread with joy, reckoning they were upon good terms with the lord of the land. If God accept our works, our present, we have reason to be cheerful. Joseph showed special regard for Benjamin, that he might try whether his brethren would envy him. It must be our rule, to be content with what we have, and not to grieve at what others have. Thus Jesus shows those whom he loves, more and more of their need. He makes them see that he is their only refuge from destruction. He overcomes their unwillingness, and brings them to himself. Then, as he sees good, he gives them some taste of his love, and welcomes them to the provisions of his house, as an earnest of what he further intends for them.

Chapter 44

Verses 1–17

Joseph tried how his brethren felt towards Benjamin. Had they envied and hated the other son of Rachel as they had hated him, and if they had the same want of feeling towards their father Jacob as heretofore, they would now have shown it. When the cup was found upon Benjamin, they would have a pretext for leaving him to be a slave. But we cannot judge what men are now, by what they have been formerly; nor what they will do, by what they have done. The steward charged them with being ungrateful, rewarding evil for good; with folly, in taking away the cup of daily use, which would soon be missed, and diligent search made for it; for so it may be read, Is not this it in which my lord drinketh, as having a particular fondness for it, and for which he would search thoroughly? Or, By which, leaving it carelessly at your table, he would make trial whether you were honest men or not? They throw themselves upon Joseph's mercy, and acknowledge the righteousness of God, perhaps thinking of the injury they had formerly done to Joseph, for which they thought God was now reckoning with them. Even in afflictions wherein we believe ourselves wronged by men, we must own that God is righteous, and finds out our sin.

Verses 18–34

Had Joseph been, as Judah supposed him, an utter stranger to the family, he could not but be wrought upon by his powerful reasonings. But neither Jacob nor Benjamin need an intercessor with Joseph; for he himself loved them. Judah's faithful cleaving to Benjamin, now, in his distress, was recompensed long afterwards by the tribe of Benjamin keeping with the tribe of Judah, when the other tribes deserted it. The apostle, when discoursing of the mediation of Christ, observes, that our Lord sprang out of Judah, Heb **7**:**14**; and he not only made intercession for the transgressors, but he became a Surety for them, testifying therein tender concern, both for his Father and for his brethren. Jesus, the great antitype of Joseph, humbles and proves his people, even after they have had some tastes of his loving-kindness. He brings their sins to their remembrance, that they may exercise and show repentance, and feel how much they owe to his mercy.

Chapter 45

Verses 1–15

Joseph let Judah go on, and heard all he had to say. He found his brethren humbled for their sins, mindful of himself, for Judah had mentioned him twice in his speech, respectful to their father, and very tender of their brother Benjamin. Now they were ripe for the comfort he designed, by making himself known. Joseph ordered all his attendants to withdraw. Thus Christ makes himself and his loving-kindness known to his people, out of the sight and hearing of the world. Joseph shed tears of tenderness and strong affection, and with these threw off that austerity with which he had hitherto behaved toward his brethren. This represents the Divine compassion toward returning penitents. "I am Joseph, your brother." This would humble them yet more for their sin in selling him, but would encourage them to hope for kind treatment. Thus, when Christ would convince Paul, he said, I am Jesus; and when he would comfort his disciples, he said, It is I, be not afraid. When Christ manifests himself to his people, he encourages them to draw near to him with a true heart. Joseph does so, and shows them, that whatever they thought to do against him, God had brought good out of it. Sinners must grieve and be angry with themselves for their sins, though God brings good out of it, for that is no thanks to them. The agreement between all this, and the case of a sinner, on Christ's manifesting himself to his soul, is very striking. He does not, on this account, think sin a less, but a greater evil; and yet he is so armed against despair, as even to rejoice in what God hath wrought, while he trembles in thinking of the dangers and destruction from which he has escaped. Joseph promises to take care of his father and all the family. It is the duty of children, if the necessity of their parents at any time require it, to support and supply them to the utmost of their ability; this is showing piety at home, **1**Ti **5**:**4**. After Joseph had embraced Benjamin, he caressed them all, and then his brethren talked with him freely of all the affairs of their father's house. After the tokens of true reconciliation with the Lord Jesus, sweet communion with him follows.

Verses 16–24

Pharaoh was kind to Joseph, and to his relations for his sake. Egypt would make up the losses of their removal. Thus those for whom Christ intends his heavenly glory, ought not to regard the things of this world. The best of its enjoyments are but lumber; we cannot make sure of them while here, much less can we carry them away with us. Let us not set our eyes or hearts upon the world; there are better things for us in that blessed land, whither Christ, our Joseph, is gone to prepare a place. Joseph dismissed his brethren with a seasonable caution, "See that ye fall not out by the way." He knew they were too apt to be quarrelsome; and having forgiven them all, he lays this charge upon them, not to upbraid one another. This command our Lord Jesus has given to us, that we love one another, and that whatever happens, or has happened, we fall not out. For we are brethren, we have all one Father. We are all guilty, and instead of quarrelling with one another, have reason to fall out with ourselves. We are, or hope to be, forgiven of God, whom we have all offended, and, therefore, should be ready to forgive one another. We are "by the way," a way through the land of Egypt, where we have many eyes upon us, that seek advantage against us; a way that leads to the heavenly Canaan, where we hope to be for ever in perfect peace.

Verses 25–28

To hear that Joseph is alive, is too good news to be true; Jacob faints, for he believes it not. We faint, because we do not believe. At length, Jacob is convinced of the truth. Jacob was old, and did not expect to live long. He says, Let my eyes be refreshed with this sight before they are closed, and then I need no more to make me happy in this world. Behold Jesus manifesting himself as a Brother and a Friend to those who once were his despisers, his enemies. He assures them of his love and the riches of his grace. He commands them to lay aside envy, anger, malice, and strife, and to live in peace with each other. He teaches them to give up the world for him and his fulness. He supplies all that is needful to bring them home to himself, that where he is they may be also. And though, when he at last sends for his people, they may for a time feel some doubts and fears, yet the thought of seeing his glory and of being with him, will enable them to say, It is enough, I am willing to die; and I go to see, and to be with the Beloved of my soul.

Chapter 46

Verses 1–4

Even as to those events and undertakings which appear most joyful, we should seek counsel, assistance, and a blessing from the Lord.

Attending on his ordinances, and receiving the pledges of his covenant love, we expect his presence, and that peace which it confers. In all removals we should be reminded of our removal out of this world. Nothing can encourage us to fear no evil when passing through the valley of the shadow of death, but the presence of Christ.

Verses 5–27

We have here a particular account of Jacob's family. Though the fulfilling of promises is always sure, yet it is often slow. It was now **215** years since God had promised Abraham to make of him a great nation, ch. **12**:**2**; yet that branch of his seed, to which the promise was made sure, had only increased to seventy, of whom this particular account is kept, to show the power of God in making these seventy become a vast multitude.

Verses 28–34

It was justice to Pharaoh to let him know that such a family was come to settle in his dominions. If others put confidence in us, we must not be so base as to abuse it by imposing upon them. But how shall Joseph dispose of his brethren? Time was, when they were contriving to be rid of him; now he is contriving to settle them to their advantage; this is rendering good for evil. He would have them live by themselves, in the land of Goshen, which lay nearest to Canaan. Shepherds were an abomination to the Egyptians. Yet Joseph would have them not ashamed to own this as their occupation before Pharaoh. He might have procured places for them at court or in the army. But such preferments would have exposed them to the envy of the Egyptians, and might have tempted them to forget Canaan and the promise made unto their fathers. An honest calling is no disgrace, nor ought we to account it so, but rather reckon it a shame to be idle, or to have nothing to do. It is generally best for people to abide in the callings they have been bred to and used to. Whatever employment and condition God in his providence has allotted for us, let us suit ourselves to it, satisfy ourselves with it, and not mind high things. It is better to be the credit of a mean post, than the shame of a high one. If we wish to destroy our souls, or the souls of our children, then let us seek for ourselves, and for them, great things; but if not, it becomes us, having food and raiment, therewith to be content.

Chapter 47

Verses 1–6

Though Joseph was a great man, especially in Egypt, yet he owned his brethren. Let the rich and great in the world not overlook or despise poor relations. Our Lord Jesus is not ashamed to call us brethren. In answer to Pharaoh's inquiry, What is your calling? they told him that they were shepherds, adding that they were come to sojourn in the land for a time, while the famine prevailed in Canaan. Pharaoh offered to employ them as shepherds, provided they were active men. Whatever our business or employment is, we should aim to excel in it, and to prove ourselves clever and industrious.

Verses 7–12

With the gravity of old age, the piety of a true believer, and the authority of a patriarch and a prophet, Jacob besought the Lord to bestow a blessing upon Pharaoh. He acted as a man not ashamed of his religion; and who would express gratitude to the benefactor of himself and his family. We have here a very uncommon answer given to a very common question. Jacob calls his life a pilgrimage; the sojourning of a stranger in a foreign country, or his journey home to his own country. He was not at home upon earth; his habitation, his inheritance, his treasures were in heaven. He reckons his life by days; even by days life is soon reckoned, and we are not sure of the continuance of it for a day. Let us therefore number our days. His days were few. Though he had now lived one hundred and thirty years, they seemed but a few days, in comparison with the days of eternity, and the eternal state. They were evil; this is true concerning man. He is of few days and full of trouble; since his days are evil, it is well they are few. Jacob's life had been made up of evil days. Old age came sooner upon him than it had done upon some of his fathers. As the young man should not be proud of his strength or beauty, so the old man should not be proud of his age, and his hoary hairs, though others justly reverence them; for those who are accounted very old, attain not to the years of the patriarchs. The hoary head is only a crown of glory, when found in the way of righteousness. Such an answer could not fail to impress the heart of Pharaoh, by reminding him that worldly prosperity and happiness could not last long, and was not enough to satisfy. After a life of vanity and vexation, man goes down into the grave, equally from the throne as the cottage. Nothing can make us happy, but the prospect of an everlasting home in heaven, after our short and weary pilgrimage on earth.

Verses 13–26

Care being taken of Jacob and his family, which mercy was especially designed by Providence in Joseph's advancement, an account is given of the saving the kingdom of Egypt from ruin. There was no bread, and the people were ready to die. See how we depend upon God's providence. All our wealth would not keep us from starving, if rain were withheld for two or three years. See how much we are at God's mercy, and let us keep ourselves always in his love. Also see how much we smart by our own want of care. If all the Egyptians had laid up corn for themselves in the seven years of plenty, they had not been in these straits; but they regarded not the warning. Silver and gold would not feed them: they must have corn. All that a man hath will he give for his life. We cannot judge this matter by modern rules. It is plain that the Egyptians regarded Joseph as a public benefactor. The whole is consistent with Joseph's character, acting between Pharaoh and his subjects, in the fear of God. The Egyptians confessed concerning Joseph, Thou hast saved our lives. What multitudes will gratefully say to Jesus, at the last day, Thou hast saved our souls from the most tremendous destruction, and in the season of uttermost distress! The Egyptians parted with all their property, and even their liberty, for the saving of their lives: can it then be too much for us to count all but loss, and part with all, at His command, and for His sake, who will both save our souls, and give us an hundredfold, even here, in this present world? Surely if saved by Christ, we shall be willing to become his servants.

Verses 27–31

At last the time drew nigh that Israel must die. Israel, a prince with God, had power over the Angel, and prevailed, yet must die. Joseph supplied him with bread, that he might not die by famine, but that did not secure him from dying by age or sickness. He died by degrees; his candle gradually burnt down to the socket, so that he saw the time drawing nigh. It is an advantage to see the approach of death, before we feel it, that we may be quickened to do, with all our might, what our hands find to do. However, death is not far from any of us. Jacob's care, as he saw the day approach, was about his burial; not the pomp of it, but he would be buried in Canaan, because it was the land of promise. It was a type of heaven, that better country, which he declared plainly he expected, Heb **11**:**14**. Nothing will better help to make a death-bed easy, than the certain prospect of rest in the heavenly Canaan after death. When this was done, Israel bowed himself upon the bed's head, worshipping God, as it is explained, see Heb **11**:**21**, giving God thanks for all his favours; in feebleness thus supporting himself, expressing his willingness to leave the world. Even those who lived on Joseph's provision, and Jacob who was so dear to him, must die. But Christ Jesus gives us the true bread, that we may eat and live for ever. To Him let us come and yield ourselves, and when we draw near to death, he who supported us through life, will meet us and assure us of everlasting salvation.

Chapter 48

Verses 1–7

The death-beds of believers, with the prayers and counsels of dying persons, are suited to make serious impressions upon the young, the gay, and the prosperous: we shall do well to take children on such occasions, when it can be done properly. If the Lord please, it is very desirable to bear our dying testimony to his truth, to his faithfulness, and the pleasantness of his ways. And one would wish so to live, as to give energy and weight to our dying exhortations. All true believers are blessed at their death, but all do not depart equally full of spiritual consolations. Jacob adopted Joseph's two sons. Let them not succeed their father, in his power and grandeur in Egypt; but let them succeed in the inheritance of the promise made to Abraham. Thus the aged dying patriarch teaches these young persons to take their lot with the people of God. He appoints each of them to be the head of a tribe. Those are worthy of double honour, who, through God's grace, break through the temptations of worldly wealth and preferment, to embrace religion in disgrace and poverty. Jacob will have Ephraim and Manasseh to know, that it is better to be low, and in the church, than high, and out of it.

Verses 8–22

The two good men own God in their comforts. Joseph says, They are my sons whom God has given me. Jacob says, God hath showed me thy seed. Comforts are doubly sweet to us when we see them coming from God's hand. He not only prevents our fears, but exceeds our hopes. Jacob mentions the care the Divine providence had taken of him all his days. A great deal of hardship he had known in his time, but God kept him from the evil of his troubles. Now he was dying, he looked upon himself as redeemed from all sin and sorrow for ever. Christ, the Angel of the covenant, redeems from all evil. Deliverances from misery and dangers, by the Divine power, coming through the ransom of the blood of Christ, in Scripture are often called redemption. In blessing Joseph's sons, Jacob crossed hands. Joseph was willing to support his first-born, and would have removed his father's hands. But Jacob acted neither by mistake, nor from a partial affection to one more than the other; but from a spirit of prophecy, and by the Divine counsel. God, in bestowing blessings upon his people, gives more to some than to others, more gifts, graces, and comforts, and more of the good things of this life. He often gives most to those that are least likely. He chooses the weak things of the world; he raises the poor out of the dust. Grace observes not the order of nature, nor does God prefer those whom we think fittest to be preferred, but as it pleases him. How poor are they who have no riches but those of this world! How miserable is a death-bed to those who have no well-grounded hope of good, but dreadful apprehensions of evil, and nothing but evil for ever!

Chapter 49

Verses 1, 2

All Jacob's sons were living. His calling them together was a precept for them to unite in love, not to mingle with the Egyptians; and foretold that they should not be separated, as Abraham's sons and Isaac's were, but should all make one people. We are not to consider this address as the expression of private feelings of affection, resentment, or partiality; but as the language of the Holy Ghost, declaring the purpose of God respecting the character, circumstances, and situation of the tribes which descended from the sons of Jacob, and which may be traced in their histories.

Verses 3–7

Reuben was the first-born; but by gross sin, he forfeited the birthright. The character of Reuben is, that he was unstable as water. Men do not thrive, because they do not fix. Reuben's sin left a lasting infamy upon his family. Let us never do evil, then we need not fear being told of it. Simeon and Levi were passionate and revengeful. The murder of the Shechemites is a proof of this. Jacob protested against that barbarous act. Our soul is our honour; by its powers we are distinguished from, and raised above, the beasts that perish. We ought, from our hearts, to abhor all bloody and mischievous men. Cursed be their anger. Jacob does not curse their persons, but their lusts. I will divide them. The sentence as it respects Levi was turned into a blessing. This tribe performed an acceptable service in their zeal against the worshippers of the golden calf, Ex 32. Being set apart to God as priests, they were in that character scattered through the nation of Israel.

Verses 8–12

Judah's name signifies praise. God was praised for him, chap. **29:35**, praised by him, and praised in him; therefore his brethren shall praise him. Judah should be a strong and courageous tribe. Judah is compared, not to a lion raging and ranging, but to a lion enjoying the satisfaction of his power and success, without creating vexation to others; this is to be truly great. Judah should be the royal tribe, the tribe from which Messiah the Prince should come. Shiloh, that promised Seed in whom the earth should be blessed, "that peaceable and prosperous One," or "Saviour," he shall come of Judah. Thus dying Jacob at a great distance saw Christ's day, and it was his comfort and support on his death-bed. Till Christ's coming, Judah possessed authority, but after his crucifixion this was shortened, and according to what Christ foretold, Jerusalem was destroyed, and all the poor harassed remnant of Jews were confounded together. Much which is here said concerning Judah, is to be applied to our Lord Jesus. In him there is plenty of all which is nourishing and refreshing to the soul, and which maintains and cheers the Divine life in it. He is the true Vine; wine is the appointed symbol of his blood, which is drink indeed, as shed for sinners, and applied in faith; and all the blessings of his gospel are wine and milk, without money and without price, to which every thirsty soul is welcome. Isa **55:1**.

Verses 13–18

Concerning Zebulun: if prophecy says, Zebulun shall be a haven of ships, be sure Providence will so plant him. God appoints the bounds of our habitation. It is our wisdom and duty to accommodate ourselves to our lot, and to improve it; if Zebulun dwell at the heaven of the sea, let him be for a haven of ships. Concerning Issachar: he saw that the land was pleasant, yielding not only pleasant prospects, but pleasant fruits to recompense his toils. Let us, with an eye of faith, see the heavenly rest to be good, and that land of promise to be pleasant; this will make our present services easy. Dan should, by art, and policy, and surprise, gain advantages against his enemies, like a serpent biting the heel of the traveller. Jacob, almost spent, and ready to faint, relieves himself with those words, "I have waited for thy salvation, O Lord!" The salvation he waited for was Christ, the promised Seed; now that he was going to be gathered to his people, he breathes after Him to whom the gathering of the people shall be. He declared plainly that he sought heaven, the better country, Heb **11**:**13**, **14**. Now he is going to enjoy the salvation, he comforts himself that he had waited for the salvation. Christ, as our way to heaven, is to be waited on; and heaven, as our rest in Christ, is to be waited for. It is the comfort of a dying saint thus to have waited for the salvation of the Lord; for then he shall have what he has been waiting for.

Verses 19–21

Concerning Gad, Jacob alludes to his name, which signifies a troop, and foresees the character of that tribe. The cause of God and his people, though for a time it may seem to be baffled and run down, will be victorious at last. It represents the Christian's conflict. Grace in the soul is often foiled in its conflicts; troops of corruption overcome it, but the cause is God's, and grace will in the end come off conqueror, yea, more than conqueror, Ro **8**:**37**. Asher should be a rich tribe. His inheritance bordered upon Carmel, which was fruitful to a proverb. Naphtali, is a hind let loose. We may consider it as a description of the character of this tribe. Unlike the laborious ox and ass; desirous of ease and liberty; active, but more noted for quick despatch than steady labour and perseverance. Like the suppliant who, with goodly words, craves mercy. Let not those of different tempers and gifts censure or envy one another.

Verses 22–27

The blessing of Joseph is very full. What Jacob says of him, is history as well as prophecy. Jacob reminds him of the difficulties and fiery darts of temptations he had formerly struggled through. His faith did not fail, but through his trials he bore all his burdens with firmness, and did not do anything unbecoming. All our strength for resisting temptations, and bearing afflictions, comes from God; his grace is sufficient. Joseph became the shepherd of Israel, to take care of his father and family; also the stone of Israel, their foundation and strong support. In this, as in many other things, Joseph was a remarkable type of the Good Shepherd, and tried Corner Stone of the whole church of God. Blessings are promised to Joseph's posterity, typical of the vast and everlasting blessings which come upon the spiritual seed of Christ. Jacob blessed all his sons, but especially Joseph, "who was separated from his brethren." Not only separated in Egypt, but, possessing eminent dignity, and more devoted to God. Of Benjamin it is said, He shall ravin as a wolf. Jacob was guided in what he said by the Spirit of prophecy, and not by natural affection; else he would have spoken with more tenderness of his beloved son Benjamin. Concerning him he only foresees and foretells, that his posterity should be a warlike tribe, strong and daring, and that they should enrich themselves with the spoils of their enemies; that they should be active. Blessed Paul was of this tribe, Ro **11**:**1**; Php **3**:**5**; he, in the morning of his day, devoured the prey as a persecutor, but in the evening divided the spoils as a preacher; he shared the blessings of Judah's Lion, and assisted in his victories.

Verses 28–33

Jacob blessed every one according to the blessings God in after-times intended to bestow upon them. He spoke about his burial-place, from a principle of faith in the promise of God, that Canaan should be the inheritance of his seed in due time. When he had finished both his blessing and his charge, and so had finished his testimony, he addressed himself to his dying work. He gathered up his feet into the bed, not only as one patiently submitting to the stroke, but as one cheerfully composing himself to rest, now that he was weary. He freely gave up his spirit into the hand of God, the Father of spirits. If God's people be our people, death will gather us to them. Under the care of the Shepherd of Israel, we shall lack nothing for body or soul. We shall remain unmoved until our work is finished; then, breathing out our souls into His hands for whose salvation we have waited, we shall depart in peace, and leave a blessing for our children after us.

Chapter 50

Verses 1–6

Though pious relatives and friends have lived to a good old age, and we are confident they are gone to glory, yet we may regret our own loss, and pay respect to their memory by lamenting them. Grace does not destroy, but it purifies, moderates, and regulates natural affection. The departed soul is out of the reach of any tokens of our affection; but it is proper to show respect to the body, of which we look for a glorious and joyful resurrection, whatever may become of its remains in this world. Thus Joseph showed his faith in God, and love to his father. He ordered the body to be embalmed, or wrapped up with spices, to preserve it. See how vile our bodies are, when the soul has forsaken them; they will in a very little time become noisome, and offensive.

Verses 7–14

Jacob's body was attended, not only by his own family, but by the great men of Egypt. Now that they were better acquainted with the Hebrews, they began to respect them. Professors of religion should endeavour by wisdom and love to remove the prejudices many have against them. Standers-by took notice of it as a grievous mourning. The death of good men is a loss to any place, and ought to be greatly lamented.

Verses 15–21

Various motives might cause the sons of Jacob to continue in Egypt, notwithstanding the prophetic vision Abraham had of their bondage there. Judging of Joseph from the general temper of human nature, they thought he would now avenge himself on those who hated and injured him without cause. Not being able to resist, or to flee away, they attempted to soften him by humbling themselves. They pleaded with him as the servants of Jacob's God. Joseph was much affected at seeing this complete fulfilment of his dreams. He directs them not to fear him, but to fear God; to humble themselves before the Lord, and to seek the Divine forgiveness. He assures them of his own kindness to them. See what an excellent spirit Joseph was of, and learn of him to render good for evil. He comforted them, and, to banish all their fears, he spake kindly to them. Broken spirits must be bound up and encouraged. Those we love and forgive, we must not only do well for, but speak kindly to.

Verses 22–26

Joseph having honoured his father, his days were long in the land, which, for the present, God had given him. When he saw his death approaching, he comforted his brethren with the assurance of their return to Canaan in due time. We must comfort others with the same comforts with which we have been comforted of God, and encourage them to rest on the promises which are our support. For a confession of his own faith, and a confirmation of theirs, he charges them to keep his remains unburied till that glorious day, when they should be settled in the land of promise. Thus Joseph, by faith in the doctrine of the resurrection, and the promise of Canaan, gave commandment concerning his bones. This would keep up their expectation of a speedy departure from Egypt, and keep Canaan continually in their minds. This would also attach Joseph's posterity to their brethren. The death, as well as the life of this eminent saint, was truly excellent; both furnish us with strong encouragement to persevere in the service of God. How happy to set our early in the heavenly race, to continue stedfastly, and to finish the course with joy! This Joseph did, this we also may do. Even when the pains of death are upon us, if we have trusted in Him upon whom the patriarchs, prophets, and apostles depended, we need not fear to say, "My flesh and my heart faileth, but God is the strength of my heart, and my portion for ever."

Exodus

The Book of Exodus relates the forming of the children of Israel into a church and a nation. We have hitherto seen true religion shown in domestic life, now, we begin to trace its effects upon the concerns of kingdoms and nations. Exodus signifies "the departure;" the chief event therein recorded is the departure of Israel from Egypt and Egyptian bondage; it plainly points out the fulfilling of several promises and prophecies to Abraham respecting his seed, and shadows forth the state of the church, in the wilderness of this world, until her arrival at the heavenly Canaan, an eternal rest.

Chapter 1

Verses 1–7

During more than **200** years, while Abraham, Isaac, and Jacob lived at liberty, the Hebrews increased slowly; only about seventy persons went down into Egypt. There, in about the same number of years, though under cruel bondage, they became a large nation. This wonderful increase was according to the promise long before made unto the fathers. Though the performance of God's promises is sometimes slow, it is always sure.

Verses 8–14

The land of Egypt became to Israel a house of bondage. The place where we have been happy, may soon become the place of our affliction; and that may prove the greatest cross to us, of which we said, This same shall comfort us. Cease from man, and say not of any place on this side heaven, This is my rest. All that knew Joseph, loved him, and were kind to his brethren for his sake; but the best and most useful services a man does to others, are soon forgotten after his death. Our great care should be, to serve God, and to please him who is not unrighteous, whatever men are, to forget our work and labour of love. The offence of Israel is, that he prospers. There is no sight more hateful to a wicked man than the prosperity of the righteous. The Egyptians feared lest the children of Israel should join their enemies, and get them up out of the land. Wickedness is ever cowardly and unjust; it makes a man fear, where no fear is, and flee, when no one pursues him. And human wisdom often is foolishness, and very sinful. God's people had task-masters set over them, not only to burden them, but to afflict them with their burdens. They not only made them serve for Pharaoh's profit, but so that their lives became bitter. The Israelites wonderfully increased. Christianity spread most when it was persecuted: the blood of the martyrs was the seed of the church. They that take counsel against the Lord and his Israel, do but imagine a vain thing, and create greater vexation to themselves.

Verses 15–22

The Egyptians tried to destroy Israel by the murder of their children. The enmity that is in the seed of the serpent, against the Seed of the woman, makes men forget all pity. It is plain that the Hebrews were now under an uncommon blessing. And we see that the services done for God's Israel are often repaid in kind. Pharaoh gave orders to drown all the male children of the Hebrews. The enemy who, by Pharaoh, attempted to destroy the church in this its infant state, is busy to stifle the rise of serious reflections in the heart of man. Let those who would escape, be afraid of sinning, and cry directly and fervently to the Lord for assistance.

Chapter 2

Verses 1–4

Observe the order of Providence: just at the time when Pharaoh's cruelty rose to its height by ordering the Hebrew children to be drowned, the deliverer was born. When men are contriving the ruin of the church, God is preparing for its salvation. The parents of Moses saw he was a goodly child. A lively faith can take encouragement from the least hint of the Divine favour. It is said, Heb **11**:**23**, that the parents of Moses hid him by faith; they had the promise that Israel should be preserved, which they relied upon. Faith in God's promise quickens to the use of lawful means for obtaining mercy. Duty is ours, events are God's. Faith in God will set us above the fear of man. At three months' end, when they could not hide the infant any longer, they put him in an ark of bulrushes by the river's brink, and set his sister to watch. And if the weak affection of a mother were thus careful, what shall we think of Him, whose love, whose compassion is, as himself, boundless. Moses never had a stronger protection about him, no, not when all the Israelites were round his tent in the wilderness, than now, when he lay alone, a helpless babe upon the waves. No water, no Egyptian can hurt him. When we seem most neglected and forlorn, God is most present with us.

Verses 5–10

Come, see the place where that great man, Moses, lay, when he was a little child; it was in a bulrush basket by the river's side. Had he been left there long, he must have perished. But Providence brings Pharaoh's daughter to the place where this poor forlorn infant lay, and inclines her heart to pity it, which she dares do, when none else durst. God's care of us in our infancy ought to be often mentioned by us to his praise. Pharaoh cruelly sought to destroy Israel, but his own daughter had pity on a Hebrew child, and not only so, but, without knowing it, preserved Israel's deliverer, and provided Moses with a good nurse, even his own mother. That he should have a Hebrew nurse, the sister of Moses brought the mother into the place of a nurse. Moses was treated as the son of Pharoah's daughter. Many who, by their birth, are obscure and poor, by surprising events of Providence, are raised high in the world, to make men know that God rules.

Verses 11–15

Moses boldly owned the cause of God's people. It is plain from Heb **11**. that this was done in faith, with the full purpose of leaving the honours, wealth, and pleasures of his rank among the Egyptians. By the grace of God he was a partaker of faith in Christ, which overcomes the world. He was willing, not only to risk all, but to suffer for his sake; being assured that Israel were the people of God. By special warrant from Heaven, which makes no rule for other cases, Moses slew an Egyptian, and rescued an oppressed Israelites. Also, he tried to end a dispute between two Hebrews. The reproof Moses gave, may still be of use. May we not apply it to disputants, who, by their fierce debates, divide and weaken the Christian church? They forget that they are brethren. He that did wrong quarreled with Moses. It is a sign of guilt to be angry at reproof. Men know not what they do, nor what enemies they are to themselves, when they resist and despise faithful reproofs and reprovers. Moses might have said, if this be the spirit of the Hebrews, I will go to court again, and be the son of Pharaoh's daughter. But we must take heed of being set against the ways and people of God, by the follies and peevishness of some persons that profess religion. Moses was obliged to flee into the land of Midian. God ordered this for wise and holy ends.

Verses 16–22

Moses found shelter in Midian. He was ready to help Reuel's daughters to water their flocks, although bred in learning and at court. Moses loved to be doing justice, and to act in defence of such as he saw injured, which every man ought to do, as far as it is in his power. He loved to be doing good; wherever the providence of God casts us, we should desire and try to be useful; and when we cannot do the good we would, we must be ready to do the good we can. Moses commended himself to the prince of Midian; who married one of his daughters to Moses, by whom he had a son, called Gershom, "a stranger there," that he might keep in remembrance the land in which he had been a stranger.

Verses 23–25

The Israelites' bondage in Egypt continued, though the murdering of their infants did not continue. Sometimes the Lord suffers the rod of the wicked to lie very long and very heavy on the lot of the righteous. At last they began to think of God under their troubles. It is a sign that the Lord is coming towards us with deliverance, when he inclines and enables us to cry to him for it. God heard their groaning; he made it to appear that he took notice of their complaints. He remembered his covenant, of which he is ever mindful. He considered this, and not any merit of theirs. He looked upon the children of Israel. Moses looked upon them, and pitied them; but now God looked upon them, and helped them. He had respect unto them. His eyes are now fixed upon Israel, to show himself in their behalf. God is ever thus, a very present help in trouble. Take courage then, ye who, conscious of guilt and thraldom, are looking to Him for deliverance. God in Christ Jesus is also looking upon you. A call of love is joined with a promise of the Redeemer. Come unto me, all ye that labour and are heavy laden, and I will give you rest, Mt **11**:**28**.

Chapter 3

Verses 1–6

The years of the life of Moses are divided into three forties; the first forty he spent as a prince in Pharaoh's court, the second as a shepherd in Midian, the third as a king in Jeshurun. How changeable is the life of man! The first appearance of God to Moses, found him tending sheep. This seems a poor employment for a man of his parts and education, yet he rests satisfied with it; and thus learns meekness and contentment, for which he is more noted in sacred writ, than for all his learning. Satan loves to find us idle; God is pleased when he finds us employed. Being alone, is a good friend to our communion with God. To his great surprise, Moses saw a bush burning without fire to kindle it. The bush burned, and yet did not burn away; an emblem of the church in bondage in Egypt. And it fitly reminds us of the church in every age, under its severest persecutions kept by the presence of God from being destroyed. Fire is an emblem, in Scripture, of the Divine holiness and justice, also of the afflictions and trials with which God proves and purifies his people, and even of that baptism of the Holy Ghost, by which sinful affections are consumed, and the soul changed into the Divine nature and image. God gave Moses a gracious call, to which he returned a ready answer. Those that would have communion with God, must attend upon him in the ordinances wherein he is pleased to manifest himself and his glory, though it be in a bush. Putting off the shoe was a token of respect and submission. We ought to draw nigh to God with a solemn pause and preparation, carefully avoiding every thing that looks light and rude, and unbecoming his service. God does not say, I was the God of Abraham, Isaac, and Jacob, but I am. The patriarchs still live, so many years after their bodies have been in the grave. No length of time can separate the souls of the just from their Maker. By this, God instructed Moses as to another world, and strengthened his belief of a future state. Thus it is interpreted by our Lord Jesus, who, from hence, proves that the dead are raised, Lu **20**:**37**. Moses hid his face, as if both ashamed and afraid to look upon God. The more we see of God, and his grace, and covenant love, the more cause we shall see to worship him with reverence and godly fear.

Verses 7–10

God notices the afflictions of Israel. Their sorrows; even the secret sorrows of God's people are known to him. Their cry; God hears the cries of his afflicted people. The oppression they endured; the highest and greatest of their oppressors are not above him. God promises speedy deliverance by methods out of the common ways of providence. Those whom God, by his grace, delivers out of a spiritual Egypt, he will bring to a heavenly Canaan. (Ex **3**:**11-15**)

Verses 11–15

Formerly Moses thought himself able to deliver Israel, and set himself to the work too hastily. Now, when the fittest person on earth for it, he knows his own weakness. This was the effect of more knowledge of God and of himself. Formerly, self-confidence mingled with strong faith and great zeal, now sinful distrust of God crept in under the garb of humility; so defective are the strongest graces and the best duties of the most eminent saints. But all objections are answered in, Certainly I will be with thee. That is enough. Two names God would now be known by. A name that denotes what he is in himself, I AM THAT I AM. This explains his name Jehovah, and signifies, **1**. That he is self-existent: he has his being of himself. **2**. That he is eternal and unchangeable, and always the same, yesterday, to-day, and for ever. **3**. That he is incomprehensible; we cannot by searching find him out: this name checks all bold and curious inquiries concerning God. **4**. That he is faithful and true to all his promises, unchangeable in his word as well as in his nature; let Israel know this, I AM hath sent me unto you. I am, and there is none else besides me. All else have their being from God, and are wholly dependent upon him. Also, here is a name that denotes what God is to his people. The Lord God of your fathers sent me unto you. Moses must revive among them the religion of their fathers, which was almost lost; and then they might expect the speedy performance of the promises made unto their fathers.

Verses 16–22

Moses' success with the elders of Israel would be good. God, who, by his grace, inclines the heart, and opens the ear, could say beforehand, They shall hearken to thy voice; for he would make them willing in this day of power. As to Pharaoh, Moses is here told that petitions and persuasions, and humble complaints, would not prevail with him; nor a mighty hand stretched out in signs and wonders. But those will certainly be broken by the power of God's hand, who will not bow to the power of his word. Pharaoh's people should furnish Israel with riches at their departure. In Pharaoh's tyranny and Israel's oppression, we see the miserable, abject state of sinners. However galling the yoke, they drudge on till the Lord sends redemption. With the invitations of the gospel, God sends the teaching of his Spirit. Thus are men made willing to seek and to strive for deliverance. Satan loses his power to hold them, they come forth with all they have and are, and apply all to the glory of God and the service of his church.

Chapter 4

Verses 1–9

Moses objects, that the people would not take his word, unless he showed them some sign. God gives him power to work miracles. But those who are now employed to deliver God's messages to men, need not the power to work miracles: their character and their doctrines are to be tried by that word of God to which they appeal. These miracles especially referred to the miracles of the Lord Jesus Christ. It belonged to Him only, to cast the power of the devil out of the soul, and to heal the soul of the leprosy of sin; and so it was for Him first to cast the devil out of the body, and to heal the leprosy of the body.

Verses 10–17

Moses continued backward to the work God designed him for; there was much of cowardice, slothfulness, and unbelief in him. We must not judge of men by the readiness of their discourse. A great deal of wisdom and true worth may be with a slow tongue. God sometimes makes choice of those as his messengers, who have the least of the advantages of art or nature, that his grace in them may appear the more glorious. Christ's disciples were no orators, till the Holy Spirit made them such. God condescends to answer the excuse of Moses. Even self-diffidence, when it hinders us from duty, or clogs us in duty, is very displeasing to the Lord. But while we blame Moses for shrinking from this dangerous service, let us ask our own hearts if we are not neglecting duties more easy, and less perilous. The tongue of Aaron, with the head and heart of Moses, would make one completely fit for this errand. God promises, I will be with thy mouth, and with his mouth. Even Aaron, who could speak well, yet could not speak to purpose, unless God gave constant teaching and help; for without the constant aid of Divine grace, the best gifts will fail.

Verses 18–23

After God had appeared in the bush, he often spake to Moses. Pharaoh had hardened his own heart against the groans and cries of the oppressed Israelites; and now God, in the way of righteous judgment, hardens his heart against the teaching of the miracles, and the terror of the plagues. But whether Pharaoh will hear, or whether he will forbear, Moses must tell him, Thus saith the Lord. He must demand a discharge for Israel, Let my son go; not only my servant, whom thou hast no right to detain, but my son. It is my son that serves me, and therefore must be spared, must be pleaded for. In case of refusal I will slay thy son, even thy first-born. As men deal with God's people, let them expect so to be dealt with.

Verses 24–31

God met Moses in anger. The Lord threatened him with death or sent sickness upon him, as the punishment of his having neglected to circumcise his son. When God discovers to us what is amiss in our lives, we must give all diligence to amend it speedily. This is the voice of every rod; it calls us to return to Him that smites us. God sent Aaron to meet Moses. The more they saw of God's bringing them together, the more pleasant their interview was. The elders of Israel met them in faith, and were ready to obey them. It often happens, that less difficulty is found than was expected, in such undertakings as are according to the will of God, and for his glory. Let us but arise and try at our proper work, the Lord will be with us and prosper us. If Israel welcomed the tidings of their deliverance, and worshipped the Lord, how should we welcome the glad tidings of redemption, embrace it in faith, and adore the Redeemer!

Chapter 5

Verses 1–9

God will own his people, though poor and despised, and will find a time to plead their cause. Pharaoh treated all he had heard with contempt. He had no knowledge of Jehovah, no fear of him, no love to him, and therefore refused to obey him. Thus Pharaoh's pride, ambition, covetousness, and political knowledge, hardened him to his own destruction. What Moses and Aaron ask is very reasonable, only to go three days' journey into the desert, and that on a good errand. We will sacrifice unto the Lord our God. Pharaoh was very unreasonable, in saying that the people were idle, and therefore talked of going to sacrifice. He thus misrepresents them, that he might have a pretence to add to their burdens. To this day we find many who are more disposed to find fault with their neighbours, for spending in the service of God a few hours spared from their wordly business, than to blame others, who give twice the time to sinful pleasures. Pharaoh's command was barbarous. Moses and Aaron themselves must get to the burdens. Persecutors take pleasure in putting contempt and hardship upon ministers. The usual tale of bricks must be made, without the usual allowance of straw to mix with the clay. Thus more work was to be laid upon the men, which, if they performed, they would be broken with labour; and if not, they would be punished.

Verses 10–23

The Egyptian task-masters were very severe. See what need we have to pray that we may be delivered from wicked men. The head-workmen justly complained to Pharaoh: but he taunted them. The malice of Satan has often represented the service and worship of God, as fit employment only for those who have nothing else to do, and the business only of the idle; whereas, it is the duty of those who are most busy in the world. Those who are diligent in doing sacrifice to the Lord, will, before God, escape the doom of the slothful servant, though with men they do not. The Israelites should have humbled themselves before God, and have taken to themselves the shame of their sin; but instead of that, they quarrel with those who were to be their deliverers. Moses returned to the Lord. He knew that what he had said and done, was by God's direction; and therefore appeals to him. When we find ourselves at any time perplexed in the way of our duty, we ought to go to God, and lay open our case before him by fervent prayer. Disappointments in our work must not drive us from our God, but still we must ponder why they are sent.

Chapter 6

Verses 1–9

We are most likely to prosper in attempts to glorify God, and to be useful to men, when we learn by experience that we can do nothing of ourselves; when our whole dependence is placed on him, and our only expectation is from him. Moses had been expecting what God would do; but now he shall see what he will do. God would now be known by his name Jehovah, that is, a God performing what he had promised, and finishing his own work. God intended their happiness: I will take you to me for a people, a peculiar people, and I will be to you a God. More than this we need not ask, we cannot have, to make us happy. He intended his own glory: Ye shall know that I am the Lord. These good words, and comfortable words, should have revived the drooping Israelites, and have made them forget their misery; but they were so taken up with their troubles, that they did not heed God's promises. By indulging discontent and fretfulness, we deprive ourselves of the comfort we might have, both from God's word and from his providence, and go comfortless.

Verses 10–13

The faith of Moses was so feeble that he could scarcely be kept to his work. Ready obedience is always according to the strength of our faith. Though our weaknesses ought to humble us, yet they ought not to discourage us from doing our best in any service we have to do for God. When Moses repeats his baffled arguments, he is argued with no longer, but God gives him and Aaron a charge, both to the children of Israel, and to Pharaoh. God's authority is sufficient to answer all objections, and binds all to obey, without murmuring or disputing, Php **2**:**14**.

Verses 14–30

Moses and Aaron were Israelites; raised up unto them of their brethren, as Christ also should be, who was to be the Prophet and Priest, the Redeemer and Lawgiver of the people of Israel. Moses returns to his narrative, and repeats the charge God had given him to deliver his message to Pharaoh, and his objection against it. Those who have spoken unadvisedly with their lips ought to reflect upon it with regret, as Moses seems to do here. "Uncircumcised," is used in Scripture to note the unsuitableness there may be in any thing to answer its proper purpose; as the carnal heart and depraved nature of fallen man are wholly unsuited to the services of God, and to the purposes of his glory. It is profitable to place no confidence in ourselves, all our sufficiency must be in the Lord. We never can trust ourselves too little, or our God too much. I can do nothing by myself, said the apostle, but I can do all things through Christ which strengtheneth me.

Chapter 7

Verses 1–7

God glorifies himself. He makes people know that he is Jehovah. Israel is made to know it by the performance of his promises to them, and the Egyptians by the pouring out of his wrath upon them. Moses, as the ambassador of Jehovah, speaking in his name, laid commands upon Pharaoh, denounced threatenings against him, and called for judgments upon him. Pharaoh, proud and great as he was, could not resist. Moses stood not in awe of Pharaoh, but made him tremble. This seems to be meant in the words, Thou shalt be a god unto Pharaoh. At length Moses is delivered from his fears. He makes no more objections, but, being strengthened in faith, goes about his work with courage, and proceeds in it with perseverance.

Verses 8–13

What men dislike, because it opposes their pride and lusts, they will not be convinced of; but it is easy to cause them to believe things they wish to be true. God always sends with his word full proofs of its Divine authority; but when men are bent to disobey, and willing to object, he often permits a snare to be laid wherein they are entangled. The magicians were cheats, trying to copy the real miracles of Moses by secret sleights or jugglings, which to a small extent they succeeded in doing, so as to deceive the bystanders, but they were at length obliged to confess they could not any longer imitate the effects of Divine power. None assist more in the destruction of sinners, than such as resist the truth by amusing men with a counterfeit resemblance of it. Satan is most to be dreaded when transformed into an angel of light.

Verses 14–25

Here is the first of the ten plagues, the turning of the water into blood. It was a dreadful plague. The sight of such vast rolling streams of blood could not but strike horror. Nothing is more common than water: so wisely has Providence ordered it, and so kindly, that what is so needful and serviceable to the comfort of human life, should be cheap and almost every where to be had; but now the Egyptians must either drink blood, or die for thirst. Egypt was a pleasant land, but the dead fish and blood now rendered it very unpleasant. It was a righteous plague, and justly sent upon the Egyptians; for Nile, the river of Egypt, was their idol. That creature which we idolize, God justly takes from us, or makes bitter to us. They had stained the river with the blood of the Hebrews' children, and now God made that river all blood. Never any thirsted after blood, but sooner or later they had enough of it. It was a significant plague; Egypt had great dependence upon their river, Zec **14**:**18**; so that in smiting the river, they were warned of the destruction of all the produce of their country. The love of Christ to his disciples changes all their common mercies into spiritual blessings; the anger of God towards his enemies, renders their most valued advantages a curse and a misery to them. Aaron is to summon the plague by smiting the river with his rod. It was done in the sight of Pharaoh and his attendants, for God's true miracles were not performed as Satan's lying wonders; truth seeks no corners. See the almighty power of God. Every creature is that to us which he makes it to be water or blood. See what changes we may meet with in the things of this world; what is always vain, may soon become vexatious. See what mischievous work sin makes. If the things that have been our comforts prove our crosses, we must thank ourselves. It is sin that turns our waters into blood. The plague continued seven days; and in all that time Pharaoh's proud heart would not let him desire Moses to pray for the removal of it. Thus the hypocrites in heart heap up wrath. No wonder that God's anger is not turned away, but that his hand is stretched out still.

Chapter 8

Verses 1–15

Pharaoh is plagued with frogs; their vast numbers made them sore plagues to the Egyptians. God could have plagued Egypt with lions, or bears, or wolves, or with birds of prey, but he chose to do it by these despicable creatures. God, when he pleases, can arm the smallest parts of the creation against us. He thereby humbled Pharaoh. They should neither eat, nor drink, nor sleep in quiet; but wherever they were, they should be troubled by the frogs. God's curse upon a man will pursue him wherever he goes, and lie heavy upon him whatever he does. Pharaoh gave way under this plague. He promises that he will let the people go. Those who bid defiance to God and prayer, first or last, will be made to see their need of both. But when Pharaoh saw there was respite, he hardened his heart. Till the heart is renewed by the grace of God, the thoughts made by affliction do not abide; the convictions wear off, and the promises that were given are forgotten. Till the state of the air is changed, what thaws in the sun will freeze again in the shade.

Verses 16–19

These lice were produced out of the dust of the earth; out of any part of the creation God can fetch a scourge, with which to correct those who rebel against him. Even the dust of the earth obeys him. These lice were very troublesome, as well as disgraceful to the Egyptians, whose priests were obliged to take much pains that no vermin ever should be found about them. All the plagues inflicted on the Egyptians, had reference to their national crimes, or were rendered particularly severe by their customs. The magicians attempted to imitate it, but they could not. It forced them to confess, This is the finger of God! The check and restraint put upon us, must needs be from a Divine power. Sooner or later God will force even his enemies to acknowledge his own power. Pharaoh, notwithstanding this, was more and more obstinate.

Verses 20–32

Pharaoh was early at his false devotions to the river; and shall we be for more sleep and more slumber, when any service to the Lord is to be done? The Egyptians and the Hebrews were to be marked in the plague of flies. The Lord knows them that are his, and will make it appear, perhaps in this world, certainly in the other, that he has set them apart for himself. Pharaoh unwillingly entered into a treaty with Moses and Aaron. He is content they should sacrifice to their God, provided they would do it in the land of Egypt. But it would be an abomination to God, should they offer the Egyptian sacrifices; and it would be an abomination to the Egyptians, should they offer to God the objects of the worship of the Egyptians, namely, their calves or oxen. Those who would offer acceptable sacrifice to God, must separate themselves from the wicked and profane. They must also retire from the world. Israel cannot keep the feast of the Lord, either among the brick-kilns or among the flesh-pots of Egypt. And they must sacrifice as God shall command, not otherwise. Though they were in slavery to Pharaoh, yet they must obey God's commands. Pharaoh consents for them to go into the wilderness, provided they do not go so far but that he might fetch them back again. Thus, some sinners, in a pang of conviction, part with their sins, yet are loth they should go very far away; for when the fright is over, they will turn to them again. Moses promised the removal of this plague. But let not Pharaoh deal deceitfully any more. Be not deceived; God is not mocked: if we think to cheat God by a sham repentance and a false surrender of ourselves to him, we shall put a fatal cheat upon our own souls. Pharaoh returned to his hardness. Reigning lusts break through the strongest bonds, and make men presume and go from their word. Many seem in earnest, but there is some reserve, some beloved, secret sin. They are unwilling to look upon themselves as in danger of everlasting misery. They will refrain from other sins; they do much, give much, and even punish themselves much. They will leave it off sometimes, and, as it were, let their sin depart a little way; but will not make up their minds to part with all and follow Christ, bearing the cross. Rather than that, they venture all. They are sorrowful, but depart from Christ, determined to keep the world at present, and they hope for some future season, when salvation may be had without such costly sacrifices; but, at length, the poor sinner is driven away in his wickedness, and left without hope to lament his folly.

Chapter 9

Verses 1–7

God will have Israel released, Pharaoh opposes it, and the trial is, whose word shall stand. The hand of the Lord at once is upon the cattle, many of which, some of all kinds, die by a sort of murrain. This was greatly to the loss of the owners; they had made Israel poor, and now God would make them poor. The hand of God is to be seen, even in the sickness and death of cattle; for a sparrow falls not to the ground without our Father. None of the Israelites' cattle should die; the Lord shall sever. The cattle died. The Egyptians worshipped their cattle. What we make an idol of, it is just with God to remove from us. This proud tyrant and cruel oppressor deserved to be made an example by the just Judge of the universe. None who are punished according to what they deserve, can have any just cause to complain. Hardness of heart denotes that state of mind upon which neither threatenings nor promise, neither judgements nor mercies, make any abiding impression. The conscience being stupified, and the heart filled with pride and presumption, they persist in unbelief and disobedience. This state of mind is also called the stony heart. Very different is the heart of flesh, the broken and contrite heart. Sinners have none to blame but themselves, for that pride and ungodliness which abuse the bounty and patience of God. For, however the Lord hardens the hearts of men, it is always as a punishment of former sins.

Verses 8–12

When the Egyptians were not wrought upon by the death of their cattle, God sent a plague that seized their own bodies. If lesser judgments do not work, God will send greater. Sometimes God shows men their sin in their punishment. They had oppressed Israel in the furnaces, and now the ashes of the furnace are made a terror to them. The plague itself was very grievous. The magicians themselves were struck with these boils. Their power was restrained before; but they continued to withstand Moses, and to confirm Pharaoh in his unbelief, till they were forced to give way. Pharaoh continued obstinate. He had hardened his own heart, and now God justly gave him up to his own heart's lusts, permitting Satan to blind and harden him. If men shut their eyes against the light, it is just with God to close their eyes. This is the sorest judgment a man can be under out of hell.

Verses 13–21

Moses is here ordered to deliver a dreadful message to Pharaoh. Providence ordered it, that Moses should have a man of such a fierce and stubborn spirit as this Pharaoh to deal with; and every thing made it a most signal instance of the power of God has to humble and bring down the proudest of his enemies. When God's justice threatens ruin, his mercy at the same time shows a way of escape from it. God not only distinguished between Egyptians and Israelites, but between some Egyptians and others. If Pharaoh will not yield, and so prevent the judgment itself, yet those that will take warning, may take shelter. Some believed the things which were spoken, and they feared, and housed their servants and cattle, and it was their wisdom. Even among the servants of Pharaoh, some trembled at God's word; and shall not the sons of Israel dread it? But others believed not, and left their cattle in the field. Obstinate unbelief is deaf to the fairest warnings, and the wisest counsels, which leaves the blood of those that perish upon their own heads.

Verses 22–35

Woful havoc this hail made: it killed both men and cattle; the corn above ground was destroyed, and that only preserved which as yet was not come up. The land of Goshen was preserved. God causes rain or hail on one city and not on another, either in mercy or in judgment. Pharaoh humbled himself to Moses. No man could have spoken better: he owns himself wrong; he owns that the Lord is righteous; and God must be justified when he speaks, though he speaks in thunder and lightning. Yet his heart was hardened all this while. Moses pleads with God: though he had reason to think Pharaoh would repent of his repentance, and he told him so, yet he promises to be his friend. Moses went out of the city, notwithstanding the hail and lightning which kept Pharaoh and his servants within doors. Peace with God makes men thunder-proof. Pharaoh was frightened by the tremendous judgment; but when that was over, his fair promises were forgotten. Those that are not bettered by judgments and mercies, commonly become worse.

Chapter 10

Verses 1–11

The plagues of Egypt show the sinfulness of sin. They warn the children of men not to strive with their Maker. Pharaoh had pretended to humble himself; but no account was made of it, for he was not sincere therein. The plague of locusts is threatened. This should be much worse than any of that kind which had ever been known. Pharaoh's attendants persuade him to come to terms with Moses. Hereupon Pharaoh will allow the men to go, falsely pretending that this was all they desired. He swears that they shall not remove their little ones. Satan does all he can to hinder those that serve God themselves, from bringing their children to serve him. He is a sworn enemy to early piety. Whatever would put us from engaging our children in God's service, we have reason to suspect Satan in it. Nor should the young forget that the Lord's counsel is, Remember thy Creator in the days of thy youth; but Satan's counsel is, to keep children in a state of slavery to sin and to the world. Mark that the great foe of man wishes to retain him by the ties of affection, as Pharaoh would have taken hostages from the Israelites for their return, by holding their wives and children in captivity. Satan is willing to share our duty and our service with the Saviour, because the Saviour will not accept those terms.

Verses 12–20

God bids Moses stretch out his hand; locusts came at the call. An army might more easily have been resisted than this host of insects. Who then is able to stand before the great God? They covered the face of the earth, and ate up the fruit of it. Herbs grow for the service of man; yet when God pleases, insects shall plunder him, and eat the bread out of his mouth. Let our labour be, not for the habitation and meat thus exposed, but for those which endure to eternal life. Pharaoh employs Moses and Aaron to pray for him. There are those, who, in distress, seek the help of other people's prayers, but have no mind to pray for themselves. They show thereby that they have no true love to God, nor any delight in communion with him. Pharaoh desires only that this death might be taken away, not this sin. He wishes to get rid of the plague of locusts, not the plague of a hard heart, which was more dangerous. An east wind brought the locusts, a west wind carries them off. Whatever point the wind is in, it is fulfilling God's word, and turns by his counsel. The wind bloweth where it listeth, as to us; but not so as it respects God. It was also an argument for their repentance; for by this it appeared that God is ready to forgive, and swift to show mercy. If he does this upon the outward tokens of humiliation, what will he do if we are sincere! Oh that this goodness of God might lead us to repentance! Pharaoh returned to his resolution again, not to let the people go. Those who have often baffled their convictions, are justly given up to the lusts of their hearts.

Verses 21–29

The plague of darkness brought upon Egypt was a dreadful plague. It was darkness which might be felt, so thick were the fogs. It astonished and terrified. It continued three days; six nights in one; so long the most lightsome palaces were dungeons. Now Pharaoh had time to consider, if he would have improved it. Spiritual darkness is spiritual bondage; while Satan blinds men's eyes that they see not, he binds their hands and feet, that they work not for God, nor move toward heaven. They sit in darkness. It was righteous with God thus to punish. The blindness of their minds brought upon them this darkness of the air; never was mind so blinded as Pharaoh's, never was air so darkened as Egypt. Let us dread the consequences of sin; if three days of darkness were so dreadful, what will everlasting darkness be? The children of Israel, at the same time, had light in their dwellings. We must not think we share in common mercies as a matter of course, and therefore that we owe no thanks to God for them. It shows the particular favour he bears to his people. Wherever there is an Israelite indeed, though in this dark world, there is light, there is a child of light. When God made this difference between the Israelites and the Egyptians, who would not have preferred the poor cottage of an Israelite to the fine palace of an Egyptian? There is a real difference between the house of the wicked, which is under a curse, and the habitation of the just, which is blessed. Pharaoh renewed the treaty with Moses and Aaron, and consented they should take their little ones, but would have their cattle left. It is common for sinners to bargain with God Almighty; thus they try to mock him, but they deceive themselves. The terms of reconciliation with God are so fixed, that though men dispute them ever so long, they cannot possibly alter them, or bring them lower. We must come to the demand of God's will; we cannot expect he should condescend to the terms our lusts would make. With ourselves and our children, we must devote all our worldly possessions to the service of God; we know not what use he will make of any part of what we have. Pharaoh broke off the conference abruptly, and resolved to treat no more. Had he forgotten how often he had sent for Moses to ease him of his plagues? and must he now be bid to come no more? Vain malice! to threaten him with death, who was armed with such power! What will not hardness of heart, and contempt of God's word and commandments, bring men to! After this, Moses came no more till he was sent for. When men drive God's word from them, he justly gives them up to their own delusions.

Chapter 11

Verses 1–3

A secret revelation was made to Moses while in the presence of Pharaoh, that he might give warning of the last dreadful judgment, before he went out. This was the last day of the servitude of Israel; they were about to go away. Their masters, who had abused them in their work, would have sent them away empty; but God provided that the labourers should not lose their hire, and ordered them to demand it now, at their departure, and it was given to them. God will right the injured, who in humble silence commit their cause to him; and none are losers at last by patient suffering. The Lord gave them favour in the sight of the Egyptians, by making it appear how much he favoured them. He also changed the spirit of the Egyptians toward them, and made them to be pitied of their oppressors. Those that honour God, he will honour.

Verses 4–10

The death of all the first-born in Egypt at once: this plague had been the first threatened, but is last executed. See how slow God is to wrath. The plague is foretold, the time is fixed; all their first-born should sleep the sleep of death, not silently, but so as to rouse the families at midnight. The prince was not too high to be reached by it, nor the slaves at the mill too low to be noticed. While angels slew the Egyptians, not so much as a dog should bark at any of the children of Israel. It is an earnest of the difference there shall be in the great day, between God's people and his enemies. Did men know what a difference God puts, and will put to eternity, between those that serve him and those that serve him not, religion would not seem to them an indifferent thing; nor would they act in it with so much carelessness as they do. When Moses had thus delivered his message, he went out from Pharaoh in great anger at his obstinacy;

though he was the meekest of the men of the earth. The Scripture has foretold the unbelief of many who hear the gospel, that it might not be a surprise or stumbling-block to us, Ro **10**:**16**. Let us never think the worse of the gospel of Christ for the slights men put upon it. Pharaoh was hardened, yet he was compelled to abate his stern and haughty demands, till the Israelites got full freedom. In like manner the people of God will find that every struggle against their spiritual adversary, made in the might of Jesus Christ, every attempt to overcome him by the blood of the Lamb, and every desire to attain increasing likeness and love to that Lamb, will be rewarded by increasing freedom from the enemy of souls.

Chapter 12

Verses 1–20

The Lord makes all things new to those whom he delivers from the bondage of Satan, and takes to himself to be his people. The time when he does this is to them the beginning of a new life. God appointed that, on the night wherein they were to go out of Egypt, each family should kill a lamb, or that two or three families, if small, should kill one lamb. This lamb was to be eaten in the manner here directed, and the blood to be sprinkled on the door-posts, to mark the houses of the Israelites from those of the Egyptians. The angel of the Lord, when destroying the first-born of the Egyptians, would pass over the houses marked by the blood of the lamb: hence the name of this holy feast or ordinance. The passover was to be kept every year, both as a remembrance of Israel's preservation and deliverance out of Egypt, and as a remarkable type of Christ. Their safety and deliverance were not a reward of their own righteousness, but the gift of mercy. Of this they were reminded, and by this ordinance they were taught, that all blessings came to them through the shedding and sprinkling of blood. Observe, **1**. The paschal lamb was typical. Christ is our passover, **1**Co **5**:**7**. Christ is the Lamb of God, Joh **1**:**29**; often in the Revelation he is called the Lamb. It was to be in its prime; Christ offered up himself in the midst of his days, not when a babe at Bethlehem. It was to be without blemish; the Lord Jesus was a Lamb without spot: the judge who condemned Christ declared him innocent. It was to be set apart four days before, denoting the marking out of the Lord Jesus to be a Saviour, both in the purpose and in the promise. It was to be slain, and roasted with fire, denoting the painful sufferings of the Lord Jesus, even unto death, the death of the cross. The wrath of God is as fire, and Christ was made a curse for us. Not a bone of it must be broken, which was fulfilled in Christ, Joh **19**:**33**, denoting the unbroken strength of the Lord Jesus. **2**. The sprinkling of the blood was typical. The blood of the lamb must be sprinkled, denoting the applying of the merits of Christ's death to our souls; we must receive the atonement, Ro **5**:**11**. Faith is the bunch of hyssop, by which we apply the promises, and the benefits of the blood of Christ laid up in them, to ourselves. It was to be sprinkled on the door-posts, denoting the open profession we are to make of faith in Christ. It was not to be sprinkled upon the threshold; which cautions us to take heed of trampling under foot the blood of the covenant. It is precious blood, and must be precious to us. The blood, thus sprinkled, was a means of preserving the Israelites from the destroying angel, who had nothing to do where the blood was. The blood of Christ is the believer's protection from the wrath of God, the curse of the law, and the damnation of hell, Ro **8**:**1**. **3**. The solemn eating of the lamb was typical of our gospel duty to Christ. The paschal lamb was not to be looked upon only, but to be fed upon. So we must by faith make Christ our own; and we must receive spiritual strength and nourishment from him, as from our food, see Joh **6**:**53**, **55**. It was all to be eaten; those who by faith feed upon Christ, must feed upon a whole Christ; they must take Christ and his yoke, Christ and his cross, as well as Christ and his crown. It was to be eaten at once, not put by till morning. To-day Christ is offered, and is to be accepted while it is called to-day, before we sleep the sleep of death. It was to be eaten with bitter herbs, in remembrance of the bitterness of their bondage in Egypt; we must feed upon Christ with sorrow and brokenness of heart, in remembrance of sin. Christ will be sweet to us, if sin be bitter. It was to be eaten standing, with their staves in their hands, as being ready to depart. When we feed upon Christ by faith, we must forsake the rule and the dominion of sin; sit loose to the world, and every thing in it; forsake all for Christ, and reckon it no bad bargain, Heb **13**:**13**, **14**. **4**. The feast of unleavened bread was typical of the Christian life, **1**Co **5**:**7**, **8**. Having received Christ Jesus the Lord, we must continually delight ourselves in Christ Jesus. No manner of work must be done, that is, no care admitted and indulged, which does not agree with, or would lessen this holy joy. The Jews were very strict as to the passover, so that no leaven should be found in their houses. It must be a feast kept in charity, without the leaven of malice; and in sincerity, without the leaven of hypocrisy. It was by an ordinance for ever; so long as we live we must continue feeding upon Christ, rejoicing in him always, with thankful mention of the great things he has done for us.

Verses 21–28

That night, when the first-born were to be destroyed, no Israelite must stir out of doors till called to march out of Egypt. Their safety was owing to the blood of sprinkling. If they put themselves from under the protection of that, it was at their peril. They must stay within, to wait for the salvation of the Lord; it is good to do so. In after-times they should carefully teach their children the meaning of this service. It is good for children to ask about the things of God; they that ask for the way will find it. The keeping of this solemnity every year was, **1**. To look backward, that they might remember what great things God had done for them and their fathers. Old mercies, to ourselves, or to our fathers, must not be forgotten, that God may be praised, and our faith in him encouraged. **2**. It was designed to look forward, as an earnest of the great sacrifice of the Lamb of God in the fulness of time. Christ our passover was sacrificed for us; his death was our life.

Verses 29–36

The Egyptians had been for three days and nights kept in anxiety and horror by the darkness; now their rest is broken by a far more terrible calamity. The plague struck their first-born, the joy and hope of their families. They had slain the Hebrews' children, now God slew theirs. It reached from the throne to the dungeon: prince and peasant stand upon the same level before God's judgments. The destroying angel entered every dwelling unmarked with blood, as the messenger of woe. He did his dreadful errand, leaving not a house in which there was not one dead. Imagine then the cry that rang through the land of Egypt, the long, loud shriek of agony that burst from every dwelling. It will be thus in that dreadful hour when the Son of man shall visit sinners with the last judgment. God's sons, his first-born, were now released. Men had better come to God's terms at first, for he will never come to theirs. Now Pharaoh's pride is abased, and he yields. God's word will stand; we get nothing by disputing, or delaying to submit. In this terror the Egyptians would purchase the favour and the speedy departure of Israel. Thus the Lord took care that their hard-earned wages should be paid, and the people provided for their journey.

Verses 37–42

The children of Israel set forward without delay. A mixed multitude went with them. Some, perhaps, willing to leave their country, laid waste by plagues; others, out of curiosity; perhaps a few out of love to them and their religion. But there were always those among the Israelites who were not Israelites. Thus there are still hypocrites in the church. This great event was **430** years from the promise made to Abraham: see Ga **3**:**17**. So long the promise of a settlement was unfulfilled. But though God's promises are not performed quickly, they will be, in their season. This is that night of the Lord, that remarkable night, to be celebrated in all generations. The great things

God does for his people, are to be not only a few days' wonder, but to be remembered throughout all ages; especially the work of our redemption by Christ. This first passover-night was a night of the Lord, much to be observed; but the last passover-night, in which Christ was betrayed and in which the first passover, with the rest of the Jewish ceremonies, was done away, was a night of the Lord, much more to be observed. Then a yoke, heavier than that of Egypt, was broken from off our necks, and a land, better than that of Canaan, set before us. It was a redemption to be celebrated in heaven, for ever and ever.

Verses 43–51

In times to come, all the congregation of Israel must keep the passover. All that share in God's mercies should join in thankful praises for them. The New Testament passover, the Lord's supper, ought not to be neglected by any. Strangers, if circumcised, might eat of the passover. Here is an early indication of favour to the gentiles. This taught the Jews that their being a nation favoured by God, entitled them to their privileges, not their descent from Abraham. Christ our passover is sacrificed for us, **1**Co **5**:**7**; his blood is the only ransom for our souls; without the shedding of it there is no remission; without the sprinkling of it there can be no salvation. Have we, by faith in him, sheltered our souls from deserved vengeance under the protection of his atoning blood? Do we keep close to him, constantly depending upon him? Do we so profess our faith in the Redeemer, and our obligations to him, that all who pass by may know to whom we belong? Do we stand prepared for his service, ready to walk in his ways, and to separate ourselves from his enemies? These are questions of vast importance to the soul; may the Lord direct our consciences honestly to answer them.

Chapter 13

Verses 1–10

In remembrance of the destruction of the first-born of Egypt, both of man and of beast, and the deliverance of the Israelites out of bondage, the first-born males of the Israelites were set apart to the Lord. By this was set before them, that their lives were preserved through the ransom of the atonement, which in due time was to be made for sin. They were also to consider their lives, thus ransomed from death, as now to be consecrated to the service of God. The parents were not to look upon themselves as having any right in their first-born, till they solemnly presented them to God, and allowed his title to them. That which is, by special mercy, spared to us, should be applied to God's honour; at least, some grateful acknowledgment, in works of piety and charity, should be made. The remembrance of their coming out of Egypt must be kept up every year. The day of Christ's resurrection is to be remembered, for in it we were raised up with Christ out of death's house of bondage. The Scripture tells us not expressly what day of the year Christ rose, but it states particularly what day of the week it was; as the more valuable deliverance, it should be remembered weekly. The Israelites must keep the feast of unleavened bread. Under the gospel, we must not only remember Christ, but observe his holy supper. Do this in remembrance of him. Also care must be taken to teach children the knowledge of God. Here is an old law for catechising. It is of great use to acquaint children betimes with the histories of the Bible. And those who have God's law in their heart should have it in their mouth, and often speak of it, to affect themselves, and to teach others.

Verses 11–16

The firstlings of beast not used in sacrifice, were to be changed for others so used, or they were to be destroyed. Our souls are forfeited to God's justice, and unless ransomed by the sacrifice of Christ, will certainly perish. These institutions would continually remind them of their duty, to love and serve the Lord. In like manner, baptism and the Lord's supper, if explained and attended to, would remind us, and give us occasion to remind one another of our profession and duty.

Verses 17–20

There were two ways from Egypt to Canaan. One was only a few days' journey; the other was much further about, through the wilderness, and that was the way in which God chose to lead his people Israel. The Egyptians were to be drowned in the Red sea; the Israelites were to be humbled and proved in the wilderness. God's way is the right way, though it seems about. If we think he leads not his people the nearest way, yet we may be sure he leads them the best way, and so it will appear when we come to our journey's end. The Philistines were powerful enemies; it was needful that the Israelites should be prepared for the wars of Canaan, by passing through the difficulties of the wilderness. Thus God proportions his people's trials to their strength, **1**Co **10**:**13**. They went up in good order. They went up in five in a rank, some; in five bands, so others, which it seems rather to their faith and hope, that God would bring them to Canaan, in expectation of which they carried these bones with them while in the desert.

Verses 21, 22

The Lord went before them in a pillar, or appearance of the Divine Majesty. Christ was with the church in the wilderness, **1**Co **10**:**9**. Those whom God brings into a wilderness, he will not leave nor lose there, but will take care to lead them through it. It was great satisfaction to Moses and the pious Israelites, to be sure that they were under Divine guidance. Those who make the glory of God their end, and the word of God their rule, the Spirit of God the guide of their affections, and the providence of God the guide of their affairs, may be sure that the Lord goes before them, though they cannot see it with their eyes: we must now live by faith. When Israel marched, this pillar went before, and pointed out the place of encampment, as Divine Wisdom saw fit. It sheltered by day from the heat, and gave light by night. The Bible is a light to our feet, a lantern to our paths, with which the Saviour's love has provided us. It testifies of Christ. It is to us like the pillar to the Israelites. Listen to that voice which cries, I am the Light of the world; he that followeth me shall not walk in darkness, but shall have the Light of life, Joh **8**:**12**. Jesus Christ alone, as shown in the Bible, and as the Holy Spirit, in answer to prayer, recommends him to the soul, is the Way, the Truth, and the Life, Joh **14**:**6**.

Chapter 14

Verses 1–9

Pharaoh would think that all Israel was entangled in the wilderness, and so would become an easy prey. But God says, I will be honoured upon Pharaoh. All men being made for the honour of their Maker, those whom he is not honoured by, he will be honoured upon. What seems to tend to the church's ruin, is often overruled to the ruin of the church's enemies. While Pharaoh gratified his malice and revenge, he furthered the bringing to pass God's counsels concerning him. Though with the greatest reason he had let Israel go, yet now he was angry with himself for it. God makes the envy and rage of men against his people, a torment to themselves. Those who set their faces heavenward, and will live godly in Christ Jesus, must expect to be set upon by Satan's temptations and terrors. He will not tamely part with any out of his service.

Verses 10–14

There was no way open to Israel but upward, and thence their deliverance came. We may be in the way of duty, following God, and hastening toward heaven, yet may be troubled on every side. Some cried out unto the Lord; their fear led them to pray, and that was well. God brings us into straits, that he may bring us to our knees. Others cried out against Moses; fear set them murmuring as if God were not still able to work miracles. They quarrel with Moses for bringing them out of Egypt; and so were angry with God for the greatest kindness ever done them; thus gross are the absurdities of unbelief. Moses says, Fear ye not. It is always our duty and interest, when we cannot get out of troubles, yet to get above our fears; let them quicken our prayers and endeavours, but not silence our faith and hope. "Stand still," think not to save yourselves either by fighting or flying; wait God's orders, and observe them. Compose yourselves, by confidence in God, into peaceful thoughts of the great salvation God is about to work for you. If God brings his people into straits, he will find a way to bring them out.

Verses 15–20

Moses' silent prayers of faith prevailed more with God than Israel's loud outcries of fear. The pillar of cloud and fire came behind them, where they needed a guard, and it was a wall between them and their enemies. The word and providence of God have a black and dark side toward sin and sinners, but a bright and pleasant side toward the people of the Lord. He, who divided between light and darkness, Ge **1**:**4**, allotted darkness to the Egyptians, and light to the Israelites. Such a difference there will be between the inheritance of the saints in light, and that utter darkness which will be the portion of hypocrites for ever.

Verses 21–31

The dividing the Red sea was the terror of the Canaanites, Jos **2**:**9**; the praise and triumph of the Israelites, Ps **114**:**3**; **106**:**9**; **136**:**13**. It was a type of baptism, **1**Co **10**:**1**, **2**. Israel's passage through it was typical of the conversion of souls, Isa **11**:**15**; and the Egyptians being drowned in it was typical of the final ruin of all unrepenting sinners. God showed his almighty power, by opening a passage through the waters, some miles over. God can bring his people through the greatest difficulties, and force a way where he does not find it. It was an instance of his wonderful favour to his Israel. They went through the sea, they walked upon dry land in the midst of the sea. This was done, in order to encourage God's people in all ages to trust him in the greatest straits. What cannot he do who did this? What will not he do for those that fear and love him, who did this for these murmuring, unbelieving Israelites? Then followed the just and righteous wrath of God upon his and his people's enemies. The ruin of sinners is brought on by their own rage and presumption. They might have let Israel alone, and would not; now they would flee from the face of Israel, and cannot. Men will not be convinced, till it is too late, that those who meddle with God's people, meddle to their own hurt. Moses was ordered to stretch out his hand over the sea; the waters returned, and overwhelmed all the host of the Egyptians. Pharaoh and his servants, who had hardened one another in sin, now fell together, not one escaped. The Israelites saw the Egyptians dead upon the sands. The sight very much affected them. While men see God's works, and feel the benefit, they fear him and trust in him. How well were it for us, if we were always in as good a frame as sometimes! Behold the end to which a Christian may look forward. His enemies rage, and are mighty; but while he holds fast by God, he shall pass the waves in safety guarded by that very power of his Saviour, which shall come down on every spiritual foe. The enemies of his soul whom he hath seen to-day, he shall see no more for ever.

Chapter 15

Verses 1–21

This song is the most ancient we know of. It is a holy song, to the honour of God, to exalt his name, and celebrate his praise, and his only, not in the least to magnify any man. Holiness to the Lord is in every part of it. It may be considered as typical, and prophetical of the final destruction of the enemies of the church. Happy the people whose God is the Lord. They have work to do, temptations to grapple with, and afflictions to bear, and are weak in themselves; but his grace is their strength. They are often in sorrow, but in him they have comfort; he is their song. Sin, and death, and hell threaten them, but he is, and will be their salvation. The Lord is a God of almighty power, and woe to those that strive with their Maker! He is a God of matchless perfection; he is glorious in holiness; his holiness is his glory. His holiness appears in the hatred of sin, and his wrath against obstinate sinners. It appears in the deliverance of Israel, and his faithfulness to his own promise. He is fearful in praises; that which is matter of praise to the servants of God, is very dreadful to his enemies. He is doing wonders, things out of the common course of nature; wondrous to those in whose favour they are wrought, who are so unworthy, that they had no reason to expect them. There were wonders of power and wonders of grace; in both, God was to be humbly adored.

Verses 22–27

In the wilderness of Shur the Israelites had no water. At Marah they had water, but it was bitter; so that they could not drink it. God can make bitter to us that from which we promise ourselves most, and often does so in the wilderness of this world, that our wants, and disappointments in the creature, may drive us to the Creator, in whose favour alone true comfort is to be had. In this distress the people fretted, and quarrelled with Moses. Hypocrites may show high affections, and appear earnest in religious exercises, but in the time of temptation they fall away. Even true believers, in seasons of sharp trial, will be tempted to fret, distrust, and murmur. But in every trial we should cast our care upon the Lord, and pour out our hearts before him. We shall then find that a submissive will, a peaceful conscience, and the comforts of the Holy Ghost, will render the bitterest trial tolerable, yea, pleasant. Moses did what the people had neglected to do; he cried unto the Lord. And God provided graciously for them. He directed Moses to a tree which he cast into the waters, when, at once, they were made sweet. Some make this tree typical of the cross of Christ, which sweetens the bitter waters of affliction to all the faithful, and enables them to rejoice in tribulation. But a rebellious Israelite shall fare no better than a rebellious Egyptian. The threatening is implied only, the promise is expressed. God is the great Physician. If we are kept well, it is he that keeps us; if we are made well, it is he that recovers us. He is our life and the length of our days. Let us not forget that we are kept from destruction, and delivered from our enemies, to be the Lord's servants. At Elim they had good water, and enough of it. Though God may, for a time, order his people to encamp by the bitter waters of Marah, that shall not always be their lot. Let us not faint at tribulations.

Chapter 16

Verses 1–12

The provisions of Israel, brought from Egypt, were spent by the middle of the second month, and they murmured. It is no new thing for the greatest kindness to be basely represented as the greatest injuries. They so far undervalue their deliverance, that they wished they had died in Egypt; and by the hand of the Lord, that is, by the plagues which cut off the Egyptians. We cannot suppose they had plenty in Egypt, nor could they fear dying for want in the wilderness, while they had flocks and herds: none talk more absurdly than murmurers. When we begin to fret, we ought to consider, that God hears all our murmurings. God promises a speedy and constant supply. He tried whether they would trust him, and rest satisfied with the bread of the day in its day. Thus he tried if they would serve him, and it appeared how ungrateful they were. When God plagued the Egyptians, it was to make them know he was their Lord; when he provided for the Israelites, it was to make them know he was their God.

Verses 13–21

At evening the quails came up, and the people caught with ease as many as they needed. The manna came down in dew. They called it "Manna, Manhu," which means, "What is this?" "It is a portion; it is that which our God has allotted us, and we will take it, and be thankful." It was pleasant food; it was wholesome food. The manna was rained from heaven; it appeared, when the dew was gone, as a small round thing, as small as the hoar frost, like coriander seed, in colour like pearls. The manna fell only six days in the week, and in double quantity on the sixth day; it bred worms and became offensive if kept more than one day, excepting on the sabbath. The people had never seen it before. It could be ground in a mill, or beaten in a mortar, and was then made into cakes and baked. It continued the forty years the Israelites were in the wilderness, wherever they went, and ceased when they arrived in Canaan. All this shows how different it was from any thing found before, or found now. They were to gather the manna every morning. We are hereby taught, **1**. To be prudent and diligent in providing food for ourselves and our households; with quietness working, and eating our own bread, not the bread of idleness or deceit. God's bounty leaves room for man's duty; it did so even when manna was rained; they must not eat till they have gathered. **2**. To be content with enough. Those that have most, have for themselves but food and raiment; those that have least, generally have these; so that he who gathers much has nothing over, and he who gathers little has no lack. There is not such a disproportion between one and another in the enjoyment of the things of this life, as in the mere possession of them. **3**. To depend upon Providence: let them sleep quietly, though they have no bread in their tents, nor in all their camp, trusting that God, with the following day, would bring them in their daily bread. It was surer and safer in God's storehouse than their own, and would come thence sweeter and fresher. See here the folly of hoarding. The manna laid up by some, who thought themselves wiser, and better managers, than their neighbours, and who would provide lest it should fail next day, bred worms, and became good for nothing. That will prove to be most wasted, which is covetously and distrustfully spared. Such riches are corrupted, Jas **5**:**2**, **3**. The same wisdom, power, and goodness that brought food daily from above for the Israelites in the wilderness, brings food yearly out of the earth in the constant course of nature, and gives us all things richly to enjoy.

Verses 22–31

Here is mention of a seventh-day sabbath. It was known, not only before the giving of the law upon mount Sinai, but before the bringing of Israel out of Egypt, even from the beginning, Ge **2**:**3**. The setting apart one day in seven for holy work, and, in order to that, for holy rest, was ever since God created man upon the earth, and is the most ancient of the Divine laws. Appointing them to rest on the seventh day, he took care that they should be no losers by it; and none ever will be losers by serving God. On that day they were to fetch in enough for two days, and to make it ready. This directs us to contrive family affairs, so that they may hinder us as little as possible in the work of the sabbath. Works of necessity are to be done on that day; but it is desirable to have as little as may be to do, that we may apply ourselves the more closely to prepare for the life that is to come. When they kept manna against a command, it stank; when they kept it by a command, it was sweet and good; every thing is sanctified by the word of God and prayer. On the seventh day God did not send the manna, therefore they must not expect it, nor go out to gather. This showed that it was produced by miracle.

Verses 32–36

God having provided manna to be his people's food in the wilderness, the remembrance of it was to be preserved. Eaten bread must not be forgotten. God's miracles and mercies are to be had in remembrance. The word of God is the manna by which our souls are nourished, Mt **4**:**4**. The comforts of the Spirit are hidden manna, Re **2**:**17**. These come from heaven, as the manna did, and are the support and comfort of the Divine life in the soul, while we are in the wilderness of this world. Christ in the word is to be applied to the soul, and the means of grace are to be used. We must every one of us gather for ourselves, and gather in the morning of our days, the morning of our opportunities; which if we let slip, it may be too late to gather. The manna must not be hoarded up, but eaten; those who have received Christ, must by faith live upon him, and not receive his grace in vain. There was manna enough for all, enough for each, and none had too much; so in Christ there is enough, but not more than we need. But those who ate manna, hungered again, died at last, and with many of them God was not well pleased; whereas they that feed on Christ by faith, shall never hunger, and shall die no more, and with them God will be for ever well pleased. Let us seek earnestly for the grace of the Holy Spirit, to turn all our knowledge of the doctrine of Christ crucified, into the spiritual nourishment of our souls by faith and love.

Chapter 17

Verses 1–7

The children of Israel journeyed according to the commandment of the Lord, led by the pillar of cloud and fire, yet they came to a place where there was no water for them to drink. We may be in the way of duty, yet may meet with troubles, which Providence brings us into, for the trial of our faith, and that God may be glorified in our relief. They began to question whether God was with them or not. This is called their "tempting God," which signifies distrust of him after they had received such proofs of his power and goodness. Moses mildly answered them. It is folly to answer passion with passion; that makes bad worse. God graciously appeared to help them. How wonderful the patience and forbearance of God toward provoking sinners! That he might show his power as well as his pity, and make it a miracle of mercy, he gave them water out of a rock. God can open fountains for us where we least expect them. Those who, in this wilderness, keep to God's way, may trust him to provide for them. Also, let this direct us to depend on Christ's grace. The apostle says, that Rock was Christ, **1**Co **10**:**4**, it was a type of him. While the curse of God might justly have been executed upon our guilty souls, behold the Son of God is smitten for us. Let us ask and receive. There was a constant, abundant supply of this water. Numerous as believers are, the supply of the Spirit of Christ is enough for all. The water flowed from the rock in streams to refresh the wilderness, and attended them on their way towards Canaan; and this water flows from Christ, through the ordinances, in the barren wilderness of this world, to refresh our souls, until we come to glory. A new name was given to the place, in remembrance, not of the mercy of their supply, but of the sin of their murmuring: "Massah," Temptation, because they tempted God; "Meribah," Strife, because they chid with Moses. Sin leaves a blot upon the name.

Verses 8–16

Israel engaged with Amalek in their own necessary defence. God makes his people able, and calls them to various services for the good of his church. Joshua fights, Moses prays, both minister to Israel. The rod was held up, as the banner to encourage the soldiers. Also to God, by way of appeal to him. Moses was tired. The strongest arm will fail with being long held out; it is God only whose hand is stretched out still. We do not find that Joshua's hands were heavy in fighting, but Moses' hands were heavy in praying; the more spiritual any service is, the more apt we are to fail and flag in it. To convince Israel that the hand of Moses, whom they had been chiding, did more for their safety than their own hands, his rod than their sword, the success rises and falls as Moses lifts up or lets down his hands. The church's cause is more or less successful, as her friends are more or less strong in faith, and fervent in prayer. Moses, the man of God, is glad of help. We should not be shy, either of asking help from others, or of giving help to others. The hands of Moses being thus stayed, were steady till the going down of the sun. It was great encouragement to the people to see Joshua before them in the field of battle, and Moses above them on the hill. Christ is both to us; our Joshua, the Captain of our salvation, who fights our battles, and our Moses, who ever lives, making intercession above, that our faith fail not. Weapons formed against God's Israel cannot prosper long, and shall be broken at last. Moses must write what had been done, what Amalek had done against Israel; write their bitter hatred; write their cruel attempts; let them never be forgotten, nor what God had done for Israel in saving them from Amalek. Write what should be done; that in process of time Amalek should be totally ruined and rooted out. Amalek's destruction was typical of the destruction of all the enemies of Christ and his kingdom.

Chapter 18

Verses 1–6

Jethro came to rejoice with Moses in the happiness of Israel, and to bring his wife and children to him. Moses must have his family with him, that while he ruled the church of God, he might set a good example in family government, **1**Ti **3**:**5**.

Verses 7–12

Conversation concerning God's wondrous works is good, and edifies. Jethro not only rejoiced in the honour done to his son-in-law, but in all the goodness done to Israel. Standers-by were more affected with the favours God had showed to Israel, than many were who received them. Jethro gave the glory to Israel's God. Whatever we have the joy of, God must have the praise. They joined in a sacrifice of thanksgiving. Mutual friendship is sanctified by joint worship. It is very good for relations and friends to join in the spiritual sacrifice of prayer and praise, as those that meet in Christ. This was a temperate feast; they did eat bread, manna. Jethro must see and taste that bread from heaven, and though a gentile, is welcome: the gentiles are welcomed to Christ the Bread of life.

Verses 13–27

Here is the great zeal and the toil of Moses as a magistrate. Having been employed to redeem Israel out of the house of bondage, he is a further type of Christ, that he is employed as a lawgiver and a judge among them. If the people were as quarrelsome one with another as they were with God, no doubt Moses had many causes brought before him. This business Moses was called to; it appears that he did it with great care and kindness. The meanest Israelite was welcome to bring his cause before him. Moses kept to his business from morning to night. Jethro thought it was too much for him to undertake alone; also it would make the administration of justice tiresome to the people. There may be over-doing even in well-doing. Wisdom is profitable to direct, that we may neither content ourselves with less than our duty, nor task ourselves beyond our strength. Jethro advised Moses to a better plan. Great men should not only study to be useful themselves, but contrive to make others useful. Care must be taken in the choice of the persons admitted into such a trust. They should be men of good sense, that understood business, and that would not be daunted by frowns or clamours, but abhorred the thought of a bribe. Men of piety and religion; such as fear God, who dare not to do a base thing, though they could do it secretly and securely. The fear of God will best fortify a man against temptations to injustice. Moses did not despise this advice. Those are not wise, who think themselves too wise to be counselled.

Chapter 19

Verses 1–8

Moses was called up the mountain, and was employed as the messenger of this covenant. The Maker and first Mover of the covenant, is God himself. This blessed charter was granted out of God's own free grace. The covenant here mentioned was the national covenant, by which the Israelites were a people under the government of Jehovah. It was a type of the new covenant made with true believers in Christ Jesus; but, like other types, it was only a shadow of good things to come. As a nation they broke this covenant; therefore the Lord declared that he would make a new covenant with Israel, writing his law, not upon tables of stone, but in their hearts, Jer **31**:**33**; Heb **8**:**7**–**10**. The covenant spoken of in these places as ready to vanish away, is the national covenant with Israel, which they forfeited by their sins. Unless we carefully attend to this, we shall fall into mistakes while reading the Old Testament. We must not suppose that the nation of the Jews were under the covenant of works, which knows nothing of repentance, faith in a Mediator, forgiveness of sins, or grace; nor yet that the whole nation of Israel bore the character, and possessed the privileges of true believers, as being actually sharers in the covenant of grace. They were all under a dispensation of mercy; they had outward privileges and advantages for salvation; but, like professing Christians, most rested therein, and went no further. Israel consented to the conditions. They answered as one man, All that the Lord hath spoken we will do. Oh that there had been such a heart in them! Moses, as a mediator, returned the words of the people to God. Thus Christ, the Mediator, as a Prophet, reveals God's will to us, his precepts and promises; and then, as a Priest, offers up to God our spiritual sacrifices, not only of prayer and praise, but of devout affections, and pious resolutions, the work of his own Spirit in us.

Verses 9–15

The solemn manner in which the law was delivered, was to impress the people with a right sense of the Divine majesty. Also to convince them of their own guilt, and to show that they could not stand in judgment before God by their own obedience. In the law, the sinner discovers what he ought to be, what he is, and what he wants. There he learns the nature, necessity, and glory of redemption, and of being made holy. Having been taught to flee to Christ, and to love him, the law is the rule of his obedience and faith.

Verses 16–25

Never was there such a sermon preached, before or since, as this which was preached to the church in the wilderness. It might be supposed that the terrors would have checked presumption and curiosity in the people; but the hard heart of an unawakened sinner can trifle with the most terrible threatenings and judgments. In drawing near to God, we must never forget his holiness and greatness, nor our own meanness and pollution. We cannot stand in judgment before him according to his righteous law. The convinced transgressor asks, What must I do to be saved? and he hears the voice, Believe in the Lord Jesus Christ, and thou shalt be saved. The Holy Ghost, who made the law to convince of sin, now takes of the things of Christ, and shows them to us. In the gospel we read, Christ hath redeemed us from the curse of the law, being made a curse for us. We have redemption through his blood, even the forgiveness of sins. Through him we are justified from all things, from which we could not be justified by the law of Moses. But the Divine law is binding as a rule of life. The Son of God came down from heaven, and suffered poverty, shame, agony, and death, not only to redeem us from its curse, but to bind us more closely to keep its commands.

Chapter 20

Verses 1, 2

God speaks many ways to the children of men; by conscience, by providences, by his voice, to all which we ought carefully to attend; but he never spake at any time so as he spake the TEN COMMANDMENTS. This law God had given to man before; it was written in his heart; but sin so defaced it, that it was necessary to revive the knowledge of it. The law is spiritual, and takes knowledge of the secret thoughts, desires, and dispositions of the heart. Its grand demand is love, without which outward obedience is mere hypocrisy. It requires perfect, unfailing, constant obedience; no law in the world admits disobedience to itself. Whosoever shall keep the whole law, and yet offend in one point, he is guilty of all, Jas **2**:**10**. Whether in the heart or the conduct, in thought, word, or deed, to omit or to vary any thing, is sin, and the wages of sin is death.

Verses 3–11

The first four of the ten commandments, commonly called the FIRST table, tell our duty to God. It was fit that those should be put first, because man had a Maker to love, before he had a neighbour to love. It cannot be expected that he should be true to his brother, who is false to his God. The first commandment concerns the object of worship, JEHOVAH, and him only. The worship of creatures is here forbidden. Whatever comes short of perfect love, gratitude, reverence, or worship, breaks this commandment. Whatsoever ye do, do all the glory of God. The second commandment refers to the worship we are to render to the Lord our God. It is forbidden to make any image or picture of the Deity, in any form, or for any purpose; or to worship any creature, image, or picture. But the spiritual import of this command extends much further. All kinds of superstition are here forbidden, and the using of mere human inventions in the worship of God. The third commandment concerns the manner of worship, that it be with all possible reverence and seriousness. All false oaths are forbidden. All light appealing to God, all profane cursing, is a horrid breach of this command. It matters not whether the word of God, or sacred things, all such-like things break this commandment, and there is no profit, honour, or pleasure in them. The Lord will not hold him guiltless that taketh his name in vain. The form of the fourth commandment, "Remember," shows that it was not now first given, but was known by the people before. One day in seven is to be kept holy. Six days are allotted to worldly business, but not so as to neglect the service of God, and the care of our souls. On those days we must do all our work, and leave none to be done on the sabbath day. Christ allowed works of necessity, charity, and piety; for the sabbath was made for man, and not man for the sabbath, Mr **2**:**27**; but all works of luxury, vanity, or self-indulgence in any form, are forbidden. Trading, paying wages, settling accounts, writing letters of business, worldly studies, trifling visits, journeys, or light conversation, are not keeping this day holy to the Lord. Sloth and indolence may be a carnal, but not a holy rest. The sabbath of the Lord should be a day of rest from worldly labour, and a rest in the service of God. The advantages from the due keeping of this holy day, were it only to the health and happiness of mankind, with the time it affords for taking care of the soul, show the excellency of this commandment. The day is blessed; men are blessed by it, and in it. The blessing and direction to keep holy are not limited to the seventh day, but are spoken of the sabbath day.

Verses 12–17

The laws of the SECOND table, that is, the last six of the ten commandments, state our duty to ourselves and to one another, and explain the great commandment, Thou shalt love thy neighbour as thyself, Lu **10**:**27**. Godliness and honesty must go together. The fifth commandment concerns the duties we owe to our relations. Honour thy father and thy mother, includes esteem of them, shown in our conduct; obedience to their lawful commands; come when they call you, go where they send you, do what they bid you, refrain from what they forbid you; and this, as children, cheerfully, and from a principle of love. Also submission to their counsels and corrections. Endeavouring, in every thing, to comfort parents, and to make their old age easy; maintaining them if they need support, which our Saviour makes to be particularly intended in this commandment, Mt **15**:**4**–**6**. Careful observers have noted a peculiar blessing in temporal things on obedient, and the re**verse** on disobedient children. The sixth commandment requires that we regard the life and the safety of others as we do our own. Magistrates and their officers, and witnesses testifying the truth, do not break this command. Self-defence is lawful; but much which is not deemed murder by the laws of man, is such before God. Furious passions, stirred up by anger or by drunkenness, are no excuse: more guilty is murder in duels, which is a horrible effect of a haughty, revengeful spirit. All fighting, whether for wages, for renown, or out of anger and malice, breaks this command, and the bloodshed therein is murder. To tempt men to vice and crimes which shorten life, may be included. Misconduct, such as may break the heart, or shorten the lives of parents, wives, or other relatives, is a breach of this command. This command forbids all envy, malice, hatred, or anger, all provoking or insulting language. The destruction of our own lives is here forbidden. This commandment requires a spirit of kindness, longsuffering, and forgiveness. The seventh commandment concerns chastity. We should be as much afraid of that which defiles the body, as of that which destroys it. Whatever tends to pollute the imagination, or to raise the passions, falls under this law, as impure pictures, books, conversation, or any other like matters. The eighth commandment is the law of love as it respects the property of others. The portion of worldly things allotted us, as far as it is obtained in an honest way, is the bread which God hath given us; for that we ought to be thankful, to be contented with it, and, in the use of lawful means, to trust Providence for the future. Imposing upon the ignorance, easiness, or necessity of others, and many other things, break God's law, though scarcely blamed in society. Plunderers of kingdoms though above human justice, will be included in this sentence. Defrauding the public, contracting debts without prospect of paying them, or evading payment of just debts, extravagance, all living upon charity when not needful, all squeezing the poor in their wages; these, and such things, break this command; which requires industry, frugality, and content, and to do to others, about worldly property, as we would they should do to us. The ninth commandment concerns our own and our neighbour's good name. This forbids speaking falsely on any matter, lying, equivocating, and any way devising or designing to deceive our neighbour. Speaking unjustly against our neighbour, to hurt his reputation. Bearing false witness against him, or in common conversation slandering, backbiting, and tale-bearing; making what is done amiss, worse than it is, and in any way endeavouring to raise our reputation upon the ruin of our neighbour's. How much this command is every day broken among persons of all ranks! The tenth commandment strikes at the root; Thou shalt not covet. The others forbid all desire of doing what will be an injury to our neighbour; this forbids all wrong desire of having what will gratify ourselves.

Verses 18–21

This law, which is so extensive that we cannot measure it, so spiritual that we cannot evade it, and so reasonable that we cannot find fault with it, will be the rule of the future judgment of God, as it is for the present conduct of man. If tried by this rule, we shall find our lives have been passed in transgressions. And with this holy law and an awful judgment before us, who can despise the gospel of Christ? And the knowledge of the law shows our need of repentance. In every believer's heart sin is dethroned and crucified, the law of God is written, and the image of God renewed. The Holy Spirit enables him to hate sin and flee from it, to love and keep this law in sincerity and truth; nor will he cease to repent.

Verses 22–26

Moses having entered into the thick darkness, God there spake in his hearing all that follows from hence to the end of chap. **23**, which is mostly an exposition of the ten commandments. The laws in these **verses** relate to God's worship. The Israelites are assured of God's gracious acceptance of their devotions. Under the gospel, men are encouraged to pray every where, and wherever God's people meet in his name to worship him, he will be in the midst of them; there he will come unto them, and will bless them.

Chapter 21

Verses 1–11

The laws in this chapter relate to the fifth and sixth commandments; and though they differ from our times and customs, nor are they binding on us, yet they explain the moral law, and the rules of natural justice. The servant, in the state of servitude, was an emblem of that state of bondage to sin, Satan, and the law, which man is brought into by robbing God of his glory, by the transgression of his precepts. Likewise in being made free, he was an emblem of that liberty wherewith Christ, the Son of God, makes free from bondage his people, who are free indeed; and made so freely, without money and without price, of free grace.

Verses 12–21

God, who by his providence gives and maintains life, by his law protects it. A wilful murderer shall be taken even from God's altar. But God provided cities of refuge to protect those whose unhappiness it was, and not their fault, to cause the death of another; for such as by accident, when a man is doing a lawful act, without intent of hurt, happens to kill another. Let children hear the sentence of God's word upon the ungrateful and disobedient; and remember that God will certainly requite it, if they have ever cursed their parents, even in their hearts, or have lifted up their hands against them, except they repent, and flee for refuge to the Saviour. And let parents hence learn to be very careful in training up their children, setting them a good example, especially in the government of their passions, and in praying for them; taking heed not to provoke them to wrath. Through poverty the Israelites sometimes sold themselves or their children; magistrates sold some persons for their crimes, and creditors were in some cases allowed to sell their debtors who could not pay. But "man-stealing," the object of which is to force another into slavery, is ranked in the New Testament with the greatest crimes. Care is here taken, that satisfaction be made for hurt done to a person, though death do not follow. The gospel teaches masters to forbear, and to moderate threatenings, Eph **6**:**9**, considering with Job, What shall I do, when God riseth up? Job **31**:**13**, **14**.

Verses 22–36

The cases here mentioned give rules of justice then, and still in use, for deciding similar matters. We are taught by these laws, that we must be very careful to do no wrong, either directly or indirectly. If we have done wrong, we must be very willing to make it good, and be desirous that nobody may lose by us.

Chapter 22

Judicial laws.

—The people of God should ever be ready to show mildness and mercy, according to the spirit of these laws. We must answer to God, not only for what we do maliciously, but for what we do heedlessly. Therefore, when we have done harm to our neighbour, we should make restitution, though not compelled by law. Let these scriptures lead our souls to remember, that if the grace of God has indeed appeared to us, then it has taught us, and enabled us so to conduct ourselves by its holy power, that denying ungodliness and wordly lusts, we should live soberly, righteously, and godly in this present world, Tit **2**:**12**. And the grace of God teaches us, that as the Lord is our portion, there is enough in him to satisfy all the desires of our souls.

Chapter 23

Verses 1–9

In the law of Moses are very plain marks of sound moral feeling, and of true political wisdom. Every thing in it is suited to the desired and avowed object, the worship of one only God, and the separation of Israel from the pagan world. Neither parties, friends, witnesses, nor common opinions, must move us to lessen great faults, to aggravate small ones, excuse offenders, accuse the innocent, or misrepresent any thing.

Verses 10–19

Every seventh year the land was to rest. They must not plough or sow it; what the earth produced of itself, should be eaten, and not laid up. This law seems to have been intended to teach dependence on Providence, and God's faithfulness in sending the larger increase while they kept his appointments. It was also typical of the heavenly rest, when all earthly labours, cares, and interests shall cease for ever. All respect to the gods of the heathen is strictly forbidden. Since idolatry was a sin to which the Israelites leaned, they must blot out the remembrance of the gods of the heathen. Solemn religious attendance on God, in the place which he should choose, is strictly required. They must come together before the Lord. What a good Master do we serve, who has made it our duty to rejoice before him! Let us devote with pleasure to the service of God that portion of our time which he requires, and count his sabbaths and ordinances to be a feast unto our souls. They were not to come empty-handed; so now, we must not come to worship God empty-hearted; our souls must be filled with holy desires toward him, and dedications of ourselves to him; for with such sacrifices God is well pleased.

Verses 20–33

It is here promised that they should be guided and kept in their way through the wilderness to the land of promise, Behold, I send an angel before thee, mine angel. The precept joined with this promise is, that they be obedient to this angel whom God would send before them. Christ is the Angel of Jehovah; this is plainly taught by St. Paul, **1**Co **10**:**9**. They should have a comfortable settlement in the land of Canaan. How reasonable are the conditions of this promise; that they should serve the only true God; not the gods of the nations, which are no gods at all. How rich are the particulars of this promise! The comfort of their food, the continuance of their health, the increase of their wealth, the prolonging their lives to old age. Thus hath godliness the promise of the life that now is. It is promised that they should subdue their enemies. Hosts of hornets made way for the hosts of Israel; such mean creatures can God use for chastising his people's enemies. In real kindness to the church, its enemies are subdued by little and little; thus we are kept on our guard, and in continual dependence on God. Corruptions are driven out of the hearts of God's people, not all at once, but by little and little. The precept with this promise is, that they should not make friendship with idolaters. Those that would keep from bad courses, must keep from bad company. It is dangerous to live in a bad neighbourhood; others' sins will be our snares. Our greatest danger is from those who would make us sin against God.

Chapter 24

Verses 1–8

A solemn covenant was made between God and Israel. Very solemn it was, typifying the covenant of grace between God and believers, through Christ. As soon as God separated to himself a peculiar people, he governed them by a written word, as he has done ever since. God's covenants and commands are so just in themselves, and so much for our good, that the more we think of them, and the more plainly and fully they are set before us, the more reason we may see to comply with them. The blood of the sacrifice was sprinkled on the altar, on the book, and on the people. Neither their persons, their moral obedience, nor religious services, would meet with acceptance from a holy God, except through the shedding and sprinkling' of blood. Also the blessings granted unto them were all of mercy; and the Lord would deal with them in kindness. Thus the sinner, by faith in the blood of Christ, renders willing and acceptable obedience. (Ex **24**:**9-11**)

Verses 9–11

The elders saw the God of Israel; they had some glimpse of his glory, though whatever they saw, it was something of which no image or picture could be made, yet enough to satisfy them that God was with them of a truth. Nothing is described but what was under his feet. The sapphires are the pavement under his feet; let us put all the wealth of this world under our feet, and not in our hearts. Thus the believer sees in the face of Jesus Christ, far clearer discoveries of the glorious justice and holiness of God, than ever he saw under terrifying convictions; and through the Saviour, holds communion with a holy God.

Verses 12–18

A cloud covered the mount six days; a token of God's special presence there. Moses was sure that he who called him up would protect him. Even those glorious attributes of God which are most terrible to the wicked, the saints with humble reverence rejoice in. And through faith in the atoning Sacrifice, we hope for greater honour than Moses ever enjoyed on earth. Now we see through a glass darkly, but when he shall appear, then face to face. This vision of God will continue with equal, if not increasing brightness of joy; not for a few days only, but through eternity.

Chapter 25

Verses 1–9

God chose the people of Israel to be a peculiar people to himself, above all people, and he himself would be their King. He ordered a royal palace to be set up among them for himself, called a sanctuary, or holy place, or habitation. There he showed his presence among them. And because in the wilderness they dwelt in tents, this royal palace was ordered to be a tabernacle, that it might move with them. The people were to furnish Moses with the materials, by their own free will. The best use we can make of our worldly wealth, is to honour God with it in works of piety and charity. We should ask, not only, What must we do? but, What may we do for God? Whatever they gave, they must give it cheerfully, not grudgingly, for God loves a cheerful giver, **2**Co **9**:**7**. What is laid out in the service of God, we must reckon well bestowed; and whatsoever is done in God's service, must be done by his direction. (Ex **25**:**10-22**)

Verses 10–22

The ark was a chest, overlaid with gold, in which the two tables of the law were to be kept. These tables are called the testimony; God in them testified his will. This law was a testimony to the Israelites, to direct them in their duty, and would be a testimony against them, if they transgressed. This ark was placed in the holy of holies; the blood of the sacrifices was sprinkled, and the incense burned, before it, by the high priest; and above it appeared the visible glory, which was the symbol of the Divine presence. This was a type of Christ in his sinless nature, which saw no corruption, in personal union with his Divine nature, atoning for our sins against it, by his death. The cherubim of gold looked one towards another, and both looked downward toward the ark. It denotes the angels' attendance on the Redeemer, their readiness to do his will, their presence in the assemblies of saints, and their desire to look into the mysteries of the gospel. It was covered with a covering of gold, called the mercy-seat. God is said to dwell, or sit between the cherubim, on the mercy-seat. There he would give his law, and hear supplicants, as a prince on his throne.

Verses 23–30

A table was to be made of wood, overlaid with gold, to stand in the outer tabernacle, to be always furnished with the shew-bread. This table, with the articles on it, and its use, seems to typify the communion which the Lord holds with his redeemed people in his ordinances, the provisions of his house, the feasts they are favoured with. Also the food for their souls, which they always find when they hunger after it; and the delight he takes in their persons and services, as presented before him in Christ.

Verses 31–40

The candlestick represents the light of God's word and Spirit, in and through Christ Jesus, afforded in this dark world to his believing people, to direct their worship and obedience, and to afford them consolations. The church is still dark, as the tabernacle was, in comparison with what it will be in heaven; but the word of God is a light shining in a dark place, **2**Pe **1**:**19**, and a dark place indeed the world would be without it. In ver. #(**40**) is an express caution to Moses. Nothing was left to his own fancy, or to that of the workmen, or the people; but the will of God must be observed in every particular. Christ's instruction to his disciples, Mt **28**:**20**, is like this, Observe all things whatsoever I have commanded you. Let us remember that we are the temples of the Holy Ghost, that we have the law of God in our hearts, that we are to live a life of communion with God, feast on his ordinances, and are the light of the world, if indeed we are followers of Christ. May the Lord help us to try ourselves by this view of religion, and to walk according thereto.

Chapter 26

Verses 1–6

God manifested his presence among the Israelites in a tabernacle or tent, because of their condition in the wilderness. God suits the tokens of his favour, and the gifts of his grace, to his people's state and wants. The curtains of the tabernacle were to be very rich. They were to be embroidered with cherubim, signifying that the angels of God pitch their tents round about the church, Ps **34**:**7**. (Ex **26**:**7-14**)

Verses 7–14

The curtains of meaner materials, being made both longer and broader, covered the others, and were defended by coverings of skins. The whole represents the person and doctrine of Christ, and the church of true Christians, and all heavenly things, which outwardly are mean, but inwardly, and in the sight of God, are glorious and precious.

Verses 15–30

The sockets of silver each weighed about **115** pounds; they were placed in rows on the ground. In every pair of these sockets, a strong board of shittim-wood, covered with plates of gold, was fitted by mortises and tenons. Thus walls were formed for the two sides, and for the west end. The wall was further held together by bars, which passed through rings of gold. Over this the curtains were spread. Though movable, it was strong and firm. The materials were very costly. In all this it was a type of the church of God, built upon the foundation of the apostles and prophets, Jesus Christ himself being the chief Corner-stone, Eph **2**:**20**, **21**.

Verses 31–37

A vail, or curtain, separated the holy place from the most holy place. It was hung upon pillars. This vail was for a partition between the holy place and the most holy; which forbade any to look into the holiest of all. The apostle tells what was the meaning of this vail, Heb **9**:**8**. That the ceremonial law could not make the comers thereunto perfect, nor would the observance of it bring men to heaven; the way into the holiest of all was not made manifest, while the first tabernacle was standing. Life and immortality lay hidden till they were brought to light by the gospel; which was signified by the rending of this vail at the death of Christ, Mt **27**:**51**. We have now boldness to enter into the holiest, in all acts of worship, by the blood of Jesus; yet such as obliges us to holy reverence. Another vail was for the outer door of the tabernacle. This vail was all the defence the tabernacle had. God takes care of his church on earth. A curtain shall be, if God please to make it so, as strong a defence to his house, as gates of brass and bars of iron. With this typical description of Christ and his church before us, what is our judgment of these matters? Do we see any glory in the person of Christ? any excellence in his character? any thing precious in his salvation? or any wisdom in the doctrine of the cross? Will our religion bear examination? and are we more careful to approve our hearts to God than our characters toward men?

Chapter 27

Verses 1–8

In the court before the tabernacle, where the people attended, was an altar, to which they must bring their sacrifices, and on which their priests must offer them to God. It was of wood overlaid with brass. A grate of brass was let into the hollow of the altar, about the middle of which the fire was kept, and the sacrifice burnt. It was made of net-work like a sieve, and hung hollow, that the ashes might fall through. This brazen altar was a type of Christ dying to make atonement for our sins. The wood had been consumed by the fire from heaven, if it had not been secured by the brass: nor could the human nature of Christ have borne the wrath of God, if it had not been supported by Divine power.

Verses 9–19

The tabernacle was enclosed in a court, about sixty yards long and thirty broad, formed by curtains hung upon brazen pillars, fixed in brazen sockets. Within this enclosure the priests and Levites offered the sacrifices, and thither the Jewish people were admitted. These distinctions represented the difference between the visible nominal church, and the true spiritual church, which alone has access to God, and communion with him.

Verses 20, 21

The pure oil signified the gifts and graces of the Spirit, which all believers receive from Christ, the good Olive, and without which our light cannot shine before men. The priests were to light the lamps, and tend them. It is the work of ministers, by preaching and expounding the Scriptures, which are as a lamp, to enlighten the church, God's tabernacle upon earth. Blessed be God, this light is not now confined to the Jewish tabernacle, but is a light to lighten the gentiles, and for salvation unto the ends of the earth.

Chapter 28

Verses 1–5

Hitherto the heads of families were the priests, and offered sacrifices; but now this office was confined to the family of Aaron only; and so continued till the gospel dispensation. The holy garments not only distinguished the priests from the people, but were emblems of that holy conduct which should ever be the glory and beauty, the mark of the ministers of religion, without which their persons and ministrations will be had in contempt. They also typified the glory of the Divine majesty, and the beauty of complete holiness, which rendered Jesus Christ the great High Priest. But our adorning under the gospel, is not to be of gold and costly array, but the garments of salvation, the robe of righteousness.

Verses 6–14

This richly-wrought ephod was the outmost garment of the high priest; plain linen ephods were worn by the inferior priests. It was a short coat without sleeves, fastened close to the body with a girdle. The shoulder-pieces were buttoned together with precious stones set in gold, one on each shoulder, on which were engraven the names of the children of Israel. Thus Christ, our High Priest, presents his people before the Lord for a memorial. As Christ's coat had no seam, but was woven from the top throughout, so it was with the ephod.

The golden bells on this ephod, by their preciousness and pleasant sound, well represent the good profession that the saints make, and the pomegranates the fruit they bring forth.

Verses 15–30

The chief ornament of the high priest, was the breastplate, a rich piece of cloth, curiously worked. The name of each tribe was graven in a precious stone, fixed in the breastplate, to signify how precious, in God's sight, believers are, and how honourable. How small and poor soever the tribe was, it was as a precious stone in the breastplate of the high priest; thus are all the saints dear to Christ, however men esteem them. The high priest had the names of the tribes, both on his shoulders and on his breast, which reminds us of the power and the love with which our Lord Jesus pleads for those that are his. He not only bears them up in his arms with almighty strength, but he carries them in his bosom with tender affection. What comfort is this to us in all our addresses to God! The Urim and Thummim, by which the will of God was made known in doubtful cases, were put in this breastplate. Urim and Thummim signify light and integrity. There are many conjectures what these were; the most probable opinion seems to be, that they were the twelve precious stones in the high priest's breastplate. Now, Christ is our Oracle. By him God, in these last days, makes known himself and his mind to us, Heb **1**:**1**, **2**; Joh **1**:**18**. He is the true Light, the faithful Witness, the Truth itself, and from him we receive the Spirit of Truth, who leads into all truth.

Verses 31–39

The robe of the ephod was under the ephod, and reached down to the knees, without sleeves. Aaron must minister in the garments appointed. We must serve the Lord with holy fear, as those who know they deserve to die. A golden plate was fixed on Aaron's forehead, engraven with "Holiness to the Lord." Aaron was hereby reminded that God is holy, and that his priests must be holy, devoted to the Lord. This must appear in their forehead, in open profession of their relation to God. It must be engraven like the engravings of a signet; deep and durable; not painted so as to be washed off, but firm and lasting; such must our holiness to the Lord be. Christ is our High Priest; through him sins are forgiven to us, and not laid to our charge. Our persons, our doings, are pleasing to God upon the account of Christ, and not otherwise.

Verses 40–43

The priest's garments typify the righteousness of Christ. If we appear not before God in that, we shall bear our iniquity, and die. Blessed is he, therefore, that watcheth, and keepeth his garments, Re **16**:**15**. And blessed be God that we have a High Priest, appointed of God, and set apart for his work; furnished for his high office by the glory of his Divine majesty, and the beauty of perfect holiness. Happy are we, if by the law spiritually understood, we see that such a High Priest became us; that we cannot draw near to a holy God, or be accepted, but by him. There is no light, no wisdom, no perfection, but from him; no glory, no beauty, but in being like unto him. Let us take encouragement from the power, love, and compassion of our High Priest, to draw near with boldness to the throne of grace, that we may obtain mercy, and find grace to help in time of need.

Chapter 29

Verses 1–37

Aaron and his sons were to be set apart for the priest's office, with ceremony and solemnity. Our Lord Jesus is the great High Priest of our profession, called of God to be so; anointed with the Spirit, whence he is called Messiah, the Christ; clothed with glory and beauty; sanctified by his own blood; made perfect, or consecrated through sufferings, Heb **2**:**10**. All believers are spiritual priests, to offer spiritual sacrifices, **1**Pe **2**:**5**, washed in the blood of Christ, and so made to our God priests, Re **1**:**5**, **6**. They also are clothed with the beauty of holiness, and have received the anointing, **1**Jo **2**:**27**. The Spirit of God is called the finger of God, (Lu **11**:**20**, compared with Mt **12**:**28**,) and by him the merit of Christ is applied to our souls. This consecration signifies the admission of a sinner into the spiritual priesthood, to offer spiritual sacrifices, acceptable to God through Jesus Christ.

Verses 38–46

A lamb was to be offered upon the altar every morning, and a lamb every evening. This typified the continual intercession which Christ ever lives to make for his church. Though he offered himself but once for all, that one offering thus becomes a continual offering. This also teaches us to offer to God the spiritual sacrifices of prayer and praise every day, morning and evening. Our daily devotions are the most needful of our daily works, and the most pleasant of our daily comforts. Prayer-time must be kept up as duly as meal-time. Those starve their own souls, who keep not up constant attendance on the throne of grace; constancy in religion brings in the comfort of it.

Chapter 30

Verses 1–10

The altar of incense represented the Son of God in his human nature, and the incense burned thereon typified his pleading for his people. The continual intercession of Christ was represented by the daily burning of incense thereon, morning and evening. Once every year the blood of the atonement was to be applied to it, denoting that the intercession of Christ has all its virtue from his sufferings on earth, and that we need no other sacrifice or intercessor but Christ alone.

Verses 11–16

The tribute was half a shekel, about fifteen pence of our money. The rich were not to give more, nor the poor less; the souls of the rich and poor are alike precious, and God is no respecter of persons, Ac **10**:**34**; Job **34**:**19**. In other offerings men were to give according to their wordly ability; but this, which was the ransom of the soul, must be alike for all. The souls of all are of equal value, equally in danger, and all equally need a ransom. The money raised was to be used in the service of the tabernacle. Those who have the benefit, must not grudge the necessary charges of God's public worship. Money cannot make atonement for the soul, but it may be used for the honour of Him who has made the atonement, and for the maintenance of the gospel by which the atonement is applied.

Verses 17–21

A large vessel of brass, holding water, was to be set near the door of the tabernacle. Aaron and his sons must wash their hands and feet at this laver, every time they went in to minister. This was to teach them purity in all their services, and to dread the pollution of sin. They must not only wash and be made clean, when first made priests, but must wash and be kept clean, whenever they went to minister. It teaches us daily to attend upon God, daily to renew our repentance for sin, and our looking to the blood of Christ for remission; for in many things we daily offend.

Verses 22–38

Directions are here given for making the holy anointing oil, and the incense to be used in the service of the tabernacle. To show the excellency of holiness, there was this spiced oil in the tabernacle, which was grateful to the sight and to the smell. Christ's name is as ointment poured forth, So **1**:**3**, and the good name of Christians is like precious ointment, Ec **7**:**1**. The incense burned upon the golden altar was prepared of sweet spices. When it was used, it was to be beaten very small; thus it pleased the Lord to bruise the Redeemer, when he offered himself for a sacrifice of a sweet-smelling savour. The like should not be made for any common use. Thus God would keep in the people's minds reverence for his own services, and teach us not to profane or abuse any thing whereby God makes himself known. It is a great affront to God to jest with sacred things, and to make sport with his word and ordinances. It is most dangerous and fatal to use professions of the gospel of Christ to forward wordly interests.

Chapter 31

Verses 1–11

The Israelites, who had been masons and bricklayers in Egypt, were not qualified for curious workmanship; but the Spirit who gave the apostles utterance in divers tongues, miraculously gave Bezaleel and Aholiab the skill that was wanting. The honour which comes from God, is always attended with a work to be done; to be employed for God is high honour. Those whom God calls to any service, he will find or make fit for it. The Lord gives different gifts to different persons; let each mind his proper work, diligently remembering that whatever wisdom any one possesses, the Lord put it in the heart, to do his commandments.

Verses 12–17

Orders were now given that a tabernacle should be set up for the service of God. But they must not think that the nature of the work, and the haste that was required, would justify them in working at it on sabbath days. The Hebrew word /shabath/ signifies rest, or ceasing from labour. The thing signified by the sabbath is that rest in glory which remains for the people of God; therefore the moral obligation of the sabbath must continue, till time is swallowed up in eternity.

Verse 18

The law was written in tables of stone, to show how lasting it is: to denote likewise the hardness of our hearts; one might more easily write on stone, than write any thing good on our corrupt natural hearts. It was written with the finger of God; by his will and power. God only can write his law in the heart: he gives a heart of flesh; then, by his Spirit, which is the finger of God, writes his will in the heart, **2**Co **3**:**3**.

Chapter 32

Verses 1–6

While Moses was in the mount, receiving the law from God, the people made a tumultuous address to Aaron. This giddy multitude were weary of waiting for the return of Moses. Weariness in waiting betrays to many temptations. The Lord must be waited for till he comes, and waited for though he tarry. Let their readiness to part with their ear-rings to make an idol, shame our niggardliness in the service of the true God. They did not draw back on account of the cost of their idolatry; and shall we grudge the expenses of religion? Aaron produced the shape of an ox or calf, giving it some finish with a graving tool. They offered sacrifice to this idol. Having set up an image before them, and so changed the truth of God into a lie, their sacrifices were abomination. Had they not, only a few days before, in this very place, heard the voice of the Lord God speaking to them out of the midst of the fire, Thou shalt not make to thyself any graven image? Had they not themselves solemnly entered into covenant with God, that they would do all he had said to them, and would be obedient? ch. **24**:**7**. Yet before they stirred from the place where this covenant had been solemnly made, they brake an express command, in defiance of an express threatening. It plainly shows, that the law was no more able to make holy, than it was to justify; by it is the knowledge of sin, but not the cure of sin. Aaron was set apart by the Divine appointment to the office of the priesthood; but he, who had once shamed himself so far as to build an altar to a golden calf, must own himself unworthy of the honour of attending at the altar of God, and indebted to free grace alone for it. Thus pride and boasting were silenced.

Verses 7–14

God says to Moses, that the Israelites had corrupted themselves. Sin is the corruption of the sinner, and it is a self-corruption; every man is tempted when he is drawn aside of his own lust. They had turned aside out of the way. Sin is a departing from the way of duty into a by-path. They soon forgot God's works. He sees what they cannot discover, nor is any wickedness of the world hid from him. We could not bear to see the thousandth part of that evil which God sees every day. God expresses the greatness of his just displeasure, after the manner of men who would have prayer of Moses could save them from ruin; thus he was a type of Christ, by whose mediation alone, God would reconcile the world to himself. Moses pleads God's glory. The glorifying God's name, as it ought to be our first petition, and it is so in the Lord's prayer, so it ought to be our great plea. And God's promises are to be our pleas in prayer; for what he has promised he is able to perform. See the power of prayer. In answer to the prayers of Moses, God showed his purpose of sparing the people, as he had before seemed determined on their destruction; which change of the outward discovery of his purpose, is called repenting of the evil.

Verses 15–20

What a change it is, to come down from the mount of communion with God, to converse with a wicked world. In God we see nothing but what is pure and pleasing; in the world nothing but what is sinful and provoking. That it might appear an idol is nothing in the world, Moses ground the calf to dust. Mixing this powder with their drink, signified that the backslider in heart should be filled with his own ways.

Verses 21–29

Never did any wise man make a more frivolous and foolish excuse than that of Aaron. We must never be drawn into sin by any thing man can say or do to us; for men can but tempt us to sin, they cannot force us. The approach of Moses turned the dancing into trembling. They were exposed to shame by their sin. The course Moses took to roll away this reproach, was, not by concealing the sin, or putting any false colour upon it, but by punishing it. The Levites were to slay the ringleaders in this wickedness; yet none were executed but those who openly stood forth. Those are marked for ruin who persist in sin: those who in the morning were shouting and dancing, before night were dying. Such sudden changes do the judgments of the Lord sometimes make with sinners that are secure and jovial in their sin.

Verses 30–35

Moses calls it a great sin. The work of ministers is to show people the greatness of their sins. The great evil of sin appears in the price of pardon. Moses pleads with God for mercy; he came not to make excuses, but to make atonement. We are not to suppose that Moses means that he would be willing to perish for ever, for the people's sake. We are to love our neighbour as ourselves, and not more than ourselves. But having that mind which was in Christ, he was willing to lay down his life in the most painful manner, if he might thereby preserve the people. Moses could not wholly turn away the wrath of God; which shows that the law of Moses was not able to reconcile men to God, and to perfect our peace with him. In Christ alone, God so pardons sin as to remember it no more. From this history we see, that no unhumbled, carnal heart, can long endure the holy precepts, the humbling truths, and the spiritual worship of God. But a god, a priest, a worship, a doctrine, and a sacrifice, suited to the carnal mind, will ever meet with abundance of worshippers. The very gospel itself may be so perverted as to suit a worldly taste. Well is it for us, that the Prophet like unto Moses, but who is beyond compare more powerful and merciful, has made atonement for our souls, and now intercedes in our behalf. Let us rejoice in his grace.

Chapter 33

Verses 1–6

Those whom God pardons, must be made to know what their sin deserved. "Let them go forward as they are;" this was very expressive of God's displeasure. Though he promises to make good his covenant with Abraham, in giving them Canaan, yet he denies them the tokens of his presence they had been blessed with. The people mourned for their sin. Of all the bitter fruits and consequences of sin, true penitents most lament, and dread most, God's departure from them. Canaan itself would be no pleasant land without the Lord's presence. Those who parted with ornaments to maintain sin, could do no less than lay aside ornaments, in token of sorrow and shame for it.

Verses 7–11

Moses took the tabernacle, and pitched it without the camp. This seems to have been a temporary building, set up for worship, and at which he judged disputes among the people. The people looked after him; they were very desirous to be at peace with God, and concerned to know what would come to pass. The cloudy pillar which had withdrawn from the camp when it was polluted with idolatry, now returned. If our hearts go forth toward God to meet him, he will graciously come to meet us.

Verses 12–23

Moses is very earnest with God. Thus, by the intercession of Christ, we are not only saved from ruin, but become entitled to everlasting happiness. Observe here how he pleads. We find grace in God's sight, if we find grace in our hearts to guide and quicken us in the way of our duty. Moses speaks as one who dreaded the thought of going forward without the Lord's presence. God's gracious promises, and mercy towards us, should not only encourage our faith, but also excite our fervency in prayer. Observe how he speeds. See, in a type, Christ's intercession, which he ever lives to make for all that come to God by him; and that it is not by any thing in those for whom he intercedes. Moses then entreats a sight of God's glory, and is heard in that also. A full discovery of the glory of God, would overwhelm even Moses himself. Man is mean, and unworthy of it; weak, and could not bear it; guilty, and could not but dread it. The merciful display which is made in Christ Jesus, alone can be borne by us. The Lord granted that which would abundantly satisfy. God's goodness is his glory; and he will have us to know him by the glory of his mercy, more than by the glory of his majesty. Upon the rock there was a fit place for Moses to view the goodness and glory of God. The rock in Horeb was typical of Christ the Rock; the Rock of refuge, salvation, and strength. Happy are they who stand upon this Rock. The cleft may be an emblem of Christ, as smitten, crucified, wounded, and slain. What follows, denotes the imperfect knowledge of God in the present state, even as revealed in Christ; for this, when compared with the heavenly sight of him. is but like seeing a man that is gone by, whose back only is to be seen. God in Christ, as he is, even the fullest and brightest displays of his glory, grace, and goodness, are reserved to another state.

Chapter 34

Verses 1–4

When God made man in his own image, the moral law was written in his heart, by the finger of God, without outward means. But since the covenant then made with man was broken, the Lord has used the ministry of men, both in writing the law in the Scriptures, and in writing it in the heart. When God was reconciled to the Israelites, he ordered the tables to be renewed, and wrote his law in them. Even under the gospel of peace by Christ, the moral law continues to bind believers. Though Christ has redeemed us from the curse of the law, yet not from the commands of it. The first and the best evidence of the pardon of sin, and peace with God, is the writing the law in the heart.

Verses 5–9

The Lord descended by some open token of his presence and manifestation of his glory in a cloud, and thence proclaimed his NAME; that is, the perfections and character which are denoted by the name JEHOVAH. The Lord God is merciful; ready to forgive the sinner, and to relieve the needy. Gracious; kind, and ready to bestow undeserved benefits. Long-suffering; slow to anger, giving time for repentance, only punishing when it is needful. He is abundant in goodness and truth; even sinners receive the riches of his bounty abundantly, though they abuse them. All he reveals is infallible truth, all he promises is in faithfulness. Keeping mercy for thousands; he continually shows mercy to sinners, and has treasures, which cannot be exhausted, to the end of time. Forgiving iniquity, and transgression, and sin; his mercy and goodness reach to the full and free forgiveness of sin. And will by no means clear the guilty; the holiness and justice of God are part of his goodness and love towards all his creatures. In Christ's sufferings, the Divine holiness and justice are fully shown, and the evil of sin is made known. God's forgiving mercy is always attended by his converting, sanctifying grace. None are pardoned but those who repent and forsake the allowed practice of every sin; nor shall any escape, who abuse, neglect, or despise this great salvation. Moses bowed down, and worshipped reverently. Every perfection in the name of God, the believer may plead with Him for the forgiveness of his sins, the making holy of his heart, and the enlargement of the Redeemer's kingdom.

Verses 10–17

The Israelites are commanded to destroy every monument of idolatry, however curious or costly; to refuse all alliance, friendship, or marriage with idolaters, and all idolatrous feasts; and they were reminded not with idolaters, and all idolatrous feats; and they were reminded not to repeat the crime of making molten images. Jealously is called the rage of a man, Pr **6**:**34**; but in God it is holy and just displeasure. Those cannot worship God aright, who do not worship him only.

Verses 18–27

Once a week they must rest, even in ploughing time, and in harvest. All worldly business must give way to that holy rest; even harvest work will prosper the better, for the religious observance of the sabbath day in harvest time. We must show that we prefer our communion with God, and our duty to him, before the business or the joy of harvest. Thrice a year they must appear before the Lord God, the God of Israel. Canaan was a desirable land, and the neighbouring nations were greedy; yet God says, They shall not desire it. Let us check all sinful desires against God and his glory, in our hearts, and then trust him to check all sinful desires in the hearts of others against us. The way of duty is the way of safety. Those who venture for him never lose by him. Three feasts are here mentioned: **1**. The Passover, in remembrance of the deliverance out of Egypt. **2**. The feast of weeks, or the feast of Pentecost; added to it is the law of the first-fruits. **3**. The feast of in-gathering, or the feast of Tabernacles. Moses is to write these words, that the people might know them better. We can never be enough thankful to God for the written word. God would make a covenant with Israel, in Moses as a mediator. Thus the covenant of grace is made with believers through Christ.

Verses 28–35

Near and spiritual communion with God improves the graces of a renewed and holy character. Serious godliness puts a lustre upon a man's countenance, such as commands esteem and affection. The vail which Moses put on, marked the obscurity of that dispensation, compared with the gospel dispensation of the New Testament. It was also an emblem of the natural vail on the hearts of men respecting spiritual things. Also the vail that was and is upon the nation of Israel, which can only be taken away by the Spirit of the Lord showing to them Christ, as the end of the law for righteousness to every one that believeth. Fear and unbelief would put the vail before us, they would hinder our free approach to the mercy-seat above. We should spread our wants, temporal and spiritual, fully before our heavenly Father; we should tell him our hinderances, struggles, trails, and temptations; we should acknowledge our offences.

Chapter 35

Verses 1–3

The mild and easy yoke of Christ has made our sabbath duties more delightful, and our sabbath restraints less irksome, than those of the Jews; but we are the more guilty by neglecting them. Surely God's wisdom in giving us the sabbath, with all the mercy of its purposes, are sinfully disregarded. Is it nothing to pour contempt upon the blessed day, which a bounteous God has given to us for our growth in grace with the church below, and to prepare us for happiness with the church above?

Verses 4–19

The tabernacle was to be dedicated to the honour of God, and used in his service; and therefore what was brought for it, was an offering to the Lord. The rule is, Whosoever is of a willing heart, let him bring. All that were skilful must work. God dispenses his gifts; and as every man hath received, so he must minister, **1**Pe **4**:**10**. Those that were rich, must bring in materials to work on; those that were skilful, must serve the tabernacle with their skill: as they needed one another, so the tabernacle needed them both, **1**Co **12**:**7**–**21**.

Verses 20–29

Without a willing mind, costly offerings would be abhorred; with it, the smallest will be accepted. Our hearts are willing, when we cheerfully assist in promoting the cause of God. Those who are diligent and contented in employments considered mean, are as much accepted of God as those engaged in splendid services. The women who spun the goats' hair were wise-hearted, because they did it heartily to the Lord. Thus the labourer, mechanic, or servant who attends to his work in the faith and fear of God, may be as wise, for his place, as the most useful minister, and be equally accepted of the Lord. Our wisdom and duty consist in giving God the glory and use of our talents, be they many or few.

Verses 30–35

Here is the Divine appointment of the master-workmen, that there might be no strife for the office, and that all who were employed in the work might take direction from, and give account to them. Those whom God called by name to his service, he filled with the Spirit of God. Skill, even in worldly employments, is God's gift, and comes from above. But many are ready enough in cutting out work for other people, and can tell what this man or that man should do; but the burdens they bind on others, they themselves will not touch with one of their fingers. Such will fall under the character of slothful servants. These men were not only to devise and to work themselves, but they were to teach others. Those that rule should teach; and those to whom God has given knowledge, should be willing to make it known for the benefit of others.

Chapter 36

The making of the tabernacle, The liberality of the people restrained.

—The readiness and zeal with which these builders set about their work, the exactness with which they performed it, and the faithfulness with which they objected to receive more contributions, are worthy of our imitation. Thus should we serve God, and our superiors also, in all things lawful. Thus should all who are in public trusts abhor filthy lucre, and avoid all occasions and temptations to covetousness. Where have we the representation of God's love towards us, that we by love dwell in him and he in us, save in Emmanuel? Mt **1**:**23**. This is the sum of the ministry of reconciliation, **2**Co **5**:**18**, **19**. This was the design of the "tabernacle of witness," a visible testimony of the love of God to the race of men, however they were fallen from their first state. And this love was shown by Christ's taking up his abode on earth; by the Word being made flesh, Joh **1**:**14**, wherein, as the original expresses it, he did tabernacle among us.

Chapter 37

The making of the ark, and the furniture of the tabernacle.

—In the furniture of the tabernacle were emblems of a spiritual and acceptable service. The incense represented the prayers of the saints. The sacrifice of the alter represented the Lamb of God that taketh away the sins of the world. The golden pot with manna, or bread from heaven, the flesh of Jesus Christ, which he gave for the life of the world. The candlestick, with its lights, the teaching and enlightening of the Holy Spirit. The shew-bread represented that provision for those who hunger and thirst after righteousness, which the gospel, the ordinances and the sacraments of the house of prayer, abundantly bestow. The exactness of the workmen to their rule, should be followed by us; seeking for the influences of the Holy Spirit, that we may rejoice in and glorify God while in this world, and at length be with him for ever.

Chapter 38

Verses 1–8

In all ages of the church there have been some persons more devoted to God, more constant in their attendance upon his ordinances, and more willing to part even with lawful things, for his sake, than others. Some women, devoted to God and zealous for the tabernacle worship, expressed zeal by parting with their mirrors, which were polished plates of brass. Before the invention of looking-glasses, these served the same purposes. (Ex **38**:**9-20**)

Verses 9–20

The walls of the court being of curtains only, intimated that the state of the Jewish church itself was movable and changeable; and in due time to be taken down and folded up, when the place of the tent should be enlarged, and its cords lengthened, to make room for the Gentile world.

Verses 21–31

The foundation of massy pieces of silver showed the solidity and purity of the truth upon which the church is founded. Let us regard the Lord Jesus Christ while reading of the furniture of the tabernacle. While looking at the altar of burnt-offering, let us see Jesus. In him, his righteousness, and salvation, is a full and sufficient offering for sin. In the laver of regeneration, by his Holy Spirit, let our souls be washed, and they shall be clean; and as the people offered willingly, so may our souls be made willing. Let us be ready to part with any thing, and count all but loss to win Christ.

Chapter 39

Verses 1–31

The priests' garments were rich and splendid. The church in its infancy was thus taught by shadows of good things to come; but the substance is Christ, and the grace of the gospel. Christ is our great High Priest. When he undertook the work of our redemption, he put on the clothes of service, he arrayed himself with the gifts and graces of the Spirit, girded himself with resolution to go through the undertaking, took charge of all God's spiritual Israel, laid them near his heart, engraved them on the palms of his hands, and presented them to his Father. And he crowned himself with holiness to the Lord, consecrating his whole undertaking to the honour of his Father's holiness. True believers are spiritual priests. The clean linen with which all their clothes of service must be made, is the righteousness of saints, Re **19**:**8**.

Verses 32–43

The tabernacle was a type or emblem of Jesus Christ. As the Most High dwelt visibly within the sanctuary, even on the ark, so did he reside in the human nature and tabernacle of his dear Son; in Christ dwelt all the fulness of the Godhead bodily, Col **2**:**9**. The tabernacle was a symbol of every real Christian. In the soul of every true follower of the Saviour the Father dwells, the object of his worship, and the author of his blessings. The tabernacle also typified the church of the Redeemer. The meanest and the mightiest are alike dear to the Father's love, freely exercised through faith in Christ. The tabernacle was a type and emblem of the heavenly temple, Re **21**:**3**. What, then, will be the splendour of His appearance, when the cloud shall be withdrawn, and his faithful worshippers shall see him as he is!

Chapter 40

Verses 1–15

When a new year begins, we should seek to serve God better than the year before. In half a year the tabernacle was completed. When the hearts of numbers are earnest in a good cause, much may be done in a short time; and when the commandments of God are continually attended to, as the rule of working, all will be done well. The high-priesthood was in the family of Aaron till Christ came, and in Him, the substance of all these shadows, it continues for ever.

Verses 16–33

When the tabernacle and the furniture of it were prepared, they did not put off rearing it till they came to Canaan; but, in obedience to the will of God, they set it up in the midst of their camp. Those who are unsettled in the world, must not think that this will excuse want of religion; as if it were enough to begin to serve God when they begin to be settled in the world. No; a tabernacle for God is very needful, even in a wilderness, especially as we may be in another world before we come to fix in this. And we may justly fear lest we should deceive ourselves with a form of godliness. The thought that so few entered Canaan, should warn young persons especially, not to put off the care of their souls.

Verses 34–38

The cloud covered the tabernacle even in the clearest day; it was not a cloud which the sun scatters. This cloud was a token of God's presence to be seen day and night, by all Israel, that they might never again question, Is the Lord among us, or is he not? It guided the camp of Israel through the wilderness. While the cloud rested on the tabernacle, they rested; when it removed, they followed it. The glory of the Lord filled the tabernacle. In light and fire the Shechinah made itself visible: God is Light; our God is a consuming Fire. Yet so dazzling was the light, and so dreadful the fire, that Moses was not able to enter into the tent of the congregation, till the splendour was abated. But what Moses could not do, our Lord Jesus has done, whom God caused to draw near; and who has invited us to come boldly, even to the mercy-seat. Being taught by the Holy Spirit to follow the example of Christ, as well as to depend upon him, to attend his ordinances, and obey his precepts, we shall be kept from losing our way, and be led in the midst of the paths of judgment, till we come to heaven, the habitation of his holiness. BLESSED BE GOD FOR JESUS CHRIST!

Leviticus

God ordained divers kinds of oblations and sacrifices, to assure his people of the forgiveness of their offences, if they offered them in true faith and obedience. Also he appointed the priests and Levites, their apparel, offices, conduct, and portion. He showed what feasts they should observe, and at what times. He declared by these sacrifices and ceremonies, that the reward of sin is death, and that without the blood of Christ, the innocent Lamb of God, there can be no forgiveness of sins.

Chapter 1

Verses 1, 2

The offering of sacrifices was an ordinance of true religion, from the fall of man unto the coming of Christ. But till the Israelites were in the wilderness, no very particular regulations seem to have been appointed. The general design of these laws is plain. The sacrifices typified Christ; they also shadowed out the believer's duty, character, privilege, and communion with God. There is scarcely any thing spoken of the Lord Jesus in Scripture which has not also a reference to his people. This book begins with the laws concerning sacrifices; the most ancient were the burnt-offerings, about which God here gives Moses directions. It is taken for granted that the people would be willing to bring offerings to the Lord. The very light of nature directs man, some way or other, to do honour to his Maker, as his Lord. Immediately after the fall, sacrifices were ordained.

Verses 3–9

In the due performance of the Levitical ordinances, the mysteries of the spiritual world are represented by corresponding natural objects; and future events are exhibited in these rites. Without this, the whole will seem unmeaning ceremonies. There is in these things a type of the sufferings of the Son of God, who was to be a sacrifice for the sins of the whole world? The burning body of an animal was but a faint representation of that everlasting misery, which we all have deserved; and which our blessed Lord bore in his body and in his soul, when he died under the load of our iniquities. Observe, **1**. The beast to be offered must be without blemish. This signified the strength and purity that were in Christ, and the holy life that should be in his people. **2**. The owner must offer it of his own free will. What is done in religion, so as to please God, must be done by love. Christ willingly offered himself for us. **3**. It must be offered at the door of the tabernacle, where the brazen altar of burnt-offerings stood, which sanctified the gift: he must offer it at the door, as one unworthy to enter, and acknowledging that a sinner can have no communion with God, but by sacrifice. **4**. The offerer must put his hand upon the head of his offering, signifying thereby, his desire and hope that it might be accepted from him, to make atonement for him. **5**. The sacrifice was to be killed before the Lord, in an orderly manner, and to honour God. It signified also, that in Christians the flesh must be crucified with its corrupt affections and lust. **6**. The priests were to sprinkle the blood upon the altar; for the blood being the life, that was it which made atonement. This signified the pacifying and purifying of our consciences, by the sprinkling of the blood of Jesus Christ upon them by faith. **7**. The beast was to be divided into several pieces, and then to be burned upon the altar. The burning of the sacrifice signified the sharp sufferings of Christ, and the devout affections with which, as a holy fire, Christians must offer up themselves, their whole spirit, soul, and body, unto God. **8**. This is said to be an offering of a sweet savour. As an act of obedience to a Divine command, and a type of Christ, this was well-pleasing to God; and the spiritual sacrifices of Christians are acceptable to God, through Christ, **1**Pe **2**:**5**.

Verses 10–17

Those who could not offer a bullock, were to bring a sheep or a goat; and those who were not able to do that, were accepted of God, if they brought a turtle-dove, or a pigeon. Those creatures were chosen for sacrifice which were mild, and gentle, and harmless; to show the innocence and meekness that were in Christ, and that should be in Christians. The offering of the poor was as typical of Christ's atonement as the more costly sacrifices, and expressed as fully repentance, faith, and devotedness to God. We have no excuse, if we refuse the pleasant and reasonable service now required. But we can no more offer the sacrifice of a broken heart, or of praise and thanksgiving, than an Israelite could offer a bullock or a goat, except as God hath first given to us. The more we do in the Lord's service, the greater are our obligations to him, for the will, for the ability, and opportunity. In many things God leaves us to fix what shall be spent in his service, whether of our time or our substance; yet where God's providence has put much into a man's power, scanty offerings will not be accepted, for they are not proper expressions of a willing mind. Let us be devoted in body and soul to his service, whatever he may call us to give, venture, do, or suffer for his sake.

Chapter 2

Verses 1–11

Meat-offerings may typify Christ, as presented to God for us, and as being the Bread of life to our souls; but they rather seem to denote our obligation to God for the blessings of providence, and those good works which are acceptable to God. The term "meat" was, and still is, properly given to any kind of provision, and the greater part of this offering was to be eaten for food, not burned. These meat-offerings are mentioned after the burnt-offerings: without an interest in the sacrifice of Christ, and devotedness of heart to God, such services cannot be accepted. Leaven is the emblem of pride, malice, and hypocrisy, and honey of sensual pleasure. The former are directly opposed to the graces of humility, love, and sincerity, which God approves; the latter takes men from the exercises of devotion, and the practice of good works. Christ, in his character and sacrifice, was wholly free from the things denoted by leaven; and his suffering life and agonizing death were the very opposites to worldly pleasure. His people are called to follow, and to be like him.

Verses 12–16

Salt is required in all the offerings. God hereby intimates to them that their sacrifices, in themselves, were unsavoury. All religious services must be seasoned with grace. Christianity is the salt of the earth. Directions are given about offering their first-fruits at harvest. If a man, with a thankful sense of God's goodness in giving him a plentiful crop, was disposed to present an offering to God, let him bring the first ripe and full ears. Whatever was brought to God must be the best in its kind, though it were but green ears of corn. Oil and frankincense must be put upon it. Wisdom and humility soften and sweeten the spirits and services of young people, and their green ears of corn shall be acceptable. God takes delight in the first ripe fruits of the Spirit, and the expressions of early piety and devotion. Holy love to God is the fire by which all our offerings must be made. The frankincense denotes the mediation and intercession of Christ, by which our services are accepted. Blessed be God that we have the substance, of which these observances were but shadows. There is that excellency in Christ, and in his work as Mediator, which no types and shadows can fully represent. And our dependence thereon must be so entire, that we must never lose sight of it in any thing we do, if we would be accepted of God.

Chapter 3

Verses 1–5

The peace-offerings had regard to God as the giver of all good things. These were divided between the altar, the priest, and the owner. They were called peace-offering, because in them God and his people did, as it were, feast together, in token of friendship. The peace-offerings were offered by way of supplication. If a man were in pursuit of any mercy, he would add a peace-offering to his prayer for it. Christ is our Peace, our Peace-offering; for through him alone it is that we can obtain an answer of peace to our prayers. Or, the peace-offering was offered by way of thanksgiving for some mercy received. We must offer to God the sacrifice of praise continually, by Christ our Peace; and then this shall please the Lord better than an ox or bullock.

Verses 6–17

Here is a law that they should eat neither fat nor blood. As for the fat, it means the fat of the inwards, the suet. The blood was forbidden for the same reason; because it was God's part of every sacrifice. God would not permit the blood that made atonement to be used as a common thing, Heb **10**:**29**; nor will he allow us, though we have the comfort of the atonement made, to claim for ourselves any share in the honour of making it. This taught the Jews to observe distinction between common and sacred things; it kept them separate from idolaters. It would impress them more deeply with the belief of some important mystery in the shedding of the blood and the burning the fat of their solemn sacrifices. Christ, as the Prince of peace, "made peace with the blood of his cross." Through him the believer is reconciled to God; and having the peace of God in his heart, he is disposed to follow peace with all men. May the Lord multiply grace, mercy, and peace, to all who desire to bear the Christian character.

Chapter 4

Verses 1–12

Burnt-offerings, meat-offerings, and peace-offerings, had been offered before the giving of the law upon mount Sinai; and in these the patriarchs had respect to sin, to make atonement for it. But the Jews were now put into a way of making atonement for sin, more particularly by sacrifice, as a shadow of good things to come; yet the substance is Christ, and that one offering of himself, by which he put away sin. The sins for which the sin-offerings were appointed are supposed to be open acts. They are supposed to be sins of commission, things which ought not to have been done. Omissions are sins, and must come into judgment: yet what had been omitted at one time, might be done at another; but a sin committed was past recall. They are supposed to be sins committed through ignorance. The law begins with the case of the anointed priest. It is evident that God never had any infallible priest in his church upon earth, when even the high priest was liable to fall into sins of ignorance. All pretensions to act without error are sure marks of Antichrist. The beast was to be carried without the camp, and there burned to ashes. This was a sign of the duty of repentance, which is the putting away sin as a detestable thing, which our soul hates. The sin-offering is called sin. What they did to that, we must do to our sins; the body of sin must be destroyed, Ro **6**:**6**. The apostle applies the carrying this sacrifice without the camp to Christ, Heb **13**:**11**–**13**.

Verses 13–21

If the leaders of the people, through mistake, caused them to err, an offering must be brought, that wrath might not come upon the whole congregation. When sacrifices were offered, the persons, on whose behalf they were devoted, were to lay their hands on the heads of the victims, and to confess their sins. The elders were to do so, when the sacrifices were offered for the whole congregation. The load of sin was supposed then to be borne by the guiltless animal. When the offering is completed, it is said, atonement is made, and the sin shall be forgiven. The saving of churches and kingdoms from ruin, is owing to the satisfaction and mediation of Christ.

Verses 22–26

Those who have power to call others to account, are themselves accountable to the Ruler of rulers. The sin of the ruler, committed through ignorance, must come to his knowledge, either by the check of his own conscience, or by the reproof of his friends; both which even the best and greatest, not only should submit to, but be thankful for. That which I see not, teach thou me, and, Show me wherein I have erred, are prayers we should put up to God every day; that if, through ignorance, we fall into sin, we may not through ignorance abide in it.

Verses 27–35

Here is the law of the sin-offering for a common person. To be able to plead, when charged with sin, that we did it ignorantly, and through the surprise of temptation, will not bring us off, if we have no interest in that great plea, Christ hath died. The sins of ignorance committed by a common person, needed a sacrifice; the greatest are not above, the meanest are not below Divine justice. None, if offenders, were overlooked. Here rich and poor meet together; they are alike sinners, and welcome to Christ. From all these laws concerning the sin-offerings, we may learn to hate sin, and to watch against it; and to value Christ, the great and true Sin-offering, whose blood cleanses from all sin, which it was not possible that the blood of bulls and of goats should take away. For us to err, with the Bible in our hands, is the effect of pride, sloth, and carelessness. We need to use frequent self-examination, with serious study of the Scriptures, and earnest prayer for the convincing influences of God the Holy Spirit; that we may detect our sins of ignorance, repent, and obtain forgiveness through the blood of Christ.

Chapter 5

Verses 1–13

The offences here noticed are, **1**. A man's concealing the truth, when he was sworn as a witness to speak the truth, the whole truth, and nothing but the truth. If, in such a case, for fear of offending one that has been his friend, or may be his enemy, a man refuses to give evidence, or gives it but in part, he shall bear his iniquity. And that is a heavy burden, which, if some course be not taken to get it removed, will sink a man to hell. Let all that are called at any time to be witnesses, think of this law, and be free and open in their evidence, and take heed of prevaricating. An oath of the Lord is a sacred thing, not to be trifled with. **2**. A man's touching any thing that was ceremonially unclean. Though his touching the unclean thing only made him ceremonially defiled, yet neglecting to wash himself according to the law, was either carelessness or contempt, and contracted moral guilt. As soon as God, by his Spirit, convinces our consciences of any sin or duty, we must follow the conviction, as not ashamed to own our former mistake. **3**. Rash swearing, that a man will do or not do such a thing. As if the performance of his oath afterward prove unlawful, or what cannot be done. Wisdom and watchfulness beforehand would prevent these difficulties. In these cases the offender must confess his sin, and bring his offering; but the offering was not accepted, unless accompanied with confession and humble prayer for pardon. The confession must be particular; that he hath sinned in that thing. Deceit lies in generals; many will own they have sinned, for that all must own; but their sins in any one particular they are unwilling to allow. The way to be assured of pardon, and armed against sin for the future, is to confess the exact truth. If any were very poor, they might bring some flour, and that should be accepted. Thus the expense of the sin-offering was brought lower than any other, to teach that no man's poverty shall ever bar the way of his pardon. If the sinner brought two doves, one was to be offered for a sin-offering, and the other for a burnt-offering. We must first see that our peace be made with God, and then we may expect that our services for his glory will be accepted by him. To show the loathsomeness of sin, the flour, when offered, must not be made grateful to the taste by oil, or to the smell by frankincense. God, by these sacrifices, spoke comfort to those who had offended, that they might not despair, nor pine away in their sins. Likewise caution not to offend any more, remembering how expensive and troublesome it was to make atonement.

Verses 14–19

Here are offerings to atone for trespasses against a neighbour. If a man put to his own use unwittingly, any thing dedicated to God, he was to bring this sacrifice. We are to be jealous over ourselves, to ask pardon for the sin, and make satisfaction for the wrong, which we do but suspect ourselves guilty of. The law of God is so very broad, the occasions of sin in this guilty of. The law of God is so very broad, the occasions of sin in this world are so numerous, and we are so prone to evil, that we need to fear always, and to pray always, that we may be kept from sin. Also we should look before us at every step. The true Christian daily pleads guilty before God, and seeks forgiveness through the blood of Christ. And the gospel salvation is so free, that the poorest is not shut out; and so full, that the most burdened conscience may find relief from it. Yet the evil of sin is so displayed as to cause every pardoned sinner to abhor and dread it.

Chapter 6

Verses 1–7

Though all the instances relate to our neighbour, yet it is called a trespass against the Lord. Though the person injured be mean, and even despicable, yet the injury reflects upon that God who has made the command of loving our neighbour next to that of loving himself. Human laws make a difference as to punishments; but all methods of doing wrong to others, are alike violations of the Divine law, even keeping what is found, when the owner can be discovered. Frauds are generally accompanied with lies, often with false oaths. If the offender would escape the vengeance of God, he must make ample restitution, according to his power, and seek forgiveness by faith in that one Offering which taketh away the sin of the world. The trespasses here mentioned, still are trespasses against the law of Christ, which insists as much upon justice and truth, as the law of nature, or the law of Moses.

Verses 8–13

The daily sacrifice of a lamb is chiefly referred to. The priest must take care of the fire upon the altar. The first fire upon the altar came from heaven, ch. **9**:**24**; by keeping that up continually, all their sacrifices might be said to be consumed with the fire from heaven, in token of God's acceptance. Thus should the fire of our holy affections, the exercise of our faith and love, of prayer and praise, be without ceasing.

Verses 14–23

The law of the burnt-offerings put upon the priests a great deal of care and work; the flesh was wholly burnt, and the priests had nothing but the skin. But most of the meat-offering was their own. It is God's will that his ministers should be provided with what is needful.

Verses 24–30

The blood of the sin-offering was to be washed out of the clothes on which it should happen to be sprinkled, which signified the regard we ought to have to the blood of Christ, not counting it a common thing. The vessel in which the flesh of the sin-offering was boiled must be broken, if it were an earthen one; but if a brazen one, well washed. This showed that the defilement was not wholly taken away by the offering; but the blood of Christ thoroughly cleanses from all sin. All these rules set forth the polluting nature of sin, and the removal of guilt from the sinner to the sacrifice. Behold and wonder at Christ's love, in that he was content to be made a sin-offering for us, and so to procure our pardon for continual sins and failings. He that knew no sin was made sin (that is, a sin-offering) for us, **2**Co **5**:**21**. Hence we have pardon, and not only pardon, but power also, against sin, Ro **8**:**3**.

Chapter 7

Verses 1–10

In the sin-offering and the trespass-offering, the sacrifice was divided between the altar and the priest; the offerer had no share, as he had in the peace-offerings. The former expressed repentance and sorrow for sin, therefore it was more proper to fast than feast; the peace-offerings denoted communion with a reconciled God in Christ, the joy and gratitude of a pardoned sinner, and the privileges of a true believer.

Verses 11–27

As to the peace-offerings, in the expression of their sense of mercy, God left them more at liberty, than in the expression of their sense of sin; that their sacrifices, being free-will offerings, might be the more acceptable, while, by obliging them to bring the sacrifices of atonement, God shows the necessity of the great Propitiation. The main reason why blood was forbidden of old, was because the Lord had appointed blood for an atonement. This use, being figurative, had its end in Christ, who by his death and blood-shedding caused the sacrifices to cease. Therefore this law is not now in force on believers.

Verses 28–34

The priest who offered, was to have the breast and the right shoulder. When the sacrifice was killed, the offerer himself must present God's part of it; that he might signify his cheerfully giving it up to God. He was with his own hands to lift it up, in token of his regard to God as the God of heaven; and then to wave it to and fro, in token of his regard to God as the Lord of the whole earth. Be persuaded and encouraged to feed and feast upon Christ, our Peace-offering. This blessed Peace-offering is not for the priests only, for saints of the highest rank and greatest eminence, but for the common people also. Take heed of delay. Many think to repent and return to God when they are dying and dropping into hell; but they should eat the peace-offering, and eat it now. Stay not till the day of the Lord's patience be run out, for eating the third day will not be accepted, nor will catching at Christ when thou art gone to hell! (Le **7**:**35-38**)

Verses 35–38

Solemn acts of religious worship are not things which we may do or not do at our pleasure; it is at our peril if we omit them. An observance of the laws of Christ cannot be less necessary than of the laws of Moses.

Chapter 8

Verses 1–13

The consecration of Aaron and his sons had been delayed until the tabernacle had been prepared, and the laws of the sacrifices given. Aaron and his sons were washed with water, to signify that they ought to purify themselves from all sinful dispositions, and ever after to keep themselves pure. Christ washes those from their sins in his own blood whom he makes kings and priests to our God, Re **1**:**5**, **6**; and those that draw near to God must be washed in pure water, Heb **10**:**22**. The anointing of Aaron was to typify the anointing of Christ with the Spirit, which was not given by measure to him. All believers have received the anointing.

Verses 14–36

In these types we see our great High Priest, even Christ Jesus, solemnly appointed, anointed, and invested with his sacred office, by his own blood, and the influences of his Holy Spirit. He sanctifies the ordinances of religion, to the benefit of his people and the honour of God the Father; who for his sake accepts our worship, though it is polluted with sin. We may also rejoice, that he is a merciful and faithful High Priest, full of compassion to the feeble-minded and tempest-tossed soul. All true Christians are consecrated to be spiritual priests. We should seriously ask ourselves, whether in our daily walk we study to maintain this character? and abound in spiritual sacrifices, acceptable to God through Christ? If so, still there is no cause for boasting. Let us not despise our fellow-sinners; but remembering what we have done, and how we are saved, let us seek and pray for their salvation.

Chapter 9

Verses 1–21

These many sacrifices, which were all done away by the death of Christ, teach us that our best services need washing in his blood, and that the guilt of our best sacrifices needs to be done away by one more pure and more noble than they. Let us be thankful that we have such a High Priest. The priests had not a day's respite from service allowed. God's spiritual priests have constant work, which the duty of every day requires; they that would give up their account with joy, must redeem time. The glory of God appeared in the sight of the people, and owned what they had done. We are not now to expect such appearances, but God draws nigh to those who draw nigh to him, and the offerings of faith are acceptable to him; though the sacrifices being spiritual, the tokens of the acceptance are spiritual likewise. When Aaron had done all that was to be done about the sacrifices, he lifted up his hands towards the people, and blessed them. Aaron could but crave a blessing, God alone can command it.

Verses 22–24

When the solemnity was finished, and the blessing pronounced, God testified his acceptance. There came a fire out from before the Lord, and consumed the sacrifice. This fire might justly have fastened upon the people, and have consumed them for their sins; but its consuming the sacrifice signified God's acceptance of it, as an atonement for the sinner. This also was a figure of good things to come. The Spirit descended upon the apostles in fire. And the descent of this holy fire into our souls, to kindle in them pious and devout affections toward God, and such a holy zeal as burns up the flesh and the lusts of it, is a certain token of God's gracious acceptance of our persons and performances. Nothing goes to God, but what comes from him. We must have grace, that holy fire, from the God of grace, else we cannot serve him acceptably, Heb **12**:**28**. The people were affected with this discovery of God's glory and grace. They received it with the highest joy; triumphing in the assurance given them that they had God nigh unto them. And with the lowest reverence; humbly adoring the majesty of that God, who vouchsafed thus to manifest himself to them. That is a sinful fear of God, which drives us from him; a gracious fear makes us bow before him.

Chapter 10

Verses 1, 2

Next to Moses and Aaron, none were more likely to be honourable in Israel than Nadab and Abihu. There is reason to think that they were puffed up with pride, and that they were heated with wine. While the people were prostrate before the Lord, adoring his presence and glory, they rushed into the tabernacle to burn incense, though not at the appointed time; both together, instead of one alone, and with fire not taken from the altar. If it had been done through ignorance, they had been allowed to bring a sin-offering. But the soul that doeth presumptuously, and in contempt of God's majesty and justice, that soul shall be cut off. The wages of sin is death. They died in the very act of their sin. The sin and punishment of these priests showed the imperfection of that priesthood from the very beginning, and that it could not shelter any from the fire of God's wrath, otherwise than as it was typical of Christ's priesthood.

Verses 3–7

The most quieting considerations under affliction are fetched from the word of God. What was it that God spake? Though Aaron's heart must have been filled with anguish and dismay, yet with silent submission he revered the justice of the stroke. When God corrects us or ours for sin, it is our duty to accept the punishment, and say, It is the Lord, let him do what seemeth him good. Whenever we worship God, we come nigh unto him, as spiritual priests. This ought to make us very serious in all acts of devotion. It concerns us all, when we come nigh to God, to do every religious exercise, as those who believe that the God with whom we have to do, is a holy God. He will take vengeance on those that profane his sacred name by trifling with him.

Verses 8–11

Do not drink wine or strong drink. During the time they ministered, the priests were forbidden it. It is required of gospel ministers, that they be not given to wine, **1**Ti **3**:**3**. It is, Lest ye die; die when ye are in drink. The danger of death, to which we are continually exposed, should engage all to be sober.

Verses 12–20

Afflictions should rather quicken us to our duty, than take us from it. But our unfitness for duty, when it is natural and not sinful, will have great allowances made for it; God will have mercy, and not sacrifice. Let us profit by the solemn warning this history conveys. When professing worshippers come with zeal without knowledge, carnal affections, earthly, light, vain, trifling thoughts, the devices of will-worship, instead of the offering of soul and spirit; then the incense is kindled by a flame which never came down from heaven, which the Spirit of a holy God never sent within their hearts.

Chapter 11

What animals were clean and unclean.

—These laws seem to have been intended, **1**. As a test of the people's obedience, as Adam was forbidden to eat of the tree of knowledge; and to teach them self-denial, and the government of their appetites. **2**. To keep the Israelites distinct from other nations. Many also of these forbidden animals were objects of superstition and idolatry to the heathen. **3**. The people were taught to make distinctions between the holy and unholy in their companions and intimate connexions. **4**. The law forbad, not only the eating of the unclean beasts, but the touching of them. Those who would be kept from any sin, must be careful to avoid all temptations to it, or coming near it. The exceptions are very minute, and all were designed to call forth constant care and exactness in their obedience; and to teach us to obey. Whilst we enjoy our Christian liberty, and are free from such burdensome observances, we must be careful not to abuse our liberty. For the Lord hath redeemed and called his people, that they may be holy, even as he is holy. We must come out, and be separate from the world; we must leave the company of the ungodly, and all needless connexions with those who are dead in sin; we must be zealous of good works devoted followers of God, and companions of his people.

Chapter 12

Ceremonial purification.

—After the laws concerning clean and unclean food, come the laws concerning clean and unclean persons. Man imparts his depraved nature to his offspring, so that, excepting as the atonement of Christ and the sanctification of the Spirit prevent, the original blessing, "Increase and multiply," Ge **1**:**28**, is become to the fallen race a direful curse, and communicates sin and misery. Let those women who have received mercy from God in child-bearing, with all thankfulness own God's goodness to them; and this shall please the Lord better than sacrifices.

Chapter 13

Verses 1–17

The plague of leprosy was an uncleanness, rather than a disease. Christ is said to cleanse lepers, not to cure them. Common as the leprosy was among the Hebrews, during and after their residence in Egypt, we have no reason to believe that it was known among them before. Their distressed state and employment in that land must have rendered them liable to disease. But it was a plague often inflicted immediately by the hand of God. Miriam's leprosy, and Gehazi's, and king Uzziah's, were punishments of particular sins; no marvel there was care taken to distinguish it from a common distemper. The judgment of it was referred to the priests. And it was a figure of the moral pollutions of men's minds by sin, which is the leprosy of the soul, defiling to the conscience, and from which Christ alone can cleanse. The priest could only convict the leper, (by the law is the knowledge of sin,) but Christ can cure the sinner, he can take away sin. It is a work of great importance, but of great difficulty, to judge of our spiritual state. We all have cause to suspect ourselves, being conscious of sores and spots; but whether clean or unclean is the question. As there were certain marks by which to know it was leprosy, so there are marks of such as are in the gall of bitterness. The priest must take time in making his judgment. This teaches all, both ministers and people, not to be hasty in censures, nor to judge anything before the time. If some men's sins go before unto judgment, the sins of others follow after, and so do men's good works. If the person suspected were found to be clean, yet he must wash his clothes, because there had been ground for the suspicion. We have need to be washed in the blood of Christ from our spots, though not leprosy spots; for who can say, I am pure from sin?

Verses 18–44

The priest is told what judgment to make, if there were any appearance of a leprosy in old sores; and such is the danger of those who having escaped the pollutions of the world are again entangled therein. Or, in a burn by accident, ver. #(**24**). The burning of strife and contention often occasions the rising and breaking out of that corruption, which proves that men are unclean. Human life lies exposed to many grievances. With what troops of diseases are we beset on every side; and thy all entered by sin! If the constitution be healthy, and the body lively and easy, we are bound to glorify God with our bodies. Particular note was taken of the leprosy, if in the head. If the leprosy of sin has seized the head; if the judgment be corrupted, and wicked principles, which support wicked practices, are embraced, it is utter uncleanness, from which few are cleansed. Soundness in the faith keeps leprosy from the head.

Verses 45, 46

When the priest had pronounced the leper unclean, it put a stop to his business in the world, cut him off from his friends and relations, and ruined all the comfort he could have in the world. He must humble himself under the mighty hand of God, not insisting upon his cleanness, when the priest had pronounced him unclean, but accepting the punishment. Thus must we take to ourselves the shame that belongs to us, and with broken hearts call ourselves "Unclean, unclean;" heart unclean, life unclean; unclean by original corruption, unclean by actual transgression; unclean, therefore deserving to be for ever shut out from communion with God, and all hope of happiness in him; unclean, therefore undone, if infinite mercy do not interpose. The leper must warn others to take heed of coming near him. He must then be shut out of the camp, and afterward, when they came to Canaan, be shut out of the city, town, or village where he lived, and dwell with none but those that were lepers like himself. This typified the purity which ought to be in the gospel church.

Verses 47–59

The garment suspected to be tainted with leprosy was not to be burned immediately. If, upon search, it was found that there was a leprous spot, it must be burned, or at least that part of it. If it proved to be free, it must be washed, and then might be used. This also sets forth the great evil there is in sin. It not only defiles the sinner's conscience, but it brings a stain upon all he has and all that he does. And those who make their clothes servants to their pride and lust, may see them thereby tainted with leprosy. But the robes of righteousness never fret, nor are moth-eaten.

Chapter 14

Verses 1–9

The priests could not cleanse the lepers; but when the Lord removed the plague, various rules were to be observed in admitting them again to the ordinances of God, and the society of his people. They represent many duties and exercises of truly repenting sinners, and the duties of ministers respecting them. If we apply this to the spiritual leprosy of sin, it intimates that when we withdraw from those who walk disorderly, we must not count them as enemies, but admonish them as brethren. And also that when God by his grace has brought to repentance, they ought with tenderness and joy, and sincere affection, to be received again. Care should always be taken that sinners may not be encouraged, nor penitents discouraged. If it were found that the leprosy was healed, the priest must declare it with the particular solemnities here described. The two birds, one killed, and the other dipped in the blood of the bird that was killed, and then let loose, may signify Christ shedding his blood for sinners, and rising and ascending into heaven. The priest having pronounced the leper clean from the disease, he must make himself clean from all remains of it. Thus those who have comfort of the remission of their sins, must with care and caution cleanse themselves from sins; for every one that has this hope in him, will be concerned to purify himself.

Verses 10–32

The cleansed leper was to be presented to the Lord, with his offerings. When God has restored us to enjoy public worship again, after sickness, distance, or otherwise, we should testify our thanksgiving by our diligent use of the liberty. And both we and our offerings must be presented before the Lord, by the Priest that made us clean, even our Lord Jesus. Beside the usual rites of the trespass-offering, some of the blood, and some of the oil, was to be put upon him that was to be cleansed. Wherever the blood of Christ is applied for justification, the oil of the Spirit is applied for sanctification; these two cannot be separated. We have here the gracious provision the law made for poor lepers. The poor are as welcome to God's altar as the rich. But though a meaner sacrifice was accepted from the poor, yet the same ceremony was used for the rich; their souls are as precious, and Christ and his gospel are the same to both. Even for the poor one lamb was necessary. No sinner could be saved, had it not been for the Lamb that was slain, and hath redeemed us to God with his blood.

Verses 33–53

The leprosy in a house is unaccountable to us, as well as the leprosy in a garment; but now sin, where that reigns in a house, is a plague there, as it is in a heart. Masters of families should be aware, and afraid of the first appearance of sin in their families, and put it away, whatever it is. If the leprosy is got into the house, the infected part must be taken out. If it remain in the house, the whole must be pulled down. The owner had better be without a dwelling, than live in one that was infected. The leprosy of sin ruins families and churches. Thus sin is so interwoven with the human body, that it must be taken down by death.

Verses 54–57

When that God who is rich in mercy, for his great love wherewith he loved us, even when we were dead in sins, hath quickened us by his grace, Eph **2**:**4**, **5**, we shall manifest the change by repenting, and forsaking former sins. Let us follow after holiness, and let us compassionate other poor lepers, and desire, seek, and pray for their cleansing.

Chapter 15

Laws concerning ceremonial uncleanness.

—We need not be curious in explaining these laws; but have reason to be thankful that we need fear no defilement, except that of sin, nor need ceremonial and burdensome purifications. These laws remind us that God sees all things, even those which escape the notice of men. The great gospel duties of faith and repentance are here signified, and the great gospel privileges of the application of Christ's blood to our souls for our justification, and his grace for our sanctification.

Chapter 16

Verses 1–14

Without entering into particulars of the sacrifices on the great day of atonement, we may notice that it was to be a statute for ever, till that dispensation be at an end. As long as we are continually sinning, we continually need the atonement. The law of afflicting our souls for sin, is a statue which will continue in force till we arrive where all tears, even those of repentance, will be wiped from our eyes. The apostle observes it as a proof that the sacrifices could not take away sin, and cleanse the conscience from it, that in them there was a remembrance made of sin every year, upon the day of atonement, Heb **10**:**1**, **3**. The repeating the sacrifices, showed there was in them but a feeble effort toward making atonement; this could be done only by offering up the body of Christ once for all; and that sacrifice needed not to be repeated. (Le **16**:**15-34**)

Verses 15–34

Here are typified the two great gospel privileges, of the remission of sin, and access to God, both of which we owe to our Lord Jesus. See the expiation of guilt. Christ is both the Maker and the Matter of the atonement; for he is the Priest, the High Priest, that makes reconciliation for the sins of the people. And as Christ is the High Priest, so he is the Sacrifice with which atonement is made; for he is all in all in our reconciliation to God. Thus he was figured by the two goats. The slain goat was a type of Christ dying for our sins; the scape-goat a type of Christ rising again for our justification. The atonement is said to be completed by putting the sins of Israel upon the head of the goat, which was sent away into a wilderness, a land not inhabited; and the sending away of the goat represented the free and full remission of their sins. He shall bear upon him all their iniquities. Thus Christ, the Lamb of God, takes away the sin of the world, by taking it upon himself, Joh **1**:**29**. The entrance into heaven, which Christ made for us, was typified by the high priest's entrance into the most holy place. See Heb **9**:**7**. The high priest was to come out again; but our Lord Jesus ever lives, making intercession, and always appears in the presence of God for us. Here are typified the two great gospel duties of faith and repentance. By faith we put our hands upon the head of the offering; relying on Christ as the Lord our Righteousness, pleading his satisfaction, as that which alone is able to atone for our sins, and procure us a pardon. By repentance we afflict our souls; not only fasting for a time from the delights of the body, but inwardly sorrowing for sin, and living a life of self-denial, assuring ourselves, that if we confess our sins, God is faithful and just to forgive us our sins, and to cleanse us from all unrighteousness. By the atonement we obtain rest for our souls, and all the glorious liberties of the children of God. Sinner, get the blood of Christ effectually applied to thy soul, or else thou canst never look God in the face with any comfort or acceptance. Take this blood of Christ, apply it by faith, and see how it atones with God.

Chapter 17

Verses 1–9

All the cattle killed by the Israelites, while in the wilderness, were to be presented before the door of the tabernacle, and the flesh to be returned to the offerer, to be eaten as a peace-offering, according to the law. When they entered Canaan, this only continued in respect of sacrifices. The spiritual sacrifices we are now to offer, are not confined to any one place. We have now no temple or altar that sanctifies the gift; nor does the gospel unity rest only in one place, but in one heart, and the unity of the Spirit. Christ is our Altar, and the true Tabernacle; in him God dwells among men. It is in him that our sacrifices are acceptable to God, and in him only. To set up other mediators, or other altars, or other expiatory sacrifices, is, in effect, to set up other gods. And though God will graciously accept our family offerings, we must not therefore neglect attending at the tabernacle.

Verses 10–16

Here is a confirmation of the law against eating blood. They must eat no blood. But this law was ceremonial, and is now no longer in force; the coming of the substance does away the shadow. The blood of beasts is no longer the ransom, but Christ's blood only; therefore there is not now the reason for abstaining there then was. The blood is now allowed for the nourishment of our bodies; it is no longer appointed to make an atonement for the soul. Now the blood of Christ makes atonement really and effectually; to that, therefore, we must have regard, and not consider it as a common thing, or treat it with indifference.

Chapter 18

Unlawful marriages and fleshly lusts.

—Here is a law against all conformity to the corrupt usages of the heathen. Also laws against incest, against brutal lusts, and barbarous idolatries; and the enforcement of these laws from the ruin of the Canaanites. God here gives moral precepts. Close and constant adherence to God's ordinances is the most effectual preservative from gross sin. The grace of God only will secure us; that grace is to be expected only in the use of the means of grace. Nor does He ever leave any to their hearts' lusts, till they have left him and his services.

Chapter 19

laws.

—There are some ceremonial precepts in this chapter, but most of these precepts are binding on us, for they are explanations of the ten commandments. It is required that Israel be a holy people, because the God of Israel is a holy God, ver. #(**2**). To teach real separation from the world and the flesh, and entire devotedness to God. This is now the law of Christ; may the Lord bring every thought within us into obedience to it! Children are to be obedient to their parents, ver. #(**3**). The fear here required includes inward reverence and esteem, outward respect and obedience, care to please them and to make them easy. God only is to be worshipped, ver. #(**4**). Turn not from the true God to false ones, from the God who will make you holy and happy, to those that will deceive you, and make you for ever miserable. Turn not your eyes to them, much less your heart. They should leave the gleanings of their harvest and vintage for the poor, ver. #(**9**). Works of piety must be always attended with works of charity, according to our ability. We must not be covetous, griping, and greedy of every thing we can lay claim to, nor insist upon our right in all things. We are to be honest and true in all our dealings, ver. #(**11**). Whatever we have in the world, we must see that we get it honestly, for we cannot be truly rich, or long rich, with that which is not so. Reverence to the sacred name of God must be shown, ver. #(**12**). We must not detain what belongs to another, particularly the wages of the hireling, ver. #(**13**). We must be tender of the credit and safety of those that cannot help themselves, ver. #(**14**). Do no hurt to any, because they are unwilling or unable to avenge themselves. We ought to take heed of doing any thing which may occasion our weak brother to fall. The fear of God should keep us from doing wrong things, though they will not expose us to men's anger. Judges, and all in authority, are commanded to give judgment without partiality, ver. #(**15**). To be a tale-bearer, and to sow discord among neighbours, is as bad an office as a man can put himself into. We are to rebuke our neighbour in love, ver. #(**17**). Rather rebuke him than hate him, for an injury done to thyself. We incur guilt by not reproving; it is hating our brother. We should say, I will do him the kindness to tell him of his faults. We are to put off all malice, and to put on brotherly love, ver. #(**18**). We often wrong ourselves, but we soon forgive ourselves those wrongs, and they do not at all lessen our love to ourselves; in like manner we should love our neighbour. We must in many cases deny ourselves for the good of our neighbour. Ver. #(**31**): For Christians to have their fortunes told, to use spells and charms, or the like, is a sad affront to God. They must be grossly ignorant who ask, "What harm is there in these things?" Here is a charge to young people to show respect to the aged, ver. #(**32**). Religion teaches good manners, and obliges us to honour those to whom honour is due. A charge was given to the Israelites to be very tender of strangers, ver. #(**33**). Strangers, and the widows and fatherless, are God's particular care. It is at our peril, if we do them any wrong. Strangers shall be welcome to God's grace; we should do what we can to recommend religion to them. Justice in weights and measures is commanded, ver. #(**35**). We must make conscience of obeying God's precepts. We are not to pick and choose our duty, but must aim at standing complete in all the will of God. And the nearer our lives and tempers are to the precepts of God's law, the happier shall we be, and the happier shall we make all around us, and the better shall we adorn the gospel.

Chapter 20

Verses 1–9

Are we shocked at the unnatural cruelty of the ancient idolaters in sacrificing their children? We may justly be so. But are there not very many parents, who, by bad teaching and wicked examples, and by the mysteries of iniquity which they show their children, devote them to the service of Satan, and forward their everlasting ruin, in a manner even more to be lamented? What an account must such parents render to God, and what a meeting will they have with their children at the day of judgment! On the other hand, let children remember that he who cursed father or mother was surely put to death. This law Christ confirmed. Laws which were made before are repeated, and penalties annexed to them. If men will not avoid evil practices, because the law has made these practices sin, and it is right that we go on that principle, surely they should avoid them when the law has made them death, from a principle of self-preservation. In the midst of these laws comes in a general charge, Sanctify yourselves, and be ye holy. It is the Lord that sanctifies, and his work will be done, though it be difficult. Yet his grace is so far from doing away our endeavours, that it strongly encourages them. Work out your salvation, for it is God that worketh in you.

Verses 10–27

These **verse**s repeat what had been said before, but it was needful there should be line upon line. What praises we owe to God that he has taught the evil of sin, and the sure way of deliverance from it! May we have grace to adorn the doctrine of God our Saviour in all things; may we have no fellowship with unfruitful works of darkness, but reprove them.

Chapter 21

Laws concerning the priests.

—As these priests were types of Christ, so all ministers must be followers of him, that their example may teach others to imitate the Saviour. Without blemish, and separate from sinners, He executed his priestly office on earth. What manner of persons then should his ministers be! But all are, if Christians, spiritual priests; the minister especially is called to set a good example, that the people may follow it. Our bodily infirmities, blessed be God, cannot now shut us out from his service, from these privileges, or from his heavenly glory. Many a healthful, beautiful soul is lodged in a feeble, deformed body. And those who may not be suited for the work of the ministry, may serve God with comfort in other duties in his church.

Chapter 22

Laws concerning the priests and sacrifices.

—In this chapter we have divers laws concerning the priests and sacrifices, all for preserving the honour of the sanctuary. Let us recollect with gratitude that our great High Priest cannot be hindered by any thing from the discharge of his office. Let us also remember, that the Lord requires us to reverence his name, his truths, his ordinances, and commandments. Let us beware of hypocrisy, and examine ourselves concerning our sinful defilements, seeking to be purified from them in the blood of Christ, and by his sanctifying Spirit. Whoever attempts to expiate his own sin, or draws near in the pride of self-righteousness, puts as great an affront on Christ, as he who comes to the Lord's table from the gratification of sinful lusts. Nor can the minister who loves the souls of the people, suffer them to continue in this dangerous delusion. He must call upon them, not only to repent of their sins, and forsake them; but to put their whole trust in the atonement of Christ, by faith in his name, for pardon and acceptance with God; thus only will the Lord make them holy, as his own people.

Chapter 23

Verses 1–3

In this chapter we have the institution of holy times; many of which have been mentioned before. Though the yearly feasts were made more remarkable by general attendance at the sanctuary, yet these must not be observed more than the sabbath. On that day they must withdraw from all business of the world. It is a sabbath of rest, typifying spiritual rest from sin, and rest in God. God's sabbaths are to be religiously observed in every private house, by every family apart, as well as by families together, in holy assemblies. The sabbath of the Lord in our dwellings will be their beauty, strength, and safety; it will sanctify, build up, and glorify them.

Verses 4–14

The feast of the Passover was to continue seven days; not idle days, spent in sport, as many that are called Christians spend their holy-days. Offerings were made to the Lord at his altar; and the people were taught to employ their time in prayer, and praise, and godly meditation. The sheaf of first-fruits was typical of the Lord Jesus, who is risen from the dead as the First-fruits of them that slept. Our Lord Jesus rose from the dead on the very day that the first-fruits were offered. We are taught by this law to honour the Lord with our substance, and with the first-fruits of all our increase, Pr **3**:**9**. They were not to eat of their new corn, till God's part was offered to him out of it; and we must always begin with God: begin every day with him, begin every meal with him, begin every affair and business with him; seek first the kingdom of God.

Verses 15–22

The feast of Weeks was held in remembrance of the giving of the law, fifty days after the departure from Egypt; and looked forward to the outpouring of the Holy Ghost, fifty days after Christ our Passover was sacrificed for us. On that day the apostles presented the first-fruits of the Christian church to God. To the institution of the feast of Pentecost, is added a repetition of that law, by which they were required to leave the gleanings of their fields. Those who are truly sensible of the mercy they received from God, will show mercy to the poor without grudging.

Verses 23–32

the blowing of trumpets represented the preaching of the gospel, by which men are called to repent of sin, and to accept the salvation of Christ, which was signified by the day of atonement. Also it invited to rejoice in God, and become strangers and pilgrims on earth, which was denoted by the feast of Tabernacles, observed in the same month. At the beginning of the year, they were called by this sound of trumpet to shake off spiritual drowsiness, to search and try their ways, and to amend them. The day of atonement was the ninth day after this; thus they were awakened to prepare for that day, by sincere and serious repentance, that it might indeed be to them a day of atonement. The humbling of our souls for sin, and the making our peace with God, is work that requires the whole man, and the closest application of mind. On that day God spake peace to his people, and to his saints; therefore they must lay aside all their wordly business, that they might the more clearly hear that voice of joy and gladness.

Verses 33–44

In the feast of Tabernacles there was a remembrance of their dwelling in tents, or booths, in the wilderness, as well as their fathers dwelling in tents in Canaan; to remind them of their origin and their deliverance. Christ's tabernacling on earth in human nature, might also be prefigured. And it represents the believer's life on earth: a stranger and pilgrim here below, his home and heart are above with his Saviour. They would the more value the comforts and conveniences of their own houses, when they had been seven days dwelling in the booths. It is good for those who have ease and plenty, sometimes to learn what it is to endure hardness. The joy of harvest ought to be improved for the furtherance of our joy in God. The earth is the Lord's, and the fullness thereof; therefore whatever we have the comfort of, he must have the glory of, especially when any mercy is perfected. God appointed these feasts, "Beside the sabbaths and your free-will offerings." Calls to extraordinary services will not excuse from constant and stated ones.

Chapter 24

Verses 1–9

The loaves of bread typify Christ as the Bread of life, and the food of the souls of his people. He is the Light of his church, the Light of the world; in and through his word this light shines. By this light we discern the food prepared for our souls; and we should daily, but especially from sabbath to sabbath, feed thereon in our hearts with thanksgiving. And as the loaves were left in the sanctuary, so should we abide with God till he dismiss us.

Verses 10–23

This offender was the son of an Egyptian father, and an Israelitish mother. The notice of his parents shows the common ill effect of mixed marriages. A standing law for the stoning of blasphemers was made upon this occasion. Great stress is laid upon this law. It extends to the strangers among them, as well as to those born in the land. Strangers, as well as native Israelites, should be entitled to the benefit of the law, so as not to suffer wrong; and should be liable to the penalty of this law, in case they did wrong. If those who profane the name of God escape punishment from men, yet the Lord our God will not suffer them to escape his righteous judgments. What enmity against God must be in the heart of man, when blasphemies against God proceed out of his mouth. If he that despised Moses' law, died without mercy, of what punishment will they be worthy, who despise and abuse the gospel of the Son of God! Let us watch against anger, do no evil, avoid all connexions with wicked people, and reverence that holy name which sinners blaspheme.

Chapter 25

Verses 1–7

All labour was to cease in the seventh year, as much as daily labour on the seventh day. These statues tell us to beware of covetousness, for a man's life consists not in the abundance of his possessions. We are to exercise willing dependence on God's providence for our support; to consider ourselves the Lord's tenants or stewards, and to use our possessions accordingly. This year of rest typified the spiritual rest which all believers enter into through Christ. Through Him we are eased of the burden of wordly care and labour, both being sanctified and sweetened to us; and we are enabled and encouraged to live by faith.

Verses 8–22

The word "jubilee" signifies a peculiarly animated sound of the silver trumpets. This sound was to be made on the evening of the great day of atonement; for the proclamation of gospel liberty and salvation results from the sacrifice of the Redeemer. It was provided that the lands should not be sold away from their families. They could only be disposed of, as it were, by leases till the year of jubilee, and then returned to the owner or his heir. This tended to preserve their tribes and families distinct, till the coming of the Messiah. The liberty every man was born to, if sold or forfeited, should return at the year of jubilee. This was typical of redemption by Christ from the slavery of sin and Satan, and of being brought again to the liberty of the children of God. All bargains ought to be made by this rule, "Ye shall not oppress one another," not take advantage of one another's ignorance or necessity, "but thou shalt fear thy God." The fear of God reigning in the heart, would restrain from doing wrong to our neighbour in word or deed. Assurance was given that they should be great gainers, by observing these years of rest. If we are careful to do our duty, we may trust God with our comfort. This was a miracle for an encouragement to all neither sowed or reaped. This was a miracle for an encouragement to all God's people, in all ages, to trust him in the way of duty. There is nothing lost by faith and self-denial in obedience. Some asked, What shall we eat the seventh year? Thus many Christians anticipate evils, questioning what they shall do, and fearing to proceed in the way of duty. But we have no right to anticipate evils, so as to distress ourselves about them. To carnal minds we may appear to act absurdly, but the path of duty is ever the path of safety.

Verses 23–34

If the land were not redeemed before the year of jubilee, it then returned to him that sold or mortgaged it. This was a figure of the free grace of God in Christ; by which, and not by any price or merit of our own, we are restored to the favour of God. Houses in walled cities were more the fruits of their own industry than land in the country, which was the direct gift of God's bounty; therefore if a man sold a house in a city, he might redeem it only within a year after the sale. This encouraged strangers and proselytes to come and settle among them.

Verses 35–38

Poverty and decay are great grievances, and very common; the poor ye have always with you. Thou shalt relieve him; by sympathy, pitying the poor; by service, doing for them; and by supply, giving to them according to their necessity, and thine ability. Poor debtors must not be oppressed. Observe the arguments here used against extortion: "Fear thy God." Relieve the poor, "that they may live with thee;" for they may be serviceable to thee. The rich can as ill spare the poor, as the poor can the rich. It becomes those that have received mercy to show mercy.

Verses 39–55

A native Israelite, if sold for debt, or for a crime, was to serve but six years, and to go out the seventh. If he sold himself, through poverty, both his work and his usage must be such as were fitting for a son of Abraham. Masters are required to give to their servants that which is just and equal, Col **4**:**1**. At the year of jubilee the servant should go out free, he and his children, and should return to his own family. This typified redemption from the service of sin and Satan, by the grace of God in Christ, whose truth makes us free, Joh

8:**32**. We cannot ransom our fellow-sinners, but we may point out Christ to them; while by his grace our lives may adorn his gospel, express our love, show our gratitude, and glorify his holy name.

Chapter 26

Verses 1–13

This chapter contains a general enforcement of all the laws given by Moses; by promises of reward in case of obedience, on the one hand; and threatenings of punishment for disobedience, on the other. While Israel maintained a national regard to God's worship, sabbaths, and sanctuary, and did not turn aside to idolatry, the Lord engaged to continue to them temporal mercies and religious advantages. These great and precious promises, though they relate chiefly to the life which now is, were typical of the spiritual blessings made sure by the covenant of grace to all believers, through Christ. **1**. Plenty and abundance of the fruits of the earth. Every good and perfect gift must be expected from above, from the Father of lights. **2**. Peace under the Divine protection. Those dwell in safety, that dwell in God. **3**. Victory and success in their wars. It is all one with the Lord to save by many or by few. **4**. The increase of their people. The gospel church shall be fruitful. **5**. The favour of God, which is the fountain of all Good. **6**. Tokens of his presence in and by his ordinances. The way to have God's ordinances fixed among us, is to cleave closely to them. **7**. The grace of the covenant. All covenant blessings are summed up in the covenant relation, I will be your God, and ye shall be my people; and they are all grounded upon their redemption. Having purchased them, God would own them, and never cast them off till they cast him off. (Le **26**:**14-39**)

Verses 14–39

After God has set the blessing before them which would make them a happy people if they would be obedient, he here sets the curse before them, the evils which would make them miserable, if they were disobedient. Two things would bring ruin. **1**. A contempt of God's commandments. They that reject the precept, will come at last to renounce the covenant. **2**. A contempt of his corrections. If they will not learn obedience by the things they suffer, God himself would be against them; and this is the root and cause of all their misery. And also, The whole creation would be at war with them. All God's sore judgments would be sent against them. The threatenings here are very particular, they were prophecies, and He that foresaw all their rebellions, knew they would prove so. TEMPORAL judgments are threatened. Those who will not be parted from their sins by the commands of God, shall be parted from them by judgments. Those wedded to their lusts, will have enough of them. SPIRITUAL judgments are threatened, which should seize the mind. They should find no acceptance with God. A guilty conscience would be their continual terror. It is righteous with God to leave those to despair of pardon, who presume to sin; and it is owing to free grace, if we are not left to pine away in the iniquity we were born in, and have lived in.

Verses 40–46

Among the Israelites, persons were not always prosperous or afflicted according to their obedience or disobedience. But national prosperity was the effect of national obedience, and national judgments were brought on by national wickedness. Israel was under a peculiar covenant. National wickedness will end in the ruin of any people, especially where the word of God and the light of the gospel are enjoyed. Sooner or later, sin will be the ruin, as well as the reproach, of every people. Oh that, being humbled for our sins, we might avert the rising storm before it bursts upon us! God grant that we may, in this our day, consider the things which belong to our eternal peace.

Chapter 27

Verses 1–13

Zeal for the service of God disposed the Israelites, on some occasions, to dedicate themselves or their children to the service of the Lord, in his house for life. Some persons who thus dedicated themselves might be employed as assistants; in general they were to be redeemed for a value. It is good to be zealously affected and liberally disposed for the Lord's service; but the matter should be well weighed, and prudence should direct as to what we do; else rash vows and hesitation in doing them will dishonour God, and trouble our own minds.

Verses 14–25

Our houses, lands, cattle, and all our substance, must be used to the glory of God. It is acceptable to him that a portion be given to support his worship, and to promote his cause. But God would not approve such a degree of zeal as ruined a man's family.

Verses 26–33

Things or persons devoted, are distinguished from things or persons that were only sanctified. Devoted things were most holy to the Lord, and could neither be taken back nor applied to other purposes. Whatever productions they had the benefit, God must be honoured with the tenth of, if it could be applied. Thus they acknowledge God to be the Owner of their land, the Giver of its fruits, and themselves to be his tenants, and dependants upon him. Thus they gave him thanks for the plenty they enjoyed, and besought his favour in the continuance of it. We are taught to honour the Lord with our substance.

Verse 34

The last **verse** seems to have reference to this whole book. Many of the precepts in it are moral, and always binding; others are ceremonial, and peculiar to the Jewish nation; yet they have a spiritual meaning, and so teach us; for unto us, by these institutions, is the gospel preached, as well as unto them, Heb **4**:**2**. The doctrine of reconciliation to God by a Mediator, is not clouded with the smoke of burning sacrifice, but cleared by the knowledge of Christ and him crucified. We are under the sweet and easy institutions of the gospel, which pronounces those true worshippers, who worship the Father in spirit and truth, by Christ only, and in his name. Yet, let us not think, because we are not tied to the ceremonial rites and oblations, that a little care, time, and expense, will serve to honour God with. Having boldness to enter into the holiest by the blood of Jesus, let us draw near with a true heart, and in full assurance of faith, worshipping God with the more cheerfulness and humble confidence, still saying, BLESSED BE GOD FOR JESUS CHRIST.

Numbers

This book is called NUMBERS from the several numberings of the people contained in it. It extends from the giving of the law at Sinai, till their arrival in the plains of Jordan. An account is given of their murmuring and unbelief, for which they were sentenced to wander in the wilderness nearly forty years; also some laws, both, moral and ceremonial. Their trials greatly tended to distinguish the wicked and hypocrites from the faithful and true servants of God, who served him with a pure heart.

Chapter 1

Verses 1–43

The people were numbered to show God's faithfulness in thus increasing the seed of Jacob, that they might be the better trained for the wars and conquest of Canaan, and to ascertain their families in order to the division of the land. It is said of each tribe, that those were numbered who were able to go forth to war; they had wars before them, though now they met with no opposition. Let the believer be prepared to withstand the enemies of his soul, though all may appear to be peace.

Verses 44–46

We have here the sum total. How much was required to maintain all these in the wilderness! They were all provided for by God every day. When we observe the faithfulness of God, however unlikely the performance of his promise may appear, we may take courage as to those which yet remain to be fulfilled to the church of God.

Verses 47–54

Care is here taken to distinguish the tribe of Levi, which, in the matter of the golden calf, had distinguished itself. Singular services shall be recompensed by singular honours. It was to the honour of the Levites, that to them was committed the care of the tabernacle and its treasures, in their camps and in their marches. It was for the honour of the holy things that none should see them, or touch them, but those who were called of God to the service. We all are unfit and unworthy to have fellowship with God, till called by his grace into the fellowship of his Son Jesus Christ our Lord; and so, being the spiritual seed of that great High Priest, we are made priests to our God. Great care must be taken to prevent sin, for preventing sin is preventing wrath. Being a holy tribe, they were not reckoned among other Israelites. They that minister about holy things, should neither entangle themselves, nor be entangled, in worldly affairs. And let every believer seek to do what the Lord has commanded.

Chapter 2

The order of the tribes in their tents.

—The tribes were to encamp about the tabernacle, which was to be in the midst of them. It was a token of God's gracious presence. Yet they were to pitch their tents afar off, in reverence to the sanctuary. The children of Israel put themselves in their posts, without murmuring or disputing; and as it was their safety, so it was their beauty. It is our duty and interest to be contented with the place allotted to us, and to endeavour to occupy it in a proper manner, without envying or murmuring; without ambition or covetousness. Thus the gospel church ought to be compact, according to the Scripture model, every one knowing and keeping his place; and then all that wish well to the church rejoice, beholding their order, Col **2**:**5**.

Chapter 3

Verses 1–13

There was much work belonging to the priests' office, and there were now only Aaron and his two sons to do it; God appoints the Levites to attend them. Those whom God finds work for, he will find help for. The Levites were taken instead of the first-born. When He that made us, saves us, as the first-born of Israel were saved, we are laid under further obligations to serve him faithfully. God's right to us by redemption, confirms the right he has to us by creation.

Verses 14–39

The Levites were in three classes, according to the sons of Levi; Gershon, Kohath, and Merari; and these were subdivided into families. The posterity of Moses were not at all honoured or privileged, but stood upon the level with other Levites; thus it was plain, that Moses did not seek the advancement of his own family, or to secure any honours to it. The tribe of Levi was by much the least of all the tribes. God's chosen are but a little flock in comparison with the world.

Verses 40–51

The number of the first-born, and that of the Levites, came near to each other. Known unto God are all his works beforehand; there is an exact proportion between them, and so it will appear, when they are compared together. The small number of first-born, over and above the number of the Levites, were to be redeemed, and the redemption-money given to Aaron. The church is called the church of the first-born, which is redeemed, not as they were, with silver and gold; but, being devoted by sin to the justice of God, is ransomed with the precious blood of the Son of God. All men are the Lord's by creation, and all true christians are his by redemption. Each should know his own post and duty; nor can any service required by such a Master be rightly accounted mean or hard.

Chapter 4

Verses 1–3

The middle-aged men of the tribe of Levi, all from thirty years old to fifty, were to be employed in the service of the tabernacle. The service of God requires the best of our strength, and the prime portion of our time, which cannot be better spent than to the honour of Him who is the First and Best. And the service of God should be done when we are most lively and active. Those do not consider this who put off repentance to old age, and so leave the best work to be done in the worst time.

Verses 4–20

The Kohathites were to carry the holy things of the tabernacle. All the holy things were to be covered; not only for security and respect, but to keep them from being seen. This not only marked the reverence due to holy things, but the mystery of the things signified by those types, and the darkness of the dispensation. But now, through Christ, the case is altered, and we are encouraged to come boldly to the throne of grace.

Verses 21–33

We have here the charge of the other two families of the Levites, which, though not so honourable as the first, yet was necessary, and to be done regularly. All the things were delivered them by name. It intimates the care God takes of his church and every member of it. The death of the saints is represented as the taking down of the tabernacle, **2**Co **5**:**1**, and the putting it off, **2**Pe **1**:**14**. All shall be raised up in the great day, when these vile bodies shall be made like the glorious body of Jesus Christ, and so shall be for ever with the Lord.

Verses 34–49

God so ordered it, that though the Merarites were the fewest in number, yet they should have most able men among them; for whatever service God calls men to, he will furnish them for it, give strength in proportion to the work, and grace sufficient. The least of the tribes had many more able men than the Levites: those who engage in the service of this world, are many more than those devoted to the service of God. May our souls be wholly devoted to his service.

Chapter 5

Verses 1–10

The camp was to be cleansed. The purity of the church must be kept as carefully as the peace and order of it. Every polluted Israelite must be separated. The wisdom from above is first pure, then peaceable. The greater profession of religion any house or family makes, the more they are obliged to put away iniquity far from them. If a man overreach or defraud his brother in any matter, it is a trespass against the Lord, who strictly charges and commands us to do justly. What is to be done when a man's awakened conscience charges him with guilt of this kind, though done long ago? He must confess his sin, confess it to God, confess it to his neighbour, and take shame to himself; though it go against him to own himself in a lie, yet he must do it. Satisfaction must be made for the offence done to God, as well as for the loss sustained by the neighbour; restitution in that case is not enough without faith and repentance. While that which is wrongly gotten is knowingly kept, the guilt remains on the conscience, and is not done away by sacrifice or offering, prayers or tears; for it is the same act of sin persisted in. This is the doctrine of right reason, and of the word of God. It detects hypocrites, and directs the tender conscience to proper conduct, which, springing from faith in Christ, will make way for inward peace.

Verses 11–31

This law would make the women of Israel watch against giving cause for suspicion. On the other hand, it would hinder the cruel treatment such suspicions might occasion. It would also hinder the guilty from escaping, and the innocent from coming under just suspicion. When no proof could be brought, the wife was called on to make this solemn appeal to a heart-searching God. No woman, if she were guilty, could say "Amen" to the adjuration, and drink the water after it, unless she disbelieved the truth of God, or defied his justice. The water is called the bitter water, because it caused the curse. Thus sin is called an evil and a bitter thing. Let all that meddle with forbidden pleasures, know that they will be bitterness in the latter end. From the whole learn, **1**. Secret sins are known to God, and sometimes are strangely brought to light in this life; and that there is a day coming when God will, by Christ, judge the secrets of men according to the gospel, Ro **2**:**16**. **2** In particular, Whoremongers and adulterers God will surely judge. Though we have not now the waters of jealousy, yet we have God's word, which ought to be as great a terror. Sensual lusts will end in bitterness. **3**. God will manifest the innocency of the innocent. The same providence is for good to some, and for hurt to others. And it will answer the purposes which God intends.

Chapter 6

Verses 1–21

The word Nazarite signifies separation. Some were appointed of God, before their birth, to be Nazarites all their days, as Samson and John the Baptist. But, in general, it was a vow of separation from the world and devotedness to the services of religion, for a limited time, and under certain rules, which any person might make if they pleased. A Nazarite is spoken of as well known; but his obligation is brought to a greater certainty than before. That the fancies of superstitious men might not multiply the restraints endlessly, God gives them rules. They must not drink wine or strong drink, nor eat grapes. Those who separate themselves to God, must not gratify the desires of the body, but keep it under. Let all Christians be very moderate in the use of wine and strong drink; for if the love of these once gets the mastery of a man, he becomes an easy prey to Satan. The Nazarites were to eat nothing that came of the vine; this may teach the utmost care to avoid sin, and all that borders upon it, and leads to it, or may be a temptation to us. They must not cut their hair. They must neither poll their heads, nor shave their beards; this was the mark of Samson being a Nazarite. This signified neglect of the body, and of the ease and ornament of it. Those who separate themselves to God, must keep their consciences pure from dead works, and not touch unclean things. All the days of their separation they must be holy to the Lord. This was the meaning of those outward observances, and without this they were of no account. No penalty or sacrifice was appointed for those who wilfully broke their vow of being Nazarites; they must answer another day for such profane trifling with the Lord their God; but those were to be relieved who did not sin wilfully. There is nothing in Scripture that bears the least resemblance to the religious orders of the church of Rome, except these Nazarites. But mark the difference, or rather how completely opposed! The religious of that church are forbidden to marry; but no such restriction is laid upon the Nazarites. They are commanded to abstain from meats; but the Nazarites might eat any food allowed other Israelites. They are not generally forbidden wine, not even on their fasting days; but the Nazarites might not have wine at any time. Their vow is lasting, even to the end of their lives; the Nazarites' vow was only for a limited time, at their own will; and in certain cases not unless allowed by husbands or parents. Such a thorough difference there is between rules of man's invention and those directed in Scripture, Let us not forget that the Lord Jesus is not only our Surety, but also our example. For his sake we must renounce worldly pleasures, abstain from fleshy lusts, be separate from sinners, make open profession of our faith, moderate natural affections, be spiritually-minded, and devoted to God's service, and desirous to be an example all around us. (Nu **6**:**22-27**)

Verses 22–27

The priests were solemnly to bless the people in the name of the Lord. To be under the almighty protection of God our Saviour; to enjoy his favour as the smile of a loving Father, or as the cheering beams of the sun; while he mercifully forgives our sins, supplies our wants, consoles the heart, and prepares us by his grace for eternal glory; these things form the substance of this blessing, and the sum total of all blessings. In so rich a list of mercies worldly joys are not worthy to be mentioned. Here is a form of prayer. The name Jehovah is three times repeated. The Jews think there is some mystery; and we know what it is, the New Testament having explained it. There we are directed to expect the blessing from the grace of our Lord Jesus Christ, the love of the Father, and the communion of the Holy Ghost, 2Co **13**:**14**; each of which Persons is Jehovah, and yet they are not three Lords, but one Lord.

Chapter 7

Verses 1–9

The offering of the princes to the service of the tabernacle was not made till it was fully set up. Necessary observances must always take place of free-will offerings. The more any are advanced, the greater opportunity they have of serving God and their generation. No sooner was the tabernacle set up, than provision is made for the removal of it. Even when but just settled in the world, we must be preparing for changes and removes, especially for the great change.

Verses 10–89

The princes and great men were most forward in the service of God. Here is an example to those in authority, and of the highest rank; they ought to use their honour and power, their estate and interest, to promote religion and the service of God in the places where they live. Though it was a time of joy and rejoicing, yet still, in the midst of their sacrifices, we find a sin-offering. As, in our best services, we are conscious that there is sin, there should be repentance, even in our most joyful services. In all approaches to God we must by faith look to Christ as the Sin-offering. They brought their offerings each on a day. God's work should not be done confusedly, or in a hurry; take time, and we shall have done the sooner, or, at least, we shall have done the better. If services are to be done for twelve days together, we must not call it a task and a burden. All their offerings were the same; all the tribes of Israel had an equal share in the altar, and an equal interest in the sacrifices offered upon it. He who now spake to Moses, as the Shechinah or Divine Majesty, from between the Cherubim, was the Eternal Word, the second Person in the Trinity; for all God's communion with man is by his Son, by whom he made the world, and rules the church, who is the same yesterday, to-day, and for ever.

Chapter 8

Verses 1–4

Aaron himself lighted the lamps, thus representing his Divine Master. The Scripture is a light shining in a dark place, 2Pe **1**:**19**. A dark place even the church would be without it; as the tabernacle, which had no window, would have been without the lamps. The work of ministers is to light these lamps, by expounding and applying the word of God. Jesus Christ is the only Light of our dark, sinful world; and by his atonement, by his word and the Holy Spirit, he diffuses light around.

Verses 5–26

Here we have directions for the solemn ordination of the Levites. All Israel must know that they took not this honour to themselves, but were called of God to it; nor was it enough that they were distinguished from others. All who are employed for God, must be dedicated to him, according to the employment. Christians must be baptized, ministers must be ordained; we must first give ourselves unto the Lord, and then our services. The Levites must be cleansed. They must be clean that bear the vessels of the Lord. Moses must sprinkle the water of purifying upon them. This signifies the application of the blood of Christ to our souls by faith, that we may be fit to serve the living God. God declares his acceptance of them. All who expect to share in the privileges of the tabernacle, must resolve to do the service of the tabernacle. As, on the one hand, none of God's creatures are his necessary servants, he needs not the service of any of them; so none are merely honorary servants, to do nothing. All whom God owns, he employs; angels themselves have their services.

Chapter 9

Verses 1–14

God gave particular orders for the keeping of this passover, and, for aught that appears, after this, they kept no passover till they came to Canaan, Jos **5**:**10**. It early showed that the ceremonial institutions were not to continue always, as so soon after they were appointed, some were suffered to sleep for many years. But the ordinance of the Lord's Supper was not thus set aside in the first days of the Christian church, although those were days of greater difficulty and distress than Israel knew in the wilderness; nay, in the times of persecution, the Lord's Supper was celebrated more frequently than afterward. Israelites in the wilderness could not forget the deliverance out of Egypt. There was danger of this when they came to Canaan. Instructions were given concerning those who were ceremonially unclean, when they were to eat the passover. Those whose minds and consciences are defiled by sin, are unfit for communion with God, and cannot partake with comfort of the gospel passover, till they are cleansed by true repentance and faith. Observe with what trouble and concern these men complained that they were kept back from offering to the Lord. It should be a trouble to us, when by any occasion we are kept back from the solemnities of a sabbath or a sacrament. Observe the deliberation of Moses in resolving this case. Ministers must ask counsel of God's mouth, not determine according to their own fancy or affection, but according to the word of God to the best of their knowledge. And if, in difficult cases, time is taken to spread the matter before God by humble, believing prayer, the Holy Spirit assuredly will direct in the good and right way. God gave directions in this case, and in other similar cases, explanatory of the law of the passover. As those who, against their minds, are forced to absent themselves from God's ordinances, may expect the favours of God's grace under their affliction, so those who, of choice, absent themselves, may expect God's wrath for their sin. Be not deceived: God is not mocked.

Verses 15–23

This cloud was appointed to be the visible sign and symbol of God's presence with Israel. Thus we are taught to see God always near us, both night and day. As long as the cloud rested on the tabernacle, so long they continued in the same place. There is no time lost, while we are waiting God's time. When the cloud was taken up, they removed, however comfortably they were encamped. We are kept at uncertainty concerning the time of our putting off the earthly house of this tabernacle, that we may be always ready to remove at the command of the Lord. It is very safe and pleasant going when we see God before us, and resting where he appoints us to rest. The leading of this cloud is spoken of as signifying the guidance of the blessed Spirit. We are not now to expect such tokens of the Divine presence and guidance; but the promise is sure to all God's spiritual Israel, that he will guide them by his counsel. Ps **73**:**24**, even unto death, Ps **48**:**14**. All the children of God shall be led by the Spirit of God, Ro **8**:**14**. He will direct the paths of those who in all their ways acknowledge him, Pr **3**:**6**. At the commandment of the Lord, our hearts should always move and rest, saying, Father, thy will be done; dispose of me and mine as thou pleasest. What thou wilt, and where thou wilt; only let me be thine, and always in the way of my duty. In applying general precepts to particular circumstances, there should be good counsel and fervent prayer. When any undertaking is evidently wrong, or doubtfully right, and yet the mind leans that way, in such a case "the moving of the cloud," as men sometimes miscall it, is generally no more than a temptation Satan is permitted to propose; and men fancy they are following the Lord, when they are following their own wayward inclinations. The record of his mercy will conduct us with unerring truth, through Christ, to everlasting peace. Follow the pillar of the cloud and of fire. Lay the BIBLE to heart, and receive with meekness the ingrafted word, which is able to save your souls.

Chapter 10

Verses 1–10

Here are directions concerning the public notices to be given the people by sound of trumpet. Their laws in every case were to be Divine, therefore, even in this matter Moses is directed. These trumpets typify the preached gospel. It sounds an alarm to sinners, calls them to repent, proclaims liberty to the captives and slaves of Satan, and collects the worshippers of God. It directs and encourages their heavenly journey; stirs them up to combat against the world and sin, encouraging them with the assurance of victory. It leads their attention to the sacrifice of Christ, and shows the Lord's presence for their protection. It is also necessary that the gospel trumpet give a distinct sound, according to the persons addressed, or the end proposed; whether to convince, humble, console, exhort, reprove, or teach. The sounding of the trumpet of the gospel is God's ordinance, and demands the attention of all to whom it is sent. (Nu **10**:**11-28**)

Verses 11–28

After the Israelites had continued nearly a year at mount Sinai, and all was settled respecting their future worship, they began their march to Canaan. True religion begins with the knowledge of the holy law of God, and humiliation for sin, but we must go on towards perfection, in acquaintance with Christ and his gospel, and those effectual encouragements, motives, and assistances to holiness, which it proposes. They took their journey according to the commandment of the Lord, De **1**:**6**–**8**, and as the cloud led them. Those who give themselves to the direction of God's word and Spirit, steer a steady course, even when they seem bewildered. While they are sure they cannot lose their God and Guide, they need not fear losing their way. They went out of the wilderness of Sinai, and rested in the wilderness of Paran. All our removes in this world are but from one wilderness to another. The changes we think will be for the better do not always prove so. We shall never be at rest, never at home, till we come to heaven, but all will be well there.

Verses 29–32

Moses invites his kindred to go to Canaan. Those that are bound for the heavenly Canaan, should ask and encourage their friends to go with them: we shall have none the less of the joys of heaven, for others coming to share with us. It is good having fellowship with those who have fellowship with God. But the things of this world, which are seen, draw strongly from the pursuit of the things of the other world, which are not seen. Moses urges that Hobab might be serviceable to them. Not to show where they must encamp, nor what way they must march, the cloud was to direct that; but to show the conveniences of the place they marched through, and encamped in. It well consists with our trust in God's providence, to use the help of our friends.

Verses 33–36

Their going out and coming in, gives an example to us to begin and end every day's journey and every day's work with prayer. Here is Moses's prayer when the ark set forward, "Rise up, and let thine enemies be scattered." There are those in the world who are enemies to God and haters of him; secret and open enemies; enemies to his truths, his laws, his ordinances, his people. But for the scattering and defeating of God's enemies, there needs no more than God's arising. Observe also the prayer of Moses when the ark rested, that God would cause his people to rest. The welfare and happiness of the Israel of God, consist in the continual presence of God among them. Their safety is not in their numbers, but in the favour of God, and his gracious return to them, and resting with them. Upon this account, Happy art thou, O Israel! who is like unto thee, O people! God will go before them, to find them resting-places by the way. His promise is, and their prayers are, that he will never leave them nor forsake them.

Chapter 11

Verses 1–3

Here is the people's sin; they complained. See the sinfulness of sin, which takes occasion from the commandment to be provoking. The weakness of the law discovered sin, but could not destroy it; checked, but could not conquer it. They complained. Those who are of a discontented spirit, will always find something to quarrel or fret about, though the circumstances of their outward condition be ever so favourable. The Lord heard it, though Moses did not. God knows the secret frettings and murmurings of the heart, though concealed from men. What he noticed, he was much displeased with, and he chastised them for this sin. The fire of their wrath against God burned in their minds; justly did the fire of God's wrath fasten on their bodies; but God's judgments came on them gradually, that they might take warning. It appeared that God delights not in punishing; when he begins, he is soon prevailed with to let it fall.

Verses 4–9

Man, having forsaken his proper rest, feels uneasy and wretched, though prosperous. They were weary of the provision God had made for them, although wholesome food and nourishing. It cost no money or care, and the labour of gathering it was very little indeed; yet they talked of Egypt's cheapness, and the fish they ate there freely; as if that cost them nothing, when they paid dearly for it with hard service! While they lived on manna, they seemed exempt from the curse sin has brought on man, that in the sweat of his face he should eat bread; yet they speak of it with scorn. Peevish, discontented minds will find fault with that which has no fault in it, but that it is too good for them. Those who might be happy, often make themselves miserable by discontent. They could not be satisfied unless they had flesh to eat. It is evidence of the dominion of the carnal mind, when we want to have the delights and satisfaction of sense. We should not indulge in any desire which we cannot in faith turn into prayer, as we cannot when we ask meat for our lust. What is lawful of itself becomes evil, when God does not allot it to us, yet we desire it.

Verses 10–15

The provocation was very great; yet Moses expressed himself otherwise than became him. He undervalued the honour God had put upon him. He magnified his own performances, while he had the Divine wisdom to direct him, and Almighty power to dispense rewards and punishments. He speaks distrustfully of the Divine grace. Had the work been much less he could not have gone through it in his own strength; but had it been much greater, through God strengthening him, he might have done it. Let us pray, Lord, lead us not into temptation.

Verses 16–23

Moses is to choose such as he knew to be elders, that is, wise and experienced men. God promises to qualify them. If they were not found fit for the employ, they should be made fit. Even the discontented people shall be gratified too, that every mouth may be stopped. See here, I. The vanity of all the delights of sense; they will cloy, but they will not satisfy. Spiritual pleasures alone will satisfy and last. As the world passes away, so do the lusts of it. **2**. What brutish sins gluttony and drunkenness are! they make that to hurt the body which should be its health. Moses objects. Even true and great believers sometimes find it hard to trust God under the discouragements of second causes, and against hope to believe in hope. God here brings Moses to this point, The Lord God is Almighty; and puts the proof upon the issue, Thou shalt see whether my word shall come to pass or not. If he speaks, it is done.

Verses 24–30

We have here the fulfilment of God's word to Moses, that he should have help in the government of Israel. He gave of his Spirit to the seventy elders. They discoursed to the people of the things of God, so that all who heard them might say, that God was with them of a truth. Two of the elders, Eldad and Medad, went not out unto the tabernacle, as the rest, being sensible of their own weakness and unworthiness. But the Spirit of God found them in the camp, and there they exercised their gift of praying, preaching, and praising God; they spake as moved by the Holy Ghost. The Spirit of God is not confined to the tabernacle, but, like the wind, blows where He listeth. And they that humble themselves shall be exalted; and those who are most fit for government, are least ambitious of it. Joshua does not desire that they should be punished, but only restrained for the future. This motion he made out of zeal for what he thought to be the unity of the church. He would have them silenced, lest they should occasion a schism, or should rival Moses; but Moses was not afraid of any such effects from that Spirit which God had put upon them. Shall we reject those whom Christ has owned, or restrain any from doing good, because they are not in every thing of our mind? Moses wishes all the Lord's people were prophets, that he would put his Spirit upon all of them. Let the testimony of Moses be believed by those who desire to be in power; that government is a burden. It is a burden of care and trouble to those who make conscience of the duty of it; and to those who do not, it will prove a heavier burden in the day of account. Let the example of Moses be followed by those in power; let them not despise the advice and assistance of others, but desire it, and be thankful for it. If all the present number of the Lord's people were rendered prophets, or ministers, by the Spirit of Christ, though not all agreed in outward matters, there is work enough for all, in calling sinners to repentance, and faith in our Lord Jesus.

Verses 31–35

God performed his promise to the people, in giving them flesh. How much more diligent men are in collecting the meat that perishes, than in labouring for meat which endures to everlasting life! We are quick-sighted in the affairs of time; but stupidity blinds us as to the concerns of eternity. To pursue worldly advantages, we need no arguments; but when we are to secure the true riches, then we are all forgetfulness. Those who are under the power of a carnal mind, will have their lusts fulfilled, though it be to the certain damage and ruin of their precious souls. They paid dearly for their feasts. God often grants the desires of sinners in wrath, while he denies the desires of his own people in love. What we unduly desire, if we obtain it, we have reason to fear, will be some way or other a grief and cross to us. And what multitudes there are in all places, who shorten their lives by excess of one kind or other! Let us seek for those pleasures which satisfy, but never surfeit; and which will endure for evermore.

Chapter 12

Verses 1–9

The patience of Moses was tried in his own family, as well as by the people. The pretence was, that he had married a foreign wife; but probably their pride was hurt, and their envy stirred up, by his superior authority. Opposition from our near relations, and from religious friends, is most painful. But this is to be looked for, and it will be well if in such circumstances we can preserve the gentleness and meekness of Moses. Moses was thus fitted to the work he was called to. God not only cleared Moses, but praised him. Moses had the spirit of prophecy in a way which set him far above all other prophets; yet he that is least in the kingdom of heaven, is greater than he; and our Lord Jesus infinitely excels him, Heb **3**:**1**. Let Miriam and Aaron consider whom it was they insulted. We have reason to be afraid of saying or doing any thing against the servants of God. And those are presumptuous indeed who are not afraid to speak evil of dignities, **2**Pe **2**:**10**. The removal of God's presence is the surest and saddest token of God's displeasure. Woe to us, if he depart! he never departs, till by sin and folly we drive him from us.

Verses 10–16

The cloud departed, and Miriam became leprous. When God goes, evil comes: expect no good when God departs. Her foul tongue, as Bishop Hall says, was justly punished with a foul face. Aaron, as priest, was judge of the leprosy. He could not pronounce her leprous without trembling, knowing himself to be equally guilty. But if she was thus punished for speaking against Moses, what will become of those who sin against Christ? Aaron, who joined his sister in speaking against Moses, is forced for himself and his sister, to beseech him, and to speak highly of him whom he had so lately blamed. Those who trample upon the saints and servants of God, will one day be glad to make court to them. It is well when rebukes produce confession of sin and repentance. Such offenders, though corrected and disgraced, shall be pardoned. Moses made it appear, that he forgave the injury done him. To this pattern of Moses, and that of our Saviour, who said, "Father, forgive them," we must conform. A reason is given for Miriam's being put out of the camp for seven days; because thus she ought to accept the punishment of her sin. When under the tokens of God's displeasure for sin, it becomes us to take shame to ourselves. This hindered the people's progress in their march forward towards Canaan. Many things oppose us, but nothing so hinders us in the way to heaven, as sin.

Chapter 13

Verses 1–20

A memorable and melancholy history is related in this and the following chapter, of the turning back of Israel from the borders of Canaan, and the sentencing them to wander and perish in the wilderness, for their unbelief and murmuring. It appears, De **1**:**22**, that the motion to search out the land came from the people. They had a better opinion of their own policy than of God's wisdom. Thus we ruin ourselves by believing the reports and representations of sense rather than Divine revelation. We walk by sight not by faith. Moses gave the spies this charge, Be of good courage. It was not only a great undertaking they were put upon, which required good management and resolution; but a great trust was reposed in them, which required that they should be faithful. Courage in such circumstances can only spring from strong faith, which Caleb and Joshua alone possessed.

Verses 21–25

The searchers of the land brought a bunch of grapes with them, and other fruits, as proofs of the goodness of the country; which was to Israel both the earnest and the specimen of all the fruits of Canaan. Such are the present comforts we have in communion with God, foretastes of the fulness of joy we expect in the heavenly Canaan. We may see by them what heaven is.

Verses 26–33

We may wonder that the people of Israel staid forty days for the return of their spies, when they were ready to enter Canaan, under all the assurances of success they could have from the Divine power, and the miracles that had hitherto attended them. But they distrusted God's power and promise. How much we stand in our own light by our unbelief! At length the messengers returned; but the greater part discouraged the people from going forward to Canaan. Justly are the Israelites left to this temptation, for putting confidence in the judgment of men, when they had the word of God to trust in. Though they had found the land as good as God had said, yet they would not believe it to be as sure as he had said, but despaired of having it, though Eternal Truth had engaged it to them. This was the representation of the evil spies. Caleb, however, encouraged them to go forward, though seconded by Joshua only. He does not say, Let us go up and conquer it; but, Let us go and possess it. Difficulties that are in the way of salvation, dwindle and vanish before a lively, active faith in the power and promise of God. All things are possible, if they are promised, to him that believes; but carnal sense and carnal professors are not to be trusted. Unbelief overlooks the promises and power of God, magnifies every danger and difficulty, and fills the heart with discouragement. May the Lord help us to believe! we shall then find all things possible.

Chapter 14

Verses 1–4

Those who do not trust God, continually vex themselves. The sorrow of the world worketh death. The Israelites murmured against Moses and Aaron, and in them reproached the Lord. They look back with causeless discontent. See the madness of unbridled passions, which makes men prodigal of what nature accounts most dear, life itself. They wish rather to die criminals under God's justice, than to live conquerors in his favour. At last they resolve, that, instead of going forward to Canaan, they would go back to Egypt. Those who walk not in God's counsels, seek their own ruin. Could they expect that God's cloud would lead them, or his manna attend them? Suppose the difficulties of conquering Canaan were as they imagined, those of returning to Egypt were much greater. We complain of our place and lot, and we would change; but is there any place or condition in this world, that has not something in it to make us uneasy, if we are disposed to be so? The way to better our condition, is to get our spirits in a better frame. See the folly of turning from the ways of God. But men run on the certain fatal consequences of a sinful course.

Verses 5–10

Moses and Aaron were astonished to see a people throw away their own mercies. Caleb and Joshua assured the people of the goodness of the land. They made nothing of the difficulties in the way of their gaining it. If men were convinced of the desirableness of the gains of religion, they would not stick at the services of it. Though the Canaanites dwell in walled cities, their defence was departed from them. The other spies took notice of their strength, but these of their wickedness. No people can be safe, when they have provoked God to leave them. Though Israel dwell in tents, they are fortified. While we have the presence of God with us, we need not fear the most powerful force against us. Sinners are ruined by their own rebellion. But those who, like Caleb and Joshua, faithfully expose themselves for God, are sure to be taken under his special protection, and shall be hid from the rage of men, either under heaven or in heaven. (Nu **14**:**11-19**)

Verses 11–19

Moses made humble intercession for Israel. Herein he was a type of Christ, who prayed for those that despitefully used him. The pardon of a nation's sin, is the turning away the nation's punishment; and for that Moses is here so earnest. Moses argued that, consistently with God's character, in his abundant mercies, he could forgive them.

Verses 20–35

The Lord granted the prayer of Moses so far as not at once to destroy the congregation. But disbelief of the promise forbids the benefit. Those who despise the pleasant land shall be shut out of it. The promise of God should be fulfilled to their children. They wished to die in the wilderness; God made their sin their ruin, took them at their word, and their carcases fell in the wilderness. They were made to groan under the burden of their own sin, which was too heavy for them to bear. Ye shall know my breach of promise, both the causes of it, that it is procured by your sin, for God never leaves any till they first leave him; and the consequences of it, that will produce your ruin. But your little ones, now under twenty years old, which ye, in your unbelief, said should be a prey, them will I bring in. God will let them know that he can put a difference between the guilty and the innocent, and cut them off without touching their children. Thus God would not utterly take away his loving kindness.

Verses 36–39

Here is the sudden death of the ten evil spies. They sinned in bringing a slander upon the land of promise. Those greatly provoke God, who misrepresent religion, raise dislike in men's minds toward it, or give opportunity to those to do so, who seek occasion. Justly are murmurers made mourners. If they had mourned for the sin, when they were faithfully reproved, the sentence had been prevented; but as they mourned for the judgment only, it did them no service. There is in hell such mourning as this; but tears will not quench the flames, nor cool the tongue.

Verses 40–45

Some of the Israelites were now earnest to go forward toward Canaan. But it came too late. If men would but be as earnest for heaven while their day of grace lasts, as they will be when it is over, how well would it be for them! That which has been duty in its season, when mistimed, may be turned into sin. Those who are out of the way of their duty, are not under God's protection, and go at their peril. God bade them go, and they would not; he forbade them, and they would go. Thus is the carnal mind enmity against God. They had distrusted God's strength; they now presume upon their own without his. And the expedition fails accordingly; now the sentence began to be executed, that their carcases should fall in the wilderness. That affair can never end well, which begins with sin. The way to obtain peace with our friends, and success against our enemies, is, to have God, as our Friend, and to keep in his love. Let us take warning from the fate of Israel, lest we perish after the same example of unbelief. Let us go forth, depending on God's mercy, power, promise, and truth; he will be with us, and bring our souls to everlasting rest.

Chapter 15

Verses 1–21

Full instructions are given about the meat-offerings and drink-offerings. The beginning of this law is very encouraging, When ye come into the land of your habitation which I give unto you. This was a plain intimation that God would secure the promised land to their seed. It was requisite, since the sacrifices of acknowledgment were intended as the food of God's table, that there should be a constant supply of bread, oil, and wine, whatever the flesh-meat was. And the intent of this law is to direct the proportions of the meat-offering and drink-offering. Natives and strangers are placed on a level in this as in other like matters. It was a happy forewarning of the calling of the Gentiles, and of their admission into the church. If the law made so little difference between Jew and Gentile, much less would the gospel, which broke down the partition-wall, and reconciled both to God.

Verses 22–29

Though ignorance will in a degree excuse, it will not justify those who might have known their Lord's will, yet did it not. David prayed to be cleansed from his secret faults, those sins which he himself was not aware of. Sins committed ignorantly, shall be forgiven through Christ the great Sacrifice, who, when he offered up himself once for all upon the cross, seemed to explain one part of the intention of his offering, in that prayer, Father, forgive them, for they know not what they do. It looked favourably upon the Gentiles, that this law of atoning for sins of ignorance, is expressly made to extend to those who were strangers to Israel.

Verses 30–36

Those are to be reckoned presumptuous sinners, who sin designedly against God's will and glory. Sins thus committed are exceedingly sinful. He that thus breaks the commandment reproaches the Lord. He also despises the word of the Lord. Presumptuous sinners despise it, thinking themselves too great, too good, and too wise, to be ruled by it. A particular instance of presumption in the sin of sabbath-breaking is related. The offence was gathering sticks on the sabbath day, to make a fire, whereas the people were to bake and seethe what they had occasion for, the day before, Ex **16**:**23**. This was done as an affront both to the law and to the Lawgiver. God is jealous for the honour of his sabbaths, and will not hold him guiltless who profanes them, whatever men may do. God intended this punishment for a warning to all, to make conscience of keeping holy the sabbath. And we may be assured that no command was ever given for the punishment of sin, which, at the judgment day, shall not prove to have come from perfect love and justice. The right of God to a day of devotion to himself, will be disputed and denied only by such as listen to the pride and unbelief of their hearts, rather than to the teaching of the Spirit of truth and life. Wherein consists the difference between him who was detected gathering sticks in the wilderness on the day of God, and the man who turns his back upon the blessings of sabbath appointments, and the promises of sabbath mercies, to use his time, his cares, and his soul, in heaping up riches; and waste his hours, his property, and his strength in sinful pleasure? Wealth may come by the unhallowed effort, but it will not come alone; it will have its awful reward. Sinful pursuits lead to ruin.

Verses 37–41

The people are ordered by the Lord to make fringes on the borders of their garments. The Jews were distinguished from their neighbours in their dress, as well as in their diet, and thus taught not to be conformed to the way of the heathen in other things. They proclaimed themselves Jews wherever they were, as not ashamed of God and his law. The fringes were not appointed for trimming and adorning their clothes, but to stir up their minds by way of remembrance, 2Pe **3**:**1**. If they were tempted to sin, the fringe would warn them not to break God's commandments. We should use every means of refreshing our memories with the truths and precepts of God's word, to strengthen and quicken our obedience, and arm our minds against temptation. Be holy unto your God; cleansed from sin, and sincerely devoted to his service; and that great reason for all the commandments is again and again repeated, "I am the Lord your God."

Chapter 16

Verses 1–11

Pride and ambition occasion a great deal of mischief both in churches and states. The rebels quarrel with the settlement of the priesthood upon Aaron and his family. Small reason they had to boast of the people's purity, or of God's favour, as the people had been so often and so lately polluted with sin, and were now under the marks of God's displeasure. They unjustly charge Moses and Aaron with taking honour to themselves; whereas they were called of God to it. See here, **1**. What spirit levellers are of; those who resist the powers God has set over them. **2**. What usage they have been serviceable. Moses sought instruction from God. The heart of the wise studies to answer, and asks counsel of God. Moses shows their privileges as Levites, and convicts them of the sin of undervaluing these privileges. It will help to keep us from envying those above us, duly to consider how many there are below us.

Verses 12–15

Moses summoned Dathan and Abiram to bring their complaints; but they would not obey. They bring very false charges against Moses. Those often fall under the heaviest censures, who in truth deserve the highest praise. Moses, though the meekest man, yet, finding God reproached in him, was very wroth; he could not bear to see the people ruining themselves. He appeals to God as to his own integrity. He bade them appear with Aaron next morning, at the time of offering the morning incense. Korah undertook thus to appear. Proud ambitious men, while projecting their own advancement, often hurry on their own shameful fall.

Verses 16–22

The same glory of the Lord that appeared to place Aaron in his office at first, Le **9**:**23**, now appeared to confirm him in it; and to confound those who set up against him. Nothing is more terrible to those who are conscious of guilt, than the appearance of the Divine glory. See how dangerous it is to have fellowship with sinners, and to partake with them. Though the people had treacherously deserted them, yet Moses and Aaron approved themselves faithful shepherds of Israel. If others fail in their duty to us, that does not take away the obligations we are under to seek their welfare. Their prayer was a pleading prayer, and it proved a prevailing one.

Verses 23–34

The seventy elders of Israel attend Moses. It is our duty to do what we can to countenance and support lawful authority when it is opposed. And those who would not perish with sinners, must come out from among them, and be separate. It was in answer to the prayer of Moses, that God stirred up the hearts of the congregation to remove for their own safety. Grace to separate from evil-doers is one of the things that accompany salvation. God, in justice, left the rebels to the obstinacy and hardness of their own hearts. Moses, by Divine direction, when all Israel were waiting the event, declares that if the rebels die a common death, he will be content to be called and counted an imposter. As soon as Moses had spoken the word, God caused the earth to open and swallow them all up. The children perished with their parents; in which, though we cannot tell how bad they might be to deserve it, or how good God might be otherwise to them; yet of this we are sure, that Infinite Justice did them no wrong. It was altogether miraculous. God has, when he pleases, strange punishments for the workers of iniquity. It was very significant. Considering how the earth is still in like manner loaded with the weight of man's sins, we have reason to wonder that it does not now sink under its load. The ruin of others should be our warning. Could we, by faith, hear the outcries of those that are gone down to the bottomless pit, we should give more diligence than we do to escape for our lives, lest we also come into their condemnation.

Verses 35–40

A fire went out from the Lord, and consumed the two hundred and fifty men that offered incense, while Aaron, who stood with them, was preserved alive. God is jealous of the honour of his own institutions, and will not have them invaded. The sacrifice of the wicked is an abomination to the Lord. The censers are devoted, and, as all devoted things, must be made serviceable to the glory of God. This covering of the altar would remind the children of Israel of this event, that others might hear and fear, and do no more presumptuously. They brought destruction on themselves both in body and soul. Thus all who break the law and neglect the gospel choose and love death.

Verses 41–50

The gaping earth was scarcely closed, before the same sins are again committed, and all these warnings slighted. They called the rebels the people of the Lord; and find fault with Divine justice. The obstinacy of Israel notwithstanding the terrors of God's law, as given on mount Sinai, and the terrors of his judgments, shows how necessary the grace of God is to change men's hearts and lives. Love will do what fear cannot. Moses and Aaron interceded with God for mercy, knowing how great the provocation was. Aaron went, and burned incense between the living and the dead, not to purify the air, but to pacify an offended God. As one tender of the life of every Israelite, Aaron made all possible speed. We must render good for evil. Observe especially, that Aaron was a type of Christ. There is an infection of sin in the world, which only the cross and intercession of Jesus Christ can stay and remove. He enters the defiled and dying camp. He stands between the dead and the living; between the eternal Judge and the souls under condemnation. We must have redemption through His blood, even the remission of sins. We admire the ready devotion of Aaron: shall we not bless and praise the unspeakable grace and love which filled the Saviour's heart, when he placed himself in our stead, and bought us with his life? Greatly indeed hath God commended his love towards us, in that while we were yet sinners, Christ died for us, Ro **5**:**8**.

Chapter 17

Verses 1–7

It is an instance of the grace of God, that, having wrought divers miracles to punish sin, he would work one more to prevent it. Twelve rods or staves were to be brought in. It is probable that they were the staves which the princes used as ensigns of their authority; old dry staves, that had no sap in them. They were to expect that the rod of the tribe, or prince, whom God chose to the priesthood, should bud and blossom. Moses did not object that the matter was sufficiently settled already; he did not undertake to determine it; but left the case before the Lord.

Verses 8–13

While all the other rods remained as they were. Aaron's rod became a living branch. In some places there were buds, in others blossoms, in others fruit, at the same time; all this was miraculous. Thus Aaron was manifested to be under the special blessing of Heaven. Fruitfulness is the best evidence of a Divine call; and the plants of God's setting, and the boughs cut off them, will flourish. This rod was preserved, to take away the murmurings of the people, that they might not die. The design of God, in all his providences, and in the memorials of them, is to take away sin. Christ was manifested to take away sin. Christ is expressly called a rod out of the stem of Jesse: little prospect was there, according to human views, that he should ever flourish. But the dry rod revived and blossomed to the confusion of his adversaries. The people cry, Behold, we die, we perish, we all perish! This was the language of a repining people, quarrelling with the judgments of God, which by their own pride and obstinacy they brought upon themselves. It is very wicked to fret against God when we are in affliction, and in our distress thus to trespass yet more. If we die, if we perish, it is of ourselves, and the blame will be upon our own heads. When God judges, he will overcome, and will oblige the most obstinate gainsayers to confess their folly. And how great are our mercies, that we have a clearer and a better dispensation, established upon better promises!

Chapter 18

Verses 1–7

The people complained of their difficulty and peril in drawing near to God. God here gives them to understand, that the priests should come near for them. Aaron would see reason not to be proud of his preferment, when he considered the great care and charge upon him. Be not high-minded, but fear. The greater the trust of work and power that is committed to us, the greater danger there is of betraying that trust. This is a good reason why we should neither envy others' honours, nor desire high places.

Verses 8–19

All believers are spiritual priests, and God has promised to take care of them. Godliness has the promise of the life that now is. And from the provision here made for the priests, the apostle shows that it is the duty of christian churches to maintain their ministers. Scandalous maintenance makes scandalous ministers. The priests were to be wholly devoted to their ministry, not diverted from it, or disturbed in it, by worldly care or business. Also, that they might be examples of living by faith, not only in God's providence, but in his ordinances. The best should be offered for the first-fruits unto the Lord. Those who think to save, by putting God off with the refuse, deceive themselves, for God is not mocked.

Verses 20–32

As Israel was a people not to be numbered among the nations, so Levi was a tribe to be distinguished from the rest. Those who have God for their Inheritance and their Portion for ever, ought to look with holy contempt and indifference upon the possessions of this world. The Levites were to give God his dues out of their tithes, as well as the Israelites out of their increase. See, in ver. #(**31**), the way to have comfort in all our worldly possessions, so as to bear no sin by reason of them. **1**. We must be sure that what we have is got honestly and in the service of God. That meat is best eaten which is first earned; but if any will not work, neither shall he eat, **2**Th **3**:**10**. **2**. We must be sure that God has his dues out of it. We have the comfort of our substance, when we have honoured the Lord with it. Ye shall bear no sin by reason of it, when ye have heaved the best from it. We should give alms of such things as we have, that all may be holy and comfortable to us.

Chapter 19

Verses 1–10

The heifer was to be wholly burned. This typified the painful sufferings of our Lord Jesus, both in soul and body, as a sacrifice made by fire, to satisfy God's justice for man's sin. These ashes are said to be laid up as a purification for sin, because, though they were only to purify from ceremonial uncleanness, yet they were a type of that purification for sin which our Lord Jesus made by his death. The blood of Christ is laid up for us in the word and sacraments, as a fountain of merit, to which by faith we may have constant recourse, for cleansing our consciences.

Verses 11–22

Why did the law make a corpse a defiling thing? Because death is the wages of sin, which entered into the world by it, and reigns by the power of it. The law could not conquer death, nor abolish it, as the gospel does, by bringing life and immortality to light, and so introducing a better hope. As the ashes of the heifer signified the merit of Christ, so the running water signified the power and grace of the blessed Spirit, who is compared to rivers of living water; and it is by his work that the righteousness of Christ is applied to us for our cleansing. Those who promise themselves benefit by the righteousness of Christ, while they submit not to the grace and influence of the Holy Spirit, do but deceive themselves; we cannot be purified by the ashes, otherwise than in the running water. What use could there be in these appointments, if they do not refer to the doctrines concerning the sacrifice of Christ? But comparing them with the New Testament, the knowledge to be got from them is evident. The true state of fallen man is shown in these institutions. Here we learn the defiling nature of sin, and are warned to avoid evil communications.

Chapter 20

Verses 1–13

After thirty-eight years' tedious abode in the wilderness, the armies of Israel advanced towards Canaan again. There was no water for the congregation. We live in a wanting world, and wherever we are, must expect to meet with something to put us out. It is a great mercy to have plenty of water, a mercy which, if we found the want of, we should more own the worth of. Hereupon they murmured against Moses and Aaron. They spake the same absurd and brutish language their fathers had done. It made their crime the worse, that they had smarted so long for the discontent and distrusts of their fathers, yet they venture in the same steps. Moses must again, in God's name, command water out of a rock for them; God is as able as ever to supply his people with what is needful for them. But Moses and Aaron acted wrong. They took much of the glory of this work of wonder to themselves; "Must we fetch water?" As if it were done by some power or worthiness of their own. They were to speak to the rock, but they smote it. Therefore it is charged upon them, that they did not sanctify God, that is, they did not give to him alone that glory of this miracle which was due unto his name. And being provoked by the people, Moses spake unadvisedly with his lips. The same pride of man would still usurp the office of the appointed Mediator; and become to ourselves wisdom, righteousness, and sanctification, and redemption. Such a state of sinful independence, such a rebellion of the soul against its Saviour, the voice of God condemns in every page of the gospel.

Verses 14–21

The nearest way to Canaan from the place where Israel encamped, was through the country of Edom. The ambassadors who were sent returned with a denial. The Edomites feared to receive damage by the Israelites. And had this numerous army been under any other discipline than that of the righteous God himself, there might have been cause for this jealousy. But Esau hated Jacob because of the blessing; and now the hatred revived, when the blessing was about to be inherited. We must not think it strange, if reasonable requests be denied by unreasonable men, and if those whom God favours be affronted by men.

Verses 22–29

God bids Aaron prepare to die. There is something of displeasure in these orders. Aaron must not enter Canaan, because he had failed in his duty at the waters of strife. There is much of mercy in them. Aaron, though he dies for his transgression, dies with ease, and in honour. He is gathered to his people, as one who dies in the arms of Divine grace. There is much significancy in these orders. Aaron must not enter Canaan, to show that the Levitical priesthood could make nothing perfect; that must be done by bringing in a better hope. Aaron submits, and dies in the method and manner appointed; and, for aught that appears, with as much cheerfulness as if he had been going to bed. It was a great satisfaction to Aaron to see his son, who was dear to him, preferred; and his office preserved and secured: especially, to see in this a figure of Christ's everlasting priesthood. A good man would desire, if it were the will of God, not to outlive his usefulness. Why should we covet to continue any longer in this world, than while we may do some service in it for God and our generation?

Chapter 21

Verses 1–3

Before the people began their march round the country of Edom, the king of Arad, a Canaanite, who inhabited the southern part of the country, attacked them in the wilderness, and took some prisoners. This was to lead the Israelites to look more thoroughly to the Lord.

Verses 4–9

The children of Israel were wearied by a long march round the land of Edom. They speak discontentedly of what God had done for them, and distrustfully of what he would do. What will they be pleased with, whom manna will not please? Let not the contempt which some cast on the word of God, make us value it less. It is the bread of life, substantial bread, and will nourish those who by faith feed upon it, to eternal life, whoever may call it light bread. We see the righteous judgment God brought upon them for murmuring. He sent fiery serpents among them, which bit or stung many to death. It is to be feared that they would not have owned the sin, if they had not felt the smart; but they relent under the rod. And God made a wonderful provision for their relief. The Jews themselves say it was not the sight of the brazen serpent that cured; but in looking up to it, they looked up to God as the Lord that healed them. There was much gospel in this. Our Saviour declared, Joh **3**:**14**, **15**, that as Moses lifted up the serpent in the wilderness, so the Son of man must be lifted up, that whatsoever believeth in him, should not perish. Compare their disease and ours. Sin bites like a serpent, and stings like an adder. Compare the application of their remedy and ours. They looked and lived, and we, if we believe, shall not perish. It is by faith that we look unto Jesus, Heb **12**:**2**. Whosoever looked, however desperate his case, or feeble his sight, or distant his place, was certainly and perfectly cured. The Lord can relieve us from dangers and distresses, by means which human reason never would have devised. Oh that the venom of the old serpent, inflaming men's passions, and causing them to commit sins which end in their eternal destruction, were as sensibly felt, and the danger as plainly seen, as the Israelites felt pain from the bite of the fiery serpents, and feared the death which followed! Then none would shut their eyes to Christ, or turn from his gospel. Then a crucified Saviour would be so valued, that all things else would be accounted loss for him; then, without delay, and with earnestness and simplicity, all would apply to him in the appointed way, crying, Lord, save us; we perish! Nor would any abuse the freeness of Christ's salvation, while they reckoned the price which it cost him.

Verses 10–20

We have here the removes of the children of Israel, till they came to the plains of Moab, from whence they passed over Jordan into Canaan. The end of their pilgrimage was near. "They set forward." It were well if we did thus; and the nearer we come to heaven, were so much the more active and abundant in the work of the Lord. The wonderful success God granted to his people, is here spoken of, and, among the rest, their actions on the river Arnon, at Vaheb in Suphah, and other places on that river. In every stage of our lives, nay, in every step, we should notice what God has wrought for us; what he did at such a time, and what in such a place, ought to be distinctly remembered. God blessed his people with a supply of water. When we come to heaven, we shall remove to the well of life, the fountain of living waters. They received it with joy and thankfulness, which made the mercy doubly sweet. With joy must we draw water out of the wells of salvation, Isa **12**:**3**. As the brazen serpent was a figure of Christ, who is lifted up for our cure, so is this well a figure of the Spirit, who is poured forth for our comfort, and from whom flow to us rivers of living waters, Joh **7**:**38**, **39**. Does this well spring up in our souls? If so, we should take the comfort to ourselves, and give the glory to God. God promised to give water, but they must open the ground. God's favours must be expected in the use of such means as are within our power, but still the power is only of God.

Verses 21–35

Sihon went with his forces against Israel, out of his own borders, without provocation, and so ran upon his own ruin. The enemies of God's church often perish by the counsels they think most wisely taken. Og, king of Bashan, instead of being warned by the fate of his neighbours, to make peace with Israel, makes war with them, which proves in like manner his destruction. Wicked men do their utmost to secure themselves and their possessions against the judgments of God; but all in vain, when the day comes on which they must fall. God gave Israel success, while Moses was with them, that he might see the beginning of the glorious work, though he must not live to see it finished. This was, in comparison, but as the day of small things, yet it was an earnest of great things. We must prepare for fresh conflicts and enemies. We must make no peace or truce with the powers of darkness, nor even treat with them; nor should we expect any pause in our contest. But, trusting in God, and obeying his commands, we shall be more than conquerors over every enemy.

Chapter 22

Verses 1–14

The king of Moab formed a plan to get the people of Israel cursed; that is, to set God against them, who had hitherto fought for them. He had a false notion, that if he could get some prophet to pray for evil upon them, and to pronounce a blessing upon himself and his forces, that then he should be able to deal with them. None had so great a reputation as Balaam; and Balak will employ him, though he send a great way for him. It is not known whether the Lord had ever spoken to Balaam, or by him, before this; though it is probable he had, and it is certain he did afterwards. Yet we have abundant proof that he lived and died a wicked man, an enemy to God and his people. And the curse shall not come upon us if there is not a cause, even though men utter it. To prevail with Balaam, they took the wages of unrighteousness, but God laid restraint upon Balaam, forbidding him to curse Israel. Balaam was no stranger to Israel's cause; so that he ought to have answered the messengers at once, that he would never curse a people whom God had blessed; but he takes a night's time to consider what he should do. When we parley with temptations, we are in great danger of being overcome. Balaam was not faithful in returning God's answer to the messengers. Those are a fair mark for Satan's temptation, who lessen Divine restraints; as if to go against God's law were only to go without his leave. The messengers also are not faithful in returning Balaam's answer to Balak. Thus many are abused by the flatteries of those about them, and are prevented from seeing their own faults and follies.

Verses 15–21

A second embassy was sent to Balaam. It were well for us, if we were as earnest and constant in prosecuting a good work, notwithstanding disappointments. Balak laid a bait, not only for Balaam's covetousness, but for his pride and ambition. How earnestly should we beg of God daily to mortify such desires in us! Thus sinners stick at no pains, spare no cost, and care not how low they stoop, to gratify their luxury, or their malice. Shall we then be unwilling to do what is right? God forbid! Balaam's convictions charged him to keep to the command of God; nor could any man have spoken better. But many call God theirs, who are not his, not truly because not only his. There is no judging men by their words; God knows the heart. Balaam's corruptions at the same time inclined him to go contrary to the command. He seemed to refuse the temptation; but he expressed no abhorrence of it. He had a strong desire to accept the offer, and hoped that God might give him leave to go. He had already been told what the will of God was. It is a certain evidence of the ruling of corruption in the heart, to beg leave to sin. God gave Balaam up to his own heart's lusts. As God sometimes denies the prayers of his people in love, so sometimes he grants the desires of the wicked in wrath.

Verses 22–35

We must not think, that because God does not always by his providence restrain men from sin, therefore he approves of it, or that it is not hateful to him. The holy angels oppose sin, and perhaps are employed in preventing it more than we are aware. This angel was an adversary to Balaam, because Balaam counted him his adversary; those are really our best friends, and we ought so to reckon them, who stop our progress in sinful ways. Balaam has notice of God's displeasure by the ass. It is common for those whose hearts are fully set in them to do evil, to push on violently, through the difficulties Providence lays in their way. The Lord opened the mouth of the ass. This was a great miracle wrought by the power of God. He who made man speak, could, when he pleased, make the ass to speak with man's voice. The ass complained of Balaam's cruelty. The righteous God does not allow the meanest or weakest to be abused; but they shall be able to speak in their own defence, or he will some way or other speak for them. Balaam at length has his eyes opened. God has many ways to bring down the hard and unhumbled heart. When our eyes are opened, we shall see the danger of sinful ways, and how much it was for our advantage to be crossed. Balaam seemed to relent; I have sinned; but it does not appear that he was sensible of this wickedness of his heart, or willing to own it. If he finds he cannot go forward, he will be content, since there is no remedy, to go back. Thus many leave their sins, only because their sins have left them. The angel declared that he should not only be unable to curse Israel, but should be forced to bless them: this would be more for the glory of God, and to his own confusion, than if he had turned back.

Verses 36–41

Balak has now nothing to complain of, but that Balaam did not come sooner. Balaam bids Balak not depend too much upon him. He seems to speak with vexation; but is really as desirous to please Balak, as ever he had pretended to be to please God. See what need we have to pray every day, Our Father which art in heaven, lead us not into temptation. Let us be jealous over our own hearts, seeing how far men may go in the knowledge of God, and yet come short of Divine grace.

Chapter 23

Verses 1–10

With the camps of Israel full in view, Balaam ordered seven altars to be built, and a bullock and a ram to be offered on each. Oh the sottishness of superstition, to imagine that God will be at man's beck! The curse is turned into a blessing, by the overruling power of God, in love to Israel. God designed to serve his own glory by Balaam, and therefore met him. If God put a word into the mouth of Balaam, who would have defied God and Israel, surely he will not be wanting to those who desire to glorify God, and to edify his people; it shall be given what they should speak. He who opened the mouth of the ass, caused the mouth of this wicked man to speak words as contrary to the desire of his heart, as those of the ass were to the powers of the brute. The miracle was as great in the one case as in the other. Balaam pronounces Israel safe. He owns he could do no more than God suffered him to do. He pronounces them happy in their distinction from the rest of the nations. Happy in their numbers, which made them both honourable and formidable. Happy in their last end. Death is the end of all men; even the righteous must die, and it is good for us to think of this with regard to ourselves, as Balaam does here, speaking of his own death. He pronounces the righteous truly blessed, not only while they live, but when they die; which makes their death even more desirable than life itself. But there are many who desire to die the death of the righteous, but do not endeavour to live the life of the righteous; gladly would they have an end like theirs, but not a way like theirs. They would be saints in heaven, but not saints on earth. This saying of Balaam's is only a wish, not a prayer; it is a vain wish, being only a wish for the end, without any care for the means. Many seek to quiet their consciences with the promise of future amendment, or take up with some false hope, while they neglect the only way of salvation, by which a sinner can be righteous before God.

Verses 11–30

Balak was angry with Balaam. Thus a confession of God's overruling power is extorted from a wicked prophet, to the confusion of a wicked prince. A second time the curse is turned into a blessing; and this blessing is both larger and stronger than the former. Men change their minds, and break their words; but God never changes his mind, and therefore never recalls his promise. And when in Scripture he is said to repent, it does not mean any change of his mind; but only a change of his way. There was sin in Jacob, and God saw it; but there was not such as might provoke him to give them up to ruin. If the Lord sees that we trust in his mercy, and accept of his salvation; that we indulge no secret lust, and continue not in rebellion, but endeavour to serve and glorify him; we may be sure that he looks upon us as accepted in Christ, that our sins are all pardoned. Oh the wonders of providence and grace, the wonders of redeeming love, of pardoning mercy, of the new-creating Spirit! Balak had no hope of ruining Israel, and Balaam showed that he had more reason to fear being ruined by them. Since Balaam cannot say what he would have him, Balak wished him to say nothing. But though there are many devices in man's heart, God's counsels shall stand. Yet they resolve to make another attempt, though they had no promise on which to build their hopes. Let us, who have a promise that the vision at the end shall speak and not lie, continue earnest in prayer, Lu **18**:**1**.

Chapter 24

Verses 1–9

Now Balaam spake not his own sense, but the language of the Spirit that came upon him. Many have their eyes open who have not their hearts open; are enlightened, but not sanctified. That knowledge which puffs men up with pride, will but serve to light them to hell, whither many go with their eyes open. The blessing is nearly the same as those given before. He admires in Israel, their beauty. The righteous, doubtless, is more excellent than his neighbour. Their fruitfulness and increase. Their honour and advancement. Their power and victory. He looks back upon what had been done for them. Their power and victory. He looks back upon what had been done for them. Their courage and security. The righteous are bold as a lion, not when assaulting others, but when at rest, because God maketh them to dwell in safety. Their influence upon their neighbours. God takes what is done to them, whether good or evil, as done to himself. (Nu **24**:**10-14**)

Verses 10–14

This vain attempt to curse Israel is ended. Balak broke out into a rage against Balaam, and expressed great vexation. Balaam has a very full excuse; God restrained him from saying what he would have said, and constrained him to say what he would not have uttered.

Verses 15–25

Under the powerful influence of the Spirit of prophecy, Balaam foretold the future prosperity and extensive dominion of Israel. Balaam boasts that his eyes are open. The prophets were in old times called seers. He had heard the words of God, which many do who neither heed them, nor hear God in them. He knew the knowledge of the Most High. A man may be full of the knowledge of God, yet utterly destitute of the grace of God. He calls God the Most High and the Almighty. No man could seem to express a greater respect to God; yet he had no true fear of him, love to him, nor faith in him; so far a man may go toward heaven, and yet come short of it at last. Here is Balaam's prophecy concerning Him who should be the crown and glory of his people Israel; who is David in the type; but our Lord Jesus, the promised Messiah, is chiefly pointed at, and of him it is an illustrious prophecy. Balaam, a wicked man, shall see Christ, but shall not see him nigh; not see him as Job, who saw him as his Redeemer, and saw him for himself. When he comes in the clouds, every eye shall see him; but many will see him, as the rich man in hell saw Abraham, afar off. He shall come out of Jacob, and Israel, as a Star and a Sceptre; the former denoting his glory and lustre; the latter his power and authority. Christ shall be King, not only of Jacob and Israel, but of all the world; so that all shall be either governed by his golden sceptre, or dashed in pieces by his iron rod. Balaam prophesied concerning the Amalekites and Kenites, part of whose country he had now in view. Even a nest in a rock will not be a lasting security. Here is a prophecy that looks as far forward as to the Greeks and Romans. He acknowledges all the revolutions of states and kingdoms to be the Lord's doing. These events will make such desolations, that scarcely any will escape. They that live then, will be as brands plucked out of the fire. May God fit us for the worst of times! Thus Balaam, instead of cursing the church, curses Amalek the first, and Rome the last enemy of the church. Not Rome pagan only, but Rome papal also; antichrist and all the antichristian powers. Let us ask ourselves, Do we in knowledge, experience, or profession, excel Balaam? No readiness of speech, even in preaching or prayer, no gifts of knowledge or prophecy, are in themselves different from, or superior to the boasted gifts of him who loved the wages of unrighteousness, and died the enemy of God. Simple dependence on the Redeemer's atoning blood and sanctifying grace, cheerful submission to the Divine will, constant endeavours to glorify God and benefit his people, these are less splendid, but far more excellent gifts, and always accompany salvation. No boasting hypocrite ever possessed these; yet the feeblest believer has something of them, and is daily praying for more of them.

Chapter 25

Verses 1–5

The friendship of the wicked is more dangerous than their enmity; for none can prevail against God's people if they are not overcome by their inbred lusts; nor can any enchantment hurt them, but the enticements of worldly interests and pleasures. Here is the sin of Israel, to which they are enticed by the daughters of Moab and Midian. Those are our worst enemies who draw us to sin, for that is the greatest mischief any man can do us. Israel's sin did that which all Balaam's enchantments could not do; it set God against them. Diseases are the fruits of God's anger, and the just punishments of prevailing sins; one infection follows the other. Ringleaders in sin ought to be made examples of justice.

Verses 6–15

Phinehas, in the courage of zeal and faith, executed vengeance on Zimri and Cozbi. This act can never be an example for private revenge, or religious persecution, or for irregular public vengeance.

Verses 16–18

We read not that any Midianites died of the plague; God punished them with the sword of an enemy, not with the rod of a father. We must set ourselves against whatever is an occasion of sin to us, Mt **5**:**29**, **30**. Whatever draws us to sin, should be a vexation to us, as a thorn in the flesh. And none will be more surely and severely punished than those who, after Satan's example, and with his subtlety, tempt others to sin.

Chapter 26

Verses 1–51

Moses did not number the people but when God commanded him. We have here the families registered, as well as the tribes. The total was nearly the same as when numbered at mount Sinai. Notice is here taken of the children of Korah; they died not, as the children of Dathan and Abiram; they seem not to have joined even their own father in rebellion. If we partake not of the sins of sinners, we shall not partake of their plagues. (Nu **26**:**52-56**)

Verses 52–56

In distributing these tribes, the general rule of equity is prescribed; that to many should be given more, and to fewer less. Though it seems left to the prudence of their prince, the matter at last must be settled by the providence of God, with which all must be satisfied.

Verses 57–62

Levi was God's tribe; therefore it was not numbered with the rest, but alone. It came not under the sentence, that none of them should enter Canaan excepting Caleb and Joshua.

Verses 63–65

The execution of the sentence passed on the murmurers, chap. **14**:**29**, is observable. There was not one man numbered now, who was numbered then, but Caleb and Joshua. Here appeared the righteousness of God, and his faithfulness to his threatenings. Especially observe the truth of God, in performing his promise to Caleb and Joshua. Death makes awful havoc of the human species, and causes surprising changes in families and nations; yet all is appointed in perfect wisdom, justice, and truth, by the Lord himself. This should stir us up to think upon the hateful nature of sin, the cause of all these devastations. We should renew our repentance, seek forgiveness, value the salvation of Christ, remember how frail we are, prepare for the summons of death, and fill up our days in serving our generation according to the will of God.

Chapter 27

Verses 1–11

The five daughters of Zelophehad considered themselves as left destitute, having neither father nor brother to inherit any land. Their believing expectation that the word of the Lord would be performed in due season, and their desire of an interest in the promised inheritance; and the modest, candid manner in which they asked, without secret murmurs or discontents, are a good example. They ask for a possession in the land of Canaan. Herein they discovered, **1**. Strong faith in the power and promise of God, concerning the giving of the land of Canaan to Israel. **2**. And earnest desire of a place and name in the land of promise, which was a type of heaven. **3**. Respect and honour for their father, whose name was dear to them now he was gone. He never had done any thing that might bar his children's claim. It is a comfort to parents when they come to die, if though they have smarted for their own sin, yet they are not conscious of any of those iniquities which God will visit on their children. God himself gives judgment. He takes notice of the affairs, not only of nations, but of private families, and orders them according to his will. The petition is granted. Those who seek an inheritance in the land of promise, shall have what they seek for, and other things shall be added to them.

Verses 12–14

Moses must die, but he shall have the satisfaction of seeing the land of promise. This sight of Canaan signified his believing prospect of the better country, that is, the heavenly. Moses must die, but death does not cut him off; it only brings him to rest with the holy patriarchs. It is but to die as they died, having lived as they lived; and as their end was peace, why should we fear any evil in the passage of that dark valley? (Nu **27**:**15-23**)

Verses 15–23

Envious spirits do not love their successors; but Moses was not one of these. We should concern ourselves, both in our prayers and in our endeavours, for the rising generation, that religion may be maintained and advanced, when we are in our graves. God appoints a successor, even Joshua; who had signalized himself by his courage in fighting Amalek, his humility in ministering to Moses, and his faith and sincerity in witnessing against the report of the evil spies. This man God appoints to succeed Moses; a man in whom is the Spirit, the Spirit of grace. He is a good man, fearing God and hating covetousness, and acting from principle. He has the spirit of government; he is fit to do the work and discharge the trusts of his place. He has a spirit of conduct and courage; he had also the Spirit of prophecy. That man is not fully qualified for any service in the church of Christ, who is destitute of the graces and gifts of the Holy Spirit, whatever human abilities he may possess. And in Joshua's succession we are reminded "that the law was given by Moses," who by reason of our transgression could not bring us to heaven; but "grace and truth came by Jesus Christ," for the salvation of every believer.

Chapter 28

Verses 1–8

God saw fit now to repeat the law of sacrifices. This was a new generation of men; and they were concerned to keep their peace with God when at war with their enemies. The daily sacrifice is called a continual burnt-offering; when we are bid to pray always, at least every morning and evening we should offer up solemn prayers and praises to God. Nothing is added here but that the wine poured out in the drink-offering is to be strong wine, to teach us to serve God with the best we have. It was a figure of the blood of Christ, the memorial of which is still left to the church in wine; and of the blood of the martyrs, which was poured out as a drink-offering on the sacrifice and service of our faith, Php **2**:**17**.

Verses 9–15

Every sabbath day, beside the two lambs offered for the daily burnt-offering, there must be two more offered. This teaches us to double our devotions on sabbath days, for so the duty of the day requires. The sabbath rest is to be observed, in order more closely to apply ourselves to the sabbath work, which ought to fill up the sabbath time. The offerings in the new moons showed thankfulness for the renewing of earthly blessings: when we rejoice in the gifts of providence, we must make the sacrifice of Christ, that great gift of special grace, the fountain and spring-head of our joy. And the worship performed in the new moons is made typical of gospel solemnities, Isa **66**:**23**. As the moon borrows light from the sun, and is renewed by its influences; so the church borrows her light from Jesus Christ, who is the Sun of righteousness, renewing the state of the church, especially under the gospel. (Nu **28**:**16-31**)

Verses 16–31

By the sacrifices enjoined in this chapter, we are reminded of the continued power of the sacrifice of Christ, and of our continual need to depend thereon. No hurrying employments, or perilous situations, or prosperous circumstances, should cause slackness in our religious exercises; but should rather stir us up to greater diligence in seeking help from, or giving thanks to the Lord. And all is to be accompanied with repentance, faith is the Lord Jesus, and love to him, and to produce true holiness in our conduct towards all men; otherwise God will abhor our most solemn services and abundant devotions. And Christ is able to supply the wants of every day, every week, every month, every year, every ordinance, every case.

Chapter 29

Verses 1–11

There were more sacred solemnities in the seventh month than in any other. It was the space between harvest and seed-time. The more leisure we have from the pressing occupations of this life, the more time we should spend in the immediate service of God. The blowing of the trumpets was appointed, Le **22**:**24**. Here they are directed what sacrifices to offer on that day. Those who would know the mind of God in the Scriptures, must compare one part with another. The latter discoveries of Divine light explain what was dark, and supply what was wanting, in the former, that the man of God may be perfect.

Verses 12–40

Soon after the day of atonement, the day in which men were to afflict their souls, followed the feast of Tabernacles, in which they were to rejoice before the Lord. Their days of rejoicing were to be days of sacrifices. A disposition to be cheerful does us good, when it encourages our hearts in the duties of God's service. All the days of dwelling in booths they must offer sacrifices; while we are here in a tabernacle state, it is our interest, as well as our duty, constantly to keep up communion with God. The sacrifices for each of the seven days are appointed. Every day there must be a sin-offering, as in the other feasts. Our burnt-offerings of praise cannot be accepted of God, unless we have an interest in the great sacrifice which Christ offered, when he made himself a Sin-offering for us. And no extraordinary services should put aside stated devotions. Every thing here reminds us of our sinfulness. The life that we live in the flesh must be by the faith of the Son of God; until we go to be with him, to behold his glory, and praise his mercy, who hath loved us and washed us from our sins in his own blood. To whom be honour and glory for ever. Amen.

Chapter 30

Verses 1, 2

No man can be bound by his own promise to do what he is already, by the Divine precept, forbidden to do. In other matters the command is, that he shall not break his words, through he may change his mind.

Verses 3–16

Two cases of vows are determined. The case of a daughter in her father's house. When her vow comes to his knowledge, it is in his power either to confirm it or do it away. The law is plain in the case of a wife. If her husband allows her vow, though only by silence, it stands. If he disallows it, her obligation to her husband takes place of it; for to him she ought to be in subjection, as unto the Lord. The Divine law consults the good order of families. It is fit that every man should bear rule in his own house, and have his wife and children in subjection; rather than that this great rule should be broken, or any encouragement be given to inferior relations to break those bonds asunder, God releases the obligation even of a solemn vow. So much does religion secure the welfare of all societies; and in it the families of the earth have a blessing.

Chapter 31

Verses 1–6

All who, without commission from God, dare to execute private revenge, and who, from ambition, covetousness, or resentment, wage war and desolate kingdoms, must one day answer for it. But if God, instead of sending an earthquake, a pestilence, or a famine, be pleased to authorize and command any people to avenge his cause, such a commission surely is just and right. The Israelites could show such a commission, though no persons now can do so. Their wars were begun and carried on expressly by Divine direction, and they were enabled to conquer by miracles. Unless it can be proved that the wicked Canaanites did not deserve their doom, objectors only prove their dislike to God, and their love to his enemies. Man makes light of the evil of sin, but God abhors it. This explains the terrible executions of the nations which had filled the measure of their sins.

Verses 7–12

The Israelites slew the Kings of Midian. They slew Balaam. God's overruling providence brought him thither, and their just vengeance found him. Had he himself rightly believed what he had said of the happy state of Israel, he would not have thus herded with the enemies of Israel. The Midianites' wicked wiles were Balaam's projects: it was just that he should perish with them, Ho **4**:**5**. They took the women and children captives. They burnt their cities and castles, and returned to the camp.

Verses 13–18

The sword of war should spare women and children; but the sword of justice should know no distinction, but that of guilty or not guilty. This war was the execution of a righteous sentence upon a guilty nation, in which the women were the worst criminals. The female children were spared, who, being brought up among the Israelites, would not tempt them to idolatry. The whole history shows the hatefulness of sin, and the guilt of tempting others; it teaches us to avoid all occasions of evil, and to give no quarter to inward lusts. The women and children were not kept for sinful purposes, but for slaves, a custom every where practised in former times, as to captives. In the course of providence, when famine and plagues visit a nation for sin, children suffer in the common calamity. In this case parents are punished in their children; and for children dying before actual sin, full provision is made as to their eternal happiness, by the mercy of God in Christ.

Verses 19–24

The Israelites had to purify themselves according to the law, and to abide without the camp seven days, though they had not contracted any moral guilt, the war being just and lawful, and commanded by God. Thus God would preserve in their minds a dread and detestation of shedding blood. The spoil had been used by Midianites, and being now come into the possession of Israelites, it was fit that it should be purified.

Verses 25–47

Whatever we have, God justly claims a part. Out of the people's share God required one in fifty, but out of the soldiers' share only one in five hundred. The less opportunity we have of honouring God with personal services, the more should we give in money or value.

Verses 48–54

The success of the Israelites had been very remarkable, so small a company overcoming such multitudes, but it was still more wonderful that not one was slain or missing. They presented the gold they found among the spoils, as an offering to the Lord. Thus they confessed, that instead of claiming a reward for their service, they needed forgiveness of much that had been amiss, and desired to be thankful for the preservation of their lives, which might justly have been taken away.

Chapter 32

Verses 1–5

Here is a proposal made by the Reubenites and Gadites, that the land lately conquered might be allotted to them. Two things common in the world might lead these tribes to make this choice; the lust of the eye, and the pride of life. There was much amiss in the principle they went upon; they consulted their own private convenience more than the public good. Thus to the present time, many seek their own things more than the things of Jesus Christ; and are led by worldly interests and advantages to take up short of the heavenly Canaan.

Verses 6–15

The proposal showed disregard to the land of Canaan, distrust of the Lord's promise, and unwillingness to encounter the difficulties and dangers of conquering and driving out the inhabitants of that land. Moses is wroth with them. It will becomes any of God's Israel to sit down unconcerned about the difficult and perilous concerns of their brethren, whether public or personal. He reminds them of the fatal consequences of the unbelief and faint-heartedness of their fathers, when they were, as themselves, just ready to enter Canaan. If men considered as they ought what would be the end of sin, they would be afraid of the beginning of it.

Verses 16–27

Here is the good effect of plain dealing. Moses, by showing their sin, and the danger of it, brought them to their duty, without murmuring or disputing. All men ought to consider the interests of others as well as their own; the law of love requires us to labour, venture, or suffer for each other as there may be occasion. They propose that their men of war should go ready armed before the children of Israel into the land of Canaan, and that they should not return till the conquest of Canaan was ended. Moses grants their request, but he warns them of the danger of breaking their word. If you fail, you sin against the Lord, and not against your brethren only; God will certainly reckon with you for it. Be sure your sin will find you out. Sin will surely find out the sinner sooner or later. It concerns us now to find our sins out, that we may repent of them, and forsake them, lest they find us out to our ruin.

Verses 28–42

Concerning the settlement of these tribes, observe, that they built the cities, that is, repaired them. They changed the names of them; probably they were idolatrous, therefore they should be forgotten. A spirit of selfishness, of seeking our own, not the things of Christ, when each one ought to assist others, is as dangerous as it is common. It is impossible to be sincere in the faith, sensible of the goodness of God, constrained by the love of Christ, sanctified by the power of the Holy Ghost, and yet be indifferent to the progress of religion, and the spiritual success of others, through love of ease, or fear of conflict. Let then your light so shine before men, that they may see your good works, and glorify your Father which is in heaven.

Chapter 33

Verses 1–49

This is a brief review of the travels of the children of Israel through the wilderness. It is a memorable history. In their travels towards Canaan they were continually on the remove. Such is our state in this world; we have here no continuing city, and all our removes in this world are but from one part a desert to another. They were led to and fro, forward and backward, yet were all the while under the direction of the pillar of cloud and fire. God led them about, yet led them the right way. The way God takes in bringing his people to himself is always the best way, though it does not always seem to us the nearest way. Former events are mentioned. Thus we ought to keep in mind the providences of God concerning us and families, us and our land, and the many instances of that Divine care which has led us, and fed us, and kept us all our days hitherto. Few periods of our lives can be thought upon, without reminding us of the Lord's goodness, and our own ingratitude and disobedience: his kindness leaves us without excuse for our sins. We could not wish to travel over again the stages we have passed, unless we could hope, by the grace of God, to shun the sins we then committed, and to embrace such opportunities of doing good as we have let slip. Soon will our wanderings end, and our eternal state be fixed beyond recall; how important then is the present moment! Happy are those whom the Lord now guides with his counsel, and will at length receive to his glory. To this happiness the gospel calls us. Behold now is the accepted time, now is the day of salvation. Let sinners seize the opportunity, and flee for refuge to the hope set before them. Let us redeem our time, to glorify God and serve our generation; and he will carry us safely through all, to his eternal kingdom.

Verses 50–56

Now that they were to pass over Jordan, they were entering again into temptation to follow idols; and they are threatened that, if they spared either the idols or the idolaters, their sin would certainly be their punishment. They would foster vipers in their own bosoms. The remnant of the Canaanites, if they made any peace with them, though but for a time, would be pricks in their eyes, and thorns in their sides. We must expect trouble and affliction from whatever sin we indulge; that which we are willing should tempt us, will vex us. It was intended that the Canaanites should be put out of the land; but if the Israelites learned their wicked ways, they also would be put out. Let us hear this and fear. If we do not drive out sin, sin will drive us out. If we are not the death of our lusts, our lusts will be the death of our souls.

Chapter 34

Verses 1–15

Canaan was of small extent; as it is here bounded, it is but about **160** miles in length, and about **50** in breadth; yet this was the country promised to the father of the faithful, and the possession of the seed of Israel. This was that little spot of ground, in which alone, for many ages, God was known. This was the vineyard of the Lord, the garden enclosed; but as it is with gardens and vineyards, the narrowness of the space was made up by the fruitfulness of the soil. Though the earth is the Lord's, and the fulness thereof, yet few know him, and serve him; but those few are happy, because fruitful to God. Also, see how little a share of the world God gives to his own people. Those who have their portion in heaven, have reason to be content with a small pittance of this earth. Yet a little that a righteous man has, having it from the love of God, and with his blessing, is far better and more comfortable than the riches of many wicked. (Nu **34**:**16-29**)

Verses 16–29

God here appoints men to divide the land to them. So sure must they feel of victory and success while God fought for them, that the persons are named who should be intrusted with the dividing of the land.

Chapter 35

Verses 1–8

The cities of the priests and Levites were not only to accommodate them, but to place them, as religious teachers, in several parts of the land. For though the typical service of the tabernacle or temple was only in one place, the preaching of the word of God, and prayer and praise, were not thus confined. These cities were to be given out of each tribe. Each thus made a grateful acknowledgement to God. Each tribe had the benefit of the Levites dwelling amongst them, to teach them the knowledge of the Lord; thus no parts of the country were left to sit in darkness. The gospel provides that he who is taught in the word, should communicate to him that teaches, in all good things, Ga **6**:**6**. We are to free God's ministers from distracting cares, and to leave them at leisure for the duties of their station; so that they may be wholly employed therein, and avail themselves of every opportunity, by acts of kindness, to gain the good-will of the people, and to draw their attention.

Verses 9–34

To show plainly the abhorrence of murder, and to provide the more effectually for the punishment of the murderer, the nearest relation of the deceased, under the title of avenger of blood, (or the redeemer of blood,) in notorious cases, might pursue, and execute vengeance. A distinction is made, not between sudden anger and malice aforethought, both which are the crime of murder; but between intentionally striking a man with any weapon likely to cause death, and an unintentional blow. In the latter case alone, the city of refuge afforded protection. Murder in all its forms, and under all disguises, pollutes a land. Alas! that so many murders, under the name of duels, prize-fights, &c. should pass unpunished. There were six cities of refuge; one or other might be reached in less than a day's journey from any part of the land. To these, man-slayers might flee for refuge, and be safe, till they had a fair trial. If acquitted from the charge, they were protected from the avenger of blood; yet they must continue within the bounds of the city till the death of the high priest. Thus we are reminded that the death of the great High Priest is the only means whereby sins are pardoned, and sinners set at liberty. These cities are plainly alluded to, both in the Old and New Testament, we cannot doubt the typical character of their appointment. Turn ye to the strong hold, ye prisoners of hope, saith the voice of mercy, Zec **9**:**12**, alluding to the city of refuge. St. Paul describes the strong consolation of fleeing for refuge to the hope set before us, in a passage always applied to the gracious appointment of the cities of refuge, Heb **6**:**18**. The rich mercies of salvation, through Christ, prefigured by these cities, demand our regard. **1**. Did the ancient city rear its towers of safety on high? See Christ raised up on the cross; and is he not exalted at the right hand of his Father, to be a Prince and a Saviour, to give repentance and remission of sins? **2**. Does not the highway of salvation, resemble the smooth and plain path to the city of refuge? Survey the path that leads to the Redeemer. Is there any stumbling-block to be found therein, except that which an evil heart of unbelief supplies for its own fall? **3**. Waymarks were set up pointing to the city. And is it not the office of the ministers of the gospel to direct sinners to Him? **4**. The gate of the city stood open night and day. Has not Christ declared, Him that cometh unto me I will in nowise cast out? **5**. The city of refuge afforded support to every one who entered its walls. Those who have reached the refuge, may live by faith on Him whose flesh is meat indeed, and whose blood is drink indeed. **6**. The city was a refuge for all. In the gospel there is no respect of persons. That soul lives not which deserves not Divine wrath; that soul lives not which may not in simple faith hope for salvation and life eternal, through the Son of God.

Chapter 36

Verses 1–4

The heads of the tribe of Manasseh represent the evil which might follow, if the daughters of Zelophehad should marry into any other tribes. They sought to preserve the Divine appointment of inheritances, and that contests and quarrels should not rise among those who should come afterwards. It is the wisdom and duty of those who have estates in the world, to settle them, and to dispose of them, so that no strife and contention may arise. (Nu **36**:**5-12**)

Verses 5–12

Those who consult the oracles of God, concerning the making of their heavenly inheritance sure, shall not only be directed what to do, but their inquiries shall be graciously accepted. God would not have one tribe enriched at the expense of another. Each tribe was to keep to its own inheritance. The daughters of Zelophehad submitted to this appointment. How could they fail to marry well, when God himself directed them? Let the people of God learn how suitable and proper it is, like the daughters of Israel, to be united only to their own people. Ought not every true believer Israel, to be united only to their own people. Ought not every true believer in Jesus, to be very attentive in the near and tender relations of life, to be united only to such as are united to the Lord? All our intentions and inclinations ought to be subjected to the will of God, when that is made known to us, and especially in contracting marriage. Although the word of God allows affection and preference in this important relation, it does not sanction that foolish, ungovernable, and idolatrous passion, which cares not what may be the end; but in defiance of authority, determines upon self-gratification. All such conduct, however disguised, is against common sense, the interests of society, the happiness of the marriage relation, and, what is still more evil, against the religion of Christ.

Verse 13

These are the judgments the Lord commanded in the plains of Moab. Most of them related to the settlement in Canaan, into which the Israelites were now entering. Whatever new condition God, by his providence, brings us into, we must beg him to teach us the duties of it, and to enable us to do them, that we may do the work of the day in its day, the duty of a place in its place.

Deuteronomy

This book repeats much of the history and of the laws contained in the three foregoing books: Moses delivered it to Israel a little before his death, both by word of mouth, that it might affect, and by writing, that it might abide. The men of that generation to which the law was first given were all dead, and a new generation was sprung up, to whom God would have it repeated by Moses himself, now they were going to possess the land of Canaan. The wonderful love of God to his church is set forth in this book; how he ever preserved his church for his own mercies sake, and would still have his name called upon among them. Such are the general outlines of this book, the whole of which shows Moses' love for Israel, and marks him an eminent type of the Lord Jesus Christ. Let us apply the exhortations and persuasions to our own consciences, to excite our minds to a believing, grateful obedience to the commands of God.

Chapter 1

Verses 1–8

Moses spake to the people all the Lord had given him in commandment. Horeb was but eleven days distant from Kadesh-barnea. This was to remind them that their own bad conduct had occasioned their tedious wanderings; that they might the more readily understand the advantages of obedience. They must now go forward. Though God brings his people into trouble and affliction, he knows when they have been tried long enough. When God commands us to go forward in our Christian course, he sets the heavenly Canaan before us for our encouragement.

Verses 9–18

Moses reminds the people of the happy constitution of their government, which might make them all safe and easy, if it was not their own fault. He owns the fulfilment of God's promise to Abraham, and prays for the further accomplishment of it. We are not straitened in the power and goodness of God; why should we be straitened in our own faith and hope? Good laws were given to the Israelites, and good men were to see to the execution of them, which showed God's goodness to them, and the care of Moses.

Verses 19–46

Moses reminds the Israelites of their march from Horeb to Kadesh-barnea, through that great and terrible wilderness. He shows how near they were to a happy settlement in Canaan. It will aggravate the eternal ruin of hypocrites, that they were not far from the kingdom of God. As if it were not enough that they were sure of their God before them, they would send men before them. Never any looked into the Holy Land, but they must own it to be a good land. And was there any cause to distrust this God? An unbelieving heart was at the bottom of all this. All disobedience to God's laws, and distrust of his power and goodness, flow from disbelief of his word, as all true obedience springs from faith. It is profitable for us to divide our past lives into distinct periods; to give thanks to God for the mercies we have received in each, to confess and seek the forgiveness of all the sins we can remember; and thus to renew our acceptance of God's salvation, and our surrender of ourselves to his service. Our own plans seldom avail to good purpose; while courage in the exercise of faith, and in the path of duty, enables the believer to follow the Lord fully, to disregard all that opposes, to triumph over all opposition, and to take firm hold upon the promised blessings.

Chapter 2

Verses 1–7

Only a short account of the long stay of Israel in the wilderness is given. God not only chastised them for their murmuring and unbelief, but prepared them for Canaan; by humbling them for sin, teaching them to mortify their lusts, to follow God, and to comfort themselves in him. Though Israel may be long kept waiting for deliverance and enlargement, it will come at last. Before God brought Israel to destroy their enemies in Canaan, he taught them to forgive their enemies in Edom. They must not, under pretence of God's covenant and conduct, think to seize all they could lay hands on. Dominion is not founded in grace. God's Israel shall be well placed, but must not expect to be placed alone in the midst of the earth. Religion must never be made a cloak for injustice. Scorn to be beholden to Edomites, when thou hast an all-sufficient God to depend upon. Use what thou hast, use it cheerfully. Thou hast experienced the care of the Divine providence, never use any crooked methods for thy supply. All this is equally to be applied to the experience of the believer.

Verses 8–23

We have the origin of the Moabites, Edomites, and Ammonites. Moses also gives an instance older than any of these; the Caphtorims drove the Avims out of their country. These revolutions show what uncertain things wordly possessions are. It was so of old, and ever will be so. Families decline, and from them estates are transferred to families that increase; so little continuance is there in these things. This is recorded to encourage the children of Israel. If the providence of God has done this for Moabites and Ammonites, much more would his promise do it for Israel, his peculiar people. Cautions are given not to meddle with Moabites and Ammonites. Even wicked men must not be wronged. God gives and preserves outward blessings to wicked men; these are not the best things, he has better in store for his own children.

Verses 24–37

God tried his people, by forbidding them to meddle with the rich countries of Moab and Ammon. He gives them possession of the country of the Amorites. If we keep from what God forbids, we shall not lose by our obedience. The earth is the Lord's and the fulness thereof; and he gives it to whom he pleases; but when there is no express direction, none can plead his grant for such proceedings. Though God assured the Israelites that the land should be their own, yet they must contend with the enemy. What God gives we must endeavour to get. What a new world did Israel now come into! Much more joyful will the change be, which holy souls will experience, when they remove out of the wilderness of this world to the better country, that is, the heavenly, to the city that has foundations. Let us, by reflecting upon God's dealings with his people Israel, be led to meditate upon our years spent in vanity, through our transgressions. But happy are those whom Jesus has delivered from the wrath to come. To whom he hath given the earnest of his Spirit in their hearts. Their inheritance cannot be affected by revolutions of kingdoms, or changes in earthly possessions.

Chapter 3

Verses 1–11

Og was very powerful, but he did not take warning by the ruin of Sihon, and desire conditions of peace. He trusted his own strength, and so was hardened to his destruction. Those not awakened by the judgments of God on others, ripen for the like judgments on themselves.

Verses 12–20

This country was settled on the Reubenites, Gadites, and half the tribe of Manasseh: see Nu **32**. Moses repeats the condition of the grant to which they agreed. When at rest, we should desire to see our brethren at rest too, and should be ready to do what we can towards it; for we are not born for ourselves, but are members one of another.

Verses 21–29

Moses encouraged Joshua, who was to succeed him. Thus the aged and experienced in the service of God, should do all they can to strengthen the hands of those who are young, and setting out in religion. Consider what God has done, what God has promised. If God be for us, who can be against us, so as to prevail? We reproach our Leader if we follow him trembling. Moses prayed, that, if it were God's will, he might go before Israel, over Jordan into Canaan. We should never allow any desires in our hearts, which we cannot in faith offer up to God by prayer. God's answer to this prayer had a mixture of mercy and judgment. God sees it good to deny many things we desire. He may accept our prayers, yet not grant us the very things we pray for. It God does not by his providence give us what we desire, yet if by his grace he makes us content without, it comes to much the same. Let it suffice thee to have God for thy Father, and heaven for thy portion, though thou hast not every thing thou wouldst have in the world. God promised Moses a sight of Canaan from the top of Pisgah. Though he should not have the possession of it, he should have the prospect of it. Even great believers, in this present state, see heaven but at a distance. God provided him a successor. It is a comfort to the friends of the church of Christ, to see God's work likely to be carried on by others, when they are silent in the dust. And if we have the earnest and prospect of heaven, let these suffice us; let us submit to the Lord's will, and speak no more to Him of matters which he sees good to refuse us.

Chapter 4

Verses 1–23

The power and love of God to Israel are here made the ground and reason of a number of cautions and serious warnings; and although there is much reference to their national covenant, yet all may be applied to those who live under the gospel. What are laws made for but to be observed and obeyed? Our obedience as individuals cannot merit salvation; but it is the only evidence that we are partakers of the gift of God, which is eternal life through Jesus Christ, Considering how many temptations we are compassed with, and what corrupt desires we have in our bosoms, we have great need to keep our hearts with all diligence. Those cannot walk aright, who walk carelessly.

Moses charges particularly to take heed of the sin of idolatry. He shows how weak the temptation would be to those who thought aright; for these pretended gods, the sun, moon, and stars, were only blessings which the Lord their God had imparted to all nations. It is absurd to worship them; shall we serve those that were made to serve us? Take heed lest ye forget the covenant of the Lord your God. We must take heed lest at any time we forget our religion. Care, caution, and watchfulness, are helps against a bad memory.

Verses 24–40

Moses urged the greatness, glory, and goodness of God. Did we consider what a God he is with whom we have to do, we should surely make conscience of our duty to him, and not dare to sin against him. Shall we forsake a merciful God, who will never forsake us, if we are faithful unto him? Whither can we go? Let us be held to our duty by the bonds of love, and prevailed with by the mercies of God to cleave to him. Moses urged God's authority over them, and their obligations to him. In keeping God's commandments they would act wisely for themselves. The fear of the Lord, that is wisdom. Those who enjoy the benefit of Divine light and laws, ought to support their character for wisdom and honour, that God may be glorified thereby. Those who call upon God, shall certainly find him within call, ready to give an answer of peace to every prayer of faith. All these statutes and judgments of the Divine law are just and righteous, above the statutes and judgments of any of the nations. What they saw at mount Sinai, gave an earnest of the day of judgment, in which the Lord Jesus shall be revealed in flaming fire. They must also remember what they heard at mount Sinai. God manifests himself in the works of the creation, without speech or language, yet their voice is heard, Ps **19**:**1**, **3**; but to Israel he made himself known by speech and language, condescending to their weakness. The rise of this nation was quite different from the origin of all other nations. See the reasons of free grace; we are not beloved for our own sakes, but for Christ's sake. Moses urged the certain benefit and advantage of obedience. This argument he had begun with, ver. #(**1**), That ye may live, and go in and possess the land; and this he concludes with, ver. #(**40**), That it may go well with thee, and with thy children after thee. He reminds them that their prosperity would depend upon their piety. Apostacy from God would undoubtedly be the ruin of their nation. He foresees their revolt from God to idols. Those, and those only, shall find God to their comfort, who seek him with all their heart. Afflictions engage and quicken us to seek God; and, by the grace of God working with them, many are thus brought back to their right mind. When these things are come upon thee, turn to the Lord thy God, for thou seest what comes of turning from him. Let all the arguments be laid together, and then say, if religion has not reason on its side. None cast off the government of their God, but those who first abandon the understanding of a man.

Verses 41–49

Here is the introduction to another discourse, or sermon, Moses preached to Israel, which we have in the following chapters. He sets the law before them, as the rule they were to work by, the way they were to walk in. He sets it before them, as the glass in which they were to see their natural face, that, looking into this perfect law of liberty, they might continue therein. These are the laws, given when Israel was newly come out of Egypt; and they were now repeated. Moses gave these laws in charge, while they encamped over against Beth-peor, an idol place of the Moabites. Their present triumphs were a powerful argument for obedience. And we should understand our own situation as sinners, and the nature of that gracious covenant to which we are invited. Therein greater things are shown to us than ever Israel saw from mount Sinai; greater mercies are given to us than they experienced in the wilderness, or in Canaan. One speaks to us, who is of infinitely greater dignity than Moses; who bare our sins upon the cross; and pleads with us by His dying love.

Chapter 5

Verses 1–5

Moses demands attention. When we hear the word of God we must learn it; and what we have learned we must put in practice, for that is the end of hearing and learning; not to fill our heads with notions, or our mouths with talk, but to direct our affections and conduct.

Verses 6–22

There is some variation here from Ex **20** as between the Lord's prayer in Mt **6** and Lu **11**. It is more necessary that we tie ourselves to the things, than to the words unalterably. The original reason for hallowing the sabbath, taken from God's resting from the work of creation on the seventh day, is not here mentioned. Though this ever remains in force, it is not the only reason. Here it is taken from Israel's deliverance out of Egypt; for that was typical of our redemption by Jesus Christ, in remembrance of which the Christian sabbath was to be observed. In the resurrection of Christ we were brought into the glorious liberty of the children of God, with a mighty hand, and an outstretched arm. How sweet is it to a soul truly distressed under the terrors of a broken law, to hear the mild and soul-reviving language of the gospel!

Verses 23–33

Moses refers to the consternation caused by the terror with which the law was given. God's appearances have always been terrible to man, ever since the fall; but Christ, having taken away sin, invites us to come boldly to the throne of grace. They were in a good mind, under the strong convictions of the word they heard. Many have their consciences startled by the law who have them not purified; fair promises are extorted from them, but no good principles are fixed and rooted in them. God commended what they said. He desires the welfare and salvation of poor sinners. He has given abundant proof that he does so; he gives us time and space to repent. He has sent his Son to redeem us, promised his Spirit to those who pray for him, and has declared that he has no pleasure in the ruin of sinners. It would be well with many, if there were always such a heart in them, as there seems to be sometimes; when they are under conviction of sin, or the rebukes of providence, or when they come to look death in the face. The only way to be happy, is to be holy. Say to the righteous, It shall be well with them. Let believers make it more and more their study and delight, to do as the Lord God hath commanded.

Chapter 6

Verses 1–3

In this and the like passages, the "commandments" seem to denote the moral law, the "statues" the ceremonial law, and the "judgments" the law by which the judges decided. Moses taught the people all that, and that only, which God commanded him to teach. Thus Christ's ministers are to teach his churches all he has commanded, neither more nor less, Mt **28**:**20**. The fear of God in the heart will be the most powerful principle of obedience. It is highly desirable that not we only, but our children, and our children's children, may fear the Lord. Religion and righteousness advance and secure the prosperity of any people.

Verses 4, 5

Here is a brief summary of religion, containing the first principles of faith and obedience. Jehovah our God is the only living and true

God; he only is God, and he is but One God. Let us not desire to have any other. The three-fold mention of the Divine names, and the plural number of the word translated God, seem plainly to intimate a Trinity of persons, even in this express declaration of the unity of the Godhead. Happy those who have this one Lord for their God. It is better to have one fountain than a thousand cisterns; one all-sufficient God than a thousand insufficient friends. This is the first and great commandment of God's law, that we love him; and that we do all parts of our duty to him from a principle of love; My son, give me thine heart. We are to love God with all our heart, and soul, and might. That is, **1**. With a sincere love; not in word and tongue only, but inwardly in truth. **2**. With a strong love. He that is our All, must have our all, and none but he. **3**. With a superlative love; we must love God above any creature whatever, and love nothing but what we love for him. **4**. With an intelligent love. To love him with all the heart, and with all the understanding, we must see good cause to love him. **5**. With an entire love; he is ONE, our hearts must be united in his love. Oh that this love of God may be shed abroad in our hearts!

Verses 6–16

Here are means for maintaining and keeping up religion in our hearts and houses. **1**. Meditation. God's words must be laid up in our hearts, that our thoughts may be daily employed about them. **2**. The religious education of children. Often repeat these things to them. Be careful and exact in teaching thy children. Teach these truths to all who are any way under thy care. **3**. Pious discourse. Thou shalt talk of these things with due reverence and seriousness, for the benefit not only of thy children, but of thy servants, thy friends and companions. Take all occasions to discourse with those about thee, not of matters of doubtful disputation, but of the plain truths and laws of God, and the things that belong to our peace. **4**. Frequent reading of the word. God appointed them to write sentences of the law upon their walls, and in scrolls of parchment to be worn about their wrists. This seems to have been binding in the letter of it to the Jews, as it is to us in the intent of it; which is, that we should by all means make the word of God familiar to us; that we may have it ready to use upon all occasions, to restrain us from sin, and direct us in duty. We must never be ashamed to own our religion, nor to own ourselves under its check and government. Here is a caution not to forget God in a day of prosperity and plenty. When they came easily by the gift, they would be apt to grow secure, and unmindful of the Giver. Therefore be careful, when thou liest safe and soft, lest thou forget the Lord. When the world smiles, we are apt to make court to it, and expect our happiness in it, and so we forget Him who is our only portion and rest. There is need of great care and caution at such a time. Then beware; being warned of your danger, stand upon your guard. Thou shalt not tempt the Lord thy God; neither by despairing of his power and goodness, while we keep in the way of our duty; nor by presuming upon it, when we turn aside out of that way.

Verses 17–25

Moses gives charge to keep God's commandments. Negligence will ruin us; but we cannot be saved without diligence. It is our interest, as well as our duty, to be religious. It will be our life. Godliness has the promise of the continuance and comfort of the life that now is, as far as it is for God's glory. It will be our righteousness. It is only through the Mediator we can be righteous before God. The knowledge of the spirituality and excellency of the holy law of God, is suited to show sinful man his need of a Saviour, and to prepare his heart to welcome a free salvation. The gospel honours the law, not only in the perfect obedience of the Son of God, the Lord Jesus Christ; but in that it is a plan for bringing back apostate rebels and enemies, by repentance, faith, forgiveness, and renewing grace, to love God above all things, even in this world; and in the world above, to love him perfectly, even as angels love him.

Chapter 7

Verses 1–11

Here is a strict caution against all friendship and fellowship with idols and idolaters. Those who are in communion with God, must have no communication with the unfruitful works of darkness. Limiting the orders to destroy, to the nations here mentioned, plainly shows that after ages were not to draw this into a precedent. A proper understanding of the evil of sin, and of the mystery of a crucified Saviour, will enable us to perceive the justice of God in all his punishments, temporal and eternal. We must deal decidedly with our lusts that war against our souls; let us not show them any mercy, but mortify, and crucify, and utterly destroy them. Thousands in the world that now is, have been undone by ungodly marriages; for there is more likelihood that the good will be perverted, than that the bad will be converted. Those who, in choosing yoke-fellows, keep not within the bounds of a profession of religion, cannot promise themselves helps meet for them.

Verses 12–26

We are in danger of having fellowship with the works of darkness if we take pleasure in fellowship with those who do such works. Whatever brings us into a snare, brings us under a curse. Let us be constant to our duty, and we cannot question the constancy of God's mercy. Diseases are God's servants; they go where he sends them, and do what he bids them. It is therefore good for the health of our bodies, thoroughly to mortify the sin of our souls; which is our rule of duty. Yet sin is never totally destroyed in this world; and it actually prevails in us much more than it would do, if we were watchful and diligent. In all this the Lord acts according to the counsel of his own will; but that counsel being hid from us, forms no excuse for our sloth and negligence, of which it is in no degree the cause. We must not think, that because the deliverance of the church, and the destruction of the enemies of the soul, are not done immediately, therefore they will never be done. God will do his own work in his own method and time; and we may be sure that they are always the best. Thus corruption is driven out of the hearts of believers by little and little. The work of sanctification is carried on gradually; but at length there will be a complete victory. Pride, security, and other sins that are common effects of prosperity, are enemies more dangerous than beasts of the field, and more apt to increase upon us.

Chapter 8

Verses 1–9

Obedience must be, **1**. Careful, observe to do; **2**. Universal, to do all the commandments; and **3**. From a good principle, with a regard to God as the Lord, and their God, and with a holy fear of him. To engage them to this obedience. Moses directs them to look back. It is good to remember all the ways, both of God's providence and grace, by which he has led us through this wilderness, that we may cheerfully serve him and trust in him. They must remember the straits they were sometimes brought into, for mortifying their pride, and manifesting their perverseness; to prove them, that they and others might know all that was in their heart, and that all might see that God chose them, not for any thing in them which might recommend them to his favour. They must remember the miraculous supplies of food and raiment granted them. Let none of God's children distrust their Father, nor take any sinful course for the supply of their necessities. Some way or other, God will provide for them in the way of duty and honest diligence, and verily they shall be fed. It may be applied spiritually; the word of God is the food of the soul. Christ is the word of God; by him we live. They must also remember the rebukes they had been under, and not without need. This use we should make of all our afflictions; by them let us be quickened to our duty. Moses also directs them to look forward to Canaan. Look which way we will, both to look back and to look forward, to Canaan. Look which way we will, both to look back and to look forward will furnish us with arguments for obedience. Moses saw in that land a type of the better country. The gospel church is the New Testament Canaan, watered with the Spirit in his gifts and graces, planted with trees of righteousness, bearing fruits of righteousness. Heaven is the good land, in which nothing is wanting, and where is fulness of joy.

Verses 10–20

Moses directs to the duty of a prosperous condition. Let them always remember their Benefactor. In everything we must give thanks. Moses arms them against the temptations of a prosperous condition. When men possess large estates, or are engaged in profitable business, they find the temptation to pride, forgetfulness of God, and carnal-mindedness, very strong; and they are anxious and troubled about many things. In this the believing poor have the advantage; they more easily perceive their supplies coming from the Lord in answer to the prayer of faith; and, strange as it may seem, they find less difficulty in simply trusting him for daily bread. They taste a sweetness therein, which is generally unknown to the rich, while they are also freed from many of their temptations. Forget not God's former dealings with thee. Here is the great secret of Divine Providence. Infinite wisdom and goodness are the source of all the changes and trials believers experience. Israel had many bitter trials, but it was "to do them good." Pride is natural to the human heart. Would one suppose that such a people, after their slavery at the brick-kilns, should need the thorns of the wilderness to humble them? But such is man! And they were proved that they might be humbled. None of us live a single week without giving proofs of our weakness, folly, and depravity. To broken-hearted souls alone the Saviour is precious indeed. Nothing can render the most suitable outward and inward trials effectual, but the power of the Spirit of God. See here how God's giving and our getting are reconciled, and apply it to spiritual wealth. All God's gifts are in pursuance of his promises. Moses repeats the warning he had often given of the fatal consequences of forsaking God. Those who follow others in sin, will follow them to destruction. If we do as sinners do, we must expect to fare as sinners fare.

Chapter 9

Verses 1–6

Moses represents the strength of the enemies they were now to encounter. This was to drive them to God, and engage their hope in him. He assures them of victory, by the presence of God with them. He cautions them not to have the least thought of their own righteousness, as if that procured this favour at God's hand. In Christ we have both righteousness and strength; in Him we must glory, not in ourselves, nor in any sufficiency of our own. It is for the wickedness of these nations that God drives them out. All whom God rejects, are rejected for their own wickedness; but none whom he accepts are accepted for their own righteousness. Thus boasting is for ever done away: see Eph **2**:**9**, **11**, **12**.

Verses 7–29

That the Israelites might have no pretence to think that God brought them to Canaan for their righteousness, Moses shows what a miracle of mercy it was, that they had not been destroyed in the wilderness. It is good for us often to remember against ourselves, with sorrow and shame, our former sins; that we may see how much we are indebted to free grace, and may humbly own that we never merited any thing but wrath and the curse at God's hand. For so strong is our propensity to pride, that it will creep in under one pretence or another. We are ready to fancy that our righteousness has got for us the special favour of the Lord, though in reality our wickedness is more plain than our weakness. But when the secret history of every man's life shall be brought forth at the day of judgment, all the world will be proved guilty before God. At present, One pleads for us before the mercy-seat, who not only fasted, but died upon the cross for our sins; through whom we may approach, though self-condemned sinners, and beseech for undeserved mercy and for eternal life, as the gift of God in Him. Let us refer all the victory, all the glory, and all the praise, to Him who alone bringeth salvation.

Chapter 10

Verses 1–11

Moses reminded the Israelites of God's great mercy to them, notwithstanding their provocations. There were four things in and by which the Lord showed himself reconciled to Israel. God gave them his law. Thus God has intrusted us with Bibles, sabbaths, and sacraments, as tokens of his presence and favour. God led them forward toward Canaan. He appointed a standing ministry among them for holy things. And now, under the gospel, when the pouring forth of the Spirit is more plentiful and powerful, the succession is kept up by the Spirit's work on men's hearts, qualifying and making some willing for that work in every age. God accepted Moses as an advocate or intercessor for them, and therefore appointed him to be their prince and leader. Moses was a type of Christ, who ever lives, pleading for us, and has all power in heaven and in earth.

Verses 12–22

We are here taught our duty to God in our principles and our practices. We must fear the Lord our God. We must love him, and delight in communion with him. We must walk in the ways in which he has appointed us to walk. We must serve him with all our heart and soul. What we do in his service we must do cheerfully, and with good will. We must keep his commandments. There is true honour and pleasure in obedience. We must give honour to God; and to him we must cleave, as one we love and delight in, trust in, and from whom we have great expectations. We are here taught our duty to our neighbour. God's common gifts to mankind oblige us to honour all men. And those who have themselves been in distress, and have found mercy with God, should be ready to show kindness to those who are in the like distress. We are here taught our duty to ourselves. Circumcise your hearts. Cast away all corrupt affections and inclinations, which hinder you from fearing and loving God. By nature we do not love God. This is original sin, the source whence our wickedness proceeds; and the carnal mind is enmity against God, for it is not subject to the law of God, neither indeed can be; so then they that are in the flesh cannot please God, Ro **8**:**5**–**9**. Let us, without delay or reserve, come and cleave to our reconciled God in Jesus Christ, that we may love, serve, and obey him acceptably, and be daily changed into his image, from glory to glory, by the Spirit of the Lord. Consider the greatness and glory of God; and his goodness and grace; these persuade us to our duty. Blessed Spirit! Oh for thy purifying, persevering, and renewing influences, that being called out of the state of strangers, such as our fathers were, we may be found among the number of the children of God, and that our lot may be among the saints.

Chapter 11

Verses 1–7

Observe the connexion of these two; Thou shalt love the Lord, and keep his charge. Love will work in obedience, and that only is acceptable obedience which flows from a principle of love, 1Jo **5**:**3**. Moses recounts some of the great and terrible works of God which their eyes had seen. What our eyes have seen, especially in our early days, should affect us, and make us better long afterwards.

Verses 8–17

Moses sets before them, for the future, life and death, the blessing and the curse, according as they did or did not keep God's commandment. Sin tends to shorten the days of all men, and to shorten the days of a people's prosperity. God will bless them with an abundance of all good things, if they would love him and serve him. Godliness has the promise of the life that now is; but the favour of God shall put gladness into the heart, more than the increase of corn, and wine, and oil. Revolt from God to idols would certainly be their ruin. Take heed that your hearts be not deceived. All who forsake God to set their affection upon any creature, will find themselves wretchedly deceived, to their own destruction; and this will make it worse, that it was for want of taking heed.

Verses 18–25

Let all be directed by the three rules here given. **1**. Let our hearts be filled with the word of God. There will not be good practices in the life, unless there be good thoughts, good affections, and good principles in the heart. **2**. Let our eyes be fixed upon the word of God, having constant regard to it as the guide of our way, as the rule of our work, Ps **119**:**30**. **3**. Let our tongues be employed about the word of God. Nor will any thing do more to cause prosperity, and keeping up religion in a nation, than the good education of children.

Verses 26–32

Moses sums up all the arguments for obedience in two words, the blessing and the curse. He charged the people to choose which they would have. Moses then appointed a public and solemn proclamation of the blessing and curse, to be made upon the two mountains of Gerizim and Ebal. We have broken the law, and are under its curse, without remedy from ourselves. In mercy, the gospel again sets before us a blessing and a curse. A blessing, if we obey the call to repentance, to faith in Christ, and newness of heart and life through him; an awful curse, if we neglect so great salvation. Let us thankfully welcome these glad tidings of great joy; and let us not harden our hearts, but hear this voice of God while it is called to-day, and while he invites us to come to him upon a mercy-seat. Let us be diligent to make our calling and election sure.

Chapter 12

Verses 1–4

Moses comes to the statutes he had to give in charge to Israel; and begins with such as relate to the worship of God. The Israelites are charged not to bring the rites and usages of idolaters into the worship of God; not under colour of making it better. We cannot serve God and mammon; nor worship the true God and idols; nor depend upon Christ Jesus and upon superstitious or self-righteous confidences.

Verses 5–32

The command to bring ALL the sacrifices to the door of the tabernacle, was now explained with reference to the promised land. As to moral service, then, as now, men might pray and worship every where, as they did in their synagogues. The place which God would choose, is said to be the place where he would put his name. It was to be his habitation, where, as King of Israel, he would be found by all who reverently sought him. Now, under the gospel, we have no temple or altar that sanctifies the gift but Christ only: and as to the places of worship, the prophets foretold that in every place the spiritual incense should be offered, Mal **1**:**11**. Our Saviour declared, that those are accepted as true worshippers, who worship God in sincerity and truth, without regard either to this mountain or Jerusalem, Joh **4**:**21**. And a devout Israelite might honour God, keep up communion with him, and obtain mercy from him, though he had no opportunity of bringing a sacrifice to his altar. Work for God should be done with holy joy and cheerfulness. Even children and servants must rejoice before God; the services of religion are to be a pleasure, and not a task or drudgery. It is the duty of people to be kind to their ministers, who teach them well, and set them good examples. As long as we live, we need their assistance, till we come to that world where ordinances will not be needed. Whether we eat or drink, or whatever we do, we are commanded to do all to the glory of God. And we must do all in the name of the Lord Jesus Christ, giving thanks to the Father through him. They must not even inquire into the modes and forms of idolatrous worship. What good would it do them to know those depths of Satan? And our inward satisfaction will be more and more, as we abound in love and good works, which spring from faith and the in-dwelling Spirit of Christ.

Chapter 13

Verses 1–5

Moses had cautioned against the peril that might arise from the Canaanites. Here he cautions against the rise of idolatry among themselves. It is needful for us to be well acquainted with the truths and precepts of the Bible; for we may expect to be proved by temptations of evil under the appearance of good, of error in the guise of truth; nor can any thing rightly oppose such temptations, but the plain, express testimony of God's word to the contrary. And it would be a proof of sincere affection for God, that, notwithstanding specious pretences, they should not be wrought upon the forsake God, and follow other gods to serve them.

Verses 6–11

It is the policy of Satan to try to lead us to evil by those whom we love, whom we least suspect of any ill design, and whom we are desirous to please, and apt to conform to. The enticement here is supposed to come from a brother or child, who are near by nature; from a wife or friend, who are near by choice, and are to us as our souls. But it is our duty to prefer God and religion, before the nearest and dearest friends we have in the world. We must not, to please our friends, break God's law. Thou shalt not consent to him, nor go with him, not for company, or curiosity, not to gain his affections. It is a general rule, If sinners entice thee, consent thou not, Pr **1**:**10**. And we must not hinder the course of God's justice.

Verses 12–18

Here is the case of a city revolting from the God of Israel, and serving other gods. The crime is supposed to be committed by one of the cities of Israel. Even when they were ordered to preserve their religion by force, yet they were not allowed to bring others to it by fire and sword. Spiritual judgments under the Christian dispensation are more terrible than the execution of criminals; we have not less cause than the Israelites had, to fear the Divine wrath. Let us then fear the spiritual idolatry of covetousness, and the love of worldly pleasure; and be careful not to countenance them in our families, by our example or by the education of our children. May the Lord write his law and truth in our hearts, there set up his throne, and shed abroad his love!

Chapter 14

Verses 1–21

Moses tells the people of Israel how God had given them three distinguishing privileges, which were their honour, and figures of those spiritual blessings in heavenly things, with which God has in Christ blessed us. Here is election; "The Lord hath chosen thee." He did not choose them because they were by their own acts a peculiar people to him above other nations, but he chose them that they might be so by his grace; and thus were believers chosen, Eph **1**:**4**. Here is adoption; "Ye are the children of the Lord your God;" not because God needed children, but because they were orphans, and needed a father. Every spiritual Israelite is indeed a child of God, a partaker of his nature and favour. Here is sanctification; "Thou art a holy people." God's people are required to be holy, and if they are holy, they are indebted to the grace God which makes them so. Those whom God chooses to be his children, he will form to be a holy people, and zealous of good works. They must be careful to avoid every thing which might disgrace their profession, in the sight of those who watch for their halting. Our heavenly Father forbids nothing but for our welfare. Do thyself no harm; do not ruin thy health, thy reputation, thy domestic comforts, thy peace of mind. Especially do not murder thy soul. Do not be the vile slave of thy appetites and passions. Do not render all around thee miserable, and thyself wretched; but aim at that which is most excellent and useful. The laws which regarded many sorts of flesh as unclean, were to keep them from mingling with their idolatrous neighbours. It is plain in the gospel, that these laws are now done away. But let us ask our own hearts, Are we of the children of the Lord our God? Are we separate from the ungodly world, in being set apart to God's glory, the purchase of Christ's blood? Are we subjects of the work of the Holy Ghost? Lord, teach us from these precepts how pure and holy all thy people ought to live!

Verses 22–29

A second portion from the produce of their land was required. The whole appointment evidently was against the covetousness, distrust, and selfishness of the human heart. It promoted friendliness, liberality, and cheerfulness, and raised a fund for the relief of the poor. They were taught that their worldly portion was most comfortably enjoyed, when shared with their brethren who were in want. If we thus serve God, and do good with what we have, it is promised that the Lord our God will bless us in all the works of our land. The blessing of God is all to our outward prosperity; and without that blessing, the work of our hands will bring nothing to pass. The blessing descends upon the working hand. Expect not that God should bless thee in thy idleness and love of ease. And it descends upon the giving hand. He who thus scatters, certainly increases; and to be free and generous in the support of religion, and any good work, is the surest and safest way of thriving.

Chapter 15

Verses 1–11

This year of release typified the grace of the gospel, in which is proclaimed the acceptable year of the Lord; and by which we obtain the release of our debts, that is, the pardon of our sins. The law is spiritual, and lays restraints upon the thoughts of the heart. We mistake, if we think thoughts are free from God's knowledge and check. That is a wicked heart indeed, which raises evil thoughts from the good law of God, as theirs did, who, because God had obliged them to the charity of forgiving, denied the charity of giving. Those who would keep from the act of sin, must keep out of their minds the very thought of sin. It is a dreadful thing to have the cry of the poor justly against us. Grudge not a kindness to thy brother; distrust not the providence of God. What thou doest, do freely, for God loves a cheerful giver, **2**Co **9**:**7**.

Verses 12–18

Here the law concerning Hebrew servants is repeated. There is an addition, requiring the masters to put some small stock into their servants' hands to set up with for themselves, when sent out of their servitude, wherein they had received no wages. We may expect family blessings, the springs of family prosperity, when we make conscience of our duty to our family relations. We are to remember that we are debtors to Divine justice, and have nothing to pay with. That we are slaves, poor, and perishing. But the Lord Jesus Christ, by becoming poor, and by shedding his blood, has made a full and free provision for the payment of our debts, the ransom of our souls, and the supply of all our wants. When the gospel is clearly preached, the acceptable year of the Lord is proclaimed; the year of release of our debts, of the deliverance of our souls, and of obtaining rest in him. And as faith in Christ and love to him prevail, they will triumph over the selfishness of the heart, and over the unkindness of the world, doing away the excuses that rise from unbelief, distrust, and covetousness.

Verses 19–23

Here is a direction what to do with the firstlings. We are not now limited as the Israelites were; we make no difference between a first calf, or lamb, and the rest. Let us then look to the gospel meaning of this law, devoting ourselves and the first of our time and strength to God; and using all our comforts and enjoyments to his praise, and under the direction of his law, as we have them all by his gift.

Chapter 16

Verses 1–17

The laws for the three yearly feasts are here repeated; that of the Passover, that of the Pentecost, that of Tabernacles; and the general law concerning the people's attendance. Never should a believer forget his low estate of guilt and misery, his deliverance, and the price it cost the Redeemer; that gratitude and joy in the Lord may be mingled with sorrow for sin, and patience under the tribulations in his way to the kingdom of heaven. They must rejoice in their receivings from God, and in their returns of service and sacrifice to him; our duty must be our delight, as well as our enjoyment. If those who were under the law must rejoice before God, much more we that are under the grace of the gospel; which makes it our duty to rejoice evermore, to rejoice in the Lord always. When we rejoice in God ourselves, we should do what we can to assist others also to rejoice in him, by comforting the mourners, and supplying those who are in want. All who make God their joy, may rejoice in hope, for He is faithful that has promised.

Verses 18–22

Care is taken for the due administration of justice. All personal regards must be laid aside, so that right is done to all, and wrong to none. Care is taken to prevent following the idolatrous customs of the heathen. Nothing belies God more, or tends more to corrupt the minds of men, than representing and worshipping, by an image, that God, who is an almighty and eternal Spirit, present every where. Alas! even in gospel days, and under a better dispensation, established upon better promises, there is a tendency to set up idols, under one form or another, in the human heart.

Chapter 17

Verses 1–7

No creature which had any blemish was to be offered in sacrifice to God. We are thus called to remember the perfect, pure, and spotless sacrifice of Christ, and reminded to serve God with the best of our abilities, time, and possession, or our pretended obedience will be hateful to him. So great a punishment as death, so remarkable a death as stoning, must be inflicted on the Jewish idolater. Let all who in our day set up idols in their hearts, remember how God punished this crime in Israel.

Verses 8–13

Courts of judgment were to be set up in every city. Though their judgment had not the Divine authority of an oracle, it was the judgment of wise, prudent, experienced men, and had the advantage of a Divine promise.

Verses 14–20

God himself was in a particular manner Israel's King; and if they set another over them, it was necessary that he should choose the person. Accordingly, when the people desired a king, they applied to Samuel, a prophet of the Lord. In all cases, God's choice, if we can but know it, should direct, determine, and overrule ours. Laws are given for the prince that should be elected. He must carefully avoid every thing that would turn him from God and religion. Riches, honours, and pleasures, are three great hinderances of godliness, (the lusts of the flesh, the lusts of the eye, and the pride of life,) especially to those in high stations; against these the king is here warned. The king must carefully study the law of God, and make that his rule; and having a copy of the Scriptures of his own writing, must read therein all the days of his life. It is not enough to have Bibles, but we must use them, use them daily, as long as we live. Christ's scholars never learn above their Bibles, but will have constant occasion for them, till they come to that world where knowledge and love will be made perfect. The king's writing and reading were as nothing, if he did not practise what he wrote and read. And those who fear God and keep his commandments, will fare the better for it even in this world.

Chapter 18

Verses 1–8

Care is taken that the priests entangle not themselves with the affairs of this life, nor enrich themselves with the wealth of this world; they have better things to mind. Care is likewise taken that they want not the comforts and conveniences of this life. The people must provide for them. He that has the benefit of solemn religious assemblies, ought to give help for the comfortable support of those that minister in such assemblies.

Verses 9–14

Was it possible that a people so blessed with Divine institutions, should ever be in any danger of making those their teachers whom God had made their captives? They were in danger; therefore, after many like cautions, they are charged not to do after the abominations of the nations of Canaan. All reckoning of lucky or unlucky days, all charms for diseases, all amulets or spells to prevent evil, fortune-telling, &c. are here forbidden. These are so wicked as to be a chief cause of the rooting out of the Canaanites. It is amazing to think that there should be any pretenders of this kind in such a land, and day of light, as we live in. They are mere impostors who blind and cheat their followers.

Verses 15–22

It is here promised concerning Christ, that there should come a Prophet, great above all the prophets; by whom God would make known himself and his will to the children of men, more fully and clearly than he had ever done before. He is the Light of the world, Joh **8**:**12**. He is the World by whom God speaks to us, Joh **1**:**1**; Heb **1**:**2**. In his birth he should be one of their nation. In his resurrection he should be raised up at Jerusalem, and from thence his doctrine should go forth to all the world. Thus God, having raised up his Son Christ Jesus, sent him to bless us. He should be like unto Moses, only above him. This prophet is come, even JESUS; and is "He that should come," and we are to look for no other. The view of God which he gives, will not terrify or overwhelm, but encourages us. He speaks with fatherly affection and Divine authority united. Whoever refuses to listen to Jesus Christ, shall find it is at his peril; the same that is the Prophet is to be his Judge, Joh **12**:**48**. Woe then to those who refuse to hearken to His voice, to accept His salvation, or yield obedience to His sway! But happy they who trust in Him, and obey Him. He will lead them in the paths of safety and peace, until He brings them to the land of perfect light, purity, and happiness. Here is a caution against false prophets. It highly concerns us to have a right touchstone wherewith to try the word we hear, that we may know what that word is which the Lord has not spoken. Whatever is against the plain sense of the written word, or which gives countenance or encouragement to sin, we may be sure is not that which the Lord has spoken.

Chapter 19

Verses 1–13

Here is the law settled between the blood of the murdered, and the blood of the murderer; provision is made, that the cities of refuge should be a protection, so that a man should not die for that as a crime, which was not his willing act. In Christ, the Lord our Righteousness, refuge is provided for those who by faith flee unto him. But there is no refuge in Jesus Christ for presumptuous sinners, who go on still in their trespasses. Those who flee to Christ from their sins, shall be safe in him, but not those who expect to be sheltered by him in their sins.

Verse 14

Direction is given to fix landmarks in Canaan. It is the will of God that every one should know his own; and that means should be used to hinder the doing and suffering of wrong. This, without doubt, is a moral precept, and still binding. Let every man be content with his own lot, and be just to his neighbours in all things.

Verses 15–21

Sentence should never be passed upon the testimony of one witness alone. A false witness should suffer the same punishment which he sought to have inflicted upon the person he accused. Nor could any law be more just. Let all Christians not only be cautious in bearing witness in public, but be careful not to join in private slanders; and let all whose consciences accuse them of crime, without delay flee for refuge to the hope set before them in Jesus Christ.

Chapter 20

Verses 1–9

In the wars wherein Israel engaged according to the will of God, they might expect the Divine assistance. The Lord was to be their only confidence. In these respects they were types of the Christian's warfare. Those unwilling to fight, must be sent away. The unwillingness might arise from a man's outward condition. God would not be served by men forced against their will. Thy people shall be willing, Ps **110**:**3**. In running the Christian race, and fighting the good fight of faith, we must lay aside all that would make us unwilling. If a man's unwillingness rose from weakness and fear, he had leave to return from the war. The reason here given is, lest his brethren's heart fail as well as his heart. We must take heed that we fear not with the fear of them that are afraid, Isa **8**:**12**.

Verses 10–12

The Israelites are here directed about the nations on whom they made war. Let this show God's grace in dealing with sinners. He proclaims peace, and beseeches them to be reconciled. Let it also show us our duty in dealing with our brethren. Whoever are for war, we must be for peace. Of the cities given to Israel, none of their inhabitants must be left. Since it could not be expected that they should be cured of their idolatry, they would hurt Israel. These regulations are not the rules of our conduct, but Christ's law of love. The horrors of war must fill the feeling heart with anguish upon every recollection; and are proofs of the wickedness of man, the power of Satan, and the just vengeance of God, who thus scourges a guilty world. But how dreadful their case who are engaged in unequal conflict with their Maker, who will not submit to render him the easy tribute of worship and praise! Certain ruin awaits them. Let neither the number nor the power of the enemies of our souls dismay us; nor let even our own weakness cause us to tremble or to faint. The Lord will save us; but in this war let none engage whose hearts are fond of the world, or afraid of the cross and the conflict. Care is here taken that in besieging cities the fruit-trees should not be destroyed. God is a better friend to man than he is to himself; and God's law consults our interests and comforts; while our own appetites and passions, which we indulge, are enemies to our welfare. Many of the Divine precepts restrain us from destroying that which is for our life and food. The Jews understand this as forbidding all wilful waste upon any account whatsoever. Every creature of God is good; as nothing is to be refused, so nothing is to be abused. We may live to want what we carelessly waste.

Chapter 21

Verses 1–9

If a murderer could not be found out, great solemnity is provided for putting away the guilt from the land, as an expression of dread and detesting of that sin. The providence of God has often wonderfully brought to light these hidden works of darkness, and the sin of the guilty has often strangely found them out. The dread of murder should be deeply impressed upon every heart, and all should join in detecting and punishing those who are guilty. The elders were to profess that they had not been any way aiding or abetting the sin. The priests were to pray to God for the country and nation, that God would be merciful. We must empty that measure by our prayers, which others are filling by their sins. All would be taught by this solemnity, to use the utmost care and diligence to prevent, discover, and punish murder. We may all learn from hence to take heed of partaking in other men's sins. And we have fellowship with the unfruitful works of darkness, if we do not reprove them.

Verses 10–14

By this law a soldier was allowed to marry his captive, if he pleased. This might take place upon some occasions; but the law does not show any approval of it. It also intimates how binding the laws of justice and honour are in marriage; which is a sacred engagement.

Verses 15–17

This law restrains men from disinheriting their eldest sons without just cause. The principle in this case as to children, is still binding to parents; they must give children their right without partiality.

Verses 18–21

Observe how the criminal is here described. He is a stubborn and rebellious son. No child was to fare the worse for weakness of capacity, slowness, or dulness, but for wilfulness and obstinacy. Nothing draws men into all manner of wickedness, and hardens them in it more certainly and fatally, than drunkenness. When men take to drinking, they forget the law of honouring parents. His own father and mother must complain of him to the elders of the city. Children who forget their duty, must thank themselves, and not blame their parents, if they are regarded with less and less affection. He must be publicly stoned to death by the men of his city. Disobedience to a parent's authority must be very evil, when such a punishment was ordered; nor is it less provoking to God now, though it escapes punishment in this world. But when young people early become slaves to sensual appetites, the heart soon grows hard, and the conscience callous; and we can expect nothing but rebellion and destruction.

Verses 22, 23

By the law of Moses, the touch of a dead body was defiling, therefore dead bodies must not be left hanging, as that would defile the land. There is one reason here which has reference to Christ; "He that is hanged is accursed of God;" that is, it is the highest degree of disgrace and reproach. Those who see a man thus hanging between heaven and earth, will conclude him abandoned of both, and unworthy of either. Moses, by the Spirit, uses this phrase of being accursed of God, when he means no more than being treated most disgracefully, that it might afterward be applied to the death of Christ, and might show that in it he underwent the curse of the law for us; which proves his love, and encourages to faith in him.

Chapter 22

Verses 1–4

If we duly regard the golden rule of "doing to others as we would they should do unto us," many particular precepts might be omitted. We can have no property in any thing that we find. Religion teaches us to be neighbourly, and to be ready to do all good offices to all men. We know not how soon we may have occasion for help.

Verses 5–12

God's providence extends itself to the smallest affairs, and his precepts do so, that even in them we may be in the fear of the Lord, as we are under his eye and care. Yet the tendency of these laws, which seem little, is such, that being found among the things of God's law, they are to be accounted great things. If we would prove ourselves to be God's people, we must have respect to his will and to his glory, and not to the vain fashions of the world. Even in putting on our garments, as in eating or in drinking, all must be done with a serious regard to preserve our own and others' purity in heart and actions. Our eye should be single, our heart simple, and our behaviour all of a piece.

Verses 13–30

These and the like regulations might be needful then, and yet it is not necessary that we should curiously examine respecting them. The laws relate to the seventh commandment, laying a restraint upon fleshly lusts which war against the soul.

Chapter 23

Verses 1–8

We ought to value the privileges of God's people, both for ourselves and for our children, above all other advantages. No personal blemishes, no crimes of our forefathers, no difference of nation, shuts us out under the Christian dispensation. But an unsound heart will deprive us of blessings; and a bad example, or an unsuitable marriage, may shut our children from them.

Verses 9–14

The camp of the Lord must have nothing offensive in it. If there must be this care taken to preserve the body clean, much more should we be careful to keep the mind pure.

Verses 15–25

It is honourable to shelter and protect the weak, provided they are not wicked. Proselytes and converts to the truth, should be treated with particular tenderness, that they may have no temptation to return to the world. We cannot honour God with our substance, unless it be honestly and honourably come by. It must not only be considered what we give, but how we got it. Where the borrower gets, or hopes to get, it is just that the lender should share the gain; but to him that borrows for necessary food, pity must be showed. That which is gone out of thy lips, as a solemn and deliberate vow, must not be recalled, but thou shalt keep and perform it punctually and fully. They were allowed to pluck and eat of the corn or grapes that grew by the road side; only they must not carry any away. This law intimated what great plenty of corn and wine they should have in Canaan. It provided for the support of poor travellers, and teaches us to be kind to such, teaches us to be ready to distribute, and not to think every thing lost that is given away. Yet it forbids us to abuse the kindness of friends, or to take advantage of what is allowed. Faithfulness to their engagements should mark the people of God; and they should never encroach upon others.

Chapter 24

Verses 1–4

Where the providence of God, or his own wrong choice in marriage, has allotted to a Christian a trial instead of a help meet; he will from his heart prefer bearing the cross, to such relief as tends to sin, confusion, and misery. Divine grace will sanctify this cross, support under it, and teach so to behave, as will gradually render it more tolerable.

Verses 5–13

It is of great consequence that love be kept up between husband and wife; that they carefully avoid every thing which might make them strange one to another. Man-stealing was a capital crime, which could not be settled, as other thefts, by restitution. The laws concerning leprosy must be carefully observed. Thus all who feel their consciences under guilt and wrath, must not cover it, or endeavour to shake off their convictions; but by repentance, and prayer, and humble confession, take the way to peace and pardon. Some orders are given about pledges for money lent. This teaches us to consult the comfort and subsistence of others, as much as our own advantage. Let the poor debtor sleep in his own raiment, and praise God for thy kindness to him. Poor debtors ought to feel more than commonly they do, the goodness of creditors who do not take all the advantage of the law against them, nor should this ever be looked upon as weakness.

Verses 14–22

It is not hard to prove that purity, piety, justice, mercy, fair conduct, kindness to the poor and destitute, consideration for them, and generosity of spirit, are pleasing to God, and becoming in his redeemed people. The difficulty is to attend to them in our daily walk and conversation.

Chapter 25

Verses 1–3

Every punishment should be with solemnity, that those who see it may be filled with dread, and be warned not to offend in like manner. And though the criminals must be shamed as well as put to pain, for their warning and disgrace, yet care should be taken that they do not appear totally vile. Happy those who are chastened of the Lord to humble them, that they should not be condemned with the world to destruction.

Verse 4

This is a charge to husbandmen. It teaches us to make much of the animals that serve us. But we must learn, not only to be just, but kind to all who are employed for the good of our better part, our souls, 1Co 9:9.

Verses 5–12

The custom here regulated seems to have been in the Jewish law in order to keep inheritances distinct; now it is unlawful.

Verses 13–16

Dishonest gain always brings a curse on men's property, families, and souls. Happy those who judge themselves, repent of and forsake their sins, and put away evil things, that they may not be condemned of the Lord.

Verses 17–19

Let every persecutor and injurer of God's people take warning from the case of the Amalekites. The longer it is before judgement comes, the more dreadful will it be at last. Amalek may remind us of the foes of our souls. May we be enabled to slay all our lusts, all the corruptions both within and without, all the powers of darkness and of the world, which oppose our way to the blessed Saviour.

Chapter 26

Verses 1–11

When God has made good his promises to us, he expects we should own it to the honour of his faithfulness. And our creature comforts are doubly sweet, when we see them flowing from the fountain of the promise. The person who offered his first-fruits, must remember and own the mean origin of that nation, of which he was a member. A Syrian ready to perish was my father. Jacob is here called a Syrian. Their nation in its infancy sojourned in Egypt as strangers, they served there as slaves. They were a poor, despised, oppressed people in Egypt; and though become rich and great, had no reason to be proud, secure, or forgetful of God. He must thankfully acknowledge God's great goodness to Israel. The comfort we have in our own enjoyments, should lead us to be thankful for our share in public peace and plenty; and with present mercies we should bless the Lord for the former mercies we remember, and the further mercies we expect and hope for. He must offer his basket of first-fruits. Whatever good thing God gives us, it is his will that we make the most comfortable use we can of it, tracing the streams to the Fountain of all consolation.

Verses 12–15

How should the earth yield its increase, or, if it does, what comfort can we take in it, unless therewith our God gives us his blessing? All this represented the covenant relation between a reconciled God and every true believer, and the privileges and duties belonging to it. We must be watchful, and show that according to the covenant of grace in Christ Jesus, the Lord is our God, and we are his people, waiting in his appointed way for the performance of his gracious promises.

Verses 16–19

Moses here enforces the precepts. They are God's laws, therefore thou shalt do them, to that end were they given thee; do them, and dispute them not; do them, and draw not back; do them, not carelessly and hypocritically, but with thy heart and soul, thy whole heart and thy whole soul. We forswear ourselves, and break the most sacred engagement, if, when we have taken the Lord to be our God, we do not make conscience of obeying his commands. We are elected to obedience, **1**Pe **1**:**2**; chosen that we should be holy, Eph **1**:**4**; purified a peculiar people, that we might not only do good works, but be zealous in them, Tit **2**:**14**. Holiness is true honour, and the only way to everlasting honour.

Chapter 27

Verses 1–10

As soon as they were come into Canaan, they must set up a monument, on which they must write the words of this law. They must set up an altar. The word and prayer must go together. Though they might not, of their own heads, set up any altar besides that at the tabernacle; yet, by the appointment of God, they might, upon special occasion. This altar must be made of unhewn stones, such as they found upon the field. Christ, our Altar, is a stone cut out of the mountain without hands, refused by the builders, as having no form or comeliness, but accepted of God the Father, and made the Head of the corner. In the Old Testament the words of the law are written, with the curse annexed; which would overcome us with horror, if we had not, in the New Testament, an altar erected close by, which gives consolation. Blessed be God, the printed copies of the Scriptures among us, do away the necessity of such methods as were presented to Israel. The end of the gospel ministry is, and the end of preachers ought to be, to make the word of God as plain as possible. Yet, unless the Spirit of God prosper such labours with Divine power, we shall not, even by these means, be made wise unto salvation: for this blessing we should therefore daily and earnestly pray.

Verses 11–26

The six tribes appointed for blessing, were all children of the free women, for to such the promise belongs, Ga **4**:**31**. Levi is here among the rest. Ministers should apply to themselves the blessing and curse they preach to others, and by faith set their own Amen to it. And they must not only allure people to their duty with the promises of a blessing, but awe them with the threatenings of a curse, by declaring that a curse would be upon those who do such things. To each of the curses the people were to say, Amen. It professed their faith, that these, and the like curses, were real declarations of the wrath of God against the ungodliness and unrighteousness of men, not one jot of which shall fall to the ground. It was acknowledging the equity of these curses. Those who do such things deserve to fall, and lie under the curse. Lest those who were guilty of other sins, not here mentioned, should think themselves safe from the curse, the last reaches all. Not only those who do the evil which the law forbids, but those also who omit the good which the law requires. Without the atoning blood of Christ, sinners can neither have communion with a holy God, nor do any thing acceptable to him; his righteous law condemns every one who, at any time, or in any thing, transgresses it. Under its awful curse we remain as transgressors, until the redemption of Christ is applied to our hearts. Wherever the grace of God brings salvation, it teaches the believer to deny ungodliness and wordly lusts, to live soberly, righteously, and godly in this present world, consenting to, and delighting in the words of God's law, after the inward man. In this holy walk, true peace and solid joy are to be found.

Chapter 28

Verses 1–14

This chapter is a very large exposition of two words, the blessing and the curse. They are real things and have real effects. The blessings are here put before the curses. God is slow to anger, but swift to show mercy. It is his delight to bless. It is better that we should be drawn to what is good by a child-like hope of God's favour, than that we be frightened to it by a slavish fear of his wrath. The blessing is promised, upon condition that they diligently hearken to the voice of God. Let them keep up religion, the form and power of it, in their families and nation, then the providence of God would prosper all their outward concerns.

Verses 15–44

If we do not keep God's commandments, we not only come short of the blessing promised, but we lay ourselves under the curse, which includes all misery, as the blessing all happiness. Observe the justice of this curse. It is not a curse causeless, or for some light cause. The extent and power of this curse. Wherever the sinner goes, the curse of God follows; wherever he is, it rests upon him. Whatever he has is under a curse. All his enjoyments are made bitter; he cannot take any true comfort in them, for the wrath of God mixes itself with them. Many judgments are here stated, which would be the fruits of the curse, and with which God would punish the people of the Jews, for their apostacy and disobedience. We may observe the fulfilling of these threatenings in their present state. To complete their misery, it is threatened that by these troubles they should be bereaved of all comfort and hope, and left to utter despair. Those who walk by sight, and not by faith, are in danger of losing reason itself, when every thing about them looks frightful.

Verses 45–68

If God inflicts vengeance, what miseries his curse can bring upon mankind, even in this present world! Yet these are but the beginning of sorrows to those under the curse of God. What then will be the misery of that world where their worm dieth not, and their fire is not quenched! Observe what is here said of the wrath of God, which should come and remain upon the Israelites for their sins. It is amazing to think that a people so long the favourites of Heaven, should be so cast off; and yet that a people so scattered in all nations should be kept distinct, and not mixed with others. If they would not serve God with cheerfulness, they should be compelled to serve their enemies. We may justly expect from God, that if we do not fear his fearful name, we shall feel his fearful plagues; for one way or other God will be feared. The destruction threatened is described. They have, indeed, been plucked from off the land, ver. #(**63**). Not only by the Babylonish captivity, and when Jerusalem was destroyed by the Romans; but afterwards, when they were forbidden to set foot in Jerusalem. They should have no rest; no rest of body, ver. **65**, but be continually on the remove, either in hope of gain, or fear of persecution. No rest of the mind, which is much worse. They have been banished from city to city, from country to country; recalled, and banished again. These events, compared with the favour shown to Israel in ancient times, and with the prophecies about them, should not only excite astonishment, but turn unto us for a testimony, assuring us of the truth of Scripture. And when the other prophecies of their conversion to Christ shall come to pass, the whole will be a sign and a wonder to all the nations of the earth, and the forerunner of a general spread of true christianity. The fulfilling of these prophecies upon the Jewish nation, delivered more than three thousand years ago, shows that Moses spake by the Spirit of God; who not only foresees the ruin of sinners, but warns of it, that they may prevent it by a true and timely repentance, or else be left without excuse. And let us be thankful that Christ hath redeemed us from the curse of the law, by being made a curse for us, and bearing in his own person all that punishment which our sins merit, and which we must otherwise have endured for ever. To this Refuge and salvation let sinners flee; therein let believers rejoice, and serve their reconciled God with gladness of heart, for the abundance of his spiritual blessings.

Chapter 29

Verses 1–9

Both former mercies, and fresh mercies, should be thought on by us as motives to obedience. The hearing ear, and seeing eye, and the understanding heart, are the gift of God. All that have them, have them from him. God gives not only food and raiment, but wealth and large possessions, to many to whom he does not give grace. Many enjoy the gifts, who have not hearts to perceive the Giver, nor the true design and use of the gifts. We are bound, in gratitude and interest, as well as in duty and faithfulness, to keep the words of the covenant.

Verses 10–21

The national covenant made with Israel, not only typified the covenant of grace made with true believers, but also represented the outward dispensation of the gospel. Those who have been enabled to consent to the Lord's new covenant of mercy and grace in Jesus Christ, and to give up themselves to be his people, should embrace every opportunity of renewing their open profession of relation to him, and their obligation to him, as the God of salvation, walking according thereto. The sinner is described as one whose heart turns away from his God; there the mischief begins, in the evil heart of unbelief, which inclines men to depart from the living God to dead idols. Even to this sin men are now tempted, when drawn aside by their own lusts and fancies. Such men are roots that bear gall and wormwood. They are weeds which, if let alone, overspread the whole field. Satan may for a time disguise this bitter morsel, so that thou shalt not have the natural taste of it, but at the last day, if not before, the true taste shall be discerned. Notice the sinner's security in sin. Though he hears the words of the curse, yet even then he thinks himself safe from the wrath of God. There is scarcely a threatening in all the book of God more dreadful than this. Oh that presumptuous sinners would read it, and tremble! for it is a real declaration of the wrath of God, against ungodliness and unrighteousness of man.

Verses 22–28

Idolatry would be the ruin of their nation. It is no new thing for God to bring desolating judgments on a people near to him in profession. He never does this without good reason. It concerns us to seek for the reason, that we may give glory to God, and take warning to ourselves. Thus the law of Moses leaves sinners under the curse, and rooted out of the Lord's land; but the grace of Christ toward penitent, believing sinners, plants them again in their land; and they shall no more be pulled up, being kept by the power of God.

Verse 29

Moses ends his prophecy of the Jews' rejection, just as St. Paul ends his discourse on the same subject, when it began to be fulfilled, Ro **11**:**33**. We are forbidden curiously to inquire into the secret counsels of God, and to determine concerning them. But we are directed and encouraged, diligently to seek into that which God has made known. He has kept back nothing that is profitable for us, but only that of which it is good for us to be ignorant. The end of all Divine revelation is, not to furnish curious subjects of speculation and discourse, but that we may do all the words of this law, and be blessed in our deed. This, the Bible plainly reveals; further than this, man cannot profitably go. By this light he may live and die comfortably, and be happy for ever.

Chapter 30

Verses 1–10

In this chapter is a plain intimation of the mercy God has in store for Israel in the latter days. This passage refers to the prophetic warnings of the last two chapters, which have been mainly fulfilled in the destruction of Jerusalem by the Romans, and in their dispersion to the present day; and there can be no doubt that the prophetic promise contained in these **verses** yet remain to come to pass. The Jewish nation shall in some future period, perhaps not very distant, be converted to the faith of Christ; and, many think, again settled in the land of Canaan. The language here used is in a great measure absolute promises; not merely a conditional engagement, but declaring an event assuredly to take place. For the Lord himself here engages to "circumcise their hearts;" and when regenerating grace has removed corrupt nature, and Divine love has supplanted the love of sin, they certainly will reflect, repent, return to God, and obey him; and he will rejoice in doing them good. The change that will be wrought upon them will not be only outward, or consisting in mere opinions; it will reach to their souls. It will produce in them an utter hatred of all sin, and a fervent love to God, as their reconciled God in Christ Jesus; they will love him with all their hearts, and with all their soul. They are very far from this state of mind at present, but so were the murderers of the Lord Jesus, on the day of Pentecost; who yet in one hour were converted unto God. So shall it be in the day of God's power; a nation shall be born in a day; the Lord will hasten it in his time. As a conditional promise this passage belongs to all persons and all people, not to Israel only; it assures us that the greatest sinners, if they repent and are converted, shall have their sins pardoned, and be restored to God's favour.

Verses 11–14

The law is not too high for thee. It is not only known afar off; it is not confined to men of learning. It is written in thy books, made plain, so that he who runs may read it. It is in thy mouth, in the tongue commonly used by thee, in which thou mayest hear it read, and talk of it among thy children. It is delivered so that it is level to the understanding of the meanest. This is especially true of the gospel of Christ, to which the apostle applies it. But the word is nigh us, and Christ in that word; so that if we believe with the heart, that the promises of the Messiah are fulfilled in our Lord Jesus, and confess them with our mouth, we then have Christ with us.

Verses 15–20

What could be said more moving, and more likely to make deep and lasting impressions? Every man wishes to obtain life and good, and to escape death and evil; he desires happiness, and dreads misery. So great is the compassion of the Lord, that he has favoured men, by his word, with such a knowledge of good and evil as will make them for ever happy, if it be not their own fault. Let us hear the sum of the whole matter. If they and theirs would love God, and serve him, they should live and be happy. If they or theirs should turn from God, desert his service, and worship other gods, that would certainly be their ruin. There never was, since the fall of man, more than one way to heaven; which is marked out in both Testaments, though not with equal clearness. Moses meant that same way of acceptance, which Paul more plainly described; and Paul's words mean the same obedience, on which Moses more fully treated. In both Testaments the good and right way is brought near, and plainly revealed to us.

Chapter 31

Verses 1–8

Moses assures Israel of the constant presence of God with them. This is applied by the apostle to all God's spiritual Israel, to encourage their faith and hope; unto us is this gospel preached, as well as unto them; he will never fail thee, nor forsake thee, Heb **13**:**5**. Moses commends Joshua to them for a leader; one whose wisdom, and courage, and affection they had long known; one whom God had appointed to be their leader; and therefore would own and bless. Joshua is well pleased to be admonished by Moses to be strong and of good courage. Those shall speed well, who have God with them; therefore they ought to be of good courage. Through God let us do valiantly, for through him we shall do victoriously; if we resist the devil, he will flee from us.

Verses 9–13

Though we read the word in private, we must not think it needless to hear it read in public. This solemn reading of the law must be done in the year of release. The year of release was typical of gospel grace, which is called the acceptable year of the Lord; for our pardon and liberty by Christ, engage us to keep his commandments. It must be read to all Israel, men, women, children, and to the strangers. It is the will of God that all people should acquaint themselves with his word. It is a rule to all, therefore should be read to all. Whoever has read of the pains taken by many persons to get scraps of the Scriptures, when a whole copy could not be obtained, or safely possessed, will see how thankful we should be for the thousands of copies amongst us. They will also understand the very different situation in which the Israelites were placed for many ages. But the heart of man is so careless, that all will be found too little, to keep up a knowledge of the truths, precepts, and worship of God.

Verses 14–22

Moses and Joshua attended the Divine Majesty at the door of the tabernacle. Moses is told again that he must shortly die; even those who are most ready and willing to die, need to be often reminded of its coming. The Lord tells Moses, that, after his death, the covenant he had taken so much pains to make between Israel and their God, would certainly be broken. Israel would forsake Him; then God would forsake Israel. Justly does he cast those off who so unjustly cast him off. Moses is directed to deliver them a song, which should remain a standing testimony for God, as faithful to them in giving them warning, and against them, as persons false to themselves in not taking the warning. The word of God is a discerner of the thoughts and intents of men's hearts, and meets them by reproofs and correction. Ministers who preach the word, know not the imaginations of men; but God, whose word it is, knows perfectly.

Verses 23–30

The solemn delivery of the book of the law to the Levites, to be deposited in, or rather by the side, of the ark, is again related. The song which follows in the next chapter is delivered to Moses, and by him to the people. He wrote it first, as the Holy Spirit taught him; and then spake it in the hearing of all the people. Moses tells them plainly, I know that after my death ye will utterly corrupt yourselves. Many a sad thought, no doubt, it occasioned to this good man; but his comfort was, that he had done his duty, and that God would be glorified in their dispersion, if not in their settlement, for the foundation of God stands sure.

Chapter 32

Verses 1, 2

Moses begins with a solemn appeal to heaven and earth, concerning the truth and importance of what he was about to say. His doctrine is the gospel, the speech of God, the doctrine of Christ; the doctrine of grace and mercy through him, and of life and salvation by him.

Verses 3–6

"He is a Rock." This is the first time God is called so in Scripture. The expression denotes that the Divine power, faithfulness, and love, as revealed in Christ and the gospel, form a foundation which cannot be changed or moved, on which we may build our hopes of happiness. And under his protection we may find refuge from all our enemies, and in all our troubles; as the rocks in those countries sheltered from the burning rays of the sun, and from tempests, or were fortresses from the enemy. "His work is perfect:" that of redemption and salvation, in which there is a display of all the Divine perfection, complete in all its parts. All God's dealings with his creatures are regulated by wisdom which cannot err, and perfect justice. He is indeed just and right; he takes care that none shall lose by him. A high charge is exhibited against Israel. Even God's children have their spots, while in this imperfect state; for if we say we have no sin, no spot, we deceive ourselves. But the sin of Israel was not habitual, notorious, unrepented sin; which is a certain mark of the children of Satan. They were fools to forsake their mercies for lying vanities. All wilful sinners, especially sinners in Israel, are unwise and ungrateful.

Verses 7–14

Moses gives particular instances of God's kindness and concern for them. The eagle's care for her young is a beautiful emblem of Christ's love, who came between Divine justice and our guilty souls, and bare our sins in his own body on the tree. And by the preached gospel, and the influences of the Holy Spirit, He stirs up and prevails upon sinners to leave Satan's bondage. In ver. #(**13**, **14**), are emblems of the conquest believers have over their spiritual enemies, sin, Satan, and the world, in and through Christ. Also of their safety and triumph in him; of their happy frames of soul, when they are above the world, and the things of it. This will be the blessed case of spiritual Israel in every sense in the latter day.

Verses 15–18

Here are two instances of the wickedness of Israel, each was apostacy from God. These people were called Jeshurun, "an upright people," so some; "a seeing people," so others: but they soon lost the reputation both of their knowledge and of their righteousness. They indulged their appetites, as if they had nothing to do but to make provision for the flesh to fulfil the lusts of it. Those who make a god of themselves, and a god of their bellies, in pride and wantonness, and cannot bear to be told of it, thereby forsake God, and show they esteem him lightly. There is but one way of a sinner's acceptance and sanctification, however different modes of irreligion, or false religion, may show that favourable regard for other ways, which is often miscalled candid. How mad are idolaters, who forsake the Rock of salvation, to run themselves upon the rock of perdition!

Verses 19–25

The revolt of Israel was described in the foregoing **verses**, and here follow the resolves of Divine justice as to them. We deceive ourselves, if we think that God will be mocked by a faithless people. Sin makes us hateful in the sight of the holy God. See what mischief sin does, and reckon those to be fools that mock at it.

Verses 26–38

The idolatry and rebellions of Israel deserved, and the justice of God seemed to demand, that they should be rooted out. But He spared Israel, and continues them still to be living witnesses of the truth of the Bible, and to silence unbelievers. They are preserved for wise and holy purposes and the prophecies give us some idea what those purposes are. The Lord will never disgrace the throne of his glory. It is great wisdom, and will help much to the return of sinners to God, seriously to consider their latter end, or the future state. It is here meant particularly of what God foretold by Moses, about this people in the latter days; but it may be applied generally. Oh that men would consider the happiness they will lose, and the misery they will certainly plunge into, if they go on in their trespasses! What will be in the end thereof? Jer **5**:**31**. For the Lord will in due time bring down the enemies of the church, in displeasure against their wickedness. When sinners deem themselves most secure, they suddenly fall into destruction. And God's time to appear for the deliverance of his people, is when things are at the worst with them. But those who trust to any rock but God, will find it fail them when they most need it. The rejection of the Messiah by the Jewish nation, is the continuance of their ancient idolatry, apostacy, and rebellion. They shall be brought to humble themselves before the Lord, to repent of their sins, and to trust in their long-rejected Mediator for salvation. Then he will deliver them, and make their prosperity great.

Verses 39–43

This conclusion of the song speaks, **1**. Glory to God. No escape can be made from his power. **2**. It speaks terror to his enemies. Terror indeed to those who hate him. The wrath of God is here revealed from heaven against them. **3**. It speaks comfort to his own people. The song concludes with words of joy. Whatever judgments are brought upon sinners, it shall go well with the people of God.

Verses 44–47

Here is the solemn delivery of this song to Israel, with a charge to mind all the good words Moses had said unto them. It is not a trifle, but a matter of life and death: mind it, and you are made for ever; neglect it, and you are for ever undone. Oh that men were fully persuaded that religion is their life, even the life of their souls!

Verses 48–52

Now Moses had done his work, why should he desire to live a day longer? God reminds him of the sin of which he had been guilty, for which he was kept from entering Canaan. It is good for the best of men to die repenting the infirmities of which they are conscious. But those may die with comfort and ease, whenever God calls for them, notwithstanding the sins they remember against themselves, who have a believing prospect, and a well-grounded hope of eternal life beyond death.

Chapter 33

Verses 1–5

To all his precepts, warnings, and prophecies, Moses added a solemn blessing. He begins with a description of the glorious appearances of God, in giving the law. His law works like fire. If received, it is melting, warming, purifying, and burns up the dross of corruption; if rejected, it hardens, sears, pains, and destroys. The Holy Spirit came down in cloven tongues, as of fire; for the gospel also is a fiery law. The law of God written in the heart, is a certain proof of the love of God shed abroad there: we must reckon His law one of the gifts of his grace.

Verses 6–23

The order in which the tribes are here blessed, is not the same as is observed elsewhere. The blessing of Judah may refer to the whole tribe in general, or to David as a type of Christ. Moses largely blesses the tribe of Levi. Acceptance with God is what we should all aim at, and desire, in all our devotions, whether men accept us or not, **2**Co **5**:**9**. This prayer is a prophecy, that God will keep up a ministry in his church to the end of time. The tribe of Benjamin had their inheritance close to mount Zion. To be situated near the ordinances, is a precious gift from the Lord, a privilege not to be exchanged for any worldly advantage, or indulgence. We should thankfully receive the earthly blessings sent to us, through the successive seasons. But those good gifts which come down from the Father of lights, through the rising of the Sun of righteousness, and the pouring out of his Spirit like the rain which makes fruitful, are infinitely more precious, as the tokens of his special love. The precious things here prayed for, are figures of spiritual blessing in heavenly things by Christ, the gifts, graces, and comforts of the Spirit. When Moses prays for the good will of Him that dwelt in the bush, he refers to the covenant, on which all our hopes of God's favour must be founded. The providence of God appoints men's habitations, and wisely disposes men to different employments for the public good. Whatever our place and business are, it is our wisdom and duty to apply thereto; and it is happiness to be well pleased therewith. We should not only invite others to the service of God, but abound in it. The blessing of Naphtali. The favour of God is the only favour satisfying to the soul. Those are happy indeed, who have the favour of God; and those shall have it, who reckon that in having it they have enough, and desire no more.

Verses 24, 25

All shall be sanctified to true believers; if their way be rough, their feet shall be shod with the preparation of the gospel of peace. As thy days, so shall thy strength be. The "day" is often in Scripture put for the events of the day; it is a promise that God would graciously and constantly support under trials and troubles, whatever they were. It is a promise sure to all the spiritual seed of Abraham. Have they work allotted? They shall have strength to do it. Have they burdens appointed? They shall have strength, and never be tempted above what they are able to bear.

Verses 26–29

None had such a God as Israel. There is no people like the Israel of God. What is here said of the church of Israel is to be applied to the spiritual church. Never were people so well seated and sheltered. Those who make God their habitation, shall have all the comforts and benefits of a habitation in him, Ps **91**:**1**. Never were people so well supported and borne up. How low soever the people of God are at any time brought, everlasting arms are underneath them, to keep the spirit from sinking, from fainting, and their faith from failing. Divine grace is sufficient for them, **2**Co **12**:**9**. Never were people so well commanded. Thus believers are more than conquerors over their spiritual enemies, through Christ that loved them. Never were people so well secured and protected. Israel shall dwell in safety alone. All who keep close to God, shall be kept safe by him. Never were people so well provided for. Every true Israelite looks with faith to the better country, the heavenly Canaan, which is filled with better things than corn and wine. Never were people so well helped. If in danger of any harm, or in want of any good, they had an eternal God to go to. Nothing could hurt those whom God helped, nor was it possible the people should perish who were saved by the Lord. Never were people so well armed. Those in whose hearts is the excellency of holiness, are defended by the whole armour of God, Eph **6**. Never were people so well assured of victory over their enemies. Thus shall the God of peace tread Satan under the feet of all believers, and shall do it shortly, Ro **16**:**20**. May God help us to seek and to set our affections on the things above; and to turn our souls from earthly perishing objects; that we may not have our lot with Israel's foes in the regions of darkness and despair, but with the Israel of God, in the realms of love and eternal happiness.

Chapter 34

Verses 1–4

Moses seemed unwilling to leave his work; but that being finished, he manifested no unwillingness to die. God had declared that he should not enter Canaan. But the Lord also promised that Moses should have a view of it, and showed him all that good land. Such a sight believers now have, through grace, of the bliss and glory of their future state. Sometimes God reserves the brightest discoveries of his grace to his people to support their dying moments. Those may leave this world with cheerfulness, who die in the faith of Christ, and in the hope of heaven.

Verses 5–8

Moses obeyed this command of God as willingly as any other, though it seemed harder. In this he resembled our Lord Jesus Christ. But he died in honour, in peace, and in the most easy manner; the Saviour died upon the disgraceful and torturing cross. Moses died very easily; he died "at the mouth of the Lord," according to the will of God. The servants of the Lord, when they have done all their other work, must die at last, and be willing to go home, whenever their Master sends for them, Ac **21**:**13**. The place of his burial was not known. If the soul be at rest with God, it is of little consequence where the body rests. There was no decay in the strength of his body, nor in the vigour and activity of his mind; his understanding was as clear, and his memory as strong as ever. This was the reward of his services, the effect of his extraordinary meekness. There was solemn mourning for him. Yet how great soever our losses have been, we must not give ourselves up to sorrow. If we hope to go to heaven rejoicing, why should we go to the grave mourning?

Verses 9–12

Moses brought Israel to the borders of Canaan, and then died and left them. This signifies that the law made nothing perfect, Heb **7**:**19** It brings men into a wilderness of conviction, but not into the Canaan of rest and settled peace. That honour was reserved for Joshua, our Lord Jesus, of whom Joshua was a type, (and the name is the same,) to do that for us which the law could not do, Ro **8**:**3**. Through him we enter into the spiritual rest of conscience, and eternal rest in heaven. Moses was greater than any other prophet of the Old Testament. But our Lord Jesus went beyond him, far more than the other prophets came short of him. And see a strong resemblance between the redeemer of the children of Israel and the Redeemer of mankind. Moses was sent by God, to deliver the Israelites form a cruel bondage; he led them out, and conquered their enemies. He became not only their deliverer, but their lawgiver; not only their lawgiver, but their judge; and, finally, leads them to the border of the land of promise. Our blessed Saviour came to rescue us out of the slavery of the devil, and to restore us to liberty and happiness. He came to confirm every moral precept of the first lawgiver; and to write them, not on tables of stone, but on fleshly tables of the heart. He came to be our Judge also, inasmuch as he hath appointed a day when he will judge all the secrets of men, and reward or punish accordingly. This greatness of Christ above Moses, is a reason why Christians should be obedient and faithful to the holy religion by which they profess to be Christ's followers. God, by his grace, make us all so!

Joshua

Here is the history of Israel's passing into the land of Canaan, conquering and dividing it, under the command of Joshua, and their history until his death. The power and truth of God in fulfilling his promises to Israel, and in executing his justly threatened vengeance on the Canaanites, are wonderfully displayed. This should teach us to regard the tremendous curses denounced in the word of God against impenitent sinners, and to seek refuge in Christ Jesus.

Chapter 1

Verses 1–4

Joshua had attended upon Moses. He who was called to honour, had been long used to business. Our Lord Jesus took upon him the form of a servant. Joshua was trained up under command. Those are fittest to rule, who have learned to obey. The removal of useful men should quicken survivors to be the more diligent in doing good. Arise, go over Jordan. At this place and at this time the banks were overflowed. Joshua had no bridge or boats, and yet he must believe that God, having ordered the people over, would open a way.

Verses 5–9

Joshua is to make the law of God his rule. He is charged to meditate therein day and night, that he might understand it. Whatever affairs of this world we have to mind, we must not neglect the one thing needful. All his orders to the people, and his judgments, must be according to the law of God. Joshua must himself be under command; no man's dignity or dominion sets him above the law of God. He is to encourage himself with the promise and presence of God. Let not the sense of thine own infirmities dishearten thee; God is all-sufficient. I have commanded, called, and commissioned thee to do it, and will be sure to bear thee out in it. When we are in the way of duty, we have reason to be strong and very bold. Our Lord Jesus, as Joshua here, was borne up under his sufferings by a regard to the will of God, and the commandment from his Father.

Verses 10–15

Joshua says to the people, Ye shall pass over Jordan, and shall possess the land; because God had said so to him. We honour the truth of God, when we stagger not at the promise of God. The two tribes and a half were to go over Jordan with their brethren. When God, by his providence, has given us rest, we ought to consider what service we may do to our brethren.

Verses 16–18

The people of Israel engage to obey Joshua; All that thou commandest us to do we will readily do, without murmuring or disputing, and whithersoever thou sendest us we will go. The best we can ask of God for our magistrates, is, that they may have the presence of God; that will make them blessings to us, so that in seeking this for them, we consult our own interest. May we be enabled to enlist under the banner of the Captain of our salvation, to be obedient to his commands, and to fight the good fight of faith, with all that trust in and love his name, against all who oppose his authority; for whoever refuses to obey him must be destroyed.

Chapter 2

Verses 1–7

Faith in God's promises ought not to do away, but to encourage our diligence in the use of proper means. The providence of God directed the spies to the house of Rahab. God knew where there was one that would be true to them, though they did not. Rahab appears to have been an innkeeper; and if she had formerly been one of bad life, which is doubtful, she had left her evil courses. That which seems to us most accidental, is often overruled by the Divine providence to serve great ends. It was by faith that Rahab received those with peace, against whom her king and country had war. We are sure this was a good work; it is so spoken of by the apostle, Jas **2**:**25**; and she did it by faith, such a faith as set her above the fear of man. Those only are true believers, who find in their hearts to venture for God; they take his people for their people, and cast in their lot among them. The spies were led by the special providence of God, and Rahab entertained them out of regard to Israel and Israel's God, and not for lucre or for any evil purpose. Though excuses may be offered for the guilt of Rahab's falsehood, it seems best to admit nothing which tends to explain it away. Her views of the Divine law must have been very dim: a falsehood like this, told by those who enjoy the light of revelation, whatever the motive, would deserve heavy censure.

Verses 8–21

Rahab had heard of the miracles the Lord wrought for Israel. She believed that his promises would certainly be fulfilled, and his threatenings take effect; and that there was no way of escape but by submitting to him, and joining with his people. The conduct of Rahab proved that she had the real principle of Divine faith. Observe the promises the spies made to her. The goodness of God is often expressed by his kindness and truth, Ps **117**:**2**; in both these we must be followers of him. Those who will be conscientious in keeping promises, are cautious in making them. The spies make needful conditions. The scarlet cord, like the blood upon the doorpost at the passover, recalls to remembrance the sinner's security under the atoning blood of Christ; and that we are to flee thereto for refuge from the wrath of a justly offended God. The same cord Rahab used for the saving of these Israelites, was to be used for her own safety. What we serve and honour God with, we may expect he will bless, and make useful to us.

Verses 22–24

The report the spies brought was encouraging. All the people of the country faint because of Israel; they have neither wisdom to yield, nor courage to fight. Those terrors of conscience, and that sense of Divine wrath, which dismay the ungodly, but bring not to repentance, are fearful forebodings of approaching destruction. But grace yet abounds to the chief of sinners. Let them, without delay, flee to Christ, and all shall be well.

Chapter 3

Verses 1–6

The Israelites came to Jordan in faith, having been told that they should pass it. In the way of duty, let us proceed as far as we can, and depend on the Lord. Joshua led them. Particular notice is taken of his early rising, as afterwards upon other occasions, which shows how little he sought his own ease. Those who would bring great things to pass, must rise early. Love not sleep, lest thou come to poverty. All in public stations should always attend to the duty of their place. The people were to follow the ark. Thus must we walk after the rule of the word, and the direction of the Spirit, in everything; so shall peace be upon us as upon the Israel of God; but we must follow our ministers only as they follow Christ. All their way through the wilderness was an untrodden path, but most so this through Jordan. While we are here, we must expect and prepare to pass ways that we have not passed before; but in the path of duty we may proceed with boldness and cheerfulness. Whether we are called to suffer poverty, pain, labour, persecution, reproach, or death, we are following the Author and Finisher of our faith; nor can we set our feet in any dangerous or difficult spot, through our whole journey, but faith will there see the prints of the Redeemer's feet, who trod that very path to glory above, and bids us follow him, that where he is, we may be also. They were to sanctify themselves. Would we experience the effects of God's love and power, we must put away sin, and be careful not to grieve the Holy Spirit of God.

Verses 7–13

The waters of Jordan shall be cut off. This must be done in such a way as never was done, but in the dividing of the Red sea. That miracle is here repeated; God has the same power to finish the salvation of his people, as to begin it; the WORD of the Lord was as truly with Joshua as with Moses. God's appearances for his people ought to encourage faith and hope. God's work is perfect, he will keep his people. Jordan's flood cannot keep out Israel, Canaan's force cannot turn them out again.

Verses 14–17

Jordan overflowed all its banks. This magnified the power of God, and his kindness to Israel. Although those who oppose the salvation of God's people have all advantages, yet God can and will conquer. This passage over Jordan, as an entrance to Canaan, after their long, weary wanderings in the wilderness, shadowed out the believer's passage through death to heaven, after he has finished his wanderings in this sinful world. Jesus, typified by the ark, hath gone before, and he crossed the river when it most flooded the country around. Let us treasure up experiences of His faithful and tender care, that they may help our faith and hope in the last conflict.

Chapter 4

Verses 1–9

The works of the Lord are so worthy of rememberance, and the heart of man is so prone to forget them, that various methods are needful to refresh our memories, for the glory of God, our advantage, and that of our children. God gave orders for preparing this memorial.

Verses 10–19

The priests with the ark did not stir till ordered to move. Let none be weary of waiting, while they have the tokens of God's presence with them, even the ark of the covenant, though it be in the depths of adversity. Notice is taken of the honour put upon Joshua. Those are feared in the best manner, and to the best purpose, who make it appear that God is with them, and that they set him before them.

Verses 20–24

It is the duty of parents to tell their children betimes of the words and works of God, that they may be trained up in the way they should go. In all the instruction parents give their children, they should teach them to fear God. Serious godliness is the best learning. Are we not called, as much as the Israelites, to praise the loving-kindness of our God? Shall we not raise a pillar to our God, who has brought us through dangers and distresses in so wonderful a way? For hitherto the Lord hath helped us, as much as he did his saints of old. How great the stupidity and ingratitude of men, who perceive not His hand, and will not acknowledge his goodness, in their frequent deliverances!

Chapter 5

Verses 1–9

How dreadful is their case, who see the wrath of God advancing towards them, without being able to turn it aside, or escape it! Such will be the horrible situation of the wicked; nor can words express the anguish of their feelings, or the greatness of their terror. Oh that they would now take warning, and before it be too late, flee for refuge to lay hold upon that hope set before them in the gospel! God impressed these fears on the Canaanites, and dispirited them. This gave a short rest to the Israelites, and circumcision rolled away the reproach of Egypt. They were hereby owned to be the free-born children of God, having the seal of the covenant. When God glorifies himself in perfecting the salvation of his people, he not only silences all enemies, but rolls back their reproaches upon themselves.

Verses 10–12

A solemn passover was kept, at the time appointed by the law, in the plains of Jericho, in defiance of the Canaanites round about them. It was a performance of the promise, that when they went up to keep the feasts, their land should be under the special protection of the Divine providence, Ex **34**:**24**. Notice is taken of the ceasing of the manna as soon as they had eaten the old corn of the land. For as it came just when they needed, so it continued as long as they needed it. This teaches us not to expect supplies by miracles, when they may be had in a common way. The word and ordinances of God are spiritual manna, with which God nourishes his people in this wilderness. Though often forfeited, yet they are continued while we are here; but when we come to the heavenly Canaan, this manna will cease, for we shall no longer need it.

Verses 13–15

We read not of any appearance of God's glory to Joshua till now. There appeared to him one as a man to be noticed. This Man was the Son of God, the eternal Word. Joshua gave him Divine honours: he received them, which a created angel would not have done, and he is called Jehovah, chap. **6**:**2**. To Abraham he appeared as a traveller; to Joshua as a man of war. Christ will be to his people what their faith needs. Christ had his sword drawn, which encouraged Joshua to carry on the war with vigour. Christ's sword drawn in his hand, denotes how ready he is for the defence and salvation of his people. His sword turns every way. Joshua will know whether he is a friend or a foe. The cause between the Israelites and Canaanites, between Christ and Beelzebub, will not admit of any man's refusing to take one part or the other, as he may do in worldly contests. Joshua's inquiry shows an earnest desire to know the will of Christ, and a cheerful readiness and resolution to do it. All true Christians must fight under Christ's banner, and they will conquer by his presence and assistance.

Chapter 6

Verses 1–5

Jericho resolves Israel shall not be its master. It shut itself up, being strongly fortified both by art and nature. Thus were they foolish, and their hearts hardened to their destruction; the miserable case of all that strengthen themselves against the Almighty. God resolves Israel shall be its master, and that quickly. No warlike preparations were to be made. By the uncommon method of besieging the city, the Lord honoured the ark, as the symbol of his presence, and showed that all the victories were from him. The faith and patience of the people were proved and increased.

Verses 6–16

Wherever the ark went, the people attended it. God's ministers, by the trumpet of the everlasting gospel, which proclaims liberty and victory, must encourage the followers of Christ in their spiritual warfare. As promised deliverances must be expected in God's way, so they must be expected in his time. At last the people were to shout: they did so, and the walls fell. This was a shout of faith; they believed the walls of Jericho would fall. It was a shout of prayer; they cry to Heaven for help, and help came.

Verses 17–27

Jericho was to be a solemn and awful sacrifice to the justice of God, upon those who had filled up the measure of their sins. So He appoints, from whom, as creatures, they received their lives, and to whom, as sinners, they had forfeited them. Rahab perished not with them that believed not, Heb **11**:**31**. All her kindred were saved with her; thus faith in Christ brings salvation to the house, Ac **16**:**31**. She, and they with her, were plucked as brands from the burning. With Rahab, or with the men of Jericho; our portion must be assigned, as we posses or disregard the sign of salvation; even faith in Christ, which worketh by love. Let us remember what depends upon our choice, and let us choose accordingly. God shows the weight of a Divine curse; where it rests there is no getting from under it; for it brings ruin without remedy.

Chapter 7

Verses 1–5

Achan took some of the spoil of Jericho. The love of the world is that root of bitterness, which of all others is most hardly rooted up. We should take heed of sin ourselves, lest by it many be defiled or disquieted, Heb **12**:**15**; and take heed of having fellowship with sinners, lest we share their guilt. It concerns us to watch over one another to prevent sin, because others' sins may be to our damage. The easy conquest of Jericho excited contempt of the enemy, and a disposition to expect the Lord to do all for them without their using proper means. Thus men abuse the doctrines of Divine grace, and the promises of God, into excuses for their own sloth and self-indulgence. We are to work out our own salvation, though it is God that works in us. It was a dear victory to the Canaanites, whereby Israel was awakened and reformed, and reconciled to their God, and the people of Canaan hardened to their own ruin.

Verses 6–9

Joshua's concern for the honour of God, more than even for the fate of Israel, was the language of the Spirit of adoption. He pleaded with God. He laments their defeat, as he feared it would reflect on God's wisdom and power, his goodness and faithfulness. We cannot at any time urge a better plea than this, Lord, what wilt thou do for thy great name? Let God be glorified in all, and then welcome his whole will.

Verses 10–15

God awakens Joshua to inquiry, by telling him that when this accursed thing was put away, all would be well. Times of danger and trouble should be times of reformation. We should look at home, into our own hearts, into our own houses, and make diligent search to find out if there be not some accursed thing there, which God sees and abhors; some secret lust, some unlawful gain, some undue withholding from God or from others. We cannot prosper, until the accursed thing be destroyed out of our hearts, and put out of our habitations and our families, and forsaken in our lives. When the sin of sinners finds them out, God is to be acknowledged. With a certain and unerring judgment, the righteous God does and will distinguish between the innocent and the guilty; so that though the righteous are of the same tribe, and family, and household with the wicked, yet they never shall be treated as the wicked.

Verses 16–26

See the folly of those that promise themselves secrecy in sin. The righteous God has many ways of bringing to light the hidden works of darkness. See also, how much it is our concern, when God is contending with us, to find out the cause that troubles us. We must pray with holy Job, Lord, show me wherefore thou contendest with me. Achan's sin began in the eye. He saw these fine things, as Eve saw the forbidden fruit. See what comes of suffering the heart to walk after the eyes, and what need we have to make this covenant with our eyes, that if they wander they shall be sure to weep for it. It proceeded out of the heart. They that would be kept from sinful actions, must mortify and check in themselves sinful desires, particularly the desire of worldly wealth. Had Achan looked upon these things with an eye of faith, he would have seen they were accursed things, and would have dreaded them; but looking on them with an eye of sense only, he saw them as goodly things, and coveted them. When he had committed the sin, he tried to hide it. As soon as he had got this plunder, it became his burden, and he dared not to use his ill-gotten treasure. So differently do objects of temptation appear at a distance, to what they do when they have been gotten. See the deceitfulness of sin; that which is pleasing in the commission, is bitter in the reflection. See how they will be deceived that rob God. Sin is a very troublesome thing, not only to a sinner himself, but to all about him. The righteous God will certainly recompense tribulation to them that trouble his people. Achan perished not alone in his sin. They lose their own, who grasp at more than their own. His sons and daughters were put to death with him. It is probable that they helped to hide the things; they must have known of them. What fatal consequences follow, even in this world, to the sinner himself, and to all belonging him! One sinner destroys much good. What, then, will be the wrath to come? Let us flee from it to Christ Jesus as the sinner's Friend. There are circumstances in the confession of Achan, marking the progress of sin, from its first entrance into the heart to its being done, which may serve as the history of almost every offence against the law of God, and the sacrifice of Jesus Christ.

Chapter 8

Verses 1, 2

When we have faithfully put away sin, that accursed thing which separates between us and God, then, and not till then, we may look to hear from God to our comfort; and God's directing us how to go on in our Christian work and warfare, is a good evidence of his being reconciled to us. God encouraged Joshua to proceed. At Ai the spoil was not to be destroyed as at Jericho, therefore there was no danger of the people's committing such a trespass. Achan, who caught at forbidden spoil, lost that, and life, and all; but the rest of the people, who kept themselves from the accursed thing, were quickly rewarded for their obedience. The way to have the comfort of what God allows us, is, to keep from what he forbids us. No man shall lose by self-denial.

Verses 3–22

Observe Joshua's conduct and prudence. Those that would maintain their spiritual conflicts must not love their ease. Probably he went into the valley alone, to pray to God for a blessing, and he did not seek in vain. He never drew back till the work was done. Those that have stretched out their hands against their spiritual enemies, must never draw them back.

Verses 23–29

God, the righteous Judge, had sentenced the Canaanites for their wickedness; the Israelites only executed his doom. None of their conduct can be drawn into an example for others. Especial reason no doubt there was for this severity to the king of Ai; it is likely he had been notoriously wicked and vile, and a blasphemer of the God of Israel.

Verses 30–35

As soon as Joshua got to the mountains Ebal and Gerizim, without delay, and without caring for the unsettled state of Israel, or their enemies, he confirmed the covenant of the Lord with his people, as appointed, De **11**; **27**. We must not think to defer covenanting with God till we are settled in the world; nor must any business put us from minding and pursuing the one thing needful. The way to prosper is to begin with God, Mt **6**:**33**. They built an altar, and offered sacrifice to God, in token of their dedicating themselves to God, as living sacrifices to his honour, in and by a Mediator. By Christ's sacrifice of himself for us, we have peace with God. It is a great mercy to any people to have the law of God in writing, and it is fit that the written law should be in a known tongue, that it may be seen and read of all men.

Chapter 9

Verses 1, 2

Hitherto the Canaanites had defended themselves, but here they consult to attack Israel. Their minds were blinded, and their hearts hardened to their destruction. Though often at enmity with each other, yet they united against Israel. Oh that Israel would learn of Canaanites, to sacrifice private interests to the public welfare, and to lay aside all quarrels among themselves, that they may unite against the enemies of God's kingdom! (Jos **9**:**3-13**)

Verses 3–13

Other people heard these tidings, and were driven thereby to make war upon Israel; but the Gibeonites were led to make peace with them. Thus the discovery of the glory and the grace of God in the gospel, is to some a savour of life unto life, but to others a savour of death unto death, **2**Co **2**:**16**. The same sun softens wax and hardens clay. The falsehood of the Gibeonites cannot be justified. We must not do evil that good may themselves to the God of Israel, we have reason to think Joshua would have been directed by the oracle of God to spare their lives. But when they had once said, "We are come from a far country," they were led to say it made of skins, and their clothes: one lie brings on another, and that a third, and so on. The way of that sin is especially down-hill. Yet their faith and prudence are to be commended. In submitting to Israel they submitted to the God of Israel, which implied forsaking their idolatries. And how can we do better than cast ourselves upon the mercy of a God of all goodness? The way to avoid judgment is to meet it by repentance. Let us do like these Gibeonites, seek peace with God in the rags of abasement, and godly sorrow; so our sin shall not be our ruin. Let us be servants to Jesus, our blessed Joshua, and we shall live.

Verses 14–21

The Israelites, having examined the provisions of the Gibeonites, hastily concluded that they confirmed their account. We make more haste than good speed, when we stay not to take God with us, and do not consult him by the word and prayer. The fraud was soon found out. A lying tongue is but for a moment. Had the oath been in itself unlawful, it would not have been binding; for no obligation can render it our duty to commit a sin. But it was not unlawful to spare the Canaanites who submitted, and left idolatry, desiring only that their lives might be spared. A citizen of Zion swears to his own hurt, and changes not, Ps **15**:**4**. Joshua and the princes, when they found that they had been deceived, did not apply to Eleazar the high priest to be freed from their engagement, much less did they pretend that no faith is to be kept with those to whom they had sworn. Let this convince us how we ought to keep our promises, and make good our bargains; and what conscience we ought to make of our words.

Verses 22–27

The Gibeonites do not justify their lie, but plead that they did it to save their lives. And the fear was not merely of the power of man; one might flee from that to the Divine protection; but of the power of God himself, which they saw engaged against them. Joshua sentences them to perpetual bondage. They must be servants, but any work becomes honourable, when it is done for the house of the Lord, and the offices thereof. Let us, in like manner, submit to our Lord Jesus, saying, We are in thy hand, do unto us as seemeth good and right unto thee, only save our souls; and we shall not repent it. If He appoints us to bear his cross, and serve him, that shall be neither shame nor grief to us, while the meanest office in God's service will entitle us to a dwelling in the house of the Lord all the days of our life. And in coming to the Saviour, we do not proceed upon a peradventure. We are invited to draw nigh, and are assured that him that cometh to Him, he will in nowise cast out. Even those things which sound harsh, and are humbling, and form sharp trials of our sincerity, will prove of real advantage.

Chapter 10

Verses 1–6

When sinners leave the service of Satan and the friendship of the world, that they make peace with God and join Israel, they must not marvel if the world hate them, if their former friends become foes. By such methods Satan discourages many who are convinced of their danger, and almost persuaded to be Christians, but fear the cross. These things should quicken us to apply to God for protection, help, and deliverance.

Verses 7–14

The meanest and most feeble, who have just begun to trust the Lord, are as much entitled to be protected as those who have long and faithfully been his servants. It is our duty to defend the afflicted, who, like the Gibeonites, are brought into trouble on our account, or for the sake of the gospel. Joshua would not forsake his new vassals. How much less shall our true Joshua fail those who trust in Him! We may be wanting in our trust, but our trust never can want success. Yet God's promises are not to slacken and do away, but to quicken and encourage our endeavours. Notice the great faith of Joshua, and the power of God answering it by the miraculous staying of the sun, that the day of Israel's victories might be made longer. Joshua acted on this occasion by impulse on his mind from the Spirit of God. It was not necessary that Joshua should speak, or the miracle be recorded, according to the modern terms of astronomy. The sun appeared to the Israelites over Gibeon, and the moon over the valley of Ajalon, and there they appeared to be stopped on their course for one whole day. Is any thing too hard for the Lord? forms a sufficient answer to ten thousand difficulties, which objectors have in every age started against the truth of God as revealed in his written word. Proclamation was hereby made to the neighbouring nations, Behold the works of the Lord, and say, What nation is there so great as Israel, who has God so nigh unto them?

Verses 15–27

None moved his tongue against any of the children of Israel. This shows their perfect safety. The kings were called to an account, as rebels against the Israel of God. Refuges of lies will but secure for God's judgment. God punished the abominable wickedness of these kings, the measure of whose iniquity was now full. And by this public act of justice, done upon these ringleaders of the Canaanites in sin, he would possess his people with the greater dread and detestation of the sins of the nations that God cast out from before them. Here is a type and figure of Christ's victories over the powers of darkness, and of believers' victories through him. In our spiritual conflicts we must not be satisfied with obtaining some important victory. We must pursue our scattered enemies, searching out the remains of sin as they rise up in our hearts, and thus pursue the conquest. In so doing, the Lord will afford light until the warfare be accomplished.

Verses 28–43

Joshua made speed in taking these cities. See what a great deal of work may be done in a little time, if we will be diligent, and improve our opportunities. God here showed his hatred of the idolatries and other abominations of which the Canaanites had been guilty, and shows us how great the provocation was, by the greatness of the destruction brought upon them. Here also was typified the destruction of all the enemies of the Lord Jesus, who, having slighted the riches of his grace, must for ever feel the weight of his wrath. The Lord fought for Israel. They could not have gotten the victory, if God had not undertaken the battle. We conquer when God fights for us; if he be for us, who can be against us?

Chapter 11

Verses 1–9

The wonders God wrought for the Israelites were to encourage them to act vigorously themselves. Thus the war against Satan's kingdom, carried on by preaching the gospel, was at first forwarded by miracles; but being fully proved to be of God, we are now left to the Divine grace in the usual course, in the use of the sword of the Spirit. God encouraged Joshua. Fresh dangers and difficulties make it necessary to seek fresh supports from the word of God, which we have nigh unto us for use in every time of need. God proportions our trials to our strength, and our strength to our trials. Joshua's obedience in destroying the horses and chariots, shows his self-denial in compliance with God's command. The possession of things on which the carnal heart is prone to depend, is hurtful to the life of faith, and the walk with God; therefore it is better to be without worldly advantages, than to have the soul endangered by them. (Jos **11**:**10-14**)

Verses 10–14

The Canaanites filled up the measure of their iniquity, and were, as a judgment, left to the pride, obstinacy, and enmity of their hearts, and to the power of Satan; all restraints being withdrawn, while the dispensations of Providence tended to drive them to despair. They brought on themselves the vengeance they justly merited, of which the Israelites were to be executioners, by the command the Lord gave to Moses.

Verses 15–23

Never let the sons of Anak be a terror to the Israel of God, for their day to fall will come. The land rested from war. It ended not in a peace with the Canaanites, that was forbidden, but in a peace from them. There is a rest, a rest from war, remaining for the people of God, into which they shall enter, when their warfare is accomplished. That which was now done, is compared with what had been said to Moses. God's word and his works, if viewed together, will be found mutually to set each other forth. If we make conscience of our duty, we need not question the performance of the promise. But the believer must never put off his armour, or expect lasting peace, till he closes his eyes in death; nay, as his strength and usefulness increase, he may expect more heavy trials; yet the Lord will not permit any enemies to assault the believer till he has prepared him for the battle. Christ Jesus ever lives to plead for his people, and their faith shall not fail, however Satan may be permitted to assault them. And however tedious, sharp, and difficult the believer's warfare, his patience in tribulation may be encouraged by the joyfulness of hope; for he will, ere long, rest from sin and from sorrow in the Canaan above.

Chapter 12

Verses 1–6

Fresh mercies must not drown the remembrance of former mercies, nor must the glory of the present instruments of good to the church diminish the just honour of those who went before them, since God is the same who wrought by both. Moses gave to one part of Israel a very rich and fruitful country, but it was on the outside of Jordan. Joshua gave to all Israel the holy land, within Jordan. So the law has given to some few of God's spiritual Israel worldly blessings, earnests of good things to come; but our Lord Jesus, the true Joshua, provided for all the children of promise spiritual blessings, and the heavenly Canaan.

Verses 7–24

We have here the limits of the country Joshua conquered. A list is given of the kings subdued by Israel: thirty-one in all. This shows how fruitful Canaan then was, in which so many chose to throng together. This was the land God appointed for Israel; yet in our day it is one of the most barren and unprofitable countries in the world. Such is the effect of the curse it lies under, since its possessors rejected Christ and his gospel, as was foretold by Moses, De **29**:**23**. The vengeance of a righteous God, inflicted on all these kings and their subjects, for their wickedness, should make us dread and hate sin. The fruitful land bestowed on his chosen people, should fill our hearts with hope and confidence in his mercy, and with humble gratitude.

Chapter 13

Verses 1–6

At this chapter begins the account of the dividing of the land of Canaan among the tribes of Israel by lot; a narrative showing the performance of the promise made to the fathers, that this land should be given to the seed of Jacob. We are not to pass over these chapters of hard names as useless. Where God has a mouth to speak, and a hand to write, we should find an ear to hear, and an eye to read; and may God give us a heart to profit! Joshua is supposed to have been about one hundred years old at this time. It is good for those who are old and stricken in years to be put in remembrance of their being so. God considers the frame of his people, and would not have them burdened with work above their strength. And all people, especially old people, should set to do that quickly which must be done before they die, lest death prevent them, Ec **9**:**10**. God promise that he would make the Israelites masters of all the countries yet unsubdued, through Joshua was old, and not able to do it; old, and not likely to live to see it done. Whatever becomes of us, and however we may be laid aside as despised, broken vessels, God will do his own work in his own time. We must work out our salvation, then God will work in us, and work with us; we must resist our spiritual enemies, then God will tread them under our feet; we must go forth to our Christian work and warfare, then God will go forth before us.

Verses 7–33

The land must be divided among the tribes. It is the will of God that every man should know his own, and not take that which is another's. The world must be governed, not by force, but right. Wherever our habitation is placed, and in whatever honest way our portion is assigned, we should consider them as allotted of God; we should be thankful for, and use them as such, while every prudent method should be used to prevent disputes about property, both at present and in future. Joshua must be herein a type of Christ, who has not only conquered the gates of hell for us, but has opened to us the gates of heaven, and having purchased the eternal inheritance for all believers, will put them in possession of it. Here is a general description of the country given to the two tribes and a half, by Moses. Israel must know their own, and keep to it; and may not, under pretence of their being God's peculiar people, encroach on their neighbours. Twice in this chapter it is noticed, that to the tribe of Levi Moses gave no inheritance: see Nu **18**:**20**. Their maintenance must be brought out of all the tribes. The ministers of the Lord should show themselves indifferent about worldly interests, and the people should take care they want nothing suitable. And happy are those who have the Lord God of Israel for their inheritance, though little of this world falls to their lot. His providences will supply their wants, his consolations will support their souls, till they gain heavenly joy and everlasting pleasures.

Chapter 14

Verses 1–5

The Israelites must occupy the new conquests. Canaan would have been subdued in vain, if it had not been inhabited. Yet every man might not go and settle where he pleased. God shall choose our inheritance for us. Let us survey our heritage of present mercy, our prospect for the land of promise, eternal in the heavens. Is God any respecter of persons? Is it not better that our place, as to earthly good or sorrow, should be determined by the infinite wisdom of our heavenly Father, than by our own ignorance? Should not those for whom the great mystery of godliness was exhibited, those whose redemption was purchased by Jesus Christ, thankfully refer their earthly concerns to his appointment?

Verses 6–15

Caleb's request is, "Give me this mountain," or Hebron, because it was formerly in God's promise to him, and he would let Israel knows how much he valued the promise. Those who live by faith value that which is given by God's promise, far above what is given by his providence only. It was now in the Anakims' possession, and Caleb would let Israel know how little he feared the enemy, and that he would encourage them to push on their conquests. Caleb answered to his name, which signifies "all heart." Hebron was settled on Caleb and his heirs, because he wholly followed the Lord God of Israel. Happy are we if we follow him. Singular piety shall be crowned with singular favour.

Chapter 15

Verses 1–12

Joshua allotted to Judah, Ephraim, and the half of Manasseh, their inheritances before they left Gilgal. Afterwards removing to Shiloh, another survey was made, and the other tribes had their portion assigned. In due time all God's people are settled.

Verses 13–19

Achsah obtained some land by Caleb's free grant. He gave her a south land. Land indeed, but a south land, dry and apt to be parched. She obtained more, on her request, and he gave the upper and the nether springs. Those who understand it but of one field, watered both with the rain of heaven, and the springs that issued out of the earth, countenance the allusion commonly made to this, when we pray for spiritual and heavenly blessings which relate to our souls, as blessings of the upper springs, and those which relate to the body and the life that now is, as blessings of the nether springs. All the blessings, both of the upper and the nether springs, belong to the children of God. As related to Christ, they have them freely given of the Father, for the lot of their inheritance.

Verses 20–63

Here is a list of the cities of Judah. But we do not here find Bethlehem, afterwards the city of David, and ennobled by the birth of our Lord Jesus in it. That city, which, at the best, was but little among the thousands of Judah, Mic **5**:**2**, except that it was thus honoured, was now so little as not to be accounted one of the cities.

Chapter 16

The sons of Joseph.

—This and the following chapter should not be separated. They give the lots of Ephraim and Manasseh, the children of Joseph, who, next to Judah, were to have the post of honour, and therefore had the first and best portion in the northern part of Canaan, as Judah in the southern part. God's people now, as of old, suffer his enemies to remain. Blessed Lord, when will all our enemies be subdued? 1Co **15**:**26**. Do thou drive them all out; thou alone canst do it. These settled boundaries may remind us, that our situation and provision in this life, as well as our future inheritance, are appointed by the only wise and righteous God, and we should be content with our portion, since he knows what is best for us, and all we have is more than we deserve.

Chapter 17

Verses 1–6

Manasseh was but half of the tribe of Joseph, yet it was divided into two parts. The daughters of Zelophehad now reaped the benefit of their pious zeal and prudent forecast. Those who take care in the wilderness of this world, to make sure to themselves a place in the inheritance of the saints in light, will have the comfort of it in the other world; while those who neglect it now, will lose it for ever. Lord, teach us here to believe and obey, and give us an inheritance among thy saints, in glory everlasting.

Verses 7–13

There was great communication between Manasseh and Ephraim. Though each tribe had its inheritance, yet they should intermix one with another, to do good offices one to another, as became those, who, though of different tribes, were all one Israel, and were bound to love as brethren. But they suffered the Canaanites to live among them, against the command of God, to serve their own ends.

Verses 14–18

Joshua, as a public person, had no more regard to his own tribe than to any other, but would govern without favour or affection; wherein he has left a good example to all in public trusts. Joshua tells them, that what was fallen to their share would be a sufficient lot for them, if they would but work and fight. Men excuse themselves from labour by any pretence; and nothing serves the purpose better than having rich and powerful relations, able to provide for them; and they are apt to desire a partial and unfaithful disposal of what is intrusted to those they think able to give such help. But there is more real kindness in pointing out the advantages within reach, and in encouraging men to make the best of them, than in granting indulgences to sloth and extravagance. True religion gives no countenance to these evils. The rule is, They shall not eat who will not work; and many of our "cannots" are only the language of idleness, which magnifies every difficulty and danger. This is especially the case in our spiritual work and warfare. Without Christ we can do nothing, but we are apt to sit still and attempt nothing. if we belong to Him, he will stir us up to our best endeavours, and to cry to him for help. Then our coast will be enlarged, **1**Ch **4**:**9**, **10**, and complainings silenced, or rather, turned into joyful thanksgivings.

Chapter 18

Verse 1

Shiloh was in the lot of Ephraim, the tribe to which Joshua belonged, and it was proper that the tabernacle should be near the residence of the chief governor. The name of this city is the same as that by which Jacob prophesied of the Messiah, Ge **49**:**10**. It is supposed by some that the city was thus called, when it was chosen for the resting-place of the ark, which typified our great Peace-maker, and the way by him to a reconciled God.

Verses 2–10

After a year or more, Joshua blamed their slackness, and told them how to proceed. God, by his grace, has given us a title to a good land, the heavenly Canaan, but we are slack to take possession of it; we enter not into that rest, as we might by faith, and hope, and holy joy. How long shall it be thus with us? How long shall we thus stand in our own light, and forsake our own mercies for lying vanities? Joshua stirs the Israelites up to take possession of their lots. He is ready to do his part, if they will do theirs.

Verses 11–28

The boundaries of each portion were distinctly drawn, and the inheritance of each tribe settled. All contests and selfish claims were prevented by the wise appointment of God, who allotted the hill and the valley, the corn and pasture, the brooks and rivers, the towns and cities. Is the lot of any servant of Christ cast in affliction and sorrow? It is the Lord; let him do what seemeth him good. Are we in prosperity and peace? It is from above. Be humbled when you compare the gift with your own unworthiness. Forget not Him that gave the good, and always be ready to resign it at his command.

Chapter 19

Verses 1–9

The men of Judah did not oppose taking away the cities within their border, when convinced that they had more than was right. If a true believer has obtained an unintended and improper advantage in any thing, he will give it up without murmuring. Love seeketh not her own, and doth not behave unseemly; it will induce those in whom it richly dwells, to part with their own to supply what is lacking to their brethren.

Verses 10–16

In the division to each tribe of Israel, the prophetic blessings of Jacob were fulfilled. They chose for themselves, or it was divided to them by lot, in the manner and places that he foresaw. So sure a rule to go by is the word of prophecy: we see by it what to believe, and it proves beyond all dispute the things that are of God.

Verses 17–51

Joshua waited till all the tribes were settled, before he asked any provision for himself. He was content to be unfixed, till he saw them all placed, and herein is an example to all in public places, to prefer the common welfare before private advantage. Those who labour most to do good to others, seek an inheritance in the Canaan above: but it will be soon enough to enter thereon, when they have done all the service to their brethren of which they are capable. Nor can any thing more effectually assure them of their title to it, than endeavouring to bring others to desire, to seek, and to obtain it. Our Lord Jesus came and dwelt on earth, not in pomp but poverty, providing rest for man, yet himself not having where to lay his head; for Christ pleased not himself. Nor would he enter upon his inheritance, till by his obedience to death he secured the eternal inheritance for all his people; nor will he account his own glory completed, till every ransomed sinner is put in possession of his heavenly rest.

Chapter 20

Verses 1–6

When the Israelites were settled in their promised inheritance, they were reminded to set apart the cities of refuge, whose use and typical meaning have been explained, Nu **35**; De **19**. God's spiritual Israel have, and shall have in Christ and heaven, not only rest to repose in, but refuge to secure themselves in. These cities were designed to typify the relief which the gospel provides for penitent sinners, and their protection from the curse of the law and the wrath of God, in our Lord Jesus, to whom believers flee for refuge, Heb **6**:**18**.

Verses 7–9

These cities, as those also on the other side Jordan, stood so that a man might in half a day reach one of them from any part of the country. God is ever a Refuge at hand. They were all Levites' cities. It was kindness to the poor fugitive, that when he might not go up to the house of the Lord, yet he had the servants of God with him, to instruct him, and pray for him, and to help to make up the want of public ordinances. Some observe a significance in the names of these cities with application to Christ our Refuge. Kedesh signifies holy, and our Refuge is the holy Jesus. Shechem, a shoulder, and the government is upon his shoulder. Hebron, fellowship, and believers are called into the fellowship of Christ Jesus our Lord. Bezer, a fortification, for he is a strong hold to all those that trust in him. Ramoth, high or exalted, for Him hath God exalted with his own right hand. Golan, joy or exultation, for in Him all the saints are justified, and shall glory.

Chapter 21

Verses 1–8

The Levites waited till the other tribes were provided for, before they preferred their claim to Joshua. They build their claim upon a very good foundation; not their own merits or services, but the Divine precept. The maintenance of ministers is not a thing left merely to the will of the people, that they may let them starve if they please; they which preach the gospel should live by the gospel, and should live comfortably. (Jos **21**:**9-42**)

Verses 9–42

By mixing the Levites with the other tribes, they were made to see that the eyes of all Israel were upon them, and therefore it was their concern to walk so that their ministry might not be blamed. Every tribe had its share of Levites' cities. Thus did God graciously provide for keeping up religion among them, and that they might have the word in all parts of the land. Yet, blessed be God, we have the gospel more diffused amongst us. (Jos **21**:**43-45**)

Verses 43–45

God promised to give to the seed of Abraham the land of Canaan for a possession, and now they possessed it, and dwelt therein. And the promise of the heavenly Canaan is as sure to all God's spiritual Israel; for it is the promise of Him that cannot lie. There stood not a man before them. The after-prevalence of the Canaanites was the effect of Israel's slothfulness, and the punishment of their sinful inclination to the idolatries and abominations of the heathen whom they harboured and indulged. There failed not aught of any good thing, which the Lord had spoken to the house of Israel. In due season all his promises will be accomplished; then will his people acknowledge that the Lord has exceeded their largest expectations, and made them more than conquerors, and brought them to their desired rest.

Chapter 22

Verses 1–9

Joshua dismisses the tribes with good counsel. Those who have the commandment have it in vain, unless they do the commandment; and it will not be done aright unless we take diligent heed. In particular to love the Lord our God, as the best of beings, and the best of friends; and as far as that principle rules in the heart, there will be constant care and endeavour to walk in his ways, even those that are narrow and up-hill. In every instance to keep his commandments. At all times, and in all conditions, with purpose of heart to cleave unto the Lord, and to serve him and his kingdom among men, with all our heart, and with all our soul. This good counsel is given to all; may God give us grace to take it!

Verses 10–20

Here is the care of the separated tribes to keep their hold of Canaan's religion. At first sight it seemed a design to set up an altar against the altar at Shiloh. God is jealous for his own institutions; we should be so too, and afraid of every thing that looks like, or leads to idolatry. Corruptions in religion are best dealt with at first. But their prudence in following up this zealous resolution is no less commendable. Many an unhappy strife would be prevented, or soon made up, by inquiries into the matter of the offence. The remembrance of great sins committed formerly, should engage us to stand on our guard against the beginnings of sin; for the way of sin is down-hill. We are all concerned to reprove our neighbour when he does amiss, lest we suffer sin upon him, Le **19**:**17**. The offer made that they should be welcome to come to the land where the Lord's tabernacle was, and settle there, was in the spirit of true Israelites.

Verses 21–29

The tribes took the reproofs of their brethren in good part. With solemnity and meekness they proceeded to give all the satisfaction in their power. Reverence of God is expressed in the form of their appeal. This brief confession of faith would remove their brethren's suspicion that they intended to worship other gods. Let us always speak of God with seriousness, and mention his name with a solemn pause. Those who make appeals to Heaven with a careless "God knows," take his name in vain: it is very unlike this. They express great confidence of their own uprightness in the matter of their appeal. "God knows it," for he is perfectly acquainted with the thoughts and intents of the heart. In every thing we do in religion, it highly concerns us to approve ourselves to God, remembering that he knows the heart. And if our sincerity be known to God, we should study likewise to let others know it by its fruits, especially those who, though they mistake us, show zeal for the glory of God. They disdained the design of which they were suspected to be guilty, and fully explained their true intent in building this altar. Those who have found the comfort and benefit of God's ordinances, cannot but desire to preserve them to their seed, and to use all possible care that their children may be looked upon as having a part in him. Christ is the great Altar that sanctifies every gift; the best evidence of our interest in him is the work of his Spirit in our hearts.

Verses 30–34

It is well that there was on both sides a disposition to peace, as there was a zeal for God; for quarrels about religion, for want of wisdom and love, often prove the most fierce and difficult to be made up. Proud and peevish spirits, when they have passed any unjust blame on their brethren, though full evidence be brought of its unfairness, can by no means be persuaded to withdraw it. But Israel was not so prejudiced. They looked upon their brethren's innocence as a token of God's presence. Our brethren's zeal for the power of godliness, and faith and love, notwithstanding the fears of their breaking the unity of the church, are things of which we should be very glad to be satisfied. The altar was called ED, a witness. It was a witness of their care to keep their religion pure and entire, and would witness against their descendants, if they should turn from following after the Lord. Happy will it be when all professed Christians learn to copy the example of Israel, to unite zeal and steady adherence to the cause of truth, with candour, meekness, and readiness to understand each other, to explain and to be satisfied with the explanations of their brethren. May the Lord increase the number of those who endeavour to keep the unity of the Spirit in the bond of peace! may increasing grace and consolation be with all who love Jesus Christ in sincerity!

Chapter 23

Verses 1–10

Joshua was old and dying, let them observe what he said now. He put them in mind of the great things God had done for them in his days. He exhorted them to be very courageous. Keep with care, do with diligence, and regard with sincerity what is written. Also, very cautiously to endeavour that the heathen idolatry may be forgotten, so that it may never be revived. It is sad that among Christians the names of the heathen gods are so commonly used, and made so familiar as they are. Joshua exhorts them to be very constant. There might be many things amiss among them, but they had not forsaken the Lord their God; the way to make people better, is to make the best of them.

Verses 11–16

Would we cleave to the Lord, we must always stand upon our guard, for many a soul is lost through carelessness. Love the Lord your God, and you will not leave him. Has God been thus true to you? Be not you false to him. He is faithful that has promised, Heb **10**:**23**. The experience of every Christian witnesses the same truth. Conflicts may have been severe and long, trials great and many; but at the last he will acknowledge that goodness and mercy followed him all the days of his life. Joshua states the fatal consequences of going back; know for a certainty it will be your ruin. The first step would be, friendship with idolaters; the next would be, marrying with them; the end of that would be, serving their gods. Thus the way of sin is down-hill, and those who have fellowship with sinners, cannot avoid having fellowship with sin. He describes the destruction he warns them of. The goodness of the heavenly Canaan, and the free and sure grant God has made of it, will add to the misery of those who shall for ever be shut out from it. Nothing will make them see how wretched they are, so much, as to see how happy they might have been. Let us watch and pray against temptation. Let us trust in God's faithfulness, love, and power; let us plead his promises, and cleave to his commandments, then we shall be happy in life, in death, and for ever.

Chapter 24

Verses 1–14

We must never think our work for God done, till our life is done. If he lengthen out our days beyond what we expected, like those of Joshua, it is because he has some further service for us to do. He who aims at the same mind which was in Christ Jesus, will glory in bearing the last testimony to his Saviour's goodness, and in telling to all around, the obligations with which the unmerited goodness of God has bound him. The assembly came together in a solemn religious manner. Joshua spake to them in God's name, and as from him. His sermon consists of doctrine and application. The doctrinal part is a history of the great things God had done for his people, and for their fathers before them. The application of this history of God's mercies to them, is an exhortation to fear and serve God, in gratitude for his favour, and that it might be continued.

Verses 15–28

It is essential that the service of God's people be performed with a willing mind. For LOVE is the only genuine principle whence all acceptable service of God can spring. The Father seeks only such to worship him, as worship him in spirit and in truth. The carnal mind of man is enmity against God, therefore, is not capable of such spiritual worship. Hence the necessity of being born again. But numbers rest in mere forms, as tasks imposed upon them. Joshua puts them to their choice; but not as if it were indifferent whether they served God or not. Choose you whom ye will serve, now the matter is laid plainly before you. He resolves to do this, whatever others did. Those that are bound for heaven, must be willing to swim against the stream. They must not do as the most do, but as the best do. And no one can behave himself as he ought in any station, who does not deeply consider his religious duties in family relations. The Israelites agree with Joshua, being influenced by the example of a man who had been so great a blessing to them; We also will serve the Lord. See how much good great men do, by their influence, if zealous in religion. Joshua brings them to express full purpose of heart to cleave to the Lord. They must come off from all confidence in their own sufficiency, else their purposes would be in vain. The service of God being made their deliberate choice, Joshua binds them to it by a solemn covenant. He set up a monument of it. In this affecting manner Joshua took his last leave of them; if they perished, their blood would be upon their own heads. Though the house of God, the Lord's table, and even the walls and trees before which we have uttered our solemn purposes of serving him, would bear witness against us if we deny him, yet we may trust in him, that he will put his fear into our hearts, that we shall not depart from him. God alone can give grace, yet he blesses our endeavours to engage men to his service.

Verses 29–33

Joseph died in Egypt, but gave commandment concerning his bones, that they should not rest in their grave till Israel had rest in the land of promise. Notice also the death and burial of Joshua, and of Eleazar the chief priest. The most useful men, having served their generation, according to the will of God, one after another, fall asleep and see corruption. But Jesus, having spent and ended his life on earth more effectually than either Joshua or Joseph, rose from the dead, and saw no corruption. And the redeemed of the Lord shall inherit the kingdom he prepared for them from the foundation of the world. They will say in admiration of the grace of Jesus, Unto him that loved us, and washed us from our sins in his own blood, and hath made us kings and priests unto God and his Father, to him be glory and dominion for ever and ever. Amen.

Judges

The book of Judges is the history of Israel during the government of the Judges, who were occasional deliverers, raised up by God to rescue Israel from their oppressors, to reform the state of religion, and to administer justice to the people. The state of God's people does not appear in this book so prosperous, nor their character so religious, as might have been expected; but there were many believers among them, and the tabernacle service was attended to. The history exemplifies the frequent warnings and predictions of Moses, and should have close attention. The whole is full of important instruction.

Chapter 1

Verses 1–8

The Israelites were convinced that the war against the Canaanites was to be continued; but they were in doubt as to the manner in which it was to be carried on after the death of Joshua. In these respects they inquired of the Lord. God appoints service according to the strength he has given. From those who are most able, most work is expected. Judah was first in dignity, and must be first in duty. Judah's service will not avail unless God give success; but God will not give the success, unless Judah applies to the service. Judah was the most considerable of all the tribes, and Simeon the least; yet Judah begs Simeon's friendship, and prays for aid from him. It becomes Israelites to help one another against Canaanites; and all Christians, even those of different tribes, should strengthen one another. Those who thus help one another in love, have reason to hope that God will graciously help both. Adoni-bezek was taken prisoner. This prince had been a severe tyrant. The Israelites, doubtless under the Divine direction, made him suffer what he had done to others; and his own conscience confessed that he was justly treated as he had treated others. Thus the righteous God sometimes, in his providence, makes the punishment answer the sin.

Verses 9–20

The Canaanites had iron chariots; but Israel had God on their side, whose chariots are thousands of angels, Ps **68**:**17**. Yet they suffered their fears to prevail against their faith. About Caleb we read in Jos **15**:**16–19**. The Kenites had settled in the land. Israel let them fix where they pleased, being a quiet, contented people. They that molested none, were molested by none. Blessed are the meek, for they shall inherit the earth.

Verses 21–36

The people of Israel were very careless of their duty and interest. Owing to slothfulness and cowardice, they would not be at the pains to complete their conquests. It was also owing to their covetousness: they were willing to let the Canaanites live among them, that they might make advantage of them. They had not the dread and detestation of idolatry they ought to have had. The same unbelief that kept their fathers forty years out of Canaan, kept them now out of the full possession of it. Distrust of the power and promise of God deprived them of advantages, and brought them into troubles. Thus many a believer who begins well is hindered. His graces languish, his lusts revive, Satan plies him with suitable temptations, the world recovers its hold; he brings guilt into his conscience, anguish into his heart, discredit on his character, and reproach on the gospel. Though he may have sharp rebukes, and be so recovered that he does not perish, yet he will have deeply to lament his folly through his remaining days; and upon his dying bed to mourn over the opportunities of glorifying God and serving the church he has lost. We can have no fellowship with the enemies of God within us or around us, but to our hurt; therefore our only wisdom is to maintain unceasing war against them.

Chapter 2

Verses 1–5

It was the great Angel of the covenant, the Word, the Son of God, who spake with Divine authority as Jehovah, and now called them to account for their disobedience. God sets forth what he had done for Israel, and what he had promised. Those who throw off communion with God, and have fellowship with the unfruitful works of darkness, know not what they do now, and will have nothing to say for themselves in the day of account shortly. They must expect to suffer for this their folly. Those deceive themselves who expect advantages from friendship with God's enemies. God often makes men's sin their punishment; and thorns and snares are in the way of the froward, who will walk contrary to God. The people wept, crying out against their own folly and ingratitude. They trembled at the word, and not without cause. It is a wonder sinners can ever read the Bible with dry eyes. Had they kept close to God and their duty, no voice but that of singing had been heard in their congregation; but by their sin and folly they made other work for themselves, and nothing is to be heard but the voice of weeping. The worship of God, in its own nature, is joy, praise, and thanksgiving; our sins alone render weeping needful. It is pleasing to see men weep for their sins; but our tears, prayers, and even amendment, cannot atone for sin.

Verses 6–23

We have a general idea of the course of things in Israel, during the time of the Judges. The nation made themselves as mean and miserable by forsaking God, as they would have been great and happy if they had continued faithful to him. Their punishment answered to the evil they had done. They served the gods of the nations round about them, even the meanest, and God made them serve the princes of the nations round about them, even the meanest. Those who have found God true to his promises, may be sure that he will be as true to his threatenings. He might in justice have abandoned them, but he could not for pity do it. The Lord was with the judges when he raised them up, and so they became saviours. In the days of the greatest distress of the church, there shall be some whom God will find or make fit to help it. The Israelites were not thoroughly reformed; so mad were they upon their idols, and so obstinately bent to backslide. Thus those who have forsaken the good ways of God, which they have once known and professed, commonly grow most daring and desperate in sin, and have their hearts hardened. Their punishment was, that the Canaanites were spared, and so they were beaten with their own rod. Men cherish and indulge their corrupt appetites and passions; therefore God justly leaves them to themselves, under the power of their sins, which will be their ruin. God has told us how deceitful and desperately wicked our hearts are, but we are not willing to believe it, until by making bold with temptation we find it true by sad experience. We need to examine how matters stand with ourselves, and to pray without ceasing, that we may be rooted and grounded in love, and that Christ may dwell in our hearts by faith. Let us declare war against every sin, and follow after holiness all our days.

Chapter 3

Verses 1–7

As the Israelites were a type of the church on earth, they were not to be idle and slothful. The Lord was pleased to try them by the remains of the devoted nations they spared. Temptations and trials detect the wickedness of the hearts of sinners; and strengthen he graces of believers in their daily conflict with Satan, sin, and this evil world. They must live in this world, but they are not of it, and are forbidden to conform to it. This marks the difference between the followers of Christ and mere professors. The friendship of the world is more fatal than its enmity; the latter can only kill the body, but the former murders many precious souls.

Verses 8–11

The first judge was Othniel: even in Joshua's time Othniel began to be famous. Soon after Israel's settlement in Canaan their purity began to be corrupted, and their peace disturbed. But affliction makes those cry to God who before would scarcely speak to him. God returned in mercy to them for their deliverance. The Spirit of the Lord came upon Othniel. The Spirit of wisdom and courage to qualify him for the service, and the Spirit of power to excite him to it. He first judged Israel, reproved and reformed them, and then went to war. Let sin at home be conquered, that worst of enemies, then enemies abroad will be more easily dealt with. Thus let Christ be our Judge and Lawgiver, then he will save us.

Verses 12–30

When Israel sins again, God raises up a new oppressor. The Israelites did ill, and the Moabites did worse; yet because God punishes the sins of his own people in this world, Israel is weakened, and Moab strengthened against them. If lesser troubles do not do the work, God will send greater. When Israel prays again, God raises up Ehud. As a judge, or minister of Divine justice, Ehud put to death Eglon, the king of Moab, and thus executed the judgments of God upon him as an enemy to God and Israel. But the law of being subject to principalities and powers in all things lawful, is the rule of our conduct. No such commissions are now given; to pretend to them is to blaspheme God. Notice Ehud's address to Eglon. What message from God but a message of vengeance can a proud rebel expect? Such a message is contained in the word of God; his ministers are boldly to declare it, without fearing the frown, or respecting the persons of sinners. But, blessed be God, they have to deliver a message of mercy and of free salvation; the message of vengeance belongs only to those who neglect the offers of grace. The consequence of this victory was, that the land had rest eighty years. It was a great while for the land to rest; yet what is that to the saints' everlasting rest in the heavenly Canaan.

Verse 31

The side of the country which lay south-west, was infested by the Philistines. God raised up Shamgar to deliver them; having neither sword nor spear, he took an ox-goad, the instrument next at hand. God can make those serviceable to his glory and to his church's good, whose birth, education, and employment, are mean and obscure. It is no matter what the weapon is, if God directs and strengthens the arm. Often he works by unlikely means, that the excellency of the power may appear to be of God.

Chapter 4

Verses 1–3

The land had rest for eighty years, which should have confirmed them in their religion; but it made them secure, and indulge their lusts. Thus the prosperity of fools destroys them. Jabin and his general Sisera, mightily oppressed Israel. This enemy was nearer than any of the former. Israel cried unto the Lord, when distress drove them to him, and they saw no other way of relief. Those who slight God in prosperity, will find themselves under a necessity of seeking him in trouble.

Verses 4–9

Deborah was a prophetess; one instructed in Divine knowledge by the inspiration of the Spirit of God. She judged Israel as God's mouth to them; correcting abuses, and redressing grievances. By God's direction, she ordered Barak to raise an army, and engage Jabin's forces. Barak insisted much upon her presence. Deborah promised to go with him. She would not send him where she would not go herself. Those who in God's name call others to their duty, should be ready to assist them in it. Barak values the satisfaction of his mind, and the good success of his enterprise, more than mere honour.

Verses 10–16

Siser's confidence was chiefly in his chariots. But if we have ground to hope that God goes before us, we may go on with courage and cheerfulness. Be not dismayed at the difficulties thou meetest with in resisting Satan, in serving God, or suffering for him; for is not the Lord gone before thee? Follow him then fully. Barak went down, though upon the plain the iron chariots would have advantage against him: he quitted the mountain in dependence on the Divine power; for in the Lord alone is the salvation of his people, Jer **3**:**23**. He was not deceived in his confidence. When God goes before us in our spiritual conflicts, we must bestir ourselves; and when, by his grace, he gives us some success against the enemies of our souls, we must improve it by watchfulness and resolution.

Verses 17–24

Sisera's chariots had been his pride and his confidence. Thus are those disappointed who rest on the creature; like a broken reed, it not only breaks under them, but pierces them with many sorrows. The idol may quickly become a burden, Isa **46**:**1**; what we were sick for, God can make us sick of. It is probable that Jael really intended kindness to Sisera; but by a Divine impulse she was afterwards led to consider him as the determined enemy of the Lord and of his people, and to destroy him. All our connexions with God's enemies must be broken off, if we would have the Lord for our God, and his people for our people. He that had thought to have destroyed Israel with his many iron chariots, is himself destroyed with one iron nail. Thus the weak things of the world confound the mighty. The Israelites would have prevented much mischief, if they had sooner destroyed the Canaanites, as God commanded and enabled them: but better be wise late, and buy wisdom by experience, than never be wise.

Chapter 5

Verses 1–5

No time should be lost in returning thanks to the Lord for his mercies; for our praises are most acceptable, pleasant, and profitable, when they flow from a full heart. By this, love and gratitude would be more excited and more deeply fixed in the hearts of believers; the events would be more known and longer remembered. Whatever Deborah, Barak, or the army had done, the Lord must have all the praise. The will, the power, and the success were all from Him.

Verses 6–11

Deborah describes the distressed state of Israel under the tyranny of Jabin, that their salvation might appear more gracious. She shows what brought this misery upon them. It was their idolatry. They chose new gods, with new names. But under all these images, Satan was worshipped. Deborah was a mother to Israel, by diligently promoting the salvation of their souls. She calls on those who shared the advantages of this great salvation, to offer up thanks to God for it. Let such as are restored, not only to their liberty as other Israelites, but to their rank, speak God's praises. This is the Lord's doing. In these acts of his, justice was executed on his enemies. In times of persecution, God's ordinances, the walls of salvation, whence the waters of life are drawn, are resorted to at the hazard of the lives of those who attend them. At all times Satan will endeavour to hinder the believer from drawing near to the throne of grace. Notice God's kindness to his trembling people. It is the glory of God to protect those who are most exposed, and to help the weakest. Let us notice the benefit we have from the public peace, the inhabitants of villages especially, and give God the praise.

Verses 12–23

Deborah called on her own soul to be in earnest. He that will set the hearts of other men on fire with the love of Christ, must himself burn with love. Praising God is a work we should awake to, and awake ourselves unto. She notices who fought against Israel, who fought for them, and who kept away. Who fought against them. They were obstinate enemies to God's people, therefore the more dangerous. Who fought for them. The several tribes that helped are here spoken of with honour; for though God is above all to be glorified, those who are employed must have their due praise, to encourage others. But the whole creation is at war with those to whom God is an enemy. The river of Kishon fought against their enemies. At most times it was shallow, yet now, probably by the great rain that fell, it was so swelled, and the stream so deep and strong, that those who attempted to pass, were drowned. Deborah's own soul fought against them. When the soul is employed in holy exercises, and heart-work is made of them, through the grace of God, the strength of our spiritual enemies will be trodden down, and will fall before us. She observes who kept away, and did not side with Israel, as might have been expected. Thus many are kept from doing their duty by the fear of trouble, the love of ease, and undue affection to their worldly business and advantage. Narrow, selfish spirits care not what becomes of God's church, so that they can but get, keep, and save money. All seek their own, Php **2**:**21**. A little will serve those for a pretence to stay at home, who have no mind to engage in needful services, because there is difficulty and danger in them. But we cannot keep away from the contest between the Lord and his enemies; and if we do not actively endeavour to promote his cause in this wicked world, we shall fall under the curse against the workers of iniquity. Though He needs no human help, yet he is pleased to accept the services of those who improve their talents to advance his cause. He requires every man to do so.

Verses 24–31

Jael had a special blessing. Those whose lot is cast in the tent, in a low and narrow sphere, if they serve God according to the powers he has given them, shall not lose their reward. The mother of Sisera looked for his return, not in the least fearing his success. Let us take heed of indulging eager desires towards any temporal good, particularly toward that which cherishes vain-glory, for that was what she here doted on. What a picture does she present of an ungodly and sensual heart! How shameful and childish these wishes of an aged mother and her attendants for her son! And thus does God often bring ruin on his enemies when they are most puffed up. Deborah concludes with a prayer to God for the destruction of all his foes, and for the comfort of all his friends. Such shall be the honour, and joy of all who love God in sincerity, they shall shine for ever as the sun in the firmament.

Chapter 6

Verses 1–6

Israel's sin was renewed, and Israel's troubles were repeated. Let all that sin expect to suffer. The Israelites hid themselves in dens and caves; such was the effect of a guilty conscience. Sin dispirits men. The invaders left no food for Israel, except what was taken into the caves. They prepared that for Baal with which God should have been served, now God justly sends an enemy to take it away in the season thereof.

Verses 7–10

They cried to God for a deliverer, and he sent them a prophet to teach them. When God furnishes a land with faithful ministers, it is a token that he has mercy in store for it. He charges them with rebellion against the Lord; he intends to bring them to repentance. Repentance is real when the sinfulness of sin, as disobedience to God, is chiefly lamented.

Verses 11–24

Gideon was a man of a brave, active spirit, yet in obscurity through the times: he is here stirred up to undertake something great. It was very sure that the Lord was with him, when his Angel was with him. Gideon was weak in faith, which made it hard to reconcile the assurances of the presence of God with the distress to which Israel was brought. The Angel answered his objections. He told him to appear and act as Israel's deliverer, there needed no more. Bishop Hall says, While God calls Gideon valiant, he makes him so. God delights to advance the humble. Gideon desires to have his faith confirmed. Now, under the influences of the Spirit, we are not to expect signs before our eyes such as Gideon here desired, but must earnestly pray to God, that if we have found grace in his sight, he would show us a sign in our heart, by the powerful working of his Spirit there, The Angel turned the meat into an offering made by fire; showing that he was not a man who needed meat, but the Son of God, who was to be served and honoured by sacrifice, and who in the fulness of time was to make himself a sacrifice. Hereby a sign was given to Gideon, that he had found grace in God's sight. Ever since man has by sin exposed himself to God's wrath and curse, a message from heaven has been a terror to him, as he scarcely dares to expect good tidings thence. In this world, it is very awful to have any con**verse** with that world of spirits to which we are so much strangers. Gideon's courage failed him. But God spoke peace to him.

Verses 25–32

See the power of God's grace, that he could raise up a reformer; and the kindness of his grace, that he would raise up a deliverer, out of the family of a leader in idolatry. Gideon must not think it enough not to worship at that altar; he must throw it down, and offer sacrifice on another. It was needful he should make peace with God, before he made war on Midian. Till sin be pardoned through the great Sacrifice, no good is to be expected. God, who has all hearts in his hands, influenced Joash to appear for his son against the advocates for Baal, though he had joined formerly in the worship of Baal. Let us do our duty, and trust God with our safety. Here is a challenge to Baal, to do either good or evil; the result convinced his worshippers of their folly, in praying to one to help them that could not avenge himself.

Verses 33–40

These signs are truly miraculous, and very significant. Gideon and his men were going to fight the Midianites; could God distinguish between a small fleece of Israel, and the vast floor of Midian? Gideon is made to know that God could do so. Is Gideon desirous that the dew of Divine grace might come down upon himself in particular? He sees the fleece wet with dew to assure him of it. Does he desire that God will be as the dew to all Israel? Behold, all the ground is wet. What cause we sinners of the Gentiles have, to bless the Lord that the dew of heavenly blessings, once confined to Israel, is now sent to all the inhabitants of the earth! Yet still the means of grace are in different measures, according to the purposes of God. In the same congregation, one man's soul is like Gideon's moistened fleece, another like the dry ground.

Chapter 7

Verses 1–8

God provides that the praise of victory may be wholly to himself, by appointing only three hundred men to be employed. Activity and prudence go with dependence upon God for help in our lawful undertakings. When the Lord sees that men would overlook him, and through unbelief, would shrink from perilous services, or that through pride they would vaunt themselves against him, he will set them aside, and do his work by other instruments. Pretences will be found by many, for deserting the cause and escaping the cross. But though a religious society may thus be made fewer in numbers, yet it will gain as to purity, and may expect an increased blessing from the Lord. God chooses to employ such as are not only well affected, but zealously affected in a good thing. They grudged not at the liberty of the others who were dismissed. In doing the duties required by God, we must not regard the forwardness or backwardness of others, nor what they do, but what God looks for at our hands. He is a rare person who can endure that others should excel him in gifts or blessings, or in liberty; so that we may say, it is by the special grace of God that we regard what God says to us, and not look to men what they do.

Verses 9–15

The dream seemed to have little meaning in it; but the interpretation evidently proved the whole to be from the Lord, and discovered that the name of Gideon had filled the Midianites with terror. Gideon took this as a sure pledge of success; without delay he worshipped and praised God, and returned with confidence to his three hundred men. Wherever we are, we may speak to God, and worship him. God must have the praise of that which encourages our faith. And his providence must be acknowledged in events, though small and seemingly accidental.

Verses 16–22

This method of defeating the Midianites may be alluded to, as exemplifying the destruction of the devil's kingdom in the world, by the preaching of the everlasting gospel, the sounding that trumpet, and the holding forth that light out of earthen vessels, for such are the ministers of the gospel, **2**Co **4**:**6**, **7**. God chose the foolish things of the world to confound the wise, a barley-cake to overthrow the tents of Midian, that the excellency of the power might be of God only. The gospel is a sword, not in the hand, but in the mouth: the sword of the Lord and of Gideon; of God and Jesus Christ, of Him that sits on the throne and the Lamb. The wicked are often led to avenge the cause of God upon each other, under the power of their delusions, and the fury of their passions. See also how God often makes the enemies of the church instruments to destroy one another; it is a pity that the church's friends should ever act like them.

Verses 23–25

Two chief commanders of the host of Midian were taken and slain by the men of Ephraim. It were to be wished that we all did as these did, and that where help is needed, that it were willingly and readily performed by another. And that if there were any excellent and profitable matter begun, we were willing to have fellow-labourers to the finishing and perfecting the same, and not, as often, hinder one another.

Chapter 8

Verses 1–3

Those who will not attempt or venture any thing in the cause of God, will be the most ready to censure and quarrel with such as are of a more zealous and enterprising spirit. And those who are the most backward to difficult services, will be the most angry not to have the credit of them. Gideon stands here as a great example of self-denial; and shows us that envy is best removed by humility. The Ephraimites had given vent to their passion in very wrong freedom of speech, a certain sign of a weak cause: reason runs low when chiding flies high.

Verses 4–12

Gideon's men were faint, yet pursuing; fatigued with what they had done, yet eager to do more against their enemies. It is many a time the true Christian's case, fainting, and yet pursuing. The world knows but little of the persevering and successful struggle the real believer maintains with his sinful heart. But he betakes himself to that Divine strength, in the faith of which he began his conflict, and by the supply of which alone he can finish it in triumph.

Verses 13–17

The active servants of the Lord meet with more dangerous opposition from false professors than from open enemies; but they must not care for the behaviour of those who are Israelites in name, but Midianites in heart. They must pursue the enemies of their souls, and of the cause of God, though they are ready to faint through inward conflicts and outward hardships. And they shall be enabled to persevere. The less men help, and the more they seek to hinder, the more will the Lord assist. Gideon's warning being slighted, the punishment was just. Many are taught with the briers and thorns of affliction, who would not learn otherwise.

Verses 18–21

The kings of Midian must be reckoned with. As they confessed themselves guilty of murder, Gideon acted as the avenger of blood, being the next of kin to the persons slain. Little did they think to have heard of this so long after; but murder seldom goes unpunished in this life. Sins long forgotten by man, must be accounted for to God. What poor consolation in death from the hope of suffering less pain, and of dying with less disgrace than some others! yet many are more anxious on these accounts, than concerning the future judgment, and what will follow.

Verses 22–28

Gideon refused the government the people offered him. No good man can be pleased with any honour done to himself, which belongs only to God. Gideon thought to keep up the remembrance of this victory by an ephod, made of the choicest of the spoils. But probably this ephod had, as usual, a teraphim annexed to it, and Gideon intended this for an oracle to be consulted. Many are led into false ways by one false step of a good man. It became a snare to Gideon himself, and it proved the ruin of the family. How soon will ornaments which feed the lust of the eye, and form the pride of life, as well as tend to the indulgences of the flesh, bring shame on those who are fond of them!

Verses 29–35

As soon as Gideon was dead, who kept the people to the worship of the God of Israel, they found themselves under no restraint; then they went after Baalim, and showed no kindness to the family of Gideon. No wonder if those who forget their God, forget their friends. Yet conscious of our own ingratitude to the Lord, and observing that of mankind in general, we should learn to be patient under any unkind returns we meet with for our poor services, and resolve, after the Divine example, not to be overcome of evil, but to overcome evil with good.

Chapter 9

Verses 1–6

The men of Shechem chose Abimelech king. God was not consulted whether they should have any king, much less who it should be. If parents could see what their children would do, and what they are to suffer, their joy in them often would be turned into sorrow: we may be thankful that we cannot know what shall happen. Above all, we should fear and watch against sin; for our evil conduct may produce fatal effects upon our families, after we are in our graves.

Verses 7–21

There was no occasion for the trees to choose a king, they are all the trees of the Lord which he has planted. Nor was there any occasion for Israel to set a king over them, for the Lord was their King. Those who bear fruit for the public good, are justly respected and honoured by all that are wise, more than those who merely make a figure. All these fruit-trees gave much the same reason for their refusal to be promoted over the trees; or, as the margin reads it, to go up and down for the trees. To rule, involves a man in a great deal both of toil and care. Those who are preferred to public trust and power, must forego all private interests and advantages, for the good of others. And those advanced to honour and dignity, are in great danger of losing their fruitfulness. For which reason, they that desire to do good, are afraid of being too great. Jotham compares Abimelech to the bramble or thistle, a worthless plant, whose end is to be burned. Such a one was Abimelech.

Verses 22–29

Abimelech is seated in the throne his father refused. But how long does this glory last? Stay but three years, and see the bramble withered and burned. The prosperity of the wicked is short and fickle. The Shechemites are plagued by no other hand than Abimelech's. They raised him unjustly to the throne; they first feel the weight of his sceptre.

Verses 30–49

Abimelech intended to punish the Schechemites for slighting him now, but God punished them for their serving him formerly in the murder of Gideon's sons. When God uses men as instruments in his hand to do his work, he means one thing, and they another. That, which they hoped would have been for their welfare, proved a snare and a trap, as those will certainly find, who run to idols for shelter; such will prove a refuge of lies. (Jdg **9**:**50-57**)

Verses 50–57

The Shechemites were ruined by Abimelech; now he is reckoned with, who was their leader in villany. Evil pursues sinners, and sometimes overtakes them, when not only at ease, but triumphant. Though wickedness may prosper a while, it will not prosper always. The history of mankind, if truly told, would greatly resemble that of this chapter. The records of what are called splendid events present to us such contests for power. Such scenes, though praised of men, fully explain the Scripture doctrine of the deceitfulness and desperate wickedness of the human heart, the force of men's lust, and the effect of Satan's influence. Lord, thou has given us thy word of truth and righteousness, O pour upon us thy spirit of purity, peace, and love, and write thy holy law in our hearts.

Chapter 10

Verses 1–5

Quiet and peaceable reigns, though the best to live in, yield least variety of matter to be spoken of. Such were the days of Tola and Jair. They were humble, active, and useful men, rulers appointed of God.

Verses 6–9

Now the threatening was fulfilled, that the Israelites should have no power to stand before their enemies, Le **26**:**17**, **37**. By their evil ways and their evil doings they procured this to themselves.

Verses 10–18

God is able to multiply men's punishments according to the numbers of their sins and idols. But there is hope when sinners cry to the Lord for help, and lament their ungodliness as well as their more open transgressions. It is necessary, in true repentance, that there be a full conviction that those things cannot help us which we have set in competition with God. They acknowledged what they deserved, yet prayed to God not to deal with them according to their deserts. We must submit to God's justice, with a hope in his mercy. True repentance is not only for sin, but from sin. As the disobedience and misery of a child are a grief to a tender father, so the provocations of God's people are a grief to him. From him mercy never can be sought in vain. Let then the trembling sinner, and the almost despairing backslider, cease from debating about God's secret purposes, or from expecting to find hope from former experiences. Let them cast themselves on the mercy of God our Saviour, humble themselves under his hand, seek deliverance from the powers of darkness, separate themselves from sin, and from occasions of it, use the means of grace diligently, and wait the Lord's time, and so they shall certainly rejoice in his mercy.

Chapter 11

Verses 1–11

Men ought not to be blamed for their parentage, so long as they by their personal merits roll away any reproach. God had forgiven Israel, therefore Jephthah will forgive. He speaks not with confidence of his success, knowing how justly God might suffer the Ammonites to prevail for the further punishment of Israel. Nor does he speak with any confidence at all in himself. If he succeed, it is the Lord delivers them into his hand; he thereby reminds his countrymen to look up to God as the Giver of victory. The same question as here, in fact, is put to those who desire salvation by Christ. If he save you, will ye be willing that he shall rule you? On no other terms will he save you. If he make you happy, shall he make you holy? If he be your helper, shall he be your Head? Jephthah, to obtain a little worldly honour, was willing to expose his life: shall we be discouraged in our Christian warfare by the difficulties we may meet with, when Christ has promised a crown of life to him that overcometh?

Verses 12–28

One instance of the honour and respect we owe to God, as our God, is, rightly to employ what he gives us to possess. Receive it from him, use it for him, and part with it when he calls for it. The whole of this message shows that Jephthah was well acquainted with the books of Moses. His argument was clear, and his demand reasonable. Those who possess the most courageous faith, will be the most disposed for peace, and the readiest to make advances to obtain; but rapacity and ambition often cloak their designs under a plea of equity, and render peaceful endeavours of no avail.

Verses 29–40

Several important lessons are to be learned from Jephthah's vow. **1**. There may be remainders of distrust and doubting, even in the hearts of true and great believers. **2**. Our vows to God should not be as a purchase of the favour we desire, but to express gratitude to him. **3**. We need to be very well-advised in making vows, lest we entangle ourselves. **4**. What we have solemnly vowed to God, we must perform, if it be possible and lawful, though it be difficult and grievous to us. **5**. It well becomes children, obediently and cheerfully to submit to their parents in the Lord. It is hard to say what Jephthah did in performance of his vow; but it is thought that he did not offer his daughter as a burnt-offering. Such a sacrifice would have been an abomination to the Lord; it is supposed she was obliged to remain unmarried, and apart from her family. Concerning this and some other such passages in the sacred history, about which learned men are divided and in doubt, we need not perplex ourselves; what is necessary to our salvation, thanks be to God, is plain enough. If the reader recollects the promise of Christ concerning the teaching of the Holy Spirit, and places himself under this heavenly Teacher, the Holy Ghost will guide to all truth in every passage, so far as it is needful to be understood.

Chapter 12

Verses 1–7

The Ephraimites had the same quarrel with Jephthah as with Gideon. Pride was at the bottom of the quarrel; only by that comes contention. It is ill to fasten names of reproach upon persons or countries, as is common, especially upon those under outward disadvantages. It often occasions quarrels that prove of ill consequence, as it did here. No contentions are so bitter as those between brethren or rivals for honour. What need we have to watch and pray against evil tempers! May the Lord incline all his people to follow after things which make for peace!

Verses 8–15

We have here a short account of three more of the judges of Israel. The happiest life of individuals, and the happiest state of society, is that which affords the fewest remarkable events. To live in credit and quiet, to be peacefully useful to those around us, to possess a clear conscience; but, above all, and without which nothing can avail, to enjoy communion with God our Saviour while we live, and to die at peace with God and man, form the substance of all that a wise man can desire.

Chapter 13

Verses 1–7

Israel did evil: then God delivered them again into the hands of the Philistines. When Israel was in this distress, Samson was born. His parents had been long childless. Many eminent persons were born of such mothers. Mercies long waited for, often prove signal mercies; and by them others may be encouraged to continue their hope in God's mercy. The angel notices her affliction. God often sends comfort to his people very seasonably, when they feel their troubles most. This deliverer of Israel must be devoted to God. Manoah's wife was satisfied that the messenger was of God. She gave her husband a particular account, both of the promise and of the precept. Husbands and wives should tell each other their experiences of communion with God, and their improvements in acquaintance with him, that they may help each other in the way that is holy.

Verses 8–14

Blessed are those who have not seen, and yet, as Manoah, have believed. Good men are more careful and desirous to know the duty to be done by them, than to know the events concerning them: duty is ours, events are God's. God will guide those by his counsel, who desire to know their duty, and apply to him to teach them. Pious parents, especially, will beg Divine assistance. The angel repeats the directions he had before given. There is need of much care for the right ordering both of ourselves and our children, that we may be duly separate from the world, and living sacrifices to the Lord.

Verses 15–23

What Manoah asked for instruction in his duty, he was readily told; but what he asked to gratify his curiosity, was denied. God has in his word given full directions concerning our duty, but never designed to answer other questionings. There are secret things which belong not to us, of which we must be quite contented to be ignorant, while in this world. The name of our Lord is wonderful and secret; but by his wonderful works he makes himself known as far as is needful for us. Prayer is the ascent of the soul to God. But without Christ in the heart by faith, our services are offensive smoke; in him, acceptable flame. We may apply this to Christ's sacrifice of himself for us; he ascended in the flame of his own offering, for by his own blood he entered in once into the holy place, Heb **9**:**12**. In Manoah's reflections there is great fear; We shall surely die. In his wife's reflection there is great faith. As a help meet for him, she encouraged him. Let believers who have had communion with God in the word and prayer, to whom he has graciously manifested himself, and who have had reason to think God has accepted their works, take encouragement from thence in a cloudy and dark day. God would not have done what he has done for my soul, if he had designed to forsake me, and leave me to perish at last; for his work is perfect. Learn to reason as Manoah's wife; If God designed me to perish under his wrath, he would not give me tokens of his favour.

Verses 24, 25

The Spirit of the Lord began to move Samson when a youth. This was evidence that the Lord blessed him. Where God gives his blessing, he gives his Spirit to qualify for the blessing. Those are blessed indeed in whom the Spirit of grace begins to work in the days of their childhood. Samson drank no wine or strong drink, yet excelled in strength and courage, for he had the Spirit of God moving him; therefore be not drunk with wine, but be filled with the Spirit.

Chapter 14

Verses 1–4

As far as Samson's marriage was a common case, it was weak and foolish of him to set his affections upon a daughter of the Philistines. Shall one, not only an Israelite, but a Nazarite, devoted to the Lord, covet to become one with a worshipper of Dagon? It does not appear that he had any reason to think her wise or virtuous, or any way likely to be a help meet for him; but he saw something in her agreeable to his fancy. He that, in the choice of a wife, is only guided by his eye, and governed by his fancy, must afterwards thank himself if he find a Philistine in his arms. Yet it was well done not to proceed till Samson had made his parents acquainted with the matter. Children ought not to marry, nor to move towards it, without the advice and consent of their parents. Samson's parents did well to dissuade him from yoking himself unequally with unbelievers. It seems that it pleased God to leave Samson to follow his own inclinations, intending to bring out good from his conduct; and his parents consented, because he was bent upon it. However, his example is not recorded for us to do likewise.

Verses 5–9

By enabling him to kill a lion, God let Samson know what he could do in the strength of the Spirit of the Lord, that he might never be afraid to look the greatest difficulties in the face. He was alone in the vineyards, whither he had rambled. Young people consider not how they exposed themselves to the roaring lion that seeks to devour, when they wander from their prudent, pious parents. Nor do men consider what lions lurk in the vineyards, the vineyards of red wines. Our Lord Jesus having conquered Satan, that roaring lion, believers, like Samson, find honey in the carcass abundant strength and satisfaction, enough for themselves, and for all their friends.

Verses 10–20

Samson's riddle literally meant no more than that he had got honey, for food and for pleasure, from the lion, which in its strength and fury was ready to devour him. But the victory of Christ over Satan, by means of his humiliation, agonies, and death, and the exaltation that followed to him, with the glory thence to the Father, and spiritual advantages to his people, seem directly alluded to. And even death, that devouring monster, being robbed of his sting, and stripped of his horror, forwards the soul to the realms of bliss. In these and other senses, out of the eater comes forth meat, and out of the strong, sweetness. Samson's companions obliged his wife to get the explanation from him. A worldly wife, or a worldly friend, is to a godly man as an enemy in the camp, who will watch every opportunity to betray him. No union can be comfortable or lasting, where secrets cannot be intrusted, without danger of being divulged. Satan, in his temptations, could not do us the mischief he does, if he did not plough with the heifer of our corrupt nature. His chief advantage against us arises from his correspondence with our deceitful hearts and inbred lusts. This proved an occasion of weaning Samson from his new relations. It were well for us, if the unkindness we meet with from the world, and our disappointments in it, obliged us by faith and prayer to return to our heavenly Father's house, and to rest there. See how little confidence is to be put in man. Whatever pretence of friendship may be made, a real Philistine will soon be weary of a true Israelite.

Chapter 15

Verses 1–8

When there are differences between relations, let those be reckoned the wisest and best, who are most forward to forgive or forget, and most willing to stoop and yield for the sake of peace. In the means which Samson employed, we must look at the power of God supplying them, and making them successful, to mortify the pride and punish the wickedness of the Philistines. The Philistines threatened Samson's wife that they would burn her and her father's house. She, to save herself and oblige her countrymen, betrayed her husband; and the very thing that she feared, and by sin sought to avoid, came upon her! She, and her father's house, were burnt with fire, and by her countrymen, whom she thought to oblige by the wrong she did to her husband. The mischief we seek to escape by any unlawful practices, we often pull down upon our own heads.

Verses 9–17

Sin dispirits men, it hides from their eyes the things that belong to their peace. The Israelites blamed Samson for what he had done against the Philistines, as if he had done them a great injury. Thus our Lord Jesus did many good works, and for those the Jews were ready to stone him. When the Spirit of the Lord came upon Samson, his cords were loosed: where the Spirit of the Lord is, there is liberty, and those are free indeed who are thus set free. Thus Christ triumphed over the powers of darkness that shouted against him, as if they had him in their power. Samson made great destruction among the Philistines. To take the bone of an ass for this, was to do wonders by the foolish things of the world, that the excellency of the power might be of God, not of man. This victory was not in the weapon, was not in the arm; but it was in the Spirit of God, which moved the weapon by the arm. We can do all things through Him that strengtheneth us. Seest thou a poor Christian, who is enabled to overcome a temptation by weak, feeble counsel, there is the Philistine vanquished by a sorry jaw-bone.

Verses 18–20

So little notice did the men of Judah take of their deliverer, that he was ready to perish for want of a draught of water. Thus are the greatest slights often put upon those who do the greatest services. Samson prayed to God in this distress. Those that forget to attend God their praises, may be compelled to attend him with their prayers. Past experiences of God's power and goodness, are excellent pleas in prayer for further mercy. He pleads his being exposed to God's enemies; our best pleas are taken from God's glory. The Lord sent him seasonable relief. The place of this action was, from the jaw-bone, called Lehi. And in the place thus called, God caused a fountain suddenly and seasonably to open, close by Samson. We should be more thankful for the mercy of water, did we consider how ill we can spare it. Israel submitted to him whom they had betrayed. God was with him; henceforward they were directed by him as their judge.

Chapter 16

Verses 1–3

Hitherto Samson's character has appeared glorious, though uncommon. In this chapter we find him behaving in so wicked a manner, that many question whether or not he were a godly man. But the apostle has determined this, Heb **11**:**32**. By adverting to the doctrines and examples of Scripture, the artifices of Satan, the deceitfulness of the human heart, and the methods in which the Lord frequently deals with his people, we may learn useful lessons from this history, at which some needlessly stumble, while others cavil and object. The peculiar time in which Samson lived may account for many things, which, if done in our time, and without the special appointment of Heaven, would be highly criminal. And there might have been in him many exercises of piety, which, if recorded, would have reflected a different light upon his character. Observe Samson's danger. Oh that all who indulge their sensual appetites in drunkenness, or any fleshly lusts, would see themselves thus surrounded, way-laid, and marked for ruin by their spiritual enemies! The faster they sleep, the more secure they feel, the greater their danger. We hope it was with a pious resolution not to return to his sin, that he rose under a fear of the danger he was in. Can I be safe under this guilt? It was bad that he lay down without such checks; but it would have been worse, if he had laid still under them.

Verses 4–17

Samson had been more than once brought into mischief and danger by the love of women, yet he would not take warning, but is again taken in the same snare, and this third time is fatal. Licentiousness is one of the things that take away the heart. This is a deep pit into which many have fallen; but from which few have escaped, and those by a miracle of mercy, with the loss of reputation and usefulness, of almost all, except their souls. The anguish of the suffering is ten thousand times greater than all the pleasures of the sin.

Verses 18–21

See the fatal effects of false security. Satan ruins men by flattering them into a good opinion of their own safety, and so bringing them to mind nothing, and fear nothing; and then he robs them of their strength and honour, and leads them captive at his will. When we sleep our spiritual enemies do not. Samson's eyes were the inlets of his sin, (ver. #(**1**),) and now his punishment began there. Now the Philistines blinded him, he had time to remember how his own lust had before blinded him. The best way to preserve the eyes, is, to turn them away from beholding vanity. Take warning by his fall, carefully to watch against all fleshly lusts; for all our glory is gone, and our defence departed from us, when our separation to God, as spiritual Nazarites, is profaned.

Verses 22–24

Samson's afflictions were the means of bringing him to deep repentance. By the loss of his bodily sight the eyes of his understanding were opened; and by depriving him of bodily strength, the Lord was pleased to renew his spiritual strength. The Lord permits some few to wander wide and sink deep, yet he recovers them at last, and marking his displeasure at sin in their severe temporal sufferings, preserves them from sinking into the pit of destruction. Hypocrites may abuse these examples, and infidels mock at them, but true Christians will thereby be rendered more humble, watchful, and circumspect; more simple in their dependence on the Lord, more fervent in prayer to be kept from falling, and in praise for being preserved; and, if they fall, they will be kept from sinking into despair.

Verses 25–31

Nothing fills up the sins of any person or people faster than mocking and misusing the servants of God, even thought it is by their own folly that they are brought low. God put it into Samson's heart, as a public person, thus to avenge on them God's quarrel, Israel's, and his own. That strength which he had lost by sin, he recovers by prayer. That it was not from passion or personal revenge, but from holy zeal for the glory of God and Israel, appears from God's accepting and answering the prayer. The house was pulled down, not by the natural strength of Samson, but by the almighty power of God. In his case it was right he should avenge the cause of God and Israel. Nor is he to be accused of self-murder. He sought not his own death, but Israel's deliverance, and the destruction of their enemies. Thus Samson died in bonds, and among the Philistines, as an awful rebuke for his sins; but he died repentant. The effects of his death typified those of the death of Christ, who, of his own will, laid down his life among transgressors, and thus overturned the foundation of Satan's kingdom, and provided for the deliverance of his people. Great as was the sin of Samson, and justly as he deserved the judgments he brought upon himself, he found mercy of the Lord at last; and every penitent shall obtain mercy, who flees for refuge to that Saviour whose blood cleanses from all sin. But here is nothing to encourage any to indulge sin, from a hope they shall at last repent and be saved.

Chapter 17

Verses 1–6

What is related in this, and the rest of the chapters to the end of this book, was done soon after the death of Joshua: see chap. Jud **20**:**28**. That it might appear how happy the nation was under the Judges, here is showed how unhappy they were when there was no Judge. The love of money made Micah so undutiful to his mother as to rob her, and made her so unkind to her son, as to curse him. Outward losses drive good people to their prayers, but bad people to their curses. This woman's silver was her god, before it was made into a graven or a molten image. Micah and his mother agreed to turn their money into a god, and set up idol worship in their family. See the cause of this corruption. Every man did that which was right in his own eyes, and then they soon did that which was evil in the sight of the Lord.

Verses 7–13

Micah thought it was a sign of God's favour to him and his images, that a Levite should come to his door. Thus those who please themselves with their own delusions, if Providence unexpectedly bring any thing to their hands that further them in their evil way, are apt from thence to think that God is pleased with them.

Chapter 18

The Danites seek to enlarge their inheritance, and rob Micah.

—The Danites determined to take Micah's gods with them. Oh the folly of these Danites! How could they imagine those gods should protect them, that could not keep themselves from being stolen! To take them for their own use, was a double crime; it showed they neither feared God, nor regarded man, but were lost both to godliness and honesty. What a folly was it for Micah to call those his gods, which he had made, when He only is to be worshipped by us as God, that made us! That is put in God's place, which we are concerned about, as if our all were bound up in it. If people will walk in the name of their false gods, much more should we love and serve the true God!

Chapter 19

The wickedness of the men of Gibeah.

—The three remaining chapters of this book contain a very sad history of the wickedness of the men of Gibeah, in Benjamin. The righteous Lord permits sinners to execute just vengeance on one another, and if the scene here described is horrible, what will the discoveries of the day of judgment be! Let each of us consider how to escape from the wrath to come, how to mortify the sins of our own hearts, to resist Satan's temptations, and to avoid the pollutions there are in the world.

Chapter 20

The tribe of Benjamin nearly extirpated.

—The Israelites' abhorrence of the crime committed at Gibeah, and their resolution to punish the criminals, were right; but they formed their resolves with too much haste and self-confidence. The eternal ruin of souls will be worse, and more fearful, than these desolations of a tribe.

Chapter 21

The Israelites lament for the Benjamites.

—Israel lamented for the Benjamites, and were perplexed by the oath they had taken, not to give their daughters to them in marriage. Men are more zealous to support their own authority than that of God. They would have acted better if they had repented of their rash oaths, brought sin-offerings, and sought forgiveness in the appointed way, rather than attempt to avoid the guilt of perjury by actions quite as wrong. That men can advise others to acts of treachery or violence, out of a sense of duty, forms a strong proof of the blindness of the human mind when left to itself, and of the fatal effects of a conscience under ignorance and error.

Ruth

We find in this book excellent examples of faith, piety, patience, humility, industry, and loving-kindness, in the common events of life. Also we see the special care which God's providence take of our smallest concerns, encouraging us to full trust therein. We may view this book as a beautiful, because natural representation of human life; as a curious detail of important facts; and as a part of the plan of redemption.

Chapter 1

Verses 1–5

Elimelech's care to provide for his family, was not to be blamed; but his removal into the country of Moab could not be justified. And the removal ended in the wasting of his family. It is folly to think of escaping that cross, which, being laid in our way, we ought to take up. Changing our place seldom is mending it. Those who bring young people into bad acquaintance, and take them out of the way of public ordinances, thought they may think them well-principled, and armed against temptation, know not what will be the end. It does not appear that the women the sons of Elimelech married, were proselyted to the Jewish religion. Earthly trials or enjoyments are of short continuance. Death continually removes those of every age and situation, and mars all our outward comforts: we cannot too strongly prefer those advantages which shall last for ever.

Verses 6–14

Naomi began to think of returning, after the death of her two sons. When death comes into a family, it ought to reform what is amiss there. Earth is made bitter to us, that heaven may be made dear. Naomi seems to have been a person of faith and piety. She dismissed her daughters-in-law with prayer. It is very proper for friends, when they part, to part with them thus part in love. Did Naomi do well, to discourage her daughters from going with her, when she might save them from the idolatry of Moab, and bring them to the faith and worship of the God of Israel? Naomi, no doubt, desired to do that; but if they went with her, she would not have them to go upon her account. Those that take upon them a profession of religion only to oblige their friends, or for the sake of company, will be converts of small value. If they did come with her, she would have them make it their deliberate choice, and sit down first and count the cost, as it concerns those to do who make a profession of religion. And more desire "rest in the house of a husband," or some wordly settlement or earthly satisfaction, than the rest to which Christ invites our souls; therefore when tried they will depart from Christ, though perhaps with some sorrow.

Verses 15–18

See Ruth's resolution, and her good affection to Naomi. Orpah was loth to part from her; yet she did not love her well enough to leave Moab for her sake. Thus, many have a value and affection for Christ, yet come short of salvation by him, because they will not forsake other things for him. They love him, yet leave him, because they do not love him enough, but love other things better. Ruth is an example of the grace of God, inclining the soul to choose the better part. Naomi could desire no more than the solemn declaration Ruth made. See the power of resolution; it silences temptation. Those that go in religious ways without a stedfast mind, stand like a door half open, which invites a thief; but resolution shuts and bolts the door, resists the devil and forces him to flee.

Verses 19–22

Naomi and Ruth came to Bethlehem. Afflictions will make great and surprising changes in a little time. May God, by his grace, fit us for all such changes, especially the great change!, Naomi signifies "pleasant," or "amiable;" Mara, "bitter," or "bitterness." She was now a woman of a sorrowful spirit. She had come home empty, poor, a widow and childless. But there is a fulness for believers of which they never can be emptied; a good part which shall not be taken from those who have it. The cup of affliction is a "bitter" cup, but she owns that the affliction came from God. It well becomes us to have our hearts humbled under humbling providences. It is not affliction itself, but affliction rightly borne, that does us good.

Chapter 2

Verses 1–3

Observe Ruth's humility. When Providence had made her poor, she cheerfully stoops to her lot. High spirits will rather starve than stoop; not so Ruth. Nay, it is her own proposal. She speaks humbly in her expectation of leave to glean. We may not demand kindness as a debt, but ask, and take it as a favour, though in a small matter. Ruth also was an example of industry. She loved not to eat the bread of idleness. This is an example to young people. Diligence promises well, both for this world and the other. We must not be shy of any honest employment. No labour is a reproach. Sin is a thing below us, but we must not think any thing else so, to which Providence call us. She was an example of regard to her mother, and of trust in Providence. God wisely orders what seem to us small events; and those that appear altogether uncertain, still are directed to serve his own glory, and the good of his people.

Verses 4–16

The pious and kind language between Boaz and his reapers shows that there were godly persons in Israel. Such language as this is seldom heard in our field; too often, on the contrary, what is immoral and corrupt. A stranger would form a very different opinion of our land, from that which Ruth would form of Israel from the converse and conduct of Boaz and his reapers. But true religion will teach a man to behave aright in all states and conditions; it will form kind masters and faithful servants, and cause harmony in families. True religion will cause mutual love and kindness among persons of different ranks. It had these effects on Boaz and his men. When he came to them he prayed for them. They did not, as soon as he was out of hearing curse him, as some ill-natured servants that hate their master's eye, but they returned his courtesy. Things are likely to go on well where there is such good-will as this between masters and servants. They expressed their kindness to each other by praying one for another. Boaz inquired concerning the stranger he saw, and ordered her to be well treated. Masters must take care, not only that they do no hurt themselves, but that they suffer not their servants and those under them to do wrong. Ruth humbly owned herself unworthy of favours, seeing she was born and brought up a heathen. It well becomes us all to think humbly of ourselves, esteeming others better than ourselves. And let us, in the kindness of Boaz to Ruth, note the kindness of the Lord Jesus Christ to poor sinners.

Verses 17–23

It encourages industry, that in all labour, even that of gleaning, there is profit. Ruth was pleased with what she gained by her own industry, and was careful to secure it. Let us thus take care that we lose not those things which we have wrought, which we have gained for our souls' good, 2Jo **1**:**8**. Parents should examine their children, as Naomi did, not to frighten or discourage them, so as to make them hate home, or tempt them to tell a lie; but to commend them if they have done well, and with mildness to reprove and caution them if they have done otherwise. It is a good question for us to ask ourselves every night, Where have I gleaned to-day? What improvement have I made in knowledge and grace? What have I done that will turn to a good account? When the Lord deals bountifully with us, let us not be found in any other field, nor seeking for happiness and satisfaction in the creature. We lose Divine favours, if we slight them. Ruth dutifully observed her mother's directions. And when the harvest was ended, she kept her aged mother company at home. Dinah went out to see the daughters of the land; her vanity ended in disgrace, Ge **34**. Ruth kept at home, and helped to maintain her mother, and went out on no other errand than to get provision for her; her humility and industry ended in preferment.

Chapter 3

Verses 1–5

The married state should be a rest, as much as any thing upon earth can be so, as it ought to fix the affections and form a connexion for life. Therefore it should be engaged in with great seriousness, with earnest prayers for direction, for the blessing of God, and with regard to his precepts. Parents should carefully advise their children in this important concern, that it may be well with them as to their souls. Be it always remembered, That is best for us which is best for our souls. The course Naomi advised appears strange to us; but it was according to the laws and usages of Israel. If the proposed measure had borne the appearance of evil, Naomi would not have advised it. Law and custom gave Ruth, who was now proselyted to the true religion, a legal claim upon Boaz. It was customary for widows to assert this claim, De **25**:**5**–**10**. But this is not recorded for imitation in other times, and is not to be judged by modern rules. And if there had been any evil in it, Ruth was a woman of too much virtue and too much sense to have listened to it.

Verses 6–13

What in one age or nation would be improper, is not always so in another age or another nation. Being a judge of Israel, Boaz would tell Ruth what she should do; also whether he had the right of redemption, and what methods must be taken, and what rites used, in order to accomplishing her marriage with him or another person. The conduct of Boaz calls for the highest praise. He attempted not to take advantage of Ruth; he did not disdain her as a poor, destitute stranger, nor suspect her of any ill intentions. He spoke honourably of her as a virtuous woman, made her a promise, and as soon as the morning arrived, sent her away with a present to her mother-in-law. Boaz made his promise conditional, for there was a kinsman nearer than he, to whom the right of redemption belonged.

Verses 14–18

Ruth had done all that was fit for her to do, she must patiently wait the event. Boaz, having undertaken this matter, would be sure to manage it well. Much more reason have true believers to cast their care on God, because he has promised to care for them. Our strength is to sit still, Isa **30**:**7**. This narrative may encourage us to lay ourselves by faith at the feet of Christ: He is our near Kinsman; having taken our nature upon him. He has the right to redeem. Let us seek to receive from him his directions: Lord, what wilt thou have me to do? Ac **9**:**6**. He will never blame us as doing this unseasonably. And let us earnestly desire and seek the same rest for our children and friends, that it may be well with them also.

Chapter 4

Verses 1–8

This matter depended on the laws given by Moses about inheritances, and doubtless the whole was settled in the regular and legal manner. This kinsman, when he heard the conditions of the bargain, refused it. In like manner many are shy of the great redemption; they are not willing to espouse religion; they have heard well of it, and have nothing to say against it; they will give it their good word, but they are willing to part with it, and cannot be bound to it, for fear of marring their own inheritance in this world. The right was resigned to Boaz. Fair and open dealing in all matters of contract and trade, is what all must make conscience of, who would approve themselves true Israelites, without guile. Honesty will be found the best policy.

Verses 9–12

Men are ready to seize opportunities for increasing their estates, but few know the value of godliness. Such are the wise men of this world, whom the Lord charges with folly. They attend not to the concerns of their souls, but reject the salvation of Christ, for fear of marring their inheritance. But God did Boaz the honour to bring him into the line of the Messiah, while the kinsman, who was afraid of lessening himself, and marring his inheritance, has his name, family, and inheritance forgotten.

Verses 13–22

Ruth bore a son, through whom thousands and myriads were born to God; and in being the lineal ancestor of Christ, she was instrumental in the happiness of all that shall be saved by him; even of us Gentiles, as well as those of Jewish descent. She was a witness for God to the Gentile world, that he had not utterly forsaken them, but that in due time they should become one with his chosen people, and partake of his salvation. Prayer to God attended the marriage, and praise to him attended the birth of the child. What a pity it is that pious language should not be more used among Christians, or that it should be let fall into formality! Here is the descent of David from Ruth. And the period came when Bethlehem-Judah displayed greater wonders than those in the history of Ruth, when the outcast babe of another forlorn female of the same race appeared, controlling the counsels of the Roman master of the world, and drawing princes and wise men from the east, with treasures of gold, and frankincense, and myrrh to his feet. His name shall endure for ever, and all nations shall call Him blessed. In that Seed shall all the nations of the earth be blessed.

Samuel

In this book we have an account of Eli, and the wickedness of his sons; also of Samuel, his character and actions. Then of the advancement of Saul to be the king of Israel, and his ill behaviour, until his death made way for David's succession to the throne, who was an eminent type of Christ. David's patience, modesty, constancy, persecution by open enemies and feigned friends, are a pattern and example to the church, and to every member of it. Many things in this book encourage the faith, hope, and patience of the suffering believer. It contains also many useful cautions and awful warnings.

Chapter 1

Verses 1–8

Elkanah kept up his attendance at God's altar, notwithstanding the unhappy differences in his family. If the devotions of a family prevail not to put an end to its divisions, yet let not the divisions put a stop to the devotions. To abate our just love to any relation for the sake of any infirmity which they cannot help, and which is their affliction, is to make God's providence quarrel with his precept, and very unkindly to add affliction to the afflicted. It is evidence of a base disposition, to delight in grieving those who are of a sorrowful spirit, and in putting those out of humour who are apt to fret and be uneasy. We ought to bear one another's burdens, not add to them. Hannah could not bear the provocation. Those who are of a fretful spirit, and are apt to lay provocations too much to heart, are enemies to themselves, and strip themselves of many comforts both of life and godliness. We ought to notice comforts, to keep us from grieving for crosses. We should look at that which is for us, as well as what is against us.

Verses 9–18

Hannah mingled tears with her prayers; she considered the mercy of our God, who knows the troubled soul. God gives us leave, in prayer, not only to ask good things in general, but to mention that special good thing we most need and desire. She spoke softly, none could hear her. Hereby she testified her belief of God's knowledge of the heart and its desires. Eli was high priest, and judge in Israel. It ill becomes us to be rash and hasty in censures of others, and to think people guilty of bad things while the matter is doubtful and unproved. Hannah did not retort the charge, and upbraid Eli with the wicked conduct of his own sons. When we are at any time unjustly censured, we have need to set a double watch before the door of our lips, that we do not return censure for censure. Hannah thought it enough to clear herself, and so must we. Eli was willing to acknowledge his mistake. Hannah went away with satisfaction of mind. She had herself by prayer committed her case to God, and Eli had prayed for her. Prayer is heart's ease to a gracious soul. Prayer will smooth the countenance; it should do so. None will long remain miserable, who use aright the privilege of going to the mercy-seat of a reconciled God in Christ Jesus.

Verses 19–28

Elkanah and his family had a journey before them, and a family of children to take with them, yet they would not move till they had worshipped God together. Prayer and provender do not hinder a journey. When men are in such haste to set out upon journeys, or to engage in business, that they have not time to worship God, they are likely to proceed without his presence and blessing. Hannah, though she felt a warm regard for the courts of God's house, begged to stay at home. God will have mercy, and not sacrifice. Those who are detained from public ordinances, by the nursing and tending of little children, may take comfort from this instance, and believe, that if they do that duty in a right spirit, God will graciously accept them therein. Hannah presented her child to the Lord with a grateful acknowledgment of his goodness in answer to prayer. Whatever we give to God, it is what we have first asked and received from him. All our gifts to him were first his gifts to us. The child Samuel early showed true piety. Little children should be taught to worship God when very young. Their parents should teach them in it, bring them to it, and put them on doing it as well as they can; God will graciously accept them, and will teach them to do better.

Chapter 2

Verses 1–10

Hannah's heart rejoiced, not in Samuel, but in the Lord. She looks beyond the gift, and praises the Giver. She rejoiced in the salvation of the Lord, and in expectation of His coming, who is the whole salvation of his people. The strong are soon weakened, and the weak are soon strengthened, when God pleases. Are we poor? God made us poor, which is a good reason why we should be content, and make up our minds to our condition. Are we rich? God made us rich, which is a good reason why we should be thankful, and serve him cheerfully, and do good with the abundance he gives us. He respects not man's wisdom or fancied excellences, but chooses those whom the world accounts foolish, teaching them to feel their guilt, and to value his free and precious salvation. This prophecy looks to the kingdom of Christ, that kingdom of grace, of which Hannah speaks, after having spoken largely of the kingdom of providence. And here is the first time that we meet with the name MESSIAH, or his Anointed. The subjects of Christ's kingdom will be safe, and the enemies of it will be ruined; for the Anointed, the Lord Christ, is able to save, and to destroy.

Verses 11–26

Samuel, being devoted to the Lord in a special manner, was from a child employed about the sanctuary in the services he was capable of. As he did this with a pious disposition of mind, it was called ministering unto the Lord. He received a blessing from the Lord. Those young people who serve God as well as they can, he will enable to improve, that they may serve him better. Eli shunned trouble and exertion. This led him to indulge his children, without using parental authority to restrain and correct them when young. He winked at the abuses in the service of the sanctuary till they became customs, and led to abominations; and his sons, who should have taught those that engaged in the service of the sanctuary what was good, solicited them to wickedness. Their offence was committed even in offering the sacrifices for sins, which typified the atonement of the Saviour! Sins against the remedy, the atonement itself, are most dangerous, they tread under foot the blood of the covenant. Eli's reproof was far too mild and gentle. In general, none are more abandoned than the degenerate children of godly persons, when they break through restraints.

Verses 27–36

Those who allow their children in any evil way, and do not use their authority to restrain and punish them, in effect honour them more than God. Let Eli's example excite parents earnestly to strive against the beginnings of wickedness, and to train up their children in the nurture and admonition of the Lord. In the midst of the sentence against the house of Eli, mercy is promised to Israel. God's work shall never fall to the ground for want of hands to carry it on. Christ is that merciful and faithful High Priest, whom God raised up when the Levitical priesthood was thrown off, who in all things did his Father's mind, and for whom God will build a sure house, build it on a rock, so that hell cannot prevail against it.

Chapter 3

Verses 1–10

The call which Divine grace designs shall be made effectual; will be repeated till it is so, till we come to the call. Eli, perceiving that it was the voice of God that Samuel heard, instructed him what to say. Though it was a disgrace to Eli, for God's call to be directed to Samuel, yet he told him how to meet it. Thus the elder should do their utmost to assist and improve the younger that are rising up. Let us never fail to teach those who are coming after us, even such as will soon be preferred before us, Joh **1**:**30**. Good words should be put into children's mouths betimes, by which they may be prepared to learn Divine things, and be trained up to regard them.

Verses 11–18

What a great deal of guilt and corruption is there in us, concerning which we may say, It is the iniquity which our own heart knoweth; we are conscious to ourselves of it! Those who do not restrain the sins of others, when it is in their power to do it, make themselves partakers of the guilt, and will be charged as joining in it. In his remarkable answer to this awful sentence, Eli acknowledged that the Lord had a right to do as he saw good, being assured that he would do nothing wrong. The meekness, patience, and humility contained in those words, show that he was truly repentant; he accepted the punishment of his sin.

Verses 19–21

All increase in wisdom and grace, is owing to the presence of God with us. God will graciously repeat his visits to those who receive them aright. Early piety will be the greatest honour of young people. Those who honour God he will honour. Let young people consider the piety of Samuel, and from him they will learn to remember their Creator in the days of their youth. Young children are capable of religion. Samuel is a proof that their waiting upon the Lord will be pleasing to him. He is a pattern of all those amiable tempers, which are the brightest ornament of youth, and a sure source of happiness.

Chapter 4

Verses 1–9

Israel is smitten before the Philistines. Sin, the accursed thing, was in the camp, and gave their enemies all the advantage they could wish for. They own the hand of God in their trouble; but, instead of submitting, they speak angrily, as not aware of any just provocation they had given him. The foolishness of man perverts his way, and then his heart frets against the Lord, Pr **19**:**3**, and finds fault with him. They supposed that they could oblige God to appear for them, by bringing the ark into their camp. Those who have gone back in the life of religion, sometimes discover great fondness for the outward observances of it, as if those would save them; and as if the ark, God's throne, in the camp, would bring them to heaven, though the world and the flesh are on the throne in the heart.

Verses 10, 11

The taking of the ark was a great judgment upon Israel, and a certain token of God's displeasure. Let none think to shelter themselves from the wrath of God, under the cloak of outward profession.

Verses 12–18

The defeat of the army was very grievous to Eli as a judge; the tidings of the death of his two sons, to whom he had been so indulgent, and who, as he had reason to fear, died impenitent, touched him as a father; yet there was a greater concern on his spirit. And when the messenger concluded his story with, "The ark of God is taken," he is struck to the heart, and died immediately. A man may die miserably, yet not die eternally; may come to an untimely end, yet the end be peace.

Verses 19–22

The wife of Phinehas seems to have been a person of piety. Her dying regret was for the loss of the ark, and the departure of the glory from Israel. What is any earthly joy to her that feels herself dying? No joy but that which is spiritual and divine, will stand in any stead then; death is too serious a thing to admit the relish of any earthly joy. What is it to one that is lamenting the loss of the ark? What pleasure can we take in our creature comforts and enjoyments, if we want God's word and ordinances; especially if we want the comfort of his gracious presence, and the light of his countenance? If God go, the glory goes, and all good goes. Woe unto us if he depart! But though the glory is withdrawn from one sinful nation, city, or village after another, yet it shall never depart altogether, but shines forth in one place when eclipsed in another.

Chapter 5

Verses 1–5

See the ark's triumph over Dagon. Thus the kingdom of Satan will certainly fall before the kingdom of Christ, error before truth, profaneness before godliness, and corruption before grace in the hearts of the faithful. When the interests of religion seem to be ready to sink, even then we may be confident that the day of their triumph will come. When Christ, the true Ark of the covenant, really enters the heart of fallen man, which is indeed Satan's temple, all idols will fall, every endeavour to set them up again will be vain, sin will be forsaken, and unrighteous gain restored; the Lord will claim and possess the throne. But pride, self-love, and worldly lusts, though dethroned and crucified, still remain within us, like the stump of Dagon. Let us watch and pray that they may not prevail. Let us seek to have them more entirely destroyed.

Verses 6–12

The hand of the Lord was heavy upon the Philistines; he not only convinced them of their folly, but severely chastised their insolence. Yet they would not renounce Dagon; and instead of seeking God's mercy, they desired to get clear of his ark. Carnal hearts, when they smart under the judgments of God, would rather, if it were possible, put him far from them, than enter into covenant or communion with him, and seek him for their friend. But their devices to escape the Divine judgments only increase them. Those that fight against God will soon have enough of it.

Chapter 6

Verses 1–9

Seven months the Philistines were punished with the presence of the ark; so long it was a plague to them, because they would not send it home sooner. Sinners lengthen out their own miseries by refusing to part with their sins. The Israelites made no effort to recover the ark. Alas! where shall we find concern for religion prevail above all other matters? In times of public calamity we fear for ourselves, for our families, and for our country; but who cares for the ark of God? We are favoured with the gospel, but it is treated with neglect or contempt. We need not wonder if it should be taken from us; to many persons this, though the heavies of calamities, would occasion no grief. There are multitudes whom any profession would please as well as that of Christianity. But there are those who value the house, the word, and the ministry of God above their richest possessions, who dread the loss of these blessings more than death. How willing bad men are to shift off their convictions, and when they are in trouble, to believe it is a chance that happens; and that the rod has no voice which they should hear or heed!

Verses 10–18

These two kine knew their owner, their great Owner, whom Hophin and Phinehas knew not. God's providence takes notice even of brute creatures, and serves its own purposes by them. When the reapers saw the ark, they rejoiced; their joy for that was greater than the joy of harvest. The return of the ark, and the revival of holy ordinances, after days of restraint and trouble, are matters of great joy.

Verses 19–21

It is a great affront to God, for vain men to pry into, and meddle with the secret things which belong not to them, De **29**:**29**; Col **2**:**18**. Man was ruined by desiring forbidden knowledge. God will not suffer his ark to be profaned. Be not deceived, God is not mocked. Those that will not fear his goodness, and reverently use the tokens of his grace, shall be made to feel his justice. The number smitten is expressed in an unusual manner in the original, and it is probable that it means **1170**. They desire to be rid of the ark. Foolish men run from one extreme to the other. They should rather have asked, How may we have peace with God, and recover his favor? Mic **6**:**6**, **7**. Thus, when the word of God works with terror on sinners' consciences, they, instead of taking the blame and shame to themselves, quarrel with the word, and put that from them. Many stifle their convictions, and put salvation away from them.

Chapter 7

Verses 1–4

God will find a resting-place for his ark; if some thrust it from them, the hearts of others shall be inclined to receive it. It is no new thing for God's ark to be in a private house. Christ and his apostles preached from house to house, when they could not have public places. Twenty years passed before the house of Israel cared for the want of the ark. During this time the prophet Samuel laboured to revive true religion. The few words used are very expressive; and this was one of the most effectual revivals of religion which ever took place in Israel.

Verses 5, 6

Israel drew water and poured it out before the Lord; signifying their humiliation and sorrow for sin. They pour out their hearts in repentance before the Lord. They were free and full in their confession, and fixed in their resolution to cast away from them all their wrong doings. They made a public confession, We have sinned against the Lord; thus giving glory to God, and taking shame to themselves. And if we thus confess our sins, we shall find our God faithful and just to forgive us our sins.

Verses 7–12

The Philistines invaded Israel. When sinners begin to repent and reform, they must expect that Satan will muster all his force against them, and set his instruments at work to the utmost, to oppose and discourage them. The Israelites earnestly beg Samuel to pray for them. Oh what a comfort it is to all believers, that our great Intercessor above never ceases, is never silent! for he always appears in the presence of God for us. Samuel's sacrifice, without his prayer, had been an empty shadow. God gave a gracious answer. And Samuel erected a memorial of this victory, to the glory of God, and to encourage Israel. Through successive generations, the church of God has had cause to set up Eben-ezers for renewed deliverances; neither outward persecutions nor inward corruptions have prevailed against her, because "hitherto the Lord hath helped her:" and he will help, even to the end of the world.

Verses 13–17

In this great revival of true religion, the ark was neither removed to Shiloh, nor placed with the tabernacle any where else. This disregard to the Levitical institutions showed that their typical meaning formed their chief use; and when that was overlooked, they became a lifeless service, not to be compared with repentance, faith, and the love of God and man.

Chapter 8

Verses 1–3

It does not appear that Samuel's sons were so profane and vicious as Eli's sons; but they were corrupt judges, they turned aside after lucre. Samuel took no bribes, but his sons did, and then they perverted judgment. What added to the grievance of the people was, that they were threatened by an invasion from Nahash, king of the Ammonites.

Verses 4–9

Samuel was displeased; he could patiently bear what reflected on himself, and his own family; but it displeased him when they said, Give us a king to judge us, because that reflected upon God. It drove him to his knees. When any thing disturbs us, it is our interest, as well as our duty, to show our trouble before God. Samuel is to tell them that they shall have a king. Not that God was pleased with their request, but as sometimes he opposes us from loving-kindness, so at other times he gratifies us in wrath; he did so here. God knows how to bring glory to himself, and serves his own wise purposes, even by men's foolish counsels.

Verses 10–22

If they would have a king to rule them, as the eastern kings ruled their subjects, they would find the yoke exceedingly heavy. Those that submit to the government of the world and the flesh, are told plainly, what hard masters they are, and what tyranny the dominion of sin is. The law of God and the manner of men widely differ from each other; the former should be our rule in the several relations of life; the latter should be the measure of our expectations from others. These would be their grievances, and, when they complained to God, he would not hear them. When we bring ourselves into distress by our own wrong desires and projects, we justly forfeit the comfort of prayer, and the benefit of Divine aid. The people were obstinate and urgent in their demand. Sudden resolves and hasty desires make work for long and leisurely repentance. Our wisdom is, to be thankful for the advantages, and patient under the disadvantages of the government we may live under; and to pray continually for our rulers, that they may govern us in the fear of God, and that we may live under them in all godliness and honesty. And it is a hopeful symptom when our desires of worldly objects can brook delay; and when we can refer the time and manner of their being granted to God's providence.

Chapter 9

Verses 1–10

Saul readily went to seek his father's asses. His obedience to his father was praise-worthy. His servant proposed, that since they were now at Ramah, they should call on Samuel, and take his advice. Wherever we are, we should use our opportunities of acquainting ourselves with those who are wise and good. Many will consult a man of God, if he comes in their way, that would not go a step out of their way to get wisdom. We sensibly feel worldly losses, and bestow much pains to make them up; but how little do we attempt, and how soon are we weary, in seeking the salvation of our souls! If ministers could tell men how to secure their property, or to get wealth, they would be more consulted and honoured than they now are, though employed in teaching them how to escape eternal misery, and to obtain eternal life. Most people would rather be told their fortune than their duty. Samuel needed not their money, nor would he have denied his advice, if they had not brought it; but they gave it to him as a token of respect, and of the value they put upon his office, and according to the general usage of those times, always to bring a present to those in authority.

Verses 11–17

The very maid-servants of the city could direct to the prophet. They had heard of the sacrifice, and could tell of the necessity for Samuel's presence. It is no small benefit to live in religious and holy places. And we should always be ready to help those who are seeking after God's prophets. Though God had, in displeasure, granted Israel's request for a king, yet he sends them a man to be captain over them, to save them out of the hand of the Philistines. He does it, listening graciously to their cry.

Verses 18–27

Samuel, that good prophet, was so far from envying Saul, or bearing him any ill-will, that he was the first and most forward to do him honour. Both that evening and early the next morning, Samuel communed with Saul upon the flat roof of the house. We may suppose Samuel now convinced Saul that he was the person God had fixed upon for the government, and of his own willingness to resign. How different are the purposes of the Lord for us, from our intentions for ourselves! Perhaps Saul was the only one who ever went out to seek asses, and literally found a kingdom; but many have set out and moved their dwellings to seek riches and pleasures, who have been guided to places where they found salvation for their souls. Thus they have met with those who addressed them as if aware of the secrets of their lives and hearts, and have been led seriously to regard the word of the Lord. If this has been our case, though our worldly plans have not prospered, let us not care for that; the Lord has given us, or has prepared us for, what is far better.

Chapter 10

Verses 1–8

The sacred anointing, then used, pointed at the great Messiah, or Anointed One, the King of the church, and High Priest of our profession, who was anointed with the oil of the Spirit, not by measure, but without measure, and above all the priests and princes of the Jewish church. For Saul's further satisfaction, Samuel gives him some signs which should come to pass the same day. The first place he directs him to, was the sepulchre of one of his ancestors; there he must be reminded of his own mortality, and now that he had a crown before him, must think of his grave, in which all his honour would be laid in the dust. From the time of Samuel there appears to have been schools, or places where pious young men were brought up in the knowledge of Divine things. Saul should find himself strongly moved to join with them, and should be turned into another man from what he had been. The Spirit of God changes men, wonderfully transforms them. Saul, by praising God in the communion of saints, became another man, but it may be questioned if he became a new man.

Verses 9–16

The signs Samuel had given Saul, came to pass punctually; he found that God had given him another heart, another disposition of mind. Yet let not an outward show of devotion, and a sudden change for the present, be too much relied on; Saul among the prophets was Saul still. His being anointed was kept private. He leaves it to God to carry on his own work by Samuel, and sits still, to see how the matter will fall.

Verses 17–27

Samuel tells the people, Ye have this day rejected your God. So little fond was Saul now of that power, which soon after, when he possessed it, he could not think of parting with, that he hid himself. It is good to be conscious of our unworthiness and insufficiency for the services to which we are called; but men should not go into the contrary extreme, by refusing the employments to which the

Lord and the church call them. The greater part of the people treated the matter with indifference. Saul modestly went home to his own house, but was attended by a band of men whose hearts God disposed to support his authority. If the heart bend at any time the right way, it is because He has touched it. One touch is enough when it is Divine. Others despised him. Thus differently are men affected to our exalted Redeemer. There is a remnant who submit to him, and follow him wherever he goes; they are those whose hearts God has touched, whom he has made willing. But there are others who despise him, who ask, How shall this man save us? They are offended in him, and they will be punished.

Chapter 11

Verses 1–11

The first fruit of Saul's government was the rescue of Jabesh-gilead from the Ammonites. To save their lives, men will part with liberty, and even consent to have their eyes put out; is it then no wisdom to part with that sin which is as dear to us as our right eye, rather than to be cast into hell-fire? See the faith and confidence of Saul, and, grounded thereon, his courage and resolution. See also his activity in this business. When the Spirit of the Lord comes upon men, it will make them expert, even without experience. When zeal for the glory of God, and love for the brethren, urge men to earnest efforts, and when God is pleased to help, great effects may speedily be produced.

Verses 12–15

They now honoured Saul whom they had despised; and if an enemy be made a friend, that is more to our advantage than to have him slain. The once despised Saviour will at length be acknowledged by all as the Lord's own anointed king. As yet, upon his mercy-seat, he receives the submission of rebels, and even pleads their cause; but shortly, from his righteous tribunal, he will condemn all who persist in opposing him.

Chapter 12

Verses 1–5

Samuel not only cleared his own character, but set an example before Saul, while he showed the people their ingratitude to God and to himself. There is a just debt which all men to their own good name, especially men in public stations, which is, to guard it against unjust blame and suspicions, that they may finish their course with honour, as well as with joy. And that we have in our places lived honestly, will be our comfort, under any slights and contempt that may be put upon us.

Verses 6–15

The work of ministers is to reason with people; not only to exhort and direct, but to persuade, to convince men's judgments, and so to gain their wills and affections. Samuel reasons of the righteous acts of the Lord. Those who follow God faithfully, he will enable to continue following him. Disobedience would certainly be the ruin of Israel. We mistake if we think that we can escape God's justice, by trying to shake off his dominion. If we resolve that God shall not rule us, yet he will judge us.

Verses 16–25

At Samuel's word, God sent thunder and rain, at a season of the year when, in that country, the like was not seen. This was to convince them they had done wickedly in asking a king; not only by its coming at an unusual time, in wheat harvest, and on a clear day, but by the prophet's giving notice of it before. He showed their folly in desiring a king to save them, rather than God, or Samuel; promising themselves more from an arm of flesh, than from the arm of God, or from the power of prayer. Could their prince command such forces as the prophet could do by his prayers? It startled them very much. Some will not be brought to see their sins by any gentler methods than storms and thunders. They entreat Samuel to pray for them. Now they see their need of him whom shortly before they slighted. Thus many who will not have Christ to reign over them, would yet be glad to have him intercede for them, to turn away the wrath of God. Samuel aims to confirm the people in their religion. Whatever we make a god of, we shall find it deceive us. Creatures in their own places are good; but when put in God's place, they are vain things. We sin if we restrain prayer, and in particular if we cease praying for the church. They only asked him to pray for them; but he promises to do more, to teach them. He urges that they were bound in gratitude to serve God, considering what great things he had done for them; and that they were bound in interest to serve him, considering what he would do against them, if they should still do wickedly. Thus, as a faithful watchman, he gave them warning, and so delivered his own soul. If we consider what great things the Lord hath done for us, especially in the great work of redemption, we can neither want motive, encouragement, nor assistance in serving him.

Chapter 13

Verses 1–7

Saul reigned one year, and nothing particular happened; but in his second year the events recorded in this chapter took place. For above a year he gave the Philistine time to prepare for war, and to weaken and to disarm the Israelites. When men are lifted up in self-sufficiency, they are often led into folly. The chief advantages of the enemies of the church are derived from the misconduct of its professed friends. When Saul at length sounded an alarm, the people, dissatisfied with his management, or terrified by the power of the enemy, did not come to him, or speedily deserted him.

Verses 8–14

Saul broke the order expressly given by Samuel, see ch. **1**Sa **10**:**8**, as to what should be done in cases of extremity. Saul offered sacrifice without Samuel, and did it himself, though he was neither priest nor prophet. When charged with disobedience, he justified himself in what he had done, and gave no sign of repentance for it. He would have this act of disobedience pass for an instance of his prudence, and as a proof of his piety. Men destitute of inward piety, often lay great stress on the outward performances of religion. Samuel charges Saul with being an enemy to himself. Those that disobey the commandments of God, do foolishly for themselves. Sin is folly, and the greatest sinners are the greatest fools. Our disposition to obey or disobey God, will often be proved by our behaviour in things which appear small. Men see nothing but Saul's outward act, which seems small; but God saw that he did this with unbelief and distrust of his providence, with contempt of his authority and justice, and with rebellion against the light of his own conscience. Blessed Saviour, may we never, like Saul, bring our poor offerings, or fancied peace-offerings, without looking to thy precious, thy all-sufficient sacrifice! Thou only, O Lord, canst make, or hast made, our peace in the blood of the cross.

Verses 15–23

See how politic the Philistines were when they had power; they not only prevented the people of Israel from making weapons of war, but obliged them to depend upon their enemies, even for instruments of husbandry. How impolitic Saul was, who did not, in the beginning of his reign, set himself to redress this. Want of true sense always accompanies want of grace. Sins which appear to us very little, have dangerous consequences. Miserable is a guilty, defenceless nation; much more those who are destitute of the whole armour of God.

Chapter 14

Verses 1–15

Saul seems to have been quite at a loss, and unable to help himself. Those can never think themselves safe who see themselves out of God's protection. Now he sent for a priest and the ark. He hopes to make up matters with the Almighty by a partial reformation, as many do whose hearts are unhumbled and unchanged. Many love to have ministers who prophesy smooth things to them. Jonathan felt a Divine impulse and impression, putting him upon this bold adventure. God will direct the steps of those that acknowledge him in all their ways, and seek to him for direction, with full purpose of heart to follow his guidance. Sometimes we find most comfort in that which is least our own doing, and into which we have been led by the unexpected but well-observed turns of Divine providence. There was trembling in the host. It is called a trembling of God, signifying, not only a great trembling they could not resist, nor reason themselves out of, but that it came at once from the hand of God. He that made the heart, knows how to make it tremble.

Verses 16–23

The Philistines were, by the power of God, set against one another. The more evident it was that God did all, the more reason Saul had to inquire whether God would give him leave to do any thing. But he was in such haste to fight a fallen enemy, that he would not stay to end his devotions, nor hear what answer God would give him. He that believeth, will not make such haste, nor reckon any business so urgent, as not to allow time to take God with him.

Verses 24–35

Saul's severe order was very unwise; if it gained time, it lost strength for the pursuit. Such is the nature of our bodies, that daily work cannot be done without daily bread, which therefore our Father in heaven graciously gives. Saul was turning aside from God, and now he begins to build altars, being then most zealous, as many are, for the form of godliness when he was denying the power of it.

Verses 36–46

If God turns away our prayer, we have reason to suspect it is for some sin harboured in our hearts, which we should find out, that we may put it away, and put it to death. We should always first suspect and examine ourselves; but an unhumbled heart suspects every other person, and looks every where but at home for the sinful cause of calamity. Jonathan was discovered to be the offender. Those most indulgent to their own sins are most severe upon others; those who most disregard God's authority, are most impatient when their own commands are slighted. Such as cast abroad curses, endanger themselves and their families. What do we observe in the whole of Saul's behaviour on this occasion, but an impetuous, proud, malignant, impious disposition? And do we not in every instance perceive that man, left to himself, betrays the depravity of his nature, and is enslaved to the basest tempers.

Verses 47–52

Here is a general account of Saul's court and camp. He had little reason to be proud of his royal dignity, nor had any of his neighbours cause to envy him, for he had but little enjoyment after he took the kingdom. And often men's earthly glory makes a blaze just before the dark night of disgrace and woe comes on them.

Chapter 15

Verses 1–9

The sentence of condemnation against the Amalekites had gone forth long before, Ex **17**:14; De **25**:**19**, but they had been spared till they filled up the measure of their sins. We are sure that the righteous Lord does no injustice to any. The remembering the kindness of the ancestors of the Kenites, in favour to them, at the time God was punishing the injuries done by the ancestors of the Amalekites, tended to clear the righteousness of God in this dispensation. It is dangerous to be found in the company of God's enemies, and it is our duty and interest to come out from among them, lest we share in their sins and plagues, Re **18**:**4**. As the commandment had been express, and a test of Saul's obedience, his conduct evidently was the effect of a proud, rebellious spirit. He destroyed only the refuse, that was good for little. That which was now destroyed was sacrificed to the justice of God.

Verses 10–23

Repentance in God is not a change of mind, as it is in us, but a change of method. The change was in Saul; "He is turned back from following me." Hereby he made God his enemy. Samuel spent a whole night in pleading for Saul. The rejection of sinners is the grief of believers: God delights not in their death, nor should we. Saul boasts to Samuel of his obedience. Thus sinners think, by justifying themselves, to escape being judged of the Lord. The noise the cattle made, like the rust of the silver, Jas **5**:**3**, witnessed against him. Many boast of obedience to the command of God; but what means then their indulgence of the flesh, their love of the world, their angry and unkind spirit, and their neglect of holy duties, which witness against them? See of what evil covetousness is the root; and see what is the sinfulness of sin, and notice that in it which above any thing else makes it evil in the sight of the Lord; it is disobedience: "Thou didst not obey the voice of the Lord." Carnal, deceitful hearts, like Saul, think to excuse themselves from God's commandments by what pleases themselves. It is hard to convince the children of disobedience. But humble, sincere, and conscientious obedience to the will of God, is more pleasing and acceptable to him than all burnt-offering and sacrifices. God is more glorified and self more denied, by obedience than by sacrifice. It is much easier to bring a bullock or lamb to be burned upon the altar, than to bring every high thought into obedience to God, and to make our will subject to his will. Those are unfit and unworthy to rule over men, who are not willing that God should rule over them.

Verses 24–31

There were several signs of hypocrisy in Saul's repentance. **1**. He besought Samuel only, and seemed most anxious to stand right in his opinion, and to gain his favour. **2**. He excuses his fault, even when confessing it; that is never the way of a true penitent. **3**. All his care was to save his credit, and preserve his interest in the people. Men are fickle and alter their minds, feeble and cannot effect their purposes; something happens they could not foresee, by which their measures are broken; but with God it is not so. The Strength of Israel will not lie.

Verses 32–35

Many think the bitterness of death is past when it is not gone by; they put that evil day far from them, which is very near. Samuel calls Agag to account for his own sins. He followed the example of his ancestors' cruelty, justly therefore is all the righteous blood shed by Amalek required. Saul seems unconcerned at the token of God's displeasure which he lay under, yet Samuel mourns day and night for him. Jerusalem was carnally secure while Christ wept over it. Do we desire to do the whole will of God? Turn to him, not in form and appearance, but with sincerity.

Chapter 16

Verses 1–5

It appears that Saul was grown very wicked. Of what would he not be guilty, who durst think to kill Samuel? The elders of Bethlehem trembled at Samuel's coming. It becomes us to stand in awe of God's messengers, and to tremble at his word. His answer was, I come peaceably, for I come to sacrifice. When our Lord Jesus came into the world, though men had reason to fear that his errand was to condemn the world, yet he gave full assurance that he came peaceably, for he came to sacrifice, and he brought his offering with him; A body hast thou prepared me. Let us sanctify ourselves, and depend upon His sacrifice.

Verses 6–13

It was strange that Samuel, who had been so disappointed in Saul, whose countenance and stature recommended him, should judge of another man by that rule. We can tell how men look, but God can tell what they are. He judges of men by the heart. We often form a mistaken judgment of characters; but the Lord values only the faith, fear, and love, which are planted in the heart, beyond human discernment. And God does not favour our children according to our fond partiality, but often most honours and blesses those who have been least regarded. David at length was pitched upon. He was the youngest of the sons of Jesse; his name signifies Beloved; he was a type of God's beloved Son. It should seem, David was least set by of all the sons of Jesse. But the Spirit of the Lord came upon David from that day forward. His anointing was not an empty ceremony, a Divine power went with that instituted sign; he found himself advanced in wisdom and courage, with all the qualifications of a prince, though not advanced in his outward circumstances. This would satisfy him that his election was of God. The best evidence of our being predestinated to the kingdom of glory, is, our being sealed with the Spirit of promise, and experience of a work of grace in our hearts.

Verses 14–23

Saul is made a terror to himself. The Spirit of the Lord departed from him. If God and his grace do not rule us, sin and Satan will have possession of us. The devil, by the Divine permission, troubled and terrified Saul, by the corrupt humours of his body, and passions of his mind. He grew fretful, peevish, and discontented, and at times a madman. It is a pity that music, which may be serviceable to the good temper of the mind, should ever be abused, to support vanity and luxury, and made an occasion of drawing the heart from God and serious things. That is driving away the good Spirit, not the evil spirit. Music, diversions, company, or business, have for a time often been employed to quiet the wounded conscience; but nothing can effect a real cure but the blood of Christ, applied in faith, and the sanctifying Spirit sealing the pardon, by his holy comforts. All other plans to dispel religious melancholy are sure to add to distress, either in this world or the next.

Chapter 17

Verses 1–11

Men so entirely depend upon God in all things, that when he withdraws his help, the most valiant and resolute cannot find their hearts or hands, as daily experience shows.

Verses 12–30

Jesse little thought of sending his son to the army at that critical juncture; but the wise God orders actions and affairs, so as to serve his designs. In times of general formality and lukewarmness, every degree of zeal which implies readiness to go further, or to venture more in the cause of God than others, will be blamed as pride and ambition, and by none more than by near relations, like Eliab, or negligent superiors. It was a trial of David's meekness, patience, and constancy. He had right and reason on his side, and did not render railing for railing; with a soft answer he turned away his brother's wrath. This conquest of his own passion was more honourable than that of Goliath. Those who undertake great and public services, must not think it strange if they are spoken ill of, and opposed by those from whom they expect support and assistance. They must humbly go on with their work, in the face not only of enemies' threats, but of friends' slights and suspicions.

Verses 31–39

A shepherd lad, come the same morning from keeping sheep, had more courage than all the mighty men of Israel. Thus God often sends good words to his Israel, and does great things for them, by the weak and foolish things of the world. As he had answered his brother's passion with meekness, so David answered Saul's fear with faith. When David kept sheep, he proved himself very careful and tender of his flock. This reminds us of Christ, the good Shepherd, who not only ventured, but laid down his life for the sheep. Our experience ought to encourage us to trust in God, and be bold in the way of duty. He that has delivered, does and will continue to do so. David gained leave to fight the Philistine. Not being used to such armour as Saul put upon him, he was not satisfied to go in that manner; this was from the Lord, that it might more plainly appear he fought and conquered in faith, and that the victory was from Him who works by the feeblest and most despised means and instruments. It is not to be inquired how excellent any thing is, but how proper. Let Saul's coat be ever so rich, and his armour ever so strong, what is David the better if they fit him not? But faith, prayer, truth, and righteousness; the whole armour of God, and the mind that was in Christ; are equally needful for all the servants of the Lord, whatever may be their work.

Verses 40–47

The security and presumption of fools destroy them. Nothing can excel the humility, faith, and piety which appear in David's words. He expressed his assured expectation of success; he gloried in his mean appearance and arms, that the victory might be ascribed to the

Lord alone.

Verses 48–58

See how frail and uncertain life is, even when a man thinks himself best fortified; how quickly, how easily, and by how small a matter, the passage may be opened for life to go out, and death to enter! Let not the strong man glory in his strength, nor the armed man in his armour. God resists the proud, and pours contempt on those who defy him and his people. No one ever hardened his heart against God and prospered. The history is recorded, that all may exert themselves for the honour of God, and the support of his cause, with bold and unshaken reliance on him. There is one conflict in which all the followers of the Lamb are, and must be engaged; one enemy, more formidable than Goliath, still challenges the armies of Israel. But "resist the devil, and he will flee from you." Go forth to battle with the faith of David, and the powers of darkness shall not stand against you. But how often is the Christian foiled through an evil heart of unbelief!

Chapter 18

Verses 1–5

The friendship of David and Jonathan was the effect of Divine grace, which produces in true believers one heart and one soul, and causes them to love each other. This union of souls is from partaking in the Spirit of Christ. Where God unites hearts, carnal matters are too weak to separate them. Those who love Christ as their own souls, will be willing to join themselves to him in an everlasting covenant. It was certainly a great proof of the power of God's grace in David, that he was able to bear all this respect and honour, without being lifted up above measure.

Verses 6–11

David's troubles not only immediately follow his triumphs, but arise from them; such is the vanity of that which seems greatest in this world. It is a sign that the Spirit of God is departed from men, if, like Saul, they are peevish, envious, suspicious, and ill-natured. Compare David, with his harp in his hand, aiming to serve Saul, and Saul, with his javelin in his hand, aiming to slay David; and observe the sweetness and usefulness of God's persecuted people, and the barbarity of their persecutors. But David's safety must be ascribed to God's providence.

Verses 12–30

For a long time David was kept in continual apprehension of falling by the hand of Saul, yet he persevered in meek and respectful behaviour towards his persecutor. How uncommon is such prudence and discretion, especially under insults and provocations! Let us inquire if we imitate this part of the exemplary character before us. Are we behaving wisely in all our ways? Is there no sinful omission, no rashness of spirit, nothing wrong in our conduct? Opposition and perverseness in others, will not excuse wrong tempers in us, but should increase our care, and attention to the duties of our station. Consider Him that endured contradiction of sinners against himself, lest ye be weary and faint in your minds, Heb **12**:**3**. If David magnified the honour of being son-in-law to king Saul, how should we magnify the honour of being sons to the King of kings!

Chapter 19

Verses 1–10

How forcible are right words! Saul was, for a time, convinced of the unreasonableness of his enmity to David; but he continued his malice against David. So incurable is the hatred of the seed of the serpent against that of the woman; so deceitful and desperately wicked is the heart of man without the grace of God, Jer **17**:**9**.

Verses 11–24

Michal's stratagem to gain time till David got to a distance was allowable, but her falsehood had not even the plea of necessity to excuse it, and manifests that she was not influenced by the same spirit of piety which had dictated Jonathan's language to Saul. In flying to Samuel, David made God his refuge. Samuel, as a prophet, was best able to advise him what to do in this day of distress. He met with little rest or satisfaction in Saul's court, therefore went to seek it in Samuel's church. What little pleasure is to be had in this world, those have who live a life of communion with God; to that David returned in the time of trouble. So impatient was Saul after David's blood, so restless against him, that although baffled by one providence after another, he could not see that David was under the special protection of God. And when God will take this way to protect David, even Saul prophesies. Many have great gifts, yet no grace; they may prophesy in Christ's name, yet are disowned by him. Let us daily seek for renewing grace, which shall be in us as a well of water springing up into everlasting life. Let us cleave to truth and holiness with full purpose of heart. In every danger and trouble, let us seek protection, comfort, and direction in God's ordinances.

Chapter 20

Verses 1–10

The trials David met with, prepared him for future advancement. Thus the Lord deals with those whom he prepares unto glory. He does not put them into immediate possession of the kingdom, but leads them to it through much tribulation, which he makes the means of fitting them for it. Let them not murmur at his gracious appointment, nor distrust his care; but let them look forward with joyful expectation to the crown which is laid up for them. Sometimes it appears to us that there is but a step between us and death; at all times it may be so, and we should prepare for the event. But though dangers appear most threatening, we cannot die till the purpose of God concerning us is accomplished; nor till we have served our generation according to his will, if we are believers. Jonathan generously offers David his services. This is true friendship. Thus Christ testifies his love to us, Ask, and it shall be done for you; and we must testify our love to him, by keeping his commandments.

Verses 11–23

Jonathan faithfully promises that he would let David know how he found his father affected towards him. It will be kindness to ourselves and to ours, to secure an interest in those whom God favours, and to make his friends ours. True friendship rests on a firm basis, and is able to silence ambition, self-love, and undue regard for others. But who can fully understand the love of Jesus, who gave himself as a sacrifice for rebellious, polluted sinners! how great then ought to be the force and effects of our love to him, to his cause, and his people!

Verses 24–34

None were more constant than David in attending holy duties; nor had he been absent, but self-preservation obliged him to withdraw. In great peril present opportunities for Divine ordinances may be waved. But it is bad for us, except in case of necessity, to omit any opportunity of statedly attending on them. Jonathan did wisely and well for himself and family, to secure an interest in David, yet for this he is blamed. It is good to take God's people for our people. It will prove to our advantage at last, however it may now be thought against our interest. Saul was outrageous. What savage beasts, and worse, does anger make men!

Verses 35–42

The separation of two such faithful friends was grievous to both, but David's case was the more deplorable, for David was leaving all his comforts, even those of God's sanctuary. Christians need not sorrow, as men without hope; but being one with Christ, they are one with each other, and will meet in his presence ere long, to part no more; to meet where all tears shall be wiped from their eyes.

Chapter 21

Verses 1–9

David, in distress, fled to the tabernacle of God. It is great comfort in a day of trouble, that we have a God to go to, to whom we may open our cases, and from whom we may ask and expect direction. David told Ahimelech a gross untruth. What shall we say to this? The Scripture does not conceal it, and we dare not justify it; it was ill done, and proved of bad consequence; for it occasioned the death of the priests of the Lord. David thought upon it afterward with regret. David had great faith and courage, yet both failed him; he fell thus foully through fear and cowardice, and owing to the weakness of his faith. Had he trusted God aright, he would not have used such a sorry, sinful shift for his own preservation. It is written, not for us to do the like, no, not in the greatest straits, but for our warning. David asked of Ahimelech bread and a sword. Ahimelech supposed they might eat the shew-bread. The Son of David taught from it, that mercy is to be preferred to sacrifice; that ritual observances must give way to moral duties. Doeg set his foot as far within the tabernacle as David did. We little know with what hearts people come to the house of God, nor what use they will make of pretended devotion. If many come in simplicity of heart to serve their God, others come to observe their teachers and to prove accusers. Only God and the event can distinguish between a David and a Doeg, when both are in the tabernacle. (**1**Sa **21**:**10-15**)

Verses 10–15

God's persecuted people have often found better usage from Philistines than from Israelites. David had reason to put confidence in Achish, yet he began to be afraid. His conduct was degrading, and discovered wavering in his faith and courage. The more simply we depend on God, and obey him, the more comfortably and surely we shall walk through this troublesome world.

Chapter 22

Verses 1–5

See what weak instruments God sometimes uses, to bring about his own purposes. The Son of David is ready to receive distressed souls, who will be commanded by him. He receives all who come unto Him, however vile and miserable; he changes them into a holy people, and employs them in his service: those who would reign with him must be contented first to suffer with and for him. Observe with what tender concern David provided for his aged parents. The first thing he does is to find them a quiet habitation, whatever became of himself. Let children learn to honour their parents, in every thing consulting their ease and satisfaction. Though highly preferred, and much employed, let them not forget their aged parents. The steps of a good man are ordered by the Lord. And the Lord will preserve his people for their appointed work, however they may be hated and exposed.

Verses 6–19

See the nature of jealous malice and its pitiful arts. Saul looks upon all about him as his enemies, because they do not just say as he says. In Ahimelech's answer to Saul we have the language of conscious innocence. But what wickedness will not the evil spirit hurry men to when he gets the dominion! Saul alleges that which was utterly false and unproved. But the most bloody tyrants have found instruments of their cruelty as barbarous as themselves. Doeg, having murdered the priests, went to the city, Nob, and put all to the sword there. Nothing so vile but those may do it, who have provoked God to give them up to their hearts' lusts. Yet this was the accomplishment of the threatenings against the house of Eli. Though Saul was unrighteous in doing this, yet God was righteous in permitting it. No word of God shall fall to the ground.

Verses 20–23

David greatly lamented the calamity. It is great trouble to a good man to find himself any way the cause of evil to others. He must have been much pained, when he considered that his falsehood was one cause of this fatal event. David speaks with assurance of his own safety, and promises that Abiathar should have his protection. With the Son of David, all who are his may be sure they shall be in safeguard, Ps **91**:**1**. In the hurry and distraction David was continually in, he found time for communion with God, and found comfort in it.

Chapter 23

Verses 1–6

When princes persecute God's people, let them expect vexation on all sides. The way for any country to be quiet, is to let God's church be quiet in it: if Saul fight against David, the Philistines fight against his country. David considered himself the protector of the land. Thus did the Saviour Jesus, and left us an example. Those are unlike David, who sullenly decline to do good, if they are not rewarded for services.

Verses 7–13

Well might David complain of his enemies, that they rewarded him evil for good, and that for his love they were his adversaries. Christ was used thus basely. David applied to his great Protector for direction. No sooner was the ephod brought him than he made use of it. We have the Scriptures in our hands, let us take advice from them in doubtful cases. Say, Bring hither the Bible. David's address to God is very solemn, also very particular. God allows us to be so in our addresses to him; Lord, direct me in this matter, about which I am now at a loss. God knows not only what will be, but what would be, if it were not hindered; therefore he knows how to deliver the godly out of temptation, and how to render to every man according to his works.

Verses 14–18

David made no attempt against Saul; he kept God's way, waited God's time, and was content to secure himself in woods and wildernesses. Let it make us think the worse of this world, which often gives such bad treatment to its best men: let it make us long for that kingdom where goodness shall for ever be in glory, and holiness in honour. We find Jonathan comforting David. As a pious friend, he directed him to God, the Foundation of his comfort. As a self-denying friend, he takes pleasure in the prospect of David's advancement to the throne. As a constant friend, he renewed his friendship with him. Our covenant with God should be often renewed, and therein our communion with him kept up. If the con**verse** of one friend, at one meeting, gives comfort and strengthens our hearts, what may not be expected from the continual supports and powerful love of the Saviour of sinners, the covenanted Friend of believers!

Verses 19–29

In the midst of his wickedness, Saul affected to speak the language of piety. Such expressions, without suitable effects, can only amuse or deceive those who hear, and those who use them. This mountain was an emblem of the Divine Providence coming between David and the destroyer. Let us not be dismayed at the prospect of future difficulties, but stay ourselves upon Him who is wonderful in counsel and excellent in working. Sooner than his promise shall fail, he will commission Philistines to effect our escape, at the very moment when our case appears most desperate. God requires entire dependence on him, If ye will not believe, surely ye shall not be established, Isa **7**:**9**.

Chapter 24

Verses 1–7

God delivered Saul into David's hand. It was an opportunity given to David to exercise faith and patience. He had a promise of the kingdom, but no command to slay the king. He reasons strongly, both with himself and with his men, against doing Saul any hurt. Sin is a thing which it becomes us to startle at, and to resist temptations thereto. He not only would not do this bad thing himself, but he would not suffer those about him to do it. Thus he rendered good for evil, to him from whom he received evil for good; and was herein an example to all who are called Christians, not to be overcome of evil, but to overcome evil with good.

Verses 8–15

David was falsely charged with seeking Saul's hurt; he shows Saul that God's providence had given him opportunity to do it. And it was upon a good principle that he refused to do it. He declares his fixed resolution never to be his own avenger. If men wrong us, God will right us, at farthest, in the judgment of the great day.

Verses 16–22

Saul speaks as quite overcome with David's kindness. Many mourn for their sins, who do not truly repent of them; weep bitterly for them, yet continue in love and in league with them. Now God made good to David that word on which he had caused him to hope, that he would bring forth his righteousness as the light, Ps **37**:**6**. Those who take care to keep a good conscience, may leave it to God to secure them the credit of it. Sooner or later, God will force even those who are of the synagogue of Satan to know and to own those whom he has loved. They parted in peace. Saul went home convinced, but not converted; ashamed of his envy to David, yet retaining in his breast that root of bitterness; vexed that when at last he had found David, he could not find in his heart to destroy him, as he had designed. Malice often seems dead when it is only asleep, and will revive with double force. Yet, whether the Lord bind men's hands, or affect their hearts, so that they do not hurt us, the deliverance is equally from him; it is an evidence of his love, and an earnest of our salvation, and should make us thankful.

Chapter 25

Verse 1

All Israel lamented Samuel, and they had reason. He prayed daily for them. Those have hard hearts, who can bury faithful ministers without grief; who do not feel their loss of those who have prayed for them, and taught them the way of the Lord.

Verses 2–11

We should not have heard of Nabal, if nothing had passed between him and David. Observe his name, Nabal, "A fool;" so it signifies. Riches make men look great in the eye of the world; but to one that takes right views, Nabal looked very mean. He had no honour or honesty; he was churlish, cross, and ill-humoured; evil in his doings, hard and oppressive; a man that cared not what fraud and violence he used in getting and saving. What little reason have we to value the wealth of this world, when so great a churl as Nabal abounds, and so good a man as David suffers want!, David pleaded the kindness Nabal's shepherds had received. Considering that David's men were in distress and debt, and discontented, and the scarcity of provisions, it was by good management that they were kept from plundering. Nabal went into a passion, as covetous men are apt to do, when asked for any thing, thinking thus to cover one sin with another; and, by abusing the poor, to excuse themselves from relieving them. But God will not thus be mocked. Let this help us to bear reproaches and misrepresentations with patience and cheerfulness, and make us easy under them; it has often been the lot of the excellent ones of the earth. Nabal insists much on the property he had in the provisions of his table. May he not do what he will with his own? We mistake, if we think we are absolute lords of what we have, and may do what we please with it. No; we are but stewards, and must use it as we are directed, remembering it is not our own, but His who intrusted us with it.

Verses 12–17

God is kind to the evil and unthankful, and why may not we be so? David determined to destroy Nabal, and all that belonged to him. Is this thy voice, O David? Has he been so long in the school of affliction, where he should have learned patience, and yet is so passionate? He at other times was calm and considerate, but is put into such a heat by a few hard words, that he seeks to destroy a whole family. What are the best of men, when God leaves them to themselves, that they may know what is in their hearts? What need to pray, Lord, lead us not into temptation!

Verses 18–31

By a present Abigail atoned for Nabal's denial of David's request. Her behaviour was very submissive. Yielding pacifies great offences. She puts herself in the place of a penitent, and of a petitioner. She could not excuse her husband's conduct. She depends not upon her own reasonings, but on God's grace, to soften David, and expects that grace would work powerfully. She says that it was below him to take vengeance on so weak and despicable an enemy as Nabal, who, as he would do him no kindness, so he could do him no hurt. She foretells the glorious end of David's present troubles. God will preserve thy life; therefore it becomes not thee unjustly and unnecessarily to take away the lives of any, especially of the people of thy God and Saviour. Abigail keeps this argument for the last, as very powerful with so good a man; that the less he indulged his passion, the more he consulted his peace and the repose of his own conscience. Many have done that in a heat, which they have a thousand times wished undone again. The sweetness of revenge is soon turned into bitterness. When tempted to sin, we should consider how it will appear when we think upon it afterwards.

Verses 32–39

David gives God thanks for sending him this happy check in a sinful way. Whoever meet us with counsel, direction, comfort, caution, or seasonable reproof, we must see God sending them. We ought to be very thankful for those happy providences which are the means of keeping us from sinning. Most people think it enough, if they take reproof patiently; but few will take it thankfully, and commend those who give it, and accept it as a favour. The nearer we are to committing sin, the greater is the mercy of a seasonable restraint. Sinners are often most secure when most in danger. He was very drunk. A sign he was Nabal, a fool, that could not use plenty without abusing it; who could not be pleasant with his friends without making a beast of himself. There is not a surer sign that a man has but little wisdom, nor a surer way to destroy the little he has, than drinking to excess. Next morning, how he is changed! His heart overnight merry with wine, next morning heavy as a stone; so deceitful are carnal pleasures, so soon passes the laughter of the fool; the end of that mirth is heaviness. Drunkards are sad, when they reflect upon their own folly. About ten days after, the Lord smote Nabal, that he died. David blessed God that he had been kept from killing Nabal. Worldly sorrow, mortified pride, and an affrighted conscience, sometimes end the joys of the sensualist, and separate the covetous man from his wealth; but, whatever the weapon, the Lord smites men with death when it pleases him.

Verses 39–44

Abigail believed that David would be king over Israel, and greatly esteemed his pious and excellent character. She deemed his proposal of marriage honourable, and advantageous to her, notwithstanding his present difficulties. With great humility, and doubtless agreeably to the customs of those times, she consented, being willing to share his trails. Thus those who join themselves to Christ, must be willing now to suffer with him, believing that hereafter they shall reign with him.

Chapter 26

Verses 1–12

How soon do unholy hearts lose the good impressions convictions have made upon them! How helpless were Saul and all his men! All as though disarmed and chained, yet nothing is done to them; they are only asleep. How easily can God weaken the strongest, befool the wisest, and baffle the most watchful! David still resolved to wait till God thought fit to avenge him on Saul. He will by no means force his way to the promised crown by any wrong methods. The temptation was very strong; but if he yielded, he would sin against God, therefore he resisted the temptation, and trusted God with the event.

Verses 13–20

David reasoned seriously and affectionately with Saul. Those who forbid our attendance on God's ordinances, do what they can to estrange us from God, and to make us heathens. We are to reckon that which exposes us to sin the greatest injury that can be done us. If the Lord stirred thee up against me, either in displeasure to me, taking this way to punish me for my sins against him, or in displeasure to thee, if it be the effect of that evil spirit from the Lord which troubles thee; let Him accept an offering from us both. Let us join in seeking peace, and to be reconciled with God by sacrifice.

Verses 21–25

Saul repeated his good words and good wishes. But he showed no evidence of true repentance towards God. David and Saul parted to meet no more. No reconciliation among men is firm, which is not founded in an cemented by peace with God through Jesus Christ. In sinning against God, men play the fool, and err exceedingly. Many obtain a passing view of these truths, who hate and close their eyes against the light. Fair professions do not entitle those to confidence who have long sinned against the light, yet the confessions of obstinate sinners may satisfy us that we are in the right way, and encourage us to persevere, expecting our recompence from the Lord alone.

Chapter 27

Verses 1–7

Unbelief is a sin that easily besets even good men, when without are fightings, and within are fears; and it is a hard matter to get over them. Lord, increase our faith! We may blush to think that the word of a Philistine should go further than the word of an Israelite, and that the city of Gath should be a place of refuge for a good man, when the cities of Israel refuse him a safe abode. David gained a comfortable settlement, not only at a distance from Gath, but bordering upon Israel, where he might keep up a correspondence with his own countrymen.

Verses 8–12

While David was in the land of the Philistines, he attacked some remains of the devoted nations. The people whom he cut off were long before doomed to destruction. It is often wisdom to shun public notice, but we must in no situation be idle. We must always try to do somewhat in the cause of God. This expedition David hid from Achish. But an equivocation which serves the purpose of a lie, is as like to it as a hypocrite is to a profane person, it is only better in appearance, therefore more dangerous. Yet, though believers often manifest imperfections, they can never be prevailed upon to renounce the service of God, and to unite interests with his enemies, or finally to become the servants of sin and Satan. But what a train of evils follow from unbelief! When we forget the Lord's past mercies, and his gracious assurances, we shall be overwhelmed with desponding fears, and probably be led to adopt some dishonourable method to get rid of our troubles. Nothing can so effectually establish us in holy tempers and practices, and preserve us from perplexities, as firm, unshaken dependence upon the promises of God in Christ Jesus.

Chapter 28

Verses 1–6

David could not refuse Achish without danger. If he promised assistance, and then stood neuter, or went over to the Israelites, he would behave with ingratitude and treachery. If he fought against Israel, he would sin greatly. It seemed impossible that he should get out of this difficulty with a clear conscience; but his evasive answer, intended to gain time, was not consistent with the character of an Israelite indeed. Troubles are terrors to the children of disobedience. In his distress, Saul inquired of the Lord. He did not seek in faith, but with a double, unstable mind. Saul had put the law in force against those that had familiar spirits, Ex **22**:**18**. Many seem zealous against, sin, when they are any way hurt by it, who have no concern for the glory of God, nor any dislike of sin as sin. Many seem enemies to sin in others, while they indulge it in themselves. Saul will drive the devil out of his kingdom, yet harbours him in his heart by envy and malice. How foolish to consult those whom, according to God's law, he had endeavoured to root out!

Verses 7–19

When we go from the plain path of duty, every thing draws us further aside, and increases our perplexity and temptation. Saul desires the woman to bring one from the dead, with whom he wished to speak; this was expressly forbidden, De **18**:**11**. All real or pretended witchcraft or conjuration, is a malicious or an ignorant attempt to gain knowledge or help from some creature, when it cannot be had from the Lord in the path of duty. While Samuel was living, we never read of Saul's going to advise with him in any difficulties; it had been well for him if he had. But now he is dead, "Bring me up Samuel." Many who despise and persecute God's saints and ministers when living, would be glad to have them again, when they are gone. The whole shows that it was no human fraud or trick. Though the woman could not cause Samuel's being sent, yet Saul's inquiry might be the occasion of it. The woman's surprise and terror proved that it was an unusual and unexpected appearance. Saul had despised Samuel's solemn warnings in his lifetime, yet now that he hoped, as in defiance of God, to obtain some counsel and encouragement from him, might not God permit the soul of his departed prophet to appear to Saul, to confirm his former sentence, and denounce his doom? The expression, "Thou and thy sons shall be with me," means no more than that they shall be in the eternal world. There appears much solemnity in God's permitting the soul of a departed prophet to come as a witness from heaven, to confirm the word he had spoken on earth.

Verses 20–25

Those that expect any good counsel or comfort, otherwise than from God, and in the way of his institutions, will be as wretchedly disappointed as Saul. Though terrified even to despair, he was not humbled. He confessed not his sins, offered no sacrifices, and presented no supplications. He does not seem to have cared about his sons or his people, or to have attempted any escape; but in sullen despair he rushed upon his doom. God sets up a few such beacons, to warn men not to stifle convictions, or despise his word. But while one repenting thought remains, let no sinner suppose himself in this case. Let him humble himself before God, determined to live and die beseeching his favour, and he will succeed.

Chapter 29

Verses 1–5

David waited with a secret hope that the Lord would help him out of his difficulty. But he seems to have been influenced too much by the fear of man, in consenting to attend Achish. It is hard to come near to the brink of sin, and not to fall in. God inclined the princes of the Philistines to oppose David's being employed in the battle. Thus their dislike befriended him, when no friend could do him such a kindness.

Verses 6–11

David scarcely ever had a greater deliverance than when dismissed from such insnaring service. God's people should always behave themselves so, as, if possible, to get the good word of all they have dealings with: and it is due to those who have acted well, to speak well of them.

Chapter 30

Verses 1–6

When we go abroad in the way of our duty, we may comfortably hope that God will take care of our families in our absence, but not otherwise. If, when we come off a journey, we find our abode in peace, and not laid waste, as David here found his, let the Lord be praised for it. David's men murmured against him. Great faith must expect such severe trials. But, observe, that David was brought thus low, only just before he was raised to the throne. When things are at the worst with the church and people of God, then they begin to mend. David encouraged himself in the Lord his God. His men fretted at their loss, the soul of the people was bitter; their own discontent and impatience added to the affliction and misery. But David bore it better, though he had more reason than any of them to lament it. They gave liberty to their passions, but he set his graces to work; and while they dispirited each other, he, by encouraging himself in God, kept his spirit calm. Those who have taken the Lord for their God, may take encouragement from him in the worst times.

Verses 7–15

If in all our ways, even when, as in this case, there can be no doubt they are just, we acknowledge God, we may expect that he will direct our steps, as he did those of David. David, in tenderness to his men, would by no means urge them beyond their strength. The Son of David thus considers the frames of his followers, who are not all alike strong and vigorous in their spiritual pursuits and conflicts; but, where we are weak, there he is kind; nay more, there he is strong, 2Co **12**:**9**, **10**. A poor Egyptian lad, scarcely alive, is made the means of a great deal of good to David. Justly did Providence make this poor servant, who was basely used by his master, an instrument in the destruction of the Amalekites; for God hears the cry of the oppressed. Those are unworthy the name of true Israelites, who shut up their compassion from persons in distress. We should neither do an injury nor deny a kindness to any man; some time or other it may be in the power of the lowest to return a kindness or an injury.

Verses 16–20

Sinners are nearest to ruin, when they cry, Peace and safety, and put the evil day far from them. Nor does any thing give our spiritual enemies more advantage than sensuality and indulgence. Eating and drinking, and dancing, have been the soft and pleasant way in which many have gone down to the congregation of the dead. The spoil was recovered, and brought off; nothing was lost, but a great deal gained.

Verses 21–31

What God gives us, he designs we should do good with. In distributing the spoil, David was just and kind. Those are men of Belial indeed, who delight in putting hardships upon their brethren, and care not who is starved, so that they may be fed to the full. David was generous and kind to all his friends. Those who consider the Lord as the Giver of their abundance, will dispose of it with fairness and liberality.

Chapter 31

Verses 1–7

We cannot judge of the spiritual or eternal state of any by the manner of their death; for in that, there is one event to the righteous and to the wicked. Saul, when sorely wounded, and unable to resist or to flee, expressed no concern about his never-dying soul; but only desired that the Philistines might not insult over him, or put him to pain, and he became his own murderer. As it is the grand deceit of the devil, to persuade sinners, under great difficulties, to fly to this last act of desperation, it is well to fortify the mind against it, by a serious consideration of its sinfulness before God, and its miserable consequences in society. But our security is not in ourselves. Let us seek protection from Him who keepeth Israel. Let us watch and pray; and take unto us the whole armour of God, that we may be able to withstand in the evil day, and having done all, to stand.

Verses 8–13

The Scripture makes no mention what became of the souls of Saul and his sons, after they were dead; but of their bodies only: secret things belong not to us. It is of little consequence by what means we die, or what is done with our dead bodies. If our souls are saved, our bodies will be raised incorruptible and glorious; but not to fear His wrath, who is able to destroy both body and soul in hell, is the extreme of folly and wickedness. How useless is the respect of fellow-creatures to those who are suffering the wrath of God! While pompous funerals, grand monuments, and he praises of men, honour the memory of the deceased, the soul may be suffering in the regions of darkness and despair! Let us seek that honour which cometh from God only.

Samuel

This book is the history of the reign of king David. It relates his victories, the growth of the prosperity of Israel, and his reformation of the state of religion. With these events are recorded the grievous sins he committed, and the family as well as public troubles with which he was punished. We here meet with many things worthy of imitation, and many that are written for our warning. The history of king David is given in Scripture with much faithfulness, and from it he appears, to those who fairly balance his many virtues and excellent qualities against his faults, to have been a great and good man.

Chapter 1

Verses 1–10

The blow which opened David's way to the throne was given about the time he had been sorely distressed. Those who commit their concerns to the Lord, will quietly abide his will. It shows that he desired not Saul's death, and he was not impatient to come to the throne.

Verses 11–16

David was sincere in his mourning for Saul; and all with him humbled themselves under the hand of God, laid so heavily upon Israel by this defeat. The man who brought the tidings, David put to death, as a murderer of his prince. David herein did not do unjustly; the Amalekite confessed the crime. If he did as he said, he deserved to die for treason; and his lying to David, if indeed it were a lie, proved, as sooner or later that sin will prove, lying against himself. Hereby David showed himself zealous for public justice, without regard to his own private interest.

Verses 17–27

Kasheth, or "the bow," probably was the title of this mournful, funeral song. David does not commend Saul for what he was not; and says nothing of his piety or goodness. Jonathan was a dutiful son, Saul an affectionate father, therefore dear to each other. David had reason to say, that Jonathan's love to him was wonderful. Next to the love between Christ and his people, that affection which springs form it, produces the strongest friendship. The trouble of the Lord's people, and triumphs of his enemies, will always grieve true believers, whatever advantages they may obtain by them.

Chapter 2

Verses 1–7

After the death of Saul, many went to David at Ziklag, **1**Ch **12**:**22**, but he trusted in God who promised him the kingdom, to give it in his own time and manner. Yet assurance of hope in God's promise, will quicken pious endeavours. If I be chosen to the crown of life, it does not follow, Then I will do nothing; but, Then I will do all that God directs me. This good use David made of his election, and so will all whom God has chosen. In all our journeys and removes, it is comfortable to see God going before us; and we may do so, if by faith and prayer we set Him before us. God, according to the promise, directed David's path. David rose gradually: thus the kingdom of the Messiah, the Son of David, is set up by degrees; he is Lord of all, but we see not yet all things put under him.

Verses 8–17

The nation in general refused David. By this the Lord trained up his servant for future honour and usefulness; and the tendency of true godliness was shown in his behaviour while passing through various difficulties. David was herein a type of Christ, whom Israel would not submit to, though anointed of the Father to be a Prince and a Saviour to them. Abner meant, Let the young men fight before us, when he said, Let them play before us: fools thus make a mock at sin. But he is unworthy the name of a man, that can thus trifle with human blood.

Verses 18–24

Death often comes by ways we least suspect. We are often betrayed by the accomplishments we are proud of! Asahel's swiftness, which he presumed so much upon, did him no service, but hastened his end.

Verses 25–32

Abner appeals to Joab concerning the miserable consequences of a civil war. Those who make light of such unnatural contests, will find that they are bitterness to all concerned. How easy it is for men to use reason, when it makes for them, who would not use it, if it made against them! See how the issue of things alter men's minds! The same thing which looked pleasant in the morning, at night looked dismal. Those who are most forward to enter into contention, will repent before they have done with it, and had better leave it off before it be meddled with, as Solomon advises. This is true of every sin, oh that men would consider it in time, that it will be bitterness in the latter end! Asahel's funeral is here mentioned. Distinctions are made between the dust of some and that of others; but in the resurrection no difference will be made, but between the godly and ungodly, which will remain for ever.

Chapter 3

Verses 1–6

The length of this war tried the faith and patience of David, and made his settlement at last the more welcome. The contest between grace and corruption in the hearts of believers, may fitly be compared to this warfare. There is a long war between them, the flesh lusting against the spirit, and the spirit against the flesh; but as the work of holiness is carried on, corruption, like the house of Saul, grows weaker and weaker; while grace, like the house of David, grows stronger and stronger.

Verses 7–21

Many, like Abner, are not above committing base crimes, who are too proud to bear reproof, or even the suspicion of being guilty. While men go on in sin, and apparently without concern, they are often conscious that they are fighting against God. Many mean to serve their own purposes; and will betray those who trust them, when they can get any advantage. Yet the Lord serves his own designs, even by those who are thus actuated by revenge, ambition, or lust; but as they intend not to honour him, in the end they will be thrown aside with contempt. There was real generosity both to Michal and to the memory of Saul, in David's receiving the former, remembering probably how once he owed his life to her affection, and knowing that she was separated from him partly by her father's authority. Let no man set his heart on that which he is not entitled to. If any disagreement has separated husband and wife, as they expect the blessing of God, let them be reconciled, and live together in love.

Verses 22–39

Judgments are prepared for such scorners as Abner; but Joab, in what he did, acted wickedly. David laid Abner's murder deeply to heart, and in many ways expressed his detestation of it. The guilt of blood brings a curse upon families: if men do not avenge it, God will. It is a sad thing to die like a fool, as they do that any way shorten their own days, and those who make no provision for another world. Who would be fond of power, when a man may have the name of it, and must be accountable for it, yet is hampered in the use of it? David ought to have done his duty, and then trusted God with the issue. Carnal policy spared Joab. The Son of David may long delay, but never fails to punish impenitent sinners. He who now reigns upon the throne of David, has a kingdom of a nobler kind. Whatever He doeth, is noticed by all his willing people, and is pleasing to them.

Chapter 4

Verses 1–7

See how Ishbosheth was murdered! When those difficulties dispirit us, which should sharpen our endeavours, we betray both our heavenly crowns and our earthly lives. Love not sleep, lest thou come to poverty and ruin. The idle soul is an easy prey to the destroyer. We know not when and where death will meet us. When we lie down to sleep, we are not sure that we may not sleep the sleep of death before we awake; nor do we know from what hand the death-blow may come.

Verses 8–12

A person may be glad to obtain his just wishes, and yet really regret the means by which he receives them. He may be sorry for the death of a person by which he is a gainer. These men shed innocent blood, from the basest motives. David justly executed vengeance upon them. He would not be beholden to any to help him by unlawful practices. God had helped him over many a difficulty, and through many a danger, therefore he depended upon him to crown and complete his own work. He speaks of his redemption from all adversity, as a thing done; though he had many storms yet before him, he knew that He who had delivered, would deliver.

Chapter 5

Verses 1–5

David was anointed king a third time. His advances were gradual, that his faith might be tried, and that he might gain experience. Thus his kingdom typified that of the Messiah, which was to come to its height by degrees. Thus Jesus became our Brother, took upon him our nature, dwelt in it that he might become our Prince and Saviour: thus the humbled sinner takes encouragement from the endearing relation, applies for his salvation, submits to his authority, and craves his protection.

Verses 6–10

The enemies of God's people are often very confident of their own strength, and most secure when their day to fall draws nigh. But the pride and insolence of the Jebusites animated David, and the Lord God of hosts was with him. Thus in the day of God's power, Satan's strong-hold, the human heart, is changed into a habitation of God through the Spirit, and into a throne on which the Son of David rules, and brings every thought into obedience to himself. May He thus come, and claim, and cleanse, each of our hearts; and, destroying every idol, may he reign there for ever!

Verses 11–16

David's house was not the worse, nor the less fit to be dedicated to God, for being built by the sons of the stranger. It is prophesied of the gospel church, The sons of strangers shall build up thy walls, and their kings shall minister unto thee, Isa **60**:**10**. David's government was rooted and built up. David was established king; so is the Son of David, and all who, through him, are made to our God kings and priests. Never had the nation of Israel appeared so great as it began now to be. Many have the favour and love of God, yet do not perceive it, and so want the comfort of it; but to be exalted to that, and to perceive it, is happiness. David owned it was for his people's sake God had done great things for him; that he might be a blessing to them, and that they might be happy under him.

Verses 17–25

The Philistines considered not that David had the presence of God with him, which Saul had forfeited and lost. The kingdom of the Messiah, as soon as it was set up in the world, was thus attacked by the powers of darkness. The heathen raged, and the kings of the earth set themselves to oppose it; but all in vain, Ps **2**:**1**, &c. The destruction will turn, as this did, upon Satan's own kingdom. David owns dependence on God for victory; and refers himself to the good pleasure of God, Wilt thou do it? The assurance God has given us of victory over our spiritual enemies, should encourage us in our spiritual conflicts. David waited till God moved; he stirred then, but not till then. He was trained up in dependence on God and his providence. God performed his promise, and David failed not to improve his advantages. When the kingdom of the Messiah was to be set up, the apostles, who were to beat down the devil's kingdom, must not attempt any thing till they received the promise of the Spirit; who came with a sound from heaven, as of a rushing, mighty wind, Ac **2**:**2**.

Chapter 6

Verses 1–5

God is present with the souls of his people, when they want the outward tokens of his presence; but now David is settled in the throne, the honour of the ark begins to revive. Let us learn hence, to think and to speak highly of God; and to think and speak honourably of holy ordinances, which are to us as the ark was unto Israel, the tokens of God's presence, Mt **28**:**20**. Christ is our Ark; in and by him God manifests his favour, and accepts our prayers and praises. The ark especially typified Christ and his mediation, in which the name of Jehovah and all his glories are displayed. The priests should have carried the ark upon their shoulders. Philistines may carry the ark in a cart without suffering for it; but if Israelites do so, it is at their peril, because this was not what God appointed.

Verses 6–11

Uzzah was struck dead for touching the ark. God saw presumption and irreverence in Uzzah's heart. Familiarity, even with that which is most awful, is apt to breed contempt. If it were so great a crime for one to lay hold on the ark of the covenant who had no right to do so, what is it for those to lay claim to the privileges of the covenant that come not up to the terms of it? Obed-edom opened his doors without fear, knowing the ark was a savour of death unto death to those only who treated it wrong. The same hand that punished Uzzah's proud presumption, rewarded Obed-edom's humble boldness. Let none think the worse of the gospel for the judgments on those that reject it, but consider the blessings it brings to all who receive it. Let masters of families be encouraged to keep up religion in their families. It is good to live in a family that entertains the ark, for all about it will fare the better.

Verses 12–19

It became evident, that happy was the man who had the ark near him. Christ is indeed a Stone of stumbling, and a Rock of offence, to those that are disobedient; but to those that believe, he is a Corner-stone, elect, precious, **1**Pe **2**:**6**–**8**. Let us be religious. Is the ark a blessing to others' houses? We may have it, and the blessing of it, without fetching it away from our neighbours. David, at first setting out, offered sacrifices to God. We are likely to speed in our enterprises, when we begin with God, and give diligence to seek peace with him. And we are so unworthy, and our services are so defiled, that all our joy in God must be connected with repentance and faith in the Redeemer's atoning blood. David attended with high expressions of joy. We ought to serve God with our whole body and soul, and with every endowment and power we possess. On this occasion David laid aside his royal robes, and put on a plain linen dress. David prayed with and for the people, and as a prophet, solemnly blessed them in the name of the Lord.

Verses 20–23

David returned to bless his household, to pray with them, and for them, and to offer up family thanksgiving for this national mercy. It is angels' work to worship God, surely that cannot lower the greatest of men. But even the palaces of princes are not free from family troubles. Exercises of religion appear mean in the eyes of those who have little or no religion themselves. If we can approve ourselves to God in what we do in religion, and do it as before the Lord, we need not heed reproach. Piety will have its praise: let us not be indifferent in it, nor afraid or ashamed to own it. David was contented to justify himself, and he did not further reprove or blame Michal's insolence; but God punished her. Those that honour God, he will honour; but those that despise him, and his servants and service, shall be lightly esteemed.

Chapter 7

Verses 1–3

David being at rest in his palace, considered how he might best employ his leisure and prosperity in the service of God. He formed a design to build a temple for the ark. Nathan here did not speak as a prophet, but as a godly man, encouraging David by his private judgment. We ought to do all we can to encourage and promote the good purposes and designs of others, and, as we have opportunity, to forward a good work.

Verses 4–17

Blessings are promised to the family and posterity of David. These promises relate to Solomon, David's immediate successor, and the royal line of Judah. But they also relate to Christ, who is often called David and the Son of David. To him God gave all power in heaven and earth, with authority to execute judgment. He was to build the gospel temple, a house for God's name; the spiritual temple of true believers, to be a habitation of God through the Spirit. The establishing of his house, his throne, and his kingdom for ever, can be applied to no other than to Christ and his kingdom: David's house and kingdom long since came to an end. The committing iniquity cannot be applied to the Messiah himself, but to his spiritual seed; true believers have infirmities, for which they must expect to be corrected, though they are not cast off.

Verses 18–29

David's prayer is full of the breathings of devout affection toward God. He had low thoughts of his own merits. All we have, must be looked upon as Divine gifts. He speaks very highly and honourably of the Lord's favours to him. Considering what the character and condition of man is, we may be amazed that God should deal with him as he does. The promise of Christ includes all; if the Lord God be ours, what more can we ask, or think of? Eph **3**:**20**. He knows us better than we know ourselves; therefore let us be satisfied with what he has done for us. What can we say more for ourselves in our prayers, than God has said for us in his promises? David ascribes all to the free grace of God. Both the great things He had done for him, and the great things He had made known to him. All was for his word's sake, that is, for the sake of Christ the eternal Word. Many, when they go to pray, have their hearts to seek, but David's heart was found, that is, it was fixed; gathered in from its wanderings, entirely engaged to the duty, and employed in it. That prayer which is from the tongue only, will not please God; it must be found in the heart: that must be lifted up and poured out before God. He builds his faith, and hopes to speed, upon the sureness of God's promise. David prays for the performance of the promise. With God, saying and doing are not two things, as they often are with men; God will do as he hath said. The promises of God are not made to us by name, as to David, but they belong to all who believe in Jesus Christ, and plead them in his name.

Chapter 8

Verses 1–8

David subdued the Philistines. They had long been troublesome to Israel. And after the long and frequent struggles the saints have with the powers of darkness, like Israel with the Philistines, the Son of David shall tread them all under foot, and make the saints more than conquerors. He smote the Moabites, and made them tributaries to Israel. Two parts he destroyed, the third part he spared. The line that was to keep alive, though it was but one, is ordered to be a full line. Let the line of mercy be stretched to the utmost. He smote the Syrians. In all these wars David was protected, for this in his psalms he often gives glory to God.

Verses 9–14

All the precious things David was master of, were dedicated things; they were designed for building the temple. The idols of gold David destroyed, 2Sa **5**:**21**, but the vessels of gold he dedicated. Thus, in the conquest of a soul by the grace of the Son of David, what stands in opposition to God must be destroyed, every lust must be mortified and crucified, but what may glorify him must be dedicated; thus the property of it is altered. God employs his servants in various ways; some, as David, in spiritual battles; others, as Solomon, in spiritual buildings; and one prepares work for the other, that God may have the glory of all.

Verses 15–18

David neither did wrong, nor denied or delayed right to any. This speaks his close application to business; also his readiness to admit all addresses and appeals made to him. He had no respect of persons in judgment. Herein he was a type of Christ. To Him let us submit, his friendship let us seek, his service let us count our pleasure, diligently attending to the work he assigns to each of us. David made his sons chief rulers; but all believers, Christ's spiritual seed, are better preferred, for they are made kings and priests to our God, Re **1**:**6**.

Chapter 9

Verses 1–8

Amidst numerous affairs we are apt to forget the gratitude we owe, and the engagements we are under, not only to our friends, but to God himself. Yet persons of real godliness will have no rest till they have discharged them. And the most proper objects of kindness and charity, frequently will not be found without inquiry. Jonathan was David's sworn friend, therefore he shows kindness to his son Mephibosheth. God is faithful to us; let us not be unfaithful to one another. If Providence has raised us, and our friends and their families are brought low, we must look upon that as giving us the fairer opportunity of being kind to them.

Verses 9–13

As David was a type of Christ, his Lord and Son, his Root and Offspring, let his kindness to Mephibosheth remind us of the kindness and love of God our Saviour to fallen man, to whom he was under no obligation, as David was to Jonathan. The Son of God seeks this lost and ruined race, who sought not after him. He comes to seek and to save them!

Chapter 10

Verses 1–5

Nahash had been an enemy to Israel, yet had showed kindness to David. David therefore resolves gratefully to return it. If a Pharisee gives alms in pride, though God will not reward it, yet he that receives the alms ought to return thanks for it. Those who bear ill-will to their neighbours, are resolved not to believe that their neighbours bear any good-will to them. There is nothing so well meant, but it may be ill interpreted, and is wont to be so, by men who love nobody but themselves. The best men must not think it strange if they are thus misrepresented. Charity thinketh no evil. According to the usages of those days and countries, Hanun treated David's ambassadors in the most contemptuous manner. David showed much concern for his servants. Let us learn not to lay unjust reproaches to heart; they will wear off, and turn only to the shame of those who utter or do them; while the reputation wrongfully hurt in a little time grows again, as these beards did. God will bring forth thy righteousness as the light, therefore wait patiently for him, Ps **37**:**6**, **7**.

Verses 6–14

They that are at war with the Son of David, not only give the provocation, but begin the war. God has forces to send against those that set his wrath at defiance, Isa **5**:**19**, which will convince them that none ever hardened his heart against God, and prospered. Christ's soldiers should strengthen one another's hands in their spiritual warfare. Let nothing be wanting in us, whatever the success be. When we make conscience of doing our duty, we may, with satisfaction, leave the event with God, assuredly hoping for his salvation in his own way and time.

Verses 15–19

Here is a new attempt of the Syrians. Even the baffled cause will make head as long as there is any life in it; the enemies of the Son of David do so. But now the promise made to Abraham, Ge **15**:**18**, and repeated to Joshua, Jos **1**:**4**, that the borders of Israel should extend to the river Euphrates, was performed. Learn hence, that it is dangerous to help those who have God against them; for when they fall, their helpers will fall with them.

Chapter 11

Verses 1–5

Observe the occasions of David's sin; what led to it. **1**. Neglect of his business. He tarried at Jerusalem. When we are out of the way of our duty, we are in temptation. **2**. Love of ease: idleness gives great advantage to the tempter. **3**. A wandering eye. He had not, like Job, made a covenant with his eyes, or, at this time, he had forgotten it. And observe the steps of the sin. See how the way of sin is down-hill; when men begin to do evil, they cannot soon stop. Observe the aggravations of the sin. How could David rebuke or punish that in others, of which he was conscious that he himself was guilty?

Verses 6–13

Giving way to sin hardens the heart, and provokes the departure of the Holy Spirit. Robbing a man of his reason, is worse than robbing him of his money; and drawing him into sin, is worse than drawing him into any wordly trouble whatever.

Verses 14–27

Adulteries often occasion murders, and one wickedness is sought to be covered by another. The beginnings of sin are much to be dreaded; for who knows where they will end? Can a real believer ever tread this path? Can such a person be indeed a child of God? Though grace be not lost in such an awful case, the assurance and consolation of it must be suspended. All David's life, spirituality, and comfort in religion, we may be sure were lost. No man in such a case can have evidence to be satisfied that he is a believer. The higher a man's confidence is, who has sunk in wickedness, the greater his presumption and hypocrisy. Let not any one who resembles David in nothing but his transgressions, bolster up his confidence with this example. Let him follow David in his humiliation, repentance, and his other eminent graces, before he thinks himself only a backslider, and not a hypocrite. Let no opposer of the truth say, These are the fruits of faith! No; they are the effects of corrupt nature. Let us all watch against the beginnings of self-indulgence, and keep at the utmost distance from all evil. But with the Lord there is mercy and plenteous redemption. He will cast out no humble, penitent believer; nor will he suffer Satan to pluck his sheep out of his hand. Yet the Lord will recover his people, in such a way as will mark his abhorrence of their crimes, to hinder all who regard his word from abusing the encouragements of his mercy.

Chapter 12

Verses 1–14

God will not suffer his people to lie still in sin. By this parable Nathan drew from David a sentence against himself. Great need there is of prudence in giving reproofs. In his application, he was faithful. He says in plain terms, Thou art the man. God shows how much he hates sin, even in his own people; and wherever he finds it, he will not let it go unpunished. David says not a word to excuse himself or make light of his sin, but freely owns it. When David said, I have sinned, and Nathan perceived that he was a true penitent, he assured him his sin was forgiven. Thou shalt not die: that is, not die eternally, nor be for ever put away from God, as thou wouldest have been, if thou hadst not put away the sin. Though thou shalt all thy days be chastened of the Lord, yet thou shalt not be condemned with the world. There is this great evil in the sins of those who profess religion and relation to God, that they furnish the enemies of God and religion with matter for reproach and blasphemy. And it appears from David's case, that even where pardon is obtained, the Lord will visit the transgression of his people with the rod, and their iniquity with stripes. For one momentary gratification of a vile lust, David had to endure many days and years of extreme distress.

Verses 15–25

David now penned the **51**st Psalm, in which, though he had been assured that his sin was pardoned, he prays earnestly for pardon, and greatly laments his sin. He was willing to bear the shame of it, to have it ever before him, to be continually upbraided with it. God gives us leave to be earnest with him in prayer for particular blessings, from trust in his power and general mercy, though we have no particular promise to build upon. David patiently submitted to the will of God in the death of one child, and God made up the loss to his advantage, in the birth of another. The way to have creature comforts continued or restored, or the loss made up some other way, is cheerfully to resign them to God. God, by his grace, particularly owned and favoured that son, and ordered him to be called Jedidiah, Beloved of the Lord. Our prayers for our children are graciously and as fully answered when some of them die in their infancy, for they are well taken care of, and when others live, "beloved of the Lord."

Verses 26–31

To be thus severe in putting the children of Ammon to slavery was a sign that David's heart was not yet made soft by repentance, at the time when this took place. We shall be most compassionate, kind, and forgiving to others, when we most feel our need of the Lord's forgiving love, and taste the sweetness of it in our own souls.

Chapter 13

Verses 1–20

From henceforward David was followed with one trouble after another. Adultery and murder were David's sins, the like sins among his children were the beginnings of his punishment: he was too indulgent to his children. Thus David might trace the sins of his children to his own misconduct, which must have made the anguish of the chastisement worse. Let no one ever expect good treatment from those who are capable of attempting their seduction; but it is better to suffer the greatest wrong than to commit the least sin.

Verses 21–29

Observe the aggravations of Absalom's sin: he would have Ammon slain, when least fit to go out of the world. He engaged his servants in the guilt. Those servants are ill-taught who obey wicked masters, against God's commands. Indulged children always prove crosses to godly parents, whose foolish love leads them to neglect their duty to God.

Verses 30–39

Jonadab was as guilty of Ammon's death, as of his sin; such false friends do they prove, who counsel us to do wickedly. Instead of loathing Absalom as a murderer, David, after a time, longed to go forth to him. This was David's infirmity: God saw something in his heart that made a difference, else we should have thought that he, as much as Eli, honoured his sons more than God.

Chapter 14

Verses 1–20

We may notice here, how this widow pleads God's mercy, and his clemency toward poor guilty sinners. The state of sinners is a state of banishment from God. God pardons none to the dishonour of his law and justice, nor any who are impenitent; nor to the encouragement of crimes, or the hurt of others.

Verses 21–24

David was inclined to favour Absalom, yet, for the honour of his justice, he could not do it but upon application made for him, which may show the methods of Divine grace. It is true that God has thoughts of compassion toward poor sinners, not willing that any should perish; yet he is only reconciled to them through a Mediator, who pleads on their behalf. God was in Christ reconciling the world to himself, and Christ came to this land of our banishment, to bring us to God.

Verses 25–27

Nothing is said of Absalom's wisdom and piety. All here said of him is, that he was very handsome. A poor commendation for a man that had nothing else in him valuable. Many a polluted, deformed soul dwells in a fair and comely body. And we read that he had a very fine head of hair. It was a burden to him, but he would not cut it as long as he could bear the weight. That which feeds and gratifies pride, is not complained of, though uneasy. May the Lord grant us the beauty of holiness, and the adorning of a meek and quiet spirit! Only those who fear God are truly happy.

Verses 28–33

By his insolent carriage toward Joab, Absalom brought Joab to plead for him. By his insolent message to the king, he gained his wishes. When parents and rulers countenance such characters, they will soon suffer the most fatal effects. But did the compassion of a father prevail to reconcile him to an impenitent son, and shall penitent sinners question the compassion of Him who is the Father of mercies?

Chapter 15

Verses 1–6

David allows Absalom's pomp. Those parents know not what they do, who indulge a proud humour in their children: many young people are ruined by pride. And those commonly are most eager for authority who least understand its duties.

Verses 7–12

See how willing tender parents are to believe the best concerning their children. But how easy and how wicked is it, for children to take advantage of good parents, and to deceive them with the show of religion! The principal men of Jerusalem joined Absalom's feast upon his sacrifice. Pious persons are glad to see others appear religious, and this gives occasion for deceptions. The policy of wicked men, and the subtlety of Satan, are exerted to draw good persons to countenance base designs.

Verses 13–23

David determined to quit Jerusalem. He took this resolve, as a penitent submitting to the rod. Before unrighteous Absalom he could justify himself, and stand out; but before the righteous God he must condemn himself, and yield to his judgments. Thus he accepts the punishment of his sin. And good men, when they themselves suffer, are anxious that others should not be led to suffer with them. He compelled none; those whose hearts were with Absalom, to Absalom let them go, and so shall their doom be. Thus Christ enlists none but willing followers. David cannot bear to think that Ittai, a stranger and an exile, a proselyte and a new convert, who ought to be encouraged and made easy, should meet with hard usage. But such value has Ittai for David's wisdom and goodness, that he will not leave him. He is a friend indeed, who loves at all times, and will adhere to us in adversity. Let us cleave to the Son of David, with full purpose of heart, and neither life nor death shall separate us from his love.

Verses 24–30

David is very careful for the safety of the ark. It is right to be more concerned for the church's prosperity than our own; to prefer the success of the gospel above our own wealth, credit, ease, and safety. Observe with what satisfaction and submission David speaks of the Divine disposal. It is our interest, as well as our duty, cheerfully to acquiesce in the will of God, whatever befalls us. Let us see God's hand in all events; and that we may not be afraid of what shall be, let us see all events in God's hand. David's sin was ever before him, Ps **51**:**3**; but never so plain, nor ever appearing so black as now. He never wept thus when Saul hunted him, but a wounded conscience makes troubles lie heavy, Ps **38**:**4**.

Verses 31–37

David prays not against Ahithophel's person, but against his counsel. He prayed this, in firm belief that God has all hearts in his hand, and tongues also. But we must second our prayers with endeavours, and David did so, else we tempt God. But we do not find wisdom and simplicity so united in any mere man, that we can perceive nothing which needs forgiveness. Yet, when the Son of David was treated with all possible treachery and cruelty, his wisdom, meekness, candour, and patience, were perfect. Him let us follow, cleave to, and serve, in life and in death.

Chapter 16

Verses 1–4

Ziba belied Mephibosheth. Great men ought always to be jealous of flatterers, and to be careful that they hear both sides.

Verses 5–14

David bore Shimei's curses much better than Ziba's flatteries; by these he was brought to pass a wrong judgment on another, by those to pass a right judgment on himself: the world's smiles are more dangerous than its frowns. Once and again David spared Saul's life, while Saul sought his. But innocence is no defence against malice and falsehood; nor are we to think it strange, if we are charged with that which we have been most careful to keep ourselves from. It is well for us, that men are not to be our judges, but He whose judgment is according to truth. See how patient David was under this abuse. Let this remind us of Christ, who prayed for those who reviled and crucified him. A humble spirit will turn reproaches into reproofs, and get good from them, instead of being provoked by them. David the hand of God in it, and comforts himself that God would bring good out of his affliction. We may depend upon God to repay, not only our services, but our sufferings.

Verses 15–23

The wisest counsellors of that age were Ahithophel and Hushai: Absalom thinks himself sure of success, when he has both; on them he relies, and consults not the ark, though he had that with him. But miserable counsellors were they both. Hushai would never counsel him to do wisely. Ahithophel counselled him to do wickedly; and so did as effectually betray him, as he did, who was designedly false to him: for they that advise men to sin, certainly advise them to their hurt. After all, honesty is the best policy, and will be found so in the long run. Ahithophel gave wicked counsel to Absalom; to render himself so hateful to his father, that he would never be reconciled to him; this cursed policy was of the devil. How desperately wicked is the human heart!

Chapter 17

Verses 1–21

Here was a wonderful effect of Divine Providence blinding Absalom's mind and influencing his heart, that he could not rest in Ahithophel's counsel, and that he should desire Hushai's advice. But there is no contending with that God who can arm a man against himself, and destroy him by his own mistakes and passions. Ahithophel's former counsel was followed, for God intended to correct David; but his latter counsel was not followed, for God meant not to destroy him. He can overrule all counsels. Whatever wisdom or help any man employs or affords, the success is from God alone, who will not let his people perish.

Verses 22–29

Ahithophel hanged himself for vexation that his counsel was not followed. That will break a proud man's heart which will not break a humble man's sleep. He thought himself in danger, concluding, that, because his counsel was not followed, Absalom's cause would fail; and to prevent a possible public execution, he does justice upon himself. Thus the breath is stopped, and the head laid low, from which nothing could be expected but mischief. Absalom chased his father. But observe how God sometimes makes up to his people that comfort from strangers, which they are disappointed of in their own families. Our King needs not our help; but he assures us, that what we do for the least of his brethren, who are sick, poor, and destitute, shall be accepted and recompensed as if done to himself

Chapter 18

Verses 1–8

How does David render good for evil! Absalom would have only David smitten; David would have only Absalom spared. This seems to be a resemblance of man's wickedness towards God, and God's mercy to man, of which it is hard to say which is most amazing. Now the Israelites see what it is to take counsel against the Lord and his anointed.

Verses 9–18

Let young people look upon Absalom, hanging on a tree, accursed, forsaken of heaven and earth; there let them read the Lord's abhorrence of rebellion against parents. Nothing can preserve men from misery and contempt, but heavenly wisdom and the grace of God.

Verses 19–33

By directing David to give God thanks for his victory, Ahimaaz prepared him for the news of his son's death. The more our hearts are fixed and enlarged, in thanksgiving to God for our mercies, the better disposed we shall be to bear with patience the afflictions mixed with them. Some think David's wish arose from concern about Absalom's everlasting state; but he rather seems to have spoken without due thought. He is to be blamed for showing so great fondness for a graceless son. Also for quarrelling with Divine justice. And for opposing the justice of the nation, which, as king, he had to administer, and which ought to be preferred before natural affection. The best men are not always in a good frame; we are apt to over-grieve for what we over-loved. But while we learn from this example to watch and pray against sinful indulgence, or neglect of our children, may we not, in David, perceive a shadow of the Saviour's love, who wept over, prayed for, and even suffered death for mankind, though vile rebels and enemies.

Chapter 19

Verses 1–8

To continue to lament for so bad a son as Absalom, was very unwise, and very unworthy. Joab censures David, but not with proper respect and deference to his sovereign. A plain case may be fairly pleaded with those above us, and they may be reproved for what they do amiss, but it must not be with rudeness and insolence. Yet David took the reproof and the counsel, prudently and mildly. Timely giving way, usually prevents the ill effects of mistaken measures.

Verses 9–15

God's providence, by the priests' persuasions and Amasa's interest, brought the people to resolve the recall of the king. David stirred not till he received this invitation. Our Lord Jesus will rule in those that invite him to the throne in their hearts, and not till he is invited. He first bows the heart, and makes it willing in the day of his power, then rules in the midst of his enemies, Ps **110**:**2**, **3**.

Verses 16–23

Those who now slight and abuse the Son of David, would be glad to make their peace when he shall come in his glory; but it will be too late. Shimei lost no time. His abuse had been personal, and with the usual right feeling of good men, David could more easily forgive it.

Verses 24–30

David recalls the forfeiture of Mephibosheth's estate; and he expressed joy for the king's return. A good man contentedly bears his own losses, while he sees Israel in peace, and the Son of David exalted.

Verses 31–39

Barzillai thought he had done himself honour in doing the king any service. Thus, when the saints shall be called to inherit the kingdom, they will be amazed at the recompence being so very far beyond the service, Mt **25**:**37**. A good man would not go any where to be burdensome; or, will rather be so to his own house than to another's. It is good for all, but especially becomes old people, to think and speak much of dying. The grave is ready for me, let me go and get ready for it.

Verses 40–43

The men of Israel though themselves despised, and the fiercer words of the men of Judah produced very bad effects. Much evil might be avoided, if men would watch against pride, and remember that a soft answer turneth away wrath. Though we have right and reason on our side, if we speak it with fierceness, God is displeased.

Chapter 20

Verses 1–3

One trial arises after another for our good, till we reach the place where sin and sorrow are for ever done away. Angry disputers misunderstand or misconstrue one another's words; proud men will have every thing their own way, or wholly refuse their assistance. The favour of the many is not to be depended upon; and what have others to expect, when Hosanna to the Son of David was soon changed to Crucify him, crucify him?

Verses 4–13

Joab barbarously murdered Amasa. The more plot there is in a sin, the worse it is. Joab contentedly sacrificed the interest both of the king and the kingdom to his personal revenge. But one would wonder with what face a murderer could pursue a traitor; and how, under such a load of guilt, he had courage to enter upon danger: his conscience was seared.

Verses 14–22

Justly is that place attacked, which dares to harbour a traitor; nor will the heart fare better which indulges rebellious lusts, that will not have Christ to reign over them. A discreet woman, by her prudent management, satisfied Joab, and yet saved the city. Wisdom is not confined to rank or sex; it consists not in deep knowledge; but in understanding how to act as matters arise, that troubles may be turned away and benefits secured. A great deal of mischief would be prevented, if contending parties would understand one another. Let both sides be undeceived. The single condition of peace is, the surrender of the traitor. It is so in God's dealing with the soul, when besieged by conviction and distress; sin is the traitor; the beloved lust is the rebel: part with that, cast away the transgression, and all shall be well. There is no peace on any other terms.

Verses 23–26

Here is the state of David's court, after his restoration. It is well when able men are appointed to discharge public duties; let all seek to perform those duties, as faithful servants to the Son of David.

Chapter 21

Verses 1–9

Every affliction arises from sin, and should lead us to repent and humble ourselves before God; but some troubles especially show that they are sent to bring sin to remembrance. God's judgments often look a great way back, which requires us to do so, when we are under his rebukes. It is not for us to object against the people's smarting for the sin of their king; perhaps they helped him. Nor against this generation suffering for the sin of the last. God often visits the sins of the fathers upon the children, and he gives no account of any matters. Time does not wear out the guilt of sin; nor can we build hopes of escape upon the delay of judgments. If we cannot understand all the reasons of Providence in this matter, still we have no right to demand that God should acquaint us with those reasons. It must be right, because it is the will of God, and in the end it will be proved to be so. Money is no satisfaction for blood. It should seem, Saul's posterity trod in his steps, for it is called a bloody house. It was the spirit of the family, therefore they are justly reckoned with for his sin, as well as for their own. The Gibeonites did not require this out of malice against Saul or his family. It was not to gratify any revenge, but for the public good. They were put to death at the beginning of harvest; they were thus sacrificed to turn away the wrath of Almighty God, who had withheld the harvest-mercies for some years past, and to obtain his favour in the present harvest. In vain do we expect mercy from God, unless we do justice upon our sins. Executions must not be thought cruel, which are for the public welfare.

Verses 10–14

That a guilty land should enjoy many years of plenty, calls for gratitude; and we need not wonder misused abundance should be punished with scarcity; yet how few are disposed to ask of the Lord concerning the sinful cause, while numbers search for the second causes by which he is pleased to work! But the Lord will plead the cause of those who cannot or will not avenge themselves; and the prayers of the poor are of great power. When God sent rain to water the earth, these bodies were buried, for then it appeared that God was entreated for the land. When justice is done on earth, vengeance from heaven ceases. God is pacified, and is entreated for us through Christ, who was hanged on a tree, and so made a curse for us, to do away our guilt, though he was himself guiltless.

Verses 15–22

These events seem to have taken place towards the end of David's reign. David fainted, but he did not flee, and God sent help in the time of need. In spiritual conflicts, even strong saints sometimes wax faint; then Satan attacks them furiously; but those who stand their ground and resist him, shall be relieved and made more than conquerors. Death is a Christian's last enemy, and a son of Anak; but through Him that triumphed for us, believers shall be more than conquerors at last, even over that enemy.

Chapter 22

David's psalm of thanksgiving.

—This chapter is a psalm of praise; we find it afterwards nearly as Ps **18**. They that trust God in the way of duty, shall find him a present help in their greatest dangers: David did so. Remarkable preservations should be particularly mentioned in our praises. We shall never be delivered from all enemies till we get to heaven. God will preserve all his people, 2Ti **4**:**18**. Those who receive signal mercies from God, ought to give him the glory. In the day that God delivered David, he sang this song. While the mercy is fresh, and we are most affected with it, let the thank-offering be brought, to be kindled with the fire of that affection. All his joys and hopes close, as all our hopes should do, in the great Redeemer.

Chapter 23

Verses 1–7

These words of David are very worthy of regard. Let those who have had long experience of God's goodness, and the pleasantness of heavenly wisdom, when they come to finish their course, bear their testimony to the truth of the promise. David avows his Divine inspiration, that the Spirit of God spake by him. He, and other holy men, spake and wrote as they were moved by the Holy Ghost. In many things he had his own neglect and wrong conduct to blame. But David comforted himself that the Lord had made with him an everlasting covenant. By this he principally intended the covenant of mercy and peace, which the Lord made with him as a sinner, who believed in the promised Saviour, who embraced the promised blessing, who yielded up himself to the Lord, to be his redeemed servant. Believers shall for ever enjoy covenant blessings; and God the Father, Son, and Holy Ghost, shall be for ever glorified in their salvation. Thus pardon, righteousness, grace, and eternal life, are secured as the gift of God through Jesus Christ. There is an infinite fulness of grace and all blessings treasured up in Christ, for those who seek his salvation. This covenant was all David's salvation, he so well knew the holy law of God and the extent of his own sinfulness, that he perceived what was needful for his own case in this salvation. It was therefore all his desire. In comparison, all earthly objects lost their attractions; he was willing to give them up, or to die and leave them, that he might enjoy full happiness, Ps **73**:**24**–**28**. Still the power of evil, and the weakness of his faith, hope, and love, were his grief and burden. Doubtless he would have allowed that his own slackness and want of care were the cause; but the hope that he should soon be made perfect in glory, encouraged him in his dying moments.

Verses 8–39

David once earnestly longed for the water at the well of Bethlehem. It seems to be an instance of weakness. He was thirsty; with the water of that well he had often refreshed himself when a youth, and it was without due thought that he desired it. Were his valiant men so forward to expose themselves, upon the least hint of their prince's mind, and so eager to please him, and shall not we long to approve ourselves to our Lord Jesus, by ready compliance with his will, as shown us by his word, Spirit, and providence? But David poured out the water as a drink-offering to the Lord. Thus he would cross his own foolish fancy, and punish himself for indulging it, and show that he had sober thoughts to correct his rash ones, and knew how to deny himself. Did David look upon that water as very precious which was got at the hazard of these men's blood, and shall not we much more value those benefits for purchasing which our blessed Saviour shed his blood? Let all beware of neglecting so great salvation.

Chapter 24

Verses 1–9

For the people's sin David was left to act wrong, and in his chastisement they received punishment. This example throws light upon God's government of the world, and furnishes a useful lesson. The pride of David's heart, was his sin in numbering of the people. He thought thereby to appear the more formidable, trusting in an arm of flesh more than he should have done, and though he had written so much of trusting in God only. God judges not of sin as we do. What appears to us harmless, or, at least, but a small offence, may be a great sin in the eye of God, who discerns the thoughts and intents of the heart. Even ungodly men can discern evil tempers and wrong conduct in believers, of which they themselves often remain unconscious. But God seldom allows those whom he loves the pleasures they sinfully covet.

Verses 10–15

It is well, when a man has sinned, if he has a heart within to smite him for it. If we confess our sins, we may pray in faith that God would forgive them, and take away, by pardoning mercy, that sin which we cast away by sincere repentance. What we make the matter of our pride, it is just in God to take from us, or make bitter to us, and make it our punishment. This must be such a punishment as the people have a large share in, for though it was David's sin that opened the sluice, the sins of the people all contributed to the flood. In this difficulty, David chose a judgment which came immediately from God, whose mercies he knew to be very great, rather than from men, who would have triumphed in the miseries of Israel, and have been thereby hardened in their idolatry. He chose the pestilence; he and his family would be as much exposed to it as the poorest Israelite; and he would continue for a shorter time under the Divine rebuke, however severe it was. The rapid destruction by the pestilence shows how easily God can bring down the proudest sinners, and how much we owe daily to the Divine patience.

Verses 16, 17

Perhaps there was more wickedness, especially more pride, and that was the sin now chastised, in Jerusalem than elsewhere, therefore the hand of the destroyer is stretched out upon that city; but the Lord repented him of the evil, changed not his mind, but his way. In the very place where Abraham was stayed from slaying his son, this angel, by a like countermand, was stayed from destroying Jerusalem. It is for the sake of the great Sacrifice, that our forfeited lives are preserved from the destroying angel. And in David is the spirit of a true shepherd of the people, offering himself as a sacrifice to God, for the salvation of his subjects.

Verses 18–25

God's encouraging us to offer to him spiritual sacrifices, is an evidence of his reconciling us to himself. David purchased the ground to build the altar. God hates robbery for burnt-offering. Those know not what religion is, who chiefly care to make it cheap and easy to themselves, and who are best pleased with that which costs them least pains or money. For what have we our substance, but to honour God with it; and how can it be better bestowed? See the building of the altar, and the offering proper sacrifices upon it. Burnt-offerings to the glory of God's justice; peace-offerings to the glory of his mercy. Christ is our Altar, our Sacrifice; in him alone we may expect to escape his wrath, and to find favour with God. Death is destroying all around, in so many forms, and so suddenly, that it is madness not to expect and prepare for the close of life.

1.Kings

The history now before us accounts for the affairs of the kingdoms of Judah and Israel, yet with special regard to the kingdom of God among them; for it is a sacred history. It is earlier as to time, teaches much more, and is more interesting than any common histories.

Chapter 1

Verses 1–4

We have David sinking under infirmities. He was chastised for his recent sins, and felt the effects of his former toils and hardships.

Verses 5–10

Indulgent parents are often chastised with disobedient children, who are anxious to possess their estates. No worldly wisdom, nor experience, nor sacredness of character, can insure the continuance in any former course of those who remain under the power of self-love. But we may well wonder by what arts Joab and Abiathar could be drawn aside.

Verses 11–31

Observe Nathan's address to Bathsheba. Let me give thee counsel how to save thy own life, and the life of thy son. Such as this is the counsel Christ's ministers give us in his name, to give all diligence, not only that no man take our crown, Re **3**:**11**, but that we save our lives, even the lives of our souls. David made a solemn declaration of his firm cleaving to his former resolution, that Solomon should be his successor. Even the recollection of the distresses from which the Lord redeemed him, increased his comfort, inspired his hopes, and animated him to his duty, under the decays of nature and the approach of death.

Verses 32–53

The people expressed great joy and satisfaction in the elevation of Solomon. Every true Israelite rejoices in the exaltation of the Son of David. Combinations formed upon evil principles will soon be dissolved, when self-interest calls another way. How can those who do evil deeds expect to have good tidings? Adonijah had despised Solomon, but soon dreaded him. We see here, as in a glass, Jesus, the Son of David and the Son of God, exalted to the throne of glory, notwithstanding all his enemies. His kingdom is far greater than that of his father David, and therein all the true people of God cordially rejoice. The prosperity of his cause is vexation and terror to his enemies. No horns of the altar, nor forms of godliness, nor pretences to religion, can profit those who will not submit to His authority, and accept of his salvation; and if their submission be hypocritical, they shall perish without remedy.

Chapter 2

Verses 1–4

David's charge to Solomon is, to keep the charge of the Lord. The authority of a dying father is much, but nothing to that of a living God. God promised David that the Messiah should come from his descendants, and that promise was absolute; but the promise, that there should not fail of them a man on the throne of Israel, was conditional; if he walks before God in sincerity, with zeal and resolution: in order hereunto, he must take heed to his way. (**1**Ki **2**:**5**-**11**)

Verses 5–11

These dying counsels concerning Joab and Shimei, did not come from personal anger, but for the security of Solomon's throne, which was the murders he had committed, but would readily repeat them to carry any purpose; though long reprieved, he shall be reckoned with at last. Time does not wear out the guilt of any sin, particularly of murder. Concerning Shimei, Hold him not guiltless; do not think him any true friend to thee, or thy government, or fit to be trusted; he has no less malice now than he had then. David's dying sentiments are recorded, as delivered under the influence of the Holy Ghost, **2**Sa **23**:**1**–**7**. The Lord discovered to him the offices and the salvation of that glorious personage, the Messiah, whose coming he then foretold, and from whom he derived all his comforts and expectations. That passage gives a decided proof that David died under the influence of the Holy Ghost, in the exercise of faith and hope.

Verses 12–25

Solomon received Bathsheba with all the respect that was owing to a mother; but let none be asked for that which they ought not to grant. It ill becomes a good man to prefer a bad request, or to appear in a bad cause. According to eastern customs it was plain that Adonijah sought to be king, by his asking for Abishag as his wife, and Solomon could not be safe while he lived. Ambitious, turbulent spirits commonly prepare death for themselves. Many a head has been lost by catching at a crown.

Verses 26–34

Solomon's words to Abiathar, and his silence, imply that some recent conspiracies had been entered into. Those that show kindness to God's people shall have it remembered to their advantage. For this reason Solomon spares Abiathar's life, but dismisses him from his offices. In case of such sins as the blood of beasts would atone for, the altar was a refuge, but not in Joab's case. Solomon looks upward to God as the Author of peace, and forward to eternity as the perfection of it. The Lord of peace himself gives us that peace which is everlasting.

Verses 35–46

The old malignity remains in the unconverted heart, and a watchful eye should be kept on those who, like Shimei, have manifested their enmity, but have given no evidence of repentance. No engagements or dangers will restrain worldly men; they go on, though they forfeit their lives and souls. Let us remember, God will not accommodate his judgment to us. His eye is over us; and let us strive to walk as in his presence. Let our every act, word, and thought, be governed by this great truth, that the hour is quickly coming when the smallest circumstances of our lives shall be brought to light, and our eternal state be fixed by a righteous and unerring God. Thus Solomon's throne was established in peace, as the type of the Redeemer's kingdom of peace and righteousness. And it is a comfort, in reference to the enmity of the church's enemies, that, how much soever they rage, it is a vain thing they imagine. Christ's throne is established, and they cannot shake it.

Chapter 3

Verses 1–4

He that loved the Lord, should, for his sake, have fixed his love upon one of the Lord's people. Solomon was a wise man, a rich man, a great man; yet the brightest praise of him, is that which is the character of all the saints, even the poorest, "He loved the Lord." Where God sows plentifully, he expects to reap accordingly; and those that truly love God and his worship, will not grudge the expenses of their religion. We must never think that wasted which is laid out in the service of God.

Verses 5–15

Solomon's dream was not a common one. While his bodily powers were locked up in sleep, the powers of his soul were strengthened; he was enabled to receive the Divine vision, and to make a suitable choice. God, in like manner, puts us in the ready way to be happy, by assuring us we shall have what we need, and pray for. Solomon's making such a choice when asleep, and the powers of reason least active, showed it came from the grace of God. Having a humble sense of his own wants and weakness, he pleads, Lord, I am but a little child. The more wise and considerate men are, the better acquainted they are with their own weakness, and the more jealous of themselves. Solomon begs of God to give him wisdom. We must pray for it, Jas **1**:**5**, that it may help us in our particular calling, and the various occasions we have. Those are accepted of God, who prefer spiritual blessings to earthly good. It was a prevailing prayer, and prevailed for more than he asked. God gave him wisdom, such as no other prince was ever blessed with; and also gave him riches and honour. If we make sure of wisdom and grace, these will bring outward prosperity with them, or sweeten the want of it. The way to get spiritual blessings, is to wrestle with God in prayer for them. The way to get earthly blessings, is to refer ourselves to God concerning them. Solomon has wisdom given him, because he did ask it, and wealth, because he did not.

Verses 16–28

An instance of Solomon's wisdom is given. Notice the difficulty of the case. To find out the true mother, he could not try which the child loved best, and therefore tried which loved the child best: the mother's sincerity will be tried, when the child is in danger. Let parents show their love to their children, especially by taking care of their souls, and snatching them as brands out of the burning. By this and other instances of the wisdom with which God endued him, Solomon had great reputation among his people. This was better to him than weapons of war; for this he was both feared and loved.

Chapter 4

Verses 1–19

In the choice of the great officers of Solomon's court, no doubt, his wisdom appeared. Several are the same that were in his father's time. A plan was settled by which no part of the country was exhausted to supply his court, though each sent its portion.

Verses 20–28

Never did the crown of Israel shine so bright, as when Solomon wore it. He had peace on all sides. Herein, his kingdom was a type of the Messiah's; for to Him it is promised that he shall have the heathen for his inheritance, and that princes shall worship him. The spiritual peace, and joy, and holy security, of all the faithful subjects of the Lord Jesus, were typified by that of Israel. The kingdom of God is not, as Solomon's was, meat and drink, but, what is infinitely better, righteousness, and peace, and joy in the Holy Ghost. The vast number of his attendants, and the great resort to him, are shown by the provision daily made. Herein Christ far outdoes Solomon, that he feeds all his subjects, not with the bread that perishes, but with that which endures to eternal life.

Verses 29–34

Solomon's wisdom was more his glory than his wealth. He had what is here called largeness of heart, for the heart is often put for the powers of the mind. He had the gift of utterance, as well as wisdom. It is very desirable, that those who have large gifts of any kind, should have large hearts to use them for the good of others. What treasures of wisdom and knowledge are lost! But every sort of knowledge that is needful for salvation is to be found in the holy Scriptures. There came persons from all parts, who were more eager after knowledge than their neighbours, to hear the wisdom of Solomon. Solomon was herein a type of Christ, in whom are hid all treasures of wisdom and knowledge; and hid for us, for he is made of God to us, wisdom. Christ's fame shall spread through all the earth, and men of all nations shall come to him, learn of him, and take upon them his easy yoke, and find rest for their souls.

Chapter 5

Verses 1–9

Here is Solomon's design to build a temple. There is no adversary, no Satan, so the word is; no instrument of Satan to oppose it, or to divert from it. Satan does all he can, to hinder temple work. When there is no evil abroad, then let us be ready and active in that which is good, and get forward. Let God's promises quicken our endeavours. And all outward skill and advantages should be made serviceable to the interests of Christ's kingdom. If Tyre supplies Israel with craftsmen, Israel will supply Tyre with corn, Eze **27**:**17**. Thus, by the wise disposal of Providence, one country has need of another, and is benefitted by another, that there may be dependence on one another, to the glory of God.

Verses 10–18

The temple was chiefly built by the riches and labour of Gentiles, which typified their being called into the church. Solomon commanded, and they brought costly stones for the foundation. Christ, who is laid for a Foundation, is a chosen and precious Stone. We should lay our foundation firm, and bestow most pains on that part of our religion which lies out of the sight of men. And happy those who, as lively stones, are built up a spiritual house, for a habitation of God through the Spirit. Who among us will build in the house of the Lord?

Chapter 6

Verses 1–10

The temple is called the house of the Lord, because it was directed and modelled by him, and was to be employed in his service. This gave it the beauty of holiness, that it was the house of the Lord, which was far beyond all other beauties. It was to be the temple of the God of peace, therefore no iron tool must be heard; quietness and silence suit and help religious exercises. God's work should be done with much care and little noise. Clamour and violence often hinder, but never further the work of God. Thus the kingdom of God in the heart of man grows up in silence, Mr **5**:**27**.

Verses 11–14

None employ themselves for God, without having his eye upon them. But God plainly let Solomon know that all the charge for building this temple, would neither excuse from obedience to the law of God, nor shelter from his judgments, in case of disobedience.

Verses 15–38

See what was typified by this temple. **1**. Christ is the true Temple. In him dwells all the fulness of the Godhead; in him meet all God's spiritual Israel; through him we have access with confidence to God. **2**. Every believer is a living temple, in whom the Spirit of God dwells, **1**Co **3**:**16**. This living temple is built upon Christ as its Foundation, and will be perfect in due time. **3**. The gospel church is the mystical temple. It grows to a holy temple in the Lord, enriched and beautified with the gifts and graces of the Spirit. This temple is built firm, upon a Rock. **4**. Heaven is the everlasting temple. There the church will be fixed. All that shall be stones in that building, must, in the present state of preparation, be fitted and made ready for it. Let sinners come to Jesus as the living Foundation, that they may be built on him, a part of this spiritual house, consecrated in body and soul to the glory of God.

Chapter 7

Verses 1–12

All Solomon's buildings, though beautiful, were intended for use. Solomon began with the temple; he built for God first, and then his other buildings. The surest foundations of lasting prosperity are laid in early piety. He was thirteen years building his house, yet he built the temple in little more than seven years; not that he was more exact, but less eager in building his own house, than in building God's. We ought to prefer God's honour before our own ease and satisfaction.

Verses 13–47

The two brazen pillars in the porch of the temple, some think, were to teach those that came to worship, to depend upon God only, for strength and establishment in all their religious exercises. "Jachin," God will fix this roving mind. It is good that the heart be established with grace. "Boaz," In him is our strength, who works in us both to will and to do. Spiritual strength and stability are found at the door of God's temple, where we must wait for the gifts of grace, in use of the means of grace. Spiritual priests and spiritual sacrifices must be washed in the laver of Christ's blood, and of regeneration. We must wash often, for we daily contract pollution. There are full means provided for our cleansing; so that if we have our lot for ever among the unclean it will be our own fault. Let us bless God for the fountain opened by the sacrifice of Christ for sin and for uncleanness.

Verses 48–51

Christ is now the Temple and the Builder; the Altar and the Sacrifice; the Light of our souls, and the Bread of life; able to supply all the wants of all that have applied or shall apply to him. Outward images cannot represent, words cannot express, the heart cannot conceive, his preciousness or his love. Let us come to him, and wash away our sins in his blood; let us seek for the purifying grace of his Spirit; let us maintain communion with the Father through his intercession, and yield up ourselves and all we have to his service. Being strengthened by him, we shall be accepted, useful, and happy.

Chapter 8

Verses 1–11

The bringing in the ark, is the end which must crown the work: this was done with great solemnity. The ark was fixed in the place appointed for its rest in the inner part of the house, whence they expected God to speak to them, even in the most holy place. The staves of the ark were drawn out, so as to direct the high priest to the mercy-seat over the ark, when he went in, once a year, to sprinkle the blood there; so that they continued of use, though there was no longer occasion to carry it by them. The glory of God appearing in a cloud may signify, **1**. The darkness of that dispensation, in comparison with the light of the gospel, by which, with open face, we behold, as in a glass, the glory of the Lord. **2**. The darkness of our present state, in comparison with the sight of God, which will be the happiness of heaven, where the Divine glory is unveiled.

Verses 12–21

Solomon encouraged the priests, who were much astonished at the dark cloud. The dark dispensations of Providence should quicken us in fleeing for refuge to the hope of the gospel. Nothing can more reconcile us to them, than to consider what God has said, and to compare his word and works together. Whatever good we do, we must look on it as the performance of God's promise to us, not of our promises to him.

Verses 22–53

In this excellent prayer, Solomon does as we should do in every prayer; he gives glory to God. Fresh experiences of the truth of God's promises call for larger praises. He sues for grace and favour from God. The experiences we have of God's performing his promises, should encourage us to depend upon them, and to plead them with him; and those who expect further mercies, must be thankful for former mercies. God's promises must be the guide of our desires, and the ground of our hopes and expectations in prayer. The sacrifices, the incense, and the whole service of the temple, were all typical of the Redeemer's offices, oblation, and intercession. The temple, therefore, was continually to be remembered. Under one word, "forgive," Solomon expressed all that he could ask in behalf of his people. For, as all misery springs from sin, forgiveness of sin prepares the way for the removal of every evil, and the receiving of every good. Without it, no deliverance can prove a blessing. In addition to the teaching of the word of God, Solomon entreated the Lord himself to teach the people to profit by all, even by their chastisements. They shall know every man the plague of his own heart, what it is that pains him; and shall spread their hands in prayer toward this house; whether the trouble be of body or mind, they shall represent it before God. Inward burdens seem especially meant. Sin is the plague of our own hearts; our in-dwelling corruptions are our spiritual diseases: every true Israelite endeavours to know these, that he may mortify them, and watch against the risings of them. These drive him to his knees; lamenting these, he spreads forth his hands in prayer. After many particulars, Solomon concludes with the general request, that God would hearken to his praying people. No place, now, under the gospel, can add to the prayers made in or towards it. The substance is Christ; whatever we ask in his name, it shall be given us. In this manner the Israel of God is established and sanctified, the backslider is recovered and healed. In this manner the stranger is brought nigh, the mourner is comforted, the name of God is glorified. Sin is the cause of all our troubles; repentance and forgiveness lead to all human happiness.

Verses 54–61

Never was a congregation dismissed with what was more likely to affect them, and to abide with them. What Solomon asks for in this prayer, is still granted in the intercession of Christ, of which his supplication was a type. We shall receive grace sufficient, suitable, and seasonable, in every time of need. No human heart is of itself willing to obey the gospel call to repentance, faith, and newness of life, walking in all the commandments of the Lord, yet Solomon exhorts the people to be perfect. This is the scriptural method, it is our duty to obey the command of the law and the call of the gospel, seeing we have broken the law. When our hearts are inclined thereto, feeling our sinfulness and weakness, we pray for Divine assistance; thus are we made able to serve God through Jesus Christ.

Verses 62–66

Solomon offered a great sacrifice. He kept the feast of tabernacles, as it seems, after the feast of dedication. Thus should we go home, rejoicing, from holy ordinances, thankful for God's Goodness

Chapter 9

Verses 1–9

God warned Solomon, now he had newly built and dedicated the temple, that he and his people might not be high-minded, but fear. After all the services we can perform, we stand upon the same terms with the Lord as before. Nothing can purchase for us liberty to sin, nor would the true believer desire such a licence. He would rather be chastened of the Lord, than be allowed to go on with ease and prosperity in sin.

Verses 10–14

Solomon gave Hiram twenty cities. Hiram did not like them. If Solomon would gratify him, let it be in his own element, by becoming his partner in trade, as he did. See how the providence of God suits this earth to the various tempers of men, and the dispositions of men to the earth, and all for the good of mankind in general.

Verses 15–28

Here is a further account of Solomon's greatness. He began at the right end, for he built God's house first, and finished that before he began his own; then God blessed him, and he prospered in all his other buildings. Let piety begin, and profit follow; leave pleasure to the last. Whatever pains we take for the glory of God, and to profit others, we are likely to have the advantage. Canaan, the holy land, the glory of all lands, had no gold in it; which shows that the best produce is that which is for the present support of life, our own and others; such things did Canaan produce. Solomon got much by his merchandise, and yet has directed us to a better trade, within reach of the poorest. Wisdom is better than the merchandise of silver, and the gain thereof than fine gold, Pr **3**:**14**.

Chapter 10

Verses 1–13

The queen of Sheba came to Solomon to hear his wisdom, thereby to improve her own. Our Saviour mentions her inquiries after God, by Solomon, as showing the stupidity of those who inquire not after God, by our Lord Jesus Christ. By waiting and prayer, by diligently searching the Scriptures, by consulting wise and experienced Christians, and by practising what we have learned, we shall be delivered from difficulties. Solomon's wisdom made more impression upon the queen of Sheba than all his prosperity and grandeur. There is a spiritual excellence in heavenly things, and in consistent Christians, to which no reports can do justice. Here the truth exceeded; and all who, through grace, are brought to commune with God, will say the one half was not told them of the pleasures and the advantages of wisdom's ways. Glorified saints, much more, will say of heaven, that the thousandth part was not told them, **1**Co **2**:**9**. She pronounced them happy that constantly attended Solomon. With much more reason may we say of Christ's servants, Blessed are they that dwell in his house; they will be still praising him. She made a noble present to Solomon. What we present to Christ, he needs not, but will have us do so to express our gratitude. The believer who has been with Jesus, will return to his station, discharge his duties with readiness, and from better motives; looking forward to the day when, being absent from the body, he shall be present with the Lord.

Verses 14–29

Solomon increased his wealth. Silver was nothing accounted of. Such is the nature of worldly wealth, plenty of it makes it the less valuable; much more should the enjoyment of spiritual riches lessen our esteem of all earthly possessions. If gold in abundance makes silver to be despised, shall not wisdom, and grace, and the foretastes of heaven, which are far better than gold, make gold to be lightly esteemed? See in Solomon's greatness the performance of God's promise, and let it encourage us to seek first the righteousness of God's kingdom. This was he, who, having tasted all earthly enjoyments, wrote a book, to show the vanity of all worldly things, the vexation of spirit that attends them, and the folly of setting our hearts upon them: and to recommend serious godliness, as that which will do unspeakably more to make us happy, that all the wealth and power he was master of; and, through the grace of God, it is within our reach.

Chapter 11

Verses 1–8

There is not a more melancholy and astonishing instance of human depravity in the sacred Scriptures, than that here recorded. Solomon became a public worshipper of abominable idols! Probably he by degrees gave way to pride and luxury, and thus lost his relish for true wisdom. Nothing forms in itself a security against the deceitfulness and depravity of the human heart. Nor will old age cure the heart of any evil propensity. If our sinful passions are not crucified and mortified by the grace of God, they never will die of themselves, but will last even when opportunities to gratify them are taken away. Let him that thinks he stands, take heed lest he fall. We see how weak we are of ourselves, without the grace of God; let us therefore live in constant dependence on that grace. Let us watch and be sober: ours is a dangerous warfare, and in an enemy's country, while our worst foes are the traitors in our own hearts. (**1**Ki **11**:**9-13**)

Verses 9–13

The Lord told Solomon, it is likely by a prophet, what he must expect for his apostacy. Though we have reason to hope that he repented, and found mercy, yet the Holy Ghost did not expressly record it, but left it doubtful, as a warning to others not to sin. The guilt may be taken away, but not the reproach; that will remain. Thus it must remain uncertain to us till the day of judgment, whether or not Solomon was left to suffer the everlasting displeasure of an offended God.

Verses 14–25

While Solomon kept close to God and to his duty, there was no enemy to give him uneasiness; but here we have an account of two. If against us, he can make us fear even the least, and the very grasshopper shall be a burden. Though they were moved by principles of ambition or revenge, God used them to correct Solomon.

Verses 26–40

In telling the reason why God rent the kingdom from the house of Solomon, Ahijah warned Jeroboam to take heed of sinning away his preferment. Yet the house of David must be supported; out of it the Messiah would arise. Solomon sought to kill his successor. Had not he taught others, that whatever devices are in men's hearts, the counsel of the Lord shall stand? Yet he himself thinks to defeat that counsel. Jeroboam withdrew into Egypt, and was content to live in exile and obscurity for awhile, being sure of a kingdom at last. Shall not we be content, who have a better kingdom in reserve?

Verses 41–43

Solomon's reign was as long as his father's, but his life was not so. Sin shortened his days. If the world, with all its advantages, could satisfy the soul, and afford real joy, Solomon would have found it so. But he was disappointed in all, and to warn us, has left this record of all earthly enjoyments, "Vanity and vexation of spirit." The New Testament declares that one greater than Solomon is come to reign over us, and to possess the throne of his father David. May we not see something of Christ's excellency faintly represented to us in this figure?

Chapter 12

Verses 1–15

The tribes complained not to Rehoboam of his father's idolatry, and revolt from God. That which was the greatest grievance, was none to them; so careless were they in matters of religion, if they might live at ease, and pay no taxes. Factious spirits will never want something to complain of. And when we see the Scripture account of Solomon's reign; the peace, wealth, and prosperity Israel then enjoyed; we cannot doubt but that their charges were false, or far beyond the truth. Rehoboam answered the people according to the counsel of the young men. Never was man more blinded by pride, and desire of arbitrary power, than which nothing is more fatal. God's counsels were hereby fulfilled. He left Rehoboam to his own folly, and hid from his eyes the things which belonged to his peace, that the kingdom might be rent from him. God serves his own wise and righteous purposes by the imprudences and sins of men. Those that lose the kingdom of heaven, throw it away, as Rehoboam, by wilfulness and folly.

Verses 16–24

The people speak unbecomingly of David. How soon are good men, and their good services to the public, forgotten ! These considerations should reconcile us to our losses and troubles, that God is the Author of them, and our brethren the instruments: let us not meditate revenge. Rehoboam and his people hearkened to the word of the Lord. When we know God's mind, we must submit, how much soever it crosses our own mind. If we secure the favour of God, not all the universe can hurt us.

Verses 25–33

Jeroboam distrusted the providence of God; he would contrive ways and means, and sinful ones too, for his own safety. A practical disbelief of God's all-sufficiency is at the bottom of all our departures from him. Though it is probable he meant his worship for Jehovah the God of Israel, it was contrary to the Divine law, and dishonourable to the Divine majesty to be thus represented. The people might be less shocked at worshipping the God of Israel under an image, than if they had at once been asked to worship Baal; but it made way for that idolatry. Blessed Lord, give us grace to reverence thy temple, thine ordinances, thine house of prayer, thy sabbaths, and never more, like Jeroboam, to set up in our hearts any idol of abomination. Be thou to us every thing precious; do thou reign and rule in our hearts, the hope of glory.

Chapter 13

Verses 1–10

In threatening the altar, the prophet threatens the founder and worshippers. Idolatrous worship will not continue, but the word of the Lord will endure for ever. The prediction plainly declared that the family of David would continue, and support true religion, when the ten tribes would not be able to resist them. If God, in justice, harden the hearts of sinners, so that the hand they have stretched out in sin they cannot pull in again by repentance, that is a spiritual judgment, represented by this, and much more dreadful. Jeroboam looked for help, not from his calves, but from God only, from his power, and his favour. The time may come when those that hate the preaching, would be glad of the prayers of faithful ministers. Jeroboam does not desire the prophet to pray that his sin might be pardoned, and his heart changed, but only that his hand might be restored. He seemed affected for the present with both the judgment and the mercy, but the impression wore off. God forbade his messenger to eat or drink in Bethel, to show his detestation of their idolatry and apostacy from God, and to teach us not to have fellowship with the works of darkness. Those have not learned self-denial, who cannot forbear one forbidden meal.

Verses 11–22

The old prophet's conduct proves that he was not really a godly man. When the change took place under Jeroboam, he preferred his ease and interest to his religion. He took a very bad method to bring the good prophet back. It was all a lie. Believers are most in danger of being drawn from their duty by plausible pretences of holiness. We may wonder that the wicked prophet went unpunished, while the holy man of God was suddenly and severely punished. What shall we make of this? The judgments of God are beyond our power to fathom; and there is a judgment to come. Nothing can excuse any act of wilful disobedience. This shows what they must expect who hearken to the great deceiver. They that yield to him as a tempter, will be terrified by him as a tormentor. Those whom he now fawns upon, he will afterwards fly upon; and whom he draws into sin, he will try to drive to despair.

Verses 23–34

God is displeased at the sins of his own people; and no man shall be protected in disobedience, by his office, his nearness to God, or any services he has done for him. God warns all whom he employs, strictly to observe their orders. We cannot judge of men by their sufferings, nor of sins by present punishments; with some, the flesh is destroyed, that the spirit may be saved; with others, the flesh is pampered, that the soul may ripen for hell. Jeroboam returned not from his evil way. He promised himself that the calves would secure the crown to his family, but they lost it, and sunk his family. Those betray themselves who think to support themselves by any sin whatever. Let us dread prospering in sinful ways; pray to be kept from every delusion and temptation, and to be enabled to walk with self-denying perseverance in the way of God's commands.

Chapter 14

Verses 1–6

"At that time," when Jeroboam did evil, his child sickened. When sickness comes into our families, we should inquire whether there may not be some particular sin harboured in our houses, which the affliction is sent to convince us of, and reclaim us from. It had been more pious if he had desired to know wherefore God contended with him; had begged the prophet's prayers, and cast away his idols from him; but most people would rather be told their fortune, than their faults or their duty. He sent to Ahijah, because he had told him he should be king. Those who by sin disqualify themselves for comfort, yet expect that their ministers, because they are good men, should speak peace and comfort to them, greatly wrong themselves and their ministers. He sent his wife in disguise, that the prophet might only answer her question concerning her son. Thus some people would limit their ministers to smooth things, and care not for having the whole counsel of God declared to them, lest it should prophesy no good concerning them, but evil. But she shall know, at the first word, what she has to trust to. Tidings of a portion with hypocrites will be heavy tidings. God will judge men according to what they are, not by what they seem to be.

Verses 7–20

Whether we keep an account of God's mercies to us or not, he does; and he will set them in order before us, if we are ungrateful, to our greater confusion. Ahijah foretells the speedy death of the child then sick, in mercy to him. He only in the house of Jeroboam had affection for the true worship of God, and disliked the worship of the calves. To show the power and sovereignty of his grace, God saves some out of the worst families, in whom there is some good thing towards the Lord God of Israel. The righteous are removed from the evil to come in this world, to the good to come in a better world. It is often a bad sign for a family, when the best in it are buried out of it. Yet their death never can be a loss to themselves. It was a present affliction to the family and kingdom, by which both ought to have been instructed. God also tells the judgments which should come upon the people of Israel, for conforming to the worship Jeroboam established. After they left the house of David, the government never continued long in one family, but one undermined and destroyed another. Families and kingdoms are ruined by sin. If great men do wickedly, they draw many others, both into the guilt and punishment. The condemnation of those will be severest, who must answer, not only for their own sins, but for sins others have been drawn into, and kept in, by them.

Verses 21–31

Here is no good said of Rehoboam, and much said to the disadvantage of his subjects. The abounding of the worst crimes, of the worst of the heathen, in Jerusalem, the city the Lord had chosen for his temple and his worship, shows that nothing can mend the hearts of fallen men but the sanctifying grace of the Holy Spirit. On this alone may we depend; for this let us daily pray, in behalf of ourselves and all around us. The splendour of their temple, the pomp of their priesthood, and all the advantages with which their religion was attended, could not prevail to keep them close to it; nothing less than the pouring out the Spirit will keep God's Israel in their allegiance to him. Sin exposes, makes poor, and weakens any people. Shishak, king of Egypt, came and took away the treasures. Sin makes the gold become dim, changes the most fine gold, and turns it into brass.

Chapter 15

Verses 1–8

Abijam's heart was not perfect with the Lord his God; he wanted sincerity; he began well, but he fell off, and walked in all the sins of his father, following his bad example, though he had seen the bad consequences of it. David's family was continued as a lamp in Jerusalem, to maintain the true worship of God there, when the light of Divine truth was extinguished in all other places. The Lord has still taken care of his cause, while those who ought to have been serviceable thereto have lived and perished in their sins. The Son of David will still continue a light to his church, to establish it in truth and righteousness to the end of time. There are two kinds of fulfilling the law, one legal, the other by the gospel. Legal is, when men do all things required in the law, and that by themselves. None ever thus fulfilled the law but Christ, and Adam before his fall. The gospel manner of fulfilling the law is, to believe in Christ who fulfilled the law for us, and to endeavour in the whole man to obey God in all his precepts. And this is accepted of God, as to all those that are in Christ. Thus David and others are said to fulfil the law.

Verses 9–24

Asa did what was right in the eyes of the Lord. That is right indeed which is so in God's eyes. Asa's times were times of reformation. He removed that which was evil; there reformation begins, and a great deal he found to do. When Asa found idolatry in the court, he rooted it out thence. Reformation must begin at home. Asa honours and respects his mother; he loves her well, but he loves God better. Those that have power are happy when thus they have hearts to use it well. We must not only cease to do evil, but learn to do well; not only cast away the idols of our iniquity, but dedicate ourselves and our all to God's honour and glory. Asa was cordially devoted to the service of God, his sins not arising from presumption. But his league with Benhadad arose from unbelief. Even true believers find it hard, in times of urgent danger, to trust in the Lord with all their heart. Unbelief makes way for carnal policy, and thus for one sin after another. Unbelief has often led Christians to call in the help of the Lord's enemies in their contests with their brethren; and some who once shone brightly, have thus been covered with a dark cloud towards the end of their days.

Verses 25–34

During the single reign of Asa in Judah, the government of Israel was in six or seven different hands. Observe the ruin of the family of Jeroboam; no word of God shall fall to the ground. Divine threatenings are not designed merely to terrify. Ungodly men execute the just judgments of God upon each other. But in the midst of dreadful sins and this apparent confusion, the Lord carries on his own plan: when it is fully completed, the glorious justice, wisdom, truth, and mercy therein displayed, shall be admired and adored through all the ages of eternity.

Chapter 16

Verses 1–14

This chapter relates wholly to the kingdom of Israel, and the revolutions of that kingdom. God calls Israel his people still, though wretchedly corrupted. Jehu foretells the same destruction to come upon Baasha's family, which that king had been employed to bring upon the family of Jeroboam. Those who resemble others in their sins, may expect to resemble them in the plagues they suffer, especially those who seem zealous against such sins in others as they allow in themselves. Baasha himself dies in peace, and is buried with honour. Herein plainly appears that there are punishments after death, which are most to be dreaded. Let Elah be a warning to drunkards, who know not but death may surprise them. Death easily comes upon men when they are drunk. Besides the diseases which men bring themselves into by drinking, when in that state, men are easily overcome by an enemy, and liable to bad accidents. Death comes terribly upon men in such a state, finding them in the act of sin, and unfitted for any act of devotion; that day comes upon them unawares. The word of God was fulfilled, and the sins of Baasha and Elah were reckoned for, with which they provoked God. Their idols are called their vanities, for idols cannot profit nor help; miserable are those whose gods are vanities.

Verses 15–28

When men forsake God, they will be left to plague one another. Proud aspiring men ruin one another. Omri struggled with Tibni some years. Though we do not always understand the rules by which God governs nations and individuals in his providence, we may learn useful lessons from the history before us. When tyrants succeed each other, and massacres, conspiracies, and civil wars, we may be sure the Lord has a controversy with the people for their sins; they are loudly called to repent and reform. Omri made himself infamous by his wickedness. Many wicked men have been men of might and renown; have built cities, and their names are found in history; but they have no name in the book of life.

Verses 29–34

Ahab did evil above all that reigned before him, and did it with a particular enmity both against Jehovah and Israel. He was not satisfied with breaking the second commandment by image-worship, he broke the first by worshipping other gods: making light of lesser sins makes way for greater. Marriages with daring offenders also imbolden in wickedness, and hurry men on to the greatest excesses. One of Ahab's subjects, following the example of his presumption, ventured to build Jericho. Like Achan, he meddled with the accursed thing; turned that to his own use, which was devoted to God's honour: he began to build, in defiance of the curse well devoted to God's honour: he began to build, in defiance of the curse well known in Israel; but none ever hardened his heart against God, and prospered. Let the reading of this chapter cause us to mark the dreadful end of all the workers of iniquity. And what does the history of all ungodly men furnish, what ever rank or situation they move in, but sad examples of the same?

Chapter 17

Verses 1–7

God wonderfully suits men to the work he designs them for. The times were fit for an Elijah; an Elijah was fit for them. The Spirit of the Lord knows how to fit men for the occasions. Elijah let Ahab know that God was displeased with the idolaters, and would chastise them by the want of rain, which it was not in the power of the gods they served to bestow. Elijah was commanded to hide himself. If Providence calls us to solitude and retirement, it becomes us to go: when we cannot be useful, we must be patient; and when we cannot work for God, we must sit still quietly for him. The ravens were appointed to bring him meat, and did so. Let those who have but from hand to mouth, learn to live upon Providence, and trust it for the bread of the day, in the day. God could have sent angels to minister to him; but he chose to show that he can serve his own purposes by the meanest creatures, as effectually as by the mightiest. Elijah seems to have continued thus above a year. The natural supply of water, which came by common providence, failed; but the miraculous supply of food, made sure to him by promise, failed not. If the heavens fail, the earth fails of course; such are all our creature-comforts: we lose them when we most need them, like brooks in summer. But there is a river which makes glad the city of God, that never runs dry, a well of water that springs up to eternal life. Lord, give us that living water! (1Ki **17**:**8-16**)

Verses 8–16

Many widows were in Israel in the days of Elias, and some, it is likely, would have bidden him welcome to their houses; yet he is sent to honour and bless with his presence a city of Sidon, a Gentile city, and so becomes the first prophet of the Gentiles. Jezebel was Elijah's greatest enemy; yet, to show her how powerless was her malice, God will find a hiding-place for him even in her own country. The person appointed to entertain Elijah is not one of the rich or great men of Sidon; but a poor widow woman, in want, and desolate, is made both able and willing to sustain him. It is God's way, and it is his glory, to make use of, and put honour upon, the weak and foolish things of the world. O woman, great was thy faith; one has not found the like, no not in Israel. She took the prophet's word, that she should not lose by it. Those who can venture upon the promise of God, will make no difficulty to expose and empty themselves in his service, by giving him his part first. Surely the increase of this widow's faith, so as to enable her thus readily to deny herself, and to depend upon the Divine promise, was as great a miracle in the kingdom of grace, as the increase of her meal and oil in the kingdom of providence. Happy are all who can thus, against hope, believe and obey in hope. One poor meal's meat this poor widow gave the prophet; in recompence of it, she and her son did eat above two years, in a time of famine. To have food from God's special favour, and in such good company as Elijah, made it more than doubly sweet. It is promised to those who trust in God, that they shall not be ashamed in evil time; in days of famine they shall be satisfied.

Verses 17–24

Neither faith nor obedience shut out afflictions and death. The child being dead, the mother spake to the prophet, rather to give vent to her sorrow, than in hope of relief. When God removes our comforts from us, he remembers our sins against us, perhaps the sins of our youth, though long since past. When God remembers our sins against us, he designs to teach us to remember them against ourselves, and to repent of them. Elijah's prayer was doubtless directed by the Holy Spirit. The child revived. See the power of prayer, and the power of Him who hears prayer.

Chapter 18

Verses 1–16

The severest judgments, of themselves, will not humble or change the hearts of sinners; nothing, except the blood of Jesus Christ, can atone for the guilt of sin; nothing, except the sanctifying Spirit of God, can purge away its pollution. The priests and the Levites were gone to Judah and Jerusalem, **2**Ch **11**:**13**, **14**, but instead of them God raised up prophets, who read and expounded the word. They probably were from the schools of the prophets, first set up by Samuel. They had not the spirit of prophecy as Elijah, but taught the people to keep close to the God of Israel. These Jezebel sought to destroy. The few that escaped death were forced to hide themselves. God has his remnant among all sorts, high and low; and that faith, fear, and love of his name, which are the fruits of the Holy Spirit, will be accepted through the Redeemer. See how wonderfully God raises up friends for his ministers and people, for their shelter in difficult times. Bread and water were now scarce, yet Obadiah will find enough for God's prophets, to keep them alive. Ahab's care was not to lose all the beasts; but he took no care about his soul, not to lose that. He took pains to seek grass, but none to seek the favour of God; fencing against the effect, but not inquiring how to remove the cause. But it bodes well with a people, when God calls his ministers to stand forth, and show themselves. And we may the better endure the bread of affliction, while our eyes see our teachers.

Verses 17–20

One may guess how people stand affected to God, by observing how they stand affected to his people and ministers. It has been the lot of the best and most useful men, like Elijah, to be called and counted the troublers of the land. But those who cause God's judgments do the mischief, not he that foretells them, and warns the nation to repent.

Verses 21–40

Many of the people wavered in their judgment, and varied in their practice. Elijah called upon them to determine whether Jehovah or Baal was the self-existent, supreme God, the Creator, Governor, and Judge of the world, and to follow him alone. It is dangerous to halt between the service of God and the service of sin, the dominion of Christ and the dominion of our lusts. If Jesus be the only Saviour, let us cleave to him alone for every thing; if the Bible be the world of God, let us reverence and receive the whole of it, and submit our understanding to the Divine teaching it contains. Elijah proposed to bring the matter to a trial. Baal had all the outward advantages, but the event encourages all God's witnesses and advocates never to fear the face of man. The God that answers by fire, let him be God: the atonement was to be made by sacrifice, before the judgment could be removed in mercy. The God therefore that has power to pardon sin, and to signify it by consuming the sin-offering, must needs be the God that can relieve from the calamity. God never required his worshippers to honour him in the manner of the worshippers of Baal; but the service of the devil, though sometimes it pleases and pampers the body, yet, in other things, really is cruel to it, as in envy and drunkenness. God requires that we mortify our lusts and corruptions; but bodily penances and severities are no pleasure to him. Who has required these things at your hands? A few words uttered in assured faith, and with fervent affection for the glory of God, and love to the souls of men, or thirstings after the Lord's image and his favour, form the effectual, fervent prayer of the righteous man, which availeth much. Elijah sought not his own glory, but that of God, for the good of the people. The people are all agreed, convinced, and satisfied; Jehovah, he is the God. Some, we hope, had their hearts turned, but most of them were convinced only, not converted. Blessed are they that have not seen what these saw, yet have believed, and have been wrought upon by it, more than they that saw it.

Verses 41–46

Israel, being so far reformed as to acknowledge the Lord to be God, and to consent to the execution of Baal's prophets, was so far accepted, that God poured out blessing upon the land. Elijah long continued praying. Though the answer of our fervent and believing supplications does not come quickly, we must continue earnest in prayer, and not faint or give over. A little cloud at length appeared, which soon overspread the heavens, and watered the earth. Great blessings often arise from small beginnings, showers of plenty from a cloud of span long. Let us never despise the day of small things, but hope and wait for great things from it. From what small beginnings have great matters arisen! It is thus in all the gracious proceedings of God with the soul. Scarcely to be perceived are the first workings of his Spirit in the heart, which grow up at last to the wonder of men, and applause of angels. Elijah hastened Ahab home, and attended him. God will strengthen his people for every service to which his commandments and providence call them. The awful displays of Divine justice and holiness dismay the sinner, extort confessions, and dispose to outward obedience while the impression lasts; but the view of these, with mercy, love, and truth in Christ Jesus, is needful to draw the soul to self-abasement, trust, and love. The Holy Spirit employs both in the conversion of sinners; when sinners are impressed with Divine truths, they should be exhorted to set about the duties to which the Saviour calls his disciples.

Chapter 19

Verses 1–8

Jezebel sent Elijah a threatening message. Carnal hearts are hardened and enraged against God, by that which should convince and conquer them. Great faith is not always alike strong. He might be serviceable to Israel at this time, and had all reason to depend upon God's protection, while doing God's work; yet he flees. His was not the deliberate desire of grace, as Paul's, to depart and be with Christ. God thus left Elijah to himself, to show that when he was bold and strong, it was in the Lord, and the power of his might; but of himself he was no better than his fathers. God knows what he designs us for, though we do not, what services, what trials, and he will take care that we are furnished with grace sufficient.

Verses 9–13

The question God put, What doest thou here, Elijah? is a reproof. It concerns us often to ask whether we are in our place, and in the way of our duty. Am I where I should be? whither God calls me, where my business lies, and where I may be useful? He complained of the people, and their obstinacy in sin; I only am left. Despair of success hinders many a good enterprise. Did Elijah come hither to meet with God? he shall find that God will meet him. The wind, and earthquake, and fire, did not make him cover his face, but the still voice did. Gracious souls are more affected by the tender mercies of the Lord, than by his terrors. The mild voice of Him who speaks from the cross, or the mercy-seat, is accompanied with peculiar power in taking possession of the heart.

Verses 14–18

God repeated the question, What doest thou here? Then he complained of his discouragement; and whither should God's prophets go with their complaints of that kind, but to their Master? The Lord gave him an answer. He declares that the wicked house of Ahab shall be rooted out, that the people of Israel shall be punished for their sins; and he shows that Elijah was not left alone as he had supposed, and also that a helper should at once be raised up for him. Thus all his complaints are answered and provided for. God's faithful ones are often his hidden ones, Ps **83**:**3**, and the visible church is scarcely to be seen: the wheat is lost in chaff, and the gold in dross, till the sifting, refining, separating day comes. The Lord knows them that are his, though we do not; he sees in secret. When we come to heaven we shall miss many whom we thought to have met there; we shall meet many whom we little thought to have met there. God's love often proves larger than man's charity, and far more extended.

Verses 19–21

Elijah found Elisha by Divine direction, not in the schools of the prophets, but in the field; not reading, or praying, or sacrificing, but ploughing. Idleness is no man's honour, nor is husbandry any man's disgrace. An honest calling in the world, does not put us out of the way of our heavenly calling, any more than it did Elisha. His heart was touched by the Holy Spirit, and he was ready to leave all to attend Elijah. It is in a day of power that Christ's subjects are made willing; nor would any come to Christ unless they were thus drawn. It was a discouraging time for prophets to set out in. A man that had consulted with flesh and blood, would not be fond of Elijah's mantle; yet Elisha cheerfully leaves all to accompany him. When the Saviour said to one and to another, Follow me, the dearest friends and most profitable occupations were cheerfully left, and the most arduous duties done from love to his name. May we, in like manner, feel the energy of his grace working in us mightily, and by unreserved submission at once, may we make our calling and election sure.

Chapter 20

Verses 1–11

Benhadad sent Ahab a very insolent demand. Ahab sent a very disgraceful submission; sin brings men into such straits, by putting them out of the Divine protection. If God do not rule us, our enemies shall: guilt dispirits men, and makes them cowards. Ahab became desperate. Men will part with their most pleasant things, those they most love, to save their lives; yet they lose their souls rather than part with any pleasure or interest to prevent it. Here is one of the wisest sayings that ever Ahab spake, and it is a good lesson to all. It is folly to boast of any day to come, since we know not what it may bring forth. Apply it to our spiritual conflicts. Peter fell by self-confidence. Happy is the man who is never off his watch.

Verses 12–21

The proud Syrians were beaten, and the despised Israelites were conquerors. The orders of the proud, drunken king disordered his troops, and prevented them from attacking the Israelites. Those that are most secure, are commonly least courageous. Ahab slew the Syrians with a great slaughter. God often makes one wicked man a scourge to another.

Verses 22–30

Those about Benhadad advised him to change his ground. They take it for granted that it was not Israel, but Israel's gods, that beat them; but they speak very ignorantly of Jehovah. They supposed that Israel had many gods, to whom they ascribed limited power within a certain district; thus vain were the Gentiles in their imaginations concerning God. The greatest wisdom in worldly concerns is often united with the most contemptible folly in the things of God.

Verses 31–43

This encouragement sinners have to repent and humble themselves before God; Have we not heard, that the God of Israel is a merciful God? Have we not found him so? That is gospel repentance, which flows from an apprehension of the mercy of God, in Christ; there is forgiveness with him. What a change is here! The most haughty in prosperity often are most abject in adversity; an evil spirit will thus affect a man in both these conditions. There are those on whom, like Ahab, success is ill bestowed; they know not how to serve either God or their generation, or even their own true interests with their prosperity: Let favour be showed to the wicked, yet will he not learn righteousness. The prophet designed to reprove Ahab by a parable. If a good prophet were punished for sparing his friend and God's when God said, Smite, of much sorer punishment should a wicked king be thought worthy, who spared his enemy and God's, when God said, Smite. Ahab went to his house, heavy and displeased, not truly penitent, or seeking to undo what he had done amiss; every way out of humour, notwithstanding his victory. Alas! many that hear the glad tidings of Christ, are busy and there till the day of salvation is gone.

Chapter 21

Verses 1–4

Naboth, perhaps, had been pleased that he had a vineyard situated so near the palace, but the situation proved fatal to him; many a man's possessions have been his snare, and his neighbourhood to greatness, of bad consequence. Discontent is a sin that is its own punishment, and makes men torment themselves. It is a sin that is its own parent; it arises not from the condition, but from the mind: as we find Paul contented in a prison, so Ahab was discontented in a palace. He had all the delights of Canaan, that pleasant land, at command; the wealth of a kingdom, the pleasures of a court, and the honours and powers of a throne; yet all avails him nothing without Naboth's vineyard. Wrong desires expose men to continual vexations, and those that are disposed to fret, however well off, may always find something or other to fret at.

Verses 5–16

When, instead of a help meet, a man has an agent for Satan, in the form of an artful, unprincipled, yet beloved wife, fatal effects may be expected. Never were more wicked orders given by any prince, than those Jezebel sent to the rulers of Jezreel. Naboth must be murdered under colour of religion. There is no wickedness so vile, so horrid, but religion has sometimes been made a cover for it. Also, it must be done under colour of justice, and with the formalities of legal process. Let us, from this sad story, be amazed at the wickedness of the wicked, and the power of Satan in the children of disobedience. Let us commit the keeping of our lives and comforts to God, for innocence will not always be our security; and let us rejoice in the knowledge that all will be set to rights in the great day.

Verses 17–29

Blessed Paul complains that he was sold under sin, Ro **7**:**14**, as a poor captive against his will; but Ahab was willing, he sold himself to sin; of choice, and as his own act and deed, he loved the dominion of sin. Jezebel his wife stirred him up to do wickedly. Ahab is reproved, and his sin set before his eyes, by Elijah. That man's condition is very miserable, who has made the word of God his enemy; and very desperate, who reckons the ministers of that word his enemies, because they tell him the truth. Ahab put on the garb and guise of a penitent, yet his heart was unhumbled and unchanged. Ahab's repentance was only what might be seen of men; it was outward only. Let this encourage all that truly repent, and unfeignedly believe the holy gospel, that if a pretending partial penitent shall go to his house reprieved, doubtless, a sincere believing penitent shall go to his house justified.

Chapter 22

Verses 1–14

The same easiness of temper, which betrays some godly persons into friendship with the declared enemies of religion, renders it very dangerous to them. They will be drawn to wink at and countenance such conduct and conversation as they ought to protest against with abhorrence. Whithersoever a good man goes, he ought to take his religion with him, and not be ashamed to own it when he is with those who have no regard for it. Jehoshaphat had not left behind him, at Jerusalem, his affection and reverence for the word of the Lord, but avowed it, and endeavoured to bring it into Ahab's court. And Ahab's prophets, to please Jehoshaphat, made use of the name of Jehovah: to please Ahab, they said, Go up. But the false prophets cannot so mimic the true, but that he who has spiritual senses exercised, can discern the fallacy. One faithful prophet of the Lord was worth them all. Wordly men have in all ages been alike absurd in their views of religion. They would have the preacher fit his doctrine to the fashion of the times, and the taste of the hearers, and yet to add. Thus saith the Lord, to words that men would put into their mouths. They are ready to cry out against a man as rude and foolish, who scruples thus to try to secure his own interests, and to deceive others.

Verses 15–28

The greatest kindness we can do to one that is going in a dangerous way, is, to tell him of his danger. To leave the hardened criminal without excuse, and to give a useful lesson to others, Micaiah related his vision. This matter is represented after the manner of men: we are not to imagine that God is ever put upon new counsels; or that he needs to consult with angels, or any creature, about the methods he should take; or that he is the author of sin, or the cause of any man's telling or believing a lie. Micaiah returned not the blow of Zedekiah, yet, since he boasted of the Spirit, as those commonly do that know least of the Holy Spirit's operations, the true prophet left him to be convinced of his error by the event. Those that will not have their mistakes set right in time, by the word of God, will be undeceived, when it is too late, by the judgments of God. We should be ashamed of what we call trials, were we to consider what the servants of God have endured. Yet it will be well, if freedom from trouble prove not more hurtful to us; we are more easily allured and bribed into unfaithfulness and conformity to the world, than driven to them.

Verses 29–40

Ahab basely intended to betray Johoshaphat to danger, that he might secure himself. See what they get that join with wicked men. How can it be expected that he should be true to his friend, who has been false to his God! He had said in compliment to Ahab, I am as thou art, and now he was indeed taken for him. Those that associate with evil-doers, are in danger of sharing in their plagues. By Jehoshaphat's deliverance, God let him know, that though he was displeased with him, yet he had not deserted him. God is a friend that will not fail us when other friends do. Let no man think to hide himself from God's judgment. God directed the arrow to hit Ahab; those cannot escape with life, whom God has doomed to death. Ahab lived long enough to see part of Micaiah's prophecy accomplished. He had time to feel himself die; with what horror must he have thought upon the wickedness he had committed!

Verses 41–50

Jehoshaphat's reign appears to have been one of the best, both as to piety and prosperity. He pleased God, and God blessed him.

Verses 51–53

Ahaziah's reign was very short, not two years; some sinners God makes quick work with. A very bad character is given of him; he listened not to instruction, took no warning, but followed the example of his wicked father, and the counsel of his more wicked mother, Jezebel, who was still living. Miserable are the children who not only derive a sinful nature from their parents, but are taught by them to increase it; and most unhappy parents are they, that help to damn their children's souls. Hardened sinners rush forward, unawed and unmoved, in the ways from which others before them have been driven into everlasting misery.

2 Kings

Verses 1–8

When Ahaziah rebelled against the Lord, Moab revolted from him. Sin weakens and impoverishes us. Man's revolt from God is often punished by the rebellion of those who owe subjection to him. Ahaziah fell through a lattice, or railing. Wherever we go, there is but a step between us and death. A man's house is his castle, but not to secure him against God's judgments. The whole creation, which groans under the burden of man's sin, will, at length, sink and break under the weight like this lattice. He is never safe that has God for his enemy. Those that will not inquire of the word of God for their comfort, shall hear it to their terror, whether they will or no.

Verses 9–18

Elijah called for fire from heaven, to consume the haughty, daring sinners; not to secure himself, but to prove his mission, and to reveal the wrath of God from heaven, against the ungodliness and unrighteousness of men. Elijah did this by a Divine impulse, yet our Saviour would not allow the disciples to do the like, Lu **9**:**54**. The dispensation of the Spirit and of grace by no means allowed it. Elijah was concerned for God's glory, those for their own reputation. The Lord judges men's practices by their principles, and his judgment is according to truth. The third captain humbled himself, and cast himself upon the mercy of God and Elijah. There is nothing to be got by contending with God; and those are wise for themselves, who learn submission from the fatal end of obstinacy in others. The courage of faith has often struck terror into the heart of the proudest sinner. So thunderstruck is Ahaziah with the prophet's words, that neither he, nor any about him, offer him violence. Who can harm those whom God shelters? Many who think to prosper in sin, are called hence like Ahaziah, when they do not expect it. All warns us to seek the Lord while he may be found.

Chapter 2

Verses 1–8

The Lord had let Elijah know that his time was at hand. He therefore went to the different schools of the prophets to give them his last exhortations and blessing. The removal of Elijah was a type and figure of the ascension of Christ, and the opening of the kingdom of heaven to all believers. Elisha had long followed Elijah, and he would not leave him now when he hoped for the parting blessing. Let not those who follow Christ come short by tiring at last. The waters of Jordan, of old, yielded to the ark; now, to the prophet's mantle, as a token of God's presence. When God will take up his faithful ones to heaven, death is the Jordan which they must pass through, and they find a way through it. The death of Christ has divided those waters, that the ransomed of the Lord may pass over. O death, where is thy sting, thy hurt, thy terror!

Verses 9–12

That fulness, from whence prophets and apostles had all their supply, still exists as of old, and we are told to ask large supplies from it. Diligent attendance upon Elijah, particularly in his last hours, would be proper means for Elisha to obtain much of his spirit. The comforts of departing saints, and their experiences, help both to gild our comforts and to strengthen our resolutions. Elijah is carried to heaven in a fiery chariot. Many questions might be asked about this, which could not be answered. Let it suffice that we are told, what his Lord, when he came, found him doing. He was engaged in serious discourse, encouraging and directing Elisha about the kingdom of God among men. We mistake, if we think preparation for heaven is carried on only by contemplation and acts of devotion. The chariot and horses appeared like fire, something very glorious, not for burning, but brightness. By the manner in which Elijah and Enoch were taken from this world, God gave a glimpse of the eternal life brought to light by the gospel, of the glory reserved for the bodies of the saints, and of the opening of the kingdom of heaven to all believers. It was also a figure of Christ's ascension. Though Elijah was gone triumphantly to heaven, yet this world could ill spare him. Surely their hearts are hard, who feel not, when God, by taking away faithful, useful men, calls for weeping and mourning. Elijah was to Israel, by his counsels, reproofs, and prayers, better than the strongest force of chariot and horse, and kept off the judgments of God. Christ bequeathed to his disciples his precious gospel, like Elijah's mantle; the token of the Divine power being exerted to overturn the empire of Satan, and to set up the kingdom of God in the world. The same gospel remains with us, though the miraculous powers are withdrawn, and it has Divine strength for the conversion and salvation of sinners.

Verses 13–18

Elijah left his mantle to Elisha; as a token of the descent of the Spirit upon him; it was more than if he had left him thousands of gold and silver. Elisha took it up, not as a sacred relic to be worshipped, but as a significant garment to be worn. Now that Elijah was taken to heaven, Elisha inquired, **1**. After God; when our creature-comforts are removed, we have a God to go to, who lives for ever. **2**. After the God that Elijah served, and honoured, and pleaded for. The Lord God of the holy prophets is the same yesterday, to-day, and for ever; but what will it avail us to have the mantles of those that are gone, their places, their books, if we have not their spirit, their God? See Elisha's dividing the river; God's people need not fear at last passing through the Jordan of death as on dry ground. The sons of the prophets made a needless search for Elijah. Wise men may yield to that, for the sake of peace, and the good opinion of others, which yet their judgment is against, as needless and fruitless. Traversing hills and valleys will never bring us to Elijah, but following the example of his holy faith and zeal will, in due time.

Verses 19–25

Observe the miracle of healing the waters. Prophets should make every place to which they come better for them, endeavouring to sweeten bitter spirits, and to make barren souls fruitful, by the word of God, which is like the salt cast into the water by Elisha. It was an apt emblem of the effect produced by the grace of God on the sinful heart of man. Whole families, towns, and cities, sometimes have a new appearance through the preaching of the gospel; wickedness and evil have been changed into fruitfulness in the works of righteousness, which are, through Christ, to the praise and glory of God. Here is a curse on the youths of Bethel, enough to destroy them; it was not a curse causeless, for it was Elisha's character, as God's prophet, that they abused. They bade him "go up," reflecting on the taking up of Elijah into heaven. The prophet acted by Divine impulse. If the Holy Spirit had not directed Elisha's solemn curse, the providence of God would not have followed it with judgment. The Lord must be glorified as a righteous God who hates sin, and will reckon for it. Let young persons be afraid of speaking wicked words, for God notices what they say. Let them not mock at any for defects in mind or body; especially it is at their peril, if they scoff at any for well doing. Let parents that would have comfort in their children, train them up well, and do their utmost betimes to drive out the foolishness that is bound up in their hearts. And what will be the anguish of those parents, at the day of judgment, who witness the everlasting condemnation of their offspring, occasioned by their own bad example, carelessness, or wicked teaching!

Chapter 3

Verses 1–5

Jehoram took warning by God's judgment, and put away the image of Baal, yet he maintained the worship of the calves. Those do not truly repent or reform, who only part with the sins they lose by, but continue to love the sins that they think to gain by.

Verses 6–19

The king of Israel laments their distress, and the danger they were in. He called these kings together, yet he charges it upon Providence. Thus the foolishness of man perverteth his way, and then his heart fretteth against the Lord, Pr **19**:**3**. It was well that Jehoshaphat inquired of the Lord now, but it had been much better if he had done it before he engaged in this war. Good men sometimes neglect their duty, till necessity and affliction drive them to it. Wicked people often fare the better for the friendship and society of the godly. To try their faith and obedience, Elisha bids them make the valley full of pits to receive water. Those who expect God's blessings, must dig pools for the rain to fill, as in the valley of Baca, and thus make even that a well, Ps **84**:**6**. We need not inquire whence the water came. God is not tied to second causes. They that sincerely seek for the dew of God's grace, shall have it, and by it be made more than conquerors.

Verses 20–27

It is a blessing to be favoured with the company of those who have power with God, and can prevail by their prayers. A kingdom may be upheld and prosper, in consequence of the fervent prayers of those who are dear to God. May we place our highest regard upon such as are most precious in his account. When sinners are saying Peace, peace, destruction comes upon them: despair will follow their mad presumption. In Satan's service and at his suggestion, such horrid deeds have been done, as cause the natural feelings of the heart to shudder; like the king of Moab's sacrificing his son. It is well not to urge the worst of men to extremities; we should rather leave them to the judgment of God.

Chapter 4

Verses 1–7

Elisha's miracles were acts of real charity: Christ's were so; not only great wonders, but great favours to those for whom they were wrought. God magnifies his goodness with his power. Elisha readily received a poor widow's complaint. Those that leave their families under a load of debt, know not what trouble they cause. It is the duty of all who profess to follow the Lord, while they trust to God for daily bread, not to tempt him by carelessness or extravagance, nor to contract debts; for nothing tends more to bring reproach upon the gospel, or distresses their families more when they are gone. Elisha put the widow in a way to pay her debt, and to maintain herself and her family. This was done by miracle, but so as to show what is the best method to assist those who are in distress, which is, to help them to improve by their own industry what little they have. The oil, sent by miracle, continued flowing as long as she had empty vessels to receive it. We are never straitened in God, or in the riches of his grace; all our straitness is in ourselves. It is our faith that fails, not his promise. He gives more than we ask: were there more vessels, there is enough in God to fill them; enough for all, enough for each; and the Redeemer's all-sufficiency will only be stayed from the supplying the wants of sinners and saving their souls, when no more apply to him for salvation. The widow must pay her debt with the money she received for her oil. Though her creditors were too hard with her, yet they must be paid, even before she made any provision for her children. It is one of the main laws of the Christian religion, that we pay every just debt, and give every one his own, though we leave ever so little for ourselves; and this, not of constraint, but for conscience' sake. Those who bear an honest mind, cannot with pleasure eat their daily bread, unless it be their own bread. She and her children must live upon the rest; that is, upon the money received for the oil, with which they must put themselves into a way to get an honest livelihood. We cannot now expect miracles, yet we may expect mercies, if we wait on God, and seek to him. Let widows in particular depend upon him. He that has all hearts in his hand, can, without a miracle, send as effectual a supply.

Verses 8–17

Elisha was well thought of by the king of Israel for his late services; a good man can take as much pleasure in serving others, as in raising himself. But the Shunammite needed not any good offices of this kind. It is a happiness to dwell among our own people, that love and respect us, and to whom we are able to do good. It would be well with many, if they did but know when they are really well off. The Lord sees the secret wish which is suppressed in obedience to his will, and he will hear the prayers of his servants in behalf of their benefactors, by sending unasked-for and unexpected mercies; nor must the professions of men of God be supposed to be delusive like those of men of the world.

Verses 18–37

Here is the sudden death of the child. All the mother's tenderness cannot keep alive a child of promise, a child of prayer, one given in love. But how admirably does the prudent, pious mother, guard her lips under this sudden affliction! Not one peevish word escapes from her. Such confidence had she of God's goodness, that she was ready to believe that he would restore what he had now taken away. O woman, great is thy faith! He that wrought it, would not disappoint it. The sorrowful mother begged leave of her husband to go to the prophet at once. She had not thought it enough to have Elisha's help sometimes in her own family, but, though a woman of rank, attended on public worship. It well becomes the men of God, to inquire about the welfare of their friends and their families. The answer was, It is well. All well, and yet the child dead in the house! Yes! All is well that God does; all is well with them that are gone, if they are gone to heaven; and all well with us that stay behind, if, by the affliction, we are furthered in our way thither. When any creature-comfort is taken from us, it is well if we can say, through grace, that we did not set our hearts too much upon it; for if we did, we have reason to fear it was given in anger, and taken away in wrath. Elisha cried unto God in faith; and the beloved son was restored alive to his mother. Those who would convey spiritual life to dead souls, must feel deeply for their case, and labour fervently in prayer for them. Though the minister cannot give Divine life to his fellow-sinners, he must use every means, with as much earnestness as if he could do so.

Verses 38–44

There was a famine of bread, but not of hearing the word of God, for Elisha had the sons of the prophets sitting before him, to hear his wisdom. Elisha made hurtful food to become safe and wholesome. If a mess of pottage be all our dinner, remember that this great prophet had no better for himself and his guests. The table often becomes a snare, and that which should be for our welfare, proves a trap: this is a good reason why we should not feed ourselves without fear. When we are receiving the supports and comforts of life, we must keep up an expectation of death, and a fear of sin. We must acknowledge God's goodness in making our food wholesome and nourishing; I am the Lord that healeth thee. Elisha also made a little food go a great way. Having freely received, he freely gave. God has promised his church, that he will abundantly bless her provision, and satisfy her poor with bread, Ps **132**:**15**; whom he feeds, he fills; and what he blesses, comes to much. Christ's feeding his hearers was a miracle far beyond this, but both teach us that those who wait upon God in the way of duty, may hope to be supplied by Divine Providence.

Chapter 5

Verses 1–8

Though the Syrians were idolaters, and oppressed God's people, yet the deliverance of which Naaman had been the means, is here ascribed to the Lord. Such is the correct language of Scripture, while those who write common history, plainly show that God is not in all their thoughts. No man's greatness, or honour, can place him our of the reach of the sorest calamities of human life: there is many a sickly, crazy body under rich and gay clothing. Every man has some but or other, something that blemishes and diminishes him, some allay to his grandeur, some damp to his joy. This little maid, though only a girl, could give an account of the famous prophet the Israelites had among them. Children should be early told of the wondrous works of God, that, wherever they go, they may talk of them. As became a good servant, she desired the health and welfare of her master, though she was a captive, a servant by force; much more should servants by choice, seek their masters' good. Servants may be blessings to the families where they are, by telling what they know of the glory of God, and the honour of his prophets. Naaman did not despise what she told, because of her meanness. It would be well if men were as sensible of the burden of sin as they are of bodily disease. And when they seek the blessings which the Lord sends in answer to the prayers of his faithful people, they will find nothing can be had, except they come as beggars for a free gift, not as lords to demand or purchase.

Verses 9–14

Elisha knew Naaman to be a proud man, and he would let him know, that before the great God all men stand upon the same level. All God's commands make trial of men's spirits, especially those which direct a sinner how to apply for the blessings of salvation. See in Naaman the folly of pride; a cure will not content him, unless he be cured with pomp and parade. He scorns to be healed, unless he be humoured. The way by which a sinner is received and made holy, through the blood, and by the Spirit of Christ, through faith alone in his name, does not sufficiently humour or employ self, to please the sinner's heart. Human wisdom thinks it can supply wiser and better methods of cleansing. Observe, masters should be willing to hear reason. As we should be deaf to the counsel of the ungodly, though given by great and respected names, so we are to have our ears open to good advice, though brought by those below us. Wouldst thou not do any thing? When diseased sinners are content to do any thing, to submit to any thing, to part with any thing, for a cure, then, and not till then, is there any hope of them. The methods for the healing of the leprosy of sin, are so plain, that we are without excuse if we do not observe them. It is but, Believe, and be saved; Repent, and be pardoned; Wash, and be clean. The believer applies for salvation, not neglecting, altering, or adding to the Saviour's directions; he is thus made clean from guilt, while others, who neglect them, live and die in the leprosy of sin.

Verses 15–19

The mercy of the cure affected Naaman more than the miracle. Those are best able to speak of the power of Divine grace, who themselves experience it. He also shows himself grateful to Elisha the prophet. Elijah refused any recompence, not because he thought it unlawful, for he received presents from others, but to show this new convert that the servants of the God of Israel looked upon worldly wealth with a holy contempt. The whole work was from God, in such a manner, that the prophet would not give counsel when he had no directions from the Lord. It is not well violently to oppose the lesser mistakes which unite with men's first convictions; we cannot bring men forward any faster than the Lord prepares them to receive instruction. Yet as to us, if, in covenanting with God, we desire to reserve any known sin, to continue to indulge ourselves in it, that is a breach of his covenant. Those who truly hate evil, will make conscience of abstaining from all appearances of evil.

Verses 20–27

Naaman, a Syrian, a courtier, a soldier, had many servants, and we read how wise and good they were. Elisha, a holy prophet, a man of God, has but one servant, and he proves a base liar. The love of money, that root of all evil, was at the bottom of Gehazi's sin. He thought to impose upon the prophet, but soon found that the Spirit of prophecy could not be deceived, and that it was in vain to lie to the Holy Ghost. It is folly to presume upon sin, in hopes of secrecy. When thou goest aside into any by-path, does not thy own conscience go with thee? Does not the eye of God go with thee? He that covers his sin, shall not prosper; particularly, a lying tongue is but for a moment. All the foolish hopes and contrivances of carnal worldlings are open before God. It is not a time to increase our wealth, when we can only do it in such ways as are dishonourable to God and religion, or injurious to others. Gehazi was punished. If he will have Naaman's money, he shall have his disease with it. What was Gehazi profited, though he gained two talents, when thereby he lost his health, his honour, his peace, his service, and, if repentance prevented not, his soul for ever? Let us beware of hypocrisy and covetousness, and dread the curse of spiritual leprosy remaining on our souls.

Chapter 6

Verses 1–7

There is that pleasantness in the converse of servants of God, which can make those who listen to them forget the pain and the weariness of labour. Even the sons of the prophets must not be unwilling to labour. Let no man think an honest employment a burden or a disgrace. And labour of the head, is as hard, and very often harder, than labour with the hands. We ought to be careful of that which is borrowed, as of our own, because we must do as we would be done by. This man was so respecting the axe-head. And to those who have an honest mind, the sorest grievance of poverty is, not so much their own want and disgrace, as being rendered unable to pay just debts. But the Lord cares for his people in their smallest concerns. And God's grace can thus raise the stony iron heart, which is sunk into the mud of this world, and raise up affections, naturally earthly.

Verses 8–12

The king of Israel regarded the warnings Elisha gave him, of danger from the Syrians, but would not heed the warnings of danger from his sins. Such warnings are little heeded by most; they would save themselves from death, but will not from hell. Nothing that is done, said, or thought, by any person, in any place, at any time, is out of God's knowledge.

Verses 13–23

What Elisha said to his servant is spoken to all the faithful servants of God, when without are fightings, and within are fears. Fear not, with that fear which has torment and amazement; for they that are with us, to protect us, are more than they that are against us, to destroy us. The eyes of his body were open, and with them he saw the danger. Lord, open the eyes of our faith, that with them we may see thy protecting hand. The clearer sight we have of the sovereignty and power of Heaven, the less we shall fear the troubles of earth. Satan, the god of this world, blinds men's eyes, and so deludes them unto their own ruin; but when God enlightens their eyes, they see themselves in the midst of their enemies, captives to Satan, and in danger of hell, though, before, they thought their condition good. When Elisha had the Syrians at his mercy, he made it appear that he was influenced by Divine goodness as well as Divine power. Let us not be overcome of evil, but overcome evil with good. The Syrians saw it was to no purpose to try to assault so great and so good a man.

Verses 24–33

Learn to value plenty, and to be thankful for it; see how contemptible money is, when in time of famine it is so freely parted with for any thing that is eatable! The language of Jehoram to the woman may be the language of despair. See the word of God fulfilled; among the threatenings of God's judgments upon Israel for their sins, this was one, that they should eat the flesh of their own children, De **28:53–57**. The truth and the awful justice of God were displayed in this horrible transaction. Alas! what miseries sin has brought upon the world! But the foolishness of man perverts his way, and then his heart frets against the Lord. The king swears the death of Elisha. Wicked men will blame any one as the cause of their troubles, rather than themselves, and will not leave their sins. If rending the clothes, without a broken and contrite heart, would avail, if wearing sackcloth, without being renewed in the spirit of their mind, would serve, they would not stand out against the Lord. May the whole word of God increase in us reverent fear and holy hope, that we may be stedfast and immovable, always abounding in the work of the Lord, knowing that our labour is not in vain in the Lord.

Chapter 7

Verses 1, 2

Man's extremity is God's opportunity of making his own power to be glorious: his time to appear for his people is when their strength is gone. Unbelief is a sin by which men greatly dishonour and displease God, and deprive themselves of the favours he designed for them. Such will be the portion of those that believe not the promise of eternal life; they shall see it at a distance, but shall never taste of it. But no temporal deliverances and mercies will in the end profit sinners, unless they are led to repentance by the goodness of God.

Verses 3–11

God can, when he pleases, make the stoutest heart to tremble; and as for those who will not fear God, he can make them fear at the shaking of a leaf. Providence ordered it, that the lepers came as soon as the Syrians were fled. Their consciences told them that mischief would befall them, if they took care of themselves only. Natural humanity, and fear of punishment, are powerful checks on the selfishness of the ungodly. These feelings tend to preserve order and kindness in the world; but they who have found the unsearchable riches of Christ, will not long delay to report the good tidings to others. From love to him, not from selfish feelings, they will gladly share their earthly good things with their brethren.

Verses 12–20

Here see the wants of Israel supplied in a way they little thought of, which should encourage us to depend upon the power and goodness of God in our greatest straits. God's promise may be safely relied on, for no word of his shall fall to the ground. The nobleman that questioned the truth of Elisha's word, saw the plenty, to silence and shame his unbelief, and therein saw his own folly; but he did not eat of the plenty he saw. Justly do those find the world's promises fail them, who think that the promises of God will disappoint them. Learn how deeply God resents distrust of his power, providence, and promise: how uncertain life is, and the enjoyments of it: how certain God's threatenings are, and how sure to come on the guilty. May God help us to inquire whether we are exposed to his threatenings, or interested in his promises.

Chapter 8

Verses 1–6

The kindness of the good Shunammite to Elisha, was rewarded by the care taken of her in famine. It is well to foresee an evil, and wisdom, when we foresee it, to hide ourselves if we lawfully may do so. When the famine was over, she returned out of the land of the Philistines; that was no proper place for an Israelite, any longer than there was necessity for it. Time was when she dwelt so securely among her own people, that she had no occasion to be spoken for to the king; but there is much uncertainty in this life, so that things or persons may fail us which we most depend upon, and those befriend us which we think we shall never need. Sometimes events, small in themselves, prove of consequence, as here; for they made the king ready to believe Gehazi's narrative, when thus confirmed. It made him ready to grant her request, and to support a life which was given once and again by miracle.

Verses 7–15

Among other changes of men's minds by affliction, it often gives other thoughts of God's ministers, and teaches to value the counsels and prayers of those whom they have hated and despised. It was not in Hazael's countenance that Elisha read what he would do, but God revealed it to him, and it fetched tears from his eyes: the more foresight men have, the more grief they are liable to. It is possible for a man, under the convictions and restraints of natural conscience, to express great abhorrence of a sin, yet afterwards to be reconciled to it. Those that are little and low in the world, cannot imagine how strong the temptations of power and prosperity are, which, if ever they arrive at, they will find how deceitful their hearts are, how much worse than they suspected. The devil ruins men, by saying they shall certainly recover and do well, so rocking them asleep in security. Hazael's false account was an injury to the king, who lost the benefit of the prophet's warning to prepare for death, and an injury to Elisha, who would be counted a false prophet. It is not certain that Hazael murdered his master, or if he caused his death it may have been without any design. But he was a dissembler, and afterwards proved a persecutor to Israel.

Verses 16–24

A general idea is given of Jehoram's badness. His father, no doubt, had him taught the true knowledge of the Lord, but did ill to marry him to the daughter of Ahab; no good could come of union with an idolatrous family.

Verses 25–29

Names do not make natures, but it was bad for Jehoshaphat's family to borrow names from Ahab's. Ahaziah's relation to Ahab's family was the occasion of his wickedness and of his fall. When men choose wives for themselves, let them remember they are choosing mothers for their children. Providence so ordered it, that Ahaziah might be cut off with the house of Ahab, when the measure of their iniquity was full. Those who partake with sinners in their sin, must expect to partake with them in their plagues. May all the changes, troubles, and wickedness of the world, make us more earnest to obtain an interest in the salvation of Christ.

Chapter 9

Verses 1–10

In these and the like events, we must acknowledge the secret working of God, disposing men to fulfil his purposes respecting them. Jehu was anointed king over Israel, by the Lord's special choice. The Lord still had a remnant of his people, and would yet preserve his worship among them. Of this Jehu was reminded. He was commanded to destroy the house of Ahab, and, as far as he acted in obedience to God, and upon right principles, he needed not to regard reproach or opposition. The murder of God's prophets is strongly noticed. Jezebel persisted in idolatry and enmity to Jehovah and his servants, and her iniquity was now full.

Verses 11–15

Those who faithfully deliver the Lord's message to sinners, have in all ages been treated as madmen. Their judgment, speech, and conduct are contrary to those of other men; they endure much in pursuit of objects, and are influenced by motives, into which the others cannot enter. But above all, the charge is brought by the worldly and ungodly of all sorts, who are mad indeed; while the principles and practice of the devoted servants of God, prove to be wise and reasonable. Some faith in the word of God, seems to have animated Jehu to this undertaking.

Verses 16–29

Jehu was a man of eager spirit. The wisdom of God is seen in the choice of those employed in his work. But it is not for any man's reputation to be known by his fury. He that has rule over his own spirit, is better than the mighty. Joram met Jehu in the portion of Naboth. The circumstances of events are sometimes ordered by Divine Providence to make the punishment answer to the sin, as face answers to face in a glass. The way of sin can never be the way of peace, Isa **57**:**21**. What peace can sinners have with God? No peace so long as sin is persisted in; but when it is repented of and forsaken, there is peace. Joram died as a criminal, under the sentence of the law. Ahaziah was joined with the house of Ahab. He was one of them; he had made himself so by sin. It is dangerous to join evil-doers; we shall be entangled in guilt and misery by it.

Verses 30–37

Instead of hiding herself, as one afraid of Divine vengeance, Jezebel mocked at fear. See how a heart, hardened against God, will brave it out to the last. There is not a surer presage of ruin, than an unhumbled heart under humbling providences. Let those look at Jezebel's conduct and fate, who use arts to seduce others to commit wickedness, and to draw them aside from the ways of truth and righteousness. Jehu called for aid against Jezebel. When reformation-work is on foot, it is time to ask, Who sides with it? Her attendants delivered her up. Thus she was put to death. See the end of pride and cruelty, and say, The Lord is righteous. When we pamper our bodies, let us think how vile they are; shortly they will be a feast for worms under ground, or beasts above ground. May we all flee from that wrath which is revealed from heaven, against all ungodliness and unrighteousness of men.

Chapter 10

Verses 1–14

In the most awful events, though attended by the basest crimes of man, the truth and justice of God are to be noticed; and he never did nor can command any thing unjust or unreasonable. Jehu destroyed all that remained of the house of Ahab; all who had been partners in his wickedness. When we think upon the sufferings and miseries of mankind, when we look forward to the resurrection and last judgment, and think upon the vast number of the wicked waiting their awful sentence of everlasting fire; when the whole sum of death and misery has been considered, the solemn question occurs, Who slew all these? The answer is, SIN. Shall we then harbour sin in our bosoms, and seek for happiness from that which is the cause of all misery?

Verses 15–28

Is thine heart right? This is a question we should often put to ourselves. I make a fair profession, have gained a reputation among men, but, is my heart right? Am I sincere with God? Jehonadab owned Jehu in the work, both of revenge and of reformation. An upright heart approves itself to God, and seeks no more than his acceptance; but if we aim at the applause of men, we are upon a false foundation. Whether Jehu looked any further we cannot judge. The law of God was express, that idolaters were to be put to death. Thus idolatry was abolished for the present out of Israel. May we desire that it be rooted out of our hearts.

Verses 29–36

It is justly questionable whether Jehu acted from a good principle, and whether he did not take some false steps in doing it; yet no services done for God shall go unrewarded. But true conversion is not only from gross sin, but from all sin; not only from false gods, but from false worships. True conversion is not only from wasteful sins, but from gainful sins; not only from sins which hurt our worldly interests, but from those that support and befriend them; in forsaking which is the great trial whether we can deny ourselves and trust God. Jehu showed great care and zeal for rooting out a false religion, but in the true religion he cared not, took no heed to please God and do his duty. Those that are heedless, it is to be feared, are graceless. The people were also careless, therefore it is not strange that in those days the Lord began to cut Israel short. They were short in their duty to God, therefore God cut them short in their extent, wealth, and power.

Chapter 11

Verses 1–12

Athaliah destroyed all she knew to be akin to the crown. Jehoash, one of the king's sons, was hid. Now was the promise made to David bound up in one life only, and yet it did not fail. Thus to the Son of David, the Lord, according to his promise, will secure a spiritual seed, hidden sometimes, and unseen, but hidden in God's pavilion, and unhurt. Six years Athaliah tyrannized. Then the king was brought forward. A child indeed, but he had a good guardian, and, what was better, a good God to go to With such joy and satisfaction must the kingdom of Christ be welcomed into our hearts, when his throne is set up there, and Satan the usurper is cast out. Say, Let the King, even Jesus, live, for ever live and reign in my soul, and in all the world.

Verses 13–16

Athaliah hastened her own destruction. She herself was the greatest traitor, and yet was first and loudest in crying, Treason, treason! The most guilty are commonly the most forward to reproach others.

Verses 17–21

King and people would cleave most firmly to each other, when both had joined themselves to the Lord. It is well with a people, when all the changes that pass over them help to revive, strengthen, and advance the interests of religion among them. Covenants are of use, both to remind us of, and bind us to, the duties already binding on us. They immediately abolished idolatry; and, pursuant to the covenant with one another, they expressed mutual readiness to help each other. The people rejoiced, and Jerusalem was quiet. The way for people to be joyful and at peace, is to engage fully in the service of God; for the voice of joy and thanksgiving is in the dwellings of the righteous, but there is no peace for the wicked.

Chapter 12

Verses 1–16

It is a great mercy to young people, especially to all young men of rank, like Jehoash, to have those about them who will instruct them to do what is right in the sight of the Lord; and they do wisely and well for themselves, when willing to be counselled and ruled. The temple was out of repair; Jehoash orders the repair of the temple. The king was zealous. God requires those who have power, to use it for the support of religion, the redress of grievances, and repairing of decays. The king employed the priests to manage, as most likely to be hearty in the work. But nothing was done effectually till the twenty-third year of his reign. Another method was therefore taken. When public distributions are made faithfully, public contributions will be made cheerfully. While they were getting all they could for the repair of the temple, they did not break in upon the stated maintenance of the priests. Let not the servants of the temple be starved, under colour of repairing the breaches of it. Those that were intrusted did the business carefully and faithfully. They did not lay it out in ornaments for the temple, till the other work was completed; hence we may learn, in all our expenses, to prefer that which is most needful, and, in dealing for the public, to deal as we would for ourselves.

Verses 17–21

Let us review the character of Jehoash, and consider what we may learn from it. When we see what a sad conclusion there was to so promising a beginning, it ought to make us seek into our spiritual declinings. If we know any thing of Christ as the foundation of our faith and hope, let us desire to know nothing but Christ. May the work of the blessed Spirit on our souls be manifest; may we see, feel, and be earnest, in seeking after Jesus in all his fulness, suitableness, and grace, that our souls may be brought over from dead works to serve the living and true God.

Chapter 13

Verses 1–9

It was the ancient honour of Israel that they were a praying people. Jehoahaz, their king, in his distress, besought the Lord; applied himself for help, but not to the calves; what help could they give him? He sought the Lord. See how swift God is to show mercy; how ready to hear prayer; how willing to find a reason to be gracious; else he would not look so far back as the ancient covenant Israel had so often broken, and forfeited. Let this invite and engage us for ever to him; and encourage even those who have forsaken him, to return and repent; for there is forgiveness with him, that he may be feared. And if the Lord answer the mere cry of distress for temporal relief, much more will he regard the prayer of faith for spiritual blessings.

Verses 10–19

Jehoash, the king, came to Elisha, to receive his dying counsel and blessing. It may turn much to our spiritual advantage, to attend the sick-beds and death-beds of good men, that we may be encouraged in religion by the living comforts they have from it in a dying hour. Elisha assured the king of his success; yet he must look up to God for direction and strength; must reckon his own hands not enough, but go on, in dependence upon Divine aid. The trembling hands of the dying prophet, as they signified the power of God, gave this arrow more force than the hands of the king in his full strength. By contemning the sign, the king lost the thing signified, to the grief of the dying prophet. It is a trouble to good men, to see those to whom they wish well, forsake their own mercies, and to see them lose advantages against spiritual enemies.

Verses 20–25

God has many ways to chastise a provoking people. Trouble comes sometimes from that point whence we least feared it. The mention of this invasion on the death of Elisha, shows that the removal of God's faithful prophets is a presage of coming judgments. His dead body was a means of giving life to another dead body. This miracle was a confirmation of his prophecies. And it may have reference to Christ, by whose death and burial, the grave is made a safe and happy passage to life to all believers. Jehoash was successful against the Syrians, just as often as he had struck the ground with the arrows, then a stop was put to his victories. Many have repented, when too late, of distrusts and the straitness of their desires.

Chapter 14

Verses 1–7

Amaziah began well, but did not go on so. It is not enough to do that which our pious predecessors did, merely to keep up the common usage, but we must do it as they did, from the same principle of faith and devotion, and with the same sincerity and resolution.

Verses 8–14

For some time after the division of the kingdoms, Judah suffered much from the enmity of Israel. After Asa's time, it suffered more by the friendship of Israel, and by the alliance made with them. Now we meet with hostility between them again. How may a humble man smile to hear two proud and scornful men set their wits on work, to vilify and undervalue one another! Unholy success excites pride; pride excites contentions. The effects of pride in others, are insufferable to those who are proud themselves. These are the sources of trouble and sin in private life; but when they arise between princes, they become the misery of their whole kingdoms. Jehoash shows Amaziah the folly of his challenge; Thine heart has lifted thee up. The root of all sin is in the heart, thence it flows. It is not Providence, the event, the occasion, whatever it is, that makes men proud, secure, discontented, or the like, but their own hearts do it. (**2Ki 14:15-22**)

Verses 15–22

Amaziah survived his conqueror fifteen years. He was slain by his own subjects. Azariah, or Uzziah, seems to have been very young when his father was slain. Though the years of his reign are reckoned from that event, he was not fully made king till eleven years afterwards.

Verses 23–29

God raised up the prophet Jonah, and by him declared the purposes of his favour to Israel. It is a sign that God has not cast off his people, if he continues faithful ministers among them. Two reasons are given why God blessed them with those victories: **1**. Because the distress was very great, which made them objects of his compassion. **2**. Because the decree was not yet gone forth for their destruction. Many prophets there had been in Israel, but none left prophecies in writing till this age, and their prophecies are part of the Bible. Hosea began to prophesy in the reign of this Jeroboam. At the same time Amos prophesied; soon after Micah, then Isaiah, in the days of Ahaz and Hezekiah. Thus God, in the darkest and most degenerate ages of the church, raised up some to be burning and shining lights in it; to their own age, by their preaching and living, and a few by their writings, to reflect light upon us in the last times.

Chapter 15

Verses 1–7

Uzziah did for the most part that which was right. It was happy for the kingdom that a good reign was a long one.

Verses 8–31

This history shows Israel in confusion. Though Judah was not without troubles, yet that kingdom was happy, compared with the state of Israel. The imperfections of true believers are very different from the allowed wickedness of ungodly men. Such is human nature, such are our hearts, if left to themselves, deceitful above all things, and desperately wicked. We have reason to be thankful for restraints, for being kept out of temptation, and should beg of God to renew a right spirit within us.

Verses 32–38

Jotham showed great respect to the temple. If magistrates cannot do all they would, for the suppressing of vice and profaneness, let them do the more to support and advance piety and virtue.

Chapter 16

Verses 1–9

Few and evil were the days of Ahaz. Those whose hearts condemn them, will go any where in a day of distress, rather than to God. The sin was its own punishment. It is common for those who bring themselves into straits by one sin, to try to help themselves out by another.

Verses 10–16

God's altar had hitherto been kept in its place, and in use; but Ahaz put another in the room of it. The natural regard of the mind of man to some sort of religion, is not easily extinguished; but except it be regulated by the word, and by the Spirit of God, it produces absurd superstitions, or detestable idolatries. Or, at best, it quiets the sinner's conscience with unmeaning ceremonies. Infidels have often been remarkable for believing ridiculous falsehoods.

Verses 17–20

Ahaz put contempt upon the sabbath, and thus opened a wide inlet to all manner of sin. This he did for the king of Assyria. When those who have had a ready passage to the house of the Lord, turn it another way to please their neighbours, they are going down-hill apace to ruin.

Chapter 17

Verses 1–6

When the measure of sin is filled up, the Lord will forbear no longer. The inhabitants of Samaria must have endured great affliction. Some of the poor Israelites were left in the land. Those who were carried captives to a great distance, were mostly lost among the nations.

Verses 7–23

Though the destruction of the kingdom of the ten tribes was but briefly related, it is in these **verse**s largely commented upon, and the reasons of it given. It was destruction from the Almighty: the Assyrian was but the rod of his anger, Isa **10**:**5**. Those that bring sin into a country or family, bring a plague into it, and will have to answer for all the mischief that follows. And vast as the outward wickedness of the world is, the secret sins, evil thoughts, desires, and purposes of mankind are much greater. There are outward sins which are marked by infamy; but ingratitude, neglect, and enmity to God, and the idolatry and impiety which proceed therefrom, are far more malignant. Without turning from every evil way, and keeping God's statutes, there can be no true godliness; but this must spring from belief of his testimony, as to wrath against all ungodliness and unrighteousness, and his mercy in Christ Jesus.

Verses 24–41

The terror of the Almighty will sometimes produce a forced or feigned submission in unconverted men; like those brought from different countries to inhabit Israel. But such will form unworthy thoughts of God, will expect to please him by outward forms, and will vainly try to reconcile his service with the love of the world and the indulgence of their lusts. May that fear of the Lord, which is the beginning of wisdom, possess our hearts, and influence our conduct, that we may be ready for every change. Wordly settlements are uncertain; we know not whither we may be driven before we die, and we must soon leave the world; but the righteous hath chosen that good part which shall not be taken from him.

Chapter 18

Verses 1–8

Hezekiah was a true son of David. Some others did that which was right, but not like David. Let us not suppose that when times and men are bad, they must needs grow worse and worse: that does not follow: after many bad kings, God raised one up like David himself. The brazen serpent had been carefully preserved, as a memorial of God's goodness to their fathers in the wilderness; but it was idle and wicked to burn incense to it. All helps to devotion, not warranted by the word of God, interrupt the exercise of faith; they always lead to superstition and other dangerous evils. Human nature perverts every thing of this kind. True faith needs not such aids; the word of God, daily thought upon and prayed over, is all the outward help we need.

Verses 9–16

The descent Sennacherib made upon Judah, was a great calamity to that kingdom, by which God would try the faith of Hezekiah, and chastise the people. The secret dislike, the hypocrisy, and lukewarmness of numbers, require correction; such trials purify the faith and hope of the upright, and bring them to simple dependence on God.

Verses 17–37

Rabshakeh tries to convince the Jews, that it was to no purpose for them to stand it out. What confidence is this wherein thou trustest? It were well if sinners would submit to the force of this argument, in seeking peace with God. It is, therefore, our wisdom to yield to him, because it is in vain to contend with him: what confidence is that which those trust in who stand out against him? A great deal of art there is in this speech of Rabshakeh; but a great deal of pride, malice, falsehood, and blasphemy. Hezekiah's nobles held their peace. There is a time to keep silence, as well as a time to speak; and there are those to whom to offer any thing religious or rational, is to cast pearls before swine. Their silence made Rabshakeh yet more proud and secure. It is often best to leave such persons to rail and blaspheme; a decided expression of abhorrence is the best testimony against them. The matter must be left to the Lord, who has all hearts in his hands, committing ourselves unto him in humble submission, believing hope, and fervent prayer.

Chapter 19

Verses 1–7

Hezekiah discovered deep concern at the dishonour done to God by Rabshakeh's blasphemy. Those who speak from God to us, we should in a particular manner desire to speak to God for us. The great Prophet is the great Intercessor. Those are likely to prevail with God, who lift up their hearts in prayer. Man's extremity is God's opportunity. While his servants can speak nothing but terror to the profane, the proud, and the hypocritical, they have comfortable words for the discouraged believer.

Verses 8–19

Prayer is the never-failing resource of the tempted Christian, whether struggling with outward difficulties or inward foes. At the mercy-seat of his almighty Friend he opens his heart, spreads his case, like Hezekiah, and makes his appeal. When he can discern that the glory of God is engaged on his side, faith gains the victory, and he rejoices that he shall never be moved. The best pleas in prayer are taken from God's honour. (**2Ki 19**:**20-34**)

Verses 20–34

All Sennacherib's motions were under the Divine cognizance. God himself undertakes to defend the city; and that person, that place, cannot but be safe, which he undertakes to protect. The invasion of the Assyrians probably had prevented the land from being sown that year. The next is supposed to have been the sabbatical year, but the Lord engaged that the produce of the land should be sufficient for their support during those two years. As the performance of this promise was to be after the destruction of Sennacherib's army, it was a sign to Hezekiah's faith, assuring him of that present deliverance, as an earnest of the Lord's future care of the kingdom of Judah. This the Lord would perform, not for their righteousness, but his own glory. May our hearts be as good ground, that his word may strike root therein, and bring forth fruit in our lives.

Verses 35–37

That night which followed the sending of this message to Hezekiah, the main body of their army was slain. See how weak the mightiest men are before Almighty God. Who ever hardened himself against Him and prospered? The king of Assyria's own sons became his murderers. Those whose children are undutiful, ought to consider whether they have not been so to their Father in heaven? This history exhibits a strong proof of the good of firm trust and confidence in God. He will afflict, but not forsake his people. It is well when our troubles drive us to our knees. But does it not reprove our unbelief? How unwilling are we to rest on the declaration of Jehovah! How desirous to know in what way he will save us! How impatient when relief is delayed! But we must wait for the fulfilling of his word. Lord, help our unbelief.

Chapter 20

Verses 1–11

Hezekiah was sick unto death, in the same year in which the king of Assyria besieged Jerusalem. A warning to prepare for death was brought to Hezekiah by Isaiah. Prayer is one of the best preparations for death, because by it we fetch in strength and grace from God, to enable us to finish well. He wept sorely: some gather from hence that he was unwilling to die; it is in the nature of man to dread the separation of soul and body. There was also something peculiar in Hezekiah's case; he was now in the midst of his usefulness. Let Hezekiah's prayer, see Isa **38**. interpret his tears; in that is nothing which is like his having been under that fear of death, which has bondage or torment. Hezekiah's piety made his sick-bed easy. "O Lord, remember now;" he does not speak as if God needed to be put in mind of any thing by us; nor, as if the reward might be demanded as due; it is Christ's righteousness only that is the purchase of mercy and grace. Hezekiah does not pray, Lord, spare me; but, Lord, remember me; whether I live or die, let me be thine. God always hears the prayers of the broken in heart, and will give health, length of days, and temporal deliverances, as much and as long as is truly good for them. Means were to be used for Hezekiah's recovery; yet, considering to what a height the disease was come, and how suddenly it was checked, the cure was miraculous. It is our duty, when sick, to use such means as are proper to help nature, else we do not trust God, but tempt him. For the confirmation of his faith, the shadow of the sun was carried back, and the light was continued longer than usual, in a miraculous manner. This work of wonder shows the power of God in heaven as well as on earth, the great notice he takes of prayer, and the great favour he bears to his chosen.

Verses 12–21

The king of Babylon was at this time independent of the king of Assyria, though shortly after subdued by him. Hezekiah showed his treasures and armour, and other proofs of his wealth and power. This was the effect of pride and ostentation, and departing from simple reliance on God. He also seems to have missed the opportunity of speaking to the Chaldeans, about Him who had wrought the miracles which excited their attention, and of pointing out to them the absurdity and evil of idolatry. What is more common than to show our friends our houses and possessions? But if we do this in the pride of ours hearts, to gain applause from men, not giving praise to God, it becomes sin in us, as it did in Hezekiah. We may expect vexation from every object with which we are unduly pleased. Isaiah, who had often been Hezekiah's comforter, is now is reprover. The blessed Spirit is both, Joh **16**:**7**, **8**. Ministers must be both, as there is occasion. Hezekiah allowed the justice of the sentence, and God's goodness in the respite. Yet the prospect respecting his family and nation must have given him many painful feelings. Hezekiah was indeed humbled for the pride of his heart. And blessed are the dead who die in the Lord; for they rest from their labours, and their works do follow them.

Chapter 21

Verses 1–9

Young persons generally desire to become their own masters, and to have early possession of riches and power. But this, for the most part, ruins their future comfort, and causes mischief to others. It is much happier when young persons are sheltered under the care of parents or guardians, till age gives experience and discretion. Though such young persons are less indulged, they will afterwards be thankful. Manasseh wrought much wickedness in the sight of the Lord, as if on purpose to provoke him to anger; he did more evil than the nations whom the Lord destroyed. Manasseh went on from bad to worse, till carried captive to Babylon. The people were ready to comply with his wishes, to obtain his favour and because it suited their depraved inclinations. In the reformation of large bodies, numbers are mere time-servers, and in temptation fall away.

Verses 10–18

Here is the doom of Judah and Jerusalem. The words used represent the city emptied and utterly desolate, yet not destroyed thereby, but cleansed, and to be kept for the future dwelling of the Jews: forsaken, yet not finally, and only as to outward privileges, for individual believers were preserved in that visitation. The Lord will cast off any professing people who dishonour him by their crimes, but never will desert his cause on earth. In the book of Chronicles we read of Manasseh's repentance, and acceptance with God; thus we may learn not to despair of the recovery of the greatest sinners. But let none dare to persist in sin, presuming that they may repent and reform when they please. There are a few instances of the conversion of notorious sinners, that none may despair; and but few, that none may presume.

Verses 19–26

Amon profaned God's house with his idols; and God suffered his house to be polluted with his blood. How unrighteous soever they were that did it, God was righteous who suffered it to be done. Now was a happy change from one of the worst, to one of the best of the kings of Judah. Once more Judah was tried with a reformation. Whether the Lord bears long with presumptuous offenders, or speedily cuts them off in their sins, all must perish who persist in refusing to walk in his ways.

Chapter 22

Verses 1–10

The different event of Josiah's early succession from that of Manasseh, must be ascribed to the distinguishing grace of God; yet probably the persons that trained him up were instruments in producing this difference. His character was most excellent. Had the people joined in the reformation as heartily as he persevered in it, blessed effects would have followed. But they were wicked, and had become fools in idolatry. We do not obtain full knowledge of the state of Judah from the historical records, unless we refer to the writings of the prophets who lived at the time. In repairing the temple, the book of the law was found, and brought to the king. It seems, this book of the law was lost and missing; carelessly mislaid and neglected, as some throw their Bibles into corners, or maliciously concealed by some of the idolaters. God's care of the Bible plainly shows his interest in it. Whether this was the only copy in being or not, the things contained in it were new, both to the king and to the high priest. No summaries, extracts, or collections out of the Bible, can convey and preserve the knowledge of God and his will, like the Bible itself. It was no marvel that the people were so corrupt, when the book of the law was so scarce; they that corrupted them, no doubt, used arts to get that book out of their hands. The abundance of Bibles we possess aggravates our national sins; for what greater contempt of God can we show, than to refuse to read his word when put into our hands, or, reading it, not to believe and obey it? By the holy law is the knowledge of sin, and by the blessed gospel is the knowledge of salvation. When the former is understood in its strictness and excellence, the sinner begins to inquire, What must I do to be saved? And the ministers of the gospel point out to him Jesus Christ, as the end of the law for righteousness to every one that believeth.

Verses 11–20

The book of the law is read before the king. Those best honour their Bibles, who study them; daily feed on that bread, and walk by that light. Convictions of sin and wrath should put us upon this inquiry, What shall we do to be saved? Also, what we may expect, and must provide for. Those who are truly apprehensive of the weight of God's wrath, cannot but be very anxious how they may be saved. Huldah let Josiah know what judgments God had in store for Judah and Jerusalem. The generality of the people were hardened, and their hearts unhumbled, but Josiah's heart was tender. This is tenderness of heart, and thus he humbled himself before the Lord. Those who most fear God's wrath, are least likely to feel it. Though Josiah was mortally wounded in battle, yet he died in peace with God, and went to glory. Whatever such persons suffer or witness, they are gathered to the grave in peace, and shall enter into the rest which remaineth for the people of God.

Chapter 23

Verses 1–3

Josiah had received a message from God, that there was no preventing the ruin of Jerusalem, but that he should only deliver his own soul; yet he does his duty, and leaves the event to God. He engaged the people in the most solemn manner to abolish idolatry, and to serve God in righteousness and true holiness. Though most were formal or hypocritical herein, yet much outward wickedness would be prevented, and they were accountable to God for their own conduct.

Verses 4–14

What abundance of wickedness in Judah and Jerusalem! One would not have believed it possible, that in Judah, where God was known, in Israel, where his name was great, in Salem, in Zion, where his dwelling-place was, such abominations should be found. Josiah had reigned eighteen years, and had himself set the people a good example, and kept up religion according to the Divine law; yet, when he came to search for idolatry, the depth and extent were very great. Both common history, and the records of God's word, teach, that all the real godliness or goodness ever found on earth, is derived from the new-creating Spirit of Jesus Christ.

Verses 15–24

Josiah's zeal extended to the cities of Israel within his reach. He carefully preserved the sepulchre of that man of God, who came from Judah to foretell the throwing down of Jeroboam's altar. When they had cleared the country of the old leaven of idolatry, then they applied themselves to the keeping of the feast. There was not holden such a passover in any of the foregoing reigns. The revival of a long-neglected ordinance, filled them with holy joy; and God recompensed their zeal in destroying idolatry with uncommon tokens of his presence and favour. We have reason to think that during the remainder of Josiah's reign, religion flourished.

Verses 25–30

Upon reading these **verse**s, we must say, Lord, though thy righteousness be as the great mountains, evident, plainly to be seen, and past dispute; yet thy judgments are a great deep, unfathomable, and past finding out. The reforming king is cut off in the midst of his usefulness, in mercy to him, that he might not see the evil coming upon his kingdom: but in wrath to his people, for his death was an inlet to their desolations. (**2**Ki **23**:**31-37**)

Verses 31–37

After Josiah was laid in his grave, one trouble came on another, till, in twenty-two years, Jerusalem was destroyed. The wicked perished in great numbers, the remnant were purified, and Josiah's reformation had raised up some to join the few who were the precious seed of their future church and nation. A little time, and slender abilities, often suffice to undo the good which pious men have, for a course of years, been labouring to effect. But, blessed be God, the good work which he begins by his regenerating Spirit, cannot be done away, but withstands all changes and temptations.

Chapter 24

Verses 1–7

If Jehoiakim had served the Lord, he had not been servant to Nebuchadnezzar. If he had been content with his servitude, and true to his word, his condition had been no worse; but, rebelling against Babylon, he plunged himself into more trouble. See what need nations have to lament the sins of their fathers, lest they smart for them. Threatenings will be fulfilled as certainly as promises, if the sinner's repentance prevent not. (**2**Ki **24**:**8-20**)

Verses 8–20

Jehoiachin reigned but three months, yet long enough to show that he justly smarted for his fathers' sins, for he trod in their steps. His uncle was intrusted with the government. This Zedekiah was the last of the kings of Judah. Though the judgments of God upon the three kings before him might have warned him, he did that which was evil, like them. When those intrusted with the counsels of a nation act unwisely, and against their true interest, we ought to notice the displeasure of God in it. It is for the sins of a people that God hides from them the things that belong to the public peace. And in fulfilling the secret purposes of his justice, the Lord needs only leave men to the blindness of their own minds, or to the lusts of their own hearts. The gradual approach of Divine judgments affords sinners space for repentance, and believers leisure to prepare for meeting the calamity, while it shows the obstinacy of those who will not forsake their sins.

Chapter 25

Verses 1–7

Jerusalem was so fortified, that it could not be taken till famine rendered the besieged unable to resist. In the prophecy and Lamentations of Jeremiah, we find more of this event; here it suffices to say, that the impiety and misery of the besieged were very great. At length the city was taken by storm. The king, his family, and his great men escaped in the night, by secret passages. But those deceive themselves who think to escape God's judgments, as much as those who think to brave them. By what befell Zedekiah, two prophecies, which seemed to contradict each other, were both fulfilled. Jeremiah prophesied that Zedekiah should be brought to Babylon, Jer **32**:**5**; **34**:**3**; Ezekiel, that he should not see Babylon, Eze **12**:**13**. He was brought thither, but his eyes being put out, he did not see it.

Verses 8–21

The city and temple were burnt, and, it is probable, the ark in it. By this, God showed how little he cares for the outward pomp of his worship, when the life and power of religion are neglected. The walls of Jerusalem were thrown down, and the people carried captive to Babylon. The vessels of the temple were carried away. When the things signified were sinned away, what should the signs stand there for? It was righteous with God to deprive those of the benefit of his worship, who had preferred false worships before it; those that would have many altars, now shall have none. As the Lord spared not the angels that sinned, as he doomed the whole race of fallen men to the grave, and all unbelievers to hell, and as he spared not his own Son, but delivered him up for us all, we need not wonder at any miseries he may bring upon guilty nations, churches, or persons.

Verses 22–30

The king of Babylon appointed Gedaliah to be the governor and protector of the Jews left their land. But the things of their peace were so hidden from their eyes, that they knew not when they were well off. Ishmael basely slew him and all his friends, and, against the counsel of Jeremiah, the rest went to Egypt. Thus was a full end made of them by their own folly and disobedience; see Jeremiah chap. **40** to **45** Jehoiachin was released out of prison, where he had been kept **37** years. Let none say that they shall never see good again, because they have long seen little but evil: the most miserable know not what turn Providence may yet give to their affairs, nor what comforts they are reserved for, according to the days wherein they have been afflicted. Even in this world the Saviour brings a release from bondage to the distressed sinner who seeks him, bestowing foretastes of the pleasures which are at his right hand for evermore. Sin alone can hurt us; Jesus alone can do good to sinners.

1 Chronicles

The books of Chronicles are, in a great measure, repetitions of what is in the books of Samuel and of the Kings, yet there are some excellent useful things in them which we find not elsewhere. The FIRST BOOK traces the rise of the Jewish people from Adam, and afterward gives an account of the reign of David. In the SECOND BOOK the narrative is continued, and relates the progress and end of the kingdom of Judah; also it notices the return of the Jews from the Babylonish captivity. Jerome says, that whoever supposes himself to have knowledge of the Scriptures without being acquainted with the books of Chronicles, deceives himself. Historical facts passed over elsewhere, names, and the connexion of passages are to be found here, and many questions concerning the gospel are explained.

Chapter 1

Verses 1–27

This chapter, and many that follow, repeat the genealogies, or lists of fathers and children in the Bible history, and put them together, with many added. When compared with other places, there are some differences found; yet we must not therefore stumble at the word, but bless God that the things necessary to salvation are plain enough. The original of the Jewish nation is here traced from the first man that God created, and is thereby distinguished from the obscure, fabulous, and absurd origins assigned to other nations. But the nations now are all so mingled with one another, that no one nation, nor the greatest part of any, is descended entirely from any of one nation, nor the greatest part of any, is descended entirely from any of these fountains. Only this we are sure of, that God has created of one blood all nations of men; they are all descended from one Adam, one Noah. Have we not all one father? Has not one God created us? Mal **2**:**10**.

Verses 28–54

The genealogy is from hence confined to the posterity of Abraham. Let us take occasion from reading these lists of names, to think of the multitudes that have gone through this world, have done their parts in it, and then quitted it. As one generation, even of sinful men, passes away, another comes. Ec **1**:**4**; Nu **32**:**14**, and will do so while the earth remains. Short is our passage through time into eternity. May we be distinguished as the Lord's people.

Chapter 2

Genealogies.

—We are now come to the register of the children of Israel, that distinguished people, who were to dwell alone, and not be reckoned among the nations. But now, in Christ, all are welcome to his salvation who come to him; all have equal privileges according to their faith in him, their love and devotedness to him. All that is truly valuable consists in the favour, peace, and image of God, and a life spent to his glory, in promoting the welfare of our fellow-creatures.

Chapter 3

Genealogies.

—Of all the families of Israel, none were so illustrious as the family of David: here we have a full account of it. From this family, as concerning the flesh, Christ came. The attentive observer will perceive that the children of the righteous enjoy many advantages.

Chapter 4

Genealogies.

—In this chapter we have a further account of Judah, the most numerous and most famous of all the tribes; also an account of Simeon. The most remarkable person in this chapter is Jabez. We are not told upon what account Jabez was more honourable than his brethren; but we find that he was a praying man. The way to be truly great, is to seek to do God's will, and to pray earnestly. Here is the prayer he made. Jabez prayed to the living and true God, who alone can hear and answer prayer; and, in prayer he regarded him as a God in covenant with his people. He does not express his promise, but leaves it to be understood; he was afraid to promise in his own strength, and resolved to devote himself entirely to God. Lord, if thou wilt bless me and keep me, do what thou wilt with me; I will be at thy command and disposal for ever. As the text reads it, this was the language of a most ardent and affectionate desire, Oh that thou wouldest bless me! Four things Jabez prayed for. **1**. That God would bless him indeed. Spiritual blessings are the best blessings: God's blessings are real things, and produce real effects. **2**. That He would enlarge his coast. That God would enlarge our hearts, and so enlarge our portion in himself, and in the heavenly Canaan, ought to be our desire and prayer. **3**. That God's hand might be with him. God's hand with us, to lead us, protect us, strengthen us, and to work all our works in us and for us, is a hand all-sufficient for us. **4**. That he would keep him from evil, the evil of sin, the evil of trouble, all the evil designs of his enemies, that they might not hurt, nor make him a Jabez indeed, a man of sorrow. God granted that which he requested. God is ever ready to hear prayer: his ear is not now heavy.

Chapter 5

Genealogies.

—This chapter gives some account of the two tribes and a half seated on the east side of Jordan. They were made captives by the king of Assyria, because they had forsaken the Lord. Only two things are here recorded concerning these tribes. **1**. They all shared in a victory. Happy is that people who live in harmony together, who assist each other against the common enemies of their souls, trusting in the Lord, and calling upon him. **2**. They shared in captivity. They would have the best land, not considering that it lay most exposed. The desire of earthly objects draws to a distance from God's ordinances, and prepares men for destruction.

Chapter 6

Genealogies.

—We have an account of Levi in this chapter. The priests and Levites were more concerned than any other Israelites, to preserve their descent clear, and to be able to prove it; because all the honours and privileges of their office depended upon their descent. Now, the Spirit of God calls ministers to their work, without any limit as to the families they came from; and then, as now, though believers and ministers may be very useful to the church, none but our great High Priest can make atonement for sin, nor can any be accepted but through his atonement.

Chapter 7

Genealogies.

—Here is no account either of Zebulun or Dan. We can assign no reason why they only should be omitted; but it is the disgrace of the tribe of Dan, that idolatry began in that colony which fixed in Laish, and called it Dan, Jud **18** and there one of the golden calves was set up by Jeroboam. Dan is omitted, Re **7**. Men become abominable when they forsake the worship of the true God, for any creature object.

Chapter 8

Genealogies.

—Here is a larger list of Benjamin's tribe. We may suppose that many things in these genealogies, which to us seem difficult, abrupt, and perplexed, were plain and easy at that time, and fully answered the intention for which they were published. Many great and mighty nations then were in being upon earth, and many illustrious men, whose names are now wholly forgotten; while the names of multitudes of the Israel of God are here kept in everlasting remembrance. The memory of the just is blessed.

Chapter 9

Genealogies.

—This chapter expresses that one end of recording all these genealogies was, to direct the Jews, when they returned out of captivity, with whom to unite, and where to reside. Here is an account of the good state into which the affairs of religion were put, on the return from Babylon. Every one knew his charge. Work is likely to be done well when every one knows the duty of his place, and makes a business of it. God is the God of order. Thus was the temple a figure of the heavenly one, where they rest not day nor night from praising God, Re **4**:**8**. Blessed be His name, believers there shall, not in turn, but all together, without interruption, praise him night and day: may the Lord make each of us fit for the inheritance of the saints in light.

Chapter 10

The death of Saul.

—The design chiefly in view in these books of the Chronicles, appears to be to preserve the records of the house of David. Therefore the writer repeats not the history of Saul's reign, but only of his death, by which a way was made for David to the throne. And from the ruin of Saul, we may learn, **1**. That the sin of sinners will certainly find them out, sooner or later; Saul died for his transgression. **2**. That no man's greatness can exempt him from the judgments of God. **3**. Disobedience is a killing thing. Saul died for not keeping the word of the Lord. May be delivered from unbelief, impatience, and despair. By waiting on the Lord we shall obtain a kingdom that cannot be moved.

Chapter 11

Verses 1–9

David was brought to possess the throne of Israel after he had reigned seven years in Hebron, over Judah only. God's counsels will be fulfilled at last, whatever difficulties lie in the way. The way to be truly great, is to be really useful, to devote all our talents to the Lord.

Verses 10–47

An account is given of David's worthies, the great men who served him. Yet David reckoned his success, not as from the mighty men that were with him, but from the mighty God, whose presence is all in all. In strengthening him, they strengthened themselves and their own interest, for his advancement was theirs. We shall gain by what we do in our places for the support of the kingdom of the Son of David; and those that are faithful to Him, shall find their names registered much more to their honour, than these are in the records of fame.

Chapter 12

Verses 1–22

Here is an account of those who appeared and acted as David's friends, while he was persecuted. No difficulties or dangers should keep the sinner from coming to the Savior, nor drive the believer from the path of duty. Those who break through, and overcome in these attempts, will find abundant recompence. From the words of Amasai we may learn how to testify our affection and allegiance to the Lord Jesus; his we must be throughly; on his side we must be forward to appear and act. If we are under the influence of the Spirit, we shall desire to have our lot among them, and to declare ourselves on their side; if in faith and love we embrace the cause of Christ, he will receive, employ, and advance us.

Verses 23–40

When the throne of Christ is set up in a soul, there is, or ought to be, great joy in that soul; and provision is made, not as here, for a few days, but for the whole life, and for eternity. Happy are those who wisely perceive it to be their duty and interest, to submit to the Saviour Jesus Christ, the Son of David; who renounce for his sake all that is not consistent; whose earnest endeavours to do good are directed by the wisdom that God giveth, through acquaintance with his word, experience, and observation. If any man lack this wisdom, let him ask it of God, who giveth to all men liberally, and upbraideth not, and it shall be given him.

Chapter 13

Verses 1–5

David said not, What magnificent thing shall I do now? or, What pleasant thing? but, What pious thing? that he might have the comfort and benefit of that sacred oracle. Let us bring the ark to us, that it may be a blessing to us. Those who honour God, profit themselves. It is the wisdom of those setting out in the world, to take God's ark with them. Those are likely to go on in the favour of God, who begin in the fear of God. (**1**Ch **13**:**6-14**)

Verses 6–14

Let the sin of Uzza warn all to take heed of presumption, rashness, and irreverence, in dealing with holy things; and let none think that a good design will justify a bad action. Let the punishment of Uzza teach us not to dare to trifle with God in our approaches to him; yet let us, through Christ, come boldly to the throne of grace. If the gospel be to some a savour of death unto death, as the ark was to Uzza, yet let us receive it in the love of it, and it will be to us a savour of life unto life.

Chapter 14

David's victories.

—In this chapter we have an account of, **1**. David's kingdom established. **2**. His family built up. **3**. His enemies defeated. This is repeated from **2**Sa **5**. Let the fame of David be looked upon as a type and figure of the exalted honour of the Son of David.

Chapter 15

Verses 1–24

Wise and good men may be guilty of oversights, which they will correct, as soon as they are aware of them. David does not try to justify what had been done amiss, nor to lay the blame on others; but he owns himself guilty, with others, of not seeking God in due order

Verses 25–29

It is good to notice the assistance of Divine Providence, even in things which fall within the compass of our natural powers; if God did not help us, we could not stir a step. If we do our religious duties in any degree aright, we must own it was God that helped us; had we been left to ourselves, we should have been guilty of some fatal errors. And every thing in which we engage, must be done in dependence on the mercy of God through the sacrifice of the Redeemer.

Chapter 16

Verses 1–6

Though God's word and ordinances may be clouded and eclipsed for a time, they shall shine out of obscurity. This was but a tent, a humble dwelling, yet this was the tabernacle which David, in his psalms, often speaks of with so much affection. David showed himself generous to his subjects, as he had found God gracious to him. Those whose hearts are enlarged with holy joy, should show it by being open-handed.

Verses 7–36

Let God be glorified in our praises. Let others be edified and taught, that strangers to him may be led to adore him. Let us ourselves triumph and trust in God. Those that give glory to God's name are allowed to glory in it. Let the everlasting covenant be the great matter of our joy his people of old, be remembered by us with thankfulness to him. Show forth from day to day his salvation, his promised salvation by Christ. We have reason to celebrate that from day to day; for we daily receive the benefit, and it is a subject that can never be exhausted. In the midst of praises, we must not forget to pray for the servants of God in distress.

Verses 37–43

The worship of God ought to be the work of every day. David put it into order. At Jerusalem, where the ark was, Asaph and his brethren were to minister before the ark continually, with songs of praise. No sacrifices were offered there, nor incense burnt, because the altars were not there; but David's prayers were directed as incense, and the lifting up of his hands as the evening sacrifice. So early did spiritual worship take place of ceremonial. Yet the ceremonial worship, being of Divine institution, must by no means be omitted; therefore at Gibeon, at the altars, the priests attended; for their work was to sacrifice and burn incense; and that they did continually, morning and evening, according to the law of Moses. As the ceremonies were types of the mediation of Christ, the observance of them was of great consequence. The attendance of his appointed ministers is right in itself, and encourages the people.

Chapter 17

David's purposes; God's gracious promises.

—This chapter is the same as **2**Sa **7**. See what is there said upon it. It is very observable that what in Samuel is said to be, "for thy word's sake," is here said to be, "for thy servant's sake," ver. #(**19**). Jesus Christ is both the Word of God, Re **19**:**13**, and the Servant of God, Isa **42**:**1**; and it is for his sake, upon account of his mediation, that the promises are made good to all believers; it is in him, that they are yea and amen. For His sake it is done, for his sake it is made known; to him we owe all this greatness, from him we are to expect all these great things. They are the unsearchable riches of Christ, which, if by faith we see in themselves, and see in the Lord Jesus, we cannot but magnify as the only true greatness, and speak honourably of them. For this blessedness may we look amidst the trials of life, and when we feel the hand of death upon us; and seek it for our children after us.

Chapter 18

David's victories.

—This chapter is the same as **2**Sa **8**. Our good fight of faith, under the Captain of our salvation, will end in everlasting triumph and peace. The happiness of Israel, through David's victories, and just government, faintly shadowed forth the happiness of the redeemed in the realms above.

Chapter 19

David's wars.

—The history is here repeated which we read **2**Sa **10**. The only safety of sinners consists in submitting to the Lord, seeking peace with him, and becoming his servants. Let us assist each other in a good cause; but let us fear lest, while made instruments of good to others, we should come short of salvation, through unbelief and sin.

Chapter 20

David's wars.

—Though the Lord will severely correct the sins of his believing people, he will not leave them in the hands of their enemies. His assistance will overcome all advantages of number and strength of those that defy his Israel. All that trust in Christ, shall be made more than conquerors through him that loveth them.

Chapter 21

David's numbering the people.

—No mention is made in this book of David's sin in the matter of Uriah, neither of the troubles that followed it: they had no needful connexion with the subjects here noted. But David's sin, in numbering the people, is related: in the atonement made for that sin, there was notice of the place on which the temple should be built. The command to David to build an altar, was a blessed token of reconciliation. God testified his acceptance of David's offerings on this altar. Thus Christ was made sin, and a curse for us; it pleased the Lord to bruise him, that through him, God might be to us, not a consuming Fire, but a reconciled God. It is good to continue attendance on those ordinances in which we have experienced the tokens of God's presence, and have found that he is with us of a truth. Here God graciously met me, therefore I will still expect to meet him.

Chapter 22

Verses 1–5

On occasion of the terrible judgment inflicted on Israel for the sin of David, God pointed out the place where he would have the temple built; upon which, David was excited to make preparations for the great work. David must not build, but he would do all he could; he prepared abundantly before his death. What our hands find to do for God, and our souls, and those round us, let us do it with all our might, before our death; for after death there is no device nor working. And when the Lord refuses to employ us in those services which we desired, we must not be discouraged or idle, but do what we can, though in a humbler sphere.

Verses 6–16

David gives Solomon the reason why he should build the temple. Because God named him. Nothing is more powerful to engage us in any service for God, than to know that we are appointed thereto. Because he would have leisure and opportunity to do it. He should have peace and quietness. Where God gives rest, he expects work. Because God had promised to establish his kingdom. God's gracious promises should quicken and strengthen our religious service. David delivered to Solomon an account of the vast preparations he had made for this building; not from pride and vain-glory, but to encourage Solomon to engage cheerfully in the great work. He must not think, by building the temple, to purchase a dispensation to sin; on the contrary, his doing that would not be accepted, if he did not take heed to fulfil the statutes of the Lord. In our spiritual work, as well as in our spiritual warfare, we have need of courage and resolution.

(1Ch 22:17-19)

Verses 17–19

Whatever is done towards rendering the word of God generally known and attended to, is like bringing a stone, or an ingot of gold, towards erecting the temple. This should encourage us when we grieve that we do not see more fruit of our labours; much good may appear after our death, which we never thought of. Let us not then be weary of well doing. The work is in the hands of the Prince of peace. As he, the Author and Finisher of the work, is pleased to employ us as his instruments, let us arise and be doing, encouraging and helping one another; working by his rule, after his example, in dependence on his grace, assured that he will be with us, and that our labour shall not be in vain in the Lord.

Chapter 23

Verses 1–23

David, having given charge concerning the building of the temple, settles the method of the temple service, and orders the officers of it. When those of the same family were employed together, it would engage them to love and assist one another.

Verses 24–32

Now the people of Israel were so many, there should be more employed in the temple service, that every Israelite who brought an offering might find a Levite ready to help him. When more work is to be done, it is pity but there should be more workmen. A new heart, a spiritual mind, which delights greatly in God's commandments, and can find a refreshing feast in his ordinances, forms the great distinction between the true Christian and all other men in the world. To the spiritual man every service will yield satisfaction. He will be ever abounding in the work of the Lord; being never so happy as when employed for such a good Master, in so pleasant a service. He will not regard whether he is called to take the lead, or to keep the charge of others who are placed over him. May we seek and serve the Lord uprightly, and leave all the rest to his disposal, by faith in his word.

Chapter 24

The divisions of the priests and Levites.

—When every one has, knows, and keeps his place and work, the more there are the better. In the mystical body of Christ, every member has its use, for the good of the whole. Christ is High Priest over the house of God, to whom all believers, being made priests, are to be in subjection. In Christ, no difference is made between bond and free, elder and younger. The younger brethren, if faithful and sincere, shall be no less acceptable to Christ than the fathers. May we all be children of the Lord, fitted to sing his praises for ever in his temple above.

Chapter 25

The singers and musicians.

—David put those in order who were appointed to be singers and musicians in the temple. To prophesy, in this place, means praising God with great earnestness and devout affections, under the influences of the Holy Spirit. In raising these affections, poetry and music were employed. If the Spirit of God do not put life and fervour into our devotions, they will, however ordered, be a lifeless, worthless form.

Chapter 26

The offices of the Levites.

—The porters and treasurers of the temple, had occasion for strength and valour to oppose those who wrongly attempted to enter the sanctuary, and to guard the sacred treasures. Much was expended daily upon the altar; flour, wine, oil, salt, fuel, beside the lamps; quantities of these were kept beforehand, besides the sacred vestments and utensils. These were the treasures of the house of God. These treasures typified the plenty there is in our heavenly Father's house, enough and to spare. From those sacred treasuries, the unsearchable riches of Christ, all our wants are supplied; and receiving from his fulness, we must give him the glory, and endeavour to dispose of our abilities and substance according to his will. We have an account of those employed as officers and judges. The magistracy is an ordinance of God for the good of the church, as truly as the ministry, and must not be neglected. None of the Levites who were employed in the service of the sanctuary, none of the singers or porters, were concerned in this outward business; one duty was enough to engage the whole man. Wisdom, courage, strength of faith, holy affections, and constancy of mind in doing our duty, are requisite or useful for every station.

Chapter 27

Verses 1–15

In the kingdoms of this world readiness for war forms a security for peace; in like manner, nothing so much encourages Satan's assaults as to be unwatchful. So long as we stand armed with the whole armour of God, in the exercise of faith, and preparation of heart for the conflict, we shall certainly be safe, and probably enjoy inward peace.

Verses 16–34

The officers of the court, or the rulers of the king's substance, had the oversight and charge of the king's tillage, his vineyards, his herds, his flocks, which formed the wealth of eastern kings. Much of the wisdom of princes is seen in the choice of their ministry, and common persons show it in the choice of their advisers. David, though he had all these about him, preferred the word of God before them all. Thy testimonies are my delight and my counsellors.

Chapter 28

Verses 1–10

During David's last sickness, many chief priests and Levites were at Jerusalem. Finding himself able, David spoke of his purpose to build a temple for God, and of God's disallowing that purpose. He opened to them God's gracious purposes concerning Solomon. David charged them to cleave stedfastly to God and their duty. We cannot do our work as we should, unless we put on resolution, and fetch in strength from Divine grace. Religion or piety has two distinct parts. The first is knowledge of God, the second is worship of God. David says, Know thou the God of thy father, and serve him with a perfect heart and a willing mind. God is made known by his works and word. Revelation alone shows the whole character of God, in his providence, his holy law, his condemnation of sinners, his blessed gospel, and the ministration of the Spirit to all true believers. The natural man cannot receive this knowledge of God. But thus we learn the value of the Saviour's atonement, and of the sanctification of the Holy Spirit, and are influenced to walk in all his commandments. It brings a sinner to his proper place at the foot of the cross, as a poor, guilty, helpless worm, deserving wrath, yet expecting every thing needful from the free mercy and grace of God our Father, and the Lord Jesus Christ. Having been forgiven much, the pardoned sinner learns to love much.

Verses 11–21

The temple must be a sacred thing, and a type of Christ; it must be framed by Divine teaching. Christ is the true temple, the church is the gospel temple, and heaven the everlasting temple; all are framed according to the Divine counsels, and the plan laid in the Divine wisdom, ordained before the world, for God's glory and our good. David gave this pattern to Solomon, that he might go by rule. Materials were provided for the most costly utensils of the temple. Directions were given which way to look for help in this great undertaking. Be not dismayed; God will help thee, and thou must look up to him in the first place. We may be sure that God, who owned our fathers, and carried them through the services of their day, will, in like manner, never leave us, while he has any work to do in us, or by us. Good work is likely to go on, when all concerned are hearty in furthering it. Let us hope in God's mercy; if we seek him, he will be found of us.

Chapter 29

Verses 1–9

What is done in works of piety and charity, should be done willingly, not by constraint; for God loves a cheerful giver. David set a good example. This David offered, not from constraint, or for show; but because he had set his affection to the house of God, and thought he could never do enough towards promoting that good work. Those who would draw others to good, must lead the way themselves.

Verses 10–19

We cannot form a right idea of the magnificence of the temple, and the buildings around it, about which such quantities of gold and silver were employed. But the unsearchable riches of Christ exceed the splendour of the temple, infinitely more than that surpassed the meanest cottage on earth. Instead of boasting of these large oblations, David gave solemn thanks to the Lord. All they gave for the Lord's temple was his own; if they attempted to keep it, death would soon have removed them from it. They only use they could make of it to their real advantage, was, to consecrate it to the service of Him who gave it.

Verses 20–25

This great assembly joined with David in adoring God. Whoever is the mouth of the congregation, those only have the benefit who join him, not by bowing down the head, so much as by lifting up the soul. Solomon sat on the throne of the Lord. Solomon's kingdom typified the kingdom of the Messiah, whose throne is the throne of the Lord.

Verses 26–30

When we read the second book of Samuel, we could scarcely have expected to behold David appear so illustrious in his closing scene. But his repentance had been as remarkable as his sin; and his conduct during his afflictions, and towards the end of his life, appears to have had a good effect on his subjects. Blessed be God, even the chief of sinners may hope for a glorious departure, when brought to repent and flee for refuge to the Saviour's atoning blood. Let us mark the difference between the spirit and character of the man after God's own heart, living and dying, and those of worthless professors, who resemble him in nothing but their sins, and who wickedly try to excuse their crimes by his sins. Let us watch and pray, lest we be overcome by temptation, and overtaken by sin, to the dishonour of God, and the wounding of our own consciences. When we feel that we have offended, let us follow David's example of repentance and patience, looking for a glorious resurrection, through our Lord Jesus Christ.

2 Chronicles

Solomon's choice of wisdom, His strength and wealth.

—SOLOMON began his reign with a pious, public visit to God's altar. Those that pursue present things most eagerly, are likely to be disappointed; while those that refer themselves to the providence of God, if they have not the most, have the most comfort. Those that make this world their end, come short of the other, and are disappointed in this also; but those that make the other world their end, shall not only obtain that, and full satisfaction in it, but shall have as much of this world as is good for them, in their way. Let us then be contented, without those great things which men generally covet, but which commonly prove fatal snares to the soul.

Chapter 2

Solomon's message to Huram respecting the temple, His treaty with Huram.

—Solomon informs Huram of the particular services to be performed in the temple. The mysteries of the true religion, unlike those of the Gentile superstitions, sought not concealment. Solomon endeavoured to possess Huram with great and high thoughts of the God of Israel. We should not be afraid or ashamed to embrace every opportunity to speak of God, and to impress others with a deep sense of the importance of his favour and service. Now that the people of Israel kept close to the law and worship of God, the neighbouring nations were willing to be taught by them in the true religion, as the Israelites had been willing in the days of their apostacy, to be infected with the idolatries and superstitions of their neighbours. A wise and pious king is an evidence of the Lord's special love for his people. How great then was God's love to his believing people, in giving his only-begotten Son to be their Prince and their Saviour.

Chapter 3

The building of the temple.

—There is a more particular account of the building of the temple in **1**Ki **6**. It must be in the place David had prepared, not only which he had purchased, but which he had fixed on by Divine direction. Full instructions enable us to go about our work with certainty and to proceed therein with comfort. Blessed be God, the Scriptures are enough to render the man of God thoroughly furnished for every good work. Let us search the Scriptures daily, beseeching the Lord to enable us to understand, believe, and obey his word, that our work and our way may be made plain, and that all may be begun, continued, and ended in him. Beholding God, in Christ, his true Temple, more glorious than that of Solomon's, may we become a spiritual house, a habitation of God through the Spirit.

Chapter 4

The furniture of the temple.

—Here is a further account of the furniture of God's house. Both without doors and within, there was that which typified the grace of the gospel, and shadowed out good things to come, of which the substance is Christ. There was the brazen altar. The making of this was not mentioned in the book of Kings. On this all the sacrifices were offered, and it sanctified the gift. The people who worshipped in the courts might see the sacrifices burned. They might thus be led to consider the great Sacrifice, to be offered in the fulness of time, to take away sin, and put an end to death, which the blood of bulls and goats could not possibly do. And, with the smoke of the sacrifices, their hearts might ascend to heaven, in holy desires towards God and his favour. In all our devotions we must keep the eye of faith fixed upon Christ. The furniture of the temple, compared with that of the tabernacle, showed that God's church would be enlarged, and his worshippers multiplied. Blessed be God, there is enough in Christ for all.

Chapter 5

Verses 1–10

The ark was a type of Christ, and, as such, a token of the presence of God. That gracious promise, Lo, I am with you alway, even unto the end of the world, does, in effect, bring the ark into our religious assemblies, if we by faith and prayer plead that promise; and this we should be most earnest for. When Christ is formed in a soul, the law written in the heart, the ark of the covenant settled there, so that it becomes the temple of the Holy Ghost, there is true satisfaction in that soul.

Verses 11–14

God took possession of the temple; he filled it with a cloud. Thus he signified his acceptance of this temple, to be the same to him that the tabernacle of Moses was, and assured his people that he would be the same in it. Would we have God dwell in our hearts, we must leave room for him; every thing else must give way. The Word was made flesh; and when he comes to his temple, like a refiner's fire, who may abide the day of his coming? May he prepare us for that day.

Chapter 6

Solomon's prayer at the dedication of the temple.

—The order of Solomon's prayer is to be observed. First and chiefly, he prays for repentance and forgiveness, which is the chief blessing, and the only solid foundation of other mercies: he then prays for temporal mercies; thereby teaching us what things to mind and desire most in our prayers. This also Christ hath taught us in his perfect pattern and form of prayer, where there is but one prayer for outward, and all the rest are for spiritual blessings. The temple typified the human nature of Christ, in whom dwelleth all the fulness of the Godhead bodily. The ark typified his obedience and sufferings, by which repenting sinners have access to a reconciled God, and communion with him. Jehovah has made our nature his resting-place for ever, in the person of Emmanuel, and through him he dwells with, and delights in his church of redeemed sinners. May our hearts become his resting-place; may Christ dwell therein by faith, consecrating them as his temples, and shedding abroad his love therein. May the Father look upon us in and through his Anointed; and may he remember and bless us in all things, according to his mercy to sinners, in and through Christ.

Chapter 7

God's answer to Solomon's prayer.

—God gave a gracious answer to Solomon's prayer. The mercies of God to sinners are made known in a manner well suited to impress all who receive them, with his majesty and holiness. The people worshipped and praised God. When he manifests himself as a consuming Fire to sinners, his people can rejoice in him as their Light. Nay, they had reason to say, that God was good in this. It is of the Lord's mercies we are not consumed, but the sacrifice in our stead, for which we should be very thankful. And whoever beholds with true faith, the Saviour agonizing and dying for man's sin, will, by that view, find his godly sorrow enlarged, his hatred of sin increased, his soul made more watchful, and his life more holy. Solomon prosperously effected all he designed, for adorning both God's house and his own. Those who begin with the service of God, are likely to go on successfully in their own affairs. It was Solomon's praise, that what he undertook, he went through with; it was by the grace of God that he prospered in it. Let us then stand in awe, and sin not. Let us fear the Lord's displeasure, hope in his mercy, and walk in his commandments.

Chapter **8**

Solomon's buildings and trade.

—It sometimes requires more wisdom and resolution to govern a family in the fear of God, than to govern a kingdom with reputation. The difficulty is increased, when a man has a hinderance instead of a help meet in the wife of his bosom. Solomon kept up the holy sacrifices, according to the law of Moses. In vain had the altar been built, in vain had fire come down from heaven, if sacrifices had not been constantly brought. Spiritual sacrifices are required of us, which we are to bring daily and weekly; it is good to be in a settled method of devotion. When the service of the temple was put into good order, it is said, The house of the Lord was perfected. The work was the main matter, not the place; the temple was unfinished till all this was done. Canaan was a rich country, and yet must send to Ophir for gold The Israelites were a wise people, but must be beholden to the king of Tyre for men that had knowledge of the seas. Grace, and not gold, is the best riches, and acquaintance with God and his law, the best knowledge. Leaving the children of this world to scramble for the toys of this world, may we, as the children of God, lay up our treasure in heaven, that where our treasure is, our hearts also may be.

Chapter 9

Verses 1–12

This history has been considered, **1Ki 10**; yet because our Saviour has proposed it as an example in seeking after him, Mt **12**:**42**, we must not pass it over without observing, that those who know the worth of true wisdom will grudge no pains or cost to obtain it. The queen of Sheba put herself to a great deal of trouble and expense to hear the wisdom of Solomon; and yet, learning from him to serve God, and do her duty, she thought herself well paid for her pains. Heavenly wisdom is that pearl of great price, for which, if we part with all, we make a good bargain.

Verses 13–31

The imports here mentioned, would show that prosperity drew the minds of Solomon and his subjects to the love of things curious and uncommon, though useless in themselves. True wisdom and happiness are always united together; but no such alliance exists between wealth and the enjoyment of the things of this life. Let us then acquaint ourselves with the Saviour, that we may find rest for our souls. Here is Solomon reigning in wealth and power, in ease and fulness, the like of which could never since be found; for the most known of the great princes of the earth were famed for their wars; whereas Solomon reigned forty years in profound peace. The promise was fulfilled, that God would give him riches and honour, such as no kings have had or shall have. The lustre wherein he appeared, was typical of the spiritual glory of the kingdom of the Messiah, and but a faint representation of His throne, which is above every throne. Here is Solomon dying, and leaving all his wealth and power to one who he knew would be a fool! Ec **2**:**18**, **19**. This was not only vanity, but vexation of spirit. Neither power, wealth, nor wisdom, can ward off or prepare for the stroke of death. But thanks be to God who giveth the victory to the true believer, even over this dreaded enemy, through Jesus Christ our Lord.

Chapter 10

The ten tribes revolt from Rehoboam.

—Moderate counsels are wisest and best. Gentleness will do what violence will not do. Most people like to be accosted mildly. Good words cost only a little self-denial, yet they purchase great things. No more needs to be done to ruin men, than to leave them to their own pride and passion. Thus, whatever are the devices of men, God is doing his own work by all, and fulfilling the word which he has spoken. No man can bequeath his prosperity to his heirs any more than his wisdom; though our children will generally be affected by our conduct, whether good or bad. Let us then seek those good things which will be our own for ever; and crave the blessing of God upon our posterity, in preference to wealth or worldly exaltation.

Chapter 11

Verses 1–12

A few good words might have prevented the rebellion of Rehoboam's subjects; but all the force of his kingdom cannot bring them back. And it is in vain to contend with the purpose of God, when it is made known to us. Even those who are destitute of true faith, will at times pay some regard to the word of God, and be kept by it from wrong actions, to which they are prone by nature.

Verses 13–23

When the priests and Levites came to Jerusalem, the devout, pious Israelites followed them. Such as set their hearts to seek the Lord God of Israel, left the inheritance of their fathers, and went to Jerusalem, that they might have free access to the altar of God, and be out of the temptation to worship the calves. That is best for us, which is best for our souls; in all our choices, religious advantages must be sought before all outward conveniences. Where God's faithful priests are, his faithful people should be. And when it has been proved that we are willing to renounce our worldly interests, so far as we are called to do so for the sake of Christ and his gospel, we have good evidence that we are truly his disciples. And it is the interest of a nation to protect religion and religious people.

Chapter 12

Rehoboam, forsaking the Lord, is punished.

—When Rehoboam was so strong that he supposed he had nothing to fear from Jeroboam, he cast off his outward profession of godliness. It is very common, but very lamentable, that men, who in distress or danger, or near death, seem much engaged in seeking and serving God, throw aside all their religion when they have received a merciful deliverance. God quickly brought troubles upon Judah, to awaken the people to repentance, before their hearts were hardened. Thus it becomes us, when we are under the rebukes of Providence, to justify God, and to judge ourselves. If we have humbled hearts under humbling providences, the affliction has done its work; it shall be removed, or the property of it be altered. The more God's service is compared with other services, the more reasonable and easy it will appear. Are the laws of temperance thought hard? The effects of intemperance will be found much harder. The service of God is perfect liberty; the service of our lusts is complete slavery. Rehoboam was never rightly fixed in his religion. He never quite cast off God; yet he engaged not his heart to seek the Lord. See what his fault was; he did not serve the Lord, because he did not seek the Lord. He did not pray, as Solomon, for wisdom and grace; he did not consult the word of God, did not seek to that as his oracle, nor follow its directions. He made nothing of his religion, because he did not set his heart to it, nor ever came up to a steady resolution in it. He did evil, because he never was determined for good.

Chapter 13

Abijah overcomes Jeroboam.

—Jeroboam and his people, by apostacy and idolatry, merited the severe punishment Abijah was permitted to execute upon them. It appears from the character of Abijah, **1Ki 15**:**3**, that he was not himself truly religious, yet he encouraged himself from the religion of his people. It is common for those that deny the power of godliness, to boast of the form of it. Many that have little religion themselves, value it in others. But it was true that there were numbers of pious worshippers in Judah, and that theirs was the more righteous cause. In their distress, when danger was on every side, which way should they look for deliverance unless upward? It is an unspeakable comfort, that our way thither is always open. They cried unto the Lord. Earnest prayer is crying. To the cry of prayer they added the shout of faith, and became more than conquerors. Jeroboam escaped the sword of Abijah, but God struck him; there is no escaping his sword.

Chapter 14

Asa's piety, He strengthens his kingdom.

—Asa aimed at pleasing God, and studied to approve himself to him. Happy those that walk by this rule, not to do that which is right in their own eyes, or in the eye of the world, but which is so in God's sight. We find by experience that it is good to seek the Lord; it gives us rest; while we pursue the world, we meet with nothing but vexation. Asa consulted with his people how to make a good use of the peace they enjoyed; and concluded with them that they must not be idle, nor secure. A formidable army of Ethiopians invaded Asa's kingdom. This evil came upon them, that their faith in God might be tried. Asa's prayer is short, but it is the real language of faith and expectation from God. When we go forth in God's name, we cannot but prosper, and all things work together for the good of those whom he favours.

Chapter 15

The people make a solemn covenant with God.

—The work of complete reformation appeared so difficult, that Asa had not courage to attempt it, till assured of Divine assistance and acceptance. He and his people offered sacrifices to God; thanksgiving for the favours they had received, and supplication for further favours. Prayers and praises are now our spiritual sacrifices. The people, of their own will, covenanted to seek the Lord, each for himself, with earnestness. What is religion but seeking God, inquiring after him, applying to him upon all occasions? We make nothing of our religion, if we do not make heart-work of it; God will have all the heart, or none. Our devotedness to God our Saviour, should be avowed and shown in the most solemn and public manner. What is done in hypocrisy is a mere drudgery.

Chapter 16

Asa seeks the aid of the Syrians, His death.

—A plain and faithful reproof was given to Asa by a prophet of the Lord, for making a league with Syria. God is displeased when he is distrusted, and when an arm of flesh is relied on, more than his power and goodness. It is foolish to lean on a broken reed, when we have the Rock of ages to rely upon. To convince Asa of his folly, the prophet shows that he, of all men, had no reason to distrust God, who had found him such a powerful Helper. The many experiences we have had of the goodness of God to us, aggravate our distrust of him. But see how deceitful our hearts are! we trust in God when we have nothing else to trust to, when need drives us to him; but when we have other things to stay on, we are apt to depend too much on them. Observe Asa's displeasure at this reproof. What is man, when God leaves him to himself! He that abused his power for persecuting God's prophet, was left to himself, to abuse it further for crushing his own subjects. Two years before he died, Asa was diseased in his feet. Making use of physicians was his duty; but trusting to them, and expecting that from them which was to be had from God only, were his sin and folly. In all conflicts and sufferings we need especially to look to our own hearts, that they may be perfect towards God, by faith, patience, and obedience.

Chapter 17

Jehoshaphat promotes religion in Judah, His prosperity.

—Jehoshaphat found his people generally very ignorant, and therefore endeavoured to have them well taught. The public teaching of the word of God forms, in all ages, the great method of promoting the power of godliness. Thereby the understanding is informed, the conscience is awakened and directed. We have a particular account of Jehoshaphat's prosperity. But it was not his formidable army that restrained the neighbouring nations from attempting any thing against Israel, but the fear of God which fell upon them, when Jehoshaphat reformed his country, and set up a preaching ministry in it. The ordinances of God are more the strength and safety of a kingdom, than soldiers and weapons of war. The Bible requires use to notice the hand of God in every event, yet this is little regarded. But let all employ the talents they have: be faithful, even in that which is little. Set up the worship of God in your houses. The charge of a family is important. Why should you not instruct them as Jehoshaphat did his subjects, in the book of the law of the Lord. But be consistent. Do not recommend one thing, and practise another. Begin with yourselves. Seek to the Lord God of Israel, then call upon children and servants to follow your example.

Chapter 18

Jehoshaphat's alliance with Ahab.

—This history we read in **1**Ki **22**. Abundant riches and honour give large opportunities of doing good, but they are attended with many snares and temptations. Men do not know much of the artifices of Satan and the deceitfulness of their own hearts, when they covet riches with the idea of being able to do good with them. What can hurt those whom God will protect? What can shelter those whom God will destroy? Jehoshaphat is safe in his robes, Ahab killed in his armour; for the race is not to the swift, nor the battle to the strong. We should be cautious of entangling ourselves in the worldly undertakings of evil men; and still more we should avoid engaging in their sinful projects. But, when they call upon him, God can and will bring his faithful people out of the difficulties and dangers into which they have sinfully run themselves. He has all hearts in his hand, so that he easily rescues them. Blessed is the man that putteth his trust in the Lord.

Chapter 19

Jehoshaphat visits his kingdom.

—Whenever we return in peace to our houses, we ought to acknowledge God's providence in preserving our going out and coming in. And if we have been kept through more than common dangers, we are, in a special manner, bound to be thankful. Distinguishing mercies lay us under strong obligations. The prophet tells Jehoshaphat he had done very ill in joining Ahab. He took the reproof well. See the effect the reproof had upon him. He strictly searched his own kingdom. By what the prophet said, Jehoshaphat perceived that his former attempts for reformation were well-pleasing to God; therefore he did what was then left undone. It is good when commendations quicken us to our duty. There are diversities of gifts and operations, but all from the same Spirit, and for the public good; and as every one has received the gift, so let him minister the same. Blessed be God for magistrates and ministers, scribes and statesmen, men of books, and men of business. Observe the charge the king gave. They must do all in the fear of the Lord, with a perfect, upright heart. And they must make it their constant care to prevent sin, as an offence to God, and what would bring wrath on the people.

Chapter 20

Verses 1–13

In all dangers, public or personal, our first business should be to seek help from God. Hence the advantage of days for national fasting and prayer. From the first to the last of our seeking the Lord, we must approach him with humiliation for our sins, trusting only in his mercy and power. Jehoshaphat acknowledges the sovereign dominion of the Divine Providence. Lord, exert it on our behalf. Whom should we seek to, whom should we trust to for relief, but the God we have chosen and served. Those that use what they have for God, may comfortably hope he will secure it to them. Every true believer is a son of Abraham, a friend of God; with such the everlasting covenant is established, to such every promise belongs. We are assured of God's love, by his dwelling in human nature in the person of the Saviour. Jehoshaphat mentions the temple, as a token of God's favourable presence. He pleads the injustice of his enemies. We may well appeal to God against those that render us evil for good. Though he had a great army, he said, We have no might without thee; we rely upon thee.

Verses 14–19

The Spirit of prophecy came upon a Levite in the midst of the congregation. The Spirit, like the wind, blows where and on whom He listeth. He encouraged them to trust in God. Let the Christian soldier go out against his spiritual enemies, and the God of peace will make him more than a conqueror. Our trials will prove our gain. The advantage will be all our own, but the whole glory must be given to God.

Verses 20–30

Jehoshaphat exhorted his troops to firm faith in God. Faith inspires a man with true courage; nor will any thing help more to the establishing of the heart in shaking times, than a firm belief of the power, and mercy, and promise of God. In all our trust in the Lord, and our praises of him, let us especially look at his everlasting mercy to sinners through Jesus Christ. Never was an army so destroyed as that of the enemy. Thus God often makes wicked people destroy one another. And never was a victory celebrated with more solemn thanksgivings.

Verses 31–37

Jehoshaphat kept close to the worship of God, and did what he could to keep his people close to it. But after God had done such great things for him, given him not only victory, but wealth; after this, to go and join himself with a wicked king, was very ungrateful. What could he expect but that God would be angry with him? Yet it seems, he took the warning; for when Ahaziah afterward pressed him to join him, he would not, **1**Ki **22**:**49**. Thus the alliance was broken, and the Divine rebuke had its effect, at least for a season. Let us be thankful for any losses which may have prevented the loss of our immortal souls. Let us praise the Lord, who sought after us, and left us not to perish in our sins.

Chapter 21

Verses 1–11

Jehoram hated his brethren, and slew them, for the same reason that Cain hated Abel, and slew him, because their piety condemned his impiety. In the mystery of Providence such men sometimes prosper for a time; but the Lord has righteous purposes in permitting such events, part of which may now be made out, and the rest will be seen hereafter.

Verses 12–20

A warning from God was sent to Jehoram. The Spirit of prophecy might direct Elijah to prepare this writing in the foresight of Jehoram's crimes. He is plainly told that his sin should certainly ruin him. But no marvel that sinners are not frightened from sin, and to repentance, by the threatenings of misery in another world, when the certainty of misery in this world, the sinking of their estates, and the ruin of their health, will not restrain them from vicious courses. See Jehoram here stripped of all his comforts. Thus God plainly showed that the controversy was with him, and his house. He had slain all his brethren to strengthen himself; now, all his sons are slain but one. David's house must not be wholly destroyed, like those of Israel's kings, because a blessing was in it; that of the Messiah. Good men may be afflicted with diseases; but to them they are fatherly chastisements, and by the support of Divine consolations the soul may dwell at ease, even when the body lies in pain. To be sick and poor, sick and solitary, but especially to be sick and in sin, sick and under the curse of God, sick and without grace to bear it, is a most deplorable case. Wickedness and profaneness make men despicable, even in the eyes of those who have but little religion.

Chapter 22

The reign of Ahaziah, Athaliah destroys the royal family.

—The counsel of the ungodly ruins many young persons when they are setting out in the world. Ahaziah gave himself up to be led by evil men. Those who advise us to do wickedly, counsel us to our destruction; while they pretend to be friends, they are our worst enemies. See and dread the mischief of bad company. If not the infection, yet let the destruction be feared, Re **18**:**4**. We have here, a wicked woman endeavouring to destroy the house of David, and a good woman preserving it. No word of God shall fall to the ground. The whole truth of the prophecies that the Messiah was to come from David, and thereby the salvation of the world, appeared to be now hung upon the brittle thread of the life of a single infant, to destroy whom was the interest of the reigning power. But God had purposed, and vain were the efforts of earth and hell.

Chapter 23

Joash crowned, and Athaliah slain.

—To look upon ourselves and each other as the Lord's people, should make us earnest in the discharge of our duty both to God and man. Thus was this happy revolution brought about, and the people rejoiced. When the Son of David is enthroned in the soul, all is quiet, and joyful. See **2**Ki **11**.

Chapter 24

Verses 1–14

Joash is more zealous about the repair of the temple than Jehoiada himself. It is easier to build temples, than to be temples to God. But the repairing of places for public worship is a good work, which all should promote. And many a good work would be done that now lies undone, if active men would put it forward.

Verses 15–27

See what a great judgment on any prince or people, the death of godly, zealous, useful men is. See how necessary it is that we act in religion from inward principle. Then the loss of a parent, a minister, or a friend, will not be losing our religion. Often both princes and inferior people have been flattered to their ruin. True grace alone will enable a man to bring forth fruit unto the end. Zechariah, the son of Jehoiada, being filled with the Spirit of prophecy, stood up, and told the people of their sin. This is the work of ministers, by the word of God, as a lamp and a light, to discover the sin of men, and expound the providences of God. They stoned Zechariah to death in the court of the house of the Lord. Observe the dying martyr's words: The Lord look upon it, and require it! This came not from a spirit of revenge, but a spirit of prophecy. God smote Joash with great diseases, of body, or mind, or both, before the Syrians departed from him. If vengeance pursue men, the end of one trouble will be but the beginning of another. His own servants slew him. These judgments are called the burdens laid upon him, for the wrath of God is a heavy burden, too heavy for any man to bear. May God help us to take warning, to be upright in heart, and to persevere in his ways to the end.

Chapter 25

Verses 1–13

Amaziah was no enemy to religion, but cool and indifferent friend. Many do what is good, but not with a perfect heart. Rashness makes work for repentance. But Amaziah's obedience to the command of God was to his honour. A firm belief of God's all-sufficiency to bear us out in our duty, and to make up all the loss and damage was sustain in his service, will make his yoke very easy, and his burden very light. When we are called to part with any thing for God and our religion, it should satisfy us, that God is able to give us much more than this. Convinced sinners, who have not true faith, always object to self-denying obedience. They are like Amaziah; they say, But what shall we do for the hundred talents? What shall we do if by keeping the sabbath holy we lose so many good customers? What shall we do without this gain? What shall we do if we lose the friendship of the world? Many endeavour to quiet their consciences by the pretence that forbidden practices are necessary. The answer is, as here, The Lord is able to give thee much more than this. He makes up, even in this world, for all that is given up for his sake.

Verses 14–16

To worship the gods of those whom Amaziah had conquered, who could not help their own worshippers, was the greatest absurdity. If men would consider how unable all those things are to help them, to which they look whenever they forsake God, they would not be such enemies to themselves. The reproof God sent by a prophet was too just to be answered; themselves. The reproof God sent by a prophet was too just to be answered; but he was bidden not to say a word more. The secure sinner rejoices to have silenced his reprovers and monitors; but what comes of it? Those that are deaf to reproof, are ripening for destruction.

Verses 17–28

Never was a proud prince more thoroughly mortified than Amaziah by Joash king of Israel. A man's pride will bring him low, Pr **29**:**23**; it goes before his destruction, and deservedly brings it on. He that exalteth himself shall be abased. He that goes forth hastily to strive, will not know what he shall do in the end thereof, when his neighbour has put him to shame, Pr **25**:**8**. And what are we when we offer to establish our own righteousness, or presume to justify ourselves before the Most High God, but despicable thistles, that fancy themselves stately cedars? And are not various temptations, is not every corruption, a wild beast of the desert, which will trample on the wretched boaster, and tread his haughty pretensions to the dust? A man's pride shall bring him low; his ruin may be dated from his turning from the Lord.

Chapter 26

Verses 1–15

As long as Uzziah sought the Lord, and minded religion, God made him to prosper. Those only prosper whom God makes to prosper; for prosperity is his gift. Many have owned, that as long as they sought the Lord, and kept close to their duty, they prospered; but when they forsook God, every thing went cross. God never continues either to bless the indolent or to withhold his blessing from the diligent. He will never suffer any to seek his face in vain. Uzziah's name was famed throughout all the neighbouring countries. A name with God and good people makes truly honourable. He did not delight in war, nor addict himself to sports, but delighted in husbandry.

Verses 16–23

The transgression of the kings before Uzziah was, forsaking the temple of the Lord, and burning incense upon idolatrous altars. But his transgression was, going into the holy place, and attempting to burn incense upon the altar of God. See how hard it is to avoid one extreme, and not run into another. Pride of heart was at the bottom of his sin; a lust that ruins many. Instead of lifting up the name God in gratitude to him who had done so much for him, his heart was lifted up to his hurt. Men's pretending to forbidden knowledge, and seeking things too high for them, are owing to pride of heart. The incense of our prayers must be, by faith, put into the hands of our Lord Jesus, the great High Priest of our profession, else we cannot expect it to be accepted by God, Re **8**:**3**. Though Uzziah strove with the priests, he would not strive with his Maker. But he was punished for his transgression; he continued a leper to his death, shut out from society. The punishment answered the sin as face to face in a glass. Pride was at the bottom of his transgression, and thus God humbled him, and put dishonour upon him. Those that covet forbidden honours, forfeit allowed ones. Adam, by catching at the tree of knowledge which he might not eat of, debarred himself of the tree of life which he might have eaten of. Let all that read say, The Lord is righteous. And when the Lord sees good to throw prosperous and useful men aside, as broken vessels, if he raises up others to fill their places, they may rejoice to renounce all worldly concerns, and employ their remaining days in preparation for death.

Chapter 27

Jotham's reign in Judah.

—The people did corruptly. Perhaps Jotham was wanting towards the reformation of the land. Men may be very good, and yet not have courage and zeal to do what they might. It certainly casts blame upon the people. Jotham prospered, and became mighty. The more stedfast we are in religion, the more mighty we are, both to resist evil, and to do good. The Lord often removes wise and pious rulers, and sends others, whose follies and vices punish a people that valued not their mercies.

Chapter 28

The wicked reign of Ahaz in Judah.

—Israel gained this victory because God was wroth with Judah, and made them the rod of his indignation. He reminds them of their own sins. It ill becomes sinners to be cruel. Could they hope for the mercy of God, if they neither showed mercy nor justice to their brethren? Let it be remembered, that every man is our neighbour, our brother, our fellow man, if not our fellow Christian. And no man who is acquainted with the word of God, need fear to maintain that slavery is against the law of love and the gospel of grace. Who can hold his brother in bondage, without breaking the rule of doing to others as he would they should do unto him? But when sinners are left to their own heart's lusts, they grow more desperate in wickedness. God commands them to release the prisoners, and they obeyed. The Lord brought Judah low. Those who will not humble themselves under the word of God, will justly be humbled by his judgments. It is often found, that wicked men themselves have no real affection for those that revolt to them, nor do they care to do them a kindness. This is that king Ahaz! that wretched man! Those are wicked and vile indeed, that are made worse by their afflictions, instead of being made better by them; who, in their distress, trespass yet more, and have their hearts more fully set in them to do evil. But no marvel that men's affections and devotions are misplaced, when they mistake the author of their trouble and of their help. The progress of wickedness and misery is often rapid; and it is awful to reflect upon a sinner's being driven away in his wickedness into the eternal world.

Chapter 29

Verses 1–19

When Hezekiah came to the crown, he applied at once to work reform. Those who begin with God, begin at the right end of their work, and it will prosper accordingly. Those that turn their backs upon God's ordinances, may truly be said to forsake God himself. There are still such neglects, if the word be not duly read and opened, for that was signified by the lighting the lamps, and also if prayers and praise be not offered up, for that was signified by the burning incense. Neglect of God's worship was the cause of the calamities they had lain under. The Lord alone can prepare the heart of man for vital godliness: when much good is done in a little time, the glory must be ascribed to him; and all who love him or the souls of men, will rejoice therein. Let those that do good work, learn to do it well.

Verses 20–36

As soon as Hezekiah heard that the temple was ready, he lost no time. Atonement must be made for the sins of the last reign. It was not enough to lament and forsake those sins; they brought a sin-offering. Our repentance and reformation will not obtain pardon but in and through Christ, who was made sin, that is, a sin-offering for us. While the offerings were on the altar, the Levites sang. Sorrow for sin must not prevent us from praising God. The king and the congregation gave their consent to all that was done. It is not enough for us to be where God is worshipped, if we do not ourselves worship with the heart. And we should offer up our spiritual sacrifices of praise and thanksgiving, and devote ourselves and all we have, as sacrifices, acceptable to the Father only through the Redeemer.

Chapter 30

Verses 1–12

Hezekiah made Israel as welcome to the passover, as any of his own subjects. Let us yield ourselves unto the Lord. Say not, you will do what you please, but resolve to do what he pleases. We perceive in the carnal mind a stiffness, an obstinacy, an unaptness to compel with God; we have it from our fathers: this must be overcome. Those who, through grace, have turned to God themselves, should do all they can to bring others to him. Numbers will be scorners, but some will be humbled and benefited; perhaps where least expected. The rich mercy of God is the great argument by which to enforce repentance; the vilest who submit and yield themselves to the Lord, seek his grace, and give themselves to his service, shall certainly be saved. Oh that messengers were sent forth to carry these glad tidings to every city and every village, through every land!

Verses 13–20

The great thing needful in attendance upon God in solemn ordinances, is, that we make heart-work of it; all is nothing without this. Where this sincerity and fixedness of heart are, there may yet be many things short of the purification of the sanctuary. These defects need pardoning, healing grace; for omissions in duty are sins, as well as omissions of duty. If God should deal with us in strict justice, even as to the very best of our doings, we should be undone. The way to obtain pardon, is to seek it of God by prayer; it must be gotten by petition through the blood of Christ. Yet every defect is sin, and needs forgiveness; and should be matter to humble, but not to discourage us, though nothing can make up for the want of a heart prepared to seek the Lord.

Verses 21–27

Many prayers were put up to God with the peace-offerings. In these Israel looked to God as the God of their fathers, a God in covenant with them. There was also abundance of good preaching. The Levites read and explained the Scriptures. Faith cometh by hearing, and true religion preaching has abounded. They sang psalms every day: praising God should be much of our work in religious assemblies. Having kept the seven days of the feast in this religious manner, they had so much comfort in it, that they kept other seven days also. This they did with gladness. Holy duties should be done with holy gladness. And when sinners humble themselves before the Lord, they may expect gladness in his ordinances. Those who taste this happiness will not soon grow weary of it, but will be glad to prolong their enjoyment.

Chapter 31

Hezekiah destroys idolatry.

—After the passover, the people of Israel applied with vigour to destroy the monuments of idolatry. Public ordinances should stir us up to cleanse our hearts, our houses, and shops, from the filth of sin, and the idolatry of covetousness, and to excite others to do the same. The after-improvement of solemn ordinances, is of the greatest importance to personal, family, and public religion. When they had tasted the sweetness of God's ordinance in the late passover, they were free in maintaining the temple service. Those who enjoy the benefit of a settled ministry, will not grudge the expense of it. In all that Hezekiah attempted in God's service, he was earnest and single in his aim and dependence, and was prospered accordingly. Whether we have few or many talents intrusted to us, may we thus seek to improve them, and encourage others to do the same. What is undertaken with a sincere regard to the glory of God, will succeed to our own honour and comfort at last.

Chapter 32

Verses 1–23

Those who trust God with their safety, must use proper means, else they tempt him. God will provide, but so must we also. Hezekiah gathered his people together, and spake comfortably to them. A believing confidence in God, will raise us above the prevailing fear of man. Let the good subjects and soldiers of Jesus Christ, rest upon his word, and boldly say, Since God is for us, who can be against us? By the favour of God, enemies are lost, and friends gained.

Verses 24–33

God left Hezekiah to himself, that, by this trial and his weakness in it, what was in his heart might be known; that he was not so perfect in grace as he thought he was. It is good for us to know ourselves, and our own weakness and sinfulness, that we may not be conceited, or self-confident, but may always live in dependence upon Divine grace. We know not the corruption of our own hearts, nor what we shall do if God leaves us to ourselves. His sin was, that his heart was lifted up. What need have great men, and good men, and useful men, to study their own infirmities and follies, and their obligations to free grace, that they may never think highly of themselves; but beg earnestly of God, that he will always keep them humble! Hezekiah made a bad return to God for his favours, by making even those favours the food and fuel of his pride. Let us shun the occasions of sin: let us avoid the company, the amusements, the books, yea, the very sights that may administer to sin. Let us commit ourselves continually to God's care and protection; and beg of him never to leave us nor forsake us. Blessed be God, death will soon end the believer's conflict; then pride and every sin will be abolished. He will no more be tempted to withhold the praise which belongs to the God of his salvation.

Chapter 33

Verses 1–20

We have seen Manasseh's wickedness; here we have his repentance, and a memorable instance it is of the riches of God's pardoning mercy, and the power of his renewing grace. Deprived of his liberty, separated from his evil counsellors and companions, without any prospect but of ending his days in a wretched prison, Manasseh thought upon what had passed; he began to cry for mercy and deliverance. He confessed his sins, condemned himself, was humbled before God, loathing himself as a monster of impiety and wickedness. Yet he hoped to be pardoned through the abundant mercy of the Lord. Then Manasseh knew that Jehovah was God, able to deliver. He knew him as a God of salvation; he learned to fear, trust in, love, and obey him. From this time he bore a new character, and walked in newness of life. Who can tell what tortures of conscience, what pangs of grief, what fears of wrath, what agonizing remorse he endured, when he looked back on his many years of apostacy and rebellion against God; on his having led thousands into sin and perdition; and on his blood-guiltiness in the persecution of a number of God's children? And who can complain that the way of heaven is blocked up, when he sees such a sinner enter? Say the worst against thyself, here is one as bad who finds the way to repentance. Deny not to thyself that which God hath not denied to thee; it is not thy sin, but thy impenitence, that bars heaven against thee. **(2**Ch **33**:**21-25)**

Verses 21–25

Amon's father did ill, but he did worse. Whatever warnings or convictions he had, he never humbled himself. He was soon cut off in his sins, and made a warning for all men not to abuse the example of God's patience and mercy to Manasseh, as an encouragement to continue in sin. May God help us to be honest to ourselves, and to think aright respecting our own character, before death fixes us in an unchangeable state.

Chapter 34

Josiah's good reign in Judah.

—As the years of infancy cannot be useful to our fellow-creatures, our earliest youth should be dedicated to God, that we may not waste any of the remaining short space of life. Happy and wise are those who seek the Lord and prepare for usefulness at an early age, when others are pursuing sinful pleasures, contracting bad habits, and forming ruinous connexions. Who can express the anguish prevented by early piety, and its blessed effects? Diligent self-examination and watchfulness will convince us of the deceitfulness and wickedness of our own hearts, and the sinfulness of our lives. We are here encouraged to humble ourselves before God, and to seek unto him, as Josiah did. And believers are here taught, not to fear death, but to welcome it, when it takes them away from the evil to come. Nothing hastens the ruin of a people, nor ripens them for it, more than their disregard of the attempts made for their reformation. Be not deceived, God is not mocked. The current and tide of affections only turns at the command of Him who raises up those that are dead in trespasses and sins. We behold peculiar loveliness, in the grace the Lord bestows on those, who in tender years seek to know and to love the Saviour. Hath Jesus, the Day-spring from on high, visited you? Can you trace your knowledge of this light and life of man, like Josiah, from your youth? Oh the unspeakable happiness of becoming acquainted with Jesus from our earliest years!

Chapter 35

Verses 1–19

The destruction Josiah made of idolatry, was more largely related in the book of Kings. His solemnizing the passover is related here. The Lord's supper resembles the passover more than any other of the Jewish festivals; and the due observance of that ordinance, is a proof of growing piety and devotion. God alone can truly make our hearts holy, and prepare them for his holy services; but there are duties belonging to us, in doing which we obtain this blessing from the Lord.

Verses 20–27

The Scripture does not condemn Josiah's conduct in opposing Pharaoh. Yet Josiah seems to deserve blame for not inquiring of the Lord after he was warned; his death might be a rebuke for his rashness, but it was a judgment on a hypocritical and wicked people. He that lives a life of repentance, faith, and obedience, cannot be affected by the sudden manner in which he is removed. The people lamented him. Many mourn over sufferings, who will not forsake the sins that caused God to send them. Yet this alone can turn away judgments. If we blame Josiah's conduct, we should be watchful, lest we be cut down in a way dishonourable to our profession.

Chapter 36

Verses 1–21

The ruin of Judah and Jerusalem came on by degrees. The methods God takes to call back sinners by his word, by ministers, by conscience, by providences, are all instances of his compassion toward them, and his unwillingness that any should perish. See here what woful havoc sin makes, and, as we value the comfort and continuance of our earthly blessings, let us keep that worm from the root of them. They had many times ploughed and sowed their land in the seventh year, when it should have rested, and now it lay unploughed and unsown for ten times seven years. God will be no loser in his glory at last, by the disobedience of men. If they refused to let the land rest, God would make it rest. What place, O God, shall thy justice spare, if Jerusalem has perished? If that delight of thine were cut off for wickedness, let us not be high-minded, but fear.

Verses 22, 23

God had promised the restoring of the captives, and the rebuilding of Jerusalem, at the end of seventy years; and that time to favour Zion, that set time, came at last. Though God's church be cast down, it is not cast off; though his people be corrected, they are not abandoned; though thrown into the furnace, they are not lost there, nor left there any longer than till the dross be separated. Though God contend long, he will not contend always. Before we close the books of the Chronicles, which contain a faithful register of events, think what desolation sin introduced into the world, nay, even into the church of God. Let us tremble at what is here recorded, while in the character of some few gracious souls, we discover that the Lord left not himself without witness. And when we have looked at this faithful portrait of man by nature, let us contrast with it that same nature, when recovered by Almighty grace, through the justifying and soul-adorning righteousness of Christ our Saviour.

Ezra

The history of this book is the accomplishment of Jeremiah's prophecy concerning the return of the Jews out of Babylon. From its contents we especially learn, that every good work will meet with opposition from enemies, and be hurt by the misconduct of friends; but that God will make his cause to prevail, notwithstanding all obstacles and adversaries. The restoration of the Jews was an event of the highest consequence, tending to preserve religion in the world, and preparing the way for the appearance of the Great Deliverer, the Lord Jesus Christ.

Chapter 1

Verses 1–4

The Lord stirred up the spirit of Cyrus. The hearts of kings are in the hand of the Lord. God governs the world by his influence on the spirits of men; whatever good they do, God stirs up their spirits to do it. It was during the captivity of the Jews, that God principally employed them as the means of calling the attention of the heathen to him. Cyrus took it for granted, that those among the Jews who were able, would offer free-will offerings for the house of God. He would also have them supplied out of his kingdom. Well-wishers to the temple should be well-doers for it.

Verses 5–11

The same God that raised up the spirit of Cyrus to proclaim liberty to the Jews, raised up their spirits to take the benefit. The temptation was to some to stay in Babylon; but some feared not to return, and they were those whose spirits God raised, by his Spirit and grace. Whatever good we do, is owing to the grace of God. Our spirits naturally bow down to this earth and the things of it; if they move upward in any good affections or good actions, it is God who raises them. The calls and offers of the gospel are like the proclamation of Cyrus. Those bound under the power of sin, may be made free by Jesus Christ. Whosoever will, by repentance and faith, return to God, Jesus Christ has opened the way for him, and raises him out of the slavery of sin into the glorious liberty of the children of God. Many that hear this joyful sound, choose to sit still in Babylon, are in love with their sins, and will not venture upon a holy life; but some break through all discouragements, whatever it cost them; they are those whose spirit God has raised above the world and the flesh, whom he has made willing. Thus will the heavenly Canaan be filled, though many perish in Babylon; and the gospel offer will not have been made in vain. The bringing back the Jews from captivity, represents the redemption of sinners by Jesus Christ.

Chapter 2

Verses 1–35

An account was kept of the families that came up out of captivity. See how sin lowers a nation, which righteousness would exalt!

Verses 36–63

Those who undervalue their relation to the Lord in times of reproach, persecution, or distress, will have no benefit from it when it becomes honourable or profitable. Those who have no evidence that they are, by the new birth, spiritual priests unto God, through Jesus Christ, have no right to the comforts and privileges of Christians.

Verses 64–70

Let none complain of the needful expenses of their religion. Seek first the kingdom of God, his favour and his glory, then will all other things be added unto them. Their offerings were nothing, compared with the offerings of the princes in David's time; yet, being according to their ability, were as acceptable to God. The Lord will carry us through all undertakings entered on according to his will, with an aim to his glory, and dependence on his assistance. Those who, at the call of the gospel, renounce sin and return to the Lord, shall be guarded and guided through all perils of the way, and arrive safely at the mansions provided in the holy city of God.

Chapter 3

Verses 1–7

From the proceedings of the Jews on their arrival, let us learn to begin with God, and to do what we can in the worship of God, when we cannot do what we would. They could not at once have a temple, but they would not be without an altar. Fear of danger should stir us to our duty. Have we many enemies? Then it is good to have God our Friend, and to keep up communion with him. Our fears should drive us to our knees. The sacrifices for all these solemnities were a heavy expense for so poor a company; yet besides those expressly appointed, many brought free-will offerings to the Lord. And they made preparation for the building of the temple without delay: whatever God calls us to do, we may depend upon his providence to furnish us with the needful means.

Verses 8–13

There was a remarkable mixture of affections upon laying the foundation of the temple. Those that only knew the misery of having no temple at all, praised the Lord with shouts of joy. To them, even this foundation seemed great. We ought to be thankful for the beginnings of mercy, though it be not yet perfect. But those who remembered the glory of the first temple, and considered how far inferior this was likely to be, wept with a loud voice. There was reason for it, and if they bewailed the sin that was the cause of this melancholy change, they did well. Yet it was wrong to cast a damp upon the common joys. They despised the day of small things, and were unthankful for the good they enjoyed. Let not the remembrance of former afflictions drown the sense of present mercies.

Chapter 4

Verses 1–5

Every attempt to revive true religion will stir up the opposition of Satan, and of those in whom he works. The adversaries were the Samaritans, who had been planted in the land of Israel, **2**Ki **17**. It was plain that they did not mean to unite in the worship of the Lord, according to his word. Let those who discourage a good work, and weaken them that are employed in it, see whose pattern they follow. (Ezr **4**:**6-24**)

Verses 6–24

It is an old slander, that the prosperity of the church would be hurtful to kings and princes. Nothing can be more false, for true godliness teaches us to honour and obey our sovereign. But where the command of God requires one thing and the law of the land another, we must obey God rather than man, and patiently submit to the consequences. All who love the gospel should avoid all appearance of evil, lest they should encourage the adversaries of the church. The world is ever ready to believe any accusation against the people of God, and refuses to listen to them. The king suffered himself to be imposed upon by these frauds and falsehoods. Princes see and hear with other men's eyes and ears, and judge things as represented to them, which are often done falsely. But God's judgment is just; he sees things as they are.

Chapter 5

Verses 1, 2

The building of the temple was stopped about fifteen years. Then they had two good ministers, who urged them to go on with the work. It is a sign that God has mercy in store for a people, when he raises up prophets to be helpers in the way and work of God, as guides, overseers, and rulers. In Haggai, we see what great things God does by his word, which he magnifies above all his name, and by his Spirit working with it.

Verses 3–17

While employed in God's work, we are under his special protection; his eye is upon us for good. This should keep us to our duty, and encourage us therein, when difficulties are ever so discouraging. The elders of the Jews gave the Samaritans an account of their proceedings. Let us learn hence, with meekness and fear, to give a reason of the hope that is in us; let us rightly understand, and then readily declare, what we do in God's service, and why we do it. And while in this world, we always shall have to confess, that our sins have provoked the wrath of God. All our sufferings spring from thence, and all our comforts from his unmerited mercy. However the work may seem to be hindered, yet the Lord Jesus Christ is carrying it on, his people are growing unto a holy temple in the Lord, for a habitation of God through the Spirit.

Chapter 6

Verses 1–12

When God's time is come for fulfilling his gracious purposes concerning his church, he will raise up instruments to do it, from whom such good service was not expected. While our thoughts are directed to this event, we are led by Zechariah to fix our regard on a nobler, a spiritual building. The Lord Jesus Christ continues to lay one stone upon another: let us assist the great design. Difficulties delay the progress of this sacred edifice. Yet let not opposition discourage us, for in due season it will be completed to his abundant praise. He shall bring forth the head-stone thereof with shoutings, crying, Grace, grace unto it.

Verses 13–22

The gospel church, that spiritual temple, is long in the building, but it will be finished at last, when the mystical body is completed. Every believer is a living temple, building up himself in his most holy faith: much opposition is given to this work by Satan and our own corruptions. We trifle, and proceed in it with many stops and pauses; but He that has begun the good work, will see it performed. Then spirits of just men will be made perfect. By getting their sins taken away, the Jews would free themselves from the sting of their late troubles. Their service was with joy. Let us welcome holy ordinances with joy, and serve the Lord with gladness.

Chapter 7

Verses 1–10

Ezra went from Babylon to Jerusalem, for the good of his country. The king was kind to him; he granted all his requests, whatever Ezra desired to enable him to serve his country. When he went, many went with him; he obtained favour from his king, by the Divine favour. Every creature is that to us, which God makes it to be. We must see the hand of God in the events that befal us, and acknowledge him with thankfulness.

Verses 11–26

The liberality of heathen kings to support the worship of God, reproached the conduct of many kings of Judah, and will rise up in judgment against the covetousness of wealthy professed Christians, who will not promote the cause of God. But the weapons of Christian ministers are not carnal. Faithful preaching, holy lives, fervent prayers, and patient suffering when called to it, are the means to bring men into obedience to Christ.

Verses 27, 28

Two things Ezra blessed God for: **1**. For his commission. If any good appear in our hearts, or in the hearts of others, we must own that God put it there, and bless him; it is he that worketh in us, both to will and to do that which is good. **2**. For his encouragement: God has extended mercy to me. Ezra was a man of courage, yet he ascribed this not to his own heart, but to God's hand. If God give us his hand, we are bold and cheerful; if he withdraw it, we are weak as water. Whatever we are enabled to do for God and those around us, God must have all the glory.

Chapter 8

Verses 1–20

Ezra assembles the outcasts of Israel, and the dispersed of Judah. God raised up the spirits of a small remnant to accompany him. What a pity that good men should omit a good work, for want of being spoken to!

Verses 21–23

Ezra procured Levites to go with him; but what will that avail, unless he have God with him? Those who seek God, are safe under the shadow of his wings, even in their greatest dangers; but those who forsake him, are always exposed. When entering upon any new state of life, our care should be, to bring none of the guilt of the sins of our former condition into it. When we are in any peril, let us be at peace with God, and then nothing can do us any real hurt. All our concerns about ourselves, our families, and our estates, it is our wisdom and duty, by prayer to commit to God, and to leave the care of them with him. And, on some occasions, we should decline advantages which are within our reach, lest we should cause others to stumble, and so our God be dishonoured. Let us ask wisdom of God, that we may know how to use or to refuse lawful things. We shall be no losers by venturing, suffering, or giving up for the Lord's sake. Their prayers were answered, and the event declared it. Never have any that sought God in earnest, found that they sought him in vain. In times of difficulty and danger, to set a season apart for secret or for social prayer, is the best method for relief we can take.

Verses 24–30

Do we expect that God should, by his providence, keep that which belongs to us, let us, by his grace, keep that which belongs to him. Let God's honour and interest be our care; and then we may expect that our lives and comforts will be his.

Verses 31–36

Enemies laid wait for the Jews, but God protected them. Even the common perils of journeys, call us to go out with prayer, and to return with praise and thanksgiving. But what shall we render when the Lord has led us safely through the pilgrimage of life, through the gloomy vale of death, out of the reach of all our enemies, into everlasting happiness! Among their sacrifices they had a sin-offering. The atonement sweetens and secures every mercy to us, which will not be truly comfortable, unless sin be taken away, and our peace made with God. Then had the church rest. The expressions here used, direct us to the deliverance of sinners from spiritual bondage, and their pilgrimage to the heavenly Jerusalem, under the care and protection of their God and Saviour.

Chapter 9

Verses 1–4

Many corruptions lurk out of the view of the most careful rulers. Some of the people disobeyed the express command of God, which forbade all marriages with the heathen, De **7**. Disbelief of God's all-sufficiency, is at the bottom of the sorry shifts we make to help ourselves. They exposed themselves and their children to the peril of idolatry, that had ruined their church and nation. Carnal professors may make light of such connexions, and try to explain away the exhortations to be separate; but those who are best acquainted with the word of God, will treat the subject in another manner. They must forebode the worst from such unions. The evils excused, and even pleaded for; by many professors, astonish and cause regret in the true believer. All who profess to be God's people, ought to strengthen those that appear and act against vice and profaneness.

Verses 5–15

The sacrifice, especially the evening sacrifice, was a type of the blessed Lamb of God, who in the evening of the world, was to take away sin by the sacrifice of himself. Ezra's address is a penitent confession of sin, the sin of his people. But let this be the comfort of true penitents, that though their sins reach to the heavens, God's mercy is in the heavens. Ezra, speaking of sin, speaks as one much ashamed. Holy shame is as necessary in true repentance as holy sorrow. Ezra speaks as much amazed. The discoveries of guilt cause amazement; the more we think of sin, the worse it looks. Say, God be merciful to me sinner. Ezra speaks as one much afraid. There is not a surer or saddler presage of ruin, than turning to sin, after great judgments, and great deliverances. Every one in the church of God, has to wonder that he has not wearied out the Lord's patience, and brought destruction upon himself. What then must be the case of the ungodly? But though the true penitent has nothing to plead in his own behalf, the heavenly Advocate pleads most powerfully for him.

Chapter 10

Verses 1–5

Shechaniah owned the national guilt. The case is sad, but it is not desperate; the disease threatening, but not incurable. Now that the people begin to lament, a spirit of repentance seems to be poured out; now there is hope that God will forgive, and have mercy. The sin that rightly troubles us, shall not ruin us. In melancholy times we must observe what makes for us, as well as against us. And there may be good hopes through grace, even where there is the sense of great guilt before God. The case is plain; what has been done amiss, must be undone again as far as possible; nothing less than this is true repentance. Sin must be put away, with a resolution never to have any thing more to do with it. What has been unjustly got, must be restored. Arise, be of good courage. Weeping, in this case, is good, but reforming is better. As to being unequally yoked with unbelievers, such marriages, it is certain, are sinful, and ought not to be made; but now they are not null, as they were before the gospel did away the separation between Jews and Gentiles.

Verses 6–14

There is hope concerning people, when they are convinced, not only that it is good to part with their sins, but that it is necessary; we must do it, or we are undone. So rich is the mercy, and so plenteous the redemption of God, that there is hope for the vilest who hear the gospel, and are willing to accept of free salvation. When sinners mourn for their sins, and tremble at the word of God, there is hope that they will forsake them. To affect others with godly sorrow or love to God, we must ourselves be affected. It was carefully agreed how this affair should be carried on. That which is hastily resolved on seldom proves lasting.

Verses 15–44

The best reformers can but do their endeavour; when the Redeemer himself shall come to Zion, he shall effectually turn away ungodliness from Jacob. And when sin is repented of and forsaken, God will forgive it; but the blood of Christ, our Sin-offering, is the only atonement which takes away our guilt. No seeming repentance or amendment will benefit those who reject Him, for self-dependence proves them still unhumbled. All the names written in the book of life, are those of penitent sinners, not of self-righteous persons, who think they have no need of repentance.

Nehemiah

The Old Testament history closes with the book of Nehemiah, wherein is recorded the workings of his heart, in the management of public affairs; with many devout reflections.

Chapter 1

Nehemiah's distress for the misery of Jerusalem, His prayer.

—Nehemiah was the Persian king's cup-bearer. When God has work to do, he will never want instruments to do it with. Nehemiah lived at ease, and in honour, but does not forget that he is an Israelite, and that his brethren are in distress. He was ready to do them all the good offices he could; and that he might know how best to do them a kindness, he makes inquiries about them. We should inquire especially concerning the state of the church and religion. Every Jerusalem on this side the heavenly one will have some defect, which will require the help and services of its friends. Nehemiah's first application was to God, that he might have the fuller confidence in his application to the king. Our best pleas in prayer are taken from the promise of God, the word on which he has caused us to hope. Other means must be used, but the effectual fervent prayer of a righteous man avails most. Communion with God will best prepare us for our dealings with men. When we have intrusted our concerns to God, the mind is set at liberty; it feels satisfaction and composure, and difficulties vanish. We know that if the affair be hurtful, he can easily hinder it; and if it be good for us, he can as easily forward it.

Chapter 2

Verses 1–8

Our prayers must be seconded with serious endeavours, else we mock God. We are not limited to certain moments in our addresses to the King of kings, but have liberty to go to him at all times; approaches to the throne of grace are never out of season. But the sense of God's displeasure and the afflictions of his people, are causes of sorrow to the children of God, under which no earthly delights can comfort. The king encouraged Nehemiah to tell his mind. This gave him boldness to speak; much more may the invitation Christ has given us to pray, and the promise that we shall speed, encourage us to come boldly to the throne of grace. Nehemiah prayed to the God of heaven, as infinitely above even this mighty monarch. He lifted up his heart to that God who understands the language of the heart. Nor should we ever engage in any pursuit in which it would be wrong for us thus to seek and expect the Divine direction, assistance, and blessing. There was an immediate answer to his prayer; for the seed of Jacob never sought the God of Jacob in vain.

Verses 9–18

When Nehemiah had considered the matter, he told the Jews that God had put it into his heart to build the wall of Jerusalem. He does not undertake to do it without them. By stirring up ourselves and one another to that which is good, we strengthen ourselves and one another for it. We are weak in our duty, when we are cold and careless.

Verses 19, 20

The enmity of the serpent's seed against the cause of Christ is confined to no age or nation. The application to ourselves is plain. The church of God asks for our help. Is it not desolate, and exposed to assaults? Does the consideration of its low estate cause you any grief? Let not business, pleasure, or the support of a party so engage attention, as that Zion and her welfare shall be nothing to you.

Chapter 3

The rebuilding the walls of Jerusalem.

—The work was divided, so that every one might know what he had to do, and mind it, with a desire to excel; yet without contention, or separate interests. No strife appears among them, but which should do most for the public good. Every Israelite should lend a hand toward the building up of Jerusalem. Let not nobles think any thing below them, by which they may advance the good of their country. Even some females helped forward the work. Some repaired over against their houses, and one repaired over against his chamber. When a general good work is to be done, each should apply himself to that part which is within his reach. If every one will sweep before his own door, the street will be clean; if every one will mend one, we shall all be mended. Some that had first done helped their fellows. The walls of Jerusalem, in heaps of rubbish, represent the desperate state of the world around, while the number and malice of those who hindered the building, give some faint idea of the enemies we have to contend with, while executing the work of God. Every one must begin at home; for it is by getting the work of God advanced in our own souls that we shall best contribute to the good of the church of Christ. May the Lord thus stir up the hearts of his people, to lay aside their petty disputes, and to disregard their worldly interests, compared with building the walls of Jerusalem, and defending the cause of truth and godliness against the assaults of avowed enemies.

Chapter 4

Verses 1–6

Many a good work has been looked upon with contempt by proud and haughty scorners. Those who disagree in almost every thing, will unite in persecution. Nehemiah did not answer these fools according to their folly, but looked up to God by prayer. God's people have often been a despised people, but he hears all the slights that are put upon them, and it is their comfort that he does so. Nehemiah had reason to think that the hearts of those sinners were desperately hardened, else he would not have prayed that their sins might never be blotted out. Good work goes on well, when people have a mind to it. The reproaches of enemies should quicken us to our duty, not drive us from it.

Verses 7–15

The hindering good work is what bad men aim at, and promise themselves success in; but good work is God's work, and it shall prosper. God has many ways of bringing to light, and so of bringing to nought, the devices and designs of his church's enemies. If our enemies cannot frighten us from duty, or deceive us into sin, they cannot hurt us. Nehemiah put himself and his cause under the Divine protection. It was the way of this good man, and should be our way. All his cares, all his griefs, all his fears, he spread before God. Before he used any means, he made his prayer to God. Having prayed, he set a watch against the enemy. If we think to secure ourselves by prayer, without watchfulness, we are slothful, and tempt God; if by watchfulness, without prayer, we are proud, and slight God: either way, we forfeit his protection. God's care of our safety, should engage and encourage us to go on with vigour in our duty. As soon as a danger is over, let us return to our work, and trust God another time.

Verses 16–23

We must watch always against spiritual enemies, and not expect that our warfare will be over till our work is ended. The word of God is the sword of the Spirit, which we ought to have always at hand, and never to have to seek for it, either in our labours, or in our conflicts, as Christians. Every true Christian is both a labourer and a soldier, working with one hand, and fighting with the other. Good work is likely to go on with success, when those who labour in it, make a business of it. And Satan fears to assault the watchful Christian; or, if attacked, the Lord fights for him. Thus must we wait to the close of life, never putting off our armour till our work and warfare are ended; then we shall be welcomed to the rest and joy of our Lord.

Chapter 5

Verses 1–5

Men prey upon their fellow-creatures: by despising the poor they reproach their Maker. Such conduct is a disgrace to any, but who can sufficiently abhor it when adopted by professing Christians? With compassion for the oppressed, we should lament the hardships which many in the world are groaning under; putting our souls into their souls' stead, and remembering in our prayers and succours those who are burdened. But let those who show no mercy, expect judgment without mercy.

Verses 6–13

Nehemiah knew that, if he built Jerusalem's walls ever so high, so thick, or so strong, the city could not be safe while there were abuses. The right way to reform men's lives, is to convince their consciences. If you walk in the fear of God, you will not be either covetous of worldly gain, or cruel toward your brethren. Nothing exposes religion more to reproach, than the worldliness and hard-heartedness of the professors of it. Those that rigorously insist upon their right, with a very ill grace try to persuade others to give up theirs. In reasoning with selfish people, it is good to contrast their conduct with that of others who are liberal; but it is best to point to His example, who though he was rich, yet for our sakes became poor, that we, through his poverty, might be rich, **2Co 8:9**. They did according to promise. Good promises are good things, but good performances are better.

Verses 14–19

Those who truly fear God, will not dare to do any thing cruel or unjust. Let all who are in public places remember that they are so placed to do good, not to enrich themselves. Nehemiah mentions it to God in prayer, not as if he had merited any favour from God, but to show that he depended upon God only, to make up to him what he had lost and laid out for his honour. Nehemiah evidently spake and acted as one that knew himself to be a sinner. He did not mean to claim a reward as of debt, but in the manner that the Lord rewards a cup of cold water given to a disciple for his sake. The fear and love of God in the heart, and true love of the brethren, will lead to every good work. These are proper evidences of justifying faith; and our reconciled God will look upon persons of this character for good, according to all they have done for his people.

Chapter 6

Verses 1–9

Let those who are tempted to idle merry meetings by vain companions, thus answer the temptation, We have work to do, and must not neglect it. We must never suffer ourselves to be overcome, by repeated urgency, to do anything sinful or imprudent; but when attacked with the same temptation, must resist it with the same reason and resolution. It is common for that which is desired only by the malicious, to be falsely represented by them as desired by the many. But Nehemiah knew at what they aimed, he not only denied that such things were true, but that they were reported; he was better known than to be thus suspected. We must never omit any known duty for fear it should be misconstrued; but, while we keep a good conscience, let us trust God with our good name. God's people, though loaded with reproach, are not really fallen so low in reputation as some would have them thought to be. Nehemiah lifted up his heart to Heaven in a short prayer. When, in our Christian work and warfare, we enter upon any service or conflict, this is a good prayer, I have such a duty to do, such a temptation to grapple with; now, therefore, O God, strengthen my hands. Every temptation to draw us from duty, should quicken us the more to duty.

Verses 10–14

The greatest mischief our enemies can do us, is, to frighten us from our duty, and to lead us to do what is sinful. Let us never decline a good work, never do a bad one. We ought to try all advice, and to reject what is contrary to the word of God. Every man should study to be consistent. Should I, a professed Christian, called to be a saint, a child of God, a member of Christ, a temple of the Holy Ghost, should I be covetous, sensual, proud, or envious? Should I yield to impatience, discontent, or anger? Should I be slothful, unbelieving, or unmerciful? What effects will such conduct have upon others? All that God has done for us, or by us, or given to us, should lead us to watchfulness, self-denial, and diligence. Next to the sinfulness of sin, we should dread the scandal.

Verses 15–19

The wall was begun and finished in fifty-two days, though they rested on the sabbaths. A great deal of work may be done in a little time, if we set about it in earnest, and keep close to it. See the mischief of marrying with strangers. When men once became akin to Tobiah, they soon became sworn to him. A sinful love leads to a sinful league. The enemy of souls employs many instruments, and forms many projects, to bring reproach on the active servants of God, or to take them from their work. But we should follow the example of Him who laid down his life for the sheep. Those that simply cleave to the Lord and his work will be supported.

Chapter 7

Verses 1–4

Nehemiah, having finished the wall, returned to the Persian court, and came to Jerusalem again with a new commission. The public safety depends on every one's care to guard himself and his family against sin.

Verses 5–73

Nehemiah knew that the safety of a city, under God, depends more upon the inhabitants than upon its walls. Every good gift and every good work are from above. God gives knowledge, he gives grace; all is of him, and therefore all must be to him. What is done by human prudence, must be ascribed to the direction of Divine Providence. But woe to those who turn back from the Lord, loving this present world! and happy those who dedicate themselves, and their substance, to his service and glory!

Chapter 8

Verses 1–8

Sacrifices were to be offered only at the door of the temple; but praying and preaching were, and are, services of religion, as acceptably performed in one place as in another. Masters of families should bring their families with them to the public worship of God. Women and children have souls to save, and are therefore to acquaint themselves with the word of God, and to attend on the means of grace. Little ones, as they come to reason, must be trained up in religion. Ministers when they go to the pulpit, should take their Bibles with them; Ezra did so. Thence they must fetch their knowledge; according to that rule they must speak, and must show that they do so. Reading the Scriptures in religious assemblies is an ordinance of God, whereby he is honoured, and his church edified. Those who hear the word, should understand it, else it is to them but an empty sound of words. It is therefore required of teachers that they explain the word, and give the sense of it. Reading is good, and preaching is good, but expounding makes reading the better understood, and preaching the more convincing. It has pleased God in almost every age of the church to raise up, not only those who have preached the gospel, but also those who have given their views of Divine truth in writing; and though many who have attempted to explain Scripture, have darkened counsel by words without knowledge, yet the labours of others are of excellent use. All that we hear must, however, be brought to the test of Scripture. They heard readily, and minded every word. The word of God demands attention. If through carelessness we let much slip in hearing, there is danger that through forgetfulness we shall let all slip after hearing.

Verses 9–12

It was a good sign that their hearts were tender, when they heard the words of the law. The people were to send portions to those for whom nothing was prepared. It is the duty of a religious feast, as well as of a religious fast, to draw out the soul to the hungry; God's bounty should make us bountiful. We must not only give to those that offer themselves, but send to those out of sight. Their strength consisted in joy in the Lord. The better we understand God's word, the more comfort we find in it; the darkness of trouble arises from the darkness of ignorance.

Verses 13–18

They found written in the law about the feast of tabernacles. Those who diligently search the Scriptures, find things written there which they have forgotten. This feast of tabernacles was a representation of the believer's tabernacle state in this world, and a type of the holy joy of the gospel church. The conversion of the nations to the faith of Christ, is foretold under the figure of this feast, Zec **14:16**. True religion will render us strangers and pilgrims upon earth. We read and hear the word acceptably and profitably, when we do according to what is written therein; when what appears to be our duty is revived, after it has been neglected. They minded the substance; else the ceremony had been of no use. They did it, rejoicing in God and his goodness. These are the means which the Spirit of God crowns with success, in bringing the hearts of sinners to tremble and to become humbled before God. But those are enemies to their own growth in holiness, who always indulge sorrow, even for sin, and put away from them the consolations tendered by the word and Spirit of God.

Chapter 9

Verses 1–3

The word will direct and quicken prayer, for by it the Spirit helps our infirmities in prayer. The careful study of God's word will more and more discover to us our own sinfulness, and the plenteousness of his salvation; thus it calls us to mourn for sin, and to rejoice in him. Every discovery of the truth of God, should render us more unwearied in attendance on his sacred word, and on his worship.

Verses 4–38

The summary of their prayers we have here upon record. Much more, no doubt, was said. Whatever ability we have to do any thing in the way of duty, we are to serve and glorify God according to the utmost of it. When confessing our sins, it is good to notice the mercies of God, that we may be the more humbled and ashamed. The dealings of the Lord showed his goodness and long-suffering, and the hardness of their hearts. The testimony of the prophets was the testimony of the Spirit in the prophets, and it was the Spirit of Christ in them. They spake as they were moved by the Holy Ghost, and what they said is to be received accordingly. The result was, wonder at the Lord's mercies, and the feeling that sin had brought them to their present state, from which nothing but unmerited love could rescue them. And is not their conduct a specimen of human nature? Let us study the history of our land, and our own history. Let us recollect our advantages from childhood, and ask what were our first returns? Let us frequently do so, that we may be kept humble, thankful, and watchful. Let all remember that pride and obstinacy are sins which ruin the soul. But it is often as hard to persuade the broken-hearted to hope, as formerly it was to bring them to fear. Is this thy case? Behold this sweet promise, A God ready to pardon! Instead of keeping away from God under a sense of unworthiness, let us come boldly to the throne of grace, that we may obtain mercy, and find grace to help in time of need. He is a God ready to pardon.

Chapter 10

Verses 1–31

Conversion is separating from the course and custom of this world, devoting ourselves to the conduct directed by the word of God. When we bind ourselves to do the commandments of God, it is to do all his commandments, and to look to him as the Lord, and our Lord.

Verses 32–39

Having covenanted against the sins of which they had been guilty, they obliged themselves to observe the duties they had neglected. We must not only cease to do evil, but learn to do well. Let not any people expect the blessing of God, unless they keep up public worship. It is likely to go well with our houses, when care is taken that the work of God's house goes on well. When every one helps, and every one gives, though but little, toward a good work, the whole will come to be a large sum. We must do what we can in works of piety and charity; and whatever state we are placed in, cheerfully perform our duty to God, which will be the surest way to ease and liberty. As the ordinances of God are the appointed means of support to our souls, the believer will not grudge the expense; yet most people leave their souls to starve.

Chapter 11

The distribution of the people.

—In all ages, men have preferred their own ease and advantage to the public good. Even the professors of religion too commonly seek their own, and not the things of Christ. Few have had such attachment to holy things and holy places, as to renounce pleasure for their sake. Yet surely, our souls should delight to dwell where holy persons and opportunities of spiritual improvement most abound. If we have not this love to the city of our God, and to every thing that assists our communion with the Saviour, how shall we be willing to depart hence; to be absent from the body, that we may be present with the Lord? To the carnal-minded, the perfect holiness of the New Jerusalem would be still harder to bear than the holiness of God's church on earth. Let us seek first the favour of God, and his glory; let us study to be patient, contented, and useful in our several stations, and wait, with cheerful hope, for admission into the holy city of God.

Chapter 12

Verses 1–26

It is a debt we owe to faithful ministers, to remember our guides, who have spoken to us the word of God. It is good to know what our godly predecessors were, that we may learn what we should be.

Verses 27–43

All our cities, all our houses, must have holiness to the Lord written upon them. The believer should undertake nothing which he does not dedicate to the Lord. We are concerned to cleanse our hands, and purify our hearts, when any work for God is to pass through them. Those that would be employed to sanctify others, must sanctify themselves, and set themselves apart for God. To those who are sanctified, all their creature-comforts and enjoyments are made holy. The people greatly rejoiced. All that share in public mercies, ought to join in public thanksgivings.

Verses 44–47

When the solemnities of a thanksgiving day leave such impressions on ministers and people, that both are more careful and cheerful in doing their duty, they are indeed acceptable to the Lord, and turn to good account. And whatever we do, must be purified by the blood of sprinkling, and by the grace of the Holy Spirit, or it cannot be acceptable to God.

Chapter 13

Verses 1–9

Israel was a peculiar people, and not to mingle with the nations. See the benefit of publicly reading the word of God; when it is duly attended to, it discovers to us sin and duty, good and evil, and shows wherein we have erred. We profit, when we are thus wrought upon to separate from evil. Those that would drive sin out of their hearts, the living temples, must throw out its household stuff, and all the provision made for it; and take away all the things that are the food and fuel of lust; this is really to mortify it. When sin is cast out of the heart by repentance, let the blood of Christ be applied to it by faith, then let it be furnished with the graces of God's Spirit, for every good work.

Verses 10–14

If a sacred character will not keep men from setting an evil example, it must not shelter any one from deserved blame and punishment. The Levites had been wronged; their portions had not been given them. They were gone to get livelihoods for themselves and their families, for their profession would not maintain them. A maintenance not sufficient, makes a poor ministry. The work is neglected, because the workmen are. Nehemiah laid the fault upon the rulers. Both ministers and people, who forsake religion and the services of it, and magistrates, who do not what they can to keep them to it, will have much to answer for. He delayed not to bring the Levites to their places again, and that just payment should be made. Nehemiah on every occasion looked up to God, and committed himself and all his affairs to Him. It pleased him to think that he had been of use to revive and support religion in his country. He here refers to God, not in pride, but with a humble appeal concerning his honest intention in what he had done. He prays, "Remember me;" not, Reward me. "Wipe not out my good deeds;" not, Publish them, or record them. Yet he was rewarded, and his good deeds recorded. God does more than we are able to ask.

Verses 15–22

The keeping holy the Lord's day forms an important object for their attention who would promote true godliness. Religion never prospers while sabbaths are trodden under foot. No wonder there was a general decay of religion, and corruption of manners among the Jews, when they forsook the sanctuary and profaned the sabbath. Those little consider what an evil they do, who profane the sabbath. We must answer for the sins others are led to commit by our example. Nehemiah charges it on them as an evil thing, for so it is, proceeding from contempt of God and our own souls. He shows that sabbath-breaking was one of the sins for which God had brought judgments upon them; and if they did not take warning, but returned to the same sins again, they had to expect further judgments. The courage, zeal, and prudence of Nehemiah in this matter, are recorded for us to do likewise; and we have reason to think, that the cure he wrought was lasting. He felt and confessed himself a sinner, who could demand nothing from God as justice, when he thus cried unto him for mercy.

Verses 23–31

If either parent be ungodly, corrupt nature will incline the children to take after that one; which is a strong reason why Christians should not be unequally yoked. In the education of children, great care should be taken about the government of their tongues; that they learn not the language of Ashdod, no impious or impure talk, no corrupt communication. Nehemiah showed the evil of these marriages. Some, more obstinate than the rest, he smote, that is, ordered them to be beaten by the officers according to the law, De **25**:**2**, **3**. Here are Nehemiah's prayers on this occasion He prays, "Remember them, O my God." Lord, convince and convert them; put them in mind of what they should be and do. The best services to the public have been forgotten by those for whom they were done, therefore Nehemiah refers himself to God, to recompense him. This may well be the summary of our petitions; we need no more to make us happy than this; Remember me, O my God, for good. We may humbly hope that the Lord will remember us and our services, although, after lives of unwearied activity and usefulness, we shall still see cause to abhor ourselves and repent in dust and ashes, and to cry out with Nehemiah, Spare me, O my God, according to the greatness of they mercy.

Esther

We find in this book, that even those Jews who were scattered in the province of the heathen, were taken care of, and were wonderfully preserved, when threatened with destruction. Though the name of God be not in this book, the finger of God is shown by minute events for the bringing about his people's deliverance. This history comes in between Ezr **6**; **7**.

Chapter 1

Verses 1–9

The pride of Ahasuerus's heart rising with the grandeur of his kingdom, he made an extravagant feast. This was vain glory. Better is a dinner of herbs with quietness, than this banquet of wine, with all the noise and tumult that must have attended it. But except grace prevails in the heart, self-exaltation and self-indulgence, in one form or another, will be the ruling principle. Yet none did compel; so that if any drank to excess, it was their own fault. This caution of a heathen prince, even when he would show his generosity, may shame many called Christians, who, under pretence of sending the health round, send sin round, and death with it. There is a woe to them that do so; let them read it, and tremble, Hab **2**:**15**, **16**.

Verses 10–22

Ahasuerus's feast ended in heaviness, by his own folly. Seasons of peculiar festivity often end in vexation. Superiors should be careful not to command what may reasonably be disobeyed. But when wine is in, men's reason departs from them. He that had rule over **127** provinces, had no rule over his own spirit. But whether the passion or the policy of the king was served by this decree, God's providence made way for Esther to the crown, and defeated Haman's wicked project, even before it had entered into his heart, and he arrived at his power. Let us rejoice that the Lord reigns, and will overrule the madness or folly of mankind to promote his own glory, and the safety and happiness of his people.

Chapter 2

Verses 1–20

We see to what absurd practices those came, who were destitute of Divine revelation, and what need there was of the gospel of Christ, to purify men from the lusts of the flesh, and to bring them back to the original institution of marriage. Esther was preferred as queen. Those who suggest that Esther committed sin to come at this dignity, do not consider the custom of those times and countries. Every one that the king took was married to him, and was his wife, though of a lower rank. But how low is human nature sunk, when such as these are the leading pursuits and highest worldly happiness of men! Disappointment and vexation must follow; and he most wisely consults his enjoyment, even in this present life, who most exactly obeys the precepts of the Divine law. But let us turn to consider the wise and merciful providence of God, carrying on his deep but holy designs in the midst of all this. And let no change in our condition be a pretext for forgetting our duties to parents, or the friends who have stood in their place.

Verses 21–23

Good subjects must not conceal any bad design they know of against the prince, or the public peace. Mordecai was not rewarded at the time, but a remembrance was written. Thus, with respect to those who serve Christ, though their recompence is not till the resurrection of the just, yet an account is kept of their work of faith and labour of love, which God is not unrighteous to forget. The servant of God must be faithful to every trust, and watchful for those who employ him. If he appear to be neglected now, he will be remembered hereafter. None of our actions can be forgotten; even our most secret thoughts are written in lasting registers, Re **20**:**12**.

Chapter 3

Verses 1–6

Mordecai refused to reverence Haman. The religion of a Jew forbade him to give honours to any mortal man which savoured of idolatry, especially to so wicked a man as Haman. By nature all are idolaters; self is our favourite idol, we are pleased to be treated as if every thing were at our disposal. Though religion by no means destroys good manners, but teaches us to render honour to whom honour is due, yet by a citizen of Zion, not only in his heart, but in his eyes, such a vile person as Haman was, is contemned, Ps **15**:**4**. The true believer cannot obey edicts, or conform to fashions, which break the law of God. He must obey God rather than man, and leave the consequences to him. Haman was full of wrath. His device was inspired by that wicked spirit, who has been a murderer from the beginning; whose enmity to Christ and his church, governs all his children.

Verses 7–15

Without some acquaintance with the human heart, and the history of mankind, we should not think that any prince could consent to a dreadful proposal, so hurtful to himself. Let us be thankful for mild and just government. Haman inquires, according to his own superstitions, how to find a lucky day for the designed massacre! God's wisdom serves its own purposes by men's folly. Haman has appealed to the lot, and the lot, by delaying the execution, gives judgment against him. The event explains the doctrine of a particular providence over all the affairs of men, and the care of God over his church. Haman was afraid lest the king's conscience should smite him for what he had done; to prevent which, he kept him drinking. This cursed method many often take to drown convictions, and to harden their own hearts, and the hearts of others, in sin. All appeared in a favourable train to accomplish the project. But though sinners are permitted to proceed to the point they aim at, an unseen but almighty Power turns them back. How vain and contemptible are the strongest assaults against Jehovah! Had Haman obtained his wish, and the Jewish nation perished, what must have become of all the promises? How could the prophecies concerning the great Redeemer of the world have been fulfilled? Thus the everlasting covenant itself must have failed, before this diabolical project could take place.

Chapter 4

Verses 1–4

Mordecai avowed his relation to the Jews. Public calamities, that oppress the church of God, should affect our hearts more than any private affliction, and it is peculiarly distressing to occasion sufferings to others. God will keep those that are exposed to evil by the tenderness of their consciences.

Verses 5–17

We are prone to shrink from services that are attended with peril or loss. But when the cause of Christ and his people demand it, we must take up our cross, and follow him. When Christians are disposed to consult their own ease or safety, rather than the public good, they should be blamed. The law was express, all knew it. It is not thus in the court of the King of kings: to the footstool of his throne of grace we may always come boldly, and may be sure of an answer of peace to the prayer of faith. We are welcome, even into the holiest, through the blood of Jesus. Providence so ordered it, that, just then, the king's affections had cooled toward Esther; her faith and courage thereby were the more tried; and God's goodness in the favour she now found with the king, thereby shone the brighter. Haman no doubt did what he could to set the king against her. Mordecai suggests, that it was a cause which, one way or other, would certainly be carried, and which therefore she might safely venture in. This was the language of strong faith, which staggered not at the promise when the danger was most threatening, but against hope believed in hope. He that by sinful devices will save his life, and will not trust God with it in the way of duty, shall lose it in the way of sin. Divine Providence had regard to this matter, in bringing Esther to be queen. Therefore thou art bound in gratitude to do this service for God and his church, else thou dost not answer the end of thy being raised up. There is wise counsel and design in all the providences of God, which will prove that they are all intended for the good of the church. We should, every one, consider for what end God has put us in the place where we are, and study to answer that end: and take care that we do not let it slip. Having solemnly commended our souls and our cause to God, we may venture upon his service. All dangers are trifling compared with the danger of losing our souls. But the trembling sinner is often as much afraid of casting himself, without reserve, upon the Lord's free mercy, as Esther was of coming before the king. Let him venture, as she did, with earnest prayer and supplication, and he shall fare as well and better than she did. The cause of God must prevail: we are safe in being united to it.

Chapter 5

Verses 1–8

Esther having had power with God, and prevailing, like Jacob, had power with men too. He that will lose his life for God, shall save it, or find it in a better life. The king encouraged her. Let us from this be encouraged to pray always to our God, and not to faint. Esther came to a proud, imperious man; but we come to the God of love and grace. She was not called, but we are; the Spirit says, Come, and the Bride says, Come. She had a law against her, we have a promise, many a promise, in favour of us; Ask, and it shall be given you. She had no friend to go with her, or to plead for her; on the contrary, he that was then the king's favourite, was her enemy; but we have an Advocate with the Father, in whom he is well pleased. Let us therefore come boldly to the throne of grace. God put it into Esther's heart to delay her petition a day longer; she knew not, but God did, what was to happen in that very night.

Verses 9–14

This account of Haman is a comment upon Pr **21**:**24**. Self-admirers and self-flatterers are really self-deceivers. Haman, the higher he is lifted up, the more impatient he is of contempt, and the more enraged at it. The affront from Mordecai spoiled all. A slight affront, which a humble man would scarcely notice, will torment a proud man, even to madness, and will mar all his comforts. Those disposed to be uneasy, will never want something to be uneasy at. Such are proud men; though they have much to their mind, if they have not all to their mind, it is as nothing to them. Many call the proud happy, who display pomp and make a show; but this is a mistaken thought. Many poor cottagers feel far less uneasiness than the rich, with all their fancied advantages around them. The man who knows not Christ, is poor though he be rich, because he is utterly destitute of that which alone is true riches.

Chapter 6

Verses 1–3

The providence of God rules over the smallest concerns of men. Not a sparrow falls to the ground without him. Trace the steps which Providence took towards the advancement of Mordecai. The king could not sleep when Providence had a design to serve, in keeping him awake. We read of no illness that broke his sleep, but God, whose gift sleep is, withheld it from him. He who commanded a hundred and twenty-seven provinces, could not command one hour's sleep.

Verses 4–11

See how men's pride deceives them. The deceitfulness of our own hearts appears in nothing more than in the conceit we have of ourselves and our own performances: against which we should constantly watch and pray. Haman thought the king loved and valued no one but himself, but he was deceived. We should suspect that the esteem which others profess for us, is not so great as it seems to be, that we may not think too well of ourselves, nor trust too much in others. How Haman is struck, when the king bids him do honour to Mordecai the Jew, the very man whom he hated above all men, whose ruin he was now designing!

Verses 12–14

Mordecai was not puffed up with his honours, he returned to his place and the duty of it. Honour is well bestowed on those that do not think themselves above their business. But Haman could not bear it. What harm had it done him? But that will break a proud man's heart, which will not break a humble man's sleep. His doom was, out of this event, read to him by his wife and his friends. They plainly confessed that the Jews, though scattered through the nations, were special objects of Divine care. Miserable comforters are they all; they did not advise Haman to repent, but foretold his fate as unavoidable. The wisdom of God is seen, in timing the means of his church's deliverance, so as to manifest his own glory.

Chapter 7

Verses 1–6

If the love of life causes earnest pleadings with those that can only kill the body, how fervent should our prayers be to Him, who is able to destroy both body and soul in hell! How should we pray for the salvation of our relatives, friends, and all around us! When we petition great men, we must be cautious not to give them offence; even just complaints must often be kept back. But when we approach the King of kings with reverence, we cannot ask or expect too much. Though nothing but wrath be our due, God is able and willing to do exceeding abundantly, even beyond all we can ask or think.

Verses 7–10

The king was angry: those that do things with self-will, reflect upon them afterward with self-reproach. When angry, we should pause before we come to any resolution, and thus rule our own spirits, and show that we are governed by reason. Those that are most haughty and insolent when in power and prosperity, commonly, like Haman, are the most abject and poor-spirited when brought down. The day is coming when those that hate and persecute God's chosen ones, would gladly be beholden to them. The king returns yet more angry against Haman. Those about him were ready to put his wrath into execution. How little can proud men be sure of the interest they think they have! The enemies of God's church have often been thus taken in their own craftiness. The Lord is known by such judgments. Then was the king's wrath pacified, and not till then. And who pities Haman hanged on his own gallows? who does not rather rejoice in the Divine righteousness displayed in the destruction his own art brought upon him? Let the workers of iniquity tremble, turn to the Lord, and seek pardon through the blood of Jesus.

Chapter 8

Verses 1, 2

What Haman would have done mischief with, Esther will do good with. All the trust the king had reposed in Haman, he now placed in Mordecai: a happy change. See the vanity of laying up treasure upon earth; he that heapeth up riches, knoweth not who shall gather them. With what little pleasure, nay, with what constant vexation, would Haman have looked upon his estate, if he could have foreseen that Mordecai, the man he hated above all men in the world, should have rule over all that wherein he had laboured! It is our interest to make sure of those riches which will not be left behind, but which will go with us to another world.

Verses 3–14

It was time to be earnest, when the church of God was at stake. Esther, though safe herself, fell down and begged for the deliverance of her people. We read of no tears when she begged for her own life, but although she was sure of that, she wept for her people. Tears of pity and tenderness are the most Christ-like. According to the constitution of the Persian government, no law or decree could be repealed or recalled. This is so far from speaking to the wisdom and honour of the Medes and Persians, that it clearly shows their pride and folly. This savours of that old presumption which ruined all, We will be as gods! It is God's prerogative not to repent, or to say what can never be altered or unsaid. Yet a way was found, by another decree, to authorize the Jews to stand upon their defence. The decree was published in the languages of all the provinces. Shall all the subjects of an earthly prince have his decrees in languages they understand, and shall God's oracles and laws be locked up from any of his servants in an unknown tongue?

Verses 15–17

Mordecai's robes now were rich. These things are not worth notice, but as marks of the king's favour, and the fruit of God's favour to his church. It is well with a land, when ensigns of dignity are made the ornaments of serious piety. When the church prospers, many will join it, who will be shy of it when in trouble. When believers have rest, and walk in the fear of the Lord, and the comfort of the Holy Ghost, they will be multiplied. And the attempts of Satan to destroy the church, always tend to increase the number of true Christians.

Chapter 9

Verses 1–19

The enemies of the Jews hoped to have power over them by the former edict. If they had attempted nothing against the people of God, they would not themselves have suffered. The Jews, acting together, strengthened one another. Let us learn to stand fast in one spirit, and with one mind, striving together against the enemies of our souls, who endeavour to rob us of our faith, which is more precious than our lives. The Jews, to the honour of their religion, showed contempt of wordly wealth, that they might make it appear they desired nothing except their own preservation. In every case the people of God should manifest humanity and disinterestedness, frequently refusing advantages which might lawfully be obtained. The Jews celebrated their festival the day after they had finished their work. When we have received great mercies from God, we ought to be speedy in making thankful returns to him.

Verses 20–32

The observance of the Jewish feasts, is a public declaration of the truth of the Old Testament Scriptures. And as the Old Testament Scriptures are true, the Messiah expected by the Jews is come long ago; and none but Jesus of Nazareth can be that Messiah. The festival was appointed by authority, yet under the direction of the Spirit of God. It was called the feast of Purim, from a Persian word, which signifies a lot. The name of this festival would remind them of the almighty power of the God of Israel, who served his own purposes by the superstitions of the heathen. In reviewing our mercies, we should advert to former fears and distresses. When our mercies are personal, we should not by forgetfulness lose the comfort of them, or withhold from the Lord the glory due to his name. May the Lord teach us to rejoice, with that holy joy which anticipates and prepares for the blessedness of heaven. Every instance of Divine goodness to ourselves, is a new obligation laid on us to do good, to those especially who most need our bounty. Above all, redemption by Christ binds us to be merciful, **2Co 8:9**.

Chapter 10

Greatness of Ahasuerus—Mordecai's advancement.

—Many instances of the grandeur of Ahasuerus might have been given: these were written in the Persian chronicles, which are long since lost, while the sacred writings will live till time shall be no more. The concerns of the despised worshippers of the Lord are deemed more important by the Holy Spirit, than the exploits of the most illustricus monarch on earth. Mordecai was truly great, and his greatness gave him opportunities of doing the more good. He did not disown his people the Jews, and no doubt kept to the true religion. He did not seek his own wealth, but the welfare of his people. Few have it in their power to do so much good as Mordecai; but all have it in their power to do hurt, and who has it not in his power to do some good? We are not required to do what is not in our power, or is unsuited to our station; but all are bound to live under the influence of the tempers displayed in the saints, whose examples are recorded in the Bible. If we live by the faith of Christ, we shall be active according to the ability and opportunities he gives us, in promoting his glory and the best interests of men. If our faith be genuine, it will work by love. Wait in faith and prayer, and the event will be safe and glorious; our salvation is sure, through our Lord Jesus Christ.

Job

This book is so called from Job, whose prosperity, afflictions, and restoration, are here recorded. He lived soon after Abraham, or perhaps before that patriarch. Most likely it was written by Job himself, and it is the most ancient book in existence. The instructions to be learned from the patience of Job, and from his trials, are as useful now, and as much needed as ever. We live under the same Providence, we have the same chastening Father, and there is the same need for correction unto righteousness. The fortitude and patience of Job, though not small, gave way in his severe troubles; but his faith was fixed upon the coming of his Redeemer, and this gave him stedfastness and constancy, though every other dependence, particularly the pride and boast of a self-righteous spirit, was tried and consumed. Another great doctrine of the faith, particularly set forth in the book of Job, is that of Providence. It is plain, from this history, that the Lord watched over his servant Job with the affection of a wise and loving father.

Chapter 1

Verses 1–5

Job was prosperous, and yet pious. Though it is hard and rare, it is not impossible for a rich man to enter into the kingdom of heaven. By God's grace the temptations of worldly wealth may be overcome. The account of Job's piety and prosperity comes before the history of his great afflictions, showing that neither will secure from troubles. While Job beheld the harmony and comforts of his sons with satisfaction, his knowledge of the human heart made him fearful for them. He sent and sanctified them, reminding them to examine themselves, to confess their sins, to seek forgiveness; and as one who hoped for acceptance with God through the promised Saviour, he offered a burnt-offering for each. We perceive his care for their souls, his knowledge of the sinful state of man, his entire dependence on God's mercy in the way he had appointed.

Verses 6–12

Job's afflictions began from the malice of Satan, by the Lord's permission, for wise and holy purposes. There is an evil spirit, the enemy of God, and of all righteousness, who is continually seeking to distress, to lead astray, and, if possible, to destroy those who love God. How far his influence may extend, we cannot say; but probably much unsteadiness and unhappiness in Christians may be ascribed to him. While we are on this earth we are within his reach. Hence it concerns us to be sober and vigilant, **1**Pe **5**:**8**. See how Satan censures Job. This is the common way of slanderers, to suggest that which they have no reason to think is true. But as there is nothing we should dread more than really being hypocrites, so there is nothing we need dread less than being called and counted so without cause. It is not wrong to look at the eternal recompence in our obedience; but it is wrong to aim at worldly advantages in our religion. God's people are taken under his special protection; they, and all that belong to them. The blessing of the Lord makes rich; Satan himself owns it. God suffered Job to be tried, as he suffered Peter to be sifted. It is our comfort that God has the devil in a chain, Re **20**:**1**. He has no power to lead men to sin, but what they give him themselves; nor any power to afflict men, but what is given him from above. All this is here described to us after the manner of men. The Scripture speaks thus to teach us that God directs the affairs of the world.

Verses 13–19

Satan brought Job's troubles upon him on the day that his children began their course of feasting. The troubles all came upon Job at once; while one messenger of evil tidings was speaking, another followed. His dearest and most valuable possessions were his ten children; news is brought him that they are killed. They were taken away when he had most need of them to comfort him under other losses. In God only have we a help present at all times. (Job **1**:**20-22**)

Verses 20–22

Job humbled himself under the hand of God. He reasons from the common state of human life, which he describes. We brought nothing of this world's goods into the world, but have them from others; and it is certain we can carry nothing out, but must leave them to others. Job, under all his losses, is but reduced to his first state. He is but where he must have been at last, and is only unclothed, or unloaded rather, a little sooner than he expected. If we put off our clothes before we go to bed, it is some inconvenience, but it may be the better borne when it is near bed-time. The same who gave hath taken away. See how Job looks above instruments, and keeps his eye upon the First Cause. Afflictions must not divert us from, but quicken us to religion. If in all our troubles we look to the Lord, he will support us. The Lord is righteous. All we have is from his gift; we have forfeited it by sin, and ought not to complain if he takes any part from us. Discontent and impatience charge God with folly. Against these Job carefully watched; and so must we, acknowledging that as God has done right, but we have done wickedly, so God has done wisely, but we have done very foolishly. And may the malice and power of Satan render that Saviour more precious to our souls, who came to destroy the works of the devil; who, for our salvation, suffered from that enemy far more than Job suffered, or we can think.

Chapter 2

Verses 1–6

How well is it for us, that neither men nor devils are to be our judges! but all our judgment comes from the Lord, who never errs. Job holds fast his integrity still, as his weapon. God speaks with pleasure of the power of his own grace. Self-love and self-preservation are powerful in the hearts of men. But Satan accuses Job, representing him as wholly selfish, and minding nothing but his own ease and safety. Thus are the ways and people of God often falsely blamed by the devil and his agents. Permission is granted to Satan to make trial, but with a limit. If God did not chain up the roaring lion, how soon would he devour us! Job, thus slandered by Satan, was a type of Christ, the first prophecy of whom was, that Satan should bruise his heel, and be foiled.

Verses 7–10

The devil tempts his own children, and draws them to sin, and afterwards torments, when he has brought them to ruin; but this child of God he tormented with affliction, and then tempted to make a bad use of his affliction. He provoked Job to curse God. The disease was very grievous. If at any time we are tried with sore and grievous distempers, let us not think ourselves dealt with otherwise than as God sometimes deals with the best of his saints and servants. Job humbled himself under the mighty hand of God, and brought his mind to his condition. His wife was spared to him, to be a troubler and tempter to him. Satan still endeavours to draw men from God, as he did our first parents, by suggesting hard thoughts of Him, than which nothing is more false. But Job resisted and overcame the temptation. Shall we, guilty, polluted, worthless creatures, receive so many unmerited blessings from a just and holy God, and shall we refuse to accept the punishment of our sins, when we suffer so much less than we deserve? Let murmuring, as well as boasting, be for ever done away. Thus far Job stood the trial, and appeared brightest in the furnace of affliction. There might be risings of corruption in his heart, but grace had the upper hand.

Verses 11–13

The friends of Job seem noted for their rank, as well as for wisdom and piety. Much of the comfort of this life lies in friendship with the prudent and virtuous. Coming to mourn with him, they vented grief which they really felt. Coming to comfort him, they sat down with him. It would appear that they suspected his unexampled troubles were judgments for some crimes, which he had vailed under his professions of godliness. Many look upon it only as a compliment to visit their friends in sorrow; we must look life. And if the example of Job's friends is not enough to lead us to pity the afflicted, let us seek the mind that was in Christ.

Chapter 3

Verses 1–10

For seven days Job's friends sat by him in silence, without offering consolidation: at the same time Satan assaulted his mind to shake his confidence, and to fill him with hard thoughts of God. The permission seems to have extended to this, as well as to torturing the body. Job was an especial type of Christ, whose inward sufferings, both in the garden and on the cross, were the most dreadful; and arose in a great degree from the assaults of Satan in that hour of darkness. These inward trials show the reason of the change that took place in Job's conduct, from entire submission to the will of God, to the impatience which appears here, and in other parts of the book. The believer, who knows that a few drops of this bitter cup are more dreadful than the sharpest outward afflictions, while he is favoured with a sweet sense of the love and presence of God, will not be surprised to find that Job proved a man of like passions with others; but will rejoice that Satan was disappointed, and could not prove him a hypocrite; for though he cursed the day of his birth, he did not curse his God. Job doubtless was afterwards ashamed of these wishes, and we may suppose what must be his judgment of them now he is in everlasting happiness.

Verses 11–19

Job complained of those present at his birth, for their tender attention to him. No creature comes into the world so helpless as man. God's power and providence upheld our frail lives, and his pity and patience spared our forfeited lives. Natural affection is put into parents' hearts by God. To desire to die that we may be with Christ, that we may be free from sin, is the effect and evidence of grace; but to desire to die, only that we may be delivered from the troubles of this life, savours of corruption. It is our wisdom and duty to make the best of that which is, be it living or dying; and so to live to the Lord, and die to the Lord, as in both to be his, Ro **14**:**8**. Observe how Job describes the repose of the grave; There the wicked cease from troubling. When persecutors die, they can no longer persecute. There the weary are at rest: in the grave they rest from all their labours. And a rest from sin, temptation, conflict, sorrows, and labours, remains in the presence and enjoyment of God. There believers rest in Jesus, nay, as far as we trust in the Lord Jesus and obey him, we here find rest to our souls, though in the world we have tribulation.

Verses 20–26

Job was like a man who had lost his way, and had no prospect of escape, or hope of better times. But surely he was in an ill frame for death when so unwilling to live. Let it be our constant care to get ready for another world, and then leave it to God to order our removal thither as he thinks fit. Grace teaches us in the midst of life's greatest comforts, to be willing to die, and in the midst of its greatest crosses, to be willing to live. Job's way was hid; he knew not wherefore God contended with him. The afflicted and tempted Christian knows something of this heaviness; when he has been looking too much at the things that are seen, some chastisement of his heavenly Father will give him a taste of this disgust of life, and a glance at these dark regions of despair. Nor is there any help until God shall restore to him the joys of his salvation. Blessed be God, the earth is full of his goodness, though full of man's wickedness. This life may be made tolerable if we attend to our duty. We look for eternal mercy, if willing to receive Christ as our Saviour.

Chapter 4

Verses 1–6

Satan undertook to prove Job a hypocrite by afflicting him; and his friends concluded him to be one because he was so afflicted, and showed impatience. This we must keep in mind if we would understand what passed. Eliphaz speaks of Job, and his afflicted condition, with tenderness; but charges him with weakness and faint-heartedness. Men make few allowances for those who have taught others. Even pious friends will count that only a touch which we feel as a wound. Learn from hence to draw off the mind of a sufferer from brooding over the affliction, to look at the God of mercies in the affliction. And how can this be done so well as by looking to Christ Jesus, in whose unequalled sorrows every child of God soonest learns to forget his own?

Verses 7–11

Eliphaz argues, **1**. That good men were never thus ruined. But there is one event both to the righteous and to the wicked, Ec **9**:**2**, both in life and death; the great and certain difference is after death. Our worst mistakes are occasioned by drawing wrong views from undeniable truths. **2**. That wicked men were often thus ruined: for the proof of this, Eliphaz vouches his own observation. We may see the same every day.

Verses 12–21

Eliphaz relates a vision. When we are communing with our own hearts, and are still, Ps **4**:**4**, then is a time for the Holy Spirit to commune with us. This vision put him into very great fear. Ever since man sinned, it has been terrible to him to receive communications from Heaven, conscious that he can expect no good tidings thence. Sinful man! shall he pretend to be more just, more pure, than God, who being his Maker, is his Lord and Owner? How dreadful, then, the pride and presumption of man! How great the patience of God! Look upon man in his life. The very foundation of that cottage of clay in which man dwells, is in the dust, and it will sink with its own weight. We stand but upon the dust. Some have a higher heap of dust to stand upon than others but still it is the earth that stays us up, and will shortly swallow us up. Man is soon crushed; or if some lingering distemper, which consumes like a moth, be sent to destroy him, he cannot resist it. Shall such a creature pretend to blame the appointments of God? Look upon man in his death. Life is short, and in a little time men are cut off. Beauty, strength, learning, not only cannot secure them from death, but these things die with them; nor shall their pomp, their wealth, or power, continue after them. Shall a weak, sinful, dying creature, pretend to be more just than God, and more pure than his Maker? No: instead of quarrelling with his afflictions, let him wonder that he is out of hell. Can a man be cleansed without his Maker? Will God justify sinful mortals, and clear them from guilt? or will he do so without their having an interest in the righteousness and gracious help of their promised Redeemer, when angels, once ministering spirits before his throne, receive the just recompence of their sins? Notwithstanding the seeming impunity of men for a short time, though living without God in the world, their doom is as certain as that of the fallen angels, and is continually overtaking them. Yet careless sinners note it so little, that they expect not the change, nor are wise to consider their latter end.

Chapter 5

Verses 1–5

Eliphaz here calls upon Job to answer his arguments. Were any of the saints or servants of God visited with such Divine judgments as Job, or did they ever behave like him under their sufferings? The term, "saints," holy, or more strictly, consecrated ones, seems in all ages to have been applied to the people of God, through the Sacrifice slain in the covenant of their reconciliation. Eliphaz doubts not that the sin of sinners directly tends to their ruin. They kill themselves by some lust or other; therefore, no doubt, Job has done some foolish thing, by which he has brought himself into this condition. The allusion was plain to Job's former prosperity; but there was no evidence of Job's wickedness, and the application to him was unfair and severe.

Verses 6–16

Eliphaz reminds Job, that no affliction comes by chance, nor is to be placed to second causes. The difference between prosperity and adversity is not so exactly observed, as that between day and night, summer and winter; but it is according to the will and counsel of God. We must not attribute our afflictions to fortune, for they are from God; nor our sins to fate, for they are from ourselves. Man is born in sin, and therefore born to trouble. There is nothing in this world we are born to, and can truly call our own, but sin and trouble. Actual transgressions are sparks that fly out of the furnace of original corruption. Such is the frailty of our bodies, and the vanity of all our enjoyments, that our troubles arise thence as the sparks fly upward; so many are they, and so fast does one follow another. Eliphaz reproves Job for not seeking God, instead of quarrelling with him. Is any afflicted? let him pray. It is heart's ease, a salve for every sore. Eliphaz speaks of rain, which we are apt to look upon as a little thing; but if we consider how it is produced, and what is produced by it, we shall see it to be a great work of power and goodness. Too often the great Author of all our comforts, and the manner in which they are conveyed to us, are not noticed, because they are received as things of course. In the ways of Providence, the experiences of some are encouragements to others, to hope the best in the worst of times; for it is the glory of God to send help to the helpless, and hope to the hopeless. And daring sinners are confounded, and forced to acknowledge the justice of God's proceedings.

Verses 17–27

Eliphaz gives to Job a word of caution and exhortation: Despise not thou the chastening of the Almighty. Call it a chastening, which comes from the Father's love, and is for the child's good; and notice it as a messenger from Heaven. Eliphaz also encourages Job to submit to his condition. A good man is happy though he be afflicted, for he has not lost his enjoyment of God, nor his title to heaven; nay, he is happy because he is afflicted. Correction mortifies his corruptions, weans his heart from the world, draws him nearer to God, brings him to his Bible, brings him to his knees. Though God wounds, yet he supports his people under afflictions, and in due time delivers them. Making a wound is sometimes part of a cure. Eliphaz gives Job precious promises of what God would do for him, if he humbled himself. Whatever troubles good men may be in, they shall do them no real harm. Being kept from sin, they are kept from the evil of trouble. And if the servants of Christ are not delivered from outward troubles, they are delivered by them, and while overcome by one trouble, they conquer all. Whatever is maliciously said against them shall not hurt them. They shall have wisdom and grace to manage their concerns. The greatest blessing, both in our employments and in our enjoyments, is to be kept from sin. They shall finish their course with joy and honour. That man lives long enough who has done his work, and is fit for another world. It is a mercy to die seasonably, as the corn is cut and housed when fully ripe; not till then, but then not suffered to stand any longer. Our times are in God's hands; it is well they are so. Believers are not to expect great wealth, long life, or to be free from trials. But all will be ordered for the best. And remark from Job's history, that steadiness of mind and heart under trial, is one of the highest attainments of faith. There is little exercise for faith when all things go well. But if God raises a storm, permits the enemy to send wave after wave, and seemingly stands aloof from our prayers, then, still to hang on and trust God, when we cannot trace him, this is the patience of the saints. Blessed Saviour! how sweet it is to look unto thee, the Author and Finisher of faith, in such moments!

Chapter 6

Verses 1–7

Job still justifies himself in his complaints. In addition to outward troubles, the inward sense of God's wrath took away all his courage and resolution. The feeling sense of the wrath of God is harder to bear than any outward afflictions. What then did the Saviour endure in the garden and on the cross, when he bare our sins, and his soul was made a sacrifice to Divine justice for us! Whatever burden of affliction, in body or estate, God is pleased to lay upon us, we may well submit to it as long as he continues to us the use of our reason, and the peace of our conscience; but if either of these is disturbed, our case is very pitiable. Job reflects upon his friends for their censures. He complains he had nothing offered for his relief, but what was in itself tasteless, loathsome, and burdensome.

Verses 8–13

Job had desired death as the happy end of his miseries. For this, Eliphaz had reproved him, but he asks for it again with more vehemence than before. It was very rash to speak thus of God destroying him. Who, for one hour, could endure the wrath of the Almighty, if he let loose his hand against him? Let us rather say with David, O spare me a little. Job grounds his comfort upon the testimony of his conscience, that he had been, in some degree, serviceable to the glory of God. Those who have grace in them, who have the evidence of it, and have it in exercise, have wisdom in them, which will be their help in the worst of times.

Verses 14–30

In his prosperity Job formed great expectations from his friends, but now was disappointed. This he compares to the failing of brooks in summer. Those who rest their expectations on the creature, will find it fail when it should help them; whereas those who make God their confidence, have help in the time of need, Heb **4**:**16**. Those who make gold their hope, sooner or later will be ashamed of it, and of their confidence in it. It is our wisdom to cease from man. Let us put all our confidence in the Rock of ages, not in broken reeds; in the Fountain of life, not in broken cisterns. The application is very close; "for now ye are nothing." It were well for us, if we had always such convictions of the vanity of the creature, as we have had, or shall have, on a sick-bed, a death-bed, or in trouble of conscience. Job upbraids his friends with their hard usage. Though in want, he desired no more from them than a good look and a good word. It often happens that, even when we expect little from man, we have less; but from God, even when we expect much, we have more. Though Job differed from them, yet he was ready to yield as soon as it was made to appear that he was in error. Though Job had been in fault, yet they ought not to have given him such hard usage. His righteousness he holds fast, and will not let it go. He felt that there had not been such iniquity in him as they supposed. But it is best to commit our characters to Him who keeps our souls; in the great day every upright believer shall have praise of God.

Chapter 7

Verses 1–6

Job here excuses what he could not justify, his desire of death. Observe man's present place: he is upon earth. He is yet on earth, not in hell. Is there not a time appointed for his abode here? yes, certainly, and the appointment is made by Him who made us and sent us here. During that, man's life is a warfare, and as day-labourers, who have the work of the day to do in its day, and must make up their account at night. Job had as much reason, he thought, to wish for death, as a poor servant that is tired with his work, has to wish for the shadows of the evening, when he shall go to rest. The sleep of the labouring man is sweet; nor can any rich man take so much satisfaction in his wealth, as the hireling in his day's wages. The comparison is plain; hear his complaint: His days were useless, and had long been so; but when we are not able to work for God, if we sit still quietly for him, we shall be accepted. His nights were restless. Whatever is grievous, it is good to see it appointed for us, and as designed for some holy end. When we have comfortable nights, we must see them also appointed to us, and be thankful for them. His body was noisome. See what vile bodies we have. His life was hastening apace. While we are living, every day, like the shuttle, leaves a thread behind: many weave the spider's web, which will fail, ch. **8**:**14**. But if, while we live, we live unto the Lord, in works of faith and labours of love, we shall have the benefit, for every man shall reap as he sowed, and wear as he wove.

Verses 7–16

Plain truths as to the shortness and vanity of man's life, and the certainty of death, do us good, when we think and speak of them with application to ourselves. Dying is done but once, and therefore it had need be well done. An error here is past retrieve. Other clouds arise, but the same cloud never returns: so a new generation of men is raised up, but the former generation vanishes away. Glorified saints shall return no more to the cares and sorrows of their houses; nor condemned sinners to the gaieties and pleasures of their houses. It concerns us to secure a better place when we die. From these reasons Job might have drawn a better conclusion than this, I will complain. When we have but a few breaths to draw, we should spend them in the holy, gracious breathings of faith and prayer; not in the noisome, noxious breathings of sin and corruption. We have much reason to pray, that He who keeps Israel, and neither slumbers nor sleeps, may keep us when we slumber and sleep. Job covets to rest in his grave. Doubtless, this was his infirmity; for though a good man would choose death rather than sin, yet he should be content to live as long as God pleases, because life is our opportunity of glorifying him, and preparing for heaven.

Verses 17–21

Job reasons with God concerning his dealings with man. But in the midst of this discourse, Job seems to have lifted up his thoughts to God with some faith and hope. Observe the concern he is in about his sins. The best men have to complain of sin; and the better they are, the more they will complain of it. God is the Preserver of our lives, and the Saviour of the souls of all that believe; but probably Job meant the Observer of men, whose eyes are upon the ways and hearts of all men. We can hide nothing from Him; let us plead guilty before his throne of grace, that we may not be condemned at his judgment-seat. Job maintained, against his friends, that he was not a hypocrite, not a wicked man, yet he owns to his God, that he had sinned. The best must so acknowledge, before the Lord. He seriously inquires how he might be at peace with God, and earnestly begs forgiveness of his sins. He means more than the removing of his outward trouble, and is earnest for the return of God's favour. Wherever the Lord removes the guilt of sin, he breaks the power of sin. To strengthen his prayer for pardon, Job pleads the prospect he had of dying quickly. If my sins be not pardoned while I live, I am lost and undone for ever. How wretched is sinful man without a knowledge of the Saviour!

Chapter 8

Verses 1–7

Job spake much to the purpose; but Bildad, like an eager, angry disputant, turns it all off with this, How long wilt thou speak these things? Men's meaning is not taken aright, and then they are rebuked, as if they were evil-doers. Even in disputes on religion, it is too common to treat others with sharpness, and their arguments with contempt. Bildad's discourse shows that he had not a favourable opinion of Job's character. Job owned that God did not pervert judgment; yet it did not therefore follow that his children were cast-aways, or that they did for some great transgression. Extraordinary afflictions are not always the punishment of extraordinary sins, sometimes they are the trials of extraordinary graces: in judging of another's case, we ought to take the favorable side. Bildad puts Job in hope, that if he were indeed upright, he should yet see a good end of his present troubles. This is God's way of enriching the souls of his people with graces and comforts. The beginning is small, but the progress is to perfection. Dawning light grows to noon-day.

Verses 8–19

Bildad discourses well of hypocrites and evil-doers, and the fatal end of all their hopes and joys. He proves this truth of the destruction of the hopes and joys of hypocrites, by an appeal to former times. Bildad refers to the testimony of the ancients. Those teach best that utter words out of their heart, that speak from an experience of spiritual and divine things. A rush growing in fenny ground, looking very green, but withering in dry weather, represents the hypocrite's profession, which is maintained only in times of prosperity. The spider's web, spun with great skill, but easily swept away, represents a man's pretensions to religion when without the grace of God in his heart. A formal professor flatters himself in his own eyes, doubts not of his salvation, is secure, and cheats the world with his vain confidences. The flourishing of the tree, planted in the garden, striking root to the rock, yet after a time cut down and thrown aside, represents wicked men, when most firmly established, suddenly thrown down and forgotten. This doctrine of the vanity of a hypocrite's confidence, or the prosperity of a wicked man, is sound; but it was not applicable to the case of Job, if confined to the present world.

Verses 20–22

Bildad here assures Job, that as he was so he should fare; therefore they concluded, that as he fared so he was. God will not cast away an upright man; he may be cast down for a time, but he shall not be cast away for ever. Sin brings ruin on persons and families. Yet to argue, that Job was an ungodly, wicked man, was unjust and uncharitable. The mistake in these reasonings arose from Job's friends not distinguishing between the present state of trial and discipline, and the future state of final judgment. May we choose the portion, possess the confidence, bear the cross, and die the death of the righteous; and, in the mean time, be careful neither to wound others by rash judgments, nor to distress ourselves needlessly about the opinions of our fellow-creatures.

Chapter 9

Verses 1–13

In this answer Job declared that he did not doubt the justice of God, when he denied himself to be a hypocrite; for how should man be just with God? Before him he pleaded guilty of sins more than could be counted; and if God should contend with him in judgment, he could not justify one out of a thousand, of all the thoughts, words, and actions of his life; therefore he deserved worse than all his present sufferings. When Job mentions the wisdom and power of God, he forgets his complaints. We are unfit to judge of God's proceedings, because we know not what he does, or what he designs. God acts with power which no creature can resist. Those who think they have strength enough to help others, will not be able to help themselves against it.

Verses 14–21

Job is still righteous in his own eyes, ch. **32**:**1**, and this answer, though it sets forth the power and majesty of God, implies that the question between the afflicted and the Lord of providence, is a question of might, and not of right; and we begin to discover the evil fruits of pride and of a self-righteous spirit. Job begins to manifest a disposition to condemn God, that he may justify himself, for which he is afterwards reproved. Still Job knew so much of himself, that he durst not stand a trial. If we say, We have no sin, we not only deceive ourselves, but we affront God; for we sin in saying so, and give the lie to the Scripture. But Job reflected on God's goodness and justice in saying his affliction was without cause.

Verses 22–24

Job touches briefly upon the main point now in dispute. His friends maintained that those who are righteous and good, always prosper in this world, and that none but the wicked are in misery and distress: he said, on the contrary, that it is a common thing for the wicked to prosper, and the righteous to be greatly afflicted. Yet there is too much passion in what Job here says, for God doth not afflict willingly. When the spirit is heated with dispute or with discontent, we have need to set a watch before our lips.

Verses 25–35

What little need have we of pastimes, and what great need to redeem time, when it runs on so fast towards eternity! How vain the enjoyments of time, which we may quite lose while yet time continues! The remembrance of having done our duty will be pleasing afterwards; so will not the remembrance of having got worldly wealth, when it is all lost and gone. Job's complaint of God, as one that could not be appeased and would not relent, was the language of his corruption. There is a Mediator, a Daysman, or Umpire, for us, even God's own beloved Son, who has purchased peace for us with the blood of his cross, who is able to save to the uttermost all who come unto God through him. If we trust in his name, our sins will be buried in the depths of the sea, we shall be washed from all our filthiness, and made whiter than snow, so that none can lay any thing to our charge. We shall be clothed with the robes of righteousness and salvation, adorned with the graces of the Holy Spirit, and presented faultless before the presence of his glory with exceeding joy. May we learn the difference between justifying ourselves, and being thus justified by God himself. Let the tempest-tossed soul consider Job, and notice that others have passed this dreadful gulf; and though they found it hard to believe that God would hear or deliver them, yet he rebuked the storm, and brought them to the desired haven. Resist the devil; give not place to hard thoughts of God, or desperate conclusions about thyself. Come to Him who invites the weary and heavy laden; who promises in nowise to cast them out.

Chapter 10

Verses 1–7

Job, being weary of his life, resolves to complain, but he will not charge God with unrighteousness. Here is a prayer that he might be delivered from the sting of his afflictions, which is sin. When God afflicts us, he contends with us; when he contends with us, there is always a reason; and it is desirable to know the reason, that we may repent of and forsake the sin for which God has a controversy with us. But when, like Job, we speak in the bitterness of our souls, we increase guilt and vexation. Let us harbour no hard thoughts of God; we shall hereafter see there was no cause for them. Job is sure that God does not discover things, nor judge of them, as men do; therefore he thinks it strange that God continues him under affliction, as if he must take time to inquire into his sin.

Verses 8–13

Job seems to argue with God, as if he only formed and preserved him for misery. God made us, not we ourselves. How sad that those bodies should be instruments of unrighteousness, which are capable of being temples of the Holy Ghost! But the soul is the life, the soul is the man, and this is the gift of God. If we plead with ourselves as an inducement to duty, God made me and maintains me, we may plead as an argument for mercy, Thou hast made me, do thou new-make me; I am thine, save me.

Verses 14–22

Job did not deny that as a sinner he deserved his sufferings; but he thought that justice was executed upon him with peculiar rigour. His gloom, unbelief, and hard thoughts of God, were as much to be ascribed to Satan's inward temptations, and his anguish of soul, under the sense of God's displeasure, as to his outward trials, and remaining depravity. Our Creator, become in Christ our Redeemer also, will not destroy the work of his hands in any humble believer; but will renew him unto holiness, that he may enjoy eternal life. If anguish on earth renders the grave a desirable refuge, what will be their condition who are condemned to the blackness of darkness for ever? Let every sinner seek deliverance from that dreadful state, and every believer be thankful to Jesus, who delivereth from the wrath to come.

Chapter 11

Verses 1–6

Zophar attacked Job with great vehemence. He represented him as a man that loved to hear himself speak, though he could say nothing to the purpose, and as a man that maintained falsehoods. He desired God would show Job that less punishment was exacted than he deserved. We are ready, with much assurance, to call God to act in our quarrels, and to think that if he would but speak, he would take our part. We ought to leave all disputes to the judgment of God, which we are sure is according to truth; but those are not always right who are most forward to appeal to the Divine judgment.

Verses 7–12

Zophar speaks well concerning God and his greatness and glory, concerning man and his vanity and folly. See here what man is; and let him be humbled. God sees this concerning vain man, that he would be wise, would be thought so, though he is born like a wild ass's colt, so unteachable and untameable. Man is a vain creature; empty, so the word is. Yet he is a proud creature, and self-conceited. He would be wise, would be thought so, though he will not submit to the laws of wisdom. He would be wise, he reaches after forbidden wisdom, and, like his first parents, aiming to be wise above what is written, loses the tree of life for the tree of knowledge. Is such a creature as this fit to contend with God?

Verses 13–20

Zophar exhorts Job to repentance, and gives him encouragement, yet mixed with hard thoughts of him. He thought that worldly prosperity was always the lot of the righteous, and that Job was to be deemed a hypocrite unless his prosperity was restored. Then shalt thou lift up thy face without spot; that is, thou mayst come boldly to the throne of grace, and not with the terror and amazement expressed in ch. **9**:**34**. If we are looked upon in the face of the Anointed, our faces that were cast down may be lifted up; though polluted, being now washed with the blood of Christ, they may be lifted up without spot. We may draw near in full assurance of faith, when we are sprinkled from an evil conscience, Heb **10**:**22**.

Chapter 12

Verses 1–5

Job upbraids his friends with the good opinion they had of their own wisdom compared with his. We are apt to call reproofs reproaches, and to think ourselves mocked when advised and admonished; this is our folly; yet here was colour for this charge. He suspected the true cause of their conduct to be, that they despised him who was fallen into poverty. It is the way of the world. Even the just, upright man, if he comes under a cloud, is looked upon with contempt.

Verses 6–11

Job appeals to facts. The most audacious robbers, oppressors, and impious wretches, often prosper. Yet this is not by fortune or chance; the Lord orders these things. Worldly prosperity is of small value in his sight: he has better things for his children. Job resolves all into the absolute proprietorship which God has in all the creatures. He demands from his friends liberty to judge of what they had said; he appeals to any fair judgment. (Job **12**:**12-25**)

Verses 12–25

This is a noble discourse of Job concerning the wisdom, power, and sovereignty of God, in ordering all the affairs of the children of men, according to the counsel of His own will, which none can resist. It were well if wise and good men, who differ about lesser things, would see how it is for their honour and comfort, and the good of others, to dwell most upon the great things in which they agree. Here are no complaints, or reflections. He gives many instances of God's powerful management of the children of men, overruling all their counsels, and overcoming all their oppositions. Having all strength and wisdom, God knows how to make use, even of those who are foolish and bad; otherwise there is so little wisdom and so little honesty in the world, that all had been in confusion and ruin long ago. These important truths were suited to convince the disputants that they were out of their depth in attempting to assign the Lord's reasons for afflicting Job; his ways are unsearchable, and his judgments past finding out. Let us remark what beautiful illustrations there are in the word of God, confirming his sovereignty, and wisdom in that sovereignty: but the highest and infinitely the most important is, that the Lord Jesus was crucified by the malice of the Jews; and who but the Lord could have known that this one event was the salvation of the world?

Chapter 13

Verses 1–12

With self-preference, Job declared that he needed not to be taught by them. Those who dispute are tempted to magnify themselves, and lower their brethren, more than is fit. When dismayed or distressed with the fear of wrath, the force of temptation, or the weight of affliction, we should apply to the Physician of our souls, who never rejects any, never prescribes amiss, and never leaves any case uncured. To Him we may speak at all times. To broken hearts and wounded consciences, all creatures, without Christ, are physicians of no value. Job evidently speaks with a very angry spirit against his friends. They had advanced some truths which nearly concerned Job, but the heart unhumbled before God, never meekly receives the reproofs of men.

Verses 13–22

Job resolved to cleave to the testimony his own conscience gave of his uprightness. He depended upon God for justification and salvation, the two great things we hope for through Christ. Temporal salvation he little expected, but of his eternal salvation he was very confident; that God would not only be his Saviour to make him happy, but his salvation, in the sight and enjoyment of whom he should be happy. He knew himself not to be a hypocrite, and concluded that he should not be rejected. We should be well pleased with God as a Friend, even when he seems against us as an enemy. We must believe that all shall work for good to us, even when all seems to make against us. We must cleave to God, yea, though we cannot for the present find comfort in him. In a dying hour, we must derive from him living comforts; and this is to trust in him, though he slay us.

Verses 23–28

Job begs to have his sins discovered to him. A true penitent is willing to know the worst of himself; and we should all desire to know what our transgressions are, that we may confess them, and guard against them for the future. Job complains sorrowfully of God's severe dealings with him. Time does not wear out the guilt of sin. When God writes bitter things against us, his design is to make us bring forgotten sins to mind, and so to bring us to repent of them, as to break us off from them. Let young persons beware of indulging in sin. Even in this world they may so possess the sins of their youth, as to have months of sorrow for moments of pleasure. Their wisdom is to remember their Creator in their early days, that they may have assured hope, and sweet peace of conscience, as the solace of their declining years. Job also complains that his present mistakes are strictly noticed. So far from this, God deals not with us according to our deserts. This was the language of Job's melancholy views. If God marks our steps, and narrowly examines our paths, in judgment, both body and soul feel his righteous vengeance. This will be the awful case of unbelievers, yet there is salvation devised, provided, and made known in Christ.

Chapter 14

Verses 1–6

Job enlarges upon the condition of man, addressing himself also to God. Every man of Adam's fallen race is short-lived. All his show of beauty, happiness, and splendour falls before the stroke of sickness or death, as the flower before the scythe; or passes away like the shadow. How is it possible for a man's conduct to be sinless, when his heart is by nature unclean? Here is a clear proof that Job understood and believed the doctrine of original sin. He seems to have intended it as a plea, why the Lord should not deal with him according to his own works, but according to His mercy and grace. It is determined, in the counsel and decree of God, how long we shall live. Our times are in his hands, the powers of nature act under him; in him we live and move. And it is very useful to reflect seriously on the shortness and uncertainty of human life, and the fading nature of all earthly enjoyments. But it is still more important to look at the cause, and remedy of these evils. Until we are born of the Spirit, no spiritually good thing dwells in us, or can proceed from us. Even the little good in the regenerate is defiled with sin. We should therefore humble ourselves before God, and cast ourselves wholly on the mercy of God, through our Divine Surety. We should daily seek the renewing of the Holy Ghost, and look to heaven as the only place of perfect holiness and happiness.

Verses 7–15

Though a tree is cut down, yet, in a moist situation, shoots come forth, and grow up as a newly planted tree. But when man is cut off by death, he is for ever removed from his place in this world. The life of man may fitly be compared to the waters of a land flood, which spread far, but soon dry up. All Job's expressions here show his belief in the great doctrine of the resurrection. Job's friends proving miserable comforters, he pleases himself with the expectation of a change. If our sins are forgiven, and our hearts renewed to holiness, heaven will be the rest of our souls, while our bodies are hidden in the grave from the malice of our enemies, feeling no more pain from our corruptions, or our corrections.

Verses 16–22

Job's faith and hope spake, and grace appeared to revive; but depravity again prevailed. He represents God as carrying matters to extremity against him. The Lord must prevail against all who contend with him. God may send disease and pain, we may lose all comfort in those near and dear to us, every hope of earthly happiness may be destroyed, but God will receive the believer into realms of eternal happiness. But what a change awaits the prosperous unbeliever! How will he answer when God shall call him to his tribunal? The Lord is yet upon a mercy-seat, ready to be gracious. Oh that sinners would be wise, that they would consider their latter end! While man's flesh is upon him, that is, the body he is so loth to lay down, it shall have pain; and while his soul is within him, that is, the spirit he is so loth to resign, it shall mourn. Dying work is hard work; dying pangs often are sore pangs. It is folly for men to defer repentance to a death-bed, and to have that to do which is the one thing needful, when unfit to do anything.

Chapter 15

Verses 1–16

Eliphaz begins a second attack upon Job, instead of being softened by his complaints. He unjustly charges Job with casting off the fear of God, and all regard to him, and restraining prayer. See in what religion is summed up, fearing God, and praying to him; the former the most needful principle, the latter the most needful practice. Eliphaz charges Job with self-conceit. He charges him with contempt of the counsels and comforts given him by his friends. We are apt to think that which we ourselves say is important, when others, with reason, think little of it. He charges him with opposition to God. Eliphaz ought not to have put harsh constructions upon the words of one well known for piety, and now in temptation. It is plain that these disputants were deeply convinced of the doctrine of original sin, and the total depravity of human nature. Shall we not admire the patience of God in bearing with us? and still more his love to us in the redemption of Christ Jesus his beloved Son?

Verses 17–35

Eliphaz maintains that the wicked are certainly miserable: whence he would infer, that the miserable are certainly wicked, and therefore Job was so. But because many of God's people have prospered in this world, it does not therefore follow that those who are crossed and made poor, as Job, are not God's people. Eliphaz shows also that wicked people, particularly oppressors, are subject to continual terror, live very uncomfortably, and perish very miserably. Will the prosperity of presumptuous sinners end miserably as here described? Then let the mischiefs which befal others, be our warnings. Though no chastening for the present seemeth to be joyous, but grievous, nevertheless, afterward it yieldeth the peaceable fruits of righteousness to them that are exercised thereby. No calamity, no trouble, however heavy, however severe, can rob a follower of the Lord of his favour. What shall separate him from the love of Christ?

Chapter 16

Verses 1–5

Eliphaz had represented Job's discourses as unprofitable, and nothing to the purpose; Job here gives his the same character. Those who pass censures, must expect to have them retorted; it is easy, it is endless, but what good does it do? Angry answers stir up men's passions, but never convince their judgments, nor set truth in a clear light. What Job says of his friends is true of all creatures, in comparison with God; one time or other we shall be made to see and own that miserable comforters are they all. When under convictions of sin, terrors of conscience, or the arrests of death, only the blessed Spirit can comfort effectually; all others, without him, do it miserably, and to no purpose. Whatever our brethren's sorrows are, we ought by sympathy to make them our own; they may soon be so.

Verses 6–16

Here is a doleful representation of Job's grievances. What reason we have to bless God, that we are not making such complaints! Even good men, when in great troubles, have much ado not to entertain hard thoughts of God. Eliphaz had represented Job as unhumbled under his affliction: No, says Job, I know better things; the dust is now the fittest place for me. In this he reminds us of Christ, who was a man of sorrows, and pronounced those blessed that mourn, for they shall be comforted.

Verses 17–22

Job's condition was very deplorable; but he had the testimony of his conscience for him, that he never allowed himself in any gross sin. No one was ever more ready to acknowledge sins of infirmity. Eliphaz had charged him with hypocrisy in religion, but he specifies prayer, the great act of religion, and professes that in this he was pure, though not from all infirmity. He had a God to go to, who he doubted not took full notice of all his sorrows. Those who pour out tears before God, though they cannot plead for themselves, by reason of their defects, have a Friend to plead for them, even the Son of man, and on him we must ground all our hopes of acceptance with God. To die, is to go the way whence we shall not return. We must all of us, very certainly, and very shortly, go this journey. Should not then the Saviour be precious to our souls? And ought we not to be ready to obey and to suffer for his sake? If our consciences are sprinkled with his atoning blood, and testify that we are not living in sin or hypocrisy, when we go the way whence we shall not return, it will be a release from prison, and an entrance into everlasting happiness.

Chapter 17

Verses 1–9

Job reflects upon the harsh censures his friends had passed upon him, and, looking on himself as a dying man, he appeals to God. Our time is ending. It concerns us carefully to redeem the days of time, and to spend them in getting ready for eternity. We see the good use the righteous should make of Job's afflictions from God, from enemies, and from friends. Instead of being discouraged in the service of God, by the hard usage this faithful servant of God met with, they should be made bold to proceed and persevere therein. Those who keep their eye upon heaven as their end, will keep their feet in the paths of religion as their way, whatever difficulties and discouragements they may meet with.

Verses 10–16

Job's friends had pretended to comfort him with the hope of his return to a prosperous estate; he here shows that those do not go wisely about the work of comforting the afflicted, who fetch their comforts from the possibility of recovery in this world. It is our wisdom to comfort ourselves, and others, in distress, with that which will not fail; the promise of God, his love and grace, and a well-grounded hope of eternal life. See how Job reconciles himself to the grave. Let this make believers willing to die; it is but going to bed; they are weary, and it is time that they were in their beds. Why should not they go willingly when their Father calls them? Let us remember our bodies are allied to corruption, the worm and the dust; and let us seek for that lively hope which shall be fulfilled, when the hope of the wicked shall be put out in darkness; that when our bodies are in the grave, our souls may enjoy the rest reserved for the people of God.

Chapter 18

Verses 1–4

Bildad had before given Job good advice and encouragement; here he used nothing but rebukes, and declared his ruin. And he concluded that Job shut out the providence of God from the management of human affairs, because he would not admit himself to be wicked.

Verses 5–10

Bildad describes the miserable condition of a wicked man; in which there is much certain truth, if we consider that a sinful condition is a sad condition, and that sin will be men's ruin, if they do not repent. Though Bildad thought the application of it to Job was easy, yet it was not safe nor just. It is common for angry disputants to rank their opponents among God's enemies, and to draw wrong conclusions from important truths. The destruction of the wicked is foretold. That destruction is represented under the similitude of a beast or bird caught in a snare, or a malefactor taken into custody. Satan, as he was a murderer, so he was a robber, from the beginning. He, the tempter, lays snares for sinners wherever they go. If he makes them sinful like himself, he will make them miserable like himself. Satan hunts for the precious life. In the transgression of an evil man there is a snare for himself, and God is preparing for his destruction. See here how the sinner runs himself into the snare.

Verses 11–21

Bildad describes the destruction wicked people are kept for, in the other world, and which in some degree, often seizes them in this world. The way of sin is the way of fear, and leads to everlasting confusion, of which the present terrors of an impure conscience are earnests, as in Cain and Judas. Miserable indeed is a wicked man's death, how secure soever his life was. See him dying; all that he trusts to for his support shall be taken from him. How happy are the saints, and how indebted to the lord Jesus, by whom death is so far done away and changed, that this king of terrors is become a friend and a servant! See the wicked man's family sunk and cut off. His children shall perish, either with him or after him. Those who consult the true honour of their family, and its welfare, will be afraid of withering all by sin. The judgments of God follow the wicked man after death in this world, as a proof of the misery his soul is in after death, and as an earnest of that everlasting shame and contempt to which he shall rise in the great day. The memory of the just is blessed, but the name of the wicked shall rot, Pr **10**:**7**. It would be well if this report of wicked men would cause any to flee from the wrath to come, from which their power, policy, and riches cannot deliver them. But Jesus ever liveth to deliver all who trust in him. Bear up then, suffering believers. Ye shall for a little time have sorrow, but your Beloved, your Saviour, will see you again; your hearts shall rejoice, and your joy no man taketh away.

Chapter 19

Verses 1–7

Job's friends blamed him as a wicked man, because he was so afflicted; here he describes their unkindness, showing that what they condemned was capable of excuse. Harsh language from friends, greatly adds to the weight of afflictions: yet it is best not to lay it to heart, lest we harbour resentment. Rather let us look to Him who endured the contradiction of sinners against himself, and was treated with far more cruelty than Job was, or we can be. (Job **19**:**8-22**)

Verses 8–22

How doleful are Job's complaints! What is the fire of hell but the wrath of God! Seared consciences will feel it hereafter, but do not fear it now: enlightened consciences fear it now, but shall not feel it hereafter. It is a very common mistake to think that those whom God afflicts he treats as his enemies. Every creature is that to us which God makes it to be; yet this does not excuse Job's relations and friends. How uncertain is the friendship of men! but if God be our Friend, he will not fail us in time of need. What little reason we have to indulge the body, which, after all our care, is consumed by diseases it has in itself. Job recommends himself to the compassion of his friends, and justly blames their harshness. It is very distressing to one who loves God, to be bereaved at once of outward comfort and of inward consolation; yet if this, and more, come upon a believer, it does not weaken the proof of his being a child of God and heir of glory.

Verses 23–29

The Spirit of God, at this time, seems to have powerfully wrought on the mind of Job. Here he witnessed a good confession; declared the soundness of his faith, and the assurance of his hope. Here is much of Christ and heaven; and he that said such things are these, declared plainly that he sought the better country, that is, the heavenly. Job was taught of God to believe in a living Redeemer; to look for the resurrection of the dead, and the life of the world to come; he comforted himself with the expectation of these. Job was assured, that this Redeemer of sinners from the yoke of Satan and the condemnation of sin, was his Redeemer, and expected salvation through him; and that he was a living Redeemer, though not yet come in the flesh; and that at the last day he would appear as the Judge of the world, to raise the dead, and complete the redemption of his people. With what pleasure holy Job enlarges upon this! May these faithful sayings be engraved by the Holy Spirit upon our hearts. We are all concerned to see that the root of the matter be in us. A living, quickening, commanding principle of grace in the heart, is the root of the matter; as necessary to our religion as the root of the tree, to which it owes both its fixedness and its fruitfulness. Job and his friends differed concerning the methods of Providence, but they agreed in the root of the matter, the belief of another world.

Chapter 20

Verses 1–9

Zophar's discourse is upon the certain misery of the wicked. The triumph of the wicked and the joy of the hypocrite are fleeting. The pleasures and gains of sin bring disease and pain; they end in remorse, anguish, and ruin. Dissembled piety is double iniquity, and the ruin that attends it will be accordingly.

Verses 10–22

The miserable condition of the wicked man in this world is fully set forth. The lusts of the flesh are here called the sins of his youth. His hiding it and keeping it under his tongue, denotes concealment of his beloved lust, and delight therein. But He who knows what is in the heart, knows what is under the tongue, and will discover it. The love of the world, and of the wealth of it, also is wickedness, and man sets his heart upon these. Also violence and injustice, these sins bring God's judgments upon nations and families. Observe the punishment of the wicked man for these things. Sin is turned into gall, than which nothing is more bitter; it will prove to him poison; so will all unlawful gains be. In his fulness he shall be in straits, through the anxieties of his own mind. To be led by the sanctifying grace of God to restore what was unjustly gotten, as Zaccheus was, is a great mercy. But to be forced to restore by the horrors of a despairing conscience, as Judas was, has no benefit and comfort attending it.

Verses 23–29

Zophar, having described the vexations which attend wicked practices, shows their ruin from God's wrath. There is no fence against this, but in Christ, who is the only Covert from the storm and tempest, Isa **32**:**2**. Zophar concludes, "This is the portion of a wicked man from God;" it is allotted him. Never was any doctrine better explained, or worse applied, than this by Zophar, who intended to prove Job a hypocrite. Let us receive the good explanation, and make a better application, for warning to ourselves, to stand in awe and sin not. One view of Jesus, directed by the Holy Spirit, and by him suitably impressed upon our souls, will quell a thousand carnal reasonings about the suffering of the faithful.

Chapter 21

Verses 1–6

Job comes closer to the question in dispute. This was, Whether outward prosperity is a mark of the true church, and the true members of it, so that ruin of a man's prosperity proves him a hypocrite? This they asserted, but Job denied. If they looked upon him, they might see misery enough to demand compassion, and their bold interpretations of this mysterious providence should be turned into silent wonder.

Verses 7–16

Job says, Remarkable judgments are sometimes brought upon notorious sinners, but not always. Wherefore is it so? This is the day of God's patience; and, in some way or other, he makes use of the prosperity of the wicked to serve his own counsels, while it ripens them for ruin; but the chief reason is, because he will make it appear there is another world. These prospering sinners make light of God and religion, as if because they have so much of this world, they had no need to look after another. But religion is not a vain thing. If it be so to us, we may thank ourselves for resting on the outside of it. Job shows their folly.

Verses 17–26

Job had described the prosperity of wicked people; in these **verses** he opposes this to what his friends had maintained about their certain ruin in this life. He reconciles this to the holiness and justice of God. Even while they prosper thus, they are light and worthless, of no account with God, or with wise men. In the height of their pomp and power, there is but a step between them and ruin. Job refers the difference Providence makes between one wicked man and another, into the wisdom of God. He is Judge of all the earth, and he will do right. So vast is the disproportion between time and eternity, that if hell be the lot of every sinner at last, it makes little difference if one goes singing thither, and another sighing. If one wicked man die in a palace, and another in a dungeon, the worm that dies not, and the fire that is not quenched, will be the same to them. Thus differences in this world are not worth perplexing ourselves about.

Verses 27–34

Job opposes the opinion of his friends, That the wicked are sure to fall into visible and remarkable ruin, and none but the wicked; upon which principle they condemned Job as wicked. Turn to whom you will, you will find that the punishment of sinners is designed more for the other world than for this, Jude **1**:**14**, **15**. The sinner is here supposed to live in a great deal of power. The sinner shall have a splendid funeral: a poor thing for any man to be proud of the prospect of. He shall have a stately monument. And a valley with springs of water to keep the turf green, was accounted an honourable burial place among eastern people; but such things are vain distinctions. Death closes his prosperity. It is but a poor encouragement to die, that others have died before us. That which makes a man die with true courage, is, with faith to remember that Jesus Christ died and was laid in the grave, not only before us, but for us. That He hath gone before us, and died for us, who is alive and liveth for us, is true consolation in the hour of death.

Chapter 22

Verses 1–4

Eliphaz considers that, because Job complained so much of his afflictions, he thought God was unjust in afflicting him; but Job was far from thinking so. What Eliphaz says, is unjustly applied to Job, but it is very true, that when God does us good it is not because he is indebted to us. Man's piety is no profit to God, no gain. The gains of religion to men are infinitely greater than the losses of it. God is a Sovereign, who gives no account of his conduct; but he is perfectly wise, just, faithful, good, and merciful. He approves the likeness of his own holiness, and delights in the fruits of his Spirit; he accepts the thankful services of the humble believer, while he rejects the proud claim of the self-confident.

Verses 5–14

Eliphaz brought heavy charges against Job, without reason for his accusations, except that Job was visited as he supposed God always visited every wicked man. He charges him with oppression, and that he did harm with his wealth and power in the time of his prosperity.

Verses 15–20

Eliphaz would have Job mark the old way that wicked men have trodden, and see what the end of their way was. It is good for us to mark it, that we may not walk therein. But if others are consumed, and we are not, instead of blaming them, and lifting up ourselves, as Eliphaz does here, we ought to be thankful to God, and take it for a warning.

Verses 21–30

The answer of Eliphaz wrongly implied that Job had hitherto not known God, and that prosperity in this life would follow his sincere conversion. The counsel Eliphaz here gives is good, though, as to Job, it was built upon a false supposition that he was a stranger and enemy to God. Let us beware of slandering our brethren; and if it be our lot to suffer in this manner, let us remember how Job was treated; yea, how Jesus was reviled, that we may be patient. Let us examine whether there may not be some colour for the slander, and walk watchfully, so as to be clear of all appearances of evil.

Chapter 23

Verses 1–7

Job appeals from his friends to the just judgement of God. He wants to have his cause tried quickly. Blessed be God, we may know where to find him. He is in Christ, reconciling the world unto himself; and upon a mercy-seat, waiting to be gracious. Thither the sinner may go; and there the believer may order his cause before Him, with arguments taken from his promises, his covenant, and his glory. A patient waiting for death and judgment is our wisdom and duty, and it cannot be without a holy fear and trembling. A passionate wishing for death or judgement is our sin and folly, and ill becomes us, as it did Job.

Verses 8–12

Job knew that the Lord was every where present; but his mind was in such confusion, that he could get no fixed view of God's merciful presence, so as to find comfort by spreading his case before him. His views were all gloomy. God seemed to stand at a distance, and frown upon him. Yet Job expressed his assurance that he should be brought forth, tried, and approved, for he had obeyed the precepts of God. He had relished and delighted in the truths and commandments of God. Here we should notice that Job justified himself rather than God, or in opposition to him, ch. **32**:**2**. Job might feel that he was clear from the charges of his friends, but boldly to assert that, though visited by the hand of God, it was not a chastisement of sin, was his error. And he is guilty of a second, when he denies that there are dealings of Providence with men in this present life, wherein the injured find redress, and the evil are visited for their sins.

Verses 13–17

As Job does not once question but that his trials are from the hand of God, and that there is no such thing as chance, how does he account for them? The principle on which he views them is, that the hope and reward of the faithful servants of God are only laid up in another life; and he maintains that it is plain to all, that the wicked are not treated according to their deserts in this life, but often directly the re**verse**. But though the obtaining of mercy, the first-fruits of the Spirit of grace, pledges a God, who will certainly finish the work which he has began; yet the afflicted believer is not to conclude that all prayer and entreaty will be in vain, and that he should sink into despair, and faint when he is reproved of Him. He cannot tell but the intention of God in afflicting him may be to produce penitence and prayer in his heart. May we learn to obey and trust the Lord, even in tribulation; to live or die as he pleases: we know not for what good ends our lives may be shortened or prolonged.

Chapter 24

Verses 1–12

Job discourses further about the prosperity of the wicked. That many live at ease who are ungodly and profane, he had showed, ch. xxi. Here he shows that many who live in open defiance of all the laws of justice, succeed in wicked practices; and we do not see them reckoned with in this world. He notices those that do wrong under pretence of law and authority; and robbers, those that do wrong by force. He says, "God layeth not folly to them;" that is, he does not at once send his judgments, nor make them examples, and so manifest their folly to all the world. But he that gets riches, and not by right, at his end shall be a fool, Jer **17**:**11**.

Verses 13–17

See what care and pains wicked men take to compass their wicked designs; let it shame our negligence and slothfulness in doing good. See what pains those take, who make provision for the flesh to fulfil the lusts of it: pains to compass, and then to hide that which will end in death and hell at last. Less pains would mortify and crucify the flesh, and be life and heaven at last. Shame came in with sin, and everlasting shame is at the end of it. See the misery of sinners; they are exposed to continual frights: yet see their folly; they are afraid of coming under the eye of men, but have no dread of God's eye, which is always upon them: they are not afraid of doing things which they are afraid of being known to do.

Verses 18–25

Sometimes how gradual is the decay, how quiet the departure of a wicked person, how is he honoured, and how soon are all his cruelties and oppressions forgotten! They are taken off with other men, as the harvestman gathers the ears of corn as they come to hand. There will often appear much to resemble the wrong view of Providence Job takes in this chapter. But we are taught by the word of inspiration, that these notions are formed in ignorance, from partial views. The providence of God, in the affairs of men, is in every thing a just and wise providence. Let us apply this whenever the Lord may try us. He cannot do wrong. The unequalled sorrows of the Son of God when on earth, unless looked at in this view, perplex the mind. But when we behold him, as the sinner's Surety, bearing the curse, we can explain why he should endure that wrath which was due to sin, that Divine justice might be satisfied, and his people saved.

Chapter 25

Bildad shows that man cannot be justified before God.

—Bildad drops the question concerning the prosperity of wicked men; but shows the infinite distance there is between God and man. He represents to Job some truths he had too much overlooked. Man's righteousness and holiness, at the best, are nothing in comparison with God's, Ps **89**:**6**. As God is so great and glorious, how can man, who is guilty and impure, appear before him? We need to be born again of water and of the Holy Ghost, and to be bathed again and again in the blood of Christ, that Fountain opened, Zec **13**:**1**. We should be humbled as mean, guilty, polluted creatures, and renounce self-dependence. But our vileness will commend Christ's condescension and love; the riches of his mercy and the power of his grace will be magnified to all eternity by every sinner he redeems.

Chapter 26

Verses 1–4

Job derided Bildad's answer; his words were a mixture of peevishness and self-preference. Bildad ought to have laid before Job the consolations, rather than the terrors of the Almighty. Christ knows how to speak what is proper for the weary, Isa **50**:**4**; and his ministers should not grieve those whom God would not have made sad. We are often disappointed in our expectations from our friends who should comfort us; but the Comforter, the Holy Ghost, never mistakes, nor fails of his end.

Verses 5–14

Many striking instances are here given of the wisdom and power of God, in the creation and preservation of the world. If we look about us, to the earth and waters here below, we see his almighty power. If we consider hell beneath, though out of our sight, yet we may conceive the discoveries of God's power there. If we look up to heaven above, we see displays of God's almighty power. By his Spirit, the eternal Spirit that moved upon the face of the waters, the breath of his mouth, Ps **33**:**6**, he has not only made the heavens, but beautified them. By redemption, all the other wonderful works of the Lord are eclipsed; and we may draw near, and taste his grace, learn to love him, and walk with delight in his ways. The ground of the controversy between Job and the other disputants was, that they unjustly thought from his afflictions that he must have been guilty of heinous crimes. They appear not to have duly considered the evil and just desert of original sin; nor did they take into account the gracious designs of God in purifying his people. Job also darkened counsel by words without knowledge. But his views were more distinct. He does not appear to have alleged his personal righteousness as the ground of his hope towards God. Yet what he admitted in a general view of his case, he in effect denied, while he complained of his sufferings as unmerited and severe; that very complaint proving the necessity for their being sent, in order to his being further humbled in the sight of God.

Chapter 27

Verses 1–6

Job's friends now suffered him to speak, and he proceeded in a grave and useful manner. Job had confidence in the goodness both of his cause and of his God; and cheerfully committed his cause to him. But Job had not due reverence when he spake of God as taking away his judgment, and vexing his soul. To resolve that our hearts shall not reproach us, while we hold fast our integrity, baffles the designs of the evil spirit.

Verses 7–10

Job looked upon the condition of a hypocrite and a wicked man, to be most miserable. If they gained through life by their profession, and kept up their presumptuous hope till death, what would that avail when God required their souls? The more comfort we find in our religion, the more closely we shall cleave to it. Those who have no delight in God, are easily drawn away by the pleasures, and easily overcome by the crosses of this life. (Job **27**:**11-23**)

Verses 11–23

Job's friends, on the same subject, spoke of the misery of wicked men before death as proportioned to their crimes; Job considered that if it were not so, still the consequences of their death would be dreadful. Job undertook to set this matter in a true light. Death to a godly man, is like a fair gale of wind to convey him to the heavenly country; but, to a wicked man, it is like a storm, that hurries him away to destruction. While he lived, he had the benefit of sparing mercy; but now the day of God's patience is over, and he will pour out upon him his wrath. When God casts down a man, there is no flying from, nor bearing up under his anger. Those who will not now flee to the arms of Divine grace, which are stretched out to receive them, will not be able to flee from the arms of Divine wrath, which will shortly be stretched out to destroy them. And what is a man profited if he gain the whole world, and thus lose his own soul?

Chapter 28

Verses 1–11

Job maintained that the dispensations of Providence were regulated by the highest wisdom. To confirm this, he showed of what a great deal of knowledge and wealth men may make themselves masters. The caverns of the earth may be discovered, but not the counsels of Heaven. Go to the miners, thou sluggard in religion, consider their ways, and be wise. Let their courage and diligence in seeking the wealth that perishes, shame us out of slothfulness and faint-heartedness in labouring for the true riches. How much better is it to get wisdom than gold! How much easier, and safer! Yet gold is sought for, but grace neglected. Will the hopes of precious things out of the earth, so men call them, though really they are paltry and perishing, be such a spur to industry, and shall not the certain prospect of truly precious things in heaven be much more so?

Verses 12–19

Job here speaks of wisdom and understanding, the knowing and enjoying of God and ourselves. Its worth is infinitely more than all the riches in this world. It is a gift of the Holy Ghost which cannot be bought with money. Let that which is most precious in God's account, be so in ours. Job asks after it as one that truly desired to find it, and despaired of finding it any where but in God; any way but by Divine revelation. (Job **28**:**20-28**)

Verses 20–28

There is a two-fold wisdom; one hid in God, which is secret, and belongs not to us; the other made known by him, and revealed to man. One day's events, and one man's affairs, have such reference to, and so hang one upon another, that He only, to whom all is open, and who sees the whole at one view, can rightly judge of every part. But the knowledge of God's revealed will is within our reach, and will do us good. Let man look upon this as his wisdom, To fear the Lord, and to depart from evil. Let him learn that, and he is learned enough. Where is this wisdom to be found? The treasures of it are hid in Christ, revealed by the word, received by faith, through the Holy Ghost. It will not feed pride or vanity, or amuse our vain curiosity. It teaches and encourages sinners to fear the Lord, and to depart from evil, in the exercise of repentance and faith, without desiring to solve all difficulties about the events of this life.

Chapter 29

Verses 1–6

Job proceeds to contrast his former prosperity with his present misery, through God's withdrawing from him. A gracious soul delights in God's smiles, not in the smiles of this world. Four things were then very pleasant to holy Job. **1**. The confidence he had in the Divine protection. **2**. The enjoyment he had of the Divine favour. **3**. The communion he had with the Divine word. **4**. The assurance he had of the Divine presence. God's presence with a man in his house, though it be but a cottage, makes it a castle and a palace. Then also he had comfort in his family. Riches and flourishing families, like a candle, may be soon extinguished. But when the mind is enlightened by the Holy Spirit, when a man walks in the light of God's countenance, every outward comfort is doubled, every trouble is diminished, and he may pass cheerfully by this light through life and through death. Yet the sensible comfort of this state is often withdrawn for a season; and commonly this arises from sinful neglect, and grieving the Holy Spirit: sometimes it may be a trial of a man's faith and grace. But it is needful to examine ourselves, to seek for the cause of such a change by fervent prayer, and to increase our watchfulness.

Verses 7–17

All sorts of people paid respect to Job, not only for the dignity of his rank, but for his personal merit, his prudence, integrity, and good management. Happy the men who are blessed with such gifts as these! They have great opportunities of honouring God and doing good, but have great need to watch against pride. Happy the people who are blessed with such men! it is a token for good to them. Here we see what Job valued himself by, in the day of his prosperity. It was by his usefulness. He valued himself by the check he gave to the violence of proud and evil men. Good magistrates must thus be a restraint to evil-doers, and protect the innocent; in order to this, they should arm themselves with zeal and resolution. Such men are public blessings, and resemble Him who rescues poor sinners from Satan. How many who were ready to perish, now are blessing Him! But who can show forth His praises? May we trust in His mercy, and seek to imitate His truth, justice, and love.

Verses 18–25

Being thus honoured and useful, Job had hoped to die in peace and honour, in a good old age. If such an expectation arise from lively faith in the providence and promise of God, it is well; but if from conceit of our own wisdom, and dependence on changeable, earthly things, it is ill grounded, and turns to sin. Every one that has the spirit of wisdom, has not the spirit of government; but Job had both. Yet he had the tenderness of a comforter. This he thought upon with pleasure, when he was himself a mourner. Our Lord Jesus is a King who hates iniquity, and upon whom the blessing of a world ready to perish comes. To Him let us give ear.

Chapter 30

Verses 1–14

Job contrasts his present condition with his former honour and authority. What little cause have men to be ambitious or proud of that which may be so easily lost, and what little confidence is to be put in it! We should not be cast down if we are despised, reviled, and hated by wicked men. We should look to Jesus, who endured the contradiction of sinners.

Verses 15–31

Job complains a great deal. Harbouring hard thoughts of God was the sin which did, at this time, most easily beset Job. When inward temptations join with outward calamities, the soul is hurried as in a tempest, and is filled with confusion. But woe be to those who really have God for an enemy! Compared with the awful state of ungodly men, what are all outward, or even inward temporal afflictions? There is something with which Job comforts himself, yet it is but a little. He foresees that death will be the end of all his troubles. God's wrath might bring him to death; but his soul would be safe and happy in the world of spirits. If none pity us, yet our God, who corrects, pities us, even as a father pitieth his own children. And let us look more to the things of eternity: then the believer will cease from mourning, and joyfully praise redeeming love.

Chapter 31

Verses 1–8

Job did not speak the things here recorded by way of boasting, but in answer to the charge of hypocrisy. He understood the spiritual nature of God's commandments, as reaching to the thoughts and intents of the heart. It is best to let our actions speak for us; but in some cases we owe it to ourselves and to the cause of God, solemnly to protest our innocence of the crimes of which we are falsely accused. The lusts of the flesh, and the love of the world, are two fatal rocks on which multitudes split; against these Job protests he was always careful to stand upon his guard. And God takes more exact notice of us than we do of ourselves; let us therefore walk circumspectly. He carefully avoided all sinful means of getting wealth. He dreaded all forbidden profit as much as all forbidden pleasure. What we have in the world may be used with comfort, or lost with comfort, if honestly gotten. Without strict honestly and faithfulness in all our dealings, we can have no good evidence of true godliness. Yet how many professors are unable to abide this touchstone!

Verses 9–15

All the defilements of the life come from a deceived heart. Lust is a fire in the soul: those that indulge it, are said to burn. It consumes all that is good there, and lays the conscience waste. It kindles the fire of God's wrath, which, if not quenched by the blood of Christ, will consume even to eternal destruction. It consumes the body; it consumes the substance. Burning lusts bring burning judgments. Job had a numerous household, and he managed it well. He considered that he had a Master in heaven; and as we are undone if God should be severe with us, we ought to be mild and gentle towards all with whom we have to do.

Verses 16–23

Job's conscience gave testimony concerning his just and charitable behaviour toward the poor. He is most large upon this head, because in this matter he was particularly accused. He was tender of all, and hurtful to none. Notice the principles by which Job was restrained from being uncharitable and unmerciful. He stood in awe of the Lord, as certainly against him, if he should wrong the poor. Regard to worldly interests may restrain a man from actual crimes; but the grace of God alone can make him hate, dread, and shun sinful thoughts and desires.

Verses 24–32

Job protests, **1**. That he never set his heart upon the wealth of this world. How few prosperous professors can appeal to the Lord, that they have not rejoiced because their gains were great! Through the determination to be rich, numbers ruin their souls, or pierce themselves with many sorrows. **2**. He never was guilty of idolatry. The source of idolatry is in the heart, and it corrupts men, and provokes God to send judgments upon a nation. **3**. He neither desired nor delighted in the hurt of the worst enemy he had. If others bear malice to us, that will not justify us in bearing malice to them. **4**. He had never been unkind to strangers. Hospitality is a Christian duty, **1**Pe **4**:**9**.

Verses 33–40

Job clears himself from the charge of hypocrisy. We are loth to confess our faults, willing to excuse them, and to lay the blame upon others. But he that thus covers his sins, shall not prosper, Pr **28**:**13**. He speaks of his courage in what is good, as an evidence of his sincerity in it. When men get estates unjustly, they are justly deprived of comfort from them; it was sown wheat, but shall come up thistles. What men do not come honestly by, will never do them any good. The words of Job are ended. They end with a bold assertion, that, with respect to accusation against his moral and religious character as the cause for his sufferings, he could appeal to God. But, however confident Job was, we shall see he was mistaken, chap. **40**:4, **5**; **1**Jo **1**:**8**. Let us all judge ourselves; wherein we are guilty, let us seek forgiveness in that blood which cleanseth from all sin; and may the Lord have mercy upon us, and write his laws in our hearts!

Chapter 32

Verses 1–5

Job's friends were silenced, but not convinced. Others had been present. Elihu was justly displeased with Job, as more anxious to clear his own character than the justice and goodness of God. Elihu was displeased with Job's friends because they had not been candid to Job. Seldom is a quarrel begun, more seldom is a quarrel carried on, in which there are not faults on both sides. Those that seek for truth, must not reject what is true and good on either side, nor approve or defend what is wrong.

Verses 6–14

Elihu professes to speak by the inspiration of the Holy Spirit, and corrects both parties. He allowed that those who had the longest experience should speak first. But God gives wisdom as he pleases; this encouraged him to state his opinion. By attention to the word of God, and dependence upon the Holy Spirit, young men may become wiser than the aged; but this wisdom will render them swift to hear, slow to speak, and disposed to give others a patient hearing.

Verses 15–22

If we are sure that the Spirit of God suggested what we are about to say, still we ought to refrain, till it comes to our turn to speak. God is the God of order, not of confusion. It is great refreshment to a good man, to speak for the glory of the Lord, and to edify others. And the more we consider the majesty of God, as our Maker, and the more we dread his wrath and justice, the less shall we sinfully fear or flatter men. Could we set the wrath Lord always before us, in his mercies and his terrors, we should not be moved from doing our duty in whatever we are called to do.

Chapter 33

Verses 1–7

Job had desired a judge to decide his appeal. Elihu was one according to his wish, a man like himself. If we would rightly convince men, it must be by reason, not by terror; by fair argument, not by a heavy hand.

Verses 8–13

Elihu charges Job with reflecting upon the justice and goodness of God. When we hear any thing said to God's dishonour, we ought to bear our testimony against it. Job had represented God as severe in marking what he did amiss. Elihu urges that he had spoken wrong, and that he ought to humble himself before God, and by repentance to unsay it. God is not accountable to us. It is unreasonable for weak, sinful creatures, to strive with a God of infinite wisdom, power, and goodness. He acts with perfect justice, wisdom, and goodness, where we cannot perceive it.

Verses 14–18

God speaks to us by conscience, by providences, and by ministers; of all these Elihu discourses. There was not then, that we know of, any Divine revelation in writing, though now it is our principal guide. When God designs men's good, by the convictions and dictates of their own consciences, he opens the heart, as Lydia's, and opens the ears, so that conviction finds or forces its way in. The end and design of these admonitions are to keep men from sin, particularly the sin of pride. While sinners are pursuing evil purposes, and indulging their pride, their souls are hastening to destruction. That which turns men from sin, saves them from hell. What a mercy it is to be under the restraints of an awakened conscience!

Verses 19–28

Job complained of his diseases, and judged by them that God was angry with him; his friends did so too: but Elihu shows that God often afflicts the body for good to the soul. This thought will be of great use for our getting good from sickness, in and by which God speaks to men. Pain is the fruit of sin; yet, by the grace of God, the pain of the body is often made a means of good to the soul. When afflictions have done their work, they shall be removed. A ransom or propitiation is found. Jesus Christ is the Messenger and the Ransom, so Elihu calls him, as Job had called him his Redeemer, for he is both the Purchaser and the Price, the Priest and the sacrifice. So high was the value of souls, that nothing less would redeem them; and so great the hurt done by sin, that nothing less would atone for it, than the blood of the Son of God, who gave his life a ransom for many. A blessed change follows. Recovery from sickness is a mercy indeed, when it proceeds from the remission of sin. All that truly repent of their sins, shall find mercy with God. The works of darkness are unfruitful works; all the gains of sin will come far short of the damage. We must, with a broken and contrite heart, confess our sins to God, **1**Jo **1**:**9**. We must confess the fact of sin; and not try to justify or excuse ourselves. We must confess the fault of sin; I have perverted that which was right. We must confess the folly of sin; So foolish have I been and ignorant. Is there not good reason why we should make such a confession?

Verses 29–33

Elihu shows that God's great and gracious design toward the children of men, is, to save them from being for ever miserable, and to bring them to be for ever happy. By whatever means we are kept back from the we shall bless the Lord for them at least, and should bless him for them though they be painful and distressing. Those that perish for ever are without excuse, for they would not be healed.

Chapter 34

Verses 1–9

Elihu calls upon those present to decide with him upon Job's words. The plainest Christian, whose mind is enlightened, whose heart is sanctified by the Spirit of God, and who is **verse**d in the Scriptures, can say how far matters, words, or actions, agree with true religion, better than any that lean to their own understandings. Job had spoken as if he meant wholly to justify himself. He that say, I have cleansed my hands in vain, does not only offend against God's children, Ps **73**:**13**–**15**, but gratifies his enemies, and says as they say.

Verses 10–15

Elihu had showed Job, that God meant him no hurt by afflicting him, but intended his spiritual benefit. Here he shows, that God did him no wrong by afflicting him. If the former did not satisfy him, this ought to silence him. God cannot do wickedness, nor the Almighty commit wrong. If services now go unrewarded, and sins now go unpunished, yet there is a day coming, when God will fully render to every man according to his works. Further, though the believer's final condemnation is done away through the Saviour's ransom, yet he has merited worse than any outward afflictions; so that no wrong is done to him, however he may be tried.

Verses 16–30

Elihu appeals directly to Job himself. Could he suppose that God was like those earthly princes, who hate right, who are unfit to rule, and prove the scourges of mankind? It is daring presumption to condemn God's proceedings, as Job had done by his discontents. Elihu suggests divers considerations to Job, to produce in him high thoughts of God, and so to persuade him to submit. Job had often wished to plead his cause before God. Elihu asks, To what purpose? All is well that God does, and will be found so. What can make those uneasy, whose souls dwell at ease in God? The smiles of all the world cannot quiet those on whom God frowns.

Verses 31–37

When we reprove for what is amiss, we must direct to what is good. Job's friends would have had him own himself a wicked man. Let will only oblige him to own that he spoke unadvisedly with his lips. Let us, in giving reproof, not make a matter worse than it is. Elihu directs Job to humble himself before God for his sins, and to accept the punishment. Also to pray to God to discover his sins to him. A good man is willing to know the worst of himself; particularly, under affliction, he desires to be told wherefore God contends with him. It is not enough to be sorry for our sins, but we must go and sin no more. And if we are affectionate children, we shall love to speak with our Father, and to tell him all our mind. Elihu reasons with Job concerning his discontent under affliction. We are ready to think every thing that concerns us should be just as we would have it; but it is not reasonable to expect this. Elihu asks whether there was not sin and folly in what Job said. God is righteous in all his ways, and holy in all his works, Ps **145**:**17**. The believer saith, Let my Saviour, my wise and loving Lord, choose every thing for me. I am sure that will be wisest, and the best for his glory and my good.

Chapter 35

Verses 1–8

Elihu reproves Job for justifying himself more than God, and called his attention to the heavens. They are far above us, and God is far above them; how much then is he out of the reach, either of our sins or of our services! We have no reason to complain if we have not what we expect, but should be thankful that we have better than we deserve.

Verses 9–13

Job complained that God did not regard the cries of the oppressed against their oppressors. This he knew not how to reconcile the justice of God and his government. Elihu solves the difficulty. Men do not notice the mercies they enjoy in and under their afflictions, nor are thankful for them, therefore they cannot expect that God should deliver them out of affliction. He gives songs in the night; when our condition is dark and melancholy, there is that in God's providence and promise, which is sufficient to support us, and to enable us even to rejoice in tribulation. When we only pore upon our afflictions, and neglect the consolations of God which are treasured up for us, it is just in God to reject our prayers. Even the things that will kill the body, cannot hurt the soul. If we cry to God for the removal of an affliction, and it is not removed, the reason is, not because the Lord's hand is shortened, or his ear heavy; but because we are not sufficiently humbled.

Verses 14–16

As in prosperity we are ready to think our mountain will never be brought low; so when in adversity, we are ready to think our valley will never be filled up. But to conclude that to-morrow must be as this day, is as absurd as to think that the weather, when either fair or foul, will be always so. When Job looked up to God, he had no reason to speak despairingly. There is a day of judgment, when all that seems amiss will be found to be right, and all that seems dark and difficult will be cleared up and set straight. And if there is Divine wrath in our troubles, it is because we quarrel with God, are fretful, and distrust Divine Providence. This was Job's case. Elihu was directed by God to humble Job, for as to some things he had both opened his mouth in vain, and had multiplied words without knowledge. Let us be admonished, in our afflictions, not so much to set forth the greatness of our suffering, as the greatness of the mercy of God.

Chapter 36

Verses 1–4

Elihu only maintained that the affliction was sent for his trial; and lengthened because Job was not yet thoroughly humbled under it. He sought to ascribe righteousness to his Maker; to clear this truth, that God is righteous in all his ways. Such knowledge must be learned from the word and Spirit of God, for naturally we are estranged from it. The fitness of Elihu's discourse to the dispute between Job and his friends is plain. It pointed out to Job the true reason of those trials with which he had been pointed out to Job the true reason of those trials with which he had been visited. It taught that God had acted in mercy towards him, and the spiritual benefit he was to derive from them. It corrected the mistake of his friends, and shewed that Job's calamities were for good.

Verses 5–14

Elihu here shows that God acts as righteous Governor. He is always ready to defend those that are injured. If our eye is ever toward God in duty, his eye will be ever upon us in mercy, and, when we are at the lowest, will not overlook us. God intends, when he afflicts us, to discover past sins to us, and to bring them to our remembrance. Also, to dispose our hearts to be taught: affliction makes people willing to learn, through the grace of God working with and by it. And further, to deter us from sinning for the future. It is a command, to have no more to do with sin. If we faithfully serve God, we have the promise of the life that now is, and the comforts of it, as far as is for God's glory and our good: and who would desire them any further? We have the possession of inward pleasures, the great peace which those have that love God's law. If the affliction fail in its work, let men expect the furnace to be heated till they are consumed. Those that die without knowledge, die without grace, and are undone for ever. See the nature of hypocrisy; it lies in the heart: that is for the world and the flesh, while perhaps the outside seems to be for God and religion. Whether sinners die in youth, or live long to heap up wrath, their case is dreadful. The souls of the wicked live after death, but it is in everlasting misery.

Verses 15–23

Elihu shows that Job caused the continuance of his own trouble. He cautions him not to persist in frowardness. Even good men need to be kept to their duty by the fear of God's wrath; the wisest and best have enough in them to deserve his stroke. Let not Job continue his unjust quarrel with God and his providence. And let us never dare to think favourably of sin, never indulge it, nor allow ourselves in it. Elihu thinks Job needed this caution, he having chosen rather to gratify his pride and humour by contending with God, than to mortify them by submitting, and accepting the punishment. It is absurd for us to think to teach Him who is himself the Fountain of light, truth, knowledge, and instruction. He teaches by the Bible, and that is the best book; teaches by his Son, and he is the best Master. He is just in all proceedings.

Verses 24–33

Elihu endeavours to fill Job with high thought of God, and so to persuade him into cheerful submission to his providence. Man may see God's works, and is capable of discerning his hand in them, which the beasts are not, therefore they ought to give him the glory. But while the worker of iniquity ought to tremble, the true believer should rejoice. Children should hear with pleasure their Father's voice, even when he speaks in terror to his enemies. There is no light but there may be a cloud to intercept it. The light of the favour of God, the light of his countenance, the most blessed light of all, even that light has many a cloud. The clouds of our sins cause the Lord to his face, and hinder the light of his loving-kindness from shining on our souls.

Chapter 37

Verses 1–13

The changes of the weather are the subject of a great deal of our thoughts and common talk; but how seldom do we think and speak of these things, as Elihu, with a regard to God, the director of them! We must notice the glory of God, not only in the thunder and lightning, but in the more common and less awful changes of the weather; as the snow and rain. Nature directs all creatures to shelter themselves from a storm; and shall man only be unprovided with a refuge? Oh that men would listen to the voice of God, who in many ways warns them to flee from the wrath to come; and invites them to accept his salvation, and to be happy. The ill opinion which men entertain of the Divine direction, peculiarly appears in their murmurs about the weather, though the whole result of the year proves the folly of their complaints. Believers should avoid this; no days are bad as God makes them, though we make many bad by our sins. (Job **37**:**14-20**)

Verses 14–20

Due thoughts of the works of God will help to reconcile us to all his providences. As God has a powerful, freezing north wind, so he has a thawing, composing south wind: the Spirit is compared to both, because he both convinces and comforts, So **4**:**16**. The best of men are much in the dark concerning the glorious perfections of the Divine nature and the Divine government. Those who, through grace, know much of God, know nothing, in comparison with what is to be known, and of what will be known, when that which is perfect is come.

Verses 21–24

Elihu concludes his discourse with some great sayings concerning the glory of God. Light always is, but is not always to be seen. When clouds come between, the sun is darkened in the clear day. The light of God's favour shines ever towards his faithful servants, though it be not always seen. Sins are clouds, and often hinder us from seeing that bright light which is in the face of God. Also, as to those thick clouds of sorrow which often darken our minds, the Lord hath a wind which passes and clears them away. What is that wind? It is his Holy Spirit. As the wind dispels and sweeps away the clouds which are gathered in the air, so the Spirit of God clears our souls from the clouds and fogs of ignorance and unbelief, of sin and lust. From all these clouds the Holy Spirit of God frees us in the work of regeneration. And from all the clouds which trouble our consciences, the Holy Spirit sets us free in the work of consolation. Now that God is about to speak, Elihu delivers a few words, as the sum of all his discourse. With God is terrible majesty. Sooner or later all men shall fear him.

Chapter 38

Verses 1–3

Job had silenced, but had not convinced his friends. Elihu had silenced Job, but had not brought him to admit his guilt before God. It pleased the Lord to interpose. The Lord, in this discourse, humbles Job, and brings him to repent of his passionate expressions concerning God's providential dealings with him; and this he does, by calling upon Job to compare God's being from everlasting to everlasting, with his own time; God's knowledge of all things, with his own ignorance; and God's almighty power, with his own weakness. Our darkening the counsels of God's wisdom with our folly, is a great provocation to God. Humble faith and sincere obedience see farthest and best into the will of the Lord.

Verses 4–11

For the humbling of Job, God here shows him his ignorance, even concerning the earth and the sea. As we cannot find fault with God's work, so we need not fear concerning it. The works of his providence, as well as the work of creation, never can be broken; and the work of redemption is no less firm, of which Christ himself is both the Foundation and the Corner-stone. The church stands as firm as the earth.

Verses 12–24

The Lord questions Job, to convince him of his ignorance, and shame him for his folly in prescribing to God. If we thus try ourselves, we shall soon be brought to own that what we know is nothing in comparison with what we know not. By the tender mercy of our God, the Day-spring from on high has visited us, to give light to those that sit in darkness, whose hearts are turned to it as clay to the seal, **2**Co **4**:**6**. God's way in the government of the world is said to be in the sea; this means, that it is hid from us. Let us make sure that the gates of heaven shall be opened to us on the other side of death, and then we need not fear the opening of the gates of death. It is presumptuous for us, who perceive not the breadth of the earth, to dive into the depth of God's counsels. We should neither in the brightest noon count upon perpetual day, nor in the darkest midnight despair of the return of the morning; and this applies to our inward as well as to our outward condition. What folly it is to strive against God! How much is it our interest to seek peace with him, and to keep in his love!

Verses 25–41

Hitherto God had put questions to Job to show him his ignorance; now God shows his weakness. As it is but little that he knows, he ought not to arraign the Divine counsels; it is but little he can do, therefore he ought not to oppose the ways of Providence. See the all-sufficiency of the Divine Providence; it has wherewithal to satisfy the desire of every living thing. And he that takes care of the young ravens, certainly will not be wanting to his people. This being but one instance of the Divine compassion out of many, gives us occasion to think how much good our God does, every day, beyond what we are aware of. Every view we take of his infinite perfections, should remind us of his right to our love, the evil of sinning against him, and our need of his mercy and salvation.

Chapter 39

God inquires of Job concerning several animals.

—In these questions the Lord continued to humble Job. In this chapter several animals are spoken of, whose nature or situation particularly show the power, wisdom, and manifold works of God. The wild ass. It is better to labour and be good for something, than to ramble and be good for nothing. From the untameableness of this and other creatures, we may see, how unfit we are to give law to Providence, who cannot give law even to a wild ass's colt. The unicorn, a strong, stately, proud creature. He is able to serve, but not willing; and God challenges Job to force him to it. It is a great mercy if, where God gives strength for service, he gives a heart; it is what we should pray for, and reason ourselves into, which the brutes cannot do. Those gifts are not always the most valuable that make the finest show. Who would not rather have the voice of the nightingale, than the tail of the peacock; the eye of the eagle and her soaring wing, and the natural affection of the stork, than the beautiful feathers of the ostrich, which can never rise above the earth, and is without natural affection? The description of the war-horse helps to explain the character of presumptuous sinners. Every one turneth to his course, as the horse rushes into the battle. When a man's heart is fully set in him to do evil, and he is carried on in a wicked way, by the violence of his appetites and passions, there is no making him fear the wrath of God, and the fatal consequences of sin. Secure sinners think themselves as safe in their sins as the eagle in her nest on high, in the clefts of the rocks; but I will bring thee down from thence, saith the Lord, Jer **49**:**16**. All these beautiful references to the works of nature, should teach us a right view of the riches of the wisdom of Him who made and sustains all things. The want of right views concerning the wisdom of God, which is ever present in all things, led Job to think and speak unworthily of Providence.

Chapter 40

Verses 1–5

Communion with the Lord effectually convinces and humbles a saint, and makes him glad to part with his most beloved sins. There is need to be thoroughly convinced and humbled, to prepare us for remarkable deliverances. After God had shown Job, by his manifest ignorance of the works of nature, how unable he was to judge of the methods and designs of Providence, he puts a convincing question to him; Shall he that contendeth with the Almighty instruct him? Now Job began to melt into godly sorrow: when his friends reasoned with him, he did not yield; but the voice of the Lord is powerful. When the Spirit of truth is come, he shall convince. Job yields himself to the grace of God. He owns himself an offender, and has nothing to say to justify himself. He is now sensible that he has sinned; and therefore he calls himself vile. Repentance changes men's opinion of themselves. Job is now convinced of his error. Those who are truly sensible of their own sinfulness and vileness, dare not justify themselves before God. He perceived that he was a poor, mean, foolish, and sinful creature, who ought not to have uttered one word against the Divine conduct. One glimpse of God's holy nature would appal the stoutest rebel. How, then will the wicked bear the sight of his glory at the day of judgment? But when we see this glory revealed in Jesus Christ, we shall be humbled without being terrified; self-abasement agrees with filial love. (Job **40**:**6-14**)

Verses 6–14

Those who profit by what they have heard from God, shall hear more from him. And those who are truly convinced of sin, yet need to be more thoroughly convinced and more humbled. No doubt God, and he only, has power to humble and bring down proud men; he has wisdom to know when and how to do it, and it is not for us to teach him how to govern the world. Our own hands cannot save us by recommending us to God's grace, much less rescuing us from his justice; and therefore into his hand we must commit ourselves. The renewal of a believer proceeds in the same way of conviction, humbling, and watchfulness against remaining sin, as his first conversion. When convinced of many evils in our conduct, we still need convincing of many more.

Verses 15–24

God, for the further proving of his own power, describes two vast animals, far exceeding man in bulk and strength. Behemoth signifies beasts. Most understand it of an animal well known in Egypt, called the river-horse, or hippopotamus. This vast animal is noticed as an argument to humble ourselves before the great God; for he created this vast animal, which is so fearfully and wonderfully made. Whatever strength this or any other creature has, it is derived from God. He that made the soul of man, knows all the ways to it, and can make the sword of justice, his wrath, to approach and touch it. Every godly man has spiritual weapons, the whole armour of God, to resist, yea, to overcome the tempter, that his never-dying soul may be safe, whatever becomes of his frail flesh and mortal body.

Chapter 41

Concerning Leviathan.

—The description of the Leviathan, is yet further to convince Job of his own weakness, and of God's almighty power. Whether this Leviathan be a whale or a crocodile, is disputed. The Lord, having showed Job how unable he was to deal with the Leviathan, sets forth his own power in that mighty creature. If such language describes the terrible force of Leviathan, what words can express the power of God's wrath? Under a humbling sense of our own vileness, let us revere the Divine Majesty; take and fill our allotted place, cease from our own wisdom, and give all glory to our gracious God and Saviour. Remembering from whom every good gift cometh, and for what end it was given, let us walk humbly with the Lord.

Chapter 42

Verses 1–6

Job was now sensible of his guilt; he would no longer speak in his own excuse; he abhorred himself as a sinner in heart and life, especially for murmuring against God, and took shame to himself. When the understanding is enlightened by the Spirit of grace, our knowledge of Divine things as far exceeds what we had before, as the sight of the eyes excels report and common fame. By the teachings of men, God reveals his Son to us; but by the teachings of his Spirit he reveals his Son in us, Ga **1**:**16**, and changes us into the same image, **2Co 3**:**18**. It concerns us to be deeply humbled for the sins of which we are convinced. Self-loathing is ever the companion of true repentance. The Lord will bring those whom he loveth, to adore him in self-abasement; while true grace will always lead them to confess their sins without self-justifying.

Verses 7–9

After the Lord had convinced and humbled Job, and brought him to repentance, he owned him, comforted him, and put honour upon him. The devil had undertaken to prove Job a hypocrite, and his three friends had condemned him as a wicked man; but if God say, Well done, thou good and faithful servant, it is of little consequence who says otherwise. Job's friends had wronged God, by making prosperity a mark of the true church, and affliction a certain proof of God's wrath. Job had referred things to the future judgment and the future state, more than his friends, therefore he spake of God that which was right, better than his friends had done. And as Job prayed and offered sacrifice for those that had grieved and wounded his spirit, so Christ prayed for his persecutors, and ever lives, making intercession for the transgressors. Job's friends were good men, and belonged to God, and He would not let them be in their mistake any more than Job; but having humbled him by a discourse out of the whirlwind, he takes another way to humble them. They are not to argue the matter again, but they must agree in a sacrifice and a prayer, and that must reconcile them, Those who differ in judgment about lesser things, yet are one in Christ the great Sacrifice, and ought therefore to love and bear with one another. When God was angry with Job's friends, he put them in a way to make peace with him. Our quarrels with God always begin on our part, but the making peace begins on his. Peace with God is to be had only in his own way, and upon his own terms. These will never seem hard to those who know how to value this blessing: they will be glad of it, like Job's friends, upon any terms, though ever so humbling. Job did not insult over his friends, but God being graciously reconciled to him, he was easily reconciled to them. In all our prayers and services we should aim to be accepted of the Lord; not to have praise of men, but to please God. (Job **42**:**10-17**)

Verses 10–17

In the beginning of this book we had Job's patience under his troubles, for an example; here, for our encouragement to follow that example, we have his happy end. His troubles began in Satan's malice, which God restrained; his restoration began in God's mercy, which Satan could not oppose. Mercy did not return when Job was disputing with his friends, but when he was praying for them. God is served and pleased with our warm devotions, not with our warm disputes. God doubled Job's possessions. We may lose much for the Lord, but we shall not lose any thing by him. Whether the Lord gives us health and temporal blessings or not, if we patiently suffer according to his will, in the end we shall be happy. Job's estate increased. The blessing of the Lord makes rich; it is he that gives us power to get wealth, and gives success in honest endeavours. The last days of a good man sometimes prove his best, his last works his best works, his last comforts his best comforts; for his path, like that of the morning light, shines more and more unto the perfect day.

Psalms

David was the penman of most of the psalms, but some evidently were composed by other writers, and the writers of some are doubtful. But all were written by the inspiration of the Holy Ghost; and no part of the Old Testament is more frequently quoted or referred to in the New. Every psalm either points directly to Christ, in his person, his character, and offices; or may lead the believer's thoughts to Him. And the psalms are the language of the believer's heart, whether mourning for sin, thirsting after God, or rejoicing in Him. Whether burdened with affliction, struggling with temptation, or triumphing in the hope or enjoyment of deliverance; whether admiring the Divine perfections, thanking God for his mercies, mediating on his truths, or delighting in his service; they form a Divinely appointed standard of experience, by which we may judge ourselves. Their value, in this view, is very great, and the use of them will increase with the growth of the power of true religion in the heart. By the psalmist's expressions, the Spirit helps us to pray. If we make the psalms familiar to us, whatever we have to ask at the throne of grace, by way of confession, petition, or thanksgiving, we may be assisted from thence. Whatever devout affection is working in us, holy desire or hope, sorrow or joy, we may here find words to clothe it; sound speech which cannot be condemned. In the language of this Divine book, the prayers and praises of the church have been offered up to the throne of grace from age to age.

Chapter 1

Verses 1–3

To meditate in God's word, is to discourse with ourselves concerning the great things contained in it, with close application of mind and fixedness of thought. We must have constant regard to the word of God, as the rule of our actions, and the spring of our comforts; and have it in our thoughts night and day. For this purpose no time is amiss.

Verses 4–6

The ungodly are the re**verse** of the righteous, both in character and condition. The ungodly are not so, ver. **4**; they are led by the counsel of the wicked, in the way of sinners, to the seat of the scornful; they have no delight in the law of God; they bring forth no fruit but what is evil. The righteous are like useful, fruitful trees: the ungodly are like the chaff which the wind drives away: the dust which the owner of the floor desires to have driven away, as not being of any use. They are of no worth in God's account, how highly soever they may value themselves. They are easily driven to and fro by every wind of temptation. The chaff may be, for a while, among the wheat, but He is coming, whose fan is in his hand, and who will thoroughly purge his floor. Those that, by their own sin and folly, make themselves as chaff, will be found so before the whirlwind and fire of Divine wrath. The doom of the ungodly is fixed, but whenever the sinner becomes sensible of this guilt and misery, he may be admitted into the company of the righteous by Christ the living way, and become in Christ a new creature. He has new desires, new pleasures, hopes, fears, sorrows, companions, and employments. His thoughts, words, and actions are changed. He enters on a new state, and bears a new character. Behold, all things are become new by Divine grace, which changes his soul into the image of the Redeemer. How different the character and end of the ungodly!

Chapter 2

Verses 1–6

We are here told who would appear as adversaries to Christ. As this world is the kingdom of Satan, unconverted men, of every rank, party, and character, are stirred up by him to oppose the cause of God. But the rulers of the earth generally have been most active. The truths and precepts of Christianity are against ambitious projects and worldly lusts. We are told what they aim at in this opposition. They would break asunder the bands of conscience, and the cords of God's commandments; they will not receive, but cast them away as far as they can. These enemies can show no good cause for opposing so just and holy a government, which, if received by all, would bring a heaven upon earth. They can hope for no success in so opposing so powerful a kingdom. The Lord Jesus has all power both in heaven and in earth, and is Head over all things to the church, notwithstanding the restless endeavours of his enemies. Christ's throne is set up in his church, that is, in the hearts of all believers.

Verses 7–9

The kingdom of the Messiah is founded upon an eternal decree of God the Father. This our Lord Jesus often referred to, as what he governed himself by. God hath said unto him, Thou art my Son, and it becomes each of us to say to him, Thou art my Lord, my Sovereign'. The Son, in asking the heathen for his inheritance, desires their happiness in him; so that he pleads for them, ever lives to do so, and is able to save to the uttermost, and he shall have multitudes of willing, loyal subjects, among them. Christians are the possession of the Lord Jesus; they are to him for a name and a praise. God the Father gives them to him, when, by his Spirit and grace, he works upon them to submit to the Lord Jesus.

Verses 10–12

Whatever we rejoice in, in this world, it must always be with trembling, because of the uncertainty of all things in it. To welcome Jesus Christ, and to submit to him, is our wisdom and interest. Let him be very dear and precious; love him above all, love him in sincerity, love him much, as she did, to whom much was forgiven, and, in token of it, kissed his feet, Lu **7**:**38**. And with a kiss of loyalty take this yoke upon you, and give up yourselves to be governed by his laws, disposed of by his providence, and entirely devoted to his cause. Unbelief is a sin against the remedy. It will be utter destruction to yourselves; lest ye perish in the way of your sins, and from the way of your vain hopes; lest your way perish, lest you prove to have missed the way of happiness. Christ is the way; take heed lest ye be cut off from Him as your way to God. They thought themselves in the way; but neglecting Christ, they perish from it. Blessed will those be in the day of wrath, who, by trusting in Christ, have made him their Refuge.

Chapter 3

Verses 1–3

An active believer, the more he is beaten off from God, either by the rebukes of providence, or the reproaches of enemies, the faster hold he will take, and the closer will he cleave to him. A child of God startles at the very thought of despairing of help in God. See what God is to his people, what he will be, what they have found him, what David found in him. **1**. Safety; a shield for me; which denotes the advantage of that protection. **2**. Honour; those whom God owns for his, have true honour put upon them. **3**. Joy and deliverance. If, in the worst of times, God's people can lift up their heads with joy, knowing that all shall work for good to them, they will own God as giving them both cause and hearts to rejoice.

Verses 4–8

Care and grief do us good, when they engage us to pray to God, as in earnest. David had always found God ready to answer his prayers. Nothing can fix a gulf between the communications of God's grace towards us, and the working of his grace in us; between his favour and our faith. He had always been very safe under the Divine protection. This is applicable to the common mercies of every night, for which we ought to give thanks every morning. Many lie down, and cannot sleep, through pain of body, or anguish of mind, or the continual alarms of fear in the night. But it seems here rather to be meant of the calmness of David's spirit, in the midst of his dangers. The Lord, by his grace and the consolations of his Spirit, made him easy. It is a great mercy, when we are in trouble, to have our minds stayed upon God. Behold the Son of David composing himself to his rest upon the cross, that bed of sorrows; commending his Spirit into the Father's hands in full confidence of a joyful resurrection. Behold this, O Christian: let faith teach thee how to sleep, and how to die; while it assures thee that as sleep is a short death, so death is only a longer sleep; the same God watches over thee, in thy bed and in thy grave. David's faith became triumphant. He began the psalm with complaints of the strength and malice of his enemies; but concludes with rejoicing in the power and grace of his God, and now sees more with him than against him. Salvation belongeth unto the Lord; he has power to save, be the danger ever so great. All that have the Lord for their God, are sure of salvation; for he who is their God, is the God of Salvation.

Chapter 4

Verses 1–5

Hear me for thy mercy-sake, is our best plea. He who will not ask such blessings as pardon, and justifying righteousness, and eternal life, must perish for the want of them. Alas! that so many should make so fearful a choice. The psalmist warns against sin. Keep up holy reverence of the glory and majesty of God. You have a great deal to say to your hearts, they may be spoken with, let it not be unsaid. Examine them by serious self-reflection; let your thoughts fasten upon that which is good, and keep close to it. Consider your ways, and before you turn to sleep at night, examine your consciences with respect to what you have done in the day; particularly what you have done amiss, that you may repent of it. when you awake in the night, meditate upon God, and the things that belong to your peace. Upon a sick-bed, particularly, we should consider our ways. Be still. when you have asked conscience a question, be serious, be silent, wait for an answer. Open not the mouth to excuse sin. All confidence must be pan answer. Open not the mouth to excuse sin. All confidence only: therefore, after commanding the sacrifices of righteousness, the psalmist says, Put your trust in the Lord.

Verses 6–8

Wordly people inquire for good, not for the chief good; all they want is outward good, present good, partial good, good meat, good drink, a good trade, and a good estate; but what are all these worth? Any good will serve the turn of most men, but a gracious soul will not be put off so. Lord, let us have thy favour, and let us know that we have it, we desire no more; let us be satisfied of thy loving-kindness, and will be satisfied with it. Many inquire after happiness, but David had found it. When God puts grace in the heart, he puts gladness in the heart. Thus comforted, he pitied, but neither envied nor feared the most prosperous sinner. He commits all his affairs to God, and is prepared to welcome his holy will. But salvation is in Christ alone; where will those appear who despise him as their Mediator, and revile him in his disciples? May they stand in awe, and no longer sin against the only remedy.

Chapter 5

Verses 1–6

God is a prayer-hearing God. Such he has always been, and he is still as ready to hear prayer as ever. The most encouraging principle of prayer, and the most powerful plea in prayer, is, to look upon him as our King and our God. David also prays to a sin-hating God. sin is folly, and sinners are the greatest of all fools; fools of their own making. Wicked people hate God; justly are they hated of him, and this will be their endless misery and ruin. Let us learn the importance of truth and sincerity, in all the affairs of life. Liars and murderers resemble the devil, and are his children, therefore it may well be expected that God should abhor them. These were the characters of David's enemies; and such as these are still the enemies of Christ and his people.

Verses 7–12

David prayed often alone, yet was very constant in attendance on public worship. The mercy of God should ever be the foundation both of our hope and of our joy, in every thing wherein we have to do with him. Let us learn to pray, not for ourselves only, but for others; grace be with all that love Christ in sincerity. The Divine blessing comes down upon us through Jesus Christ, the righteous or just One, as of old it did upon Israel through David, whom God protected, and placed upon the throne. Thou, O Christ, art the righteous Saviour, thou art the King of Israel, thou art the Fountain of blessing to all believers; thy favour is the defence and protection of thy church.

Chapter 6

Verses 1–7

These **verses** speak the language of a heart truly humbled, of a broken and contrite spirit under great afflictions, sent to awaken conscience and mortify corruption. Sickness brought sin to his remembrance, and he looked upon it as a token of God's displeasure against him. The affliction of his body will be tolerable, if he has comfort in his soul. Christ's sorest complaint, in his sufferings, was of the trouble of his soul, and the want of his Father's smiles. Every page of Scripture proclaims the fact, that salvation is only of the Lord. Man is a sinner, his case can only be reached by mercy; and never is mercy more illustrious than in restoring backsliders. With good reason we may pray, that if it be the will of God, and he has any further work for us or our friends to do in this world, he will yet spare us or them to serve him. To depart and be with Christ is happiest for the saints; but for them to abide in the flesh is more profitable for the church.

Verses 8–10

What a sudden change is here! Having made his request known to God, the psalmist is confident that his sorrow will be turned into joy. By the workings of God's grace upon his heart, he knew his prayer was accepted, and did not doubt but it would, in due time, be answered. His prayers will be accepted, coming up out of the hands of Christ the Mediator. The word signifies prayer made to God, the righteous Judge, as the God of his righteousness, who would plead his cause, and right his wrongs. A believer, through the blood and righteousness of Christ, can go to God as a righteous God, and plead with him for pardon and cleansing, who is just and faithful to grant both. He prays for the conversion of his enemies, or foretells their ruin.

Chapter 7

Verses 1–9

David flees to God for succour. But Christ alone could call on Heaven to attest his uprightness in all things. All His works were wrought in righteousness; and the prince of this world found nothing whereof justly to accuse him. Yet for our sakes, submitting to be charged as guilty, he suffered all evils, but, being innocent, he triumphed over them all. The plea is, "For the righteous God trieth the hearts and the reins." He knows the secret wickedness of the wicked, and how to bring it to an end; he is witness to the secret sincerity of the just, and has ways of establishing it. When a man has made peace with God about all his sins, upon the terms of grace and mercy, through the sacrifice of the Mediator, he may, in comparison with his enemies, appeal to God's justice to decide.

Verses 10–17

David is confident that he shall find God his powerful Saviour. The destruction of sinners may be prevented by their conversion; for it is threatened, If he turn not from his evil way, let him expect it will be his ruin. But amidst the threatenings of wrath, we have a gracious offer of mercy. God gives sinners warning of their danger, and space to repent, and prevent it. He is slow to punish, and long-suffering to us-ward, not willing that any should perish. The sinner is described, ver. #(**14–16**), as taking more pains to ruin his soul than, if directed aright, would save it. This is true, in a sense, of all sinners. Let us look to the Saviour under all our trials. Blessed Lord, give us grace to look to thee in the path of tribulation, going before thy church and people, and marking the way by thine own spotless example. Under all the persecutions which in our lesser trials mark our way, let the looking to Jesus animate our minds and comfort our hearts.

Chapter 8

Verses 1, 2

The psalmist seeks to give unto God the glory due to his name. How bright this glory shines even in this lower world! He is ours, for he made us, protects us, and takes special care of us. The birth, life, preaching, miracles, suffering, death, resurrection, and ascension of Jesus are known through the world. No name is so universal, no power and influence so generally felt, as those of the Saviour of mankind. But how much brighter it shines in the upper world! We, on this earth, only hear God's excellent name, and praise that; the angels and blessed spirits above, see his glory, and praise that; yet he is exalted far above even their blessing and praise. Sometimes the grace of God appears wonderfully in young children. Sometimes the power of God brings to pass great things in his church, by very weak and unlikely instruments, that the excellency of the power might the more evidently appear to be of God, and not of man. This he does, because of his enemies, that he may put them to silence.

Verses 3–9

We are to consider the heavens, that man thus may be directed to set his affections on things above. What is man, so mean a creature, that he should be thus honoured! so sinful a creature, that he should be thus favoured! Man has sovereign dominion over the inferior creatures, under God, and is appointed their lord. This refers to Christ. In Heb **2**:**6–8**, the apostle, to prove the sovereign dominion of Christ, shows he is that Man, that Son of man, here spoken of, whom God has made to have dominion over the works of his hands. The greatest favour ever showed to the human race, and the greatest honour ever put upon human nature, were exemplified in the Lord Jesus. With good reason does the psalmist conclude as he began, Lord, how excellent is thy name in all the earth, which has been honoured with the presence of the Redeemer, and is still enlightened by his gospel, and governed by his wisdom and power! What words can reach his praises, who has a right to our obedience as our Redeemer?

Chapter 9

Verses 1–10

If we would praise God acceptably, we must praise him in sincerity, with our whole heart. When we give thanks for some one particular mercy, we should remember former mercies. Our joy must not be in the gift, so much as in the Giver. The triumphs of the Redeemer ought to be the triumphs of the redeemed. The almighty power of God is that which the strongest and stoutest of his enemies are no way able to stand before. We are sure that the judgment of God is according to truth, and that with him there is no unrighteousness. His people may, by faith, flee to him as their Refuge, and may depend on his power and promise for their safety, so that no real hurt shall be done to them. Those who know him to be a God of truth and faithfulness, will rejoice in his word of promise, and rest upon that. Those who know him to be an everlasting Father, will trust him with their souls as their main care, and trust in him at all times, even to the end; and by constant care seek to approve themselves to him in the whole course of their lives. Who is there that would not seek him, who never hath forsaken those that seek Him?

Verses 11–20

Those who believe that God is greatly to be praised, not only desire to praise him better themselves, but desire that others may join with them. There is a day coming, when it will appear that he has not forgotten the cry of the humble; neither the cry of their blood, or the cry of their prayers. We are never brought so low, so near to death, but God can raise us up. If he has saved us from spiritual and eternal death, we may thence hope, that in all our distresses he will be a very present help to us. The overruling providence of God frequently so orders it, that persecutors and oppressors are brought to ruin by the projects they formed to destroy the people of God. Drunkards kill themselves; prodigals beggar themselves; the contentious bring mischief upon themselves: thus men's sins may be read in their punishment, and it becomes plain to all, that the destruction of sinners is of themselves. All wickedness came originally with the wicked one from hell; and those who continue in sin, must go to that place of torment. The true state, both of nations and of individuals, may be correctly estimated by this one rule, whether in their doings they remember or forget God. David encourages the people of God to wait for his salvation, though it should be long deferred. God will make it appear that he never did forget them: it is not possible he should. Strange that man, dust in his and about him, should yet need some sharp affliction, some severe visitation from God, to bring him to the knowledge of himself, and make him feel who and what he is.

Chapter 10

Verses 1–11

God's withdrawings are very grievous to his people, especially in times of trouble. We stand afar off from God by our unbelief, and then complain that God stands afar off from us. Passionate words against bad men do more hurt than good; if we speak of their badness, let it be to the Lord in prayer; he can make them better. The sinner proudly glories in his power and success. Wicked people will not seek after God, that is, will not call upon him. They live without prayer, and that is living without God. They have many thoughts, many objects and devices, but think not of the Lord in any of them; they have no submission to his will, nor aim for his glory. The cause of this is pride. Men think it below them to be religious. They could not break all the laws of justice and goodness toward man, if they had not first shaken off all sense of religion.

Verses 12–18

The psalmist speaks with astonishment, at the wickedness of the wicked, and at the patience and forbearance of God. God prepares the heart for prayer, by kindling holy desires, and strengthening our most holy faith, fixing the thoughts, and raising the affections, and then he graciously accepts the prayer. The preparation of the heart is from the Lord, and we must seek unto him for it. Let the poor, afflicted, persecuted, or tempted believer recollect, that Satan is the prince of this world, and that he is the father of all the ungodly. The children of God cannot expect kindness, truth, or justice from such persons as crucified the Lord of glory. But this once suffering Jesus, now reigns as King over all the earth, and of his dominion there shall be no end. Let us commit ourselves unto him, humbly trusting in his mercy. He will rescue the believer from every temptation, and break the arm of every wicked oppressor, and bruise Satan under our feet shortly. But in heaven alone will all sin and temptation be shut out, though in this life the believer has a foretaste of deliverance.

Chapter 11

David's struggle with, and triumph over a strong temptation to distrust God, and betake himself to indirect means for his own safety, in a time of danger.

—Those that truly fear God and serve him, are welcome to put their trust in him. The psalmist, before he gives an account of his temptation to distrust God, records his resolution to trust in Him, as that by which he was resolved to live and die. The believer, though not terrified by his enemies, may be tempted, by the fears of his friends, to desert his post, or neglect his work. They perceive his danger, but not his security; they give him counsel that savours of worldly policy, rather than of heavenly wisdom. The principles of religion are the foundations on which the faith and hope of the righteous are built. We are concerned to hold these fast against all temptations to unbelief; for believers would be undone, if they had not God to go to, God to trust in, and future bliss to hope for. The prosperity of wicked people in their wicked, evil ways, and the straits and distresses which the best men are sometimes brought into, tried David's faith. We need not say, Who shall go up to heaven, to fetch us thence a God to trust in? The word is nigh us, and God in the word; his Spirit is in his saints, those living temples, and the Lord is that Spirit. This God governs the world. We may know what men seem to be, but God knows what they are, as the refiner knows the value of gold when he has tried it. God is said to try with his eyes, because he cannot err, or be imposed upon. If he afflicts good people, it is for their trial, therefore for their good. However persecutors and oppressors may prosper awhile, they will for ever perish. God is a holy God, and therefore hates them. He is a righteous Judge, and will therefore punish them. In what a horrible tempest are the wicked hurried away at death! Every man has the portion of his cup assigned him. Impenitent sinner, mark your doom! The last call to repentance is about to be addressed to you, judgement is at hand; through the gloomy shade of death you pass into the region of eternal wrath. Hasten then, O sinner, to the cross of Christ. How stands the case between God and our souls? Is Christ our hope, our consolation, our security? Then, not otherwise, will the soul be carried through all its difficulties and conflicts.

Chapter 12

The psalmist begs help of God, because there were none among men whom he durst trust.

—This psalm furnishes good thoughts for bad times; a man may comfort himself with such meditations and prayers. Let us see what makes the times bad, and when they may be said to be so. Ask the children of this world, What makes the times bad? they will tell you, Scarcity of money, decay of trade, and the desolations of war, make the times bad: but the Scripture lays the badness of the times on causes of another nature, **2**Ti **3**:**1**, &c.: perilous times shall come, for sin shall abound; and of this David complains. When piety decays times really are bad. He who made man's mouth will call him to an account for his proud, profane, dissembling, or even useless words. When the poor and needy are oppressed, then the times are very bad. God himself takes notice of the oppression of the poor, and the sighing of the needy. When wickedness abounds, and is countenanced by those in authority, then the times are very bad. See with what good things we are here furnished for such bad times; and we cannot tell what times we may be reserved for. **1**. We have a God to go to, from whom we may ask and expect the redress of all our grievances. **2**. God will certainly punish and restrain false and proud men. **3**. God will work deliverance for his oppressed people. His help is given in the fittest time. Though men are false, God is faithful; though they are not to be trusted, God is. The preciousness of God's word is compared to silver refined to the highest degree. How many proofs have been given of its power and truth! God will secure his chosen remnant, however bad the times are. As long as the world stands, there will be a generation of proud and wicked men. But all God's people are put into the hands of Christ our Saviour; there they are in safety, for none can pluck them thence; being built on Him, the Rock, they are safe, notwithstanding temptation or persecution come with ever so much force upon them.

Chapter 13

The psalmist complains that God had long withdrawn. He earnestly prays for comfort. He assures himself of an answer of peace.

—God sometimes hides his face, and leaves his own children in the dark concerning their interest in him: and this they lay to heart more than any outward trouble whatever. But anxious cares are heavy burdens with which believers often load themselves more than they need. The bread of sorrows is sometimes the saint's daily bread; our Master himself was a man of sorrows. It is a common temptation, when trouble lasts long, to think that it will last always. Those who have long been without joy, begin to be without hope. We should never allow ourselves to make any complaints but what drive us to our knees. Nothing is more killing to a soul than the want of God's favour; nothing more reviving than the return of it. The sudden, delightful changes in the book of Psalms, are often very remarkable. We pass from depth of despondency to the height of religious confidence and joy. It is thus, ver. **5**. All is gloomy dejection in ver. **4**; but here the mind of the despondent worshipper rises above all its distressing fears, and throws itself, without reserve, on the mercy and care of its Divine Redeemer. See the power of faith, and how good it is to draw near to God. If we bring our cares and griefs to the throne of grace, and leave them there, we may go away like Hannah, and our countenances will be no more said, **1**Sa **1**:**18**. God's mercy is the support of the psalmist's faith. Finding I have that to trust to, I am comforted, though I have no merit of my own. His faith in God's mercy filled his heart with joy in his salvation; for joy and peace come by believing. He has dealt bountifully with me. By faith he was as confident of salvation, as if it had been completed already. In this way believers pour out their prayers, renouncing all hopes but in the mercy of God through the Saviour's blood: and sometimes suddenly, at others gradually, they will find their burdens removed, and their comforts restored; they then allow that their fears and complaints were unnecessary, and acknowledge that the Lord hath dealt bountifully with them.

Chapter 14

A description of the depravity of human nature, and the deplorable corruption of a great part of mankind.

—The fool hath said in his heart, There is no God. The sinner here described is an atheist, one that saith there is no Judge or Governor of the world, no Providence ruling over the affairs of men. He says this in his heart. He cannot satisfy himself that there is none, but wishes there were none, and pleases himself that it is possible there may be none; he is willing to think there is none. This sinner is a fool; he is simple and unwise, and this is evidence of it: he is wicked and profane, and this is the cause. The word of God is a discerner of these thoughts. No man will say, There is no God, till he is so hardened in sin, that it is become his interest that there should be none to call him to an account. The disease of sin has infected the whole race of mankind. They are all gone aside, there is none that doeth good, no, not one. Whatever good is in any of the children of men, or is done by them, it is not of themselves, it is God's work in them. They are gone aside from the right way of their duty, the way that leads to happiness, and are turned into the paths of the destroyer. Let us lament the corruption of our nature, and see what need we have of the grace of God: let us not marvel that we are told we must be born again. And we must not rest in any thing short of union with Christ, and a new creation to holiness by his Spirit. The psalmist endeavours to convince sinners of the evil and danger of their way, while they think themselves very wise, and good, and safe. Their wickedness is described. Those that care not for God's people, for God's poor, care not for God himself. People run into all manner of wickedness, because they do not call upon God for his grace. What good can be expected from those that live without prayer? But those that will not fear God, may be made to fear at the shaking of a leaf. All our knowledge of the depravity of human nature should endear to us salvation out of Zion. But in heaven alone shall the whole company of the redeemed rejoice fully, and for evermore. The world is bad; oh that the Messiah would come and change its character! There is universal corruption; oh for the times of reformation! The triumphs of Zion's King will be the joys of Zion's children. The second coming of Christ, finally to do away the dominion of sin and Satan, will be the completing of this salvation, which is the hope, and will be the joy of every Israelite indeed. With this assurance we should comfort ourselves and one another, under the sins of sinners and sufferings of saints.

Chapter 15

The way to heaven, if we would be happy, we must be holy. We are encouraged to walk in that way.

—Here is a very serious question concerning the character of a citizen of Zion. It is the happiness of glorified saints, that they dwell in the holy hill; they are at home there, they shall be for ever there. It concerns us to make it sure to ourselves that we have a place among them. A very plain and particular answer is here given. Those who desire to know their duty, will find the Scripture a very faithful director, and conscience a faithful monitor. A citizen of Zion is sincere in his religion. He is really what he professes to be, and endeavours to stand complete in all the will of God. He is just both to God and man; and, in speaking to both, speaks the truth in his heart. He scorns and abhors wrong and fraud; he cannot reckon that a good bargain, nor a saving one, which is made with a lie; and knows that he who wrongs his neighbour will prove, in the end, to have most injured himself. He is very careful to do hurt to no man. He speaks evil of no man, makes not others' faults the matter of his common talk; he makes the best of every body, and the worst of nobody. If an ill-natured story be told him, he will disprove it if he can; if not, it goes no further. He values men by their virtue and piety. Wicked people are vile people, worthless, and good for nothing; so the word signifies. He thinks the worse of no man's piety for his poverty and mean condition. He reckons that serious piety puts honour upon a man, more than wealth, or a great name. He honours such, desires their conversation and an interest in their prayers, is glad to show them respect, or do them a kindness. By this we may judge of ourselves in some measure. Even wise and good men may swear to their own hurt: but see how strong the obligation is, a man must rather suffer loss to himself and his family, than wrong his neighbour. He will not increase his estate by extortion, or by bribery. He will not, for any gain, or hope of it to himself, do any thing to hurt a righteous cause. Every true living member of the church, like the church itself, is built upon a Rock. He that doeth these things shall not be moved for ever. The grace of God shall always be sufficient for him. The union of these tempers and this conduct, can only spring from repentance for sin, faith in the Saviour, and love to him. In these respects let us examine and prove our own selves.

Chapter 16

This psalm begins with expressions of devotion, which may be applied to Christ; but ends with such confidence of a resurrection, as must be applied to Christ, and to him only.

—David flees to God's protection, with cheerful, believing confidence. Those who have avowed that the Lord is their Lord, should often put themselves in mind of what they have done, take the comfort of it, and live up to it. He devotes himself to the honour of God, in the service of the saints. Saints on earth we must be, or we shall never be saints in heaven. Those renewed by the grace of God, and devoted to the glory of God, are saints on earth. The saints in the earth are excellent ones, yet some of them so poor, that they needed to have David's goodness extended to them. David declares his resolution to have no fellowship with the works of darkness; he repeats the solemn choice he had made of God for his portion and happiness, takes to himself the comfort of the choice, and gives God the glory of it. This is the language of a devout and pious soul. Most take the world for their chief good, and place their happiness in the enjoyments of it; but how poor soever my condition is in this world, let me have the love and favour of God, and be accepted of him; let me have a title by promise to life and happiness in the future state; and I have enough. Heaven is an inheritance; we must take that for our home, our rest, our everlasting good, and look upon this world to be no more ours, than the country through which is our road to our Father's house. Those that have God for their portion, have a goodly heritage. Return unto thy rest, O my soul, and look no further. Gracious persons, though they still covet more of God, never covet more than God; but, being satisfied of his loving-kindness, are abundantly satisfied with it: they envy not any their carnal mirth and delights. But so ignorant and foolish are we, that if left to ourselves, we shall forsake our own mercies for lying vanities. God having given David counsel by his word and Spirit, his own thoughts taught him in the night season, and engaged him by faith to live to God. **Verses** #(**8**–**11**), are quoted by St. Peter in his first sermon, after the pouring out of the Spirit on the day of Pentecost, Ac **2**:**25**–**31**; he declared that David in them speaks concerning Christ, and particularly of his resurrection. And Christ being the Head of the body, the church, these **verse**s may be applied to all Christians, guided and animated by the Spirit of Christ; and we may hence learn, that it is our wisdom and duty to set the Lord always before us. And if our eyes are ever toward God, our hearts and tongues may ever rejoice in him. Death destroys the hope of man, but not the hope of a real Christian. Christ's resurrection is an earnest of the believer's resurrection. In this world sorrow is our lot, but in heaven there is joy, a fulness of joy; our pleasures here are for a moment, but those at God's right hand are pleasures for evermore. Through this thy beloved Son, and our dear Saviour, thou wilt show us, O Lord, the path of life; thou wilt justify our souls now, and raise our bodies by thy power at the last day; when earthly sorrow shall end in heavenly joy, pain in everlasting happiness.

Chapter 17

Verses 1–7

This psalm is a prayer. Feigned prayers are fruitless; but if our hearts lead our prayers, God will meet them with his favour. The psalmist had been used to pray, so that it was not his distress and danger that now first brought him to his duty. And he was encouraged by his faith to expect God would notice his prayers. Constant resolution and watchfulness against sins of the tongue, will be a good evidence of our integrity. Aware of man's propensity to wicked works, and of his own peculiar temptations, David had made God's word his preservative from the paths of Satan, which lead to destruction. If we carefully avoid the paths of sin, it will be very lead to destruction. If we carefully avoid the paths of sin, it will be very comfortable in the reflection, when we are in trouble. Those that are, through grace, going in God's paths, should pray that their goings may be held up in those paths. David prays, Lord, still hold me up. Those who would proceed and persevere in the ways of God, must, by faith prayer, get daily fresh supplies of grace and strength from him. Show thy marvellous loving-kindness, distinguishing favours, not common mercies, but be gracious to me; do as thou usest to do to those who love thy name.

Verses 8–15

Being compassed with enemies, David prays to God to keep him in safety. This prayer is a prediction that Christ would be preserved, through all the hardships and difficulties of his humiliation, to the glories and joys of his exalted state, and is a pattern to Christians to commit the keeping of their souls to God, trusting him to preserve them to his heavenly kingdom. Those are our worst enemies, that are enemies to our souls. They are God's sword, which cannot move without him, and which he will sheathe when he has done his work with it. They are his hand, by which he chastises his people. There is no fleeing from God's hand, but by fleeing to it. It is very comfortable, when we are in fear of the power of man, to see it dependent upon, and in subjection to the power of God. Most men look on the things of this world as the best things; and they look no further, nor show any care to provide for another life. The things of this world are called treasures, they are so accounted; but to the soul, and when compared with eternal blessings, they are trash. The most afflicted Christian need not envy the most prosperous men of the world, who have their portion in this life. Clothed with Christ's righteousness, having through his grace a good heart and a good life, may we by faith behold God's face, and set him always before us. When we awake every morning, may we be satisfied with his likeness set before us in his word, and with his likeness stamped upon us by his renewing grace. Happiness in the other world is prepared only for those that are justified and sanctified: they shall be put in possession of it when the soul awakes, at death, out of its slumber in the body, and when the body awakes, at the resurrection, out of its slumber in the grave. There is no satisfaction for a soul but in God, and in his good will towards us, and his good work in us; yet that satisfaction will not be perfect till we come to heaven.

Chapter 18

Verses 1–19

The first words, "I will love thee, O Lord, my strength," are the scope and contents of the psalm. Those that truly love God, may triumph in him as their Rock and Refuge, and may with confidence call upon him. It is good for us to observe all the circumstances of a mercy which magnify the power of God and his goodness to us in it. David was a praying man, and God was found a prayer-hearing God. If we pray as he did, we shall speed as he did. God's manifestation of his presence is very fully described, ver. #(**7**–**15**). Little appeared of man, but much of God, in these deliverances. It is not possible to apply to the history of the son of Jesse those awful, majestic, and stupendous words which are used through this description of the Divine manifestation. Every part of so solemn a scene of terrors tells us, a greater than David is here. God will not only deliver his people out of their troubles in due time, but he will bear them up under their troubles in the mean time. Can we meditate on ver. **18**, without directing one thought to Gethsemane and Calvary? Can we forget that it was in the hour of Christ's deepest calamity, when Judas betrayed, when his friends forsook, when the multitude derided him, and the smiles of his Father's love were withheld, that the powers of darkness prevented him? The sorrows of death surrounded him, in his distress he prayed, Heb **5**:**7**. God made the earth to shake and tremble, and the rocks to cleave, and brought him out, in his resurrection, because he delighted in him and in his undertaking.

Verses 20–28

Those that forsake the ways of the Lord, depart from their God. But though conscious to ourselves of many a false step, let there not be a wicked departure from our God. David kept his eye upon the rule of God's commands. Constant care to keep from that sin, whatever it be, which most easily besets us, proves that we are upright before God. Those who show mercy to others, even they need mercy. Those who are faithful to God, shall find him all that to them which he has promised to be. The words of the Lord are pure words, very sure to be depended on, and very sweet to be delighted in. Those who resist God, and walk contrary to him, shall find that he will walk contrary to them, Le **26**:**21**–**24**. The gracious recompence of which David spoke, may generally be expected by those who act from right motives. Hence he speaks comfort to the humble, and terror to the proud; "Thou wilt bring down high looks." And he speaks encouragement to himself; "Thou wilt light my candle:" thou wilt revive and comfort my sorrowful spirit; thou wilt guide my way, that I may avoid the snares laid for me. Thou wilt light my candle to work by, and give me an opportunity of serving thee. Let those that walk in darkness, and labour under discouragements, take courage; God himself will be a Light to them.

Verses 29–50

When we praise for one mercy, we must observe the many more, with which we have been compassed all our days. Many things had contributed to David's advancement, and he owns the hand of God in them all, to teach us to do likewise. In **verse** #(**32**), and the following **verses**, are the gifts of God to the spiritual warrior, whereby he is prepared for the contest, after the example of his victorious Leader. Learn that we must seek release being made through Christ, shall be rejected. In David the type, we behold out of trouble through Christ. The prayer put up, without reconciliation Jesus our Redeemer, conflicting with enemies, compassed with sorrows and with floods of ungodly men, enduring not only the pains of death, but the wrath of God for us; yet calling upon the Father with strong cries and tears; rescued from the grave; proceeding to reconcile, or to put under his feet all other enemies, till death, the last enemy, shall be destroyed. We should love the Lord, our Strength, and our Salvation; we should call on him in every trouble, and praise him for every deliverance; we should aim to walk with him in all righteousness and true holiness, keeping from sin. If we belong to him, he conquers and reigns for us, and we shall conquer and reign through him, and partake of the mercy of our anointed King, which is promised to all his seed for evermore. Amen.

Chapter 19

Verses 1–6

The heavens so declare the glory of God, and proclaim his wisdom, power, and goodness, that all ungodly men are left without excuse. They speak themselves to be works of God's hands; for they must have a Creator who is eternal, infinitely wise, powerful, and good. The counter-changing of day and night is a great proof of the power of God, and calls us to observe, that, as in the kingdom of nature, so in that of providence, he forms the light, and creates the darkness, Isa **45**:**7**, and sets the one against the other. The sun in the firmament is an emblem of the Sun of righteousness, the Bridegroom of the church, and the Light of the world, diffusing Divine light and salvation by his gospel to the nations of the earth. He delights to bless his church, which he has espoused to himself; and his course will be unwearied as that of the sun, till the whole earth is filled with his light and salvation. Let us pray for the time when he shall enlighten, cheer, and make fruitful every nation on earth, with the blessed salvation. They have no speech or language, so some read it, and yet their voice is heard. All people may hear these preachers speak in their own tongue the wonderful works of God. Let us give God the glory of all the comfort and benefit we have by the lights of heaven, still looking above and beyond them to the Sun of righteousness.

Verses 7–10

The Holy Scripture is of much greater benefit to us than day or night, than the air we breathe, or the light of the sun. To recover man out of his fallen state, there is need of the word of God. The word translated "law," may be rendered doctrine, and be understood as meaning all that teaches us true religion. The whole is perfect; its tendency is to convert or turn the soul from sin and the world, to God and holiness. It shows our sinfulness and misery in departing from God, and the necessity of our return to him. This testimony is sure, to be fully depended on: the ignorant and unlearned believing what God saith, become wise unto salvation. It is a sure direction in the way of duty. It is a sure fountain of living comforts, and a sure foundation of lasting hopes. The statues of the Lord are right, just as they should be; and, because they are right, they rejoice the heart. The commandments of the Lord are pure, holy, just, and good. By them we discover our need of a Saviour; and then learn how to adorn his gospel. They are the means which the Holy Spirit uses in enlightening the eyes; they bring us to a sight and sense of our sin and misery, and direct us in the way of duty. The fear of the Lord, that is, true religion and godliness, is clean, it will cleanse our way; and it endureth for ever. The ceremonial law is long since done away, but the law concerning the fear of God is ever the same. The judgments of the Lord, his precepts, are true; they are righteous, and they are so altogether; there is no unrighteousness in any of them. Gold is only for the body, and the concerns of time; but grace is for the soul, and the concerns of eternity. The word of God, received by faith, is more precious than gold; it is sweet to the soul, sweeter than honey. The pleasure of sense soon surfeit, yet never satisfy; but those of religion are substantial and satisfying; there is no danger of excess.

Verses 11–14

God's word warns the wicked not to go on in his wicked way, and warns the righteous not to turn from his good way. There is a reward, not only after keeping, but in keeping God's commandments. Religion makes our comforts sweet, and our crosses easy, life truly valuable, and death itself truly desirable. David not only desired to be pardoned and cleansed from the sins he had discovered and confessed, but from those he had forgotten or overlooked. All discoveries of sin made to us by the law, should drive us to the throne of grace, there to pray. His dependence was the same with that of every Christian who says, Surely in the Lord Jesus have I righteousness and strength. No prayer can be acceptable before God which is not offered in the strength of our Redeemer or Divine Kinsman, through Him who took our nature upon him, that he might redeem us unto God, and restore the long-lost inheritance. May our hearts be much affected with the excellence of the word of God; and much affected with the evil of sin, and the danger we are in of it, and the danger we are in by it.

Chapter 20

This psalm is a prayer for the kings of Israel, but with relation to Christ.

—Even the greatest of men may be much in trouble. Neither the crown on the king's head, nor the grace in his heart, would make him free from trouble. Even the greatest of men must be much in prayer. Let none expect benefit by the prayers of the church, or their friends, who are capable of praying for themselves, yet neglect it. Pray that God would protect his person, and preserve his life. That God would enable him to go on in his undertakings for the public good. We may know that God accepts our spiritual sacrifices, if by his Spirit he kindles in our souls a holy fire of piety and love to God. Also, that the Lord would crown his enterprises with success. Our first step to victory in spiritual warfare is to trust only in the mercy and grace of God; all who trust in themselves will soon be cast down. Believers triumph in God, and his revelation of himself to them, by which they distinguish themselves from those that live without God in the world. Those who make God and his name their praise, may make God and his name their trust. This was the case when the pride and power of Jewish unbelief, and pagan idolatry, fell before the sermons and lives of the humble believers in Jesus. This is the case in every conflict with our spiritual enemies, when we engage them in the name, the spirit, and the power of Christ; and this will be the case at the last day, when the world, with the prince of it, shall be brought down and fall; but believers, risen-from the dead, through the resurrection of the Lord, shall stand, and sing his praises in heaven. In Christ's salvation let us rejoice; and set up our banners in the name of the Lord our God, assured that by the saving strength of his right hand we shall be conquerors over every enemy.

Chapter 21

Verses 1–6

Happy the people whose king makes God's strength his confidence, and God's salvation his joy; who is pleased with all the advancements of God kingdom, and trusts God to support him in all he does for the service of it. All our blessings are blessings of goodness, and are owing, not to any merit of ours, but only to God's goodness. But when God's blessings come sooner, and prove richer than we imagine; when they are given before we prayed for them, before we were ready for them, nay, when we feared the contrary; then it may be truly said that he prevented, or went before us, with them. Nothing indeed prevented, or went before Christ, but to mankind never was any favour more preventing than our redemption by Christ. Thou hast made him to be a universal, everlasting blessing to the world, in whom the families of the earth are, and shall be blessed; and so thou hast made him exceeding glad with the countenance thou hast given to his undertaking, and to him in the prosecution of it. The Spirit of prophecy rises from what related to the king, to that which is peculiar to Christ; none other is blessed for ever, much less a blessing for ever.

Verses 7–13

The psalmist teaches to look forward with faith, and hope, and prayer upon what God would further do. The success with which God blessed David, was a type of the total overthrow of all Christ's enemies. Those who might have had Christ to rule and save them, but rejected him and fought against him, shall find the remembrance of it a worm that dies not. God makes sinners willing by his grace, receives them to his favour, and delivers them from the wrath to come. May he exalt himself, by his all-powerful grace, in our hearts, destroying all the strong-holds of sin and Satan. How great should be our joy and praise to behold our Brother and Friend upon the throne, and for all the blessings we may expect from him! yet he delights in his exalted state, as enabling him to confer happiness and glory on poor sinners, who are taught to love and trust in him.

Chapter 22

Verses 1–10

The Spirit of Christ, which was in the prophets, testifies in this psalm, clearly and fully, the sufferings of Christ, and the glory that should follow. We have a sorrowful complaint of God's withdrawings. This may be applied to any child of God, pressed down, overwhelmed with grief and terror. Spiritual desertions are the saints' sorest afflictions; but even their complaint of these burdens is a sign of spiritual life, and spiritual senses exercised. To cry our, My God, why am I sick? why am I poor? savours of discontent and worldliness. But, "Why hast thou forsaken me?" is the language of a heart binding up its happiness in God's favour. This must be applied to Christ. In the first words of this complaint, he poured out his soul before God when he was upon the cross, Mt **27**:**46**. Being truly man, Christ felt a natural unwillingness to pass through such great sorrows, yet his zeal and love prevailed. Christ declared the holiness of God, his heavenly Father, in his sharpest sufferings; nay, declared them to be a proof of it, for which he would be continually praised by his Israel, more than for all other deliverances they received. Never any that hoped in thee, were made ashamed of their hope; never any that sought thee, sought thee in vain. Here is a complaint of the contempt and reproach of men. The Saviour here spoke of the abject state to which he was reduced. The history of Christ's sufferings, and of his birth, explains this prophecy.

Verses 11–21

In these **verse**s we have Christ suffering, and Christ praying; by which we are directed to look for crosses, and to look up to God under them. The very manner of Christ's death is described, though not in use among the Jews. They pierced his hands and his feet, which were nailed to the accursed tree, and his whole body was left so to hang as to suffer the most severe pain and torture. His natural force failed, being wasted by the fire of Divine wrath preying upon his spirits. Who then can stand before God's anger? or who knows the power of it? The life of the sinner was forfeited, and the life of the Sacrifice must be the ransom for it. Our Lord Jesus was stripped, when he was crucified, that he might clothe us with the robe of his righteousness. Thus it was written, therefore thus it behoved Christ to suffer. Let all this confirm our faith in him as the true Messiah, and excite our love to him as the best of friends, who loved us, and suffered all this for us. Christ in his agony prayed, prayed earnestly, prayed that the cup might pass from him. When we cannot rejoice in God as our song, yet let us stay ourselves upon him as our strength; and take the comfort of spiritual supports, when we cannot have spiritual delights. He prays to be delivered from the Divine wrath. He that has delivered, doth deliver, and will do so. We should think upon the sufferings and resurrection of Christ, till we feel in our souls the power of his resurrection, and the fellowship of his sufferings.

Verses 22–31

The Saviour now speaks as risen from the dead. The first words of the complaint were used by Christ himself upon the cross; the first words of the triumph are expressly applied to him, Heb **2**:**12**. All our praises must refer to the work of redemption. The suffering of the Redeemer was graciously accepted as a full satisfaction for sin. Though it was offered for sinful men, the Father did not despise or abhor it for our sakes. This ought to be the matter of our thanksgiving. All humble, gracious souls should have a full satisfaction and happiness in him. Those that hunger and thirst after righteousness in Christ, shall not labour for that which satisfies not. Those that are much in praying, will be much in thanksgiving. Those that turn to God, will make conscience of worshipping before him. Let every tongue confess that he is Lord. High and low, rich and poor, bond and free, meet in Christ. Seeing we cannot keep alive our own souls, it is our wisdom, by obedient faith, to commit our souls to Christ, who is able to save and keep them alive for ever. A seed shall serve him. God will have a church in the world to the end of time. They shall be accounted to him for a generation; he will be the same to them that he was to those who went before them. His righteousness, and not any of their own, they shall declare to be the foundation of all their hopes, and the fountain of all their joys. Redemption by Christ is the Lord's own doing. Here we see the free love and compassion of God the Father, and of our Lord Jesus Christ, for us wretched sinners, as the source of all grace and consolation; the example we are to follow, the treatment as Christians we are to expect, and the conduct under it we are to adopt. Every lesson may here be learned that can profit the humbled soul. Let those who go about to establish their own righteousness inquire, why the beloved Son of God should thus suffer, if their own doings could atone for sin? Let the ungodly professor consider whether the Saviour thus honoured the Divine law, to purchase him the privilege of despising it. Let the careless take warning to flee from the wrath to come, and the trembling rest their hopes upon this merciful Redeemer. Let the tempted and distressed believer cheerfully expect a happy end of every trial.

Chapter 23

Confidence in God's grace and care.

—"The Lord is my shepherd." In these words, the believer is taught to express his satisfaction in the care of the great Pastor of the uni**verse**, the Redeemer and Preserver of men. With joy he reflects that he has a shepherd, and that shepherd is Jehovah. A flock of sheep, gentle and harmless, feeding in verdant pastures, under the care of a skilful, watchful, and tender shepherd, forms an emblem of believers brought back to the Shepherd of their souls. The greatest abundance is but a dry pasture to a wicked man, who relishes in it only what pleases the senses; but to a godly man, who by faith tastes the goodness of God in all his enjoyments, though he has but little of the world, it is a green pasture. The Lord gives quiet and contentment in the mind, whatever the lot is. Are we blessed with the green pastures of the ordinances, let us not think it enough to pass through them, but let us abide in them. The consolations of the Holy Spirit are the still waters by which the saints are led; the streams which flow from the Fountain of living waters. Those only are led by the still waters of comfort, who walk in the paths of righteousness. The way of duty is the truly pleasant way. The work of righteousness in peace. In these paths we cannot walk, unless. God lead us into them, and lead us on in them. Discontent and distrust proceed from unbelief; an unsteady walk is the consequence: let us then simply trust our Shepherd's care, and hearken to his voice. The valley of the shadow of death may denote the most severe and terrible affliction, or dark dispensation of providence, that the psalmist ever could come under. Between the part of the flock on earth and that which is gone to heaven, death lies like a dark valley that must be passed in going from one to the other. But even in this there are words which lessen the terror. It is but the shadow of death: the shadow of a serpent will not sting, nor the shadow of a sword kill. It is a valley, deep indeed, and dark, and miry; but valleys are often fruitful, and so is death itself fruitful of comforts to God's people. It is a walk through it: they shall not be lost in this valley, but get safe to the mountain on the other side. Death is a king of terrors, but not to the sheep of Christ. When they come to die, God will rebuke the enemy; he will guide them with his rod, and sustain them with his staff. There is enough in the gospel to comfort the saints when dying, and underneath them are the everlasting arms. The Lord's people feast at his table, upon the provisions of his love. Satan and wicked men are not able to destroy their comforts, while they are anointed with the Holy Spirit, and drink of the cup of salvation which is ever full. Past experience teaches believers to trust that the goodness and mercy of God will follow them all the days of their lives, and it is their desire and determination, to seek their happiness in the service of God here, and they hope to enjoy his love for ever in heaven. While here, the Lord can make any situation pleasant, by the anointing of his Spirit and the joys of his salvation. But those that would be satisfied with the blessings of his house, must keep close to the duties of it.

Chapter 24

Verses 1–6

We ourselves are not our own; our bodies, our souls, are not. Even those of the children of men are God's, who know him not, nor own their relation to him. A soul that knows and considers its own nature, and that it must live for ever, when it has viewed the earth and the fulness thereof, will sit down unsatisfied. It will think of ascending toward God, and will ask, What shall I do, that I may abide in that happy, holy place, where he makes his people holy and happy? We make nothing of religion, if we do not make heart-work of it. We can only be cleansed from our sins, and renewed unto holiness, by the blood of Christ and the washing of the Holy Ghost. Thus we become his people; thus we receive blessing from the Lord, and righteousness from the God of our salvation. God's peculiar people shall be made truly and for ever happy. Where God gives righteousness, he designs salvation. Those that are made meet for heaven, shall be brought safe to heaven, and will find what they have been seeking.

Verses 7–10

The splendid entry here described, refers to the solemn bringing in of the ark into the tent David pitched for it, or the temple Solomon built for it. We may also apply it to the ascension of Christ into heaven, and the welcome given to him there. Our Redeemer found the gates of heaven shut, but having by his blood made atonement for sin, as one having authority, he demanded entrance. The angels were to worship him, Heb **1**:**6**: they ask with wonder, Who is he? It is answered, that he is strong and mighty; mighty in battle to save his people, and to subdue his and their enemies. We may apply it to Christ's entrance into the souls of men by his word and Spirit, that they may be his temples. Behold, he stands at the door, and knocks, Rev **3**:**20**. The gates and doors of the heart are to be opened to him, as possession is delivered to the rightful owner. We may apply it to his second coming with glorious power. Lord, open the everlasting door of our souls by thy grace, that we may now receive thee, and be wholly thine; and that, at length, we may be numbered with thy saints in glory.

Chapter 25

Verses 1–7

In worshipping God, we must lift up our souls to him. It is certain that none who, by a believing attendance, wait on God, and, by a believing hope, wait for him, shall be ashamed of it. The most advanced believer both needs and desires to be taught of God. If we sincerely desire to know our duty, with resolution to do it, we may be sure that God will direct us in it. The psalmist is earnest for the pardon of his sins. When God pardons sin, he is said to remember it no more, which denotes full remission. It is God's goodness, and not ours, his mercy, and not our merit, that must be our plea for the pardon of sin, and all the good we need. This plea we must rely upon, feeling our own unworthiness, and satisfied of the riches of God's mercy and grace. How boundless is that mercy which covers for ever the sins and follies of a youth spent without God and without hope! Blessed be the Lord, the blood of the great Sacrifice can wash away every stain.

Verses 8–14

We are all sinners; and Christ came into the world to save sinners, to teach sinners, to call sinners to repentance. We value a promise by the character of him that makes it; we therefore depend upon God's promises. All the paths of the Lord, that is, all his promises and all his providences, are mercy and truth. In all God's dealings his people may see his mercy displayed, and his word fulfilled, whatever afflictions they are now exercised with. All the paths of the Lord are mercy and truth; and so it will appear when they come to their journey's end. Those that are humble, that distrust themselves, and desire to be taught and to follow Divine guidance, these he will guide in judgment, that is, by the rule of the written word, to find rest for their souls in the Saviour. Even when the body is sick, and in pain, the soul may be at ease in God.

Verses 15–22

The psalmist concludes, as he began, with expressing dependence upon God, and desire toward him. It is good thus to hope, and quietly to wait for the salvation of the Lord. And if God turns to us, no matter who turns from us. He pleads his own integrity. Though guilty before God, yet, as to his enemies, he had the testimony of conscience that he had done them no wrong. God would, at length, give Israel rest from all their enemies round about. In heaven, God's Israel will be perfectly redeemed from all troubles. Blessed Saviour, thou hast graciously taught us that without thee we can do nothing. Do thou teach us how to pray, how to appear before thee in the way which thou shalt choose, and how to lift up our whole hearts and desires after thee, for thou art the Lord our righteousness.

Chapter 26

David, in this psalm, appeals to God touching his integrity.

—David here, by the Spirit of prophecy, speaks of himself as a type of Christ, of whom what he here says of his spotless innocence was fully and eminently true, and of Christ only, and to Him we may apply it. We are complete in him. The man that walks in his integrity, yet trusting wholly in the grace of God, is in a state of acceptance, according to the covenant of which Jesus was the Mediator, in virtue of his spotless obedience even unto death. This man desires to have his inmost soul searched and proved by the Lord. He is aware of the deceitfulness of his own heart; he desires to detect and mortify every sin; and he longs to be satisfied of his being a true believer, and to practise the holy commands of God. Great care to avoid bad company, is both a good evidence of our integrity, and a good means to keep us in it. Hypocrites and dissemblers may be found attending on God's ordinances; but it is a good sign of sincerity, if we attend upon them, as the psalmist here tells us he did, in the exercise of repentance and conscientious obedience. He feels his ground firm under him; and, as he delights in blessing the Lord with his congregations on earth, he trusts that shortly he shall join the great assembly in heaven, in singing praises to God and to the Lamb for evermore.

Chapter 27

Verses 1–6

The Lord, who is the believer's light, is the strength of his life; not only by whom, but in whom he lives and moves. In God let us strengthen ourselves. The gracious presence of God, his power, his promise, his readiness to hear prayer, the witness of his Spirit in the hearts of his people; these are the secret of his tabernacle, and in these the saints find cause for that holy security and peace of mind in which they dwell at ease. The psalmist prays for constant communion with God in holy ordinances. All God's children desire to dwell in their Father's house. Not to sojourn there as a wayfaring man, to tarry but for a night; or to dwell there for a time only, as the servant that abides not in the house for ever; but to dwell there all the days of their life, as children with a father. Do we hope that the praising of God will be the blessedness of our eternity? Surely then we ought to make it the business of our time. This he had at heart more than any thing. Whatever the Christian is as to this life, he considers the favour and service of God as the one thing needful. This he desires, prays for and seeks after, and in it he rejoices.

Verses 7–14

Wherever the believer is, he can find a way to the throne of grace by prayer. God calls us by his Spirit, by his word, by his worship, and by special providences, merciful and afflicting. When we are foolishly making court to lying vanities, God is, in love to us, calling us to seek our own mercies in him. The call is general, "Seek ye my face;" but we must apply it to ourselves, "I will seek it." The word does us no good, when we do not ourselves accept the exhortation: a gracious heart readily answers to the call of a gracious God, being made willing in the day of his power. The psalmist requests the favour of the Lord; the continuance of his presence with him; the benefit of Divine guidance, and the benefit of Divine protection. God's time to help those that trust in him, is, when all other helpers fail. He is a surer and better Friend than earthly parents are, or can be. What was the belief which supported the psalmist? That he should see the goodness of the Lord. There is nothing like the believing hope of eternal life, the foresights of that glory, and foretastes of those pleasures, to keep us from fainting under all calamities. In the mean time he should be strengthened to bear up under his burdens. Let us look unto the suffering Saviour, and pray in faith, not to be delivered into the hands of our enemies. Let us encourage each other to wait on the Lord, with patient expectation, and fervent prayer.

Chapter 28

Verses 1–5

David is very earnest in prayer. Observe his faith in prayer; God is my rock, on whom I build my hope. Believers should not rest till they have received some token that their prayers are heard. He prays that he may not be numbered with the wicked. Save me from being entangled in the snares they have laid for me. Save me from being infected with their sins, and from doing as they do. Lord, never leave me to use such arts of deceit and treachery for my safety, as they use for my ruin. Believers dread the way of sinners; the best are sensible of the danger they are in of being drawn aside: we should all pray earnestly to God for his grace to keep us. Those who are careful not to partake with sinners in their sins, have reason to hope that they shall not receive their plagues. He speaks of the just judgments of the Lord on the workers of iniquity, ver. #(**4**). This is not the language of passion or revenge. It is a prophecy that there will certainly come a day, when God will punish every man who persists in his evil deeds. Sinners shall be reckoned with, not only for the mischief they have done, but for the mischief they designed, and did what they could to effect. Disregard of the works of the Lord, is the cause of the sin of sinners, and becomes the cause of their ruin.

Verses 6–9

Has God heard our supplications? Let us then bless his name. The Lord is my strength, to support me, and carry me on through all my services and sufferings. The heart that truly believes, shall in due time greatly rejoice: we are to expect joy and peace in believing. God shall have the praise of it: thus must we express our gratitude. The saints rejoice in others' comfort as well as their own: we have the less benefit from the light of the sun, nor from the light of God's countenance, for others' sharing therein. The psalmist concludes with a short, but comprehensive prayer. God's people are his inheritance, and precious in his eyes. He prays that God would save them; that he would bless them with all good, especially the plenty of his ordinances, which are food to the soul. And direct their actions and overrule their affairs for good. Also, lift them up for ever; not only those of that age, but his people in every age to come; lift them up as high as heaven. There, and there only, will saints be lifted up for ever, never more to sink, or be depressed. Save us, Lord Jesus, from our sins; bless us, thou Son of Abraham, with the blessing of righteousness; feed us, thou good Shepherd of the sheep, and lift us up for ever from the dust, O thou, who art the Resurrection and the Life.

Chapter 29

Exhortation to give glory to God.

—The mighty and honourable of the earth are especially bound to honour and worship him; but, alas, few attempt to worship him in the beauty of holiness. When we come before him as the Redeemer of sinners, in repentance faith, and love, he will accept our defective services, pardon the sin that cleaves to them, and approve of that measure of holiness which the Holy Spirit enables us to exercise. We have here the nature of religious worship; it is giving to the Lord the glory due to his name. We must be holy in all our religious services, devoted to God, and to his will and glory. There is a beauty in holiness, and that puts beauty upon all acts of worship. The psalmist here sets forth God's dominion in the kingdom of nature. In the thunder, and lightning, and storm, we may see and hear his glory. Let our hearts be thereby filled with great, and high, and honourable thoughts of God, in the holy adoring of whom, the power of godliness so much consists. O Lord our God, thou art very great! The power of the lightning equals the terror of the thunder. The fear caused by these effects of the Divine power, should remind us of the mighty power of God, of man's weakness, and of the defenceless and desperate condition of the wicked in the day of judgment. But the effects of the Divine word upon the souls of men, under the power of the Holy Spirit, are far greater than those of thunder storms in the nature world. Thereby the stoutest are made to tremble, the proudest are cast down, the secrets of the heart are brought to light, sinners are converted, the savage, sensual, and unclean, become harmless, gentle, and pure. If we have heard God's voice, and have fled for refuge to the hope set before us, let us remember that children need not fear their Father's voice, when he speaks in anger to his enemies. While those tremble who are without shelter, let those who abide in his appointed refuge bless him for their security, looking forward to the day of judgment without dismay, safe as Noah in the ark.

Chapter 30

Verses 1–5

The great things the Lord has done for us, both by his providence and by his grace, bind us in gratitude to do all we can to advance his kingdom among men, though the most we can do is but little. God's saints in heaven sing to him; why should not those on earth do the same? Not one of all God's perfections carries in it more terror to the wicked, or more comfort to the godly, than his holiness. It is a good sign that we are in some measure partakers of his holiness, if we can heartily rejoice at the remembrance of it. Our happiness is bound up in the Divine favour; if we have that, we have enough, whatever else we want; but as long as God's anger continues, so long the saints' weeping continues.

Verses 6–12

When things are well with us, we are very apt to think that they will always be so. When we see our mistake, it becomes us to think with shame upon our carnal security as our folly. If God hide his face, a good man is troubled, though no other calamity befal him. But if God, in wisdom and justice, turn from us, it will be the greatest folly if we turn from him. No; let us learn to pray in the dark. The sanctified spirit, which returns to God, shall praise him, shall be still praising him; but the services of God's house cannot be performed by the dust; it cannot praise him; there is none of that device or working in the grave, for it is the land of silence. We ask aright for life, when we do so that we may live to praise him. In due time God delivered the psalmist out of his troubles. Our tongue is our glory, and never more so than when employed in praising God. He would persevere to the end in praise, hoping that he should shortly be where this would be the everlasting work. But let all beware of carnal security. Neither outward prosperity, nor inward peace, here, are sure and lasting. The Lord, in his favour, has fixed the believer's safety firm as the deep-rooted mountains, but he must expect to meet with temptations and afflictions. When we grow careless, we fall into sin, the Lord hides his face, our comforts droop, and troubles assail us.

Chapter 31

Verses 1–8

Faith and prayer must go together, for the prayer of faith is the prevailing prayer. David gave up his soul in a special manner to God. And with the words, ver. **5**, our Lord Jesus yielded up his last breath on the cross, and made his soul a free-will offering for sin, laying down his life as a ransom. But David is here as a man in distress and trouble. And his great care is about his soul, his spirit, his better part. Many think that while perplexed about their worldly affairs, and their cares multiply, they may be excused if they neglect their souls; but we are the more concerned to look to our souls, that, though the outward man perish, the inward man may suffer no damage. The redemption of the soul is so precious, that it must have ceased for ever, if Christ had not undertaken it. Having relied on God's mercy, he will be glad and rejoice in it. God looks upon our souls, when we are in trouble, to see whether they are humbled for sin, and made better by the affliction. Every believer will meet with such dangers and deliverances, until he is delivered from death, his last enemy.

Verses 9–18

David's troubles made him a man of sorrows. Herein he was a type of Christ, who was acquainted with grief. David acknowledged that his afflictions were merited by his own sins, but Christ suffered for ours. David's friends durst not give him any assistance. Let us not think it strange if thus deserted, but make sure of a Friend in heaven who will not fail. God will be sure to order and dispose all for the best, to all those who commit their spirits also into his hand. The time of life is in God's hands, to lengthen or shorten, make bitter or sweet, according to the counsel of his will. The way of man is not in himself, nor in our friend's hands, nor in our enemies' hands, but in God's. In this faith and confidence he prays that the Lord would save him for his mercies's sake, and not for any merit of his own. He prophesies the silencing of those that reproach and speak evil of the people of God. There is a day coming, when the Lord will execute judgment upon them. In the mean time, we should engage ourselves by well-doing, if possible, to silence the ignorance of foolish men.

Verses 19–24

Instead of yielding to impatience or despondency under our troubles, we should turn our thoughts to the goodness of the Lord towards those who fear and trust in Him. All comes to sinners through the wondrous gift of the only-begotten Son of God, to be the atonement for their sins. Let not any yield to unbelief, or think, under discouraging circumstances, that they are cut off from before the eyes of the Lord, and left to the pride of men. Lord, pardon our complaints and fears; increase our faith, patience, love, and gratitude; teach us to rejoice in tribulation and in hope. The deliverance of Christ, with the destruction of his enemies, ought to strengthen and comfort the hearts of believers under all their afflictions here below, that having suffered courageously with their Master, they may triumphantly enter into his joy and glory.

Chapter 32

Verses 1, 2

Sin is the cause of our misery; but the true believer's transgressions of the Divine law are all forgiven, being covered with the atonement. Christ bare his sins, therefore they are not imputed to him. The righteousness of Christ being reckoned to us, and we being made the righteousness of God in him, our iniquity is not imputed, God having laid upon him the iniquity of us all, and made him a sin-offering for us. Not to impute sin, is God's act, for he is the Judge. It is God that justifies. Notice the character of him whose sins are pardoned; he is sincere, and seeks sanctification by the power of the Holy Ghost. He does not profess to repent, with an intention to indulge in sin, because the Lord is ready to forgive. He will not abuse the doctrine of free grace. And to the man whose iniquity is forgiven, all manner of blessings are promised.

Verses 3–7

It is very difficult to bring sinful man humbly to accept free mercy, with a full confession of his sins and self-condemnation. But the true and only way to peace of conscience, is, to confess our sins, that they may be forgiven; to declare them that we may be justified. Although repentance and confession do not merit the pardon of transgression, they are needful to the real enjoyment of forgiving mercy. And what tongue can tell the happiness of that hour, when the soul, oppressed by sin, is enabled freely to pour forth its sorrows before God, and to take hold of his covenanted mercy in Christ Jesus! Those that would speed in prayer, must seek the Lord, when, by his providence, he calls them to seek him, and, by his Spirit, stirs them up to seek him. In a time of finding, when the heart is softened with grief, and burdened with guilt; when all human refuge fails; when no rest can be found to the troubled mind, then it is that God applies the healing balm by his Spirit.

Verses 8–11

God teaches by his word, and guides with the secret intimations of his will. David gives a word of caution to sinners. The reason for this caution is, that the way of sin will certainly end in sorrow. Here is a word of comfort to saints. They may see that a life of communion with God is far the most pleasant and comfortable. Let us rejoice, O Lord Jesus, in thee, and in thy salvation; so shall we rejoice indeed.

Chapter 33

Verses 1–11

Holy joy is the heart and soul of praise, and that is here pressed upon the righteous. Thankful praise is the breath and language of holy joy. Religious songs are proper expressions of thankful praise. Every endowment we possess, should be employed with all our skill and earnestness in God's service. His promises are all wise and good. His word is right, and therefore we are only in the right when we agree with it. His works are all done in truth. He is the righteous Lord, therefore loveth righteousness. What a pity it is that this earth, which is so full of the proofs and instances of God's goodness, should be so empty of his praises; and that of the multitudes who live upon his bounty, there are so few who live to his glory! What the Lord does, he does to purpose; it stands fast. He overrules all the counsels of men, and makes them serve his counsels; even that is fulfilled, which to us is most surprising, the eternal counsel of God, nor can any thing prevent its coming to pass.

Verses 12–22

All the motions and operations of the souls of men, which no mortals know but themselves, God knows better than they do. Their hearts, as well as their times, are all in his hand; he formed the spirit of each man within him. All the powers of the creature depend upon him, and are of no account, of no avail at all, without him. If we make God's favour sure towards us, then we need not fear whatever is against us. We are to give to him the glory of his special grace. All human devices for the salvation of our souls are vain; but the Lord's watchful eye is over those whose conscientious fear of his name proceeds from a believing hope in his mercy. In difficulties they shall be helped; in dangers they shall not receive any real damage. Those that fear God and his wrath, must hope in God and his mercy; for there is no flying from him, but by flying to him. Let thy mercy, O Lord, be upon us; let us always have the comfort and benefit, not according to our merits, but according to the promise which thou hast in thy word given to us, and according to the faith thou hast by thy Spirit and grace wrought in us.

Chapter 34

Verses 1–10

If we hope to spend eternity in praising God, it is fit that we should spend much of our time here in this work. He never said to any one, Seek ye me in vain. David's prayers helped to silence his fears; many besides him have looked unto the Lord by faith and prayer, and it has wonderfully revived and comforted them. When we look to the world, we are perplexed, and at a loss. But on looking to Christ depends our whole salvation, and all things needful thereunto do so also. This poor man, whom no man looked upon with any respect, or looked after with any concern, was yet welcome to the throne of grace; the Lord heard him, and saved him out of all his troubles. The holy angels minister to the saints, and stand for them against the powers of darkness. All the glory be to the Lord of the angels. By taste and sight we both make discoveries, and have enjoyment; Taste and see God's goodness; take notice of it, and take the comfort of it. He makes all truly blessed that trust in him. As to the things of the other world, they shall have grace sufficient for the support of spiritual life. And as to this life, they shall have what is necessary from the hand of God. Paul had all, and abounded, because he was content, Php **4**:**11**–**18**. Those who trust to themselves, and think their own efforts sufficient for them, shall want; but they shall be fed who trust in the Lord. Those shall not want, who with quietness work, and mind their own business.

Verses 11–22

Let young persons set out in life with learning the fear of the Lord, if they desire true comfort here, and eternal happiness hereafter. Those will be most happy who begin the soonest to serve so good a Master. All aim to be happy. Surely this must look further than the present world; for man's life on earth consists but of few days, and those full of trouble. What man is he that would see the good of that where all bliss is perfect? Alas! few have this good in their thoughts. That religion promises best which creates watchfulness over the heart and over the tongue. It is not enough not to do hurt, we must study to be useful, and to live to some purpose; we must seek peace and pursue it; be willing to deny ourselves a great deal for peace' sake. It is the constant practice of real believers, when in distress, to cry unto God, and it is their constant comfort that he hears them. The righteous are humbled for sin, and are low in their own eyes. Nothing is more needful to true godliness than a contrite heart, broken off from every self-confidence. In this soil every grace will flourish, and nothing can encourage such a one but the free, rich grace of the gospel of Jesus Christ. The righteous are taken under the special protection of the Lord, yet they have their share of crosses in this world, and there are those that hate them. Both from the mercy of Heaven, and the malice of hell, the afflictions of the righteous must be many. But whatever troubles befall them, shall not hurt their souls, for God keeps them from sinning in troubles. No man is desolate, but he whom God has forsaken.

Chapter 35

Verses 1–10

It is no new thing for the most righteous men, and the most righteous cause, to meet with enemies. This is a fruit of the old enmity in the seed of the serpent against the Seed of the woman. David in his afflictions, Christ in his sufferings, the church under persecution, and the Christian in the hour temptation, all beseech the Almighty to appear in their behalf, and to vindicate their cause. We are apt to justify uneasiness at the injuries men do us, by our never having given them cause to use us so ill; but this should make us easy, for then we may the more expect that God will plead our cause. David prayed to God to manifest himself in his trial. Let me have inward comfort under all outward troubles, to support my soul. If God, by his Spirit, witness to our spirits that he is our salvation, we need desire no more to make us happy. If God is our Friend, no matter who is our enemy. By the Spirit of prophecy, David foretells the just judgments of God that would come upon his enemies for their great wickedness. These are predictions, they look forward, and show the doom of the enemies of Christ and his kingdom. We must not desire or pray for the ruin of any enemies, except our lusts and the evil spirits that would compass our destruction. A traveller benighted in a bad road, is an expressive emblem of a sinner walking in the slippery and dangerous ways of temptation. But David having committed his cause to God, did not doubt of his own deliverance. The bones are the strongest parts of the body. The psalmist here proposes to serve and glorify God with all his strength. If such language may be applied to outward salvation, how much more will it apply to heavenly things in Christ Jesus!

Verses 11–16

Call a man ungrateful, and you can call him no worse: this was the character of David's enemies. Herein he was a type of Christ. David shows how tenderly he had behaved towards them in afflictions. We ought to mourn for the sins of those who do not mourn for themselves. We shall not lose by the good offices we do to any, how ungrateful soever they may be. Let us learn to possess our souls in patience and meekness like David, or rather after Christ's example.

Verses 17–28

Though the people of God are, and study to be, quiet, yet it has been common for their enemies to devise deceitful matters against them. David prays, My soul is in danger, Lord, rescue it; it belongs to thee the Father of spirits, therefore claim thine own; it is thine, save it! Lord, be not far from me, as if I were a stranger. He who exalted the once suffering Redeemer, will appear for all his people: the roaring lion shall not destroy their souls, any more than he could that of Christ, their Surety. They trust their souls in his hands, they are one with him by faith, are precious in his sight, and shall be rescued from destruction, that they may give thanks in heaven.

Chapter 36

Verses 1–4

From this psalm our hearts should be duly affected with hatred of sin, and seek satisfaction in God's loving-kindness. Here is the root of bitterness, from which all the wickedness of wicked men comes. It takes rise from contempt of God, and the want of due regard to him. Also from the deceit they put upon their own souls. Let us daily beg of God to preserve us from self-flattery. Sin is very hurtful to the sinner himself, and therefore ought to be hateful; but it is not so. It is no marvel, if those that deceive themselves, seek to deceive all mankind; to whom will they be true, who are false to their own souls? It is bad to do mischief, but worse to devise it, to do it with plot and management. If we willingly banish holy meditations in our solitary hours, Satan will soon occupy our minds with sinful imaginations. Hardened sinners stand to what they have done, as though they could justify it before God himself.

Verses 5–12

Men may shut up their compassion, yet, with God we shall find mercy. This is great comfort to all believers, plainly to be seen, and not to be taken away. God does all wisely and well; but what he does we know not now, it is time enough to know hereafter. God's loving-kindness is precious to the saints. They put themselves under his protection, and then are safe and easy. Gracious souls, though still desiring more of God, never desire more than God. The gifts of Providence so far satisfy them, that they are content with such things as they have. The benefit of holy ordinances is sweet to a sanctified soul, and strengthening to the spiritual and Divine life. But full satisfaction is reserved for the future state. Their joys shall be constant. God not only works in them a gracious desire for these pleasures, but by his Spirit fills their souls with joy and peace in believing. He quickens whom he will; and whoever will, may come, and take from him of the waters of life freely. May we know, and love, and uprightly serve the Lord; then no proud enemy, on earth or from hell, shall separate us from his love. Faith calleth things that are not, as though they were. It carries us forward to the end of time; it shows us the Lord, on his throne of judgment; the empire of sin fallen to rise no more.

Chapter 37

David persuades to patience and confidence in God, by the state of the godly and of the wicked.

Verses 1–6

When we look abroad we see the world full of evil-doers, that flourish and live in ease. So it was seen of old, therefore let us not marvel at the matter. We are tempted to fret at this, to think them the only happy people, and so we are prone to do like them: but this we are warned against. Outward prosperity is fading. When we look forward, with an eye of faith, we shall see no reason to envy the wicked. Their weeping and wailing will be everlasting. The life of religion is a believing trust in the Lord, and diligent care to serve him according to his will. It is not trusting God, but tempting him, if we do not make conscience of our duty to him. A man's life consists not in abundance, but, Thou shalt have food convenient for thee. This is more than we deserve, and it is enough for one that is going to heaven. To delight in God is as much a privilege as a duty. He has not promised to gratify the appetites of the body, and the humours of the fancy, but the desires of the renewed, sanctified soul. What is the desire of the heart of a good man? It is this, to know, and love, and serve God. Commit thy way unto the Lord; roll thy way upon the Lord, so the margin reads it. Cast thy burden upon the Lord, the burden of thy care. We must roll it off ourselves, not afflict and perplex ourselves with thoughts about future events, but refer them to God. By prayer spread thy case and all thy cares before the Lord, and trust in him. We must do our duty, and then leave the event with God. The promise is very sweet: He shall bring that to pass, whatever it is, which thou has committed to him.

Verses 7–20

Let us be satisfied that God will make all to work for good to us. Let us not discompose ourselves at what we see in this world. A fretful, discontented spirit is open to many temptations. For, in all respects, the little which is allotted to the righteous, is more comfortable and more profitable than the ill-gotten and abused riches of ungodly men. It comes from a hand of special love. God provides plentifully and well, not only for his working servants, but for his waiting servants. They have that which is better than wealth, peace of mind, peace with God, and then peace in God; that peace which the world cannot give, and which the world cannot have. God knows the believer's days. Not one day's work shall go unrewarded. Their time on earth is reckoned by days, which will soon be numbered; but heavenly happiness shall be for ever. This will be a real support to believers in evil times. Those that rest on the Rock of ages, have no reason to envy the wicked the support of their broken reeds.

Verses 21–33

The Lord our God requires that we do justly, and render to all their due. It is a great sin for those that are able, to deny the payment of just debts; it is a great misery not to be able to pay them. He that is truly merciful, will be ever merciful. We must leave our sins; learn to do well, and cleave to it. This is true religion. The blessing of God is the spring, sweetness, and security of all earthly enjoyments. And if we are sure of this, we are sure not to want any thing good for us in this world. By his grace and Holy Spirit, he directs the thoughts, affections, and designs of good men. By his providence he overrules events, so as to make their way plain. He does not always show them his way for a distance, but leads them step by step, as children are led. God will keep them from being ruined by their falls, either into sin or into trouble, though such as fall into sin will be sorely hurt. Few, if any, have known the consistent believer, or his children, reduced to abject, friendless want. God forsakes not his saints in affliction; and in heaven only the righteous shall dwell for ever; that will be their everlasting habitation. A good man may fall into the hands of a messenger of Satan, and be sorely buffeted, but God will not leave him in his enemy's hands.

Verses 34–40

Duty is ours, and we must mind it; but events are God's, we must refer the disposal of them to him. What a striking picture is in ver. #(**35**, **36**), of many a prosperous enemy of God! But God remarkably blights the projects of the prosperous wicked, especially persecutors. None are perfect in themselves, but believers are so in Christ Jesus. If all the saint's days continue dark and cloudy, his dying day may prove comfortable, and his sun set bright; or, if it should set under a cloud, yet his future state will be everlasting peace. The salvation of the righteous will be the Lord's doing. He will help them to do their duties, to bear their burdens; help them to bear their troubles well, and get good by them, and, in due time, will deliver them out of their troubles. Let sinners then depart from evil, and do good; repent of and forsake sin, and trust in the mercy of God through Jesus Christ. Let them take his yoke upon them, and learn of him, that they may dwell for evermore in heaven. Let us mark the closing scenes of different characters, and always depend on God's mercy.

Chapter 38

Verses 1–11

Nothing will disquiet the heart of a good man so much as the sense of God's anger. The way to keep the heart quiet, is to keep ourselves in the love of God. But a sense of guilt is too heavy to bear; and would sink men into despair and ruin, unless removed by the pardoning mercy of God. If there were not sin in our souls, there would be no pain in our bones, no illness in our bodies. The guilt of sin is a burden to the whole creation, which groans under it. It will be a burden to the sinners themselves, when they are heavy-laden under it, or a burden of ruin, when it sinks them to hell. When we perceive our true condition, the Good Physician will be valued, sought, and obeyed. Yet many let their wounds rankle, because they delay to go to their merciful Friend. When, at any time, we are distempered in our bodies, we ought to remember how God has been dishonoured in and by our bodies. The groanings which cannot be uttered, are not hid from Him that searches the heart, and knows the mind of the Spirit. David, in his troubles, was a type of Christ in his agonies, of Christ on his cross, suffering and deserted.

Verses 12–22

Wicked men hate goodness, even when they benefit by it. David, in the complaints he makes of his enemies, seems to refer to Christ. But our enemies do us real mischief only when they drive us from God and our duty. The true believer's trouble will be made useful; he will learn to wait for his God, and will not seek relief from the world or himself. The less we notice the unkindness and injuries that are done us, the more we consult the quiet of our own minds. David's troubles were the chastisement and the consequence of his transgressions, whilst Christ suffered for our sins and ours only. What right can a sinner have to yield to impatience or anger, when mercifully corrected for his sins? David was very sensible of the present workings of corruption in him. Good men, by setting their sorrow continually before them, have been ready to fall; but by setting God always before them, they have kept their standing. If we are truly penitent for sin, that will make us patient under affliction. Nothing goes nearer to the heart of a believer when in affliction, than to be under the apprehension of God's deserting him; nor does any thing come more feelingly from his heart than this prayer, "Be not far from me." The Lord will hasten to help those who trust in him as their salvation.

Chapter 39

Verses 1–6

If an evil thought should arise in the mind, suppress it. Watchfulness in the habit, is the bridle upon the head; watchfulness in acts, is the hand upon the bridle. When not able to separate from wicked men, we should remember they will watch our words, and turn them, if they can, to our disadvantage. Sometimes it may be necessary to keep silence, even from good words; but in general we are wrong when backward to engage in edifying discourse. Impatience is a sin that has its cause within ourselves, and that is, musing; and its ill effects upon ourselves, and that is no less than burning. In our greatest health and prosperity, every man is altogether vanity, he cannot live long; he may die soon. This is an undoubted truth, but we are very unwilling to believe it. Therefore let us pray that God would enlighten our minds by his Holy Spirit, and fill our hearts with his grace, that we may be ready for death every day and hour.

Verses 7–13

There is no solid satisfaction to be had in the creature; but it is to be found in the Lord, and in communion with him; to him we should be driven by our disappointments. If the world be nothing but vanity, may God deliver us from having or seeking our portion in it. When creature-confidences fail, it is our comfort that we have a God to go to, a God to trust in. We may see a good God doing all, and ordering all events concerning us; and a good man, for that reason, says nothing against it. He desires the pardoning of his sin, and the preventing of his shame. We must both watch and pray against sin. When under the correcting hand of the Lord, we must look to God himself for relief, not to any other. Our ways and our doings bring us into trouble, and we are beaten with a rod of our own making. What a poor thing is beauty! and what fools are those that are proud of it, when it will certainly, and may quickly, be consumed! The body of man is as a garment to the soul. In this garment sin has lodged a moth, which wears away, first the beauty, then the strength, and finally the substance of its parts. Whoever has watched the progress of a lingering distemper, or the work of time alone, in the human frame, will feel at once the force of this comparison, and that, surely every man is vanity. Afflictions are sent to stir up prayer. If they have that effect, we may hope that God will hear our prayer. The believer expects weariness and ill treatment on his way to heaven; but he shall not stay here long : walking with God by faith, he goes forward on his journey, not diverted from his course, nor cast down by the difficulties he meets. How blessed it is to sit loose from things here below, that while going home to our Father's house, we may use the world as not abusing it! May we always look for that city, whose Builder and Maker is God.

Chapter 40

Verses 1–5

Doubts and fears about the eternal state, are a horrible pit and miry clay, and have been so to many a dear child of God. There is power enough in God to help the weakest, and grace enough to help the unworthiest of all that trust in him. The psalmist waited patiently; he continued believing, hoping, and praying. This is applicable to Christ. His agony, in the garden and on the cross, was a horrible pit and miry clay. But those that wait patiently for God do not wait in vain. Those that have been under religious melancholy, and by the grace of God have been relieved, may apply ver. #(**2**) very feelingly to themselves; they are brought up out of a horrible pit. Christ is the Rock on which a poor soul can alone stand fast. Where God has given stedfast hope, he expects there should be a steady, regular walk and conduct. God filled the psalmist with joy, as well as peace in believing. Multitudes, by faith beholding the sufferings and glory of Christ, have learned to fear the justice and trust in the mercy of God through Him. Many are the benefits with which we are daily loaded, both by the providence and by the grace of God.

Verses 6–10

The psalmist foretells that work of wonder, redemption by our Lord Jesus Christ. The Substance must come, which is Christ, who must bring that glory to God, and that grace to man, which it was impossible the sacrifices should ever do. Observe the setting apart of our Lord Jesus to the work and office of Mediator. In the volume, or roll, of the book it was written of him. In the close rolls of the Divine decrees and counsel, the covenant of redemption was recorded. Also, in all the volumes of the Old Testament something was written of him, Joh **19**:**28**. Now the purchase of our salvation is made, the proclamation is sent forth, calling us to come and accept it. It was preached freely and openly. Whoever undertook to preach the gospel of Christ, would be under great temptation to conceal it; but Christ, and those he calls to that work, are carried on in it. May we believe his testimony, trust his promise, and submit to his authority.

Verses 11–17

The best saints see themselves undone, unless continually preserved by the grace of God. But see the frightful view the psalmist had of sin. This made the discovery of a Redeemer so welcome. In all his reflections upon each step of his life, he discovered something amiss. The sight and sense of our sins in their own colours, must distract us, if we have not at the same time some sight of a Saviour. If Christ has triumphed over our spiritual enemies, then we, through him, shall be more than conquerors. This may encourage all that seek God and love his salvation, to rejoice in him, and to praise him. No griefs nor poverty can render those miserable who fear the Lord. Their God, and all that he has or does, is the ground of their joy. The prayer of faith can unlock his fulness, which is adapted to all their wants. The promises are sure, the moment of fulfilment hastens forward. He who once came in great humility, shall come again in glorious majesty.

Chapter 41

Verses 1–4

The people of God are not free from poverty, sickness, or outward affliction, but the Lord will consider their case, and send due supplies. From his Lord's example the believer learns to consider his poor and afflicted brethren. This branch of godliness is usually recompensed with temporal blessings. But nothing is so distressing to the contrite believer, as a fear or sense of the Divine displeasure, or of sin in his heart. Sin is the sickness of the soul; pardoning mercy heals it, renewing grace heals it, and for this spiritual healing we should be more earnest than for bodily health.

Verses 5–13

We complain, and justly, of the want of sincerity, and that there is scarcely any true friendship to be found among men; but the former days were no better. One particularly, in whom David had reposed great confidence, took part with his enemies. And let us not think it strange, if we receive evil from those we suppose to be friends. Have not we ourselves thus broken our words toward God? We eat of his bread daily, yet lift up the heel against him. But though we may not take pleasure in the fall of our enemies, we may take pleasure in the making vain their designs. When we can discern the Lord's favour in any mercy, personal or public, that doubles it. If the grace of God did not take constant care of us, we should not be upheld. But let us, while on earth, give heartfelt assent to those praises which the redeemed on earth and in heaven render to their God and Saviour.

Chapter 42

The conflict in the soul of a believer.

Verses 1–5

The psalmist looked to the Lord as his chief good, and set his heart upon him accordingly; casting anchor thus at first, he rides out the storm. A gracious soul can take little satisfaction in God's courts, if it do not meet with God himself there. Living souls never can take up their rest any where short of a living God. To appear before the Lord is the desire of the upright, as it is the dread of the hypocrite. Nothing is more grievous to a gracious soul, than what is intended to shake its confidence in the Lord. It was not the remembrance of the pleasures of his court that afflicted David; but the remembrance of the free access he formerly had to God's house, and his pleasure in attending there. Those that commune much with their own hearts, will often have to chide them. See the cure of sorrow. When the soul rests on itself, it sinks; if it catches hold on the power and promise of God, the head is kept above the billows. And what is our support under present woes but this, that we shall have comfort in Him. We have great cause to mourn for sin; but being cast down springs from unbelief and a rebellious will; we should therefore strive and pray against it.

Verses 6–11

The way to forget our miseries, is to remember the God of our mercies. David saw troubles coming from God's wrath, and that discouraged him. But if one trouble follow hard after another, if all seem to combine for our ruin, let us remember they are all appointed and overruled by the Lord. David regards the Divine favour as the fountain of all the good he looked for. In the Saviour's name let us hope and pray. One word from him will calm every storm, and turn midnight darkness into the light of noon, the bitterest complaints into joyful praises. Our believing expectation of mercy must quicken our prayers for it. At length, is faith came off conqueror, by encouraging him to trust in the name of the Lord, and to stay himself upon his God. He adds, And my God; this thought enabled him to triumph over all his griefs and fears. Let us never think that the God of our life, and the Rock of our salvation, has forgotten us, if we have made his mercy, truth, and power, our refuge. Thus the psalmist strove against his despondency: at last his faith and hope obtained the victory. Let us learn to check all unbelieving doubts and fears. Apply the promise first to ourselves, and then plead it to God.

Chapter 43

David endeavours to still his spirit, with hope and confidence in God.

—As to the quarrel God had with David for sin, he prays, Enter not into judgment with me, if Thou doest so I shall be condemned; but as to the quarrel his enemies had with him, he prays, Lord, judge me, and in thy providence appear on my behalf. If we cannot comfort ourselves in God, we may stay ourselves upon him, and may have spiritual supports, when we want spiritual delights. He never cast off any that trusted in him, whatever fears they may have had of their own state. We need desire no more to make us happy, than the good that flow from God's favour, and is included in his promise. Those whom God leads, he leads to his holy hill; those, therefore, who pretend to be led by the Spirit, and yet turn their backs upon ordinance, deceive themselves. We are still to pray for the Spirit of light and truth, who supplies the want of Christ's bodily presence, to guide us in the way to heaven. Whatever we rejoice or triumph in, the Lord must be the joy of it. David applies to God as his never-failing hope. Let us pray earnestly, that the Lord would send forth the truth of his word, and the light of his Spirit, to guide us into the way of holiness, peace, and salvation. The desire of the Christian, like that of the prophet in distress, is to be saved from sin as well as sorrow; to be taught in the way of righteousness by the light of heavenly wisdom, shining in Jesus Christ, and to be led by this light and truth to the New Jerusalem.

Chapter 44

A petition for succour and relief.

Verses 1–8

Former experiences of God's power and goodness are strong supports to faith, and powerful pleas in prayer under present calamities. The many victories Israel obtained, were not by their own strength or merit, but by God's favour and free grace. The less praise this allows us, the more comfort it affords, that we may see all as coming from the favour of God. He fought for Israel, else they had fought in vain. This is applicable to the planting of the Christian church in the world, which was not by any human policy or power. Christ, by his Spirit, went forth conquering and to conquer; and he that planted a church for himself in the world, will support it by the same power and goodness. They trusted and triumphed in and through him. Let him that glories, glory in the Lord. But if they have the comfort of his name, let them give unto him the glory due unto it.

Verses 9–16

The believer must have times of temptation, affliction, and discouragement; the church must have seasons of persecution. At such times the people of God will be ready to fear that he has cast them off, and that his name and truth will be dishonoured. But they should look above the instruments of their trouble, to God, well knowing that their worst enemies have no power against them, but what is permitted from above.

Verses 17–26

In afflictions, we must not seek relief by any sinful compliance; but should continually meditate on the truth, purity, and knowledge of our heart-searching God. Hearts sins and secret sins are known to God, and must be reckoned for. He knows the secret of the heart, therefore judges of the words and actions. While our troubles do not drive us from our duty to God, we should not suffer them to drive us from our comfort in God. Let us take care that prosperity and ease do not render us careless and lukewarm. The church of God cannot be prevailed on by persecution to forget God; the believer's heart does not turn back from God. The Spirit of prophecy had reference to those who suffered unto death, for the testimony of Christ. Observe the pleas used, ver. #(**25**, **26**). Not their own merit and righteousness, but the poor sinner's pleas. None that belong to Christ shall be cast off, but every one of them shall be saved, and that for ever. The mercy of God, purchased, promised, and constantly flowing forth, and offered to believers, does away every doubt arising from our sins; while we pray in faith, Redeem us for thy mercies' sake.

Chapter 45

This psalm is a prophecy of Messiah the Prince, and points to him as a Bridegroom espousing the church to himself, and as a King ruling in it, and for it.

Verses 1–5

The psalmist's tongue was guided by the Spirit of God, as the pen is by the hand of a ready writer. This psalm is touching the King Jesus, his kingdom and government. It is a shame that this good matter is not more the subject of our discourse. There is more in Christ to engage our love, than there is or can be in any creature. This world and its charms are ready to draw away our hearts from Christ; therefore we are concerned to understand how much more worthy he is of our love. By his word, his promise, his gospel, the good will of God is made known to us, and the good work of God is begun and carried on in us. The psalmist, ver. #(**3**–**5**), joyfully foretells the progress and success of the Messiah. The arrows of conviction are very terrible in the hearts of sinners, till they are humbled and reconciled; but the arrows of vengeance will be more so to his enemies who refuse to submit. All who have seen his glory and tasted his grace, rejoice to see him, by his word and Spirit, bring enemies and strangers under his dominion.

Verses 6–9

The throne of this almighty King is established for ever. While the Holy Spirit leads Christ's people to look to his cross, he teaches them to see the evil of sin and the beauty of holiness; so that none of them can feel encouragement to continue in sin. The Mediator is God, else he had been neither able to do the Mediator's work, nor fit to wear the Mediator's crown. God the Father, as his God in respect to his human nature and mediatorial offices, has given to him the Holy Spirit without measure. Thus anointed to be a Prophet, Priest, and King, Christ has pre-eminence in the gladdening gifts and graces of the spirit, and from his fulness communicates them to his brethren in human nature. The Spirit is called the oil of gladness, because of the delight wherewith Christ was filled, in carrying on his undertakings. The salvation of sinners is the joy of angels, much more of the Son. And in proportion as we are conformed to his holy image, we may expect the gladdening gifts influences of the Comforter. The excellences of the Messiah, the suitableness of his offices, and the sufficiency of his grace, seem to be intended by the fragrance of his garments. The church formed of true believers, is here compared to the queen, whom, by an everlasting covenant, the Lord Jesus has betrothed to himself. This is the bride, the Lamb's wife, whose graces are compared to fine linen, for their purity; to gold, for their costliness: for as we owe our redemption, so we owe our adorning, to the precious blood of the Son of God.

Verses 10–17

If we desire to share these blessings, we must hearken to Christ's word. We must forget our carnal and sinful attachments and pursuits. He must be our Lord as well as our Saviour; all idols must be thrown away, that we may give him our whole heart. And here is good encouragement, thus to break off from former alliances. The beauty of holiness, both on the church and on particular believers, is, in the sight of Christ, of great price, and very amiable. The work of grace is the workmanship of the Spirit, it is the image of Christ upon the soul, a partaking of the Divine nature. It is clear of all sin, there is none in it, nor any comes from it. There is nothing glorious in the old man or corrupt nature; but in the new man, or work of grace upon the soul, every thing is glorious. The robe of Christ's righteousness, which he has wrought out for his church, the Father imputes unto her, and bestows upon her. None are brought to Christ, but those whom the Father brings. This notes the conversion of souls to him. The robe of righteousness, and garments of salvation, the change of raiment Christ has put upon her. Such as strictly cleave to Christ, loving him in singleness of heart, are companions of the bride, who partake of the very same grace, enjoy the same privileges, and share in one common salvation. These, every one, shall be brought to the King; not one lost or left behind. Instead of the Old Testament church, there shall be a New Testament church, a Gentile church. In the believing hope of our everlasting happiness in the other world, let us always keep up the remembrance of Christ, as our only way thither; and transmit the remembrance of him to succeeding generations, that his name may endure for ever.

Chapter 46

Verses 1–5

This psalm encourages to hope and trust in God; in his power and providence, and his gracious presence with his church in the worst of times. We may apply it to spiritual enemies, and the encouragement we have that, through Christ, we shall be conquerors over them. He is a Help, a present Help, a Help found, one whom we have found to be so; a Help at hand, one that is always near; we cannot desire a better, nor shall we ever find the like in any creature. Let those be troubled at the troubling of the waters, who build their confidence on a floating foundation; but let not those be alarmed who are led to the Rock, and there find firm footing. Here is joy to the church, even in sorrowful times. The river alludes to the graces and consolations of the Holy Spirit, which flow through every part of the church, and through God's sacred ordinances, gladdening the heart of every believer. It is promised that the church shall not be moved. If God be in our hearts, by his word dwelling richly in us, we shall be established, we shall be helped; let us trust and not be afraid.

Verses 6–11

Come and see the effects of desolating judgments, and stand in awe of God. This shows the perfect security of the church, and is an assurance of lasting peace. Let us pray for the speedy approach of these glorious days, and in silent submission let us worship and trust in our almighty Sovereign. Let all believers triumph in this, that the Lord of hosts, the God of Jacob, has been, is, and will be with us; and will be our Refuge. Mark this, take the comfort, and say, If God be for us, who can be against us? With this, through life and in death, let us answer every fear.

Chapter 47

The people exhorted to praise God.

Verses 1–4

The God with whom we have to do, is a God of awful majesty. The universal and absolute sovereignty of a holy God would be too terrible for us even to think of, were it not exercised by his Son from a mercy-seat; but now it is only terrible to the workers of iniquity. While his people express confidence and joy, and animate each other in serving him, let sinners submit to his authority, and accept his salvation. Jesus Christ shall subdue the Gentiles; he shall bring them as sheep into the fold, not for slaughter, but for preservation. He shall subdue their affections, and make them a willing people in the day of his power. Also it speaks of his giving them rest and settlement. Apply this spiritually; the Lord himself has undertaken to be the inheritance of his people. It shows the faith and submission of the saints. This is the language of every gracious soul, The Lord shall choose my inheritance for me; he knows what is good for me better than I do.

Verses 5–9

Praise is a duty in which we ought to be frequent and abundant. But here is a needful rule; Sing ye praises with understanding. As those that understand why and for what reasons they praise God, and what is the meaning of the service. It is not an acceptable service, if it is not a reasonable service. We are never to forget the end of Messiah's exaltation, so continually do the prophets dwell upon the conversion of the nations to the gospel of Christ. Why do we vainly fancy that we belong to him, unless the Spirit reign in our hearts by faith? Lord, is it not thy glory and delight to give repentance to Israel and remission of sins, now that thou art exalted as a Prince and a Saviour? Set up thy kingdom in our hearts. Bring into captivity every thought to the obedience of Christ. And so sweetly constrain all the powers and faculties of the souls of thy redeemed, into holy love, fear, and delight in thee, that praise with the understanding may rise from every heart, both here and for ever, to Thee, our God.

Chapter 48

The glories of the church of Christ.

Verses 1–7

Jerusalem is the city of our God: none on earth render him due honour except the citizens of the spiritual Jerusalem. Happy the kingdom, the city, the family, the heart, in which God is great, in which he is all. There God is known. The clearer discoveries are made to us of the Lord and his greatness, the more it is expected that we should abound in his praises. The earth is, by sin, covered with deformity, therefore justly might that spot of ground, which was beautified with holiness, be called the joy of the whole earth; that which the whole earth has reason to rejoice in, that God would thus in very deed dwell with man upon the earth. The kings of the earth were afraid of it. Nothing in nature can more fitly represent the overthrow of heathenism by the Spirit of the gospel, than the wreck of a fleet in a storm. Both are by the mighty power of the Lord.

Verses 8–14

We have here the improvement which the people of God are to make of his glorious and gracious appearances for them. Let our faith in the word of God be hereby confirmed. Let our hope of the stability of the church be encouraged. Let our minds be filled with good thoughts of God. All the streams of mercy that flow down to us, must be traced to the fountain of His loving-kindness. Let us give to God the glory of the great things he has done for us. Let all the members of the church take comfort from what the Lord does for his church. Let us observe the beauty, strength, and safety of the church. Consider its strength; see it founded on Christ the Rock, fortified by the Divine power, guarded by Him who neither slumbers nor sleeps. See what precious ordinances are its palaces, what precious promises are its bulwarks, that you may be encouraged to join yourselves to it: and tell this to others. This God, who has now done such great things for us, is unchangeable in his love to us, and his care for us. If he is our God, he will lead and keep us even to the last. He will so guide us, as to set us above the reach of death, so that it shall not do us any real hurt. He will lead us to a life in which there shall be no more death.

Chapter 49

Verses 1–5

We seldom meet with a more solemn introduction: there is no truth of greater importance. Let all hear this with application to ourselves. The poor are in danger from undue desire toward the wealth of the world, as rich people from undue delight in it. The psalmist begins with applying it to himself, and that is the right method in which to treat of Divine things. Before he sets down the folly of carnal security, he lays down, from his own experience, the benefit and comfort of a holy, gracious security, which they enjoy who trust in God, and not in their worldly wealth. In the day of judgment, the iniquity of our heels, or of our steps, our past sins, will compass us. In those days, worldly, wicked people will be afraid; but wherefore should a man fear death who has God with him?

Verses 6–14

Here is a description of the spirit and way of worldly people. A man may have wealth, and may have his heart enlarged in love, thankfulness, and obedience, and may do good with it. Therefore it is not men's having riches that proves them to be worldly, but their setting their hearts upon them as the best things. Worldly men have only some floating thoughts of the things of God, while their fixed thoughts, their inward thoughts, are about the world; that lies nearest the heart. But with all their wealth they cannot save the life of the dearest friend they have. This looks further, to the eternal redemption to be wrought out by the Messiah. The redemption of the soul shall cost very dear; but, being once wrought, it shall never need to be repeated. And he, the Redeemer, shall rise again before he sees corruption, and then shall live for evermore, Re **1**:**18**. This likewise shows the folly of worldly people, who sell their souls for that which will never buy them. With all their wealth they cannot secure themselves from the stroke of death. Yet one generation after another applaud their maxims; and the character of a fool, as drawn by heavenly Wisdom itself, Lu **12**:**16**–**21**, continues to be followed even among professed Christians. Death will ask the proud sinner, Where is thy wealth, thy pomp? And in the morning of the resurrection, when all that sleep in the dust shall awake, the upright shall be advanced to the highest honour, when the wicked shall be filled with everlasting shame and contempt, Da **12**:**2**. Let us now judge of things as they will appear in that day. The beauty of holiness is that alone which the grave cannot touch, or damage.

Verses 15–20

Believers should not fear death. The distinction of men's outward conditions, how great soever in life, makes none at death; but the difference of men's spiritual states, though in this life it may seem of small account, yet at and after death is very great. The soul is often put for the life. The God of life, who was its Creator at first, can and will be its Redeemer at last. It includes the salvation of the soul from eternal ruin. Believers will be under strong temptation to envy the prosperity of sinners. Men will praise thee, and cry thee up, as having done well for thyself in raising an estate and family. But what will it avail to be approved of men, if God condemn us? Those that are rich in the graces and comforts of the Spirit, have something of which death cannot strip them, nay, which death will improve; but as for worldly possessions, as we brought nothing into the world, so it is certain that we shall carry nothing out; we must leave all to others. The sum of the whole matter is, that it can profit a man nothing to gain the whole world, to become possessed of all its wealth and all its power, if he lose his own soul, and is cast away for want of that holy and heavenly wisdom which distinguishes man from the brutes, in his life and at his death. And are there men who can prefer the lot of the rich sinner to that of poor Lazarus, in life and death, and to eternity? Assuredly there are. What need then we have of the teaching of the Holy Ghost; when, with all our boasted powers, we are prone to such folly in the most important of all concerns!

Chapter 50

Verses 1–6

This psalm is a psalm of instruction. It tells of the coming of Christ and the day of judgment, in which God will call men to account; and the Holy Ghost is the Spirit of judgement. All the children of men are concerned to know the right way of worshipping the Lord, in spirit and in truth. In the great day, our God shall come, and make those hear his judgement who would not hearken to his law. Happy are those who come into the covenant of grace, by faith in the Redeemer's atoning sacrifice, and show the sincerity of their love by fruits of righteousness. When God rejects the services of those who rest in outside performances, he will graciously accept those who seek him aright. It is only by sacrifice, by Christ, the great Sacrifice, from whom the sacrifices of the law derived what value they had, that we can be accepted of God. True and righteous are his judgments; even sinners' own consciences will be forced to acknowledge the righteousness of God.

Verses 7–15

To obey is better than sacrifice, and to love God and our neighbour better than all burnt-offerings. We are here warned not to rest in these performances. And let us beware of resting in any form. God demands the heart, and how can human inventions please him, when repentance, faith, and holiness are neglected? In the day of distress we must apply to the Lord by fervent prayer. Our troubles, though we see them coming from God's hand, must drive us to him, not drive us from him. We must acknowledge him in all our ways, depend upon his wisdom, power, and goodness, and refer ourselves wholly to him, and so give him glory. Thus must we keep up communion with God; meeting him with prayers under trials, and with praises in deliverances. A believing supplicant shall not only be graciously answered as to his petition, and so have cause for praising God, but shall also have grace to praise him.

Verses 16–23

Hypocrisy is wickedness, which God will judge. And it is too common, for those who declare the Lord's statutes to others, to live in disobedience to them themselves. This delusion arises from the abuse of God's long-suffering, and a wilful mistake of his character and the intention of his gospel. The sins of sinners will be fully proved on them in the judgment of the great day. The day is coming when God will set their sins in order, sins of childhood and youth, of riper age and old age, to their everlasting shame and terror. Let those hitherto forgetful of God, given up to wickedness, or in any way negligent of salvation, consider their urgent danger. The patience of the Lord is very great. It is the more wonderful, because sinners make such ill use of it; but if they turn not, they shall be made to see their error when it is too late. Those that forget God, forget themselves; and it will never be right with them till they consider. Man's chief end is to glorify God: whoso offers praise, glorifies him, and his spiritual sacrifices shall be accepted. We must praise God, sacrifice praise, put it into the hands of the Priest, our Lord Jesus, who is also the altar: we must be fervent in spirit, praising the Lord. Let us thankfully accept God's mercy, and endeavour to glorify him in word and deed.

Chapter 51

Verses 1–6

David, being convinced of his sin, poured out his soul to God in prayer for mercy and grace. Whither should backsliding children return, but to the Lord their God, who alone can heal them? he drew up, by Divine teaching, an account of the workings of his heart toward God. Those that truly repent of their sins, will not be ashamed to own their repentance. Also, he instructs others what to do, and what to say. David had not only done much, but suffered much in the cause of God; yet he flees to God's infinite mercy, and depends upon that alone for pardon and peace. He begs the pardon of sin. The blood of Christ, sprinkled upon the conscience, blots out the transgression, and, having reconciled us to God, reconciles us to ourselves. The believer longs to have the whole debt of his sins blotted out, and every stain cleansed; he would be thoroughly washed from all his sins; but the hypocrite always has some secret reserve, and would have some favorite lust spared. David had such a deep sense of his sin, that he was continually thinking of it, with sorrow and shame. His sin was committed against God, whose truth we deny by wilful sin; with him we deal deceitfully. And the truly penitent will ever trace back the streams of actual sin to the fountain of original depravity. He confesses his original corruption. This is that foolishness which is bound in the heart of a child, that proneness to evil, and that backwardness to good, which is the burden of the regenerate, and the ruin of the unregenerate. He is encouraged, in his repentance, to hope that God would graciously accept him. Thou desirest truth in the inward part; to this God looks, in a returning sinner. Where there is truth, God will give wisdom. Those who sincerely endeavour to do their duty shall be taught their duty; but they will expect good only from Divine grace overcoming their corrupt nature.

Verses 7–15

Purge me with hyssop, with the blood of Christ applied to my soul by a lively faith, as the water of purification was sprinkled with a bunch of hyssop. The blood of Christ is called the blood of sprinkling, Heb **12**:**24**. If this blood of Christ, which cleanses from all sin, cleanse us from our sin, then we shall be clean indeed, Heb **10**:**2**. He asks not to be comforted, till he is first cleansed; if sin, the bitter root of sorrow, be taken away, he can pray in faith, Let me have a well-grounded peace, of thy creating, so that the bones broken by convictions may rejoice, may be comforted. Hide thy face from my sins; blot out all mine iniquities out of thy book; blot them out, as a cloud is blotted out and dispelled by the beams of the sun. And the believer desires renewal to holiness as much as the joy of salvation. David now saw, more than ever, what an unclean heart he had, and sadly laments it; but he sees it is not in his own power to amend it, and therefore begs God would create in him a clean heart. When the sinner feels this change is necessary, and reads the promise of God to that purpose, he begins to ask it. He knew he had by his sin grieved the Holy Spirit, and provoked him to withdraw. This he dreads more than anything. He prays that Divine comforts may be restored to him. When we give ourselves cause to doubt our interest in salvation, how can we expect the joy of it? This had made him weak; he prays, I am ready to fall, either into sin or into despair, therefore uphold me with thy Spirit. Thy Spirit is a free Spirit, a free Agent himself, working freely. And the more cheerful we are in our duty, the more constant we shall be to it. What is this but the liberty wherewith Christ makes his people free, which is contrasted with the yoke of bondage? Ga **5**:**1**. It is the Spirit of adoption spoken to the heart. Those to whom God is the God of salvation, he will deliver from guilt; for the salvation he is the God of, is salvation from sin. We may therefore plead with him, Lord, thou art the God of my salvation, therefore deliver me from the dominion of sin. And when the lips are opened, what should they speak but the praises of God for his forgiving mercy?

Verses 16–19

Those who are thoroughly convinced of their misery and danger by sin, would spare no cost to obtain the remission of it. But as they cannot make satisfaction for sin, so God cannot take any satisfaction in them, otherwise than as expressing love and duty to him. The good work wrought in every true penitent, is a broken spirit, a broken and a contrite heart, and sorrow for sin. It is a heart that is tender, and pliable to God's word. Oh that there were such a heart in every one of us! God is graciously pleased to accept this; it is instead of all burnt-offering and sacrifice. The broken heart is acceptable to God only through Jesus Christ; there is no true repentance without faith in him. Men despise that which is broken, but God will not. He will not overlook it, he will not refuse or reject it; though it makes God no satisfaction for the wrong done to him by sin. Those who have been in spiritual troubles, know how to pity and pray for others afflicted in like manner. David was afraid lest his sin should bring judgements upon the city and kingdom. No personal fears or troubles of conscience can make the soul, which has received grace, careless about the interests of the church of God. And let this be the continued joy of all the redeemed, that they have redemption through the blood of Christ, the forgiveness of sins according to the riches of his grace.

Chapter 52

Verses 1–5

Those that glory in sin, glory in their shame. The patience and forbearance of God are abused by sinners, to the hardening of their hearts in their wicked ways. But the enemies in vain boast in their mischief, while we have God's mercy to trust in. It will not save us from the guilt of lying, to be able to say, there was some truth in what we said, if we make it appear otherwise than it was. The more there is of craft and contrivance in any wickedness, the more there is of Satan in it. When good men die, they are transplanted from the land of the living on earth, to heaven, the garden of the Lord, where they shall take root for ever; but when wicked men die, they are rooted out, to perish for ever. The believer sees that God will destroy those who make not him their strength.

Verses 6–9

Those wretchedly deceive themselves, who think to support themselves in power and wealth without God. The wicked man trusted in the abundance of his riches; he thought his wickedness would help him to keep his wealth. Right or wrong, he would get what he could, and keep what he had, and ruin any one that stood in his way; this he thought would strengthen him; but see what it comes to! Those who by faith and love dwell in the house of God, shall be like green olive-trees there. And that we may be as green olive-trees, we must live a life of faith and holy confidence in God and his grace. It adds much to the beauty of our profession, and to fruitfulness in every grace, to be much in praising God; and we never can want matter for praise. His name alone can be our refuge and strong tower. It is very good for us to wait on that saving name; there is nothing better to calm and quiet our spirits, when disturbed, and to keep us in the way of duty, when tempted to use any crooked courses for our relief, than to hope, and quietly wait for the salvation of the Lord. None ever followed his guidance but it ended well.

Chapter 53

The corruption of man by nature.

—This psalm is almost the same as the **14**th. The scope of it is to convince us of our sins. God, by the psalmist, here shows us how bad we are, and proves this by his own certain knowledge. He speaks terror to persecutors, the worst of sinners. He speaks encouragement to God's persecuted people. How comes it that men are so bad? Because there is no fear of God before their eyes. Men's bad practices flow from their bad principles; if they profess to know God, yet in works, because in thoughts, they deny him. See the folly of sin; he is a fool, in the account of God, whose judgment we are sure is right, that harbours such corrupt thoughts. And see the fruit of sin; to what it brings men, when their hearts are hardened through the deceitfulness of sin. See also the faith of the saints, and their hope and power as to the cure of this great evil. There will come a Saviour, a great salvation, a salvation from sin. God will save his church from its enemies. He will save all believers from their own sins, that they may not be led captive by them, which will be everlasting joy to them. From this work the Redeemer had his name JESUS, for he shall save his people from their sins, Mt **1**:**21**.

Chapter 54

Verses 1–3

God is faithful, though men are not to be trusted, and it is well for us it is so. David has no other plea to depend upon than God's name, no other power to depend upon than God's strength, and these he makes his refuge and confidence. This would be the effectual answer to his prayers. Looking unto David, betrayed by the men of Judah, and to Jesus, betrayed by one of his apostles, what can we expect from any who have not set God before them, save ingratitude, treachery, malice, and cruelty? What bonds of nature, or friendship, or gratitude, or covenant, will hold those that have broken through the fear of God? Selah; Mark this. Let us set God before us at all times; for if we do not, we are in danger of despair.

Verses 4–7

Behold, God is mine Helper. If we are for him, he is for us; and if he is for us, we need not fear. Every creature is that to us, and no more, which God makes it to be. The Lord will in due time save his people, and in the mean time he sustains them, and bears them up, so that the spirit he has made shall not fail. There is truth in God's threatenings, as well as in his promises; sinners that repent not, will find it so to their cost. David's present deliverance was an earnest of further deliverance. He speaks of the completion of his deliverance as a thing done, though he had as yet many troubles before him; because, having God's promise for it, he was as sure of it as if it was done already. The Lord would deliver him out of all his troubles. May he help us to bear our cross without repining, and at length bring us to share his victories and glory. Christians never should suffer the voice of praise and thanksgiving to cease in the church of the redeemed.

Chapter 55

Verses 1–8

In these **verse**s we have, **1**. David praying. Prayer is a salve for every sore, and a relief to the spirit under every burden. **2**. David weeping. Griefs are thus, in some measure, lessened, while those increase that have no vent given them. David in great alarm. We may well suppose him to be so, upon the breaking out of Absalom's conspiracy, and the falling away of the people. Horror overwhelmed him. Probably the remembrance of his sin in the matter of Uriah added much to the terror. When under a guilty conscience we must mourn in our complaint, and even strong believers have for a time been filled with horror. But none ever was so overwhelmed as the holy Jesus, when it pleased the Lord to put him to grief, and to make his soul an offering for our sins. In his agony he prayed more earnestly, and was heard and delivered; trusting in him, and following him, we shall be supported under, and carried through all trials. See how David was weary of the treachery and ingratitude of men, and the cares and disappointments of his high station: he longed to hide himself in some desert from the fury and fickleness of his people. He aimed not at victory, but rest; a barren wilderness, so that he might be quiet. The wisest and best of men most earnestly covet peace and quietness, and the more when vexed and wearied with noise and clamour. This makes death desirable to a child of God, that it is a final escape from all the storms and tempests of this world, to perfect and everlasting rest.

Verses 9–15

No wickedness so distresses the believer, as that which he witnesses in those who profess to be of the church of God. Let us not be surprised at the corruptions and disorders of the church on earth, but long to see the New Jerusalem. He complains of one that had been very industrious against him. God often destroys the enemies of the church by dividing them. And an interest divided against itself cannot long stand. The true Christian must expect trials from professed friends, from those with whom he has been united; this will be very painful; but by looking unto Jesus we shall be enabled to bear it. Christ was betrayed by a companion, a disciple, an apostle, who resembled Ahithophel in his crimes and doom. Both were speedily overtaken by Divine vengeance. And this prayer is a prophecy of the utter, the everlasting ruin, of all who oppose and rebel against the Messiah.

Verses 16–23

In every trial let us call upon the Lord, and he will save us. He shall hear us, and not blame us for coming too often; the oftener the more welcome. David had thought all were against him; but now he sees there were many with him, more than he supposed; and the glory of this he gives to God, for it is he that raises us up friends, and makes them faithful to us. There are more true Christians, and believers have more real friends, than in their gloomy hours they suppose. His enemies should be reckoned with, and brought down; they could not ease themselves of their fears, as David could, by faith in God. Mortal men, though ever so high and strong, will easily be crushed by an eternal God. Those who are not reclaimed by the rod of affliction, will certainly be brought down to the pit of destruction. The burden of afflictions is very heavy, especially when attended with the temptations of Satan; there is also the burden of sin and corruption. The only relief under it is, to look to Christ, who bore it. Whatever it is that thou desirest God should give thee, leave it to him to give it in his own way and time. Care is a burden, it makes the heart stoop. We must commit our ways and works to the Lord; let him do as seemeth him good, and let us be satisfied. To cast our burden upon God, is to rest upon his providence and promise. And if we do so, he will carry us in the arms of his power, as a nurse carries a child; and will strengthen our spirits by his Spirit, so that they shall sustain the trial. He will never suffer the righteous to be moved; to be so shaken by any troubles, as to quit their duty to God, or their comfort in him. He will not suffer them to be utterly cast down. He, who bore the burden of our sorrows, desires us to leave to him to bear the burden of our cares, that, as he knows what is best for us, he may provide it accordingly. Why do not we trust Christ to govern the world which he redeemed?

Chapter 56

Verses 1–7

Be merciful unto me, O God. This petition includes all the good for which we come to throne of grace. If we obtain mercy there, we need no more to make us happy. It implies likewise our best plea, not our merit, but God's mercy, his free, rich mercy. We may flee to, and trust the mercy of God, when surrounded on all sides by difficulties and dangers. His enemies were too hard for him, if God did not help him. He resolves to make God's promises the matter of his praises, and so we have reason to make them. As we must not trust an arm of flesh when engaged for us, so we must not be afraid of an arm of flesh when stretched out against us. The sin of sinners will never be their security. Who knows the power of God's anger; how high it can reach, how forcibly it can strike?

Verses 8–13

The heavy and continued trials through which many of the Lord's people have passed, should teach us to be silent and patient under lighter crosses. Yet we are often tempted to repine and despond under small sorrows. For this we should check ourselves. David comforts himself, in his distress and fear, that God noticed all his grievances and all his griefs. God has a bottle and a book for his people's tears, both the tears for their sins, and those for their afflictions. He observes them with tender concern. Every true believer may boldly say, The Lord is my helper, and then I will not fear what man shall do unto me; for man has no power but what is given him from above. Thy vows are upon me, O Lord; not as a burden, but as that by which I am known to be thy servant; as a bridle that restrains me from what would be hurtful, and directs me in the way of my duty. And vows of thankfulness properly accompany prayers for mercy. If God deliver us from sin, either from doing it, or by his pardoning mercy, he has delivered our souls from death, which is the wages of sin. Where the Lord has begun a good work he will carry it on and perfect it. David hopes that God would keep him even from the appearance of sin. We should aim in all our desires and expectations of deliverance, both from sin and trouble, that we may do the better service to the Lord; that we may serve him without fear. If his grace has delivered our souls from the death of sin, he will bring us to heaven, to walk before him for ever in light.

Chapter 57

Verses 1–6

All David's dependence is upon God. The most eminent believers need often repeat the publican's prayer, "God be merciful to me a sinner." But if our souls trust in the Lord, this may assure us, in our utmost dangers, that our calamities will at length be overpast, and in the mean time, by faith and prayer, we must make him our refuge. Though God be most high, yet he condescends so low, as to take care that all things are made to work for good to his people. This is a good reason why we should pray earnestly. Look which way we will on this earth, refuge fails, no help appears; but we may look for it from heaven. If we have fled from the wrath to come, unto Jesus Christ, he that performed all things needful to purchase the salvation of his people, will do for us and in us all things needful for our enjoyment of it. It made David droop to think there should be those that bore him so much ill-will. But the mischief they designed against him, returned on themselves. And when David was in the greatest distress and disgrace, he did not pray, Lord, exalt me, but, Lord, exalt thine own name. Our best encouragement in prayer, is taken from the glory of God, and to that, more than to our own comfort, we should have regard in all our petitions for mercy.

Verses 7–11

By lively faith, David's prayers and complaints are at once turned into praises. His heart is fixed; it is prepared for every event, being stayed upon God. If by the grace of God we are brought into this even, composed frame of mind, we have great reason to be thankful. Nothing is done to purpose, in religion, unless it is done with the heart. The heart must be fixed for the duty, put in frame for it; fixed in the duty by close attention. Our tongue is our glory, and never more so than when praising God; dull and sleepy devotions will never be acceptable to God. Let us awake early in the morning, to begin the day with God; early in the beginning of a mercy. When God comes toward us with his favours, let us go forth to meet him with our praises. David desired to bring others to join in praising God; and in his psalms, he is still praising God among the people, singing to Him among the nations. Let us seek to have our hearts fixed to praise his boundless mercy and unfailing faithfulness; and to glorify him with body, soul, and spirit, which are his. Let us earnestly pray that the blessings of the gospel may be sent through every land.

Chapter 58

Verses 1–5

When wrong is done under the form of law, it is worse than any other; especially it is grievous to behold those who profess to be children of God, joining together against any of his people. We should thank the Lord for merciful restraints; we should be more earnest in seeking renewing grace, more watchful over ourselves, and more patient under the effects of fallen nature in others. The corruption of their nature was the root of bitterness. We may see in children the wickedness of the world beginning. They go astray from God and their duty as soon as possibly they can. And how soon will little children tell lies! It is our duty to take pains to teach them, and above all, earnestly to pray for converting grace to make our children new creatures. Though the poison be within, much of it may be kept from breaking forth to injure others. When the Saviour's words are duly regarded, the serpent becomes harmless. But those who refuse to hear heavenly wisdom, must perish miserably, for ever.

Verses 6–11

David prayed that the enemies of God's church and people might be disabled to do further mischief. We may, in faith, pray against the designs of the enemies of the church. He foretells their ruin. And who knows the power of God's anger? The victories of the Just One, in his own person and that of his servants, over the enemies of man's salvation, produce a joy which springs not from revenge, but from a view of the Divine mercy, justice, and truth, shown in the redemption of the elect, the punishment of the ungodly, and the fulfilment of the promises. Whoever duly considers these things, will diligently seek the reward of righteousness, and adore the Providence which orders all thing aright in heaven and in earth.

Chapter 59

Verses 1–7

In these words we hear the voice of David when a prisoner in his own house; the voice of Christ when surrounded by his merciless enemies; the voice of the church when under bondage in the world; and the voice of the Christian when under temptation, affliction, and persecution. And thus earnestly should we pray daily, to be defended and delivered from our spiritual enemies, the temptations of Satan, and the corruptions of our own hearts. We should fear suffering as evil-doers, but not be ashamed of the hatred of workers of iniquity. It is not strange, if those regard not what they themselves say, who have made themselves believe that God regards not what they say. And where there is no fear of God, there is nothing to secure proper regard to man.

Verses 8–17

It is our wisdom and duty, in times of danger and difficulty, to wait upon God; for he is our defence, in whom we shall be safe. It is very comfortable to us, in prayer, to look to God as the God of our mercy, the Author of all good in us, and the Giver of all good to us. The wicked can never be satisfied, which is the greatest misery in a poor condition. A contented man, if he has not what he would have, yet he does not quarrel with Providence, nor fret within himself. It is not poverty, but discontent that makes a man unhappy. David would praise God because he had many times, and all along, found Him his refuge in the day of trouble. He that is all this to us, is certainly worthy of our best affections, praises, and services. The trials of his people will end in joy and praise. When the night of affliction is over, they will sing of the Lord's power and mercy in the morning. Let believers now, in assured faith and hope, praise Him for those mercies, for which they will rejoice and praise him for ever.

Chapter 60

Verses 1–5

David owns God's displeasure to be the cause of all the hardships he had undergone. And when God is turning his hand in our favour, it is good to remember our former troubles. In God's displeasure their troubles began, therefore in his favour their prosperity must begin. Those breaches and divisions which the folly and corruption of man make, nothing but the wisdom and grace of God can repair, by pouring out a spirit of love and peace, by which only a kingdom is saved from ruin. The anger of God against sin, is the only cause of all misery, private or public, that has been, is, or shall be. In all these cases there is no remedy, but by returning to the Lord with repentance, faith, and prayer; beseeching him to return to us. Christ, the Son of David, is given for a banner to those that fear God; in him they are gathered together in one, and take courage. In his name and strength they wage war with the powers of darkness.

Verses 6–12

If Christ be ours, all things, one way or another, shall be for our eternal good. The man who is a new creature in Christ, may rejoice in all the precious promises God has spoken in his holiness. His present privileges, and the sanctifying influences of the Spirit, are sure earnests of heavenly glory. David rejoices in conquering the neighbouring nations, which had been enemies to Israel. The Israel of God are through Christ more than conquerors. Though sometimes they think that the Lord has cast them off, yet he will bring them into the strong city at last. Faith in the promise will assure us that it is our Father's good pleasure to give us the kingdom: But we are not yet made complete conquerors, and no true believer will abuse these truths to indulge sloth, or vain confidence. Hope in God is the best principle of true courage, for what need those fear who have God on their side? All our victories are from him, and while those who willingly submit to our anointed King shall share his glories, all his foes shall be put under his feet.

Chapter 61

Verses 1–4

David begins with prayers and tears, but ends with praise. Thus the soul, being lifted up to God, returns to the enjoyment of itself. Wherever we are, we have liberty to draw near to God, and may find a way open to the throne of grace. And that which separates us from other comforts, should drive us nearer to God, the fountain of all comfort. Though the heart is overwhelmed, yet it may be lifted up to God in prayer. Nay, I will cry unto thee, for by that means it will be supported and relieved. Weeping must quicken praying, and not deaden it. God's power and promise are a rock that is higher than we are. This rock is Christ. On the Divine mercy, as on a rock, David desired to rest his soul; but he was like a ship-wrecked sailor, exposed to the billows at the bottom of a rock too high for him to climb without help. David found that he could not be fixed on the Rock of salvation, unless the Lord placed him upon it. As there is safety in Him, and none in ourselves, let us pray to be led to and fixed upon Christ our Rock. The service of God shall be his constant work and business: all must make it so who expect to find God their shelter and strong tower. The grace of God shall be his constant comfort.

Verses 5–8

There is a people in the world that fear God's name. There is a heritage peculiar to that people; present comforts in the soul, earnests of future bliss. Those that fear God have enough in him, and must not complain. We need desire no better heritage than that of those who fear God. Those abide to good purpose in this world, who abide before God, serve him, and walk in his fear; those who do so, shall abide before him for ever. And these words are to be applied to Him of whom the angel said, the Lord shall give unto him the throne of his father David, and of his kingdom there shall be no end, Lu **1**:**32**. God's promises, and our faith in them, are not to do away, but to encourage prayer. We need not desire to be better secured than under the protection of God's mercy and truth. And if we partake of that grace and truth which came by Jesus Christ, we may praise him, whatever be our outward circumstances. But renewed experience of God's mercy and truth towards his people in Christ, is the main matter of our joy in him, and our praise unto him.

Chapter 62

Verses 1–7

We are in the way both of duty and comfort, when our souls wait upon God; when we cheerfully give up ourselves, and all our affairs, to his will and wisdom; when we leave ourselves to all the ways of his providence, and patiently expect the event, with full satisfaction in his goodness. See the ground and reason of this dependence. By his grace he has supported me, and by his providence delivered me. He only can be my Rock and my salvation; creatures are nothing without him, therefore I will look above them to him. Trusting in God, the heart is fixed. If God be for us, we need not fear what man can do against us. David having put his confidence in God, foresees the overthrow of his enemies. We have found it good to wait upon the Lord, and should charge our souls to have such constant dependence upon him, as may make us always easy. If God will save my soul, I may well leave every thing else to his disposal, knowing all shall turn to my salvation. And as David's faith in God advances to an unshaken stedfastness, so his joy in God improves into a holy triumph. Meditation and prayer are blessed means of strengthening faith and hope.

Verses 8–12

Those who have found the comfort of the ways of God themselves, will invite others into those ways; we shall never have the less for others sharing with us. the good counsel given is, to trust wholly in God. We must so trust in him at all times, as not at any time to put that trust in ourselves, or in any creature, which is to be put in him only. Trust in him to guide us when in doubt, to protect us when in danger, to supply us when in want, to strengthen us for every good word and work. We must lay out wants and our wishes before him, and then patiently submit our wills to his: this is pouring out our hearts. God is a refuge for all, even for as many as will take shelter in him. The psalmist warns against trusting in men. The multitude, those of low degree, are changeable as the wind. The rich and noble seem to have much in their power, and lavish promises; but those that depend on them, are disappointed. Weighed in the balance of Scripture, all that man can do to make us happy is lighter than vanity itself. It is hard to have riches, and not to trust in them if they increase, though by lawful and honest means; but we must take heed, lest we set our affections unduly upon them. A smiling world is the most likely to draw the heart from God, on whom alone it should be set. The consistent believer receives all from God as a trust; and he seeks to use it to his glory, as a steward who must render an account. God hath spoken as it were once for all, that power belongs to him alone. He can punish and destroy. Mercy also belongs to him; and his recompensing the imperfect services of those that believe in him, blotting out their transgressions for the Redeemer's sake, is a proof of abundant mercy, and encourages us to trust in him. Let us trust in his mercy and grace, and abound in his work, expecting mercies from him alone.

Chapter 63

Verses 1, 2

Early will I seek thee. The true Christian devotes to God the morning hour. He opens the eyes of his understanding with those of his body, and awakes each morning to righteousness. He arises with a thirst after those comforts which the world cannot give, and has immediate recourse by prayer to the Fountain of the water of life. The true believer is convinced, that nothing in this sinful world can satisfy the wants and desires of his immortal soul; he expects his happiness from God, as his portion. When faith and hope are most in exercise, the world appears a weary desert, and the believer longs for the joys of heaven, of which he has some foretastes in the ordinances of God upon earth.

Verses 3–6

Even in affliction we need not want matter for praise. When this is the regular frame of a believer's mind, he values the loving-kindness of God more than life. God's loving-kindness is our spiritual life, and that is better than temporal life. We must praise God with joyful lips; we must address ourselves to the duties of religion with cheerfulness, and speak forth the praises of God from a principle of holy joy. Praising lips must be joyful lips. David was in continual danger; care and fear held his eyes waking, and gave him wearisome nights; but he comforted himself with thoughts of God. The mercies of God, when called to mind in the night watches, support the soul, making darkness cheerful. How happy will be that last morning, when the believer, awaking up after the Divine likeness, shall be satisfied with all the fulness of God, and praise him with joyful lips, where there is no night, and where sorrow and sighing flee away!

Verses 7–11

True Christians can, in some measure, and at some times, make use of the strong language of David, but too commonly our souls cleave to the dust. Having committed ourselves to God, we must be easy and pleased, and quiet from the fear of evil. Those that follow hard after God, would soon fail, if God's right hand did not uphold them. It is he that strengthens us and comforts us. The psalmist doubts not but that though now sowing in tears, he should reap in joy. Messiah the Prince shall rejoice in God; he is already entered into the joy set before him, and his glory will be completed at his second coming. Blessed Lord, let our desire towards thee increase every hour; let our love be always upon thee; let all our enjoyment be in thee, and all our satisfaction from thee. Be thou all in all to us while we remain in the present wilderness state, and bring us home to the everlasting enjoyment of thee for ever.

Chapter 64

Verses 1–6

The psalmist earnestly begs of God to preserve him from disquieting fear. The tongue is a little member, but it boasts great things. The upright man is the mark at which the wicked aim, they cannot speak peaceably either of him or to him. There is no guard against a false tongue. It is bad to do wrong, but worse to encourage ourselves and one another in it. It is a sign that the heart is hardened to the greatest degree, when it is thus fully set to do evil. A practical disbelief of God's knowledge of all things, is at the bottom of every wickedness. The benefit of a good cause and a good conscience, appears most when nothing can help a man against his enemies, save God alone, who is always a present help.

Verses 7–10

When God brings upon men the mischiefs they have desired on others, it is weight enough to sink a man to the lowest hell. Those who love cursing, it shall come upon them. Those who behold this shall understand, and observe God's hand in all; unless we do so, we are not likely to profit by the dispensations of Providence. The righteous shall be glad in the Lord; not glad of the misery and ruin of their fellow-creatures, but glad that God is glorified, and his word fulfilled, and the cause of injured innocence pleaded effectually. They rejoice not in men, nor in themselves, nor in any creature, or creature enjoyments, nor in their wisdom, strength, riches, or righteousness; but in Christ, in whom all the seed of Israel are justified and glory, and in what he is to them, and has done for them.

Chapter 65

Verses 1–5

All the praise the Lord receives from this earth is from Zion, being the fruit of the Spirit of Christ, and acceptable through him. Praise is silent unto thee, as wanting words to express the great goodness of God. He reveals himself upon a mercy-seat, ready to hear and answer the prayers of all who come unto him by faith in Jesus Christ. Our sins prevail against us; we cannot pretend to balance them with any righteousness of our own: yet, as for our transgressions, of thine own free mercy, and for the sake of a righteousness of thine own providing, we shall not come into condemnation for them. Observe what it is to come into communion with God in order to blessedness. It is to con**verse** with him as one we love and value; it is to apply ourselves closely to religion as to the business of our dwelling-place. Observe how we come into communion with God; only by God's free choice. There is abundance of goodness in God's house, and what is satisfying to the soul; there is enough for all, enough for each: it is always ready; and all without money and without price. By faith and prayer we may keep up communion with God, and bring in comfort from him, wherever we are. But it is only through that blessed One, who approaches the Father as our Advocate and Surety, that sinners may expect or can find this happiness.

Verses 6–13

That Almighty strength which sets fast the mountains, upholds the believer. That word which stills the stormy ocean, and speaks it into a calm, can silence our enemies. How contrary soever light and darkness are to each other, it is hard to say which is most welcome. Does the watchman wait for the morning? so does the labourer earnestly desire the shades of evening. Some understand it of the morning and evening sacrifices. We are to look upon daily worship, both alone and with our families, to be the most needful of our daily occupations, the most delightful of our daily comforts. How much the fruitfulness of this lower part of the creation depends upon the influence of the upper, is easy to observe; every good and perfect gift is from above. He who enriches the earth, which is filled with man's sins, by his abundant and varied bounty, can neither want power nor will to feed the souls of his people. Temporal mercies to us unworthy creatures, shadow forth more important blessings. The rising of the Sun of righteousness, and the pouring forth of the influences of the Holy Spirit, that river of God, full of the waters of life and salvation, render the hard, barren, worthless hearts of sinners fruitful in every good work, and change the face of nations more than the sun and rain change the face of nature. Wherever the Lord passes, by his preached gospel, attended by his Holy Spirit, his paths drop fatness, and numbers are taught to rejoice in and praise him. They will descend upon the pastures of the wilderness, all the earth shall hear and embrace the gospel, and bring forth abundantly the fruits of righteousness which are, through Jesus Christ, to the glory of the Father. Manifold and marvellous, O Lord, are thy works, whether of nature or of grace; surely in loving-kindness hast thou made them all.

Chapter 66

Verses 1–7

The holy church throughout all the world lifts up her voice, to laud that Name which is above every name, to make the praise of Jesus glorious, both by word and deed; that others may be led to glorify him also. But nothing can bring men to do this aright, unless his effectual grace create their hearts anew unto holiness; and in the redemption by the death of Christ, and the glorious deliverances it effects, are more wondrous works than Israel's deliverance from Egyptian bondage.

Verses 8–12

The Lord not only preserves our temporal life, but maintains the spiritual life which he has given to believers. By afflictions we are proved, as silver in the fire. The troubles of the church will certainly end well. Through various conflicts and troubles, the slave of Satan escapes from his yoke, and obtains joy and peace in believing: through much tribulation the believer must enter into the kingdom of God.

Verses 13–20

We should declare unto those that fear God, what he has done for our souls, and how he has heard and answered our prayers, inviting them to join us in prayer and praise; this will turn to our mutual comfort, and to the glory of God. We cannot share these spiritual privileges, if we retain the love of sin in our hearts, though we refrain from the gross practice, Sin, regarded in the heart, will spoil the comfort and success of prayer; for the sacrifice of the wicked is an abomination of the Lord. But if the feeling of sin in the heart causes desires to be rid of it; if it be the presence of one urging a demand we know we must not, cannot comply with, this is an argument of sincerity. And when we pray in simplicity and godly sincerity, our prayers will be answered. This will excite gratitude to Him who hath not turned away our prayer nor his mercy from us. It was not prayer that fetched the deliverance, but his mercy that sent it. That is the foundation of our hopes, the fountain of our comforts; and ought to be the matter of our praises.

Chapter 67

A prayer for the enlargement of Christ's kingdom.

—All our happiness comes from God's mercy; therefore the first thing prayed for is, God be merciful to us, to us sinners, and pardon our sins. Pardon is conveyed by God's blessing, and secured in that. If we, by faith, walk with God, we may hope that his face will shine on us. The psalmist passes on to a prayer for the conversion of the Gentiles, which shows that the Old Testament saints desired that their advantages might also be enjoyed by others. And many Scripture prophecies and promises are wrapped up in prayers: the answer to the prayer of the church is as sure as the performance of God's promises. The joy wished to the nations, is holy joy. Let them be glad that by his providence the Lord will overrule the affairs of kingdoms; that even the kingdoms of this world shall became the kingdom of the Lord, and of his Christ. Then is declared a joyful prospect of all good when God shall do this. The success of the gospel brings outward mercies with it; righteousness exalts a nation. The blessing of the Lord sweetens all our creature-comforts to us, and makes them comforts indeed. All the world shall be brought to worship Him. When the gospel begins to spread, it shall go forward more and more, till it reaches to the ends of the earth. It is good to cast in our lot with those that are the blessed of the Lord. If nothing had been spoken in Scripture respecting the conversion of the heathen, we might think it vain to attempt so hopeless a work. But when we see with what confidence it is declared in the Scriptures, we may engage in missionary labours, assured that God will fulfil his own word. And shall we be backward to make known to the heathen the knowledge with which we are favoured, and the salvation we profess to glory in? They cannot learn unless they are taught. Then let us go forward in the strength of the Lord, and look to him to accompany the word the Holy Ghost; then Satan's kingdom shall be destroyed, and the kingdom of our Redeemer established.

Chapter 68

Verses 1–6

None ever hardened his heart against God, and prospered. God is the joy of his people, then let them rejoice when they come before him. He who derives his being from none, but gives being to all, is engaged by promise and covenant to bless his people. He is to be praised as a God of mercy and tender compassion. He ever careth for the afflicted and oppressed: repenting sinners, who are helpless and exposed more than any fatherless children, are admitted into his family, and share all their blessings.

Verses 7–14

Fresh mercies should put us in mind of former mercies. If God bring his people into a wilderness, he will be sure to go before them in it, and to bring them out of it. He provided for them, both in the wilderness and in Canaan. The daily manna seems here meant. And it looks to the spiritual provision for God's Israel. The Spirit of grace and the gospel of grace are the plentiful rain, with which God confirms his inheritance, and from which their fruit is found. Christ shall come as showers that water the earth. The account of Israel's victories is to be applied to the victories over death and hell, by the exalted Redeemer, for those that are his. Israel in Egypt among the kilns appeared wretched, but possessed of Canaan, during the reigns of David and Solomon, appeared glorious. Thus the slaves of Satan, when converted to Christ, when justified and sanctified by him, look honourable. When they reach heaven, all remains of their sinful state disappear, they shall be as the wings of the dove, covered with silver, and her feathers as gold. Full salvation will render those white as snow, who were vile and loathsome through the guilt and defilement of sin.

Verses 15–21

The ascension of Christ must here be meant, and thereto it is applied, Eph **4**:**8**. He received as the purchase of his death, the gifts needful for the conversion of sinners, and the salvation of believers. These he continually bestows, even on rebellious men, that the Lord God might dwell among them, as their Friend and Father. He gave gifts to men. Having received power to give eternal life, the Lord Jesus bestows it on as many as were given him, Joh **17**:**2**. Christ came to a rebellious world, not to condemn it, but that through him it might be saved. The glory of Zion's King is, that he is a Saviour and Benefactor to all his willing people, and a consuming fire to all that persist in rebellion against him. So many, so weighty are the gifts of God's bounty, that he may be truly said to load us with them. He will not put us off with present things for a portion, but will be the God of our salvation. The Lord Jesus has authority and power to rescue his people from the dominion of death, by taking away the sting of it from them when they die, and giving them complete victory over it when they rise again. The crown of the head, the chief pride and glory of the enemy, shall be smitten; Christ shall crush the head of the serpent.

Verses 22–28

The victories with which God blessed David over the enemies of Israel, are types of Christ's victory, for himself and for all believers. Those who take him for theirs, may see him acting as their God, as their King, for their good, and in answer to their prayers; especially in and by his word and ordinances. The kingdom of the Messiah shall be submitted to by all the rulers and learned in the world. The people seem to address the king, ver. #(**28**). But the words are applicable to the Redeemer, to his church, and every true believer. We pray, that thou, O God the Son, wilt complete thine undertaking for us, by finishing thy good work in us.

Verses 29–31

A powerful invitation is given to those that are without, to join the church. Some shall submit from fear; overcome by their consciences, and the checks of Providence, they are brought to make peace with the church. Others will submit willingly, ver. #(**29**, **31**). There is that beauty and benefit in the service of God, and in the gospel of Christ which went forth from Jerusalem, which is enough to invite sinners out of all nations.

Verses 32–35

God is to be admired and adored with reverence and godly fear, by all that attend in his holy places. The God of Israel gives strength and power unto his people. Through Christ strengthening us we can do all things, not otherwise; therefore he must have the glory of all we do, with our humble thanks for enabling us to do it, and for accepting the work of his hands in us.

Chapter 69

Verses 1–12

We should frequently consider the person of the Sufferer here spoken of, and ask why, as well as what he suffered, that, meditating thereon, we may be more humbled for sin, and more convinced of our danger, so that we may feel more gratitude and love, constraining us to live to His glory who died for our salvation. Hence we learn, when in affliction, to commit the keeping of our souls to God, that we may not be soured with discontent, or sink into despair. David was hated wrongfully, but the words far more fully apply to Christ. In a world where unrighteousness reigns so much, we must not wonder if we meet with those that are our enemies wrongfully. Let us take care that we never do wrong; then if we receive wrong, we may the better bear it. By the satisfaction Christ made to God for our sin by his blood, he restored that which he took not away, he paid our debt, suffered for our offences. Even when we can plead Not guilty, as to men's unjust accusations, yet before God we must acknowledge ourselves to deserve all that is brought upon us. All our sins take rise from our foolishness. They are all done in God's sight. David complains of the unkindness of friends and relations. This was fulfilled in Christ, whose brethren did not believe on him, and who was forsaken by his disciples. Christ made satisfaction for us, not only by putting off the honours due to God, but by submitting to the greatest dishonours that could be done to any man. We need not be discouraged if our zeal for the truths, precepts, and worship of God, should provoke some, and cause others to mock our godly sorrow and deadness to the world.

Verses 13–21

Whatever deep waters of affliction or temptation we sink into, whatever floods of trouble or ungodly men seem ready to overwhelm us, let us persevere in prayer to our Lord to save us. The tokens of God's favour to us are enough to keep our spirits from sinking in the deepest outward troubles. If we think well of God, and continue to do so under the greatest hardships, we need not fear but he will do well for us. And if at any time we are called on to suffer reproach and shame, for Christ's sake, this may be our comfort, that he knows it. It bears hard on one that knows the worth of a good name, to be oppressed with a bad one; but when we consider what a favour it is to be accounted worthy to suffer shame for the name of Jesus, we shall see that there is no reason why it should be heart-breaking to us. The sufferings of Christ were here particularly foretold, which proves the Scripture to be the word of God; and how exactly these predictions were fulfilled in Jesus Christ, which proves him to be the true Messiah. The vinegar and the gall given to him, were a faint emblem of that bitter cup which he drank up, that we might drink the cup of salvation. We cannot expect too little from men, miserable comforters are they all; nor can we expect too much from the God of all comfort and consolation.

Verses 22–29

These are prophecies of the destruction of Christ's persecutors. **Verses** #(**22**, **23**), are applied to the judgments of God upon the unbelieving Jews, in Ro **11**:**9**, **10**. When the supports of life and delights of sense, through the corruption of our nature, are made the food and fuel of sin, then our table is a snare. Their sin was, that they would not see, but shut their eyes against the light, loving darkness rather; their punishment was, that they should not see, but should be given up to their own hearts' lusts which hardened them. Those who reject God's great salvation proffered to them, may justly fear that his indignation will be poured out upon them. If men will sin, the Lord will reckon for it. But those that have multiplied to sin, may yet find mercy, through the righteousness of the Mediator. God shuts not out any from that righteousness; the gospel excludes none who do not, by unbelief, shut themselves out. But those who are proud and self-willed, so that they will not come in to God's righteousness, shall have their doom accordingly; they themselves decide it. Let those not expect any benefit thereby, who are not glad to be beholden to it. It is better to be poor and sorrowful, with the blessing of the Lord, than rich and jovial, and under his curse. This may be applied to Christ. He was, when on earth, a man of sorrows that had not where to lay his head; but God exalted him. Let us call upon the Lord, and though poor and sorrowful, guilty and defiled, his salvation will set us up on high.

Verses 30–36

The psalmist concludes the psalm with holy joy and praise, which he began with complaints of his grief. It is a great comfort to us, that humble and thankful praises are more pleasing to God than the most costly, pompous sacrifices. The humble shall look to him, and be glad; those that seek him through Christ shall live and be comforted. God will do great things for the gospel church, in which let all who wish well to it rejoice. A seed shall serve him on earth, and his servants shall inherit his heavenly kingdom. Those that love his name shall dwell before him for ever. He that spared not his own Son, but delivered him up for us all, how shall he not with him also freely give us all things? Arise, thou great Restorer of the ancient places to dwell in, and turn away ungodliness from thy people.

Chapter 70

The speedy destruction of the wicked, and the preservation of the godly.

—This psalm is almost the same as the last five **verses** of Ps **40**. While here we behold Jesus Christ set forth in poverty and distress, we also see him denouncing just and fearful punishment on his Jewish, heathen, and antichristian enemies; and pleading for the joy and happiness of his friends, to his Father's honour. Let us apply these things to our own troubled circumstances, and in a believing manner bring them, and the sinful causes thereof, to our remembrance. Urgent trials should always awake fervent prayers.

Chapter 71

Verses 1–13

David prays that he might never be made ashamed of dependence upon God. With this petition every true believer may come boldly to the throne of grace. The gracious care of Divine providence in our birth and infancy, should engage us to early piety. He that was our Help from our birth, ought to be our Hope from our youth. Let none expect ease or comfort from the world. Those who love the Lord, often are hated and persecuted; men wondered at for their principles and conduct; but the Lord has been their strong refuge. The faithful servants of God may be assured that he will not cast them off in old age, nor forsake them when their strength fails.

Verses 14–24

The psalmist declares that the righteousness of Christ, and the great salvation obtained thereby, shall be the chosen subject of his discourse. Not on a sabbath only, but on every day of the week, of the year, of his life. Not merely at stated returns of solemn devotion, but on every occasion, all the day long. Why will he always dwell on this? Because he knew not the numbers thereof. It is impossible to measure the value or the fulness of these blessings. The righteousness is unspeakable, the salvation everlasting. God will not cast off his grey-headed servants when no longer capable of labouring as they have done. The Lord often strengthens his people in their souls, when nature is sinking into decay. And it is a debt which the old disciples of Christ owe to succeeding generations, to leave behind them a solemn testimony to the advantage of religion, and the truth of God's promises; and especially to the everlasting righteousness of the Redeemer. Assured of deliverance and victory, let us spend our days, while waiting the approach of death, in praising the Holy One of Israel with all our powers. And while speaking of his righteousness, and singing his praises, we shall rise above fears and infirmities, and have earnests of the joys of heaven. The work of redemption ought, above all God's works, to be spoken of by us in our praises. The Lamb that was slain, and has redeemed us to God, is worthy of all blessing and praise.

Chapter 72

Verse 1

This psalm belongs to Solomon in part, but to Christ more fully and clearly. Solomon was both the king and the king's son, and his pious father desired that the wisdom of God might be in him, that his reign might be a remembrance of the kingdom of the Messiah. It is the prayer of a father for his child; a dying blessing. The best we can ask of God for our children is, that God would give them wisdom and grace to know and to do their duty.

Verses 2–17

This is a prophecy of the kingdom of Christ; many passages in it cannot be applied to the reign of Solomon. There were righteousness and peace at first in the administration of his government; but, before the end of his reign, there were troubles and unrighteousness. The kingdom here spoken of is to last as long as the sun, but Solomon's was soon at an end. Even the Jewish expositors understood it of the kingdom of the Messiah. Observe many great and precious promises here made, which were to have full accomplishment only in the kingdom of Christ. As far as his kingdom is set up, discord and contentions cease, in families, churches, and nations. The law of Christ, written in the heart, disposes men to be honest and just, and to render to all their due; it likewise disposes men to live in love, and so produces abundance of peace. Holiness and love shall be lasting in Christ's kingdom. Through all the changes of the world, and all the changes of life, Christ's kingdom will support itself. And he shall, by the graces and comforts of his Spirit, come down like rain upon the mown grass; not on that cut down, but that which is left growing, that it may spring again. His gospel has been, or shall be, preached to all nations. Though he needs not the services of any, yet he must be served with the best. Those that have the wealth of this world, must serve Christ with it, do good with it. Prayer shall be made through him, or for his sake; whatever we ask of the Father, should be in his name. Praises shall be offered to him: we are under the highest obligations to him. Christ only shall be feared throughout all generations. To the end of time, and to eternity, his name shall be praised. All nations shall call HIM blessed.

Verses 18–20

We are taught to bless God in Christ, for all he has done for us by him. David is earnest in prayer for the fulfilment of this prophecy and promise. It is sad to think how empty the earth is of the glory of God, how little service and honour he has from a world to which he is so bountiful. May we, like David, submit to Christ's authority, and partake of his righteousness and peace. May we bless him for the wonders of redeeming love. May we spend our days, and end our lives, praying for the spread of his gospel.

Chapter 73

Verses 1–14

The psalmist was strongly tempted to envy the prosperity of the wicked; a common temptation, which has tried the graces of many saints. But he lays down the great principle by which he resolved to abide. It is the goodness of God. This is a truth which cannot be shaken. Good thoughts of God will fortify against Satan's temptations. The faith even of strong believers may be sorely shaken, and ready to fail. There are storms that will try the firmest anchors. Foolish and wicked people have sometimes a great share of outward prosperity. They seem to have the least share of the troubles of this life; and they seem to have the greatest share of its comforts. They live without the fear of God, yet they prosper, and get on in the world. Wicked men often spend their lives without much sickness, and end them without great pain; while many godly persons scarcely know what health is, and die with great sufferings. Often the wicked are not frightened, either by the remembrance of their sins, or the prospect of their misery, but they die without terror. We cannot judge men's state beyond death, by what passes at their death. He looked abroad, and saw many of God's people greatly at a loss. Because the wicked are so very daring, therefore his people return hither; they know not what to say to it, and the rather, because they drink deep of the bitter cup of affliction. He spoke feelingly when he spoke of his own troubles; there is no disputing against sense, except by faith. From all this arose a strong temptation to cast off religion. But let us learn that the true course of sanctification consists in cleansing a man from all pollution both of soul and body. The heart is cleansed by the blood of Christ laid hold upon by faith; and by the begun works of the Lord's Spirit, manifested in the hearty resolution, purpose, and study of holiness, and a blameless course of life and actions, the hands are cleansed. It is not in vain to serve God and keep his ordinances.

Verses 15–20

The psalmist having shown the progress of his temptation, shows how faith and grace prevailed. He kept up respect for God's people, and with that he restrained himself from speaking what he had thought amiss. It is a sign that we repent of the evil thoughts of the heart, if we suppress them. Nothing gives more offence to God's children, than to say it is vain to serve God; for there is nothing more contrary to their universal experience. He prayed to God to make this matter plain to him; and he understood the wretched end of wicked people; even in the height of their prosperity they were but ripening for ruin. The sanctuary must be the resort of a tempted soul. The righteous man's afflictions end in peace, therefore he is happy; the wicked man's enjoyments end in destruction, therefore he is miserable. The prosperity of the wicked is short and uncertain, slippery places. See what their prosperity is; it is but a vain show, it is only a corrupt imagination, not substance, but a mere shadow; it is as a dream, which may please us a little while we are slumbering, yet even then it disturbs our repose.

Verses 21–28

God would not suffer his people to be tempted, if his grace were not sufficient, not only to save them from harm, but to make them gainers by it. This temptation, the working of envy and discontent, is very painful. In reflecting upon it, the psalmist owns it was his folly and ignorance thus to vex himself. If good men, at any time, through the surprise and strength of temptation, think, or speak, or act amiss, they will reflect upon it with sorrow and shame. We must ascribe our safety in temptation, and our victory, not to our own wisdom, but to the gracious presence of God with us, and Christ's intercession for us. All who commit themselves to God, shall be guided with the counsel both of his word and of his Spirit, the best counsellors here, and shall be received to his glory in another world; the believing hopes and prospects of which will reconcile us to all dark providences. And the psalmist was hereby quickened to cleave the closer to God. Heaven itself could not make us happy without the presence and love of our God. The world and all its glory vanishes. The body will fail by sickness, age, and death; when the flesh fails, the conduct, courage, and comfort fail. But Christ Jesus, our Lord, offers to be all in all to every poor sinner, who renounces all other portions and confidences. By sin we are all far from God. And a profession Christ, if we go on in sin, will increase our condemnation. May we draw near, and keep near, to our God, by faith and prayer, and find it good to do so. Those that with an upright heart put their trust in God, shall never want matter for thanksgiving to him. Blessed Lord, who hast so graciously promised to become our portion in the next world, prevent us from choosing any other in this.

Chapter 74

Verses 1–11

This psalm appears to describe the destruction of Jerusalem and the temple by the Chaldeans. The deplorable case of the people of God, at the time, is spread before the Lord, and left with him. They plead the great things God had done for them. If the deliverance of Israel out of Egypt was encouragement to hope that he would not cast them off, much more reason have we to believe, that God will not cast off any whom Christ has redeemed with his own blood. Infidels and persecutors may silence faithful ministers, and shut up places of worship, and say they will destroy the people of God and their religion together. For a long time they may prosper in these attempts, and God's oppressed servants may see no prospect of deliverance; but there is a remnant of believers, the seed of a future harvest, and the despised church has survived those who once triumphed over her. When the power of enemies is most threatening, it is comfortable to flee to the power of God by earnest prayer.

Verses 12–17

The church silences her own complaints. What God had done for his people, as their King of old, encouraged them to depend on him. It was the Lord's doing, none besides could do it. This providence was food to faith and hope, to support and encourage in difficulties. The God of Israel is the God of nature. He that is faithful to his covenant about the day and the night, will never cast off those whom he has chosen. We have as much reason to expect affliction, as to expect night and winter. But we have no more reason to despair of the return of comfort, than to despair of day and summer. And in the world above we shall have no more changes.

Verses 18–23

The psalmist begs that God would appear for the church against their enemies. The folly of such as revile his gospel and his servants will be plain to all. Let us call upon our God to enlighten the dark nations of the earth; and to rescue his people, that the poor and needy may praise his name. Blessed Saviour, thou art the same yesterday, to-day, and for ever. Make thy people more than conquerors. Be thou, Lord, all in all to them in every situation and circumstances; for then thy poor and needy people will praise thy name.

Chapter 75

Verses 1–5

We often pray for mercy, when in pursuit of it; and shall we only once or twice give thanks, when we obtain it? God shows that he is nigh to us in what we call upon him for. Public trusts are to be managed uprightly. This may well be applied to Christ and his government. Man's sin threatened to destroy the whole creation; but Christ saved the world from utter ruin. He who is made of God to us wisdom, bids us be wise. To the proud, daring sinners he says, Boast not of your power, persist not in contempt. All the present hopes and future happiness of the human race spring from the Son of God.

Verses 6–10

No second causes will raise men to preferment without the First Cause. It comes neither from the east, nor from the west, nor from the south. He mentions not the north; the same word that signifies the north, signifies the secret place; and from the secret of God's counsel it does come. From God alone all must receive their doom. There are mixtures of mercy and grace in the cup of affliction, when it is put into the hands of God's people; mixtures of the curse, when it is put into the hands of the wicked. God's people have their share in common calamities, but the dregs of the cup are for the wicked. The exaltation of the Son of David will be the subject of the saints' everlasting praises. Then let sinners submit to the King of righteousness, and let believers rejoice in and obey him.

Chapter 76

Verses 1–6

Happy people are those who have their land filled with the knowledge of God! happy persons that have their hearts filled with that knowledge! It is the glory and happiness of a people to have God among them by his ordinances. Wherein the enemies of the church deal proudly, it will appear that God is above them. See the power of God's rebukes. With pleasure may Christians apply this to the advantages bestowed by the Redeemer.

Verses 7–12

God's people are the meek of the earth, the quiet in the land, that suffer wrong, but do none. The righteous God seems to keep silence long, yet, sooner or later, he will make judgment to be heard. We live in an angry, provoking world; we often feel much, and are apt to fear more, from the wrath of man. What will not turn to his praise, shall not be suffered to break out. He can set bounds to the wrath of man, as he does to the raging sea; hitherto it shall come, and no further. Let all submit to God. Our prayers and praises, and especially our hearts, are the presents we should bring to the Lord. His name is glorious, and he is the proper object of our fear. He shall cut off the spirit of princes; he shall slip it off easily, as we slip off a flower from the stalk, or a bunch of grapes from the vine; so the word signifies. He can dispirit the most daring: since there is no contending with God, it is our wisdom, as it is our duty, to submit to him. Let us seek his favour as our portion, and commit all our concerns to him.

Chapter 77

Verses 1–10

Days of trouble must be days of prayer; when God seems to have withdrawn from us, we must seek him till we find him. In the day of his trouble the psalmist did not seek for the diversion of business or amusement, but he sought God, and his favor and grace. Those that are under trouble of mind, must pray it away. He pored upon the trouble; the methods that should have relieved him did but increase his grief. When he remembered God, it was only the Divine justice and wrath. His spirit was overwhelmed, and sank under the load. But let not the remembrance of the comforts we have lost, make us unthankful for those that are left. Particularly he called to remembrance the comforts with which he supported himself in former sorrows. Here is the language of a sorrowful, deserted soul, walking in darkness; a common case even among those that fear the Lord, Isa **50**:**10**. Nothing wounds and pierces like the thought of God's being angry. God's own people, in a cloudy and dark day, may be tempted to make wrong conclusions about their spiritual state, and that of God's kingdom in the world. But we must not give way to such fears. Let faith answer them from the Scripture. The troubled fountain will work itself clear again; and the recollection of former times of joyful experience often raises a hope, tending to relief. Doubts and fears proceed from the want and weakness of faith. Despondency and distrust under affliction, are too often the infirmities of believers, and, as such, are to be thought upon by us with sorrow and shame. When, unbelief is working in us, we must thus suppress its risings.

Verses 11–20

The remembrance of the works of God, will be a powerful remedy against distrust of his promise and goodness; for he is God, and changes not. God's way is in the sanctuary. We are sure that God is holy in all his works. God's ways are like the deep waters, which cannot be fathomed; like the way of a ship, which cannot be tracked. God brought Israel out of Egypt. This was typical of the great redemption to be wrought out in the fulness of time, both by price and power. If we have harboured doubtful thoughts, we should, without delay, turn our minds to meditate on that God, who spared not his own Son, but delivered him up for us all, that with him, he might freely give us all things.

Chapter 78

Verses 1–8

These are called dark and deep sayings, because they are carefully to be looked into. The law of God was given with a particular charge to teach it diligently to their children, that the church may abide for ever. Also, that the providences of God, both in mercy and in judgment, might encourage them to conform to the will of God. The works of God much strengthen our resolution to keep his commandments. Hypocrisy is the high road to apostacy; those that do not set their hearts right, will not be stedfast with God. Many parents, by negligence and wickedness, become murderers of their children. But young persons, though they are bound to submit in all things lawful, must not obey sinful orders, or copy sinful examples.

Verses 9–39

Sin dispirits men, and takes away the heart. Forgetfulness of God's works is the cause of disobedience to his laws. This narrative relates a struggle between God's goodness and man's badness. The Lord hears all our murmurings and distrusts, and is much displeased. Those that will not believe the power of God's mercy, shall feel the fire of his indignation. Those cannot be said to trust in God's salvation as their happiness at last, who can not trust his providence in the way to it. To all that by faith and prayer, ask, seek, and knock, these doors of heaven shall at any time be opened; and our distrust of God is a great aggravation of our sins. He expressed his resentment of their provocation; not in denying what they sinfully lusted after, but in granting it to them. Lust is contented with nothing. Those that indulge their lust, will never be estranged from it. Those hearts are hard indeed, that will neither be melted by the mercies of the Lord, nor broken by his judgments. Those that sin still, must expect to be in trouble still. And the reason why we live with so little comfort, and to so little purpose, is, because we do not live by faith. Under these rebukes they professed repentance, but they were not sincere, for they were not constant. In Israel's history we have a picture of our own hearts and lives. God's patience, and warnings, and mercies, imbolden them to harden their hearts against his word. And the history of kingdoms is much the same. Judgments and mercies have been little attended to, until the measure of their sins has been full. And higher advantages have not kept churches from declining from the commandments of God. Even true believers recollect, that for many a year they abused the kindness of Providence. When they come to heaven, how will they admire the Lord's patience and mercy in bringing them to his kingdom!

Verses 40–55

Let not those that receive mercy from God, be thereby made bold to sin, for the mercies they receive will hasten its punishment; yet let not those who are under Divine rebukes for sin, be discouraged from repentance. The Holy One of Israel will do what is most for his own glory, and what is most for their good. Their forgetting former favours, led them to limit God for the future. God made his own people to go forth like sheep; and guided them in the wilderness, as a shepherd his flock, with all care and tenderness. Thus the true Joshua, even Jesus, brings his church out of the wilderness; but no earthly Canaan, no worldly advantages, should make us forget that the church is in the wilderness while in this world, and that there remaineth a far more glorious rest for the people of God.

Verses 56–72

After the Israelites were settled in Canaan, the children were like their fathers. God gave them his testimonies, but they turned back. Presumptuous sins render even Israelites hateful to God's holiness, and exposed to his justice. Those whom the Lord forsakes become an easy prey to the destroyer. And sooner or later, God will disgrace his enemies. He set a good government over his people; a monarch after his own heart. With good reason does the psalmist make this finishing, crowning instance of God's favour to Israel; for David was a type of Christ, the great and good Shepherd, who was humbled first, and then exalted; and of whom it was foretold, that he should be filled with the Spirit of wisdom and understanding. On the uprightness of his heart, and the skilfulness of his hands, all his subjects may rely; and of the increase of his government and peace there shall be no end. Every trial of human nature hitherto, confirms the testimony of Scripture, that the heart is deceitful above all things, and desperately wicked, and nothing but being created anew by the Holy Ghost can cure the ungodliness of any.

Chapter 79

Verses 1–5

God is complained to: whither should children go but to a Father able and willing to help them? See what a change sin made in the holy city, when the heathen were suffered to pour in upon them. God's own people defiled it by their sins, therefore he suffered their enemies to defile it by their insolence. They desired that God would be reconciled. Those who desire God's favour as better than life, cannot but dread his wrath as worse than death. In every affliction we should first beseech the Lord to cleanse away the guilt of our sins; then he will visit us with his tender mercies.

Verses 6–13

Those who persist in ignorance of God, and neglect of prayer, are the ungodly. How unrighteous soever men were, the Lord was righteous in permitting them to do what they did. Deliverances from trouble are mercies indeed, when grounded upon the pardon of sin; we should therefore be more earnest in prayer for the removal of our sins than for the removal of afflictions. They had no hopes but from God's mercies, his tender mercies. They plead no merit, they pretend to none, but, Help us for the glory of thy name; pardon us for thy name's sake. The Christian forgets not that he is often bound in the chain of his sins. The world to him is a prison; sentence of death is passed upon him, and he knows not how soon it may be executed. How fervently should he at all times pray, O let the sighing of a prisoner come before thee, according to the greatness of thy power preserve thou those that are appointed to die! How glorious will the day be, when, triumphant over sin and sorrow, the church beholds the adversary disarmed for ever! while that church shall, from age to age, sing the praises of her great Shepherd and Bishop, her King and her God.

Chapter 80

Verses 1–7

He that dwelleth upon the mercy-seat, is the good Shepherd of his people. But we can neither expect the comfort of his love, nor the protection of his arm, unless we partake of his converting grace. If he is really angry at the prayers of his people, it is because, although they pray, their ends are not right, or there is some secret sin indulged in them, or he will try their patience and perseverance in prayer. When God is displeased with his people, we must expect to see them in tears, and their enemies in triumph. There is no salvation but from God's favour; there is no conversion to God but by his own grace.

Verses 8–16

The church is represented as a vine and a vineyard. The root of this vine is Christ, the branches are believers. The church is like a vine, needing support, but spreading and fruitful. If a vine do not bring forth fruit, no tree is so worthless. And are not we planted as in a well-cultivated garden, with every means of being fruitful in works of righteousness? But the useless leaves of profession, and the empty boughs of notions and forms, abound far more than real piety. It was wasted and ruined. There was a good reason for this change in God's way toward them. And it is well or ill with us, according as we are under God's smiles or frowns. When we consider the state of the purest part of the visible church, we cannot wonder that it is visited with sharp corrections. They request that God would help the vine. Lord, it is formed by thyself, and for thyself, therefore it may, with humble confidence, be committed to thyself.

Verses 17–19

The Messiah, the Protector and Saviour of the church, is the Man of God's right hand; he is the Arm of the Lord, for all power is given to him. In him is our strength, by which we are enabled to persevere to the end. The vine, therefore, cannot be ruined, nor can any fruitful branch perish; but the unfruitful will be cut off and cast into the fire. The end of our redemption is, that we should serve Him who hath redeemed us, and not go back to our old sins.

Chapter 81

Verses 1–7

All the worship we can render to the Lord is beneath his excellences, and our obligations to him, especially in our redemption from sin and wrath. What God had done on Israel's behalf, was kept in remembrance by public solemnities. To make a deliverance appear more gracious, more glorious, it is good to observe all that makes the trouble we are delivered from appear more grievous. We ought never to forget the base and ruinous drudgery to which Satan, our oppressor, brought us. But when, in distress of conscience, we are led to cry for deliverance, the Lord answers our prayers, and sets us at liberty. Convictions of sin, and trials by affliction, prove his regard to his people. If the Jews, on their solemn feast-days, were thus to call to mind their redemption out of Egypt, much more ought we, on the Christian sabbath, to call to mind a more glorious redemption, wrought out for us by our Lord Jesus Christ, from worse bondage.

Verses 8–16

We cannot look for too little from the creature, nor too much from the Creator. We may have enough from God, if we pray for it in faith. All the wickedness of the world is owing to man's wilfulness. People are not religious, because they will not be so. God is not the Author of their sin, he leaves them to the lusts of their own hearts, and the counsels of their own heads; if they do not well, the blame must be upon themselves. The Lord is unwilling that any should perish. What enemies sinners are to themselves! It is sin that makes our troubles long, and our salvation slow. Upon the same conditions of faith and obedience, do Christians hold those spiritual and eternal good things, which the pleasant fields and fertile hills of Canaan showed forth. Christ is the Bread of life; he is the Rock of salvation, and his promises are as honey to pious minds. But those who reject him as their Lord and Master, must also lose him as their Saviour and their reward.

Chapter 82

Verses 1–5

Magistrates are the mighty in authority for the public good. Magistrates are the ministers of God's providence, for keeping up order and peace, and particularly in punishing evil-doers, and protecting those that do well. Good princes and good judges, who mean well, are under Divine direction; and bad ones, who mean ill, are under Divine restraint. The authority of God is to be submitted to, in those governors whom his providence places over us. But when justice is turned from what is right, no good can be expected. The evil actions of public persons are public mischiefs.

Verses 6–8

It is hard for men to have honour put upon them, and not to be proud of it. But all the rulers of the earth shall die, and all their honour shall be laid in the dust. God governs the world. There is a righteous God to whom we may go, and on whom we may depend. This also has respect to the kingdom of the Messiah. Considering the state of affairs in the world, we have need to pray that the Lord Jesus would speedily rule over all nations, in truth, righteousness, and peace.

Chapter 83

Verses 1–8

Sometimes God seems not to be concerned at the unjust treatment of his people. But then we may call upon him, as the psalmist here. All wicked people are God's enemies, especially wicked persecutors. The Lord's people are his hidden one; the world knows them not. He takes them under his special protection. Do the enemies of the church act with one consent to destroy it, and shall not the friends of the church be united? Wicked men wish that there might be no religion among mankind. They would gladly see all its restraints shaken off, and all that preach, profess, or practise it, cut off. This they would bring to pass if it were in their power. The enemies of God's church have always been many: this magnifies the power of the Lord in preserving to himself a church in the world.

Verses 9–18

All who oppose the kingdom of Christ may here read their doom. God is the same still that ever he was; the same to his people, and the same against his and their enemies. God would make their enemies like a wheel; unsettled in all their counsels and resolves. Not only let them be driven away as stubble, but burnt as stubble. And this will be the end of wicked men. Let them be made to fear thy name, and perhaps that will bring them to seek thy name. We should desire no confusion to our enemies and persecutors but what may forward their conversion. The stormy tempest of Divine vengeance will overtake them, unless they repent and seek the pardoning mercy of their offended Lord. God's triumphs over his enemies, clearly prove that he is, according to his name JEHOVAH, an almighty Being, who has all power and perfection in himself. May we fear his wrath, and yield ourselves to be his willing servants. And let us seek deliverance by the destruction of our fleshly lusts, which war against the soul.

Chapter 84

Verses 1–7

The ordinances of God are the believer's solace in this evil world; in them he enjoys the presence of the living God: this causes him to regret his absence from them. They are to his soul as the nest to the bird. Yet they are only an earnest of the happiness of heaven; but how can men desire to enter that holy habitation, who complain of Divine ordinances as wearisome? Those are truly happy, who go forth, and go on in the exercise of religion, in the strength of the grace of Jesus Christ, from whom all our sufficiency is. The pilgrims to the heavenly city may have to pass through many a valley of weeping, and many a thirsty desert; but wells of salvation shall be opened for them, and consolations sent for their support. Those that press forward in their Christian course, shall find God add grace to their graces. And those who grow in grace, shall be perfect in glory.

Verses 8–12

In all our addresses to God, we must desire that he would look on Christ, his Anointed One, and accept us for his sake: we must look to Him with faith, and then God will with favour look upon the face of the Anointed: we, without him, dare not show our faces. The psalmist pleads love to God's ordinances. Let us account one day in God's courts better than a thousand spent elsewhere; and deem the meanest place in his service preferable to the highest earthly preferment. We are here in darkness, but if God be our God, he will be to us a Sun, to enlighten and enliven us, to guide and direct us. We are here in danger, but he will be to us a Shield, to secure us from the fiery darts that fly thick about us. Through he has not promised to give riches and dignities, he has promised to give grace and glory to all that seek them in his appointed way. And what is grace, but heaven begun below, in the knowledge, love, and service of God? What is glory, but the completion of this happiness, in being made like to him, and in fully enjoying him for ever? Let it be our care to walk uprightly, and then let us trust God to give us every thing that is good for us. If we cannot go to the house of the Lord, we may go by faith to the Lord of the house; in him we shall be happy, and may be easy. That man is really happy, whatever his outward circumstances may be, who trusts in the Lord of hosts, the God of Jacob.

Chapter 85

Verses 1–7

The sense of present afflictions should not do away the remembrance of former mercies. The favour of God is the fountain of happiness to nations, as well as to particular persons. When God forgives sin, he covers it; and when he covers the sin of his people, he covers it all. See what the pardon of sin is. In compassion to us, when Christ our Intercessor has stood before thee, thou hast turned away thine anger. When we are reconciled to God, then, and not till then, we may expect the comfort of his being reconciled to us. He shows mercy to those to whom he grants salvation; for salvation is of mere mercy. The Lord's people may expect sharp and tedious afflictions when they commit sin; but when they return to him with humble prayer, he will make them again to rejoice in him.

Verses 8–13

Sooner or later, God will speak peace to his people. If he do not command outward peace, yet he will suggest inward peace; speaking to their hearts by his Spirit. Peace is spoken only to those who turn from sin. All sin is folly, especially backsliding; it is the greatest folly to return to sin. Surely God's salvation is nigh, whatever our difficulties and distresses are. Also, his honour is secured, that glory may dwell in our land. And the truth of the promises is shown by the Divine mercy in sending the Redeemer. The Divine justice is now satisfied by the great atonement. Christ, the way, truth, and life, sprang out of the earth when he took our nature upon him, and Divine justice looked upon him well pleased and satisfied. For his sake all good things, especially his Holy Spirit, are given to those who ask him. Through Christ, the pardoned sinner becomes fruitful in good works, and by looking to and trusting in the Saviour's righteousness, finds his feet set in the way of his steps. Righteousness is a sure guide, both in meeting God, and in following him

Chapter 86

Verses 1–7

Our poverty and wretchedness, when felt, powerfully plead in our behalf at the throne of grace. The best self-preservation is to commit ourselves to God's keeping. I am one whom thou favourest, hast set apart for thyself, and made partaker of sanctifying grace. It is a great encouragement to prayer, to feel that we have received the converting grace of God, have learned to trust in him, and to be his servants. We may expect comfort from God, when we keep up our communion with God. God's goodness appears in two things, in giving and forgiving. Whatever others do, let us call upon God, and commit our case to him; we shall not seek in vain.

Verses 8–17

Our God alone possesses almighty power and infinite love. Christ is the way and the truth. And the believing soul will be more desirous to be taught the way and the truth. And the believing soul will be more desirous to be taught the way and the truth of God, in order to walk therein, than to be delivered out of earthly distress. Those who set not the Lord before them, seek after believers' souls; but the compassion, mercy, and truth of God, will be their refuge and consolation. And those whose parents were the servants of the Lord, may urge this as a plea why he should hear and help them. In considering David's experience, and that of the believer, we must not lose sight of Him, who though he was rich, for our sakes became poor, that we through his poverty might be rich.

Chapter 87

Verses 1–3

Christ himself is the Foundation of the church, which God has laid. Holiness is the strength and firmness of the church. Let us not be ashamed of the church of Christ in its meanest condition, nor of those that belong to it, since such glorious things are spoken of it. Other foundation can no man lay than that is laid, even Jesus Christ. The glorious things spoken of Zion by the Spirit, were all typical of Christ, and his work and offices; of the gospel church, its privileges and members; of heaven, its glory and perfect happiness.

Verses 4–7

The church of Christ is more glorious and excellent than the nations of the earth. In the records of heaven, the meanest of those who are born again stand registered. When God renders to every man according to his works, he shall observe who enjoyed the privileges of his sanctuary. To them much was given, and of them much will be required. Let those that dwell in Zion, mark this, and live up to their profession. Zion's songs shall be sung with joy and triumph. The springs of the joy of a carnal worldling are in wealth and pleasure; but of a gracious soul, in the word of God and prayer. All grace and consolation are derived from Christ, through his ordinances, to the souls of believers.

Chapter 88

Verses 1–9

The first words of the psalmist are the only words of comfort and support in this psalm. Thus greatly may good men be afflicted, and such dismal thoughts may they have about their afflictions, and such dark conclusion may they make about their end, through the power of melancholy and the weakness of faith. He complained most of God's displeasure. Even the children of God's love may sometimes think themselves children of wrath and no outward trouble can be so hard upon them as that. Probably the psalmist described his own case, yet he leads to Christ. Thus are we called to look unto Jesus, wounded and bruised for our iniquities. But the wrath of God poured the greatest bitterness into his cup. This weighed him down into darkness and the deep.

Verses 10–18

Departed souls may declare God's faithfulness, justice, and lovingkindness; but deceased bodies can neither receive God's favours in comfort, nor return them in praise. The psalmist resolved to continue in prayer, and the more so, because deliverance did not come speedily. Though our prayers are not soon answered, yet we must not give over praying. The greater our troubles, the more earnest and serious we should be in prayer. Nothing grieves a child of God so much as losing sight of him; nor is there any thing he so much dreads as God's casting off his soul. If the sun be clouded, that darkens the earth; but if the sun should leave the earth, what a dungeon would it be! Even those designed for God's favours, may for a time suffer his terrors. See how deep those terrors wounded the psalmist. If friends are put far from us by providences, or death, we have reason to look upon it as affliction. Such was the calamitous state of a good man. But the pleas here used were peculiarly suited to Christ. And we are not to think that the holy Jesus suffered for us only at Gethsemane and on Calvary. His whole life was labour and sorrow; he was afflicted as never man was, from his youth up. He was prepared for that death of which he tasted through life. No man could share in the sufferings by which other men were to be redeemed. All forsook him, and fled. Oftentimes, blessed Jesus, do we forsake thee; but do not forsake us, O take not thy Holy Spirit from us.

Chapter 89

Verses 1–4

Though our expectations may be disappointed, yet God's promises are established in the heavens, in his eternal counsels; they are out of the reach of opposers in hell and earth. And faith in the boundless mercy and everlasting truth of God, may bring comfort even in the deepest trials.

Verses 5–14

The more God's works are known, the more they are admired. And to praise the Lord, is to acknowledge him to be such a one that there is none like him. Surely then we should feel and express reverence when we worship God. But how little of this appears in our congregations, and how much cause have we to humble ourselves on this account! That almighty power which smote Egypt, will scatter the enemies of the church, while all who trust in God's mercy will rejoice in his name; for mercy and truth direct all he does. His counsels from eternity, and their consequences to eternity, are all justice and judgment.

Verses 15–18

Happy are those who so know the joyful sound of the gospel as to obey it; who experience its power upon their hearts, and bring forth the fruit of it in their lives. Though believers are nothing in themselves, yet having all in Christ Jesus, they may rejoice in his name. May the Lord enable us to do so. The joy of the Lord is the strength of his people; whereas unbelief dispirits ourselves and discourages others. Though it steals upon us under a semblance of humility, yet it is the very essence of pride. Christ is the Holy One of Israel; and in him was that peculiar people more blessed than in any other blessing.

Verses 19–37

The Lord anointed David with the holy oil, not only as an emblem of the graces and gifts he received, but as a type of Christ, the King Priest, and Prophet, anointed with the Holy Ghost without measure. David after his anointing, was persecuted, but none could gain advantage against him. Yet all this was a faint shadow of the Redeemer's sufferings, deliverance, glory, and authority, in whom alone these predictions and promises are fully brought to pass. He is the mighty God. This is the Redeemer appointed for us, who alone is able to complete the work of our salvation. Let us seek an interest in these blessings, by the witness of the Holy Spirit in our hearts. As the Lord corrected the posterity of David for their transgressions, so his people shall be corrected for their sins. Yet it is but a rod, not a sword; it is to correct, not to destroy. It is a rod in the hand of God, who is wise, and knows what he does; gracious, and will do what is best. It is a rod which they shall never feel, but when there is need. As the sun and moon remain in heaven, whatever changes there seem to be in them, and again appear in due season; so the covenant of grace made in Christ, whatever alteration seems to come to it, should not be questioned.

Verses 38–52

Sometimes it is not easy to reconcile God's providences with his promises, yet we are sure that God's works fulfil his word. When the great Anointed One, Christ himself, was upon the cross, God seemed to have cast him off, yet did not make void his covenant, for that was established for ever. The honour of the house of David was lost. Thrones and crowns are often laid in the dust; but there is a crown of glory reserved for Christ's spiritual seed, which fadeth not away. From all this complaint learn what work sin makes with families, noble families, with families in which religion has appeared. They plead with God for mercy. God's unchangeableness and faithfulness assure us that He will not cast off those whom he has chosen and covenanted with. They were reproached for serving him. The scoffers of the latter days, in like manner, reproach the footsteps of the Messiah when they ask, Where is the promise of his coming? **2**Pe **3**:**3**, **4**. The records of the Lord's dealings with the family of David, show us his dealings with his church, and with believers. Their afflictions and distresses may be grievous, but he will not finally cast them off. Self-deceivers abuse this doctrine, and others by a careless walk bring themselves into darkness and distress; yet let the true believer rely on it for encouragement in the path of duty, and in bearing the cross. The psalm ends with praise, even after this sad complaint. Those who give God thanks for what he has done, may give him thanks for what he will do. God will follow those with his mercies, who follow him with praises.

Chapter 90

Verses 1–6

It is supposed that this psalm refers to the sentence passed on Israel in the wilderness, Nu **14**. The favour and protection of God are the only sure rest and comfort of the soul in this evil world. Christ Jesus is the refuge and dwelling-place to which we may repair. We are dying creatures, all our comforts in the world are dying comforts, but God is an ever-living God, and believers find him so. When God, by sickness, or other afflictions, turns men to destruction, he thereby calls men to return unto him to repent of their sins, and live a new life. A thousand years are nothing to God's eternity: between a minute and a million of years there is some proportion; between time and eternity there is none. All the events of a thousand years, whether past or to come, are more present to the Eternal Mind, than what was done in the last hour is to us. And in the resurrection, the body and soul shall both return and be united again. Time passes unobserved by us, as with men asleep; and when it is past, it is as nothing. It is a short and quickly-passing life, as the waters of a flood. Man does but flourish as the grass, which, when the winter of old age comes, will wither; but he may be mown down by disease or disaster.

Verses 7–11

The afflictions of the saints often come from God's love; but the rebukes of sinners, and of believers for their sins, must be seen coming from the displeasure of God. Secret sins are known to God, and shall be reckoned for. See the folly of those who go about to cover their sins, for they cannot do so. Our years, when gone, can no more be recalled than the words that we have spoken. Our whole life is toilsome and troublesome; and perhaps, in the midst of the years we count upon, it is cut off. We are taught by all this to stand in awe. The angels that sinned know the power of God's anger; sinners in hell know it; but which of us can fully describe it? Few seriously consider it as they ought. Those who make a mock at sin, and make light of Christ, surely do not know the power of God's anger. Who among us can dwell with that devouring fire?

Verses 12–17

Those who would learn true wisdom, must pray for Divine instruction, must beg to be taught by the Holy Spirit; and for comfort and joy in the returns of God's favour. They pray for the mercy of God, for they pretend not to plead any merit of their own. His favour would be a full fountain of future joys. It would be a sufficient balance to former griefs. Let the grace of God in us produce the light of good works. And let Divine consolations put gladness into our hearts, and a lustre upon our countenances. The work of our hands, establish thou it; and, in order to that, establish us in it. Instead of wasting our precious, fleeting days in pursuing fancies, which leave the possessors for ever poor, let us seek the forgiveness of sins, and an inheritance in heaven. Let us pray that the work of the Holy Spirit may appear in converting our hearts, and that the beauty of holiness may be seen in our conduct.

Chapter 91

Verses 1–8

He that by faith chooses God for his protector, shall find all in him that he needs or can desire. And those who have found the comfort of making the Lord their refuge, cannot but desire that others may do so. The spiritual life is protected by Divine grace from the temptations of Satan, which are as the snares of the fowler, and from the contagion of sin, which is a noisome pestilence. Great security is promised to believers in the midst of danger. Wisdom shall keep them from being afraid without cause, and faith shall keep them from being unduly afraid. Whatever is done, our heavenly Father's will is done; and we have no reason to fear. God's people shall see, not only God's promises fulfilled, but his threatenings. Then let sinners come unto the Lord upon his mercy-seat, through the Redeemer's name; and encourage others to trust in him also.

Verses 9–16

Whatever happens, nothing shall hurt the believer; though trouble and affliction befal, it shall come, not for his hurt, but for good, though for the present it be not joyous but grievous. Those who rightly know God, will set their love upon him. They by prayer constantly call upon him. His promise is, that he will in due time deliver the believer out of trouble, and in the mean time be with him in trouble. The Lord will manage all his worldly concerns, and preserve his life on earth, so long as it shall be good for him. For encouragement in this he looks unto Jesus. He shall live long enough; till he has done the work he was sent into this world for, and is ready for heaven. Who would wish to live a day longer than God has some work to do, either by him or upon him? A man may die young, yet be satisfied with living. But a wicked man is not satisfied even with long life. At length the believer's conflict ends; he has done for ever with trouble, sin, and temptation.

Chapter 92

Verses 1–6

It is a privilege that we are admitted to praise the Lord, and hope to be accepted in the morning, and every night; not only on sabbath days, but every day; not only in public, but in private, and in our families. Let us give thanks every morning for the mercies of the night, and every night for the mercies of the day; going out, and coming in, let us bless God. As He makes us glad, through the works of his providence for us, and of his grace in us, and both through the great work of redemption, let us hence be encouraged. As there are many who know not the designs of Providence, nor care to know them, those who through grace do so, have the more reason to be thankful. And if distant views of the great Deliverer so animated believers of old, how should we abound in love and praise!

Verses 7–15

God sometimes grants prosperity to wicked men in displeasure; yet they flourish but for a moment. Let us seek for ourselves the salvation and grace of the gospel, that being daily anointed by the Holy Spirit, we may behold and share the Redeemer's glory. It is from his grace, by his word and Spirit, that believers receive all the virtue that keeps them alive, and makes them fruitful. Other trees, when old, leave off bearing, but in God's trees the strength of grace does not fail with the strength of nature. The last days of the saints are sometimes their best days, and their last work their best work: perseverance is sure evidence of sincerity. And may every sabbath, while it shows forth the Divine faithfulness, find our souls resting more and more upon the Lord our righteousness.

Chapter 93

The majesty, power, and holiness of Christ's kingdom.

—The Lord might have displayed only his justice, holiness, and awful power, in his dealings with fallen men; but he has been pleased to display the riches of his mercy, and the power of his renewing grace. In this great work, the Father has given all power to his Son, the Lord from heaven, who has made atonement for our sins. He not only can pardon, but deliver and protect all who trust in him. His word is past, and all the saints may rely upon it. Whatever was foretold concerning the kingdom of the Messiah, must be fulfilled in due time. All his people ought to be very strictly pure. God's church is his house; it is a holy house, cleansed from sin, and employed in his service. Where there is purity, there shall be peace. Let all carefully look if this kingdom is set up in their hearts.

Chapter 94

Verses 1–11

We may with boldness appeal to God; for he is the almighty Judge by whom every man is judged. Let this encourage those who suffer wrong, to bear it with silence, committing themselves to Him who judges righteously. These prayers are prophecies, which speak terror to the sons of violence. There will come a day of reckoning for all the hard speeches which ungodly sinners have spoken against God, his truths, and ways, and people. It would hardly be believed, if we did not witness it, that millions of rational creatures should live, move, speak, hear, understand, and do what they purpose, yet act as if they believed that God would not punish the abuse of his gifts. As all knowledge is from God, no doubt he knows all the thoughts of the children of men, and knows that the imaginations of the thoughts of men's hearts are only evil, and that continually. Even in good thoughts there is a want of being fixed, which may be called vanity. It concerns us to keep a strict watch over our thoughts, because God takes particular notice of them. Thoughts are words to God.

Verses 12–23

That man is blessed, who, under the chastening of the Lord, is taught his will and his truths, from his holy word, and by the Holy Spirit. He should see mercy through his sufferings. There is a rest remaining for the people of God after the days of their adversity, which shall not last always. He that sends the trouble, will send the rest. The psalmist found succour and relief only in the Lord, when all earthly friends failed. We are beholden, not only to God's power, but to his pity, for spiritual supports; and if we have been kept from falling into sin, or shrinking from our duty, we should give him the glory, and encourage our brethren. The psalmist had many troubled thoughts concerning the case he was in, concerning the course he should take, and what was likely to be the end of it. The indulgence of such contrivances and fears, adds to care and distrust, and renders our views more gloomy and confused. Good men sometimes have perplexed and distressed thoughts concerning God. But let them look to the great and precious promises of the gospel. The world's comforts give little delight to the soul, when hurried with melancholy thoughts; but God's comforts bring that peace and pleasure which the smiles of the world cannot give, and which the frowns of the world cannot take away. God is his people's Refuge, to whom they may flee, in whom they are safe, and may be secure. And he will reckon with the wicked. A man cannot be more miserable than his own wickedness will make him, if the Lord visit it upon him.

Chapter 95

Verses 1–7

Whenever we come into God's presence, we must come with thanksgiving. The Lord is to be praised; we do not want matter, it were well if we did not want a heart. How great is that God, whose the whole earth is, and the fulness thereof; who directs and disposes of all!, The Lord Jesus, whom we are here taught to praise, is a great God; the mighty God is one of his titles, and God over all, blessed for evermore. To him all power is given, both in heaven and earth. He is our God, and we should praise him. He is our Saviour, and the Author of our blessedness. The gospel church is his flock, Christ is the great and good Shepherd of believers; he sought them when lost, and brought them to his fold.

Verses 7–11

Christ calls upon his people to hear his voice. You call him Master, or Lord; then be his willing, obedient people. Hear the voice of his doctrine, of his law, and in both, of his Spirit: hear and heed; hear and yield. Christ's voice must be heard to-day. This day of opportunity will not last always; improve it while it is called to-day. Hearing the voice of Christ is the same with believing. Hardness of heart is at the bottom of all distrust of the Lord. The sins of others ought to be warnings to us not to tread in their steps. The murmurings of Israel were written for our admonition. God is not subject to such passions as we are; but he is very angry at sin and sinners. That certainly is evil, which deserves such a recompence; and his threatenings are as sure as his promises. Let us be aware of the evils of our hearts, which lead us to wander from the Lord. There is a rest ordained for believers, the rest of everlasting refreshment, begun in this life, and perfected in the life to come. This is the rest which God calls his rest.

Chapter 96

Verses 1–9

When Christ finished his work on earth, and was received into his glory in heaven, the church began to sing a new song unto him, and to bless his name. His apostles and evangelists showed forth his salvation among the heathen, his wonders among all people. All the earth is here summoned to worship the Lord. We must worship him in the beauty of holiness, as God in Christ, reconciling the world unto himself. Glorious things are said of him, both as motives to praise and matter of praise.

Verses 10–13

We are to hope and pray for that time, when Christ shall reign in righteousness over all nations. He shall rule in the hearts of men, by the power of truth, and the Spirit of righteousness. His coming draws nigh; this King, this Judge standeth before the door, but he is not yet come. The Lord will accept the praises of all who seek to promote the kingdom of Christ. The sea can but roar, and how the trees of the wood can show that they rejoice we know not; but He that searches the heart knows what is the mind of the Spirit, and understands the words, the broken language of the weakest. Christ will come to judge the earth, to execute just vengeance on his enemies, and to fulfil his largest promises to his people. What then are we? Would that day be welcome to us? If this be not our case, let us now begin to prepare to meet our God, by seeking the pardon of our sins, and the renewal of our souls to holiness.

Chapter 97

Verses 1–7

Though many have been made happy in Christ, still there is room. And all have reason to rejoice in Christ's government. There is a depth in his counsels, which we must not pretend to fathom; but still righteousness and judgment are the habitation of his throne. Christ's government, though it might be matter of joy to all, will yet be matter of terror to some; but it is their own fault that it is so. The most resolute and daring opposition will be baffled at the presence of the Lord. And the Lord Jesus will ere long come, and put an end to idol worship of every kind.

Verses 8–12

The faithful servants of God may well rejoice and be glad, because he is glorified; and whatever tends to his honour, is his people's pleasure. Care is taken for their safety. But something more is meant than their lives. The Lord will preserve the souls of his saints from sin, from apostacy, and despair, under their greatest trials. He will deliver them out of the hands of the wicked one, and preserve them safe to his heavenly kingdom. And those that rejoice in Christ Jesus, and in his exaltation, have fountains of joy prepared for them. Those that sow in tears, shall reap in joy. Gladness is sure to the upright in heart; the joy of the hypocrite is but for a moment. Sinners tremble, but saints rejoice at God's holiness. As he hates sin, yet freely loves the person of the repentant sinner who believes in Christ, he will make a final separation between the person he loves and the sin he hates, and sanctify his people wholly, body, soul, and spirit.

Chapter 98

Verses 1–3

A song of praise for redeeming love is a new song, a mystery hidden from ages and generations. Converts sing a new song, very different from what they had sung. If the grace of God put a new heart into our breasts, it will put a new song into our mouths. Let this new song be sung to the praise of God, in consideration of the wonders he has wrought. The Redeemer has overcome all difficulties in the way of our redemption, and was not discouraged by the services or sufferings appointed him. Let us praise him for the discoveries made to the world of the work of redemption; his salvation and his righteousness fulfilling the prophecies and promises of the Old Testament. In pursuance of this design, God raised up his Son Jesus to be not only a Light to lighten the Gentiles, but the glory of his people Israel. Surely it behoves us to inquire whether his holy arm hath gotten the victory in our hearts, over the power of Satan, unbelief, and sin? If this be our happy case, we shall exchange all light songs of vanity for songs of joy and thanksgiving; our lives will celebrate the Redeemer's praise.

Verses 4–9

Let all the children of men rejoice in the setting up the kingdom of Christ, for all may benefit by it. The different orders of rational creatures in the uni**verse**, seem to be described in figurative language in the reign of the great Messiah. The kingdom of Christ will be a blessing to the whole creation. We expect his second coming to begin his glorious reign. Then shall heaven and earth rejoice, and the joy of the redeemed shall be full. But sin and its dreadful effects will not be utterly done away, till the Lord come to judge the world in righteousness. Seeing then that we look for such things, let us give diligence that we may be found of him in peace, without spot, and blameless.

Chapter 99

Verses 1–5

God governs the world by his providence, governs the church by his grace, and both by his Son. The inhabitants of the earth have cause to tremble, but the Redeemer still waits to be gracious. Let all who hear, take warning, and seek his mercy. The more we humble ourselves before God, the more we exalt him; and let us be thus reverent, for he is holy.

Verses 6–9

The happiness of Israel is made out by referring to the most useful governors of that people. They in every thing made God's word and law their rule, knowing that they could not else expect that their prayers should be answered. They all wonderfully prevailed with God in prayer; miracles were wrought at their request. They pleaded for the people, and obtained answers of peace. Our Prophet and High Priest, of infinitely greater dignity than Moses, Aaron, or Samuel, has received and declared to us the will of the Father. Let us not only exalt the Lord with our lips, but give him the throne in our heart; and while we worship him upon his mercy-seat, let us never forget that he is holy.

Chapter 100

An exhortation to praise God, and rejoice in him.

—This song of praise should be considered as a prophecy, and even used as a prayer, for the coming of that time when all people shall know that the Lord he is God, and shall become his worshippers, and the sheep of his pasture. Great encouragement is given us, in worshipping God, to do it cheerfully. If, when we strayed like wandering sheep, he has brought us again to his fold, we have indeed abundant cause to bless his name. The matter of praise, and the motives to it, are very important. Know ye what God is in himself, and what he is to you. Know it; consider and apply it, then you will be more close and constant, more inward and serious, in his worship. The covenant of grace set down in the Scriptures of the Old and New Testament, with so many rich promises, to strengthen the faith of every weak believer, makes the matter of God's praise and of his people's joys so sure, that how sad soever our spirits may be when we look to ourselves, yet we shall have reason to praise the Lord when we look to his goodness and mercy, and to what he has said in his word for our comfort.

Chapter 101

David's vow and profession of godliness.

—In this psalm we have David declaring how he intended to regulate his household, and to govern his kingdom, that he might stop wickedness, and encourage godliness. It is also applicable to private families, and is the householder's psalm. It teaches all that have any power, whether more or less, to use it so as to be a terror to evil-doers, and a praise to them that do well. The chosen subject of the psalm is God's mercy and judgment. The Lord's providences concerning his people are commonly mixed; mercy and judgment. God has set the one over against the other, both to do good, like showers and sunshine. When, in his providence, he exercises us with the mixture of mercy and judgment, we must make suitable acknowledgments to him for both. Family mercies and family afflictions are both calls to family religion. Those who are in public stations are not thereby excused from care in governing their families; they are the more concerned to set a good example of ruling their own houses well. Whenever a man has a house of his own, let him seek to have God to dwell with him; and those may expect his presence, who walk with a perfect heart, in a perfect way. David resolves to practise no evil himself. He further resolves not to keep bad servants, nor to employ those about him that are wicked. He will not admit them into his family, lest they spread the infection of sin. A froward heart, one that delights to be cross and per**verse**, is not fit for society, the bond of which is Christian love. Nor will he countenance slanderers, those who take pleasure in wounding their neighbour's reputation. Also, God resists the proud, and false, deceitful people, who scruple not to tell lies, or commit frauds. Let every one be zealous and diligent to reform his own heart and ways, and to do this early; ever mindful of that future, most awful morning, when the King of righteousness shall cut off all wicked doers from the heavenly Jerusalem.

Chapter 102

Verses 1–11

The whole word of God is of use to direct us in prayer; but here, is often elsewhere, the Holy Ghost has put words into our mouths. Here is a prayer put into the hands of the afflicted; let them present it to God. Even good men may be almost overwhelmed with afflictions. It is our duty and interest to pray; and it is comfort to an afflicted spirit to unburden itself, by a humble representation of its griefs. We must say, Blessed be the name of the Lord, who both gives and takes away. The psalmist looked upon himself as a dying man; My days are like a shadow.

Verses 12–22

We are dying creatures, but God is an everlasting God, the protector of his church; we may be confident that it will not be neglected. When we consider our own vileness, our darkness and deadness, and the manifold defects in our prayers, we have cause to fear that they will not be received in heaven; but we are here assured of the contrary, for we have an Advocate with the Father, and are under grace, not under the law. Redemption is the subject of praise in the Christian church; and that great work is described by the temporal deliverance and restoration of Israel. Look down upon us, Lord Jesus; and bring us into the glorious liberty of thy children, that we may bless and praise thy name.

Verses 23–28

Bodily distempers soon weaken our strength, then what can we expect but that our months should be cut off in the midst; and what should we do but provide accordingly? We must own God's hand in it; and must reconcile this to his love, for often those that have used their strength well, have it weakened; and those who, as we think, can very ill be spared, have their days shortened. It is very comfortable, in reference to all the changes and dangers of the church, to remember that Jesus Christ is the same yesterday, to-day, and for ever. And in reference to the death of our bodies, and the removal of friends, to remember that God is an everlasting God. Do not let us overlook the assurance this psalm contains of a happy end to all the believer's trials. Though all things are changing, dying, perishing, like a vesture folding up and hastening to decay, yet Jesus lives, and thus all is secure, for he hath said, Because I live ye shall live also.

Chapter 103

Verses 1–5

By the pardon of sin, that is taken away which kept good things from us, and we are restored to the favor of God, who bestows good things on us. Think of the provocation; it was sin, and yet pardoned: how many the provocations, yet all pardoned! God is still forgiving, as we are still sinning and repenting. The body finds the melancholy consequences of Adam's offence, it is subject to many infirmities, and the soul also. Christ alone forgives all our sins; it is he alone who heals all our infirmities. And the person who finds his sin cured, has a well-grounded assurance that it is forgiven. When God, by the graces and comforts of his Spirit, recovers his people from their decays, and fills them with new life and joy, which is to them an earnest of eternal life and joy, they may then be said to return to the days of their youth, Job **33**:**25**.

Verses 6–14

Truly God is good to all: he is in a special manner good to Israel. He has revealed himself and his grace to them. By his ways we may understand his precepts, the ways he requires us to walk in; and his promises and purposes. He always has been full of compassion. How unlike are those to God, who take every occasion to chide, and never know when to cease! What would become of us, if God should deal so with us? The Scripture says a great deal of the mercy of God, and we all have experienced it. The father pities his children that are weak in knowledge, and teaches them; pities them when they are froward, and bears with them; pities them when they are sick, and comforts them; pities them when they are fallen, and helps them to rise; pities them when they have offended, and, upon their submission, forgives them; pities them when wronged, and rights them: thus the Lord pities those that fear him. See why he pities. He considers the frailty of our bodies, and the folly of our souls, how little we can do, how little we can bear; in all which his compassion appears.

Verses 15–18

How short is man's life, and uncertain! The flower of the garden is commonly more choice, and will last the longer, for being sheltered by the garden-wall, and the gardener's care; but the flower of the field, to which life is here compared, is not only withering in itself, but exposed to the cold blasts, and liable to be cropt and trod on by the beasts of the field. Such is man. God considers this, and pities him; let him consider it himself. God's mercy is better than life, for it will outlive it. His righteousness, the truth of his promise, shall be unto children's children, who tread in the footsteps of their forefathers' piety. Then shall mercy be preserved to them.

Verses 19–22

He who made all, rules all, and both by a word of power. He disposes all persons and things to his own glory. There is a world of holy angels who are ever praising him. Let all his works praise him. Such would have been our constant delight, if we had not been fallen creatures. Such it will in a measure become, if we are born of God. Such it will be for ever in heaven; nor can we be perfectly happy till we can take unwearied pleasure in perfect obedience to the will of our God. And let the feeling of each redeemed heart be, Bless the Lord, O my soul.

Chapter 104

Verses 1–9

Every object we behold calls on us to bless and praise the Lord, who is great. His eternal power and Godhead are clearly shown by the things which he hath made. God is light, and in him is no darkness at all. The Lord Jesus, the Son of his love, is the Light of the world.

Verses 10–18

When we reflect upon the provision made for all creatures, we should also notice the natural worship they render to God. Yet man, forgetful ungrateful man, enjoys the largest measure of his Creator's kindness. the earth, varying in different lands. Nor let us forget spiritual blessings; the fruitfulness of the church through grace, the bread of everlasting life, the cup of salvation, and the oil of gladness. Does God provide for the inferior creatures, and will he not be a refuge to his people?

Verses 19–30

We are to praise and magnify God for the constant succession of day and night. And see how those are like to the wild beasts, who wait for the twilight, and have fellowship with the unfruitful works of darkness. Does God listen to the language of mere nature, even in ravenous creatures, and shall he not much more interpret favourably the language of grace in his own people, though weak and broken groanings which cannot be uttered? There is the work of every day, which is to be done in its day, which man must apply to every morning, and which he must continue in till evening; it will be time enough to rest when the night comes, in which no man can work. The psalmist wonders at the works of God. The works of art, the more closely they are looked upon, the more rough they appear; the works of nature appear more fine and exact. They are all made in wisdom, for they all answer the end they were designed to serve. Every spring is an emblem of the resurrection, when a new world rises, as it were, out of the ruins of the old one. But man alone lives beyond death. When the Lord takes away his breath, his soul enters on another state, and his body will be raised, either to glory or to misery. May the Lord send forth his Spirit, and new-create our souls to holiness.

Verses 31–35

Man's glory is fading; God's glory is everlasting: creatures change, but with the Creator there is no variableness. And if mediation on the glories of creation be so sweet to the soul, what greater glory appears to the enlightened mind, when contemplating the great work of redemption! There alone can a sinner perceive ground of confidence and joy in God. While he with pleasure upholds all, governs all, and rejoices in all his works, let our souls, touched by his grace, meditate on and praise him.

Chapter 105

Verses 1–7

Our devotion is here stirred up, that we may stir up ourselves to praise God. Seek his strength; that is, his grace; the strength of his Spirit to work in us that which is good, which we cannot do but by strength derived from him, for which he will be sought. Seek to have his favour to eternity, therefore continue seeking it while living in this world; for he will not only be found, but he will reward those that diligently seek him.

Verses 8–23

Let us remember the Redeemer's marvellous works, his wonders, and the judgments of his mouth. Though true Christians are few number, strangers and pilgrims upon earth, yet a far better inheritance than Canaan is made sure to them by the covenant of God; and if we have the anointing of the Holy Spirit, none can do us any harm. Afflictions are among our mercies. They prove our faith and love, they humble our pride, they wean us from the world, and quicken our prayers. Bread is the staff which supports life; when that staff is broken, the body fails and sinks to the earth. The word of God is the staff of spiritual life, the food and support of the soul: the sorest judgment is a famine of hearing the word of the Lord. Such a famine was sore in all lands when Christ appeared in the flesh; whose coming, and the blessed effect of it, are shadowed forth in the history of Joseph. At the appointed time Christ was exalted as Mediator; all the treasures of grace and salvation are at his disposal, perishing sinners come to him, and are relieved by him.

Verses 24–45

As the believer commonly thrives best in his soul when under the cross; so the church also flourishes most in true holiness, and increases in number, while under persecution. Yet instruments shall be raised up for their deliverance, and plagues may be expected by persecutors. And see the special care God took of his people in the wilderness. All the benefits bestowed on Israel as a nation, were shadows of spiritual blessings with which we are blessed in Christ Jesus. Having redeemed us with his blood, restored our souls to holiness, and set us at liberty from Satan's bondage, he guides and guards us all the way. He satisfies our souls with the bread of heaven, and the water of life from the Rock of salvation, and will bring us safely to heaven. He redeems his servants from all iniquity, and purifies them unto himself, to be a peculiar people, zealous of good works.

Chapter 106

Verses 1–5

None of our sins or sufferings should prevent our ascribing glory and praise to the Lord. The more unworthy we are, the more is his kindness to be admired. And those who depend on the Redeemer's righteousness will endeavour to copy his example, and by word and deed to show forth his praise. God's people have reason to be cheerful people; and need not envy the children of men their pleasure or pride.

Verses 6–12

Here begins a confession of sin; for we must acknowledge that the Lord has done right, and we have done wickedly. We are encouraged to hope that though justly corrected, yet we shall not be utterly forsaken. God's afflicted people own themselves guilty before him. God is distrusted because his favours are not remembered. If he did not save us for his own name's sake, and to the praise of his power and grace, we should all perish.

Verses 13–33

Those that will not wait for God's counsel, shall justly be given up to their own hearts' lusts, to walk in their own counsels. An undue desire, even for lawful things, becomes sinful. God showed his displeasure for this. He filled them with uneasiness of mind, terror of conscience, and self-reproach. Many that fare deliciously every day, and whose bodies are healthful, have leanness in their souls: no love to God, no thankfulness, no appetite for the Bread of life, and then the soul must be lean. Those wretchedly forget themselves, that feast their bodies and starve their souls. Even the true believer will see abundant cause to say, It is of the Lord's mercies that I am not consumed. Often have we set up idols in our hearts, cleaved to some forbidden object; so that if a greater than Moses had not stood to turn away the anger of the Lord, we should have been destroyed. If God dealt severely with Moses for unadvised words, what do those deserve who speak many proud and wicked words? It is just in God to remove those relations that are blessings to us, when we are peevish and provoking to them, and grieve their spirits.

Verses 34–48

The conduct of the Israelites in Canaan, and God's dealings with them, show that the way of sin is down-hill; omissions make way for commissions: when they neglected to destroy the heathen, they learned their works. One sin led to many more, and brought the judgments of God on them. Their sin was, in part, their own punishment. Sinners often see themselves ruined by those who led them into evil. Satan, who is a tempter, will be a tormentor. At length, God showed pity to his people for his covenant's sake. The unchangeableness of God's merciful nature and love to his people, makes him change the course of justice into mercy; and no other change is meant by God's repentance. Our case is awful when the outward church is considered. When nations professing Christianity, are so guilty as we are, no wonder if the Lord brings them low for their sins. Unless there is general and deep repentance, there can be no prospect but of increasing calamities. The psalm concludes with prayer for completing the deliverance of God's people, and praise for the beginning and progress of it. May all the people of the earth, ere long, add their Amen.

Chapter 107

Verses 1–9

In these **verse**s there is reference to the deliverance from Egypt, and perhaps that from Babylon: but the circumstances of travellers in those countries are also noted. It is scarcely possible to conceive the horrors suffered by the hapless traveller, when crossing the trackless sands, exposed to the burning rays of the sum. The words describe their case whom the Lord has redeemed from the bondage of Satan; who pass through the world as a dangerous and dreary wilderness, often ready to faint through troubles, fears, and temptations. Those who hunger and thirst after righteousness, after God, and communion with him, shall be filled with the goodness of his house, both in grace and glory.

Verses 10–16

This description of prisoners and captives intimates that they are desolate and sorrowful. In the eastern prisons the captives were and are treated with much severity. Afflicting providences must be improved as humbling providences; and we lose the benefit, if our hearts are unhumbled and unbroken under them. This is a shadow of the sinner's deliverance from a far worse confinement. The awakened sinner discovers his guilt and misery. Having struggled in vain for deliverance, he finds there is no help for him but in the mercy and grace of God. His sin is forgiven by a merciful God, and his pardon is accompanied by deliverance from the power of sin and Satan, and by the sanctifying and comforting influences of God the Holy Spirit.

Verses 17–22

If we knew no sin, we should know no sickness. Sinners are fools. They hurt their bodily health by intemperance, and endanger their lives by indulging their appetites. This their way is their folly. The weakness of the body is the effect of sickness. It is by the power and mercy of God that we are recovered from sickness, and it is our duty to be thankful. All Christ's miraculous cures were emblems of his healing diseases of the soul. It is also to be applied to the spiritual cures which the Spirit of grace works. He sends his word, and heals souls; convinces, converts them, makes them holy, and all by the word. Even in common cases of recovery from sickness, God in his providence speaks, and it is done; by his word and Spirit the soul is restored to health and holiness.

Verses 23–32

Let those who go to sea, consider and adore the Lord. Mariners have their business upon the tempestuous ocean, and there witness deliverances of which others cannot form an idea. How seasonable it is at such a time to pray! This may remind us of the terrors and distress of conscience many experience, and of those deep scenes of trouble which many pass through, in their Christian course. Yet, in answer to their cries, the Lord turns their storm into a calm, and causes their trials to end in gladness.

Verses 33–43

What surprising changes are often made in the affairs of men! Let the present desolate state of Judea, and of other countries, explain this. If we look abroad in the world, we see many greatly increase, whose beginning was small. We see many who have thus suddenly risen, as suddenly brought to nothing. Worldly wealth is uncertain; often those who are filled with it, ere they are aware, lose it again. God has many ways of making men poor. The righteous shall rejoice. It shall fully convince all those who deny the Divine Providence. When sinners see how justly God takes away the gifts they have abused, they will not have a word to say. It is of great use to us to be fully assured of God's goodness, and duly affected with it. It is our wisdom to mind our duty, and to refer our comfort to him. A truly wise person will treasure in his heart this delightful psalm. From it, he will fully understand the weakness and wretchedness of man, and the power and loving-kindness of God, not for our merit, but for his mercy's sake.

Chapter 108

—We may usefully select passages from different psalms, as here, Ps **57**; **60**, to help our devotions, and enliven our gratitude. When the heart is firm in faith and love, the tongue, being employed in grateful praises, is our glory. Every gift of the Lord honours and profits the possessor, as it is employed in God's service and to his glory. Believers may pray with assured faith and hope, for all the blessings of salvation; which are secured to them by the faithful promise and covenant of God. Then let them expect from him help in every trouble, and victory in every conflict. Whatever we do, whatever we gain, God must have all the glory. Lord, visit all our souls with this salvation, with this favour which thou bearest to thy chosen people.

Chapter 109

Verses 1–5

It is the unspeakable comfort of all believers, that whoever is against them, God is for them; and to him they may apply as to one pleased to concern himself for them. David's enemies laughed at him for his devotion, but they could not laugh him out of it.

Verses 6–20

The Lord Jesus may speak here as a Judge, denouncing sentence on some of his enemies, to warn others. When men reject the salvation of Christ, even their prayers are numbered among their sins. See what hurries some to shameful deaths, and brings the families and estates of others to ruin; makes them and theirs despicable and hateful, and brings poverty, shame, and misery upon their posterity: it is sin, that mischievous, destructive thing. And what will be the effect of the sentence, "Go, ye cursed," upon the bodies and souls of the wicked! How it will affect the senses of the body, and the powers of the soul, with pain, anguish, horror, and despair! Think on these things, sinners, tremble and repent.

Verses 21–31

The psalmist takes God's comforts to himself, but in a very humble manner. He was troubled in mind. His body was wasted, and almost worn away. But it is better to have leanness in the body, while the soul prospers and is in health, than to have leanness in the soul, while the body is feasted. He was ridiculed and reproached by his enemies. But if God bless us, we need not care who curses us; for how can they curse whom God has not cursed; nay, whom he has blessed? He pleads God's glory, and the honour of his name. Save me, not according to my merit, for I pretend to none, but according to thy-mercy. He concludes with the joy of faith, in assurance that his present conflicts would end in triumphs. Let all that suffer according to the will of God, commit the keeping of their souls to him. Jesus, unjustly put to death, and now risen again, is an Advocate and Intercessor for his people, ever ready to appear on their behalf against a corrupt world, and the great accuser.

Chapter 110

Christ's kingdom.

—Glorious things are here spoken of Christ. Not only he should be superior to all the kings of the earth, but he then existed in glory as the eternal Son of God. Sitting is a resting posture: after services and sufferings, to give law, to give judgment. It is a remaining posture: he sits like a king for ever. All his enemies are now in a chain, but not yet made his footstool. And his kingdom, being set up, shall be kept up in the world, in despite of all the powers of darkness. Christ's people are a willing people. The power of the Spirit, going with the power of the world, to the people of Christs, is effectual to make them willing. They shall attend him in the beautiful attire of holiness; which becomes his house for ever. And he shall have many devoted to him. The dew of our youth, even in the morning of our days, ought to be consecrated to our Lord Jesus. Christ shall not only be a King, but a Priest. He is God's Minister to us, and our

Advocate with the Father, and so is the Mediator between God and man. He is a Priest of the order of Melchizedek, which was before that of Aaron, and on many accounts superior to it, and a more lively representation of Christ's priesthood. Christ's sitting at the right hand of God, speaks as much terror to his enemies as happiness to his people. The effect of this victory shall be the utter ruin of his enemies. We have here the Redeemer saving his friends, and comforting them. He shall be humbled; he shall drink of the brook in the way. The wrath of God, running in the curse of the law, may be considered as the brook in the way of his undertaking. Christ drank of the waters of affliction in his way to the throne of glory. But he shall be exalted. What then are we? Has the gospel of Christ been to us the power of God unto salvation? Has his kingdom been set up in our hearts? Are we his willing subjects? Once we knew not our need of his salvation, and we were not willing that he should reign over us. Are we willing to give up every sin, to turn from a wicked, insnaring world, and rely only on his merits and mercy, to have him for our Prophet, Priest, and King? and do we desire to be holy? To those who are thus changed, the Saviour's sacrifice, intercession, and blessing belong.

Chapter 111

The Lord is to be praised for his works.

—The psalmist resolves to praise God himself. Our exhortations and our examples should agree together. He recommends the works of the Lord, as the proper subject, when we are praising him; and the dealings of his providence toward the world, the church, and particular persons. All the works of the Lord are spoken of as one, it is his work; so admirably do all the dispensations of his providence centre in one design. The works of God, humbly and diligently sought into, shall all be found just and holy. God's pardoning sin is the most wonderful of all his works, and ought to be remembered to his glory. He will ever be mindful of his covenant; he has ever been so, and he ever will be so. His works of providence were done according to the truth of the Divine promises and prophecies, and so were verity, or truth; and by him who has a right to dispose of the earth as he pleases, and so are judgment, or righteous: and this holds good of the work of grace upon the heart of man, ver. #(**7**, **8**). All God's commandments are sure; all have been fulfilled by Christ, and remain with him for a rule of walk and conversation to us. He sent redemption unto his people, out of Egypt at first, and often afterwards; and these were typical of the great redemption, which in the fulness of time was to be wrought out by the Lord Jesus. Here his everlasting righteousness shines forth in union with his boundless mercy. No man is wise who does not fear the Lord; no man acts wisely except as influenced by that fear. This fear will lead to repentance, to faith in Christ, to watchfulness and obedience. Such persons are of a good understanding, however poor, unlearned, or despised.

Chapter 112

The blessedness of the righteous.

—We have to praise the Lord that there are a people in the world, who fear him and serve him, and that they are a happy people; which is owing entirely to his grace. Their fear is not that which love casts out, but that which love brings in. It follows and flows from love. It is a fear to offend. This is both fear and trust. The heart touched by the Spirit of God, as the needle touched with the loadstone, turns direct and speedily to God, yet still with trembling, being filled with this holy fear. Blessings are laid up for the faithful and their children's children; and true riches are bestowed on them, with as much of this world's possessions as is profitable for them. In the darkest hours of affliction and trial, the light of hope and peace will spring up within them, and seasonable relief shall turn mourning into joy. From their Lord's example they learn to be kind and full of compassion, as well as just in all their dealings; they use discretion, that they may be liberal in that manner which appears most likely to do good. Envy and slander may for a time hide their true characters here, but they shall be had in everlasting remembrance. They need not fear evil tidings. A good man shall have a settled spirit. And it is the endeavour of true believers to keep their minds stayed upon God, and so to keep them calm and undisturbed; and God has promised them both cause to do so, and grace to do so. Trusting in the Lord is the best and surest way of establishing the heart. The heart of man cannot fix any where with satisfaction, but in the truth of God, and there it finds firm footing. And those whose hearts are established by faith, will patiently wait till they gain their point. Compare all this with the vexation of sinners. The happiness of the saints is the envy of the wicked. The desire of the wicked shall perish; their desire was wholly to the world and the flesh, therefore when these perish, their joy is gone. But the blessings of the gospel are spiritual and eternal, and are conferred upon the members of the Christian church, through Christ their Head, who is the Pattern of all righteousness, and the Giver of all grace.

Chapter 113

An exhortation to praise God.

—God has praise from his own people. They have most reason to praise him; for those who attend him as his servants, know him best, and receive most of his favours, and it is easy, pleasant work to speak well of their Master. God's name ought to be praised in every place, from east to west. Within this wide space the Lord's name is to be praised; it ought to be so, though it is not. Ere long it will be, when all nations shall come and worship before him. God is exalted above all blessing and praise. We must therefore say, with holy admiration, Who is like unto the Lord our God? How condescending in him to behold the things in the earth! And what amazing condescension was it for the Son of God to come from heaven to earth, and take our nature upon him, that he might seek and save those that were lost! How vast his love in taking upon him the nature of man, to ransom guilty souls! God sometimes makes glorious his own wisdom and power, when, having some great work to do, he employs those least likely, and least thought of for it by themselves or others. The apostles were sent from fishing to be fishers of men. And this is God's constant method in his kingdom of grace. He takes men, by nature beggars, and even traitors, to be his favourites, his children, kings and priests unto him; and numbers them with the princes of his chosen people. He gives us all our comforts, which are generally the more welcome when long delayed, and no longer expected. Let us pray that those lands which are yet barren, may speedily become fruitful, and produce many converts to join in praising the Lord.

Chapter 114

An exhortation to fear God.

—Let us acknowledge God's power and goodness in what he did for Israel, applying it to that much greater work of wonder, our redemption by Christ; and encourage ourselves and others to trust in God in the greatest straits. When Christ comes for the salvation of his people , he redeems them from the power of sin and Satan, separates them from an ungodly world, forms them to be his people, and becomes their King. There is no sea, no Jordan, so deep, so broad, but, when God's time is come, it shall be divided and driven back. Apply this to the planting the Christian church in the world. What ailed Satan and his idolatries, that they trembled as they did? But especially apply it to the work of grace in the heart. What turns the stream in a regenerate soul? What affects the lusts and corruptions, that they fly back; that prejudices are removed, and the whole man becomes new? It is at the presence of God's Spirit. At the presence of the Lord, not only mountains, but the earth itself may well tremble, since it has lain under a curse for man's sin. As the Israelites were protected, so they were provided for by miracles; such was that fountain of waters into which the flinty rock was turned, and that rock was Christ. The Son of God, the Rock of ages, gave himself to death, to open a fountain to wash away sins, and to supply believers with waters of life and consolation; and they need not fear that any blessing is too great to expect from his love. But let sinners fear before their just and holy Judge. Let us now prepare to meet our God, that we may have boldness before him at his coming.

Chapter 115

Verses 1–8

Let no opinion of our own merits have any place in our prayers or in our praises. All the good we do, is done by the power of his grace; and all the good we have, is the gift of his mere mercy, and he must have all the praise. Are we in pursuit of any mercy, and wrestling with God for it, we must take encouragement in prayer from God only. Lord, do so for us; not that we may have the credit and comfort of it, but that they mercy and truth may have the glory of it. The heathen gods are senseless things. They are the works of men's hands: the painter, the carver, the statuary, can put no life into them, therefore no sense. The psalmist hence shows the folly of the worshippers of idols.

Verses 9–18

It is folly to trust in dead images, but it is wisdom to trust in the living God, for he is a help and a shield to those that trust in him. Wherever there is right fear of God, there may be cheerful faith in him; those who reverence his word, may rely upon it. He is ever found faithful. The greatest need his blessing, and it shall not be denied to the meanest that fear him. God's blessing gives an increase, especially in spiritual blessings. And the Lord is to be praised: his goodness is large, for he has given the earth to the children of men for their use. The souls of the faithful, after they are delivered from the burdens of the flesh, are still praising him; but the dead body cannot praise God: death puts an end to our glorifying him in this world of trial and conflict. Others are dead, and an end is thereby put to their service, therefore we will seek to do the more for God. We will not only do it ourselves, but will engage others to do it; to praise him when we are gone. Lord, thou art the only object for faith and love. Help us to praise thee while living and when dying, that thy name may be the first and last upon our lips: and let the sweet savour of thy name refresh our souls for ever.

Chapter 116

Verses 1–9

We have many reasons for loving the Lord, but are most affected by his loving-kindness when relieved out of deep distress. When a poor sinner is awakened to a sense of his state, and fears that he must soon sink under the just wrath of God, then he finds trouble and sorrow. But let all such call upon the Lord to deliver their souls, and they will find him gracious and true to his promise. Neither ignorance nor guilt will hinder their salvation, when they put their trust in the Lord. Let us all speak of God as we have found him; and have we ever found him otherwise than just and good? It is of his mercies that we are not consumed. Let those who labour and are heavy laden come to him, that they may find rest to their souls; and if at all drawn from their rest, let them haste to return, remembering how bountifully the Lord has dealt with them. We should deem ourselves bound to walk as in his presence. It is a great mercy to be kept from being swallowed up with over-much sorrow. It is a great mercy for God to hold us by the right hand, so that we are not overcome and overthrown by a temptation. But when we enter the heavenly rest, deliverance from sin and sorrow will be complete; we shall behold the glory of the Lord, and walk in his presence with delight we cannot now conceive.

Verses 10–19

When troubled, we do best to hold our peace, for we are apt to speak unadvisedly. Yet there may be true faith where there are workings of unbelief; but then faith will prevail; and being humbled for our distrust of God's word, we shall experience his faithfulness to it. What can the pardoned sinner, or what can those who have been delivered from trouble or distress, render to the Lord for his benefits? We cannot in any way profit him. Our best is unworthy of his acceptance; yet we ought to devote ourselves and all we have to his service. I will take the cup of salvation; I will offer the drink-offerings appointed by the law, in token of thankfulness to God, and rejoice in God's goodness to me. I will receive the cup of affliction; that cup, that bitter cup, which is sanctified to the saints, so that to them it is a cup of salvation; it is a means of spiritual health. The cup of consolation; I will receive the benefits God bestows upon me, as from his hand, and taste his love in them, as the portion not only of mine inheritance in the other world, but of my cup in this. Let others serve what masters they will, truly I am thy servant. Two ways men came to be servants. By birth. Lord, I was born in thy house; I am the son of thine handmaid, and therefore thine. It is a great mercy to be children of godly parents. By redemption. Lord, thou hast loosed my bonds, thou hast discharged me from them, therefore I am thy servant. The bonds thou hast loosed shall tie me faster unto thee. Doing good is sacrifice, with which God is well pleased; and this must accompany giving thanks to his name. Why should we offer that to the Lord which cost us nothing? The psalmist will pay his vows now; he will not delay the payment: publicly, not to make a boast, but to show he is not ashamed of God's service, and to invite others to join him. Such are true saints of God, in whose lives and deaths he will be glorified.

Chapter 117

All people called upon to praise God.

—Here is a solemn call to all nations to praise the Lord, and proper matter for that praise is suggested. We are soon weary of well-doing, if we keep not up the pious and devout affections with which the spiritual sacrifice of praise ought to be kindled and kept burning. This is a gospel psalm. The apostle, Ro **15**:**11**, quotes it as a proof that the gospel was to be preached to the Gentile nations, and that it would be entertained by them. For many ages, in Judah only was God known, and his name praised; this call was not then given to any Gentiles. But the gospel of Christ is ordered to be preached to all nations, and by him those that were afar off are made nigh. We are among the persons to whom the Holy Spirit here speaks, whom he calls upon to join his ancient people in praising the Lord. Grace has thus abounded to millions of perishing sinners. Let us then listen to the offers of the grace of God, and pray for that time when all nations of the earth shall show forth his praises. And let us bless God for the unsearchable riches of gospel grace.

Chapter 118

Verses 1–18

The account the psalmist here gives of his troubles is very applicable to Christ: many hated him without a cause; nay, the Lord himself chastened him sorely, bruised him, and put him to grief, that by his stripes we might be healed. God is sometimes the strength of his people, when he is not their song; they have spiritual supports, though they want spiritual delights. Whether the believer traces back his comfort to the everlasting goodness and mercy of God, or whether he looks forward to the blessing secured to him, he will find abundant cause for joy and praise. Every answer to our prayers is an evidence that the Lord is on our side; and then we need not fear what man can do unto us; we should conscientiously do our duty to all, and trust in him alone to accept and bless us. Let us seek to live to declare the works of God, and to encourage others to serve him and trust in him. Such were the triumphs of the Son of David, in the assurance that the good pleasure of the Lord should prosper in his hand.

Verses 19–29

Those who saw Christ's day at so great a distance, saw cause to praise God for the prospect. The prophecy, ver. #(**22**, **23**), may refer to David's preferment; but principally to Christ. **1**. His humiliation; he is the Stone which the builders refused: they would go on in their building without him. This proved the ruin of those who thus made light of him. Rejecters of Christ are rejected of God. **2**. His exaltation; he is the chief Cornerstone in the foundation. He is the chief Top-stone, in whom the building is completed, who must, in all things, have the pre-eminence. Christ's name is Wonderful; and the redemption he wrought out is the most amazing of all God's wondrous works. We will rejoice and be glad in the Lord's day; not only that such a day is appointed, but in the occasion of it, Christ's becoming the Head. Sabbath days ought to be rejoicing days, then they are to us as the days of heaven. Let this Saviour be my Saviour, my Ruler. Let my soul prosper and be in health, in that peace and righteousness which his government brings. Let me have victory over the lusts that war against my soul; and let Divine grace subdue my heart. The duty which the Lord has made, brings light with it, true light. The duty this privilege calls for, is here set forth; the sacrifices we are to offer to God in gratitude for redeeming love, are ourselves; not to be slain upon the altar, but living sacrifices, to be bound to the altar; spiritual sacrifices of prayer and praise, in which our hearts must be engaged. The psalmist praises God, and calls upon all about him to give thanks to God for the glad tidings of great joy to all people, that there is a Redeemer, even Christ the Lord. In him the covenant of grace is made sure and everlasting.

Chapter 119

The general scope and design of this psalm is to magnify the Divine law, and make it honourable. There are ten words by which Divine revelation is called in this psalm, and each expresses what God expects from us, and what we may expect from him. **1**. God's law; this is enacted by him as our Sovereign. **2**. His way; this is the rule of his providence. **3**. His testimonies; they are solemnly declared to the world. **4**. His commandments; given with authority. **5**. His precepts; not left as indifferent matters to us. **6**. His word, or saying; it is the declaration of his mind. **7**. His judgments; framed in infinite wisdom. **8**. His righteousness; it is the rule and standard of what is right. **9**. His statutes; they are always binding. **10**. His truth or faithfulness; it is eternal truth, it shall endure for ever.

Verses 1–8

This psalm may be considered as the statement of a believer's experience. As far as our views, desires, and affections agree with what is here expressed, they come from the influences of the Holy Spirit, and no further. The pardoning mercy of God in Christ, is the only source of a sinner's happiness. And those are most happy, who are preserved most free from the defilement of sin, who simply believe God's testimonies, and depend on his promises. If the heart be divided between him and the world, it is evil. But the saints carefully avoid all sin; they are conscious of much evil that clogs them in the ways of God, but not of that wickedness which draws them out of those ways. The tempter would make men think they are at them out of those ways. The tempter would make men think they are at liberty to follow the word of God or not, as they please. But the desire and prayer of a good man agree with the will and command of God. If a man expects by obedience in one thing to purchase indulgence for disobedience in others, his hypocrisy will be detected; if he is not ashamed in this world, everlasting shame will be his portion. The psalmist coveted to learn the laws of God, to give God the glory. And believers see that if God forsakes them, the temper will be too hard for them.

Verses 9–16

To original corruption all have added actual sin. The ruin of the young is either living by no rule at all, or choosing false rules: let them walk by Scripture rules. To doubt of our own wisdom and strength, and to depend upon God, proves the purpose of holiness is sincere. God's word is treasure worth laying up, and there is no laying it up safe but in our hearts, that we may oppose God's precepts to the dominion of sin, his promises to its allurements, and his threatenings to its violence. Let this be our plea with Him to teach us his statutes, that, being partakers of his holiness, we may also partake of his blessedness. And those whose hearts are fed with the bread of life, should with their lips feed many. In the way of God's commandments there is the unsearchable riches of Christ. But we do not meditate on God's precepts to good purpose, unless our good thoughts produce good works. I will not only think of thy statutes, but do them with delight. And it will be well to try the sincerity of our obedience by tracing the spring of it; the reality of our love by cheerfulness in appointed duties.

Verses 17–24

If God deals in strict justice with us, we all perish. We ought to spend our lives in his service; we shall find true life in keeping his word. Those that would see the wondrous things of God's law and gospel, must beg him to give them understanding, by the light of his Spirit. Believers feel themselves strangers on earth; they fear missing their way, and losing comfort by erring from God's commandments. Every sanctified soul hungers after the word of God, as food which there is no living without. There is something of pride at the bottom of every wilful sin. God can silence lying lips; reproach and contempt may humble and do us good, and then they shall be removed. Do we find the weight of the cross is above that we are able to bear? He that bore it for us will enable us to bear it; upheld by him we cannot sink. It is sad when those who should protect the innocent, are their betrayers. The psalmist went on in duty, and he found comfort in the word of God. The comforts of the word of God are most pleasant to a gracious soul, when other comforts are made bitter; and those that would have God's testimonies to be their delight, must be advised by them. May the Lord direct us in exercising repentance of sin, and faith in Christ.

Verses 25–32

While the souls of the children of this world cleave to the earth as their portion, the children of light are greatly burdened, because of the remains of carnal affections in their hearts. It is unspeakable comfort to a gracious soul, to think with what tenderness all its complaints are received by a gracious God. We can talk of the wonders of redeeming love, when we understand the way of God's precepts, and walk in that way. The penitent melts in sorrow for sin: even the patient spirit may melt in the sense of affliction, it is then its interest to pour out its soul before God. The way of lying means all false ways by which men deceive themselves and others, or are deceived by Satan and his instruments. Those who know and love the law of the Lord, desire to know it more, and love it better. The way of serious godliness is the way of truth; the only true way to happiness: we must always have actual regard to it. Those who stick to the word of God, may in faith expect and pray for acceptance with God. Lord, never leave me to do that by which I shall shame myself, and do not thou reject my services. Those that are going to heaven, should still press forward. God, by his Spirit, enlarges the hearts of his people when he gives them wisdom. The believer prays to be set free from sin.

Verses 33–40

Teach me thy statutes, not the mere words, but the way of applying them to myself. God, by his Spirit, gives a right understanding. But the Spirit of revelation in the word will not suffice, unless we have the Spirit of wisdom in the heart. God puts his Spirit within us, causing us to walk in his statutes. The sin here prayed against is covetousness. Those that would have the love of God rooted in them, must get the love of the world rooted out; for the friendship of the world is enmity with God. Quicken me in thy way; to redeem time, and to do every duty with liveliness of spirit. Beholding vanity deadens us, and slackens our pace; a traveller must not stand gazing upon every object that presents itself to his view. The promises of God's word greatly relate to the preservation of the true believer. When Satan has drawn a child of God into worldly compliances, he will reproach him with the falls into which he led him. Victory must come from the cross of Christ. When we enjoy the sweetness of God's precepts, it will make us long for more acquaintance with them. And where God has wrought to will, he will work to do.

Verses 41–48

Lord, I have by faith thy mercies in view; let me by prayer prevail to obtain them. And when the salvation of the saints is completed, it will plainly appear that it was not in vain to trust in God's word. We need to pray that we may never be afraid or ashamed to own God's truths and ways before men. And the psalmist resolves to keep God's law, in a constant course of obedience, without backsliding. The service of sin is slavery; the service of God is liberty. There is no full happiness, or perfect liberty, but in keeping God's law. We must never be ashamed or afraid to own our religion. The more delight we take in the service of God, the nearer we come to perfection. Not only consent to his law as good, but take pleasure in it as good for us. Let me put forth all the strength I have, to do it. Something of this mind of Christ is in every true disciple.

Verses 49–56

Those that make God's promises their portion, may with humble boldness make them their plea. He that by his Spirit works faith in us, will work for us. The word of God speaks comfort in affliction. If, through grace, it makes us holy, there is enough in it to make us easy, in all conditions. Let us be certain we have the Divine law for what we believe, and then let not scoffers prevail upon us to decline from it. God's judgments of old comfort and encourage us, for he is still the same. Sin is horrible in the eyes of all that are sanctified. Ere long the believer will be absent from the body, and present with the Lord. In the mean time, the statutes of the Lord supply subjects for grateful praise. In the season of affliction, and in the silent hours of the night, he remembers the name of the Lord, and is stirred up to keep the law. All who have made religion the first thing, will own that they have been unspeakable gainers by it.

Verses 57–64

True believers take the Lord for the portion of their inheritance, and nothing less will satisfy them. The psalmist prayed with his whole heart, knowing how to value the blessing he prayed for: he desired the mercy promised, and depended on the promise for it. He turned from by-paths, and returned to God's testimonies. He delayed not. It behoves sinners to hasten to escape; and the believer will be equally in haste to glorify God. No care or grief should take away God's word out of our minds, or hinder the comfort it bestows. There is no situation on earth in which a believer has not cause to be thankful. Let us feel ashamed that others are more willing to keep from sleep to spend the time in sinful pleasures, than we are to praise God. And we should be more earnest in prayer, that our hearts may be filled with his mercy, grace, and peace.

Verses 65–72

However God has dealt with us, he has dealt with us better than we deserve; and all in love, and for our good. Many have knowledge, but little judgment; those who have both, are fortified against the snares of Satan, and furnished for the service of God. We are most apt to wander from God, when we are easy in the world. We should leave our concerns to the disposal of God, seeing we know not what is good for us. Lord, thou art our bountiful Benefactor, incline our hearts to faith and obedience. The psalmist will go on in his duty with constancy and resolution. The proud are full of the world, and its wealth and pleasures; these make them senseless, secure, and stupid. God visits his people with affliction, that they may learn his statutes. Not only God's promises, but even his law, his percepts, though hard to ungodly men, are desirable, and profitable, because they lead us with safety and delight unto eternal life.

Verses 73–80

God made us to serve him, and enjoy him; but by sin we have made ourselves unfit to serve him, and to enjoy him. We ought, therefore, continually to beseech him, by his Holy Spirit, to give us understanding. The comforts some have in God, should be matter of joy to others. But it is easy to own, that God's judgments are right, until it comes to be our own case. All supports under affliction must come from mercy and compassion. The mercies of God are tender mercies; the mercies of a father, the compassion of a mother to her son. They come to us when we are not able to go to them. Causeless reproach does not hurt, and should not move us. The psalmist could go on in the way of his duty, and find comfort in it. He valued the good will of saints, and was desirous to keep up his communion with them. Soundness of heart signifies sincerity in dependence on God, and devotedness to him.

Verses 81–88

The psalmist sought deliverance from his sins, his foes, and his fears. Hope deferred made him faint; his eyes failed by looking out for this expected salvation. But when the eyes fail, yet faith must not. His affliction was great. He was become like a leathern bottle, which, if hung up in the smoke, is dried and shrivelled up. We must ever be mindful of God's statutes. The days of the believer's mourning shall be ended; they are but for a moment, compared with eternal happiness. His enemies used craft as well as power for his ruin, in contempt of the law of God. The commandments of God are true and faithful guides in the path of peace and safety. We may best expect help from God when, like our Master, we do well and suffer for it. Wicked men may almost consume the believer upon earth, but he would sooner forsake all than forsake the word of the Lord. We should depend upon the grace of God for strength to do every good work. The surest token of God's good-will toward us, is his good work in us.

Verses 89–96

The settling of God's word in heaven, is opposed to the changes and revolutions of the earth. And the engagements of God's covenant are established more firmly than the earth itself. All the creatures answer the ends of their creation: shall man, who alone is endued with reason, be the only unprofitable burden of the earth? We may make the Bible a pleasant companion at any time. But the word, without the grace of God, would not quicken us. See the best help for bad memories, namely, good affections; and though the exact words be lost, if the meaning remain, that is well. I am thine, not my own, not the world's; save me from sin, save me from ruin. The Lord will keep the man in peace, whose mind is stayed on him. It is poor perfection which one sees and end of. Such are all things in this world, which pass for perfections. The glory of man is but as the flower of the grass. The psalmist had seen the fulness of the word of God, and its sufficiency. The word of the Lord reaches to all cases, to all times. It will take us from all confidence in man, or in our own wisdom, strength, and righteousness. Thus shall we seek comfort and happiness from Christ alone.

Verses 97–104

What we love, we love to think of. All true wisdom is from God. A good man carries his Bible with him, if not in his hands, yet in his head and in his heart. By meditation on God's testimonies we understand more than our teachers, when we understand our own hearts. The written word is a more sure guide to heaven, than all the fathers, the teachers, and ancients of the church. We cannot, with any comfort or boldness, attend God in holy duties, while under guilt, or in any by-way. It was Divine grace in his heart, that enabled the psalmist to receive these instructions. The soul has its tastes as well as the body. Our relish for the word of God will be greatest, when that for the world and the flesh is least. The way of sin is a wrong way; and the more understanding we get by the precepts of God, the more rooted will be our hatred of sin; and the more ready we are in the Scriptures, the better furnished we are with answers to temptation.

Verses 105–112

The word of God directs us in our work and way, and a dark place indeed the world would be without it. The commandment is a lamp kept burning with the oil of the Spirit, as a light to direct us in the choice of our way, and the steps we take in that way. The keeping of God's commands here meant, was that of a sinner under a dispensation of mercy, of a believer having part in the covenant of grace. The psalmist is often afflicted; but with longing desires to become more holy, offers up daily prayers for quickening grace. We cannot offer any thing to God, that he will accept but what he is pleased to teach us to do. To have our soul or life continually in our hands, implies constant danger of life; yet he did not forget God's promises nor his precepts. Numberless are the snares laid by the wicked; and happy is that servant of God, whom they have not caused to err from his Master's precepts. Heavenly treasures are a heritage for ever; all the saints accept them as such, therefore they can be content with little of this world. We must look for comfort only in the way of duty, and that duty must be done. A good man, by the grace of God, brings his heart to his work, then it is done well.

Verses 113–120

Here is a dread of the risings of sin, and the first beginnings of it. The more we love the law of God, the more watchful we shall be, lest vain thoughts draw us from what we love. Would we make progress in keeping God's commands, we must be separate from evil-doers. The believer could not live without the grace of God; but, supported by his hand, his spiritual life shall be maintained. Our holy security is grounded on Divine supports. All departure from God's statutes is error, and will prove fatal. Their cunning is falsehood. There is a day coming which will put the wicked into everlasting fire, the fit place for the dross. See what comes of sin Surely we who fall so low in devout affections, should fear, lest a promise being left us of entering into heavenly rest, any of us should be found to come short of it, Heb **4**:**1**.

Verses 121–128

Happy is the man, who, acting upon gospel principles, does justice to all around. Christ our Surety, having paid our debt and ransom, secures all the blessings of salvation to every true believer. The psalmist expects the word of God's righteousness, and no other salvation than what is secured by that word, which cannot fall to the ground. We deserve no favour form God; we are most easy when we cast ourselves upon God's mercy, and refer ourselves to it. If any man resolve to do God's will as his servant, he shall be made to know his testimonies. We must do what we can for the support of religion, and, after all, must beg of God to take the work into his own hands. It is hypocrisy to say we love God's commandments more than our worldly interests. The way of sin is a false way, being directly contrary to God's precepts, which are right: those that love and esteem God's law, hate sin, and will not be reconciled to it.

Verses 129–136

The wonders of redeeming love will fix the heart in adoration of them. The Scriptures show us what we were, what we are, and what we shall be. They show us the mercy and the justice of the Lord, the joys of heaven, and the pains of hell. Thus they give to the simple, in a few days, understanding of those matters, which philosophers for ages sought in vain. The believer, wearied with the cares of life and his conflicts with sin, pants for the consolations conveyed to him by means of the sacred word. And every one may pray, Look thou upon me, and be merciful unto me as thou usest to do unto those that love thy name. We must beg that the Holy Spirit would order our steps. The dominion of sin is to be dreaded and prayed against by every one. The oppression of men is often more than flesh and blood can bear; and He who knoweth our frame, will not refuse to remove it in answer to the prayers of his people. Whatever obscurity may appear as to the faith of the Old Testament believers, their confidence at the throne of grace can only be explained by their having obtained more distinct views of gospel privileges, through the sacrifices and services of their law, than is generally imagined. Go to the same place, plead the name and merits of Jesus, and you will not, you cannot plead in vain. Commonly, where there is a gracious heart, there is a weeping eye. Accept, O Lord, the tears our blessed Redeemer shed in the days of his flesh, for us who should weep for our brethren or ourselves.

Verses 137–144

God never did, and never can do wrong to any. The promises are faithfully performed by Him that made them. Zeal against sin should constrain us to do what we can against it, at least to do more in religion ourselves. Our love to the word of God is evidence of our love to God, because it is designed to make us partake his holiness. Men's real excellency always makes them low in their own eyes. When we are small and despised, we have the more need to remember God's precepts, that we may have them to support us. The law of God is the truth, the standard of holiness, the rule of happiness; but the obedience of Christ alone justifies the believer. Sorrows are often the lot of saints in this vale of tears; they are in heaviness through manifold temptations. There are delights in the word of God, which the saints often most sweetly enjoy when in trouble and anguish. This is life eternal, to know God and Jesus Christ whom he has sent, Joh

17:3. May we live the life of faith and grace here, and be removed to the life of glory hereafter.

Verses 145–152

Supplications with the whole heart are presented only by those who desire God's salvation, and who love his commandments. Whither should the child go but to his father? Save me from my sins, my corruptions, my temptations, all the hinderances in my way, that I may keep thy testimonies. Christians who enjoy health, should not suffer the early hours of the morning to glide away unimproved. Hope in God's word encourages us to continue in prayer. It is better to take time from sleep, than not to find time for prayer. We have access to God at all hours; and if our first thoughts in the morning are of God, they will help to keep us in his fear all the day long. Make me lively and cheerful. God knows what we need and what is good for us, and will quicken us. If we are employed in God's service, we need not fear those who try to set themselves as far as they can out of the reach of the convictions and commands of his law. When trouble is near, God is near. He is never far to seek. All his commandments are truth. And God's promises will be performed. All that ever trusted in God have found him faithful.

Verses 153–160

The closer we cleave to the word of God, both as our rule and as our stay, the more assurance we have of deliverance. Christ is the Advocate of his people, their Redeemer. Those who were quickened by his Spirit and grace, when they were dead in trespasses and sins, often need to have the work of grace revived in them, according to the word of promise. The wicked not only do not God's statutes, but they do not even seek them. They flatter themselves that they are going to heaven; but the longer they persist in sin, the further it is from them. God's mercies are tender; they are a fountain that can never be exhausted. The psalmist begs for God's reviving, quickening grace. A man, steady in the way of his duty, though he may have many enemies, needs to fear none. Those that hate sin truly, hate it as sin, as a transgression of the law of God, and a breaking of his word. Our obedience is only pleasing to God, and pleasant to ourselves, when it comes from a principle of love. All, in every age, who receive God's word in faith and love, find every saying in it faithful.

Verses 161–168

Those whose hearts stand in awe of God's word, will rather endure the wrath of man, than break the law of God. By the word of God we are unspeakable gainers. Every man hates to have a lie told him, but we should more hate telling a lie; by the latter we give an affront to God. The more we see the beauty of truth, the more we shall see the hateful deformity of a lie. We are to praise God even for afflictions; through grace we get good from them. Those that love the world have great vexation, for it does not answer what they expect; those that love God's word have great peace, for it outdoes what they expect. Those in whom this holy love reigns, will not perplex themselves with needless scruples, or take offence at their brethren. A good hope of salvation will engage the heart in doing the commandments. And our love to the word of God must subdue our lusts, and root out carnal affections: we must make heart work of it, or we make nothing of it. We must keep the commandments of God by obedience to them, and his promises by reliance on them. God's eye is on us at all times; this should make us very careful to keep his commandments.

Verses 169–176

The psalmist desired grace and strength to lift up his prayers, and that the Lord would receive and notice them. He desired to know more of God in Christ; to know more of the doctrines of the word, and the duties of religion. He had a deep sense of unworthiness, and holy fear that his prayer should not come before God; Lord, what I pray for is, what thou hast promised. We have learned nothing to purpose, if we have not learned to praise God. We should always make the word of God the rule of our discourse, so as never to transgress it by sinful speaking, or sinful silence. His own hands are not sufficient, nor can any creature lend him help; therefore he looks up to God, that the hand that had made him may help him. He had made religion his deliberate choice. There is an eternal salvation all the saints long for, and therefore they pray that God would help their way to it. Let thy judgments help me; let all ordinances and all providences, (both are God's judgments,) further me in glorifying God; let them help me for that work. He often looks back with shame and gratitude to his lost estate. He still prays for the tender care of Him who purchased his flock with his own blood, that he may receive from him the gift of eternal life. Seek me, that is, Find me; for God never seeks in vain. Turn me, and I shall be turned. Let this psalm be a touchstone by which to try our hearts, and our lives. Do our hearts, cleansed in Christ's blood, make these prayers, resolutions and confessions our own? Is God's word the standard of our faith, and the law of our practice? Do we use it as pleas with Christ for what we need? Happy those who live in such delightful exercises.

Chapter 120

Verses 1–4

The psalmist was brought into great distress by a deceitful tongue. May every good man be delivered from lying lips. They forged false charges against him. In this distress, he sought God by fervent prayer. God can bridle their tongues. He obtained a gracious answer to this prayer. Surely sinners durst not act as they do, if they knew, and would be persuaded to think, what will be in the end thereof. The terrors of the Lord are his arrows; and his wrath is compared to burning coals of juniper, which have a fierce heat, and keep fire very long. This is the portion of the false tongue; for all that love and make a lie, shall have their portion in the lake that burns eternally.

Verses 5–7

It is very grievous to a good man, to be cast into, and kept in the company of the wicked, from whom he hopes to be for ever separated. See here the character of a good man; he is for living peaceably with all men. And let us follow David as he prefigured Christ; in our distress let us cry unto the Lord, and he will hear us. Let us follow after peace and holiness, striving to overcome evil with good.

Chapter 121

The safety of the godly.

—We must not rely upon men and means, instruments and second causes. Shall I depend upon the strength of the hills? upon princes and great men? No; my confidence is in God only. Or, we must lift up our eyes above the hills; we must look to God who makes all earthly things to us what they are. We must see all our help in God; from him we must expect it, in his own way and time. This psalm teaches us to comfort ourselves in the Lord, when difficulties and dangers are greatest. It is almighty wisdom that contrives, and almighty power that works the safety of those that put themselves under God's protection. He is a wakeful, watchful Keeper; he is never weary; he not only does not sleep, but he does not so much as slumber. Under this shade they may sit with delight and assurance. He is always near his people for their protection and refreshment. The right hand is the working hand; let them but turn to their duty, and they shall find God ready to give them success. He will take care that his people shall not fall. Thou shalt not be hurt, neither by the open assaults, nor by the secret attempts of thine enemies. The Lord shall prevent the evil thou fearest, and sanctify, remove, or lighten the evil thou feelest. He will preserve the soul, that it be not defiled by sin, and disturbed by affliction; he will preserve it from perishing eternally. He will keep thee in life and death; going out to thy labour in the morning of thy days, and coming home to thy rest when the evening of old age calls thee in. It is a protection for life. The Spirit, who is their Preserver and Comforter, shall abide with them for ever. Let us be found in our work, assured that the blessings promised in this psalm are ours.

Chapter 122

Verses 1–5

The pleasure and profit from means of grace, should make us disregard trouble and fatigue in going to them; and we should quicken one another to what is good. We should desire our Christian friends, when they have any good work in hand, to call for us, and take us with them. With what readiness should we think of the heavenly Jerusalem! How cheerfully should we bear the cross and welcome death, in hopes of a crown of glory! Jerusalem is called the beautiful city. It was a type of the gospel church, which is compact together in holy love and Christian communion, so that it is all as one city. If all the disciples of Christ were of one mind, and kept the unity of the Spirit in the bond of peace, their enemies would be deprived of their chief advantages against them. But Satan's maxim always has been, to divide that he may conquer; and few Christians are sufficiently aware of his designs.

Verses 6–9

Those who can do nothing else for the peace of Jerusalem, may pray for it. Let us consider all who seek the glory of the Redeemer, as our brethren and fellow-travellers, without regarding differences which do not affect our eternal welfare. Blessed Spirit of peace and love, who didst dwell in the soul of the holy Jesus, descend into his church, and fill those who compose it with his heavenly tempers; cause bitter contentions to cease, and make us to be of one mind. Love of the brethren and love to God, ought to stir us up to seek to be like the Lord Jesus in fervent prayer and unwearied labour, for the salvation of men, and the Divine glory.

Chapter 123

Confidence in God under contempt.

—Our Lord Jesus has taught us to look unto God in prayer as our Father in heaven. In every prayer a good man lifts up his soul to God; especially when in trouble. We desire mercy from him; we hope he will show us mercy, and we will continue waiting on him till it come. The eyes of a servant are to his master's directing hand, expecting that he will appoint him his work. And also to his supplying hand. Servants look to their master or their mistress for their portion of meat in due season. And to God we must look for daily bread, for grace sufficient; from him we must receive it thankfully. Where can we look for help but to our Master? And, further, to his protecting hand. If the servant is wronged and injured in his work, who should right him, but his master? And to his correcting hand. Whither should sinners turn but to him that smote them? They humble themselves under God's mighty hand. And lastly, to his rewarding hand. Hypocrites look to the world's hand, thence they have their reward; but true Christians look to God as their Master and their Rewarder. God's people find little mercy with men; but this is their comfort, that with the Lord there is mercy. Scorning and contempt have been, are, and are likely to be, the lot of God's people in this world. It is hard to bear; but the servants of God should not complain if they are treated as his beloved Son was. Let us then, when ready to faint under trials, look unto Jesus, and by faith and prayer cast ourselves upon the mercy of God.

Chapter 124

Verses 1–5

God suffers the enemies of his people sometimes to prevail very far against them, that his power may be seen the more in their deliverance. Happy the people whose God is Jehovah, a God all-sufficient. Besides applying this to any particular deliverance wrought in our days and the ancient times, we should have in our thoughts the great work of redemption by Jesus Christ, by which believers were rescued from Satan.

Verses 6–8

God is the Author of all our deliverances, and he must have the glory. The enemies lay snares for God's people, to bring them into sin and trouble, and to hold them there. Sometimes they seem to prevail; but in the Lord let us put our trust, and we shall not be put to confusion. The believer will ascribe all the honour of his salvation, to the power, mercy, and truth of God, and look back with wonder and thanksgiving on the way in which the Lord has led him. Let us rejoice that our help for the time to come is in him who made heaven and earth.

Chapter 125

Verses 1–3

All those minds shall be truly stayed, that are stayed on God. They shall be as Mount Zion, firm as it is; a mountain supported by providence, much more as a holy mountain supported by promise. They cannot be removed from confidence in God. They abide for ever in that grace which is the earnest of their everlasting continuance in glory. Committing themselves to God, they shall be safe from their enemies. Even mountains may moulder and come to nothing, and rocks be removed, but God's covenant with his people cannot be broken, nor his care of them cease. Their troubles shall last no longer than their strength will bear them up under them. The rod of the wicked may come, may fall upon the righteous, upon their persons, their estates, their liberties, their families names, on any thing that falls to their lot; only it cannot reach their souls. And though it may come upon their lot, it shall not rest thereon. The Lord will make all work together for their good. The wicked shall only prove a correcting rod, not a destroying sword; even this rod shall not remain upon them, lest they distrust the promise, thinking God has cast them off.

Verses 4, 5

God's promises should quicken our prayers. The way of holiness is straight; there are no windings or shiftings in it. But the ways of sinners are crooked. They shift from one purpose to another, and turn hither and thither to deceive; but disappointment and misery shall befal them. Those who cleave to the ways of God, though they may have trouble in their way, their end shall be peace. The pleading of their Saviour for them, secures to them the upholding power and preserving grace of their God. Lord, number us with them, in time, and to eternity.

Chapter 126

Verses 1–3

It is good to observe how God's deliverances of the church are for us, that we may rejoice in them. And how ought redemption from the wrath to come, from the power of sin and of Satan, to be valued! The sinner convinced of his guilt and danger, when by looking to a crucified Saviour he receives peace to his conscience, and power to break off his sins, often can scarcely believe that the prospect which opens to him is a reality.

Verses 4–6

The beginnings of mercies encourage us to pray for the completion of them. And while we are in this world there will be matter for prayer, even when we are most furnished with matter for praise. Suffering saints are often in tears; they share the calamities of human life, and commonly have a greater share than others. But they sow in tears; they do the duty of an afflicted state. Weeping must not hinder sowing; we must get good from times of affliction. And they that sow, in the tears of godly sorrow, to the Spirit, shall of the Spirit reap life everlasting; and that will be a joyful harvest indeed. Blessed are those that mourn, for they shall be for ever comforted. When we mourn for our sins, or suffer for Christ's sake, we are sowing in tears, to reap in joy. And remember that God is not mocked; for whatever a man soweth that shall he reap, Ga **6:7–9**. Here, O disciple of Jesus, behold an emblem of thy present labour and future reward; the day is coming when thou shalt reap in joy, plentiful shall be thy harvest, and great shall be thy joy in the Lord.

Chapter 127

The value of the Divine blessing.

—Let us always look to God's providence. In all the affairs and business of a family we must depend upon his blessing. **1**. For raising a family. If God be not acknowledged, we have no reason to expect his blessing; and the best-laid plans fail, unless he crowns them with success. **2**. For the safety of a family or a city. Except the Lord keep the city, the watchmen, though they neither slumber nor sleep, wake but in vain; mischief may break out, which even early discoveries may not be able to prevent. **3**. For enriching a family. Some are so eager upon the world, that they are continually full of care, which makes their comforts bitter, and their lives a burden. All this is to get money; but all in vain, except God prosper them: while those who love the Lord, using due diligence in their lawful callings, and casting all their care upon him, have needful success, without uneasiness or vexation. Our care must be to keep ourselves in the love of God; then we may be easy, whether we have little or much of this world. But we must use the proper means very diligently. Children are God's gifts, a heritage, and a reward; and are to be accounted blessings, and not burdens: he who sends mouths, will send meat, if we trust in him. They are a great support and defence to a family. Children who are young, may be directed aright to the mark, God's glory, and the service of their generation; but when they are gone into the world, they are arrows out of the hand, it is too late to direct them then. But these arrows in the hand too often prove arrows in the heart, a grief to godly parents. Yet, if trained according to God's word, they generally prove the best defence in declining years, remembering their obligations to their parents, and taking care of them in old age. All earthly comforts are uncertain, but the Lord will assuredly comfort and bless those who serve him; and those who seek the conversion of sinners, will find that their spiritual children are their joy and crown in the day of Jesus Christ.

Chapter 128

The blessings of those who fear God.

—Only those who are truly holy, are truly happy. In vain do we pretend to be of those that fear God, if we do not make conscience of keeping stedfastly to his ways. Blessed is every one that fears the Lord; whether he be high or low, rich or poor in the world. If thou fear him and walk in his ways, all shall be well with thee while thou livest, better when thou diest, best of all in eternity. By the blessing of God, the godly shall get an honest livelihood. Here is a double promise; they shall have something to do, for an idle life is a miserable, uncomfortable life, and shall have health and strength, and power of mind to do it. They shall not be forced to live upon the labours of other people. It is as much a mercy as a duty, with quietness to work and eat our own bread. They and theirs shall enjoy what they get. Such as fear the Lord and walk in his ways, are the only happy persons, whatever their station in life may be. They shall have abundant comfort in their family relations. And they shall have all the good things God has promised, and which they pray for. A good man can have little comfort in seeing his children's children, unless he sees peace upon Israel. Every true believer rejoices in the prosperity of the church. Hereafter we shall see greater things, with the everlasting peace and rest that remain for the Israel of God.

Chapter 129

Verses 1–4

The enemies of God's people have very barbarously endeavoured to wear out the saints of the Most High. But the church has been always graciously delivered. Christ has built his church upon a rock. And the Lord has many ways of disabling wicked men from doing the mischief they design against his church. The Lord is righteous in not suffering Israel to be ruined; he has promised to preserve a people to himself.

Verses 5–8

While God's people shall flourish as the loaded palm-tree, or the green and fruitful olive, their enemies shall wither as the grass upon the house-tops, which in eastern countries are flat, and what grows there never ripens; so it is with the designs of God's enemies. No wise man will pray the Lord to bless these mowers or reapers. And when we remember how Jesus arose and reigns; how his people have been supported, like the burning but unconsumed bush, we shall not fear.

Chapter 130

Verses 1–4

The only way of relief for a sin-entangled soul, is by applying to God alone. Many things present themselves as diversions, many things offer themselves as remedies, but the soul finds that the Lord alone can heal. And until men are sensible of the guilt of sin, and quit all to come at once to God, it is in vain for them to expect any relief. The Holy Ghost gives to such poor souls a fresh sense of their deep necessity, to stir them up in earnest applications, by the prayer of faith, by crying to God. And as they love their souls, as they are concerned for the glory of the Lord, they are not to be wanting in this duty. Why is it that these matters are so long uncertain with them? Is it not from sloth and despondency that they content themselves with common and customary applications to God? Then let us up and be doing; it must be done, and it is attended with safety. We are to humble ourselves before God, as guilty in his sight. Let us acknowledge our sinfulness; we cannot justify ourselves, or plead not guilty. It is our unspeakable comfort that there is forgiveness with him, for that is what we need. Jesus Christ is the great Ransom; he is ever an Advocate for us, and through him we hope to obtain forgiveness. There is forgiveness with thee, not that thou mayest be presumed upon, but that thou mayest be feared. The fear of God often is put for the whole worship of God. The only motive and encouragement for sinners is this, that there is forgiveness with the Lord.

Verses 5–8

It is for the Lord that my soul waits, for the gifts of his grace, and the working of his power. We must hope for that only which he has promised in his word. Like those who wish to see the dawn, being very desirous that light would come long before day; but still more earnestly does a good man long for the tokens of God's favour, and the visits of his grace. Let all that devote themselves to the Lord, cheerfully stay themselves on him. This redemption is redemption from all sin. Jesus Christ saves his people from their sins, both from the condemning and from the commanding power of sin. It is plenteous redemption; there is an all-sufficient fulness in the Redeemer, enough for all, enough for each; therefore enough for me, says the believer. Redemption from sin includes redemption from all other evils, therefore it is a plenteous redemption, through the atoning blood of Jesus, who shall redeem his people from all their sins. All that wait on God for mercy and grace, are sure to have peace.

Chapter 131

The psalmist's humility. Believers encouraged to trust in God.

—The psalmist aimed at nothing high or great, but to be content in every condition God allotted. Humble saints cannot think so well of themselves as others think of them. The love of God reigning in the heart, will subdue self-love. Where there is a proud heart, there is commonly a proud look. To know God and our duty, is learning sufficiently high for us. It is our wisdom not to meddle with that which does not belong to us. He was well reconciled to every condition the Lord placed him in. He had been as humble as a little child about the age of weaning, and as far from aiming at high things; as entirely at God's disposal, as the child at the disposal of the mother or nurse. We must become as little children, Mt **18**:**3**. Our hearts are desirous of worldly things, cry for them, and are fond of them; but, by the grace of God, a soul that is made holy, is weaned from these things. The child is cross and fretful while in the weaning; but in a day or two it cares no longer for milk, and it can bear stronger food. Thus does a converted soul quiet itself under the loss of what it loved, and disappointments in what it hoped for, and is easy whatever happens. When our condition is not to our mind, we must bring our mind to our condition; then we are easy to ourselves and all about us; then our souls are as a weaned child. And thus the psalmist recommends confidence in God, to all the Israel of God, from his own experience. It is good to hope, and quietly to wait for the salvation of the Lord under every trial.

Chapter 132

Verses 1–10

David bound himself to find a place for the Lord, for the ark, the token of God's presence. When work is to be done for the Lord, it is good to tie ourselves to a time. It is good in the morning to fix upon work for the day, with submission to Providence, for we know not what a day may bring forth. And we should first, and without delay, seek to have our own hearts made a habitation of God through the Spirit. He prays that God would take up his dwelling in the habitation he had built; that he would give grace to the ministers of the sanctuary to do their duty. David pleads that he was the anointed of the Lord, and this he pleads as a type of Christ, the great Anointed. We have no merit of our own to plead; but, for His sake, in whom there is a fulness of merit, let us find favour. And every true believer in Christ, is an anointed one, and has received from the Holy One the oil of true grace. The request is, that God would not turn away, but hear and answer their petitions for his Son's sake.

Verses 11–18

The Lord never turns from us when we plead the covenant with his anointed Prophet, Priest, and King. How vast is the love of God to man, that he should speak thus concerning his church! It is his desire to dwell with us; yet how little do we desire to dwell with him! He abode in Zion till the sins of Israel caused him to give them up to the spoilers. Forsake us not, O God, and deliver us not in like manner, sinful though we are. God's people have a special blessing on common enjoyments, and that blessing puts peculiar sweetness into them. Zion's poor have reason to be content with a little of this world, because they have better things prepared for them. God will abundantly bless the nourishment of the new man, and satisfy the poor in spirit with the bread of life. He gives more than we ask, and when he gives salvation, he will give abundant joy. God would bring to nothing every design formed to destroy the house of David, until King Messiah should arise out of it, to sit upon the throne of his Father. In him all the promises centre. His enemies, who will not have him to reign over them, shall at the last day be clothed with shame and confusion for ever.

Chapter **133**

The excellency of brotherly love.

—We cannot say too much, it were well if enough could be said, to persuade people to live together in peace. It is good for us, for our honour and comfort; and brings constant delight to those who live in unity. The pleasantness of this is likened to the holy anointing oil. This is the fruit of the Spirit, the proof of our union with Christ, and adorns his gospel. It is profitable as well as pleasing; it brings blessings numerous as the drops of dew. It cools the scorching heat of men's passions, as the dews cool the air and refresh the earth. It moistens the heart, and makes it fit to receive the good seed of the word, and to make it fruitful. See the proof of the excellency of brotherly love: where brethren dwell together in unity, the Lord commands the blessing. God commands the blessing; man can but beg a blessing. Believers that live in love and peace, shall have the God of love and peace with them now, and they shall shortly be with him for ever, in the world of endless love and peace. May all who love the Lord forbear and forgive one another, as God, for Christ's sake, hath forgiven them.

Chapter 134

An exhortation to bless the Lord.

—We must stir up ourselves to give glory to God, and encourage ourselves to hope for mercy and grace from him. It is an excellent plan to fill up all our spare minutes with pious meditations, and prayers and praises. No time would then be a burden, nor should we murder our hours by trifling conversation and vain amusements, or by carnal indulgences. We need desire no more to make us happy, than to be blessed of the Lord. We ought to beg spiritual blessings, not only for ourselves, but for others; not only, The Lord bless me, but, The Lord bless thee; thus testifying our belief that there is enough for others as well as for us, and showing our good will to others.

Chapter 135

Verses 1–4

The subject-matter of praise, is the blessings of grace flowing from the everlasting love of God. The name of God as a covenant God and Father in Christ, blessing us with all spiritual blessings in him, is to be loved and praised. The Lord chose a people to himself, that they might be unto him for a name and a praise. If they do not praise him for this distinguishing favour, they are the most unworthy and ungrateful of all people.

Verses 5–14

God is, and will be always, the same to his church, a gracious, faithful, wonder-working God. And his church is, and will be, the same to him, a thankful, praising people: thus his name endures for ever. He will return in ways of mercy to them, and will delight to do them good.

Verses 15–21

These **verse**s arm believers against idolatry and all false worship, by showing what sort of gods the heathen worshipped. And the more deplorable the condition of the Gentile nations that worship idols, the more are we to be thankful that we know better. Let us pity, and pray for, and seek to benefit benighted heathens and deluded sinners. Let us endeavour to glorify his name, and recommend his truth, not only with our lips, but by holy lives, copying the example of Christ's goodness and truth.

Chapter 136

Verses 1–9

Forgetful as we are, things must be often repeated to us. By "mercy" we understand the Lord's disposition to save those whom sin has rendered miserable and vile, and all the provision he has made for the redemption of sinners by Jesus Christ. The counsels of this mercy have been from everlasting, and the effects of it will endure for ever, to all who are interested in it. The Lord continues equally ready to show mercy to all who seek for it, and this is the source of all our hope and comfort.

Verses 10–22

The great things God did for Israel, when he brought them out of Egypt, were mercies which endured long to them; and our redemption by Christ, which was typified thereby, endures for ever. It is good to enter into the history of God's favours, and in each to observe, and own, that his mercy endureth for ever. He put them in possession of a good land; it was a figure of the mercy of our Lord Jesus Christ.

Verses 23–26

God's everlasting mercy is here praised for the redemption of his church; in all his glories, and all his gifts. Blessed be God, who has provided and made known to us salvation through his Son. May we know and feel his redeeming power, that we may serve him in righteousness all our days. May He who giveth food to all flesh, feed our souls unto eternal life, and enliven our affections by his grace, that we may give thanks and praise to his holy name, for his mercy endureth for ever. Let us trace up all the favours we receive to this true source, and offer praise continually.

Chapter 137

Verses 1–4

Their enemies had carried the Jews captive from their own land. To complete their woes, they insulted over them; they required of them mirth and a song. This was very barbarous; also profane, for no songs would serve but the songs of Zion. Scoffers are not to be compiled with. They do not say, How shall we sing, when we are so much in sorrow? but, It is the Lord's song, therefore we dare not sing it among idolaters.

Verses 5–9

What we love, we love to think of. Those that rejoice in God, for his sake make Jerusalem their joy. They stedfastly resolved to keep up this affection. When suffering, we should recollect with godly sorrow our forfeited mercies, and our sins by which we lost them. If temporal advantages ever render a profession, the worst calamity has befallen him. Far be it from us to avenge ourselves; we will leave it to Him who has said, Vengeance is mine. Those that are glad at calamities, especially at the calamities of Jerusalem, shall not go unpunished. We cannot pray for promised success to the church of God without looking to, though we do not utter a prayer for, the ruin of her enemies. But let us call to mind to whose grace and finished salvation alone it is, that we have any hopes of being brought home to the heavenly Jerusalem.

Chapter 138

Verses 1–5

When we can praise God with our whole heart, we need not be unwilling for the whole world to witness our gratitude and joy in him. Those who rely on his loving-kindness and truth through Jesus Christ, will ever find him faithful to his word. If he spared not his own Son, how shall he not with him freely give us all things? If God gives us strength in our souls, to bear the burdens, resist the temptations, and to do the duties of an afflicted state, if he strengthens us to keep hold of himself by faith, and to wait with patience for the event, we are bound to be thankful.

Verses 6–8

Though the Lord is high, yet he has respect to every lowly, humbled sinner; but the proud and unbelieving will be banished far from his blissful presence. Divine consolations have enough in them to revive us, even when we walk in the midst of troubles. And God will save his own people that they may be revived by the Holy Spirit, the Giver of life and holiness. If we give to God the glory of his mercy, we may take to ourselves the comfort. This confidence will not do away, but quicken prayer. Whatever good there is in us, it is God works in us both to will and to do. The Lord will perfect the salvation of every true believer, and he will never forsake those whom he has created anew in Christ Jesus unto good works.

Chapter 139

Verses 1–6

God has perfect knowledge of us, and all our thoughts and actions are open before him. It is more profitable to meditate on Divine truths, applying them to our own cases, and with hearts lifted to God in prayer, than with a curious or disputing frame of mind. That God knows all things, is omniscient; that he is every where, is omnipresent; are truths acknowledged by all, yet they are seldom rightly believed in by mankind. God takes strict notice of every step we take, every right step and every by step. He knows what rule we walk by, what end we walk toward, what company we walk with. When I am withdrawn from all company, thou knowest what I have in my heart. There is not a vain word, not a good word, but thou knowest from what thought it came, and with what design it was uttered. Wherever we are, we are under the eye and hand of God. We cannot by searching find how God searches us out; nor do we know how we are known. Such thoughts should restrain us from sin.

Verses 7–16

We cannot see God, but he can see us. The psalmist did not desire to go from the Lord. Whither can I go? In the most distant corners of the world, in heaven, or in hell, I cannot go out of thy reach. No veil can hide us from God; not the thickest darkness. No disguise can save any person or action from being seen in the true light by him. Secret haunts of sin are as open before God as the most open villanies. On the other hand, the believer cannot be removed from the supporting, comforting presence of his Almighty Friend. Should the persecutor take his life, his soul will the sooner ascend to heaven. The grave cannot separate his body from the love of his Saviour, who will raise it a glorious body. No outward circumstances can separate him from his Lord. While in the path of duty, he may be happy in any situation, by the exercise of faith, hope, and prayer.

Verses 17–24

God's counsels concerning us and our welfare are deep, such as cannot be known. We cannot think how many mercies we have received from him. It would help to keep us in the fear of the Lord all the day long, if, when we wake in the morning, our first thoughts were of him: and how shall we admire and bless our God for his precious salvation, when we awake in the world of glory! Surely we ought not to use our members and senses, which are so curiously fashioned, as instruments of unrighteousness unto sin. But our immortal and rational souls are a still more noble work and gift of God. Yet if it were not for his precious thoughts of love to us, our reason and our living for ever would, through our sins, prove the occasion of our eternal misery. How should we then delight to meditate on God's love to sinners in Jesus Christ, the sum of which exceeds all reckoning! Sin is hated, and sinners lamented, by all who fear the Lord. Yet while we shun them we should pray for them; with God their conversion and salvation are possible. As the Lord knows us thoroughly, and we are strangers to ourselves, we should earnestly desire and pray to be searched and proved by his word and Spirit. if there be any wicked way in me, let me see it; and do thou root it out of me. The way of godliness is pleasing to God, and profitable to us; and will end in everlasting life. It is the good old way. All the saints desire to be kept and led in this way, that they may not miss it, turn out of it, or tire in it.

Chapter 140

Verses 1–7

The more danger appears, the more earnest we should be in prayer to God. All are safe whom the Lord protects. If he be for us, who can be against us? We should especially watch and pray, that the Lord would hold up our goings in his ways, that our footsteps slip not. God is as able to keep his people from secret fraud as from open force; and the experience we have had of his power and care, in dangers of one kind, may encourage us to depend upon him in other dangers.

Verses 8–13

Believers may pray that God would not grant the desires of the wicked, nor further their evil devices. False accusers will bring mischief upon themselves, even the burning coals of Divine vengeance. And surely the righteous shall dwell in God's presence, and give him thanks for evermore. This is true thanksgiving, even thanks-living: this use we should make of all our deliverances, we should serve God the more closely and cheerfully. Those who, though evil spoken of and ill-used by men, are righteous in the sight of God, being justified by the righteousness of Christ, which is imputed to them, and received by faith, as the effect of which, they live soberly and righteously; these give thanks to the Lord, for the righteousness whereby they are made righteous, and for every blessing of grace, and mercy of life.

Chapter 141

Verses 1–4

Make haste unto me. Those that know how to value God's gracious presence, will be the more fervent in their prayers. When presented through the sacrifice and intercession of the Saviour, they will be as acceptable to God as the daily sacrifices and burnings of incense were of old. Prayer is a spiritual sacrifice, it is the offering up the soul and its best affections. Good men know the evil of tongue sins. When enemies are provoking, we are in danger of speaking unadvisedly. While we live in an evil world, and have such evil hearts, we have need to pray that we may neither be drawn nor driven to do any thing sinful. Sinners pretend to find dainties in sin; but those that consider how soon sin will turn into bitterness, will dread such dainties, and pray to God to take them out of their sight, and by his grace to turn their hearts against them. Good men pray against the sweets of sin.

Verses 5–10

We should be ready to welcome the rebuke of our heavenly Father, and also the reproof of our brethren. It shall not break my head, if it may but help to break my heart: we must show that we take it kindly. Those who slighted the word of God before, will be glad of it when in affliction, for that opens the ear to instruction. When the world is bitter, the word is sweet. Let us lift our prayer unto God. Let us entreat him to rescue us from the snares of Satan, and of all the workers of iniquity. In language like this psalm, O Lord, would we entreat that our poor prayers should set forth our only hope, our only dependence on thee. Grant us thy grace, that we may be prepared for this employment, being clothed with thy righteousness, and having all the gifts of thy Spirit planted in our hearts.

Chapter 142

David's comfort in prayer.

—There can be no situation so distressing or dangerous, in which faith will not get comfort from God by prayer. We are apt to show our troubles too much to ourselves, poring upon them, which does us no service; whereas, by showing them to God, we might cast the cares upon him who careth for us, and thereby ease ourselves. Nor should we allow any complaint to ourselves or others, which we cannot make to God. When our spirits are overwhelmed by distress, and filled with discouragement; when we see snares laid for us on every side, while we walk in his way, we may reflect with comfort that the Lord knoweth our path. Those who in sincerity take the Lord for their God, find him all-sufficient, as a Refuge, and as a Portion: every thing else is a refuge of lies, and a portion of no value. In this situation David prayed earnestly to God. We may apply it spiritually; the souls of believers are often straitened by doubts and fears. And it is then their duty and interest to beg of God to set them at liberty, that they may run the way of his commandments. Thus the Lord delivered David from his powerful persecutors, and dealt bountifully with him. Thus he raised the crucified Redeemer to the throne of glory, and made him Head over all things for his church. Thus the convinced sinner cries for help, and is brought to praise the Lord in the company of his redeemed people; and thus all believers will at length be delivered from this evil world, from sin and death, and praise their Saviour for ever.

Chapter 143

Verses 1–6

We have no righteousness of our own to plead, therefore must plead God's righteousness, and the word of promise which he has freely given us, and caused us to hope in. David, before he prays for the removal of his trouble, prays for the pardon of his sin, and depends upon mercy alone for it. He bemoans the weight upon his mind from outward troubles. But he looks back, and remembers God's former appearance for his afflicted people, and for him in particular. He looks round, and notices the works of God. The more we consider the power of God, the less we shall fear the face or force of man. He looks up with earnest desires towards God and his favour. This is the best course we can take, when our spirits are overwhelmed. The believer will not forget, that in his best actions he is a sinner. Meditation and prayer will recover us from distresses; and then the mourning soul strives to return to the Lord as the infant stretches out its hands to the indulgent mother, and thirsts for his consolations as the parched ground for refreshing rain.

Verses 7–12

David prays that God would be well pleased with him, and let him know that he was so. He pleads the wretchedness of his case, if God withdrew from him. But the night of distress and discouragement shall end in a morning of consolation and praise. He prays that he might be enlightened with the knowledge of God's will; and this is the first work of the Spirit. A good man does not ask the way in which is the most pleasant walking, but what is the right way. Not only show me what thy will is, but teach me how to do it. Those who have the Lord for their God, have his Spirit for their Guide; they are led by the Spirit. He prays that he might be enlivened to do God's will. But we should especially seek the destruction of our sins, our worst enemies, that we may be devotedly God's servants.

Chapter 144

Verses 1–8

When men become eminent for things as to which they have had few advantages, they should be more deeply sensible that God has been their Teacher. Happy those to whom the Lord gives that noblest victory, conquest and dominion over their own spirits. A prayer for further mercy is fitly begun with a thanksgiving for former mercy. There was a special power of God, inclining the people of Israel to be subject to David; it was typical of the bringing souls into subjection to the Lord Jesus. Man's days have little substance, considering how many thoughts and cares of a never-dying soul are employed about a poor dying body. Man's life is as a shadow that passes away. In their highest earthly exaltation, believers will recollect how mean, sinful, and vile they are in themselves; thus they will be preserved from self-importance and presumption. God's time to help his people is, when they are sinking, and all other helps fail.

Verses 9–15

Fresh favours call for fresh returns of thanks; we must praise God for the mercies we hope for by his promise, as well as those we have received by his providence. To be saved from the hurtful sword, or from wasting sickness, without deliverance from the dominion of sin and the wrath to come, is but a small advantage. The public prosperity David desired for his people, is stated. It adds much to the comfort and happiness of parents in this world, to see their children likely to do well. To see them as plants, not as weeds, not as thorns; to see them as plants growing, not withered and blasted; to see them likely to bring forth fruit unto God in their day; to see them in their youth growing strong in the Spirit. Plenty is to be desired, that we may be thankful to God, generous to our friends, and charitable to the poor; otherwise, what profit is it to have our garners full? Also, uninterrupted peace. War brings abundance of mischiefs, whether it be to attack others or to defend ourselves. And in proportion as we do not adhere to the worship and service of God, we cease to be a happy people. The subjects of the Saviour, the Son of David, share the blessings of his authority and victories, and are happy because they have the Lord for their God.

Chapter 145

Verses 1–9

Those who, under troubles and temptations, abound in fervent prayer, shall in due season abound in grateful praise, which is the true language of holy joy. Especially we should speak of God's wondrous work of redemption, while we declare his greatness. For no deliverance of the Israelites, nor the punishment of sinners, so clearly proclaims the justice of God, as the cross of Christ exhibits it to the enlightened mind. It may be truly said of our Lord Jesus Christ, that his words are words of goodness and grace; his works are works of goodness and grace. He is full of compassion; hence he came into the world to save sinners. When on earth, he showed his compassion both to the bodies and souls of men, by healing the one, and making wise the other. He is of great mercy, a merciful High Priest, through whom God is merciful to sinners.

Verses 10–21

All God's works show forth his praises. He satisfies the desire of every living thing, except the unreasonable children of men, who are satisfied with nothing. He does good to all the children of men; his own people in a special manner. Many children of God, who have been ready to fall into sin, to fall into despair, have tasted his goodness in preventing their falls, or recovering them speedily by his graces and comforts. And with respect to all that are heavy laden under the burden of sin, if they come to Christ by faith, he will ease them, he will raise them. He is very ready to hear and answer the prayers of his people. He is present every where; but in a special way he is nigh to them, as he is not to others. He is in their hearts, and dwells there by faith, and they dwell in him. He is nigh to those that call upon him, to help them in all times of need. He will be nigh to them, that they may have what they ask, and find what they seek, if they call upon him in truth and sincerity. And having taught men to love his name and holy ways, he will save them from the destruction of the wicked. May we then love his name, and walk in his ways, while we desire that all flesh should bless his holy name for ever and ever.

Chapter 146

Verses 1–4

If it is our delight to praise the Lord while we live, we shall certainly praise him to all eternity. With this glorious prospect before us, how low do worldly pursuits seem! There is a Son of man in whom there is help, even him who is also the Son of God, who will not fail those that trust in him. But all other sons of men are like the man from whom they sprung, who, being in honour, did not abide. God has given the earth to the children of men, but there is great striving about it. Yet, after a while, no part of the earth will be their own, except that in which their dead bodies are laid. And when man returns to his earth, in that very day all his plans and designs vanish and are gone: what then comes of expectations from him?

Verses 5–10

The psalmist encourages us to put confidence in God. We must hope in the providence of God for all we need as to this life, and in the grace of God for that which is to come. The God of heaven became a man that he might become our salvation. Though he died on the cross for our sins, and was laid in the grave, yet his thoughts of love to us did not perish; he rose again to fulfil them. When on earth, his miracles were examples of what he is still doing every day. He grants deliverance to captives bound in the chains of sin and Satan. He opens the eyes of the understanding. He feeds with the bread of life those who hunger for salvation; and he is the constant Friend of the poor in spirit, the helpless: with him poor sinners, that are as fatherless, find mercy; and his kingdom shall continue for ever. Then let sinners flee to him, and believers rejoice in him. And as the Lord shall reign for ever, let us stir up each other to praise his holy name.

Chapter 147

Verses 1–11

Praising God is work that is its own wages. It is comely; it becomes us as reasonable creatures, much more as people in covenant with God. He gathers outcast sinners by his grace, and will bring them into his holy habitation. To those whom God heals with the consolations of his Spirit, he speaks peace, assures them their sins are pardoned. And for this, let others praise him also. Man's knowledge is soon ended; but God's knowledge is a dept that can never be fathomed. And while he telleth the number of the stars, he condescends to hear the broken-hearted sinner. While he feeds the young ravens, he will not leave his praying people destitute. Clouds look dull and melancholy, yet without them we could have no rain, therefore no fruit. Thus afflictions look black and unpleasant; but from clouds of affliction come showers that make the soul to yield the peaceable fruits of righteousness. The psalmist delights not in things wherein sinners trust and glory; but a serious and suitable regard to God is, in his sight, of very great price. We are not to be in doubt between hope and fear, but to act under the gracious influences of hope and fear united.

Verses 12–20

The church, like Jerusalem of old, built up and preserved by the wisdom, power, and goodness of God, is exhorted to praise him for all the benefits and blessings vouchsafed to her; and these are represented by his favours in the course of nature. The thawing word may represent the gospel of Christ, and the thawing wind the Spirit of Christ; for the Spirit is compared to the wind, Joh **3**:**8**. Converting grace softens the heart that was hard frozen, and melts it into tears of repentance, and makes good reflections to flow, which before were chilled and stopped up. The change which the thaw makes is very evident, yet how it is done no one can say. Such is the change wrought in the conversion of a soul, when God's word and Spirit are sent to melt it and restore it to itself.

Chapter 148

Verses 1–6

We, in this dark and sinful world, know little of the heavenly world of light. But we know that there is above us a world of blessed angels. They are always praising God, therefore the psalmist shows his desire that God may be praised in the best manner; also we show that we have communion with spirits above, who are still praising him. The heavens, with all contained in them, declare the glory of God. They call on us, that both by word and deed, we glorify with them the Creator and Redeemer of the uni**verse**.

Verses 7–14

Even in this world, dark and bad as it is, God is praised. The powers of nature, be they ever so strong, so stormy, do what God appoints them, and no more. Those that rebel against God's word, show themselves to be more violent than even the stormy winds, yet they fulfil it. View the surface of the earth, mountains and all hills; from the barren tops of some, and the fruitful tops of others, we may fetch matter for praise. And assuredly creatures which have the powers of reason, ought to employ themselves in praising God. Let all manner of persons praise God. Those of every rank, high and low. Let us show that we are his saints by praising his name continually. He is not only our Creator, but our Redeemer; who made us a people near unto him. We may by "the Horn of his people" understand Christ, whom God has exalted to be a Prince and a Saviour, who is indeed the defence and the praise of all his saints, and will be so for ever. In redemption, that unspeakable glory is displayed, which forms the source of all our hopes and joys. May the Lord pardon us, and teach our hearts to love him more and praise him better.

Chapter 149

Verses 1–5

New mercies continually demand new songs of praise, upon earth and in heaven. And the children of Zion have not only to bless the God who made them, but to rejoice in him, as having created them in Christ Jesus unto good works, and formed them saints as well as men. The Lord takes pleasure in his people; they should rejoice in Him. When the Lord has made sinners feel their wants and unworthiness, he will adorn them with the graces of his Spirit, and cause them to bear his image, and rejoice in his happiness for ever. Let his saints employ their waking hours upon their beds in songs of praise. Let them rejoice, even upon the bed of death, assured that they are going to eternal rest and glory.

Verses 6–9

Some of God's servants of old were appointed to execute vengeance according to his word. They did not do it from personal revenge or earthly politics, but in obedience to God's command. And the honour intended for all the saints of God, consists in their triumphs over the enemies of their salvation. Christ never intended his gospel should be spread by fire and sword, or his righteousness by the wrath of man. But let the high praises of God be in our mouths, while we wield the sword of the word of God, with the shield of faith, in warfare with the world, the flesh, and the devil. The saints shall be more than conquerors over the enemies of their souls, through the blood of the Lamb and the word of his testimony. The completing of this will be in the judgement of the great day. Then shall the judgement be executed. Behold Jesus, and his gospel church, chiefly in her millennial state. He and his people rejoice in each other; by their prayers and efforts they work with him, while he goes forth in the chariots of salvation, conquering sinners by grace, or in chariots of vengeance, to destroy his enemies.

Chapter 150

A psalm of praise.

—We are here stirred up to praise God. Praise God for his sanctuary, and the privileges we enjoy by having it among us; praise him because of his power and glory in the firmament. Those who praise the Lord in heaven, behold displays of his power and glory which we cannot now conceive. But the greatest of all his mighty acts is known in his earthly sanctuary. The holiness and the love of our God are more displayed in man's redemption, than in all his other works. Let us praise our God and Saviour for it. We need not care to know what instruments of music are mentioned. Hereby is meant that in serving God we should spare no cost or pains. Praise God with strong faith; praise him with holy love and delight; praise him with entire confidence in Christ; praise him with believing triumph over the powers of darkness; praise him by universal respect to all his commands; praise him by cheerful submission to all his disposals; praise him by rejoicing in his love, and comforting ourselves in his goodness; praise him by promoting the interests of the kingdom of his grace; praise him by lively hope and expectation of the kingdom of his glory. Since we must shortly breathe our last, while we have breath let us praise the Lord; then we shall breathe our last with comfort. Let every thing that hath breath praise the Lord. Praise ye the Lord. Such is the very suitable end of a book inspired by the Spirit of God, written for the work of praise; a book which has supplied the songs of the church for more than three thousand years; a book which is quoted more frequently than any other by Christ and his apostles; a book which presents the loftiest ideas of God and his government, which is fitted to every state of human life, which sets forth every state of religious experience, and which bears simple and clear marks of its Divine origin.

Proverbs

The subject of this book may be thus stated by an enlargement on the opening **verses**. **1**. The Proverbs of Solomon, the son of David, king of Israel. **2**. Which treat of the knowledge of wisdom, of piety towards God, of instruction and moral discipline, of the understanding wise and prudent counsels. **3**. Which treat of the attainment of instruction in wisdom, which wisdom is to be shown in the conduct of life, and consists in righteousness with regard to our fellow-creatures. **4**. Which treat of the giving to the simple sagacity to discover what is right, by supplying them with just principles, and correct views of virtue and vice; and to the young man knowledge, so that he need not err through ignorance; and discretion, so that by pondering well these precepts, he may not err through obstinacy. Take the proverbs of other nations, and we shall find great numbers founded upon selfishness, cunning, pride, injustice, national contempt, and animosities. The principles of the Proverbs of Solomon are piety, charity, justice, benevolence, and true prudence. Their universal purity proves that they are the word of God.

Chapter 1

Verses 1–6

The lessons here given are plain, and likely to benefit those who feel their own ignorance, and their need to be taught. If young people take heed to their ways, according to Solomon's Proverbs, they will gain knowledge and discretion. Solomon speaks of the most important points of truth, and a greater than Solomon is here. Christ speaks by his word and by his Spirit. Christ is the Word and the Wisdom of God, and he is made to us wisdom.

Verses 7–9

Fools are persons who have no true wisdom, who follow their own devices, without regard to reason, or reverence for God. Children are reasonable creatures, and when we tell them what they must do, we must tell them why. But they are corrupt and wilful, therefore with the instruction there is need of a law. Let Divine truths and commands be to us most honourable; let us value them, and then they shall be so to us.

Verses 10–19

Wicked people are zealous in seducing others into the paths of the destroyer: sinners love company in sin. But they have so much the more to answer for. How cautious young people should be! "Consent thou not." Do not say as they say, nor do as they do, or would have thee to do; have no fellowship with them. Who could think that it should be a pleasure to one man to destroy another! See their idea of worldly wealth; but it is neither substance, nor precious. It is the ruinous mistake of thousands, that they overvalue the wealth of this world. Men promise themselves in vain that sin will turn to their advantage. The way of sin is down-hill; men cannot stop themselves. Would young people shun temporal and eternal ruin, let them refuse to take one step in these destructive paths. Men's greediness of gain hurries them upon practices which will not suffer them or others to live out half their days. What is a man profited, though he gain the world, if he lose his life? much less if he lose his soul?

Verses 20–33

Solomon, having showed how dangerous it is to hearken to the temptations of Satan, here declares how dangerous it is not to hearken to the calls of God. Christ himself is Wisdom, is Wisdoms. Three sorts of persons are here called by Him: **1**. Simple ones. Sinners are fond of their simple notions of good and evil, their simple prejudices against the ways of God, and flatter themselves in their wickedness. **2**. Scorners. Proud, jovial people, that make a jest of every thing. Scoffers at religion, that run down every thing sacred and serious. **3**. Fools. Those are the worst of fools that hate to be taught, and have a rooted dislike to serious godliness. The precept is plain; Turn you at my reproof. We do not make a right use of reproofs, if we do not turn from evil to that which is good. The promises are very encouraging. Men cannot turn by any power of their own; but God answers, Behold, I will pour out my Spirit unto you. Special grace is needful to sincere conversion. But that grace shall never be denied to any who seek it. The love of Christ, and the promises mingled with his reproofs, surely should have the attention of every one. It may well be asked, how long men mean to proceed in such a perilous path, when the uncertainty of life and the consequences of dying without Christ are considered? Now sinners live at ease, and set sorrow at defiance; but their calamity will come. Now God is ready to hear their prayers; but then they shall cry in vain. Are we yet despisers of wisdom? Let us hearken diligently, and obey the Lord Jesus, that we may enjoy peace of conscience and confidence in God; be free from evil, in life, in death, and for ever.

Chapter 2

Verses 1–9

Those who earnestly seek heavenly wisdom, will never complain that they have lost their labour; and the freeness of the gift does not do away the necessity of our diligence, Joh **6**:**27** Let them seek, and they shall find it; let them ask, and it shall be given them. Observe who are thus favoured. They are the righteous, on whom the image of God is renewed, which consists in righteousness. If we depend upon God, and seek to him for wisdom, he will enable us to keep the paths of judgment.

Verses 10–22

If we are truly wise, we shall be careful to avoid all evil company and evil practices. When wisdom has dominion over us, then it not only fills the head, but enters into the heart, and will preserve, both against corruptions within and temptations without. The ways of sin are ways of darkness, uncomfortable and unsafe: what fools are those who leave the plain, pleasant, lightsome paths of uprightness, to walk in such ways! They take pleasure in sin; both in committing it, and in seeing others commit it. Every wise man will shun such company. True wisdom will also preserve from those who lead to fleshly lusts, which defile the body, that living temple, and war against the soul. These are evils which excite the sorrow of every serious mind, and cause every reflecting parent to look upon his children with anxiety, lest they should be entangled in such fatal snares. Let the sufferings of others be our warnings. Our Lord Jesus deters from sinful pleasures, by the everlasting torments which follow them. It is very rare that any who are caught in this snare of the devil, recover themselves; so much is the heart hardened, and the mind blinded, by the deceitfulness of this sin. Many think that this caution, besides the literal sense, is to be understood as a caution against idolatry, and subjecting the soul to the body, by seeking any forbidden object. The righteous must leave the earth as well as the wicked; but the earth is a very different thing to them. To the wicked it is all the heaven they ever shall have; to the righteous it is the place of preparation for heaven. And is it all one to us, whether we share with the wicked in the miseries of their latter end, or share those everlasting joys that shall crown believers?

Chapter 3

Verses 1–6

In the way of believing obedience to God's commandments health and peace may commonly be enjoyed; and though our days may not be long upon earth, we shall live for ever in heaven. Let not mercy and truth forsake thee; God's mercy in promising, and his truth in performing: live up to them, keep up thine interest in them, and take the comfort of them. We must trust in the Lord with all our hearts, believing he is able and wise to do what is best. Those who know themselves, find their own understandings a broken reed, which, if they lean upon, will fail. Do not design any thing but what is lawful, and beg God to direct thee in every case, though it may seem quite plain. In all our ways that prove pleasant, in which we gain our point, we must acknowledge God with thankfulness. In all our ways that prove uncomfortable, and that are hedged up with thorns, we must acknowledge him with submission. It is promised, He shall direct thy paths; so that thy way shall be safe and good, and happy at last.

Verses 7–12

There is not a greater enemy to the fear of the Lord in the heart, than self-conceit of our own wisdom. The prudence and sobriety which religion teaches, tend not only to the health of the soul, but to the health of the body. Worldly wealth is but poor substance, yet, such as it is, we must honour God with it; and those that do good with what they have, shall have more to do more good with. Should the Lord visit us with trials and sickness, let us not forget that the exhortation speaks to us as to children, for our good. We must not faint under an affliction, be it ever so heavy and long, not be driven to despair, or use wrong means for relief. The father corrects the son whom he loves, because he loves him, and desires that he may be wise and good. Afflictions are so far from doing God's children any hurt, that, by the grace of God, they promote their holiness.

Verses 13–20

No precious jewels or earthly treasures are worthy to be compared with true wisdom, whether the concerns of time or eternity be considered. We must make wisdom our business; we must venture all in it, and be willing to part with all for it. This Wisdom is the Lord Jesus Christ and his salvation, sought and obtained by faith and prayer. Were it not for unbelief, remaining sinfulness, and carelessness, we should find all our ways pleasantness, and our paths peace, for his are so; but we too often step aside from them, to our own hurt and grief. Christ is that Wisdom, by whom the worlds were made, and still are in being; happy are those to whom he is made of God wisdom. He has wherewithal to make good all his promises.

Verses 21–26

Let us not suffer Christ's words to depart from us, but keep sound wisdom and discretion; then shall we walk safely in his ways. The natural life, and all that belongs to it, shall be under the protection of God's providence; the spiritual life, and all its interests, under the protection of his grace, so that we shall be kept from falling into sin or trouble.

Verses 27–35

Our business is to observe the precepts of Christ, and to copy his example; to do justice, to love mercy, and to beware of covetousness; to be ready for every good work, avoiding needless strife, and bearing evils, if possible, rather than seeking redress by law. It will be found there is little got by striving. Let us not envy prosperous oppressors; far be it from the disciples of Christ to choose any of their ways. These truths may be despised by the covetous and luxurious, but everlasting contempt will be the portion of such scorners, while Divine favour is shown to the humble believer.

Chapter 4

Verses 1–13

We must look upon our teachers as our fathers: though instruction carry in it reproof and correction, bid it welcome. Solomon's parents loved him, therefore taught him. Wise and godly men, in every age of the world, and rank in society, agree that true wisdom consists in obedience, and is united to happiness. Get wisdom, take pains for it. Get the rule over thy corruptions; take more pains to get this than the wealth of this world. An interest in Christ's salvation is necessary. This wisdom is the one thing needful. A soul without true wisdom and grace is a dead soul. How poor, contemptible, and wretched are those, who, with all their wealth and power, die without getting understanding, without Christ, without hope, and without God! Let us give heed to the sayings of Him who has the words of eternal life. Thus our path will be plain before us: by taking, and keeping fast hold of instruction, we shall avoid being straitened or stumbling.

Verses 14–27

The way of evil men may seem pleasant, and the nearest way to compass some end; but it is an evil way, and will end ill; if thou love thy God and thy soul, avoid it. It is not said, Keep at a due distance, but at a great distance; never think you can get far enough from it. The way of the righteous is light; Christ is their Way, and he is the Light. The saints will not be perfect till they reach heaven, but there they shall shine as the sun in his strength. The way of sin is as darkness. The way of the wicked is dark, therefore dangerous; they fall into sin, but know not how to avoid it. They fall into trouble, but never seek to know wherefore God contends with them, nor what will be in the end of it. This is the way we are bid to shun. Attentive hearing the word of God, is a good sign of a work of grace begun in the heart, and a good means of carrying it on. There is in the word of God a proper remedy for all diseases of the soul. Keep thy heart with all diligence. We must set a strict guard upon our souls; keep our hearts from doing hurt, and getting hurt. A good reason is given; because out of it are the issues of life. Above all, we should seek from the Lord Jesus that living water, the sanctifying Spirit, issuing forth unto everlasting life. Thus we shall be enabled to put away a froward mouth and perverse lips; our eyes will be turned from beholding vanity, looking straight forward, and walking by the rule of God's word, treading in the steps of our Lord and Master. Lord, forgive the past, and enable us to follow thee more closely for the time to come.

Chapter 5

Verses 1–14

Solomon cautions all young men, as his children, to abstain from fleshly lusts. Some, by the adulterous woman, here understand idolatry, false doctrine, which tends to lead astray men's minds and manners; but the direct view is to warn against seventh-commandment sins. Often these have been, and still are, Satan's method of drawing men from the worship of God into false religion. Consider how fatal the consequences; how bitter the fruit! Take it any way, it wounds. It leads to the torments of hell. The direct tendency of this sin is to the destruction of body and soul. We must carefully avoid every thing which may be a step towards it. Those who would be kept from harm, must keep out of harm's way. If we thrust ourselves into temptation we mock God when we pray, Lead us not into temptation. How many mischiefs attend this sin! It blasts the reputation; it wastes time; it ruins the estate; it is destructive to health; it will fill the mind with horror. Though thou art merry now, yet sooner or later it will bring sorrow. The convinced sinner reproaches himself, and makes no excuse for his folly. By the frequent acts of sin, the habits of it become rooted and confirmed. By a miracle of mercy true repentance may prevent the dreadful consequences of such sins; but this is not often; far more die as they have lived. What can express the case of the self-ruined sinner in the eternal world, enduring the remorse of his conscience!

Verses 15–23

Lawful marriage is a means God has appointed to keep from these destructive vices. But we are not properly united, except as we attend to God's word, seeking his direction and blessing, and acting with affection. Ever remember, that though secret sins may escape the eyes of our fellow-creatures, yet a man's ways are before the eyes of the Lord, who not only sees, but ponders all his goings. Those who are so foolish as to choose the way of sin, are justly left of God to themselves, to go on in the way to destruction.

Chapter 6

Verses 1–5

If we live as directed by the word of God, we shall find it profitable even in this present world. We are stewards of our worldly substance, and have to answer to the Lord for our disposal of it; to waste it in rash schemes, or such plans as may entangle us in difficulties and temptations, is wrong. A man ought never to be surety for more than he is able and willing to pay, and can afford to pay, without wronging his family; he ought to look upon every sum he is engaged for, as his own debt. If we must take all this care to get our debts to men forgiven, much more to obtain forgiveness with God. Humble thyself to him, make sure of Christ as thy Friend, to plead for thee; pray earnestly that thy sins may be pardoned, and that thou mayest be kept from going down to the pit.

Verses 6–11

Diligence in business is every man's wisdom and duty, not so much that he may attain worldly wealth, as that he may not be a burden to others, or a scandal to the church. The ants are more diligent than slothful men. We may learn wisdom from the meanest insects, and be shamed by them. Habits of indolence and indulgence grow upon people. Thus life runs to waste; and poverty, though at first at a distance, gradually draws near, like a traveller; and when it arrives, is like an armed man, too strong to be resisted. All this may be applied to the concerns of our souls. How many love their sleep of sin, and their dreams of worldly happiness! Shall we not seek to awaken such? Shall we not give diligence to secure our own salvation?

Verses 12–19

If the slothful are to be condemned, who do nothing, much more those that do all the ill they can. Observe how such a man is described. He says and does every thing artfully, and with design. His ruin shall come without warning, and without relief. Here is a list of things hateful to God. Those sins are in a special manner provoking to God, which are hurtful to the comfort of human life. These things which God hates, we must hate in ourselves; it is nothing to hate them in others. Let us shun all such practices, and watch and pray against them; and avoid, with marked disapproval, all who are guilty of them, whatever may be their rank.

Verses 20–35

The word of God has something to say to us upon all occasions. Let not faithful reproofs ever make us uneasy. When we consider how much this sin abounds, how heinous adultery is in its own nature, of what evil consequence it is, and how certainly it destroys the spiritual life in the soul, we shall not wonder that the cautions against it are so often repeated. Let us notice the subjects of this chapter. Let us remember Him who willingly became our Surety, when we were strangers and enemies. And shall Christians, who have such prospects, motives, and examples, be slothful and careless? Shall we neglect what is pleasing to God, and what he will graciously reward? May we closely watch every sense by which poison can enter our minds or affections.

Chapter 7

Verses 1–5

We must lay up God's commandments safely. Not only, Keep them, and you shall live; but, Keep them as those that cannot live without them. Those that blame strict and careful walking as needless and too precise, consider not that the law is to be kept as the apple of the eye; indeed the law in the heart is the eye of the soul. Let the word of God dwell in us, and so be written where it will be always at hand to be read. Thus we shall be kept from the fatal effects of our own passions, and the snares of Satan. Let God's word confirm our dread of sin, and resolutions against it.

Verses 6–27

Here is an affecting example of the danger of youthful lusts. It is a history or a parable of the most instructive kind. Will any one dare to venture on temptations that lead to impurity, after Solomon has set before his eyes in so lively and plain a manner, the danger of even going near them? Then is he as the man who would dance on the edge of a lofty rock, when he has just seen another fall headlong from the same place. The misery of self-ruined sinners began in disregard to God's blessed commands. We ought daily to pray that we may be kept from running into temptation, else we invite the enemies of our souls to spread snares for us. Ever avoid the neighbourhood of vice. Beware of sins which are said to be pleasant sins. They are the more dangerous, because they most easily gain the heart, and close it against repentance. Do nothing till thou hast well considered the end of it. Were a man to live as long as Methuselah, and to spend all his days in the highest delights sin can offer, one hour of the anguish and tribulation that must follow, would far outweigh them.

Chapter 8

Verses 1–11

The will of God is made known by the works of creation, and by the consciences of men, but more clearly by Moses and the prophets. The chief difficulty is to get men to attend to instruction. Yet attention to the words of Christ, will guide the most ignorant into saving knowledge of the truth. Where there is an understanding heart, and willingness to receive the truth in love, wisdom is valued above silver and gold.

Verses 12–21

Wisdom, here is Christ, in whom are all the treasures of wisdom and knowledge; it is Christ in the word, and Christ in the heart; not only Christ revealed to us, but Christ revealed in us. All prudence and skill are from the Lord. Through the redemption of Christ's precious blood, the riches of his grace abound in all wisdom and prudence. Man found out many inventions for ruin; God found one for our recovery. He hates pride and arrogance, evil ways and froward conversation; these render men unwilling to hear his humbling, awakening, holy instructions. True religion gives men the best counsel in all difficult cases, and helps to make their way plain. His wisdom makes all truly happy who receive it in the love of Christ Jesus. Seek him early, seek him earnestly, seek him before any thing else. Christ never said, Seek in vain. Those who love Christ, are such as have seen his loveliness, and have had his love shed abroad in their hearts; therefore they are happy. They shall be happy in this world, or in that which is beyond compare better. Wealth gotten by vanity will soon be diminished, but that which is well got, will wear well; and that which is well spent upon works of piety and charity, will be lasting. If they have not riches and honour in this world, they shall have that which is infinitely better. They shall be happy in the grace of God. Christ, by his Spirit, guides believers into all truth, and so leads them in the way of righteousness; and they walk after the Spirit. Also, they shall be happy in the glory of God hereafter. In Wisdom's promises, believers have goods laid up, not for days and years, but for eternity; her fruit therefore is better than gold.

Verses 22–31

The Son of God declares himself to have been engaged in the creation of the world. How able, how fit is the Son of God to be the Saviour of the world, who was the Creator of it! The Son of God was ordained, before the world, to that great work. Does he delight in saving wretched sinners, and shall not we delight in his salvation?

Verses 32–36

Surely we should hearken to Christ's voice with the readiness of children. Let us all be wise, and not refuse such mercy. Blessed are those who hear the Saviour's voice, and wait on him with daily reading, meditation, and prayer. The children of the world find time for vain amusements, without neglecting what they deem the one thing needful. Does it not show contempt of Wisdom's instructions, when people professing godliness, seek excuses for neglecting the means of grace? Christ is Wisdom, and he is Life to all believers; nor can we obtain God's favour, unless we find Christ, and are found in him. Those who offend Christ deceive themselves; sin is a wrong to the soul. Sinners die because they will die, which justifies God when he judges.

Chapter 9

Verses 1–12

Christ has prepared ordinances to which his people are admitted, and by which nourishment is given here to those that believe in him, as well as mansions in heaven hereafter. The ministers of the gospel go forth to invite the guests. The call is general, and shuts out none that do not shut out themselves. Our Saviour came, not to call the righteous, but sinners; not the wise in their own eyes, who say they see. We must keep from the company and foolish pleasures of the ungodly, or we never can enjoy the pleasures of a holy life. It is vain to seek the company of wicked men in the hope of doing them good; we are far more likely to be corrupted by them. It is not enough to forsake the foolish, we must join those that walk in wisdom. There is no true wisdom but in the way of religion, no true life but in the end of that way. Here is the happiness of those that embrace it. A man cannot be profitable to God; it is for our own good. Observe the shame and ruin of those who slight it. God is not the Author of sin: and Satan can only tempt, he cannot force. Thou shalt bear the loss of that which thou scornest: it will add to thy condemnation.

Verses 13–18

How diligent the tempter is, to seduce unwary souls into sin! Carnal, sensual pleasure, stupifies conscience, and puts out the sparks of conviction. This tempter has no solid reason to offer; and where she gets dominion in a soul, all knowledge of holy things is lost and forgotten. She is very violent and pressing. We need to seek and pray for true wisdom, for Satan has many ways to withdraw our souls from Christ. Not only worldly lusts and abandoned seducers prove fatal to the souls of men; but false teachers, with doctrines that flatter pride and give liberty to lusts, destroy thousands. They especially draw off such as have received only partial serious impressions. The depths of Satan are depths of hell; and sin, without remorse, is ruin, ruin without remedy. Solomon shows the hook; those that believe him, will not meddle with the bait. Behold the wretched, empty, unsatisfying, deceitful, and stolen pleasure sin proposes; and may our souls be so desirous of the everlasting enjoyment of Christ, that on earth we may live to him, daily, by faith, and ere long be with him in glory.

Chapter 10

Through the whole of the Proverbs, we are to look for somewhat beyond the first sense the passage may imply, and this we shall find to be Christ. He is the Wisdom so often spoken of in this book.

Verse 1

The comfort of parents much depends on their children; and this suggests to both, motives to their duties.

Verses 2, 3

Though the righteous may be poor, the Lord will not suffer him to want what is needful for spiritual life.

Verse 4

Those who are fervent in spirit, serving the Lord, are likely to be rich in faith, and rich in good works.

Verse 5

Here is just blame of those who trifle away opportunities, both for here and for hereafter.

Verse 6

Abundance of blessings shall abide on good men; real blessings.

Verse 7

Both the just and the wicked must die; but between their souls there is a vast difference.

Verse 8

The wise in heart puts his knowledge in practice.

Verse 9

Dissemblers, after all their shuffling, will be exposed.

Verse 10

Trick and artifice will be no excuse for iniquity.

Verse 11

The good man's mouth is always open to teach, comfort, and correct others.

Verse 12

Where there is hatred, every thing stirs up strife. By bearing with each other, peace and harmony are preserved.

Verse 13

Those that foolishly go on in wicked ways, prepare rods for themselves.

Verse 14

Whatever knowledge may be useful, we must lay it up, that it may not be to seek when we want it. The wise gain this wisdom by reading, by hearing the word, by meditation, by prayer, by faith in Christ, who is made of God unto us wisdom.

Verse 15

This refers to the common mistakes both of rich and poor, as to their outward condition. Rich people's wealth exposes them to many dangers; while a poor man may live comfortably, if he is content, keeps a good conscience, and lives by faith.

Verse 16

Perhaps a righteous man has no more than what he works hard for, but that labour tends to life.

Verse 17

The traveller that has missed his way, and cannot bear to be told of it, and to be shown the right way, must err still.

Verse 18

He is especially a fool who thinks to hide anything from God; and malice is no better.

Verse 19

Those that speak much, speak much amiss. He that checks himself is a wise man, and therein consults his own peace.

Verses 20, 21

The tongue of the just is sincere, freed from the dross of guile and evil design. Pious discourse is spiritual food to the needy. Fools die for want of a heart, so the word is; for want of thought.

Verse 22

That wealth which is truly desirable, has no vexation of spirit in the enjoyment; no grief for the loss; no guilt by the abuse of it. What comes from the love of God, has the grace of God for its companion.

Verse 23

Only foolish and wicked men divert themselves with doing harm to others, or tempting to sin.

Verse 24

The largest desire of eternal blessings the righteous can form, will be granted.

Verse 25

The course of prosperous sinners is like a whirlwind, which soon spends itself, and is gone.

Verse 26

As vinegar sets the teeth on edge, and as the smoke causes the eyes to smart, so the sluggard vexes his employer.

Verses 27, 28

What man is he that loves life? Let him fear God, and that will secure to him life enough in this world, and eternal life in the other.

Verse 29

The believer grows stronger in faith, and obeys with increased delight.

Verse 30

The wicked would be glad to have this earth their home for ever, but it cannot be so. They must die and leave all their idols behind.

Verses 31, 32

A good man discourses wisely for the benefit of others. But it is the sin, and will be the ruin of a wicked man, that he speaks what is displeasing to God, and provoking to those he con**verse**s with. The righteous is kept by the power of God; and nothing shall be able to separate him from the love of God which is in Christ Jesus.

Chapter 11

Verse 1

However men may make light of giving short weight or measure, and however common such crimes may be, they are an abomination to the Lord.

Verse 2

Considering how safe, and quiet, and easy the humble are, we see that with the lowly is wisdom.

Verse 3

An honest man's principles are fixed, therefore his way is plain.

Verse 4

Riches will stand men in no stead in the day of death.

Verses 5, 6

The ways of wickedness are dangerous. And sin will be its own punishment.

Verse 7

When a godly man dies, all his fears vanish; but when a wicked man dies, his hopes vanish.

Verse 8

The righteous are often wonderfully kept from going into dangerous situations, and the ungodly go in their stead.

Verse 9

Hypocrites delude men into error and sin by artful objections against the truths of God's word.

Verses 10, 11

Nations prosper when wicked men are cast down.

Verse 12

A man of understanding does not judge of others by their success.

Verse 13

A faithful man will not disclose what he is trusted with, unless the honour of God and the real good of society require it.

Verse 14

We shall often find it to our advantage to advise with others.

Verse 15

The welfare of our families, our own peace, and our ability to pay just debts, must not be brought into danger. But here especially let us consider the grace of our Lord Jesus Christ in becoming Surety even for enemies.

Verse 16

A pious and discreet woman will keep esteem and respect, as strong men keep possession of wealth.

Verse 17

A cruel, froward, ill-natured man, is vexatious to those that are, and should be to him as his own flesh, and punishes himself.

Verse 18

He that makes it his business to do good, shall have a reward, as sure to him as eternal truth can make it.

Verse 19

True holiness is true happiness. The more violent a man is in sinful pursuits, the more he hastens his own destruction.

Verse 20

Nothing is more hateful to God, than hypocrisy and double dealing, which are here signified. God delights in such as aim and act with uprightness.

Verse 21

Joining together in sin shall not protect the sinners.

Verse 22

Beauty is abused by those who have not discretion or modesty with it. This is true of all bodily endowments.

Verse 23

The wicked desire mischief to others, but it shall return upon themselves.

Verse 24

A man may grow poor by not paying just debts, not relieving the poor, not allowing needful expenses. Let men be ever so saving of what they have, if God appoints, it comes to nothing.

Verse 25

Both in temporal and spiritual things, God commonly deals with his people according to the measure by which they deal with their brethren.

Verse 26

We must not hoard up the gifts of God's bounty, merely for our own advantage.

Verse 27

Seeking mischief is here set against seeking good; for those that are not doing good are doing hurt, even to themselves.

Verse 28

The true believer is a branch of the living Vine. When those that take root in the world wither, those who are grafted into Christ shall be fruitful.

Verse 29

He that brings trouble upon himself and his family, by carelessness, or by wickedness, shall be unable to keep and enjoy what he gets, as a man is unable to hold the wind, or to satisfy himself with it.

Verse 30

The righteous are as trees of life; and their influence upon earth, like the fruits of that tree, support and nourish the spiritual life in many.

Verse 31

Even the righteous, when they offend on earth, shall meet with sharp corrections; much more will the wicked meet the due reward of their sins. Let us then seek those blessings which our Surety purchased by his sufferings and death; let us seek to copy his example, and to keep his commandments.

Chapter 12

Verse 1

Those who have grace, will delight in the instructions given them. Those that stifle their convictions, are like brutes.

Verse 2

The man who covers selfish and vicious designs under a profession of religion or friendship, will be condemned.

Verse 3

Though men may advance themselves by sinful arts, they cannot settle and secure themselves. But those who by faith are rooted in Christ, are firmly fixed.

Verse 4

A wife who is pious, prudent, and looks well to the ways of her household, who makes conscience of her duty, and can bear crosses; such a one is an honour and comfort to her husband. She that is the re**verse** of this, preys upon him, and consumes him.

Verse 5

Thoughts are not free; they are under the Divine knowledge, therefore under the Divine command. It is a man's shame to act with deceit, with trick and design.

Verse 6

Wicked people speak mischief to their neighbours. A man may sometimes do a good work with one good word.

Verse 7

God's blessing is often continued to the families of godly men, while the wicked are overthrown.

Verse 8

The apostles showed wisdom by glorying in shame for the name of Christ.

Verse 9

He that lives in a humble state, who has no one to wait upon him, but gets bread by his own labour, is happier than he that glories in high birth or gay attire, and wants necessaries.

Verse 10

A godly man would not put even an animal to needless pain. But the wicked often speak of others as well used, when they would not endure like treatment for a single day.

Verse 11

It is men's wisdom to mind their business, and follow an honest calling. But it is folly to neglect business; and the grace of God teaches men to disdain nothing but sin.

Verse 12

When the ungodly see others prosper by sin, they wish they could act in the same way. But the root of Divine grace, in the heart of the righteous, produces other desires and purposes.

Verse 13

Many a man has paid dear in this world for the transgression of his lips.

Verse 14

When men use their tongues aright, to teach and comfort others, they enjoy acceptance through Christ Jesus; and the testimony of their conscience, that they in some measure answer the end of their being.

Verse 15

A fool, in the sense of Scripture, means a wicked man, one who acts contrary to the wisdom that is from above. His rule is, to do what is right in his own eyes.

Verse 16

A foolish man is soon angry, and is hasty in expressing it; he is ever in trouble and running into mischief. It is kindness to ourselves to make light of injuries and affronts, instead of making the worst of them.

Verse 17

It is good for all to dread and detest the sin of lying, and to be governed by honesty.

Verse 18

Whisperings and evil surmises, like a sword, separate those that have been dear to each other. The tongue of the wise is health, making all whole.

Verse 19

If truth be spoken, it will hold good; whoever may be disobliged, still it will keep its ground.

Verse 20

Deceit and falsehood bring terrors and perplexities. But those who consult the peace and happiness of others have joy in their own minds.

Verse 21

If men are sincerely righteous, the righteous God has engaged that no evil shall happen to them. But they that delight in mischief shall have enough of it.

Verse 22

Make conscience of truth, not only in words, but in actions.

Verse 23

Foolish men proclaim to all the folly and emptiness of their minds.

Verse 24

Those who will not take pains in an honest calling, living by tricks and dishonesty, are paltry and beggarly.

Verse 25

Care, fear, and sorrow, upon the spirits, deprive men of vigour in what is to be done, or courage in what is to be borne. A good word from God, applied by faith, makes the heart glad.

Verse 26

The righteous is abundant; though not in this world's goods, yet in the graces and comforts of the Spirit, which are the true riches. Evil men vainly flatter themselves that their ways are not wrong.

Verse 27

The slothful man makes no good use of the advantages Providence puts in his way, and has no comfort in them. The substance of a diligent man, though not great, does good to him and his family. He sees that God gives it to him in answer to prayer.

Verse 28

The way of religion is a straight, plain way; it is the way of righteousness. There is not only life at the end, but life in the way; all true comfort.

Chapter 13

Verse 1

There is great hope of those that reverence their parents. There is little hope of any who will not hear those that deal faithfully with them.

Verse 2

By our words we must be justified or condemned, Mt **12:37**.

Verse 3

He that thinks before he speaks, that suppresses evil if he have thought it, keeps his soul from a great deal both of guilt and grief. Many a one is ruined by an ungoverned tongue.

Verse 4

The slothful desire the gains the diligent get, but hate the pains the diligent take; therefore they have nothing. This is especially true as to the soul.

Verse 5

Where sin reigns, the man is loathsome. If his conscience were awake, he would abhor himself, and repent in dust and ashes.

Verse 6

An honest desire to do right, preserves a man from fatal mistakes, better than a thousand fine-drawn distinctions.

Verse 7

Some who are really poor, trade and spend as if they were rich: this is sin, and will be shame, and it will end accordingly. Some that are really rich, would be thought to be poor: in this there is want of gratitude to God, want of justice and charity to others. There are many hypocrites, empty of grace, who will not be convinced of their poverty. There are many fearing Christians, who are spiritually rich, yet think themselves poor; by their doubts, and complaints, and griefs, they make themselves poor.

Verse 8

Great riches often tempt to violence against those that possess them; but the poor are free from such perils.

Verse 9

The light of the righteous is as that of the sun, which may be eclipsed and clouded, but will continue: the Spirit is their Light, he gives a fulness of joy: that of the wicked is as a lamp of their own kindling, easily put out.

Verse 10

All contentions, whether between private persons, families, churches, or nations, are begun and carried forward by pride. Disputes would be easily prevented or ended, if it were not for pride.

Verse 11

Wealth gotten by dishonesty or vice, has a secret curse, which will speedily waste it.

Verse 12

The delay of what is anxiously hoped for, is very painful to the mind; obtaining it is very pleasant. But spiritual blessings are chiefly intended.

Verse 13

He that stands in awe of God, and reverences his word, shall escape destruction, and be rewarded for his godly fear.

Verse 14

The rule by which the wise regulate their conduct, is a fountain yielding life and happiness.

Verse 15

The way of sinners is hard upon others, and hard to the sinner himself. The service of sin is slavery; the road to hell is strewed with the thorns and thistles that followed the curse.

Verse 16

It is folly to talk of things of which we know nothing, and to undertake what we are no way fit for.

Verse 17

Those that are wicked, and false to Christ and to the souls of men, do mischief, and fall into mischief; but those that are faithful, find sound words healing to others and to themselves.

Verse 18

He that scorns to be taught, will certainly be brought down.

Verse 19

There are in man strong desires after happiness; but never let those expect any thing truly sweet to their souls, who will not be persuaded to leave their sins.

Verse 20

Multitudes are brought to ruin by bad company. And all that make themselves wicked will be destroyed.

Verse 21

When God pursues sinners he is sure to overtake them; and he will reward the righteous.

Verse 22

The servant of God who is not anxious about riches, takes the best method of providing for his children.

Verse 23

The poor, yet industrious, thrive, though in a homely manner, while those who have great riches are often brought to poverty for want of judgment.

Verse 24

He acts as if he hated his child, who, by false indulgence, permits sinful habits to gather strength, which will bring sorrow here, and misery hereafter.

Verse 25

It is the misery of the wicked, that even their sensual appetites are always craving. The righteous feeds on the word and ordinances, to the satisfying of his soul with the promises of the gospel, and the Lord Jesus Christ, who is the Bread of life.

Chapter 14

Verse 1

A woman who has no fear of God, who is wilful and wasteful, and indulges her ease, will as certainly ruin her family, as if she plucked her house down.

Verse 2

Here are grace and sin in their true colours. Those that despise God's precepts and promises, despise God and all his power and mercy.

Verse 3

Pride grows from that root of bitterness which is in the heart. The root must be plucked up, or we cannot conquer this branch. The prudent words of wise men get them out of difficulties.

Verse 4

There can be no advantage without something which, though of little moment, will affright the indolent.

Verse 5

A conscientious witness will not dare to represent anything otherwise than according to his knowledge.

Verse 6

A scorner treats Divine things with contempt. He that feels his ignorance and unworthiness will search the Scriptures in a humble spirit.

Verse 7

We discover a wicked man if there is no savour of piety in his discourse.

Verse 8

We are travellers, whose concern is, not to spy out wonders, but to get to their journey's end; to understand the rules we are to walk by, also the ends we are to walk toward. The bad man cheats himself, and goes on in his mistake.

Verse 9

Foolish and profane men consider sin a mere trifle, to be made light of rather than mourned over. Fools mock at the sin-offering; but those that make light of sin, make light of Christ.

Verse 10

We do not know what stings of conscience, or consuming passions, torment the prosperous sinner. Nor does the world know the peace of mind a serious Christian enjoys, even in poverty and sickness.

Verse 11

Sin ruins many great families; whilst righteousness often raises and strengthens even mean families.

Verse 12

The ways of carelessness, of worldliness, and of sensuality, seem right to those that walk in them; but self-deceivers prove self-destroyers. See the vanity of carnal mirth.

Verse 14

Of all sinners backsliders will have the most terror when they reflect on their own ways.

Verse 15

Eager readiness to believe what others say, has ever proved mischievous. The whole world was thus ruined at first. The man who is spiritually wise, depends on the Saviour alone for acceptance. He is watchful against the enemies of his salvation, by taking heed to God's word.

Verse 16

Holy fear guards against every thing unholy.

Verse 17

An angry man is to be pitied as well as blamed; but the revengeful is more hateful.

Verse 18

Sin is the shame of sinners; but wisdom is the honour of the wise.

Verse 19

Even bad men acknowledge the excellency of God's people.

Verse 20

Friendship in the world is governed by self-interest. It is good to have God our Friend; he will not desert us.

Verse 21

To despise a man for his employment or appearance is a sin.

Verse 22

How wisely those consult their own interest, who not only do good, but devise it!

Verse 23

Labour of the head, or of the hand, will turn to some good account. But if men's religion runs all out in talk and noise, they will come to nothing.

Verse 24

The riches of men of wisdom and piety enlarge their usefulness.

Verse 25

An upright man will venture the displeasure of the greatest, to bring truth to light.

Verses 26, 27

Those who fear the Lord so as to obey and serve him, have a strong ground of confidence, and will be preserved. Let us seek to this Fountain of life, that we may escape the snares of death.

Verse 28

Let all that wish well to the kingdom of Christ, do what they can, that many may be added to his church.

Verse 29

A mild, patient man is one that learns of Christ, who is Wisdom itself. Unbridled passion is folly made known.

Verse 30

An upright, contented, and benevolent mind, tends to health.

Verse 31

To oppress the poor is to reproach our Creator.

Verse 32

The wicked man has his soul forced from him; he dies in his sins, under the guilt and power of them. But godly men, though they have pain and some dread of death, have the blessed hope, which God, who cannot lie, has given them.

Verse 33

Wisdom possesses the heart, and thus regulates the affections and tempers.

Verse 34

Piety and holiness always promote industry, sobriety, and honesty.

Verse 35

The great King who reigns over heaven and earth, will reward faithful servants who honour his gospel by the proper discharge of the duties of their stations: he despises not the services of the lowest.

Chapter 15

Verse 1

A right cause will be better pleaded with meekness than with passion. Nothing stirs up anger like grievous words.

Verse 2

He that has knowledge, is to use it aright, for the good of others.

Verse 3

Secret sins, services, and sorrows, are under God's eye. This speaks comfort to saints, and terror to sinners.

Verse 4

A good tongue is healing to wounded consciences, by comforting them; to sin-sick souls, by convincing them; and it reconciles parties at variance.

Verse 5

If instruction is despised, reprove men rather than suffer them to go on undisturbed in the way to ruin.

Verse 6

The wealth of worldly men increases their fears and suspicions, adds strength to their passions, and renders the fear of death more distressing.

Verse 7

We use knowledge aright when we disperse it; but the heart of the foolish has nothing to disperse that is good.

Verses 8, 9

The wicked put other things in the stead of Christ's atonement, or in the place of holy obedience. Praying graces are his gift, and the work of his Spirit, with which he is well pleased.

Verse 10

He that hates reproof shall perish in his sins, since he would not be parted from them.

Verse 11

There is nothing that can be hid from the eyes of God, not even man's thoughts.

Verse 12

A scorner cannot bear to reflect seriously within his own heart.

Verse 13

A gloomy, impatient, unthankful spirit, springing from pride and undue attachment to worldly objects, renders a man uneasy to himself and others.

Verse 14

A wise man seeks to gain more wisdom, growing in grace and in the knowledge of Christ. But a carnal mind rests contented, flattering itself.

Verse 15

Some are much in affliction, and of a sorrowful spirit. Such are to be pitied, prayed for, and comforted. And others serve God with gladness of heart, and it prompts their obedience, yet they should rejoice with trembling.

Verses 16, 17

Believers often have enough when worldly eyes see little; the Lord is with them, without the cares, troubles, and temptations which are with the wealth of the wicked.

Verse 18

He that is slow to anger, not only prevents strife, but appeases it, if kindled.

Verse 19

Those who have no heart to their work, pretend that they cannot do their work without hardship and danger. And thus many live always in doubt about their state, because always in neglect of some duty.

Verse 20

Those who treat an aged mother or a father with contempt or neglect, show their own folly.

Verse 21

Such as are truly wise, study that their thoughts, words, and actions should be regular, sincere, and holy.

Verse 22

If men will not take time and pains to deliberate, they are not likely to bring any thing to pass.

Verse 23

Wisdom is needed to suit our discourse to the occasions.

Verse 24

A good man sets his affections on things above; his way leads directly thither.

Verse 25

Pride is the ruin of multitudes. But those who are in affliction God will support.

Verse 26

The thoughts of wicked men offend Him who knows the heart.

Verse 27

The covetous man lets none of his family have rest or enjoyment. And greediness of gain often tempts to projects that bring ruin.

Verse 28

A good man is proved to be a wise man by this; he governs his tongue well.

Verse 29

God sets himself at a distance from those who set him at defiance.

Verse 30

How delightful to the humbled soul to hear the good report of salvation by the Lord Jesus Christ!

Verse 31

Faithful, friendly reproofs help spiritual life, and lead to eternal life.

Verse 32

Sinners undervalue their own souls; therefore they prefer the body before the soul, and wrong the soul to please the body.

Verse 33

The fear of the Lord will dispose us to search the Scriptures with reverence; and it will cause us to follow the leadings of the Holy Spirit. While we humbly place all our dependence on the grace of God, we are exalted in the righteousness of Christ.

Chapter 16

Verse 1

The renewing grace of God alone prepares the heart for every good work. This teaches us that we are not sufficient of ourselves to think or speak any thing wise and good.

Verse 2

Ignorance, pride, and self-flattery render us partial judges respecting our own conduct.

Verse 3

Roll the burden of thy care upon God, and leave it with him, by faith and dependence on him.

Verse 4

God makes use of the wicked to execute righteous vengeance on each other; and he will be glorified by their destruction at last.

Verse 5

Though sinners strengthen themselves and one another, they shall not escape God's judgments.

Verse 6

By the mercy and truth of God in Christ Jesus, the sins of believers are taken away, and the power of sin is broken.

Verse 7

He that has all hearts in his hand, can make a man's enemies to be at peace with him.

Verse 8

A small estate, honestly come by, will turn to better account than a great estate ill-gotten.

Verse 9

If men make God's glory their end, and his will their rule, he will direct their steps by his Spirit and grace. **10**. Let kings and judges of the earth be just, and rule in the fear of God.

Verse 11

To observe justice in dealings between man and man is God's appointment.

Verse 12

The ruler that uses his power aright, will find that to be his best security.

Verse 13

Put those in power who know how to speak to the purpose.

Verses 14, 15

Those are fools, who, to obtain the favour of an earthly prince, throw themselves out of God's favour.

Verse 16

There is joy and satisfaction of spirit, only in getting wisdom.

Verse 17

A sincerely religious man keeps at a distance from every appearance of evil. Happy is the man that walks in Christ, and is led by the Spirit of Christ.

Verse 18

When men defy God's judgments, and think themselves far from them, it is a sign they are at the door. Let us not fear the pride of others, but fear pride in ourselves.

Verse 19

Humility, though it exposes to contempt in the world, is much better than high-spiritedness, which makes God an enemy. He that understands God's word shall find good.

Verse 21

The man whose wisdom dwells in his heart, will be found more truly prudent than many who possess shining talents.

Verse 22

As waters to a thirsty land, so is a wise man to his friends and neighbours.

Verse 23

The wise man's self-knowledge, always suggests something proper to be spoken to others.

Verse 24

The word of God cures the diseases that weaken our souls.

Verse 25

This is caution to all, to take heed of deceiving themselves as to their souls.

Verse 26

We must labour for the meat which endureth to everlasting life, or we must perish.

Verses 27, 28

Ungodly men bestow more pains to do mischief than would be needful to do good. The whisperer separates friends: what a hateful, but how common a character!

Verses 29, 30

Some do all the mischief they can by force and violence, and are blind to the result.

Verse 31

Old people especially should be found in the way of religion and godliness.

Verse 32

To overcome our own passions, requires more steady management, than obtaining victory over an enemy.

Verse 33

All the disposal of Providence concerning our affairs, we must look upon to be the determining what we referred to God; and we must be reconciled to them accordingly. Blessed are those that give themselves up to the will of God; for he knows what is good for them.

Chapter 17

Verse 1

These words recommend family love and peace, as needful for the comfort of human life.

Verse 2

The wise servant is more deserving, and more likely to appear one of the family, than a profligate son.

Verse 3

God tries the heart by affliction. He thus has often shown the sin remaining in the heart of the believer.

Verse 4

Flatterers, especially false teachers, are welcome to those that live in sin.

Verse 5

Those that laugh at poverty, treat God's providence and precepts with contempt.

Verse 6

It is an honour to children to have wise and godly parents continued to them, even after they are grown up and settled in the world.

Verse 7

A fool, in Solomon's Proverbs, signifies a wicked man, whom excellent speech does not become, because his conversation contradicts it.

Verse 8

Those who set their hearts upon money, will do any thing for it. What influence should the gifts of God have on our hearts!

Verse 9

The way to preserve peace is to make the best of every thing; not to notice what has been said or done against ourselves.

Verse 10

A gentle reproof will enter, not only into the head, but into the heart of a wise man.

Verse 11

Satan, and the messengers of Satan, shall be let loose upon an evil man.

Verse 12

Let us watch over our own passions, and avoid the company of furious men.

Verse 13

To render evil for good is devilish. He that does so, brings a curse upon his family.

Verse 14

What danger there is in the beginning of strife! Resist its earliest display; and leave it off, if it were possible, before you begin.

Verse 15

It is an offence to God to acquit the guilty, or to condemn those who are not guilty.

Verse 16

Man's neglect of God's favour and his own interest is very absurd.

Verse 17

No change of outward circumstances should abate our affection for our friends or relatives. But no friend, except Christ, deserves unlimited confidence. In Him this text did receive, and still receives its most glorious fulfilment.

Verse 18

Let not any wrong their families. Yet Christ's becoming Surety for men, was a glorious display of Divine wisdom; for he was able to discharge the bond.

Verse 19

If we would keep a clear conscience and a quiet mind, we must shun all excitements to anger. And a man who affects a style of living above his means, goes the way to ruin.

Verse 20

There is nothing got by ill designs. And many have paid dear for an unbridled tongue.

Verse 21

This speaks very plainly what many wise and good men feel very strongly, how grievous it is to have a foolish, wicked child.

Verse 22

It is great mercy that God gives us leave to be cheerful, and cause to be cheerful, if by his grace he gives us hearts to be cheerful.

Verse 23

The wicked are ready to part with their money, though loved, that they may not suffer for their crimes.

Verse 24

The prudent man keeps the word of God continually in view. But the foolish man cannot fix his thoughts, nor pursue any purpose with steadiness.

Verse 25

Wicked children despise the authority of their father, and the tenderness of their mother.

Verse 26

It is very wrong to find fault for doing what is duty.

Verses 27, 28

A man may show himself to be a wise man, by the good temper of his mind, and by the good government of his tongue. He is careful when he does speak, to speak to the purpose. God knows his heart, and the folly that is bound there; therefore he cannot be deceived in his judgment as men may be.

Chapter 18

Verse 1

If we would get knowledge and grace, we must try all methods of improving ourselves.

Verse 2

Those make nothing to purpose, of learning or religion, whose only design is to have something to make a show with.

Verse 3

As soon as sin entered, shame followed.

Verse 4

The well-spring of wisdom in the heart of a believer, continually supplies words of wisdom.

Verse 5

The merits of a cause must be looked to, not the person.

Verses 6, 7

What mischief bad men do to themselves by their ungoverned tongues!

Verse 8

How base are those that sow contention! and what fatal effects may be expected from small beginnings of jealousy!

Verse 9

Omissions of duty, and in duty, are fatal to the soul, as well as commissions of sin.

Verses 10, 11

The Divine power, made known in and through our Lord Jesus Christ, forms a strong tower for the believer, who relies on the Lord. How deceitful the defence of the rich man, who has his portion and treasure in this world! It is a strong city and a high wall only in his own conceit; for it will fail when most in need. They will be exposed to the just wrath of that Judge whom they despised as a Saviour.

Verse 12

After the heart has been lifted up with pride, a fall comes. But honour shall be the reward of humility.

Verse 13

Eagerness, with self-conceit, will expose to shame.

Verse 14

Firmness of mind supports under many pains and trials. But when the conscience is tortured with remorse, no human fortitude can bear the misery; what then will hell be?

Verse 15

We must get knowledge, not only into our heads, but into our hearts.

Verse 16

Blessed be the Lord, who makes us welcome to come to his throne, without money and without price. May his gifts make room for him in our souls.

Verse 17

It is well to listen to our enemies, that we may form a better judgment of ourselves.

Verse 18

It was customary sometimes to refer matters to God, by casting lots, with solemn prayer. The profaning the lot, by using it in matters of diversion, or coveting what belongs to others, forms an objection to this now.

Verse 19

Great care must be taken to prevent quarrels among relations and those under obligations to each other. Wisdom and grace make it easy to forgive; but corruption makes it difficult.

Verse 20

The belly is here put for the heart, as elsewhere; and what that is filled with, our satisfaction will be accordingly, and our inward peace.

Verse 21

Many a one has caused his own death, or the death of others, by a false or injurious tongue.

Verse 22

A good wife is a great blessing to a man, and it is a token of Divine favour.

Verse 23

Poverty tells men they must not order or demand. And at the throne of God's grace we are all poor, and must use entreaties.

Verse 24

Christ Jesus never will forsake those who trust in and love him. May we be such friends to others, for our Master's sake. Having loved his own, which were in the world, he loved them unto the end; and we are his friends if we do whatever he commands us, Joh **15**:**14**.

Chapter 19

Verse 1

A poor man who fears God, is more honourable and happy, than a man without wisdom and grace, however rich or advanced in rank.

Verse 2

What good can the soul do, if without knowledge? And he sins who will not take time to ponder the path of his feet.

Verse 3

Men run into troubles by their own folly, and then fret at the appointments of God.

Verse 4

Here we may see how strong is men's love of money.

Verse 5

Those that tell lies in discourse, are in a fair way to be guilty of bearing false-witness.

Verse 6

We are without excuse if we do not love God with all our hearts. His gifts to us are past number, and all the gifts of men to us are fruits of his bounty.

Verse 7

Christ was left by all his disciples; but the Father was with him. It encourages our faith that he had so large an experience of the sorrows of poverty.

Verse 8

Those only love their souls aright that get true wisdom.

Verse 9

Lying is a damning, destroying sin.

Verse 10

A man that has not wisdom and grace, has no right or title to true joy. It is very unseemly for one who is a servant to sin, to oppress God's free-men.

Verse 11

He attains the most true glory who endeavours most steadily to overcome evil with good.

Verse 12

Christ is a King, whose wrath against his enemies will be as the roaring of a lion, and his favour to his people as the refreshing dew.

Verse 13

It shows the vanity of the world, that we are liable to the greatest griefs where we promise ourselves the greatest comfort.

Verse 14

A discreet and virtuous wife is more valuable than house and riches.

Verse 15

A sluggish, slothful disposition makes men poor; it brings them to want. And this applies both to the present life and that which is to come.

Verse 16

If we keep God's word, God's word will keep us from every thing really hurtful. We abuse the doctrine of free grace, if we think that it does away the necessity and advantage of obedience. Those that live at random must die. This truth is clearly taught in words enough to alarm the stoutest sinner.

Verse 17

God has chosen the poor of this world, to be rich in faith, and heirs of his kingdom.

Verse 18

When parents keep under foolish tenderness, they do their best to render children a comfort to them, and happy in themselves.

Verse 19

The spared and spoiled child is likely to become a man of great wrath.

Verse 20

Those that would be wise in their latter end, must be taught and ruled when young.

Verse 21

What should we desire, but that all our purposes may agree with God's holy will?

Verse 22

It is far better to have a heart to do good, and want ability for it, than to have ability for it, and want a heart to it.

Verse 23

Those that live in the fear of God, shall get safety, satisfaction, and true and complete happiness.

Verse 24

Indolence, when indulged, so grows upon people, that they have no heart to do the most needful things for themselves.

Verse 25

A gentle rebuke goes farthest with a man of understanding.

Verse 26

The young man who wastes his father's substance, or makes his aged mother destitute, is hateful, and will come to disgrace.

Verse 27

It is the wisdom of young men to dread hearing such talk as puts loose and evil principles into the mind.

Verse 28

Those are the worst of sinners, who are glad of an opportunity to sin.

Verse 29

The unbelief of man shall not make God's threatenings of no effect. Christ himself, when bearing sins not his own, was not spared. Justice and judgment took hold of our blessed Surety; and will God spare obstinate sinners?

Chapter 20

Verse 1

It seems hard to believe that men of the greatest abilities, as well as the ignorant, should render themselves fools and madmen, merely for the taste or excitement produced by strong liquors.

Verse 2

How formidable kings are to those who provoke them! how much more foolish then is it to provoke the King of kings!

Verse 3

To engage in quarrels is the greatest folly that can be. Yield, and even give up just demands, for peace' sake.

Verse 4

He who labours and endures hardship in his seed-time for eternity, will be properly diligent as to his earthly business.

Verse 5

Though many capable of giving wise counsel are silent, yet something may be drawn from them, which will reward those who obtain it.

Verse 6

It is hard to find those that have done, and will do more good than they speak, or care to hear spoken of.

Verse 7

A good man is not liable to uneasiness in contriving what he shall do, or in reflecting on what he has done, as those who walk in deceit. And his family fare better for his sake.

Verse 8

If great men are good men, they may do much good, and prevent very much evil.

Verse 9

Some can say, Through grace, we are cleaner than we have been; but it was the work of the Holy Spirit.

Verse 10

See the various deceits men use, of which the love of money is the root. The Lord will not bless what is thus gotten.

Verse 11

Parents should observe their children, that they may manage them accordingly.

Verse 12

All our powers and faculties are from God, and are to be employed for him.

Verse 13

Those that indulge themselves, may expect to want necessaries, which should have been gotten by honest labour.

Verse 14

Men use arts to get a good bargain, and to buy cheap; whereas a man ought to be ashamed of a fraud and a lie.

Verse 15

He that prefers true knowledge to riches, follows the ways of religion and happiness. If we really believed this truth, the word of God would be valued as it deserves, and the world would lose its tempting influence.

Verse 16

Those ruin themselves who entangle themselves in rash suretiship. Also those who are in league with abandoned women. Place no confidence in either.

Verse 17

Wealth gotten by fraud may be sweet, for the carnal mind takes pleasure in the success of wicked devices; but it will be bitter in the reflection.

Verse 18

Especially we need advice in spiritual warfare. The word and Spirit of God are the best counsellors in every point.

Verse 19

Those dearly buy their own praise, who put confidence in a man because he speaks fairly.

Verse 20

An undutiful child will become very miserable. Never let him expect any peace or comfort.

Verse 21

An estate suddenly raised, is often as suddenly ruined.

Verse 22

Wait on the Lord, attend his pleasure, and he will protect thee.

Verse 23

A bargain made by fraud will prove a losing bargain in the end.

Verse 24

How can we form plans, and conduct business, independently of the Lord?

Verse 25

The evasions men often use with their own consciences show how false and deceitful man is.

Verse 26

Justice should crush the wicked, and separate them from the virtuous.

Verse 27

The rational soul and conscience are as a lamp within us, which should be used in examining our dispositions and motives with the revealed will of God.

Verse 28

Mercy and truth are the glories of God's throne.

Verse 29

Both young and old have their advantages; and let neither despise or envy the other.

Verse 30

Severe rebukes sometimes do a great deal of good. But such is the corruption of nature, that men are loth to be rebuked for their sins. If God uses severe afflictions, to purify our hearts and fit us for his service, we have cause to be very thankful.

Chapter 21

Verse 1

The believer, perceiving that the Lord rules every heart as he sees fit, like the husbandman who turns the water through his grounds as he pleases, seeks to have his own heart, and the hearts of others, directed in his faith, fear, and love.

Verse 2

We are partial in judging ourselves and our actions.

Verse 3

Many deceive themselves with a conceit that outward devotions will excuse unrighteousness.

Verse 4

Sin is the pride, the ambition, the glory, the joy, and the business of wicked men.

Verse 5

The really diligent employ foresight as well as labour.

Verse 6

While men seek wealth by unlawful practices, they seek death.

Verse 7

Injustice will return upon the sinner, and will destroy him here and for ever.

Verse 8

The way of mankind by nature is froward and strange.

Verse 9

It is best to shun bitter contention by pouring out the heart before God. For by prudence and patience, with constant prayer, the cross may be removed.

Verse 10

The evil desires of a wicked man's heart, lead to baseness in his conduct.

Verse 11

The simple may be made wise by punishments on the wicked, and by instructions to those who are willing to be taught.

Verse 12

Good men envy not the prosperity of evil-doers; they see there is a curse on them.

Verse 13

Such as oppress the poor by beating down wages, such as will not relieve according to their ability those in distress, and those in authority who neglect to do justice, stop their ears at the cry of the poor. But doubtless care is to be used in the exercise of charity.

Verse 14

If money can conquer the fury of the passions, shall reason, the fear of God, and the command of Christ, be too weak to bridle them?

Verse 15

There is true pleasure only in the practice of religion.

Verse 16

Of all wanderers in the ways of sin, those are in the most dangerous condition who turn aside into the ways of darkness. Yet there is hope even for them in the all-sufficient Saviour; but let them flee to him without delay.

Verse 17

A life of worldly pleasure brings ruin on men.

Verse 18

The righteous is often delivered out of trouble, and the wicked comes in his stead, and so seems as a ransom for him.

Verse 19

Unbridled passions spoil the comfort of all relations.

Verse 20

The plenty obtained by prudence, industry, and frugality, is desirable. But the foolish misspend what they have upon their lusts.

Verse 21

True repentance and faith will lead him that relies on the mercy of God in Christ, to follow after righteousness and mercy in his own conduct.

Verse 22

Those that have wisdom, often do great things, even against those confident of their strength.

Verse 23

It is our great concern to keep our souls from being entangled and disquieted.

Verse 24

Pride and haughtiness make men passionate; such continually deal in wrath, as if it were their trade to be angry.

Verses 25, 26

Here is the misery of the slothful; their hands refuse to labour in an honest calling, by which they might get an honest livelihood; yet their hearts cease not to covet riches, pleasures, and honours, which cannot be obtained without labour. But the righteous and industrious have their desires satisfied.

Verse 27

When holiness is pretended, but wickedness intended, that especially is an abomination.

Verse 28

The doom of a false witness is certain.

Verse 29

A wicked man bids defiance to the terrors of the law and the rebukes of Providence. But a good man asks, What does God require of me?

Verses 30, 31

Means are to be used, but, after all, our safety and salvation are only of the Lord. In our spiritual warfare we must arm ourselves with the whole armour of God; but our strength must be in the Lord, and in the power of his might.

Chapter 22

Verse 1

We should be more careful to do that by which we may get and keep a good name, than to raise or add unto a great estate.

Verse 2

Divine Providence has so ordered it, that some are rich, and others poor, but all are guilty before God; and at the throne of God's grace the poor are as welcome as the rich.

Verse 3

Faith foresees the evil coming upon sinners, and looks to Jesus Christ as the sure refuge from the storm.

Verse 4

Where the fear of God is, there will be humility. And much is to be enjoyed by it; spiritual riches, and eternal life at last.

Verse 5

The way of sin is vexatious and dangerous. But the way of duty is safe and easy.

Verse 6

Train children, not in the way they would go, that of their corrupt hearts, but in the way they should go; in which, if you love them, you would have them go. As soon as possible every child should be led to the knowledge of the Saviour.

Verse 7

This shows how important it is for every man to keep out of debt. As to the things of this life, there is a difference between the rich and the poor; but let the poor remember, it is the Lord that made the difference.

Verse 8

The power which many abuse, will soon fail them.

Verse 9

He that seeks to relieve the wants and miseries of others shall be blessed.

Verse 10

Profane scoffers and revilers disturb the peace.

Verse 11

God will be the Friend of a man in whose spirit there is no guile; this honour have all the saints.

Verse 12

God turns the counsels and designs of treacherous men to their own confusion.

Verse 13

The slothful man talks of a lion without, but considers not his real danger from the devil, that roaring lion within, and from his own slothfulness, which kills him.

Verse 14

The vile sin of licentiousness commonly besots the mind beyond recovery.

Verse 15

Sin is foolishness, it is in the heart, there is an inward inclination to sin: children bring it into the world with them; and it cleaves close to the soul. We all need to be corrected by our heavenly Father.

Verse 16

We are but stewards, and must distribute what God intrusts to our care, according to his will.

Verses 17–21

To these words, to this knowledge, the ear must be bowed down, and the heart applied by faith and love. To live a life of delight in God and dependence on him, is the foundation of all practical religion. The way to know the certainty of the word of truth, is to make conscience of our duty.

Verses 22, 23

He that robs and oppresses the poor, does so at his peril. And if men will not appear for them, God will.

Verses 24, 25

Our corrupt hearts have so much tinder in them, that it is dangerous to have to do with those that throw about the sparks of their passion.

Verses 26, 27

Every man ought to be just to himself, and his family; those are not so, who, by folly or other carelessness, waste what they have.

Verse 28

We are taught not to trespass on another man's right. And it is hard to find a truly industrious man. Such a man will rise. Seest thou a man diligent in the business of religion? He is likely to excel. Let us then be diligent in God's work.

Chapter 23

Verses 1–3

God's restraints of the appetite only say, Do thyself no harm.

Verses 4, 5

Be not of those that will be rich. The things of this world are not happiness and a portion for a soul; those that hold them ever so fast, cannot hold them always, cannot hold them long.

Verses 6–8

Do not make thyself burdensome to any, especially those not sincere. When we are called by God to his feast, and to let our souls delight themselves, Isa **25**:**6**; **55**:**2**, we may safely partake of the Bread of life.

Verse 9

It is our duty to take all fit occasions to speak of Divine things; but if what a wise man says will not be heard, let him hold his peace.

Verses 10, 11

The fatherless are taken under God's special protection. He is their Redeemer, who will take their part; and he is mighty, almighty.

Verses 12–16

Here is a parent instructing his child to give his mind to the Scriptures. Here is a parent correcting his child: accompanied with prayer, and blessed of God, it may prove a means of preventing his destruction. Here is a parent encouraging his child, telling him what would be for his good. And what a comfort it would be, if herein he answered his expectation!

Verses 17, 18

The believer's expectation shall not be disappointed; the end of his trials, and of the sinner's prosperity, is at hand.

Verses 19–28

The gracious Saviour who purchased pardon and peace for his people, with all the affection of a tender parent, counsels us to hear and be wise, and is ready to guide our hearts in his way. Here we have an earnest call to young people, to attend to the advice of their godly parents. If the heart be guided, the steps will be guided. Buy the truth, and sell it not; be willing to part with any thing for it. Do not part with it for pleasures, honours, riches, or any thing in this world. The heart is what the great God requires. We must not think to divide the heart between God and the world; he will have all or none. Look to the rule of God's word, the conduct of his providence, and the good examples of his people. Particular cautions are given against sins most destructive to wisdom and grace in the soul. It is really a shame to make a god of the belly. Drunkenness stupifies men, and then all goes to ruin. Licentiousness takes away the heart that should be given to God. Take heed of any approaches toward this sin, it is very hard to retreat from it. It bewitches men to their ruin.

Verses 29–35

Solomon warns against drunkenness. Those that would be kept from sin, must keep from all the beginnings of it, and fear coming within reach of its allurements. Foresee the punishment, what it will at last end in, if repentance prevent not. It makes men quarrel. Drunkards wilfully make woe and sorrow for themselves. It makes men impure and insolent. The tongue grows unruly; the heart utters things contrary to reason, religion, and common civility. It stupifies and besots men. They are in danger of death, of damnation; as much exposed as if they slept upon the top of a mast, yet feel secure. They fear no peril when the terrors of the Lord are before them; they feel no pain when the judgments of God are actually upon them. So lost is a drunkard to virtue and honour, so wretchedly is his conscience seared, that he is not ashamed to say, I will seek it again. With good reason we were bid to stop before the beginning. Who that has common sense would contract a habit, or sell himself to a sin, which tends to such guilt and misery, and exposes a man every day to the danger of dying insensible, and awaking in hell? Wisdom seems in these chapters to take up the discourse as at the beginning of the book. They must be considered as the words of Christ to the sinner.

Chapter 24

Verses 1, 2

Envy not sinners. And let not a desire ever come into thy mind, Oh that I could shake off restraints!

Verses 3–6

Piety and prudence in outward affairs, both go together to complete a wise man. By knowledge the soul is filled with the graces and comforts of the spirit, those precious and pleasant riches. The spirit is strengthened for the spiritual work and the spiritual warfare, by true wisdom.

Verses 7–9

A weak man thinks wisdom is too high for him, therefore he will take no pains for it. It is bad to do evil, but worse to devise it. Even the first risings of sin in the heart are sin, and must be repented of. Those that strive to make others hateful, make themselves so.

Verse 10

Under troubles we are apt to despair of relief. But be of good courage, and God shall strengthen thy heart.

Verses 11, 12

If a man know that his neighbour is in danger by any unjust proceeding, he is bound to do all in his power to deliver him. And what is it to suffer immortal souls to perish, when our persuasions and example may be the means of preventing it?

Verses 13, 14

We are quickened to the study of wisdom by considering both the pleasure and the profit of it. All men relish things that are sweet to the palate; but many have no relish for the things that are sweet to the purified soul, and that make us wise unto salvation.

Verses 15, 16

The sincere soul falls as a traveller may do, by stumbling at some stone in his path; but gets up, and goes on his way with more care and speed. This is rather to be understood of falls into affliction, than falls into actual sin.

Verses 17, 18

The pleasure we are apt to take in the troubles of an enemy is forbidden.

Verses 19, 20

Envy not the wicked their prosperity; be sure there is no true happiness in it.

Verses 21, 22

The godly in the land, will be quiet in the land. There may be cause to change for the better, but have nothing to do with them that are given change.

Verses 23–26

The wisdom God giveth, renders a man fit for his station. Every one who finds the benefit of the right answer, will be attached to him that gave it.

Verse 27

We must prefer necessaries before conveniences, and not go in debt.

Verses 28, 29

There are three defaults in a witness pointed out.

Verses 30–34

See what a blessing the husbandman's calling is, and what a wilderness this earth would be without it. See what great difference there is in the management even of worldly affairs. Sloth and self-indulgence are the bane of all good. When we see fields overgrown with thorns and thistles, and the fences broken down, we see an emblem of the far more deplorable state of many souls. Every vile affection grows in men's hearts; yet they compose themselves to sleep. Let us show wisdom by doubling our diligence in every good thing.

Chapter 25

Verses 1–3

God needs not search into any thing; nothing can be hid from him. But it is the honour of rulers to search out matters, to bring to light hidden works of darkness.

Verses 4, 5

For a prince to suppress vice, and reform his people, is the best way to support his government.

Verses 6, 7

Religion teaches us humility and self-denial. He who has seen the glory of the Lord in Christ Jesus, will feel his own unworthiness.

Verses 8–10

To be hasty in beginning strife, will bring into difficulties. War must at length end, and might better be prevented. It is so in private quarrels; do all thou canst to settle the matter.

Verses 11, 12

A word of counsel, or reproof, rightly spoken, is especially beautiful, as fine fruit becomes still more beautiful in silver baskets.

Verse 13

See what ought to be the aim of him that is trusted with any business; to be faithful. A faithful minister, Christ's messenger, should be thus acceptable to us.

Verse 14

He who pretends to have received or given that which he never had, is like the morning cloud, that disappoints those who look for rain.

Verse 15

Be patient to bear a present hurt. Be mild to speak without passion; for persuasive language is the most effectual to prevail over the hardened mind.

Verse 16

God has given us leave to use grateful things, but we are cautioned against excess.

Verse 17

We cannot be upon good terms with our neighbours, without discretion as well as sincerity. How much better a Friend is God than any other friend! The oftener we come to him, the more welcome.

Verse 18

A false testimony is dangerous in every thing.

Verse 19

Confidence in an unfaithful man is painful and vexatious; when we put any stress on him, he not only fails, but makes us feel for it.

Verse 20

We take a wrong course if we think to relieve those in sorrow by endeavouring to make them merry.

Verses 21, 22

The precept to love even our enemies is an Old Testament commandment. Our Saviour has shown his own great example in loving us when we were enemies.

Verse 23

Slanders would not be so readily spoken, if they were not readily heard. Sin, if it receives any check, becomes cowardly.

Verse 24

It is better to be alone, than to be joined to one who is a hinderance to the comfort of life.

Verse 25

Heaven is a country afar off; how refreshing is good news from thence, in the everlasting gospel, which signifies glad tidings, and in the witness of the Spirit with our spirits that we are God's children!

Verse 26

When the righteous are led into sin, it is as hurtful as if the public fountains were poisoned.

Verse 27

We must be, through grace, dead to the pleasures of sense, and also to the praises of men.

Verse 28

The man who has no command over his anger, is easily robbed of peace. Let us give up ourselves to the Lord, and pray him to put his Spirit within us, and cause us to walk in his statutes.

Chapter 26

Verse 1

Honour is out of season to those unworthy and unfit for it.

Verse 2

He that is cursed without cause, the curse shall do him no more harm than the bird that flies over his head.

Verse 3

Every creature must be dealt with according to its nature, but careless and profligate sinners never will be ruled by reason and persuasion. Man indeed is born like the wild ass's colt; but some, by the grace of God, are changed.

Verses 4, 5

We are to fit our remarks to the man, and address them to his conscience, so as may best end the debate.

Verses 6–9

Fools are not fit to be trusted, nor to have any honour. Wise sayings, as a foolish man delivers and applies them, lose their usefulness.

Verse 10

This **verse** may either declare how the Lord, the Creator of all men, will deal with sinners according to their guilt, or, how the powerful among men should disgrace and punish the wicked.

Verse 11

The dog is a loathsome emblem of those sinners who return to their vices, **2**Pe **2**:**22**.

Verse 12

We see many a one who has some little sense, but is proud of it. This describes those who think their spiritual state to be good, when really it is very bad.

Verse 13

The slothful man hates every thing that requires care and labour. But it is foolish to frighten ourselves from real duties by fancied difficulties. This may be applied to a man slothful in the duties of religion.

Verse 14

Having seen the slothful man in fear of his work, here we find him in love with his ease. Bodily ease is the sad occasion of many spiritual diseases. He does not care to get forward with his business. Slothful professors turn thus. The world and the flesh are hinges on which they are hung; and though they move in a course of outward services, yet they are not the nearer to heaven.

Verse 15

The sluggard is now out of his bed, but he might have lain there, for any thing he is likely to bring to pass in his work. It is common for men who will not do their duty, to pretend they cannot. Those that are slothful in religion, will not be at the pains to feed their souls with the bread of life, nor to fetch in promised blessings by prayer.

Verse 16

He that takes pains in religion, knows he is working for a good Master, and that his labour shall not be in vain.

Verse 17

To make ourselves busy in other men's matters, is to thrust ourselves into temptation.

Verses 18, 19

He that sins in jest, must repent in earnest, or his sin will be his ruin.

Verses 20–22

Contention heats the spirit, and puts families and societies into a flame. And that fire is commonly kindled and kept burning by whisperers and backbiters.

Verse 23

A wicked heart disguising itself, is like a potsherd covered with the dross of silver.

Verses 24–26

Always distrust when a man speaks fair unless you know him well. Satan, in his temptations, speaks fair, as he did to Eve; but it is madness to give credit to him.

Verse 27

What pains men take to do mischief to others! but it is digging a pit, it is rolling a stone, hard work; and they prepare mischief to themselves.

Verse 28

There are two sorts of lies equally detestable. A slandering lie, the mischief of this every body sees. A flattering lie, which secretly works ruin. A wise man will be more afraid of a flatterer than of a slanderer.

Chapter 27

Verse 1

We know not what a day may bring forth. This does not forbid preparing for to-morrow, but presuming upon to-morrow. We must not put off the great work of conversion, that one thing needful.

Verse 2

There may be occasion for us to justify ourselves, but not to praise ourselves.

Verses 3, 4

Those who have no command of their passions, sink under the load.

Verses 5, 6

Plain and faithful rebukes are better, not only than secret hatred, but than love which compliments in sin, to the hurt of the soul.

Verse 7

The poor have a better relish of their enjoyments, and are often more thankful for them, than the rich. In like manner the proud and self-sufficient disdain the gospel; but those who hunger and thirst after righteousness, find comfort from the meanest book or sermon that testifies of Christ Jesus.

Verse 8

Every man has his proper place in society, where he may be safe and comfortable.

Verses 9, 10

Depend not for relief upon a kinsman, merely for kindred's sake; apply to those who are at hand, and will help in need. But there is a Friend that sticketh closer than a brother, and let us place entire confidence in him.

Verse 11

An affectionate parent urges his son to prudent conduct that should gladden his heart. The good conduct of Christians is the best answer to all who find fault with the gospel.

Verse 12

Where there is temptation, if we thrust ourselves into it, there will be sin, and punishment will follow.

Verse 13

An honest man may be made a beggar, but he is not honest that makes himself one.

Verse 14

It is folly to be fond of being praised; it is a temptation to pride.

Verses 15, 16

The contentions of a neighbour may be like a sharp shower, troublesome for a time; the contentions of a wife are like constant rain.

Verse 17

We are cautioned to take heed whom we converse with. And directed to have in view, in conversation, to make one another wiser and better.

Verse 18

Though a calling be laborious and despised, yet those who keep to it, will find there is something to be got by it. God is a Master who has engaged to honour those who serve him faithfully.

Verse 19

One corrupt heart is like another; so are sanctified hearts: the former bear the same image of the earthly, the latter the same image of the heavenly. Let us carefully watch our own hearts, comparing them with the word of God.

Verse 20

Two things are here said to be never satisfied, death and sin. The appetites of the carnal mind for profit or pleasure are always desiring more. Those whose eyes are ever toward the Lord, are satisfied in him, and shall for ever be so.

Verse 21

Silver and gold are tried by putting them into the furnace and fining-pot; so is a man tried by praising him.

Verse 22

Some are so bad, that even severe methods do not answer the end; what remains but that they should be rejected? The new-creating power of God's grace alone is able to make a change.

Verses 23–27

We ought to have some business to do in this world, and not to live in idleness, and not to meddle with what we do not understand. We must be diligent and take pains. Let us do what we can, still the world cannot be secured to us, therefore we must choose a more lasting portion; but by the blessing of God upon our honest labours, we may expect to enjoy as much of earthly blessings as is good for us.

Chapter 28

Verse 1

Sin makes men cowards. Whatever difficulties the righteous meet in the way of duty, they are not daunted.

Verse 2

National sins disturb the public repose.

Verse 3

If needy persons get opportunities of oppressing, their extortion will be more severe than that of the more wealthy.

Verse 4

Wicked people strengthen one another in wicked ways.

Verse 5

If a man seeks the Lord, it is a good sign that he understands much, and it is a good means of understanding more.

Verse 6

An honest, godly, poor man, is better than a wicked, ungodly, rich man; has more comfort in himself, and is a greater blessing to the world.

Verse 7

Companions of riotous men not only grieve their parents, but shame them.

Verse 8

That which is ill got, though it may increase much, will not last long. Thus the poor are repaid, and God is glorified.

Verse 9

The sinner at whose prayers God is angry, is one who obstinately refuses to obey God's commands.

Verse 10

The success of ungodly men is their own misery.

Verse 11

Rich men are so flattered, that they think themselves superior to others.

Verse 12

There is glory in the land when the righteous have liberty.

Verse 13

It is folly to indulge sin, and excuse it. He who covers his sins, shall not have any true peace. He who humbly confesses his sins, with true repentance and faith, shall find mercy from God. The Son of God is our great atonement. Under a deep sense of our guilt and danger, we may claim salvation from that mercy which reigns through righteousness unto eternal life, by Jesus Christ our Lord.

Verse 14

There is a fear which causes happiness. Faith and love will deliver from the fear of eternal misery; but we should always fear offending God, and fear sinning against him.

Verse 15

A wicked ruler, whatever we may call him, this scripture calls a roaring lion, and a ranging bear.

Verse 16

Oppressors want understanding; they do not consult their own honour, ease, and safety.

Verse 17

The murderer shall be haunted with terrors. None shall desire to save him from deserved punishment, nor pity him.

Verse 18

Uprightness will give men holy security in the worst times; but the false and dishonest are never safe.

Verse 19

Those who are diligent, take the way to live comfortably.

Verse 20

The true way to be happy, is to be holy and honest; not to raise an estate suddenly, without regard to right or wrong.

Verse 21

Judgment is perverted, when any thing but pure right is considered.

Verse 22

He that hastens to be rich, never seriously thinks how quickly God may take his wealth from him, and leave him in poverty.

Verse 23

Upon reflection, most will have a better opinion of a faithful reprover than of a soothing flatterer.

Verse 24

Here is the wickedness of those who think it no sin to rob their parents, by wheedling them or threatening them, or by wasting what they have, and running into debt.

Verse 25

Those make themselves always easy, that live in continual dependence upon God and his grace, and live by faith.

Verse 26

A fool trusts to his own strength, merit, and righteousness. And trusts to his own heart, which is not only deceitful above all things, but which has often deceived him.

Verse 27

A selfish man not only will not look out for objects of compassion, but will look off from those that call for his attention.

Verse 28

When power is put into the hands of the wicked, wise men decline public business. If the reader will go diligently over this and the other chapters, in many places where at first he may suppose there is least of Christ, still he will find what will lead to him.

Chapter 29

Verse 1

If God wounds, who can heal? The word of God warns all to flee from the wrath to come, to the hope set before us in Jesus Christ.

Verse 2

The people have cause to rejoice or mourn, as their rulers are righteous or wicked.

Verse 3

Divine wisdom best keeps us from ruinous lusts.

Verse 4

The Lord Jesus is the King who will minister true judgment to the people.

Verse 5

Flatterers put men off their guard, which betrays them into foolish conduct.

Verse 6

Transgressions always end in vexations. Righteous men walk at liberty, and walk in safety.

Verse 7

This **verse** is applicable to compassion for the distress of the poor, and the unfeeling disregard shown by the wicked.

Verse 8

The scornful mock at things sacred and serious. Men who promote religion, which is true wisdom, turn away the wrath of God.

Verse 9

If a wise man dispute with a conceited wrangler, he will be treated with anger or ridicule; and no good is done.

Verse 10

Christ told his disciples that they should be hated of all men. The just, whom the blood-thirsty hate, gladly do any thing for their salvation.

Verse 11

He is a fool who tells every thing he knows, and can keep no counsel.

Verse 12

One who loves flatterers, and hearkens to slanderers, causes his servants to become liars and false accusers.

Verse 13

Some are poor, others have a great deal of deceitful riches. They meet in the business of this world; the Lord gives to both the comforts of this life. To some of both sorts he gives his grace.

Verse 14

The rich will look to themselves, but the poor and needy the prince must defend and plead for.

Verse 15

Parents must consider the benefit of due correction, and the mischief of undue indulgence.

Verse 16

Let not the righteous have their faith and hope shocked by the increase of sin and sinners, but let them wait with patience.

Verse 17

Children must not be suffered to go without rebuke when they do amiss.

Verse 18

How bare does a place look without Bibles and ministers! and what an easy prey is it to the enemy of souls! That gospel is an open vision, which holds forth Christ, which humbles the sinner and exalts the Saviour, which promotes holiness in the life and conversation: and these are precious truths to keep the soul alive, and prevent it from perishing.

Verse 19

Here is an unprofitable, slothful, wicked servant; one that serves not from conscience, or love, but from fear.

Verse 20

When a man is self-conceited, rash, and given to wrangling, there is more hope of the ignorant and profligate.

Verse 21

Good usage to a servant does not mean indulgence, which would ruin even a child. The body is a servant to the soul; those that humour it, and are over-tender of it, will find it forget its place.

Verse 22

An angry, passionate disposition makes men provoking to one another, and provoking to God.

Verse 23

Only those who humble themselves shall be exalted and established.

Verse 24

The receiver is as bad as the thief.

Verse 25

Many are ashamed to own Christ now; and he will not own them in the day of judgment. But he that trusts in the Lord will be saved from this snare.

Verse 26

The wisest course is, to look to God, and seek the favour of the Ruler of rulers; for every creature is that to us which God makes it to be.

Verse 27

The just man abhors the sins of the wicked, and shuns their company. Christ exposed the wickedness of men, yet prayed for the wicked when they were crucifying him. Hatred to sin in ourselves and others, is a needful branch of the Christian temper. But all that are unholy, have rooted hatred to godliness.

Chapter 30

Verses 1–6

Agur speaks of himself as wanting a righteousness, and having done very foolishly. And it becomes us all to have low thoughts of ourselves. He speaks of himself as wanting revelation to guide him in the ways of truth and wisdom. The more enlightened people are, the more they lament their ignorance; the more they pray for clearer, still clearer discoveries of God, and his rich grace in Christ Jesus. In ver.#(**4**), there is a prophetic notice of Him who came down from heaven to be our Instructor and Saviour, and then ascended into heaven to be our Advocate. The Messiah is here spoken of as a Person distinct from the Father, but his name as yet secret. The great Redeemer, in the glories of his providence and grace, cannot be found out to perfection. Had it not been for Christ, the foundations of the earth had sunk under the load of the curse upon the ground, for man's sin. Who, and what is the mighty One that doeth all this? There is not the least ground to suspect anything wanting in the word of God; adding to his words opens the way to errors and corruptions.

Verses 7–9

Agur wisely prayed for a middle state, that he might be kept at a distance from temptations; he asked daily bread suited to his station, his family, and his real good. There is a remarkable similarity between this prayer and several clauses of the Lord's prayer. If we are removed from vanity and lies; if we are interested in the pardoning love of Christ, and have him for our portion; if we walk with God, then we shall have all we can ask or think, as to spiritual things. When we consider how those who have abundance are prone to abuse the gift, and what it is to suffer want, Agur's prayer will ever be found a wise one, though seldom offered. Food convenient; what is so for one, may not be so for another; but we may be sure that our heavenly Father will supply all our need, and not suffer us to want anything good for us; and why should we wish for more?

Verse 10

Slander not a servant to his master, accuse him not in small matters, to make mischief.

Verses 11–14

In every age there are monsters of ingratitude who ill-treat their parents. Many persuade themselves they are holy persons, whose hearts are full of sin, and who practise secret wickedness. There are others whose lofty pride is manifest. There have also been cruel monsters in every age.

Verses 15–17

Cruelty and covetousness are two daughters of the horseleech, that still cry, "Give, give," and they are continually uneasy to themselves. Four things never are satisfied, to which these devourers are compared. Those are never rich that are always coveting. And many who have come to a bad end, have owned that their wicked courses began by despising their parents' authority.

Verses 18–20

Four things cannot be fully known. The kingdom of nature is full of marvels. The fourth is a mystery of iniquity; the cursed arts by which a vile seducer gains the affections of a female; and the arts which a vile woman uses to conceal her wickedness.

Verses 21–23

Four sorts of persons are very troublesome. Men of low origin and base spirit, who, getting authority, become tyrants. Foolish and violent men indulging in excesses. A woman of a contentious spirit and vicious habits. A servant who has obtained undue influence. Let those whom Providence has advanced from low beginnings, carefully watch against that sin which most easily besets them.

Verses 24–28

Four things that are little, are yet to be admired. There are those who are poor in the world, and of small account, yet wise for their souls and another world.

Verses 29–33

We may learn from animals to go well; also to keep our temper under all provocations. We must keep the evil thought in our minds from breaking out into evil speeches. We must not stir up the passions of others. Let nothing be said or done with violence, but every thing with softness and calmness. Alas, how often have we done foolishly in rising up against the Lord our King! Let us humble ourselves before him. And having found peace with Him, let us follow peace with all men.

Chapter 31

Verses 1–9

When children are under the mother's eye, she has an opportunity of fashioning their minds aright. Those who are grown up, should often call to mind the good teaching they received when children. The many awful instances of promising characters who have been ruined by vile women, and love of wine, should warn every one to avoid these evils. Wine is to be used for want or medicine. Every creature of God is good, and wine, though abused, has its use. By the same rule, due praise and consolation should be used as cordials to the dejected and tempted, not administered to the confident and self-sufficient. All in authority should be more carefully temperate even than other men; and should be protectors of those who are unable or afraid to plead their own cause. Our blessed Lord did not decline the bitterest dregs of the cup of sorrow put into his hands; but he puts the cup of consolation into the hands of his people, and causes those to rejoice who are in the deepest distress.

Verses 10–31

This is the description of a virtuous woman of those days, but the general outlines equally suit every age and nation. She is very careful to recommend herself to her husband's esteem and affection, to know his mind, and is willing that he rule over her. **1**. She can be trusted, and he will leave such a wife to manage for him. He is happy in her. And she makes it her constant business to do him good. **2**. She is one that takes pains in her duties, and takes pleasure in them. She is careful to fill up time, that none be lost. She rises early. She applies herself to the business proper for her, to women's business. She does what she does, with all her power, and trifles not. **3**. She makes what she does turn to good account by prudent management. Many undo themselves by buying, without considering whether they can afford it. She provides well for her house. She lays up for hereafter. **4**. She looks well to the ways of her household, that she may oblige all to do their duty to God and one another, as well as to her. **5**. She is intent upon giving as upon getting, and does it freely and cheerfully. **6**. She is discreet and obliging; every word she says, shows she governs herself by the rules of wisdom. She not only takes prudent measures herself, but gives prudent advice to others. The law of love and kindness is written in the heart, and shows itself in the tongue. Her heart is full of another world, even when her hands are most busy about this world. **7**. Above all, she fears the Lord. Beauty recommends none to God, nor is it any proof of wisdom and goodness, but it has deceived many a man who made his choice of a wife by it. But the fear of God reigning in the heart, is the beauty of the soul; it lasts for ever. **8**. She has firmness to bear up under crosses and disappointments. She shall reflect with comfort when she comes to be old, that she was not idle or useless when young. She shall rejoice in a world to come. She is a great blessing to her relations. If the fruit be good, the tree must have our good word. But she leaves it to her own works to praise her. Every one ought to desire this honour that cometh from God; and according to this standard we all ought to regulate our judgments. This description let all women daily study, who desire to be truly beloved and respected, useful and honourable. This passage is to be applied to individuals, but may it not also be applied to the church of God, which is described as a virtuous spouse? God by his grace has formed from among sinful men a church of true believers, to possess all the excellences here described.

Ecclesiastes

The name of this book signifies "The Preacher." The wisdom of God here preaches to us, speaking by Solomon, who it is evident was the author. At the close of his life, being made sensible of his sin and folly, he recorded here his experience for the benefit of others, as the book of his repentance; and he pronounced all earthly good to be "vanity and vexation of spirit." It convinces us of the vanity of the world, and that it cannot make us happy; of the vileness of sin, and its certain tendency to make us miserable. It shows that no created good can satisfy the soul, and that happiness is to be found in God alone; and this doctrine must, under the blessed Spirit's teaching, lead the heart to Christ Jesus.

Chapter 1

Solomon shows that all human things are vain. (Eccl. **1**:**1-3**) Man's toil and want of satisfaction. (Eccl. **1**:**4-8**) There is nothing new. (Eccl. **1**:**9-11**) The vexation in pursuit of knowledge. (Eccl. **1**:**12-18**)

Eccl. **1**:**1-3** Much is to be learned by comparing one part of Scripture with another. We here behold Solomon returning from the broken and empty cisterns of the world, to the Fountain of living water; recording his own folly and shame, the bitterness of his disappointment, and the lessons he had learned. Those that have taken warning to turn and live, should warn others not to go on and die. He does not merely say all things are vain, but that they are vanity. VANITY OF VANITIES, ALL IS VANITY. This is the text of the preacher's sermon, of which in this book he never loses sight. If this world, in its present state, were all, it would not be worth living for; and the wealth and pleasure of this world, if we had ever so much, are not enough to make us happy. What profit has a man of all his labour? All he gets by it will not supply the wants of the soul, nor satisfy its desires; will not atone for the sins of the soul, nor hinder the loss of it: what profit will the wealth of the world be to the soul in death, in judgment, or in the everlasting state?

Eccl. **1**:**4-8** All things change, and never rest. Man, after all his labour, is no nearer finding rest than the sun, the wind, or the current of the river. His soul will find no rest, if he has it not from God. The senses are soon tired, yet still craving what is untried.

Eccl. **1**:**9-11** Men's hearts and their corruptions are the same now as in former times; their desires, and pursuits, and complaints, still the same. This should take us from expecting happiness in the creature, and quicken us to seek eternal blessings. How many things and persons in Solomon's day were thought very great, yet there is no remembrance of them now!

Eccl. **1**:**12-18** Solomon tried all things, and found them vanity. He found his searches after knowledge weariness, not only to the flesh, but to the mind. The more he saw of the works done under the sun, the more he saw their vanity; and the sight often vexed his spirit. He could neither gain that satisfaction to himself, nor do that good to others, which he expected. Even the pursuit of knowledge and wisdom discovered man's wickedness and misery; so that the more he knew, the more he saw cause to lament and mourn. Let us learn to hate and fear sin, the cause of all this vanity and misery; to value Christ; to seek rest in the knowledge, love, and service of the Saviour.

Chapter 2

The vanity and vexation of mirth, sensual pleasure, riches, and pomp. (Eccl. **2**:**1-11**) Human wisdom insufficient. (Eccl. **2**:**12-17**) This world to be used according to the will of God. (Eccl. **2**:**18-26**)

Eccl. **2**:**1-11** Solomon soon found mirth and pleasure to be vanity. What does noisy, flashy mirth towards making a man happy? The manifold devices of men's hearts, to get satisfaction from the world, and their changing from one thing to another, are like the restlessness of a man in a fever. Perceiving it was folly to give himself to wine, he next tried the costly amusements of princes. The poor, when they read such a description, are ready to feel discontent. But the remedy against all such feelings is in the estimate of it all by the owner himself. All was vanity and vexation of spirit: and the same things would yield the same result to us, as to Solomon. Having food and raiment, let us therewith be content. His wisdom remained with him; a strong understanding, with great human knowledge. But every earthly pleasure, when unconnected with better blessings, leaves the mind as eager and unsatisfied as before. Happiness arises not from the situation in which we are placed. It is only through Jesus Christ that final blessedness can be attained.

Eccl. **2**:**12-17** Solomon found that knowledge and prudence were preferable to ignorance and folly, though human wisdom and knowledge will not make a man happy. The most learned of men, who dies a stranger to Christ Jesus, will perish equally with the most ignorant; and what good can commendations on earth do to the body in the grave, or the soul in hell? And the spirits of just men made perfect cannot want them. So that if this were all, we might be led to hate our life, as it is all vanity and vexation of spirit.

Eccl. **2**:**18-26** Our hearts are very loth to quit their expectations of great things from the creature; but Solomon came to this at length. The world is a vale of tears, even to those that have much of it. See what fools they are, who make themselves drudges to the world, which affords a man nothing better than subsistence for the body. And the utmost he can attain in this respect is to allow himself a sober, cheerful use thereof, according to his rank and condition. But we must enjoy good in our labour; we must use those things to make us diligent and cheerful in worldly business. And this is the gift of God. Riches are a blessing or a curse to a man, according as he has, or has not, a heart to make a good use of them. To those that are accepted of the Lord, he gives joy and satisfaction in the knowledge and love of him. But to the sinner he allots labour, sorrow, vanity, and vexation, in seeking a worldly portion, which yet afterwards comes into better hands. Let the sinner seriously consider his latter end. To seek a lasting portion in the love of Christ and the blessings it bestows, is the only way to true and satisfying enjoyment even of this present world.

Chapter 3

The changes of human affairs. (Eccl. **3**:**1-10**) The Divine counsels unchangeable. (Eccl. **3**:**11-15**) The vanity of worldly power. (Eccl. **3**:**16-22**)

Eccl. **3**:**1-10** To expect unchanging happiness in a changing world, must end in disappointment. To bring ourselves to our state in life, is our duty and wisdom in this world. God's whole plan for the government of the world will be found altogether wise, just, and good. Then let us seize the favourable opportunity for every good purpose and work. The time to die is fast approaching. Thus labour and sorrow fill the world. This is given us, that we may always have something to do; none were sent into the world to be idle.

Eccl. **3**:**11-15** Every thing is as God made it; not as it appears to us. We have the world so much in our hearts, are so taken up with thoughts and cares of worldly things, that we have neither time nor spirit to see God's hand in them. The world has not only gained possession of the heart, but has formed thoughts against the beauty of God's works. We mistake if we think we were born for ourselves; no, it is our business to do good in this life, which is short and uncertain; we have but little time to be doing good, therefore we should redeem time. Satisfaction with Divine Providence, is having faith that all things work together for good to them that love him. God doeth all, that men should fear before him. The world, as it has been, is, and will be. There has no change befallen us, nor has any temptation by it taken us, but such as is common to men.

Eccl. **3**:**16-22** Without the fear of the Lord, man is but vanity; set that aside, and judges will not use their power well. And there is another Judge that stands before the door. With God there is a time for the redressing of grievances, though as yet we see it not. Solomon seems to express his wish that men might perceive, that by choosing this world as their portion, they brought themselves to a level with the beasts, without being free, as they are, from present vexations and a future account. Both return to the dust from whence they were taken. What little reason have we to be proud of our bodies, or bodily accomplishments! But as none can fully comprehend, so few consider properly, the difference between the rational soul of man, and the spirit or life of the beast. The spirit of man goes upward, to be judged, and is then fixed in an unchangeable state of happiness or misery. It is as certain that the spirit of the beast goes downward to the earth; it perishes at death. Surely their case is lamentable, the height of whose hopes and wishes is, that they may die like beasts. Let our inquiry be, how an eternity of existence may be to us an eternity of enjoyment? To answer this, is the grand design of revelation. Jesus is revealed as the Son of God, and the Hope of sinners.

Chapter 4

Miseries from oppression. (Eccl. **4**:**1-3**) troubles from envy. (Eccl. **4**:**4-6**) The folly of covetousness. (Eccl. **4**:**7**,**8**) The advantages of mutual assistance. (Eccl. **4**:**9-12**) the changes of royalty. (Eccl. **4**:**13-16**)

Eccl. **4**:**1-3** It grieved Solomon to see might prevail against right. Wherever we turn, we see melancholy proofs of the wickedness and misery of mankind, who try to create trouble to themselves and to each other. Being thus hardly used, men are tempted to hate and despise life. But a good man, though badly off while in this world, cannot have cause to wish he had never been born, since he is glorifying the Lord, even in the fires, and will be happy at last, for ever happy. Ungodly men have most cause to wish the continuance of life with all its vexations, as a far more miserable condition awaits them if they die in their sins. If human and worldly things were our chief good, not to exist would be preferable to life, considering the various oppressions here below.

Eccl. **4**:**4-6** Solomon notices the sources of trouble peculiar to well-doers, and includes all who labour with diligence, and whose efforts are crowned with success. They often become great and prosperous, but this excites envy and opposition. Others, seeing the vexations of an active course, foolishly expect more satisfaction in sloth and idleness. But idleness is a sin that is its own punishment. Let us by honest industry lay hold on the handful, that we may not want necessaries, but not grasp at both hands full, which would only create vexation of spirit. Moderate pains and gains do best.

Eccl. **4**:**7**,**8** Frequently, the more men have, the more they would have; and on this they are so intent, that they get no enjoyment from what they have. Selfishness is the cause of this evil. A selfish man cares for nobody; there is none to take care of but himself, yet he will scarcely allow necessary rest to himself, and the people he employs. He never thinks he has enough. He has enough for his calling, for his family, but he has not enough for his eyes. Many are so set upon the world, that in pursuit of it they bereave themselves, not only of the favour of God and eternal life, but of the pleasures of this life. The distant relations or strangers who inherit such a man's wealth, never thank him. Covetousness gathers strength by time and habit; men tottering on the brink of the grave, grow more grasping and griping. Alas, and how often do we see men professing to be followers of Him, who, "though he was rich, for our sakes became poor," anxiously scraping money together and holding it fast, excusing themselves by common-place talking about the necessity of care, and the danger of extravagance!

Eccl. **4**:**9-12** Surely he has more satisfaction in life, who labours hard to maintain those he loves, than the miser has in his toil. In all things union tends to success and safety, but above all, the union of Christians. They assist each other by encouragement, or friendly reproof. They warm each other's hearts while they **converse** together of the love of Christ, or join in singing his praises. Then let us improve our opportunities of Christian fellowship. In these things all is not vanity, though there will be some alloy as long as we are under the sun. Where two are closely joined in holy love and fellowship, Christ will by his Spirit come to them; then there is a threefold cord.

Eccl. **4**:**13-16** People are never long easy and satisfied; they are fond of changes. This is no new thing. Princes see themselves slighted by those they have studied to oblige; this is vanity and vexation of spirit. But the willing servants of the Lord Jesus, our King, rejoice in him alone, and they will love Him more and more to all eternity.

Chapter 5

What renders devotion vain. (Eccl. **5**:**1-3**) Of vows, and oppression. (Eccl. **5**:**4-8**) the vanity of riches shown. (Eccl. **5**:**9-7**) The right use of riches. (Eccl. **5**:**18-20**)

Eccl. **5**:**1-3** Address thyself to the worship of God, and take time to compose thyself for it. Keep thy thoughts from roving and wandering: keep thy affections from running out toward wrong objects. We should avoid vain repetitions; copious prayers are not here condemned, but those that are unmeaning. How often our wandering thoughts render attendance on Divine ordinances little better than the sacrifice of fools! Many words and hasty ones, used in prayer, show folly in the heart, low thoughts of God, and careless thoughts of our own souls.

Eccl. **5**:**4-8** When a person made engagements rashly, he suffered his mouth to cause his flesh to sin. The case supposes a man coming to the priest, and pretending that his vow was made rashly, and that it would be wrong to fulfil it. Such mockery of God would bring the Divine displeasure, which might blast what was thus unduly kept. We are to keep down the fear of man. Set God before thee; then, if thou seest the oppression of the poor, thou wilt not find fault with Divine Providence; nor think the worse of the institution of magistracy, when thou seest the ends of it thus perverted; nor of religion, when thou seest it will not secure men from suffering wrong. But though oppressors may be secure, God will reckon for all.

Eccl. **5**:**9-17** The goodness of Providence is more equally distributed than appears to a careless observer. The king needs the common things of life, and the poor share them; they relish their morsel better than he does his luxuries. There are bodily desires which silver itself will not satisfy, much less will worldly abundance satisfy spiritual desires. The more men have, the better house they must keep, the more servants they must employ, the more guests they must entertain, and the more they will have hanging on them. The sleep of the labourer is sweet, not only because he is tired, but because he has little care to break his sleep. The sleep of the diligent Christian, and his long sleep, are sweet; having spent himself and his time in the service of God, he can cheerfully repose in God as his Rest. But those who have every thing else, often fail to secure a good night's sleep; their abundance breaks their rest. Riches do hurt, and draw away the heart from God and duty. Men do hurt with their riches, not only gratifying their own lusts, but oppressing others, and dealing hardly with them. They will see that they have laboured for the wind, when, at death, they find the profit of their labour is all gone like the wind, they know not whither. How ill the covetous worldling bears the calamities of human life! He does not sorrow to repentance, but is angry at the providence of God, angry at all about him; which doubles his affliction.

Eccl. **5**:**18-20** Life is God's gift. We must not view our calling as a drudgery, but take pleasure in the calling where God puts us. A cheerful spirit is a great blessing; it makes employments easy, and afflictions light. Having made a proper use of riches, a man will remember the days of his past life with pleasure. The manner in which Solomon refers to God as the Giver, both of life and its enjoyments, shows they ought to be received and to be used, consistently with his will, and to his glory. Let this passage recommend to all the kind words of the merciful Redeemer, "Labour not for the meat that perisheth, but for that meat which endureth unto everlasting life." Christ is the Bread of life, the only food of the soul. All are invited to partake of this heavenly provision.

Chapter 6

The vanity of riches. Also of long life and flourishing families. (Eccl. **6**:**1-6**) The little advantage any one has in outward things. (Eccl. **6**:**7-12**)

Eccl. **6**:**1-6** A man often has all he needs for outward enjoyment; yet the Lord leaves him so to covetousness or evil dispositions, that he makes no good or comfortable use of what he has. By one means or other his possessions come to strangers: this is vanity, and an evil disease. A numerous family was a matter of fond desire and of high honour among the Hebrews; and long life is the desire of mankind in general. Even with these additions a man may not be able to enjoy his riches, family, and life. Such a man, in his passage through life, seems to have been born for no end or use. And he who has entered on life only for one moment, to quit it the next, has a preferable lot to him who has lived long, but only to suffer.

Eccl. **6**:**7-12** A little will serve to sustain us comfortably, and a great deal can do no more. The desires of the soul find nothing in the wealth of the world to give satisfaction. The poor man has comfort as well as the richest, and is under no real disadvantage. We cannot say, Better is the sight of the eyes than the resting of the soul in God; for it is better to live by faith in things to come, than to live by sense, which dwells only upon present things. Our lot is appointed. We have what pleases God, and let that please us. The greatest possessions and honours cannot set us above the common events of human life. Seeing that the things men pursue on earth increase vanities, what is man the better for his worldly devices? Our life upon earth is to be reckoned by days. It is fleeting and uncertain, and with little in it to be fond of, or to be depended on. Let us return to God, trust in his mercy through Jesus Christ, and submit to his will. Then soon shall we glide through this vexatious world, and find ourselves in that happy place, where there is fulness of joy and pleasures for evermore.

Chapter 7

The benefit of a good name; of death above life; of sorrow above vain mirth. (Eccl. **7**:**1-6**) Concerning oppression, anger, and discontent. (Eccl. **7**:**7-10**) Advantages of wisdom. (Eccl. **7**:**11-22**) Experience of the evil of sin. (Eccl. **7**:**23-29**)

Eccl. **7**:**1-6** Reputation for piety and honesty is more desirable than all the wealth and pleasure in this world. It will do more good to go to a funeral than to a feast. We may lawfully go to both, as there is occasion; our Saviour both feasted at the wedding of his friend in

Cana, and wept at the grave of his friend in Bethany. But, considering how apt we are to be vain and indulge the flesh, it is best to go to the house of mourning, to learn the end of man as to this world. Seriousness is better than mirth and jollity. That is best for us which is best for our souls, though it be unpleasing to sense. It is better to have our corruptions mortified by the rebuke of the wise, than to have them gratified by the song of fools. The laughter of a fool is soon gone, the end of his mirth is heaviness.

Eccl. **7**:**7-10** The event of our trials and difficulties is often better than at first we thought. Surely it is better to be patient in spirit, than to be proud and hasty. Be not soon angry, nor quick in resenting an affront. Be not long angry; though anger may come into the bosom of a wise man, it passes through it as a way-faring man; it dwells only in the bosom of fools. It is folly to cry out upon the badness of our times, when we have more reason to cry out for the badness of our own hearts; and even in these times we enjoy many mercies. It is folly to cry up the goodness of former times; as if former ages had not the like things to complain of that we have: this arises from discontent, and aptness to quarrel with God himself.

Eccl. **7**:**11-22** Wisdom is as good as an inheritance, yea better. It shelters from the storms and scorching heat of trouble. Wealth will not lengthen out the natural life; but true wisdom will give spiritual life, and strengthen men for services under their sufferings. Let us look upon the disposal of our condition as the work of God, and at last all will appear to have been for the best. In acts of righteousness, be not carried into heats or passions, no, not by a zeal for God. Be not conceited of thine own abilities; nor find fault with every thing, nor busy thyself in other men's matters. Many who will not be wrought upon by the fear of God, and the dread of hell, will avoid sins which ruin their health and estate, and expose to public justice. But those that truly fear God, have but one end to serve, therefore act steadily. If we say we have not sinned, we deceive ourselves. Every true believer is ready to say, God be merciful to me a sinner. Forget not at the same time, that personal righteousness, walking in newness of life, is the only real evidence of an interest by faith in the righteousness of the Redeemer. Wisdom teaches us not to be quick in resenting affronts. Be not desirous to know what people say; if they speak well of thee, it will feed thy pride, if ill, it will stir up thy passion. See that thou approve thyself to God and thine own conscience, and then heed not what men say of thee; it is easier to pass by twenty affronts than to avenge one. When any harm is done to us, examine whether we have not done as bad to others.

Eccl. **7**:**23-29** Solomon, in his search into the nature and reason of things, had been miserably deluded. But he here speaks with godly sorrow. He alone who constantly aims to please God, can expect to escape; the careless sinner probably will fall to rise no more. He now discovered more than ever the evil of the great sin of which he had been guilty, the loving many strange women, I Kin. **11**:**1**. A woman thoroughly upright and godly, he had not found. How was he likely to find such a one among those he had collected? If any of them had been well disposed, their situation would tend to render them all nearly of the same character. He here warns others against the sins into which he had been betrayed. Many a godly man can with thankfulness acknowledge that he has found a prudent, virtuous woman in the wife of his bosom; but those men who have gone in Solomon's track, cannot expect to find one. He traces up all the streams of actual transgression to the fountain. It is clear that man is corrupted and revolted, and not as he was made. It is lamentable that man, whom God made upright, has found out so many ways to render himself wicked and miserable. Let us bless Him for Jesus Christ, and seek his grace, that we may be numbered with his chosen people.

Chapter 8

Commendations of wisdom. (Eccl. **8**:**1-5**) To prepare for sudden evils and death. (Eccl. **8**:**6-8**) It shall be well with the righteous, and ill with the wicked. (Eccl. **8**:**9-13**) Mysteries of Providence. (Eccl. **8**:**14-17**)

Eccl. **8**:**1-5** None of the rich, the powerful, the honourable, or the accomplished of the sons of men, are so excellent, useful, or happy, as the wise man. Who else can interpret the words of God, or teach aright from his truths and dispensations? What madness must it be for weak and dependent creatures to rebel against the Almighty! What numbers form wrong judgments, and bring misery on themselves, in this life and that to come!

Eccl. **8**:**6-8** God has, in wisdom, kept away from us the knowledge of future events, that we may be always ready for changes. We must all die, no flight or hiding-place can save us, nor are there any weapons of effectual resistance. Ninety thousand die every day, upwards of sixty every minute, and one every moment. How solemn the thought! Oh that men were wise, that they understood these things, that they would consider their latter end! The believer alone is prepared to meet the solemn summons. Wickedness, by which men often escape human justice, cannot secure from death.

Eccl. **8**:**9-13** Solomon observed, that many a time one man rules over another to his hurt, and that prosperity hardens them in their wickedness. Sinners herein deceive themselves. Vengeance comes slowly, but it comes surely. A good man's days have some substance; he lives to a good purpose: a wicked man's days are all as a shadow, empty and worthless. Let us pray that we may view eternal things as near, real, and all-important.

Eccl. **8**:**14-17** Faith alone can establish the heart in this mixed scene, where the righteous often suffer, and the wicked prosper. Solomon commended joy, and holy security of mind, arising from confidence in God, because a man has no better thing under the sun, though a good man has much better things above the sun, than soberly and thankfully to use the things of this life according to his rank. He would not have us try to give a reason for what God does. But, leaving the Lord to clear up all difficulties in his own time, we may cheerfully enjoy the comforts, and bear up under the trials of life; while peace of conscience and joy in the Holy Ghost will abide in us through all outward changes, and when flesh and heart shall fail.

Chapter 9

Good and bad men fare alike as to this world. (Eccl. **9**:**1-3**) All men must die, Their portion as to this life. (Eccl. **9**:**4-10**) Disappointments common. (Eccl. **9**:**11**,**12**) Benefits of wisdom. (Eccl. **9**:**13-18**)

Eccl. **9**:**1-3** We are not to think our searching into the word or works of God useless, because we cannot explain all difficulties. We may learn many things good for ourselves and useful to others. But man cannot always decide who are objects of God's special love, or under his wrath; and God will certainly put a difference between the precious and the vile, in the other world. The difference as to present happiness, arises from the inward supports and consolations the righteous enjoy, and the benefit they derive from varied trials and mercies. As far as the sons of men are left to themselves, their hearts are full of evil; and prosperity in sin, causes them even to set God at defiance by daring wickedness. Though, on this side death, the righteous and the wicked may often seem to fare alike, on the other side there will be a vast difference between them.

Eccl. **9**:**4-10** The most despicable living man's state, is preferable to that of the most noble who have died impenitent. Solomon exhorts the wise and pious to cheerful confidence in God, whatever their condition in life. The meanest morsel, coming from their Father's love, in answer to prayer, will have a peculiar relish. Not that we may set our hearts upon the delights of sense, but what God has given us we may use with wisdom. The joy here described, is the gladness of heart that springs from a sense of the Divine favour. This is the world of service, that to come is the world of recompence. All in their stations, may find some work to do. And above all, sinners have the salvation of their souls to seek after, believers have to prove their faith, adorn the gospel, glorify God, and serve their generation.

Eccl. **9**:**11,12** Men's success seldom equals their expectations. We must use means, but not trust to them: if we succeed, we must give God the praise; if crossed, we must submit to his will. Those who put off the great concerns of their souls, are caught in Satan's net, which he baits with some worldly object, for which they reject or neglect the gospel, and go on in sin till they suddenly fall into destruction.

Eccl. **9**:**13-18** A man may, by his wisdom, bring to pass that which he could never do by his strength. If God be for us, who can be against us, or stand before us? Solomon observes the power of wisdom, though it may labour under outward disadvantages. How forcible are right words! But wise and good men must often content themselves with the satisfaction of having done good, or, at least, endeavoured to do it, when they cannot do the good they would, nor have the praise they should. How many of the good gifts, both of nature and Providence, does one sinner destroy and make waste! He who destroys his own soul destroys much good. One sinner may draw many into his destroying ways. See who are the friends and enemies of a kingdom or a family, if one saint does much good, and one sinner destroys much good.

Chapter 10

To preserve a character for wisdom. (Eccl. **10**:**1-3**) Respecting subjects and rulers. (Eccl. **10**:**4-10**) Of foolish talk. (Eccl. **10**:**11-15**) Duties of rulers and subjects. (Eccl. **10**:**16-20**)

Eccl. **10**:**1-3** Those especially who make a profession of religion, should keep from all appearances of evil. A wise man has great advantage over a fool, who is always at a loss when he has anything to do. Sin is the reproach of sinners, wherever they go, and shows their folly.

Eccl. **10**:**4-10** Solomon appears to caution men not to seek redress in a hasty manner, nor to yield to pride and revenge. Do not, in a passion, quit thy post of duty; wait awhile, and thou wilt find that yielding pacifies great offences. Men are not preferred according to their merit. And those are often most forward to offer help, who are least aware of the difficulties, or the consequences. The same remark is applied to the church, or the body of Christ, that all the members should have the same care one for another.

Eccl. **10**:**11-15** There is a practice in the East, of charming serpents by music The babbler's tongue is an unruly evil, full of deadly poison; and contradiction only makes it the more violent. We must find the way to keep him gentle. But by rash, unprincipled, or slanderous talk, he brings open or secret vengeance upon himself. Would we duly consider our own ignorance as to future events, it would cut off many idle words which we foolishly multiply. Fools toil a great deal to no purpose. They do not understand the plainest things, such as the entrance into a great city. But it is the excellency of the way to the heavenly city, that it is a high-way, in which the simplest wayfaring men shall not err, Is. **25**:**8**. But sinful folly makes men miss that only way to happiness.

Eccl. **10**:**16-20** The happiness of a land depends on the character of its rulers. The people cannot be happy when their princes are childish, and lovers of pleasure. Slothfulness is of ill consequence both to private and public affairs. Money, of itself, will neither feed nor clothe, though it answers the occasions of this present life, as what is to be had, may generally be had for money. But the soul, as it is not redeemed, so it is not maintained with corruptible things, as silver and gold. God sees what men do, and hears what they say in secret; and, when he pleases, brings it to light by strange and unsuspected ways. If there be hazard in secret thoughts and whispers against earthly rulers, what must be the peril from every deed, word, or thought of rebellion against the King of kings, and Lord of lords! He seeth in secret. His ear is ever open. Sinner! curse not THIS KING in thy inmost thought. Your curses cannot affect Him; but his curse, coming down upon you, will sink you to the lowest hell.

Chapter 11

Exhortation to liberality. (Eccl. **11**:**1-6**) An admonition to prepare for death, and to young persons to be religious. (Eccl. **11**:**7-10**)

Eccl. **11**:**1-6** Solomon presses the rich to do good to others. Give freely, though it may seem thrown away and lost. Give to many. Excuse not thyself with the good thou hast done, from the good thou hast further to do. It is not lost, but well laid out. We have reason to expect evil, for we are born to trouble; it is wisdom to do good in the day of prosperity. Riches cannot profit us, if we do not benefit others. Every man must labour to be a blessing to that place where the providence of God casts him. Wherever we are, we may find good work to do, if we have but hearts to do it. If we magnify every little difficulty, start objections, and fancy hardships, we shall never go on, much less go through with our work. Winds and clouds of tribulation are, in God's hands, designed to try us. God's work shall agree with his word, whether we see it or not. And we may well trust God to provide for us, without our anxious, disquieting cares. Be not weary in well-doing, for in due season, in God's time, you shall reap, Gal. **6**:**9**.

Eccl. **11**:**7-10** Life is sweet to bad men, because they have their portion in this life; it is sweet to good men, because it is the time of preparation for a better; it is sweet to all. Here is a caution to think of death, even when life is most sweet. Solomon makes an effecting address to young persons. They would desire opportunity to pursue every pleasure. Then follow your desires, but be assured that God will call you into judgment. How many give loose to every appetite, and rush into every vicious pleasure! But God registers every one of their sinful thoughts and desires, their idle words and wicked words. If they would avoid remorse and terror, if they would have hope and comfort on a dying bed, if they would escape misery here and hereafter, let them remember the vanity of youthful pleasures. That Solomon means to condemn the pleasures of sin is evident. His object is to draw the young to purer and more lasting joys. This is not the language of one grudging youthful pleasures, because he can no longer partake of them; but of one who has, by a miracle of mercy, been brought back in safety. He would persuade the young from trying a course whence so few return. If the young would live a life of true happiness, if they would secure happiness hereafter, let them remember their Creator in the days of their youth.

Chapter 12

A description of the infirmities of age. (Eccl. **12**:**1-7**) All is vanity: also a warning of the judgment to come. (Eccl. **12**:**8-14**)

Eccl. **12**:**1-7** We should remember our sins against our Creator, repent, and seek forgiveness. We should remember our duties, and set about them, looking to him for grace and strength. This should be done early, while the body is strong, and the spirits active. When a man has the pain of reviewing a misspent life, his not having given up sin and worldly vanities till he is forced to say, I have no pleasure in them, renders his sincerity very questionable. Then follows a figurative description of old age and its infirmities, which has some difficulties; but the meaning is plain, to show how uncomfortable, generally, the days of old age are. As the four **verses**, **2-5**, are a figurative description of the infirmities that usually accompany old age, Eccl. **12**:**6** notices the circumstances which take place in the hour of death. If sin had not entered into the world, these infirmities would not have been known. Surely then the aged should reflect on the evil of sin.

Eccl. **12**:**8-14** Solomon repeats his text, VANITY OF VANITIES, ALL IS VANITY. These are the words of one that could speak by dear-bought experience of the vanity of the world, which can do nothing to ease men of the burden of sin. As he considered the worth of souls, he gave good heed to what he spake and wrote; words of truth will always be acceptable words. The truths of God are as goads to such as are dull and draw back, and nails to such as are wandering and draw aside; means to establish the heart, that we may never sit loose to our duty, nor be taken from it. The Shepherd of Israel is the Giver of inspired wisdom. Teachers and guides all receive their communications from him. The title is applied in Scripture to the Lord Jesus Christ, the Son of God. The prophets sought diligently, what, or what manner of time, the Spirit of Christ in them did signify, when it testified beforehand the sufferings of Christ, and the glory that should follow. To write many books was not suited to the shortness of human life, and would be weariness to the writer, and to the reader; and then was much more so to both than it is now. All things would be vanity and vexation, except they led to this conclusion, That to fear God, and keep his commandments, is the whole of man. The fear of God includes in it all the affections of the soul towards him, which are produced by the Holy Spirit. There may be terror where there is no love, nay, where there is hatred. But this is different from the gracious fear of God, as the feelings of an affectionate child. The fear of God, is often put for the whole of true religion in the heart, and includes its practical results in the life. Let us attend to the one thing needful, and now come to him as a merciful Saviour, who will soon come as an almighty Judge, when he will bring to light the things of darkness, and manifest the counsels of all hearts. Why does God record in his word, that ALL IS VANITY, but to keep us from deceiving ourselves to our ruin? He makes our duty to be our interest. May it be graven in all our hearts. Fear God, and keep his commandments, for this is all that concerns man.

Song of Solomon

This book is a Divine allegory, which represents the love between Christ and his church of true believers, under figures taken from the relation and affection that subsist between a bridegroom and his espoused bride; an emblem often employed in Scripture, as describing the nearest, firmest, and most sure relation: see Ps. **45**; Is. **54**:**5**,**6**; **62**:**5**; Jer. **2**:**2**; **3**:**1**; also in Ezekiel, Hosea, and by our Lord himself, Matt. **9**:**15**; **25**:**1**: see also Rev. **21**:**2**,**9**; Eph. **5**:**27**. There is no character in the church of Christ, and no situation in which the believer is placed, but what may be traced in this book, as humble inquirers will find, on comparing it with other Scriptures, by the assistance of God the Holy Spirit, in answer to their supplications. Much, however, of the language has been misunderstood by expositors and translators. The difference between the customs and manners of Europe, and those of the East, must especially be kept in view. The little acquaintance with eastern customs possessed by most of our early expositors and translators, has in many cases prevented a correct rendering. Also, the changes in our own language, during the last two or three centuries, affect the manner in which some expressions are viewed, and they must not be judged by modern notions. But the great outlines, rightly interpreted, fully accord with the affections and experience of the sincere Christian.

Chapter 1

The title. (Song **1**:**1**) The church confesses her deformity. (Song **1**:**2-6**) The church beseeches Christ to lead her to the resting-place of his people. (Song **1**:**7**,**8**) Christ's commendation of the church, Her esteem for Him. (Song **1**:**9-17**)

Song **1**:**1** This is "the Song of songs," excellent above any others, for it is wholly taken up with describing the excellences of Christ, and the love between him and his redeemed people.

Song **1**:**2-6** The church, or rather the believer, speaks here in the character of the spouse of the King, the Messiah. The kisses of his mouth mean those assurances of pardon with which believers are favoured, filling them with peace and joy in believing, and causing them to abound in hope by the power of the Holy Ghost. Gracious souls take most pleasure in loving Christ, and being loved of him. Christ's love is more valuable and desirable than the best this world can give. The name of Christ is not now like ointment sealed up, but like ointment poured forth; which denotes the freeness and fulness of the setting forth of his grace by the gospel. Those whom he has redeemed and sanctified, are here the virgins that love Jesus Christ, and follow him whithersoever he goes, Rev. **14**:**4**. They entreat him to draw them by the quickening influences of his Spirit. The more clearly we discern Christ's glory, the more sensible shall we be that we are unable to follow him suitably, and at the same time be more desirous of doing it. Observe the speedy answer given to this prayer. Those who wait at Wisdom's gate, shall be led into truth and comfort. And being brought into this chamber, our griefs will vanish. We have no joy but in Christ, and for this we are indebted to him. We will remember to give thanks for thy love; it shall make more lasting impressions upon us than any thing in this world. Nor is any love acceptable to Christ but love in sincerity, Eph. **6**:**24**. The daughters of Jerusalem may mean professors not yet established in the faith. The spouse was black as the tents of the wandering Arabs, but comely as the magnificent curtains in the palaces of Solomon. The believer is black, as being defiled and sinful by nature, but comely, as renewed by Divine grace to the holy image of God. He is still deformed with remains of sin, but comely as accepted in Christ. He is often base and contemptible in the esteem of men, but excellent in the sight of God. The blackness was owing to the hard usage that had been suffered. The children of the church, her mother, but not of God, her Father, were angry with her. They had made her suffer hardships, which caused her to neglect the care of her soul. Thus, under the emblem of a poor female, made the chosen partner of a prince, we are led to consider the circumstances in which the love of Christ is accustomed to find its objects. They were wretched slaves of sin, in toil, or in sorrow, weary and heavy laden, but how great the change when the love of Christ is manifested to their souls!

Song **1**:**7**,**8** Observe the title given to Christ, O Thou whom my soul loveth. Those that do so, may come to him boldly, and may humbly plead with him. Is it with God's people a noon-time of outward troubles, inward conflicts? Christ has rest for them. Those whose souls love Jesus Christ, earnestly desire to share in the privileges of his flock. Turning aside from Christ is what gracious souls dread more than anything else. God is ready to answer prayer. Follow the track, ask for the good old way, observe the footsteps of the flock, look what has been the practice of godly people. Sit under the direction of good ministers; beside the tents of the under shepherds. Bring thy charge with thee, they shall all be welcome. It will be the earnest desire and prayer of the Christian, that God would so direct him in his worldly business, and so order his situation and employment, that he may have his Lord and Saviour always before him.

Song **1**:**9-17** The Bridegroom gives high praises of his spouse. In the sight of Christ believers are the excellent of the earth, fitted to be instruments for promoting his glory. The spiritual gifts and graces which Christ bestows on every true believer, are described by the ornaments then in use, Song **1**:**10**,**11**. The graces of the saints are many, but there is dependence upon each other. He who is the Author, will be the Finisher of the good work. The grace received from Christ's fulness, springs forth into lively exercises of faith, affection, and gratitude. Yet Christ, not his gifts, is most precious to them. The word translated "camphire," signifies "atonement or propitiation." Christ is dear to all believers, because he is the propitiation for their sins. No pretender must have his place in the soul. They resolved to lodge him in their hearts all the night; during the continuance of the troubles of life. Christ takes delight in the good work which his grace has wrought on the souls of believers. This should engage all who are made holy, to be very thankful for that grace which has made those fair, who by nature were deformed. The spouse (the believer) has a humble, modest eye, discovering simplicity and godly sincerity; eyes enlightened and guided by the Holy Spirit, that blessed Dove. The church expresses her value for Christ. Thou art the great Original, but I am but a faint and imperfect copy. Many are fair to look at, yet their temper renders them unpleasant: but Christ is fair, yet pleasant. The believer, Song **1**:**16**, speaks with praise of those holy ordinances in which true believers have fellowship with Christ. Whether the believer is in the courts of the Lord, or in retirement; whether following his daily labours, or confined on the bed of sickness, or even in a dungeon, a sense of the Divine presence will turn the place into a paradise. Thus the soul, daily having fellowship with the Father, the Son, and the Holy Spirit, enjoys a lively hope of an incorruptible, undefiled, and unfading inheritance above.

Chapter 2

The mutual love of Christ and his church. (Song **2**:**1**-**7**) The hope and calling of the church. (Song **2**:**8**-**13**) Christ's care of the church, Her faith and hope. (Song **2**:**14**-**17**)

Song **2**:**1**-**7** Believers are beautiful, as clothed in the righteousness of Christ; and fragrant, as adorned with the graces of his Spirit; and they thrive under the refreshing beams of the Sun of righteousness. The lily is a very noble plant in the East; it grows to a considerable height, but has a weak stem. The church is weak in herself, yet is strong in Him that supports her. The wicked, the daughters of this world, who have no love to Christ, are as thorns, worthless and useless, noxious and hurtful. Corruptions are thorns in the flesh; but the lily now among thorns, shall be transplanted into that paradise where there is no brier or thorn. The world is a barren tree to the soul; but Christ is a fruitful one. And when poor souls are parched with convictions of sin, with the terrors of the law, or the troubles of this world, weary and heavy laden, they may find rest in Christ. It is not enough to pass by this shadow, but we must sit down under it. Believers have tasted that the Lord Jesus is gracious; his fruits are all the precious privileges of the new covenant, purchased by his blood, and communicated by his Spirit; promises are sweet to a believer, and precepts also. Pardons are sweet, and peace of conscience sweet. If our mouths are out of taste for the pleasures of sin, Divine consolations will be sweet to us. Christ brings the soul to seek and to find comforts through his ordinances, which are as a banqueting-house where his saints feast with him. The love of Christ, manifested by his death, and by his word, is the banner he displays, and believers resort to it. How much better is it with the soul when sick from love to Christ, than when surfeited with the love of this world! And though Christ seemed to have withdrawn, yet he was even then a very present help. All his saints are in his hand, which tenderly holds their aching heads. Finding Christ thus nigh to her, the soul is in great care that her communion with him is not interrupted. We easily grieve the Spirit by wrong tempers. Let those who have comfort, fear sinning it away.

Song **2**:**8**-**13** The church pleases herself with thoughts of further communion with Christ. None besides can speak to the heart. She sees him come. This may be applied to the prospect the Old Testament saints had of Christ's coming in the flesh. He comes as pleased with his own undertaking. He comes speedily. Even when Christ seems to forsake, it is but for a moment; he will soon return with everlasting loving-kindness. The saints of old saw him, appearing through the sacrifices and ceremonial institutions. We see him through a glass darkly, as he manifests himself through the lattices. Christ invites the new convert to arise from sloth and despondency, and to leave sin and worldly vanities, for union and communion with him. The winter may mean years passed in ignorance and sin, unfruitful and miserable, or storms and tempests that accompanied his conviction of guilt and danger. Even the unripe fruits of holiness are pleasant unto Him whose grace has produced them. All these encouraging tokens and evidences of Divine favour, are motives to the soul to follow Christ more fully. Arise then, and come away from the world and the flesh, come into fellowship with Christ. This blessed change is owing wholly to the approaches and influences of the Sun of righteousness.

Song **2**:**14**-**17** The church is Christ's dove; she returns to him, as her Noah. Christ is the Rock, in whom alone she can think herself safe, and find herself easy, as a dove in the hole of a rock, when struck at by the birds of prey. Christ calls her to come boldly to the throne of grace, having a great High Priest there, to tell what her request is. Speak freely, fear not a slight or a repulse. The voice of prayer is sweet and acceptable to God; those who are sanctified have the best comeliness. The first risings of sinful thoughts and desires, the beginnings of trifling pursuits which waste the time, trifling visits, small departures from truth, whatever would admit some conformity to the world; all these, and many more, are little foxes which must be removed. This is a charge to believers to mortify their sinful appetites and passions, which are as little foxes, that destroy their graces and comforts, and crush good beginnings. Whatever we find a hinderance to us in that which is good, we must put away. He feedeth among the lilies; this shows Christ's gracious presence among believers. He is kind to all his people. It becomes them to believe this, when under desertion and absence, and so to ward off temptations. The shadows of the Jewish dispensation were dispelled by the dawning of the gospel day. And a day of comfort will come after a night of desertion. Come over the mountains of Bether, "the mountains that divide," looking forward to that day of light and love. Christ will come over every separating mountain to take us home to himself.

Chapter 3

The trials of the church by the withdrawing of Christ. (Song **3**:**1**-**5**) The excellences of the church, The care of Christ for her. (Song **3**:**6**-**11**)

Song **3**:**1**-**5** It was hard to the Old Testament church to find Christ in the ceremonial law; the watchmen of that church gave little assistance to those who sought after him. The night is a time of coldness, darkness, and drowsiness, and of dim apprehensions concerning spiritual things. At first, when uneasy, some feeble efforts are made to obtain the comfort of communion with Christ. This proves in vain; the believer is then roused to increased diligence. The streets and broad-ways seem to imply the means of grace in which the Lord is to be sought. Application is made to those who watch for men's souls. Immediate satisfaction is not found. We must not rest in any means, but by faith apply directly to Christ. The holding of Christ, and not letting him go, denotes earnest cleaving to him. What prevails is a humble, ardent suing by prayer, with a lively exercise of faith on his promises. So long as the faith of believers keeps hold of Christ, he will not be offended at their earnest asking, yea, he is well pleased with it. The believer desires to make others acquainted with his Saviour. Wherever we find Christ, we must take him home with us to our houses, especially to our hearts; and we should call upon ourselves and each other, to beware of grieving our holy Comforter, and provoking the departure of the Beloved.

Song **3**:**6**-**11** A wilderness is an emblem of the world; the believer comes out of it when he is delivered from the love of its sinful pleasures and pursuits, and refuses to comply with its customs and fashions, to seek happiness in communion with the Saviour. A poor soul shall come up, at last, under the conduct of the Comforter; like a cloud of incense ascending from the altar, or the smoke of the burnt-offerings. This signifies pious and devout affections, and the mounting of the soul heaven-ward. The believer is filled with the graces of God's Spirit; his devotions now are very lively. These graces and comforts are from the heavenly Canaan. He, who is the Peace of his people, the King of the heavenly Zion, has provided for the safe conveyance of his redeemed through the wilderness of this world. The bed, or palanquin, was contrived for rest and easy conveyance, but its beauty and magnificence showed the quality of its owner. The church is well guarded; more are with her than are against her: believers, when they repose in Christ, and with him, though they have their fears in the night, are yet safe. The chariot here denotes the covenant of redemption, the way of our salvation. This is that work of Christ, which makes him loved and admired in the eyes of believers. It is framed and contrived, both for the glory of Christ, and for the comfort of believers; it is well ordered in all things and sure. The blood of the covenant, that rich purple, is the cover of this chariot, by which believers are sheltered from the wind and storms of Divine wrath, and the troubles of this world; but the midst of it is that love of Christ which passes knowledge, this is for believers to repose upon. Christ, in his gospel, manifests himself. Take special notice of his crown. Applying this to Christ, it speaks the honour put upon him, and his power and dominion.

Chapter 4

Christ sets forth the graces of the church. (Song **4**:**1**-**7**) Christ's love to the church. (Song **4**:**8**-**15**) The church desires further influences of Divine grace. (Song **4**:**16**)

Song **4**:**1**-**7** If each of these comparisons has a meaning applicable to the graces of the church, or of the faithful Christian, they are not clearly known; and great mistakes are made by fanciful guesses. The mountain of myrrh appears to mean the mountain Moriah, on which the temple was built, where the incense was burned, and the people worshipped the Lord. This was his residence till the shadows of the law given to Moses were dispersed by the breaking of the gospel day, and the rising of the Sun of righteousness. And though, in respect of his human nature, Christ is absent from his church on earth, and will continue to be so till the heavenly day break, yet he is spiritually present in his ordinances, and with his people. How fair and comely are believers, when justified in Christ's righteousness, and adorned with spiritual graces! when their thoughts, words, and deeds, though imperfect, are pure, manifesting a heart nourished by the gospel!

Song **4**:**8**-**15** Observe the gracious call Christ gives to the church. It is, **1**. A precept; so this is Christ's call to his church to come off from the world. These hills seem pleasant, but there are in them lions' dens; they are mountains of the leopards. **2**. As a promise; many shall be brought as members of the church, from every point. The church shall be delivered from her persecutors in due time, though now she dwells among lions, Ps. **57**:**4**. Christ's heart is upon his church; his treasure is therein; and he delights in the affection she has for him; its working in the heart, and its works in the life. The odours wherewith the spouse is perfumed, are as the gifts and graces of the Spirit. Love and obedience to God are more pleasing to Christ than sacrifice or incense. Christ having put upon his spouse the white raiment of his own righteousness, and the righteousness of saints, and perfumed it with holy joy and comfort, he is well pleased with it. And Christ walks in his garden unseen. A hedge of protection is made around, which all the powers of darkness cannot break through. The souls of believers are as gardens enclosed, where is a well of living water, John **4**:**14**; **7**:**38**, the influences of the Holy Spirit. The world knows not these wells of salvation, nor can any opposer corrupt this fountain. Saints in the church, and graces in the saints, are fitly compared to fruits and spices. They are planted, and do not grow of themselves. They are precious; they are the blessings of this earth. They will be kept to good purpose when flowers are withered. Grace, when ended in glory, will last for ever. Christ is the source which makes these gardens fruitful; even a well of living waters.

Song **4**:**16** The church prays for the influences of the blessed Spirit, to make this garden fruitful. Graces in the soul are as spices in these gardens, that in them which is valuable and useful. The blessed Spirit, in his work upon the soul, is as the wind. There is the north wind of conviction, and the south wind of comfort. He stirs up good affections, and works in us both to will and to do that which is good. The church invites Christ. Let him have the honour of all the garden produces, and let us have the comfort of his acceptance of it. We can invite him to nothing but what is his own already. The believer can have no joy of the fruits, unless they redound some way or other to the glory of Christ. Let us then seek to keep separate from the world, as a garden enclosed, and to avoid conformity thereto.

Chapter 5

Christ's answer. (Song **5**:**1**) The disappointments of the church from her own folly. (Song **5**:**2**-**8**) The excellences of Christ. (Song **5**:**9**-**16**)

Song **5**:**1** See how ready Christ is to accept the invitations of his people. What little good there is in us would be lost, if he did not preserve it to himself. He also invites his beloved people to eat and drink abundantly. The ordinances in which they honour him, are means of grace.

Song **5**:**2**-**8** Churches and believers, by carelessness and security, provoke Christ to withdraw. We ought to notice our spiritual slumbers and distempers. Christ knocks to awaken us, knocks by his word and Spirit, knocks by afflictions and by our consciences; thus, Rev. **3**:**20**. When we are unmindful of Christ, still he thinks of us. Christ's love to us should engage ours to him, even in the most self-denying instances; and we only can be gainers by it. Careless souls put slights on Jesus Christ. Another could not be sent to open the door. Christ calls to us, but we have no mind, or pretend we have no strength, or we have no time, and think we may be excused. Making excuses is making light of Christ. Those put contempt upon Christ, who cannot find in their hearts to bear a cold blast, or to leave a warm bed for him. See the powerful influences of Divine grace. He put in his hand to unbolt the door, as one weary of waiting. This betokens a work of the Spirit upon the soul. The believer's rising above self-indulgence, seeking by prayer for the consolations of Christ, and to remove every hinderance to communion with him; these actings of the soul are represented by the hands dropping sweet-smelling myrrh upon the handles of the locks. But the Beloved was gone! By absenting himself, Christ will teach his people to value his gracious visits more highly. Observe, the soul still calls Christ her Beloved. Every desertion is not despair. Lord, I believe, though I must say, Lord, help my unbelief. His words melted me, yet, wretch that I was, I made excuses. The smothering and stifling of convictions will be very bitter to think of, when God opens our eyes. The soul went in pursuit of him; not only prayed, but used means, sought him in the ways wherein he used to be found. The watchmen wounded me. Some refer it to those who misapply the word to awakened consciences. The charge to the daughters of Jerusalem, seems to mean the distressed believer's desire of the prayers of the feeblest Christian. Awakened souls are more sensible of Christ's withdrawings than of any other trouble.

Song **5**:**9**-**16** Even those who have little acquaintance with Christ, cannot but see amiable beauty in others who bear his image. There are hopes of those who begin to inquire concerning Christ and his perfections. Christians, who are well acquainted with Christ themselves, should do all they can to make others know something of him. Divine glory makes him truly lovely in the eyes of all who are enlightened to discern spiritual things. He is white in the spotless innocence of his life, ruddy in the bleeding sufferings he went through at his death. This description of the person of the Beloved, would form, in the figurative language of those times, a portrait of beauty of person and of grace of manners; but the aptness of some of the allusions may not appear to us. He shall come to be glorified in his saints, and to be admired in all that believe. May his love constrain us to live to his glory.

Chapter 6

Inquiry where Christ must be sought. (Song **6**:**1**) Where Christ may be found. (Song **6**:**2**,**3**) Christ's commendations of the church. (Song **6**:**4-10**) The work of grace in the believer. (Song **6**:**11-13**)

Song **6**:**1** Those made acquainted with the excellences of Christ, and the comfort of an interest in him, desire to know where they may meet him. Those who would find Christ, must seek him early and diligently.

Song **6**:**2**,**3** Christ's church is a garden, enclosed, and separated from the world; he takes care of it, delights in it, and visits it. Those who would find Christ, must attend him in his ordinances, the word, sacraments, and prayer. When Christ comes to his church, it is to entertain his friends. And to take believers to himself: he picks the lilies one by one; and at the great day he will send forth his angels to gather all his lilies, that he may be for ever admired in them. The death of a believer is not more than the owner of a garden plucking a favourite flower; and He will preserve it from withering, yea, cause it to flourish for ever, with increasing beauty. If our own hearts can witness for us that we are Christ's, question not his being ours, for the covenant never breaks on his side. It is the comfort of the church, that he feeds among the lilies, that he takes delight in his people.

Song **6**:**4-10** All the real excellence and holiness on earth centre in the church. Christ goes forth subduing his enemies, while his followers gain victories over the world, the flesh, and the devil. He shows the tenderness of a Redeemer, the delight he takes in his redeemed people, and the workings of his own grace in them. True believers alone can possess the beauty of holiness. And when their real character is known, it will be commended. Both the church and believers, at their first conversion, look forth as the morning, their light being small, but increasing. As to their sanctification, they are fair as the moon, deriving all their light, grace, and holiness from Christ; and as to justification, clear as the sun, clothed with Christ, the Sun of righteousness, and fighting the good fight of faith, under the banners of Christ, against all spiritual enemies.

Song **6**:**11-13** In retirement and in meditation the Christian character is formed and perfected. But not in the retirement of the idle, the self-indulgent, or the trifler. When the Christian is released from the discharge of his duties in life, the world has no attractions for him. His prayer is, that all things belonging to the Spirit may live and grow within him, and around him. Such are the interesting cares and employments of him whom the world wrongly deems unhappy, and lost to his true interests. In humility and self-abasement, the humble Christian would turn away from the sight of all; but the Lord delights to honour him. Chiefly, however, may the reference be to the ministering angels who shall be sent for the soul of the Christian. Their approach may startle, but the departing soul shall find the Lord its strength and its portion for ever. The church is called the Shulamite: the word signifies perfection and peace; not in herself, but in Christ, in whom she is complete, through his righteousness; and has peace, which he made for her through his blood, and gives unto her by his Spirit.

Chapter 7

The graces of the church. (Song **7**:**1-9**) The delight of the church in Christ. (Song **7**:**10-13**)

Song **7**:**1-9** The similitudes here are different from what they were before, and in the original refer to glorious and splendid clothing. Such honour have all his saints; and having put on Christ, they are distinguished by their beautiful and glorious apparel. They adorn the doctrine of God their Saviour in all things. Consistent believers honour Christ, recommend the gospel, and convince and awaken sinners. The church resembles the stately and spreading palm; while her love for Christ, and the obedience resulting therefrom, are precious fruit of the true Vine. The King is held in the galleries. Christ takes delight in the assemblies and ordinances of his people; and admires the fruit of his grace in them. When applied to the church and to each faithful Christian, all this denotes that beauty of holiness, in which they shall be presented to their heavenly Bridegroom.

Song **7**:**10-13** The church, the believing soul, triumphs in its relation to Christ, and interest in him. She humbly desires communion with him. Let us walk together, that I may receive counsel, instruction, and comfort from thee; and may make known my wants and my grievances to thee, with freedom, and without interruption. Communion with Christ is what all that are made holy earnestly breathe after. And those who would con**verse** with Christ, must go forth from the world. Wherever we are, we may keep up communion with God. Nor should we go where we cannot in faith ask him to go with us. Those who would go abroad with Christ, must begin early in the morning of their days; must begin every day with him, seek him early, seek him diligently. A gracious soul can reconcile itself to the poorest places, if it may have communion with God in them; but the most delightful fields will not satisfy, unless the Beloved is there. Let us not think to be satisfied with any earthly object. Our own souls are our vineyards; they should be planted with useful trees. We should often search whether we are fruitful in righteousness. Christ's presence will make the vine flourish, and the tender grapes appear, as the returning sun revives the gardens. If we can appeal to him, Thou knowest all things, thou knowest that I love thee; if his Spirit witness with our spirit, that our souls prosper, it is enough. And we must beg of him to search and try us, to discover us to ourselves. The fruits and exercises of graces are pleasant to the Lord Jesus. These must be laid up, and always ready; that by our bringing forth much fruit, he may be glorified. It is all from him, therefore it is fit it should be all for him.

Chapter 8

Desire for communion with Christ. (Song **8**:**1-4**) The vehemence of this desire. (Song **8**:**5-7**) The church pleads for others. (Song **8**:**8-12**) And prays for Christ's coming. (Song **8**:**13**,**14**)

Song **8**:**1-4** The church wishes for the constant intimacy and freedom with the Lord Jesus that a sister has with a brother. That they might be as his brethren, which they are, when by grace they are made partakers of a Divine nature. Christ is become as our Brother; wherever we find him, let us be ready to own our relation to him, and affection for him, and not fear being despised for it. Is there in us an ardent wish to serve Christ more and better? What then have we laid up in store, to show our affection to the Beloved of our souls? What fruit unto holiness? The church charges all her children that they never provoke Christ to withdraw. We should reason with ourselves, when tempted to do what would grieve the Spirit.

Song **8**:**5-7** The Jewish church came up from the wilderness, supported by Divine power and favour. The Christian church was raised from a low, desolate condition, by the grace of Christ relied on. Believers, by the power of grace, are brought up from the wilderness. A sinful state is a wilderness in which there is no true comfort; it is a wandering, wanting state: There is no coming out of this wilderness, but leaning on Christ as our Beloved, by faith; not leaning to our own understanding, nor trusting in any righteousness of our own; but in the strength of him, who is the Lord our Righteousness. The words of the church to Christ which follow, entreat an abiding place in his love, and protection by his power. Set me as a seal upon thine heart; let me always have a place in thine heart; let me have an impression of love upon thine heart. Of this the soul would be assured, and without a sense thereof no rest is to be found. Those who truly love Christ, are jealous of every thing that would draw them from him; especially of themselves, lest they should do any thing to provoke him to withdraw from them. If we love Christ, the fear of coming short of his love, or the temptations to forsake him, will be most painful to us. No waters can quench Christ's love to us, nor any floods drown it. Let nothing abate our love to him. Nor will life, and all its comforts, entice a believer from loving Christ. Love of Christ, will enable us to repel and triumph over temptations from the smiles of the world, as well as from its frowns.

Song **8**:**8-12** The church pleads for the Gentiles, who then had not the word of God, nor the means of grace. Those who are brought to Christ themselves, should contrive what they may do to help others to him. Babes in Christ are always seen among Christians, and the welfare of their weak brethren is an object of continual prayer with the stronger believers. If the beginning of this work were likened to a wall built upon Him the precious Foundation and Corner-stone, then the Gentile church would become as a palace for the great King, built of solid silver. If the first preaching of the gospel were as the making a door through the wall of partition, that door should be lasting, as cased with boards of durable cedar. She shall be carefully and effectually protected, enclosed so as to receive no damage. The church is full of care for those yet uncalled. Christ says, I will do all that is necessary to be done for them. See with what satisfaction we should look back upon the times and seasons, when we were in his eyes as those that find favour. Our hearts are our vineyards, which we must keep with all diligence. To Christ, and to his praise, all our fruits must be dedicated. All that work for Christ, work for themselves, and shall be unspeakable gainers by it.

Song **8**:**13**,**14** These **verses** close the conference between Christ and his church. He first addresses her as dwelling in the gardens, the assemblies and ordinances of his saints. He exhorts her to be constant and frequent in prayers, supplications, and praises, in which he delights. She replies, craving his speedy return to take her to be wholly with Him. The heavens, those high mountains of sweet spices, must contain Christ, till the times come, when every eye shall see him, in all the glory of the better world. True believers as they are looking for, so they are hastening to the coming of that day of the Lord. Let every Christian endeavour to perform the duties of his station, that men may see his good works, and glorify his heavenly Father. Continuing earnest in prayer for what we want, our thanksgivings will abound, and our joy will be full; our souls will be enriched, and our labours prospered. We shall be enabled to look forward to death and judgment without fear. Even so, come, Lord Jesus.

Isaiah

Isaiah prophesied in the reigns of Uzziah, Jotham, Ahaz, and Hezekiah. He has been well called the evangelical prophet, on account of his numerous and full prophesies concerning the coming and character, the ministry and preaching, the sufferings and death of the Messiah, and the extent and continuance of his kingdom. Under the veil of the deliverance from Babylon, Isaiah points to a much greater deliverance, which was to be effected by the Messiah; and seldom does he mention the one, without alluding at the same time to the other; nay, he is often so much enraptured with the prospect of the more distant deliverance, as to lose sight of that which was nearer, and to dwell on the Messiah's person, office, character, and kingdom.

Chapter 1

The corruptions prevailing among the Jews. (Is. **1**:**1-9**) Severe censures. (Is. **1**:**10-15**) Exhortations to repentance. (Is. **1**:**16-20**) The state of Judah is lamented; with gracious promises of the gospel times. (Is. **1**:**21-31**)

Is. **1**:**1-9** Isaiah signifies, "The salvation of the Lord;" a very suitable name for this prophet, who prophesies so much of Jesus the Saviour, and his salvation. God's professing people did not know or consider that they owed their lives and comforts to God's fatherly care and kindness. How many are very careless in the affairs of their souls! Not considering what we do know in religion, does us as much harm, as ignorance of what we should know. The wickedness was universal. Here is a comparison taken from a sick and diseased body. The distemper threatens to be mortal. From the sole of the foot even to the head; from the meanest peasant to the greatest peer, there is no soundness, no good principle, no religion, for that is the health of the soul. Nothing but guilt and corruption; the sad effects of Adam's fall. This passage declares the total depravity of human nature. While sin remains unrepented, nothing is done toward healing these wounds, and preventing fatal effects. Jerusalem was exposed and unprotected, like the huts or sheds built up to guard ripening fruits. These are still to be seen in the East, where fruits form a large part of the summer food of the people. But the Lord had a small remnant of pious servants at Jerusalem. It is of the Lord's mercies that we are not consumed. The evil nature is in every one of us; only Jesus and his sanctifying Spirit can restore us to spiritual health.

Is. **1**:**10-15** Judea was desolate, and their cities burned. This awakened them to bring sacrifices and offerings, as if they would bribe God to remove the punishment, and give them leave to go on in their sin. Many who will readily part with their sacrifices, will not be persuaded to part with their sins. They relied on the mere form as a service deserving a reward. The most costly devotions of wicked people, without thorough reformation of heart and life, cannot be acceptable to God. He not only did not accept them, but he abhorred them. All this shows that sin is very hateful to God. If we allow ourselves in secret sin, or forbidden indulgences; if we reject the salvation of Christ, our very prayers will become abomination.

Is. **1**:**16-20** Not only feel sorrow for the sin committed, but break off the practice. We must be doing, not stand idle. We must be doing the good the Lord our God requires. It is plain that the sacrifices of the law could not atone, even for outward national crimes. But, blessed be God, there is a Fountain opened, in which sinners of every age and rank may be cleansed. Though our sins have been as scarlet and crimson, a deep dye, a double dye, first in the wool of original corruption, and afterwards in the many threads of actual transgression; though we have often dipped into sin, by many backslidings; yet pardoning mercy will take out the stain, Ps. **51**:**7**. They should have all the happiness and comfort they could desire. Life and death, good and evil, are set before us. O Lord, incline all of us to live to thy glory.

Is. **1**:**21-31** Neither holy cities nor royal ones are faithful to their trust, if religion does not dwell in them. Dross may shine like silver, and the wine that is mixed with water may still have the colour of wine. Those have a great deal to answer for, who do not help the oppressed, but oppress them. Men may do much by outward restraints; but only God works effectually by the influences of his Spirit, as a Spirit of Judgment. Sin is the worst captivity, the worst slavery. The redemption of the spiritual Zion, by the righteousness and death of Christ, and by his powerful grace, most fully accord with what is here meant. Utter ruin is threatened. The Jews should become as a tree when blasted by heat; as a garden without water, which in those hot countries would soon be burned up. Thus shall they be that trust in idols, or in an arm of flesh. Even the strong man shall be as tow; not only soon broken, and pulled to pieces, but easily catching fire. When the sinner has made himself as tow and stubble, and God makes himself as a consuming fire, what can prevent the utter ruin of the sinner?

Chapter 2

The conversion of the Gentiles, Description of the sinfulness of Israel. (Is. **2**:**1-9**) The awful punishment of unbelievers. (Is. **2**:**10-22**)

Is. **2**:**1-9** The calling of the Gentiles, the spread of the gospel, and that far more extensive preaching of it yet to come, are foretold. Let Christians strengthen one another, and support one another. It is God who teaches his people, by his word and Spirit. Christ promotes peace, as well as holiness. If all men were real Christians, there could be no war; but nothing answering to these expressions has yet taken place on the earth. Whatever others do, let us walk in the light of this peace. Let us remember that when true religion flourishes, men delight in going up to the house of the Lord, and in urging others to accompany them. Those are in danger who please themselves with strangers to God; for we soon learn to follow the ways of persons whose company we keep. It is not having silver and gold, horses and chariots, that displeases God, but depending upon them, as if we could not be safe, and easy, and happy without them, and could not but be so with them. Sin is a disgrace to the poorest and the lowest. And though lands called Christian are not full of idols, in the literal sense, are they not full of idolized riches? and are not men so busy about their gains and indulgences, that the Lord, his truths, and precepts, are forgotten or despised?

Is. **2**:**10-22** The taking of Jerusalem by the Chaldeans seems first meant here, when idolatry among the Jews was done away; but our thoughts are led forward to the destruction of all the enemies of Christ. It is folly for those who are pursued by the wrath of God, to think to hide or shelter themselves from it. The shaking of the earth will be terrible to those who set their affections on things of the earth. Men's haughtiness will be brought down, either by the grace of God convincing them of the evil of pride, or by the providence of God depriving them of all the things they were proud of. The day of the Lord shall be upon those things in which they put their confidence. Those who will not be reasoned out of their sins, sooner or later shall be frightened out of them. Covetous men make money their god; but the time will come when they will feel it as much their burden. This whole passage may be applied to the case of an awakened sinner, ready to leave all that his soul may be saved. The Jews were prone to rely on their heathen neighbours; but they are here called upon to cease from depending on mortal man. We are all prone to the same sin. Then let not man be your fear, let not him be your hope; but let your hope be in the Lord your God. Let us make this our great concern.

Chapter 3

The calamities about to come upon the land. (Is. **3**:**1-9**) The wickedness of the people. (Is. **3**:**10-15**) The distress of the proud, luxurious women of Zion. (Is. **3**:**16-26**)

Is. **3**:**1-9** God was about to deprive Judah of every stay and support. The city and the land were to be made desolate, because their words and works had been rebellious against the Lord; even at his holy temple. If men do not stay themselves upon God, he will soon remove all other supports, and then they must sink. Christ is the Bread of life and the Water of life; if he be our Stay, we shall find that is a good part not to be taken away, John **6**:**27**. Here note, **1**. That the condition of sinners is exceedingly woful. **2**. It is the soul that is damaged by sin. **3**. Whatever evil befals sinners, be sure that they bring it on themselves.

Is. **3**:**10-15** The rule was certain; however there might be national prosperity or trouble, it would be well with the righteous and ill with the wicked. Blessed be God, there is abundant encouragement to the righteous to trust in him, and for sinners to repent and return to him. It was time for the Lord to show his might. He will call men to a strict account for all the wealth and power intrusted to and abused by them. If it is sinful to disregard the necessities of the poor, how odious and wicked a part do they act, who bring men into poverty, and then oppress them!

Is. **3**:**16-26** The prophet reproves and warns the daughters of Zion of the sufferings coming upon them. Let them know that God notices the folly and vanity of proud women, even of their dress. The punishments threatened answered the sin. Loathsome diseases often are the just punishment of pride. It is not material to ask what sort of ornaments they wore; many of these things, if they had not been in fashion, would have been ridiculed then as now. Their fashions differed much from those of our times, but human nature is the same. Wasting time and money, to the neglect of piety, charity, and even of justice, displease the Lord. Many professors at the present day, seem to think there is no harm in worldly finery; but were it not a great evil, would the Holy Spirit have taught the prophet to expose it so fully? The Jews being overcome, Jerusalem would be levelled with the ground; which is represented under the idea of a desolate female seated upon the earth. And when the Romans had destroyed Jerusalem, they struck a medal, on which was represented a woman sitting on the ground in a posture of grief. If sin be harboured within the walls, lamentation and mourning are near the gates.

Chapter 4

The havoc occasioned by war. (Is. **4**:**1**) The times of the Messiah. (Is. **4**:**2-6**)

Is. **4**:**1** This first **verse** belongs to the third chapter. When the troubles should come upon the land, as the unmarried state was deemed reproachful among the Jews, these women would act contrary to common usage, and seek husbands for themselves.

Is. **4**:**2-6** Not only the setting forth Christ's kingdom in the times of the apostles, but its enlargement by gathering the dispersed Jews into the church, is foretold. Christ is called the Branch of the Lord, being planted by his power, and flourishing to his praise. The gospel is the fruit of the Branch of the Lord; all the graces and comforts of the gospel spring from Christ. It is called the fruit of the earth, because it sprang up in this world, and was suited for the present state. It will be good evidence that we are distinguished from those merely called Israel, if we are brought to see all beauty in Christ, and holiness. As a type of this blessed day, Jerusalem should again flourish as a branch, and be blessed with the fruits of the earth. God will keep for himself a holy seed. When most of those that have a place and a name in Zion, and in Jerusalem, shall be cut off by their unbelief, some shall be left. Those only that are holy shall be left, when the Son of man shall gather out of his kingdom every thing which offends. By the judgment of God's providence, sinners were destroyed and consumed; but by the Spirit of grace they are reformed and converted. The Spirit herein acts as a Spirit of judgment, enlightening the mind, convincing the conscience; also as a Spirit of burning, quickening and strengthening the affections, and making men zealously affected in a good work. An ardent love to Christ and souls, and zeal against sin, will carry men on with resolution in endeavours to turn away ungodliness from Jacob. Every affliction serves believers as a furnace, to purify them from dross; and the convincing, enlightening, and powerful influences of the Holy Spirit, gradually root out their lusts, and render them holy as He is holy. God will protect his church, and all that belong to it. Gospel truths and ordinances are the glory of the church. Grace in the soul is the glory of it; and those that have it are kept by the power of God. But only those who are weary will seek rest; only those who are convinced that a storm is approaching, will look for shelter. Affected with a deep sense of the Divine displeasure, to which we are exposed by sin, let us at once have recourse to Jesus Christ, and thankfully accept the refuge he affords.

Chapter 5

The state and conduct of the Jewish nation. (Is. **5**:**1-7**) The judgments which would come. (Is. **5**:**8-23**) The executioners of these judgments. (Is. **5**:**24-30**)

Is. **5**:**1-7** Christ is God's beloved Son, and our beloved Saviour. The care of the Lord over the church of Israel, is described by the management of a vineyard. The advantages of our situation will be brought into the account another day. He planted it with the choicest vines; gave them a most excellent law, instituted proper ordinances. The temple was a tower, where God gave tokens of his presence. He set up his altar, to which the sacrifices should be brought; all the means of grace are denoted thereby. God expects fruit from those that enjoy privileges. Good purposes and good beginnings are good things, but not enough; there must be vineyard fruit; thoughts and affections, words and actions, agreeable to the Spirit. It brought forth bad fruit. Wild grapes are the fruits of the corrupt nature. Where grace does not work, corruption will. But the wickedness of those that profess religion, and enjoy the means of grace, must be upon the sinners themselves. They shall no longer be a peculiar people. When errors and vice go without check or control, the vineyard is unpruned; then it will soon be grown over with thorns. This is often shown in the departure of God's Spirit from those who have long striven against him, and the removal of his gospel from places which have long been a reproach to it. The explanation is given. It is sad with a soul, when, instead of the grapes of humility, meekness, love, patience, and contempt of the world, for which God looks, there are the wild grapes of pride, passion, discontent, and malice, and contempt of God; instead of the grapes of praying and praising, the wild grapes of cursing and swearing. Let us bring forth fruit with patience, that in the end we may obtain everlasting life.

Is. **5**:**8-23** Here is a woe to those who set their hearts on the wealth of the world. Not that it is sinful for those who have a house and a field to purchase another; but the fault is, that they never know when they have enough. Covetousness is idolatry; and while many envy the prosperous, wretched man, the Lord denounces awful woes upon him. How applicable to many among us! God has many ways to empty the most populous cities. Those who set their hearts upon the world, will justly be disappointed. Here is woe to those who dote upon the pleasures and the delights of sense. The use of music is lawful; but when it draws away the heart from God, then it becomes a sin to us. God's judgments have seized them, but they will not disturb themselves in their pleasures. The judgments are declared. Let a man be ever so high, death will bring him low; ever so mean, death will bring him lower. The fruit of these judgments shall be, that God will be glorified as a God of power. Also, as a God that is holy; he shall be owned and declared to be so, in the righteous punishment of proud men. Those are in a woful condition who set up sin, and who exert themselves to gratify their base lusts. They are daring in sin, and walk after their own lusts; it is in scorn that they call God the Holy One of Israel. They confound and overthrow distinctions between good and evil. They prefer their own reasonings to Divine revelations; their own devices to the counsels and commands of God. They deem it prudent and politic to continue profitable sins, and to neglect self-denying duties. Also, how light soever men make of drunkenness, it is a sin which lays open to the wrath and curse of God. Their judges perverted justice. Every sin needs some other to conceal it.

Is. **5**:**24-30** Let not any expect to live easily who live wickedly. Sin weakens the strength, the root of a people; it defaces the beauty, the blossoms of a people. When God's word is despised, and his law cast away, what can men expect but that God should utterly abandon them? When God comes forth in wrath, the hills tremble, fear seizes even great men. When God designs the ruin of a provoking people, he can find instruments to be employed in it, as he sent for the Chaldeans, and afterwards the Romans, to destroy the Jews. Those who would not hear the voice of God speaking by his prophets, shall hear the voice of their enemies roaring against them. Let the distressed look which way they will, all appears dismal. If God frowns upon us, how can any creature smile? Let us diligently seek the well-grounded assurance, that when all earthly helps and comforts shall fail, God himself will be the strength of our hearts, and our portion for ever.

Chapter 6

The vision which Isaiah beheld in the temple. (Is. **6**:**1-8**) The Lord declares the blindness to come upon the Jewish nation, and the destruction which would follow. (Is. **6**:**9-13**)

Is. **6**:**1-8** In this figurative vision, the temple is thrown open to view, even to the most holy place. The prophet, standing outside the temple, sees the Divine Presence seated on the mercy-seat, raised over the ark of the covenant, between the cherubim and seraphim, and the Divine glory filled the whole temple. See God upon his throne. This vision is explained, John **12**:**41**, that Isaiah now saw Christ's glory, and spake of Him, which is a full proof that our Saviour is God. In Christ Jesus, God is seated on a throne of grace; and through him the way into the holiest is laid open. See God's temple, his church on earth, filled with his glory. His train, the skirts of his robes, filled the temple, the whole world, for it is all God's temple. And yet he dwells in every contrite heart. See the blessed attendants by whom his government is served. Above the throne stood the holy angels, called seraphim, which means "burners;" they burn in love to God, and zeal for his glory against sin. The seraphim showing their faces veiled, declares that they are ready to yield obedience to all God's commands, though they do not understand the secret reasons of his counsels, government, or promises. All vain-glory, ambition, ignorance, and pride, would be done away by one view of Christ in his glory. This awful vision of the Divine Majesty overwhelmed the prophet with a sense of his own vileness. We are undone if there is not a Mediator between us and this holy God. A glimpse of heavenly glory is enough to convince us that all our righteousnesses are as filthy rags. Nor is there a man that would dare to speak to the Lord, if he saw the justice, holiness, and majesty of God, without discerning his glorious mercy and grace in Jesus Christ. The live coal may denote the assurance given to the prophet, of pardon, and acceptance in his work, through the atonement of Christ. Nothing is powerful to cleanse and comfort the soul, but what is taken from Christ's satisfaction and intercession. The taking away sin is necessary to our speaking with confidence and comfort, either to God in prayer, or from God in preaching; and those shall have their sin taken away who complain of it as a burden, and see themselves in danger of being undone by it. It is great comfort to those whom God sends, that they go for God, and may therefore speak in his name, assured that he will bear them out.

Is. **6:9-13** God sends Isaiah to foretell the ruin of his people. Many hear the sound of God's word, but do not feel the power of it. God sometimes, in righteous judgment, gives men up to blindness of mind, because they will not receive the truth in the love of it. But no humble inquirer after Christ, need to fear this awful doom, which is a spiritual judgment on those who will still hold fast their sins. Let every one pray for the enlightening of the Holy Spirit, that he may perceive how precious are the Divine mercies, by which alone we are secured against this dreadful danger. Yet the Lord would preserve a remnant, like the tenth, holy to him. And blessed be God, he still preserves his church; however professors or visible churches may be lopped off as unfruitful, the holy seed will shoot forth, from whom all the numerous branches of righteousness shall arise.

Chapter 7

Ahaz threatened by Israel and Syria; and is assured their attack would be in vain. (Is. **7:1-9**) God gives a sure sign by the promise of the long-expected Messiah. (Is. **7:10-16**) The folly and sin of seeking relief from Assyria are reproved. (Is. **7:17-25**)

Is. **7:1-9** Ungodly men are often punished by others as bad as themselves. Being in great distress and confusion, the Jews gave up all for lost. They had made God their enemy, and knew not how to make him their friend. The prophet must teach them to despise their enemies, in faith and dependence on God. Ahaz, in fear, called them two powerful princes. No, says the prophet, they are but tails of smoking firebrands, burnt out already. The two kingdoms of Syria and Israel were nearly expiring. While God has work for the firebrands of the earth, they consume all before them; but when their work is fulfilled, they will be extinguished in smoke. That which Ahaz thought most formidable, is made the ground of their defeat; because they have taken evil counsel against thee; which is an offence to God. God scorns the scorners, and gives his word that the attempt should not succeed. Man purposes, but God disposes. It was folly for those to be trying to ruin their neighbours, who were themselves near to ruin. Isaiah must urge the Jews to rely on the assurances given them. Faith is absolutely necessary to quiet and compose the mind in trials.

Is. **7:10-16** Secret disaffection to God is often disguised with the colour of respect to him; and those who are resolved that they will not trust God, yet pretend they will not tempt him. The prophet reproved Ahaz and his court, for the little value they had for Divine revelation. Nothing is more grievous to God than distrust, but the unbelief of man shall not make the promise of God of no effect; the Lord himself shall give a sign. How great soever your distress and danger, of you the Messiah is to be born, and you cannot be destroyed while that blessing is in you. It shall be brought to pass in a glorious manner; and the strongest consolations in time of trouble are derived from Christ, our relation to him, our interest in him, our expectations of him and from him. He would grow up like other children, by the use of the diet of those countries; but he would, unlike other children, uniformly refuse the evil and choose the good. And although his birth would be by the power of the Holy Ghost, yet he should not be fed with angels' food. Then follows a sign of the speedy destruction of the princes, now a terror to Judah. "Before this child," so it may be read; "this child which I have now in my arms," (Shear-jashub, the prophet's own son, Is. **7:3**.) shall be three or four years older, these enemies' forces shall be forsaken of both their kings. The prophecy is so solemn, the sign is so marked, as given by God himself after Ahaz rejected the offer, that it must have raised hopes far beyond what the present occasion suggested. And, if the prospect of the coming of the Divine Saviour was a never-failing support to the hopes of ancient believers, what cause have we to be thankful that the Word was made flesh! May we trust in and love Him, and copy his example.

Is. **7:17-25** Let those who will not believe the promises of God, expect to hear the alarms of his threatenings; for who can resist or escape his judgments? The Lord shall sweep all away; and whomsoever he employs in any service for him, he will pay. All speaks a sad change of the face of that pleasant land. But what melancholy change is there, which sin will not make with a people? Agriculture would cease. Sorrows of every kind will come upon all who neglect the great salvation. If we remain unfruitful under the means of grace, the Lord will say, Let no fruit grow on thee henceforth for ever.

Chapter 8

Exhortations and warnings. (Is. **8:1-8**) Comfort for those who fear God. (Is. **8:9-16**) Afflictions to idolaters. (Is. **8:17-22**)

Is. **8:1-8** The prophet is to write on a large roll, or on a metal tablet, words which meant, "Make speed to spoil, hasten to the prey:" pointing out that the Assyrian army should come with speed, and make great spoil. Very soon the riches of Damascus and of Samaria, cities then secure and formidable, shall be taken away by the king of Assyria. The prophet pleads with the promised Messiah, who should appear in that land in the fulness of time, and, therefore, as God, would preserve it in the mean time. As a gentle brook is an apt emblem of a mild government, so an overflowing torrent represents a conqueror and tyrant. The invader's success was also described by a bird of prey, stretching its wings over the whole land. Those who reject Christ, will find that what they call liberty is the basest slavery. But no enemy shall pluck the believer out of Emmanuel's hand, or deprive him of his heavenly inheritance.

Is. **8:9-16** The prophet challenges the enemies of the Jews. Their efforts would be vain, and themselves broken to pieces. It concerns us, in time of trouble, to watch against all such fears as put us upon crooked courses for our own security. The believing fear of God preserves against the disquieting fear of man. If we thought rightly of the greatness and glory of God, we should see all the power of our enemies restrained. The Lord, who will be a Sanctuary to those who trust in him, will be a Stone of stumbling, and a Rock of offence, to those who make the creature their fear and their hope. If the things of God be an offence to us, they will undo us. The apostle quotes this as to all who persisted in unbelief of the gospel of Christ, I Pet. **2:8**. The crucified Emmanuel, who was and is a Stumbling-stone and Rock of offence to unbelieving Jews, is no less so to thousands who are called Christians. The preaching of the cross is foolishness in their esteem; his doctrines and precepts offend them.

Is. **8:17-22** The prophet foresaw that the Lord would hide his face; but he would look for his return in favour to them again. Though not miraculous signs, the children's names were memorials from God, suited to excite attention. The unbelieving Jews were prone to seek counsel in difficulties, from diviners of different descriptions, whose foolish and sinful ceremonies are alluded to. Would we know how we may seek to our God, and come to the knowledge of his mind? To the law and to the testimony; for there you will see what is good, and what the Lord requires. We must speak of the things of God in the words which the Holy Ghost teaches, and be ruled by them. To those that seek to familiar spirits, and regard not God's law and testimony, there shall be horror and misery. Those that go away from God, go out of the way of all good; for fretfulness is a sin that is its own punishment. They shall despair, and see no way of relief, when they curse God. And their fears will represent every thing as frightful. Those that shut their eyes against the light of God's word, will justly be left to darkness. All the miseries that ever were felt or witnessed on earth, are as nothing, compared with what will overwhelm those who leave the words of Christ, to follow delusions.

Chapter 9

The Son that should be born, and his kingdom. (Is. **9**:**1-7**) The judgments to come upon Israel, and on the enemies of the kingdom of Christ. (Is. **9**:**8-21**)

Is. **9**:**1-7** The Syrians and Assyrians first ravaged the countries here mentioned, and that region was first favoured by the preaching of Christ. Those that want the gospel, walk in darkness, and in the utmost danger. But when the gospel comes to any place, to any soul, light comes. Let us earnestly pray that it may shine into our hearts, and make us wise unto salvation. The gospel brings joy with it. Those who would have joy, must expect to go through hard work, as the husbandman, before he has the joy of harvest; and hard conflict, as the soldier, before he divides the spoil. The Jews were delivered from the yoke of many oppressors; this was a shadow of the believer's deliverance from the yoke of Satan. The cleansing the souls of believers from the power and pollution of sin, would be by the influence of the Holy Spirit, as purifying fire. These great things for the church, shall be done by the Messiah, Emmanuel. The Child is born; it was certain; and the church, before Christ came in the flesh, benefitted by his undertaking. It is a prophecy of him and of his kingdom, which those that waited for the Consolation of Israel read with pleasure. This Child was born for the benefit of us men, of us sinners, of all believers, from the beginning to the end of the world. Justly is he called Wonderful, for he is both God and man. His love is the wonder of angels and glorified saints. He is the Counsellor, for he knew the counsels of God from eternity; and he gives counsel to men, in which he consults our welfare. He is the Wonderful Counsellor; none teaches like him. He is God, the mighty One. Such is the work of the Mediator, that no less power than that of the mighty God could bring it to pass. He is God, one with the Father. As the Prince of Peace, he reconciles us to God; he is the Giver of peace in the heart and conscience; and when his kingdom is fully established, men shall learn war no more. The government shall be upon him; he shall bear the burden of it. Glorious things are spoken of Christ's government. There is no end to the increase of its peace, for the happiness of its subjects shall last for ever. The exact agreement of this prophecy with the doctrine of the New Testament, shows that Jewish prophets and Christian teachers had the same view of the person and salvation of the Messiah. To what earthly king or kingdom can these words apply? Give then, O Lord, to thy people to know thee by every endearing name, and in every glorious character. Give increase of grace in every heart of thy redeemed upon earth.

Is. **9**:**8-21** Those are ripening apace for ruin, whose hearts are unhumbled under humbling providences. For that which God designs, in smiting us, is, to turn us to himself; and if this point be not gained by lesser judgments, greater may be expected. The leaders of the people misled them. We have reason to be afraid of those that speak well of us, when we do ill. Wickedness was universal, all were infected with it. They shall be in trouble, and see no way out; and when men's ways displease the Lord, he makes even their friends to be at war with them. God would take away those they thought to have help from. Their rulers were the head. Their false prophets were the tail and the rush, the most despicable. In these civil contests, men preyed on near relations who were as their own flesh. The people turn not to Him who smites them, therefore he continues to smite: for when God judges, he will overcome; and the proudest, stoutest sinner shall either bend or break.

Chapter 10

Woes against proud oppressors. (Is. **10**:**1-4**) The Assyrian but an instrument in the hand of God for the punishment of his people. (Is. **10**:**5-19**) The deliverance from him. (Is. **10**:**20-34**)

Is. **10**:**1-4** These **verse**s are to be joined with the foregoing chapter. Woe to the superior powers that devise and decree unrighteous decrees! And woe to the inferior officers that draw them up, and enter them on record! But what will sinners do? Whither will they flee?

Is. **10**:**5-19** See what a change sin made. The king of Assyria, in his pride, thought to act by his own will. The tyrants of the world are tools of Providence. God designs to correct his people for their hypocrisy, and bring them nearer to him; but is that Sennacherib's design? No; he designs to gratify his own covetousness and ambition. The Assyrian boasts what great things he has done to other nations, by his own policy and power. He knows not that it is God who makes him what he is, and puts the staff into his hand. He had done all this with ease; none moved the wing, or cried as birds do when their nests are rifled. Because he conquered Samaria, he thinks Jerusalem would fall of course. It was lamentable that Jerusalem should have set up graven images, and we cannot wonder that she was excelled in them by the heathen. But is it not equally foolish for Christians to emulate the people of the world in vanities, instead of keeping to things which are their special honour? For a tool to boast, or to strive against him that formed it, would not be more out of the way, than for Sennacherib to vaunt himself against Jehovah. When God brings his people into trouble, it is to bring sin to their remembrance, and humble them, and to awaken them to a sense of their duty; this must be the fruit, even the taking away of sin. When these points are gained by the affliction, it shall be removed in mercy. This attempt upon Zion and Jerusalem should come to nothing. God will be as a fire to consume the workers of iniquity, both soul and body. The desolation should be as when a standard-bearer fainteth, and those who follow are put to confusion. Who is able to stand before this great and holy Lord God?

Is. **10**:**20-34** By our afflictions we may learn not to make creatures our confidence. Those only can with comfort stay upon God, who return to him in truth, not in pretence and profession only. God will justly bring this wasting away on a provoking people, but will graciously set bounds to it. It is against the mind and will of God, that his people, whatever happens, should give way to fear. God's anger against his people is but for a moment; and when that is turned from us, we need not fear the fury of man. The rod with which he corrected his people, shall not only be laid aside, but thrown into the fire. To encourage God's people, the prophet puts them in mind of what God had formerly done against the enemies of his church. God's people shall be delivered from the Assyrians. Some think it looks to the deliverance of the Jews out of their captivity; and further yet, to the redemption of believers from the tyranny of sin and Satan. And this, "because of the anointing;" for his people Israel's sake, the believers among them that had received the unction of Divine grace. And for the sake of the Messiah, the Anointed of God. Here is, Is. **10**:**28-34**, a prophetical description of Sennacherib's march towards Jerusalem, when he threatened to destroy that city. Then the Lord, in whom Hezekiah trusted, cut down his army like the hewing of a forest. Let us apply what is here written, to like matters in other ages of the church of Christ. Because of the anointing of our great Redeemer, the yoke of every antichrist must be broken from off his church: and if our souls partake of the unction of the Holy Spirit, complete and eternal deliverances will be secured to us.

Chapter 11

The peaceful character of Christ's kingdom and subjects. (Is. **11**:**1-9**) The conversion of the Gentiles and Jews. (Is. **11**:**10-16**)

Is. **11**:**1-9** The Messiah is called a Rod, and a Branch. The words signify a small, tender product; a shoot, such as is easily broken off. He comes forth out of the stem of Jesse; when the royal family was cut down and almost levelled with the ground, it would sprout again. The house of David was brought very low at the time of Christ's birth. The Messiah thus gave early notice that his kingdom was not of this world. But the Holy Spirit, in all his gifts and graces, shall rest and abide upon him; he shall have the fulness of the Godhead dwelling in him, Col. **1**:**19**; **2**:**9**. Many consider that seven gifts of the Holy Spirit are here mentioned. And the doctrine of the influences of the Holy Spirit is here clearly taught. The Messiah would be just and righteous in all his government. His threatening shall be executed by the working of his Spirit according to his word. There shall be great peace and quiet under his government. The gospel changes the nature, and makes those who trampled on the meek of the earth, meek like them, and kind to them. But it shall be more fully shown in the latter days. Also Christ, the great Shepherd, shall take care of his flock, that the nature of troubles, and of death itself, shall be so changed, that they shall not do any real hurt. God's people shall be delivered, not only from evil, but from the fear of it. Who shall separate us from the love of Christ? The better we know the God of love, the more shall we be changed into the same likeness, and the better disposed to all who have any likeness to him. This knowledge shall extend as the sea, so far shall it spread. And this blessed power there have been witnesses in every age of Christianity, though its most glorious time, here foretold, is not yet arrived. Meanwhile let us aim that our example and endeavours may help to promote the honour of Christ and his kingdom of peace.

Is. **11**:**10-16** When the gospel should be publicly preached, the Gentiles would seek Christ Jesus as their Lord and Saviour, and find rest of soul. When God's time is come for the deliverance of his people, mountains of opposition shall become plains before him. God can soon turn gloomy days into glorious ones. And while we expect the Lord to gather his ancient people, and bring them home to his church, also to bring in the fulness of the Gentiles, when all will be united in holy love, let us tread the highway of holiness he has made for his redeemed. Let us wait for the mercy of our Lord Jesus Christ unto eternal life, looking to him to prepare our way through death, that river which separates this world from the eternal world.

Chapter 12

This is a hymn of praise suited to the times of the Messiah.

The song of praise in this chapter is suitable for the return of the outcasts of Israel from their long captivity, but it is especially suitable to the case of a sinner, when he first finds peace and joy in believing; to that of a believer, when his peace is renewed after corrections for backslidings; and to that of the whole company of the redeemed, when they meet before the throne of God in heaven. The promise is sure, and the blessings contained in it are very rich; and the benefits enjoyed through Jesus Christ, call for the most enlarged thanksgivings. By Jesus Christ, the Root of Jesse, the Divine anger against mankind was turned away, for he is our Peace. Those to whom God is reconciled, he comforts. They are taught to triumph in God and their interest in him. I will trust him to prepare me for his salvation, and preserve me to it. I will trust him with all my concerns, not doubting but he will make all to work for good. Faith in God is a sovereign remedy against tormenting fears. Many Christians have God for their strength, who have him not for their song; they walk in darkness: but those who have God for their strength ought to make him their song; that is, give him the glory of it, and take to themselves the comfort of it. This salvation is from the love of God the Father, it comes to us through God the Son, it is applied by the new-creating power of God the Spirit. When this is seen by faith, the trembling sinner learns to hope in God, and is delivered from fear. The purifying and sanctifying influences of the Holy Ghost often are denoted under the emblem of springing water. This work flows through the mediation of Christ, and is conveyed to our souls by means of God's ordinances. Blessed be God, we have wells of salvation opened on every side, and may draw from them the waters of life and consolation. In the second part of this gospel song, Is. **12**:**4-6**, believers encourage one another to praise God, and seek to draw others to join them in it. No difference of opinions about the times and seasons, and other such matters, ought to divide the hearts of Christians. Let it be our care that we may be placed amongst those to whom he will say, Come, ye blessed of my Father, receive the kingdom prepared for you from the beginning of the world.

Chapter 13

The armies of God's wrath. (Is. **13**:**1-5**) The conquest of Babylon. (Is. **13**:**6-18**) Its final desolation. (Is. **13**:**19-22**)

Is. **13**:**1-5** The threatenings of God's word press heavily upon the wicked, and are a sore burden, too heavy for them to bear. The persons brought together to lay Babylon waste, are called God's sanctified or appointed ones; designed for this service, and made able to do it. They are called God's mighty ones, because they had their might from God, and were now to use it for him. They come from afar. God can make those a scourge and ruin to his enemies, who are farthest off, and therefore least dreaded.

Is. **13**:**6-18** We have here the terrible desolation of Babylon by the Medes and Persians. Those who in the day of their peace were proud, and haughty, and terrible, are quite dispirited when trouble comes. Their faces shall be scorched with the flame. All comfort and hope shall fail. The stars of heaven shall not give their light, the sun shall be darkened. Such expressions are often employed by the prophets, to describe the convulsions of governments. God will visit them for their iniquity, particularly the sin of pride, which brings men low. There shall be a general scene of horror. Those who join themselves to Babylon, must expect to share her plagues, Rev. **18**:**4**. All that men have, they would give for their lives, but no man's riches shall be the ransom of his life. Pause here and wonder that men should be thus cruel and inhuman, and see how corrupt the nature of man is become. And that little infants thus suffer, which shows that there is an original guilt, by which life is forfeited as soon as it is begun. The day of the Lord will, indeed, be terrible with wrath and fierce anger, far beyond all here stated. Nor will there be any place for the sinner to flee to, or attempt an escape. But few act as though they believed these things.

Is. **13**:**19-22** Babylon was a noble city; yet it should be wholly destroyed. None shall dwell there. It shall be a haunt for wild beasts. All this is fulfilled. The fate of this proud city is a proof of the truth of the Bible, and an emblem of the approaching ruin of the New Testament Babylon; a warning to sinners to flee from the wrath to come, and it encourages believers to expect victory over every enemy of their souls, and of the church of God. The whole world changes and is liable to decay. Wherefore let us give diligence to obtain a kingdom which cannot be moved; and in this hope let us hold fast that grace whereby we may serve God acceptably with reverence and godly fear.

Chapter 14

The destruction of Babylon, and the death of its proud monarch. (Is. **14**:**1-23**) Assurance of the destruction of Assyria. (Is. **14**:**24-27**) The destruction of the Philistines. (Is. **14**:**28-32**)

Is. **14**:**1-23** The whole plan of Divine Providence is arranged with a view to the good of the people of God. A settlement in the land of promise is of God's mercy. Let the church receive those whom God receives. God's people, wherever their lot is cast, should endeavour to recommend religion by a right and winning conversation. Those that would not be reconciled to them, should be humbled by them. This may be applied to the success of the gospel, when those were brought to obey it who had opposed it. God himself undertakes to work a blessed change. They shall have rest from their sorrow and fear, the sense of their present burdens, and the dread of worse. Babylon abounded in riches. The king of Babylon having the absolute command of so much wealth, by the help of it ruled the nations. This refers especially to the people of the Jews; and it filled up the measure of the king of Babylon's sins. Tyrants sacrifice their true interest to their lusts and passions. It is gracious ambition to covet to be like the Most Holy, for he has said, Be ye holy, for I am holy; but it is sinful ambition to aim to be like the Most High, for he has said, He who exalts himself shall be abased. The devil thus drew our first parents to sin. Utter ruin should be brought upon him. Those that will not cease to sin, God will make to cease. He should be slain, and go down to the grave; this is the common fate of tyrants. True glory, that is, true grace, will go up with the soul to heaven, but vain pomp will go down with the body to the grave; there is an end of it. To be denied burial, if for righteousness' sake, may be rejoiced in, Matt. **5**:**12**. But if the just punishment of sin, it denotes that impenitent sinners shall rise to everlasting shame and contempt. Many triumphs should be in his fall. God will reckon with those that disturb the peace of mankind. The receiving the king of Babylon into the regions of the dead, shows there is a world of spirits, to which the souls of men remove at death. And that souls have con**verse** with each other, though we have none with them; and that death and hell will be death and hell indeed, to all who fall unholy, from the height of this world's pomps, and the fulness of its pleasures. Learn from all this, that the seed of evil-doers shall never be renowned. The royal city is to be ruined and forsaken. Thus the utter destruction of the New Testament Babylon is illustrated, Rev. **18**:**2**. When a people will not be made clean with the besom of reformation, what can they expect but to be swept off the face of the earth with the besom of destruction?

Is. **14**:**24-27** Let those that make themselves a yoke and a burden to God's people, see what they are to expect. Let those that are the called according to God's purpose, comfort themselves, that whatever God has purposed, it shall stand. The Lord of hosts has purposed to break the Assyrian's yoke; his hand is stretched out to execute this purpose; who has power to turn it back? By such dispensations of providence, the Almighty shows in the most convincing manner, that sin is hateful in his sight.

Is. **14**:**28-32** Assurance is given of the destruction of the Philistines and their power, by famine and war. Hezekiah would be more terrible to them than Uzziah had been. Instead of rejoicing, there would be lamentation, for the whole land would be ruined. Such destruction will come upon the proud and rebellious, but the Lord founded Zion for a refuge to poor sinners, who flee from the wrath to come, and trust in his mercy through Christ Jesus. Let us tell all around of our comforts and security, and exhort them to seek the same refuge and salvation.

Chapter 15

The Divine judgments about to come upon the Moabites.

This prophecy coming to pass within three years, would confirm the prophet's mission, and the belief in all his other prophecies. Concerning Moab it is foretold, Is. **15**:**1**. That their chief cities should be surprised by the enemy. Great changes, and very dismal ones, may be made in a very little time. Is. **15**:**2**. The Moabites would have recourse to their idols for relief. Ungodly men, when in trouble, have no comforter. But they are seldom brought by their terrors to approach our forgiving God with true sorrow and believing prayer. Is. **15**:**3**. There should be the cries of grief through the land. It is poor relief to have many fellow-sufferers, fellow-mourners. Is. **15**:**4**. The courage of their soldiers should fail. God can easily deprive a nation of that on which it most depended for strength and defence. **5**. These calamities should cause grief in the neighbouring parts. Though enemies to Israel, yet as our fellow-creatures, it should be grievous to see them in such distress. In Is. **15**:**6-9**, the prophet describes the woful lamentations heard through the country of Moab, when it became a prey to the Assyrian army. The country should be plundered. And famine is usually the sad effect of war. Those who are eager to get abundance of this world, and to lay up what they have gotten, little consider how soon it may be all taken from them. While we warn our enemies to escape from ruin, let us pray for them, that they may seek and find forgiveness of their sins.

Chapter 16

Moab is exhorted to yield obedience. (Is. **16**:**1-5**) The pride and the judgments of Moab. (Is. **16**:**6-14**)

Is. **16**:**1-5** God tells sinners what they may do to prevent ruin; so he does to Moab. Let them send the tribute they formerly engaged to pay to Judah. Take it as good advice. Break off thy sins by righteousness, it may lengthen thy quiet. And this may be applied to the great gospel duty of submission to Christ. Send him the lamb, the best you have, yourselves a living sacrifice. When you come to God, the great Ruler, come in the name of the Lamb, the Lamb of God. Those who will not submit to Christ, shall be as a bird that wanders from her nest, which shall be snatched up by the next bird of prey. Those who will not yield to the fear of God, shall be made to yield to the fear of every thing else. He advises them to be kind to the seed of Israel. Those that expect to find favour when in trouble themselves, must show favour to those in trouble. What is here said concerning the throne of Hezekiah, also belongs, in a much higher sense, to the kingdom of Jesus Christ. Though by subjection to Him we may not enjoy worldly riches or honours, but may be exposed to poverty and contempt, we shall have peace of conscience and eternal life.

Is. **16**:**6-14** Those who will not be counselled, cannot be helped. More souls are ruined by pride than by any other sin whatever. Also, the very proud are commonly very passionate. With lies many seek to gain the gratification of pride and passion, but they shall not compass proud and angry projects. Moab was famous for fields and vineyards; but they shall be laid waste by the invading army. God can soon turn laughter into mourning, and joy into heaviness. In God let us always rejoice with holy triumph; in earthly things let us always rejoice with holy trembling. The prophet looks with concern on the desolations of such a pleasant country; it causes inward grief. The false gods of Moab are unable to help; and the God of Israel, the only true God, can and will make good what he has spoken. Let Moab know her ruin is very near, and prepare. The most awful declarations of Divine wrath, discover the way of escape to those who take warning. There is no escape, but by submission to the Son of David, and devoting ourselves to him. And, at length, when the appointed time comes, all the glory, prosperity, and multitude of the wicked shall perish.

Chapter 17

Syria and Israel threatened. (Is. **17**:**1-11**) The woe of Israel's enemies. (Is. **17**:**12-14**)

Is. **17**:**1-11** Sin desolates cities. It is strange that great conquerors should take pride in being enemies to mankind; but it is better that flocks should lie down there, than that they should harbour any in open rebellion against God and holiness. The strong holds of Israel, the kingdom of the ten tribes, will be brought to ruin. Those who are partakers in sin, are justly made partakers in ruin. The people had, by sins, made themselves ripe for ruin; and their glory was as quickly cut down and taken away by the enemy, as the corn is out of the field by the husbandman. Mercy is reserved in the midst of judgment, for a remnant. But very few shall be marked to be saved. Only here and there one was left behind. But they shall be a remnant made holy. The few that are saved were awakened to return to God. They shall acknowledge his hand in all events; they shall give him the glory due to his name. To bring us to this, is the design of his providence, as he is our Maker; and the work of his grace, as he is the Holy One of Israel. They shall look off from their idols, the creatures of their own fancy. We have reason to account those afflictions happy, which part between us and our sins. The God of our salvation is the Rock of our strength; and our forgetfulness and unmindfulness of him are at the bottom of all sin. The pleasant plants, and shoots from a foreign soil, are expressions for strange and idolatrous worship, and the vile practices connected therewith. Diligence would be used to promote the growth of these strange slips, but all in vain. See the evil and danger of sin, and its certain consequences.

Is. **17**:**12**-**14** The rage and force of the Assyrians resembled the mighty waters of the sea; but when the God of Israel should rebuke them, they would flee like chaff, or like a rolling thing, before the whirlwind. In the evening Jerusalem would be in trouble, because of the powerful invader, but before morning his army would be nearly cut off. Happy are those who remember God as their salvation, and rely on his power and grace. The trouble of the believers, and the prosperity of their enemies, will be equally short; while the joy of the former, and the destruction of those that hate and spoil them, shall last for ever.

Chapter 18

God's care for his people; and the increase of the church.

This chapter is one of the most obscure in Scripture, though more of it probably was understood by those for whose use it was first intended, than by us now. Swift messengers are sent by water to a nation marked by Providence, and measured out, trodden under foot. God's people are trampled on; but whoever thinks to swallow them up, finds they are cast down, yet not deserted, not destroyed. All the dwellers on earth must watch the motions of the Divine Providence, and wait upon the directions of the Divine will. God gives assurance to his prophet, and by him to be given to his people. Zion is his rest for ever, and he will look after it. He will suit to their case the comforts and refreshments he provides for them; they will be acceptable, because seasonable. He will reckon with his and their enemies; and as God's people are protected at all seasons of the year, so their enemies are exposed at all seasons. A tribute of praise should be brought to God from all this. What is offered to God, must be offered in the way he has appointed; and we may expect him to meet us where he records his name. Thus shall the nations of the earth be convinced that Jehovah is the God, and Israel is his people, and shall unite in presenting spiritual sacrifices to his glory. Happy are those who take warning by his judgment on others, and hasten to join him and his people. Whatever land or people may be intended, we are here taught not to think that God takes no care of his church, and has no respect to the affairs of men, because he permits the wicked to triumph for a season. He has wise reasons for so doing, which we cannot now understand, but which will appear at the great day of his coming, when he will bring every work into judgment, and reward every man according to his works.

Chapter 19

Judgments upon Egypt. (Is. **19**:**1**-**17**) Its deliverance, and the conversion of the people. (Is. **19**:**18**-**25**)

Is. **19**:**1**-**17** God shall come into Egypt with his judgments. He will raise up the causes of their destruction from among themselves. When ungodly men escape danger, they are apt to think themselves secure; but evil pursues sinners, and will speedily overtake them, except they repent. The Egyptians will be given over into the hand of one who shall rule them with rigour, as was shortly after fulfilled. The Egyptians were renowned for wisdom and science; yet the Lord would give them up to their own **perverse** schemes, and to quarrel, till their land would be brought by their contests to become an object of contempt and pity. He renders sinners afraid of those whom they have despised and oppressed; and the Lord of hosts will make the workers of iniquity a terror to themselves, and to each other; and every object around a terror to them.

Is. **19**:**18**-**25** The words, "In that day," do not always refer to the passage just before. At a time which was to come, the Egyptians shall speak the holy language, the Scripture language; not only understand it, but use it. Converting grace, by changing the heart, changes the language; for out of the abundance of the heart the mouth speaks. So many Jews shall come to Egypt, that they shall soon fill five cities. Where the sun was worshipped, a place infamous for idolatry, even there shall be a wonderful reformation. Christ, the great Altar, who sanctifies every gift, shall be owned, and the gospel sacrifices of prayer and praise shall be offered up. Let the broken-hearted and afflicted, whom the Lord has wounded, and thus taught to return to, and call upon him, take courage; for He will heal their souls, and turn their sorrowing supplications into joyful praises. The Gentile nations shall not only unite with each other in the gospel fold under Christ, the great Shepherd, but they shall all be united with the Jews. They shall be owned together by him; they shall all share in one and the same blessing. Meeting at the same throne of grace, and serving with each other in the same business of religion, should end all disputes, and unite the hearts of believers to each other in holy love.

Chapter 20

The invasion and conquest of Egypt and Ethiopia.

Isaiah was a sign to the people by his unusual dress, when he walked abroad. He commonly wore sackcloth as a prophet, to show himself mortified to the world. He was to loose this from his loins; to wear no upper garments, and to go barefooted. This sign was to signify, that the Egyptians and Ethiopians should be led away captives by the king of Assyria, thus stripped. The world will often deem believers foolish, when singular in obedience to God. But the Lord will support his servants under the most trying effects of their obedience; and what they are called upon to suffer for his sake, commonly is light, compared with what numbers groan under from year to year from sin. Those who make any creature their expectation and glory, and so put it in the place of God, will, sooner or later, be ashamed of it. But disappointment in creature-confidences, instead of driving us to despair, should drive us to God, and our expectation shall not be in vain. The same lesson is in force now; and where shall we look for aid in the hour of necessity, but to the Lord our Righteousness?

Chapter 21

The taking of Babylon. (Is. **21**:**1**-**10**) Of the Edomites. (Is. **21**:**11**,**12**) Of the Arabs. (Is. **21**:**13**-**17**)

Is. **21**:**1**-**10** Babylon was a flat country, abundantly watered. The destruction of Babylon, so often prophesied of by Isaiah, was typical of the destruction of the great foe of the New Testament church, foretold in the Revelation. To the poor oppressed captives it would be welcome news; to the proud oppressors it would be grievous. Let this check vain mirth and sensual pleasures, that we know not in what heaviness the mirth may end. Here is the alarm given to Babylon, when forced by Cyrus. An ass and a camel seem to be the symbols of the Medes and Persians. Babylon's idols shall be so far from protecting her, that they shall be broken down. True believers are the corn of God's floor; hypocrites are but as chaff and straw, with which the wheat is now mixed, but from which it shall be separated. The corn of God's floor must expect to be threshed by afflictions and persecutions. God's Israel of old was afflicted. Even then God owns it is his still. In all events concerning the church, past, present, and to come, we must look to God, who has power to do any thing for his church, and grace to do every thing that is for her good.

Is. **21**:**11**,**12** God's prophets and ministers are as watchmen in the city in a time of peace, to see that all is safe. As watchmen in the camp in time of war, to warn of the motions of the enemy. After a long sleep in sin and security, it is time to rise, to awake out of sleep. We have a great deal of work to do, a long journey to go; it is time to be stirring. After a long dark night is there any hope of the day dawning? What tidings of the night? What happens to-night? We must never be secure. But many make curious inquiries of the watchmen. They would willingly have nice questions solved, or difficult prophecies interpreted; but they do not seek into the state of their own souls, about the way of salvation, and the path of duty. The watchman answers by way of prophecy. There comes first a morning of light, and peace, and opportunity; but afterward comes a night of trouble and calamity. If there be a morning of youth and health, there will come a night of sickness and old age; if a morning of prosperity in the family, in the public, yet we must look for changes. It is our wisdom to improve the present morning, in preparation for the night that is coming after it. Inquire, return, come. We are urged to do it quickly, for there is no time to trifle. Those that return and come to God, will find they have a great deal of work to do, and but little time to do it in.

Is. **21**:**13-17** The Arabians lived in tents, and kept cattle. A destroying army shall be brought upon them, and make them an easy prey. We know not what straits we may be brought into before we die. Those may know the want of necessary food who now eat bread to the full. Neither the skill of archers, nor the courage of mighty men, can protect from the judgments of God. That is poor glory, which will thus quickly come to nothing. Thus hath the Lord said to me; and no word of his shall fall to the ground. We may be sure the Strength of Israel will not lie. Happy are those only whose riches and glory are out of the reach of invaders; all other prosperity will speedily pass away.

Chapter 22

The siege and taking of Jerusalem. (Is. **22**:**1-7**) The wicked conduct of its inhabitants. (Is. **22**:**8-14**) The displacing of Shebna, and the promotion of Eliakim, applied to the Messiah. (Is. **22**:**15-25**)

Is. **22**:**1-7** Why is Jerusalem in such terror? Her slain men are not slain with the sword, but with famine; or, slain with fear, disheartened. Their rulers fled, but were overtaken. The servants of God, who foresee and warn sinners of coming miseries, are affected by the prospect. But all the horrors of a city taken by storm, faintly shadow forth the terrors of the day of wrath.

Is. **22**:**8-14** The weakness of Judah now appeared more than ever. Now also they discovered their carnal confidence and their carnal security. They looked to the fortifications. They made sure of water for the city. But they were regardless of God in all these preparations. They did not care for his glory in what they did. They did not depend upon him for a blessing on their endeavours. For every creature is to us what God makes it to be; and we must bless him for it, and use it for him. There was great contempt of God's wrath and justice, in contending with them. God's design was to humble them, and bring them to repentance. They walked contrary to this. Actual disbelief of another life after this, is at the bottom of the carnal security and brutish sensuality, which are the sin, the shame, and ruin of so great a part of mankind. God was displeased at this. It is a sin against the remedy, and it is not likely they should ever repent of it. Whether this unbelief works by presumption or despair, it produces the same contempt of God, and is a token that a man will perish wilfully.

Is. **22**:**15-25** This message to Shebna is a reproof of his pride, vanity, and security; what vanity is all earthly grandeur, which death will so soon end! What will it avail, whether we are laid in a magnificent tomb, or covered with the green sod? Those who, when in power, turn and toss others, will be justly turned and tossed themselves. Eliakim should be put into Shebna's place. Those called to places of trust and power, should seek to God for grace to enable them to do their duty. Eliakim's advancement is described. Our Lord Jesus describes his own power as Mediator, Rev. **3**:**7**, that he has the key of David. His power in the kingdom of heaven, and in ordering all the affairs of that kingdom, is absolute. Rulers should be fathers to those under their government; and the honour men bring unto their families, by their piety and usefulness, is more to be valued than what they derive from them by their names and titles. The glory of this world gives a man no real worth or excellence; it is but hung upon him, and it will soon drop from him. Eliakim was compared to a nail in a sure place; all his family are said to depend upon him. In eastern houses, rows of large spikes were built up in the walls. Upon these the moveables and utensils were hung. Our Lord Jesus is as a nail in a sure place. That soul cannot perish, nor that concern fall to the ground, which is by faith hung upon Christ. He will set before the believer an open door, which no man can shut, and bring both body and soul to eternal glory. But those who neglect so great salvation will find, that when he shutteth none can open, whether it be shutting out from heaven, or shutting up in hell for ever.

Chapter 23

The overthrow of Tyre. (Is. **23**:**1-14**) It is established again. (Is. **23**:**15-18**)

Is. **23**:**1-14** Tyre was the mart of the nations. She was noted for mirth and diversions; and this made her loth to consider the warnings God gave by his servants. Her merchants were princes, and lived like princes. Tyre being destroyed and laid waste, the merchants should abandon her. Flee to shift for thine own safety; but those that are uneasy in one place, will be so in another; for when God's judgments pursue sinners, they will overtake them. Whence shall all this trouble come? It is a destruction from the Almighty. God designed to convince men of the vanity and uncertainty of all earthly glory. Let the ruin of Tyre warn all places and persons to take heed of pride; for he who exalts himself shall be abased. God will do it, who has all power in his hand; but the Chaldeans shall be the instruments.

Is. **23**:**15-18** The desolations of Tyre were not to be for ever. The Lord will visit Tyre in mercy. But when set at liberty, she will use her old arts of temptation. The love of worldly wealth is spiritual idolatry; and covetousness is spiritual idolatry. This directs those that have wealth, to use it in the service of God. When we abide with God in our worldly callings, when we do all in our power to further the gospel, then our merchandise and hire are holiness to the Lord, if we look to his glory. Christians should carry on business as God's servants, and use riches as his stewards.

Chapter 24

The desolation of the land. (Is. **24**:**1-12**) A few shall be preserved. (Is. **24**:**13-15**) God's kingdom advanced by his judgments. (Is. **24**:**16-23**)

Is. **24**:**1-12** All whose treasures and happiness are laid up on earth, will soon be brought to want and misery. It is good to apply to ourselves what the Scripture says of the vanity and vexation of spirit which attend all things here below. Sin has turned the earth upside down; the earth is become quite different to man, from what it was when God first made it to be his habitation. It is, at the best, like a flower, which withers in the hands of those that please themselves with it, and lay it in their bosoms. The world we live in is a world of disappointment, a vale of tears; the children of men in it are but of few days, and full of trouble, See the power of God's curse, how it makes all empty, and lays waste all ranks and conditions. Sin brings these calamities upon the earth; it is polluted by the sins of men, therefore it is made desolate by God's judgments. Carnal joy will soon be at end, and the end of it is heaviness. God has many ways to imbitter wine and strong drink to those who love them; distemper of body, anguish of mind, and the ruin of the estate, will make strong drink bitter, and the delights of sense tasteless. Let men learn to mourn for sin, and rejoice in God; then no man, no event, can take their joy from them.

Is. **24**:**13-15** There shall be a remnant preserved from the general ruin, and it shall be a devout and pious remnant. These few are dispersed; like the gleanings of the olive tree, hid under the leaves. The Lord knows those that are his; the world does not. When the mirth of carnal worldlings ceases, the joy of the saints is as lively as ever, because the covenant of grace, the fountain of their comforts, and the foundation of their hopes, never fails. Those who rejoice in the Lord can rejoice in tribulation, and by faith may triumph when all about them are in tears. They encourage their fellow-sufferers to do likewise, even those who are in the furnace of affliction. Or, in the valleys, low, dark, miry places. In every fire, even the hottest, in every place, even the remotest, let us keep up our good thoughts of God. If none of these trials move us, then we glorify the Lord in the fires.

Is. **24**:**16-23** Believers may be driven into the uttermost parts of the earth; but they are singing, not sighing. Here is terror to sinners; the prophet laments the miseries he saw breaking in like a torrent; and the small number of believers. He foresees that sin would abound. The meaning is plain, that evil pursues sinners. Unsteady, uncertain are all these things. Worldly men think to dwell in the earth as in a palace, as in a castle; but it shall be removed like a cottage, like a lodge put up for the night. It shall fall and not rise again; but there shall be new heavens and a new earth, in which shall dwell nothing but righteousness. Sin is a burden to the whole creation; it is a heavy burden, under which it groans now, and will sink at last. The high ones, that are puffed up with their grandeur, that think themselves out of the reach of danger, God will visit for their pride and cruelty. Let us judge nothing before the time, though some shall be visited. None in this world should be secure, though their condition be ever so prosperous; nor need any despair, though their condition be ever so deplorable. God will be glorified in all this. But the mystery of Providence is not yet finished. The ruin of the Redeemer's enemies must make way for his kingdom, and then the Sun of Righteousness will appear in full glory. Happy are those who take warning by the sentence against others; every impenitent sinner will sink under his transgression, and rise no more, while believers enjoy everlasting bliss.

Chapter 25

A song of praise. (Is. **25**:**1-5**) A declaration of the gospel blessings. (Is. **25**:**6-8**) The destruction of the enemies of Christ's church. (Is. **25**:**9-12**)

Is. **25**:**1-5** However this might show the deliverance of the Jews out of captivity, it looked further, to the praises that should be offered up to God for Christ's victories over our spiritual enemies, and the comforts he has provided for all believers. True faith simply credits the Lord's testimony, and relies on his truth to perform his promises. As God weakens the strong who are proud and secure, so he strengthens the weak that are humble, and stay themselves upon him. God protects his people in all weathers. The Lord shelters those who trust in him from the insolence of oppressors. Their insolence is but the noise of strangers; it is like the heat of the sun scorching in the middle of the day; but where is it when the sun is set? The Lord ever was, and ever will be, the Refuge of distressed believers. Having provided them a shelter, he teaches them to flee unto it.

Is. **25**:**6-8** The kind reception of repentant sinners, is often in the New Testament likened to a feast. The guests invited are all people, Gentiles as well as Jews. There is that in the gospel which strengthens and makes glad the heart, and is fit for those who are under convictions of sin, and mourning for it. There is a veil spread over all nations, for all sat in darkness. But this veil the Lord will destroy, by the light of his gospel shining in the world, and the power of his Spirit opening men's eyes to receive it. He will raise those to spiritual life who were long dead in trespasses and sins. Christ will himself, in his resurrection, triumph over death. Grief shall be banished; there shall be perfect and endless joy. Those that mourn for sin shall be comforted. Those who suffer for Christ shall have consolations. But in the joys of heaven, and not short of them, will fully be brought to pass this saying, God shall wipe away all tears. The hope of this should now do away over-sorrow, all weeping that hinders sowing. Sometimes, in this world God takes away the reproach of his people from among men; however, it will be done fully at the great day. Let us patiently bear sorrow and shame now; both will be done away shortly.

Is. **25**:**9-12** With joy and praise will those entertain the glad tidings of the Redeemer, who looked for him; and with a triumphant song will glorified saints enter into the joy of their Lord. And it is not in vain to wait for him; for the mercy comes at last, with abundant recompence for the delay. The hands once stretched out upon the cross, to make way for our salvation, will at length be stretched forth to destroy all impenitent sinners. Moab is here put for all adversaries of God's people; they shall all be trodden down or threshed. God shall bring down the pride of the enemies by one humbling judgment after another. This destruction of Moab is typical of Christ's victory, and the pulling down of Satan's strong holds. Therefore, beloved brethren, be ye stedfast, unmovable, always abounding in the work of the Lord; for your labour is not in vain in the Lord.

Chapter 26

The Divine mercies encourage to confidence in God. (Is. **26**:**1-4**) His judgments. (Is. **26**:**5-11**) His people exhorted to wait upon Him. (Is. **26**:**12-19**) Deliverance promised. (Is. **26**:**20**,**21**)

Is. **26**:**1-4** "That day," seems to mean when the New Testament Babylon shall be levelled with the ground. The unchangeable promise and covenant of the Lord are the walls of the church of God. The gates of this city shall be open. Let sinners then be encouraged to join to the Lord. Thou wilt keep him in peace; in perfect peace, inward peace, outward peace, peace with God, peace of conscience, peace at all times, in all events. Trust in the Lord for that peace, that portion, which will be for ever. Whatever we trust to the world for, it will last only for a moment; but those who trust in God shall not only find in him, but shall receive from him, strength that will carry them to that blessedness which is for ever. Let us then acknowledge him in all our ways, and rely on him in all trials.

Is. **26**:**5-11** The way of the just is evenness, a steady course of obedience and holy conversation. And it is their happiness that God makes their way plain and easy. It is our duty, and will be our comfort, to wait for God, to keep up holy desires toward him in the darkest and most discouraging times. Our troubles must never turn us from God; and in the darkest, longest night of affliction, with our souls must we desire him; and this we must wait and pray to him for. We make nothing of our religion, whatever our profession may be, if we do not make heart-work of it. Though we come ever so early, we shall find God ready to receive us. The intention of afflictions is to teach righteousness: blessed is the man whom the Lord thus teaches. But sinners walk contrary to him. They will go on in their evil ways, because they will not consider what a God he is whose laws they persist in despising. Scorners and the secure will shortly feel, what now they will not believe, that it is a fearful thing to fall into the hands of the living God. They will not see the evil of sin; but they shall see. Oh that they would abandon their sins, and turn to the Lord, that he may have mercy upon them.

Is. **26**:**12-19** Every creature, every business, any way serviceable to our comfort, God makes to be so; he makes that work for us which seemed to make against us. They had been slaves of sin and Satan; but by the Divine grace they were taught to look to be set free from all former masters. The cause opposed to God and his kingdom will sink at last. See our need of afflictions. Before, prayer came drop by drop; now they pour it out, it comes now like water from a fountain. Afflictions bring us to secret prayer. Consider Christ as the Speaker addressing his church. His resurrection from the dead was an earnest of all the deliverance foretold. The power of his grace, like the dew or rain, which causes the herbs that seem dead to revive, would raise his church from the lowest state. But we may refer to the resurrection of the dead, especially of those united to Christ.

Is. **26**:**20,21** When dangers threaten, it is good to retire and lie hid; when we commend ourselves to God to hide us, he will hide us either under heaven or in heaven. Thus we shall be safe and happy in the midst of tribulations. It is but for a short time, as it were for a little moment; when over, it will seem as nothing. God's place is the mercy-seat; there he delights to be: when he punishes, he comes out of his place, for he has no pleasure in the death of sinners. But there is hardly any truth more frequently repeated in Scripture, than God's determined purpose to punish the workers of iniquity. Let us keep close to the Lord, and separate from the world; and let us seek comfort in secret prayer. A day of vengeance is coming on the world, and before it comes we are to expect tribulation and suffering. But because the Christian looks for these things, shall he be restless and dismayed? No, let him repose himself in his God. Abiding in him, the believer is safe. And let us wait patiently the fulfilling of God's promises.

Chapter 27

God's care over his people. (Is. **27**:**1-5**) A promise of their recall to Divine favour. (Is. **27**:**6-13**)

Is. **27**:**1-5** The Lord Jesus with his strong sword, the virtue of his death, and the preaching of his gospel, does and will destroy him that had the power of death, that is, the devil, that old serpent. The world is a fruitless, worthless wilderness; but the church is a vineyard, a place that has great care taken of it, and from which precious fruits are gathered. God will keep it in the night of affliction and persecution, and in the day of peace and prosperity, the temptations of which are not less dangerous. God also takes care of the fruitfulness of this vineyard. We need the continual waterings of Divine grace; if these be at any time withdrawn, we wither, and come to nothing. Though God sometimes contends with his people, yet he graciously waits to be reconciled unto them. It is true, when he finds briers and thorns instead of vines, and they are set in array against him, he will tread them down and burn them. Here is a summary of the doctrine of the gospel, with which the church is to be watered every moment. Ever since sin first entered, there has been, on God's part, a righteous quarrel, but, on man's part, most unrighteous. Here is a gracious invitation given. Pardoning mercy is called the power of our Lord; let us take hold on that. Christ crucified is the power of God. Let us by lively faith take hold on his strength who is a strength to the needy, believing there is no other name by which we can be saved, as a man that is sinking catches hold of a bough, or cord, or plank, that is in his reach. This is the only way, and it is a sure way, to be saved. God is willing to be reconciled to us.

Is. **27**:**6-13** In the days of the gospel, the latter days, the gospel church shall be more firmly fixed than the Jewish church, and shall spread further. May our souls be continually watered and kept, that we may abound in the fruits of the Spirit, in all goodness, righteousness, and truth. The Jews yet are kept a separate and a numerous people; they have not been rooted out as those who slew them. The condition of that nation, through so many ages, forms a certain proof of the Divine origin of the Scriptures; and the Jews live amongst us, a continued warning against sin. But though winds are ever so rough, ever so high, God can say to them, Peace, be still. And though God will afflict his people, yet he will make their afflictions to work for the good of their souls. According to this promise, since the captivity in Babylon, no people have shown such hatred to idols and idolatry as the Jews. And to all God's people, the design of affliction is to part between them and sin. The affliction has done us good, when we keep at a distance from the occasions of sin, and use care that we may not be tempted to it. Jerusalem had been defended by grace and the Divine protection; but when God withdrew, she was left like a wilderness. This has awfully come to pass. And this is a figure of the deplorable state of the vineyard, the church, when it brought forth wild grapes. Sinners flatter themselves they shall not be dealt with severely, because God is merciful, and is their Maker. We see how weak those pleas will be. **Verses 12,13**, seem to predict the restoration of the Jews after the Babylonish captivity, and their recovery from their present dispersion. This is further applicable to the preaching of the gospel, by which sinners are gathered into the grace of God; the gospel proclaims the acceptable year of the Lord. Those gathered by the sounding of the gospel trumpet, are brought in to worship God, and added to the church; and the last trumpet will gather the saints together.

Chapter 28

The desolations of Samaria. (Is. **28**:**1-4**) The prosperity of Judah; with reproofs for sinfulness and unbelief. (Is. **28**:**5-15**) Christ is pointed out as the sure Foundation for all believers. (Is. **28**:**16-22**) God's dealings with his people. (Is. **28**:**23-29**)

Is. **28**:**1-4** What men are proud of, be it ever so mean, is to them as a crown; but pride is the forerunner of destruction. How foolishly drunkards act! Those who are overcome with wine are overcome by Satan; and there is not greater drudgery in the world than hard drinking. Their health is ruined; men are broken in their callings and estates, and their families are ruined by it. Their souls are in danger of being undone for ever, and all merely to gratify a base lust. In God's professing people, like Israel, it is worse than in any other. And he is just in taking away the plenty they thus abuse. The plenty they were proud of, is but a fading flower. Like the early fruit, which, as soon as discovered, is plucked and eaten.

Is. **28**:**5-15** The prophet next turns to Judah, whom he calls the residue of his people. Happy are those alone, who glory in the Lord of hosts himself. Hence his people get wisdom and strength for every service and every conflict. But it is only in Christ Jesus that the holy God communicates with sinful man. And whether those that teach are drunk with wine, or intoxicated with false doctrines and notions concerning the kingdom and salvation of the Messiah, they not only err themselves, but lead multitudes astray. All places where such persons have taught are filled with errors. For our instruction in the things of God, it is needful that the same precept and the same line should be often repeated to us, that we may the better understand them. God, by his word, calls us to what is really for our advantage; the service of God is the only true rest for those weary of the service of sin, and there is no refreshment but under the easy yoke of the Lord Jesus. All this had little effect upon the people. Those who will not understand what is plain, but scorn and despise it as mean and trifling, are justly punished. If we are at peace with God, we have, in effect, made a covenant with death; whenever it comes, it cannot do us any real damage, if we are Christ's. But to think of making death our friend, while by sin we are making God our enemy, is absurd. And do not they make lies their refuge who trust in their own righteousness, or to a death-bed repentance? which is a resolution to sin no more, when it is no longer in their power to do so.

Is. **28**:**16-22** Here is a promise of Christ, as the only foundation of hope for escaping the wrath to come. This foundation was laid in Zion, in the eternal counsels of God. This foundation is a stone, firm and able to support his church. It is a tried stone, a chosen stone, approved of God, and never failed any who made trial of it. A corner stone, binding together the whole building, and bearing the whole weight; precious in the sight of the Lord, and of every believer; a sure foundation on which to build. And he who in any age or nation shall believe this testimony, and rest all his hopes, and his never-dying soul on this foundation, shall never be confounded. The right effect of faith in Christ is, to quiet and calm the soul, till events shall be timed by Him, who has all times in his own hand and power. Whatever men trust to for justification, except the righteousness of Christ; or for wisdom, strength, and holiness, except the influences of the Holy Ghost; or for happiness, except the favour of God; that protection in which they thought to shelter themselves, will prove not enough to answer the intention. Those who rest in a righteousness of their own, will have deceived themselves: the bed is too short, the covering too narrow. God will be glorified in the fulfilling of his counsels. If those that profess to be members of God's church, make themselves like Philistines and Canaanites, they must expect to be dealt with as such. Then dare not to ridicule the reproofs of God's word, or the approaches of judgements.

Is. **28**:**23-29** The husbandman applies to his calling with pains and prudence, in all the works of it according to their nature. Thus the Lord, who has given men this wisdom, is wonderful in counsel, and excellent in his working. As the occasion requires, he threatens, corrects, spares, shows mercy, or executes vengeance. Afflictions are God's threshing instruments, to loosen us from the world, to part between us and our chaff, and to prepare us for use. God will proportion them to our strength; they shall be no heavier than there is need. When his end is answered, the trials and sufferings of his people shall cease; his wheat shall be gathered into the garner, but the chaff shall be burned with unquenchable fire.

Chapter 29

Judgements on Jerusalem and on its enemies. (Is. **29**:**1-8**) The senselessness and hypocrisy of the Jews. (Is. **29**:**9-16**) The conversion of the Gentiles, and future blessings for the Jews. (Is. **29**:**17-24**)

Is. **29**:**1-8** Ariel may signify the altar of burnt-offerings. Let Jerusalem know that outward religious services will not make men free from judgements. Hypocrites never can please God, nor make their peace with him. God had often and long, by a host of angels, encamped round about Jerusalem for protection and deliverance; but now he fought against it. Proud looks and proud language shall be brought down by humbling providences. The destruction of Jerusalem's enemies is foretold. The army of Sennacherib went as a dream; and thus the multitudes, that through successive ages fight against God's altar and worship, shall fall. Speedily will sinners awake from their soothing dreams in the pains of hell.

Is. **29**:**9-16** The security of sinners in sinful ways, is cause for lamentation and wonder. The learned men, through prejudice, said that the Divine prophecies were obscure; and the poor urged their want of learning. The Bible is a sealed book to every man, learned or unlearned, till he begins to study it with a simple heart and a teachable spirit, that he may thence learn the truth and the will of God. To worship God, is to approach him. And if the heart be full of his love and fear, out of the abundance of it the mouth will speak; but there are many whose religion is lip-labour only. When they pretend to be speaking to God, they are thinking of a thousand foolish things. They worship the God of Israel according to their own devices. Numbers are only formal in worship. And their religion is only to comply with custom, and to serve their own interest. But the wanderings of mind, and defects in devotion, which are the believer's burden, are very different from the withdrawing of the heart from God, so severely blamed. And those who make religion no more than a pretence, to serve a turn, deceive themselves. And as those that quarrel with God, so those that think to conceal themselves from him, in effect charge him with folly. But all their perverse conduct shall be entirely done away.

Is. **29**:**17-24** The wonderful change here foretold, may refer to the affairs of Judah, though it looks further. When a great harvest of souls was gathered to Christ from among the Gentiles, then the wilderness was turned into a fruitful field; and the Jewish church, that had long been a fruitful field, became as a deserted forest. Those who, when in trouble, can truly rejoice in God, shall soon have cause greatly to rejoice in him. The grace of meekness contributes to the increase of our holy joy. The enemies who were powerful shall become mean and weak. To complete the repose of God's people, the scorners at home shall be cut off by judgements. All are apt to speak unadvisedly, and to mistake what they hear, but it is very unfair to make a man an offender for a word. They did all they could to bring those into trouble who told them of their faults. But He that redeemed Abraham out of his snares and troubles, will redeem those who are, by faith, his true seed, out of theirs. It will be the greatest comfort to godly parents to see their children renewed creatures, the work of God's grace. May those who now err in spirit, and murmur against the truth, come to understanding, and learn true doctrine. The Spirit of truth shall set right their mistakes, and lead them into all truth. This should encourage us to pray for those that have erred, and are deceived. All who murmured at the truths of God, as hard sayings, shall learn and be aware what God designed in all. See the change religion produces in the hearts of men, and the peace and pleasure of a humble and devout spirit.

Chapter 30

The Jews reproved for seeking aid from Egypt. (Is. **30**:**1-7**) Judgements in consequence of their contempt of God's word. (Is. **30**:**8-18**) God's mercies to his church. (Is. **30**:**19-26**) The ruin of the Assyrian army, and of all God's enemies. (Is. **30**:**27-33**)

Is. **30**:**1-7** It was often the fault and folly of the Jews, that when troubled by their neighbours on one side, they sought for succour from others, instead of looking up to God. Nor can we avoid the dreadful consequences of adding sin to sin, but by making the righteousness of Christ our refuge, and seeking for the sanctification of the Holy Spirit. Men have always been prone to lean to their own understandings, but this will end in their shame and misery. They would not trust in God. They took much pains to gain the Egyptians. The riches so spent turned to a bad account. See what dangers men run into who forsake God to follow their carnal confidences. The Creator is the Rock of ages, the creature a broken reed; we cannot expect too little from man, or too much from God. Our strength is to sit still, in humble dependence upon God and his goodness, and quiet submission to his will.

Is. **30**:**8-18** The Jews were the only professing people God then had in the world, yet many among them were rebellious. They had the light, but they loved darkness rather. The prophets checked them in their sinful pursuits, so that they could not proceed without fear; this they took amiss. But faithful ministers will not be driven from seeking to awaken sinners. God is the Holy One of Israel, and so they shall find him. They did not like to hear of his holy commandments and his hatred of sin; they desired that they might no more be reminded of these things. But as they despised the word of God, their sins undermined their safety. Their state would be dashed in pieces like a potter's vessel. Let us return from our evil ways, and settle in the way of duty; that is the way to be saved. Would we be strengthened, it must be in quietness and in confidence, keeping peace in our own minds, and relying upon God. They think themselves wiser than God; but the project by which they thought to save themselves was their ruin. Only here and there one shall escape, as a warning to others. If men will not repent, turn to God, and seek happiness in his favour and service, their desires will but hasten their ruin. Those who make God alone their confidence, will have comfort. God ever waits to be gracious to all that come to him by faith in Christ, and happy are those who wait for him.

Is. **30**:**19-26** God's people will soon arrive at the Zion above, and then they will weep no more for ever. Even now they would have more comfort, as well as holiness, if they were more constant in prayer. A famine of bread is not so great a judgment as a famine of the word of God. There are right-hand and left-hand errors; the tempter is busy courting us into by-paths. It is happy if, by the counsels of a faithful minister or friend, or the checks of conscience, and the strivings of God the Spirit, we are set right when doubting, and prevented from going wrong. They shall be cured of their idolatry. To all true penitents sin becomes very hateful. This is shown daily in the conversion of souls, by the power of Divine grace, to the fear and love of God. Abundant means of grace, with the influences of the Holy Spirit, would be extended to places destitute of them. The effect of this should be comfort and joy to the people of God. Light, that is, knowledge, shall increase. This is the light which the gospel brought into the world, and which proclaims healing to the broken-hearted.

Is. **30**:**27-33** God curbs and restrains from doing mischief. With a word he guides his people into the right way, but with a bridle he turns his enemies upon their own ruin. Here, in threatening the ruin of Sennacherib's army, the prophet points at the final and everlasting destruction of all impenitent sinners. Tophet was a valley near Jerusalem, where fires were continually burning to destroy things that were hurtful and offensive, and there the idolatrous Jews caused their children to pass through the fire to Moloch. This denotes the certainty of the destruction, as an awful emblem of the place of torment in the other world. No oppressor shall escape the Divine wrath. Let sinners then flee to Christ, seeking to be reconciled to Him, that they may be safe and happy, when destruction from the Almighty shall sweep away all the workers of iniquity.

Chapter 31

The sin and folly of seeking help from Egypt. (Is. **31**:**1-5**) God's care for Jerusalem. (Is. **31**:**6-9**)

Is. **31**:**1-5** God will oppose the help sought from workers of iniquity. Sinners may be convicted of folly by plain and self-evident truths, which they cannot deny, but will not believe. There is no escaping the judgments of God; and evil pursues sinners. The Lord of hosts will come down to fight for Mount Zion. The Lion of the tribe of Judah will appear for the defence of his church. And as birds hovering over their young ones to protect them, with such compassion and affection will the Lord of hosts defend Jerusalem. He will so defend it, as to secure its safety.

Is. **31**:**6-9** They have been backsliding children, yet children; let them return, and their backslidings shall be healed, though they have sunk deep into misery, and cannot easily recover. Many make an idol of their silver and gold, and by the love of that are drawn from God; but those who turn to God, will be ready to part with it. Then, when they have cast away their idols, shall the Assyrian fall by the sword of an angel, who strikes more strongly than a mighty man, yet more secretly than a mean man. God can make the stoutest heart to tremble. But if we keep up the fire of holy love and devotion in our hearts and houses, we may depend upon God to protect us and them.

Chapter 32

Times of peace and happiness. (Is. **32**:**1-8**) An interval of trouble, yet comfort and blessings in the end. (Is. **32**:**9-20**)

Is. **32**:**1-8** Christ our righteous King, and his true disciples, are evidently here intended. The consolations and graces of his Spirit are as rivers of water in this dry land; and as the overhanging rock affords refreshing shade and shelter to the weary traveller in the desert, so his power, truth, and love, yield the believer the only real protection and refreshment in the weary land through which he journeys to heaven. Christ bore the storm himself, to keep it off from us. To him let the trembling sinner flee for refuge; for he alone can protect and refresh us in every trial. See what pains sinners take in sin; they labour at it, their hearts are intent upon it, and with art they work iniquity; but this is our comfort, that they can do no more mischief than God permits. Let us seek to have our hearts more freed from selfishness. The liberal soul devises liberal things concerning God, and desires that He will grant wisdom and prudence, the comforts of his presence, the influence of his Spirit, and in due time the enjoyment of his glory.

Is. **32**:**9-20** When there was so much provocation given to the holy God, bad times might be expected. Alas! how many careless ones there are, who support self-indulgence by shameful niggardliness! We deserve to be deprived of the supports of life, when we make them the food of lusts. Let such tremble and be troubled. Blessed times shall be brought in by the pouring out of the Spirit from on high; then, and not till then, there will be good times. The present state of the Jews shall continue until a more abundant pouring out of the Spirit from on high. Peace and quietness shall be found in the way and work of righteousness. True satisfaction is to be had only in true religion. And real holiness is real happiness now, and shall be perfect happiness, that is, perfect holiness for ever. The good seed of the word shall be sown in all places, and be watered by Divine grace; and laborious, patient labourers shall be sent forth into God's husbandry.

Chapter 33

God's judgments against the enemies of his church. (Is. **33**:**1-14**) The happiness of his people. (Is. **33**:**15-24**)

Is. **33**:**1-14** Here we have the proud and false destroyer justly reckoned with for all his fraud and violence. The righteous God often pays sinners in their own coin. Those who by faith humbly wait for God, shall find him gracious to them; as the day, so let the strength be. If God leaves us to ourselves any morning, we are undone; we must every morning commit ourselves to him, and go forth in his strength to do the work of the day. When God arises, his enemies are scattered. True wisdom and knowledge lead to strength of salvation, which renders us stedfast in the ways of God; and true piety is the only treasure which can never be plundered or spent. The distress Jerusalem was brought into, is described. God's time to appear for his people, is, when all other helpers fail. Let all who hear what God has done, acknowledge that he can do every thing. Sinners in Zion will have much to answer for, above other sinners. And those that rebel against the commands of the word, cannot take its comforts in time of need. His wrath will burn those everlastingly who make themselves fuel for it. It is a fire that shall never be quenched, nor ever go out of itself; it is the wrath of an ever-living God preying on the conscience of a never-dying soul.

Is. **33**:**15-24** The true believer watches against all occasions of sin. The Divine power will keep him safe, and his faith in that power will keep him easy. He shall want nothing needful for him. Every blessing of salvation is freely bestowed on all that ask with humble, believing prayer; and the believer is safe in time and for ever. Those that walk uprightly shall not only have bread given, and their water sure, but they shall, by faith, see the King of kings in his beauty, the beauty of holiness. The remembrance of the terror they were in, shall add to the pleasure of their deliverance. It is desirable to be quiet in our own houses, but much more so to be quiet in God's house; and in every age Christ will have a seed to serve him. Jerusalem had no large river running by it, but the presence and power of God make up all wants. We have all in God, all we need, or can desire. By faith we take Christ for our Prince and Saviour; he reigns over his redeemed people. All that refuse to have Him to reign over them, make shipwreck of their souls. Sickness is taken away in mercy, when the fruit of it is the taking away of sin. If iniquity be taken away, we have little reason to complain of outward affliction. This last **verse** leads our thoughts, not only to the most glorious state of the gospel church on earth, but to heaven, where no sickness or trouble can enter. He that blotteth out our transgressions, will heal our souls.

Chapter 34

God's vengeance against the enemies of his church. (Is. **34**:**1-8**) Their desolation. (Is. **34**:**9-17**)

Is. **34**:**1-8** Here is a prophecy of the wars of the Lord, all which are both righteous and successful. All nations are concerned. And as they have all had the benefit of his patience, so all must expect to feel his resentment. The description of bloodshed suggests tremendous ideas of the Divine judgments. Idumea here denotes the nations at enmity with the church; also the kingdom of antichrist. Our thoughts cannot reach the horrors of that awful season, to those found opposing the church of Christ. There is a time fixed in the Divine counsels for the deliverance of the church, and the destruction of her enemies. We must patiently wait till then, and judge nothing before the time. Through Christ, mercy is exercised to every believer, consistently with justice, and his name is glorified.

Is. **34**:**9-17** Those who aim to ruin the church, can never do that, but will ruin themselves. What dismal changes sin can make! It turns a fruitful land into barrenness, a crowded city into a wilderness. Let us compare all we discover in the book of the Lord, with the dealings of providence around us, that we may be more diligent in seeking the kingdom of God and his righteousness. What the mouth of the Lord has commanded, his Spirit will perform. And let us observe how the evidences of the truth continually increase, as one prophecy after another is fulfilled, until these awful scenes bring in more happy days. As Israel was a figure of the Christian church, so the Edomites, their bitter enemies, represent the enemies of the kingdom of Christ. God's Jerusalem may be laid in ruins for a time, but the enemies of the church shall be desolate for ever.

Chapter 35

The flourishing state of Christ's kingdom. (Is. **35**:**1-4**) The privileges of his people. (Is. **35**:**5-10**)

Is. **35**:**1-4** Judea was prosperous in the days of Hezekiah, but the kingdom of Christ is the great subject intended. Converting grace makes the soul that was a wilderness, to rejoice with joy and singing, and to blossom abundantly. The feeble and faint-hearted are encouraged. This is the design of the gospel. Fear is weakening; the more we strive against it, the stronger we are, both for doing and suffering; and he that says to us, Be strong, has laid help for us upon One who is mighty. Assurance is given of the approach of Messiah, to take vengeance on the powers of darkness, to recompense with abundant comforts those that mourn in Zion; He will come and save. He will come again at the end of time, to punish those who have troubled his people; and to give those who were troubled such rest as will be a full reward for all their troubles.

Is. **35**:**5-10** When Christ shall come to set up his kingdom in the world, then wonders, great wonders, shall be wrought on men's souls. By the word and Spirit of Christ, the spiritually blind were enlightened; and those deaf to the calls of God were made to hear them readily. Those unable to do any thing good, by Divine grace were made active therein. Those that knew not how to speak of God or to God, had their lips opened to show forth his praise. When the Holy Ghost came upon the Gentiles that heard the word, then were the fountains of life opened. Most of the earth is still a desert; neither means of grace, spiritual worshippers, nor fruits of holiness, are to be found in it. But the way of religion and godliness shall be laid open. The way of holiness is the way of God's commandment; it is the good old way. And the way to heaven is a plain way. Those knowing but little, and unlearned, shall be kept from missing the road. It shall be a safe way; nothing can do them any real hurt. Christ, the way to God, shall be clearly made known; and the way of a believer's duty shall be plainly marked out. Let us then go forward cheerfully, assured that the end of this way shall be everlasting joy, and rest for the soul. Those who by faith are made citizens of the gospel Zion, rejoice in Christ Jesus; and their sorrows and sighs are made to flee away by Divine consolations. Thus these prophecies conclude. Our joyful hopes and prospects of eternal life should swallow up all the sorrows and all the joys of this present time. But of what avail is it to admire the excellence of God's word, unless we can call its precious promises our own? Do we love God, not only as our Creator, but because he gave his only Son to die for us? And are we walking in the ways of holiness? Let us try ourselves by such plain questions, rather than spend time on things that may be curious and amusing, but are unprofitable.

Chapter 36

See II Kin. **18**:**17-37**, and the commentary thereon.

Chapter 37

This chapter is the same as II Kin. **19**.

Chapter 38

Hezekiah's sickness and recovery. (Is. **38**:**1-8**) His thanksgiving. (Is. **38**:**9-22**)

Is. **38**:**1-8** When we pray in our sickness, though God send not to us such an answer as he here sent to Hezekiah, yet, if by his Spirit he bids us be of good cheer, assures us that our sins are forgiven, and that, whether we live or die, we shall be his, we do not pray in vain. See II Kin. **20**:**1-11**.

Is. **38**:**9-22** We have here Hezekiah's thanksgiving. It is well for us to remember the mercies we receive in sickness. Hezekiah records the condition he was in. He dwells upon this; I shall no more see the Lord. A good man wishes not to live for any other end than that he may serve God, and have communion with him. Our present residence is like that of a shepherd in his hut, a poor, mean, and cold lodging, and with a trust committed to our charge, as the shepherd has. Our days are compared to the weaver's shuttle, Job **7**:**6**, passing and repassing very swiftly, every throw leaving a thread behind it; and when finished, the piece is cut off, taken out of the loom, and showed to our Master to be judged of. A good man, when his life is cut off, his cares and fatigues are cut off with it, and he rests from his labours. But our times are in God's hand; he has appointed what shall be the length of the piece. When sick, we are very apt to calculate our time, but are still at uncertainty. It should be more our care how we shall get safe to another world. And the more we taste of the loving-kindness of God, the more will our hearts love him, and live to him. It was in love to our poor perishing souls that Christ delivered them. The pardon does not make the sin not to have been sin, but not to be punished as it deserves. It is pleasant to think of our recoveries from sickness, when we see them flowing from the pardon of sin. Hezekiah's opportunity to glorify God in this world, he made the business, and pleasure, and end of life. Being recovered, he resolves to abound in praising and serving God. God's promises are not to do away, but to quicken and encourage the use of means. Life and health are given that we may glorify God and do good.

Chapter 39

This chapter is the same as II Kin. **20**:**12-19**.

Chapter 40

The preaching of the gospel, and glad tidings of the coming of Christ. (Is. **40**:**1-11**) The almighty power of God. (Is. **40**:**12-17**) The folly of idolatry. (Is. **40**:**18-26**) Against unbelief. (Is. **40**:**27-31**)

Is. **40**:**1-11** All human life is a warfare; the Christian life is the most so; but the struggle will not last always. Troubles are removed in love, when sin is pardoned. In the great atonement of the death of Christ, the mercy of God is exercised to the glory of his justice. In Christ, and his sufferings, true penitents receive of the Lord's hand double for all their sins; for the satisfaction Christ made by his death was of infinite value. The prophet had some reference to the return of the Jews from Babylon. But this is a small event, compared with that pointed out by the Holy Ghost in the New Testament, when John the Baptist proclaimed the approach of Christ. When eastern princes marched through desert countries, ways were prepared for them, and hinderances removed. And may the Lord prepare our hearts by the teaching of his word and the convictions of his Spirit, that high and proud thoughts may be brought down, good desires planted, crooked and rugged tempers made straight and softened, and every hinderance removed, that we may be ready for his will on earth, and prepared for his heavenly kingdom. What are all that belongs to fallen man, or all that he does, but as the grass and the flower thereof! And what will all the titles and possessions of a dying sinner avail, when they leave him under condemnation! The word of the Lord can do that for us, which all flesh cannot. The glad tidings of the coming of Christ were to be sent forth to the ends of the earth. Satan is the strong man armed; but our Lord Jesus is stronger; and he shall proceed, and do all that he purposes. Christ is the good Shepherd; he shows tender care for young converts, weak believers, and those of a sorrowful spirit. By his word he requires no more service, and by his providence he inflicts no more trouble, than he will strengthen them for. May we know our Shepherd's voice, and follow him, proving ourselves his sheep.

Is. **40**:**12-17** All created beings shrink to nothing in comparison with the Creator. When the Lord, by his Spirit, made the world, none directed his Spirit, or gave advice what to do, or how to do it. The nations, in comparison of him, are as a drop which remains in the bucket, compared with the vast ocean; or as the small dust in the balance, which does not turn it, compared with all the earth. This magnifies God's love to the world, that, though it is of such small account and value with him, yet, for the redemption of it, he gave his only-begotten Son, John **3**:**16**. The services of the church can make no addition to him. Our souls must have perished for ever, if the only Son of the Father had not given himself for us.

Is. **40**:**18-26** Whatever we esteem or love, fear or hope in, more than God, that creature we make equal with God, though we do not make images or worship them. He that is so poor, that he has scarcely a sacrifice to offer, yet will not be without a god of his own. They spared no cost upon their idols; we grudge what is spent in the service of our God. To prove the greatness of God, the prophet appeals to all ages and nations. Those who are ignorant of this, are willingly ignorant. God has the command of all creatures, and of all created things. The prophet directs us to use our reason as well as our senses; to consider who created the hosts of heaven, and to pay our homage to Him. Not one fails to fulfil his will. And let us not forget, that He spake all the promises, and engaged to perform them.

Is. **40**:**27-31** The people of God are reproved for their unbelief and distrust of God. Let them remember they took the names Jacob and Israel, from one who found God faithful to him in all his straits. And they bore these names as a people in covenant with Him. Many foolish frets, and foolish fears, would vanish before inquiry into the causes. It is bad to have evil thoughts rise in our minds, but worse to turn them into evil words. What they had known, and had heard, was sufficient to silence all these fears and distrusts. Where God had begun the work of grace, he will perfect it. He will help those who, in humble dependence on him, help themselves. As the day, so shall the strength be. In the strength of Divine grace their souls shall ascend above the world. They shall run the way of God's commandments cheerfully. Let us watch against unbelief, pride, and self-confidence. If we go forth in our own strength, we shall faint, and utterly fall; but having our hearts and our hopes in heaven, we shall be carried above all difficulties, and be enabled to lay hold of the prize of our high calling in Christ Jesus.

Chapter 41

God's care of his people. (Is. **41**:**1-9**) they are encouraged not to fear. (Is. **41**:**10-20**) The vanity and folly of idolatry. (Is. **41**:**21-29**)

Is. **41**:**1-9** Can any heathen god raise up one in righteousness, make what use of him he pleases, and make him victorious over the nations? The Lord did so with Abraham, or rather, he would do so with Cyrus. Sinners encourage one another in the ways of sin; shall not the servants of the living God stir up one another in his service? God's people are the seed of Abraham his friend. This is certainly the highest title ever given to a mortal. It means that Abraham, by Divine grace, was made like to God, and that he was admitted to communion with Him. Happy are the servants of the Lord, whom he has called to be his friends, and to walk with him in faith and holy obedience. Let not such as have thus been favoured yield to fear; for the contest may be sharp, but the victory shall be sure.

Is. **41**:**10-20** God speaks with tenderness; Fear thou not, for I am with thee: not only within call, but present with thee. Art thou weak? I will strengthen thee. Art thou in want of friends? I will help thee in the time of need. Art thou ready to fall? I will uphold thee with that right hand which is full of righteousness, dealing forth rewards and punishments. There are those that strive with God's people, that seek their ruin. Let not God's people render evil for evil, but wait God's time. It is the worm Jacob; so little, so weak, so despised and trampled on by every body. God's people are as worms, in humble thoughts of themselves, and in their enemies' haughty thoughts of them; worms, but not vipers, not of the serpent's seed. Every part of God's word is calculated to humble man's pride, and to make him appear little in his own eyes. The Lord will help them, for he is their Redeemer. The Lord will make Jacob to become a threshing instrument. God will make him fit for use, new, and having sharp spikes. This has fulfilment in the triumphs of the gospel of Christ, and of all faithful followers of Christ, over the power of darkness. God has provided comforts to supply all their wants, and to answer all their prayers. Our way to heaven lies through the wilderness of this world. The soul of man is in want, and seeks for satisfaction; but becomes weary of seeking that in the world, which is not to be had in it. Yet they shall have a constant supply, where one would least expect it. I will open rivers of grace, rivers of living water, which Christ spake of the Spirit, John **7**:**38**,**39**. When God sets up his church in the Gentile wilderness, there shall be a great change, as if thorns and briers were turned into cedars, and fir-trees, and myrtles. These blessings are kept for the poor in spirit, who long for Divine enlightening, pardon, and holiness. And God will render their barren souls fruitful in the grace of his Spirit, that all who behold may consider it.

Is. **41**:**21-29** There needs no more to show the folly of sin, than to bring to notice the reasons given in defence of it. There is nothing in idols worthy of regard. They are less than nothing, and worse than nothing. Let the advocates of other doctrines than that of salvation through Christ, bring their arguments. Can they tell of a cure for human depravity? Jehovah has power which cannot be withstood; this he will make appear. But the certain knowledge of the future must be only with Jehovah, who fulfils his own plans. All prophecies, except those of the Bible, have been uncertain. In the work of redemption the Lord showed himself much more than in the release of the Jews from Babylon. The good tidings the Lord will send in the gospel, is a mystery hid from ages and generations. A Deliverer is raised up for us, of nobler name and greater power than the deliverer of the captive Jews. May we be numbered among his obedient servants and faithful friends.

Chapter 42

The character and coming of Christ. (Is. **42**:**1-4**) The blessings of his kingdom. (Is. **42**:**5-12**) The prevalence of true religion. (Is. **42**:**13-17**) Unbelief and blindness reproved. (Is. **42**:**18-25**)

Is. **42**:**1-4** This prophecy was fulfilled in Christ, Matt. **12**:**17**. Let our souls rely on him, and rejoice in him; then, for his sake, the Father will be well-pleased with us. The Holy Spirit not only came, but rested upon him, and without measure. He patiently bore the contradiction of sinners. His kingdom is spiritual; he was not to appear with earthly honours. He is tender of those oppressed with doubts and fears, as a bruised reed; those who are as smoking flax, as the wick of a lamp newly lighted, which is ready to go out again. He will not despise them, nor lay upon them more work or more suffering than they can bear. By a long course of miracles and his resurrection, he fully showed the truth of his holy religion. By the power of his gospel and grace he fixes principles in the minds of men, which tend to make them wise and just. The most distant nations wait for his law, wait for his gospel, and shall welcome it. If we would make our calling and election sure, and have the Father delight over us for good, we must behold, hear, believe in, and obey Christ.

Is. **42**:**5-12** The work of redemption brings back man to the obedience he owes to God as his Maker. Christ is the light of the world. And by his grace he opens the understandings Satan has blinded, and sets at liberty from the bondage of sin The Lord has supported his church. And now he makes new promises, which shall as certainly be fulfilled as the old ones were. When the Gentiles are brought into the church, he is glorified in them and by them. Let us give to God those things which are his, taking heed that we do not serve the creature more than the Creator.

Is. **42**:**13-17** The Lord will appear in his power and glory. He shall cry, in the preaching of his word. He shall cry aloud in the gospel woes, which must be preached with gospel blessings, to awaken a sleeping world. He shall conquer by the power of his Spirit. And those that contradict and blaspheme his gospel, he shall put to silence and shame; and that which hinders its progress shall be taken out of the way. To those who by nature were blind, God will show the way to life and happiness by Jesus Christ. They are weak in knowledge, but He will make darkness light. They are weak in duty. but their way shall be plain. Those whom God brings into the right way, he will guide in it. This passage is a prophecy, and is also applicable to every believer; for the Lord will never leave nor forsake them.

Is. **42**:**18-25** Observe the call given to this people, and the character given of them. Multitudes are ruined for want of observing that which they cannot but see; they perish, not through ignorance, but carelessness. The Lord is well-pleased in the making known his own righteousness. For their sins they were spoiled of all their possessions. This fully came to pass in the destruction of the Jewish nation. There is no resisting, nor escaping God's anger. See the mischief sin makes; it provokes God to anger. And those not humbled by lesser judgments, must expect greater. Alas! how many professed Christians are blind as the benighted heathen! While the Lord is well-pleased in saving sinners through the righteousness of Christ he will also glorify his justice, by punishing all proud despisers. Seeing God has poured out his wrath on his once-favoured people, because of their sins, let us fear, lest a promise being left us of entering into his rest, any of us should be found to come short of it.

Chapter 43

God's unchangeable love for his people. (Is. **43**:**1-7**) Apostates and idolaters addressed. (Is. **43**:**8-13**) The deliverance from Babylon, and the conversion of the Gentiles. (Is. **43**:**14-21**) Admonition to repent of sin. (Is. **43**:**22-28**)

Is. **43**:**1-7** God's favour and good-will to his people speak abundant comfort to all believers. The new creature, wherever it is, is of God's forming. All who are redeemed with the blood of his Son, he has set apart for himself. Those that have God for them need not fear who or what can be against them. What are Egypt and Ethiopia, all their lives and treasures, compared with the blood of Christ? True believers are precious in God's sight, his delight is in them, above any people. Though they went as through fire and water, yet, while they had God with them, they need fear no evil; they should be born up, and brought out. The faithful are encouraged. They were to be assembled from every quarter. And with this pleasing object in view, the prophet again dissuades from anxious fears.

Is. **43**:**8-13** Idolaters are called to appear in defence of their idols. Those who make them, and trust in them, are like unto them. They have the shape and faculties of men; but they have not common sense. But God's people know the power of his grace, the sweetness of his comforts, the kind care of his providence, and the truth of his promise. All servants of God can give such an account of what he has wrought in them, and done for them, as may lead others to know and believe his power, truth, and love

Is. **43**:**14-21** The deliverance from Babylon is foretold, but there is reference to greater events. The redemption of sinners by Christ, the conversion of the Gentiles, and the recall of the Jews, are described. All that is to be done to rescue sinners, and to bring the believer to glory, is little, compared with that wondrous work of love, the redemption of man.

Is. **43**:**22-28** Those who neglect to call upon God, are weary of him. The Master tired not the servants with his commands, but they tired him with disobedience. What were the riches of God's mercy toward them? I, even I, am he who yet blotteth out thy transgressions. This encourages us to repent, because there is forgiveness with God, and shows the freeness of Divine mercy. When God forgives, he forgets. It is not for any thing in us, but for his mercies' sake, his promise' sake; especially for his Son's sake. He is pleased to reckon it his honour. Would man justify himself before God? The attempt is desperate: our first father broke the covenant, and we all have copied his example. We have no reason to expect pardon, except we seek it by faith in Christ; and that is always attended by true repentance, and followed by newness of life, by hatred of sin, and love to God. Let us then put him in remembrance of the promises he has made to the penitent, and the satisfaction his Son has made for them. Plead these with him in wrestling for pardon; and declare these things, that thou mayest be justified freely by his grace. This is the only way, and it is a sure way to peace.

Chapter 44

Here are promises of the influences of the Holy Spirit. (Is. **44**:**1-8**) An exposure of the folly of idolatry. (Is. **44**:**9-20**) Also the deliverance of God's people. (Is. **44**:**21-28**)

Is. **44**:**1-8** Israel is here called Jeshurun, which means "the upright one." Such only are Israelites indeed, in whom is no guile. Those that serve God he will own. He will help them over difficulties, and in their services. Water is the emblem of the Holy Spirit; as water refreshes, cleanses, and makes the earth fruitful, so do his influences the soul. This gift of the Holy Ghost is the great blessing, the plentiful pouring out of which God kept for the latter days. Where God gives his Spirit, he will give all other blessings. Hereby shall be a great increase of the church; thus it shall be spread to distant places. Was there any other Rock, or Protector, that could defend them? None besides could foretell these things to come, of which God by his prophets gave notice. All was set in order in the Divine predictions, as well as in the Divine purposes. Could any other have done so? Who can compare with Israel's Redeemer and King?

Is. **44**:**9-20** Image-making is described, to expose the folly of idolaters. Though a man had used part of a log for fuel, he fell down before an image made of the remainder, praying it to deliver him. Man greatly dishonours God, when he represents him after the image of man. Satan blinds the eyes of unbelievers, causing absurd reasonings in matters of religion. Whether men seek happiness in worldly things, or run into unbelief, superstition, or any false system, they feed on ashes. A heart deceived by pride, love of sin, and departure from God, turns men aside from his holy truth and worship. While the affections are depraved, a man holds fast the lie as his best treasure. Are our hearts set upon the wealth of the world and its pleasures? They will certainly prove a lie. If we trust to outward professions and doings, as if those would save us, we deceive ourselves. Self-suspicion is the first step towards self-deliverance. He that would deliver his soul, must question his conscience, Is there not a lie in my right hand?

Is. **44**:**21-28** Return unto me. It is the great concern of those who have backslidden from God, like the Jews of old, to hasten their return to him. The work of redemption wrought for us by Christ, encourages to hope for all blessings from him. Our transgressions and our sins are as a thick cloud between heaven and earth: sins separate between us and God; they threaten a storm of wrath. When God pardons sin, he blots out, he dispels this cloud, this thick cloud, so that the way to heaven is open again. The cloud is scattered by the Sun of righteousness; it is quite gone. The comforts that flow into the soul when sin is pardoned, are like clear shining after clouds and rain. Let not Israel be discouraged; nothing is too hard for God: having made all, he can make what use he pleases of any. Those that learn to know Christ, see all knowledge to be foolishness, in comparison with the knowledge of him. And his enemies will find their counsels turned into foolishness, and themselves taken in their craftiness. The exact fulfilling the prophecies of Scripture confirms the truth of the whole, and proves its Divine origin. The particular favours God designed for his people in captivity, were foretold here, long before they went into captivity. Very great difficulties would be in the way of their deliverance; but it is promised that by Divine power they should all be removed. God knew who should be the Deliverer of his people; and let his church know it, that when they heard such a name talked of, they might know their redemption drew nigh. It is the greatest honour of the greatest men, to be employed as instruments of the Divine favour to his people. In things wherein men serve themselves, and look no further, God makes them do all his pleasure. And a nobler Shepherd than Cyrus does his Father's will, till his work is fully completed.

Chapter 45

The deliverance of the Jews by Cyrus. (Is. **45**:**1-4**) God calls for obedience to his almighty power. (Is. **45**:**5-10**) The settlement of his people. (Is. **45**:**11-19**) The conversion of the Gentiles. (Is. **45**:**20-25**)

Is. **45**:**1-4** Cyrus is called God's anointed; he was designed and qualified for his great service by the counsel of God. The gates of Babylon which led to the river, were left open the night that Cyrus marched his army into the empty channel. The Lord went before him, giving entrance to the cities he besieged. He gave him also treasures, which had been hidden in secret places. The true God was to Cyrus an unknown God; yet God foreknew him; he called him by his name. The exact fulfilment of this must have shown Cyrus that Jehovah was the only true God, and that it was for the sake of Israel that he was prospered. In all the changes of states and kingdoms, God works out the good of his church.

Is. **45**:**5-10** There is no God beside Jehovah. There is nothing done without him. He makes peace, put here for all good; and creates evil, not the evil of sin, but the evil of punishment. He is the Author of all that is true, holy, good, or happy; and evil, error, and misery, came into the world by his permission, through the wilful apostacy of his creatures, but are restrained and overruled to his righteous purpose. This doctrine is applied, for the comfort of those that earnestly longed, yet quietly waited, for the redemption of Israel. The redemption of sinners by the Son of God, and the pouring out the Spirit, to give success to the gospel, are chiefly here intended. We must not expect salvation without righteousness; together the Lord hath created them. Let not oppressors oppose God's designs for his people. Let not the poor oppressed murmur, as if God dealt unkindly with them. Men are but earthen pots; they are broken potsherds, and are very much made so by mutual contentions. To contend with Him is as senseless as for clay to find fault with the potter. Let us turn God's promises into prayers, beseeching him that salvation may abound among us, and let us rest assured that the Judge of all the earth will do right.

Is. **45**:**11-19** Believers may ask in prayer for what they need; if for their good, it will not be withheld. But how common to hear God called to account for his dealings with man! Cyrus provided for the returning Jews. Those redeemed by Christ shall be provided for. The restoration would convince many, and convert some; and all that truly join the Lord, find his service perfect freedom. Though God be his people's God and Saviour, yet sometimes he lays them under his frowns; but let them wait upon the Lord who hides his face. There is a world without end; and it will be well or ill with us, according as it shall be with us in that world. The Lord we serve and trust, is God alone. All that God has said is plain, satisfactory, and just. As God in his word calls us to seek him, so he never denied believing prayers, nor disappointed believing expectations. He gives grace sufficient, and comfort and satisfaction of soul.

Is. **45**:**20-25** The nations are exhorted to draw near to Jehovah. None besides is able to help; he is the Saviour, who can save without the assistance of any, but without whom none can save. If the heart is brought into the obedience of Christ, the knee will cheerfully obey his commands. To Christ men shall come from every nation for blessings; all that hate his cause shall be put to shame, and all believers shall rejoice in him as their Friend and Portion. All must come to him: may we now come to him as the Lord our Righteousness, walking according to his commandments.

Chapter 46

The idols could not save themselves, but God saves his people. (Is. **46**:**1-4**) The folly of worshipping idols. (Is. **46**:**5-13**)

Is. **46**:**1-4** The heathen insulted the Jews, as if their idols Bel and Nebo were too hard for Jehovah. But their worshippers cannot help them; both the idols and the idolaters are gone into captivity. Let not God's people be afraid of either. Those things from which ungodly men expect safety and happiness, will be found unable to save them from death and hell. The true God will never fail his worshippers. The history of the life of every believer is a kind of abstract of the history of Israel. Our spiritual life is upheld by his grace, as constantly as our natural life by his providence. And God will never leave them. The Author will be the Finisher of their well-being, when, by decays, they need help as much as in infancy. This promise to Israel, enfeebled and grown old as a nation, is applicable to every aged follower of Christ. When compassed about with infirmities, and perhaps those around begin to grow weary of you, yet I am He that I have promised to be, He that you would have me to be. I will bear you up; carry you on in your way, and carry you home at last. If we learn to trust in and love him, we need not be anxious about our remaining days or years; he will still provide for us and watch over us, both as the creatures of his power, and as new-created by his Spirit.

Is. **46**:**5-13** Here the folly of those who made idols, and then prayed to them, is exposed. How does the profuseness of idolaters shame the niggardliness of many who call themselves God's servants, but are for a religion which costs them nothing! The service of sin always costs a great deal. God puts it to them what senseless, helpless things idols are. Let, then, the Jews show themselves men, avoiding such abominations. Many Scripture prophecies, delivered long ago, are not yet fulfilled; but the fulfilling of some is an earnest that the rest will come to pass. Nothing can help more to make us easy, than to be assured that God will do all his pleasure. Even those who know not and mind not God's revealed will, are called and used to fulfil the counsels of his secret will. Heaven and earth shall pass away, sooner than one tittle of the word of God. Obstinate sinners are addressed. Such were far from acceptance, but they were summoned to hearken to the word of the Lord. The salvation of a sinner begins with a humble and contrite heart, that trembles at God's word, with godly sorrow working true repentance, and faith in his mercy, through the obedience unto death of our Divine Surety. Christ, as the Divine righteousness and salvation to his people, would come in the appointed time. His salvation abides in his church for all believers.

Chapter 47

God's judgments on Babylon. (Is. **47**:**1-6**) Carelessness and confidence shall not prevent the evil. (Is. **47**:**7-15**)

Is. **47**:**1-6** Babylon is represented under the emblem of a female in deep distress. She was to be degraded and endure sufferings; and is represented sitting on the ground, grinding at the handmill, the lowest and most laborious service. God was righteous in his vengeance, and none should interpose. The prophet exults in the Lord of hosts, as the Redeemer and Holy One of Israel. God often permits wicked men to prevail against his people; but those who cruelly oppress them will be punished.

Is. **47**:**7-15** Let us beware of acting and speaking as Babylon did; of trusting in tyranny and oppression; of boasting as to our abilities, relying on ourselves, and ascribing success to our own prudence and wisdom; lest we partake of her plagues. Those in the height of prosperity, are apt to fancy themselves out of the reach of adversity. It is also common for sinners to think they shall be safe, because they think to be secret in wicked ways. But their security shall be their ruin. Let us draw from such passages as the foregoing, those lessons of humility and trust in God which they convey. If we believe the word of God, we may know how it will be with the righteous and the wicked to all eternity. We may learn how to escape the wrath to come, to glorify God, to have peace through life, hope in death, and everlasting happiness. Let us then stand aloof from all delusions.

Chapter 48

The Jews reproved for their idolatry. (Is. **48**:**1-8**) Yet deliverance is promised them. (Is. **48**:**9-15**) Solemn warnings of judgment upon those who persisted in evil. (Is. **48**:**16-22**)

Is. **48**:**1-8** The Jews valued themselves on descent from Jacob, and used the name of Jehovah as their God. They prided themselves respecting Jerusalem and the temple, yet there was no holiness in their lives. If we are not sincere in religion, we do but take the name of the Lord in vain. By prophecy they were shown how God would deal with them, long before it came to pass. God has said and done enough to prevent men's boasting of themselves, which makes the sin and ruin of the proud worse; sooner or later every mouth shall be stopped, and all become silent before Him. We are all born children of disobedience. Where original sin is, actual sin will follow. Does not the conscience of every man witness to the truth of Scripture? May the Lord prove us, and render us doers of the word.

Is. **48**:**9-15** We have nothing ourselves to plead with God, why he should have mercy upon us. It is for his praise, to the honour of his mercy, to spare. His bringing men into trouble was to do them good. It was to refine them, but not as silver; not so thoroughly as men refine silver. If God should take that course, they are all dross, and, as such, might justly be put away. He takes them as refined in part only. Many have been brought home to God as chosen vessels, and a good work of grace begun in them, in the furnace of affliction. It is comfort to God's people, that God will secure his own honour, therefore work deliverance for them. And if God delivers his people, he cannot be at a loss for instruments to be employed. God has formed a plan, in which, for his own sake, and the glory of his grace, he saves all that come to Him.

Is. **48**:**16-22** The Holy Spirit qualifies for service; and those may speak boldly, whom God and his Spirit send. This is to be applied to Christ. He was sent, and he had the Spirit without measure. Whom God redeems, he teaches; he teaches to profit by affliction, and then makes them partakers of his holiness. Also, by his grace he leads them in the way of duty; and by his providence he leads in the way of deliverance. God did not afflict them willingly. If their sins had not turned them away, their peace should have been always flowing and abundant. Spiritual enjoyments are ever joined with holiness of life and regard to God's will. It will make the misery of the disobedient the more painful, to think how happy they might have been. And here is assurance given of salvation out of captivity. Those whom God designs to bring home to himself, he will take care of, that they want not for their journey. This is applicable to the grace laid up for us in Jesus Christ, from whom all good flows to us, as the water to Israel out of the rock, for that Rock was Christ. The spiritual blessings of redemption, and the rescue of the church from antichristian tyranny, are here pointed to. But whatever changes take place, the Lord warned impenitent sinners that no good would come to them; that inward anguish and outward trouble, which spring from guilt and from the Divine wrath, must be their portion for ever.

Chapter 49

The unbelief and rejection of the Jews. (Is. **49**:**1-6**) Gracious promise to the Gentiles. (Is. **49**:**7-12**) God's love to the church. (Is. **49**:**13-17**) Its increase. (Is. **49**:**18-23**) And deliverance. (Is. **49**:**24-26**)

Is. **49**:**1-6** The great Author of redemption shows the authority for his work. The sword of his word slays the lusts of his people, and all at enmity with them. His sharp arrows wound the conscience; but all these wounds will be healed, when the sinner prays to him for mercy. But even the Redeemer, who spake as never man spake in his personal ministry, often seemed to labour in vain. And if Jacob will not be brought back to God, and Israel will not be gathered, still Christ will be glorious. This promise is in part fulfilled in the calling of the Gentiles. Men perish in darkness. But Christ enlightens men, and so makes them holy and happy.

Is. **49**:**7-12** The Father is the Lord, the Redeemer, and Holy One of Israel, as sending the Son to be the Redeemer. Man, whom he came to save, put contempt upon him. To this he submitted for our salvation. He is a pledge for all the blessings of the covenant; in him God was reconciling the world to himself. Pardoning mercy is a release from the curse of the law; renewing grace is a release from the dominion of sin: both are from Christ. He saith to those in darkness, Show yourselves. Not only see, but be seen, to the glory of God, and your own comforts. Though there are difficulties in the way to heaven, yet the grace of God will carry us over them, and make even the mountains a way. This denotes the free invitations and the encouraging promises of the gospel, and the outpouring of the Spirit.

Is. **49**:**13-17** Let there be universal joy, for God will have mercy upon the afflicted, because of his compassion; upon his afflicted, because of his covenant. We have no more reason to question his promise and grace, than we have to question his providence and justice. Be assured that God has a tender affection for his church and people; he would not have them to be discouraged. Some mothers do neglect their children; but God's compassions to his people, infinitely exceed those of the tenderest parents toward their children. His setting them as a mark on his hand, or a seal upon his arm, denotes his being ever mindful of them. As far as we have scriptural evidence that we belong to his ransomed flock, we may be sure that he will never forsake us. Let us then give diligence to make our calling and election sure, and rejoice in the hope and glory of God.

Is. **49**:**18-23** Zion is addressed as an afflicted widow, bereaved of her children. Numbers flock to her, and she is assured that they come to be a comfort to her. There are times when the church is desolate and few in number; yet its desolations shall not last for ever, and God will repair them. God can raise up friends for returning Israelites, even among Gentiles. They shall bring their children, and make them thy children. Let all deal tenderly and carefully with young converts and beginners in religion. Princes shall protect the church. It shall appear that God is the sovereign Lord of all. And those who in the exercise of faith, hope, and patience, wait on God for the fulfilment of his promises, shall never be confounded.

Is. **49**:**24-26** We were lawful captives to the justice of God, yet delivered by a price of unspeakable value. Here is an express promise: Even the prey of the terrible shall be delivered. We may here view Satan deprived of his prey, bound and cast into the pit; and all the powers that have combined to enslave, persecute, or corrupt the church, are destroyed; that all the earth may know that our Saviour and Redeemer is Jehovah, the mighty One of Jacob. And every effort we make to rescue our fellow-sinners from the bondage of Satan, is, in some degree, helping forward that great change.

Chapter 50

The rejection of the Jews. (Is. **50**:**1-3**) The sufferings and exaltation of the Messiah. (Is. **50**:**4-9**) Consolation to the believer, and warning to the unbeliever. (Is. **50**:**10,11**)

Is. **50**:**1-3** Those who have professed to be people of God, and seem to be dealt severely with, are apt to complain, as if God had been hard with them. Here is an answer for such murmurings; God never deprived any of their advantages, except for their sins. The Jews were sent into Babylon for their idolatry, a sin which broke the covenant; and they were at last rejected for crucifying the Lord of glory. God called on them to leave their sins, and prevent their own ruin. Last of all, the Son came to his own, but his own received him not. When God calls men to happiness, and they will not answer, they are justly left to be miserable. To silence doubts concerning his power, proofs of it are given. The wonders which attended his sufferings and death, proclaimed that he was the Son of God, Matt. **27**:**54**.

Is. **50**:**4-9** As Jesus was God and man in one person, we find him sometimes speaking, or spoken of, as the Lord God; at other times, as man and the servant of Jehovah. He was to declare the truths which comfort the broken, contrite heart, those weary of sin, harassed with afflictions. And as the Holy Spirit was upon him, that he might speak as never man spake; so the same Divine influence daily wakened him to pray, to preach the gospel, and to receive and deliver the whole will of the Father. The Father justified the Son when he accepted the satisfaction he made for the sin of man. Christ speaks in the name of all believers. Who dares to be an enemy to those unto whom he is a Friend? or who will contend with those whom he is an Advocate? Thus St. Paul applies it, Rom. **8**:**33**.

Is. **50**:**10,11** A child of God is afraid of incurring his displeasure. This grace usually appears most in believers when in darkness, when other graces appear not. Those that truly fear God, obey the voice of Christ. A sincere servant of God may for a long time be without views of eternal happiness. What is likely to be an effectual cure in this sad case? Let him trust in the name of the Lord; and let him stay himself upon the promises of the covenant, and build his hopes on them. Let him trust in Christ, trust in that name of his, The Lord our Righteousness; stay himself upon God as his God, in and through a Mediator. Presuming sinners are warned not to trust in themselves. Their own merit and sufficiency are light and heat to them. Creature-comforts are as sparks, short-lived, and soon gone; yet the children of this world, while they last, seek to warm themselves by them, and walk with pride and pleasure in the light of them. Those that make the world their comfort, and their own righteousness their confidence, will certainly meet with bitterness in the end. A godly man's way may be dark, but his end shall be peace and everlasting light. A wicked man's way may be pleasant, but his end and abode for ever will be utter darkness.

Chapter 51

Exhortations to trust the Messiah. (Is. **51**:**1-3**) The power of God, and the weakness of man. (Is. **51**:**4-8**) Christ defends his people. (Is. **51**:**9-16**) Their afflictions and deliverances. (Is. **51**:**17-23**)

Is. **51**:**1-3** It is good for those privileged by the new birth, to consider that they were shapen in sin. This should cause low thoughts of ourselves, and high thoughts of Divine grace. It is the greatest comfort to be made serviceable to the glory of God. The more holiness men have, and the more good they do, the more gladness they have. Let us seriously reflect upon our guilt. To do so will tend to keep the heart humble, and the conscience awake and tender. They make Christ more precious to the soul, and give strength to our attempts and prayers for others.

Is. **51**:**4-8** The gospel of Christ shall be preached and published. How shall we escape if we neglect it? There is no salvation without righteousness. The soul shall, as to this world, vanish like smoke, and the body be thrown by like a worn-out garment. But those whose happiness is in Christ's righteousness and salvation, will have the comfort of it when time and days shall be no more. Clouds darken the sun, but do not stop its course. The believer will enjoy his portion, while revilers of Christ are in darkness

Is. **51**:**9-16** The people whom Christ has redeemed with his blood, as well as by his power, will obtain joyful deliverance from every enemy. He that designs such joy for us at last, will he not work such deliverance in the mean time, as our cases require? In this world of changes, it is a short step from joy to sorrow, but in that world, sorrow shall never come in view. They prayed for the display of God's power; he answers them with consolations of his grace. Did we dread to sin against God, we should not fear the frowns of men. Happy is the man that fears God always. And Christ's church shall enjoy security by the power and providence of the Almighty.

Is. **51**:**17-23** God calls upon his people to mind the things that belong to their everlasting peace. Jerusalem had provoked God, and was made to taste the bitter fruits. Those who should have been her comforters, were their own tormentors. They have no patience by which to keep possesion of their own souls, nor any confidence in God's promise, by which to keep possession of its comfort. Thou art drunken, not as formerly, with the intoxicating cup of Babylon's idolatries, but with the cup of affliction. Know, then, the cause of God's people may for a time seem as lost, but God will protect it, by convincing the conscience, or confounding the projects, of those that strive against it. The oppressors required souls to be subjected to them, that every man should believe and worship as they would have them. But all they could gain by violence was, that people were brought to outward hypocritical conformity, for consciences cannot be forced.

Chapter 52

The welcome news of Christ's kingdom. (Is. **52**:**1-12**) The humiliation of the Messiah. (Is. **52**:**13-15**)

Is. **52**:**1-12** The gospel proclaims liberty to those bound with fears. Let those weary and heavy laden under the burden of sin, find relief in Christ, shake themselves from the dust of their doubts and fears, and loose themselves from those bands. The price paid by the Redeemer for our salvation, was not silver or gold, or corruptible things, but his own precious blood. Considering the freeness of this salvation, and how hurtful to temporal comfort sins are, we shall more value the redemption which is in Christ. Do we seek victory over every sin, recollecting that the glory of God requires holiness in every follower of Christ? The good news is, that the Lord Jesus reigns. Christ himself brought these tidings first. His ministers proclaim these good tidings: keeping themselves clean from the pollutions of the world, they are beautiful to those to whom they are sent. Zion's watchmen could scarcely discern any thing of God's favour through the dark cloud of their afflictions; but now the cloud is scattered, they shall plainly see the performance. Zion's waste places shall then rejoice; all the world will have the benefit. This is applied to our salvation by Christ. Babylon is no place for Israelites. And it is a call to all in the bondage of sin and Satan, to use the liberty Christ has proclaimed. They were to go with diligent haste, not to lose time nor linger; but they were not to go with distrustful haste. Those in the way of duty, are under God's special protection; and he that believes this, will not hasten for fear.

Is. **52**:**13-15** Here begins that wonderful, minute, and faithful description of the office, character, and glory of the Messiah, which has struck conviction to many of the most hardened unbelievers. Christ is Wisdom itself; in the work of our redemption there appeared the wisdom of God in a mystery. Those that saw him, said, Surely never man looked so miserable: never was sorrow like unto his sorrow. But God highly exalted him. That shall be discovered by the gospel of Christ, which could never be told in any other way. And Christ having once shed his blood for sinners, its power still continues. May all opposers see the wisdom of ceasing from their opposition, and be made partakers of the blood of sprinkling, and the baptism of the Holy Ghost; obeying him, and praising his salvation.

Chapter 53

The person. (Is. **53**:**1-3**) sufferings. (Is. **53**:**4-9**) humiliation, and exaltation of Christ, are minutely described; with the blessings to mankind from his death. (Is. **53**:**10-12**)

Is. **53**:**1-3** No where in all the Old Testament is it so plainly and fully prophesied, that Christ ought to suffer, and then to enter into his glory, as in this chapter. But to this day few discern, or will acknowledge, that Divine power which goes with the word. The authentic and most important report of salvation for sinners, through the Son of God, is disregarded. The low condition he submitted to, and his appearance in the world, were not agreeable to the ideas the Jews had formed of the Messiah. It was expected that he should come in pomp; instead of that, he grew up as a plant, silently, and insensibly. He had nothing of the glory which one might have thought to meet with him. His whole life was not only humble as to outward condition, but also sorrowful. Being made sin for us, he underwent the sentence sin had exposed us to. Carnal hearts see nothing in the Lord Jesus to desire an interest in him. Alas! by how many is he still despised in his people, and rejected as to his doctrine and authority!

Is. **53**:**4-9** In these **verses** is an account of the sufferings of Christ; also of the design of his sufferings. It was for our sins, and in our stead, that our Lord Jesus suffered. We have all sinned, and have come short of the glory of God. Sinners have their beloved sin, their own evil way, of which they are fond. Our sins deserve all griefs and sorrows, even the most severe. We are saved from the ruin, to which by sin we become liable, by laying our sins on Christ. This atonement was to be made for our sins. And this is the only way of salvation. Our sins were the thorns in Christ's head, the nails in his hands and feet, the spear in his side. He was delivered to death for our offences. By his sufferings he purchased for us the Spirit and grace of God, to mortify our corruptions, which are the distempers of our souls. We may well endure our lighter sufferings, if He has taught us to esteem all things but loss for him, and to love him who has first loved us.

Is. **53**:**10-12** Come, and see how Christ loved us! We could not put him in our stead, but he put himself. Thus he took away the sin of the world, by taking it on himself. He made himself subject to death, which to us is the wages of sin. Observe the graces and glories of his state of exaltation. Christ will not commit the care of his family to any other. God's purposes shall take effect. And whatever is undertaken according to God's pleasure shall prosper. He shall see it accomplished in the conversion and salvation of sinners. There are many whom Christ justifies, even as many as he gave his life a ransom for. By faith we are justified; thus God is most glorified, free grace most advanced, self most abased, and our happiness secured. We must know him, and believe in him, as one that bore our sins, and saved us from sinking under the load, by taking it upon himself. Sin and Satan, death and hell, the world and the flesh, are the strong foes he has vanquished. What God designed for the Redeemer he shall certainly possess. When he led captivity captive, he received gifts for men, that he might give gifts to men. While we survey the sufferings of the Son of God, let us remember our long catalogue of transgressions, and consider him as suffering under the load of our guilt. Here is laid a firm foundation for the trembling sinner to rest his soul upon. We are the purchase of his blood, and the monuments of his grace; for this he continually pleads and prevails, destroying the works of the devil.

Chapter 54

The increase of the church by the conversion of the Jews and Gentiles. (Is. **54**:**1-5**) Its certain deliverance. (Is. **54**:**6-10**) Its triumphant state is described. (Is. **54**:**11-17**)

Is. **54**:**1-5** Observe the low state of religion in the world, for a long time before Christianity was brought in. But by preaching the gospel, multitudes were converted from idols to the living God. This is matter of great rejoicing to the church. The bounds of the church were extended. Though its state on earth is but mean and movable, like a tent or tabernacle, it is sometimes a growing state, and must be enlarged as the family increases. But the more numerous the church grows, the more she must fortify herself against errors and corruptions. Thy Maker is thy Husband. Christ is the Holy One of Israel, the Mediator of the covenant made with the Old Testament church. Long he had been called the God of Israel; but now he shall be called the God of the whole earth. And he will cleanse from sin, and cause every true believer to rejoice in this sacred union. We never can enough admire this mercy, or duly value this privilege.

Is. **54**:**6-10** As God is slow to anger, so he is swift to show mercy. And how sweet the returns of mercy would be, when God should come and comfort them! He will have mercy on them. God's gathering his people takes rise from his mercy, not any merit of theirs; and it is with great mercies, with everlasting kindness. The wrath is little, the mercies great; the wrath for a moment, the kindness everlasting. We are neither to despond under afflictions, nor to despair of relief. Mountains have been shaken and removed, but the promises of God never were broken by any event. Mountains and hills also signify great men. Creature-confidences shall fail; but when our friends fail us, our God does not. All this is alike applicable to the church at large, and to each believer. God will rebuke and correct his people for sins; but he will not cast them off. Let this encourage us to give the more diligence to make our calling and election sure.

Is. **54**:**11-17** Let the people of God, when afflicted and tossed, think they hear God speaking comfortably to them by these words, taking notice of their griefs and fears. The church is all glorious when full of the knowledge of God; for none teaches like him. It is a promise of the teaching and gifts of the Holy Spirit. All that are taught of God are taught to love one another. This seems to relate especially to the glorious times to succeed the tribulations of the church. Holiness, more than any thing, is the beauty of the church. God promises protection. There shall be no fears within; there shall be no fightings without. Military men value themselves on their splendid titles, but God calls them, "Wasters made to destroy," for they make wasting and destruction their business. He created them, therefore he will serve his own designs by them. The day is coming when God will reckon with wicked men for their hard speeches, Jude **1**:**15**. Security and final victory are the heritage of each faithful servant of the Lord. The righteousness by which they are justified, and the grace by which they are sanctified, are the gift of God, and the effect of his special love. Let us beseech him to sanctify our souls, and to employ us in his service.

Chapter 55

An invitation to receive freely the blessings of the Saviour. (Is. **55**:**1-5**) Gracious offers of pardon and peace. (Is. **55**:**6-13**)

Is. **55**:**1-5** All are welcome to the blessings of salvation, to whom those blessings are welcome. In Christ there is enough for all, and enough for each. Those satisfied with the world, that see no need of Christ, do not thirst. They are in no uneasiness about their souls: but where God gives grace, he gives a thirst after it; and where he has given a thirst after it, he will give it. Come to Christ, for he is the Fountain opened, he is the Rock smitten. Come to holy ordinances, to the streams that make glad the city of our God. Come to the healing waters, come to the living waters, Rev. **22**:**17**. Our Saviour referred to this, John **7**:**37**. Come, and buy; make it your own by application of the grace of the gospel to yourselves. Come, and eat; make it still more your own, and enjoy it. The world comes short of our expectations; we promise ourselves, at least, water in it, and we are disappointed; but Christ outdoes our expectations. We come to him, and we find wine and milk. The gifts offered to us are such as no price can be set upon. The things offered are already paid for; for Christ purchased them at the full price of his own blood, I Pet. **1**:**19**. Our wants are beyond number, and we have nothing to supply them; if Christ and heaven are ours, we see ourselves for ever indebted to free grace. Hearken diligently; let the proud heart stoop; not only come, but accept God's offers. All the wealth and pleasure in the world, will not yield solid comfort and content to the soul. They do not satisfy even the appetites of the body; for all is vanity and vexation. Let the disappointments we meet with in the world, help to drive us to Christ, and to seek for satisfaction in him only. Then, and not before, we shall find rest for our souls. Hear, and your soul shall live. On what easy terms is happiness offered us! By the sure mercies of David, we are to understand the Messiah. All his mercies are covenant mercies; they are purchased by him, they are promised in him, and out of his hand they are dispensed to us. We know not how to find the way to the waters, but Christ is given to be a Leader, a Commander, to show us what to do, and enable us to do it. Our business is to obey him, and follow him. And there is no coming to the Father but by him. He is the Holy One of Israel, true to his promises; and he has promised to glorify Christ, by giving him the heathen for his inheritance.

Is. **55**:**6-13** Here is a gracious offer of pardon, and peace, and of all happiness. It shall not be in vain to seek God, now his word is calling to us, and his Spirit is striving with us. But there is a day coming when he will not be found. There may come such a time in this life; it is certain that at death and judgment the door will be shut. There must be not only a change of the way, but a change of the mind. We must alter our judgments about persons and things. It is not enough to break off from evil practices, we must strive against evil thoughts. To repent is to return to our Lord, against whom we have rebelled. If we do so, God will multiply to pardon, as we have multiplied to offend. But let none trifle with this plenteous mercy, or use it as an occasion to sin. Men's thoughts concerning sin, Christ, and holiness, concerning this world and the other, vastly differ from God's; but in nothing more than in the matter of pardon. We forgive, and cannot forget; but when God forgives sin, he remembers it no more. The power of his word in the kingdoms of providence and grace, is as certain as in that of nature. Sacred truth produces a spiritual change in the mind of men, which neither rain nor snow can make on the earth. It shall not return to the Lord without producing important effects. If we take a special view of the church, we shall find what great things God has done, and will do for it. The Jews shall come to their own land; this shall represent the blessings promised. Gospel grace will make a great change in men. Delivered from the wrath to come, the converted sinner finds peace in his conscience; and love constrains him to devote himself to the service of his Redeemer. Instead of being profane, contentious, selfish, or sensual, behold him patient, humble, kind, and peaceable. The hope of helping in such a work should urge us to spread the gospel of salvation. And do thou help us, O Spirit of all truth, to have such views of the fulness, freeness, and greatness of the rich mercy in Christ, as may remove from us all narrow views of sovereign grace.

Chapter 56

A charge to keep the Divine precepts. (Is. **56**:**1**,**2**) Blessings promised. (Is. **56**:**3-8**) Reproof to the careless watchmen, the teachers and rulers of the Jews. (Is. **56**:**9-12**)

Is. **56**:**1**,**2** The Lord tells us what are his expectations of duty from us. Be honest and just in all dealings. Also strictly observe the sabbath day. To have the blessing of God upon employments all the week, make conscience of keeping the sabbath holy. Have nothing to do with sin. Blessed is the man that keeps his hand from all things displeasing to God and hurtful to his own soul. Those who, through the

Spirit, wait for the hope of righteousness by faith, will be found walking in ways of holy obedience.

Is. **56**:**3-8** Unbelief often suggests things to discourage believers, against which God has expressly guarded. Spiritual blessings are unspeakably better than having sons and daughters; for children are a care, and may prove a grief and shame, but the blessings we partake of in God's house, are comforts which cannot be made bitter. Those who love the Lord truly, will serve him faithfully, and then his commandments are not grievous. Three things are promised. Assistance: I will not only bid them welcome, but incline them to come. Acceptance, and comfort: though they came mourning to the house of prayer, they shall go away rejoicing. They shall find ease by casting their cares and burdens upon God. Many a sorrowful spirit has been made joyful in the house of prayer. The Gentiles shall be one body with the Jews, that, as Christ says, John **10**:**16**, there may be one fold and one Shepherd. Thanks be to God that none are separated from him except by wilful sin and unbelief; and if we come to him, we shall be accepted through the sacrifice of our great High Priest.

Is. **56**:**9-12** Desolating judgments are called for; and this severe rebuke of the rulers and teachers of the Jewish church, is applicable to other ages and places. It is bad with a people when their shepherds slumber, and are eager after the world. Let us pray the Great Shepherd to send us pastors after his own heart, who will feed us with knowledge, that we may rejoice in his holy name, and that believers may be daily added to the church.

Chapter 57

The blessed death of the righteous. (Is. **57**:**1**,**2**) The abominable idolatries of the Jewish nation. (Is. **57**:**3-12**) Promises to the humble and contrite. (Is. **57**:**13-21**)

Is. **57**:**1**,**2** The righteous are delivered from the sting of death, not from the stroke of it. The careless world disregards this. Few lament it as a public loss, and very few notice it as a public warning. They are taken away in compassion, that they may not see the evil, nor share in it, nor be tempted by it. The righteous man, when he dies, enters into peace and rest.

Is. **57**:**3-12** The Lord here calls apostates and hypocrites to appear before him. When reproved for their sins, and threatened with judgments, they ridiculed the word of God. The Jews were guilty of idolatry before the captivity; but not after that affliction. Their zeal in the worship of false gods, may shame our indifference in the worship of the true God. The service of sin is disgraceful slavery; those who thus debase themselves to hell, will justly have their portion there. Men incline to a religion that inflames their unholy passions. They are led to do any evil, however great or vile, if they think it will atone for crimes, or purchase indulgence for some favourite lust. This explains idolatry, whether pagan, Jewish, or antichristian. But those who set up anything instead of God, for their hope and confidence, never will come to a right end. Those who forsake the only right way, wander in a thousand by-paths. The pleasures of sin soon tire, but never satisfy. Those who care not for the word of God and his providences, show they have no fear of God. Sin profits not; it ruins and destroys.

Is. **57**:**13-21** The idols and their worshippers shall come to nothing; but those who trust in God's grace, shall be brought to the joys of heaven. With the Lord there is neither beginning of days, nor end of life, nor change of time. His name is holy, and all must know him as a holy God. He will have tender regard to those who bring their mind to their condition, and dread his wrath. He will make his abode with those whose hearts he has thus humbled, in order to revive and comfort them. When troubles last long, even good men are tempted to entertain hard thoughts of God. Therefore He will not contend for ever, for he will not forsake the work of his own hands, nor defeat the purchase of his Son's blood. Covetousness is a sin that particularly lays men under the Divine displeasure. See the sinfulness of sin. See also that troubles cannot reform men unless God's grace work in them. Peace shall be published, perfect peace. It is the fruit of preaching lips, and praying lips. Christ came and preached peace to Gentiles, as well as to the Jews; to after-ages, who were afar off in time, as well as to those of that age. But the wicked would not be healed by God's grace, therefore would not be healed by his comforts. Their ungoverned lusts and passions made them like the troubled sea. Also the terrors of conscience disturbed their enjoyments. God hath said it, and all the world cannot unsay it, That there is no peace to those who allow themselves in any sin. If we are recovered from such an awful state, it is only by the grace of God. And the influences of the Holy Spirit, and that new heart, from whence comes grateful praise, the fruit of our lips, are his gift. Salvation, with all its fruits, hopes, and comforts, is his work, and to him belongs all the glory. There is no peace for the wicked man; but let the wicked forsake his way, and the unrighteous man his thoughts; and let him return to the Lord, and he will have mercy upon him, and to our God, and he will abundantly pardon.

Chapter 58

Hypocrisy reproved. (Is. **58**:**1**,**2**) A counterfeit and a true fast, with promises to real godliness, and, (Is. **58**:**3-12**) to the keeping the sabbath. (Is. **58**:**13**,**14**)

Is. **58**:**1**,**2** The Holy Spirit had hypocrites of every age in view. Self-love and timid Christians may say, Spare thyself; dislike to the cross and other motives will say, "Spare the rich and powerful;" but God says, "Spare not:" and we must obey God, not men. We all need earnestly to pray for God's assistance in examining ourselves. Men may go far toward heaven, yet come short; and they may go to hell with a good reputation.

Is. **58**:**3-12** A fast is a day to afflict the soul; if it does not express true sorrow for sin, and does not promote the putting away of sin, it is not a fast. These professors had shown sorrow on stated or occasioned fasts. But they indulged pride, covetousness, and malignant passions. To be liberal and merciful is more acceptable to God than mere fasting, which, without them, is vain and hypocritical. Many who seem humble in God's house, are hard at home, and harass their families. But no man's faith justifies, which does not work by love. Yet persons, families, neighbourhoods, churches, or nations, show repentance and sorrow for sin, by keeping a fast sincerely, and, from right motives, repenting, and doing good works. The heavy yoke of sin and oppression must be removed. As sin and sorrow dry the bones and weaken the strongest human constitution; so the duties of kindness and charity strengthen and refresh both body and mind. Those who do justly and love mercy, shall have the comfort, even in this world. Good works will bring the blessing of God, provided they are done from love to God and man, and wrought in the soul by the Holy Spirit.

Is. **58**:**13**,**14** The sabbath is a sign between God and his professing people; his appointing it is a sign of his favour to them; and their observing it is a sign of their obedience to him. We must turn from travelling on that day; from doing our pleasure on that holy day, without the control and restraint of conscience; or from indulging in the pleasures of sense. On sabbath days we must not follow our callings, or our pleasures. In all we say and do, we must put a difference between this day and other days. Even in Old Testament times the sabbath was called the Lord's day, and is fitly called so still; and for a further reason, it is the Lord Christ's day, Rev. **1**:**10**. If we thus remember the sabbath day to keep it holy, we shall have the comfort and profit of it, and have reason to say, It is good to draw near to God.

Chapter 59

Reproofs of sin and wickedness. (Is. **59**:**1-8**) Confession of sin, and lamentation for the consequences. (Is. **59**:**9-15**) Promises of deliverance. (Is. **59**:**16-21**)

Is. **59**:**1-8** If our prayers are not answered, and the salvation we wait for is not wrought for us, it is not because God is weary of hearing prayer, but because we are weary of praying. See here sin in true colours, exceedingly sinful; and see sin in its consequences, exceedingly hurtful, separating from God, and so separating us, not only from all good, but to all evil. Yet numbers feed, to their own destruction, on infidel and wicked systems. Nor can their skill or craft, in devising schemes, as the spider weaves its web, deliver or save them. No schemes of self-wrought salvation shall avail those who despise the Redeemer's robe of righteousness. Every man who is destitute of the Spirit of Christ, runs swiftly to evil of some sort; but those regardless of Divine truth and justice, are strangers to peace.

Is. **59**:**9-15** If we shut our eyes against the light of Divine truth, it is just with God to hide from our eyes the things that belong to our peace. The sins of those who profess themselves God's people, are worse than the sins of others. And the sins of a nation bring public judgments, when not restrained by public justice. Men may murmur under calamities, but nothing will truly profit while they reject Christ and his gospel.

Is. **59**:**16-21** This passage is connected with the following chapters. It is generally thought to describe the coming of the Messiah, as the Avenger and Deliverer of his church. There was none to intercede with God to turn away his wrath; none to interpose for the support of justice and truth. Yet He engaged his own strength and righteousness for his people. God will make his justice upon the enemies of his church and people plainly appear. When the enemy threatens to bear down all without control, then the Spirit of the Lord shall stop him, put him to flight. He that has delivered, will still deliver. A far more glorious salvation is promised to be wrought out by the Messiah in the fulness of time, which all the prophets had in view. The Son of God shall come to us to be our Redeemer; the Spirit of God shall come to be our Sanctifier: thus the Comforter shall abide with the church for ever, John **14**:**16**. The word of Christ will always continue in the mouths of the faithful; and whatever is pretended to be the mind of the Spirit, must be tried by the Scriptures. We must lament the progress of infidelity and impiety. But the cause of the Redeemer shall gain a complete victory even on earth, and the believer will be more than conqueror when the Lord receives him to his glory in heaven.

Chapter 60

The glories of the church of God, when the fulness of the Gentiles shall come in. (Is. **60**:**1-8**) and the Jews shall be converted and gathered from their dispersions. (Is. **60**:**9-14**) and the kingdoms of this world shall become the kingdom of our Lord, and of his Christ. (Is. **60**:**15-22**)

Is. **60**:**1-8** As far as we have the knowledge of God in us, and the favour of God towards us, our light is come. And if God's glory is seen upon us to our honour, we ought, not only with our lips, but in our lives, to return its praise. We meet with nothing in the history of the Jews which can be deemed a fulfilment of the prophecy in this chapter; we must conclude it relates principally to future events. It predicts the purity and enlargement of the church. The conversion of souls is here described. They fly to Christ, to the church, to the word and ordinances, as doves to their own home; thither they fly for refuge and shelter, thither they fly for rest. What a pleasant sight to see poor souls hastening to Christ!

Is. **60**:**9-14** God will be very gracious. We must begin with his promise, thence all mercies take rise. Many shall be brought into the church, even from far countries. Christ is always ready to receive all who come to him; and the gate of mercy is always open, night and day. All that are about the church shall be made serviceable to it. But those who will not be subject to Christ's golden sceptre, to his word and Spirit, who will not be kept in by the laws and rules of his family, shall be broken in pieces by his iron rod. The peculiar advantages of every nation, and of every description of men, shall join to beautify the church of Christ. We must suppose this to be accomplished in the beauties of holiness, and the graces and comforts of the Spirit, with which gospel ordinances are adorned and enriched. Blessed be his name, the gates of Zion are ever open to returning sinners.

Is. **60**:**15-22** We must look for the full accomplishment in times and things, exceeding those of the Old Testament church. The nations and their kings shall lay themselves out for the good of the church. Such a salvation, such a redemption, shall be wrought out for thee, as discovers itself to be the work of the Lord. Every thing shall be changed for the better. In thy land shall no more be heard threats of those that do violence, nor complaints of those that suffer violence. Thy walls shall be means of safety, thy gates shall be written upon with praises to God. In the close of this chapter are images and expressions used in the description of the New Jerusalem, Rev. **21**:**23**; **22**:**5**. Nothing can answer to this but some future glorious state of the church on earth, or the state of the church triumphant in heaven. Those that make God their only light, shall have him their all-sufficient light. And the happiness shall know no change or alloy. No people on earth are all righteous; but there are no mixtures in heaven. They shall be wholly righteous. The spirits of just men shall there be made perfect. The glory of the church shall be to the honour of God. When it shall be finished, it will appear a work of wonder. It may seem too difficult to be brought about, but the God of almighty power has undertaken it. It may seem to be delayed and put off; but the Lord will hasten it in the time appointed by his wisdom, though not in the time prescribed by our folly. Let this hope cheer us under all difficulties, and stir us up to all diligence, that we may have an abundant entrance into this everlasting kingdom of our Lord and Saviour Jesus Christ.

Chapter 61

The Messiah, his character and office. (Is. **61**:**1-3**) His promises of the future blessedness of the church. (Is. **61**:**4-9**) The church praises God for these mercies. (Is. **61**:**10**,**11**)

Is. **61**:**1-3** The prophets had the Holy Spirit of God at times, teaching them what to say, and causing them to say it; but Christ had the Spirit always, without measure, to qualify him, as man, for the work to which he was appointed. The poor are commonly best disposed to receive the gospel, James **2**:**5**; and it is only likely to profit us when received with meekness. To such as are poor in spirit, Christ preached good tidings when he said, Blessed are the meek. Christ's satisfaction is accepted. By the dominion of sin in us, we are bound under the power of Satan; but the Son is ready, by his Spirit, to make us free; and then we shall be free indeed. Sin and Satan were to be destroyed; and Christ triumphed over them on his cross. But the children of men, who stand out against these offers, shall be dealt with as enemies. Christ was to be a Comforter, and so he is; he is sent to comfort all who mourn, and who seek to him, and not to the world, for comfort. He will do all this for his people, that they may abound in the fruits of righteousness, as the branches of God's planting. Neither the mercy of God, the atonement of Christ, nor the gospel of grace, profit the self-sufficient and proud. They must be humbled, and led to know their own character and wants, by the Holy Spirit, that they may see and feel their need of the sinner's Friend and Saviour. His doctrine contains glad tidings indeed to those who are humbled before God.

Is. **61**:**4-9** Promises are here made to the Jews returned out of captivity, which extend to all those who, through grace, are delivered out of spiritual thraldom. An unholy soul is like a city that is broken down, and has no walls, like a house in ruins; but by the power of Christ's gospel and grace, it is fitted to be a habitation of God, through the Spirit. When, by the grace of God, we attain to holy indifference as to the affairs of this world; when, though our hands are employed about them, our hearts are not entangled with them, but preserved entire for God and his service, then the sons of the alien are our ploughmen and vine-dressers. Those whom He sets at liberty, he sets to work. His service is perfect freedom; it is the greatest honour. All believers are made, to our God, kings and priests; and always ought to conduct themselves as such. Those who have the Lord for their portion, have reason to say, that they have worthy portion, and to rejoice in it. In the fulness of heaven's joys we shall receive more than double for all our services and sufferings. God desires truth, and therefore hates all injustice. Nor will it justify any man's robbery to say, it was for burnt-offerings; and that robbery is most hateful which is under this pretence. Let the children of godly parents be such, that all may see the fruits of a good education; an answer to the prayers for them, in the fruit of God's blessing.

Is. **61**:**10,11** Those only shall be clothed with the garments of salvation hereafter, that are covered with the robe of Christ's righteousness now, and by the sanctification of the Spirit have God's image renewed upon them. These blessings shall spring forth for ages to come, as the fruits of the earth. So duly, so constantly, and with such advantage to mankind, will the Lord God cause righteousness and praise to spring forth. They shall spread far; the great salvation shall be published and proclaimed, to the ends of the earth. Let us be earnest in prayer, that the Lord God may cause that righteousness to spring forth among us, which constitutes the excellence and glory of the Christian profession.

Chapter 62

God's care of his church and people. (Is. **62**:**1-5**) The office of ministers in preaching the gospel. (Is. **62**:**6-9**) Every hinderance shall be removed from the way of salvation. (Is. **62**:**10-12**)

Is. **62**:**1-5** The Son of God here assures his church of his unfailing love, and his pleading for her under all trails and difficulties. She shall be called by a new name, a pleasant name, such as she was never called by before. The state of true religion in the world, before the preaching of the gospel, no man seemed to have any real concern for. God, by his grace, has wrought that in his church, which makes her his delight. Let us thence learn motives to holiness. If the Lord rejoices over us, we should rejoice in his service.

Is. **62**:**6-9** God's professing people must be a praying people. He is not displeased with us for being earnest, as men commonly are; he bids us to cry after him, and give him no rest, Luke **11**:**5,6**. It is a sign that God is coming to a people in mercy, when he pours out a spirit of prayer upon them. See how uncertain our creature-comforts are. See also God's mercy in giving plenty, and peace to enjoy it. Let us delight in attending the courts of the Lord, that we may enjoy the consolations of his Spirit.

Is. **62**:**10-12** Way shall be made for Christ's salvation; all difficulties shall be removed. He brings a reward of comfort and peace with him; but a work of humiliation and reformation before him; and they shall be called, The holy people, and, The redeemed of the Lord. Holiness puts honour and beauty upon any place or person, makes them admired, beloved, and sought after. Many events may have been part fulfilments of this, as earnests of more glorious times yet to come. The close connexion between the blessedness of the Jews and of the Gentiles, runs through the Scriptures. The Lord Jesus will complete his work, and he never will forsake one whom he has redeemed and sanctified.

Chapter 63

Christ's victory over his enemies. (Is. **63**:**1-6**) His mercy toward his church. (Is. **63**:**7-14**) The prayer of the church. (Is. **63**:**15-19**)

Is. **63**:**1-6** The prophet, in vision, beholds the Messiah returning in triumph from the conquest of his enemies, of whom Edom was a type. Travelling, not as wearied by the combat, but, in the greatness of his strength, prepared to overcome every opposing power. Messiah declares that he had been treading the wine-press of the wrath of God, Rev. **14**:**19**; **19**:**13**, and by his own power, without any human help, he had crushed his obstinate opposers, for the day of vengeance was determined on, being the appointed season for rescuing his church. Once, he appeared on earth in apparent weakness, to pour out his precious blood as an atonement for our sins; but he will in due time appear in the greatness of his strength. The vintage ripens apace; the day of vengeance, fixed and determined on, approaches apace; let sinners seek to be reconciled to their righteous Judge, ere he brings down their strength to the earth. Does Christ say, "I come quickly?" let our hearts reply, "Even so, come; let the year of the redeemed come."

Is. **63**:**7-14** The latter part of this chapter, and the whole of the next, seem to express the prayers of the Jews on their conversation. They acknowledge God's great mercies and favours to their nation. They confess their wickedness and hardness of heart; they entreat his forgiveness, and deplore the miserable condition under which they have so long suffered. The only-begotten Son of the Father became the Angel or Messenger of his love; thus he redeemed and bare them with tenderness. Yet they murmured, and resisted his Holy Spirit, despising and persecuting his prophets, rejecting and crucifying the promised Messiah. All our comforts and hopes spring from the loving-kindness of the Lord, and all our miseries and fears from our sins. But he is the Saviour, and when sinners seek after him, who in other ages glorified himself by saving and feeding his purchased flock, and leading them safely through dangers, and has given his Holy Spirit to prosper the labours of his ministers, there is good ground to hope they are discovering the way of peace.

Is. **63**:**15-19** They beseech him to look down on the abject condition of their once-favoured nation. Would it not be glorious to his name to remove the veil from their hearts, to return to the tribes of his inheritance? The Babylonish captivity, and the after-deliverance of the Jews, were shadows of the events here foretold. The Lord looks down upon us in tenderness and mercy. Spiritual judgments are more to be dreaded than any other calamities; and we should most carefully avoid those sins which justly provoke the Lord to leave men to themselves and to their deceiver. "Our Redeemer from everlasting" is thy name; thy people have always looked upon thee as the God to whom they might appeal. The Lord will hear the prayers of those who belong to him, and deliver them from those not called by his name.

Chapter 64

The church prays that God's power may be manifested. (Is. **64**:**1-5**) A confession of sin, and afflictions bewailed. (Is. **64**:**6-12**)

Is. **64**:**1-5** They desire that God would manifest himself to them and for them, so that all may see it. This is applicable to the second coming of Christ, when the Lord himself shall descend from heaven. They plead what God had used to do, and had declared his gracious purpose to do, for his people. They need not fear being disappointed of it, for it is sure; or disappointed in it, for it is sufficient. The happiness of his people is bound up in what God has designed for them, and is preparing for them, and preparing them for; what he has done or will do. Can we believe this, and then think any thing too great to expect from his truth, power, and love? It is spiritual and cannot be comprehended by human understanding. It is ever ready. See what communion there is between a gracious God and a gracious soul. We must make conscience of doing our duty in every thing the Lord our God requires. Thou meetest him; this speaks his freeness and forwardness in doing them good. Though God has been angry with us for our sins, and justly, yet his anger has soon ended; but in his favour is life, which goes on and continues, and on that we depend for our salvation.

Is. **64**:**6-12** The people of God, in affliction, confess and bewail their sins, owning themselves unworthy of his mercy. Sin is that abominable thing which the Lord hates. Our deeds, whatever they may seem to be, if we think to merit by them at God's hand, are as rags, and will not cover us; filthy rags, and will but defile us. Even our few good works in which there is real excellence, as fruits of the Spirit, are so defective and defiled as done by us, that they need to be washed in the fountain open for sin and uncleanness. It bodes ill when prayer is kept back. To pray, is by faith to take hold of the promises the Lord has made of his good-will to us, and to plead them; to take hold of him, earnestly begging him not to leave us; or soliciting his return. They brought their troubles upon themselves by their own folly. Sinners are blasted, and then carried away, by the wind of their own iniquity; it withers and then ruins them. When they made themselves as an unclean thing, no wonder that God loathed them. Foolish and careless as we are, poor and despised, yet still Thou art our Father. It is the wrath of a Father we are under, who will be reconciled; and the relief our case requires is expected only from him. They refer themselves to God. They do not say, "Lord, rebuke us not," for that may be necessary; but, "Not in thy displeasure." They state their lamentable condition. See what ruin sin brings upon a people; and an outward profession of holiness will be no defence against it. God's people presume not to tell him what he shall say, but their prayer is, Speak for the comfort and relief of thy people. How few call upon the Lord with their whole hearts, or stir themselves to lay hold upon him! God may delay for a time to answer our prayers, but he will, in the end, answer those who call on his name and hope in his mercy.

Chapter 65

The calling of the Gentiles, and the rejection of the Jews. (Is. **65**:**1-7**) The Lord would preserve a remnant. (Is. **65**:**8-10**) Judgments upon the wicked. (Is. **65**:**11-16**) The future happy and flourishing state of the church. (Is. **65**:**17-25**)

Is. **65**:**1-7** The Gentiles came to seek God, and find him, because they were first sought and found of him. Often he meets some thoughtless trifler or profligate opposer, and says to him, Behold me; and a speedy change takes place. All the gospel day, Christ waited to be gracious. The Jews were bidden, but would not come. It is not without cause they are rejected of God. They would do what most pleased them. They grieved, they vexed the Holy Spirit. They forsook God's temple, and sacrificed in groves. They cared not for the distinction between clean and unclean meats, before it was taken away by the gospel. Perhaps this is put for all forbidden pleasures, and all that is thought to be gotten by sin, that abominable thing which the Lord hates. Christ denounced many woes against the pride and hypocrisy of the Jews. The proof against them is plain. And let us watch against pride and self-preference, remembering that every sin, and the most secret thoughts of man's heart, are known and will be judged by God.

Is. **65**:**8-10** In the bunch of unripe grapes, at present of no value, the new wine is contained. The Jews have been kept a distinct people, that all may witness the fulfilment of ancient prophecies and promises. God's chosen, the spiritual seed of praying Jacob, shall inherit his mountains of bliss and joy, and be carried safe to them through the vale of tears. All things are for the display of God's glory in the redemption of sinners.

Is. **65**:**11-16** Here the different states of the godly and wicked, of the Jews who believed, and of those who persisted in unbelief, are set against one another. They prepared a table for that troop of deities which the heathen worship, and poured out drink-offerings to that countless number. Their worshippers spared no cost to honour them, which should shame the worshippers of the true God. See the malignity of sin; it is doing by choice what we know will displease God. In every age and nation, the Lord leaves those who persist in doing evil, and despise the call of the gospel. God's servants shall have the bread of life, and shall want nothing good for them. But those who forsake the Lord, shall be ashamed of vain confidence in their own righteousness, and the hopes they built thereon. Wordly people bless themselves in the abundance of this world's goods; but God's servants bless themselves in him. He is their strength and portion. They shall honour him as the God of truth. And it was promised that in him should all the families of the earth be blessed. They shall think themselves happy in having him for their God, who made them forget their troubles.

Is. **65**:**17-25** In the grace and comfort believers have in and from Christ, we are to look for this new heaven and new earth. The former confusions, sins and miseries of the human race, shall be no more remembered or renewed. The approaching happy state of the church is described under a variety of images. He shall be thought to die in his youth, and for his sins, who only lives to the age of a hundred years. The event alone can determine what is meant; but it is plain that Christianity, if universal, would so do away violence and evil, as greatly to lengthen life. In those happy days, all God's people shall enjoy the fruit of their labours. Nor will children then be the trouble of their parents, or suffer trouble themselves. The evil dispositions of sinners shall be completely moritified; all shall live in harmony. Thus the church on earth shall be full of happiness, like heaven. This prophecy assures the servants of Christ, that the time approaches, wherein they shall be blessed with the undisturbed enjoyment of all that is needful for their happiness. As workers together with God, let us attend his ordinances, and obey his commands.

Chapter 66

God looks at the heart, and vengeance is threatened for guilt. (Is. **66**:**1-4**) The increase of the church, when Jew and Gentile shall be gathered to the Redeemer. (Is. **66**:**5-14**) Every enemy of the church shall be destroyed, and the final ruin of ungodly men shall be seen. (Is. **66**:**15-24**)

Is. **66**:**1-4** The Jews gloried much in their temple. But what satisfaction can the Eternal Mind take in a house made with men's hands? God has a heaven and an earth of his own making, and temples of man's making; but he overlooks them, that he may look with favour to him who is poor in spirit and serious, self-abasing and self-denying; whose heart truly sorrows for sin: such a heart is a living temple for God. The sacrifice of the wicked is not only unacceptable, but a great offence to God. And he that now offers a sacrifice after the law, does in effect set aside Christ's sacrifice. He that burns incense, puts contempt upon the incense of Christ's intercession, and is as if he blessed an idol. Men shall be deceived by the vain confidences with which they deceive themselves. Unbelieving hearts, and unpurified consciences, need no more to make them miserable, than to have their own fears brought upon them. Whatever men put in the place of the priesthood, atonement, and intercession of Christ, will be found hateful to God.

Is. **66**:**5-14** The prophet turns to those that trembled at God's word, to comfort and encourage them. The Lord will appear, to the joy of the humble believer, and to the confusion of hypocrites and persecutors. When the Spirit was poured out, and the gospel went forth from Zion, multitudes were converted in a little time. The word of God, especially his promises, and ordinances, are the consolations of the church. The true happiness of all Christians is increased by every convert brought to Christ. The gospel brings with it, wherever it is received in its power, such a river of peace, as will carry us to the ocean of boundless and endless bliss. Divine comforts reach the inward man; the joy of the Lord will be the strength of the believer. Both God's mercy and justice shall be manifested, and for ever magnified.

Is. **66**:**15-24** A prophetic declaration is given of the Lord's vengeance on all enemies of his church, especially that of all antichristian opposers of the gospel in the latter days. Is. **66**:**19**,**20**, set forth the abundance of means for conversion of sinners. These expressions are figurative, and express the plentiful and gracious helps for bringing God's elect home to Christ. All shall be welcome; and nothing shall be wanting for their assistance and encouragement. A gospel ministry shall be set up in the church; they would have solemn worship before the Lord. In the last **verse** the nature of the punishment of sinners in the world to come is represented. Then shall the righteous and wicked be separated. Our Saviour applies this to the everlasting misery and torment of impenitent sinners in the future state. To the honour of that free grace which thus distinguishes them, let the redeemed of the Lord, with humility, and not without holy trembling, sing triumphant songs. With this affecting representation of the opposite states of the righteous and wicked, characters which include the whole human race, Isaiah concludes his prophecies. May God grant, for Christ's sake, that our portion may be with those who fear and love his name, who cleave to his truths, and persevere in every good work, looking to receive from the Lord Jesus Christ the gracious invitation, Come, ye blessed of my Father, inherit the kingdom prepared for you from the foundation of the world.

Jeremiah

Jeremiah was a priest, a native of Anathoth, in the tribe of Benjamin. He was called to the prophetic office when very young, about seventy years after the death of Isaiah, and exercised it for about forty years with great faithfulness, till the sins of the Jewish nation came to their full measure and destruction followed. The prophecies of Jeremiah do not stand as they were delivered. Blayney has endeavoured to arrange them in more regular order, namely, Jer. **1-20**; **22**; **23**; **25**; **26**; **35**; **36**; **45**; **24**; **29**; **30**; **31**; **27**; **28**; **21**; **34**; **37**; **32**; **33**; **38**; **39**:**15-18**, **1-14**; **40-44**; **46-52**. The general subject of his prophecies is the idolatry and other sins of the Jews; the judgments by which they were threatened, with references to their future restoration and deliverance, and promises of the Messiah. They are remarkable for plain and faithful reproofs, affectionate expostulations, and awful warnings.

Chapter 1

Jeremiah's call to the prophetic office. (Jer. **1**:**1-10**) A vision of an almond-tree and of a seething-pot, Divine protection is promised. (Jer. **1**:**11-19**)

Jer. **1**:**1-10** Jeremiah's early call to the work and office of a prophet is stated. He was to be a prophet, not to the Jews only, but to the neighbouring nations. He is still a prophet to the whole world, and it would be well if they would attend to these warnings. The Lord who formed us, knows for what particular services and purposes he intended us. But unless he sanctify us by his new-creating Spirit, we shall neither be fit for his holy service on earth, nor his holy happiness in heaven. It becomes us to have low thoughts of ourselves. Those who are young, should consider that they are so, and not venture beyond their powers. But though a sense of our own weakness and insufficiency should make us go humbly about our work, it should not make us draw back when God calls us. Those who have messages to deliver from God, must not fear the face of man. The Lord, by a sign, gave Jeremiah such a gift as was necessary. God's message should be delivered in his own words. Whatever wordly wise men or politicians may think, the safety of kingdoms is decided according to the purpose and word of God.

Jer. **1**:**11-19** God gave Jeremiah a view of the destruction of Judah and Jerusalem by the Chaldeans. The almond-tree, which is more forward in the spring than any other, represented the speedy approach of judgments. God also showed whence the intended ruin should arise. Jeremiah saw a seething-pot boiling, representing Jerusalem and Judah in great commotion. The mouth or face of the furnace or hearth, was toward the north; from whence the fire and fuel were to come. The northern powers shall unite. The cause of these judgments was the sin of Judah. The whole counsel of God must be declared. The fear of God is the best remedy against the fear of man. Better to have all men our enemies than God our enemy; those who are sure they have God with them, need not, ought not to fear, whoever is against them. Let us pray that we may be willing to give up personal interests, and that nothing may move us from our duty.

Chapter 2

God expostulates with his people. (Jer. **2**:**1-8**) Their revolt beyond example. (Jer. **2**:**9-13**) Guilt the cause of sufferings. (Jer. **2**:**14-19**) The sins of Judah. (Jer. **2**:**20-28**) Their false confidence. (Jer. **2**:**29-37**)

Jer. **2**:**1-8** Those who begin well, but do not persevere, will justly be upbraided with their hopeful and promising beginnings. Those who desert religion, commonly oppose it more than those who never knew it. For this they could have no excuse. God's spiritual Israel must own their obligations to him for safe conduct through the wilderness of this world, so dangerous to the soul. Alas, that many, who once appeared devoted to the Lord, so live that their professions aggravate their crimes! Let us be careful that we do not lose in zeal and fervency, as we gain knowledge.

Jer. **2**:**9-13** Before God punishes sinners, he pleads with them, to bring them to repentance. He pleads with us, what we should plead with ourselves. Be afraid to think of the wrath and curse which will be the portion of those who throw themselves out of God's grace and favour. Grace in Christ is compared to water from a fountain, it being cooling and refreshing, cleansing and making fruitful: to living water, because it quickens dead sinners, revives drooping saints, supports and maintains spiritual life, and issues in eternal life, and is ever-flowing. To forsake this Fountain is the first evil; this is done when the people of God neglect his word and ordinances. They hewed them out broken cisterns, that could hold no water. Such are the world, and the things in it; such are the inventions of men when followed and depended on. Let us, with purpose of heart, cleave to the Lord only; whither else shall we go? How prone are we to forego the consolations of the Holy Spirit, for the worthless joys of the enthusiast and hypocrite!

Jer. **2**:**14-19** Is Israel a servant? No, they are the seed of Abraham. We may apply this spiritually: Is the soul of man a slave? No, it is not; but has sold its own liberty, and enslaved itself to divers lusts and passions. The Assyrian princes, like lions, prevailed against Israel. People from Egypt destroyed their glory and strength. They brought these calamities on themselves by departing from the Lord. The use and application of this is, Repent of thy sin, that thy correction may not be thy ruin. What has a Christian to do in the ways of forbidden pleasure or vain sinful mirth, or with the pursuits of covetousness and ambition?

Jer. **2**:**20-28** Notwithstanding all their advantages, Israel had become like the wild vine that bears poisonous fruit. Men are often as much under the power of their unbridled desires and their sinful lusts, as the brute beasts. But the Lord here warns them not to weary themselves in pursuits which could only bring distress and misery. As we must not despair of the mercy of God, but believe that to be sufficient for the pardon of our sins, so neither must we despair of the grace of God, but believe that it is able to subdue our corruptions, though ever so strong.

Jer. **2**:**29-37** The nation had not been wrought upon by the judgements of God, but sought to justify themselves. The world is, to those who make it their home and their portion, a wilderness and a land of darkness; but those who dwell in God, have the lines fallen to them in pleasant places. Here is the language of presumptuous sinners. The Jews had long thrown off serious thoughts of God. How many days of our lives pass without suitable remembrance of him! The Lord was displeased with their confidences, and would not prosper them therein. Men employ all their ingenuity, but cannot find happiness in the way of sin, or excuse for it. They may shift from one sin to another, but none ever hardened himself against God, or turned from him, and prospered.

Chapter 3

Exhortations to repentance. (Jer. **3**:**1-5**) Judah more guilty than Israel. (Jer. **3**:**6-11**) But pardon is promised. (Jer. **3**:**12-20**) The children of Israel express their sorrow and repentance. (Jer. **3**:**21-25**)

Jer. **3**:**1-5** In repentance, it is good to think upon the sins of which we have been guilty, and the places and companies where they have been committed. How gently the Lord had corrected them! In receiving penitents, he is God, and not man. Whatever thou hast said or done hitherto, wilt thou not from this time apply to me? Will not this grace of God overcome thee? Now pardon is proclaimed, wilt thou not take the benefit? They will hope to find in him the tender compassions of a Father towards a returning prodigal. They will come to him as the Guide of their youth: youth needs a guide. Repenting sinners may encourage themselves that God will not keep his anger to the end. All God's mercies, in every age, suggest encouragement; and what can be so desirable for the young, as to have the Lord for their Father, and the Guide of their youth? Let parents daily direct their children earnestly to seek this blessing.

Jer. **3**:**6-11** If we mark the crimes of those who break off from a religious profession, and the consequences, we see abundant reason to shun evil ways. It is dreadful to be proved more criminal than those who have actually perished in their sins; yet it will be small comfort in everlasting punishment, for them to know that others were viler than they.

Jer. **3**:**12-20** See God's readiness to pardon sin, and the blessings reserved for gospel times. These words were proclaimed toward the north; to Israel, the ten tribes, captive in Assyria. They are directed how to return. If we confess our sins, the Lord is faithful and just to forgive them. These promises are fully to come to pass in the bringing back the Jews in after-ages. God will graciously receive those that return to him; and by his grace, he takes them out from among the rest. The ark of the covenant was not found after the captivity. The whole of that dispensation was to be done away, which took place after the multitude of believers had been greatly increased by the conversion of the Gentiles, and of the Israelites scattered among them. A happy state of the church is foretold. He can teach all to call him Father; but without thorough change of heart and life, no man can be a child of God, and we have no security for not departing from Him.

Jer. **3**:**21-25** Sin is turning aside to crooked ways. And forgetting the Lord our God is at the bottom of all sin. By sin we bring ourselves into trouble. The promise to those that return is, God will heal their backslidings, by his pardoning mercy, his quieting peace, and his renewing grace. They come devoting themselves to God. They come disclaiming all expectations of relief and succour from any but the Lord. Therefore they come depending upon him only. He is the Lord, and he only can save. It points out the great salvation from sin Jesus Christ wrought out for us. They come justifying God in their troubles, and judging themselves for their sins. True penitents learn to call sin shame, even the sin they have been most pleased with. True penitents learn to call sin death and ruin, and to charge upon it all they suffer. While men harden themselves in sin, contempt and misery are their portion: for he that covereth his sins shall not prosper, but he that confesseth and forsaketh them, shall find mercy.

Chapter 4

Exhortations and promises. (Jer. **4**:**1-2**) Judah exhorted to repentance. (Jer. **4**:**3-4**) Judgements denounced. (Jer. **4**:**5-18**) The approaching ruin of Judah. (Jer. **4**:**19-31**)

Jer. **4**:**1**,**2** The first two **verse**s should be read with the last chapter. Sin must be put away out of the heart, else it is not put away out of God's sight, for the heart is open before him.

Jer. **4**:**3**,**4** An unhumbled heart is like ground untilled. It is ground which may be improved; it is our ground let out to us; but it is fallow; it is over-grown with thorns and weeds, the natural product of the corrupt heart. Let us entreat the Lord to create in us a clean heart, and to renew a right spirit within us; for except a man be born again, he cannot enter into the kingdom of heaven.

Jer. **4**:**5-18** The fierce conqueror of the neighbouring nations was to make Judah desolate. The prophet was afflicted to see the people lulled into security by false prophets. The approach of the enemy is described. Some attention was paid in Jerusalem to outward reformation; but it was necessary that their hearts should be washed, in the exercise of true repentance and faith, from the love and pollution of sin. When lesser calamities do not rouse sinners and reform nations, sentence will be given against them. The Lord's voice declares that misery is approaching, especially against wicked professors of the gospel; when it overtakes them, it will be plainly seen that the fruit of wickedness is bitter, and the end is fatal.

Jer. **4**:**19-31** The prophet had no pleasure in delivering messages of wrath. He is shown in a vision the whole land in confusion. Compared with what it was, every thing is out of order; but the ruin of the Jewish nation would not be final. Every end of our comforts is not a full end. Though the Lord may correct his people very severely, yet he will not cast them off. Ornaments and false colouring would be of no avail. No outward privileges or profession, no contrivances would prevent destruction. How wretched the state of those who are like foolish children in the concerns of their souls! Whatever we are ignorant of, may the Lord make of good understanding in the ways of godliness. As sin will find out the sinner, so sorrow will, sooner or later, find out the secure.

Chapter 5

The Jews' profession of religion was hypocritical. (Jer. **5**:**1-9**) The cruel proceedings of their enemies. (Jer. **5**:**10-18**) Their apostacy and idolatry. (Jer. **5**:**19-31**)

Jer. **5**:**1-9** None could be found who behaved as upright and godly men. But the Lord saw the true character of the people through all their disguises. The poor were ignorant, and therefore they were wicked. What can be expected but works of darkness, from people that know nothing of God and religion? There are God's poor, who, notwithstanding poverty, know the way of the Lord, walk in it, and do their duty; but these were willingly ignorant, and their ignorance would not be their excuse. The rich were insolent and haughty, and the abuse of God's favours made their sin worse.

Jer. **5**:**10-18** Multitudes are ruined by believing that God will not be so strict as his word says he will; by this artifice Satan undid mankind. Sinners are not willing to own any thing to be God's word, that tends to part them from, or to disquiet them in, their sins. Mocking and misusing the Lord's messengers, filled the measure of their iniquity. God can bring trouble upon us from places and causes very remote. He has mercy in store for his people, therefore will set bounds to this desolating judgment. Let us not overlook the "nevertheless," Jer. **5**:**18**. This is the Lord's covenant with Israel. He thereby proclaims his holiness, and his utter displeasure against sin while sparing the sinner, Ps. **89**:**30-35**.

Jer. **5**:**19-31** Unhumbled hearts are ready to charge God with being unjust in their afflictions. But they may read their sin in their punishment. If men will inquire wherefore the Lord doeth hard things unto them, let them think of their sins. The restless waves obeyed the Divine decree, that they should not pass the sandy shores, which were as much a restraint as lofty mountains; but they burst all restraints of God's law, and were wholly gone into wickedness. Neither did they consider their interest. While the Lord, year after year, reserves to us the appointed weeks of harvest, men live on his bounty; yet they transgress against him. Sin deprives us of God's blessings; it makes the heaven as brass, and the earth as iron. Certainly the things of this world are not the best things; and we are not to think, that, because evil men prosper, God allows their practices. Though sentence against evil works is not executed speedily, it will be executed. Shall I not visit for these things? This speaks the certainty and the necessity of God's judgments. Let those who walk in bad ways consider that an end will come, and there will be bitterness in the latter end.

Chapter 6

The invasion of Judea. (Jer. **6**:**1-8**) The justice of God's proceedings. (Jer. **6**:**9-17**) All methods used to amend them had been without success. (Jer. **6**:**18-30**)

Jer. **6**:**1-8** Whatever methods are used, it is vain to contend with God's judgments. The more we indulge in the pleasures of this life, the more we unfit ourselves for the troubles of this life. The Chaldean army shall break in upon the land of Judah, and in a little time devour all. The day is coming, when those careless and secure in sinful ways will be visited. It is folly to trifle when we have eternal salvation to work out, and the enemies of that salvation to fight against. But they were thus eager, not that they might fulfil God's counsels, but that they might fill their own treasures; yet God thereby served his own purposes. The corrupt heart of man, in its natural state, casts out evil thoughts, just as a fountain casts out her waters. It is always flowing, yet always full. The God of mercy is loth to depart even from a provoking people, and is earnest with them, that by repentance and reformation, they may prevent things from coming to extremity.

Jer. **6**:**9-17** When the Lord arises to take vengeance, no sinners of any age or rank, or of either sex escape. They were set upon the world, and wholly carried away by the love of it. If we judge of this sin by God's word, we find multitudes in every station and rank given up to it. Those are to be reckoned our worst and most dangerous enemies, who flatter us in a sinful way. Oh that men would be wise for their souls! Ask for the old paths; the way of godliness and righteousness has always been the way God has owned and blessed. Ask for the old paths set forth by the written word of God. When you have found the good way, go on in it, you will find abundant recompence at your journey's end. But if men will not obey the voice of God and flee to his appointed Refuge, it will plainly appear at the day of judgment, that they are ruined because they reject God's word.

Jer. **6**:**18-30** God rejects their outward services, as worthless to atone for their sins. Sacrifice and incense were to direct them to a Mediator; but when offered to purchase a license to go on in sin, they provoke God. The sins of God's professing people make them an easy prey to their enemies. They dare not show themselves. Saints may rejoice in hope of God's mercies, though they see them only in the promise: sinners must mourn for fear of God's judgments, though they see them only in the threatenings. They are the worst of revolters, and are all corrupters. Sinners soon become tempters. They are compared to ore supposed to have good metal in it, but which proves all dross. Nothing will prevail to part between them and their sins. Reprobate silver shall they be called, useless and worthless. When warnings, corrections, rebukes, and all means of grace, leave men unrenewed, they will be left, as rejected of God, to everlasting misery. Let us pray, then, that we may be refined by the Lord, as silver is refined.

Chapter 7

Confidence in the temple is vain. (Jer. **7**:**1-16**) The provocation by persisting in idolatry. (Jer. **7**:**17-20**) God justifies his dealings with them. (Jer. **7**:**21-28**) And threatens vengeance. (Jer. **7**:**29-34**)

Jer. **7**:**1-16** No observances, professions, or supposed revelations, will profit, if men do not amend their ways and their doings. None can claim an interest in free salvation, who allow themselves in the practice of known sin, or live in the neglect of known duty. They thought that the temple they profaned would be their protection. But all who continue in sin because grace has abounded, or that grace may abound, make Christ the minister of sin; and the cross of Christ, rightly understood, forms the most effectual remedy to such poisonous sentiments. The Son of God gave himself for our transgressions, to show the excellence of the Divine law, and the evil of sin. Never let us think we may do wickedness without suffering for it.

Jer. **7**:**17-20** The Jews took pride in showing zeal for their idols. Let us learn to be earnest in the service of our God, even from this bad example. Let us think it an honour to be employed in any work for God. Let us be as diligent ourselves, and as careful to teach our children the truths of God, as many are to teach the mysteries of iniquity. The direct tendency of this sin is malice against God, but it will hurt themselves. And they shall find there is no escaping. God's wrath is fire unquenchable.

Jer. **7**:**21-28** God shows that obedience was required of them. That which God commanded was, Hearken diligently to the voice of the Lord thy God. The promise is very encouraging. Let God's will be your rule, and his favour shall be your happiness. God was displeased with disobedience. We understand the gospel as little as the Jews understood the law, if we think that even the sacrifice of Christ lessens our obligation to obey.

Jer. 7:**29-34** In token both of sorrow and of slavery, Jerusalem must be degraded, and separated from God, as she had been separated to him. The heart is the place in which God has chosen to put his name; but if sin has the innermost and uppermost place there, we pollute the temple of the Lord. The destruction of Jerusalem appears here very terrible. The slain shall be many; they having made it the place of their sin. Evil pursues sinners, even after death. Those who will not, by the grace of God, be cured of vain mirth, shall, by the justice of God, be deprived of all mirth. How many ruin their health and property without complaining, when engaged in Satan's service! May we learn to relish holy joys, and to sit loose to all others though lawful.

Chapter 8

The remains of the dead exposed. (Jer. **8**:**1-3**) The stupidity of the people, compared with the instinct of the brute creation. (Jer. **8**:**4-13**) The alarm of the invasion, and lamentation. (Jer. **8**:**14-22**)

Jer. **8**:**1-3** Though no real hurt can be done to a dead body, yet disgrace to the remains of wicked persons may alarm those yet alive; and this reminds us that the Divine justice and punishments extend beyond the grave. Whatever befalls us here, let us humble ourselves before God, and seek his mercy.

Jer. **8**:**4-13** What brought this ruin? **1**. The people would not attend to reason; they would not act in the affairs of their souls with common prudence. Sin is backsliding; it is going back from the way that leads to life, to that which leads to destruction. **2**. They would not attend to the warning of conscience. They did not take the first step towards repentance: true repentance begins in serious inquiry as to what we have done, from conviction that we have done amiss. **3**. They would not attend to the ways of providence, nor understand the voice of God in them, Jer. **8**:**7**. They know not how to improve the seasons of grace, which God affords. Many boast of their religious knowledge, yet, unless taught by the Spirit of God, the instinct of brutes is a more sure guide than their supposed wisdom. **4**. They would not attend to the written word. Many enjoy abundance of the means of grace, have Bibles and ministers, but they have them in vain. They will soon be ashamed of their devices. The pretenders to wisdom were the priests and the false prophets. They flattered people in sin, and so flattered them into destruction, silencing their fears and complaints with, All is well. Selfish teachers may promise peace when there is no peace; and thus men encourage each other in committing evil; but in the day of visitation they will have no refuge to flee unto.

Jer. **8**:**14-22** At length they begin to see the hand of God lifted up. And when God appears against us, every thing that is against us appears formidable. As salvation only can be found in the Lord, so the present moment should be seized. Is there no medicine proper for a sick and dying kingdom? Is there no skilful, faithful hand to apply the medicine? Yes, God is able to help and to heal them. If sinners die of their wounds, their blood is upon their own heads. The blood of Christ is balm in Gilead, his Spirit is the Physician there, all-sufficient; so that the people may be healed, but will not. Thus men die unpardoned and unchanged, for they will not come to Christ to be saved.

Chapter 9

The people are corrected, Jerusalem is destroyed. (Jer. **9**:**1-11**) The captives suffer in a foreign land. (Jer. **9**:**12-22**) God's loving-kindness, He threatens the enemies of his people. (Jer. **9**:**23-26**)

Jer. **9**:**1-11** Jeremiah wept much, yet wished he could weep more, that he might rouse the people to a due sense of the hand of God. But even the desert, without communion with God, through Christ Jesus, and the influences of the Holy Spirit, must be a place for temptation and evil; while, with these blessings, we may live in holiness in crowded cities. The people accustomed their tongues to lies. So false were they, that a brother could not be trusted. In trading and bargaining they said any thing for their own advantage, though they knew it to be false. But God marked their sin. Where no knowledge of God is, what good can be expected? He has many ways of turning a fruitful land into barrenness for the wickedness of those that dwell therein.

Jer. **9**:**12-22** In Zion the voice of joy and praise used to be heard, while the people kept close to God; but sin has altered the sound, it is now the voice of lamentation. Unhumbled hearts lament their calamity, but not their sin, which is the cause of it. Let the doors be shut ever so fast, death steals upon us. It enters the palaces of princes and great men, though stately, strongly built, and guarded. Nor are those more safe that are abroad; death cuts off even the children from without, and the young men from the streets. Hearken to the word of the Lord, and mourn with godly sorrow. This alone can bring true comfort; and it can turn the heaviest afflictions into precious mercies.

Jer. **9**:**23-26** In this world of sin and sorrow, ending soon in death and judgement, how foolish for men to glory in their knowledge, health, strength, riches, or in any thing which leaves them under the dominion of sin and the wrath of God! and of which an account must hereafter be rendered; it will but increase their misery. Those are the true Israel who worship God in the Spirit, rejoice in Christ Jesus, and have no confidence in the flesh. Let us prize the distinction which comes from God, and will last for ever. Let us seek it diligently.

Chapter 10

The absurdity of idolatry. (Jer. **10**:**1-16**) Destruction denounced against Jerusalem. (Jer. **10**:**17-25**)

Jer. **10**:**1-16** The prophet shows the glory of Israel's God, and exposes the folly of idolaters. Charms and other attempts to obtain supernatural help, or to pry into futurity, are copied from the wicked customs of the heathen. Let us stand in awe, and not dare provoke God, by giving that glory to another which is due to him alone. He is ready to forgive, and save all who repent and believe in the name of his Son Jesus Christ. Faith learns these blessed truths from the word of God; but all knowledge not from that source, leads to doctrines of vanity.

Jer. **10**:**17-25** The Jews who continued in their own land, felt secure. But, sooner or later, sinners will find all things as the word of God has declared, and that its threatenings are not empty terrors. Submission will support the believer under every grief allotted to him; but what can render the load of Divine vengeance easy to be borne by those who fall under it in sullen despair? Those cannot expect to prosper, who do not, by faith and prayer, take God with them in all their ways. The report of the enemy's approach was very dreadful. Yet the designs which men lay deep, and think well formed, are dashed to pieces in a moment. Events are often overruled, so as to be quite contrary to what we intended and expected. If the Lord has directed our steps into the ways of peace and righteousness, let us entreat him to enable us to walk therein. Say not, Lord, do not correct me; but, Lord, do not correct me in anger. We may bear the smart of God's rod, but we cannot bear the weight of his wrath. Those who restrain prayer, prove that they know not God; for those who know him will seek him, and seek his favour. If even severe corrections lead sinners to be convinced of wholesome truths, they will have abundant cause for gratitude. And they will then humble themselves before the Lord.

Chapter 11

The disobedient Jews reproved. (Jer. **11**:**1-10**) Their utter ruin. (Jer. **11**:**11-17**) The people would be destroyed who sought the prophet's life. (Jer. **11**:**18-23**)

Jer. **11**:**1-10** God never promised to bestow blessings on his rational creatures, while they persist in wilful disobedience. Pardon and acceptance are promised freely to all believers; but no man can be saved who does not obey the command of God to repent, to believe in Christ, to separate from sin and the world, to choose self-denial and newness of life. In general, men will hearken to those who speak of doctrines, promises, and privileges; but when duties are mentioned, they will not bend their ear.

Jer. **11**:**11-17** Evil pursues sinners, and entangles them in snares, out of which they cannot free themselves. Now, in their distress, their many gods and many altars stand them in no stead. And those whose own prayers will not be heard, cannot expect benefit from the prayers of others. Their profession of religion shall prove of no use. When trouble came upon them, they made this their confidence, but God has rejected it. His altar shall yield them no satisfaction. The remembrance of God's former favours to them shall be no comfort under troubles; and his remembrance of them shall be no argument for their relief. Every sin against the Lord is a sin against ourselves, and so it will be found sooner or later.

Jer. **11**:**18-23** The prophet Jeremiah tells much concerning himself, the times he lived in being very troublesome. Those of his own city plotted how they might cause his death. They thought to end his days, but he outlived most of his enemies; they thought to blast his memory, but it lives to this day, and will be blessed while time lasts. God knows all the secret designs of his and his people's enemies, and can, when he pleases, make them known. God's justice is a terror to the wicked, but a comfort to the godly. When we are wronged, we have a God to commit our cause to, and it is our duty to commit it to him. We should also look well to our own spirits, that we are not overcome with evil, but that by patient continuance in praying for our enemies, and in kindness to them, we may overcome evil with good.

Chapter 12

Jeremiah complains of the prosperity of the wicked. (Jer. **12**:**1-6**) The heavy judgments to come upon the nation. (Jer. **12**:**7-13**) Divine mercy to them, and even to the nations around. (Jer. **12**:**14-17**)

Jer. **12**:**1-6** When we are most in the dark concerning God's dispensations, we must keep up right thoughts of God, believing that he never did the least wrong to any of his creatures. When we find it hard to understand any of his dealings with us, or others, we must look to general truths as our first principles, and abide by them: the Lord is righteous. The God with whom we have to do, knows how our hearts are toward him. He knows both the guile of the hypocrite and the sincerity of the upright. Divine judgments would pull the wicked out of their pasture as sheep for the slaughter. This fruitful land was turned into barrenness for the wickedness of those that dwelt therein. The Lord reproved the prophet. The opposition of the men of Anathoth was not so formidable as what he must expect from the rulers of Judah. Our grief that there should be so much evil is often mixed with peevishness on account of the trials it occasions us. And in this our favoured day, and under our trifling difficulties, let us consider how we should behave, if called to sufferings like those of saints in former ages.

Jer. **12**:**7-13** God's people had been the dearly-beloved of his soul, precious in his sight, but they acted so, that he gave them up to their enemies. Many professing churches become like speckled birds, presenting a mixture of religion and the world, with its vain fashions, pursuits, and pollutions. God's people are as men wondered at, as a speckled bird; but this people had by their own folly made themselves so; and the beasts and birds are called to prey upon them. The whole land would be made desolate. But until the judgments were actually inflicted, none of the people would lay the warning to heart. When God's hand is lifted up, and men will not see, they shall be made to feel. Silver and gold shall not profit in the day of the Lord's anger. And the efforts of sinners to escape misery, without repentance and works answerable thereto, will end in confusion.

Jer. **12**:**14-17** The Lord would plead the cause of his people against their evil neighbours. Yet he would afterwards show mercy to those nations, when they should learn true religion. This seems to look forward to the times when the fulness of the Gentiles shall come in. Those who would have their lot with God's people, and a last end like theirs, must learn their ways, and walk in them.

Chapter 13

The glory of the Jews should be marred. (Jer. **13**:**1-11**) All ranks should suffer misery, An earnest exhortation to repentance. (Jer. **13**:**12-17**) An awful message to Jerusalem and its king. (Jer. **13**:**18-27**)

Jer. **13**:**1-11** It was usual with the prophets to teach by signs. And we have the explanation, Jer. **13**:**9-11**. The people of Israel had been to God as this girdle. He caused them to cleave to him by the law he gave them, the prophets he sent among them, and the favours he showed them. They had by their idolatries and sins buried themselves in foreign earth, mingled among the nations, and were so corrupted that they were good for nothing. If we are proud of learning, power, and outward privileges, it is just with God to wither them. The minds of men should be awakened to a sense of their guilt and danger; yet nothing will be effectual without the influences of the Spirit.

Jer. **13**:**12-17** As the bottle was fitted to hold the wine, so the sins of the people made them vessels of wrath, fitted for the judgments of God; with which they should be filled till they caused each other's destruction. The prophet exhorts them to give glory to God, by confessing their sins, humbling themselves in repentance, and returning to his service. Otherwise they would be carried into other countries in all the darkness of idolatry and wickedness. All misery, witnessed or foreseen, will affect a feeling mind, but the pious heart must mourn most over the afflictions of the Lord's flock.

Jer. **13**:**18-27** Here is a message sent to king Jehoiakim, and his queen. Their sorrows would be great indeed. Do they ask, Wherefore come these things upon us? Let them know, it is for their obstinacy in sin. We cannot alter the natural colour of the skin; and so is it morally impossible to reclaim and reform these people. Sin is the blackness of the soul; it is the discolouring of it; we were shapen in it, so that we cannot get clear of it by any power of our own. But Almighty grace is able to change the Ethiopian's skin. Neither natural depravity, nor strong habits of sin, form an obstacle to the working of God, the new-creating Spirit. The Lord asks of Jerusalem, whether she is determined not be made clean. If any poor slave of sin feels that he could as soon change his nature as master his headstrong lusts, let him not despair; for things impossible to men are possible with God. Let us then seek help from Him who is mighty to save.

Chapter 14

A drought upon the land of Judah. (Jer. **14**:**1-7**) A confession of sin in the name of the people. (Jer. **14**:**8-9**) The Divine purpose to punish is declared. (Jer. **14**:**10-16**) The people supplicate. (Jer. **14**:**17-22**)

Jer. **14**:**1-9** The people were in tears. But it was rather the cry of their trouble, and of their sin, than of their prayer. Let us be thankful for the mercy of water, that we may not be taught to value it by feeling the want of it. See what dependence husbandmen have upon the Divine providence. They cannot plough nor sow in hope, unless God water their furrows. The case even of the wild beasts was very pitiable. The people are not forward to pray, but the prophet prays for them. Sin is humbly confessed. Our sins not only accuse us, but answer against us. Our best pleas in prayer are those fetched from the glory of God's own name. We should dread God's departure, more than the removal of our creature-comforts. He has given Israel his word to hope in. It becomes us in prayer to show ourselves more concerned for God's glory than for our own comfort. And if we now return to the Lord, he will save us to the glory of his grace.

Jer. **14**:**10-16** The Lord calls the Jews "this people," not "his people." They had forsaken his service, therefore he would punish them according to their sins. He forbade Jeremiah to plead for them. The false prophets were the most criminal. The Lord pronounces condemnation on them; but as the people loved to have it so, they were not to escape judgments. False teachers encourage men to expect peace and salvation, without repentance, faith, conversion, and holiness of life. But those who believe a lie must not plead if for an excuse. They shall feel what they say they will not fear.

Jer. **14**:**17-22** Jeremiah acknowledged his own sins, and those of the people, but pleaded with the Lord to remember his covenant. In their distress none of the idols of the Gentiles could help them, nor could the heavens give rain of themselves. The Lord will always have a people to plead with him at his mercy-seat. He will heal every truly repenting sinner. Should he not see fit to hear our prayers on behalf of our guilty land, he will certainly bless with salvation all who confess their sins and seek his mercy.

Chapter 15

The destruction of the wicked described. (Jer. **15**:**1-9**) The prophet laments such messages, and is reproved. (Jer. **15**:**10-14**) He supplicates pardon, and is promised protection. (Jer. **15**:**15-21**)

Jer. **15**:**1-9** The Lord declares that even Moses and Samuel must have pleaded in vain. The putting of this as a case, though they should stand before him, shows that they do not, and that saints in heaven do not pray for saints on earth. The Jews were condemned to different kinds of misery by the righteous judgment of God, and the remnant would be driven away, like the chaff, into captivity. Then was the populous city made desolate. Bad examples and misused authority often produce fatal effects, even after men are dead, or have repented of their crimes: this should make all greatly dread being the occasion of sin in others.

Jer. **15**:**10-14** Jeremiah met with much contempt and reproach, when they ought to have blessed him, and God for him. It is a great and sufficient support to the people of God, that however troublesome their way may be, it shall be well with them in their latter end. God turns to the people. Shall the most hardy and vigorous of their efforts be able to contend with the counsel of God, or with the army of the Chaldeans? Let them hear their doom. The enemy will treat the prophet well. But the people who had great estates would be used hardly. All parts of the country had added to the national guilt; and let each take shame to itself.

Jer. **15**:**15-21** It is matter of comfort that we have a God, to whose knowledge of all things we may appeal. Jeremiah pleads with God for mercy and relief against his enemies, persecutors, and slanderers. It will be a comfort to God's ministers, when men despise them, if they have the testimony of their own consciences. But he complains, that he found little pleasure in his work. Some good people lose much of the pleasantness of religion by the fretfulness and uneasiness of their natural temper, which they indulge. The Lord called the prophet to cease from his distrust, and to return to his work. If he attended thereto, he might be assured the Lord would deliver him from his enemies. Those who are with God, and faithful to him, he will deliver from trouble or carry through it. Many things appear frightful, which do not at all hurt a real believer in Christ.

Chapter 16

Prohibitions given to the prophet. (Jer. **16**:**1-9**) The justice of God in these judgments. (Jer. **16**:**10-13**) Future restoration of the Jews, and the conversion of the Gentiles. (Jer. **16**:**14-21**)

Jer. **16**:**1-9** The prophet must conduct himself as one who expected to see his country ruined very shortly. In the prospect of sad times, he is to abstain from marriage, mourning for the dead, and pleasure. Those who would convince others of the truths of God, must make it appear by their self-denial, that they believe it themselves. Peace, inward and outward, family and public, is wholly the work of God, and from his loving-kindness and mercy. When He takes his peace from any people, distress must follow. There may be times when it is proper to avoid things otherwise our duty; and we should always sit loose to the pleasures and concerns of this life.

Jer. **16**:**10-13** Here seems to be the language of those who quarrel at the word of God, and instead of humbling and condemning themselves, justify themselves, as though God did them wrong. A plain and full answer is given. They were more obstinate in sin than their fathers, walking every one after the devices of his heart. Since they will not hearken, they shall be hurried away into a far country, a land they know not. If they had God's favour, that would make even the land of their captivity pleasant.

Jer. **16**:**14-21** The restoration from the Babylonish captivity would be remembered in place of the deliverance from Egypt; it also typified spiritual redemption, and the future deliverance of the church from antichristian oppression. But none of the sins of sinners can be hidden from God, or shall be overlooked by him. He will find out and raise up instruments of his wrath, that shall destroy the Jews, by fraud like fishers, by force like hunters. The prophet, rejoicing at the hope of mercy to come, addressed the Lord as his strength and refuge. The deliverance out of captivity shall be a figure of the great salvation to be wrought by the Messiah. The nations have often known the power of Jehovah in his wrath; but they shall know him as the strength of his people, and their refuge in time of trouble.

Chapter 17

The fatal consequences of the idolatry of the Jews. (Jer. **17**:**1-4**) The happiness of the man that trusts in God; the end of the opposite character. (Jer. **17**:**5-11**) The malice of the prophet's enemies. (Jer. **17**:**12-18**) The observance of the sabbath. (Jer. **17**:**19-27**)

Jer. **17**:**1-4** The sins which men commit make little impression on their minds, yet every sin is marked in the book of God; they are all so graven upon the table of the heart, that they will all be remembered by the conscience. That which is graven in the heart will become plain in the life; men's actions show the desires and purposes of their hearts. What need we have to humble ourselves before God, who are so vile in his sight! How should we depend on his mercy and grace, begging of God to search and prove us; not to suffer us to be deceived by our own hearts, but to create in us a clean and holy nature by his Spirit!

Jer. **17**:**5-11** He who puts confidence in man, shall be like the heath in a desert, a naked tree, a sorry shrub, the product of barren ground, useless and worthless. Those who trust to their own righteousness and strength, and think they can do without Christ, make flesh their arm, and their souls cannot prosper in graces or comforts. Those who make God their Hope, shall flourish like a tree always green, whose leaf does not wither. They shall be fixed in peace and satisfaction of mind; they shall not be anxious in a year of drought. Those who make God their Hope, have enough in him to make up the want of all creature-comforts. They shall not cease from yielding fruit in holiness and good works. The heart, the conscience of man, in his corrupt and fallen state, is deceitful above all things. It calls evil good, and good evil; and cries peace to those to whom it does not belong. Herein the heart is desperately wicked; it is deadly, it is desperate. The case is bad indeed, if the conscience, which should set right the errors of other faculties, is a leader in the delusion. We cannot know our own hearts, nor what they will do in an hour of temptation. Who can understand his errors? Much less can we know the hearts of others, or depend upon them. He that believes God's testimony in this matter, and learns to watch his own heart, will find this is a correct, though a sad picture, and learns many lessons to direct his conduct. But much in our own hearts and in the hearts of others, will remain unknown. Yet whatever wickedness there is in the heart, God sees it. Men may be imposed upon, but God cannot be deceived. He that gets riches, and not by right, though he may make them his hope, never shall have joy of them. This shows what vexation it is to a worldly man at death, that he must leave his riches behind; but though the wealth will not follow to another world, guilt will, and everlasting torment. The rich man takes pains to get an estate, and sits brooding upon it, but never has any satisfaction in it; by sinful courses it comes to nothing. Let us be wise in time; what we get, let us get it honestly; and what we have, use it charitably, that we may be wise for eternity.

Jer. **17**:**12-18** The prophet acknowledges the favour of God in setting up religion. There is fulness of comfort in God, overflowing, ever-flowing fulness, like a fountain. It is always fresh and clear, like spring-water, while the pleasures of sin are puddle-waters. He prays to God for healing, saving mercy. He appeals to God concerning his faithful discharge of the office to which he was called. He humbly begs that God would own and protect him in the work to which he had plainly called him. Whatever wounds or diseases we find to be in our hearts and consciences, let us apply to the Lord to heal us, to save us, that our souls may praise his name. His hands can bind up the troubled conscience, and heal the broken heart; he can cure the worst diseases of our nature.

Jer. **17**:**19-27** The prophet was to lay before the rulers and the people of Judah, the command to keep holy the sabbath day. Let them strictly observe the fourth command. If they obeyed this word, their prosperity should be restored. It is a day of rest, and must not be made a day of labour, unless in cases of necessity. Take heed, watch against the profanation of the sabbath. Let not the soul be burdened with the cares of this world on sabbath days. The streams of religion run deep or shallow, according as the banks of the sabbath are kept up or neglected. The degree of strictness with which this ordinance is observed, or the neglect shown towards it, is a good test to find the state of spiritual religion in any land. Let all; by their own example, by attention to their families, strive to check this evil, that national prosperity may be preserved, and, above all, that souls may be saved.

Chapter 18

God's power over his creatures is represented by the potter. (Jer. **18**:**1-10**) The Jews exhorted to repentance, and judgments foretold. (Jer. **18**:**11-17**) The prophet appeals to God. (Jer. **18**:**18-23**)

Jer. **18**:**1-10** While Jeremiah looks upon the potter's work, God darts into his mind two great truths. God has authority, and power, to form and fashion kingdoms and nations as he pleases. He may dispose of us as he thinks fit; and it would be as absurd for us to dispute this, as for the clay to quarrel with the potter. But he always goes by fixed rules of justice and goodness. When God is coming against us in judgments, we may be sure it is for our sins; but sincere conversion from the evil of sin will prevent the evil of punishment, as to persons, and to families, and nations.

Jer. **18**:**11-17** Sinners call it liberty to live at large; whereas for a man to be a slave to his lusts, is the very worst slavery. They forsook God for idols. When men are parched with heat, and meet with cooling, refreshing streams, they use them. In these things men will not leave a certainty for an uncertainty; but Israel left the ancient paths appointed by the Divine law. They walked not in the highway, in which they might travel safely, but in a way in which they must stumble: such was the way of idolatry, and such is the way of iniquity. This made their land desolate, and themselves miserable. Calamities may be borne, if God smile upon us when under them; but if he is displeased, and refuses his help, we are undone. Multitudes forget the Lord and his Christ, and wander from the ancient paths, to walk in ways of their own devising. But what will they do in the day of judgment!

Jer. **18**:**18-23** When the prophet called to repentance, instead of obeying the call, the people devised devices against him. Thus do sinners deal with the great Intercessor, crucifying him afresh, and speaking against him on earth, while his blood is speaking for them in heaven. But the prophet had done his duty to them; and the same will be our rejoicing in a day of evil.

Chapter 19

By the type of breaking an earthen vessel, Jeremiah is to predict the destruction of Judah.

Jer. **19**:**1-9** The prophet must give notice of ruin coming upon Judah and Jerusalem. Both rulers and ruled must attend to it. That place which holiness made the joy of the whole earth, sin made the reproach and shame of the whole earth. There is no fleeing from God's justice, but by fleeing to his mercy.

Jer. **19**:**10-15** The potter's vessel, after it is hardened, can never be pieced again when it is broken. And as the bottle was broken, so shall Judah and Jerusalem be broken by the Chaldeans. No human hand can repair it; but if they return to the Lord he will heal. As they filled Tophet with the slain sacrificed to their idols, so will God fill the whole city with the slain that shall fall as sacrifices to his justice. Whatever men may think, God will appear as terrible against sin and sinners as the Scriptures state; nor shall the unbelief of men make his promise or his threatenings of no effect. The obstinacy of sinners in sinful ways, is their own fault; if they are deaf to the word of God, it is because they have stopped their ears. We have need to pray that God, by his grace, would deliver us from hardness of heart, and contempt of his word and commandments.

Chapter 20

The doom of Pashur, who ill-treated the prophet. (Jer. **20**:**1-6**) Jeremiah complains of hard usage. (Jer. **20**:**7-13**) He regrets his ever having been born. (Jer. **20**:**14-18**)

Jer. **20**:**1-6** Pashur smote Jeremiah, and put him in the stocks. Jeremiah was silent till God put a word into his mouth. To confirm this, Pashur has a name given him, "Fear on every side." It speaks a man not only in distress, but in despair; not only in danger, but in fear on every side. The wicked are in great fear where no fear is, for God can make the most daring sinner a terror to himself. And those who will not hear of their faults from God's prophets, shall be made to hear them from their consciences. Miserable is the man thus made a terror to himself. His friends shall fail him. God lets him live miserably, that he may be a monument of Divine justice.

Jer. **20**:**7-13** The prophet complains of the insult and injury he experienced. But Jer. **20**:**7** may be read, Thou hast persuaded me, and I was persuaded. Thou wast stronger than I; and didst overpower me by the influence of thy Spirit upon me. So long as we see ourselves in the way of God, and of duty, it is weakness and folly, when we meet with difficulties and discouragements, to wish we had never set out in it. The prophet found the grace of God mighty in him to keep him to his business, notwithstanding the temptation he was in to throw it up. Whatever injuries are done to us, we must leave them to that God to whom vengeance belongs, and who has said, I will repay. So full was he of the comfort of God's presence, the Divine protection he was under, and the Divine promise he had to depend upon, that he stirred up himself and others to give God the glory. Let the people of God open their cause before Him, and he will enable them to see deliverance.

Jer. **20**:**14-18** When grace has the victory, it is good to be ashamed of our folly, to admire the goodness of God, and be warned to guard our spirits another time. See how strong the temptation was, over which the prophet got the victory by Divine assistance! He is angry that his first breath was not his last. While we remember that these wishes are not recorded for us to utter the like, we may learn good lessons from them. See how much those who think they stand, ought to take heed lest they fall, and to pray daily, Lead us not into temptation. How frail, changeable, and sinful is man! How foolish and unnatural are the thoughts and wishes of our hearts, when we yield to discontent! Let us consider Him who endured the contradiction of sinners against himself, lest we should be at any time weary and faint in our minds under our lesser trials.

Chapter 21

The only way of deliverance is to be surrendering to the Babylonians. (Jer. **21**:**1-10**) The wickedness of the king and his household. (Jer. **21**:**11-14**)

Jer. **21**:**1-10** When the siege had begun, Zedekiah sent to ask of Jeremiah respecting the event. In times of distress and danger, men often seek those to counsel and pray for them, whom, at other times, they despise and oppose; but they only seek deliverance from punishment. When professors continue in disobedience, presuming upon outward privileges, let them be told that the Lord will prosper his open enemies against them. As the king and his princes would not surrender, the people are exhorted to do so. No sinner on earth is left without a Refuge, who really desires one; but the way of life is humbling, it requires self-denial, and exposes to difficulties.

Jer. **21**:**11-14** The wickedness of the king and his family was the worse because of their relation to David. They were urged to act with justice, at once, lest the Lord's anger should be unquenchable. If God be for us, who can be against us? But if he be against us, who can do any thing for us?

Chapter 22

Justice is recommended, and destruction threatened in case of disobedience. (Jer. **22**:**1-9**) The captivity of Jehoiakim, and the end of Jeconiah. (Jer. **22**:**10-19**) The doom of the royal family. (Jer. **22**:**20-30**)

Jer. **22**:**1-9** The king of Judah is spoken to, as sitting upon the throne of David, the man after God's own heart. Let him follow his example, that he may have the benefit of the promises made to him. The way to preserve a government, is to do the duty of it. But sin will be the ruin of the houses of princes, as well as of meaner men. And who can contend with destroyers of God's preparing? God destroys neither persons, cities, nor nations, except for sin; even in this world he often makes it plain for what crimes he sends punishment; and it will be clear at the day of judgement.

Jer. **22**:**10-19** Here is a sentence of death upon two kings, the wicked sons of a very pious father. Josiah was prevented from seeing the evil to come in this world, and removed to see the good to come in the other world; therefore, weep not for him, but for his son Shallum, who is likely to live and die a wretched captive. Dying saints may be justly envied, while living sinners are justly pitied. Here also is the doom of Jehoiakim. No doubt it is lawful for princes and great men to build, beautify, and furnish houses; but those who enlarge their houses, and make them sumptuous, need carefully to watch against the workings of vain-glory. He built his houses by unrighteousness, with money gotten unjustly. And he defrauded his workmen of their wages. God notices the wrong done by the greatest to poor servants and labourers, and will repay those in justice, who will not, in justice, pay those whom they employ. The greatest of men must look upon the meanest as their neighbours, and be just to them accordingly. Jehoiakim was unjust, and made no conscience of shedding innocent blood. Covetousness, which is the root of all evil, was at the bottom of all. The children who despise their parents' old fashions, commonly come short of their real excellences. Jehoiakim knew that his father found the way of duty to be the way of comfort, yet he would not tread in his steps. He shall die unlamented, hateful for oppression and cruelty.

Jer. **22**:**20-30** The Jewish state is described under a threefold character. Very haughty in a day of peace and safety. Very fearful on alarm of trouble. Very much cast down under pressure of trouble. Many never are ashamed of their sins till brought by them to the last extremity. The king shall close his days in bondage. Those that think themselves as signets on God's right hand, must not be secure, but fear lest they should be plucked thence. The Jewish king and his family shall be carried to Babylon. We know where we were born, but where we shall die we know not; it is enough that our God knows. Let it be our care that we die in Christ, then it will be well with us wherever we die, thought it may be in a far country. The Jewish king shall be despised. Time was when he was delighted in; but all those in whom God has no pleasure, some time or other, will be so lowered, that men will have no pleasure in them. Whoever are childless, it is the Lord that writes them so; and those who take no care to do good in their days, cannot expect to prosper. How little is earthly grandeur to be depended upon, or flourishing families to be rejoiced in! But those who hear the voice of Christ, and follow him, have eternal life, and shall never perish, neither shall any enemy pluck them out of his almighty hands.

Chapter 23

The restoration of the Jews to their own land. (Jer. **23**:**1-8**) The wickedness of the priests and prophets of Judah, The people exhorted not to listen to false promises. (Jer. **23**:**9-22**) The pretenders to inspiration threatened. (Jer. **23**:**23-32**) Also the scoffers at true prophecy.

(Jer. **23**:**33**-**40**)

Jer. **23**:**1**-**8** Woe be to those who are set to feed God's people, but take no concern to do them good! Here is a word of comfort to the neglected sheep. Though only a remnant of God's flock is left, he will find them out, and they shall be brought to their former habitations. Christ is spoken of as a branch from David's family. He is righteous himself, and through him all his people are made righteous. Christ shall break the usurped power of Satan. All the spiritual seed of believing Abraham and praying Jacob shall be protected, and shall be saved from the guilt and dominion of sin. In the days of Christ's government in the soul, the soul dwells at ease. He is here spoken of as "the Lord our Righteousness." He is so our Righteousness as no creature could be. His obedience unto death is the justifying righteousness of believers, and their title to heavenly happiness. And their sanctification, as the source of all their personal obedience is the effect of their union with him, and of the supply of this Spirit. By this name every true believer shall call him, and call upon him. We have nothing to plead but this, Christ has died, yea, rather is risen again; and we have taken him for our Lord. This righteousness which he has wrought out to the satisfaction of law and justice, becomes ours; being a free gift given to us, through the Spirit of God, who puts it upon us, clothes us with it, enables us to lay hold upon it, and claim an interest in it. "The Lord our Righteousness" is a sweet name to a convinced sinner; to one that has felt the guilt of sin in his conscience; seen his need of that righteousness, and the worth of it. This great salvation is far more glorious than all former deliverances of his church. May our souls be gathered to Him, and be found in him.

Jer. **23**:**9**-**22** The false prophets of Samaria had deluded the Israelites into idolatries; yet the Lord considered the false prophets of Jerusalem as guilty of more horrible wickedness, by which the people were made bold in sin. These false teachers would be compelled to suffer the most bitter part of the Lord's indignation. They made themselves believe that there was no harm in sin, and practised accordingly; then they made others believe so. Those who are resolved to go on in evil ways, will justly be given up to believe strong delusions. But which of them had received any revelation of God, or understood any thing of his word? There was a time coming when they would reflect on their folly and unbelief with remorse. The teaching and example of the true prophets led men to repentance, faith, and righteousness. The false prophets led men to rest in forms and notions, and to be quiet in their sins. Let us take heed that we do not follow unrighteousness.

Jer. **23**:**23**-**32** Men cannot be hidden from God's all-seeing eye. Will they never see what judgments they prepare for themselves? Let them consider what a vast difference there is between these prophecies and those delivered by the true prophets of the Lord. Let them not call their foolish dreams Divine oracles. The promises of peace these prophets make are no more to be compared to God's promises than chaff to wheat. The unhumbled heart of man is like a rock; if not melted by the word of God as a fire, it will be broken to pieces by it as a hammer. How can they be long safe, or at all easy, who have a God of almighty power against them? The word of God is no smooth, lulling, deceitful message. And by its faithfulness it may certainly be distinguished from false doctrines.

Jer. **23**:**33**-**40** Those are miserable indeed who are forsaken and forgotten of God; and men's jesting at God's judgments will not baffle them. God had taken Israel to be a people near to him, but they shall now be cast out of his presence. It is a mark of great and daring impiety for men to jest with the words of God. Every idle and profane word will add to the sinner's burden in the day of judgment, when everlasting shame will be his portion.

Chapter 24

Good and bad figs represent the Jews in captivity, and those who remain in their own land.

The prophet saw two baskets of figs set before the temple, as offerings of first-fruits. The figs in one basket were very good, those in the other basket very bad. What creature viler than a wicked man? and what more valuable than a godly man? This vision was to raise the spirits of those gone into captivity, by assuring them of a happy return; and to humble and awaken the proud and secure spirits of those yet in Jerusalem, by assuring them of a miserable captivity. The good figs represents the pious captives. We cannot determine as to God's love or hatred by what is before us. Early suffering sometimes proves for the best. The sooner the child is corrected, the better effect the correction is likely to have. Even this captivity was for their good; and God's intentions never are in vain. By afflictions they were convinced of sin, humbled under the hand of God, weaned from the world, taught to pray, and turned from sins, particularly from idolatry. God promises that he will own them in captivity. The Lord will own those who are his, in all conditions. God assures them of his protection in trouble, and a glorious deliverance in due time. When our troubles are sanctified to us, we may be sure that they will end well. They shall return to him with their whole heart. Thus they should have liberty to own him for their God, to pray to him, and expect blessings from him. The bad figs were Zedekiah and those of his party yet in the land. These should be removed for their hurt, and forsaken of all mankind. God has many judgments, and those that escape one, may expect another, till they are brought to repent. Doubtless, this prophecy had its fulfilment in that age; but the Spirit of prophecy may here look forward to the dispersion of the unbelieving Jews, in all the nations of the earth. Let those who desire blessings from the Lord, beg that he will give them a heart to know him.

Chapter 25

The Jews rebuked for not obeying calls to repentance. (Jer. **25**:**1**-**7**) Their captivity during seventy years is expressly foretold. (Jer. **25**:**8**-**14**) Desolations upon the nations shown by the emblem of a cup of wrath. (Jer. **25**:**15**-**29**) The judgments again declared. (Jer. **25**:**30**-**38**)

Jer. **25**:**1**-**7** The call to turn from evil ways to the worship and service of God, and for sinners to trust in Christ, and partake of his salvation, concerns all men. God keeps an account how long we possess the means of grace; and the longer we have them, the heavier will our account be if we have not improved them. Rising early, points out the earnest desire that this people should turn and live. Personal and particular reformation must be insisted on as necessary to a national deliverance; and every one must turn from his own evil way. Yet all was to no purpose. They would not take the right and only method to turn away the wrath of God.

Jer. **25**:**8**-**14** The fixing of the time during which the Jewish captivity should last, would not only confirm the prophecy, but also comfort the people of God, and encourage faith and prayer. The ruin of Babylon is foretold: the rod will be thrown into the fire when the correcting work is done. When the set time to favour Zion is come, Babylon shall be punished for their iniquity, as other nations have been punished for their sins. Every threatening of the Scripture will certainly be accomplished.

Jer. **25**:**15**-**29** The evil and the good events of life are often represented in Scripture as cups. Under this figure is represented the desolation then coming upon that part of the world, of which Nebuchadnezzar, who had just began to reign and act, was to be the instrument; but this destroying sword would come from the hand of God. The desolations the sword should make in all these kingdoms, are represented by the consequences of excessive drinking. This may make us loathe the sin of drunkenness, that the consequences of it are used to set forth such a woful condition. Drunkenness deprives men of the use of their reason, makes men as mad. It takes from them the valuable blessing, health; and is a sin which is its own punishment. This may also make us dread the judgments of war. It soon fills a nation with confusion. They will refuse to take the cup at thy hand. They will not believe Jeremiah; but he must tell them it is the word of the Lord of hosts, and it is in vain for them to struggle against Almighty power. And if God's judgments begin with backsliding professors, let not the wicked expect to escape.

Jer. **25**:**30-38** The Lord has just ground of controversy with every nation and every person; and he will execute judgment on all the wicked. Who can avoid trembling when God speaks in displeasure? The days are fully come; the time fixed in the Divine counsels, which will make the nations wholly desolate. The tender and delicate shall share the common calamity. Even those who used to live in peace, and did nothing to provoke, shall not escape. Blessed be God, there is a peaceable habitation above, for all the sons of peace. The Lord will preserve his church and all believers in all changes; for nothing can separate them from his love.

Chapter 26

The destruction of the temple and city foretold. (Jer. **26**:**1-6**) Jeremiah's life is threatened. (Jer. **26**:**7-15**) He is defended by the elders. (Jer. **26**:**16-24**)

Jer. **26**:**1-6** God's ambassadors must not seek to please men, or to save themselves from harm. See how God waits to be gracious. If they persisted in disobedience, it would ruin their city and temple. Can any thing else be expected? Those who will not be subject to the commands of God, make themselves subject to the curse of God.

Jer. **26**:**7-15** The priests and prophets charged Jeremiah as deserving death, and bore false witness against him. The elders of Israel came to inquire into this matter. Jeremiah declares that the Lord sent him to prophesy thus. As long as ministers keep close to the word they have from God, they need not fear. And those are very unjust who complain of ministers for preaching of hell and damnation; for it is from a desire to bring them to heaven and salvation. Jeremiah warns them of their danger if they go on against him. All men may know, that to hurt, or put to death, or to show hatred to their faithful reprovers, will hasten and increase their own punishment.

Jer. **26**:**16-24** When secure sinners are threatened with taking away the Spirit of God, and the kingdom of God, it is what is warranted from the word of God. Hezekiah who protected Micah, prospered. Did Jehoiakim, who slew Urijah, prosper? The examples of bad men, and the bad consequences of their sins, should deter from what is evil. Urijah was faithful in delivering his message, but faulty in leaving his work. And the Lord was pleased to permit him to lose his life, while Jeremiah was protected in danger. Those are safest who most simply trust in the Lord, whatever their outward circumstances may be; and that He has all men's hearts in his hands, encourages us to trust him in the way of duty. He will honour and recompense those who show kindness to such as are persecuted for his sake.

Chapter 27

The neighbouring nations to be subdued. (Jer. **27**:**1-11**) Zedekiah is warned to yield. (Jer. **27**:**12-18**) The vessels of the temple to be carried to Babylon, but afterwards to be restored. (Jer. **27**:**19-22**)

Jer. **27**:**1-11** Jeremiah is to prepare a sign that all the neighbouring countries would be made subject to the king of Babylon. God asserts his right to dispose of kingdoms as he pleases. Whatever any have of the good things of this world, it is what God sees fit to give; we should therefore be content. The things of this world are not the best things, for the Lord often gives the largest share to bad men. Dominion is not founded in grace. Those who will not serve the God who made them, shall justly be made to serve their enemies that seek to ruin them. Jeremiah urges them to prevent their destruction, by submission. A meek spirit, by quiet submission to the hardest turns of providence, makes the best of what is bad. Many persons may escape destroying providences, by submitting to humbling providences. It is better to take up a light cross in our way, than to pull a heavier on our own heads. The poor in spirit, the meek and humble, enjoy comfort, and avoid many miseries to which the high-spirited are exposed. It must, in all cases, be our interest to obey God's will.

Jer. **27**:**12-18** Jeremiah persuades the king of Judah to surrender to the king of Babylon. Is it their wisdom to submit to the heavy iron yoke of a cruel tyrant, that they may secure their lives; and is it not much more our wisdom to submit to the pleasant and easy yoke of our Lord and Master, Jesus Christ, that we may secure our souls? It were well if sinners would be afraid of the destruction threatened against all who will not have Christ to reign over them. Why should they die the second death, infinitely worse than that by sword and famine, when they may submit and live? And those who encourage sinners to go on in sinful ways, will perish with them.

Jer. **27**:**19-22** Jeremiah assures them that the brazen vessels should go after the golden ones. All shall be carried to Babylon. But he concludes with a gracious promise, that the time would come when they should be brought back. Though the return of the prosperity of the church does not come in our time, we must not despair, for it will come in God's time.

Chapter 28

A false prophet opposes Jeremiah. (Jer. **28**:**1-9**) The false prophet warned of his approaching death. (Jer. **28**:**10-17**)

Jer. **28**:**1-9** Hananiah spoke a false prophecy. Here is not a word of good counsel urging the Jews to repent and return to God. He promises temporal mercies, in God's name, but makes no mention of the spiritual mercies which God always promised with earthly blessings. This was not the first time Jeremiah had prayed for the people, though he prophesied against them. He appeals to the event, to prove Hananiah's falsehood. The prophet who spake only of peace and prosperity, without adding that they must not by wilful sin stop God's favours, will be proved a false prophet. Those who do not declare the alarming as well as the encouraging parts of God's word, and call men to repentance, and faith, and holiness, tread in the steps of the false prophets. The gospel of Christ encourages men to do works meet for repentance, but gives no encouragement to continue in sin.

Jer. **28**:**10-17** Hananiah is sentenced to die, and Jeremiah, when he has received direction from God, boldly tells him so; but not before he received that commission. Those have much to answer for, who tell sinners that they shall have peace, though they harden their hearts in contempt of God's word. The servant of God must be gentle to all men. He must give up even his right, and leave the Lord to plead his cause. Every attempt of ungodly men to make vain the purposes of God, will add to their miseries.

Chapter 29

Two letters to the captives in Babylon; In the first, they are recommended to be patient and composed. (Jer. **29**:**1-19**) In the second, judgments are denounced against the false prophets who deceived them. (Jer. **29**:**20-32**)

Jer. **29**:**1-7** The written word of God is as truly given by inspiration of God as his spoken word. The zealous servant of the Lord will use every means to profit those who are far off, as well as those who are near him. The art of writing is very profitable for this end; and by the art of printing it is rendered most beneficial for circulating the knowledge of the word of God. God's sending to the captives by this letter would show that he had not forsaken them, though he was displeased, and corrected them. If they live in the fear of God, they may live comfortably in Babylon. In all conditions of life, it is our wisdom and duty not to throw away the comfort of what we may have, because we have not all we would have. They are directed to seek the good of the country where they were captives. While the king of Babylon protected them, they must live quiet and peaceable lives under him, in all godliness and honesty; patiently leaving it to God to work deliverance for them in due time.

Jer. **29**:**8-19** Let men beware how they call those prophets whom they choose after their own fancies, and how they consider their fancies and dreams to be revelations from God. False prophets flatter people in their sins, because they love to be flattered; and they speak smoothly to their prophets, that their prophets may speak smoothly to them. God promises that they should return after seventy years were accomplished. By this it appears, that the seventy years of the captivity are not to be reckoned from the last captivity, but the first. It will be the bringing to pass of God's good word to them. This shall form God's purposes. We often do not know our own minds, but the Lord is never at an uncertainty. We are sometimes ready to fear that God's designs are all against us; but as to his own people, even that which seems evil, is for good. He will give them, not the expectations of their fears, or the expectations of their fancies, but the expectations of their faith; the end he has promised, which will be the best for them. When the Lord pours out an especial spirit of prayer, it is a good sign that he is coming toward us in mercy. Promises are given to quicken and encourage prayer. He never said, Seek ye me in vain. Those who remained at Jerusalem would be utterly destroyed, notwithstanding what the false prophets said to the contrary. The reason has often been given, and it justifies the eternal ruin of impenitent sinners; Because they have not hearkened to my words; I called, but they refused.

Jer. **29**:**20-32** Jeremiah foretells judgments upon the false prophets, who deceived the Jews in Babylon. Lying was bad; lying to the people of the Lord, to delude them into a false hope, was worse; but pretending to rest their own lies upon the God of truth, was worst of all. They flattered others in their sins, because they could not reprove them without condemning themselves. The most secret sins are known to God; and there is a day coming when he will bring to light all the hidden works of darkness. Shemaiah urges the priests to persecute Jeremiah. Their hearts are wretchedly hardened who justify doing mischief by having power to do it. They were in a miserable thraldom for mocking the messengers of the Lord, and misusing his prophets; yet in their distress they trespass still more against the Lord. Afflictions will not of themselves cure men of their sins, unless the grace of God works with them. Those who slight the blessings, deserve to lose the benefit of God's word, like Shemaiah. The accusations against many active Christians in all ages, amount to no more than this, that they earnestly counsel men to attend to their true interest and duties, and to wait for the performance of God's promises in his appointed way.

Chapter 30

Troubles which shall be before the restoration of Israel. (Jer. **30**:**1-11**) Encouragement to trust Divine promises. (Jer. **30**:**12-17**) The blessings under Christ, and the wrath on the wicked. (Jer. **30**:**18-24**)

Jer. **30**:**1-11** Jeremiah is to write what God had spoken to him. The very words are such as the Holy Ghost teaches. These are the words God ordered to be written; and promises written by his order, are truly his word. He must write a description of the trouble the people were now in, and were likely to be in. A happy end should be put to these calamities. Though the afflictions of the church may last long, they shall not last always. The Jews shall be restored again. They shall obey, or hearken to the Messiah, the Christ, the Son of David, their King. The deliverance of the Jews from Babylon, is pointed out in the prophecy, but the restoration and happy state of Israel and Judah, when converted to Christ their King, are foretold; also the miseries of the nations before the coming of Christ. All men must honour the Son as they honour the Father, and come into the service and worship of God by him. Our gracious Lord pardons the sins of the believer, and breaks off the yoke of sin and Satan, that he may serve God without fear, in righteousness and true holiness before him all the remainder of his days, as the redeemed subject of Christ our King.

Jer. **30**:**12-17** When God is against a people, who will be for them? Who can be for them, so as to do them any kindness? Incurable griefs are owing to incurable lusts. Yet, though the captives suffered justly, and could not help themselves, the Lord intended to appear for them, and to punish their oppressors; and he will still do so. But every effort to heal ourselves must prove fruitless, so long as we neglect the heavenly Advocate and sanctifying Spirit. The dealings of His grace with every true convert, and every returning backslider, are the same in effect as his proceedings to the Jews.

Jer. **30**:**18-24** We have here further intimations of the favour of God for them after the days of their calamity have expired. The proper work and office of Christ, as Mediator, is to draw near unto God, for us, as the High Priest of our profession. His own undertaking, in compliance with his Father's will, and in compassion to fallen man, engaged him. Jesus Christ was, in all this, truly wonderful. They shall be taken again into covenant with the Lord, according to the covenant made with their fathers. "I will be your God:" it is his good-will to us, which is the summary of that part of the covenant. The wrath of God against the wicked is very terrible, like a whirlwind. The purposes of his wrath, as well as the purposes of his love, will all be fulfilled. God will comfort all that turn to him; but those who approach him must have their hearts engaged to do it with reverence, devotion, and faith. How will they escape who neglect so great salvation?

Chapter 31

The restoration of Israel. (Jer. **31**:**1-9**) Promises of guidance and happiness; Rachel lamenting. (Jer. **31**:**10-17**) Ephraim laments his errors. (Jer. **31**:**18-20**) The promised Saviour. (Jer. **31**:**21-26**) God's care over the church. (Jer. **31**:**27-34**) Peace and prosperity in gospel time. (Jer. **31**:**35-40**)

Jer. **31**:**1-9** God assures his people that he will again take them into covenant relation to himself. When brought very low, and difficulties appear, it is good to remember that it has been so with the church formerly. But it is hard under present frowns to take comfort from former smiles; yet it is the happiness of those who, through grace, are interested in the love of God, that it is an everlasting love, from everlasting in the counsels, to everlasting in the continuance. Those whom God loves with this love, he will draw to himself, by the influences of his Spirit upon their souls. When praising God for what he has done, we must call upon him for the favours his church needs and expects. When the Lord calls, we must not plead that we cannot come; for he that calls us, will help us, will strengthen us. The goodness of God shall lead them to repentance. And they shall weep for sin with more bitterness, and more tenderness, when delivered out of their captivity, than when groaning under it. If we take God for our Father, and join the church of the first-born, we shall want nothing that is good for us. These predictions doubtless refer also to a future gathering of the Israelites from all quarters of the globe.

And they figuratively describe the conversion of sinners to Christ, and the plain and safe way in which they are led.

Jer. **31**:**10-17** He that scattered Israel, knows where to find them. It is comfortable to observe the goodness of the Lord in the gifts of providence. But our souls are never valuable as gardens, unless watered with the dews of God's Spirit and grace. A precious promise follows, which will not have full accomplishment except in the heavenly Zion. Let them be satisfied of God's loving-kindness, and they will be satisfied with it, and desire no more to make them happy. Rachel is represented as rising from her grave, and refusing to be comforted, supposing her offspring rooted out. The murder of the children at Bethlehem, by Herod, Matt. **2**:**16-18**, in some degree fulfilled this prediction, but could not be its full meaning. If we have hope in the end, concerning an eternal inheritance, for ourselves and those belonging to us, all temporal afflictions may be borne, and will be for our good.

Jer. **31**:**18-20** Ephraim (the ten tribes) is weeping for sin. He is angry at himself for his sin, and folly, and frowardness. He finds he cannot, by his own power, keep himself close with God, much less bring himself back when he is revolted. Therefore he prays, Turn thou me, and I shall be turned. His will was bowed to the will of God. When the teaching of God's Spirit went with the corrections of his providence, then the work was done. This is our comfort in affliction, that the Lord thinks upon us. God has mercy in store, rich mercy, sure mercy, suitable mercy, for all who seek him in sincerity.

Jer. **31**:**21-26** The way from the bondage of sin to the liberty of God's children, is a high-way. It is plain, it is safe; yet none are likely to walk in it, unless they set their hearts towards it. They are encouraged by the promise of a new, unheard-of, extraordinary thing; a creation, a work of Almighty power; the human nature of Christ, formed and prepared by the power of the Holy Ghost: and this is here mentioned as an encouragement to the Jews to return to their own land. And a comfortable prospect is given them of a happy settlement there. Godliness and honesty God has joined: let no man think to put them asunder, or to make the one atone for the want of the other. In the love and favour of God the weary soul shall find rest, and the sorrowful shall find joy. And what can we see with more satisfaction than the good of Jerusalem, and peace upon Israel?

Jer. **31**:**27-34** The people of God shall become numerous and prosperous. In Heb. **8**:**8**,**9**, this place is quoted as the sum of the covenant of grace made with believers in Jesus Christ. Not, I will give them a new law; for Christ came not to destroy the law, but to fulfil it; but the law shall be written in their hearts by the finger of the Spirit, as formerly written in the tables of stone. The Lord will, by his grace, make his people willing people in the day of his power. All shall know the Lord; all shall be welcome to the knowledge of God, and shall have the means of that knowledge. There shall be an outpouring of the Holy Spirit, at the time the gospel is published. No man shall finally perish, but for his own sins; none, who is willing to accept of Christ's salvation.

Jer. **31**:**35-40** As surely as the heavenly bodies will continue their settled course, according to the will of their Creator, to the end of time, and as the raging sea obeys him, so surely will the Jews be continued a separate people. Words can scarcely set forth more strongly the restoration of Israel. The rebuilding of Jerusalem, and its enlargement and establishment, shall be an earnest of the great things God will do for the gospel church. The personal happiness of every true believer, as well as the future restoration of Israel, is secured by promise, covenant, and oath. This Divine love passes knowledge; and to those who take hold upon it, every present mercy is an earnest of salvation.

Chapter 32

Jeremiah buys a field. (Jer. **32**:**1-15**) The prophet's prayer. (Jer. **32**:**16-25**) God declares that he will give up his people, but promises to restore them. (Jer. **32**:**26-44**)

Jer. **32**:**1-15** Jeremiah, being in prison for his prophecy, purchased a piece of ground. This was to signify, that though Jerusalem was besieged, and the whole country likely to be laid waste, yet the time would come, when houses, and fields, and vineyards, should be again possessed. It concerns ministers to make it appear that they believe what they preach to others. And it is good to manage even our worldly affairs in faith; to do common business with reference to the providence and promise of God.

Jer. **32**:**16-25** Jeremiah adores the Lord and his infinite perfections. When at any time we are perplexed about the methods of Providence, it is good for us to look to first principles. Let us consider that God is the fountain of all being, power, and life; that with him no difficulty is such as cannot be overcome; that he is a God of boundless mercy; that he is a God of strict justice; and that he directs every thing for the best. Jeremiah owns that God was righteous in causing evil to come upon them. Whatever trouble we are in, personal or public, we may comfort ourselves that the Lord sees it, and knows how to remedy it. We must not dispute God's will, but we may seek to know what it means.

Jer. **32**:**26-44** God's answer discovers the purposes of his wrath against that generation of the Jews, and the purposes of his grace concerning future generations. It is sin, and nothing else, that ruins them. The restoration of Judah and Jerusalem is promised. This people were now at length brought to despair. But God gives hope of mercy which he had in store for them hereafter. Doubtless the promises are sure to all believers. God will own them for his, and he will prove himself theirs. He will give them a heart to fear him. All true Christians shall have a disposition to mutual love. Though they may have different views about lesser things, they shall all be one in the great things of God; in their views of the evil of sin, and the low estate of fallen man, the way of salvation through the Saviour, the nature of true holiness, the vanity of the world, and the importance of eternal things. Whom God loves, he loves to the end. We have no reason to distrust God's faithfulness and constancy, but only our own hearts. He will settle them again in Canaan. These promises shall surely be performed. Jeremiah's purchase was the pledge of many a purchase that should be made after the captivity; and those inheritances are but faint resemblances of the possessions in the heavenly Canaan, which are kept for all who have God's fear in their hearts, and do not depart from him. Let us then bear up under our trials, assured we shall obtain all the good he has promised us.

Chapter 33

The restoration of the Jews. (Jer. **33**:**1-13**) The Messiah promised; happiness of his times. (Jer. **33**:**14-26**)

Jer. **33**:**1-13** Those who expect to receive comforts from God, must call upon him. Promises are given, not to do away, but to quicken and encourage prayer. These promises lead us to the gospel of Christ; and in that God has revealed truth to direct us, and peace to make us easy. All who by sanctifying grace are cleansed from the filth of sin, by pardoning mercy are freed from the guilt. When sinners are thus justified, washed, and sanctified in the name of the Lord Jesus, and by the Holy Spirit, they are enabled to walk before God in peace and purity. Many are led to perceive the real difference between the people of God and the world around them, and to fear the Divine wrath. It is promised that the people who were long in sorrow, shall again be filled with joy. Where the Lord gives righteousness and peace, he will give all needful supplies for temporal wants; and all we have will be comforts, as sanctified by the word and by prayer.

Jer. **33**:**14-26** To crown the blessings God has in store, here is a promise of the Messiah. He imparts righteousness to his church, for he is made of God to us righteousness; and believers are made the righteousness of God in him. Christ is our Lord God, our righteousness, our sanctification, and our redemption. His kingdom is an everlasting kingdom. But in this world prosperity and adversity succeed each other, as light and darkness, day and night. The covenant of priesthood shall be secured. And all true believers are a holy priesthood, a royal priesthood, they offer up spiritual sacrifices, acceptable to God; themselves, in the first place, as living sacrifices. The promises of that covenant shall have full accomplishment in the gospel Israel. In Gal. **6**:**16**, all that walk according to the gospel rule, are made to be the Israel of God, on whom shall be peace and mercy. Let us not despise the families which were of old the chosen people of God, though for a time they seem to be cast off.

Chapter 34

Zedekiah's death at Babylon foretold. (Jer. **34**:**1-7**) The Jews reproved for compelling their poor brethren to return to unlawful bondage. (Jer. **34**:**8-22**)

Jer. **34**:**1-7** Zedekiah is told that the city shall be taken, and that he shall die a captive, but he shall die a natural death. It is better to live and die penitent in a prison, than to live and die impenitent in a palace.

Jer. **34**:**8-22** A Jew should not be held in servitude above seven years. This law they and their fathers had broken. And when there was some hope that the siege was raised, they forced the servants they had released into their services again. Those who think to cheat God by dissembled repentance and partial reformation, put the greatest cheat upon their own souls. This shows that liberty to sin, is really only liberty to have the sorest judgments. It is just with God to disappoint expectations of mercy, when we disappoint the expectations of duty. And when reformation springs only from terror, it is seldom lasting. Solemn vows thus entered into, profane the ordinances of God; and the most forward to bind themselves by appeals to God, are commonly most ready to break them. Let us look to our hearts, that our repentance may be real, and take care that the law of God regulates our conduct.

Chapter 35

The obedience of the Rechabites. (Jer. **35**:**1-11**) The Jews' disobedience to the Lord. (Jer. **35**:**12-19**)

Jer. **35**:**1-11** Jonadab was famous for wisdom and piety. He lived nearly **300** years before, II Kin. **10**:**15**. Jonadab charged his posterity not to drink wine. He also appointed them to dwell in tents, or movable dwelling: this would teach them not to think of settling any where in this world. To keep low, would be the way to continue long in the land where they were strangers. Humility and contentment are always the best policy, and men's surest protection. Also, that they might not run into unlawful pleasures, they were to deny themselves even lawful delights. The consideration that we are strangers and pilgrims should oblige us to abstain from all fleshly lusts. Let them have little to lose, and then losing times would be the less dreadful: let them sit loose to what they had, and then they might with less pain be stript of it. Those are in the best frame to meet sufferings who live a life of self-denial, and who despise the vanities of the world. Jonadab's posterity observed these rules strictly, only using proper means for their safety in a time of general suffering.

Jer. **35**:**12-19** The trial of the Rechabites' constancy was for a sign; it made the disobedience of the Jews to God the more marked. The Rechabites were obedient to one who was but a man like themselves, and Jonadab never did for his seed what God has done for his people. Mercy is promised to the Rechabites. We are not told respecting the performance of this promise; but doubtless it was performed, and travellers say the Rechabites may be found a separate people to this day. Let us follow the counsels of our pious forefathers, and we shall find good in so doing.

Chapter 36

Baruch is to write the prophecies of Jeremiah. (Jer. **36**:**1-8**) The princes advise them to hide themselves. (Jer. **36**:**9-19**) The king having heard a part, burns the roll. (Jer. **36**:**20-32**)

Jer. **36**:**1-8** The writing of the Scriptures was by Divine appointment. The Divine wisdom directed to this as a proper means; if it failed, the house of Judah would be the more without excuse. The Lord declares to sinners the evil he purposes to do against them, that they may hear, and fear, and return from their evil ways; and whenever any one makes this use of God's warnings, in dependence on his promised mercy, he will find the Lord ready to forgive his sins. All others will be left without excuse; and the consideration that great is the anger God has pronounced against us for sin, should quicken both our prayers and our endeavours.

Jer. **36**:**9-19** Shows of piety and devotion may be found even among those, who, though they keep up forms of godliness, are strangers and enemies to the power of it. The princes patiently attended the reading of the whole book. They were in great fear. But even those who are convinced to the truth and importance of what they hear, and are disposed to favour those who preach it, often have difficulties and reserves about their safety, interest, or preferment, so that they do not act according to their convictions, and try to get rid of what they find troublesome.

Jer. **36**:**20-32** Those who despise the word of God, will soon show, as this king did, that they hate it; and, like him, they would wish it destroyed. See what enmity there is against God in the carnal mind, and wonder at his patience. The princes showed some concern, till they saw how light the king made of it. Beware of making light of God's word!

Chapter 37

The Chaldean army will return. (Jer. **37**:**1-10**) Jeremiah is imprisoned. (Jer. **37**:**11-21**)

Jer. **37**:**1-10** Numbers witness the fatal effects of other men's sins, yet heedlessly step into their places, and follow the same destructive course. When in distress, we ought to desire the prayers of ministers and Christian friends. And it is common for those to desire to be prayed for, who will not be advised; yet sinners are often hardened by a pause in judgments. But if God help us not, no creature can. Whatever instruments God has determined to use, they shall do the work, though they seem unlikely.

Jer. **37**:**11-21** There are times when it is the wisdom of good men to retire, to enter into their chambers, and to shut the doors, Is. **26**:**20**. Jeremiah was seized as a deserter, and committed to prison. But it is no new thing for the best friends of the church to be belied, as in the interests of her worst enemies. When thus falsely accused, we may deny the charge, and commit our cause to Him who judges righteously. Jeremiah obtained mercy of the Lord to be faithful, and would not, to obtain mercy of man, be unfaithful to God or to his prince; he tells the king the whole truth. When Jeremiah delivered God's message, he spake with boldness; but when he made his own request, he spake submissively. A lion in God's cause must be a lamb in his own. And God gave Jeremiah favour in the eyes of the king.

The Lord God can make even the cells of a prison become pastures to his people, and will raise up friends to provide for them, so that in the days of famine they shall be satisfied.

Chapter 38

Jeremiah is cast into a dungeon, from whence he is delivered by an Ethiopian. (Jer. **38**:**1-13**) He advises the king to surrender to the Chaldeans. (Jer. **38**:**14-28**)

Jer. **38**:**1-13** Jeremiah went on in his plain preaching. The princes went on in their malice. It is common for wicked people to look upon God's faithful ministers as enemies, because they show what enemies the wicked are to themselves while impenitent. Jeremiah was put into a dungeon. Many of God's faithful witnesses have been privately made away in prisons. Ebed-melech was an Ethiopian; yet he spoke to the king faithfully, These men have done ill in all they have done to Jeremiah. See how God can raise up friends for his people in distress. Orders were given for the prophet's release, and Ebed-melech saw him drawn up. Let this encourage us to appear boldly for God. Special notice is taken of his tenderness for Jeremiah. What do we behold in the different characters then, but the same we behold in the different characters now, that the Lord's children are conformed to his example, and the children of Satan to their master?

Jer. **38**:**14-28** Jeremiah was not forward to repeat the warnings, which seemed only to endanger his own life, and to add to the king's guilt, but asked whether he feared to do the will of God. The less men fear God, the more they fear men; often they dare not act according to their own judgments and consciences.

Chapter 39

The taking of Jerusalem. (Jer. **39**:**1-10**) Jeremiah used well. (Jer. **39**:**11-14**) Promises of safety to Ebed-melech. (Jer. **39**:**15-18**)

Jer. **39**:**1-10** Jerusalem was so strong, that the inhabitants believed the enemy could never enter it. But sin provoked God to withdraw his protection, and then it was as weak as other cities. Zedekiah had his eyes put out; so he was condemned to darkness who had shut his eyes against the clear light of God's word. Those who will not believe God's words, will be convinced by the event. Observe the wonderful changes of Providence, how uncertain are earthly possessions; and see the just dealings of Providence: but whether the Lord makes men poor or rich, nothing will profit them while they cleave to their sins.

Jer. **39**:**11-14** The servants of God alone are prepared for all events; and they are delivered and comforted, while the wicked suffer. They often meet with more kindness from the profane, than from hypocritical professors of godliness. The Lord will raise them up friends, do them good, and perform all his promises.

Jer. **39**:**15-18** Here is a message to assure Ebed-melech of a recompence for his great kindness to Jeremiah. Because thou hast put thy trust in me, saith the Lord. God recompenses men's services according to their principles. Those who trust God in the way of duty, as this good man did, will find that their hope shall not fail in times of the greatest danger.

Chapter 40

Jeremiah is directed to go to Gedaliah. (Jer. **40**:**1-6**) A conspiracy against Gedaliah. (Jer. **40**:**7-16**)

Jer. **40**:**1-6** The captain of the guard seems to glory that he had been God's instrument to fulfil, what Jeremiah had been God's messenger to foretell. Many can see God's justice and truth with regard to others, who are heedless and blind as to themselves and their own sins. But, sooner or later, all men shall be made sensible that their sin is the cause of all their miseries. Jeremiah has leave to dispose of himself; but is advised to go to Gedaliah, governor of the land under the king of Babylon. It is doubtful whether Jeremiah acted right in this decision. But those who desire the salvation of sinners, and the good of the church, are apt to expect better times from slight appearances, and they will prefer the hope of being useful, to the most secure situations without it.

Jer. **40**:**7-16** Jeremiah had never in his prophecies spoken of any good days for the Jews, to come immediately after the captivity; yet Providence seemed to encourage such an expectation. But how soon is this hopeful prospect blighted! When God begins a judgment, he will complete it. While pride, ambition, or revenge, bears rule in the heart, men will form new projects, and be restless in mischief, which commonly ends in their own ruin. Who would have thought, that after the destruction of Jerusalem, rebellion would so soon have sprung up? There can be no thorough change but what grace makes. And if the miserable, who are kept in everlasting chains for the judgment of the great day, were again permitted to come on earth, the sin and evil of their nature would be unchanged. Lord, give us new hearts, and that new mind in which the new birth consists, since thou hast said we cannot without it see thy heavenly kingdom.

Chapter 41

Ishmael murders Gedaliah. (Jer. **41**:**1-10**) Johanan recovers the captives, and purposes to retire to Egypt. (Jer. **41**:**11-18**)

Jer. **41**:**1-10** Those who hate the worshippers of God, often put on the appearance of piety, that they may the easier hurt them. As death often meets men where they least expect it, we should continually search whether we are in such a state and frame of mind, as we would wish to be found in when called to appear before our Judge. Sometimes the ransom of a man's life is his riches. But those who think to bribe death, saying, Slay us not, for we have treasures in the field, will find themselves wretchedly deceived. This melancholy history warns us, never to be secure in this world. We never can be sure of peace on this side heaven.

Jer. **41**:**11-18** The success of villany must be short, and none can prosper who harden their hearts against God. And those justly lose comfort in real fears, who excuse themselves in sin by pretended fears. The removal of a prudent and peaceable ruler, and the succession of another who is rash and ambitious, affects the welfare of many. Only those are happy and steady who fear the Lord and walk in his ways.

Chapter 42

Johanan desires Jeremiah to ask counsel of God. (Jer. **42**:**1-6**) They are assured of safety in Judea, but of destruction in Egypt. (Jer. **42**:**7-22**)

Jer. **42**:**1-6** To serve a turn, Jeremiah is sought out, and the captains ask for his assistance. In every difficult, doubtful case, we must look to God for direction; and we may still, in faith, pray to be guided by a spirit of wisdom in our hearts, and the leadings of Providence. We do not truly desire to know the mind of God, if we do not fully resolve to comply with it when we know it. Many promise to do what the Lord requires, while they hope to have their pride flattered, and their favourite lusts spared. Yet something betrays the state of their hearts.

Jer. **42**:**7-22** If we would know the mind of the Lord in doubtful cases, we must wait as well as pray. God is ever ready to return in mercy to those he has afflicted; and he never rejects any who rely on his promises. He has declared enough to silence even the causeless fears of his people, which discourge them in the way of duty. Whatever loss or suffering we may fear from obedience, is provided against in God's word; and he will protect and deliver all who trust in him and serve him. It is folly to quit our place, especially to quit a holy land, because we meet with trouble in it. And the evils we think to escape by sin, we certainly bring upon ourselves. We may apply this to the common troubles of life; and those who think to avoid them by changing their place, will find that the grievances common to men will meet them wherever they go. Sinners who dissemble with God in solemn professions especially should be rebuked with sharpness; for their actions speak more plainly than words. We know not what is good for ourselves; and what we are most fond of, and have our hearts most set upon, often proves hurtful, and sometimes fatal.

Chapter 43

The leaders carry the people to Egypt. (Jer. **43**:**1-7**) Jeremiah foretells the conquest of Egypt. (Jer. **43**:**8-13**)

Jer. **43**:**1-7** Only by pride comes contention, both with God and man. They preferred their own wisdom to the revealed will of God. Men deny the Scriptures to be the word of God, because they are resolved not to conform themselves to Scripture rules. When men will persist in sin, they charge the best actions to bad motives. These Jews deserted their own land, and threw themselves out of God's protection. It is the folly of men, that they often ruin themselves by wrong endeavours to mend their situation.

Jer. **43**:**8-13** God can find his people wherever they are. The Spirit of prophecy was not confined to the land of Israel. It is foretold that Nebuchadnezzar should destroy and carry into captivity many of the Egyptians. Thus God makes one wicked man, or wicked nation, a scourge and plague to another. He will punish those who deceive his professing people, or tempt them to rebellion.

Chapter 44

The Jews in Egypt persist in idolatry. (Jer. **44**:**1-14**) They refuse to reform. (Jer. **44**:**15-19**) Jeremiah then denounces destruction upon them. (Jer. **44**:**20-30**)

Jer. **44**:**1-14** God reminds the Jews of the sins that brought desolations upon Judah. It becomes us to warn men of the danger of sin with all seriousness: Oh, do not do it! If you love God, do not, for it is provoking to him; if you love your own souls, do not, for it is destructive to them. Let conscience do this for us in the hour of temptation. The Jews whom God sent into the land of the Chaldeans, were there, by the power of God's grace, weaned from idolatry; but those who went by their own perverse will into the land of the Egyptians, were there more attached than ever to their idolatries. When we thrust ourselves without cause or call into places of temptation, it is just with God to leave us to ourselves. If we walk contrary to God, he will walk contrary to us. The most awful miseries to which men are exposed, are occasioned by the neglect of offered salvation.

Jer. **44**:**15-19** These daring sinners do not attempt excuses, but declare they will do that which is forbidden. Those who disobey God, commonly grow worse and worse, and the heart is more hardened by the deceitfulness of sin. Here is the real language of the rebellious heart. Even the afflictions which should have parted them from their sins, were taken so as to confirm them in their sins. It is sad when those who should quicken each other to what is good, and so help one another to heaven, harden each other in sin, and so ripen one another for hell. To mingle idolatry with Divine worship, and to reject the mediation of Christ, are provoking to God, and ruinous to men. All who worship images, or honour saints, and angels, and the queen of heaven, should recollect what came from the idolatrous practices of the Jews.

Jer. **44**:**20-30** Whatever evil comes upon us, it is because we have sinned against the Lord; we should therefore stand in awe, and sin not. Since they were determined to persist in their idolatry, God would go on to punish them. What little remains of religion were among them, would be lost. The creature-comforts and confidences from which we promise ourselves most, may fail as soon as those from which we promise ourselves least; and all are what God makes them, not what we fancy them to be. Well-grounded hopes of our having a part in the Divine mercy, are always united with repentance and obedience.

Chapter 45

An encouragement sent to Baruch.

Baruch was employed in writing Jeremiah's prophecies, and reading them, see Jer. **36**, and was threatened for it by the king. Young beginners in religion are apt to be discouraged with little difficulties, which they commonly meet with at first in the service of God. These complaints and fears came from his corruptions. Baruch had raised his expectations too high in this world, and that made the distress and trouble he was in harder to be borne. The frowns of the world would not disquiet us, if we did not foolishly flatter ourselves with the hopes of its smiles, and court and covet them. What a folly is it then to seek great things for ourselves here, where every thing is little, and nothing certain! The Lord knows the real cause of our fretfulness and despondency better than we do, and we should beg of him to examine our hearts, and to repress every wrong desire in us.

Chapter 46

The defeat of the Egyptians. (Jer. **46**:**1-12**) Their overthrow after the siege of Tyre. (Jer. **46**:**13-26**) A promise of comfort to the Jews. (Jer. **46**:**27**,**28**)

Jer. **46**:**1-12** The whole word of God is against those who obey not the gospel of Christ; but it is for those, even of the Gentiles, who turn to Him. The prophecy begins with Egypt. Let them strengthen themselves with all the art and interest they have, yet it shall be all in vain. The wounds God inflicts on his enemies, cannot be healed by medicines. Power and prosperity soon pass from one to another in this changing world.

Jer. **46**:**13-28** Those who encroached on others, shall now be themselves encroached on. Egypt is now like a very fair heifer, not accustomed to the yoke of subjection; but destruction comes out of the north: the Chaldeans shall come. Comfort and peace are spoken to the Israel of God, designed to encourage them when the judgments of God were abroad among the nations. He will be with them, and only correct them in measure; and will not punish them with everlasting destruction from his presence.

Chapter 47

The calamities of the Philistines.

The Philistines had always been enemies to Israel; but the Chaldean army shall overflow their land like a deluge. Those whom God will spoil, must be spoiled. For when the Lord intends to destroy the wicked, he will cut off every helper. So deplorable are the desolations of war, that the blessings of peace are most desirable. But we must submit to His appointments who ordains all in perfect wisdom and justice.

Chapter 48

Prophecies against Moab for pride and security. (Jer. **48**:**1-13**) For carnal confidence and contempt of God. (Jer. **48**:**14-47**)

Jer. **48**:**1-13**. The Chaldeans are to destroy the Moabites. We should be thankful that we are required to seek the salvation of men's lives, and the salvation of their souls, not to shed their blood; but we shall be the more without excuse if we do this pleasant work deceitfully. The cities shall be laid in ruins, and the country shall be wasted. There will be great sorrow. There will be great hurry. If any could give wings to sinners, still they could not fly out of the reach of Divine indignation. There are many who persist in unrepented iniquity, yet long enjoy outward prosperity. They had been long corrupt and unreformed, secure and sensual in prosperity. They have no changes of their peace and prosperity, therefore their hearts and lives are unchanged, Ps. **55**:**19**.

Jer. **48**:**14-47**. The destruction of Moab is further prophesied, to awaken them by national repentance and reformation to prevent the trouble, or by a personal repentance and reformation to prepare for it. In reading this long roll of threatenings, and mediating on the terror, it will be of more use to us to keep in view the power of God's anger and the terror of his judgments, and to have our hearts possessed with a holy awe of God and of his wrath, than to search into all the figures and expressions here used. Yet it is not perpetual destruction. The chapter ends with a promise of their return out of captivity in the latter days. Even with Moabites God will not contend for ever, nor be always wroth. The Jews refer it to the days of the Messiah; then the captives of the Gentiles, under the yoke of sin and Satan, shall be brought back by Divine grace, which shall make them free indeed.

Chapter 49

Prophecies relative to the Ammonites. (Jer. **49**:**1-6**) The Edomites. (Jer. **49**:**7-22**) The Syrians. (Jer. **49**:**23-27**) The Kedarenes. (Jer. **49**:**28-33**) The Elamites. (Jer. **49**:**34-39**)

Jer. **49**:**1-6**. Might often prevails against right among men, yet that might shall be controlled by the Almighty, who judges aright; and those will find themselves mistaken, who, like the Ammonites, think every thing their own on which they can lay their hands. The Lord will call men to account for every instance of dishonesty, especially to the destitute.

Jer. **49**:**7-22** The Edomites were old enemies to the Israel of God. But their day is now at hand; it is foretold, not only to warn them, but for the sake of the Israel of God, whose afflictions were aggravated by them. Thus Divine judgments go round from nation to nation; the earth is full of commotion, and nothing can escape the ministers of Divine vengeance. The righteousness of God is to be observed amidst the violence of men.

Jer. **49**:**23-27** How easily God can dispirit those nations that have been most celebrated for valour! Damascus waxes feeble. It was a city of joy, having all the delights of the sons of men. But those deceive themselves who place their happiness in carnal joys.

Jer. **49**:**28-33** Nebuchadnezzar would make desolation among the people of Kedar, who dwelt in the deserts of Arabia. He who conquered many strong cities, will not leave those unconquered that dwell in tents. He will do this to gratify his own covetousness and ambition; but God orders it for correcting an unthankful people, and for warning a careless world to expect trouble when they seem most safe. They shall flee, get far off, and dwell deep in the deserts; they shall be dispersed. But privacy and obscurity are not always protection and security.

Jer. **49**:**34-39** The Elamites were the Persians; they acted against God's Israel, and must be reckoned with. Evil pursues sinners. God will make them know that he reigns. Yet the destruction of Elam shall not be for ever. But this promise was to have its full accomplishment in the days of the Messiah. In reading the Divine assurance of the destruction of all the enemies of the church, the believer sees that the issue of the holy war is not doubtful. It is blessed to recollect, that He who is for us, is more than all against us. And he will subdue the enemies of our souls.

Chapter 50

The ruin of Babylon. (Jer. **50**:**1-3**,**8-16**,**21-32**,**35-46**;) The redemption of God's people. (Jer. **50**:**4-7**,**17-20**,**33**,**34**)

Jer. **50**:**1-7** The king of Babylon was kind to Jeremiah, yet the prophet must foretell the ruin of that kingdom. If our friends are God's enemies, we dare not speak peace to them. The destruction of Babylon is spoken of as done thoroughly. Here is a word for the comfort of the Jews. They shall return to their God first, then to their own land; the promise of their conversion and reformation makes way for the other promises. Their tears flow not from the sorrow of the world, as when they went into captivity, but from godly sorrow. They shall seek after the Lord as their God, and have no more to do with idols. They shall think of returning to their own country. This represents the return of poor souls to God. In true converts there are sincere desires to attain the end, and constant cares to keep in the way. Their present case is lamented as very sad. The sins of professing Christians never will excuse those who rejoice in destroying them.

Jer. **50**:**8-20** The desolation that shall be brought upon Babylon is set forth in a variety of expressions. The cause of this destruction is the wrath of the Lord. Babylon shall be wholly desolated; for she hath sinned against the Lord. Sin makes men a mark for the arrows of God's judgments. The mercy promised to the Israel of God, shall not only accompany, but arise from the destruction of Babylon. These sheep shall be gathered from the deserts, and put again into good pasture. All who return to God and their duty, shall find satisfaction of soul in so doing. Deliverances out of trouble are comforts indeed, when fruits of the forgiveness of sin.

Jer. **50**:**21-32** The forces are mustered and empowered to destroy Babylon. Let them do what God demands, and they shall bring to pass what he threatens. The pride of men's hearts sets God against them, and ripens them apace for ruin. Babylon's pride must be her ruin; she has been proud against the Holy One of Israel; who can keep those up whom God will throw down?

Jer. **50**:**33-46** It is Israel's comfort in distress, that, though they are weak, their Redeemer is strong. This may be applied to believers, who complain of the dominion of sin and corruption, and of their own weakness and manifold infirmities. Their Redeemer is able to keep what they commit to him; and sin shall not have dominion over them. He will give them that rest which remains for the people of God. Also here is Babylon's sin, and their punishment. The sins are, idolatry and persecution. He that will not save his people in their sins, never will countenance the wickedness of his open enemies. The judgments of God for these sins will lay them waste. In the judgments denounced against prosperous Babylon, and the mercies promised to afflicted Israel, we learn to choose to suffer affliction with the people of God, rather than to enjoy the pleasures of sin for a season.

Chapter 51

Babylon's doom; God's controversy with her; encouragements from thence to the Israel of God. (Jer. **51**:**1-58**) The confirming of this. (Jer. **51**:**59-64**)

Jer. **51**:**1-58** The particulars of this prophecy are dispersed and interwoven, and the same things left and returned to again. Babylon is abundant in treasures, yet neither her waters nor her wealth shall secure her. Destruction comes when they did not think of it. Wherever we are, in the greatest depths, at the greatest distances, we are to remember the Lord our God; and in the times of the greatest fears and hopes, it is most needful to remember the Lord. The feeling excited by Babylon's fall is the same with the New Testament Babylon, Rev. **18**:**9**,**19**. The ruin of all who support idolatry, infidelity, and superstition, is needful for the revival of true godliness; and the threatening prophecies of Scripture yield comfort in this view. The great seat of antichristian tyranny, idolatry, and superstition, the persecutor of true Christians, is as certainly doomed to destruction as ancient Babylon. Then will vast multitudes mourn for sin, and seek the Lord. Then will the lost sheep of the house of Israel be brought back to the fold of the good Shepherd, and stray no more. And the exact fulfilment of these ancient prophecies encourages us to faith in all the promises and prophecies of the sacred Scriptures.

Jer. **51**:**59-64** This prophecy is sent to Babylon, to the captives there, by Seraiah, who is to read it to his countrymen in captivity. Let them with faith see the end of these threatening powers, and comfort themselves herewith. When we see what this world is, how glittering its shows, and how flattering its proposals, let us read in the book of the Lord that it shall shortly be desolate. The book must be thrown into the river Euphrates. The fall of the New Testament Babylon is thus represented, Rev. **18**:**21**. Those that sink under the weight of God's wrath and curse, sink for ever. Babylon, and every antichrist, will soon sink and rise no more for ever. Let us hope in God's word, and quietly wait for his salvation; then we shall see, but shall not share, the destruction of the wicked.

Chapter 52

The fate of Zedekiah. (Jer. **52**:**1-11**) The destruction of Jerusalem. (Jer. **52**:**12-23**) The captivities. (Jer. **52**:**24-30**) The advancement of Jehoiachin. (Jer. **52**:**31-34**)

Jer. **52**:**1-11** This fruit of sin we should pray against above any thing; Cast me not away from thy presence, Ps. **51**:**11**. None are cast out of God's presence but those who by sin have first thrown themselves out. Zedekiah's flight was in vain, for there is no escaping the judgments of God; they come upon the sinner, and overtake him, let him flee where he will.

Jer. **52**:**12-23** The Chaldean army made woful havoc But nothing is so particularly related here, as the carrying away of the articles in the temple. The remembrance of their beauty and value shows us the more the evil of sin.

Jer. **52**:**24-30** The leaders of the Jews caused them to err; but now they are, in particular, made monuments of Divine justice. Here is an account of two earlier captivities. This people often were wonders both of judgment and mercy.

Jer. **52**:**31-34** See this history of king Jehoiachin in II Kin. **25**:**27-30**. Those under oppression will find it is not in vain for them to hope and quietly to wait for the salvation of the Lord. Our times are in God's hand, for the hearts of all we have to deal with are so. May we be enabled, more and more, to rest on the Rock of Ages, and to look forward with holy faith to that hour, when the Lord will bring again Zion, and overthrow all the enemies of the church.

Lamentations

It is evident that Jeremiah was the author of the Lamentations which bear his name. The book was not written till after the destruction of Jerusalem by the Chaldeans. May we be led to consider sin as the cause of all our calamities, and under trials exercise submission, repentance, faith, and prayer, with the hope of promised deliverance through God's mercy.

Chapter 1

The miserable state of Jerusalem, the just consequences of its sins. (Lam. **1**:**1-11**) Jerusalem represented as a captive female, lamenting, and seeking the mercy of God. (Lam. **1**:**12-22**)

Lam. **1**:**1-11** The prophet sometimes speaks in his own person; at other times Jerusalem, as a distressed female, is the speaker, or some of the Jews. The description shows the miseries of the Jewish nation. Jerusalem became a captive and a slave, by reason of the greatness of her sins; and had no rest from suffering. If we allow sin, our greatest adversary, to have dominion over us, justly will other enemies also be suffered to have dominion. The people endured the extremities of famine and distress. In this sad condition Jerusalem acknowledged her sin, and entreated the Lord to look upon her case. This is the only way to make ourselves easy under our burdens; for it is the just anger of the Lord for man's transgressions, that has filled the earth with sorrows, lamentations, sickness, and death.

Lam. **1**:**12-22** Jerusalem, sitting dejected on the ground, calls on those that passed by, to consider whether her example did not concern them. Her outward sufferings were great, but her inward sufferings were harder to bear, through the sense of guilt. Sorrow for sin must be great sorrow, and must affect the soul. Here we see the evil of sin, and may take warning to flee from the wrath to come. Whatever may be learned from the sufferings of Jerusalem, far more may be learned from the sufferings of Christ. Does he not from the cross speak to every one of us? Does he not say, Is it nothing to you, all ye that pass by? Let all our sorrows lead us to the cross of Christ, lead us to mark his example, and cheerfully to follow him.

Chapter 2

Lamentation for the misery of Jerusalem.

Lam. **2**:**1-9** A sad representation is here made of the state of God's church, of Jacob and Israel; but the notice seems mostly to refer to the hand of the Lord in their calamities. Yet God is not an enemy to his people, when he is angry with them and corrects them. And gates and bars stand in no stead when God withdraws his protection. It is just with God to cast down those by judgments, who debase themselves by sin; and to deprive those of the benefit and comfort of sabbaths and ordinances, who have not duly valued nor observed them. What should they do with Bibles, who make no improvement of them? Those who misuse God's prophets, justly lose them. It becomes necessary, though painful, to turn the thoughts of the afflicted to the hand of God lifted up against them, and to their sins as the source of their miseries.

Lam. **2**:**10**-**22** Causes for lamentation are described. Multitudes perished by famine. Even little children were slain by their mother's hands, and eaten, according to the threatening, Deut. **28**:**53**. Multitudes fell by the sword. Their false prophets deceived them. And their neighbours laughed at them. It is a great sin to jest at others' miseries, and adds much affliction to the afflicted. Their enemies triumphed over them. The enemies of the church are apt to take its shocks for its ruins; but they will find themselves deceived. Calls to lamentation are given; and comforts for the cure of these lamentations are sought. Prayer is a salve for every sore, even the sorest; a remedy for every malady, even the most grievous. Our business in prayer is to refer our case to the Lord, and leave it with him. His will be done. Let us fear God, and walk humbly before him, and take heed lest we fall.

Chapter 3

The faithful lament their calamities, and hope in God's mercies.

Lam. **3**:**1**-**20** The prophet relates the more gloomy and discouraging part of his experience, and how he found support and relief. In the time of his trial the Lord had become terrible to him. It was an affliction that was misery itself; for sin makes the cup of affliction a bitter cup. The struggle between unbelief and faith is often very severe. But the weakest believer is wrong, if he thinks that his strength and hope are perished from the Lord.

Lam. **3**:**21**-**36** Having stated his distress and temptation, the prophet shows how he was raised above it. Bad as things are, it is owing to the mercy of God that they are not worse. We should observe what makes for us, as well as what is against us. God's compassions fail not; of this we have fresh instances every morning. Portions on earth are perishing things, but God is a portion for ever. It is our duty, and will be our comfort and satisfaction, to hope and quietly to wait for the salvation of the Lord. Afflictions do and will work very much for good: many have found it good to bear this yoke in their youth; it has made many humble and serious, and has weaned them from the world, who otherwise would have been proud and unruly. If tribulation work patience, that patience will work experience, and that experience a hope that makes not ashamed. Due thoughts of the evil of sin, and of our own sinfulness, will convince us that it is of the Lord's mercies we are not consumed. If we cannot say with unwavering voice, The Lord is my portion; may we not say, I desire to have Him for my portion and salvation, and in his word do I hope? Happy shall we be, if we learn to receive affliction as laid upon us by the hand of God.

Lam. **3**:**37**-**41** While there is life there is hope; and instead of complaining that things are bad, we should encourage ourselves with the hope they will be better. We are sinful men, and what we complain of, is far less than our sins deserve. We should complain to God, and not of him. We are apt, in times of calamity, to reflect on other people's ways, and blame them; but our duty is to search and try our own ways, that we may turn from evil to God. Our hearts must go with our prayers. If inward impressions do not answer to outward expressions, we mock God, and deceive ourselves.

Lam. **3**:**42**-**54** The more the prophet looked on the desolations, the more he was grieved. Here is one word of comfort. While they continued weeping, they continued waiting; and neither did nor would expect relief and succour from any but the Lord.

Lam. **3**:**55**-**66** Faith comes off conqueror, for in these **verse**s the prophet concludes with some comfort. Prayer is the breath of the new man, drawing in the air of mercy in petitions, and returning it in praises; it proves and maintains the spiritual life. He silenced their fears, and quieted their spirits. Thou saidst, Fear not. This was the language of God's grace, by the witness of his Spirit with their spirits. And what are all our sorrows, compared with those of the Redeemer? He will deliver his people from every trouble, and revive his church from every persecution. He will save believers with everlasting salvation, while his enemies perish with everlasting destruction.

Chapter 4

The deplorable state of the nation is contrasted with its ancient prosperity.

Lam. **4**:**1**-**12** What a change is here! Sin tarnishes the beauty of the most exalted powers and the most excellent gifts; but that gold, tried in the fire, which Christ bestows, never will be taken from us; its outward appearance may be dimmed, but its real value can never be changed. The horrors of the siege and destruction of Jerusalem are again described. Beholding the sad consequences of sin in the church of old, let us seriously consider to what the same causes may justly bring down the church now. But, Lord, though we have gone from thee in rebellion, yet turn to us, and turn our hearts to thee, that we may fear thy name. Come to us, bless us with awakening, converting, renewing, confirming grace.

Lam. **4**:**13**-**20** Nothing ripens a people more for ruin, nor fills the measure faster, than the sins of priests and prophets. The king himself cannot escape, for Divine vengeance pursues him. Our anointed King alone is the life of our souls; we may safely live under his shadow, and rejoice in Him in the midst of our enemies, for He is the true God and eternal life.

Lam. **4**:**21**,**22** Here it is foretold that an end should be put to Zion's troubles. Not the fulness of punishment deserved, but of what God has determined to inflict. An end shall be put to Edom's triumphs. All the troubles of the church and of the believer will soon be accomplished. And the doom of their enemies approaches. The Lord will bring their sins to light, and they shall lie down in eternal sorrow. Edom here represents all the enemies of the church. And the corruption, and sin of Israel, which the prophet has proved to be universal, justifies the judgments of the Lord. It shows the need of that grace in Christ Jesus, which the sin and corruption of all mankind make so necessary.

Chapter 5

The Jewish nation supplicating the Divine favour.

Lam. **5**:**1**-**16** Is any afflicted? Let him pray; and let him in prayer pour out his complaint to God. The people of God do so here; they complain not of evils feared, but of evils felt. If penitent and patient under what we suffer for the sins of our fathers, we may expect that He who punishes, will return in mercy to us. They acknowledge, Woe unto us that we have sinned! All our woes are owing to our own sin and folly. Though our sins and God's just displeasure cause our sufferings, we may hope in his pardoning mercy, his sanctifying grace, and his kind providence. But the sins of a man's whole life will be punished with vengeance at last, unless he obtains an interest in Him who bare our sins in his own body on the tree.

Lam. **5**:**17**-**22** The people of God express deep concern for the ruins of the temple, more than for any other of their calamities. But whatever changes there are on earth, God is still the same, and remains for ever wise and holy, just and good; with Him there is no variableness nor shadow of turning. They earnestly pray to God for mercy and grace; Turn us to thee, O Lord. God never leaves any till they first leave him; if he turns them to him in a way of duty, no doubt he will quickly return to them in a way of mercy. If God by his grace renew our hearts, he will by his favour renew our days. Troubles may cause our hearts to be faint, and our eyes to be dim, but the way to the mercy-seat of our reconciled God is open. Let us, in all our trials, put our whole trust and confidence in his mercy; let us confess our sins, and pour out our hearts before him. Let us watch against repinings and despondency; for we surely know, that it shall be well in the end with all that trust in, fear, love, and serve the Lord. Are not the Lord's judgments in the earth the same as in Jeremiah's days? Let Zion then be remembered by us in our prayers, and her welfare be sought above every earthly joy. Spare, Lord, spare thy people, and give not thine heritage to reproach, for the heathen to rule over them.

Ezekiel

Ezekiel was one of the priests; he was carried captive to Chaldea with Jehoiachin. All his prophecies appear to have been delivered in that country, at some place north of Babylon. Their chief object appears to have been to comfort his brethren in captivity. He is directed to warn of the dreadful calamities coming upon Judea, particularly upon the false prophets, and the neighbouring nations. Also to announce the future restoration of Israel and Judah from their several dispersions, and their happy state in their latter days, under the Messiah. Much of Christ will be found in this book, especially in the conclusion.

Chapter 1

Ezekiel's vision of God, and of the angelic host. (Ezek. **1**:**1-14**) The conduct of Divine Providence. (Ezek. **1**:**15-25**) A revelation of the Son of man upon his heavenly throne. (Ezek. **1**:**26-28**)

Ezek. **1**:**1-14** It is a mercy to have the word of God brought to us, and a duty to attend to it diligently, when we are in affliction. The voice of God came in the fulness of light and power, by the Holy Spirit. These visions seem to have been sent to possess the prophet's mind with great and high thoughts of God. To strike terror upon sinners. To speak comfort to those that feared God, and humbled themselves. In Ezek. **1**:**4-14**, is the first part of the vision, which represents God as attended and served by a vast company of angels, who are all his messengers, his ministers, doing his commandments. This vision would impress the mind with solemn awe and fear of the Divine displeasure, yet raise expectations of blessings. The fire is surrounded with a glory. Though we cannot by searching find out God to perfection, yet we see the brightness round about it. The likeness of the living creatures came out of the midst of the fire; angels derive their being and power from God. They have the understanding of a man, and far more. A lion excels in strength and boldness. An ox excels in diligence and patience, and unwearied discharge of the work he has to do. An eagle excels in quickness and piercing sight, and in soaring high; and the angels, who excel man in all these respects, put on these appearances. The angels have wings; and whatever business God sends them upon, they lose no time. They stood straight, and firm, and steady. They had not only wings for motion, but hands for action. Many persons are quick, who are not active; they hurry about, but do nothing to purpose; they have wings, but no hands. But wherever the angels' wings carried them, they carried hands with them, to be doing what duty required. Whatever service they went about, they went every one straight forward. When we go straight, we go forward; when we serve God with one heart, we perform work. They turned not when they went. They made no mistakes; and their work needed not to be gone over again. They turned not from their business to trifle with any thing. They went whithersoever the Spirit of God would have them go. The prophet saw these living creatures by their own light, for their appearance was like burning coals of fire; they are seraphim, or "burners;" denoting the ardour of their love to God, and fervent zeal in his service. We may learn profitable lessons from subjects we cannot fully enter into or understand. But let us attend to the things which relate to our peace and duty, and leave secret things to the Lord, to whom alone they belong.

Ezek. **1**:**15-25** Providence, represented by the wheels, produces changes. Sometimes one spoke of the wheel is uppermost, sometimes another; but the motion of the wheel on its own axletree is regular and steady. We need not despond in adversity; the wheels are turning round and will raise us in due time, while those who presume in prosperity know not how soon they may be cast down. The wheel is near the living creatures; the angels are employed as ministers of God's providence. The spirit of the living creatures was in the wheels; the same wisdom, power, and holiness of God, that guide and govern the angels, by them order all events in this lower world. The wheel had four faces, denoting that the providence of God exerts itself in all parts. Look every way upon the wheel of providence, it has a face toward you. Their appearance and work were as a wheel in the middle of a wheel. The disposals of Providence seem to us dark, perplexed, and unaccountable, yet are all wisely ordered for the best. The motion of these wheels was steady, regular, and constant. They went as the Spirit directed, therefore returned not. We should not have to undo that by repentance which we have done amiss, if we followed the guidance of the Spirit. The rings, or rims of the wheels were so vast, that when put in motion the prophet was afraid to look upon them. The consideration of the height and depth of God's counsel should awe us. They were full of eyes round about. The motions of Providence are all directed by infinite Wisdom. All events are determined by the eyes of the Lord, which are in every place beholding the evil and the good; for there is no such thing as chance or fortune. The firmament above was a crystal, glorious, but terribly so. That which we take to be a dark cloud, is to God clear as crystal, through which he looks upon all the inhabitants of the earth. When the angels had roused a careless world, they let down their wings, that God's voice might be plainly heard. The voice of Providence is to open men's ears to the voice of the word. Sounds on earth should awaken our attention to the voice from heaven; for how shall we escape, if we turn away from Him that speaks from thence.

Ezek. **1**:**26-28** The eternal Son, the second Person in the Trinity, who afterwards took the human nature, is here denoted. The first thing observed was a throne. It is a throne of glory, a throne of grace, a throne of triumph, a throne of government, a throne of judgment. It is good news to men, that the throne above the firmament is filled with One who appears, even there, in the likeness of a man. The throne is surrounded with a rainbow, the well-known emblem of the covenant, representing God's mercy and covenanted love to his people. The fire of God's wrath was breaking out against Jerusalem, but bounds should be set to it; he would look upon the bow, and remember the covenant. All the prophet saw was only to prepare him for what he was to hear. When he fell on his face, he heard the voice of One that spake. God delights to teach the humble. Let sinners, then, humble themselves before him. And let believers think upon his glory, that they may be gradually changed into his image by the Spirit of the Lord.

Chapter 2

The prophet is directed what he is to do. (Ezek. **2**:**1-5**) And encouraged to be resolute, faithful, and devoted. (Ezek. **2**:**6-10**)

Ezek. **2**:**1-5** Lest Ezekiel should be lifted up with the abundance of the revelations, he is put in mind that still he is a son of man, a weak, mortal creature. As Christ usually called himself the Son of man, it was also an honourable distinction. Ezekiel's posture showed reverence, but his standing up would be a posture of greater readiness and fitness for business. God will speak to us, when we stand ready to do what he commands us. As Ezekiel had not strength of his own, the Spirit entered into him. God is graciously pleased to work in us whatever he requires of us. The Holy Spirit sets us upon our feet, by inclining our wills to our duty. Thus, when the Lord calls upon the sinner to awake, and attend to the concerns of his soul, the Spirit of life and grace comes with the call. Ezekiel is sent with a message to the children of Israel. Many might treat his message with contempt, yet they should know by the event that a prophet had been sent to them. God will be glorified, and his word made honourable, whether it be a savour of life unto life, or of death unto death.

Ezek. **2**:**6-10** Those who will do any thing to purpose in the service of God, must not fear men. Wicked men are as briers and thorns; but they are nigh unto cursing, and their end is to be burned. The prophet must be faithful to the souls of those to whom he was sent. All who speak from God to others, must obey his voice. The discoveries of sin, and the warnings of wrath, should be matter of lamentation. And those acquainted with the word of God, will clearly perceive it is filled with woe to impenitent sinners; and that all the precious promises of the gospel are for the repenting, believing servants of the Lord.

Chapter 3

The preparation of the prophet for his work. (Ezek. **3**:**1-11**) His office, as that of a watchman. (Ezek. **3**:**12-2**) The restraining and restoring his speech. (Ezek. **3**:**22-27**)

Ezek. **3**:**1-11** Ezekiel was to receive the truths of God as the food for his soul, and to feed upon them by faith, and he would be strengthened. Gracious souls can receive those truths of God with delight, which speak terror to the wicked. He must speak all that, and that only, which God spake to him. How can we better speak God's mind than with his words? If disappointed as to his people, he must not be offended. The Ninevites were wrought upon by Jonah's preaching, when Israel was unhumbled and unreformed. We must leave this unto the Divine sovereignty, and say, Lord, thy judgments are a great deep. They will not regard the word of the prophet, for they will not regard the rod of God. Christ promises to strengthen him. He must continue earnest in preaching, whatever the success might be.

Ezek. **3**:**12-21** This mission made the holy angels rejoice. All this was to convince Ezekiel, that the God who sent him had power to bear him out in his work. He was overwhelmed with grief for the sins and miseries of his people, and overpowered by the glory of the vision he had seen. And however retirement, meditation, and communion with God may be sweet, the servant of the Lord must prepare to serve his generation. The Lord told the prophet he had appointed him a watchman to the house of Israel. If we warn the wicked, we are not chargeable with their ruin. Though such passages refer to the national covenant made with Israel, they are equally to be applied to the final state of all men under every dispensation. We are not only to encourage and comfort those who appear to be righteous, but they are to be warned, for many have grown high-minded and secure, have fallen, and even died in their sins. Surely then the hearers of the gospel should desire warnings, and even reproofs.

Ezek. **3**:**22-27** Let us own ourselves for ever indebted to the mediation of Christ, for the blessed intercourse between God and man; and a true believer will say, I am never less alone than when thus alone. When the Lord opened Ezekiel's mouth, he was to deliver his message boldly, to place life and death, the blessing and the curse, before the people, and leave them to their choice.

Chapter 4

The siege of Jerusalem. (Ezek. **4**:**1-8**) The famine the inhabitants would suffer. (Ezek. **4**:**9-17**)

Ezek. **4**:**1-8** The prophet was to represent the siege of Jerusalem by signs. He was to lie on his left side for a number of days, supposed to be equal to the years from the establishment of idolatry. All that the prophet sets before the children of his people, about the destruction of Jerusalem, is to show that sin is the provoking cause of the ruin of that once flourishing city.

Ezek. **4**:**9-17** The bread which was Ezekiel's support, was to be made of coarse grain and pulse mixed together, seldom used except in times of urgent scarcity, and of this he was only to take a small quantity. Thus was figured the extremity to which the Jews were to be reduced during the siege and captivity. Ezekiel does not plead, Lord, from my youth I have been brought up delicately, and never used to any thing like this; but that he had been brought up conscientiously, and never had eaten any thing forbidden by the law. It will be comfortable when we are brought to suffer hardships, if our hearts can witness that we have always been careful to keep even from the appearance of evil. See what woful work sin makes, and acknowledge the righteousness of God herein. Their plenty having been abused to luxury and excess, they were justly punished by famine. When men serve not God with cheerfulness in the abundance of all things, God will make them serve their enemies in the want of all things.

Chapter 5

A type of hair, showing the judgments about to come upon the Jews. (Ezek. **5**:**1-4**) These awful judgments are declared. (Ezek. **5**:**5-17**)

Ezek. **5**:**1-4** The prophet must shave off the hair of his head and beard, which signifies God's utter rejecting and abandoning that people. One part must be burned in the midst of the city, denoting the multitudes that should perish by famine and pestilence. Another part was to be cut in pieces, representing the many who were slain by the sword. Another part was to be scattered in the wind, denoting the carrying away of some into the land of the conqueror, and the flight of others into the neighbouring countries for shelter. A small quantity of the third portion was to be bound in his shirts, as that of which he is very careful. But few were reserved. To whatever refuge sinners flee, the fire and sword of God's wrath will consume them.

Ezek. **5**:**5-17** The sentence passed upon Jerusalem is very dreadful, the manner of expression makes it still more so. Who is able to stand in God's sight when he is angry? Those who live and die impenitent, will perish for ever unpitied; there is a day coming when the Lord will not spare. Let not persons or churches, who change the Lord's statutes, expect to escape the doom of Jerusalem. Let us endeavour to adorn the doctrine of God our Saviour in all things. Sooner or later God's word will prove itself true.

Chapter 6

The Divine judgments for idolatry. (Ezek. **6**:**1-7**) A remnant shall be saved. (Ezek. **6**:**8-10**) The calamities are to be lamented. (Ezek. **6**:**11-14**)

Ezek. **6**:**1-7**. War desolates persons, places, and things esteemed most sacred. God ruins idolatries even by the hands of idolaters. It is just with God to make that a desolation, which we make an idol. The superstitions to which many trust for safety, often cause their ruin. And the day is at hand, when idols and idolatry will be as thoroughly destroyed from the professedly Christian church as they were from among the Jews.

Ezek. **6**:**8-10** A remnant of Israel should be left; at length they should remember the Lord, their obligations to him, and rebellion against him. True penitents see sin to be that abominable thing which the Lord hates. Those who truly loathe sin, loathe themselves because of sin. They give glory to God by their repentance. Whatever brings men to remember Him, and their sins against him, should be regarded as a blessing.

Ezek. **6**:**11-14** It is our duty to be affected, not only with our own sins and sufferings, but to look with compassion upon the miseries wicked people bring upon themselves. Sin is a desolating thing; therefore, stand in awe, and sin not. If we know the worth of souls, and the danger to which unbelievers are exposed, we shall deem every sinner who takes refuge in Jesus from the wrath to come, an abundant recompence for all contempt or opposition we may meet with.

Chapter 7

The desolation of the land. (Ezek. **7**:**1-15**) The distress of the few who should escape. (Ezek. **7**:**16-22**) The captivity. (Ezek. **7**:**23-27**)

Ezek. **7**:**1-15** The abruptness of this prophecy, and the many repetitions, show that the prophet was deeply affected by the prospect of these calamities. Such will the destruction of sinners be; for none can avoid it. Oh that the wickedness of the wicked might end before it bring them to an end! Trouble is to the impenitent only an evil, it hardens their hearts, and stirs up their corruptions; but there are those to whom it is sanctified by the grace of God, and made a means of much good. The day of real trouble is near, not a mere echo or rumour of troubles. Whatever are the fruits of God's judgments, our sin is the root of them. These judgments shall be universal. And God will be glorified in all. Now is the day of the Lord's patience and mercy, but the time of the sinner's trouble is at hand.

Ezek. **7**:**16-22** Sooner or later, sin will cause sorrow; and those who will not repent of their sin, may justly be left to pine away in it. There are many whose wealth is their snare and ruin; and the gaining the world is the losing of their souls. Riches profit not in the day of wrath. The wealth of this world has not that in it which will answer the desires of the soul, or be any satisfaction to it in a day of distress. God's temple shall stand them in no stead. Those are unworthy to be honoured with the form of godliness, who will not be governed by its power.

Ezek. **7**:**23-27** Whoever break the bands of God's law, will find themselves bound and held by the chains of his judgments. Since they encouraged one another to sin, God would dishearten them. All must needs be in trouble, when God comes to judge them according to their deserts. May the Lord enable us to seek that good part which shall not be taken away.

Chapter 8

The idolatries committed by the Jewish rulers. (Ezek. **8**:**1-6**) The superstitions to which the Jews were then devoted, the Egyptian. (Ezek. **8**:**7-12**) The Phoenician. (Ezek. **8**:**13,14**) The Persian. (Ezek. **8**:**15,16**) The heinousness of their sin. (Ezek. **8**:**17,18**)

Ezek. **8**:**1-6** The glorious personage Ezekiel beheld in vision, seemed to take hold upon him, and he was conveyed in spirit to Jerusalem. There, in the inner court of the temple, was prepared a place for some base idol. The whole was presented in vision to the prophet. If it should please God to give any man a clear view of his glory and majesty, and of all the abominations committing in any one city, he would then admit the justice of the severest punishments God should inflict thereon.

Ezek. **8**:**7-12** A secret place was, as it were, opened, where the prophet saw creatures painted on the walls, and a number of the elders of Israel worshipped before them. No superiority in worldly matters will preserve men from lust, or idolatries, when they are left to their own deceitful hearts; and those who are soon wearied in the service of God, often grudge no toil nor expense when following their superstitions. When hypocrites screen themselves behind the wall of an outward profession, there is some hole or other left in the wall, something that betrays them to those who look diligently. There is a great deal of secret wickedness in the world. They think themselves out of God's sight. But those are ripe indeed for ruin, who lay the blame of their sins upon the Lord.

Ezek. **8**:**13-18** The yearly lamenting for Tammuz was attended with infamous practices; and the worshippers of the sun here described, are supposed to have been priests. The Lord appeals to the prophet concerning the heinousness of the crime; "and lo, they put the branch to their nose," denoting some custom used by idolaters in honour of the idols they served. The more we examine human nature and our own hearts, the more abominations we shall discover; and the longer the believer searches himself, the more he will humble himself before God, and the more will he value the fountain open for sin, and seek to wash therein.

Chapter 9

A vision denoting the destruction of the inhabitants of Jerusalem, and the departure of the symbol of the Divine presence.

Ezek. **9**:**1-4** It is a great comfort to believers, that in the midst of destroyers and destructions, there is a Mediator, a great High Priest, who has an interest in heaven, and in whom saints on earth have an interest. The representation of the Divine glory from above the ark, removed to the threshold, denoted that the Lord was about to leave his mercy-seat, and to pronounce judgment on the people. The distinguishing character of this remnant that is to be saved, is such as sigh and cry to God in prayer, because of the abominations in Jerusalem. Those who keep pure in times of general wickedness, God will keep safe in times of general trouble and distress.

Ezek. **9**:**5-11** The slaughter must begin at the sanctuary, that all may see and know that the Lord hates sin most in those nearest to him. He who was appointed to protect, reported the matter. Christ is faithful to the trust reposed in him. Is he commanded by his Father to secure eternal life to the chosen remnant? He says, Of all that thou hast given me, I have lost none. If others perish, and we are saved, we must ascribe the difference wholly to the mercy of our God, for we too have deserved wrath. Let us still continue to plead in behalf of others. But where the Lord shows no mercy he does no injustice; he only recompenses men's ways.

Chapter 10

A vision of the burning of the city. (Ezek. **10**:**1-7**) The Divine glory departing from the temple. (Ezek. **10**:**8-22**)

Ezek. **10**:**1-7** The fire being taken from between the wheels, under the cherubim, Ezek. **1**:**13**, seems to have signified the wrath of God to be executed upon Jerusalem. It intimated that the fire of Divine wrath, which kindles judgment upon a people, is just and holy; and in the great day, the earth, and all the works that are therein, will be burnt up.

Ezek. **10**:**8-22** Ezekiel sees the working of Divine providence in the government of the lower world, and the affairs of it. When God is leaving a people in displeasure, angels above, and all events below, further his departure. The Spirit of life, the Spirit of God, directs all creatures, in heaven and on earth, so as to make them serve the Divine purpose. God removes by degrees from a provoking people; and, when ready to depart, would return to them, if they were a repenting, praying people. Let this warn sinners to seek the Lord while he may be found, and to call on him while he is near, and cause us all to walk humbly and watchfully with our God.

Chapter 11

Divine judgments against the wicked at Jerusalem. (Ezek. **11**:**1-13**) Divine favour towards those in captivity. (Ezek. **11**:**14-21**) The Divine presence forsakes the city. (Ezek. **11**:**22-25**)

Ezek. **11**:**1-13** Where Satan cannot persuade men to look upon the judgment to come as uncertain, he gains his point by persuading them to look upon it as at a distance. These wretched rulers dare to say, We are as safe in this city as flesh in a boiling pot; the walls of the city shall be to us as walls of brass, we shall receive no more damage from the besiegers than the caldron does from the fire. When sinners flatter themselves to their own ruin, it is time to tell them they shall have no peace if they go on. None shall remain in possession of the city but those who are buried in it. Those are least safe who are most secure. God is often pleased to single out some sinners for warning to others. Whether Pelatiah died at that time in Jerusalem, or when the fulfilment of the prophecy drew near, is uncertain. Like Ezekiel, we ought to be much affected with the sudden death of others, and we should still plead with the Lord to have mercy on those who remain.

Ezek. **11**:**14-21** The pious captives in Babylon were insulted by the Jews who continued in Jerusalem; but God made gracious promises to them. It is promised, that God will give them one heart; a heart firmly fixed for God, and not wavering. All who are made holy have a new spirit, a new temper and dispositions; they act from new principles, walk by new rules, and aim at new ends. A new name, or a new face, will not serve without a new spirit. If any man be in Christ, he is a new creature. The carnal heart, like a stone, cannot be made to feel. Men live among the dead and dying, and are neither concerned nor humbled. He will make their hearts tender and fit to receive impressions: this is God's work, it is his gift by promise; and a wonderful and happy change is wrought by it, from death to life. Their practices shall be agreeable to those principles. These two must and will go together. When the sinner feels his need of these blessings, let him present the promises as prayers in the name of Christ, they will be performed.

Ezek. **11**:**22-25** Here is the departure of God's presence from the city and temple. It was from the Mount of Olives that the vision went up, typifying the ascension of Christ to heaven from that very mountain. Though the Lord will not forsake his people, yet he may be driven away from any part of his visible church by their sins, and woe will be upon them when He withdraws his presence, glory, and protection.

Chapter 12

The approaching captivity. (Ezek. **12**:**1-16**) An emblem of the consternation of the Jews. (Ezek. **12**:**17-20**) Answers to the objections of scoffers. (Ezek. **12**:**21-28**)

Ezek. **12**:**1-16** By the preparation for removal, and his breaking through the wall of his house at evening, as one desirous to escape from the enemy, the prophet signified the conduct and fate of Zedekiah. When God has delivered us, we must glorify him and edify others, by acknowledging our sins. Those who by afflictions are brought to this, are made to know that God is the Lord, and may help to bring others to know him.

Ezek. **12**:**17-20** The prophet must eat and drink in care and fear, with trembling, that he might express the condition of those in Jerusalem during the siege. When ministers speak of the ruin coming upon sinners, they must speak as those that know the terrors of the Lord. Afflictions are happy ones, however grievous to flesh and blood, that improve us in the knowledge of God.

Ezek. **12**:**21-28** From that forbearance of God, which should have led them to repent, the Jews hardened themselves in sin. It will not serve for an excuse in speaking evil, to plead that it is a common saying. There is but a step between us and an awful eternity; therefore it concerns us to get ready for a future state. No one will be able to put from himself the evil day, unless by seeking peace with the Lord.

Chapter 13

Heavy judgments against lying prophets. (Ezek. **13**:**1-9**) The insufficiency of their work. (Ezek. **13**:**10-16**) Woes against false prophetesses. (Ezek. **13**:**17-23**)

Ezek. **13**:**1-9** Where God gives a warrant to do any thing, he gives wisdom. What they delivered was not what they had seen or heard, as that is which the ministers of Christ deliver. They were not praying prophets, had no intercourse with Heaven; they contrived how to please people, not how to do them good; they stood not against sin. They flattered people into vain hopes. Such widen the breach, by causing men to think themselves deserving of eternal life, when the wrath of God abides upon them.

Ezek. **13**:**10-16** One false prophet built the wall, set up the notion that Jerusalem should be victorious, and made himself acceptable by it. Others made the matter yet more plausible and promising; they daubed the wall which the first had built; but they would, ere long, be undeceived when their work was beaten down by the storm of God's just wrath; when the Chaldean army desolated the land. Hopes of peace and happiness, not warranted by the word of God, will cheat men; like a wall well daubed, but ill built.

Ezek. **13**:**17-23** It is ill with those who had rather hear pleasing lies than unpleasing truths. The false prophetesses tried to make people secure, signified by laying them at ease, and to make them proud, signified by the finery laid on their heads. They shall be confounded in their attempts, and God's people shall be delivered out of their hands. It behoves Christians to keep close to the word of God, and in every thing to seek the teaching of the Holy Spirit. Let us so trust the promises of God as to keep his commandments.

Chapter 14

Threatenings against hypocrites. (Ezek. **14**:**1-11**) God's purpose to punish the guilty Jews, but a few should be saved. (Ezek. **14**:**12-23**)

Ezek. **14**:**1-11** No outward form or reformation can be acceptable to God, so long as any idol possesses the heart; yet how many prefer their own devices and their own righteousness, to the way of salvation! Men's corruptions are idols in their hearts, and are of their own setting up; God will let them take their course. Sin renders the sinner odious in the eyes of the pure and holy God; and in his own eyes also, whenever conscience is awakened. Let us seek to be cleansed from the guilt and pollution of sins, in that fountain which the Lord has opened.

Ezek. **14**:**12-23** National sins bring national judgments. Though sinners escape one judgment, another is waiting for them. When God's professing people rebel against him, they may justly expect all his judgments. The faith, obedience, and prayers of Noah prevailed to the saving of his house, but not of the old world. Job's sacrifice and prayer in behalf of his friends were accepted, and Daniel had prevailed for the saving his companions and the wise men of Babylon. But a people that had filled the measure of their sins, was not to expect to escape for the sake of any righteous men living among them; not even of the most eminent saints, who could be accepted in their own case only through the sufferings and righteousness of Christ. Yet even when God makes the greatest desolations by his judgments, he saves some to be monuments of his mercy. In firm belief that we shall approve the whole of God's dealings with ourselves, and with all mankind, let us silence all rebellious murmurs and objections.

Chapter 15

Jerusalem like an unfruitful vine.

If a vine be fruitful, it is valuable. But if not fruitful, it is worthless and useless, it is cast into the fire. Thus man is capable of yielding a precious fruit, in living to God; this is the sole end of his existence; and if he fails in this, he is of no use but to be destroyed. What blindness then attaches to those who live in the total neglect of God and of true religion! This similitude is applied to Jerusalem. Let us beware of an unfruitful profession. Let us come to Christ, and seek to abide in him, and to have his words abide in us.

Chapter 16

A parable showing the first low estate of the Jewish nation, its prosperity, idolatries, and punishment.

Ezek. **16**:**1-58** In this chapter God's dealings with the Jewish nation, and their conduct towards him, are described, and their punishment through the surrounding nations, even those they most trusted in. This is done under the parable of an exposed infant rescued from death, educated, espoused, and richly provided for, but afterwards guilty of the most abandoned conduct, and punished for it; yet at last received into favour, and ashamed of her base conduct. We are not to judge of these expressions by modern ideas, but by those of the times and places in which they were used, where many of them would not sound as they do to us. The design was to raise hatred to idolatry, and such a parable was well suited for that purpose.

Ezek. **16**:**59-63** After a full warning of judgments, mercy is remembered, mercy is reserved. These closing **verse**s are a precious promise, in part fulfilled at the return of the penitent and reformed Jews out of Babylon, but to have fuller accomplishment in gospel times. The Divine mercy should be powerful to melt our hearts into godly sorrow for sin. Nor will God ever leave the sinner to perish, who is humbled for his sins, and comes to trust in His mercy and grace through Jesus Christ; but will keep him by his power, through faith unto salvation.

Chapter 17

A parable relative to the Jewish nation. (Ezek. **17**:**1-10**) to which an explanation is added. (Ezek. **17**:**11-21**) A direct promise of the Messiah. (Ezek. **17**:**22-24**)

Ezek. **17**:**1-10** Mighty conquerors are aptly likened to birds or beasts of prey, but their destructive passions are overruled to forward God's designs. Those who depart from God, only vary their crimes by changing one carnal confidence for another, and never will prosper.

Ezek. **17**:**11-21** The parable is explained, and the particulars of the history of the Jewish nation at that time may be traced. Zedekiah had been ungrateful to his benefactor, which is a sin against God. In every solemn oath, God is appealed to as a witness of the sincerity of him that swears. Truth is a debt owing to all men. If the professors of the true religion deal treacherously with those of a false religion, their profession makes their sin the worse; and God will the more surely and severely punish it. The Lord will not hold those guiltless who take his name in vain; and no man shall escape the righteous judgment of God who dies under unrepented guilt.

Ezek. **17**:**22-24** The unbelief of man shall not make the promise of God of none effect. The parable of a tree, used in the threatening, is here presented in the promise. It appears only applicable to Jesus, the Son of David, the Messiah of God. The kingdom of Satan, which has borne so long, so large a sway, shall be broken, and the kingdom of Christ, which was looked upon with contempt, shall be established. Blessed be God, our Redeemer is seen even by the ends of the earth. We may find refuge from the wrath to come, and from every enemy and danger, under his shadow; and believers are fruitful in him.

Chapter 18

God has no respect of persons. (Ezek. **18**:**1-20**) The Divine providence is vindicated. (Ezek. **18**:**21-29**) A gracious invitation to repentance. (Ezek. **18**:**30-32**)

Ezek. **18**:**1-20** The soul that sinneth it shall die. As to eternity, every man was, is, and will be dealt with, as his conduct shows him to have been under the old covenant of works, or the new covenant of grace. Whatever outward sufferings come upon men through the sins of others, they deserve for their own sins all they suffer; and the Lord overrules every event for the eternal good of believers. All souls are in the hand of the great Creator: he will deal with them in justice or mercy; nor will any perish for the sins of another, who is not in some sense worthy of death for his own. We all have sinned, and our souls must be lost, if God deal with us according to his holy law; but we are invited to come to Christ. If a man who had shown his faith by his works, had a wicked son, whose character and conduct were the re**verse** of his parent's, could it be expected he should escape the Divine vengeance on account of his father's piety? Surely not. And should a wicked man have a son who walked before God as righteous, this man would not perish for his father's sins. If the son was not free from evils in this life, still he should be partaker of salvation. The question here is not about the meritorious ground of justification, but about the Lord's dealings with the righteous and the wicked.

Ezek. **18**:**21-29** The wicked man would be saved, if he turned from his evil ways. The true penitent is a true believer. None of his former transgressions shall be mentioned unto him, but in the righteousness which he has done, as the fruit of faith and the effect of conversion, he shall surely live. The question is not whether the truly righteous ever become apostates. It is certain that many who for a time were thought to be righteous, do so, while Ezek. **18**:**26,27** speaks the fulness of pardoning mercy: when sin is forgiven, it is blotted out, it is remembered no more. In their righteousness they shall live; not for their righteousness, as if that were an atonement for their sins, but in their righteousness, which is one of the blessings purchased by the Mediator. What encouragement a repenting, returning sinner has to hope for pardon and life according to this promise! In **verse 28** is the beginning and progress of repentance. True believers watch and pray, and continue to the end, and they are saved. In all our disputes with God, he is in the right, and we are in the wrong.

Ezek. **18**:**30-32** The Lord will judge each of the Israelites according to his ways. On this is grounded an exhortation to repent, and to make them a new heart and a new spirit. God does not command what cannot be done, but admonishes us to do what is in our power, and to pray for what is not. Ordinances and means are appointed, directions and promises are given, that those who desire this change may seek it from God.

Chapter 19

A parable lamenting the ruin of Jehoahaz and Jehoiakim. (Ezek. **19**:**1-9**) Another describing the desolation of the people. (Ezek. **19**:**10-14**)

Ezek. **19**:**1-9** Ezekiel is to compare the kingdom of Judah to a lioness. He must compare the kings of Judah to a lion's whelps; they were cruel and oppressive to their own subjects. The righteousness of God is to be acknowledged, when those who have terrified and enslaved others, are themselves terrified and enslaved. When professors of religion form connexions with ungodly persons, their children usually grow up following after the maxims and fashions of a wicked world. Advancement to authority discovers the ambition and selfishness of men's hearts; and those who spend their lives in mischief, generally end them by violence.

Ezek. **19**:**10-14** Jerusalem was a vine, flourishing and fruitful. This vine is now destroyed, though not plucked up by the roots. She has by wickedness made herself like tinder to the sparks of God's wrath, so that her own branches serve as fuel to burn her. Blessed be God, one Branch of the vine here alluded to, is not only become a strong rod for the sceptre of those that rule, but is Himself the true and living Vine. This shall be for a rejoicing to all the chosen people of God throughout all generations.

Chapter 20

The elders of Israel are reminded of the idolatry in Egypt. (Ezek. **20**:**1-9**) In the wilderness. (Ezek. **20**:**10-26**) In Canaan. (Ezek. **20**:**27-32**) God promises to pardon and restore them. (Ezek. **20**:**33-44**) Prophecy against Jerusalem. (Ezek. **20**:**45-49**)

Ezek. **20**:**1-9**. Those hearts are wretchedly hardened which ask God leave to go on in sin, and that even when suffering for it; see Ezek. **20**:**32**. God is justly angry with those who are resolved to go on still in their trespasses. Cause the people to know the evil deeds of their fathers, that they may see how righteous it was with God to cut them off.

Ezek. **20**:**10-26**. The history of Israel in the wilderness is referred to in the new Testament as well as in the Old, for warning. God did great things for them. He gave them the law, and revived the ancient keeping of the sabbath day. Sabbaths are privileges; they are signs of our being his people. If we do the duty of the day, we shall find, to our comfort, it is the Lord that makes us holy, that is, truly happy, here; and prepares us to be happy, that is, perfectly holy, hereafter. The Israelites rebelled, and were left to the judgments they brought upon themselves. God sometimes makes sin to be its own punishment, yet he is not the Author of sin: there needs no more to make men miserable, than to give them up to their own evil desires and passions.

Ezek. **20**:**27-32** The Jews persisted in rebellion after they settled in the land of Canaan. And these elders seem to have thought of uniting with the heathen. We make nothing by our profession if it be but a profession. There is nothing got by sinful compliances; and the carnal projects of hypocrites will stand them in no stead.

Ezek. **20**:**33-44** The wicked Israelites, notwithstanding they follow the sinful ways of other nations, shall not mingle with them in their prosperity, but shall be separated from them for destruction. There is no shaking off God's dominion; and those who will not yield to the power of his grace, shall sink under the power of his wrath. But not one of God's jewels shall be lost in the lumber of this world. He will bring the jews to the land of Israel again; and will give them true repentance. They will be overcome with his kindness: the more we know of God's holiness, the more we see the hateful nature of sin. Those who remain unaffected amidst means of grace, and would live without Christ, like the world around them, may be sure it is the way to destruction.

Ezek. **20**:**45-49** Judah and Jerusalem had been full of people, as a forest of trees, but empty of fruit. God's word prophesies against those who bring not forth the fruits of righteousness. When He will ruin a nation, who or what can save it? The plainest truths were as parables to the people. It is common for those who will not be wrought upon by the word, to blame it.

Chapter 21

The ruin of Judah under the emblem of a sharp sword. (Ezek. **21**:**1-17**) The approach of the king of Babylon described. (Ezek. **21**:**18-27**) The destruction of the Ammonites. (Ezek. **21**:**28-32**)

Ezek. **21**:**1-17** Here is an explanation of the parable in the last chapter. It is declared that the Lord was about to cut off Jerusalem and the whole land, that all might know it was his decree against a wicked and rebellious people. It behoves those who denounce the awful wrath of God against sinners, to show that they do not desire the woful day. The example of Christ teaches us to lament over those whose ruin we declare. Whatever instruments God uses in executing his judgments, he will strengthen them according to the service they are employed in. The sword glitters to the terror of those against whom it is drawn. It is a sword to others, a rod to the people of the Lord. God is in earnest in pronouncing this sentence, and the prophet must show himself in earnest in publishing it.

Ezek. **21**:**18-27** By the Spirit of prophecy Ezekiel foresaw Nebuchadnezzar's march from Babylon, which he would determine by divination. The Lord would overturn the government of Judah, till the coming of Him whose right it is. This seems to foretell the overturnings of the Jewish nation to the present day, and the troubles of states and kingdoms, which shall make way for establishing the Messiah's kingdom throughout the earth. The Lord secretly leads all to adopt his wise designs. And in the midst of the most tremendous warnings of wrath, we still hear of mercy, and some mention of Him through whom mercy is shown to sinful men.

Ezek. **21**:**28-32** The diviners of the Ammonites made false prophecies of victory. They would never recover their power, but in time would be wholly forgotten. Let us be thankful to be employed as instruments of mercy; let us use our understandings in doing good;

and let us stand aloof from men who are only skilful to destroy.

Chapter 22

The sins of Jerusalem. (Ezek. **22**:**1-16**) Israel is condemned as dross. (Ezek. **22**:**17-22**) As the corruption is general, so shall be the punishment. (Ezek. **22**:**23-31**)

Ezek. **22**:**1-16** The prophet is to judge the bloody city; the city of bloods. Jerusalem is so called, because of her crimes. The sins which Jerusalem stands charged with, are exceeding sinful. Murder, idolatry, disobedience to parents, oppression and extortion, profanation of the sabbath and holy things, seventh commandment sins, lewdness and adultery. Unmindfulness of God was at the bottom of all this wickedness. Sinners provoke God because they forget him. Jerusalem has filled the measure of her sins. Those who give up themselves to be ruled by their lusts, will justly be given up to be portioned by them. Those who resolve to be their own masters, let them expect no other happiness than their own hands can furnish; and a miserable portion it will prove.

Ezek. **22**:**17-22** Israel, compared with other nations, had been as the gold and silver compared with baser metals. But they were now as the refuse that is consumed in the furnace, or thrown away when the silver is refined. Sinners, especially backsliding professors, are, in God's account, useless and fit for nothing. When God brings his own people into the furnace, he sits by them as the refiner by his gold, to see that they are not continued there any longer than is fitting and needful. The dross shall be wholly separated, and the good metal purified. Let those who suffer pains, or lingering sickness, and find that their hearts can scarcely bear these light and momentary afflictions, take warning to flee from the wrath to come; for if these trials are not sanctified by the power of the Holy Spirit, to the cleansing their hearts and hands from sin, far worse things will come upon them.

Ezek. **22**:**23-31** All orders and degrees of men had helped to fill the measure of the nation's guilt. The people that had any power abused it, and even the buyers and sellers find some way to oppress one another. It bodes ill to a people when judgments are breaking in upon them, and the spirit of prayer is restrained. Let all who fear God, unite to promote his truth and righteousness; as wicked men of every rank and profession plot together to run them down.

Chapter 23

A history of the apostacy of God's people from him, and the aggravation thereof.

In this parable, Samaria and Israel bear the name Aholah, "her own tabernacle;" because the places of worship those kingdoms had, were of their own devising. Jerusalem and Judah bear the name of Aholibah, "my tabernacle is in her," because their temple was the place which God himself had chosen, to put his name there. The language and figures are according to those times. Will not such humbling representations of nature keep open perpetual repentance and sorrow in the soul, hiding pride from our eyes, and taking us from self-righteousness? Will it not also prompt the soul to look to God continually for grace, that by his Holy Spirit we may mortify the deeds of the body, and live in holy conversation and godliness?

Chapter 24

The fate of Jerusalem. (Ezek. **24**:**1-14**) The extent of the sufferings of the Jews. (Ezek. **24**:**15-27**)

Ezek. **24**:**1-14** The pot on the fire represented Jerusalem besieged by the Chaldeans: all orders and ranks were within the walls, prepared as a prey for the enemy. They ought to have put away their transgressions, as the scum, which rises by the heat of the fire, is taken from the top of the pot. But they grew worse, and their miseries increased. Jerusalem was to be levelled with the ground. The time appointed for the punishment of wicked men may seem to come slowly, but it will come surely. It is sad to think how many there are, on whom ordinances and providences are all lost.

Ezek. **24**:**15-27** Though mourning for the dead is a duty, yet it must be kept under by religion and right reason: we must not sorrow as men that have no hope. Believers must not copy the language and expressions of those who know not God. The people asked the meaning of the sign. God takes from them all that was dearest to them. And as Ezekiel wept not for his affliction, so neither should they weep for theirs. Blessed be God, we need not pine away under our afflictions; for should all comforts fail, and all sorrows be united, yet the broken heart and the mourner's prayer are always acceptable before God.

Chapter 25

Judgments against the Ammonites. (Ezek. **25**:**1-7**) Against the Moabites, Edomites, and Philistines. (Ezek. **25**:**8-17**)

Ezek. **25**:**1-7**. It is wicked to be glad at the calamities of any, especially of God's people; it is a sin for which he will surely reckon. God will make it appear that he is the God of Israel, though he suffers them for a time to be captives in Babylon. It is better to know Him, and to be poor, than to be rich and ignorant of him.

Ezek. **25**:**8-17** Though one event seem to the righteous and wicked, it is vastly different. Those who glory in any other defence and protection than the Divine power, providence, and promise, will, sooner or later, be ashamed of their glorying. Those who will not leave it to God to take vengeance for them, may expect that he will take vengeance on them. The equity of the Lord's judgments is to be observed, when he not only avenges injuries upon those that did them, but by those against whom they were done. Those who treasure up old hatred, and watch for the opportunity of manifesting it, are treasuring up for themselves wrath against the day of wrath.

Chapter 26

A prophecy against Tyre.

Ezek. **26**:**1-14** To be secretly pleased with the death or decay of others, when we are likely to get by it; or with their fall, when we may thrive upon it, is a sin that easily besets us, yet is not thought so bad as really it is. But it comes from a selfish, covetous principle, and from that love of the world as our happiness, which the love of God expressly forbids. He often blasts the projects of those who would raise themselves on the ruin of others. The maxims most current in the trading world, are directly opposed to the law of God. But he will show himself against the money-loving, selfish traders, whose hearts, like those of Tyre, are hardened by the love of riches. Men have little cause to glory in things which stir up the envy and rapacity of others, and which are continually shifting from one to another; and in getting, keeping, and spending which, men provoke that God whose wrath turns joyous cities into ruinous heaps.

Ezek. **26**:**15-21** See how high, how great Tyre had been. See how low Tyre is made. The fall of others should awaken us out of security. Every discovery of the fulfilment of a Scripture prophecy, is like a miracle to confirm our faith. All that is earthly is vanity and vexation.

Those who now have the most established prosperity, will soon be out of sight and forgotten.

Chapter 27

The merchandise of Tyre. (Ezek. **27**:**1-25**) Its fall and ruin. (Ezek. **27**:**26-36**)

Ezek. **27**:**1-25** Those who live at ease are to be lamented, if they are not prepared for trouble. Let none reckon themselves beautified, any further than they are sanctified. The account of the trade of Tyre intimates, that God's eye is upon men when employed in worldly business. Not only when at church, praying and hearing, but when in markets and fairs, buying and selling. In all our dealings we should keep a conscience void of offence. God, as the common Father of mankind, makes one country abound in one commodity, and another in another, serviceable to the necessity or to the comfort and ornament of human life. See what a blessing trade and merchandise are to mankind, when followed in the fear of God. Besides necessaries, an abundance of things are made valuable only by custom; yet God allows us to use them. But when riches increase, men are apt to set their hearts upon them, and forget the Lord, who gives power to get wealth.

Ezek. **27**:**26-36** The most mighty and magnificent kingdoms and states, sooner or later, come down. Those who make creatures their confidence, and rest their hopes upon them, will fall with them: happy are those who have the God of Jacob for their Help, and whose hope is in the Lord their God, who lives for ever. Those who engage in trade should learn to conduct their business according to God's word. Those who possess wealth should remember they are the Lord's stewards, and should use his goods in doing good to all. Let us seek first the kingdom of God and his righteousness.

Chapter 28

The sentence against the prince or king of Tyre. (Ezek. **28**:**1-19**) The fall of Zidon. (Ezek. **28**:**20-23**) The restoration of Israel. (Ezek. **28**:**24-26**)

Ezek. **28**:**1-19** Ethbaal, or Ithobal, was the prince or king of Tyre; and being lifted up with excessive pride, he claimed Divine honours. Pride is peculiarly the sin of our fallen nature. Nor can any wisdom, except that which the Lord gives, lead to happiness in this world or in that which is to come. The haughty prince of Tyre thought he was able to protect his people by his own power, and considered himself as equal to the inhabitants of heaven. If it were possible to dwell in the garden of Eden, or even to enter heaven, no solid happiness could be enjoyed without a humble, holy, and spiritual mind. Especially all spiritual pride is of the devil. Those who indulge therein must expect to perish.

Ezek. **28**:**20-26**. The Zidonians were borderers upon the land of Israel, and they might have learned to glorify the Lord; but, instead of that, they seduced Israel to the worship of their idols. War and pestilence are God's messengers; but he will be glorified in the restoring his people to their former safety and prosperity. God will cure them of their sins, and ease them of their troubles. This promise will at length fully come to pass in the heavenly Canaan: when all the saints shall be gathered together, every thing that offends shall be removed, all griefs and fears for ever banished. Happy, then, is the church of God, and every living member of it, though poor, afflicted, and despised; for the Lord will display his truth, power, and mercy, in the salvation and happiness of his redeemed people.

Chapter 29

The desolation of Egypt. (Ezek. **29**:**1-16**) Also a promise of mercy to Israel. (Ezek. **29**:**17-21**)

Ezek. **29**:**1-16** Worldly, carnal minds pride themselves in their property, forgetting that whatever we have, we received it from God, and should use it for God. Why, then, do we boast? Self is the great idol which all the world worships, in contempt of God and his sovereignty. God can force men out of that in which they are most secure and easy. Such a one, and all that cleave to him, shall perish together. Thus end men's pride, presumption, and carnal security. The Lord is against those who do harm to his people, and still more against those who lead them into sin. Egypt shall be a kingdom again, but it shall be the basest of the kingdoms; it shall have little wealth and power. History shows the complete fulfilment of this prophecy. God, not only in justice, but in wisdom and goodness to us, breaks the creature-stays on which we lean, that they may be no more our confidence.

Ezek. **29**:**17-21** The besiegers of Tyre obtained little plunder. But when God employs ambitious or covetous men, he will recompense them according to the desires of their hearts; for every man shall have his reward. God had mercy in store for the house of Israel soon after. The history of nations best explains ancient prophecies. All events fulfil the Scriptures. Thus, in the deepest scenes of adversity, the Lord sows the seed of our future prosperity. Happy are those who desire his favour, grace, and image; they will delight in his service, and not covet any earthly recompence; and the blessings they have chosen shall be sure to them for ever.

Chapter 30

A prophecy against Egypt. (Ezek. **30**:**1-19**) Another. (Ezek. **30**:**20-26**)

Ezek. **30**:**1-19** The prophecy of the destruction of Egypt is very full. Those who take their lot with God's enemies, shall be with them in punishment. The king of Babylon and his army shall be instruments of this destruction. God often makes one wicked man a scourge to another. No place in the land of Egypt shall escape the fury of the Chaldeans. The Lord is known by the judgments he executes. Yet these are only present effects of the Divine displeasure, not worthy of our fear, compared with the wrath to come, from which Jesus delivers his people.

Ezek. **30**:**20-26** Egypt shall grow weaker and weaker. If lesser judgments do not prevail to humble and reform sinners, God will send greater. God justly breaks that power which is abused, either to put wrongs upon people, or to put cheats upon them. Babylon shall grow stronger. In vain do men endeavour to bind up the arm the Lord is pleased to break, and to strengthen those whom he will bring down. Those who disregard the discoveries of his truth and mercy, shall know his power and justice, in the punishment for their sins.

Chapter 31

The glory of Assyria. (Ezek. **31**:**1-9**) Its fall, and the like for Egypt. (Ezek. **31**:**10-18**)

Ezek. **31**:**1-9** The falls of others, both into sin and ruin, warn us not to be secure or high-minded. The prophet is to show an instance of one whom the king of Egypt resembled in greatness, the Assyrian, compared to a stately cedar. Those who excel others, make themselves the objects of envy; but the blessings of the heavenly paradise are not liable to such alloy. The utmost security that any creature can give, is but like the shadow of a tree, a scanty and slender protection. But let us flee to God for protection, there we shall be safe. His hand must be owned in the rising of the great men of the earth, and we must not envy them. Though worldly people may seem to have firm prosperity, yet it only seems so.

Ezek. **31**:**10-18** The king of Egypt resembled the king of Assyria in his greatness: here we see he resembles him in his pride. And he shall resemble him in his fall. His own sin brings his ruin. None of our comforts are ever lost, but what have been a thousand times forfeited. When great men fall, many fall with them, as many have fallen before them. The fall of proud men is for warning to others, to keep them humble. See how low Pharaoh lies; and see what all his pomp and pride are come to. It is best to be a lowly tree of righteousness, yielding fruit to the glory of God, and to the good of men. The wicked man is often seen flourishing like the cedar, and spreading like the green bay tree, but he soon passes away, and his place is no more found. Let us then mark the perfect man, and behold the upright, for the end of that man is peace.

Chapter 32

The fall of Egypt. (Ezek. **32**:**1-16**) It is like that of other nations. (Ezek. **32**:**17-32**)

Ezek. **32**:**1-16** It becomes us to weep and tremble for those who will not weep and tremble for themselves. Great oppressors are, in God's account, no better than beasts of prey. Those who admire the pomp of this world, will wonder at the ruin of that pomp; which to those who know the vanity of all things here below, is no surprise. When others are ruined by sin, we have to fear, knowing ourselves guilty. The instruments of the desolation are formidable. And the instances of the desolation are frightful. The waters of Egypt shall run like oil, which signifies there should be universal sadness and heaviness upon the whole nation. God can soon empty those of this world's goods who have the greatest fulness of them. By enlarging the matters of our joy, we increase the occasions of our sorrow. How weak and helpless, as to God, are the most powerful of mankind! The destruction of Egypt was a type of the destruction of the enemies of Christ.

Ezek. **32**:**17-32** Divers nations are mentioned as gone down to the grave before Egypt, who are ready to give her a scornful reception; these nations had been lately ruined and wasted. But though Judah and Jerusalem were about this time ruined and laid waste, yet they are not mentioned here. Though they suffered the same affliction, and by the same hand, yet the kind design for which they were afflicted, and the mercy God reserved for them, altered its nature. It was not to them a going down to the pit, as it was to the heathen. Pharaoh shall see, and be comforted; but the comfort wicked ones have after death, is poor comfort, not real, but only in fancy. The view this prophecy gives of ruined states shows something of this present world, and the empire of death in it. Come and see the calamitous state of human life. As if men did not die fast enough, they are ingenious at finding out ways to destroy one another. Also of the other world; though the destruction of nations as such, seems chiefly intended, here is plain allusion to the everlasting ruin of impenitent sinners. How are men deceived by Satan! What are the objects they pursue through scenes of bloodshed, and their many sins? Surely man disquiets himself in vain, whether he pursues wealth, fame, power, or pleasure. The hour cometh, when all that are in their graves shall hear the voice of Christ, and shall come forth; those that have done good to the resurrection of life, and those that have done evil to the resurrection of damnation.

Chapter 33

Ezekiel's duty as a watchman. (Ezek. **33**:**1-9**) He is to vindicate the Divine government. (Ezek. **33**:**10-20**) The desolation of Judea. (Ezek. **33**:**21-29**) Judgments on the mockers of the prophets. (Ezek. **33**:**30-33**)

Ezek. **33**:**1-9** The prophet is a watchman to the house of Israel. His business is to warn sinners of their misery and danger. He must warn the wicked to turn from their way, that they may live. If souls perish through his neglect of duty, he brings guilt upon himself. See what those have to answer for, who make excuses for sin, flatter sinners, and encourage them to believe they shall have peace, though they go on. How much wiser are men in their temporal than in their spiritual concerns! They set watchmen to guard their houses, and sentinels to warn of the enemies' approach, but where the everlasting happiness or misery of the soul is at stake, they are offended if ministers obey their Master's command, and give a faithful warning; they would rather perish, listening to smooth things.

Ezek. **33**:**10-20** Those who despaired of finding mercy with God, are answered with a solemn declaration of God's readiness to show mercy. The ruin of the city and state was determined, but that did not relate to the final state of persons. God says to the righteous, that he shall surely live. But many who have made profession, have been ruined by proud confidence in themselves. Man trusts to his own righteousness, and presuming on his own sufficiency, he is brought to commit iniquity. If those who have lived a wicked life repent and forsake their wicked ways, they shall be saved. Many such amazing and blessed changes have been wrought by the power of Divine grace. When there is a settled separation between a man and sin, there shall no longer be a separation between him and God.

Ezek. **33**:**21-29** Those are unteachable indeed, who do not learn their dependence upon God, when all creature-comforts fail. Many claim an interest in the peculiar blessings to true believers, while their conduct proves them enemies of God. They call this groundless presumption strong faith, when God's testimony declares them entitled to his threatenings, and nothing else.

Ezek. **33**:**30-33** Unworthy and corrupt motives often lead men to the places where the word of God is faithfully preached. Many come to find somewhat to oppose: far more come of curiosity or mere habit. Men may have their hearts changed. But whether men hear or forbear, they will know by the event that a servant of God has been among them. All who will not know the worth of mercies by the improvement of them, will justly be made to know their worth by the want of them.

Chapter 34

The rulers reproved. (Ezek. **34**:**1-6**) The people are to be restored to their own land. (Ezek. **34**:**7-16**) The kingdom of Christ. (Ezek. **34**:**17-31**)

Ezek. **34**:**1-6** The people became as sheep without a shepherd, were given up as a prey to their enemies, and the land was utterly desolated. No rank or office can exempt from the reproofs of God's word, men who neglect their duty, and abuse the trust reposed in them.

Ezek. **34**:**7-16** The Lord declared that he intended mercy towards the scattered flock. Doubtless this, in the first place, had reference to the restoration of the Jews. It also represented the good Shepherd's tender care of the souls of his people. He finds them in their days of darkness and ignorance, and brings them to his fold. He comes to their relief in times of persecution and temptation. He leads them in the ways of righteousness, and causes them to rest on his love and faithfulness. The proud and self-sufficient, are enemies of the true gospel and of believers; against such we must guard. He has rest for disquieted saints, and terror for presumptuous sinners.

Ezek. **34**:**17-31** The whole nation seemed to be the Lord's flock, yet they were very different characters; but he knew how to distinguish between them. By good pastures and deep waters, are meant the pure word of God and the dispensing of justice. The latter **verses**, **23-31**, prophesy of Christ, and of the most glorious times of his church on earth. Under Him, as the good Shepherd, the church would be a blessing to all around. Christ, though excellent in himself, was as a tender plant out of a dry ground. Being the Tree of life, bearing all the fruits of salvation, he yields spiritual food to the souls of his people. Our constant desire and prayer should be, that there may be showers of blessings in every place where the truth of Christ is preached; and that all who profess the gospel may be filled with fruits of righteousness.

Chapter 35

A prophecy against Edom.

Ezek. **35**:**1-9** All who have God against them, have the word of God against them. Those that have a constant hatred to God and his people, as the carnal mind has, can only expect to be made desolate for ever.

Ezek. **35**:**10-15** When we see the vanity of the world in the disappointments, losses, and crosses, which others meet with, instead of showing ourselves greedy of worldly things, we should sit more loose to them. In the multitude of words, not one is unknown to God; not the most idle word; and the most daring is not above his rebuke. In the destruction of the enemies of the church, God designs his own glory; and we may be sure that he will not come short of his design. And when the fulness of the Jews and Gentiles shall come into the church, all antichristian opposers shall be destroyed.

Chapter 36

The land shall be delivered from heathen oppressors. (Ezek. **36**:**1-15**) The people are reminded of former sins, and promised deliverance. (Ezek. **36**:**16-24**) Also holiness, and gospel blessings. (Ezek. **36**:**25-38**)

Ezek. **36**:**1-15** Those who put contempt and reproach on God's people, will have them turned on themselves. God promises favour to his Israel. We have no reason to complain, if the more unkind men are, the more kind God is. They shall come again to their own border. It was a type of the heavenly Canaan, of which all God's children are heirs, and into which they all shall be brought together. And when God returns in mercy to a people who return to him in duty, all their grievances will be set right. The full completion of this prophecy must be in some future event.

Ezek. **36**:**16-24** The restoration of that people, being typical of our redemption by Christ, shows that the end aimed at in our salvation is the glory of God. The sin of a people defiles their land; renders it abominable to God, and uncomfortable to themselves. God's holy name is his great name; his holiness is his greatness, nor does any thing else make a man truly great.

Ezek. **36**:**25-38** Water is an emblem of the cleansing our polluted souls from sin. But no water can do more than take away the filth of the flesh. Water seems in general the sacramental sign of the sanctifying influences of the Holy Ghost; yet this is always connected with the atoning blood of Christ. When the latter is applied by faith to the conscience, to cleanse it from evil works, the former is always applied to the powers of the soul, to purify it from the pollution of sin. All that have an interest in the new covenant, have a new heart and a new spirit, in order to their walking in newness of life. God would give a heart of flesh, a soft and tender heart, complying with his holy will. Renewing grace works as great a change in the soul, as the turning a dead stone into living flesh. God will put his Spirit within, as a Teacher, Guide, and Sanctifier. The promise of God's grace to fit us for our duty, should quicken our constant care and endeavour to do our duty. These are promises to be pleaded by, and will be fulfilled to, all true believers in every age.

Chapter 37

God restores dried bones to life. (Ezek. **37**:**1-14**) The whole house of Israel is represented as enjoying the blessings of Christ's kingdom. (Ezek. **37**:**15-28**)

Ezek. **37**:**1-14** No created power could restore human bones to life. God alone could cause them to live. Skin and flesh covered them, and the wind was then told to blow upon these bodies; and they were restored to life. The wind was an emblem of the Spirit of God, and represented his quickening powers. The vision was to encourage the desponding Jews; to predict both their restoration after the captivity, and also their recovery from their present and long-continued dispersion. It was also a clear intimation of the resurrection of the dead; and it represents the power and grace of God, in the conversion of the most hopeless sinners to himself. Let us look to Him who will at last open our graves, and bring us forth to judgment, that He may now deliver us from sin, and put his Spirit within us, and keep us by his power, through faith, unto salvation.

Ezek. **37**:**15-28** This emblem was to show the people, that the Lord would unite Judah and Israel. Christ is the true David, Israel's King of old; and those whom he makes willing in the day of his power, he makes to walk in his judgments, and to keep his statutes. Events yet to come will further explain this prophecy. Nothing has more hindered the success of the gospel than divisions. Let us study to keep the unity of the Spirit in the bond of peace; let us seek for Divine grace to keep us from detestable things; and let us pray that all nations may be obedient and happy subjects of the Son of David, that the Lord may be our God, and we may be his people for evermore.

Chapter 38

The army and malice of Gog. (Ezek. **38**:**1-13**) God's judgments. (Ezek. **38**:**14-23**)

Ezek. **38**:**1-13** These events will be in the latter days. It is supposed these enemies will come together to invade the land of Judea, and God will defeat them. God not only sees who are now the enemies of his church, but he foresees who will be so, and lets them know by his word that he is against them; though they join together, the wicked shall not be unpunished.

Ezek. **38**:**14-23** The enemy should make a formidable descent upon the land of Israel. When Israel dwell safely under the Divine protection, shalt not thou be made to know it by finding that endeavours to destroy them are made in vain? Promises of security are treasured up in the word of God, against the troubles and dangers the church may be brought into in the latter days. In the destruction of sinners, God makes it appear that he is a great and holy God. We should desire and pray daily. Father, glorify thine own name.

Chapter 39

The destruction of Gog. (Ezek. **39**:**1-10**) Its extent. (Ezek. **39**:**11-22**) Israel again favoured. (Ezek. **39**:**23-29**)

Ezek. **39**:**1-10** The Lord will make the most careless and hardened transgressors know his holy name, either by his righteous anger, or by the riches of his mercy and grace. The weapons formed against Zion shall not prosper. Though this prophecy is to be fulfilled in the latter days, it is certain. From the language used, it seems that the army of Gog will be destroyed by miracle.

Ezek. **39**:**11-22** How numerous the enemies which God destroyed for the defence of his people Israel! Times of great deliverances should be times of reformation. Every one should help the utmost he can, toward cleansing the land from reproach. Sin is an enemy every man should strive against. Those engaged in public work, especially of cleansing and reforming a land, ought to be men who will go through with what they undertake, who will be always employed. When good work is to be done, every one should further it. Having received special favours from God, let us cleanse ourselves from all evil. It is a work which will require persevering diligence, that search may be made into the secret recesses of sin. The judgments of the Lord, brought upon sin and sinners, are a sacrifice to the justice of God, and a feast to the faith and hope of God's people. See how evil pursues sinners, even after death. After all that ambitious and covetous men do and look for, "a place of graves" is all the Lord gives them on earth, while their guilty souls are doomed to misery in another world.

Ezek. **39**:**23-29** When the Lord shall have mercy on the whole house of Israel, by converting them to Christianity, and when they shall have borne the shame of being cast off for their sins, then the nations shall learn to know, worship, and serve him. Then Israel also shall know the Lord, as revealed in and by Christ. Past events do not answer to these predictions. The pouring out of the Spirit is a pledge that God's favour will continue. He will hide his face no more from those on whom he has poured out his Spirit. When we pray that God would never cast us from his presence, we must as earnestly pray that, in order thereto, he would never take his Holy Spirit from us.

Chapter 40

The Vision of the Temple.

Here is a vision, beginning at Ezek. **40**, and continued to the end of the book, Ezek. **48**, which is justly looked upon to be one of the most difficult portions in all the book of God. When we despair to be satisfied as to any difficulty we meet with, let us bless God that our salvation does not depend upon it, but that things necessary are plain enough; and let us wait till God shall reveal even this unto us. This chapter describes two outward courts of the temple. Whether the personage here mentioned was the Son of God, or a created angel, is not clear. But Christ is both our Altar and our Sacrifice, to whom we must look with faith in all approaches to God; and he is Salvation in the midst of the earth, Ps. **74**:**12**, to be looked unto from all quarters.

Chapter 41

After the prophet had observed the courts, he was brought to the temple. If we attend to instructions in the plainer parts of religion, and profit by them, we shall be led further into an acquaintance with the mysteries of the kingdom of heaven.

Chapter 42

In this chapter are described the priests' chambers, their use, and the dimensions of the holy mount on which the temple stood. These chambers were many. Jesus said, In my Father's house are many mansions: in his house on earth there are many; multitudes, by faith, are lodging in his sanctuary, and yet there is room. These chambers, though private, were near the temple. Our religious services in our chambers, must prepare for public devotions, and further us in improving them, as our opportunities are.

Chapter 43

After Ezekiel had surveyed the temple of God, he had a vision of the glory of God. When Christ crucified, and the things freely given to us of God, through Him, are shown to us by the Holy Ghost, they make us ashamed for our sins. This frame of mind prepares us for fuller discoveries of the mysteries of redeeming love; and the whole of the Scriptures should be opened and applied, that men may see their sins, and repent of them. We are not now to offer any atoning sacrifices, for by one offering Christ has perfected for ever those that are sanctified, Heb. **10**:**14**; but the sprinkling of his blood is needful in all our approaches to God the Father. Our best services can be accepted only as sprinkled with the blood which cleanses from all sin.

Chapter 44

This chapter contains ordinances relative to the true priests. The prince evidently means Christ, and the words in Ezek. **44**:**2**, may remind us that no other can enter heaven, the true sanctuary, as Christ did; namely, by virtue of his own excellency, and his personal holiness, righteousness, and strength. He who is the Brightness of Jehovah's glory entered by his own holiness; but that way is shut to the whole human race, and we all must enter as sinners, by faith in his blood, and by the power of his grace.

Chapter 45

In the period here foretold, the worship and the ministers of God will be provided for; the princes will rule with justice, as holding their power under Christ; the people will live in peace, ease, and godliness. These things seem to be represented in language taken from the customs of the times in which the prophet wrote. Christ is our Passover that is sacrificed for us: we celebrate the memorial of that sacrifice, and feast upon it, triumphing in our deliverance out of the Egyptian slavery of sin, and our preservation from the destroying sword of Divine justice, in the Lord's supper, which is our passover feast; as the whole Christian life is, and must be, the feast of the unleavened bread of sincerity and truth.

Chapter 46

The ordinances of worship for the prince and for the people, are here described, and the gifts the prince may bestow on his sons and servants. Our Lord has directed us to do many duties, but he has also left many things to our choice, that those who delight in his commandments may abound therein to his glory, without entangling their own consciences, or prescribing rules unfit for others; but we must never omit our daily worship, nor neglect to apply the sacrifice of the Lamb of God to our souls, for pardon, peace, and salvation.

Chapter 47

These waters signify the gospel of Christ, which went forth from Jerusalem, and spread into the countries about; also the gifts and powers of the Holy Ghost which accompanied it, by virtue of which is spread far, and produced blessed effects. Christ is the Temple; and he is the Door; from him the living waters flow, out of his pierced side. They are increasing waters. Observe the progress of the gospel in the world, and the process of the work of grace in the heart; attend the motions of the blessed Spirit under Divine guidance. If we search into the things of God, we find some things plain and easy to be understood, as the waters that were but to the ankles; others more difficult, which require a deeper search, as the waters to the knees, or the loins; and some quite beyond our reach, which we cannot penetrate; but must, as St. Paul did, adore the depth, Rom. **11**. It is wisdom to begin with that which is most easy, before we proceed to that which is dark and hard to be understood. The promises of the sacred word, and the privileges of believers, as shed abroad in their souls by the quickening Spirit, abound where the gospel is preached; they nourish and delight the souls of men; they never fade nor wither, nor are exhausted. Even the leaves serve as medicines to the soul: the warnings and reproofs of the word, though less pleasant than Divine consolations, tend to heal the diseases of the soul. All who believe in Christ, and are united to him by his sanctifying Spirit, will share the privileges of Israelites. There is room in the church, and in heaven, for all who seek the blessings of that new covenant of which Christ is Mediator.

Chapter 48

Here is a description of the several portions of the land belonging to each tribe. In gospel times, behold all things are become new. Much is wrapped up in emblems and numbers. This method God has used to state mysterious truths in his word, not to be more clearly revealed till the proper time and season. But into the church of Christ, both in its state of warfare and triumph, there is free access by faith, from every side. Christ has opened the kingdom of heaven for all believers. Whoever will, may come, and take of the water of life, of the tree of life, freely. The Lord is there, in his church, to be nigh unto them in all they call upon him for. This is true of every real Christian; whatever soul has in it a living principle of grace, it may truly be said, The Lord is there. May we be found citizens of this holy city, and act agreeably to that character; and have the benefit of the Lord's presence with us, in life, in death, and for evermore.

Daniel

Daniel was of noble birth, if not one of the royal family of Judah. He was carried captive to Babylon in the fourth year of Jehoiachin, B. C. **606**, when a youth. He was there taught the learning of the Chaldeans, and held high offices, both under the Babylonian and Persian empires. He was persecuted for his religion, but was miraculously delivered; and lived to a great age, as he must have been about ninety-four years old at the time of the last of his visions. The book of Daniel is partly historical, relating various circumstances which befel himself and the Jews, at Babylon; but is chiefly prophetical, detailing visions and prophecies which foretell numerous important events relative to the four great empires of the world, the coming and death of the Messiah, the restoration of the Jews, and the conversion of the Gentiles. Though there are considerable difficulties in explaining the prophetical meaning of some passages in this book, we always find encouragement to faith and hope, examples worthy of imitation, and something to direct our thoughts to Christ Jesus upon the cross and on his glorious throne.

Chapter 1

The captivity of Daniel and his companions. (Dan. **1**:**1**-**7**) Their refusal to eat the king's meat. (Dan. **1**:**8**-**16**) Their improvement in wisdom. (Dan. **1**:**17**-**21**)

Dan. **1**:**1**-**7** Nebuchadnezzar, king of Babylon, in the first year of his reign, took Jerusalem, and carried whom and what he pleased away. From this first captivity, most think the seventy years are to be dated. It is the interest of princes to employ wise men; and it is their wisdom to find out and train up such. Nebuchadnezzar ordered that these chosen youths should be taught. All their Hebrew names had something of God in them; but to make them forget the God of their fathers, the Guide of their youth, the heathen gave them names that savoured of idolatry. It is painful to reflect how often public education tends to corrupt the principles and morals.

Dan. **1**:**8**-**16** The interest we think we make for ourselves, we must acknowledge to be God's gift. Daniel was still firm to his religion. Whatever they called him, he still held fast the spirit of an Israelite. These youths scrupled concerning the meat, lest it should be sinful. When God's people are in Babylon they need take special care that they partake not of her sins. It is much to the praise of young people, not to covet or seek the delights of sense. Those who would excel in wisdom and piety, must learn betimes to keep the body under. Daniel avoided defiling himself with sin; and we should more fear that than any outward trouble. It is easier to keep temptation at a distance, than to resist it when near. And we cannot better improve our interest in any with whom we have found favour, than to use it to keep us from sin. People will not believe the benefit of avoiding excess, and of a spare diet, nor how much they contribute to the health of the body, unless they try. Conscientious temperance will always do more, even for the comfort of this life, than sinful indulgence.

Dan. **1**:**17**-**21** Daniel and his fellows kept to their religion; and God rewarded them with eminence in learning. Pious young persons should endeavour to do better than their fellows in useful things; not for the praise of man, but for the honour of the gospel, and that they may be qualified for usefulness. And it is well for a country, and for the honour of a prince, when he is able to judge who are best fitted to serve him, and prefers them on that account. Let young men steadily attend to this chapter; and let all remember that God will honour those who honour him, but those who despise him shall be lightly esteemed.

Chapter 2

Nebuchadnezzar's dream. (Dan. **2**:**1**-**13**) It is revealed to Daniel. (Dan. **2**:**14**-**23**) He obtains admission to the king. (Dan. **2**:**24**-**30**) The dream and the interpretation. (Dan. **2**:**31**-**45**) Honours to Daniel and his friends. (Dan. **2**:**46**-**49**)

Dan. **2**:**1**-**13** The greatest men are most open to cares and troubles of mind, which disturb their repose in the night, while the sleep of the labouring man is sweet and sound. We know not the uneasiness of many who live in great pomp, and, as others vainly think, in pleasure also. The king said that his learned men must tell him the dream itself, or they should all be put to death as deceivers. Men are more eager to ask as to future events, than to learn the way of salvation or the path of duty; yet foreknowledge of future events increases anxiety and trouble. Those who deceived, by pretending to do what they could not do, were sentenced to death, for not being able to do what they did not pretend to.

Dan. **2**:**14**-**23** Daniel humbly prayed that God would discover to him the king's dream, and the meaning of it. Praying friends are valuable friends; and it well becomes the greatest and best men to desire the prayers of others. Let us show that we value our friends, and their prayers. They were particular in prayer. And whatever we pray for, we can expect nothing but as the gift of God's mercies. God gives us leave in prayer to tell our wants and burdens. Their plea with God was, the peril they were in. The mercy Daniel and his fellows prayed for, was bestowed. The fervent prayers of righteous men avail much. Daniel was thankful to God for making known that to him, which saved the lives of himself and his fellows. How much more should we be thankful to God, for making known the great salvation of the soul to those who are not among the worldly wise and prudent!

Dan. **2**:**24-30** Daniel takes away the king's opinion of his magicians and soothsayers. The insufficiency of creatures should drive us to the all-sufficiency of the Creator. There is One who can do that for us, and make known that to us, which none on earth can, particularly the work of redemption, and the secret designs of God's love to us therein. Daniel confirmed the king in his opinion, that the dream was of great consequence, relating to the affairs and changes of this lower world. Let those whom God has highly favoured and honoured, lay aside all opinion of their own wisdom and worthiness, that the Lord alone may be praised for the good they have and do.

Dan. **2**:**31-45** This image represented the kingdoms of the earth, that should successively rule the nations, and influence the affairs of the Jewish church. **1**. The head of gold signified the Chaldean empire, then in being. **2**. The breast and arms of silver signified the empire of the Medes and Persians. **3**. The belly and thighs of brass signified the Grecian empire, founded by Alexander. **4**. The legs and feet of iron signified the Roman empire. The Roman empire branched into ten kingdoms, as the toes of these feet. Some were weak as clay, others strong as iron. Endeavours have often been used to unite them, for strengthening the empire, but in vain. The stone cut out without hands, represented the kingdom of our Lord Jesus Christ, which should be set up in the kingdoms of the world, upon the ruins of Satan's kingdom in them. This was the Stone which the builders refused, because it was not cut out by their hands, but it is become the head stone of the corner. Of the increase of Christ's government and peace there shall be no end. The Lord shall reign, not only to the end of time, but when time and days shall be no more. As far as events have gone, the fulfilling this prophetic vision has been most exact and undeniable; future ages shall witness this Stone destroying the image, and filling the whole earth.

Dan. **2**:**46-49** It is our business to direct attention to the Lord, as the Author and Giver of every good gift. Many have thoughts of the Divine power and majesty, who do not think of serving God themselves. But all should strive, that God may be glorified, and the best interests of mankind furthered.

Chapter 3

Nebuchadnezzar's golden image. (Dan. **3**:**1-7**) Shadrach and his companions refuse to worship it. (Dan. **3**:**8-18**) They are cast into a furnace, but are miraculously preserved. (Dan. **3**:**19-27**) Nebuchadnezzar gives glory to Jehovah. (Dan. **3**:**28-30**)

Dan. **3**:**1-7** In the height of the image, about thirty yards, probably is included a pedestal, and most likely it was only covered with plates of gold, not a solid mass of that precious metal. Pride and bigotry cause men to require their subjects to follow their religion, whether right or wrong, and when worldly interest allures, and punishment overawes, few refuse. This is easy to the careless, the sensual, and the infidel, who are the greatest number; and most will go their ways. There is nothing so bad which the careless world will not be drawn to by a concert of music, or driven to by a fiery furnace. By such methods, false worship has been set up and maintained.

Dan. **3**:**8-18** True devotion calms the spirit, quiets and softens it, but superstition and devotion to false gods inflame men's passions. The matter is put into a little compass, Turn, or burn. Proud men are still ready to say, as Nebuchadnezzar, Who is the Lord, that I should fear his power? Shadrach, Meshach, and Abednego did not hesitate whether they should comply or not. Life or death were not to be considered. Those that would avoid sin, must not parley with temptation when that to which we are allured or affrighted is manifestly evil. Stand not to pause about it, but say, as Christ did, Get thee behind me, Satan. They did not contrive an evasive answer, when a direct answer was expected. Those who make their duty their main care, need not be anxious or fearful concerning the event. The faithful servants of God find him able to control and overrule all the powers armed against them. Lord, if thou wilt, thou canst. If He be for us, we need not fear what man can do unto us. God will deliver us, either from death or in death. They must obey God rather than man; they must rather suffer than sin; and must not do evil that good may come. Therefore none of these things moved them. The saving them from sinful compliance, was as great a miracle in the kingdom of grace, as the saving them out of the fiery furnace was in the kingdom of nature. Fear of man and love of the world, especially want of faith, make men yield to temptation, while a firm persuasion of the truth will deliver them from denying Christ, or being ashamed of him. We are to be meek in our replies, but we must be decided that we will obey God rather than man.

Dan. **3**:**19-27** Let Nebuchadnezzar heat his furnace as hot as he can, a few minutes will finish the torment of those cast into it; but hell-fire tortures, and yet does not kill. Those who worshipped the beast and his image, have no rest, no pause, no moment free from pain, Rev. **14**:**10**,**11**. Now was fulfilled in the letter that great promise, Is. **43**:**2**, When thou walkest through the fire, thou shalt not be burned. Leaving it to that God who preserved them in the fire, to bring them out, they walked up and down in the midst, supported and encouraged by the presence of the Son of God. Those who suffer for Christ, have his presence in their sufferings, even in the fiery furnace, and in the valley of the shadow of death. Nebuchadnezzar owns them for servants of the most high God; a God able to deliver them out of his hand. It is our God only is the consuming fire, Heb. **12**:**29**. Could we but see into the eternal world, we should behold the persecuted believer safe from the malice of his foes, while they are exposed to the wrath of God, and tormented in unquenchable fires.

Dan. **3**:**28-30** What God did for these his servants, would help to keep the Jews to their religion while in captivity, and to cure them of idolatry. The miracle brought deep convictions on Nebuchadnezzar. But no abiding change then took place in his conduct. He who preserved these pious Jews in the fiery furnace, is able to uphold us in the hour of temptation, and to keep us from falling into sin.

Chapter 4

Nebuchadnezzar acknowledges the power of Jehovah. (Dan. **4**:**1-18**) Daniel interprets his dream. (Dan. **4**:**19-27**) The fulfilment of it. (Dan. **4**:**28-37**)

Dan. **4**:**1-18** The beginning and end of this chapter lead us to hope, that Nebuchadnezzar was a monument of the power of Divine grace, and of the riches of Divine mercy. After he was recovered from his madness, he told to distant places, and wrote down for future ages, how God had justly humbled and graciously restored him. When a sinner comes to himself, he will promote the welfare of others, by making known the wondrous mercy of God. Nebuchadnezzar, before he related the Divine judgments upon him for his pride, told the warnings he had in a dream or vision. The meaning was explained to him. The person signified, was to be put down from honour, and to be deprived of the use of his reason seven years. This is surely the sorest of all temporal judgments. Whatever outward affliction God is pleased to lay upon us, we have cause to bear it patiently, and to be thankful that he continues the use of our reason, and the peace of our consciences. Yet if the Lord should see fit by such means to keep a sinner from multiplying crimes, or a believer from dishonouring his name, even the dreadful prevention would be far preferable to the evil conduct. God has determined it, as a righteous Judge, and the angels in heaven applaud. Not that the great God needs the counsel or concurrence of the angels, but it denotes the solemnity of this sentence. The demand is by the word of the holy ones, God's suffering people: when the oppressed cry to God, he will hear. Let us diligently seek blessings which can never be taken from us, and especially beware of pride and forgetfulness of God.

Dan. **4**:**19-27** Daniel was struck with amazement and terror at so heavy a judgment coming upon so great a prince, and gives advice with tenderness and respect. It is necessary, in repentance, that we not only cease to do evil, but learn to do good. Though it might not wholly prevent the judgment, yet the trouble may be longer before it comes, or shorter when it does come. And everlasting misery will be escaped by all who repent and turn to God.

Dan. **4**:**28-37** Pride and self-conceit are sins that beset great men. They are apt to take that glory to themselves which is due to God only. While the proud word was in the king's mouth, the powerful word came from God. His understanding and his memory were gone, and all the powers of the rational soul were broken. How careful we ought to be, not to do any thing which may provoke God to put us out of our senses! God resists the proud. Nebuchadnezzar would be more than a man, but God justly makes him less than a man. We may learn to believe concerning God, that the most high God lives for ever, and that his kingdom is like himself, everlasting, and universal. His power cannot be resisted. When men are brought to honour God, by confession of sin and acknowledging his sovereignty, then, and not till then, they may expect that God will honour them; not only restore them to the dignity they lost by the sin of the first Adam, but add excellent majesty to them, from the righteousness and grace of the Second Adam. Afflictions shall last no longer than till they have done the work for which they were sent. There can be no reasonable doubt that Nebuchadnezzar was a true penitent, and an accepted believer. It is thought that he did not live more than a year after his restoration. Thus the Lord knows how to abase those that walk in pride, but gives grace and consolation to the humble, broken-hearted sinner who calls upon Him.

Chapter 5

Belshazzar's impious feast; the hand-writing on the wall. (Dan. **5**:**1-9**) Daniel is sent for to interpret it. (Dan. **5**:**10-17**) Daniel warns the king of his destruction. (Dan. **5**:**18-31**)

Dan. **5**:**1-9** Belshazzar bade defiance to the judgments of God. Most historians consider that Cyrus then besieged Babylon. Security and sensuality are sad proofs of approaching ruin. That mirth is sinful indeed, which profanes sacred things; and what are many of the songs used at modern feasts better than the praises sung by the heathens to their gods! See how God struck terror upon Belshazzar and his lords. God's written word is enough to put the proudest, boldest sinner in a fright. What we see of God, the part of the hand that writes in the book of the creatures, and in the book of the Scriptures, should fill us with awful thoughts concerning that part which we do not see. If this be the finger of God, what is his arm when made bare? And what is He? The king's guilty conscience told him that he had no reason to expect any good news from heaven. God can, in a moment, make the heart of the stoutest sinner to tremble; and there needs no more than to let loose his own thoughts upon him; they will give him trouble enough. No bodily pain can equal the inward agony which sometimes seizes the sinner in the midst of mirth, carnal pleasures, and worldly pomp. Sometimes terrors cause a man to flee to Christ for pardon and peace; but many cry out for fear of wrath, who are not humbled for their sins, and who seek relief by lying vanities. The ignorance and uncertainty concerning the Holy Scriptures, shown by many who call themselves wise, only tend to drive sinners to despair, as the ignorance of these wise men did.

Dan. **5**:**10-17** Daniel was forgotten at court; he lived privately, and was then ninety years of age. Many consult servants of God on curious questions, or to explain difficult subjects, but without asking the way of salvation, or the path of duty. Daniel slighted the offer of reward. He spoke to Belshazzar as to a condemned criminal. We should despise all the gifts and rewards this world can give, did we see, as we may by faith, its end hastening on; but let us do our duty in the world, and do it all the real service we can.

Dan. **5**:**18-31** Daniel reads Belshazzar's doom. He had not taken warning by the judgments upon Nebuchadnezzar. And he had insulted God. Sinners are pleased with gods that neither see, nor hear, nor know; but they will be judged by One to whom all things are open. Daniel reads the sentence written on the wall. All this may well be applied to the doom of every sinner. At death, the sinner's days are numbered and finished; after death is the judgment, when he will be weighed in the balance, and found wanting; and after judgment the sinner will be cut asunder, and given as a prey to the devil and his angels. While these things were passing in the palace, it is considered that the army of Cyrus entered the city; and when Belshazzar was slain, a general submission followed. Soon will every impenitent sinner find the writing of God's word brought to pass upon him, whether he is weighed in the balance of the law as a self-righteous Pharisee, or in that of the gospel as a painted hypocrite.

Chapter 6

The malice of Daniel's enemies. (Dan. **6**:**1-5**) His constancy in prayer. (Dan. **6**:**6-10**) He is cast into the lion's den. (Dan. **6**:**11-17**) His miraculous preservation. (Dan. **6**:**18-24**) The decree of Darius. (Dan. **6**:**25-28**)

Dan. **6**:**1-5** We notice to the glory of God, that though Daniel was now very old, yet he was able for business, and had continued faithful to his religion. It is for the glory of God, when those who profess religion, conduct themselves so that their most watchful enemies may find no occasion for blaming them, save only in the matters of their God, in which they walk according to their consciences.

Dan. **6**:**6-10** To forbid prayer for thirty days, is, for so long, to rob God of all the tribute he has from man, and to rob man of all the comfort he has in God. Does not every man's heart direct him, when in want or distress, to call upon God? We could not live a day without God; and can men live thirty days without prayer? Yet it is to be feared that those who, without any decree forbidding them, present no hearty, serious petitions to God for more than thirty days together, are far more numerous than those who serve him continually, with humble, thankful hearts. Persecuting laws are always made on false pretences; but it does not become Christians to make bitter complaints, or to indulge in revilings. It is good to have hours for prayer. Daniel prayed openly and avowedly; and though a man of vast business, he did not think that would excuse him from daily exercises of devotion. How inexcusable are those who have but little to do in the world, yet will not do thus much for their souls! In trying times we must take heed, lest, under pretence of discretion, we are guilty of cowardice in the cause of God. All who throw away their souls, as those certainly do that live without prayer, even if it be to save their lives, at the end will be found to be fools. Nor did Daniel only pray, and not give thanks, cutting off some part of the service to make the time of danger shorter; but he performed the whole. In a word, the duty of prayer is founded upon the sufficiency of God as an almighty Creator and Redeemer, and upon our wants as sinful creatures. To Christ we must turn our eyes. Thither let the Christian look, thither let him pray, in this land of his captivity.

Dan. **6**:**11**-**17** It is no new thing for what is done faithfully, in conscience toward God, to be misrepresented as done obstinately, and in contempt of the civil powers. Through want of due thought, we often do that which afterwards, like Darius, we see cause a thousand times to wish undone again. Daniel, that venerable man, is brought as the vilest of malefactors, and is thrown into the den of lions, to be devoured, only for worshipping his God. No doubt the placing the stone was ordered by the providence of God, that the miracle of Daniel's deliverance might appear more plain; and the king sealed it with his own signet, probably lest Daniel's enemies should kill him. Let us commit our lives and souls unto God, in well-doing. We cannot place full confidence even in men whom we faithfully serve; but believers may, in all cases, be sure of the Divine favour and consolation.

Dan. **6**:**18**-**24** The best way to have a good night, is to keep a good conscience. We are sure of what the king doubted, that the servants of the living God have a Master well able to protect them. See the power of God over the fiercest creatures, and believe his power to restrain the roaring lion that goeth about continually seeking to devour. Daniel was kept perfectly safe, because he believed in his God. Those who boldly and cheerfully trust in God to protect them in the way of duty, shall always find him a present help. Thus the righteous is delivered out of trouble, and the wicked cometh in his stead. The short triumph of the wicked will end in their ruin.

Dan. **6**:**25**-**28** If we live in the fear of God, and walk according to that rule, peace shall be upon us. The kingdom, the power, and the glory, for ever, are the Lord's; but many are employed in making known his wonderful works to others, who themselves remain strangers to his saving grace. May we be doers, as well as believers of his word, least at the last we should be found to have deceived ourselves.

Chapter 7

Daniel's vision of the four beasts. (Dan. **7**:**1**-**8**) and of Christ's kingdom. (Dan. **7**:**9**-**14**) The interpretation. (Dan. **7**:**15**-**28**)

Dan. **7**:**1**-**8** This vision contains the same prophetic representations with Nebuchadnezzar's dream. The great sea agitated by the winds, represented the earth and the dwellers on it troubled by ambitious princes and conquerors. The four beasts signified the same four empires, as the four parts of Nebuchadnezzar's image. Mighty conquerors are but instruments of God's vengeance on a guilty world. The savage beast represents the hateful features of their characters. But the dominion given to each has a limit; their wrath shall be made to praise the Lord, and the remainder of it he will restrain.

Dan. **7**:**9**-**14** These **verses** are for the comfort and support of the people of God, in reference to the persecutions that would come upon them. Many New Testament predictions of the judgment to come, have plain allusion to this vision; especially Rev. **20**:**11**,**12**. The Messiah is here called the Son of man; he was made in the likeness of sinful flesh, and was found in fashion as a man, but he is the Son of God. The great event foretold in this passage, is Christ's glorious coming, to destroy every antichristian power, and to render his own kingdom universal upon earth. But ere the solemn time arrives, for manifesting the glory of God to all worlds in his dealings with his creatures, we may expect that the doom of each of us will be determined at the hour of our death; and before the end shall come, the Father will openly give to his incarnate Son, our Mediator and Judge, the inheritance of the nations as his willing subjects.

Dan. **7**:**15**-**28** It is desirable to obtain the right and full sense of what we see and hear from God; and those that would know, must ask by faithful and fervent prayer. The angel told Daniel plainly. He especially desired to know respecting the little horn, which made war with the saints, and prevailed against them. Here is foretold the rage of papal Rome against true Christians. St. John, in his visions and prophecies, which point in the first place at Rome, has plain reference to these visions. Daniel had a joyful prospect of the prevalence of God's kingdom among men. This refers to the second coming of our blessed Lord, when the saints shall triumph in the complete fall of Satan's kingdom. The saints of the Most High shall possess the kingdom for ever. Far be it from us to infer from hence, that dominion is founded on grace. It promises that the gospel kingdom shall be set up; a kingdom of light, holiness, and love; a kingdom of grace, the privileges and comforts of which shall be the earnest and first-fruits of the kingdom of glory. But the full accomplishment will be in the everlasting happiness of the saints, the kingdom that cannot be moved. The gathering together the whole family of God will be a blessedness of Christ's coming.

Chapter 8

Daniel's vision of the ram and the he-goat. (Dan. **8**:**1**-**14**) The interpretation of it. (Dan. **8**:**15**-**27**)

Dan. **8**:**1**-**14** God gives Daniel a foresight of the destruction of other kingdoms, which in their day were as powerful as that of Babylon. Could we foresee the changes that shall be when we are gone, we should be less affected with changes in our own day. The ram with two horns was the second empire, that of Media and Persia. He saw this ram overcome by a he-goat. This was Alexander the Great. Alexander, when about thirty-three years of age, and in his full strength, died, and showed the vanity of worldly pomp and power, and that they cannot make a man happy. While men dispute, as in the case of Alexander, respecting the death of some prosperous warrior, it is plain that the great First Cause of all had no more of his plan for him to execute, and therefore cut him off. Instead of that one great horn, there came up four notable ones, Alexander's four chief captains. A little horn became a great persecutor of the church and people of God. It seems that the Mohammedan delusion is here pointed out. It prospered, and at one time nearly destroyed the holy religion God's right hand had planted. It is just with God to deprive those of the privileges of his house who despise and profane them; and to make those know the worth of ordinances by the want of them, who would not know it by the enjoyment of them. Daniel heard the time of this calamity limited and determined; but not the time when it should come. If we would know the mind of God, we must apply to Christ, in whom are hid all the treasures of wisdom and knowledge; not hid from us, but hid for us. There is much difficulty as to the precise time here stated, but the end of it cannot be very distant. God will, for his own glory, see to the cleansing of the church in due time. Christ died to cleanse his church; and he will so cleanse it as to present it blameless to himself.

Dan. **8**:**15**-**27** The eternal Son of God stood before the prophet in the appearance of a man, and directed the angel Gabriel to explain the vision. Daniel's fainting and astonishment at the prospect of evils he saw coming on his people and the church, confirm the opinion that long-continued calamities were foretold. The vision being ended, a charge was given to Daniel to keep it private for the present. He kept it to himself, and went on to do the duty of his place. As long as we live in this world we must have something to do in it; and even those whom God has most honoured, must not think themselves above their business. Nor must the pleasure of communion with God take us from the duties of our callings, but we must in them abide with God. All who are intrusted with public business must discharge their trust uprightly; and, amidst all doubts and discouragements, they may, if true believers, look forward to a happy issue. Thus should we endeavour to compose our minds for attending to the duties to which each is appointed, in the church and in the world.

Chapter 9

Daniel considers the time of the captivity. (Dan. **9**:**1**-**3**) His confession of sin, and prayer. (Dan. **9**:**4**-**19**) The revelation concerning the coming of the Messiah. (Dan. **9**:**20**-**27**)

Dan. **9**:**1**-**3** Daniel learned from the books of the prophets, especially from Jeremiah, that the desolation of Jerusalem would continue seventy years, which were drawing to a close. God's promises are to encourage our prayers, not to make them needless; and when we see the performance of them approaching, we should more earnestly plead them with God.

Dan. **9**:**4**-**19** In every prayer we must make confession, not only of the sins we have been guilty of, but of our faith in God, and dependence upon him, our sorrow for sin, and our resolutions against it. It must be our confession, the language of our convictions. Here is Daniel's humble, serious, devout address to God; in which he gives glory to him as a God to be feared, and as a God to be trusted. We should, in prayer, look both at God's greatness and his goodness, his majesty and mercy. Here is a penitent confession of sin, the cause of the troubles the people for so many years groaned under. All who would find mercy must thus confess their sins. Here is a self-abasing acknowledgment of the righteousness of God; and it is evermore the way of true penitents thus to justify God. Afflictions are sent to bring men to turn from their sins, and to understand God's truth. Here is a believing appeal to the mercy of God. It is a comfort that God has been always ready to pardon sin. It is encouraging to recollect that mercies belong to God, as it is convincing and humbling to recollect that righteousness belongs to him. There are abundant mercies in God, not only forgiveness, but forgivenesses. Here are pleaded the reproach God's people was under, and the ruins God's sanctuary was in. Sin is a reproach to any people, especially to God's people. The desolations of the sanctuary are grief to all the saints. Here is an earnest request to God to restore the poor captive Jews to their former enjoyments. O Lord, hearken and do. Not hearken and speak only, but hearken and do; do that for us which none else can do; and defer not. Here are several pleas and arguments to enforce the petitions. Do it for the Lord Christ's sake; Christ is the Lord of all. And for his sake God causes his face to shine upon sinners when they repent, and turn to him. In all our prayers this must be our plea, we must make mention of his righteousness, even of his only. The humble, fervent, believing earnestness of this prayer should ever be followed by us.

Dan. **9**:**20**-**27** An answer was immediately sent to Daniel's prayer, and it is a very memorable one. We cannot now expect that God should send answers to our prayers by angels, but if we pray with fervency for that which God has promised, we may by faith take the promise as an immediate answer to the prayer; for He is faithful that has promised. Daniel had a far greater and more glorious redemption discovered to him, which God would work out for his church in the latter days. Those who would be acquainted with Christ and his grace, must be much in prayer. The evening offering was a type of the great sacrifice Christ was to offer in the evening of the world: in virtue of that sacrifice Daniel's prayer was accepted; and for the sake of that, this glorious discovery of redeeming love was made to him. We have, in **verses 24**-**27**, one of the most remarkable prophecies of Christ, of his coming and his salvation. It shows that the Jews are guilty of most obstinate unbelief, in expecting another Messiah, so long after the time expressly fixed for his coming. The seventy weeks mean a day for a year, or **490** years. About the end of this period a sacrifice would be offered, making full atonement for sin, and bringing in everlasting righteousness for the complete justification of every believer. Then the Jews, in the crucifixion of Jesus, would commit that crime by which the measure of their guilt would be filled up, and troubles would come upon their nation. All blessings bestowed on sinful man come through Christ's atoning sacrifice, who suffered once for sins, the just for the unjust, that he might bring us to God. Here is our way of access to the throne of grace, and of our entrance to heaven. This seals the sum of prophecy, and confirms the covenant with many; and while we rejoice in the blessings of salvation, we should remember what they cost the Redeemer. How can those escape who neglect so great salvation!

Chapter 10

Daniel's vision near the river Hiddekel. (Dan. **10**:**1**-**9**) He is to expect a discovery of future events. (Dan. **10**:**10**-**21**)

Dan. **10**:**1**-**9**. This chapter relates the beginning of Daniel's last vision, which is continued to the end of the book. The time would be long before all would be accomplished; and much of it is not yet fulfilled. Christ appeared to Daniel in a glorious form, and it should engage us to think highly and honourably of him. Let us admire his condescension for us and our salvation. There remained no strength in Daniel. The greatest and best of men cannot bear the full discoveries of the Divine glory; for no man can see it, and live; but glorified saints see Christ as he is, and can bear the sight. How dreadful soever Christ may appear to those under convictions of sin, there is enough in his word to quiet their spirits.

Dan. **10**:**10**-**21** Whenever we enter into communion with God, it becomes us to have a due sense of the infinite distance between us and the holy God. How shall we, that are dust and ashes, speak to the Lord of glory? Nothing is more likely, nothing more effectual to revive the drooping spirits of the saints, than to be assured of God's love to them. From the very first day we begin to look toward God in a way of duty, he is ready to meet us in the way of mercy. Thus ready is God to hear prayer. When the angel had told the prophet of the things to come, he was to return, and oppose the decrees of the Persian kings against the Jews. The angels are employed as God's ministering servants, Heb. **1**:**14**. Though much was done against the Jews by the kings of Persia, God permitting it, much more mischief would have been done if God had not prevented it. He would now more fully show what were God's purposes, of which the prophecies form an outline; and we are concerned to study what is written in these Scriptures of truth, for they belong to our everlasting peace. While Satan and his angels, and evil counsellors, excite princes to mischief against the church, we may rejoice that Christ our Prince, and all his mighty angels, act against our enemies; but we ought not to expect many to favour us in this evil world. Yet the whole counsel of God shall be established; and let each one pray, Lord Jesus, be our righteousness now, and thou wilt be our everlasting confidence, through life, in death, at the day of judgment, and for evermore.

Chapter 11

The vision of the Scriptures of truth.

Dan. **11**:**1**-**30** The angel shows Daniel the succession of the Persian and Grecian empires. The kings of Egypt and Syria are noticed: Judea was between their dominions, and affected by their contests. From Dan. **11**:**5**-**30**, is generally considered to relate to the events which came to pass during the continuance of these governments; and from Dan. **11**:**21**, to relate to Antiochus Epiphanes, who was a cruel and violent persecutor of the Jews. See what decaying, perishing things worldly pomp and possessions are, and the power by which they are gotten. God, in his providence, sets up one, and pulls down another, as he pleases. This world is full of wars and fightings, which come from men's lusts. All changes and revolutions of states and kingdoms, and every event, are plainly and perfectly foreseen by God. No word of God shall fall to the ground; but what he has designed, what he has declared, shall infallibly come to pass.

While the potsherds of the earth strive with each other, they prevail and are prevailed against, deceive and are deceived; but those who know God will trust in him, and he will enable them to stand their ground, bear their cross, and maintain their conflict.

Dan. **11**:**31**-**45** The remainder of this prophecy is very difficult, and commentators differ much respecting it. From Antiochus the account seems to pass to antichrist. Reference seems to be made to the Roman empire, the fourth monarchy, in its pagan, early Christian, and papal states. The end of the Lord's anger against his people approaches, as well as the end of his patience towards his enemies. If we would escape the ruin of the infidel, the idolater, the superstitious and cruel persecutor, as well as that of the profane, let us make the oracles of God our standard of truth and of duty, the foundation of our hope, and the light of our paths through this dark world, to the glorious inheritance above.

Chapter 12

The conclusion of the vision of the Scriptures of truth. (Dan. **12**:**1**-**4**) The times of the continuance of these events. (Dan. **12**:**5**-**13**)

Dan. **12**:**1**-**4**. Michael signifies, "Who is like God," and his name, with the title of "the great Prince," points out the Divine Saviour. Christ stood for the children of our people in their stead as a sacrifice, bore the curse for them, to bear it from them. He stands for them in pleading for them at the throne of grace. And after the destruction of antichrist, the Lord Jesus shall stand at the latter day upon the earth; and He shall appear for the complete redemption of all his people. When God works deliverance from persecution for them, it is as life from the dead. When his gospel is preached, many who sleep in the dust, both Jews and Gentiles, shall be awakened by it out of their heathenism of Judaism. And in the end the multitude that sleep in the dust shall awake; many shall arise to life, and many to shame. There is glory reserved for all the saints in the future state, for all that are wise, wise for their souls and eternity. Those who turn many to righteousness, who turn sinners from the errors of their ways, and help to save their souls from death, James **5**:**20**, will share in the glory of those they have helped to heaven, which will add to their own glory.

Dan. **12**:**5**-**13** One of the angels asking how long it should be to the end of these wonders, a solemn reply is made, that it would be for a time, times, and a half, the period mentioned Dan. **7**:**25**, and in the Revelation. It signifies **1260** prophetic days or years, beginning from the time when the power of the holy people should be scattered. The imposture of Mohammed, and the papal usurpation, began about the same time; and these were a twofold attack upon the church of God. But all will end well at last. All opposing rule, principality, and power, shall be put down, and holiness and love will triumph, and be in honour, to eternity. The end, this end, shall come. What an amazing prophecy is this, of so many varied events, and extending through so many successive ages, even to the general resurrection! Daniel must comfort himself with the pleasing prospect of his own happiness in death, in judgment, and to eternity. It is good for us all to think much of going away from this world. That must be our way; but it is our comfort that we shall not go till God calls us to another world, and till he has done with us in this world; till he says, Go thou thy way, thou hast done thy work, therefore now, go thy way, and leave it to others to take thy place. It was a comfort to Daniel, and is a comfort to all the saints, that whatever their lot is in the days of their lives, they shall have a happy lot in the end of the days. And it ought to be the great care and concern of every one of us to secure this. Then we may well be content with our present lot, and welcome the will of God. Believers are happy at all times; they rest in God by faith now, and a rest is reserved for them in heaven at last.

Hosea

Hosea is supposed to have been of the kingdom of Israel. He lived and prophesied during a long period. The scope of his predictions appears to be, to detect, reprove, and convince the Jewish nation in general, and the Israelites in particular, of their many sins, particularly their idolatry: the corrupt state of the kingdom is also noticed. But he invites them to repentance, with promises of mercy, and gospel predictions of the future restoration of the Israelites and of the Jews, and their final conversion to Christianity.

Chapter 1

Under a figure, is represented the shameful idolatry of the ten tribes. (Hos. **1**:**1**-**7**) The calling of the Gentiles, and the uniting Israel and Judah under the Messiah. (Hos. **1**:**8**-**11**)

Hos. **1**:**1**-**7** Israel was prosperous, yet then Hosea boldly tells them of their sins, and foretells their destruction. Men are not to be flattered in sinful ways because they prosper in the world; nor will it last long if they go on still in their trespasses. The prophet must show Israel their sin; show it to be exceedingly hateful. Their idolatry is the sin they are here charged with. Giving that glory to any creature which is due to God alone, is an injury and affront to God; such as for a wife to take a stranger, is to her husband. The Lord, doubtless, had good reasons for giving such a command to the prophet; it would form an affecting picture of the Lord's unmerited goodness and unwearied patience, and of the perverseness and ingratitude of Israel. We should be broken and wearied with half that perverseness from others, with which we try the patience and grieve the Spirit of our God. Let us also be ready to bear any cross the Lord appoints. The prophet must show the ruin of the people, in the names given to his children. He foretells the fall of the royal family in the name of his first child: call his name Jezreel, which signifies "dispersion." He foretells God's abandoning the nation in the name of the second child; Lo-ruhamah, "not beloved," or "not having obtained mercy." God showed great mercy, but Israel abused his favours. Sin turns away the mercy of God, even from Israel, his own professing people. If pardoning mercy is denied, no other mercy can be expected. Though some, through unbelief, are broken off, yet God will have a church in this world till the end of time. Our salvation is owing to God's mercy, not to any merit of our own. That salvation is sure, of which he is the Author; and if he will work, none shall hinder.

Hos. **1**:**8**-**11** The rejection of Israel for a time, is signified by the name of another child: call him Lo-ammi, "not my people." The Lord disowns all relation to them. We love him, because he first loved us; but our being cast out of covenant, is owing to ourselves and our folly. Mercy is remembered in the midst of wrath; the rejection, as it shall not be total, so it shall not be final. The same hand that wounded, is stretched forth to heal. Very precious promises are here given concerning the Israel of God, and they may be of use to us now. Some think that these promises will not have accomplishment in full, till the general conversion of the Jews in the latter days. Also this promise is applied to the gospel, and the bringing in both the Jews and Gentiles to it, by St. Paul, Rom. **9**:**25**,**26**, and by St. Peter, I Pet. **2**:**10**. To believe in Christ, is to have him for our Head, and willingly to commit ourselves to his guidance and government. And let us pray for the coming of the glorious day, when there shall be one Lord through all the earth.

Chapter 2

The idolatry of the people. (Hos. **2**:**1-5**) God's judgments against them. (Hos. **2**:**6-13**) His promises of reconciliation. (Hos. **2**:**14-23**)

Hos. **2**:**1-5** This chapter continues the figurative address to Israel, in reference to Hosea's wife and children. Let us own and love as brethren, all whom the Lord seems to put among his children, and encourage them in that they have received mercy. But every Christian, by his example and conduct, must protest against evil and abuses, even among those to whom he belongs and owes respect. Impenitent sinners will soon be stripped of the advantages they misuse, and which they consume upon their lusts.

Hos. **2**:**6-13** God threatens what he would do with this treacherous, idolatrous people. They did not turn, therefore all this came upon them; and it is written for admonition to us. If lesser difficulties be got over, God will raise greater. The most resolute in sinful pursuits, are commonly most crossed in them. The way of God and duty is often hedged about with thorns, but we have reason to think it is a sinful way that is hedged up with thorns. Crosses and obstacles in an evil course are great blessings, and are to be so accounted; they are God's hedges, to keep us from transgressing, to make the way of sin difficult, and to keep us from it. We have reason to bless God for restraining grace, and for restraining providences; and even for sore pain, sickness, or calamity, if it keeps us from sin. The disappointments we meet with in seeking for satisfaction from the creature, should, if nothing else will do it, drive us to the Creator. When men forget, or consider not that their comforts come from God, he will often in mercy take them away, to bring them to think upon their folly and danger. Sin and mirth can never hold long together; but if men will not take away sin from their mirth, God will take away mirth from their sin. And if men destroy God's word and ordinances, it is just with him to destroy their vines and fig-trees. This shall be the ruin of their mirth. Taking away the solemn seasons and the sabbaths will not do it, they will readily part with them, and think it no loss; but He will take away their sensual pleasures. Days of sinful mirth must be visited with days of mourning.

Hos. **2**:**14-23** After these judgments the Lord would deal with Israel more gently. By the promise of rest in Christ we are invited to take his yoke upon us; and the work of conversion may be forwarded by comforts as well as by convictions. But usually the Lord drives us to despair of earthly joy, and help from ourselves, that, being shut from every other door, we may knock at Mercy's gate. From that time Israel would be more truly attached to the Lord; no longer calling him Baali, or "My lord and master," alluding to authority, rather than love, but Ishi, an address of affection. This may foretell the restoration from the Babylonish captivity; and also be applied to the conversion of the Jews to Christ, in the days of the apostles, and the future general conversion of that nation; and believers are enabled to expect infinitely more tenderness and kindness from their holy God, than a beloved wife can expect from the kindest husband. When the people were weaned from idols, and loved the Lord, no creature should do them any harm. This may be understood of the blessings and privileges of the spiritual Israel, of every true believer, and their partaking of Christ's righteousness; also, of the conversion of the Jews to Christ. Here is an argument for us to walk so that God may not be dishonoured by us: Thou art my people. If a man's family walk disorderly, it is a dishonour to the master. If God call us children, we may say, Thou art our God. Unbelieving soul, lay aside discouraging thoughts; do not thus answer God's loving-kindness. Doth God say, Thou art my people? Say, Lord, thou art our God.

Chapter 3

The prophet enters into a new contract, representing the gracious manner in which God will again restore Israel under a new covenant.

Hos. **3**:**1-3** The dislike of men to true religion is because they love objects and forms, which allow them to indulge, instead of mortifying their lusts. How wonderful that a holy God should have good-will to those whose carnal mind is enmity against Him! Here is represented God's gracious dealings with the fallen race of mankind, that had gone from him. This is the covenant of grace he is willing to enter into with them, they must be to him a people, and he will be to them a God. They must accept the punishment of their sin, and must not return to folly. And it is a certain sign that our afflictions are means of good to us, when we are kept from being overcome by the temptations of an afflicted state.

Hos. **3**:**4-5** Here is the application of the parable to Israel. They must long sit like a widow, stripped of all joys and honours; but shall at length be received again. Those that would seek the Lord so as to find him, must apply to Christ, and become his willing people. Not only are we to fear the Lord and his greatness, but the Lord and his goodness; not only his majesty, but his mercy. Even Jewish writers apply this passage to the promised Messiah; doubtless it foretold their future conversion to Christ, for which they are kept a separate people. Though the first fear of God arise from a view of his holy majesty and righteous vengeance, yet the experience of mercy and grace through Jesus Christ, will lead the heart to reverence so kind and glorious a Friend and Father, and to fear offending him.

Chapter 4

God's judgments against the sins of the people. (Hos. **4**:**1-5**) and of the priests. (Hos. **4**:**6-11**) Idolatry is reproved, and Judah is admonished. (Hos. **4**:**12-19**)

Hos. **4**:**1-5** Hosea reproves for immorality, as well as idolatry. There was no truth, mercy, or knowledge of God in the land: it was full of murders, II Kin. **21**:**16**. Therefore calamities were near, which would desolate the country. Our sins, as separate persons, as a family, as a neighbourhood, as a nation, cause the Lord to have a controversy with us; let us submit and humble ourselves before Him, that he may not go on to destroy.

Hos. **4**:**6-11** Both priests and people rejected knowledge; God will justly reject them. They forgot the law of God, neither desired nor endeavoured to retain it in mind, and to transmit the remembrance to their posterity; therefore God will justly forget them and their children. If we dishonour God with that which is our honour, it will, sooner or later, be turned into shame to us. Instead of warning the people against sin, from the consideration of the sacrifices, which showed what an offence sin was to God, since it needed an atonement, the priests encouraged the people to sin, since atonement might be made at so small an expense. It is very wicked to be pleased with the sins of others, because they may turn to our advantage. What is unlawfully gained, cannot be comfortably used. The people and the priests hardened one another in sin; therefore justly shall they share in the punishment. Sharers in sin must expect to share in ruin. Any lust harboured in the heart, in time will eat out all its strength and vigour. That is the reason why many professors grow so heavy, so dull, so dead in the way of religion. They have a liking for some secret lust, which takes away their hearts.

Hos. **4**:**12-19** The people consulted images, and not the Divine word. This would lead to disorder and sin. Thus men prepare scourges for themselves, and vice is spread through a people. Let not Judah come near the idolatrous worship of Israel. For Israel was devoted to idols, and must now be let alone. When sinners cast off the easy yoke of Christ, they go on in sin till the Lord saith, Let them alone. Then they receive no more warnings, feel no more convictions: Satan takes full possession of them, and they ripen for destruction. It is a sad and sore judgment for any man to be let alone in sin. Those who are not disturbed in their sin, will be destroyed for their sin. May we be kept from this awful state; for the wrath of God, like a strong tempest, will soon hurry impenitent sinners into ruin.

Chapter 5

The Divine judgments against Israel. (Hos. **5**:**1-7**) Approaching desolations threatened. (Hos. **5**:**8-15**)

Hos. **5**:**1-7** The piercing eye of God saw secret liking and disposition to sin, the love the house of Israel had to their sins, and the dominion their sins had over them. Pride makes men obstinate in other sins. And as Judah was treading in the same steps, they would fall with Israel. By dealing treacherously with the Lord, men only deceive themselves. Those that go to seek the Lord with their flocks and their herds only, and not with their hearts and souls, cannot expect to find him; nor shall any speed who do not seek the Lord while he may be found. See how much it is our concern to seek God early, now, while it is the accepted time, and the day of salvation.

Hos. **5**:**8-15** The destruction of impenitent sinners is not mere talk, to frighten them, it is a sentence which will not be recalled. And it is a mercy that we have timely warning given us, that we may flee from the wrath to come. Compliance with the commandments of men, who thwart the commandments of God, ripens a people for ruin. The judgments of God are sometimes to a sinful people as a moth, and as rottenness, or as a worm; as these consume the clothes and the wood, so shall the judgments of God consume them. Silently, they shall think themselves safe and thriving, but when they look into their state, shall find themselves wasting and decaying. Slowly, for the Lord gives them space to repent. Many a nation; as well as many a person, dies of a consumption. Gradually, God comes upon sinners with lesser judgments, to prevent greater, if they will be wise, and take warning. When Israel and Judah found themselves in danger, they sought the protection of the Assyrians, but this only helped to make their wound the worse. They would be forced to apply to God. He will bring them home to himself, by afflictions. When men begin to complain more of their sins than of their afflictions, then there begins to be some hope of them; and when under the conviction of sin, and the corrections of the rod, we must seek the knowledge of God. Those who are led by severe trials to seek God earnestly and sincerely, will find him a present help and an effectual refuge; for with him is plenteous redemption for all who call upon him. There is solid peace, and there only, where God is.

Chapter 6

An exhortation to repentance. (Hos. **6**:**1-3**) Israel's instability and breach of the covenant. (Hos. **6**:**4-11**)

Hos. **6**:**1-3** Those who have gone from God by consent, and in a body, drawing one another to sin, should, by consent and in a body, return to him, which will be for his glory, and their good. It will be of great use for support under afflictions, and to encourage our repentance, to keep up good thoughts of God, and of his purposes and designs concerning us. Deliverance out of trouble should be to them as life from the dead. God will revive them: the assurance of this should engage them to return to him. But this seems to have a further reference to the resurrection of Jesus Christ. Let us admire the wisdom and goodness of God, that when the prophet foretold the deliverance of the church out of her troubles, he should point out our salvation by Christ; and now these words are fulfilled in the resurrection of Christ, it confirms our faith, that this is He that should come and we are to look for no other. Here is a precious blessing promised; this is life eternal, to know God. The returns of the favour of God are secured to us as firmly as the return of the morning after a dark night. He shall come to us as the latter and former rain unto the earth, which refreshes it, and makes it fruitful. The grace of God in Christ is both the latter and the former rain; and by it the good work of our fruit-bearing is begun and carried on. And as the Redeemer was raised from the grave, so will He revive the hearts and hopes of all that trust in him. The feeblest glimpse of hope in his word, is a sure earnest of increasing light and comfort, which shall be attended with purifying, comforting grace that makes fruitful.

Hos. **6**:**4-11** Sometimes Israel and Judah seemed disposed to repent under their sufferings, but their goodness vanished like the empty morning cloud, and the early dew, and they were as vile as ever. Therefore the Lord sent awful messages by the prophets. The word of God will be the death either of the sin or of the sinner. God desired mercy rather than sacrifice, and that knowledge of him which produces holy fear and love. This exposes the folly of those who trust in outward observances, to make up for their want of love to God and man. As Adam broke the covenant of God in paradise, so Israel had broken his national covenant, notwithstanding all the favours they received. Judah also was ripe for Divine judgments. May the Lord put his fear into our hearts, and set up his kingdom within us, and never leave us to ourselves, nor suffer us to be overcome by temptation.

Chapter 7

The manifold sins of Israel. (Hos. **7**:**1-7**) Their senselessness and hypocrisy. (Hos. **7**:**8-16**)

Hos. **7**:**1-7** A practical disbelief of God's government was at the bottom of all Israel's wickedness; as if God could not see it or did not heed it. Their sins appear on every side of them. Their hearts were inflamed by evil desires, like a heated oven. In the midst of their troubles as a nation, the people never thought of seeking help from God. The actual wickedness of men's lives bears a very small proportion to what is in their hearts. But when lust is inwardly cherished, it will break forth into outward sin. Those who tempt others to drunkenness never can be their real friends, and often design their ruin. Thus men execute the Divine vengeance on each other. Those are not only heated with sin, but hardened in sin, who continue to live without prayer, even when in trouble and distress.

Hos. **7**:**8-16** Israel was as a cake not turned, half burnt and half dough, none of it fit for use; a mixture of idolatry and of the worship of Jehovah. There were tokens of approaching ruin, as grey hairs are of old age, but they noticed them not. The pride which leads to break the law of God leads to self-flattery. The mercy and grace of God are the only refuge to which obstinate sinners never think of fleeing. Though they may howl forth their terrors in the form of prayers, they seldom cry to God with their hearts. Even their prayers for earthly mercies only seek fuel for their lusts. Their turning from one sect, sentiment, form, or vice, to another, still leaves them far short of Christ and holiness. Such are we by nature. And such shall we prove if left to ourselves. Create in us a clean heart, O God, and renew a right spirit within us.

Chapter 8

Destruction threatened for the impiety of Israel. (Hos. **8**:**1-4**) For their idolatry. (Hos. **8**:**5-10**) Further threatenings for the same sins. (Hos. **8**:**11-14**)

Hos. **8**:**1-4** When Israel was hard pressed, they would claim protection from God, but this would be disregarded. What stead will it stand in to say, My God, I know thee, if we cannot say, My God, I love thee, serve thee, and cleave to thee only?

Hos. **8**:**5-10** They promised themselves plenty, peace, and victory, by worshipping idols, but their expectations came to nothing. What they sow has no stalk, no blade, or, if it have, the bud shall yield no fruit, there was nothing in them. The works of darkness are unfruitful; nay, the end of those things is death. The hopes of sinners will deceive them, and their gains will be snares. In times of danger, especially in the day of judgment, all carnal devices will fail. They take a course by themselves, and like a wild ass by himself, they will be the easier and surer prey for the lion. Man is in nothing more like the wild ass's colt, than in seeking for that succour and that satisfaction in the creature, which are to be had in God only. Though men may sorrow a little, yet if it is not after a godly sort, they will be brought to sorrow everlastingly.

Hos. **8**:**11-14** It is a great sin to corrupt the worship of God, and will be charged as sin on all who do it, how plausible soever their excuses may seem to be. The Lord had caused his law to be written for them, but they cared not to know, and would not obey it. Man seems by the temples he builds to be mindful of his Maker, yet really he has forgotten him, because he has cast off all his fear; but none ever hardened his heart against God and prospered. So long as men despise the truths and precepts of God's word, and the ordinances of his worship, all the observances and offerings, however costly, of their own devising, will be unto them for sin; for those services only are acceptable to God, which are done according to his word, and through Jesus Christ.

Chapter 9

The distress to come upon Israel. (Hos. **9**:**1-6**) The approach of the day of trouble. (Hos. **9**:**7-10**) Judgments on Israel. (Hos. **9**:**11-17**)

Hos. **9**:**1-6** Israel gave rewards to their idols, in the offerings presented to them. It is common for those who are niggardly in religion, to be prodigal upon their lusts. Those are reckoned as idolaters, who love a reward in the corn-floor better than a reward in the favour of God and in eternal life. They are full of the joy of harvest, and have no disposition to mourn for sin. When we make the world, and the things of it, our idol and our portion, it is just with God to show us our folly, and correct us. None may expect to dwell in the Lord's land, who will not be subject to the Lord's laws, or be influenced by his love. When we enjoy the means of grace, we ought to consider what we shall do, if they should be taken from us. While the pleasures of communion with God are out of the reach of change, the pleasant places purchased with silver, or in which men deposit silver, are liable to be laid in ruins. No famine is so dreadful as that of the soul.

Hos. **9**:**7-10** Time had been when the spiritual watchmen of Israel were with the Lord, but now they were like the snare of a fowler to entangle persons to their ruin. The people were become as corrupt as those of Gibeah, Judg. **19**; and their crimes should be visited in like manner. At first God had found Israel pleasing to Him, as grapes to the traveller in the wilderness. He saw them with pleasure as the first ripe figs. This shows the delight God took in them; yet they followed after idolatry.

Hos. **9**:**11-17**. God departs from a people, or from a person, when he withdraws his goodness and mercy from them; and when the Lord is departed, what can the creature do? Even though, for the present, good things seem to remain, yet the blessing is gone if God is gone. Even the children should perish with the parents. The Divine wrath dries up the root, and withers the fruit of all comforts; and the scattered Jews daily warn us to beware, lest we neglect or abuse the gospel. Yet every smiting is not a drying up of the root. It may be that God intends only to smite so that the sap may be turned to the root, that there may be more of root graces, more humility, patience, faith, and self-denial. It is very just that God should bring judgments on those who slight his offered mercy.

Chapter 10

The idolatry of Israel. (Hos. **10**:**1-8**) They are exhorted to repentance. (Hos. **10**:**9-15**)

Hos. **10**:**1-8** A vine is only valuable for its fruit; but Israel now brought no fruit to perfection. Their hearts were divided. God is the Sovereign of the heart; he will have all, or none. Were the stream of the heart wholly after God, it would run strongly, and bear down all before it. Their pretences to covenant with God were false. Even the proceeding of justice was as poisonous hemlock. Alas, how empty a vine is the visible church even at this day! But all earthly prosperity is but a collection of bubbles, soon destroyed like foam upon the water. Sinners will in vain seek shelter from that Judge, whom they now despise as a Saviour.

Hos. **10**:**9-15** Because God does not desire the death and ruin of sinners, therefore in mercy he desires their chastisement. The children of iniquity still remained in Israel. The enemies would be gathered against them. It is just with God to make those know what hardships mean, who indulge themselves in ease and pleasure. Let them cleanse their hearts from all corrupt affections and lusts, and be a broken and contrite spirit. Let them abound in works of piety towards God, and of justice and charity towards one another: herein let them sow to the Spirit. Seeking the Lord is to be every day's work, but there are special occasions when to seek him. Christ shall come as the Lord our righteousness, and grant us of it abundantly. If we sow in righteousness, we shall reap according to mercy; a reward not of debt, but of grace. Even the gains of sin yield the sinner no satisfaction. As our comforts, so our confidences in the service of sin will certainly fail us. Come and seek the Lord, and thy hope in him shall not deceive thee. See what cruel work war makes. Whatever mischief is done, it is sin that does it. What miseries men's sins bring on them, even in this world!

Chapter 11

God's regard for Israel; their ingratitude. (Hos. **11**:**1-7**) The Divine mercy yet in store. (Hos. **11**:**8-12**)

Hos. **11**:**1-7** When Israel were weak and helpless as children, foolish and froward as children, then God loved them; he bore them as the nurse does the sucking child, nourished them, and suffered their manners. All who are grown up, ought often to reflect upon the goodness of God to them in their childhood. He took care of them, took pains with them, not only as a father, or a tutor, but as a mother, or nurse. When they were in the wilderness, God showed them the way in which they should go, and bore them up, taking them by the arms. He taught them the way of his commandments by the ceremonial law given by Moses. He took them by the arms, to guide them, that they might not stray, and to hold them up, that they might not stumble and fall. God's spiritual Israel are all thus supported. It is God's work to draw poor souls to himself; and none can come to him except he draw them. With bands of love; this word signifies stronger cords than the former. He eased them of the burdens they had long groaned under. Israel is very ungrateful to God. God's counsels would have saved them, but their own counsels ruined them. They backslide; there is no hold of them, no stedfastness in them. They backslide from me, from God, the chief good. They are bent to backslide; they are ready to sin; they are forward to close with every temptation. Their hearts are fully set in them to do evil. Those only are truly happy, whom the Lord teaches by his Spirit, upholds by his power, and causes to walk in his ways. By his grace he takes away the love and dominion of sin, and creates a desire for the blessed feast of the gospel, that they may feed thereon, and live for ever.

Hos. **11**:**8-12** God is slow to anger, and is loth to abandon a people to utter ruin, who have been called by his name. When God was to give a sacrifice for sin, and a Saviour for sinners, he spared not his own Son, that he might spare us. This is the language of the day of his patience; but when men sin that away, then the great day of his wrath comes. Man's compassions are nothing in comparison with the tender mercies of our God, whose thoughts and ways, in receiving returning sinners, are as much above ours as heaven is above the earth. God knows how to pardon poor sinners. He is faithful and just to forgive us our sins, and therein declares his righteousness, now Christ has purchased the pardon, and he has promised it. Holy trembling at the word of Christ will draw us to him, not drive us from him, the children tremble, and flee to him. And all that come at the gospel call, shall have a place and a name in the gospel church. The religious service of Israel were mere hypocrisy, but in Judah regard was had to God's laws, and the people followed their pious forefathers. Let us be faithful: those who thus honour God, he will honour, but such us despise Him shall be lightly esteemed.

Chapter 12

Judah and Israel reminded of the Divine favours. (Hos. **12**:**1-6**) The provocations of Israel. (Hos. **12**:**7-14**)

Hos. **12**:**1-6** Ephraim feeds himself with vain hopes of help from man, when he is at enmity with God. The Jews vainly thought to secure the Egyptians by a present of the produce of their country. Judah is contended with also. God sees the sin of his own people, and will reckon with them for it. They are put in mind of what Jacob did, and what God did for him. When his faith upon the Divine promise prevailed above his fears, then by his strength he had power with God. He is Jehovah, the same that was, and is, and is to come. What was a revelation of God to one, is his memorial to many, to all generations. Then let those who have gone from God, be turned to him. Turn thou to the Lord, by repentance and faith, as thy God. Let those that are converted to him, walk with him in all holy conversation and godliness. Let us wrestle with Him for promised blessings, determined not to give over till we prevail; and let us seek Him in his ordinances.

Hos. **12**:**7-14** Ephraim became a merchant: the word also signifies a Canaanite. They carried on trade upon Canaanitish principles, covetously and with fraud and deceit. Thus they became rich, and falsely supposed that Providence favoured them. But shameful sins shall have shameful punishments. Let them remember, not only what a mighty prince Jacob was with God, but what a servant he was to Laban. The benefits we have had from the word of God, make our sin and folly the worse, if we put any slight upon that word. We had better follow the hardest labour in poverty, than grow rich by sin. We may form a judgment of our own conduct, by comparing it with that of ancient believers in the like circumstances. Whoever despises the message of God, will perish. May we all hear his word with humble, obedient faith.

Chapter 13

The abuse of God's favour leads to punishment. (Hos. **13**:**1-8**) A promise of God's mercy. (Hos. **13**:**9-16**)

Hos. **13**:**1-8** While Ephraim kept up a holy fear of God, and worshipped Him in that fear, so long he was very considerable. When Ephraim forsook God, and followed idolatry, he sunk. Let the men that sacrifice kiss the calves, in token of their adoration of them, affection for them, and obedience to them; but the Lord will not give his glory to another, and therefore all that worship images shall be confounded. No solid, lasting comfort, is to be expected any where but in God. God not only took care of the Israelites in the wilderness, he put them in possession of Canaan, a good land; but worldly prosperity, when it feeds men's pride, makes them forgetful of God. Therefore the Lord would meet them in just vengeance, as the most terrible beast that inhabited their forests. Abused goodness calls for greater severity.

Hos. **13**:**9-16** Israel had destroyed himself by his rebellion; but he could not save himself, his help was from the Lord only. This may well be applied to the case of spiritual redemption, from that lost state into which all have fallen by wilful sins. God often gives in displeasure what we sinfully desire. It is the happiness of the saints, that, whether God gives or takes away, all is in love. But it is the misery of the wicked, that, whether God gives or takes away, it is all in wrath, nothing is comfortable. Except sinners repent and believe the gospel, anguish will soon come upon them. The prophecy of the ruin of Israel as a nation, also showed there would be a merciful and powerful interposition of God, to save a remnant of them. Yet this was but a shadow of the ransom of the true Israel, by the death, burial, and resurrection of Christ. He will destroy death and the grave. The Lord would not repent of his purpose and promise. Yet, in the mean time, Israel would be desolated for her sins. Without fruitfulness in good works, springing from the Holy Spirit, all other fruitfulness will be found as empty as the uncertain riches of the world. The wrath of God will wither its branches, its sprigs shall be dried up, it shall come to nothing. Woes, more terrible than any from the most cruel warfare, shall fall on those who rebel against God. From such miseries, and from sin, the cause of them, may the Lord deliver us.

Chapter 14

An exhortation to repentance. (Hos. **14**:**1-3**) Blessings promised, showing the rich comforts of the gospel. (Hos. **14**:**4-8**) The just and the wicked. (Hos. **14**:**9**)

Hos. **14**:**1-3** Israel is exhorted to return unto Jehovah, from their sins and idols, by faith in his mercy, and grace through the promised Redeemer, and by diligently attending on his worship and service. Take away iniquity; lift it off as a burden we are ready to sink under, or as the stumbling-block we have often fallen over. Take it all away by a free and full forgiveness, for we cannot strike any of it off. Receive our prayer graciously. They do not say what good they seek, but refer it to God. It is not good of the world's showing, but good of God's giving. They were to consider their sins, their wants, and the remedy; and they were to take, not sacrifices, but words stating the desires of their hearts, and with them to address the Lord. The whole forms a clear description of the nature and tendency of a sinner's conversion to God through Jesus Christ. As we draw near to God by the prayer of faith, we should first beseech him to teach us what to ask. We must be earnest with him to take away all iniquity.

Hos. **14**:**4-8** Israel seeks God's face, and they shall not seek it in vain. His anger is turned from them. Whom God loves, he loves freely; not because they deserve it, but of his own good pleasure. God will be to them all they need. The graces of the Spirit are the hidden manna, hidden in the dew; the grace thus freely bestowed on them shall not be in vain. They shall grow upward, and be more flourishing; shall grow as the lily. The lily, when come to its height, is a lovely flower, Matt. **6**:**28**,**29**. They shall grow downward, and be more firm. With the flower of the lily shall be the strong root of the cedar of Lebanon. Spiritual growth consists most in the growth of the root, which is out of sight. They shall also spread as the vine, whose branches extend very widely. When believers abound in good works, then their branches spread. They shall be acceptable both to God and man. Holiness is the beauty of a soul. The church is compared to the vine and the olive, which bring forth useful fruits. God's promises pertain to those only that attend on his ordinances; not such as flee to this shadow only for shelter in a hot gleam, but all who dwell under it. When a man is brought to God, all who dwell under his shadow fare the better. The sanctifying fruits shall appear in his life. Thus believers grow up into the experience and fruitfulness of the gospel. Ephraim shall say, God will put it into his heart to say it, What have I to do any more with idols! God's promises to us are more our security and our strength for mortifying sin, than our promises to God. See the power of Divine grace. God will work such a change in him, that he shall loathe the idols as much as ever he loved them. See the benefit of sanctified afflictions. Ephraim smarted for his idolatry, and this is the fruit, even the taking away his sin, Is. **27**:**9**. See the nature of repentance; it is a firm and fixed resolution to have no more to do with sin. The Lord meets penitents with mercy, as the father of the prodigal met his returning son. God will be to all true converts both a delight and a defence; they shall sit under his shadow with delight. And as the root of a tree; From me is thy fruit found: from Him we receive grace and strength to enable us to do our duty.

Hos. **14**:**9** Who profit by the truths the prophet delivered? Such as set themselves to understand and know these things. The ways of God's providence towards us are right; all is well done. Christ is a Foundation Stone to some, to others a Stone of stumbling, and a Rock of offence. That which was ordained to life, becomes, through their abuse of it, death to them. The same sun softens wax and hardens clay. But those transgressors certainly have the most dangerous, fatal falls, who fall in the ways of God, who split on the Rock of Ages, and suck poison out of the Balm of Gilead. Let sinners in Zion fear this. May we learn to walk in the right ways of God, as his righteous servants, and may none of us be disobedient and unbelieving, and stumble at the word.

Joel

From the desolations about to come upon the land of Judah, by the ravages of locusts and other insects, the prophet Joel exhorts the Jews to repentance, fasting, and prayer. He notices the blessings of the gospel, with the final glorious state of the church.

Chapter 1

A plague of locusts. (Joel **1**:**1-7**) All sorts of people are called to lament it. (Joel **1**:**8-13**) They are to look to God. (Joel **1**:**14-20**)

Joel **1**:**1-7** The most aged could not remember such calamities as were about to take place. Armies of insects were coming upon the land to eat the fruits of it. It is expressed so as to apply also to the destruction of the country by a foreign enemy, and seems to refer to the devastations of the Chaldeans. God is Lord of hosts, has every creature at his command, and, when he pleases, can humble and mortify a proud, rebellious people, by the weakest and most contemptible creatures. It is just with God to take away the comforts which are abused to luxury and excess; and the more men place their happiness in the gratifications of sense, the more severe temporal afflictions are upon them. The more earthly delights we make needful to satisfy us, the more we expose ourselves to trouble.

Joel **1**:**8-13** All who labour only for the meat that perishes, will, sooner or later, be ashamed of their labour. Those that place their happiness in the delights of sense, when deprived of them, or disturbed in the enjoyment, lose their joy; whereas spiritual joy then flourishes more than ever. See what perishing, uncertain things our creature-comforts are. See how we need to live in continual dependence upon God and his providence. See what ruinous work sin makes. As far as poverty occasions the decay of piety, and starves the cause of religion among a people, it is a very sore judgment. But how blessed are the awakening judgments of God, in rousing his people and calling home the heart to Christ, and his salvation!

Joel **1**:**14-20** The sorrow of the people is turned into repentance and humiliation before God. With all the marks of sorrow and shame, sin must be confessed and bewailed. A day is to be appointed for this purpose; a day in which people must be kept from their common employments, that they may more closely attend God's services; and there is to be abstaining from meat and drink. Every one had added to the national guilt, all shared in the national calamity, therefore every one must join in repentance. When joy and gladness are cut off from God's house, when serious godliness decays, and love waxes cold, then it is time to cry unto the Lord. The prophet describes how grievous the calamity. See even the inferior creatures suffering for our transgression. And what better are they than beasts, who never cry to God but for corn and wine, and complain of the want of the delights of sense? Yet their crying to God in those cases, shames the stupidity of those who cry not to God in any case. Whatever may become of the nations and churches that persist in ungodliness, believers will find the comfort of acceptance with God, when the wicked shall be burned up with his indignation.

Chapter 2

God's judgments. (Joel **2**:**1-14**) Exhortations to fasting and prayer; blessings promised. (Joel **2**:**15-27**) A promise of the Holy Spirit, and of future mercies. (Joel **2**:**28-32**)

Joel **2**:**1-14** The priests were to alarm the people with the near approach of the Divine judgments. It is the work of ministers to warn of the fatal consequences of sin, and to reveal the wrath from heaven against the ungodliness and unrighteousness of men. The striking description which follows, shows what would attend the devastations of locusts, but may also describe the effects from the ravaging of the land by the Chaldeans. If the alarm of temporal judgments is given to offending nations, how much more should sinners be warned to seek deliverance from the wrath to come! Our business therefore on earth must especially be, to secure an interest in our Lord Jesus Christ; and we should seek to be weaned from objects which will soon be torn from all who now make idols of them. There must be outward expressions of sorrow and shame, fasting, weeping, and mourning; tears for trouble must be turned into tears for the sin that caused it. But rending the garments would be vain, except their hearts were rent by abasement and self-abhorrence; by sorrow for their sins, and separation from them. There is no question but that if we truly repent of our sins, God will forgive them; but whether he will remove affliction is not promised, yet the probability of it should encourage us to repent.

Joel **2**:**15-27** The priests and rulers are to appoint a solemn fast. The sinner's supplication is, Spare us, good Lord. God is ready to succour his people; and he waits to be gracious. They prayed that God would spare them, and he answered them. His promises are real answers to the prayers of faith; with him saying and doing are not two things. Some understand these promises figuratively, as pointing to gospel grace, and as fulfilled in the abundant comforts treasured up for believers in the covenant of grace.

Joel **2**:**28-32** The promise began to be fulfilled on the day of Pentecost, when the Holy Spirit was poured out, and it was continued in the converting grace and miraculous gifts conferred on both Jews and Gentiles. The judgments of God upon a sinful world, only go before the judgment of the world in the last day. Calling on God supposes knowledge of him, faith in him, desire toward him, dependence on him, and, as evidence of the sincerity of all this, conscientious obedience to him. Those only shall be delivered in the great day, who are now effectually called from sin to God, from self to Christ, from things below to things above.

Chapter 3

God's judgments in the latter days. (Joel **3**:**1-8**) The extent of these judgments. (Joel **3**:**9-17**) The blessings the church shall enjoy. (Joel **3**:**18-21**)

Joel **3**:**1-8** The restoration of the Jews, and the final victory of true religion over all opposers, appear to be here foretold. The contempt and scorn with which the Jews have often been treated as a people, and the little value set upon them, are noticed. None ever hardened his heart against God or his church, and prospered long.

Joel **3**:**9-17** Here is a challenge to all the enemies of God's people. There is no escaping God's judgments; hardened sinners, in that day of wrath, shall be cut off from all comfort and joy. Most of the prophets foretell the same final victory of the church of God over all that oppose it. To the wicked it will be a terrible day, but to the righteous it will be a joyful day. What cause have those who possess an interest in Christ, to glory in their Strength and their Redeemer! The acceptable year of the Lord, a day of such great favour to some, will be a day of remarkable vengeance to others: let every one that is out of Christ awake, and flee from the wrath to come.

Joel **3**:**18-21** There shall be abundant Divine influences, and the gospel will spread speedily into the remotest corners of the earth. These events are predicted under significant emblems; there is a day coming, when every thing amiss shall be amended. The fountain of this plenty is in the house of God, whence the streams take rise. Christ is this Fountain; his sufferings, merit, and grace, cleanse, refresh, and make fruitful. Gospel grace, flowing from Christ, shall reach to the Gentile world, to the most remote regions, and make them abound in fruits of righteousness; and from the house of the Lord above, from his heavenly temple, flows all the good we daily taste, and hope to enjoy eternally.

Amos

Amos was a herdsman, and engaged in agriculture. But the same Divine Spirit influenced Isaiah and Daniel in the court, and Amos in the sheep-folds, giving to each the powers and eloquence needful for them. He assures the twelve tribes of the destruction of the neighbouring nations; and as they at that time gave themselves up to wickedness and idolatry, he reproves the Jewish nation with severity; but describes the restoration of the church by the Messiah, extending to the latter days.

Chapter 1

Judgments against the Syrians, Philistines, Tyrians, Edomites, and Ammonites.

—GOD employed a shepherd, a herdsman, to reprove and warn the people. Those to whom God gives abilities for his services, ought not to be despised for their origin, or their employment. Judgments are denounced against the neighbouring nations, the oppressors of God's people. The number of transgressions does not here mean that exact number, but many: they had filled the measure of their sins, and were ripe for vengeance. The method in dealing with these nations is, in part, the same, yet in each there is something peculiar. In all ages this bitterness has been shown against the Lord's people. When the Lord reckons with his enemies, how tremendous are his judgments!

Chapter 2

Chapter Outline	
Judgments against Moab and Judah.	(1–8)
The ingratitude and ruin of Israel.	(9–16)

Verses 1–8

The evil passions of the heart break out in various forms; but the Lord looks to our motives, as well as our conduct. Those that deal cruelly, shall be cruelly dealt with. Other nations were reckoned with for injuries done to men; Judah is reckoned with for dishonour done to God. Judah despised the law of the Lord; and he justly gave them up to strong delusion; nor was it any excuse for their sin, that they were the lies, the idols, after which their fathers walked. The worst abominations and most grievous oppressions have been committed by some of the professed worshippers of the Lord. Such conduct leads many to unbelief and vile idolatry.

Verses 9–16

We need often to be reminded of the mercies we have received; which add much to the evil of the sins we have committed. They had helps for their souls, which taught them how to make good use of their earthly enjoyments, and were therefore more valuable. Faithful ministers are great blessings to any people; but it is God that raises them up to be so. Sinners' own consciences will witness that he has not been wanting to them in the means of grace. They did what they could to lead believers aside. Satan and his agents are busy to corrupt the minds of young people who look heavenward; they overcome many by drawing them to the love of mirth and pleasure, and into drinking company. Multitudes of young men who bade fair as professors of religion, have erred through strong drink, and have been undone for ever. The Lord complains of sin, especially the sins of his professing people, as a burden to him. And though his long-suffering be tired, his power is not, and so the sinner will find to his cost. When men reject God's word, adding obstinacy to sin, and this becomes the general character of a people, they will be given up to misery, notwithstanding all their boasted power and resources. May we then humble ourselves before the Lord, for all our ingratitude and unfaithfulness.

Chapter 3

Chapter Outline	
Judgments against Israel.	(1–8)
The like to other nations.	(9–15)

Verses 1–8

The distinguishing favours of God to us, if they do not restrain from sin, shall not exempt from punishment. They could not expect communion with God, unless they first sought peace with him. Where there is not friendship, there can be no fellowship. God and man cannot walk together, except they are agreed. Unless we seek his glory, we cannot walk with him. Let us not presume on outward privileges, without special, sanctifying grace. The threatenings of the word and providence of God against the sin of man are certain, and certainly show that the judgments of God are at hand. Nor will God remove the affliction he has sent, till it has done its work. The evil of sin is from ourselves, it is our own doing; but the evil of trouble is from God, and is his doing, whoever are the instruments. This should engage us patiently to bear public troubles, and to study to answer God's meaning in them. The whole of the passage shows that natural evil, or troubles, and not moral evil, or sin, is here meant. The warning given to a careless world will increase its condemnation another day. Oh the amazing stupidity of an unbelieving world, that will not be wrought upon by the terrors of the Lord, and that despise his mercies!

Verses 9–15

That power which is an instrument of unrighteousness, will justly be brought down and broken. What is got and kept wrongfully, will not be kept long. Some are at ease, but there will come a day of visitation, and in that day, all they are proud of, and put confidence in, shall fail them. God will inquire into the sins of which they have been guilty in their houses, the robbery they have stored up, and the luxury in which they lived. The pomp and pleasantness of men's houses, do not fortify against God's judgments, but make sufferings the more grievous and vexatious. Yet a remnant, according to the election of grace, will be secured by our great and good Shepherd, as from the jaws of destruction, in the worst times.

Chapter 4

Chapter Outline	
Israel is reproved.	(1–5)
Their impenitence shown.	(6–13)

Verses 1–5

What is got by extortion is commonly used to provide for the flesh, and to fulfil the lusts thereof. What is got by oppression cannot be enjoyed with satisfaction. How miserable are those whose confidence in unscriptural observances only prove that they believe a lie! Let us see to it that our faith, hope, and worship, are warranted by the Divine word.

Verses 6–13

See the folly of carnal hearts; they wander from one creature to another, seeking for something to satisfy, and labour for that which satisfies not; yet, after all, they will not incline their ear to Him in whom they might find all they can want. Preaching the gospel is as rain, and every thing withers where this rain is wanting. It were well if people were as wise for their souls as they are for their bodies; and, when they have not this rain near, would go and seek it where it is to be had. As the Israelites persisted in rebellion and idolatry, the Lord was coming against them as an adversary. Ere long, we must meet our God in judgment; but we shall not be able to stand before him, if he tries us according to our doings. If we would prepare to meet our God with comfort, at the awful period of his coming, we must now meet him in Christ Jesus, the eternal Son of the Father, who came to save lost sinners. We must seek him while he is to be found.

Chapter 5

Chapter Outline	
Israel is called to seek the Lord.	(1–6)
Earnest exhortations to repentance.	(7–17)
Threatenings respecting idolatries.	(18–27)

Verses 1–6

The convincing, awakening word must be heard and heeded, as well as words of comfort and peace; for whether we hear or forbear, the word of God shall take effect. The Lord still proclaims mercy to men, but they often expect deliverance from such self-invented forms as make their condemnation sure. While they refuse to come to Christ and to seek mercy in and by him, that they may live, the fire of Divine wrath breaks forth upon them. Men may make an idol of the world, but will find it cannot protect.

Verses 7–17

The same almighty power can, for repenting sinners, easily turn affliction and sorrow into prosperity and joy, and as easily turn the prosperity of daring sinners into utter darkness. Evil times will not bear plain dealing; that is, evil men will not. And these men were evil men indeed, when wise and good men thought it in vain even to speak to them. Those who will seek and love that which is good, may help to save the land from ruin. It behoves us to plead God's spiritual promises, to beseech him to create in us a clean heart, and to renew a right spirit within us. The Lord is ever ready to be gracious to the souls that seek him; and then piety and every duty will be attended to. But as for sinful Israel, God's judgments had often passed by them, now they shall pass through them.

Verses 18–27

Woe unto those that desire the day of the Lord's judgments, that wish for times of war and confusion; as some who long for changes, hoping to rise upon the ruins of their country! but this should be so great a desolation, that nobody could gain by it. The day of the Lord will be a dark, dismal, gloomy day to all impenitent sinners. When God makes a day dark, all the world cannot make it light. Those who are not reformed by the judgments of God, will be pursued by them; if they escape one, another stands ready to seize them. A pretence of piety is double iniquity, and so it will be found. The people of Israel copied the crimes of their forefathers. The law of worshipping the Lord our God, is, Him only we must serve. Professors thrive so little, because they have little or no communion with God in their duties. They were led captive by Satan into idolatry, therefore God caused them to go into captivity among idolaters.

Chapter 6

Chapter Outline	
The danger of luxury and false security.	(1–7)
Punishments of sins.	(8–14)

Verses 1–7

Those are looked upon as doing well for themselves, who do well for their bodies; but we are here told what their ease is, and what their woe is. Here is a description of the pride, security, and sensuality, for which God would reckon. Careless sinners are every where in danger; but those at ease in Zion, who are stupid, vainly confident, and abusing their privileges, are in the greatest danger. Yet many fancy themselves the people of God, who are living in sin, and in conformity to the world. But the examples of others' ruin forbid us to be secure. Those who are set upon their pleasures are commonly careless of the troubles of others, but this is great offence to God. Those who placed their happiness in the pleasures of sense, and set their hearts upon them, shall be deprived of those pleasures. Those who try to put the evil day far from them, find it nearest to them.

Verses 8–14

How dreadful, how miserable, is the case of those whose eternal ruin the Lord himself has sworn; for he can execute his purpose, and none can alter it! Those hearts are wretchedly hardened that will not be brought to mention God's name, and to worship him, when the hand of God is gone out against them, when sickness and death are in their families. Those that will not be tilled as fields, shall be abandoned as rocks. When our services of God are soured with sin, his providences will justly be made bitter to us. Men should take warning not to harden their hearts, for those who walk in pride, God will destroy.

Chapter 7

Chapter Outline	
Visions of judgments to come upon Israel.	(1–9)
Amaziah threatens Amos.	(10–17)

Verses 1–9

God bears long, but he will not bear always with a provoking people. The remembrance of the mercies we formerly received, like the produce of the earth of the former growth, should make us submissive to the will of God, when we meet with disappointments in the latter growth. The Lord has many ways of humbling a sinful nation. Whatever trouble we are under, we should be most earnest with God for the forgiveness of sin. Sin will soon make a great people small. What will become of Israel, if the hand that should raise him be stretched out against him? See the power of prayer. See what a blessing praying people are to a land. See how ready, how swift God is to show mercy; how he waits to be gracious. Israel was a wall, a strong wall, which God himself reared as a defence to his sanctuary. The Lord now seems to stand upon this wall. He measures it; it appears to be a bowing, bulging wall. Thus God would bring the people of Israel to the trial, would discover their wickedness; and the time will come, when those who have been spared often, shall be spared no longer. But the Lord still calls Israel his people. The repeated prayer and success of the prophet should lead us to seek the Saviour.

Verses 10–17

It is no new thing for the accusers of the brethren, to misrepresent them as enemies to the king and kingdom, as traitors to their prince, and troublers of the land, when they are the best friends to both. Those who make gain their godliness, and are governed by the hopes of wealth and preferment, are ready to think these the most powerful motives with others also. But those who have a warrant from God, like Amos, ought not to fear the face of man. If God, that sent him, had not strengthened him, he could not thus have set his face as a flint. The Lord often chooses the weak and foolish things of the world to confound the wise and mighty. But no fervent prayers, or self-denying labours, can bring proud sinners to bear faithful reproofs and warnings. And all who oppose or despise the Divine word, must expect fatal effects to their souls, unless they repent.

Chapter 8

Chapter Outline	
The near approach of the ruin of Israel.	(1–3)
Oppression reproved.	(4–10)
A famine of the word of God.	(11–14)

Verses 1–3

Amos saw a basket of summer fruit gathered, and ready to be eaten; which signified, that the people were ripe for destruction, that the year of God's patience was drawing towards a conclusion. Such summer fruits will not keep till winter, but must be used at once. Yet these judgments shall not draw from them any acknowledgement, either of God's righteousness or their own unrighteousness. Sinners put off repentance from day to day, because they think the Lord thus delays his judgments.

Verses 4–10

The rich and powerful of the land were the most guilty of oppression, as well as the foremost in idolatry. They were weary of the restraints of the sabbaths and the new moons, and wished them over, because no common work might be done therein. This is the character of many who are called Christians. The sabbath day and sabbath work are a burden to carnal hearts. It will either be profaned or be accounted a dull day. But can we spend our time better than in communion with God? When employed in religious services, they were thinking of marketings. They were weary of holy duties, because their worldly business stood still the while. Those are strangers to God, and enemies to themselves, who love market days better than sabbath days, who would rather be selling corn than worshipping God. They have no regard to man: those who have lost the savour of piety, will not long keep the sense of common honesty. They cheat those they deal with. They take advantage of their neighbour's ignorance or necessity, in a traffic which nearly concerns the labouring poor. Could we witness the fraud and covetousness, which, in such numerous forms, render trading an abomination to the Lord, we should not wonder to see many dealers backward in the service of God. But he who thus despises the poor, reproaches his Maker; as it regards Him, rich and poor meet together. Riches that are got by the ruin of the poor, will bring ruin on those that get them. God will remember their sin against them. This speaks the case of such unjust, unmerciful men, to be miserable indeed, miserable for ever. There shall be terror and desolation every where. It shall come upon them when they little think of it. Thus uncertain are all our creature-comforts and enjoyments, even life itself; in the midst of life we are in death. What will be the wailing in the bitter day which follows sinful and sensual pleasures!

Verses 11–14

Here was a token of God's highest displeasure. At any time, and most in a time of trouble, a famine of the word of God is the heaviest judgment. To many this is no affliction, yet some will feel it very much, and will travel far to hear a good sermon; they feel the loss of the mercies others foolishly sin away. But when God visits a backsliding church, their own plans and endeavours to find out a way of salvation, will stand them in no stead. And the most amiable and zealous would perish, for want of the water of life, which Christ only can bestow. Let us value our advantages, seek to profit by them, and fear sinning them away.

Chapter 9

Chapter Outline	
The ruin of Israel.	(1–10)
The restoration of the Jews and the gospel blessing.	(11–15)

Verses 1–10

The prophet, in vision, saw the Lord standing upon the idolatrous altar at Bethel. Wherever sinners flee from God's justice, it will overtake them. Those whom God brings to heaven by his grace, shall never be cast down; but those who seek to climb thither by vain confidence in themselves, will be cast down and filled with shame. That which makes escape impossible and ruin sure, is, that God will set his eyes upon them for evil, not for good. Wretched must those be on whom the Lord looks for evil, and not for good. The Lord would scatter the Jews, and visit them with calamities, as the corn is shaken in a sieve; but he would save some from among them. The astonishing preservation of the Jews as a distinct people, seems here foretold. If professors make themselves like the world, God will level them with the world. The sinners who thus flatter themselves, shall find that their profession will not protect them.

Verses 11–15

Christ died to gather together the children of God that were scattered abroad, here said to be those who were called by his name. The Lord saith this, who doeth this, who can do it, who has determined to do it, the power of whose grace is engaged for doing it. **Verses** #(**13–15**) may refer to the early times of Christianity, but will receive a more glorious fulfilment in the events which all the prophets more or less foretold, and may be understood of the happy state when the fulness both of the Jews and the Gentiles come into the church. Let us continue earnest in prayer for the fulfilment of these prophecies, in the peace, purity, and the beauty of the church. God marvellously preserves his elect amidst the most fearful confusions and miseries. When all seems desperate, he wonderfully revives his church, and blesses her with all spiritual blessings in Christ Jesus. And great shall be the glory of that period, in which not one good thing promised shall remain unfulfilled.

Obadiah

The first part denounces the destruction of Edom, dwelling upon the injuries they inflicted upon the Jews. The second foretells the restoration of the Jews, and the latter glories of the church.

Chapter 1

Chapter Outline	
Destruction to come upon Edom. Their offences against Jacob.	(1–16)
The restoration of the Jews, and their flourishing state in the latter times.	(17–21)

Verses 1–16

This prophecy is against Edom. Its destruction seems to have been typical, as their father Esau's rejection; and to refer to the destruction of the enemies of the gospel church. See the prediction of the success of that war; Edom shall be spoiled, and brought down. All the enemies of God's church shall be disappointed in the things they stay themselves on. God can easily lay those low who magnify and exalt themselves; and will do it. Carnal security ripens men for ruin, and makes the ruin worse when it comes. Treasures on earth cannot be so safely laid up but that thieves may break through and steal; it is therefore our wisdom to lay up for ourselves treasures in heaven. Those that make flesh their trust, arm it against themselves. The God of our covenant will never deceive us: but if we trust men with whom we join ourselves, it may prove to us a wound and dishonour. God will justly deny those understanding to keep out of danger, who will not use their understandings to keep out of sin. All violence, all unrighteousness, is sin; but it makes the violence far worse, if it be done against any of God's people. Their barbarous conduct towards Judah and Jerusalem, is charged upon them. In reflecting on ourselves, it is good to consider what we should have done; to compare our practice with the Scripture rule. Sin, thus looked upon in the glass of the commandment, will appear exceedingly sinful. Those have a great deal to answer for, who are idle spectators of the troubles of their neighbours, when able to be active helpers. Those make themselves poor, who think to make themselves rich by the ruin of the people of God; and those deceive themselves, who call all that their own on which they can lay their hands in a day of calamity. Though judgment begins at the house of God, it shall not end there. Let sorrowful believers and insolent oppressors know, that the troubles of the righteous will soon end, but those of the wicked will be eternal.

Verses 17–21

There should be deliverance and holiness at Jerusalem, and the house of Jacob would again occupy their possessions. Much of this prophecy was fulfilled when the Jews returned to their own land. But the salvation and holiness of the gospel, its spread, and the conversion of the Gentiles, seem also to be intended, especially the restoration of Israel, the destruction of antichrist, and the prosperous state of the church, to which all the prophets bear witness. When Christ is come, and not till then, shall the kingdom be the Lord's in the full sense of the term. As none that exalt themselves against the Lord shall prosper, and all shall be brought down; so none that wait upon the Lord, and put their trust in him, shall ever be dismayed. Blessed be the Divine Saviour and Judge on Mount Zion! His word shall be a savour of life unto life unto numbers, while it judges and condemns obstinate unbelievers.

Jonah

Jonah was a native of Galilee, **2Ki 14:25**. His miraculous deliverance from out of the fish, rendered him a type of our blessed Lord, who mentions it, so as to show the certain truth of the narrative. All that was done was easy to the almighty power of the Author and Sustainer of life. This book shows us, by the example of the Ninevites, how great are the Divine forbearance and long-suffering towards sinners. It shows a most striking contrast between the goodness and mercy of God, and the rebellion, impatience, and peevishness of his servant; and it will be best understood by those who are most acquainted with their own hearts.

Chapter 1

Chapter Outline	
Jonah, sent to Nineveh, flees to Tarshish.	(1–3)
He is stayed by a tempest.	(4–7)
His discourse with the mariners.	(8–12)
He is cast into the sea, and miraculously preserved.	(13–17)

Verses 1–3

It is sad to think how much sin is committed in great cities. Their wickedness, as that of Nineveh, is a bold and open affront to God. Jonah must go at once to Nineveh, and there, on the spot, cry against the wickedness of it. Jonah would not go. Probably there are few among us who would not have tried to decline such a mission. Providence seemed to give him an opportunity to escape; we may be out of the way of duty, and yet may meet with a favourable gale. The ready way is not always the right way. See what the best of men are, when God leaves them to themselves; and what need we have, when the word of the Lord comes to us, to have the Spirit of the Lord to bring every thought within us into obedience.

Verses 4–7

God sent a pursuer after Jonah, even a mighty tempest. Sin brings storms and tempests into the soul, into the family, into churches and nations; it is a disquieting, disturbing thing. Having called upon their gods for help, the sailors did what they could to help themselves. Oh that men would be thus wise for their souls, and would be willing to part with that wealth, pleasure, and honour, which they cannot keep without making shipwreck of faith and a good conscience, and ruining their souls for ever! Jonah was fast asleep. Sin is stupifying, and we are to take heed lest at any time our hearts are hardened by the deceitfulness of it. What do men mean by sleeping on in sin, when the word of God and the convictions of their own consciences, warn them to arise and call on the Lord, if they would escape everlasting misery? Should not we warn each other to awake, to arise, to call upon our God, if so be he will deliver us? The sailors concluded the storm was a messenger of Divine justice sent to some one in that ship. Whatever evil is upon us at any time, there is a cause for it; and each must pray, Lord, show me wherefore thou contendest with me. The lot fell upon Jonah. God has many ways of bringing to light hidden sins and sinners, and making manifest that folly which was thought to be hid from the eyes of all living.

Verses 8–12

Jonah gave an account of his religion, for that was his business. We may hope that he told with sorrow and shame, justifying God, condemning himself, and explaining to the mariners what a great God Jehovah is. They said to him, Why hast thou done this? If thou fearest the God that made the sea and the dry land, why wast thou such a fool as to think thou couldst flee from his presence? If the professors of religion do wrong, they will hear it from those who make no such profession. When sin has raised a storm, and laid us under the tokens of God's displeasure, we must consider what is to be done to the sin that raised the storm. Jonah uses the language of true penitents, who desire that none but themselves may fare the worse for their sins and follies. Jonah sees this to be the punishment of his iniquity, he accepts it, and justifies God in it. When conscience is awakened, and a storm raised, nothing will turn it into a calm but parting with the sin that caused the disturbance. Parting with our money will not pacify the conscience, the Jonah must be thrown overboard.

Verses 13–17

The mariners rowed against wind and tide, the wind of God's displeasure, the tide of his counsel; but it is in vain to think of saving ourselves any other way than by destroying our sins. Even natural conscience cannot but dread blood-guiltiness. And when we are led by Providence God does what he pleases, and we ought to be satisfied, though it may not please us. Throwing Jonah into the sea put an end to the storm. God will not afflict for ever, He will only contend till we submit and turn from our sins. Surely these heathen mariners will rise up in judgment against many called Christians, who neither offer prayers when in distress, nor thanksgiving for signal deliverances. The Lord commands all creatures, and can make any of them serve his designs of mercy to his people. Let us see this salvation of the Lord, and admire his power, that he could thus save a drowning man, and his pity, that he would thus save one who was running from him, and had offended him. It was of the Lord's mercies that Jonah was not consumed. Jonah was alive in the fish three days and nights: to nature this was impossible, but to the God of nature all things are possible. Jonah, by this miraculous preservation, was made a type of Christ; as our blessed Lord himself declared, Mt **12**:**40**.

Chapter 2

Chapter Outline	
The prayer of Jonah.	(1–9)
He is delivered from the fish.	(10)

Verses 1–9

Observe when Jonah prayed. When he was in trouble, under the tokens of God's displeasure against him for sin: when we are in affliction we must pray. Being kept alive by miracle, he prayed. A sense of God's good-will to us, notwithstanding our offences, opens the lips in prayer, which were closed with the dread of wrath. Also, where he prayed; in the belly of the fish. No place is amiss for prayer. Men may shut us from communion with one another, but not from communion with God. To whom he prayed; to the Lord his God. This encourages even backsliders to return. What his prayer was. This seems to relate his experience and reflections, then and afterwards, rather than to be the form or substance of his prayer. Jonah reflects on the earnestness of his prayer, and God's readiness to hear and answer. If we would get good by our troubles, we must notice the hand of God in them. He had wickedly fled from the presence of the Lord, who might justly take his Holy Spirit from him, never to visit him more. Those only are miserable, whom God will no longer own and favour. But though he was perplexed, yet not in despair. Jonah reflects on the favour of God to him, when he sought to God, and trusted in him in his distress. He warns others, and tells them to keep close to God. Those who forsake their own duty, forsake their own mercy; those who run away from the work of their place and day, run away from the comfort of it. As far as a believer copies those who observe lying vanities, he forsakes his own mercy, and lives below his privileges. But Jonah's experience encourages others, in all ages, to trust in God, as the God of salvation.

Verse 10

Jonah's deliverance may be considered as an instance of God's power over all the creatures. As an instance of God's mercy to a poor penitent, who in distress prays to him: and as a type and figure of Christ's resurrection. Amidst all our varying experiences, and the changing scenes of life; we should look by faith, fixedly, upon our once suffering and dying, but now risen and ascended Redeemer. Let us confess our sins, consider Christ's resurrection as an earnest of our own, and thankfully receive every temporal and spiritual deliverance, as the pledge of our eternal redemption.

Chapter 3

Chapter Outline	
Jonah sent again to Nineveh, preaches there.	(1–4)
Nineveh is spared upon the repentance of the inhabitants.	(5–10)

Verses 1–4

God employs Jonah again in his service. His making use of us is an evidence of his being at peace with us. Jonah was not disobedient, as he had been. He neither endeavoured to avoid hearing the command, nor declined to obey it. See here the nature of repentance; it is the change of our mind and way, and a return to our work and duty. Also, the benefit of affliction; it brings those back to their place who had deserted it. See the power of Divine grace, for affliction of itself would rather drive men from God, than draw them to him. God's servants must go where he sends them, come when he calls them, and do what he bids them; we must do whatever the word of the Lord commands. Jonah faithfully and boldly delivered his errand. Whether Jonah said more, to show the anger of God against them, or whether he only repeated these words again and again, is not certain, but this was the purport of his message. Forty days is a long time for a righteous God to delay judgments, yet it is but a little time for an unrighteous people to repent and reform in. And should it not awaken us to get ready for death, to consider that we cannot be so sure that we shall live forty days, as Nineveh then was that it should stand forty days? We should be alarmed if we were sure not to live a month, yet we are careless though we are not sure to live a day.

Verses 5–10

There was a wonder of Divine grace in the repentance and reformation of Nineveh. It condemns the men of the gospel generation, Mt **12**:**41**. A very small degree of light may convince men that humbling themselves before God, confessing their sins with prayer, and turning from sin, are means of escaping wrath and obtaining mercy. The people followed the example of the king. It became a national act, and it was necessary it should be so, when it was to prevent a national ruin. Let even the brute creatures' cries and moans for want of food remind their owners to cry to God. In prayer we must cry mightily, with fixedness of thought, firmness of faith, and devout affections. It concerns us in prayer to stir up all that is within us. It is not enough to fast for sin, but we must fast from sin; and, in order to the success of our prayers, we must no more regard iniquity in our hearts, Ps **66**:**18**. The work of a fast-day is not done with the day. The Ninevites hoped that God would turn from his fierce anger; and that thus their ruin would be prevented. They could not be so confident of finding mercy upon their repentance, as we may be, who have the death and merits of Christ, to which we may trust for pardon upon repentance. They dared not presume, but they did not despair. Hope of mercy is the great encouragement to repentance and reformation. Let us boldly cast ourselves down at the footstool of free grace, and God will look upon us with compassion. God sees who turn from their evil ways, and who do not. Thus he spared Nineveh. We read of no sacrifices offered to God to make atonement for sin; but a broken and a contrite heart, such as the Ninevites then had, he will not despise.

Chapter 4

Chapter Outline	
Jonah repines at God's mercy to Nineveh, and is reproved.	(1–4)
He is taught by the withering of a gourd, that he did wrong.	(5–11)

Verses 1–4

What all the saints make matter of joy and praise, Jonah makes the subject of reflection upon God; as if showing mercy were an imperfection of the Divine nature, which is the greatest glory of it. It is to his sparing, pardoning mercy, we all owe it that we are out of hell. He wishes for death: this was the language of folly, passion, and strong corruption. There appeared in Jonah remains of a proud, uncharitable spirit; and that he neither expected nor desired the welfare of the Ninevites, but had only come to declare and witness their destruction. He was not duly humbled for his own sins, and was not willing to trust the Lord with his credit and safety. In this frame of mind, he overlooked the good of which he had been an instrument, and the glory of the Divine mercy. We should often ask ourselves, Is it well to say thus, to do thus? Can I justify it? Do I well to be so soon angry, so often angry, so long angry, and to give others ill language in my anger? Do I well to be angry at the mercy of God to repenting sinners? That was Jonah's crime. Do we do well to be angry at that which is for the glory of God, and the advancement of his kingdom? Let the conversion of sinners, which is the joy of heaven, be our joy, and never our grief.

Verses 5–11

Jonah went out of the city, yet remained near at hand, as if he expected and desired its overthrow. Those who have fretful, uneasy spirits, often make troubles for themselves, that they may still have something to complain of. See how tender God is of his people in their afflictions, even though they are foolish and froward. A thing small in itself, yet coming seasonably, may be a valuable blessing. A gourd in the right place may do us more service than a cedar. The least creatures may be great plagues, or great comforts, as God is pleased to make them. Persons of strong passions are apt to be cast down with any trifle that crosses them, or to be lifted up with a trifle that pleases them. See what our creature-comforts are, and what we may expect them to be; they are withering things. A small worm at the root destroys a large gourd: our gourds wither, and we know not what is the cause. Perhaps creature-comforts are continued to us, but are made bitter; the creature is continued, but the comfort is gone. God prepared a wind to make Jonah feel the want of the gourd. It is just that those who love to complain, should never be left without something to complain of. When afflicting providences take away relations, possessions, and enjoyments, we must not be angry at God. What should especially silence discontent, is, that when our gourd is gone, our God is not gone. Sin and death are very dreadful, yet Jonah, in his heat, makes light of both. One soul is of more value than the whole world; surely then one soul is of more value than many gourds: we should have more concern for our own and others' precious souls, than for the riches and enjoyments of this world. It is a great encouragement to hope we shall find mercy with the Lord, that he is ready to show mercy. And murmurers shall be made to understand, that how willing soever they are to keep the Divine grace to themselves and those of their own way, there is one Lord over all, who is rich in mercy to all that call upon him. Do we wonder at the forbearance of God towards his perverse servant? Let us study our own hearts and ways; let us not forget our own ingratitude and obstinacy; and let us be astonished at God's patience towards us.

Micah

Micah was raised up to support Isaiah, and to confirm his predictions, while he invited to repentance, both by threatened judgments and promised mercies. A very remarkable passage, Mic 5 contains a summary of prophecies concerning the Messiah.

Chapter 1

Chapter Outline	
The wrath of God against Israel.	(1–7)
Also against Jerusalem and other cities, Their precautions vain.	(8–16)

Verses 1–7

The earth is called upon, with all that are therein, to hear the prophet. God's holy temple will not protect false professors. Neither men of high degree, as the mountains, nor men of low degree, as the valleys, can secure themselves or the land from the judgments of God. If sin be found in God's people he will not spare them; and their sins are most provoking to him, for they are most reproaching. When we feel the smart of sin, it behoves us to seek what is the sin we smart for. Persons and places most exalted, are most exposed to spiritual diseases. The vices of leaders and rulers shall be surely and sorely punished. The punishment answers the sin. What they gave to idols, never shall prosper, nor do them any good. What is got by one lust, is wasted on another.

Verses 8–16

The prophet laments that Israel's case is desperate; but declare it not in Gath. Gratify not those that make merry with the sins or with the sorrows of God's Israel. Roll thyself in the dust, as mourners used to do; let every house in Jerusalem become a house of Aphrah, "a house of dust." When God makes the house dust it becomes us to humble ourselves to the dust under his mighty hand. Many places should share this mourning. The names have meanings which pointed out the miseries coming upon them; thereby to awaken the people to a holy fear of Divine wrath. All refuges but Christ, must be refuges of lies to those who trust in them; other heirs will succeed to every inheritance but that of heaven; and all glory will be turned into shame, except that honour which cometh from God only. Sinners may now disregard their neighbours' sufferings, yet their turn to be punished will some come.

Chapter 2

Chapter Outline	
The sins and desolations of Israel.	(1–5)
Their evil practices.	(6–11)
A promise of restoration.	(12, 13)

Verses 1–5

Woe to the people that devise evil during the night, and rise early to carry it into execution! It is bad to do mischief on a sudden thought, much worse to do it with design and forethought. It is of great moment to improve and employ hours of retirement and solitude in a proper manner. If covetousness reigns in the heart, compassion is banished; and when the heart is thus engaged, violence and fraud commonly occupy the hands. The most haughty and secure in prosperity, are commonly most ready to despair in adversity. Woe to those from whom God turns away! Those are the sorest calamities which cut us off from the congregation of the Lord, or cut us short in the enjoyment of its privileges.

Verses 6–11

Since they say, "Prophesy not," God will take them at their word, and their sin shall be their punishment. Let the physician no longer attend the patient that will not be healed. Those are enemies, not only to God, but to their country, who silence good ministers, and stop the means of grace. What bonds will hold those who have no reverence for God's word? Sinners cannot expect to rest in a land they have polluted. You shall not only be obliged to depart out of this land, but it shall destroy you. Apply this to our state in this present world. There is corruption in the world through lust, and we should keep at a distance from it. It is not our rest: it was designed for our passage, but not for our portion; our inn, but not our home; here we have no continuing city; let us therefore arise and depart, let us seek a continuing city above. Since they will be deceived, let them be deceived. Teachers who recommend self-indulgence by their doctrine and example, best suit such sinners.

Verses 12, 13

These **verse**s may refer to the captivity of Israel and Judah. But the passage is also a prophecy of the conversion of the Jews to Christ. The Lord would not only bring them from captivity, and multiply them, but the Lord Jesus would open their way to God, by taking upon him the nature of man, and by the work of his Spirit in their hearts, breaking the fetters of Satan. Thus he has gone before, and the people follow, breaking, in his strength, through the enemies that would stop their way to heaven.

Chapter 3

Chapter Outline	
The cruelty of the princes, and the falsehood of the prophets.	(1–8)
Their false security.	(9–12)

Verses 1–8

Men cannot expect to do ill, and fare well; but to find that done to them which they did to others. How seldom do wholesome truths reach the ears of those in high stations or in authority! Those who deceive others are preparing confusion for their own faces. The prophet had ardent love to God and to the souls of men; deep concern for his glory and their salvation, and zeal against sin. The difficulties he met with did not drive him from his work. He had this strength; not from and of himself, but he was full of power by the Spirit of the Lord. Those who act honestly, may act boldly. And those who come to hear the word of God, must be willing to be told of their faults, must take it kindly, and be thankful.

Verses 9–12

Zion's walls owe no thanks to those that build them up with blood and iniquity. The sin of man works not the righteousness of God. Even when men do that which in itself is good, but do it for filthy lucre, it becomes abomination both to God and man. Faith rests in the Lord as the soul's foundation: presumption only leans upon the Lord as a prop, and would use him to serve a turn. If men's having the Lord among them will not keep them from doing evil, it never can secure them from suffering evil for so doing. See the doom of wicked Jacob; Therefore shall Zion for your sake be ploughed as a field. This was exactly fulfilled at the destruction of Jerusalem by the Romans, and is so at this day. If sacred places are polluted by sin, they will be wasted and ruined by the judgments of God.

Chapter 4

Chapter Outline	
The peace of the kingdom of Christ.	(1–8)
The judgments to come upon Jerusalem, but the final triumph of Israel.	(9–13)

Verses 1–8

The nations have not yet so submitted to the Prince of Peace, as to beat their swords into ploughshares, nor has war ceased. But very precious promises these are, relating to the gospel church, which will be more and more fulfilled, for He is faithful that has promised. There shall be a glorious church for God set up in the world, in the last days, in the days of the Messiah. Christ himself will build it upon a rock. The Gentiles worshipped their idol gods; but in the period spoken of, the people will cleave to the Lord with full purpose of heart, and delight in doing his will. The word "halteth," describes those who walk not according to the Divine word. The collecting the captives from Babylon was an earnest of healing, purifying, and prospering the church; and the reign of Christ shall continue till succeeded by the everlasting kingdom of heaven. Let us stir up each other to attend the ordinances of God, that we may learn his holy ways, and walk in them, receiving the law from his hands, which, being written in our hearts by his Spirit, may show our interest in the Redeemer's righteousness.

Verses 9–13

Many nations would assemble against Zion to rejoice in her calamities. They would not understand that the Lord had collected them as sheaves are gathered to be threshed; and that Zion would be strengthened to beat them to pieces. Nothing has yet taken place in the history of the Jewish church agreeing with this prediction. When God has conquering work for his people to do, he will furnish them with strength and ability for it. Believers should cry aloud under distresses, with the prayer of faith, not with despondency.

Chapter 5

Chapter Outline	
The birth of Christ and conversion of the Gentiles.	(1–6)
The triumphs of Israel.	(7–15)

Verses 1–6

Having showed how low the house of David would be brought, a prediction of the Messiah and his kingdom is added to encourage the faith of God's people. His existence from eternity as God, and his office as Mediator, are noticed. Here is foretold that Bethlehem should be his birthplace. Hence it was universally known among the Jews, Mt **2**:**5**. Christ's government shall be very happy for his subjects; they shall be safe and easy. Under the shadow of protection from the Assyrians, is a promise of protection to the gospel church and all believers, from the designs and attempts of the powers of darkness. Christ is our Peace as a Priest, making atonement for sin, and reconciling us to God; and he is our Peace as a King, conquering our enemies: hence our souls may dwell at ease in him. Christ will find instruments to protect and deliver. Those that threaten ruin to the church of God, soon bring ruin on themselves. This may include the past powerful effects of the preached gospel, its future spread, and the ruin of all antichristian powers. This is, perhaps, the most important single prophecy in the Old Testament: it respects the personal character of the Messiah, and the discoveries of himself to the world. It distinguishes his human birth from his existing from eternity; it foretells the rejection of the Israelites and Jews for a season, their final restoration, and the universal peace to prevail through the whole earth in the latter days. In the mean time let us trust our Shepherd's care and power. If he permits the assault of our enemies, he will supply helpers and assistance for us.

Verses 7–15

The remnant of Israel, converted to Christ in the primitive times, were among many nations as the drops of dew, and were made instruments in calling a large increase of spiritual worshippers. But to those who neglected or opposed this salvation, they would, as lions, cause terror, their doctrine condemning them. The Lord also declares that he would cause not only the reformation of the Jews, but the purification of the Christian church. In like manner shall we be assured of victory in our personal conflicts, as we simply depend upon the Lord our salvation, worship him, and serve him with diligence.

Chapter 6

Chapter Outline	
God's controversy with Israel.	(1–5)
The duties God requires.	(6–8)
The wickedness of Israel.	(9–16)

Verses 1–5

The people are called upon to declare why they were weary of God's worship, and prone to idolatry. Sin causes the controversy between God and man. God reasons with us, to teach us to reason with ourselves. Let them remember God's many favours to them and their fathers, and compare with them their unworthy, ungrateful conduct toward him.

Verses 6–8

These **verses** seem to contain the substance of Balak's consultation with Balaam how to obtain the favour of Israel's God. Deep conviction of guilt and wrath will put men upon careful inquiries after peace and pardon, and then there begins to be some ground for hope of them. In order to God's being pleased with us, our care must be for an interest in the atonement of Christ, and that the sin by which we displease him may be taken away. What will be a satisfaction to God's justice? In whose name must we come, as we have nothing to plead as our own? In what righteousness shall we appear before him? The proposals betray ignorance, though they show zeal. They offer that which is very rich and costly. Those who are fully convinced of sin, and of their misery and danger by reason of it, would give all the world, if they had it, for peace and pardon. Yet they do not offer aright. The sacrifices had value from their reference to Christ; it was impossible that the blood of bulls and goats should take away sin. And all proposals of peace, except those according to the gospel, are absurd. They could not answer the demands of Divine justice, nor satisfy the wrong done to the honour of God by sin, nor would they serve at all in place of holiness of the heart and reformation of the life. Men will part with any thing rather than their sins; but they part with nothing so as to be accepted of God, unless they do part with their sins. Moral duties are commanded because they are good for man. In keeping God's commandments there is a great reward, as well as after keeping them. God has not only made it known, but made it plain. The good which God requires of us is, not the paying a price for the pardon of sin and acceptance with God, but love to himself; and what is there unreasonable, or hard, in this? Every thought within us must be brought down, to be brought into obedience to God, if we would walk comfortably with him. We must do this as penitent sinners, in dependence on the Redeemer and his atonement. Blessed be the Lord that he is ever ready to give his grace to the humble, waiting penitent.

Verses 9–16

God, having showed how necessary it was that they should do justly, here shows how plain it was that they had done unjustly. This voice of the Lord says to all, Hear the rod when it is coming, before you see it, and feel it. Hear the rod when it is come, and you are sensible of the smart; hear what counsels, what cautions it speaks. The voice of God is to be heard in the rod of God. Those who are dishonest in their dealings shall never be reckoned pure, whatever shows of devotion they may make. What is got by fraud and oppression, cannot be kept or enjoyed with satisfaction. What we hold closest we commonly lose soonest. Sin is a root of bitterness, soon planted, but not soon plucked up again. Their being the people of God in name and profession, while they kept themselves in his love, was an honour to them; but now, being backsliders, their having been once the people of God turns to their reproach.

Chapter 7

Chapter Outline	
The general prevalence of wickedness.	(1–7)
Reliance on God, and triumph over enemies.	(8–13)
Promises and encouragements for Israel.	(14–20)

Verses 1–7

The prophet bemoans himself that he lived among a people ripening apace for ruin, in which many good persons would suffer. Men had no comfort, no satisfaction in their own families or in their nearest relations. Contempt and violation of domestic duties are a sad symptom of universal corruption. Those are never likely to come to good who are undutiful to their parents. The prophet saw no safety or comfort but in looking to the Lord, and waiting on God his salvation. When under trials, we should look continually to our Divine Redeemer, that we may have strength and grace to trust in him, and to be examples to those around us.

Verses 8–13

Those truly penitent for sin, will see great reason to be patient under affliction. When we complain to the Lord of the badness of the times, we ought to complain against ourselves for the badness of our hearts. We must depend upon God to work deliverance for us in due time. We must not only look to him, but look for him. In our greatest distresses, we shall see no reason to despair of salvation, if by faith we look to the Lord as the God of our salvation. Though enemies triumph and insult, they shall be silenced and put to shame. Though Zion's walls may long be in ruins, there will come a day when they shall be repaired. Israel shall come from all the remote parts, not turning back for discouragements. Though our enemies may seem to prevail against us, and to rejoice over us, we should not despond. Though cast down, we are not destroyed; we may join hope in God's mercy, with submission to his correction. No hinderances can prevent the favours the Lord intends for his church.

Verses 14–20

When God is about to deliver his people, he stirs up their friends to pray for them. Apply spiritually the prophet's prayer to Christ, to take care of his church, as the great Shepherd of the sheep, and to go before them, while they are here in this world as in a wood, in this world but not of it. God promises in answer to this prayer, he will do that for them which shall be repeating the miracles of former ages. As their sin brought them into bondage, so God's pardoning their sin brought them out. All who find pardoning mercy, cannot but wonder at that mercy; we have reason to stand amazed, if we know what it is. When the Lord takes away the guilt of sin, that it may not condemn us, he will break the power of sin, that it may not have dominion over us. If left to ourselves, our sins will be too hard for us; but God's grace shall be sufficient to subdue them, so that they shall not rule us, and then they shall not ruin us. When God forgives sin, he takes care that it never shall be remembered any more against the sinner. He casts their sins into the sea; not near the shore-side, where they may appear again, but into the depth of the sea, never to rise again. All their sins shall be cast there, for when God forgives sin, he forgives all. He will perfect that which concerns us, and with this good work will do all for us which our case requires, and which he has promised. These engagements relate to Christ, and the success of the gospel to the end of time, the future restoration of Israel, and the final prevailing of true religion in all lands. The Lord will perform his truth and mercy, not one jot or tittle of it shall fall to the ground: faithful is He that has promised, who also will do it. Let us remember that the Lord has given the security of his covenant, for strong consolation to all who flee for refuge to lay hold on the hope set before them in Christ Jesus.

Nahum

This prophet denounces the certain and approaching destruction of the Assyrian empire, particularly of Nineveh, which is described very minutely. Together with this is consolation for his countrymen, encouraging them to trust in God.

Chapter 1

Chapter Outline	
The justice and power of the Lord.	(1–8)
The overthrow of the Assyrians.	(9–15)

Verses 1–8

About a hundred years before, at Jonah's preaching, the Ninevites repented, and were spared, yet, soon after, they became worse than ever. Nineveh knows not that God who contends with her, but is told what a God he is. It is good for all to mix faith with what is here said concerning Him, which speaks great terror to the wicked, and comfort to believers. Let each take his portion from it: let sinners read it and tremble; and let saints read it and triumph. The anger of the Lord is contrasted with his goodness to his people. Perhaps they are obscure and little regarded in the world, but the Lord knows them. The Scripture character of Jehovah agrees not with the views of proud reasoners. The God and Father of our Lord Jesus Christ is slow to wrath and ready to forgive, but he will by no means acquit the wicked; and there is tribulation and anguish for every soul that doeth evil: but who duly regards the power of his wrath?

Verses 9–15

There is a great deal plotted against the Lord by the gates of hell, and against his kingdom in the world; but it will prove in vain. With some sinners God makes quick despatch; and one way or other, he will make an utter end of all his enemies. Though they are quiet, and many very secure, and not in fear, they shall be cut down as grass and corn, when the destroying angel passes through. God would hereby work great deliverance for his own people. But those who make themselves vile by scandalous sins, God will make vile by shameful punishments. The tidings of this great deliverance shall be welcomed with abundant joy. These words are applied to the great redemption wrought out by our Lord Jesus and the everlasting gospel. Ro **10**:**15**. Christ's ministers are messengers of good tidings, that preach peace by Jesus Christ. How welcome to those who see their misery and danger by sin! And the promise they made in the day of trouble must be made good. Let us be thankful for God's ordinances, and gladly attend them. Let us look forward with cheerful hope to a world where the wicked never can enter, and sin and temptation will no more be known.

Chapter 2

Chapter Outline	
Nineveh's destruction foretold.	(1–10)
The true cause, their sinning against God, and his appearing against them.	(11–13)

Verses 1–10

Nineveh shall not put aside this judgment; there is no counsel or strength against the Lord. God looks upon proud cities, and brings them down. Particular account is given of the terrors wherein the invading enemy shall appear against Nineveh. The empire of Assyria is represented as a queen, about to be led captive to Babylon. Guilt in the conscience fills men with terror in an evil day; and what will treasures or glory do for us in times of distress, or in the day of wrath? Yet for such things how many lose their souls!

Verses 11–13

The kings of Assyria had long been terrible and cruel to their neighbours, but the Lord would destroy their power. Many plead as an excuse for rapine and fraud, that they have families to provide for; but what is thus obtained will never do them any good. Those that fear the Lord, and get honestly what they have, shall not want for themselves and theirs. It is just with God to deprive those of children, or of comfort in them, who take sinful courses to enrich them. Those are not worthy to be heard again, that have spoken reproachfully of God. Let us then come to God upon his mercy-seat, that having peace with him through our Lord Jesus Christ, we may know that he is for us, and that all things shall work together for our everlasting good.

Chapter 3

Chapter Outline	
The sins and judgments of Nineveh.	(1–7)
Its utter destruction.	(8–19)

Verses 1–7

When proud sinners are brought down, others should learn not to lift themselves up. The fall of this great city should be a lesson to private persons, who increase wealth by fraud and oppression. They are preparing enemies for themselves; and if the Lord sees good to punish them in this world, they will have none to pity them. Every man who seeks his own prosperity, safety, and peace, should not only act in an upright, honourable manner, but with kindness to all.

Verses 8–19

Strong-holds, even the strongest, are no defence against the judgments of God. They shall be unable to do any thing for themselves. The Chaldeans and Medes would devour the land like canker-worms. The Assyrians also would be eaten up by their own numerous hired troops, which seem to be meant by the word rendered "merchants." Those that have done evil to their neighbours, will find it come home to them. Nineveh, and many other cities, states, and empires, have been ruined, and should be a warning to us. Are we better, except as there are some true Christians amongst us, who are a greater security, and a stronger defence, than all the advantages of situation or strength? When the Lord shows himself against a people, every thing they trust in must fail, or prove a disadvantage; but he continues good to Israel. He is a strong-hold for every believer in time of trouble, that cannot be stormed or taken; and he knoweth those that trust in Him.

Habakkuk

The subject of this prophecy is the destruction of Judea and Jerusalem for the sins of the people, and the consolation of the faithful under national calamities.

Chapter 1

Chapter Outline	
The wickedness of the land. The fearful vengeance to be executed.	(1–11)

These judgments to be inflicted by a nation more wicked than themselves.	(12–17)

Verses 1–11

The servants of the Lord are deeply afflicted by seeing ungodliness and violence prevail; especially among those who profess the truth. No man scrupled doing wrong to his neighbour. We should long to remove to the world where holiness and love reign for ever, and no violence shall be before us. God has good reasons for his long-suffering towards bad men, and the rebukes of good men. The day will come when the cry of sin will be heard against those that do wrong, and the cry of prayer for those that suffer wrong. They were to notice what was going forward among the heathen by the Chaldeans, and to consider themselves a nation to be scourged by them. But most men presume on continued prosperity, or that calamities will not come in their days. They are a bitter and hasty nation, fierce, cruel, and bearing down all before them. They shall overcome all that oppose them. But it is a great offence, and the common offence of proud people, to take glory to themselves. The closing words give a glimpse of comfort.

Verses 12–17

However matters may be, yet God is the Lord our God, our Holy One. We are an offending people, he is an offended God, yet we will not entertain hard thoughts of him, or of his service. It is great comfort that, whatever mischief men design, the Lord designs good, and we are sure that his counsel shall stand. Though wickedness may prosper a while, yet God is holy, and does not approve the wickedness. As he cannot do iniquity himself, so he is of purer eyes than to behold it with any approval. By this principle we must abide, though the dispensations of his providence may for a time, in some cases, seem to us not to agree with it. The prophet complains that God's patience was abused; and because sentence against these evil works and workers was not executed speedily, their hearts were the more fully set in them to do evil. Some they take up as with the angle, one by one; others they catch in shoals, as in their net, and gather them in their drag, their enclosing net. They admire their own cleverness and contrivance: there is great proneness in us to take the glory of outward prosperity to ourselves. This is idolizing ourselves, sacrificing to the drag-net because it is our own. God will soon end successful and splendid robberies. Death and judgment shall make men cease to prey on others, and they shall be preyed on themselves. Let us remember, whatever advantages we possess, we must give all the glory to God.

Chapter 2

Chapter Outline	
Habakkuk must wait in faith.	(1–4)
Judgments upon the Chaldeans.	(5–14)
Also upon drunkenness and idolatry.	(15–20)

Verses 1–4

When tossed and perplexed with doubts about the methods of Providence, we must watch against temptations to be impatient. When we have poured out complaints and requests before God, we must observe the answers God gives by his word, his Spirit, and providences; what the Lord will say to our case. God will not disappoint the believing expectations of those who wait to hear what he will say unto them. All are concerned in the truths of God's word. Though the promised favour be deferred long, it will come at last, and abundantly recompense us for waiting. The humble, broken-hearted, repenting sinner, alone seeks to obtain an interest in this salvation. He will rest his soul on the promise, and on Christ, in and through whom it is given. Thus he walks and works, as well as lives by faith, perseveres to the end, and is exalted to glory; while those who distrust or despise God's all-sufficiency will not walk uprightly with him. The just shall live by faith in these precious promises, while the performance of them is deferred. Only those made just by faith, shall live, shall be happy here and for ever.

Verses 5–14

The prophet reads the doom of all proud and oppressive powers that bear hard upon God's people. The lusts of the flesh, the lust of the eye, and the pride of life, are the entangling snares of men; and we find him that led Israel captive, himself led captive by each of these. No more of what we have is to be reckoned ours, than what we come honestly by. Riches are but clay, thick clay; what are gold and silver but white and yellow earth? Those who travel through thick clay, are hindered and dirtied in their journey; so are those who go through the world in the midst of abundance of wealth. And what fools are those that burden themselves with continual care about it; with a great deal of guilt in getting, saving, and spending it, and with a heavy account which they must give another day! They overload themselves with this thick clay, and so sink themselves down into destruction and perdition. See what will be the end hereof; what is gotten by violence from others, others shall take away by violence. Covetousness brings disquiet and uneasiness into a family; he that is greedy of gain troubles his own house; what is worse, it brings the curse of God upon all the affairs of it. There is a lawful gain, which, by the blessing of God, may be a comfort to a house; but what is got by fraud and injustice, will bring poverty and ruin upon a family. Yet that is not the worst; Thou hast sinned against thine own soul, hast endangered it. Those who wrong their neighbours, do much greater wrong to their own souls. If the sinner thinks he has managed his frauds and violence with art and contrivance, the riches and possessions he heaped together will witness against him. There are not greater drudges in the world than those who are slaves to mere wordly pursuits. And what comes of it? They find themselves disappointed of it, and disappointed in it; they will own it is worse than vanity, it is vexation of spirit. By staining and sinking earthly glory, God manifests and magnifies his own glory, and fills the earth with the knowledge of it, as plentifully as waters cover the sea, which are deep, and spread far and wide.

Verses 15–20

A severe woe is pronounced against drunkenness; it is very fearful against all who are guilty of drunkenness at any time, and in any place, from the stately palace to the paltry ale-house. To give one drink who is in want, who is thirsty and poor, or a weary traveller, or ready to perish, is charity; but to give a neighbour drink, that he may expose himself, may disclose secret concerns, or be drawn into a bad bargain, or for any such purpose, this is wickedness. To be guilty of this sin, to take pleasure in it, is to do what we can towards the murder both of soul and body. There is woe to him, and punishment answering to the sin. The folly of worshipping idols is exposed.

The Lord is in his holy temple in heaven, where we have access to him in the way he has appointed. May we welcome his salvation, and worship him in his earthly temples, through Christ Jesus, and by the influence of the Holy Spirit.

Chapter 3

Chapter Outline	
The prophet beseeches God for his people.	(1, 2)
He calls to mind former deliverances.	(3–15)
His firm trust in the Divine mercy.	(16–19)

Verses 1, 2

The word prayer seems used here for an act of devotion. The Lord would revive his work among the people in the midst of the years of adversity. This may be applied to every season when the church, or believers, suffer under afflictions and trials. Mercy is what we must flee to for refuge, and rely upon as our only plea. We must not say, Remember our merit, but, Lord, remember thy own mercy.

Verses 3–15

God's people, when in distress, and ready to despair, seek help by considering the days of old, and the years of ancient times, and by pleading them with God in prayer. The resemblance between the Babylonish and Egyptian captivities, naturally presents itself to the mind, as well as the possibility of a like deliverance through the power of Jehovah. God appeared in his glory. All the powers of nature are shaken, and the course of nature changed, but all is for the salvation of God's own people. Even what seems least likely, shall be made to work for their salvation. Hereby is given a type and figure of the redemption of the world by Jesus Christ. It is for salvation with thine anointed. Joshua who led the armies of Israel, was a figure of Him whose name he bare, even Jesus, our Joshua. In all the salvations wrought for them, God looked upon Christ the Anointed, and brought deliverances to pass by him. All the wonders done for Israel of old, were nothing to that which was done when the Son of God suffered on the cross for the sins of his people. How glorious his resurrection and ascension! And how much more glorious will be his second coming, to put an end to all that opposes him, and all that causes suffering to his people!

Verses 16–19

When we see a day of trouble approach, it concerns us to prepare. A good hope through grace is founded in holy fear. The prophet looked back upon the experiences of the church in former ages, and observed what great things God had done for them, and so was not only recovered, but filled with holy joy. He resolved to delight and triumph in the Lord; for when all is gone, his God is not gone. Destroy the vines and the fig-trees, and you make all the mirth of a carnal heart to cease. But those who, when full, enjoyed God in all, when emptied and poor, can enjoy all in God. They can sit down upon the heap of the ruins of their creature-comforts, and even then praise the Lord, as the God of their salvation, the salvation of the soul, and rejoice in him as such, in their greatest distresses. Joy in the Lord is especially seasonable when we meet with losses and crosses in the world. Even when provisions are cut off, to make it appear that man lives not by bread alone, we may be supplied by the graces and comforts of God's Spirit. Then we shall be strong for spiritual warfare and work, and with enlargement of heart may run the way of his commandments, and outrun our troubles. And we shall be successful in spiritual undertakings. Thus the prophet, who began his prayer with fear and trembling, ends it with joy and triumph. And thus faith in Christ prepares for every event. The name of Jesus, when we can speak of Him as ours, is balm for every wound, a cordial for every care. It is as ointment poured forth, shedding fragrance through the whole soul. In the hope of a heavenly crown, let us sit loose to earthly possessions and comforts, and cheerfully bear up under crosses. Yet a little while, and He that shall come will come, and will not tarry; and where he is, we shall be also.

Zephaniah

Zephaniah excites to repentance, foretells the destruction of the enemies of the Jews, and comforts the pious among them with promises of future blessings, the restoration of their nation, and the prosperity of the church in the latter days.

Chapter 1

Chapter Outline	
Threatenings against sinners.	(1–6)
More threatenings.	(7–13)
Distress from the approaching judgments.	(14–18)

Verses 1–6

Ruin is coming, utter ruin; destruction from the Almighty. The servants of God all proclaim, There is no peace for the wicked. The expressions are figurative, speaking every where desolation; the land shall be left without inhabitants. The sinners to be consumed are, the professed idolaters, and those that worship Jehovah and idols, or swear to the Lord, and to Malcham. Those that think to divide their affections and worship between God and idols, will come short of acceptance with God; for what communion can there be between light and darkness? If Satan have half, he will have all; if the Lord have but half, he will have none. Neglect of God shows impiety and contempt. May none of us be among those who draw back unto perdition, but of those who believe to the saving of the soul.

Verses 7–13

God's day is at hand; the punishment of presumptuous sinners is a sacrifice to the justice of God. The Jewish royal family shall be reckoned with for their pride and vanity; and those that leap on the threshold, invading their neighbours' rights, and seizing their possessions. The trading people and the rich merchants are called to account. Secure and careless people are reckoned with. They are secure and easy; they say in their heart, the Lord will not do good, neither will he do evil; that is, they deny his dispensing rewards and punishments. But in the day of the Lord's judgment, it will clearly appear that those who perish, fall a sacrifice to Divine justice for breaking God's law, and because they have no interest by faith in the Redeemer's atoning sacrifice.

Verses 14–18

This warning of approaching destruction, is enough to make the sinners in Zion tremble; it refers to the great day of the Lord, the day in which he will show himself by taking vengeance on them. This day of the Lord is very near; it is a day of God's wrath, wrath to the utmost. It will be a day of trouble and distress to sinners. Let them not be laid asleep by the patience of God. What is a man profited if he gain the whole world, and lose his own soul? And what shall a man give in exchange for his soul? Let us flee from the wrath to come, and choose the good part that shall never be taken from us; then we shall be prepared for every event; nothing shall separate us from the love of God in Christ Jesus our Lord.

Chapter 2

Chapter Outline	
An exhortation to repentance.	(1–3)
Judgments upon other nations.	(4–15)

Verses 1–3

The prophet calls to national repentance, as the only way to prevent national ruin. A nation not desiring, that has not desires toward God, is not desirous of his favour and grace, has no mind to repent and reform. Or, not desirable, not having any thing to recommend them to God; to whom God might justly say, Depart from me; but he says, Gather together to me that you may seek my face. We know what God's decree will bring against impenitent sinners, therefore it highly concerns all to repent in the accepted time. How careful should we all be to seek peace with God, before the Holy Spirit withdraws from us, or ceases to strive with us; before the day of grace is over, or the day of life; before our everlasting state is determined! Let the poor, despised, and afflicted, seek the Lord, and seek to understand and keep his commandments better, that they may be more humbled for their sins. The chief hope of deliverance from national judgments rests upon prayer.

Verses 4–15

Those are really in a woful condition who have the word of the Lord against them, for no word of his shall fall to the ground. God will restore his people to their rights, though long kept from them. It has been the common lot of God's people, in all ages, to be reproached and reviled. God shall be worshipped, not only by all Israel, and the strangers who join them, but by the heathen. Remote nations must be reckoned with for the wrongs done to God's people. The sufferings of the insolent and haughty in prosperity, are unpitied and unlamented. But all the desolations of flourishing nations will make way for the overturning Satan's kingdom. Let us improve our advantages, and expect the performance of every promise, praying that our Father's name may be hallowed every where, over all the earth.

Chapter 3

Chapter Outline	
Further reproofs for sin.	(1–7)
Encouragement to look for mercy.	(8–13)
Promises of future favour and prosperity.	(14–20)

Verses 1–7

The holy God hates sin most in those nearest to him. A sinful state is, and will be, a woful state. Yet they had the tokens of God's presence, and all the advantages of knowing his will, with the strongest reasons to do it; still they persisted in disobedience. Alas, that men often are more active in doing wickedness than believers are in doing good.

Verses 8–13

The preaching of the gospel is predicted, when vengeance would be executed on the Jewish nation. The purifying doctrines of the gospel, or the pure language of the grace of the Lord, would teach men to use the language of humility, repentance, and faith. Purity and piety in common conversation is good. The pure and happy state of the church in the latter days seems intended. The Lord will shut out boasting, and leave men nothing to glory in, save the Lord Jesus, as made of God to them wisdom, righteousness, sanctification, and redemption. Humiliation for sin, and obligations to the Redeemer, will make true believers upright and sincere, whatever may be the case among mere professors.

Verses 14–20

After the promises of taking away sin, follow promises of taking away trouble. When the cause is removed, the effect will cease. What makes a people holy, will make them happy. The precious promises made to the purified people, were to have full accomplishment in the gospel. These **verse**s appear chiefly to relate to the future conversion and restoration of Israel, and the glorious times which are to follow. They show the abundant peace, comfort, and prosperity of the church, in the happy times yet to come. He will save; he will be Jesus; he will answer the name, for he will save his people from their sins. Before the glorious times foretold, believers would be sorrowful, and objects of reproach. But the Lord will save the weakest believer, and cause true Christians to be greatly honoured where they had been treated with contempt. One act of mercy and grace shall serve, both to gather Israel out of their dispersions and to lead them to their own land. Then will God's Israel be made a name and a praise to eternity. The events alone can fully answer the language of this prophecy. Many are the troubles of the righteous, but they may rejoice in God's love. Surely our hearts should honour the Lord, and rejoice in him, when we hear such words of condescension and grace. If now kept from his ordinances, it is our trial and grief; but in due time we shall be gathered into his temple above. The glory and happiness of the believer will be perfect, unchangeable, and eternal, when he is freed from earthly sorrows, and brought to heavenly bliss.

Haggai

After the return from captivity, Haggai was sent to encourage the people to rebuild the temple, and to reprove their neglect. To encourage their undertaking, the people are assured that the glory of the second temple shall far exceed that of the first, by the appearing therein of Christ, the Desire of all nations.

Chapter 1

Chapter Outline	
Haggai reproves the Jews for neglecting the temple.	(1–11)
He promises God's assistance to them.	(12–15)

Verses 1–11

Observe the sin of the Jews, after their return from captivity in Babylon. Those employed for God may be driven from their work by a storm, yet they must go back to it. They did not say that they would not build a temple, but, Not yet. Thus men do not say they will never repent and reform, and be religious, but, Not yet. And so the great business we were sent into the world to do, is not done. There is a proneness in us to think wrongly of discouragements in our duty, as if they were a discharge from our duty, when they are only for the trial of our courage and faith. They neglected the building of God's house, that they might have more time and money for worldly affairs. That the punishment might answer to the sin, the poverty they thought to prevent by not building the temple, God brought upon them for not building it. Many good works have been intended, but not done, because men supposed the proper time was not come. Thus believers let slip opportunities of usefulness, and sinners delay the concerns of their souls, till too late. If we labour only for the meat that perishes, as the Jews here, we are in danger of losing our labour; but we are sure it shall not be in vain in the Lord, if we labour for the meat which lasts to eternal life. If we would have the comfort and continuance of temporal enjoyments, we must have God as our Friend. See also Lu **12:33**. When God crosses our temporal affairs, and we meet with trouble and disappointment, we shall find the cause is, that the work we have to do for God and our own souls is left undone, and we seek our own things more than the things of Christ. How many, who plead that they cannot afford to give to pious or charitable designs, often lavish ten times as much in needless expenses on their houses and themselves! But those are strangers to their own interests, who are full of care to adorn and enrich their own houses, while God's temple in their hearts lies waste. It is the great concern of every one, to apply to the necessary duty of self-examination and communion with our own hearts concerning our spiritual state. Sin is what we must answer for; duty is what we must do. But many are quick-sighted to pry into other people's ways, who are careless of their own. If any duty has been neglected, that is no reason why it should still be so. Whatever God will take pleasure in when done, we ought to take pleasure in doing. Let those who have put off their return to God, return with all their heart, while there is time.

Verses 12–15

The people returned to God in the way of duty. In attending to God's ministers, we must have respect to him that sent them. The word of the Lord has success, when by his grace he stirs up our spirits to comply with it. It is in the day of Divine power we are made willing. When God has work to be done, he will either find or make men fit to do it. Every one helped, as his ability was; and this they did with a regard to the Lord as their God. Those who have lost time, need to redeem time; and the longer we have loitered in folly, the more haste we should make. God met them in a way of mercy. Those who work for him, have him with them; and if he be for us, who can be against us? This should stir us up to be diligent.

Chapter 2

Chapter Outline	
Greater glory promised to the second temple than to the first.	(1–9)
Their sins hindered the work.	(10–19)
The kingdom of Christ foretold.	(20–23)

Verses 1–9

Those who are hearty in the Lord's service shall receive encouragement to proceed. But they could not build such a temple then, as Solomon built. Though our gracious God is pleased if we do as well as we can in his service, yet our proud hearts will scarcely let us be pleased, unless we do as well as others, whose abilities are far beyond ours. Encouragement is given the Jews to go on in the work notwithstanding. They have God with them, his Spirit and his special presence. Though he chastens their transgressions, his faithfulness does not fail. The Spirit still remained among them. And they shall have the Messiah among them shortly; "He that should come." Convulsions and changes would take place in the Jewish church and state, but first should come great revolutions and commotions among the nations. He shall come, as the Desire of all nations; desirable to all nations, for in him shall all the earth be blessed with the best of blessings; long expected and desired by all believers. The house they were building should be filled with glory, very far beyond Solomon's temple. This house shall be filled with glory of another nature. If we have silver and gold, we must serve and honour God with it, for the property is his. If we have not silver and gold, we must honour him with such as we have, and he will accept us. Let them be comforted that the glory of this latter house shall be greater than that of the former, in what would be beyond all the glories of the first house, the presence of the Messiah, the Son of God, the Lord of glory, personally, and in human nature. Nothing but the presence of the Son of God, in human form and nature, could fulfil this. Jesus is the Christ, is He that should come, and we are to look for no other. This prophecy alone is enough to silence the Jews, and condemn their obstinate rejection of Him, concerning whom all their prophets spake. If God be with us, peace is with us. But the Jews under the latter temple had much trouble; but this promise is fulfilled in that spiritual peace which Jesus Christ has by his blood purchased for all believers. All changes shall make way for Christ to be desired and valued by all nations. And the Jews shall have their eyes opened to behold how precious He is, whom they have hitherto rejected.

Verses 10–19

Many spoiled this good work, by going about it with unholy hearts and hands, and were likely to gain no advantage by it. The sum of these two rules of the law is, that sin is more easily learned from others than holiness. The impurity of their hearts and lives shall make the work of their hands, and all their offerings, unclean before God. The case is the same with us. When employed in any good work, we should watch over ourselves, lest we render it unclean by our corruptions. When we begin to make conscience of duty to God, we may expect his blessing; and whoso is wise will understand the loving-kindness of the Lord. God will curse the blessings of the wicked, and make bitter the prosperity of the careless; but he will sweeten the cup of affliction to those who diligently serve him.

Verses 20–23

The Lord will preserve Zerubbabel and the people of Judah, amidst their enemies. Here is also foretold the establishment and continuance of the kingdom of Christ; by union with whom his people are sealed with the Holy Ghost, sealed with his image, thus distinguished from all others. Here also is foretold the changes, even to that time when the kingdom of Christ shall overthrow and occupy the place of all the empires which opposed his cause. The promise has special reference to Christ, who descended from Zerubbabel in a direct line, and is the sole Builder of the gospel temple. Our Lord Jesus is the Signet on God's right hand, for all power is given to him, and derived from him. By him, and in him, all the promises of God are yea and amen. Whatever changes take place on earth, all will promote the comfort, honour, and happiness of his servants.

Zechariah

This prophecy is suitable to all, as the scope is to reprove for sin, and threaten God's judgments against the impenitent, and to encourage those that feared God, with assurances of the mercy God had in store for his church, and especially of the coming of the Messiah, and the setting up his kingdom in the world.

Chapter 1

Chapter Outline	
An exhortation to repentance.	(1–6)
A vision of the ministry of angels.	(7–17)
The security of the Jews and the destruction of their enemies.	(18–21)

Verses 1–6

God's almighty power and sovereign dominion, should engage and encourage sinners to repent and turn to Him. It is very desirable to have the Lord of hosts for our friend, and very dreadful to have him for our enemy. Review what is past, and observe the message God sent by his servants, the prophets, to your fathers. Turn ye now from your evil ways, and from your evil doings. Be persuaded to leave your sins, as the only way to prevent approaching ruin. What is become of our fathers, and of the prophets that preached to them? They are all dead and gone. Here they were, in the towns and countries where we live, passing and repassing in the same streets, dwelling in the same houses, trading in the same shops and exchanges, worshipping God in the same places. But where are they? When they died, there was not an end of them; they are in eternity, in the world of spirits, the unchangeable world to which we hasten apace. Where are they? Those of them who lived and died in sin, are in torment. Those who lived and died in Christ, are in heaven; and if we live and die as they did, we shall be with them shortly and eternally. If they minded not their own souls, is that a reason why their posterity should ruin theirs also? The prophets are gone. Christ is a Prophet that lives for ever, but all other prophets have a period put to their office. Oh that this consideration had its due weight; that dying ministers are dealing with dying people about their never-dying souls, and an awful eternity, upon the brink of which both are standing! In another world, both we and our prophets shall live for ever: to prepare for that world ought to be our great care in this. The preachers died, and the hearers died, but the word of God died not; not one jot or title of it fell to the ground; for he is righteous.

Verses 7–17

The prophet saw a dark, shady grove, hidden by hills. This represented the low, melancholy condition of the Jewish church. A man like a warrior sat on a red horse, in the midst of this shady myrtle-grove. Though the church was in a low condition, Christ was present in the midst, ready to appear for the relief of his people. Behind him were angels ready to be employed by him, some in acts of judgment, others of mercy, others in mixed events. Would we know something of the mysteries of the kingdom of heaven, we must apply, not to angels, for they are themselves learners, but to Christ himself. He is ready to teach those humbly desirous to learn the things of God. The nations near Judea enjoyed peace at that time, but the state of the Jews was unsettled, which gave rise to the pleading that followed; but mercy must only be hoped for through Christ. His intercession for his church prevails. The Lord answered the Angel, this Angel of the covenant, with promises of mercy and deliverance. All the good words and comfortable words of the gospel we receive from Jesus Christ, as he received them from the Father, in answer to the prayer of his blood; and his ministers are to preach them to all the world. The earth sat still, and was at rest. It is not uncommon for the enemies of God to be at rest in sin, while his people are enduring correction, harassed by temptation, disquieted by fears of wrath, or groaning under oppression and persecution. Here are predictions which had reference to the revival of the Jews after the captivity, but those events were shadows of what shall take place in the church, after the oppression of the New Testament Babylon is ended.

Verses 18–21

The enemies of the church threaten to cut off the name of Israel. They are horns, emblems of power, strength, and violence. The prophet saw them so formidable that he began to despair of the safety of every good man, and the success of every good work; but the Lord showed him four workmen empowered to cut off these horns. With an eye of sense we see the power of the enemies of the church; look which way we will, the world shows us that; but it is only with an eye of faith that we see it safe. The Lord shows us that. When God has work to do, he will raise up some to do it, and others to defend it, and to protect those employed in doing it. What cause there is to look up in love and praise to the holy and eternal Spirit, who has the same care over the present and eternal interests of believers, by the holy word bringing the church to know the wonderful things of salvation!

Chapter 2

Chapter Outline	
The prosperity of Jerusalem.	(1–5)
The Jews called to return to their own land.	(6–9)
A promise of God's presence.	(10–13)

Verses 1–5

The Son of David, even the Man Christ Jesus, whom the prophet sees with a measuring line in his hand, is the Master-Builder of his church. God notices the extent of his church, and will take care that whatever number of guests are brought to the wedding-supper, there shall be room. This vision means well to Jerusalem. The walls of a city, as they defend it, so they straiten its inhabitants; but Jerusalem shall be extended as freely as if it had no walls at all, yet shall be as safe as if it had the strongest walls. In the church of God there yet is room for other multitudes, more than man can number. None shall be refused who trust in Christ; and He never shuts out from heaven one true member of the church on earth. God will be a Wall of fire round them, which can neither be broken through nor undermined, nor can it be assailed without danger to those who attack. This vision was to have its full accomplishment in the gospel church, which is extended by admitting the Gentiles into it; and which has the Son of God for its Prince and Protector; especially in the glorious times yet to come.

Verses 6–9

If God will build Jerusalem for the people and their comfort, they must inhabit it for him and his glory. The promises and privileges with which God's people are blessed, should engage us to join them, whatever it costs us. When Zion is enlarged to make room for all God's Israel, it is the greatest madness for any of them to stay in Babylon. The captivity of a sinful state is by no means to be continued in, though a man may be easy in worldly matters. Escape for thy life, look not behind thee. Christ has proclaimed that deliverance to the captives, which he has himself wrought out, and it concerns every one to resolve that sin shall not have dominion over him. Those who would be found among God's children, must save themselves from this world, see Ac **2**:**40**. What Christ will do for his church, shall be an evident proof of God's care and affection. He that touches you, touches the apple of his eye. This is a strong expression of God's love to his church. He takes what is done against her as done against the tenderest part of the eye, to which the least touch is a great offence. Christ is sent to be the Protector of his church.

Verses 10–13

Here is a prediction of the coming of Christ in human nature. Many nations in that day would renounce idolatry, and God will own those for his people who join him with purpose of heart. Glorious times are foretold as a prophecy of our Lord's coming and kingdom. God is about to do something unexpected, and very surprising, and to plead his people's cause, which had long seemed neglected. Silently submit to his holy will, and patiently wait the event; assured that God will complete all his work. He will ere long come to judgment, to complete the salvation of his people, and to punish the inhabitants of the earth for their sins.

Chapter 3

Chapter Outline	
The restoration of the church.	(1–5)
A promise concerning the Messiah.	(6–10)

Verses 1–5

The angel showed Joshua, the high priest, to Zechariah, in a vision. Guilt and corruption are great discouragements when we stand before God. By the guilt of the sins committed by us, we are liable to the justice of God; by the power of sin that dwells in us, we are hateful to the holiness of God. Even God's Israel are in danger on these accounts; but they have relief from Jesus Christ, who is made of God to us both righteousness and sanctification. Joshua, the high priest, is accused as a criminal, but is justified. When we stand before God, to minister to him, or stand up for God, we must expect to meet all the resistance Satan's subtlety and malice can give. Satan is checked by one that has conquered him, and many times silenced him. Those who belong to Christ, will find him ready to appear for them, when Satan appears most strongly against them. A converted soul is a brand plucked out of the fire by a miracle of free grace, therefore shall not be left a prey to Satan. Joshua appears as one polluted, but is purified; he represents the Israel of God, who are all as an unclean thing, till they are washed and sanctified in the name of the Lord Jesus, and by the Spirit of our God. Israel now were free from idolatry, but there were many things amiss in them. There were spiritual enemies warring against them, more dangerous than any neighbouring nations. Christ loathed the filthiness of Joshua's garments, yet did not put him away. Thus God by his grace does with those whom he chooses to be priests to himself. The guilt of sin is taken away by pardoning mercy, and the power of it is broken by renewing grace. Thus Christ washes those from their sins in his own blood, whom he makes kings and priests to our God. Those whom Christ makes spiritual priests, are clothed with the spotless robe of his righteousness, and appear before God in that; and with the graces of his Spirit, which are ornaments to them. The righteousness of saints, both imputed and implanted, is the fine linen, clean and white, with which the bride, the Lamb's wife, is arrayed, Re **19**:**8**. Joshua is restored to former honours and trusts. The crown of the priesthood is put on him. When the Lord designs to restore and revive religion, he stirs up prophets and people to pray for it.

Verses 6–10

All whom God calls to any office he finds fit, or makes so. The Lord will cause the sins of the believer to pass away by his sanctifying grace, and will enable him to walk in newness of life. As the promises made to David often pass into promises of the Messiah, so the promises to Joshua look forward to Christ, of whose priesthood Joshua's was a shadow. Whatever trials we pass through, whatever services we perform, our whole dependence must rest on Christ, the Branch of righteousness. He is God's servant, employed in his work, obedient to his will, devoted to his honour and glory. He is the Branch from which all our fruit must be gathered. The eye of his Father was upon him, especially in his sufferings, and when he was buried in the grave, as the foundation-stones are under ground, out of men's sight. But the prophecy rather denotes the attention paid to this precious Corner-stone. All believers, from the beginning, had looked forward to it in the types and predictions. All believers, after Christ's coming, would look to it with faith, hope, and love. Christ shall appear for all his chosen, as the high priest when before the Lord, with the names of all Israel graven in the precious stones of his breastplate. When God gave a remnant to Christ, to be brought through grace to glory, then he engraved this precious stone. By him sin shall be taken away, both the guilt and the dominion of it; he did it in one day, that day in which he suffered and died. What should terrify when sin is taken away? Then nothing can hurt, and we sit down under Christ's shadow with delight, and are sheltered by it. And gospel grace, coming with power, makes men forward to draw others to it.

Chapter 4

Chapter Outline	
A vision of a candlestick, with two olive trees.	(1–7)
Further encouragement.	(8–10)
An explanation respecting the olive trees.	(11–14)

Verses 1–7

The prophet's spirit was willing to attend, but the flesh was weak. We should beg of God that, whenever he speaks to us, he would awaken us, and we should then stir up ourselves. The church is a golden candlestick, or lamp-bearer, set up for enlightening this dark world, and holding forth the light of Divine revelation. Two olive trees were seen, one on each side the candlestick, from which oil flowed into the bowl without ceasing. God brings to pass his gracious purposes concerning his church, without any art or labour of man; sometimes he makes use of his instruments, yet he needs them not. This represented the abundance of Divine grace, for the enlightening and making holy the ministers and members of the church, and which cannot be procured or prevented by any human power. The vision assures us that the good work of building the temple, should be brought to a happy end. The difficulty is represented as a great mountain. But all difficulties shall vanish, and all the objections be got over. Faith will remove mountains, and make them plains. Christ is our Zerubbabel; mountains of difficulty were in the way of his undertaking, but nothing is too hard for him. What comes from the grace of God, may, in faith, be committed to the grace of God, for he will not forsake the work of his own hands.

Verses 8–10

The exact fulfilment of Scripture prophecies is a convincing proof of their Divine original. Though the instruments be weak and unlikely, yet God often chooses such, to bring about great things by them. Let not the dawning light be despised; it will shine more and more to the perfect day. Those who despaired of finishing the work, shall rejoice when they see Zerubbabel giving directions what to do, and taking care that the work be done. It is a comfort to us that the same all-wise, almighty Providence, which governs the earth, is in particular conversant about the church. All that have the plummet in their hands, must look up to the eyes of the Lord, have constant regard to Divine Providence, act in dependence on its guidance and submission to its disposals. Let us fix our faith on Christ, and view Him carrying on his work according to his own glorious plan, and daily bringing his spiritual building nearer to completion. (Zec **4**:**11-14**)

Verses 11–14

Zechariah desires to know what are the two olive trees. Zerubbabel and Joshua, this prince and this priest, were endued with the gifts and graces of God's Spirit. They lived at the same time, and both were instruments in the work and service of God. Christ's offices of King and Priest were shadowed forth by them. From the union of these two offices in his person, both God and man, the fullness of grace is received and imparted. They built the temple, the church of God. So does Christ spiritually. Christ is not only the Messiah, the Anointed One himself, but he is the Good Olive to his church; and from his fulness we receive. And the Holy Spirit is the unction or anointing which we have received. From Christ the Olive Tree, by the Spirit the Olive Branch, all the golden oil of grace flows to believers, which keeps their lamps burning. Let us seek, through the intercession and bounty of the Saviour, supplies from that fulness which has hitherto sufficed for all his saints, according to their trials and employments. Let us wait on him in his ordinances, desiring to be sanctified wholly in body, soul, and spirit.

Chapter 5

Chapter Outline	
The vision of a flying roll.	(1–4)
The vision of a woman and an ephah.	(5–11)

Verses 1–4

The Scriptures of the Old and New Testament are rolls, in which God has written the great things of his law and gospel; they are flying rolls. God's word runs very swiftly, Ps **147:15**. This flying roll contains a declaration of the righteous wrath of God against sinners. Oh that we saw with an eye of faith the flying roll of God's curse hanging over the guilty world as a thick cloud, not only keeping off the sunbeams of God's favour, but big with thunders, lightnings, and storms, ready to destroy them! How welcome then would the tidings of a Saviour be, who came to redeem us from the curse of the law, being himself made a curse for us! Sin is the ruin of houses and families; especially the doing hurt to others and false witness. Who knows the power of God's anger? God's curse cannot be kept out by bars or locks. While one part of the curse of God ruins the substance of the sinner, another part will rest on the soul, and sink it to everlasting punishment. All are transgressors of the law, so we cannot escape this wrath of God, except we flee for refuge to lay hold on the hope set before us in the gospel.

Verses 5–11

In this vision the prophet sees an ephah, something in the shape of a corn measure. This betokened the Jewish nation. They are filling the measure of their iniquity; and when it is full, they shall be delivered into the hands of those to whom God sold them for their sins. The woman sitting in the midst of the ephah represents the sinful church and nation of the Jews, in their latter and corrupt age. Guilt is upon the sinner as a weight of lead, to sink him to the lowest hell. This seems to mean the condemnation of the Jews, after they filled the measure of their iniquities by crucifying Christ and rejecting his gospel. Zechariah sees the ephah, with the woman thus pressed in it, carried away to some far country. This intimates that the Jews should be hurried out of their own land, and forced to dwell in far countries, as they had been in Babylon. There the ephah shall be firmly placed, and their sufferings shall continue far longer than in their late captivity. Blindness is happened unto Israel, and they are settled upon their own unbelief. Let sinners fear to treasure up wrath against the day of wrath; for the more they multiply crimes, the faster the measure fills.

Chapter 6

Chapter Outline	
The vision of the chariots.	(1–8)
Joshua, the high priest, crowned as a type of Christ.	(9–15)

Verses 1–8

This vision may represent the ways of Providence in the government of this lower world. Whatever the providences of God about us are, as to public or private affairs, we should see them all as coming from between the mountains of brass, the immoveable counsels and decrees of God; and therefore reckon it as much our folly to quarrel with them, as it is our duty to submit to them. His providences move swiftly and strongly as chariots, but all are directed and governed by his infinite wisdom and sovereign will. The red horses signify war and bloodshed. The black, signify the dismal consequences of war, famines, pestilences, and desolations. The white, signify the return of comfort, peace, and prosperity. The mixed colour, signify events of different complexions, a day of prosperity and a day of adversity. The angels go forth as messengers of God's counsels, and ministers of his justice and mercy. And the secret motions and impulses upon the spirits of men, by which the designs of Providence are carried on, are these four spirits of the heavens, which go forth from God, and fulfil what the God of the spirits of all flesh appoints. All the events which take place in the world spring from the unchangeable counsels of the Lord, which are formed in unerring wisdom, perfect justice, truth, and goodness; and from history it is found that events happened about the period when this vision was sent to the prophet, which seem referred to therein.

Verses 9–15

Some Jews from Babylon brought an offering to the house of God. Those who cannot forward a good work by their persons, must, as they are able, forward it by their purses: if some find hands, let others fill them. Crowns are to be made, and put upon the head of Joshua. The sign was used, to make the promise more noticed, that God will, in the fulness of time, raise up a great High Priest, like Joshua, who is but the figure of one that is to come. Christ is not only the Foundation, but the Founder of this temple, by his Spirit and grace. Glory is a burden, but not too heavy for Him to bear who upholds all things. The cross was His glory, and he bore that; so is the crown an exceeding weight of glory, and he bears that. The counsel of peace should be between the priest and the throne, between the priestly and kingly offices of Jesus Christ. The peace and welfare of the gospel church, and of all believers, shall be wrought, though not by two several persons, yet by two several offices meeting in one; Christ, purchasing all peace by his priesthood, maintaining and defending it by his kingdom. The crowns used in this solemnity must be kept in the temple, as evidence of this promise of the Messiah. Let us not think of separating what God has joined in his counsel of peace. We cannot come to God by Christ as our Priest, if we refuse to have him rule over us as our King. We have no real ground to think our peace is made with God, unless we try to keep his commandments.

Chapter 7

Chapter Outline	
The captives' inquiry respecting fasting.	(1–7)
Sin the cause of their captivity.	(8–14)

Verses 1–7

If we truly desire to know the will of God in doubtful matters, we must not only consult his word and ministers, but seek his direction by fervent prayer. Those who would know God's mind should consult God's ministers; and, in doubtful cases, ask advice of those whose special business it is to search the Scriptures. The Jews seemed to question whether they ought to continue their fasts, seeing that the city and temple were likely to be finished. The first answer to their inquiry is a sharp reproof of hypocrisy. These fasts were not acceptable to God, unless observed in a better manner, and to better purpose. There was the form of duty, but no life, or soul, or power in it. Holy exercises are to be done to God, looking to his word as our rule, and his glory as our end, seeking to please him and obtain his favour; but self was the centre of all their actions. And it was not enough to weep on fast days; they should have searched the Scriptures of the prophets, that they might have seen what was the ground of God's controversy with their fathers. Whether people are in prosperity or adversity, they must be called upon to leave their sins, and to do their duty.

Verses 8–14

God's judgements upon Israel of old for their sins, were written to warn Christians. The duties required are, not keeping fasts and offering sacrifices, but doing justly and loving mercy, which tend to the public welfare and peace. The law of God lays restraint upon the heart. But they filled their minds with prejudices against the word of God. Nothing is harder than the heart of a presumptuous sinner. See the fatal consequences of this to their fathers. Great sins against the Lord of hosts, bring great wrath from his power, which cannot be resisted. Sin, if regarded in the heart, will certainly spoil the success of prayer. The Lord always hears the cry of the broken-hearted penitent; yet all who die impenitent and unbelieving, will find no remedy or refuge from miseries which while here they despised and defied, but which they then will not be able to bear.

Chapter 8

Chapter Outline	
The restoration of Jerusalem.	(1–8)
The people encouraged by promises of God's favour, and exhorted to holiness.	(9–17)
The Jews in the latter days.	(18–23)

Verses 1–8

The sins of Zion were her worst enemies. God will take away her sins, and then no other enemies shall hurt her. Those who profess religion must adorn their profession by godliness and honesty. When become a city of truth and a mountain of holiness, Jerusalem is peaceable and prosperous. **Verses** #(**4**, **5**), beautifully describe a state of great outward peace, attended with plenty, temperance, and contentment. The scattered Israelites shall be brought together from all parts. God will never leave nor forsake them in a way of mercy, for this he has promised them; and they shall never leave nor forsake him in a way of duty, as they have promised him. These promises were partly fulfilled in the Jewish church, betwixt the captivity and the time of Christ's coming; and they had fuller accomplishment in the gospel church; but the full import must be as to the future times of the Christian church, or the future restoration of the Jews. With men this is impossible, but with God all things are possible; so far are God's thoughts and ways above ours. In the present low state of vital godliness, we can hardly conceive that so complete a change can be made; but a change thus extensive and glorious, can be brought to pass by the almighty power of the new-creating Spirit, in less time than he was pleased to employ in creating the world. Let the hands of all who labour in the cause of the gospel be strong, serving the Lord in true holiness, assured that their labour shall not be in vain.

Verses 9–17

Those only who lay their hands to the plough of duty, shall have them strengthened with the promises of mercy: those who avoid their fathers' faults have the curse turned into a blessing. Those who believed the promises, were to show their faith by their works, and to wait the fulfilment. When God is displeased, he can cause trade to decay, and set every man against his neighbour; but when he returns in mercy, all is happy and prosperous. Surely believers in Christ must not trifle with the exhortation to put away lying, and to speak every man peace with his neighbour, to hate what the Lord hates, and to love that wherein he delights.

Verses 18–23

When God comes towards us in ways of mercy, we must meet him with joy and thankfulness. Therefore be faithful and honest in all your dealings; and let it be a pleasure to you to be so, though thereby you come short of the gains others get dishonestly; and, as much as in you lies, live peaceably with all men. Let the truths of God rule in your heads, and let the peace of God rule in your hearts. Thus the ancient servants of God drew the notice of heathen neighbours, whose prejudices were softened. A great increase to the church shall be made. Hitherto the Jews had been prone to learn the idolatries of other nations: what more unlikely than that they should teach religion to their conquerors, and to all the principal nations of the earth! Yet this is expressly foretold, and it came to pass. Hitherto the prophecy has been wonderfully fulfilled, and no doubt future events will explain it further. It is good to be with those who have God with them; if we take God for our God, we must take his people for our people, and be willing to take our lot with them. But let not any one think that mere zeal, either for Jews or Gentiles, will stand in the place of personal religion. Let us be living epistles of Christ, known and read of all men, so that others may wish to go with us, and to have their portion with us in the realms of bliss.

Chapter 9

Chapter Outline	
God's defence of his church.	(1–8)
Christ's coming and his kingdom.	(9–11)
Promises to the church.	(12–17)

Verses 1–8

Here are judgements foretold on several nations. While the Macedonians and Alexander's successors were in warfare in these countries, the Lord promised to protect his people. God's house lies in the midst of an enemy's country; his church is as a lily among thorns. God's power and goodness are seen in her special preservation. The Lord encamps about his church, and while armies of proud opposers shall pass by and return, his eyes watch over her, so that they cannot prevail, and shortly the time will come when no exactor shall pass by her any more.

Verses 9–17

The prophet breaks forth into a joyful representation of the coming of the Messiah, of whom the ancient Jews explained this prophecy. He took the character of their King, when he entered Jerusalem amidst the hosannas of the multitude. But his kingdom is a spiritual kingdom. It shall not be advanced by outward force or carnal weapons. His gospel shall be preached to the world, and be received among the heathen. A sinful state is a state of bondage; it is a pit, or dungeon, in which there is no water, no comfort; and we are all by nature prisoners in this pit. Through the precious blood of Christ, many prisoners of Satan have been set at liberty from the horrible pit in which they must otherwise have perished, without hope or comfort. While we admire Him, let us seek that his holiness and truth may be shown in our own spirits and conduct. These promises have accomplishment in the spiritual blessings of the gospel which we enjoy by Jesus Christ. As the deliverance of the Jews was typical of redemption by Christ, so this invitation speaks to all the language of the gospel call. Sinners are prisoners, but prisoners of hope; their case is sad, but not desperate; for there is hope in Israel concerning them. Christ is a Strong-hold, a strong Tower, in whom believers are safe from the fear of the wrath of God, the curse of the law, and the assaults of spiritual enemies. To him we must turn with lively faith; to him we must flee, and trust in his name under all trials and sufferings. It is here promised that the Lord would deliver his people. This passage also refers to the apostles, and the preachers of the gospel in the early ages. God was evidently with them; his words from their lips pierced the hearts and consciences of the hearers. They were wondrously defended in persecution, and were filled with the influences of the Holy Spirit. They were saved by the Good Shepherd as his flock, and honoured as jewels of his crown. The gifts, graces, and consolations of the Spirit, poured forth on the day of Pentecost, Ac **2** and in succeeding times, are represented. Sharp have been, and still will be, the conflicts of Zion's sons, but their God will give them success. The more we are employed, and satisfied with his goodness, the more we shall admire the beauty revealed in the Redeemer. Whatever gifts God bestows on us, we must serve him cheerfully with them; and, when refreshed with blessings, we must say, How great is his goodness!

Chapter 10

Chapter Outline	
Blessings to be sought from the Lord.	(1–5)
God will restore his people.	(6–12)

Verses 1–5

Spiritual blessings had been promised under figurative allusions to earthly plenty. Seasonable rain is a great mercy, which we may ask of God when there is most need of it, and we may look for it to come. We must in our prayers ask for mercies in their proper time. The Lord would make bright clouds, and give showers of rain. This may be an exhortation to seek the influences of the Holy Spirit, in faith and by prayer, through which the blessings held forth in the promises are obtained and enjoyed. The prophet shows the folly of making addresses to idols, as their fathers had done. The Lord visited the remnant of his flock in mercy, and was about to renew their courage and strength for conflict and victory. Every creature is to us what God makes it to be. Every one raised to support the nation, as a corner-stone does the building, or to unite those that differ, as nails join the different timbers, must come from the Lord; and those employed to overcome their enemies, must have strength and success from him. This may be applied to Christ; to him we must look to raise up persons to unite, support, and defend his people. He never will say, Seek ye me in vain.

Verses 6–12

Here are precious promises to the people of God, which look to the state of the Jews, and even to the latter days of the church. Preaching the gospel is God's call for souls to come to Jesus Christ. Those whom Christ redeemed by his blood, God will gather by his grace. Difficulties shall be got over easily, and effectually, as those in the way of the deliverance out of Egypt. God himself will be their strength, and their song. When we resist, and so overcome our spiritual enemies, then our hearts shall rejoice. If God strengthen us, we must bestir ourselves in all the duties of the Christian life, must be active in the work of God; and we must do all in the name of the Lord Jesus.

Chapter 11

Chapter Outline	
Destruction to come upon the Jews.	(1–3)
The Lord's dealing with the Jews.	(4–14)
The emblem and curse of a foolish shepherd.	(15–17)

Verses 1–3

In figurative expressions, that destruction of Jerusalem, and of the Jewish church and nation, is foretold, which our Lord Jesus, when the time was at hand, prophesied plainly and expressly. How can the fir trees stand, if the cedars fall? The falls of the wise and good into sin, and the falls of the rich and great into trouble, are loud alarms to those every way their inferiors. It is sad with a people, when those who should be as shepherds to them, are as young lions. The pride of Jordan was the thickets on the banks; and when the river overflowed the banks, the lions came up from them roaring. Thus the doom of Jerusalem may alarm other churches.

Verses 4–14

Christ came into this world for judgment to the Jewish church and nation, which were wretchedly corrupt and degenerate. Those have their minds wofully blinded, who do ill, and justify themselves in it; but God will not hold those guiltless who hold themselves so. How can we go to God to beg a blessing on unlawful methods of getting wealth, or to return thanks for success in them? There was a general decay of religion among them, and they regarded it not. The Good Shepherd would feed his flock, but his attention would chiefly be directed to the poor. As an emblem, the prophet seems to have taken two staves; Beauty, denoted the privileges of the Jewish nation, in their national covenant; the other he called Bands, denoting the harmony which hitherto united them as the flock of God. But they chose to cleave to false teachers. The carnal mind and the friendship of the world are enmity to God; and God hates all the workers of iniquity: it is easy to foresee what this will end in. The prophet demanded wages, or a reward, and received thirty pieces of silver. By Divine direction he cast it to the potter, as in disdain for the smallness of the sum. This shadowed forth the bargain of Judas to betray Christ, and the final method of applying it. Nothing ruins a people so certainly, as weakening the brotherhood among them. This follows the dissolving of the covenant between God and them: when sin abounds, love waxes cold, and civil contests follow. No wonder if those fall out among themselves, who have provoked God to fall out with them. Wilful contempt of Christ is the great cause of men's ruin. And if professors rightly valued Christ, they would not contend about little matters.

Verses 15–17

God, having showed the misery of this people in their being justly left by the Good Shepherd, shows their further misery in being abused by foolish shepherds. The description suits the character Christ gives of the scribes and Pharisees. They never do any thing to support the weak, or comfort the feeble-minded; but seek their own ease, while they are barbarous to the flock. The idol shepherd has the garb and appearance of a shepherd, receives submission, and is supported at much expense; but he leaves the flock to perish through neglect, or leads them to ruin by his example. This suits many in different churches and nations, but the warning had an awful fulfilment in the Jewish teachers. And while such deceive others to their ruin, they will themselves have the deepest condemnation.

Chapter 12

Chapter Outline	
Punishment of the enemies of Judah.	(1–8)
Repentance and sorrow of the Jews.	(9–14)

Verses 1–8

Here is a Divine prediction, which will be a heavy burden to all the enemies of the church. But it is for Israel; for their comfort and benefit. It is promised that God will make foolish the counsels, and weaken the courage of the enemies of the church. The exact meaning is not clear; but God often begins by calling the poor and despised; and in that day even the feeblest will resemble David, and be as eminent in courage and every thing good. Desirable indeed is it that the examples and labours of Christians should render them as fire among wood, as a torch in a sheaf, to kindle the flame of Divine love, to spread religion on the right hand and on the left.

Verses 9–14

The day here spoken of, is the day of Jerusalem's defence and deliverance, that glorious day when God will appear for the salvation of his people. In Christ's first coming he bruised the serpent's head, and broke all the powers of darkness that fought against God's kingdom among men. In his second coming he will complete their destruction, when he shall put down all opposing rule, principality, and power; and death itself shall be swallowed up in that victory. The Holy Spirit is gracious and merciful, and is the Author of all grace or holiness. He, also, is the Spirit of supplications, and shows men their ignorance, want, guilt, misery, and danger. At the time here foretold, the Jews will know who the crucified Jesus was; then they shall look by faith to him, and mourn with the deepest sorrow, not only in public, but in private, even each one separately. There is a holy mourning, the effect of the pouring out of the Spirit; a mourning for sin, which quickens faith in Christ, and qualifies for joy in God. This mourning is a fruit of the Spirit of grace, a proof of a work of grace in the soul, and of the Spirit of supplications. It is fulfilled in all who sorrow for sin after a godly sort; they look to Christ crucified, and mourn for him. Looking by faith upon the cross of Christ will cause us to mourn for sin after a godly sort.

Chapter 13

Chapter Outline	
The Fountain for the remission of sins, The conviction of the false prophets.	(1–6)
The death of Christ, and the saving of a remnant of the people.	(7–9)

Verses 1–6

In the time mentioned at the close of the foregoing chapter, a fountain would be opened to the rulers and people of the Jews, in which to wash away their sins. Even the atoning blood of Christ, united with his sanctifying grace. It has hitherto been closed to the unbelieving nation of Israel; but when the Spirit of grace shall humble and soften their hearts, he will open it to them also. This fountain opened is the pierced side of Christ. We are all as an unclean thing. Behold a fountain opened for us to wash in, and streams flowing to us from that fountain. The blood of Christ, and God's pardoning mercy in that blood, made known in the new covenant, are a fountain always flowing, that never can be emptied. It is opened for all believers, who as the spiritual seed of Christ, are of the house of David, and, as living members of the church, are inhabitants of Jerusalem. Christ, by the power of his grace, takes away the dominion of sin, even of beloved sins. Those who are washed in the fountain opened, as they are justified, so they are sanctified. Souls are brought off from the world and the flesh, those two great idols, that they may cleave to God only. The thorough reformation which will take place on the conversion of Israel to Christ, is here foretold. False prophets shall be convinced of their sin and folly, and return to their proper employments. When convinced that we are gone out of the way of duty, we must show the truth of our repentance by returning to it again. It is well to acknowledge those to be friends, who by severe discipline are instrumental in bringing us to a sight of error; for faithful are the wounds of a friend, Pr **27**:**6**. And it is always well for us to recollect the wounds of our Saviour. Often has he been wounded by professed friends, nay, even by his real disciples, when they act contrary to his word.

Verses 7–9

Here is a prophecy of the sufferings of Christ. God the Father gave order to the sword of his justice to awake against his Son, when he freely made his soul an offering for sin. As God, he is called "my Fellow." Christ and the Father are one. He is the Shepherd who was to lay down his life for the sheep. If a Sacrifice, he must be slain, for without shedding of the life-blood there was no remission. This sword must awake against him, yet he had no sin of his own to answer for. It may refer to the whole of Christ's sufferings, especially his agonies in the garden and on the cross, when he endured unspeakable anguish till Divine justice was fully satisfied. Smite the Shepherd, and the sheep shall be scattered. This passage our Lord Jesus declares was fulfilled, when all his disciples, in the night wherein he was betrayed, forsook him and fled. It has, and shall have its accomplishment, in the destruction of the corrupt and hypocritical part of the professed church. Because of the sin of the Jews in rejecting and crucifying Christ, and in opposing his gospel, the Romans would destroy the greater part. But a remnant would be saved. And if we are his people, we shall be refined as gold; he will be God, and the end of all our trials and sufferings will be praise, and honour, and glory, at the appearing of our Lord Jesus Christ.

Chapter 14

Chapter Outline	
The sufferings of Jerusalem.	(1–7)
Encouraging prospects, and the destruction of her enemies.	(8–15)
The holiness of the latter days.	(16–21)

Verses 1–7

The Lord Jesus often stood upon the Mount of Olives when on earth. He ascended from thence to heaven, and then desolations and distresses came upon the Jewish nation. Such is the view taken of this figuratively; but many consider it as a notice of events yet unfulfilled, and that it relates to troubles of which we cannot now form a full idea. Every believer, being related to God as his God, may triumph in the expectation of Christ's coming in power, and speak of it with pleasure. During a long season, the state of the church would be deformed by sin; there would be a mixture of truth and error, of happiness and misery. Such is the experience of God's people, a mingled state of grace and corruption. But, when the season is at the worst, and most unpromising, the Lord will turn darkness into light; deliverance comes when God's people have done looking for it.

Verses 8–15

Some consider that the progress of the gospel, beginning from Jerusalem, is referred to by the living waters flowing from that city. Neither shall the gospel and means of grace, nor the graces of the Spirit wrought in the hearts of believers by those means, ever fail, by reason either of the heat of persecution, or storms of temptation, or the blasts of any other affliction. Tremendous judgments appear to be foretold, to be sent upon those who should oppose the settlement of the Jews in their own land. How far they are to be understood literally, events alone can determine. The furious rage and malice which stir up men against each other, are faint shadows of the enmity which reigns among those who have perished in their sins. Even the inferior creatures often suffer for the sin of man, and in his plagues. Thus God will show his displeasure against sin.

Verses 16–21

As it is impossible for all nations literally to come to Jerusalem once a year, to keep a feast, it is evident that a figurative meaning must here be applied. Gospel worship is represented by the keeping of the feast of tabernacles. Every day of a Christian's life is a day of the feast of tabernacles; every Lord's day especially is the great day of the feast; therefore every day let us worship the Lord of hosts, and keep every Lord's day with peculiar solemnity. It is just for God to withhold the blessings of grace from those who do not attend the means of grace. It is a sin that is its own punishment; those who forsake the duty, forfeit the privilege of communion with God. A time of complete peace and purity of the church will arrive. Men will carry on their common affairs, and their sacred services, upon the same holy principles of faith, love and obedience. Real holiness shall be more diffused, because there shall be a more plentiful pouring forth of the Spirit of holiness than ever before. There shall be holiness even in common things. Every action and every enjoyment of the believer, should be so regulated according to the will of God, that it may be directed to his glory. Our whole lives should be as one constant sacrifice, or act of devotion; no selfish motive should prevail in any of our actions. But how far is the Christian church from this state of purity! Other times, however, are at hand, and the Lord will reform and enlarge his church, as he has promised. Yet in heaven alone will perfect holiness and happiness be found.

Malachi

Malachi was the last of the prophets, and is supposed to have prophesied B.C. **420**. He reproves the priests and the people for the evil practices into which they had fallen, and invites them to repentance and reformation, with promises of the blessings to be bestowed at the coming of the Messiah. And now that prophecy was to cease, he speaks clearly of the Messiah, as nigh at hand, and directs the people of God to keep in rememberance the law of Moses, while they were in expectation of the gospel of Christ.

Chapter 1

Chapter Outline	
The ingratitude of Israel.	(1–5)
They are careless in God's institutions.	(6–14)

Verses 1–5

All advantages, either as to outward circumstances, or spiritual privileges, come from the free love of God, who makes one to differ from another. All the evils sinners feel and fear, are the just recompence of their crimes, while all their hopes and comforts are from the unmerited mercy of the Lord. He chose his people that they might be holy. If we love him, it is because he has first loved us; yet we all are prone to undervalue the mercies of God, and to excuse our own offences.

Verses 6–14

We may each charge upon ourselves what is here charged upon the priests. Our relation to God, as our Father and Master, strongly obliges us to fear and honour him. But they were so scornful that they derided reproof. Sinners ruin themselves by trying to baffle their convictions. Those who live in careless neglect of holy ordinances, who attend on them without reverence, and go from them under no concern, in effect say, The table of the Lord is contemptible. They despised God's name in what they did. It is evident that these understood not the meaning of the sacrifices, as shadowing forth the unblemished Lamb of God; they grudged the expense, thinking all thrown away which did not turn to their profit. If we worship God ignorantly, and without understanding, we bring the blind for sacrifice; if we do it carelessly, if we are cold, dull, and dead in it, we bring the sick; if we rest in the bodily exercise, and do not make heart-work of it, we bring the lame; and if we suffer vain thoughts and distractions to lodge within us, we bring the torn. And is not this evil? Is it not a great affront to God, and a great wrong and injury to our own souls? In order to the acceptance of our actions with God, it is not enough to do that which, for the matter of it, is good; but we must do it from a right principle, in a right manner, and for a right end. Our constant mercies from God, make worse our slothfulness and niggardliness, in our returns of duty to God. A spiritual worship shall be established. Incense shall be offered to God's name, which signifies prayer and praise. And it shall be a pure offering. When the hour came, in which the true worshippers worshipped the Father in Spirit and in truth, then this incense was offered, even this pure offering. We may rely on God's mercy for pardon as to the past, but not for indulgence to sin in future. If there be a willing mind, it will be accepted, though defective; but if any be a deceiver, devoting his best to Satan and to his lusts, he is under a curse. Men now, though in a different way, profane the name of the Lord, pollute his table, and show contempt for his worship.

Chapter 2

Chapter Outline	
The priests reproved for neglecting their covenant.	(1–9)
The people reproved for their evil practices.	(10–17)

Verses 1–9

What is here said of the covenant of priesthood, is true of the covenant of grace made with all believers, as spiritual priests. It is a covenant of life and peace; it assures all believers of all happiness, both in this world and in that to come. It is an honour to God's servants to be employed as his messengers. The priest's lips should not keep knowledge from his people, but keep it for them. The people are all concerned to know the will of the Lord. We must not only consult the written word, but desire instruction and advice from God's messengers, in the affairs of our souls. Ministers must exert themselves to the utmost for the conversion of sinners; and even among those called Israelites, there are many to be turned from iniquity. Those ministers, and those only, are likely to turn men from sin, who preach sound doctrine, and live holy lives according to the Scripture. Many departed from this way; thus they misled the people. Such as walk with God in peace and righteousness, and turn others from sin, honour God; he will honour them, while those who despise him shall be lightly esteemed.

Verses 10–17

Corrupt practices are the fruit of corrupt principles; and he who is false to his God, will not be true to his fellow mortals. In contempt of the marriage covenant, which God instituted, the Jews put away the wives they had of their own nation, probably to make room for strange wives. They made their lives bitter to them; yet, in the sight of others, they pretend to be tender of them. Consider she is thy wife; thy own; the nearest relation thou hast in the world. The wife is to be looked on, not as a servant, but as a companion to the husband. There is an oath of God between them, which is not to be trifled with. Man and wife should continue to their lives' end, in holy love and peace. Did not God make one, one Eve for one Adam? Yet God could have made another Eve. Wherefore did he make but one woman for one man? It was that the children might be made a seed to serve him. Husbands and wives must live in the fear of God, that their seed may be a godly seed. The God of Israel saith that he hateth putting away. Those who would be kept from sin, must take heed to their spirits, for there all sin begins. Men will find that their wrong conduct in their families springs from selfishness, which disregards the welfare and happiness of others, when opposed to their own passions and fancies. It is wearisome to God to hear people justify themselves in wicked practices. Those who think God can be a friend to sin, affront him, and deceive themselves. The scoffers said, Where is the God of judgement? but the day of the Lord will come.

Chapter 3

Chapter Outline	
The coming of Christ.	(1–6)
The Jews reproved for their corruptions.	(7–12)
God's care of his people; The distinction between the righteous and the wicked.	(13–18)

Verses 1–6

The first words of this chapter seem an answer to the scoffers of those days. Here is a prophecy of the appearing of John the Baptist. He is Christ's harbinger. He shall prepare the way before him, by calling men to repentance. The Messiah had been long called, "He that should come," and now shortly he will come. He is the Messenger of the covenant. Those who seek Jesus, shall find pleasure in him, often when not looked for. The Lord Jesus, prepares the sinner's heart to be his temple, by the ministry of his word and the convictions of his Spirit, and he enters it as the Messenger of peace and consolation. No hypocrite or formalist can endure his doctrine, or stand before his tribunal. Christ came to distinguish men, to separate between the precious and the vile. He shall sit as a Refiner. Christ, by his gospel, shall purify and reform his church, and by his Spirit working with it, shall regenerate and cleanse souls. He will take away the dross found in them. He will separate their corruptions, which render their faculties worthless and useless. The believer needs not fear the fiery trial of afflictions and temptations, by which the Saviour refines his gold. He will take care it is not more intense or longer than is needful for his good; and this trial will end far otherwise than that of the wicked. Christ will, by interceding for them, make them accepted. Where no fear of God is, no good is to be expected. Evil pursues sinners. God is unchangeable. And though the sentence against evil works be not executed speedily, yet it will be executed; the Lord is as much an enemy to sin as ever. We may all apply this to ourselves. Because we have to do with a God that changes not, therefore it is that we are not consumed; because his compassions fail not.

Verses 7–12

The men of that generation turned away from God, they had not kept his ordinances. God gives them a gracious call. But they said, Wherein shall we return? God notices what returns our hearts make to the calls of his word. It shows great perverseness in sin, when men make afflictions excuses for sin, which are sent to part between them and their sins. Here is an earnest exhortation to reform. God must be served in the first place; and the interest of our souls ought to be preferred before that of our bodies. Let them trust God to provide for their comfort. God has blessings ready for us, but through the weakness of our faith and the narrowness of our desires, we have not room to receive them. He who makes trial will find nothing is lost by honouring the Lord with his substance.

Verses 13–18

Among the Jews at this time, some plainly discovered themselves to be children of the wicked one. The yoke of Christ is easy. But those who work wickedness, tempt God by presumptuous sins. Judge of things as they will appear when the doom of these proud sinners comes to be executed. Those that feared the Lord, spake kindly, for preserving and promoting mutual love, when sin thus abounded. They spake one to another, in the language of those that fear the Lord, and think on his name. As evil communications corrupt good minds and manners, so good communications confirm them. A book of remembrance was written before God. He will take care that his children perish not with those that believe not. They shall be vessels of mercy and honour, when the rest are made vessels of wrath and dishonour. The saints are God's jewels; they are dear to him. He will preserve them as his jewels, when the earth is burned up like dross. Those who now own God for theirs, he will then own for his. It is our duty to serve God with the disposition of children; and he will not have his children trained up in idleness; they must do him service from a principle of love. Even God's children stand in need of sparing mercy. All are righteous or wicked, such as serve God, or such as serve him not: all are going to heaven or to hell. We are often deceived in our opinions concerning both the one and the other; but at the bar of Christ, every man's character will be known. As to ourselves, we have need to think among which we shall have our lot; and, as to others, we must judge nothing before the time. But in the end all the world will confess that those alone were wise and happy, who served the Lord and trusted in Him.

Chapter 4

Chapter Outline	
The judgements on the wicked, and the happiness of the righteous.	(1–3)
Regard to be had to the law; John the Baptist promised as the forerunner of Messiah.	(4–6)

Verses 1–3

Here is a reference to the first and to the second coming of Christ: God has fixed the day of both. Those who do wickedly, who do not fear God's anger, shall feel it. It is certainly to be applied to the day of judgment, when Christ shall be revealed in flaming fire; to execute judgment on the proud, and all that do wickedly. In both, Christ is a rejoicing Light to those who serve him faithfully. By the Sun of Righteousness we understand Jesus Christ. Through him believers are justified and sanctified, and so are brought to see light. His influences render the sinner holy, joyful, and fruitful. It is applicable to the graces and comforts of the Holy Spirit, brought into the souls of men. Christ gave the Spirit to those who are his, to shine in their hearts, and to be a Comforter to them, a Sun and a Shield. That day which to the wicked will burn as an oven, will to the righteous be bright as the morning; it is what they wait for, more than those that wait for the morning. Christ came as the Sun, to bring, not only light to a dark world, but health to a distempered world. Souls shall increase in knowledge and spiritual strength. Their growth is as that of calves of the stall, not as the flower of the field, which is slender and weak, and soon withers. The saints' triumphs are all owing to God's victories; it is not they that do this, but God who does it for them. Behold another day is coming, far more dreadful to all that work wickedness than any which is gone before. How great then the happiness of the believer, when he goes from the darkness and misery of this world, to rejoice in the Lord for evermore!

Verses 4–6

Here is a solemn conclusion, not only of this prophecy, but of the Old Testament. Conscience bids us remember the law. Though we have not prophets, yet, as long as we have Bibles, we may keep up our communion with God. Let others boast in their proud reasoning, and call it enlightening, but let us keep near to that sacred word, through which this Sun of Righteousness shines upon the souls of his people. They must keep up a believing expectation of the gospel of Christ, and must look for the beginning of it. John the Baptist preached repentance and reformation, as Elijah had done. The turning of souls to God and their duty, is the best preparation of them for the great and dreadful day of the Lord. John shall preach a doctrine that shall reach men's hearts, and work a change in them. Thus he shall prepare the way for the kingdom of heaven. The Jewish nation, by wickedness, laid themselves open to the curse. God was ready to bring ruin upon them; but he will once more try whether they will repent and return; therefore he sent John the Baptist to preach repentance to them. Let the believer wait with patience for his release, and cheerfully expect the great day, when Christ shall come the second time to complete our salvation. But those must expect to be smitten with a sword, with a curse, who turn not to Him that smites them with a rod. None can expect to escape the curse of God's broken law, nor to enjoy the happiness of his chosen and redeemed people, unless their hearts are turned from sin and the world, to Christ and holiness. The grace of our Lord Jesus Christ be with us all. Amen.

Matthew

Matthew, surnamed Levi, before his conversion was a publican, or tax-gatherer under the Romans at Capernaum. He is generally allowed to have written his Gospel before any other of the evangelists. The contents of this Gospel, and the evidence of ancient writers, show that it was written primarily for the use of the Jewish nation. The fulfilment of prophecy was regarded by the Jews as strong evidence, therefore this is especially dwelt upon by St. Matthew. Here are particularly selected such parts of our Saviour's history and discourses as were best suited to awaken the Jewish nation to a sense of their sins; to remove their erroneous expectations of an earthly kingdom; to abate their pride and self-conceit; to teach them the spiritual nature and extent of the gospel; and to prepare them for the admission of the Gentiles into the church.

Chapter 1

Chapter Outline	
The genealogy of Jesus.	(1–17)
An angel appears to Joseph.	(18–25)

Verses 1–17

Concerning this genealogy of our Saviour, observe the chief intention. It is not a needless genealogy. It is not a vain-glorious one, as those of great men often are. It proves that our Lord Jesus is of the nation and family out of which the Messiah was to arise. The promise of the blessing was made to Abraham and his seed; of the dominion, to David and his seed. It was promised to Abraham that Christ should descend from him, Ge **12**:**3**; **22**:**18**; and to David that he should descend from him, **2**Sa **7**:**12**; Ps **89**:**3**, &c.; **132**:**11**; and, therefore, unless Jesus is a son of David, and a son of Abraham, he is not the Messiah. Now this is here proved from well-known records. When the Son of God was pleased to take our nature, he came near to us, in our fallen, wretched condition; but he was perfectly free from sin: and while we read the names in his genealogy, we should not forget how low the Lord of glory stooped to save the human race.

Verses 18–25

Let us look to the circumstances under which the Son of God entered into this lower world, till we learn to despise the vain honours of this world, when compared with piety and holiness. The mystery of Christ's becoming man is to be adored, not curiously inquired into. It was so ordered that Christ should partake of our nature, yet that he should be pure from the defilement of original sin, which has been communicated to all the race of Adam. Observe, it is the thoughtful, not the unthinking, whom God will guide. God's time to come with instruction to his people, is when they are at a loss. Divine comforts most delight the soul when under the pressure of perplexed thoughts. Joseph is told that Mary should bring forth the Saviour of the world. He was to call his name Jesus, a Saviour. Jesus is the same name with Joshua. And the reason of that name is clear, for those whom Christ saves, he saves from their sins; from the guilt of sin by the merit of his death, and from the power of sin by the Spirit of his grace. In saving them from sin, he saves them from wrath and the curse, and all misery, here and hereafter. Christ came to save his people, not in their sins, but from their sins; and so to redeem them from among men, to himself, who is separate from sinners. Joseph did as the angel of the Lord had bidden him, speedily, without delay, and cheerfully, without dispute. By applying the general rules of the written word, we should in all the steps of our lives, particularly the great turns of them, take direction from God, and we shall find this safe and comfortable.

Chapter 2

Chapter Outline	
The wise men's search after Christ.	(1–8)
The wise men worship Jesus.	(9–12)
Jesus carried into Egypt.	(13–15)
Herod causes the infants of Bethlehem to be massacred.	(16–18)
Death of Herod, Jesus brought to Nazareth.	(19–23)

Verses 1–8

Those who live at the greatest distance from the means of grace often use most diligence, and learn to know the most of Christ and his salvation. But no curious arts, or mere human learning, can direct men unto him. We must learn of Christ by attending to the word of God, as a light that shineth in a dark place, and by seeking the teaching of the Holy Spirit. And those in whose hearts the day-star is risen, to give them any thing of the knowledge of Christ, make it their business to worship him. Though Herod was very old, and never had shown affection for his family, and was not himself likely to live till a new-born infant had grown up to manhood, he began to be troubled with the dread of a rival. He understood not the spiritual nature of the Messiah's kingdom. Let us beware of a dead faith. A man may be persuaded of many truths, and yet may hate them, because they interfere with his ambition, or sinful indulgences. Such a belief will make him uneasy, and the more resolved to oppose the truth and the cause of God; and he may be foolish enough to hope for success therein.

Verses 9–12

What joy these wise men felt upon this sight of the star, none know so well as those who, after a long and melancholy night of temptation and desertion, under the power of a spirit of bondage, at length receive the Spirit of adoption, witnessing with their spirits that they are the children of God. We may well think what a disappointment it was to them, when they found a cottage was his palace, and his own poor mother the only attendant he had. However, these wise men did not think themselves baffled; but having found the King they sought, they presented their gifts to him. The humble inquirer after Christ will not be stumbled at finding him and his disciples in obscure cottages, after having in vain sought them in palaces and populous cities. Is a soul busy, seeking after Christ? Would it worship him, and does it say, Alas! I am a foolish and poor creature, and have nothing to offer? Nothing! Hast thou not a heart, though unworthy of him, dark, hard, and foul? Give it to him as it is, and be willing that he use and dispose of it as it pleases him; he will take it, and will make it better, and thou shalt never repent having given it to him. He shall frame it to his own likeness, and will give thee himself, and be thine for ever. The gifts the wise men presented were gold, frankincense, and myrrh. Providence sent these as a seasonable relief to Joseph and Mary in their present poor condition. Thus our heavenly Father, who knows what his children need, uses some as stewards to supply the wants of others, and can provide for them, even from the ends of the earth.

Verses 13–15

Egypt had been a house of bondage to Israel, and particularly cruel to the infants of Israel; yet it is to be a place of refuge to the holy Child Jesus. God, when he pleases, can make the worst of places serve the best of purposes. This was a trial of the faith of Joseph and Mary. But their faith, being tried, was found firm. If we and our infants are at any time in trouble, let us remember the straits in which Christ was when an infant.

Verses 16–18

Herod killed all the male children, not only in Bethlehem, but in all the villages of that city. Unbridled wrath, armed with an unlawful power, often carries men to absurd cruelties. It was no unrighteous thing with God to permit this; every life is forfeited to his justice as soon as it begins. The diseases and deaths of little children are proofs of original sin. But the murder of these infants was their martyrdom. How early did persecution against Christ and his kingdom begin! Herod now thought that he had baffled the Old Testament prophecies, and the efforts of the wise men in finding Christ; but whatever crafty, cruel devices are in men's hearts, the counsel of the Lord shall stand.

Verses 19–23

Egypt may serve to sojourn in, or take shelter in, for awhile, but not to abide in. Christ was sent to the lost sheep of the house of Israel, to them he must return. Did we but look upon the world as our Egypt, the place of our bondage and banishment, and heaven only as our Canaan, our home, our rest, we should as readily arise and depart thither, when we are called for, as Joseph did out of Egypt. The family must settle in Galilee. Nazareth was a place held in bad esteem, and Christ was crucified with this accusation, Jesus the Nazarene. Wherever Providence allots the bounds of our habitation, we must expect to share the reproach of Christ; yet we may glory in being called by his name, sure that if we suffer with him, we shall also be glorified with him.

Chapter 3

Chapter Outline	
John the Baptist, His preaching, manner of life, and baptism.	(1–6)
John reproves the Pharisees and Sadducees.	(7–12)
The baptism of Jesus.	(13–17)

Verses 1–6

After Malachi there was no prophet until John the Baptist came. He appeared first in the wilderness of Judea. This was not an uninhabited desert, but a part of the country not thickly peopled, nor much enclosed. No place is so remote as to shut us out from the visits of Divine grace. The doctrine he preached was repentance; "Repent ye." The word here used, implies a total alteration in the mind, a change in the judgment, disposition, and affections, another and a better bias of the soul. Consider your ways, change your minds: you have thought amiss; think again, and think aright. True penitents have other thoughts of God and Christ, sin and holiness, of this world and the other, than they had. The change of the mind produces a change of the way. That is gospel repentance, which flows from a sight of Christ, from a sense of his love, and from hopes of pardon and forgiveness through him. It is a great encouragement to us to repent; repent, for your sins shall be pardoned upon your repentance. Return to God in a way of duty, and he will, through Christ, return unto you in the way of mercy. It is still as necessary to repent and humble ourselves, to prepare the way of the Lord, as it then was. There is a great deal to be done, to make way for Christ into a soul, and nothing is more needful than the discovery of sin, and a conviction that we cannot be saved by our own righteousness. The way of sin and Satan is a crooked way; but to prepare a way for Christ, the paths must be made straight, Heb **12**:**13**. Those whose business it is to call others to mourn for sin, and to mortify it, ought themselves to live a serious life, a life of self-denial, and contempt of the world. By giving others this example, John made way for Christ. Many came to John's baptism, but few kept to the profession they made. There may be many forward hearers, where there are few true believers. Curiosity, and love for novelty and variety, may bring many to attend on good preaching, and to be affected for a while, who never are subject to the power of it. Those who received John's doctrine, testified their repentance by confessing their sins. Those only are ready to receive Jesus Christ as their righteousness, who are brought with sorrow and shame to own their guilt. The benefits of the kingdom of heaven, now at hand, were thereupon sealed to them by baptism. John washed them with water, in token that God would cleanse them from all their iniquities, thereby intimating, that by nature and practice all were polluted, and could not be admitted among the people of God, unless washed from their sins in the fountain Christ was to open, Zec **13**:**1**.

Verses 7–12

To make application to the souls of the hearers, is the life of preaching; so it was of John's preaching. The Pharisees laid their chief stress on outward observances, neglecting the weightier matters of the moral law, and the spiritual meaning of their legal ceremonies. Others of them were detestable hypocrites, making their pretences to holiness a cloak for iniquity. The Sadducees ran into the opposite extreme, denying the existence of spirits, and a future state. They were the scornful infidels of that time and country. There is a wrath to come. It is the great concern of every one to flee from that wrath. God, who delights not in our ruin, has warned us; he warns by the written word, by ministers, by conscience. And those are not worthy of the name of penitents, or their privileges, who say they are sorry for their sins, yet persist in them. It becomes penitents to be humble and low in their own eyes, to be thankful for the least mercy, patient under the greatest affliction, to be watchful against all appearances of sin, to abound in every duty, and to be charitable in judging others. Here is a word of caution, not to trust in outward privileges. There is a great deal which carnal hearts are apt to say within themselves, to put aside the convincing, commanding power of the word of God. Multitudes, by resting in the honours and mere advantages of their being members of an outward church, come short of heaven. Here is a word of terror to the careless and secure. Our corrupt hearts cannot be made to produce good fruit, unless the regenerating Spirit of Christ graft the good word of God upon them. And every tree, however high in gifts and honours, however green in outward professions and performances, if it bring not forth good fruit, the fruits meet for repentance, is hewn down and cast into the fire of God's wrath, the fittest place for barren trees: what else are they good for? If not fit for fruit, they are fit for fuel. John shows the design and intention of Christ's appearing, which they were now speedily to expect. No outward forms can make us clean. No ordinances, by whomsoever administered, or after whatever mode, can supply the want of the baptism of the Holy Ghost and of fire. The purifying and cleansing power of the Holy Spirit alone can produce that purity of heart, and those holy affections, which accompany salvation. It is Christ who baptizes with the Holy Ghost. This he did in the extraordinary gifts of the Spirit sent upon the apostles, Ac **2**:**4**. This he does in the graces and comforts of the Spirit, given to those that ask him, Lu **11**:**13**; Joh **7**:**38**, **39**; see Ac **11**:**16**. Observe here, the outward church is Christ's floor, Isa **21**:**10**. True believers are as wheat, substantial, useful, and valuable; hypocrites are as chaff, light and empty, useless and worthless, carried about with every wind; these are mixed, good and bad, in the same outward communion. There is a day coming when the wheat and chaff shall be separated. The last judgment will be the distinguishing day, when saints and sinners shall be parted for ever. In heaven the saints are brought together, and no longer scattered; they are safe, and no longer exposed; separated from corrupt neighbours without, and corrupt affections within, and there is no chaff among them. Hell is the unquenchable fire, which will certainly be the portion and punishment of hypocrites and unbelievers. Here life and death, good and evil, are set before us: according as we now are in the field, we shall be then in the floor.

Verses 13–17

Christ's gracious condescensions are so surprising, that even the strongest believers at first can hardly believe them; so deep and mysterious, that even those who know his mind well, are apt to start objections against the will of Christ. And those who have much of the Spirit of God while here, see that they need to apply to Christ for more. Christ does not deny that John had need to be baptized of him, yet declares he will now be baptized of John. Christ is now in a state of humiliation. Our Lord Jesus looked upon it as well becoming him to fulfil all righteousness, to own every Divine institution, and to show his readiness to comply with all God's righteous precepts. In and through Christ, the heavens are opened to the children of men. This descent of the Spirit upon Christ, showed that he was endued with his sacred influences without measure. The fruit of the Spirit is love, joy, peace, long-suffering, gentleness, goodness, faith, meekness, temperance. At Christ's baptism there was a manifestation of the three Persons in the sacred Trinity. The Father confirming the Son to be Mediator; the Son solemnly entering upon the work; the Holy Spirit descending on him, to be through his mediation communicated to his people. In Him our spiritual sacrifices are acceptable, for He is the altar that sanctifies every gift, **1**Pe **2**:**5**. Out of Christ, God is a consuming fire, but in Christ, a reconciled Father. This is the sum of the gospel, which we must by faith cheerfully embrace.

Chapter 4

Chapter Outline	
The temptation of Christ.	(1–11)
The opening of Christ's ministry in Galilee.	(12–17)
Call of Simon and others.	(18–22)
Jesus teaches and works miracles.	(23–25)

Verses 1–11

Concerning Christ's temptation, observe, that directly after he was declared to be the Son of God, and the Saviour of the world, he was tempted; great privileges, and special tokens of Divine favour, will not secure any from being tempted. But if the Holy Spirit witness to our being adopted as children of God, that will answer all the suggestions of the evil spirit. Christ was directed to the combat. If we presume upon our own strength, and tempt the devil to tempt us, we provoke God to leave us to ourselves. Others are tempted, when drawn aside of their own lust, and enticed, Jas **1**:**14**; but our Lord Jesus had no corrupt nature, therefore he was tempted only by the devil. In the temptation of Christ it appears that our enemy is subtle, spiteful, and very daring; but he can be resisted. It is a comfort to us that Christ suffered, being tempted; for thus it appears that our temptations, if not yielded to, are not sins, they are afflictions only. Satan aimed in all his temptations, to bring Christ to sin against God. **1**. He tempted him to despair of his Father's goodness, and to distrust his Father's care concerning him. It is one of the wiles of Satan to take advantage of our outward condition; and those who are brought into straits have need to double their guard. Christ answered all the temptations of Satan with "It is written;" to set us an example, he appealed to what was written in the Scriptures. This method we must take, when at any time we are tempted to sin. Let us learn not to take any wrong courses for our supply, when our wants are ever so pressing: in some way or other the Lord will provide. **2**. Satan tempted Christ to presume upon his Father's power and protection, in a point of safety. Nor are any extremes more dangerous than despair and presumption, especially in the affairs of our souls. Satan has no objection to holy places as the scene of his assaults. Let us not, in any place, be off our watch. The holy city is the place, where he does, with the greatest advantage, tempt men to pride and presumption. All high places are slippery places; advancements in the world makes a man a mark for Satan to shoot his fiery darts at. Is Satan so well **verse**d in Scripture as to be able to quote it readily? He is so. It is possible for a man to have his head full of Scripture notions, and his mouth full of Scripture expressions, while his heart is full of bitter enmity to God and to all goodness. Satan misquoted the words. If we go out of our way, out of the way of our duty, we forfeit the promise, and put ourselves out of God's protection. This passage, De **8**:**3**, made against the tempter, therefore he left out part. This promise is firm and stands good. But shall we continue in sin, that grace may abound? No. **3**. Satan tempted Christ to idolatry with the offer of the kingdoms of the world, and the glory of them. The glory of the world is the most charming temptation to the unthinking and unwary; by that men are most easily imposed upon. Christ was tempted to worship Satan. He rejected the proposal with abhorrence. "Get thee hence, Satan!" Some temptations are openly wicked; and they are not merely to be opposed, but rejected at once. It is good to be quick and firm in resisting temptation. If we resist the devil he will flee from us. But the soul that deliberates is almost overcome. We find but few who can decidedly reject such baits as Satan offers; yet what is a man profited if he gain the whole world, and lose his own soul? Christ was succoured after the temptation, for his encouragement to go on in his undertaking, and for our encouragement to trust in him; for as he knew, by experience, what it was to suffer, being tempted, so he knew what it was to be succoured, being tempted; therefore we may expect, not only that he will feel for his tempted people, but that he will come to them with seasonable relief.

Verses 12–17

It is just with God to take the gospel and the means of grace, from those that slight them and thrust them away. Christ will not stay long where he is not welcome. Those who are without Christ, are in the dark. They were sitting in this condition, a contented posture; they chose it rather than light; they were willingly ignorant. When the gospel comes, light comes; when it comes to any place, when it comes to any soul, it makes day there. Light discovers and directs; so does the gospel. The doctrine of repentance is right gospel doctrine. Not only the austere John Baptist, but the gracious Jesus, preached repentance. There is still the same reason to do so. The kingdom of heaven was not reckoned to be fully come, till the pouring out of the Holy Spirit after Christ's ascension.

Verses 18–22

When Christ began to preach, he began to gather disciples, who should be hearers, and afterwards preachers of his doctrine, who should be witnesses of his miracles, and afterwards testify concerning them. He went not to Herod's court, not to Jerusalem, among the chief priests and the elders, but to the sea of Galilee, among the fishermen. The same power which called Peter and Andrew, could have wrought upon Annas and Caiaphas, for with God nothing is impossible. But Christ chooses the foolish things of the world to confound the wise. Diligence in an honest calling is pleasing to Christ, and it is no hinderance to a holy life. Idle people are more open to the temptations of Satan than to the calls of God. It is a happy and hopeful thing to see children careful of their parents, and dutiful. When Christ comes, it is good to be found doing. Am I in Christ? is a very needful question to ask ourselves; and, next to that, Am I in my calling? They had followed Christ before, as common disciples, Joh **1**:**37**; now they must leave their calling. Those who would follow Christ aright, must, at his command, leave all things to follow him, must be ready to part with them. This instance of the power of the Lord Jesus encourages us to depend upon his grace. He speaks, and it is done.

Verses 23–25

Wherever Christ went, he confirmed his Divine mission by miracles, which were emblems of the healing power of his doctrine, and the influences of the Spirit which accompanied it. We do not now find the Saviour's miraculous healing power in our bodies; but if we are cured by medicine, the praise is equally his. Three general words are here used. He healed every sickness or disease; none was too bad; none too hard, for Christ to heal with a word. Three diseases are named; the palsy, which is the greatest weakness of the body; lunacy, which is the greatest malady of the mind; and possession of the devil, which is the greatest misery and calamity of both; yet Christ healed all, and by thus curing bodily diseases, showed that his great errand into the world was to cure spiritual maladies. Sin is the sickness, disease, and torment of the soul: Christ came to take away sin, and so to heal the soul.

Chapter 5

Chapter Outline	
Christ's sermon on the mount.	(1, 2)
Who are blessed.	(3–12)
Exhortations and warnings.	(13–16)
Christ came to confirm the law.	(17–20)
The sixth commandment.	(21–26)
The seventh commandment.	(27–32)
The third commandment.	(33–37)
The law of retaliation.	(38–42)
The law of love explained.	(43–48)

Verses 1, 2

None will find happiness in this world or the next, who do not seek it from Christ by the rule of his word. He taught them what was the evil they should abhor, and what the good they should seek and abound in.

Verses 3–12

Our Saviour here gives eight characters of blessed people, which represent to us the principal graces of a Christian. **1**. The poor in spirit are happy. These bring their minds to their condition, when it is a low condition. They are humble and lowly in their own eyes. They see their want, bewail their guilt, and thirst after a Redeemer. The kingdom of grace is of such; the kingdom of glory is for them. **2**. Those that mourn are happy. That godly sorrow which worketh true repentance, watchfulness, a humble mind, and continual dependence for acceptance on the mercy of God in Christ Jesus, with constant seeking the Holy Spirit, to cleanse away the remaining evil, seems here to be intended. Heaven is the joy of our Lord; a mountain of joy, to which our way is through a vale of tears. Such mourners shall be comforted by their God. **3**. The meek are happy. The meek are those who quietly submit to God; who can bear insult; are silent, or return a soft answer; who, in their patience, keep possession of their own souls, when they can scarcely keep possession of anything else. These meek ones are happy, even in this world. Meekness promotes wealth, comfort, and safety, even in this world. **4**. Those who hunger and thirst after righteousness are happy. Righteousness is here put for all spiritual blessings. These are purchased for us by the righteousness of Christ, confirmed by the faithfulness of God. Our desires of spiritual blessings must be earnest. Though all desires for grace are not grace, yet such a desire as this, is a desire of God's own raising, and he will not forsake the work of his own hands. **5**. The merciful are happy. We must not only bear our own afflictions patiently, but we must do all we can to help those who are in misery. We must have compassion on the souls of others, and help them; pity those who are in sin, and seek to snatch them as brands out of the burning. **6**. The pure in heart are happy; for they shall see God. Here holiness and happiness are fully described and put together. The heart must be purified by faith, and kept for God. Create in me such a clean heart, O God. None but the pure are capable of seeing God, nor would heaven be happiness to the impure. As God cannot endure to look upon their iniquity, so they cannot look upon his purity. **7**. The peace-makers are happy. They love, and desire, and delight in peace; and study to be quiet. They keep the peace that it be not broken, and recover it when it is broken. If the peace-makers are blessed, woe to the peace-breakers! **8**. Those who are persecuted for righteousness' sake are happy. This saying is peculiar to Christianity; and it is more largely insisted upon than any of the rest. Yet there is nothing in our sufferings that can merit of God; but God will provide that those who lose for him, though life itself, shall not lose by him in the end. Blessed Jesus! how different are thy maxims from those of men of this world! They call the proud happy, and admire the gay, the rich, the powerful, and the victorious. May we find mercy from the Lord; may we be owned as his children, and inherit his kingdom. With these enjoyments and hopes, we may cheerfully welcome low or painful circumstances.

Verses 13–16

Ye are the salt of the earth. Mankind, lying in ignorance and wickedness, were as a vast heap, ready to putrify; but Christ sent forth his disciples, by their lives and doctrines to season it with knowledge and grace. If they are not such as they should be, they are as salt that has lost its savour. If a man can take up the profession of Christ, and yet remain graceless, no other doctrine, no other means, can make him profitable. Our light must shine, by doing such good works as men may see. What is between God and our souls, must be kept to ourselves; but that which is of itself open to the sight of men, we must study to make suitable to our profession, and praiseworthy. We must aim at the glory of God.

Verses 17–20

Let none suppose that Christ allows his people to trifle with any commands of God's holy law. No sinner partakes of Christ's justifying righteousness, till he repents of his evil deeds. The mercy revealed in the gospel leads the believer to still deeper self-abhorrence. The law is the Christian's rule of duty, and he delights therein. If a man, pretending to be Christ's disciple, encourages himself in any allowed disobedience to the holy law of God, or teaches others to do the same, whatever his station or reputation among men may be, he can be no true disciple. Christ's righteousness, imputed to us by faith alone, is needed by every one that enters the kingdom of grace or of glory; but the new creation of the heart to holiness, produces a thorough change in a man's temper and conduct.

Verses 21–26

The Jewish teachers had taught, that nothing except actual murder was forbidden by the sixth commandment. Thus they explained away its spiritual meaning. Christ showed the full meaning of this commandment; according to which we must be judged hereafter, and therefore ought to be ruled now. All rash anger is heart murder. By our brother, here, we are to understand any person, though ever so much below us, for we are all made of one blood. "Raca," is a scornful word, and comes from pride: "Thou fool," is a spiteful word, and comes from hatred. Malicious slanders and censures are poison that kills secretly and slowly. Christ told them that how light soever they made of these sins, they would certainly be called into judgment for them. We ought carefully to preserve Christian love and peace with all our brethren; and if at any time there is a quarrel, we should confess our fault, humble ourselves to our brother, making or offering satisfaction for wrong done in word or deed: and we should do this quickly; because, till this is done, we are unfit for communion with God in holy ordinances. And when we are preparing for any religious exercises, it is good for us to make that an occasion of serious reflection and self-examination. What is here said is very applicable to our being reconciled to God through Christ. While we are alive, we are in the way to his judgement-seat; after death, it will be too late. When we consider the importance of the case, and the uncertainty of life, how needful it is to seek peace with God, without delay!

Verses 27–32

Victory over the desires of the heart, must be attended with painful exertions. But it must be done. Every thing is bestowed to save us from our sins, not in them. All our senses and powers must be kept from those things which lead to transgression. Those who lead others into temptation to sin, by dress or in other ways, or leave them in it, or expose them to it, make themselves guilty of their sin, and will be accountable for it. If painful operations are submitted to, that our lives may be saved, what ought our minds to shrink from, when the salvation of our souls is concerned? There is tender mercy under all the Divine requirements, and the grace and consolations of the Spirit will enable us to attend to them.

Verses 33–37

There is no reason to consider that solemn oaths in a court of justice, or on other proper occasions, are wrong, provided they are taken with due reverence. But all oaths taken without necessity, or in common conversation, must be sinful, as well as all those expressions which are appeals to God, though persons think thereby to evade the guilt of swearing. The worse men are, the less they are bound by oaths; the better they are, the less there is need for them. Our Lord does not enjoin the precise terms wherein we are to affirm or deny, but such a constant regard to truth as would render oaths unnecessary.

Verses 38–42

The plain instruction is, Suffer any injury that can be borne, for the sake of peace, committing your concerns to the Lord's keeping. And the sum of all is, that Christians must avoid disputing and striving. If any say, Flesh and blood cannot pass by such an affront, let them remember, that flesh and blood shall not inherit the kingdom of God; and those who act upon right principles will have most peace and comfort.

Verses 43–48

The Jewish teachers by "neighbour" understood only those who were of their own country, nation, and religion, whom they were pleased to look upon as their friends. The Lord Jesus teaches that we must do all the real kindness we can to all, especially to their souls. We must pray for them. While many will render good for good, we must render good for evil; and this will speak a nobler principle than most men act by. Others salute their brethren, and embrace those of their own party, and way, and opinion, but we must not so confine our respect. It is the duty of Christians to desire, and aim at, and press towards perfection in grace and holiness. And therein we must study to conform ourselves to the example of our heavenly Father, **1Pe 1**:**15**, **16**. Surely more is to be expected from the followers of Christ than from others; surely more will be found in them than in others. Let us beg of God to enable us to prove ourselves his children.

Chapter 6

Chapter Outline	
Against hypocrisy in almsgiving.	(1–4)
Against hypocrisy in prayer.	(5–8)
How to pray.	(9–15)
Respecting fasting.	(16–18)
Evil of being worldly-minded.	(19–24)
Trust in God commended.	(25–34)

Verses 1–4

Our Lord next warned against hypocrisy and outward show in religious duties. What we do, must be done from an inward principle, that we may be approved of God, not that we may be praised of men. In these **verses** we are cautioned against hypocrisy in giving alms. Take heed of it. It is a subtle sin; and vain-glory creeps into what we do, before we are aware. But the duty is not the less necessary and excellent for being abused by hypocrites to serve their pride. The doom Christ passes, at first may seem a promise, but it is their reward; not the reward God promises to those who do good, but the reward hypocrites promise themselves, and a poor reward it is; they did it to be seen of men, and they are seen of men. When we take least notice of our good deeds ourselves, God takes most notice of them. He will reward thee; not as a master who gives his servant what he earns, and no more, but as a Father who gives abundantly to his son that serves him.

Verses 5–8

It is taken for granted that all who are disciples of Christ pray. You may as soon find a living man that does not breathe, as a living Christian that does not pray. If prayerless, then graceless. The Scribes and Pharisees were guilty of two great faults in prayer, vain-glory and vain repetitions. "Verily they have their reward;" if in so great a matter as is between us and God, when we are at prayer, we can look to so poor a thing as the praise of men, it is just that it should be all our reward. Yet there is not a secret, sudden breathing after God, but he observes it. It is called a reward, but it is of grace, not of debt; what merit can there be in begging? If he does not give his people what they ask, it is because he knows they do not need it, and that it is not for their good. So far is God from being wrought upon by the length or words of our prayers, that the most powerful intercessions are those which are made with groanings that cannot be uttered. Let us well study what is shown of the frame of mind in which our prayers should be offered, and learn daily from Christ how to pray.

Verses 9–15

Christ saw it needful to show his disciples what must commonly be the matter and method of their prayer. Not that we are tied up to the use of this only, or of this always; yet, without doubt, it is very good to use it. It has much in a little; and it is used acceptably no further than it is used with understanding, and without being needlessly repeated. The petitions are six; the first three relate more expressly to God and his honour, the last three to our own concerns, both temporal and spiritual. This prayer teaches us to seek first the kingdom of God and his righteousness, and that all other things shall be added. After the things of God's glory, kingdom, and will, we pray for the needful supports and comforts of this present life. Every word here has a lesson in it. We ask for bread; that teaches us sobriety and temperance: and we ask only for bread; not for what we do not need. We ask for our bread; that teaches us honesty and industry: we do not ask for the bread of others, nor the bread of deceit, Pr **20**:**17**; nor the bread of idleness, Pr **31**:**27**, but the bread honestly gotten. We ask for our daily bread; which teaches us constantly to depend upon Divine Providence. We beg of God to give it us; not sell it us, nor lend it us, but give it. The greatest of men must be beholden to the mercy of God for their daily bread. We pray, Give it to us. This teaches us a compassion for the poor. Also that we ought to pray with our families. We pray that God would give it us this day; which teaches us to renew the desires of our souls toward God, as the wants of our bodies are renewed. As the day comes we must pray to our heavenly Father, and reckon we could as well go a day without food, as without prayer. We are taught to hate and dread sin while we hope for mercy, to distrust ourselves, to rely on the providence and grace of God to keep us from it, to be prepared to resist the tempter, and not to become tempters of others. Here is a promise. If you forgive, your heavenly Father will also forgive. We must forgive, as we hope to be forgiven. Those who desire to find mercy with God, must show mercy to their brethren. Christ came into the world as the great Peace-maker, not only to reconcile us to God, but one to another.

Verses 16–18

Religious fasting is a duty required of the disciples of Christ, but it is not so much a duty itself, as a means to dispose us for other duties. Fasting is the humbling of the soul, Ps **35**:**13**; that is the inside of the duty; let that, therefore, be thy principal care, and as to the outside of it, covet not to let it be seen. God sees in secret, and will reward openly.

Verses 19–24

Worldly-mindedness is a common and fatal symptom of hypocrisy, for by no sin can Satan have a surer and faster hold of the soul, under the cloak of a profession of religion. Something the soul will have, which it looks upon as the best thing; in which it has pleasure and confidence above other things. Christ counsels to make our best things the joys and glories of the other world, those things not seen which are eternal, and to place our happiness in them. There are treasures in heaven. It is our wisdom to give all diligence to make our title to eternal life sure through Jesus Christ, and to look on all things here below, as not worthy to be compared with it, and to be content with nothing short of it. It is happiness above and beyond the changes and chances of time, an inheritance incorruptible. The worldly man is wrong in his first principle; therefore all his reasonings and actions therefrom must be wrong. It is equally to be applied to false religion; that which is deemed light is thick darkness. This is an awful, but a common case; we should therefore carefully examine our leading principles by the word of God, with earnest prayer for the teaching of his Spirit. A man may do some service to two masters, but he can devote himself to the service of no more than one. God requires the whole heart, and will not share it with the world. When two masters oppose each other, no man can serve both. He who holds to the world and loves it, must despise God; he who loves God, must give up the friendship of the world.

Verses 25–34

There is scarcely any sin against which our Lord Jesus more warns his disciples, than disquieting, distracting, distrustful cares about the things of this life. This often insnares the poor as much as the love of wealth does the rich. But there is a carefulness about temporal things which is a duty, though we must not carry these lawful cares too far. Take no thought for your life. Not about the length of it; but refer it to God to lengthen or shorten it as he pleases; our times are in his hand, and they are in a good hand. Not about the comforts of this life; but leave it to God to make it bitter or sweet as he pleases. Food and raiment God has promised, therefore we may expect them. Take no thought for the morrow, for the time to come. Be not anxious for the future, how you shall live next year, or when you are old, or what you shall leave behind you. As we must not boast of tomorrow, so we must not care for to-morrow, or the events of it. God has given us life, and has given us the body. And what can he not do for us, who did that? If we take care about our souls and for eternity, which are more than the body and its life, we may leave it to God to provide for us food and raiment, which are less. Improve this as an encouragement to trust in God. We must reconcile ourselves to our worldly estate, as we do to our stature. We cannot alter the disposals of Providence, therefore we must submit and resign ourselves to them. Thoughtfulness for our souls is the best cure of thoughtfulness for the world. Seek first the kingdom of God, and make religion your business: say not that this is the way to starve; no, it is the way to be well provided for, even in this world. The conclusion of the whole matter is, that it is the will and command of the Lord Jesus, that by daily prayers we may get strength to bear us up under our daily troubles, and to arm us against the temptations that attend them, and then let none of these things move us. Happy are those who take the Lord for their God, and make full proof of it by trusting themselves wholly to his wise disposal. Let thy Spirit convince us of sin in the want of this disposition, and take away the worldliness of our hearts.

Chapter 7

Chapter Outline	
Christ reproves rash judgment.	(1–6)
Encouragements to prayer.	(7–11)
The broad and narrow way.	(12–14)
Against false prophets.	(15–20)
To be doers of the word, not hearers only.	(21–29)

Verses 1–6

We must judge ourselves, and judge of our own acts, but not make our word a law to everybody. We must not judge rashly, nor pass judgment upon our brother without any ground. We must not make the worst of people. Here is a just reproof to those who quarrel with their brethren for small faults, while they allow themselves in greater ones. Some sins are as motes, while others are as beams; some as a gnat, others as a camel. Not that there is any sin little; if it be a mote, or splinter, it is in the eye; if a gnat, it is in the throat; both are painful and dangerous, and we cannot be easy or well till they are got out. That which charity teaches us to call but a splinter in our brother's eye, true repentance and godly sorrow will teach us to call a beam in our own. It is as strange that a man can be in a sinful, miserable condition, and not be aware of it, as that a man should have a beam in his eye, and not consider it; but the god of this world blinds their minds. Here is a good rule for reprovers; first reform thyself.

Verses 7–11

Prayer is the appointed means for obtaining what we need. Pray; pray often; make a business of prayer, and be serious and earnest in it. Ask, as a beggar asks alms. Ask, as a traveller asks the way. Seek, as for a thing of value that we have lost; or as the merchantman that seeks goodly pearls. Knock, as he that desires to enter into the house knocks at the door. Sin has shut and barred the door against us; by prayer we knock. Whatever you pray for, according to the promise, shall be given you, if God see it fit for you, and what would you have more? This is made to apply to all that pray aright; every one that asketh receiveth, whether Jew or Gentile, young or old, rich or poor, high or low, master or servant, learned or unlearned, all are alike welcome to the throne of grace, if they come in faith. It is explained by a comparison taken from earthly parents, and their readiness to give their children what they ask. Parents are often foolishly fond, but God is all-wise; he knows what we need, what we desire, and what is fit for us. Let us never suppose our heavenly Father would bid us pray, and then refuse to hear, or give us what would be hurtful.

Verses 12–14

Christ came to teach us, not only what we are to know and believe, but what we are to do; not only toward God, but toward men; not only toward those of our party and persuasion, but toward men in general, all with whom we have to do. We must do that to our neighbour which we ourselves acknowledge to be fit and reasonable. We must, in our dealings with men, suppose ourselves in the same case and circumstances with those we have to do with, and act accordingly. There are but two ways right and wrong, good and evil; the way to heaven and the way to hell; in the one or other of these all are walking: there is no middle place hereafter, no middle way now. All the children of men are saints or sinners, godly or ungodly. See concerning the way of sin and sinners, that the gate is wide, and stands open. You may go in at this gate with all your lusts about you; it gives no check to appetites or passions. It is a broad way; there are many paths in it; there is choice of sinful ways. There is a large company in this way. But what profit is there in being willing to go to hell with others, because they will not go to heaven with us? The way to eternal life is narrow. We are not in heaven as soon as we are got through the strait gate. Self must be denied, the body kept under, and corruptions mortified. Daily temptations must be resisted; duties must be done. We must watch in all things, and walk with care; and we must go through much tribulation. And yet this way should invite us all; it leads to life: to present comfort in the favour of God, which is the life of the soul; to eternal bliss, the hope of which at the end of our way, should make all the difficulties of the road easy to us. This plain declaration of Christ has been disregarded by many who have taken pains to explain it away; but in all ages the real disciple of Christ has been looked on as a singular, unfashionable character; and all that have sided with the greater number, have gone on in the broad road to destruction. If we would serve God, we must be firm in our religion. Can we often hear of the strait gate and the narrow way, and how few there are that find it, without being in pain for ourselves, or considering whether we are entered on the narrow way, and what progress we are making in it?

Verses 15–20

Nothing so much prevents men from entering the strait gate, and becoming true followers of Christ, as the carnal, soothing, flattering doctrines of those who oppose the truth. They may be known by the drift and effects of their doctrines. Some part of their temper and conduct is contrary to the mind of Christ. Those opinions come not from God that lead to sin.

Verses 21–29

Christ here shows that it will not be enough to own him for our Master, only in word and tongue. It is necessary to our happiness that we believe in Christ, that we repent of sin, that we live a holy life, that we love one another. This is his will, even our sanctification. Let us take heed of resting in outward privileges and doings, lest we deceive ourselves, and perish eternally, as multitudes do, with a lie in our right hand. Let every one that names the name of Christ, depart from all sin. There are others, whose religion rests in bare hearing, and it goes no further; their heads are filled with empty notions. These two sorts of hearers are represented as two builders. This parable teaches us to hear and do the sayings of the Lord Jesus: some may seem hard to flesh and blood, but they must be done. Christ is laid for a foundation, and every thing besides Christ is sand. Some build their hopes upon worldly prosperity; others upon an outward profession of religion. Upon these they venture; but they are all sand, too weak to bear such a fabric as our hopes of heaven. There is a storm coming that will try every man's work. When God takes away the soul, where is the hope of the hypocrite? The house fell in the storm, when the builder had most need of it, and expected it would be a shelter to him. It fell when it was too late to build another. May the Lord make us wise builders for eternity. Then nothing shall separate us from the love of Christ Jesus. The multitudes were astonished at the wisdom and power of Christ's doctrine. And this sermon, ever so often read over, is always new. Every word proves its Author to be Divine. Let us be more and more decided and earnest, making some one or other of these blessednesses and Christian graces the main subject of our thoughts, even for weeks together. Let us not rest in general and confused desires after them, whereby we grasp at all, but catch nothing.

Chapter 8

Chapter Outline	
Multitudes follow Christ.	(1)
He heals a leper.	(2–4)
A centurion's servant healed.	(5–13)
Cure of Peter's wife's mother.	(14–17)
The scribe's zealous proposal.	(18–22)
Christ in a storm.	(23–27)
He heals two possessed with devils.	(28–34)

Verse 1

This **verse** refers to the close of the foregoing sermon. Those to whom Christ has made himself known, desire to know more of him.

Verses 2–4

In these **verse**s we have an account of Christ's cleansing a leper, who came and worshipped him, as one clothed with Divine power. This cleansing directs us, not only to apply to Christ, who has power over bodily diseases, for the cure of them, but it also teaches us in what manner to apply to him. When we cannot be sure of God's will, we may be sure of his wisdom and mercy. No guilt is so great, but there is that in Christ's blood which atones for it; no corruption so strong, but there is that in his grace which can subdue it. To be made clean we must commend ourselves to his pity; we cannot demand it as a debt, but we must humbly request it as a favour. Those who by faith apply to Christ for mercy and grace, may be sure that he is freely willing to give them the mercy and grace they thus seek. And those afflictions are blessed that bring us to know Christ, and cause us to seek help and salvation from him. Let those who are cleansed from their spiritual leprosy, go to Christ's ministers and open their case, that they may advise, comfort, and pray for them.

Verses 5–13

This centurion was a heathen, a Roman soldier. Though he was a soldier, yet he was a godly man. No man's calling or place will be an excuse for unbelief and sin. See how he states his servant's case. We should concern ourselves for the souls of our children and servants, who are spiritually sick, who feel not spiritual evils, who know not that which is spiritually good; and we should bring them to Christ by faith and prayers. Observe his self-abasement. Humble souls are made more humble by Christ's gracious dealings with them. Observe his great faith. The more diffident we are of ourselves, the stronger will be our confidence in Christ. Herein the centurion owns him to have Divine power, and a full command of all the creatures and powers of nature, as a master over his servants. Such servants we all should be to God; we must go and come, according to the directions of his word and the disposals of his providence. But when the Son of man comes he finds little faith, therefore he finds little fruit. An outward profession may cause us to be called children of the kingdom; but if we rest in that, and have nothing else to show, we shall be cast out. The servant got a cure of his disease, and the master got the approval of his faith. What was said to him, is said to all, Believe, and ye shall receive; only believe. See the power of Christ, and the power of faith. The healing of our souls is at once the effect and evidence of our interest in the blood of Christ.

Verses 14–17

Peter had a wife, yet was an apostle of Christ, who showed that he approved of the married state, by being thus kind to Peter's wife's relations. The church of Rome, which forbids ministers to marry, goes contrary to that apostle upon whom they rest so much. He had his wife's mother with him in his family, which is an example to be kind to our relations. In spiritual healing, the Scripture speaks the word, the Spirit gives the touch, touches the heart, touches the hand. Those who recover from fevers, commonly are weak and feeble some time after; but to show that this cure was above the power of nature, the woman was at once so well as to go about the business of the house. The miracles which Jesus did being noised abroad, many thronged to him. He healed all that were sick, though the patient was ever so mean, and the case ever so bad. Many are the diseases and calamities to which we are liable in the body; and there is more, in those words of the gospel, that Jesus Christ bore our sicknesses and carried our sorrows, to support and comfort us under them, than in all the writings of the philosophers. Let us not grudge labour, trouble, or expense in doing good to others.

Verses 18–22

One of the scribes was too hasty in promising; he proffers himself to be a close follower of Christ. He seems to be very resolute. Many resolutions for religion are produced by sudden conviction, and taken up without due consideration; these come to nothing. When this scribe offered to follow Christ, one would think he should have been encouraged; one scribe might do more credit and service than twelve fishermen; but Christ saw his heart, and answered to its thoughts, and therein teaches all how to come to Christ. His resolve seems to have been from a worldly, covetous principle; but Christ had not a place to lay his head on, and if he follows him, he must not expect to fare better than he fared. We have reason to think this scribe went away. Another was too slow. Delay in doing is as bad on the one hand, as hastiness in resolving is on the other. He asked leave to attend his father to his grave, and then he would be at Christ's service. This seemed reasonable, yet it was not right. He had not true zeal for the work. Burying the dead, especially a dead father, is a good work, but it is not thy work at this time. If Christ requires our service, affection even for the nearest and dearest relatives, and for things otherwise our duty, must give way. An unwilling mind never wants an excuse. Jesus said to him, Follow me; and, no doubt, power went with this word to him as to others; he did follow Christ, and cleaved to him. The scribe said, I will follow thee; to this man Christ said, Follow me; comparing them together, it shows that we are brought to Christ by the force of his call to us, Ro **9**:**16**.

Verses 23–27

It is a comfort to those who go down to the sea in ships, and are often in perils there, to reflect that they have a Saviour to trust in and pray to, who knows what it is to be on the water, and to be in storms there. Those who are passing with Christ over the ocean of this world, must expect storms. His human nature, like to ours in every thing but sin, was wearied, and he slept at this time to try the faith of his disciples. They, in their fear, came to their Master. Thus is it in a soul; when lusts and temptations are swelling and raging, and God is, as it were, asleep to it, this brings it to the brink of despair. Then it cries for a word from his mouth, Lord Jesus, keep not silence to me, or I am undone. Many that have true faith, are weak in it. Christ's disciples are apt to be disquieted with fears in a stormy day; to torment themselves that things are bad with them, and with dismal thoughts that they will be worse. Great storms of doubt and fear in the soul, under the power of the spirit of bondage, sometimes end in a wonderful calm, created and spoken by the Spirit of adoption. They were astonished. They never saw a storm so turned at once into a perfect calm. He that can do this, can do any thing, which encourages confidence and comfort in him, in the most stormy day, within or without, Isa **26**:**4**.

Verses 28–34

The devils have nothing to do with Christ as a Saviour; they neither have, nor hope for any benefit from him. Oh the depth of this mystery of Divine love; that fallen man has so much to do with Christ, when fallen angels have nothing to do with him! Heb **2**:**16**. Surely here was torment, to be forced to own the excellence that is in Christ, and yet they had no part in him. The devils desire not to have any thing to do with Christ as a Ruler. See whose language those speak, who will have nothing to do with the gospel of Christ. But it is not true that the devils have nothing to do with Christ as a Judge; for they have, and they know it, and thus it is with all the children of men. Satan and his instruments can go no further than he permits; they must quit possession when he commands. They cannot break his hedge of protection about his people; they cannot enter even a swine without his leave. They had leave. God often, for wise and holy ends, permits the efforts of Satan's rage. Thus the devil hurries people to sin; hurries them to what they have resolved against, which they know will be shame and grief to them: miserable is the condition of those who are led captive by him at his will. There are a great many who prefer their swine before the Saviour, and so come short of Christ and salvation by him. They desire Christ to depart out of their hearts, and will not suffer his word to have place in them, because he and his word would destroy their brutish lusts, those swine which they give themselves up to feed. And justly will Christ forsake all that are weary of him; and say hereafter, Depart, ye cursed, to those who now say to the Almighty, Depart from us.

Chapter 9

Chapter Outline	
Jesus returns to Capernaum, and heals a paralytic.	(1–8)
Matthew called.	(9)
Matthew, or Levi's feast.	(10–13)
Objections of John's disciples.	(14–17)
Christ raises the daughter of Jairus, He heals the issue of blood.	(18–26)
He heals two blind men.	(27–31)
Christ casts out a dumb spirit.	(32–34)
He sends forth the apostles.	(35–38)

Verses 1–8

The faith of the friends of the paralytic in bringing him to Christ, was a strong faith; they firmly believed that Jesus Christ both could and would heal him. A strong faith regards no obstacles in pressing after Christ. It was a humble faith; they brought him to attend on Christ. It was an active faith. Sin may be pardoned, yet the sickness not be removed; the sickness may be removed, yet the sin not pardoned: but if we have the comfort of peace with God, with the comfort of recovery from sickness, this makes the healing a mercy indeed. This is no encouragement to sin. If thou bring thy sins to Jesus Christ, as thy malady and misery to be cured of, and delivered from, it is well; but to come with them, as thy darlings and delight, thinking still to retain them and receive him, is a gross mistake, a miserable delusion. The great intention of the blessed Jesus in the redemption he wrought, is to separate our hearts from sin. Our Lord Jesus has perfect knowledge of all that we say within ourselves. There is a great deal of evil in sinful thoughts, which is very offensive to the Lord Jesus. Christ designed to show that his great errand to the world was, to save his people from their sins. He turned from disputing with the scribes, and spake healing to the sick man. Not only he had no more need to be carried upon his bed, but he had strength to carry it. God must be glorified in all the power that is given to do good.

Verse 9

Matthew was in his calling, as the rest of those whom Christ called. As Satan comes with his temptations to the idle, so Christ comes with his calls to those who are employed. We are all naturally **averse** from thee, O God; do thou bid us to follow thee; draw us by thy powerful word, and we shall run after thee. Speak by the word of the Spirit to our hearts, the world cannot hold us down, Satan cannot stop our way, we shall arise and follow thee. A saving change is wrought in the soul, by Christ as the author, and his word as the means. Neither Matthew's place, nor his gains by it, could detain him, when Christ called him. He left it, and though we find the disciples, who were fishers, occasionally fishing again afterwards, we never more find Matthew at his sinful gain.

Verses 10–13

Some time after his call, Matthew sought to bring his old associates to hear Christ. He knew by experience what the grace of Christ could do, and would not despair concerning them. Those who are effectually brought to Christ, cannot but desire that others also may be brought to him. Those who suppose their souls to be without disease will not welcome the spiritual Physician. This was the case with the Pharisees; they despised Christ, because they thought themselves whole; but the poor publicans and sinners felt that they wanted instruction and amendment. It is easy, and too common, to put the worst constructions upon the best words and actions. It may justly be suspected that those have not the grace of God themselves, who are not pleased with others' obtaining it. Christ's conversing with sinners is here called mercy; for to promote the conversion of souls is the greatest act of mercy. The gospel call is a call to repentance; a call to us to change our minds, and to change our ways. If the children of men had not been sinners, there had been no need for Christ to come among them. Let us examine whether we have found out our sickness, and have learned to follow the directions of our great Physician.

Verses 14–17

John was at this time in prison; his circumstances, his character, and the nature of the message he was sent to deliver, led those who were peculiarly attached to him, to keep frequent fasts. Christ referred them to John's testimony of him, Joh **3**:**29**. Though there is no doubt that Jesus and his disciples lived in a spare and frugal manner, it would be improper for his disciples to fast while they had the comfort of his presence. When he is with them, all is well. The presence of the sun makes day, and its absence produces night. Our Lord further reminded them of common rules of prudence. It was not usual to take a piece of rough woolen cloth, which had never been prepared, to join to an old garment, for it would not join well with the soft, old garment, but would tear it further, and the rent would be made worse. Nor would men put new wine into old leathern bottles, which were going to decay, and would be liable to burst from the fermenting of the wine; but putting the new wine into strong, new, skin bottles, both would be preserved. Great caution and prudence are necessary, that young converts may not receive gloomy and forbidding ideas of the service of our Lord; but duties are to be urged as they are able to bear them.

Verses 18–26

The death of our relations should drive us to Christ, who is our life. And it is high honour to the greatest rulers to attend on the Lord Jesus; and those who would receive mercy from Christ, must honour him. The variety of methods Christ took in working his miracles, perhaps was because of the different frames and tempers of mind, which those were in who came to him, and which He who searches the heart perfectly knew. A poor woman applied herself to Christ, and received mercy from him by the way. If we do but touch, as it were, the hem of Christ's garment by living faith, our worst evils will be healed; there is no other real cure, nor need we fear his knowing things which are a grief and burden to us, but which we would not tell to any earthly friend. When Christ entered the ruler's house, he said, Give place. Sometimes, when the sorrow of the world prevails, it is difficult for Christ and his comforts to enter. The ruler's daughter was really dead, but not so to Christ. The death of the righteous is in a special manner to be looked on as only a sleep. The words and works of Christ may not at first be understood, yet they are not therefore to be despised. The people were put forth. Scorners who laugh at what they do not understand, are not proper witnesses of the wonderful works of Christ. Dead souls are not raised to spiritual life, unless Christ take them by the hand: it is done in the day of his power. If this single instance of Christ's raising one newly dead so increased his fame, what will be his glory when all that are in their graves shall hear his voice, and come forth; those that have done good to the resurrection of life, and those that have done evil to the resurrection of damnation!

Verses 27–31

At this time the Jews expected Messiah would appear; these blind men knew and proclaimed in the streets of Capernaum that he was come, and that Jesus was he. Those who, by the providence of God, have lost their bodily sight, may, by the grace of God, have the eyes of their understanding fully enlightened. And whatever our wants and burdens are, we need no more for supply and support, than to share in the mercy of our Lord Jesus. In Christ is enough for all. They followed him crying aloud. He would try their faith, and would teach us always to pray, and not to faint, though the answer does not come at once. They followed Christ, and followed him crying; but the great question is, Do ye believe? Nature may make us earnest, but it is only grace that can work faith. Christ touched their eyes. He gives sight to blind souls by the power of his grace going with his word, and he puts the cure upon their faith. Those who apply to Jesus Christ, shall be dealt with, not according to their fancies, nor according to their profession, but according to their faith. Christ sometimes concealed his miracles, because he would not indulge the conceit which prevailed among the Jews, that their Messiah should be a temporal prince, and so give occasion to the people to attempt tumults and seditions.

Verses 32–34

Of the two, better a dumb devil than a blaspheming one. Christ's cures strike at the root, and remove the effect by taking away the cause; they open the lips, by breaking Satan's power in the soul. Nothing can convince those who are under the power of pride. They will believe anything, however false or absurd, rather than the Holy Scriptures; thus they show the enmity of their hearts against a holy God.

Verses 35–38

Jesus visited not only the great and wealthy cities, but the poor, obscure villages; and there he preached, there he healed. The souls of the meanest in the world are as precious to Christ, and should be so to us, as the souls of those who make the greatest figure. There were priests, Levites, and scribes, all over the land; but they were idol shepherds, Zec **11**:**17**; therefore Christ had compassion on the people as sheep scattered, as men perishing for lack of knowledge. To this day vast multitudes are as sheep not having a shepherd, and we should have compassion and do all we can to help them. The multitudes desirous of spiritual instruction formed a plenteous harvest, needing many active labourers; but few deserved that character. Christ is the Lord of the harvest. Let us pray that many may be raised up and sent forth, who will labour in bringing souls to Christ. It is a sign that God is about to bestow some special mercy upon a people, when he stirs them up to pray for it. And commissions given to labourers in answer to prayer, are most likely to be successful.

Chapter 10

Chapter Outline	
The apostles called.	(1–4)
The apostles instructed and sent forth.	(5–15)
Directions to the apostles.	(16–42)

Verses 1–4

The word "apostle" signifies messenger; they were Christ's messengers, sent forth to proclaim his kingdom. Christ gave them power to heal all manner of sickness. In the grace of the gospel there is a slave for every sore, a remedy for every malady. There is no spiritual disease, but there is power in Christ for the cure of it. There names are recorded, and it is their honour; yet they had more reason to rejoice that their names were written in heaven, while the high and mighty names of the great ones of the earth are buried in the dust.

Verses 5–15

The Gentiles must not have the gospel brought them, till the Jews have refused it. This restraint on the apostles was only in their first mission. Wherever they went they must proclaim, The kingdom of heaven is at hand. They preached, to establish the faith; the kingdom, to animate the hope; of heaven, to inspire the love of heavenly things, and the contempt of earthly; which is at hand, that men may prepare for it without delay. Christ gave power to work miracles for the confirming of their doctrine. This is not necessary now that the kingdom of God is come. It showed that the intent of the doctrine they preached, was to heal sick souls, and to raise those that were dead in sin. In proclaiming the gospel of free grace for the healing and saving of men's souls, we must above all avoid the appearance of the spirit of an hireling. They are directed what to do in strange towns and cities. The servant of Christ is the ambassador of peace to whatever place he is sent. His message is even to the vilest sinners, yet it behoves him to find out the best persons in every place. It becomes us to pray heartily for all, and to conduct ourselves courteously to all. They are directed how to act as to those that refused them. The whole counsel of God must be declared, and those who will not attend to the gracious message, must be shown that their state is dangerous. This should be seriously laid to heart by all that hear the gospel, lest their privileges only serve to increase their condemnation.

Verses 16–42

Our Lord warned his disciples to prepare for persecution. They were to avoid all things which gave advantage to their enemies, all meddling with worldly or political concerns, all appearance of evil or selfishness, and all underhand measures. Christ foretold troubles, not only that the troubles might not be a surprise, but that they might confirm their faith. He tells them what they should suffer, and from whom. Thus Christ has dealt fairly and faithfully with us, in telling us the worst we can meet with in his service; and he would have us deal so with ourselves, in sitting down and counting the cost. Persecutors are worse than beasts, in that they prey upon those of their own kind. The strongest bonds of love and duty, have often been broken through from enmity against Christ. Sufferings from friends and relations are very grievous; nothing cuts more. It appears plainly, that all who will live godly in Christ Jesus must suffer persecution; and we must expect to enter into the kingdom of God through many tribulations. With these predictions of trouble, are counsels and comforts for a time of trial. The disciples of Christ are hated and persecuted as serpents, and their ruin is sought, and they need the serpent's wisdom. Be ye harmless as doves. Not only, do nobody any hurt, but bear nobody any ill-will. Prudent care there must be, but not an anxious, perplexing thought; let this care be cast upon God. The disciples of Christ must think more how to do well, than how to speak well. In case of great peril, the disciples of Christ may go out of the way of danger, though they must not go out of the way of duty. No sinful, unlawful means may be used to escape; for then it is not a door of God's opening. The fear of man brings a snare, a perplexing snare, that disturbs our peace; an entangling snare, by which we are drawn into sin; and, therefore, it must be striven and prayed against. Tribulation, distress, and persecution cannot take away God's love to them, or theirs to him. Fear Him, who is able to destroy both soul and body in hell. They must deliver their message publicly, for all are deeply concerned in the doctrine of the gospel. The whole counsel of God must be made known, Ac **20**:**27**. Christ shows them why they should be of good cheer. Their sufferings witnessed against those who oppose his gospel. When God calls us to speak for him, we may depend on him to teach us what to say. A believing prospect of the end of our troubles, will be of great use to support us under them. They may be borne to the end, because the sufferers shall be borne up under them. The strength shall be according to the day. And it is great encouragement to those who are doing Christ's work, that it is a work which shall certainly be done. See how the care of Providence extends to all creatures, even to the sparrows. This should silence all the fears of God's people; Ye are of more value than many sparrows. And the very hairs of your head are all numbered. This denotes the account God takes and keeps of his people. It is our duty, not only to believe in Christ, but to profess that faith, in suffering for him, when we are called to it, as well as in serving him. That denial of Christ only is here meant which is persisted in, and that confession only can have the blessed recompence here promised, which is the real and constant language of faith and love. Religion is worth every thing; all who believe the truth of it, will come up to the price, and make every thing else yield to it. Christ will lead us through sufferings, to glory with him. Those are best prepared for the life to come, that sit most loose to this present life. Though the kindness done to Christ's disciples be ever so small, yet if there be occasion for it, and ability to do no more, it shall be accepted. Christ does not say that they deserve a reward; for we cannot merit any thing from the hand of God; but they shall receive a reward from the free gift of God. Let us boldly confess Christ, and show love to him in all things.

Chapter 11

Chapter Outline	
Christ's preaching.	(1)
Christ's answer to John's disciples.	(2–6)
Christ's testimony to John the Baptist.	(7–15)
The perverseness of the Jews.	(16–24)
The gospel revealed to the simple. The heavy-laden invited.	(25–30)

Verse 1

Our Divine Redeemer never was weary of his labour of love; and we should not be weary of well-doing, for in due season we shall reap, if we faint not.

Verses 2–6

Some think that John sent this inquiry for his own satisfaction. Where there is true faith, yet there may be a mixture of unbelief. The remaining unbelief of good men may sometimes, in an hour of temptation; call in question the most important truths. But we hope that John's faith did not fail in this matter, and that he only desired to have it strengthened and confirmed. Others think that John sent his disciples to Christ for their satisfaction. Christ points them to what they heard and saw. Christ's gracious condescensions and compassions to the poor, show that it was he that should bring to the world the tender mercies of our God. Those things which men see and hear, if compared with the Scriptures, direct in what way salvation is to be found. It is difficult to conquer prejudices, and dangerous not to conquer them; but those who believe in Christ, their faith will be found so much the more to praise, and honour, and glory.

Verses 7–15

What Christ said concerning John, was not only for his praise, but for the people's profit. Those who attend on the word will be called to give an account of their improvements. Do we think when the sermon is done, the care is over? No, then the greatest of the care begins. John was a self-denying man, dead to all the pomps of the world and the pleasures of sense. It becomes people, in all their appearances, to be consistent with their character and their situation. John was a great and good man, yet not perfect; therefore he came short of glorified saints. The least in heaven knows more, loves more, and does more in praising God, and receives more from him, than the greatest in this world. But by the kingdom of heaven here, is rather to be understood the kingdom of grace, the gospel dispensation in its power and purity. What reason we have to be thankful that our lot is cast in the days of the kingdom of heaven, under such advantages of light and love! Multitudes were wrought upon by the ministry of John, and became his disciples. And those strove for a place in this kingdom, that one would think had no right nor title to it, and so seemed to be intruders. It shows us what fervency and zeal are required of all. Self must be denied; the bent, the frame and temper of the mind must be altered. Those who will have an interest in the great salvation, will have it upon any terms, and not think them hard, nor quit their hold without a blessing. The things of God are of great and common concern. God requires no more from us than the right use of the faculties he has given us. People are ignorant, because they will not learn.

Verses 16–24

Christ reflects on the scribes and Pharisees, who had a proud conceit of themselves. He likens their behaviour to children's play, who being out of temper without reason, quarrel with all the attempts of their fellows to please them, or to get them to join in the plays for which they used to assemble. The cavils of worldly men are often very trifling and show great malice. Something they have to urge against every one, however excellent and holy. Christ, who was undefiled, and separate from sinners, is here represented as in league with them, and polluted by them. The most unspotted innocence will not always be a defence against reproach. Christ knew that the hearts of the Jews were more bitter and hardened against his miracles and doctrines, than those of Tyre and Sidon would have been; therefore their condemnation would be the greater. The Lord exercises his almighty power, yet he punishes none more than they deserve, and never withholds the knowledge of the truth from those who long after it.

Verses 25–30

It becomes children to be grateful. When we come to God as a Father, we must remember that he is Lord of heaven and earth, which obliges us to come to him with reverence as to the sovereign Lord of all; yet with confidence, as one able to defend us from evil, and to supply us with all good. Our blessed Lord added a remarkable declaration, that the Father had delivered into his hands all power, authority, and judgment. We are indebted to Christ for all the revelation we have of God the Father's will and love, ever since Adam sinned. Our Saviour has invited all that labour and are heavy-laden, to come unto him. In some senses all men are so. Worldly men burden themselves with fruitless cares for wealth and honours; the gay and the sensual labour in pursuit of pleasures; the slave of Satan and his own lusts, is the merest drudge on earth. Those who labour to establish their own righteousness also labour in vain. The convinced sinner is heavy-laden with guilt and terror; and the tempted and afflicted believer has labours and burdens. Christ invites all to come to him for rest to their souls. He alone gives this invitation; men come to him, when, feeling their guilt and misery, and believing his love and power to help, they seek him in fervent prayer. Thus it is the duty and interest of weary and heavy-laden sinners, to come to Jesus Christ. This is the gospel call; Whoever will, let him come. All who thus come will receive rest as Christ's gift, and obtain peace and comfort in their hearts. But in coming to him they must take his yoke, and submit to his authority. They must learn of him all things, as to their comfort and obedience. He accepts the willing servant, however imperfect the services. Here we may find rest for our souls, and here only. Nor need we fear his yoke. His commandments are holy, just, and good. It requires self-denial, and exposes to difficulties, but this is abundantly repaid, even in this world, by inward peace and joy. It is a yoke that is lined with love. So powerful are the assistances he gives us, so suitable the encouragements, and so strong the consolations to be found in the way of duty, that we may truly say, it is a yoke of pleasantness. The way of duty is the way of rest. The truths Christ teaches are such as we may venture our souls upon. Such is the Redeemer's mercy; and why should the labouring and burdened sinner seek for rest from any other quarter? Let us come to him daily, for deliverance from wrath and guilt, from sin and Satan, from all our cares, fears, and sorrows. But forced obedience, far from being easy and light, is a heavy burden. In vain do we draw near to Jesus with our lips, while the heart is far from him. Then come to Jesus to find rest for your souls.

Chapter 12

Chapter Outline	
Jesus defends his disciples for plucking corn on the sabbath day.	(1–8)
Jesus heals a man with a withered hand on the sabbath.	(9–13)
The malice of the Pharisees.	(14–21)
Jesus heals a demoniac.	(22–30)
Blasphemy of the Pharisees.	(31, 32)
Evil words proceed from an evil heart.	(33–37)
The scribes and Pharisees reproved for seeking a sign.	(38–45)
The disciples of Christ are his nearest relations.	(46–50)

Verses 1–8

Being in the corn-fields, the disciples began to pluck the ears of corn: the law of God allowed it, De **23**:**25**. This was slender provision for Christ and his disciples; but they were content with it. The Pharisees did not quarrel with them for taking another man's corn, but for doing it on the sabbath day. Christ came to free his followers, not only from the corruptions of the Pharisees, but from their unscriptural rules, and justified what they did. The greatest shall not have their lusts indulged, but the meanest shall have their wants considered. Those labours are lawful on the sabbath day which are necessary, and sabbath rest is to froward, not to hinder sabbath worship. Needful provision for health and food is to be made; but when servants are kept at home, and families become a scene of hurry and confusion on the Lord's day, to furnish a feast for visitors, or for indulgence, the case is very different. Such things as these, and many others common among professors, are to be blamed. The resting on the sabbath was ordained for man's good, De **5**:**14**. No law must be understood so as to contradict its own end. And as Christ is the Lord of the sabbath, it is fit the day and the work of it should be dedicated to him.

Verses 9–13

Christ shows that works of mercy are lawful and proper to be done on the Lord's day. There are more ways of doing well upon sabbath days, than by the duties of worship: attending the sick, relieving the poor, helping those who need speedy relief, teaching the young to care for their souls; these are doing good: and these must be done from love and charity, with humility and self-denial, and shall be accepted, Ge **4**:**7**. This, like other cures which Christ wrought, had a spiritual meaning. By nature our hands are withered, and we are unable of ourselves to do any thing that is good. Christ only, by the power of his grace, cures us; he heals the withered hand by putting life into the dead soul, works in us both to will and to do: for, with the command, there is a promise of grace given by the word.

Verses 14–21

The Pharisees took counsel to find some accusation, that Jesus might be condemned to death. Aware of their design, as his time was not come, he retired from that place. Face does not more exactly answer to face in water, than the character of Christ drawn by the prophet, to his temper and conduct as described by the evangelists. Let us with cheerful confidence commit our souls to so kind and faithful a Friend. Far from breaking, he will strengthen the bruised reed; far from quenching the smoking flax, or wick nearly out, he will rather blow it up into a flame. Let us lay aside contentious and angry debates; let us receive one another as Christ receives us. And while encouraged by the gracious kindness of our Lord, we should pray that his Spirit may rest upon us, and make us able to copy his example.

Verses 22–30

A soul under Satan's power, and led captive by him, is blind in the things of God, and dumb at the throne of grace; sees nothing, and says nothing to the purpose. Satan blinds the eyes by unbelief, and seals up the lips from prayer. The more people magnified Christ, the more desirous the Pharisees were to vilify him. It was evident that if Satan aided Jesus in casting out devils, the kingdom of hell was divided against itself; how then could it stand! And if they said that Jesus cast out devils by the prince of the devils, they could not prove that their children cast them out by any other power. There are two great interests in the world; and when unclean spirits are cast out by the Holy Spirit, in the conversion of sinners to a life of faith and obedience, the kingdom of God is come unto us. All who do not aid or rejoice in such a change are against Christ.

Verses 31, 32

Here is a gracious assurance of the pardon of all sin upon gospel terms. Christ herein has set an example to the sons of men, to be ready to forgive words spoken against them. But humble and conscientious believers, at times are tempted to think they have committed the unpardonable sin, while those who have come the nearest to it, seldom have any fear about it. We may be sure that those who indeed repent and believe the gospel, have not committed this sin, or any other of the same kind; for repentance and faith are the special gifts of God, which he would not bestow on any man, if he were determined never to pardon him; and those who fear they have committed this sin, give a good sign that they have not. The trembling, contrite sinner, has the witness in himself that this is not his case.

Verses 33–37

Men's language discovers what country they are of, likewise what manner of spirit they are of. The heart is the fountain, words are the streams. A troubled fountain, and a corrupt spring, must send forth muddy and unpleasant streams. Nothing but the salt of grace, cast into the spring, will heal the waters, season the speech, and purify the corrupt communication. An evil man has an evil treasure in his heart, and out of it brings forth evil things. Lusts and corruptions, dwelling and reigning in the heart, are an evil treasure, out of which the sinner brings forth bad words and actions, to dishonour God, and hurt others. Let us keep constant watch over ourselves, that we may speak words agreeable to the Christian character.

Verses 38–45

Though Christ is always ready to hear and answer holy desires and prayers, yet those who ask amiss, ask and have not. Signs were granted to those who desired them to confirm their faith, as Abraham and Gideon; but denied to those who demanded them to excuse their unbelief. The resurrection of Christ from the dead by his own power, called here the sign of the prophet Jonah, was the great proof of Christ's being the Messiah. As Jonah was three days and three nights in the whale, and then came out again alive, thus Christ would be so long in the grave, and then rise again. The Ninevites would shame the Jews for not repenting; the queen of Sheba, for not believing in Christ. And we have no such cares to hinder us, we come not to Christ upon such uncertainties. This parable represents the case of the Jewish church and nation. It is also applicable to all those who hear the word of God, and are in part reformed, but not truly converted. The unclean spirit leaves for a time, but when he returns, he finds Christ is not there to shut him out; the heart is swept by outward reformation, but garnished by preparation to comply with evil suggestions, and the man becomes a more decided enemy of the truth. Every heart is the residence of unclean spirits, except those which are temples of the Holy Ghost, by faith in Christ.

Verses 46–50

Christ's preaching was plain, easy, and familiar, and suited to his hearers. His mother and brethren stood without, desiring to speak with him, when they should have been standing within, desiring to hear him. Frequently, those who are nearest to the means of knowledge and grace are most negligent. We are apt to neglect that which we think we may have any day, forgetting that to-morrow is not ours. We often meet with hinderances in our work from friends about us, and are taken off by care for the things of this life, from the concerns of our souls. Christ was so intent on his work, that no natural or other duty took him from it. Not that, under pretence of religion, we may be disrespectful to parents, or unkind to relations; but the lesser duty must stand by, while the greater is done. Let us cease from men, and cleave to Christ; let us look upon every Christian, in whatever condition of life, as the brother, sister, or mother of the Lord of glory; let us love, respect, and be kind to them, for his sake, and after his example.

Chapter 13

Chapter Outline	
The parable of the sower.	(1–23)
The parable of the tares.	(24–30; 36–43)
The parables of the mustard-seed and the leaven.	(31–35)
The parables of the hidden treasure, the pearl of great price, the net cast into the sea, and the householder.	(44–52)
Jesus is again rejected at Nazareth.	(53–58)

Verses 1–23

Jesus entered into a boat that he might be the less pressed, and be the better heard by the people. By this he teaches us in the outward circumstances of worship not to covet that which is stately, but to make the best of the conveniences God in his providence allots to us. Christ taught in parables. Thereby the things of God were made more plain and easy to those willing to be taught, and at the same time more difficult and obscure to those who were willingly ignorant. The parable of the sower is plain. The seed sown is the word of God. The sower is our Lord Jesus Christ, by himself, or by his ministers. Preaching to a multitude is sowing the corn; we know not where it will light. Some sort of ground, though we take ever so much pains with it, brings forth no fruit to purpose, while the good soil brings forth plentifully. So it is with the hearts of men, whose different characters are here described by four sorts of ground. Careless, trifling hearers, are an easy prey to Satan; who, as he is the great murderer of souls, so he is the great thief of sermons, and will be sure to rob us of the word, if we take not care to keep it. Hypocrites, like the stony ground, often get the start of true Christians in the shows of profession. Many are glad to hear a good sermon, who do not profit by it. They are told of free salvation, of the believer's privileges, and the happiness of heaven; and, without any change of heart, without any abiding conviction of their own depravity, their need of a Saviour, or the excellence of holiness, they soon profess an unwarranted assurance. But when some heavy trial threatens them, or some sinful advantage may be had, they give up or disguise their profession, or turn to some easier system. Worldly cares are fitly compared to thorns, for they came in with sin, and are a fruit of the curse; they are good in their place to stop a gap, but a man must be well armed that has much to do with them; they are entangling, vexing, scratching, and their end is to be burned, Heb **6:8**. Worldly cares are great hinderances to our profiting by the word of God. The deceitfulness of riches does the mischief; they cannot be said to deceive us unless we put our trust in them, then they choke the good seed. What distinguished the good ground was fruitfulness. By this true Christians are distinguished from hypocrites. Christ does not say that this good ground has no stones in it, or no thorns; but none that could hinder its fruitfulness. All are not alike; we should aim at the highest, to bring forth most fruit. The sense of hearing cannot be better employed than in hearing God's word; and let us look to ourselves that we may know what sort of hearers we are.

Verses 24–30

, **36–43** This parable represents the present and future state of the gospel church; Christ's care of it, the devil's enmity against it, the mixture there is in it of good and bad in this world, and the separation between them in the other world. So prone is fallen man to sin, that if the enemy sow the tares, he may go his way, they will spring up, and do hurt; whereas, when good seed is sown, it must be tended, watered, and fenced. The servants complained to their master; Sir, didst thou not sow good seed in thy field? No doubt he did; whatever is amiss in the church, we are sure it is not from Christ. Though gross transgressors, and such as openly oppose the gospel, ought to be separated from the society of the faithful, yet no human skill can make an exact separation. Those who oppose must not be cut off, but instructed, and that with meekness. And though good and bad are together in this world, yet at the great day they shall be parted; then the righteous and the wicked shall be plainly known; here sometimes it is hard to distinguish between them. Let us, knowing the terrors of the Lord, not do iniquity. At death, believers shall shine forth to themselves; at the great day they shall shine forth before all the world. They shall shine by reflection, with light borrowed from the Fountain of light. Their sanctification will be made perfect, and their justification published. May we be found of that happy number.

Verses 31–35

The scope of the parable of the seed sown, is to show that the beginnings of the gospel would be small, but its latter end would greatly increase; in this way the work of grace in the heart, the kingdom of God within us, would be carried on. In the soul where grace truly is, it will grow really; though perhaps at first not to be discerned, it will at last come to great strength and usefulness. The preaching of the gospel works like leaven in the hearts of those who receive it. The leaven works certainly, so does the word, yet gradually. It works silently, and without being seen, Mr **4**:**26**–**29**, yet strongly; without noise, for so is the way of the Spirit, but without fail. Thus it was in the world. The apostles, by preaching the gospel, hid a handful of leaven in the great mass of mankind. It was made powerful by the Spirit of the Lord of hosts, who works, and none can hinder. Thus it is in the heart. When the gospel comes into the soul, it works a thorough change; it spreads itself into all the powers and faculties of the soul, and alters the property even of the members of the body, Ro **6**:**13**. From these parables we are taught to expect a gradual progress; therefore let us inquire, Are we growing in grace? and in holy principles and habits?

Verses 44–52

Here are four parables. **1**. That of the treasure hid in the field. Many slight the gospel, because they look only upon the surface of the field. But all who search the Scriptures, so as in them to find Christ and eternal life, Joh **5**:**39**, will discover such treasure in this field as makes it unspeakably valuable; they make it their own upon any terms. Though nothing can be given as a price for this salvation, yet much must be given up for the sake of it. **2**. All the children of men are busy; one would be rich, another would be honourable, another would be learned; but most are deceived, and take up with counterfeits for pearls. Jesus Christ is a Pearl of great price; in having him, we have enough to make us happy here and for ever. A man may buy gold too dear, but not this Pearl of great price. When the convinced sinner sees Christ as the gracious Saviour, all things else become worthless to his thoughts. **3**. The world is a vast sea, and men, in their natural state, are like the fishes. Preaching the gospel is casting a net into this sea, to catch something out of it, for His glory who has the sovereignty of this sea. Hypocrites and true Christians shall be parted: miserable is the condition of those that shall then be cast away. **4**. A skilful, faithful minister of the gospel, is a scribe, well **verse**d in the things of the gospel, and able to teach them. Christ compares him to a good householder, who brings forth fruits of last year's growth and this year's gathering, abundance and variety, to entertain his friends. Old experiences and new observations, all have their use. Our place is at Christ's feet, and we must daily learn old lessons over again, and new ones also.

Verses 53–58

Christ repeats his offer to those who have repulsed them. They upbraid him, Is not this the carpenter's son? Yes, it is true he was reputed to be so; and no disgrace to be the son of an honest tradesman; they should have respected him the more because he was one of themselves, but therefore they despised him. He did not many mighty works there, because of their unbelief. Unbelief is the great hinderance to Christ's favours. Let us keep faithful to him as the Saviour who has made our peace with God.

Chapter 14

Chapter Outline	
Death of John the Baptist.	(1–12)
Five thousand people miraculously fed.	(13–21)
Jesus walks upon the sea.	(22–33)
Jesus healing the sick.	(34–36)

Verses 1–12

The terror and reproach of conscience, which Herod, like other daring offenders, could not shake off, are proofs and warnings of a future judgment, and of future misery to them. But there may be the terror of convictions, where there is not the truth of conversion. When men pretend to favour the gospel, yet live in evil, we must not favour their self-delusion, but must deliver our consciences as John did. The world may call this rudeness and blind zeal. False professors, or timid Christians, may censure it as want of civility; but the most powerful enemies can go no further than the Lord sees good to permit. Herod feared that the putting of John to death might raise a rebellion among the people, which it did not; but he never feared it might stir up his own conscience against him, which it did. Men fear being hanged for what they do not fear being damned for. And times of carnal mirth and jollity are convenient times for carrying on bad designs against God's people. Herod would profusely reward a worthless dance, while imprisonment and death were the recompence of the man of God who sought the salvation of his soul. But there was real malice to John beneath his consent, or else Herod would have found ways to get clear of his promise. When the under shepherds are smitten, the sheep need not be scattered while they have the Great Shepherd to go to. And it is better to be drawn to Christ by want and loss, than not to come to him at all.

Verses 13–21

When Christ and his word withdraw, it is best for us to follow, seeking the means of grace for our souls before any worldly advantages. The presence of Christ and his gospel, makes a desert not only tolerable, but desirable. This little supply of bread was increased by Christ's creating power, till the whole multitude were satisfied. In seeking the welfare of men's souls, we should have compassion on their bodies likewise. Let us also remember always to crave a blessing on our meals, and learn to avoid all waste, as frugality is the proper source of liberality. See in this miracle an emblem of the Bread of life, which came down from heaven to sustain our perishing souls. The provisions of Christ's gospel appear mean and scanty to the world, yet they satisfy all that feed on him in their hearts by faith with thanksgiving.

Verses 22–33

Those are not Christ's followers who cannot enjoy being alone with God and their own hearts. It is good, upon special occasions, and when we find our hearts enlarged, to continue long in secret prayer, and in pouring out our hearts before the Lord. It is no new thing for Christ's disciples to meet with storms in the way of duty, but he thereby shows himself with the more grace to them and for them. He can take what way he pleases to save his people. But even appearances of deliverance sometimes occasion trouble and perplexity to God's people, from mistakes about Christ. Nothing ought to affright those that have Christ near them, and know he is theirs; not death itself. Peter walked upon the water, not for diversion or to boast of it, but to go to Jesus; and in that he was thus wonderfully borne up. Special supports are promised, and are to be expected, but only in spiritual pursuits; nor can we ever come to Jesus, unless we are upheld by his power. Christ bade Peter come, not only that he might walk upon the water, and so know his Lord's power, but that he might know his own weakness. And the Lord often lets his servants have their choice, to humble and prove them, and to show the greatness of his power and grace. When we look off from Christ, and look at the greatness of opposing difficulties, we shall begin to fall; but when we call to him, he will stretch out his arm, and save us. Christ is the great Saviour; those who would be saved, must come to him, and cry to him, for salvation; we are never brought to this, till we find ourselves sinking: the sense of need drives us to him. He rebuked Peter. Could we but believe more, we should suffer less. The weakness of faith, and the prevailing of our doubts, displease our Lord Jesus, for there is no good reason why Christ's disciples should be of a doubtful mind. Even in a stormy day he is to them a very present help. None but the world's Creator could multiply the loaves, none but its Governor could tread upon the waters of the sea: the disciples yield to the evidence, and confess their faith. They were suitably affected, and worshipped Christ. He that comes to God, must believe; and he that believes in God, will come, Heb **11**:**6**.

Verses 34–36

Whithersoever Christ went, he was doing good. They brought unto him all that were diseased. They came humbly beseeching him to help them. The experiences of others may direct and encourage us in seeking for Christ. As many as touched, were made perfectly whole. Those whom Christ heals, he heals perfectly. Were men more acquainted with Christ, and with the diseased state of their souls, they would flock to receive his healing influences. The healing virtue was not in the finger, but in their faith; or rather, it was in Christ, whom their faith took hold upon.

Chapter 15

Chapter Outline	
Jesus discourses about human traditions.	(1–9)
He warns against things which really defile.	(10–20)
He heals the daughter of a Syrophenician woman.	(21–28)
Jesus heals the sick, and miraculously feeds four thousand.	(29–39)

Verses 1–9

Additions to God's laws reflect upon his wisdom, as if he had left out something which was needed, and which man could supply; in one way or other they always lead men to disobey God. How thankful ought we to be for the written word of God! Never let us think that the religion of the Bible can be improved by any human addition, either in doctrine or practice. Our blessed Lord spoke of their traditions as inventions of their own, and pointed out one instance in which this was very clear, that of their transgressing the fifth commandment. When a parent's wants called for assistance, they pleaded, that they had devoted to the temple all they could spare, even though they did not part with it, and therefore their parents must expect nothing from them. This was making the command of God of no effect. The doom of hypocrites is put in a little compass; "In vain do they worship me." It will neither please God, nor profit themselves; they trust in vanity, and vanity will be their recompence.

Verses 10–20

Christ shows that the defilement they ought to fear, was not from what entered their mouths as food, but from what came out of their mouths, which showed the wickedness of their hearts. Nothing will last in the soul but the regenerating graces of the Holy Spirit; and nothing should be admitted into the church but what is from above; therefore, whoever is offended by a plain, seasonable declaration of the truth, we should not be troubled at it. The disciples ask to be better taught as to this matter. Where a weak head doubts concerning any word of Christ, an upright heart and a willing mind seek for instruction. It is the heart that is desperately wicked, Jer **17**:**9**, for there is no sin in word or deed, which was not first in the heart. They all come out of the man, and are fruits of that wickedness which is in the heart, and is wrought there. When Christ teaches, he will show men the deceitfulness and wickedness of their own hearts; he will teach them to humble themselves, and to seek to be cleansed in the Fountain opened for sin and uncleanness.

Verses 21–28

The dark corners of the country, the most remote, shall share Christ's influences; afterwards the ends of the earth shall see his salvation. The distress and trouble of her family brought a woman to Christ; and though it is need that drives us to Christ, yet we shall not therefore be driven from him. She did not limit Christ to any particular instance of mercy, but mercy, mercy, is what she begged for: she pleads not merit, but depends upon mercy. It is the duty of parents to pray for their children, and to be earnest in prayer for them, especially for their souls. Have you a son, a daughter, grievously vexed with a proud devil, an unclean devil, a malicious devil, led captive by him at his will? this is a case more deplorable than that of bodily possession, and you must bring them by faith and prayer to Christ, who alone is able to heal them. Many methods of Christ's providence, especially of his grace, in dealing with his people, which are dark and perplexing, may be explained by this story, which teaches that there may be love in Christ's heart while there are frowns in his face; and it encourages us, though he seems ready to slay us, yet to trust in him. Those whom Christ intends most to honour, he humbles to feel their own unworthiness. A proud, unhumbled heart would not have borne this; but she turned it into an argument to support her request.

The state of this woman is an emblem of the state of a sinner, deeply conscious of the misery of his soul. The least of Christ is precious to a believer, even the very crumbs of the Bread of life. Of all graces, faith honours Christ most; therefore of all graces Christ honours faith most. He cured her daughter. He spake, and it was done. From hence let such as seek help from the Lord, and receive no gracious answer, learn to turn even their unworthiness and discouragements into pleas for mercy.

Verses 29–39

Whatever our case is, the only way to find ease and relief, is to lay it at Christ's feet, to submit it to him, and refer it to his disposal. Those who would have spiritual healing from Christ, must be ruled as he pleases. See what work sin has made; what various diseases human bodies are subject to. Here were such diseases as fancy could neither guess the cause nor the cure of, yet these were subject to the command of Christ. The spiritual cures that Christ works are wonderful. When blind souls are made to see by faith, the dumb to speak in prayer, the maimed and the lame to walk in holy obedience, it is to be wondered at. His power was also shown to the multitude, in the plentiful provision he made for them: the manner is much the same as before. All did eat, and were filled. Those whom Christ feeds, he fills. With Christ there is bread enough, and to spare; supplies of grace for more than seek it, and for those that seek for more. Christ sent away the people. Though he had fed them twice, they must not look for miracles to find their daily bread. Let them go home to their callings and their own tables. Lord, increase our faith, and pardon our unbelief, teaching us to live upon thy fulness and bounty, for all things pertaining to this life, and that which is to come.

Chapter 16

Chapter Outline	
The Pharisees and Sadducees ask a sign.	(1–4)
Jesus cautions against the doctrine of the Pharisees.	(5–12)
Peter's testimony that Jesus was the Christ.	(13–20)
Christ foretells his sufferings, and rebukes Peter.	(21–23)
The necessity of self-denial.	(24–28)

Verses 1–4

The Pharisees and Sadducees were opposed to each other in principles and in conduct; yet they joined against Christ. But they desired a sign of their own choosing: they despised those signs which relieved the necessity of the sick and sorrowful, and called for something else which would gratify the curiosity of the proud. It is great hypocrisy, when we slight the signs of God's ordaining, to seek for signs of our own devising.

Verses 5–12

Christ speaks of spiritual things under a similitude, and the disciples misunderstand him of carnal things. He took it ill that they should think him as thoughtful about bread as they were; that they should be so little acquainted with his way of preaching. Then understood they what he meant. Christ teaches by the Spirit of wisdom in the heart, opening the understanding to the Spirit of revelation in the word.

Verses 13–20

Peter, for himself and his brethren, said that they were assured of our Lord's being the promised Messiah, the Son of the living God. This showed that they believed Jesus to be more than man. Our Lord declared Peter to be blessed, as the teaching of God made him differ from his unbelieving countrymen. Christ added that he had named him Peter, in allusion to his stability or firmness in professing the truth. The word translated "rock," is not the same word as Peter, but is of a similar meaning. Nothing can be more wrong than to suppose that Christ meant the person of Peter was the rock. Without doubt Christ himself is the Rock, the tried foundation of the church; and woe to him that attempts to lay any other! Peter's confession is this rock as to doctrine. If Jesus be not the Christ, those that own him are not of the church, but deceivers and deceived. Our Lord next declared the authority with which Peter would be invested. He spoke in the name of his brethren, and this related to them as well as to him. They had no certain knowledge of the characters of men, and were liable to mistakes and sins in their own conduct; but they were kept from error in stating the way of acceptance and salvation, the rule of obedience, the believer's character and experience, and the final doom of unbelievers and hypocrites. In such matters their decision was right, and it was confirmed in heaven. But all pretensions of any man, either to absolve or retain men's sins, are blasphemous and absurd. None can forgive sins but God only. And this binding and loosing, in the common language of the Jews, signified to forbid and to allow, or to teach what is lawful or unlawful.

Verses 21–23

Christ reveals his mind to his people gradually. From that time, when the apostles had made the full confession of Christ, that he was the Son of God, he began to show them of his sufferings. He spake this to set right the mistakes of his disciples about the outward pomp and power of his kingdom. Those that follow Christ, must not expect great or high things in this world. Peter would have Christ to dread suffering as much as he did; but we mistake, if we measure Christ's love and patience by our own. We do not read of any thing said or done by any of his disciples, at any time, that Christ resented so much as this. Whoever takes us from that which is good, and would make us fear to do too much for God, speaks Satan's language. Whatever appears to be a temptation to sin, must be resisted with abhorrence, and not be parleyed with. Those that decline suffering for Christ, savour more of the things of man than of the things of God.

Verses 24–28

A true disciple of Christ is one that does follow him in duty, and shall follow him to glory. He is one that walks in the same way Christ walked in, is led by his Spirit, and treads in his steps, whithersoever he goes. “Let him deny himself.” If self-denial be a hard lesson, it is no more than what our Master learned and practised, to redeem us, and to teach us. “Let him take up his cross.” The cross is here put for every trouble that befalls us. We are apt to think we could bear another’s cross better than our own, but that is best which is appointed us, and we ought to make the best of it. We must not by our rashness and folly pull crosses down upon our own heads, but must take them up when they are in our way. If any man will have the name and credit of a disciple, let him follow Christ in the work and duty of a disciple. If all worldly things are worthless when compared with the life of the body, how forcible the same argument with respect to the soul and its state of never-ending happiness or misery! Thousands lose their souls for the most trifling gain, or the most worthless indulgence, nay, often from mere sloth and negligence. Whatever is the object for which men forsake Christ, that is the price at which Satan buys their souls. Yet one soul is worth more than all the world. This is Christ’s judgment upon the matter; he knew the price of souls, for he redeemed them; nor would he underrate the world, for he made it. The dying transgressor cannot purchase one hour’s respite to seek mercy for his perishing soul. Let us then learn rightly to value our souls, and Christ as the only Saviour of them.

Chapter 17

Chapter Outline	
The transfiguration of Christ.	(1–13)
Jesus casts out a dumb and deaf spirit.	(14–21)
He again foretells his sufferings.	(22, 23)
He works a miracle to pay the tribute money.	(24–27)

Verses 1–13

Now the disciples beheld somewhat of Christ’s glory, as of the only begotten of the Father. It was intended to support their faith, when they would have to witness his crucifixion; and would give them an idea of the glory prepared for them, when changed by his power and made like him. The apostles were overcome by the glorious sight. Peter thought that it was most desirable to continue there, and to go no more down to meet the sufferings of which he was so unwilling to hear. In this he knew not what he said. We are wrong, if we look for a heaven here upon earth. Whatever tabernacles we propose to make for ourselves in this world, we must always remember to ask Christ’s leave. That sacrifice was not yet offered, without which the souls of sinful men could not have been saved; and important services were to be done by Peter and his brethren. While Peter spoke, a bright cloud overshadowed them, an emblem of the Divine presence and glory. Ever since man sinned, and heard God’s voice in the garden, unusual appearances of God have been terrible to man. They fell prostrate to the earth, till Jesus encouraged them; when looking round, they beheld only their Lord as they commonly saw him. We must pass through varied experiences in our way to glory; and when we return to the world after an ordinance, it must be our care to take Christ with us, and then it may be our comfort that he is with us.

Verses 14–21

The case of afflicted children should be presented to God by faithful and fervent prayer. Christ cured the child. Though the people were perverse, and Christ was provoked, yet care was taken of the child. When all other helps and succours fail, we are welcome to Christ, may trust in him, and in his power and goodness. See here an emblem of Christ’s undertaking as our Redeemer. It encourages parents to bring children to Christ, whose souls are under Satan’s power; he is able to heal them, and as willing as he is able. Not only bring them to Christ by prayer, but bring them to the word of Christ; to means by which Satan’s strong-holds in the soul are beaten down. It is good for us to distrust ourselves and our own strength; but it is displeasing to Christ when we distrust any power derived from him, or granted by him. There was also something in the malady which rendered the cure difficult. The extraordinary power of Satan must not discourage our faith, but quicken us to more earnestness in praying to God for the increase of it. Do we wonder to see Satan’s bodily possession of this young man from a child, when we see his spiritual possession of every son of Adam from the fall!

Verses 22, 23

Christ perfectly knew all things that should befall him, yet undertook the work of our redemption, which strongly shows his love. What outward debasement and Divine glory was the life of the Redeemer! And all his humiliation ended in his exaltation. Let us learn to endure the cross, to despise riches and worldly honours, and to be content with his will.

Verses 24–27

Peter felt sure that his Master was ready to do what was right. Christ spoke first to give him proof that no thought can be withholden from him. We must never decline our duty for fear of giving offence; but we must sometimes deny ourselves in our worldly interests, rather than give offence. However the money was lodged in the fish, He who knows all things alone could know it, and only almighty power could bring it to Peter’s hook. The power and the poverty of Christ should be mentioned together. If called by providence to be poor, like our Lord, let us trust in his power, and our God shall supply all our need, according to his riches in glory by Christ Jesus. In the way of obedience, in the course, perhaps, of our usual calling, as he helped Peter, so he will help us. And if any sudden call should occur, which we are not prepared to meet, let us not apply to others, till we first seek Christ.

Chapter 18

Chapter Outline	
The importance of humility.	(1–6)
Caution against offences.	(7–14)
The removal of offences.	(15–20)

Conduct towards brethren, The parable of the unmerciful servant.	(21–35)

Verses 1–6

Christ spoke many words of his sufferings, but only one of his glory; yet the disciples fasten upon that, and overlook the others. Many love to hear and speak of privileges and glory, who are willing to pass by the thoughts of work and trouble. Our Lord set a little child before them, solemnly assuring them, that unless they were converted and made like little children, they could not enter his kingdom. Children, when very young, do not desire authority, do not regard outward distinctions, are free from malice, are teachable, and willingly dependent on their parents. It is true that they soon begin to show other dispositions, and other ideas are taught them at an early age; but these are marks of childhood, and render them proper emblems of the lowly minds of true Christians. Surely we need to be daily renewed in the spirit of our minds, that we may become simple and humble, as little children, and willing to be the least of all. Let us daily study this subject, and examine our own spirits.

Verses 7–14

Considering the cunning and malice of Satan, and the weakness and depravity of men's hearts, it is not possible but that there should be offences. God permits them for wise and holy ends, that those who are sincere, and those who are not, may be made known. Being told before, that there will be seducers, tempters, persecutors, and bad examples, let us stand on our guard. We must, as far as lawfully we may, part with what we cannot keep without being entangled by it in sin. The outward occasions of sin must be avoided. If we live after the flesh, we must die. If we, through the Spirit, mortify the deeds of the body, we shall live. Christ came into the world to save souls, and he will reckon severely with those who hinder the progress of others who are setting their faces heavenward. And shall any of us refuse attention to those whom the Son of God came to seek and to save? A father takes care of all his children, but is particularly tender of the little ones.

Verses 15–20

If a professed Christian is wronged by another, he ought not to complain of it to others, as is often done merely upon report, but to go to the offender privately, state the matter kindly, and show him his conduct. This would generally have all the desired effect with a true Christian, and the parties would be reconciled. The principles of these rules may be practised every where, and under all circumstances, though they are too much neglected by all. But how few try the method which Christ has expressly enjoined to all his disciples! In all our proceedings we should seek direction in prayer; we cannot too highly prize the promises of God. Wherever and whenever we meet in the name of Christ, we should consider him as present in the midst of us.

Verses 21–35

Though we live wholly on mercy and forgiveness, we are backward to forgive the offences of our brethren. This parable shows how much provocation God has from his family on earth, and how untoward his servants are. There are three things in the parable: **1**. The master's wonderful clemency. The debt of sin is so great, that we are not able to pay it. See here what every sin deserves; this is the wages of sin, to be sold as a slave. It is the folly of many who are under strong convictions of their sins, to fancy they can make God satisfaction for the wrong they have done him. **2**. The servant's unreasonable severity toward his fellow-servant, notwithstanding his lord's clemency toward him. Not that we may make light of wronging our neighbour, for that is also a sin against God; but we should not aggravate our neighbour's wronging us, nor study revenge. Let our complaints, both of the wickedness of the wicked, and of the afflictions of the afflicted, be brought to God, and left with him. **3**. The master reproved his servant's cruelty. The greatness of sin magnifies the riches of pardoning mercy; and the comfortable sense of pardoning mercy, does much to dispose our hearts to forgive our brethren. We are not to suppose that God actually forgives men, and afterwards reckons their guilt to them to condemn them; but this latter part of the parable shows the false conclusions many draw as to their sins being pardoned, though their after-conduct shows that they never entered into the spirit, or experienced the sanctifying grace of the gospel. We do not forgive our offending brother aright, if we do not forgive from the heart. Yet this is not enough; we must seek the welfare even of those who offend us. How justly will those be condemned, who, though they bear the Christian name, persist in unmerciful treatment of their brethren! The humbled sinner relies only on free, abounding mercy, through the ransom of the death of Christ. Let us seek more and more for the renewing grace of God, to teach us to forgive others as we hope for forgiveness from him.

Chapter 19

Chapter Outline	
Jesus enters Judea.	(1, 2)
The Pharisees' question about divorces.	(3–12)
Young children brought to Jesus.	(13–15)
The rich young man's inquiry	(16–22)
The recompence of Christ's followers.	(23–30)

Verses 1, 2

Great multitudes followed Christ. When Christ departs, it is best for us to follow him. They found him as able and ready to help elsewhere, as he had been in Galilee; wherever the Sun of Righteousness arose, it was with healing in his wings.

Verses 3–12

The Pharisees were desirous of drawing something from Jesus which they might represent as contrary to the law of Moses. Cases about marriage have been numerous, and sometimes perplexed; made so, not by the law of God, but by the lusts and follies of men; and often people fix what they will do, before they ask for advice. Jesus replied by asking whether they had not read the account of the creation, and the first example of marriage; thus pointing out that every departure therefrom was wrong. That condition is best for us, and to be chosen and kept to accordingly, which is best for our souls, and tends most to prepare us for, and preserve us to, the kingdom of heaven. When the gospel is really embraced, it makes men kind relatives and faithful friends; it teaches them to bear the burdens, and to bear with the infirmities of those with whom they are connected, to consider their peace and happiness more than their own. As to ungodly persons, it is proper that they should be restrained by laws, from breaking the peace of society. And we learn that the married state should be entered upon with great seriousness and earnest prayer.

Verses 13–15

It is well when we come to Christ ourselves, and bring our children. Little children may be brought to Christ as needing, and being capable of receiving blessings from him, and having an interest in his intercession. We can but beg a blessing for them: Christ only can command the blessing. It is well for us, that Christ has more love and tenderness in him than the best of his disciples have. And let us learn of him not to discountenance any willing, well-meaning souls, in their seeking after Christ, though they are but weak. Those who are given to Christ, as part of his purchase, he will in no wise cast out. Therefore he takes it ill of all who forbid, and try to shut out those whom he has received. And all Christians should bring their children to the Saviour that he may bless them with spiritual blessings.

Verses 16–22

Christ knew that covetousness was the sin which most easily beset this young man; though he had got honestly what he possessed, yet he could not cheerfully part with it, and by this his want of sincerity was shown. Christ's promises make his precepts easy, and his yoke pleasant and very comfortable; yet this promise was as much a trial of the young man's faith, as the precept was of his charity and contempt of the world. It is required of us in following Christ, that we duly attend his ordinances, strictly follow his pattern, and cheerfully submit to his disposals; and this from love to him, and in dependence on him. To sell all, and give to the poor, will not serve, but we are to follow Christ. The gospel is the only remedy for lost sinners. Many abstain from gross vices who do not attend to their obligations to God. Thousands of instances of disobedience in thought, word, and deed, are marked against them in the book of God. Thus numbers forsake Christ, loving this present world: they feel convictions and desires, but they depart sorrowful, perhaps trembling. It behoves us to try ourselves in these matters, for the Lord will try us.

Verses 23–30

Though Christ spoke so strongly, few that have riches do not trust in them. How few that are poor are not tempted to envy! But men's earnestness in this matter is like their toiling to build a high wall to shut themselves and their children out of heaven. It should be satisfaction to those who are in a low condition, that they are not exposed to the temptations of a high and prosperous condition. If they live more hardly in this world than the rich, yet, if they get more easily to a better world, they have no reason to complain. Christ's words show that it is hard for a rich man to be a good Christian, and to be saved. The way to heaven is a narrow way to all, and the gate that leads into it, a strait gate; particularly so to rich people. More duties are expected from them than from others, and more sins easily beset them. It is hard not to be charmed with a smiling world. Rich people have a great account to make up for their opportunities above others. It is utterly impossible for a man that sets his heart upon his riches, to get to heaven. Christ used an expression, denoting a difficulty altogether unconquerable by the power of man. Nothing less than the almighty grace of God will enable a rich man to get over this difficulty. Who then can be saved? If riches hinder rich people, are not pride and sinful lusts found in those not rich, and as dangerous to them? Who can be saved? say the disciples. None, saith Christ, by any created power. The beginning, progress, and perfecting the work of salvation, depend wholly on the almighty power of God, to which all things are possible. Not that rich people can be saved in their worldliness, but that they should be saved from it. Peter said, We have forsaken all. Alas! it was but a poor all, only a few boats and nets; yet observe how Peter speaks, as if it had been some mighty thing. We are too apt to make the most of our services and sufferings, our expenses and losses, for Christ. However, Christ does not upbraid them; though it was but little that they had forsaken, yet it was their all, and as dear to them as if it had been more. Christ took it kindly that they left it to follow him; he accepts according to what a man hath. Our Lord's promise to the apostles is, that when the Son of man shall sit on the throne of his glory, he will make all things new, and they shall sit with him in judgement on those who will be judged according to their doctrine. This sets forth the honour, dignity, and authority of their office and ministry. Our Lord added, that every one who had forsaken possessions or comforts, for his sake and the gospel, would be recompensed at last. May God give us faith to rest our hope on this his promise; then we shall be ready for every service or sacrifice. Our Saviour, in the last **verse**, does away a mistake of some. The heavenly inheritance is not given as earthly ones are, but according to God's pleasure. Let us not trust in promising appearances or outward profession. Others may, for aught we know, become eminent in faith and holiness.

Chapter 20

Chapter Outline	
The parable of the labourers in the vineyard.	(1–16)
Jesus again foretells his sufferings.	(17–19)
The ambition of James and John.	(20–28)
Jesus gives sight to two blind men near Jericho.	(29–34)

Verses 1–16

The direct object of this parable seems to be, to show that though the Jews were first called into the vineyard, at length the gospel should be preached to the Gentiles, and they should be admitted to equal privileges and advantages with the Jews. The parable may also be applied more generally, and shows, **1**. That God is debtor to no man. **2**. That many who begin last, and promise little in religion, sometimes, by the blessing of God, arrive at a great deal of knowledge, grace, and usefulness. **3**. That the recompense of reward will be given to the saints, but not according to the time of their conversion. It describes the state of the visible church, and explains the declaration that the last shall be first, and the first last, in its various references. Till we are hired into the service of God, we are standing all the day idle: a sinful state, though a state of drudgery to Satan, may be called a state of idleness. The market-place is the world, and from that we are called by the gospel. Come, come from this market-place. Work for God will not admit of trifling. A man may go idle to hell, but he that will go to heaven, must be diligent. The Roman penny was sevenpence halfpenny in our money, wages then enough for the day's support. This does not prove that the reward of our obedience to God is of works, or of debt; when we have done all, we are unprofitable servants; but it signifies that there is a reward set before us, yet let none, upon this presumption, put off repentance till they are old. Some were sent into the vineyard at the eleventh hour; but nobody had hired them before. The Gentiles came in at the eleventh hour; the gospel had not been before preached to them. Those that have had gospel offers made them at the third or sixth hour, and have refused them, will not have to say at the eleventh hour, as these had, No man has hired us. Therefore, not to discourage any, but to awaken all, be it remembered, that now is the accepted time. The riches of Divine grace are loudly murmured at, among proud Pharisees and nominal Christians. There is great proneness in us to think that we have too little, and others too much of the tokens of God's favour; and that we do too much, and others too little in the work of God. But if God gives grace to others, it is kindness to them, and no injustice to us. Carnal worldlings agree with God for their penny in this world; and choose their portion in this life. Obedient believers agree with God for their penny in the other world, and must remember they have so agreed. Didst not thou agree to take up with heaven as thy portion, thy all; wilt thou seek for happiness in the creature? God punishes none more than they deserve, and recompenses every service done for him; he therefore does no wrong to any, by showing extraordinary grace to some. See here the nature of envy. It is an evil eye, which is displeased at the good of others, and desires their hurt. It is a grief to ourselves, displeasing to God, and hurtful to our neighbours: it is a sin that has neither pleasure, profit, nor honour. Let us forego every proud claim, and seek for salvation as a free gift. Let us never envy or grudge, but rejoice and praise God for his mercy to others as well as to ourselves.

Verses 17–19

Christ is more particular here in foretelling his sufferings than before. And here, as before, he adds the mention of his resurrection and his glory, to that of his death and sufferings, to encourage his disciples, and comfort them. A believing view of our once crucified and now glorified Redeemer, is good to humble a proud, self-justifying disposition. When we consider the need of the humiliation and sufferings of the Son of God, in order to the salvation of perishing sinners, surely we must be aware of the freeness and richness of Divine grace in our salvation.

Verses 20–28

The sons of Zebedee abused what Christ said to comfort the disciples. Some cannot have comforts but they turn them to a wrong purpose. Pride is a sin that most easily besets us; it is sinful ambition to outdo others in pomp and grandeur. To put down the vanity and ambition of their request, Christ leads them to the thoughts of their sufferings. It is a bitter cup that is to be drunk of; a cup of trembling, but not the cup of the wicked. It is but a cup, it is but a draught, bitter perhaps, but soon emptied; it is a cup in the hand of a Father, Joh **18**:**11**. Baptism is an ordinance by which we are joined to the Lord in covenant and communion; and so is suffering for Christ, Eze **20**:**37**; Isa **48**:**10**. Baptism is an outward and visible sign of an inward and spiritual grace; and so is suffering for Christ, for unto us it is given, Php **1**:**29**. But they knew not what Christ's cup was, nor what his baptism. Those are commonly most confident, who are least acquainted with the cross. Nothing makes more mischief among brethren, than desire of greatness. And we never find Christ's disciples quarrelling, but something of this was at the bottom of it. That man who labours most diligently, and suffers most patiently, seeking to do good to his brethren, and to promote the salvation of souls, most resembles Christ, and will be most honoured by him to all eternity. Our Lord speaks of his death in the terms applied to the sacrifices of old. It is a sacrifice for the sins of men, and is that true and substantial sacrifice, which those of the law faintly and imperfectly represented. It was a ransom for many, enough for all, working upon many; and, if for many, then the poor trembling soul may say, Why not for me?

Verses 29–34

It is good for those under the same trial, or infirmity of body or mind, to join in prayer to God for relief, that they may quicken and encourage one another. There is mercy enough in Christ for all that ask. They were earnest in prayer. They cried out as men in earnest. Cold desires beg denials. They were humble in prayer, casting themselves upon, and referring themselves cheerfully to, the Mediator's mercy. They showed faith in prayer, by the title they gave to Christ. Surely it was by the Holy Ghost that they called Jesus, Lord. They persevered in prayer. When they were in pursuit of such mercy, it was no time for timidity or hesitation: they cried earnestly. Christ encouraged them. The wants and burdens of the body we are soon sensible of, and can readily relate. Oh that we did as feelingly complain of our spiritual maladies, especially our spiritual blindness! Many are spiritually blind, yet say they see. Jesus cured these blind men; and when they had received sight, they followed him. None follow Christ blindly. He first by his grace opens men's eyes, and so draws their hearts after him. These miracles are our call to Jesus; may we hear it, and make it our daily prayer to grow in grace and in the knowledge of the Lord and Saviour Jesus Christ.

Chapter 21

Chapter Outline	
Christ enters Jerusalem.	(1–11)
He drives out those who profaned the temple.	(12–17)
The barren fig-tree cursed.	(18–22)
Jesus' discourse in the temple.	(23–27)
The parable of the two sons.	(28–32)
The parable of the wicked husbandmen.	(33–46)

Verses 1–11

This coming of Christ was described by the prophet Zechariah, Zec **9**:**9**. When Christ would appear in his glory, it is in his meekness, not in his majesty, in mercy to work salvation. As meekness and outward poverty were fully seen in Zion's King, and marked his triumphal entrance to Jerusalem, how wrong covetousness, ambition, and the pride of life must be in Zion's citizens! They brought the ass, but Jesus did not use it without the owner's consent. The trappings were such as came to hand. We must not think the clothes on our backs too dear to part with for the service of Christ. The chief priests and the elders afterwards joined with the multitude that abused him upon the cross; but none of them joined the multitude that did him honour. Those that take Christ for their King, must lay their all under his feet. Hosanna signifies, Save now, we beseech thee! Blessed is he that cometh in the name of the Lord! But of how little value is the applause of the people! The changing multitude join the cry of the day, whether it be Hosanna, or Crucify him. Multitudes often seem to approve the gospel, but few become consistent disciples. When Jesus was come into Jerusalem all the city was moved; some perhaps were moved with joy, who waited for the Consolation of Israel; others, of the Pharisees, were moved with envy. So various are the motions in the minds of men upon the approach of Christ's kingdom.

Verses 12–17

Christ found some of the courts of the temple turned into a market for cattle and things used in the sacrifices, and partly occupied by the money-changers. Our Lord drove them from the place, as he had done at his entering upon his ministry. Joh **2**:**13**–**17**. His works testified of him more than the hosannas; and his healing in the temple was the fulfilling the promise, that the glory of the latter house should be greater than the glory of the former. If Christ came now into many parts of his visible church, how many secret evils he would discover and cleanse! And how many things daily practised under the cloak of religion, would he show to be more suitable to a den of thieves than to a house of prayer!

Verses 18–22

This cursing of the barren fig-tree represents the state of hypocrites in general, and so teaches us that Christ looks for the power of religion in those who profess it, and the savour of it from those that have the show of it. His just expectations from flourishing professors are often disappointed; he comes to many, seeking fruit, and finds leaves only. A false profession commonly withers in this world, and it is the effect of Christ's curse. The fig-tree that had no fruit, soon lost its leaves. This represents the state of the nation and people of the Jews in particular. Our Lord Jesus found among them nothing but leaves. And after they rejected Christ, blindness and hardness grew upon them, till they were undone, and their place and nation rooted up. The Lord was righteous in it. Let us greatly fear the doom denounced on the barren fig-tree.

Verses 23–27

As our Lord now openly appeared as the Messiah, the chief priests and scribes were much offended, especially because he exposed and removed the abuses they encouraged. Our Lord asked what they thought of John's ministry and baptism. Many are more afraid of the shame of lying than of the sin, and therefore scruple not to speak what they know to be false, as to their own thoughts, affections, and intentions, or their remembering and forgetting. Our Lord refused to answer their inquiry. It is best to shun needless disputes with wicked opposers.

Verses 28–32

Parables which give reproof, speak plainly to the offenders, and judge them out of their own mouths. The parable of the two sons sent to work in the vineyard, is to show that those who knew not John's baptism to be of God, were shamed by those who knew it, and owned it. The whole human race are like children whom the Lord has brought up, but they have rebelled against him, only some are more plausible in their disobedience than others. And it often happens, that the daring rebel is brought to repentance and becomes the Lord's servant, while the formalist grows hardened in pride and enmity.

Verses 33–46

This parable plainly sets forth the sin and ruin of the Jewish nation; and what is spoken to convict them, is spoken to caution all that enjoy the privileges of the outward church. As men treat God's people, they would treat Christ himself, if he were with them. How can we, if faithful to his cause, expect a favourable reception from a wicked world, or from ungodly professors of Christianity! And let us ask ourselves, whether we who have the vineyard and all its advantages, render fruits in due season, as a people, as a family, or as separate persons. Our Saviour, in his question, declares that the Lord of the vineyard will come, and when he comes he will surely destroy the wicked. The chief priests and the elders were the builders, and they would not admit his doctrine or laws; they threw him aside as a despised stone. But he who was rejected by the Jews, was embraced by the Gentiles. Christ knows who will bring forth gospel fruits in the use of gospel means. The unbelief of sinners will be their ruin. But God has many ways of restraining the remainders of wrath, as he has of making that which breaks out redound to his praise. May Christ become more and more precious to our souls, as the firm Foundation and Cornerstone of his church. May we be willing to follow him, though despised and hated for his sake.

Chapter 22

Chapter Outline	
The parable of the marriage feast.	(1–14)
The Pharisees question Jesus as to the tribute.	(15–22)
The question of the Sadducees as to the resurrection.	(23–33)
The substance of the commandments.	(34–40)
Jesus questions the Pharisees.	(41–46)

Verses 1–14

The provision made for perishing souls in the gospel, is represented by a royal feast made by a king, with eastern liberality, on the marriage of his son. Our merciful God has not only provided food, but a royal feast, for the perishing souls of his rebellious creatures.

There is enough and to spare, of every thing that can add to our present comfort and everlasting happiness, in the salvation of his Son Jesus Christ. The guests first invited were the Jews. When the prophets of the Old Testament prevailed not, nor John the Baptist, nor Christ himself, who told them the kingdom of God was at hand, the apostles and ministers of the gospel were sent, after Christ's resurrection, to tell them it was come, and to persuade them to accept the offer. The reason why sinners come not to Christ and salvation by him, is, not because they cannot, but because they will not. Making light of Christ, and of the great salvation wrought out by him, is the damning sin of the world. They were careless. Multitudes perish for ever through mere carelessness, who show no direct aversion, but are careless as to their souls. Also the business and profit of worldly employments hinder many in closing with the Saviour. Both farmers and merchants must be diligent; but whatever we have of the world in our hands, our care must be to keep it out of our hearts, lest it come between us and Christ. The utter ruin coming upon the Jewish church and nation, is here represented. Persecution of Christ's faithful ministers fills up the measure of guilt of any people. The offer of Christ and salvation to the Gentiles was not expected; it was such a surprise as it would be to wayfaring men, to be invited to a royal wedding-feast. The design of the gospel is to gather souls to Christ; all the children of God scattered abroad, Joh **10**:**16**; **11**:**52**. The case of hypocrites is represented by the guest that had not on a wedding-garment. It concerns all to prepare for the scrutiny; and those, and those only, who put on the Lord Jesus, who have a Christian temper of mind, who live by faith in Christ, and to whom he is all in all, have the wedding-garment. The imputed righteousness of Christ, and the sanctification of the Spirit, are both alike necessary. No man has the wedding-garment by nature, or can form it for himself. The day is coming, when hypocrites will be called to account for all their presumptuous intruding into gospel ordinances, and usurpation of gospel privileges. Take him away. Those that walk unworthy of Christianity, forfeit all the happiness they presumptuously claimed. Our Saviour here passes out of the parable into that which it teaches. Hypocrites go by the light of the gospel itself down to utter darkness. Many are called to the wedding-feast, that is, to salvation, but few have the wedding-garment, the righteousness of Christ, the sanctification of the Spirit. Then let us examine ourselves whether we are in the faith, and seek to be approved by the King.

Verses 15–22

The Pharisees sent their disciples with the Herodians, a party among the Jews, who were for full subjection to the Roman emperor. Though opposed to each other, they joined against Christ. What they said of Christ was right; whether they knew it or not, blessed be God we know it. Jesus Christ was a faithful Teacher, and a bold reprover. Christ saw their wickedness. Whatever mask the hypocrite puts on, our Lord Jesus sees through it. Christ did not interpose as a judge in matters of this nature, for his kingdom is not of this world, but he enjoins peaceable subjection to the powers that be. His adversaries were reproved, and his disciples were taught that the Christian religion is no enemy to civil government. Christ is, and will be, the wonder, not only of his friends, but of his enemies. They admire his wisdom, but will not be guided by it; his power, but will not submit to it.

Verses 23–33

The doctrines of Christ displeased the infidel Sadducees, as well as the Pharisees and Herodians. He carried the great truths of the resurrection and a future state, further than they had yet been reveled. There is no arguing from the state of things in this world, as to what will take place hereafter. Let truth be set in a clear light, and it appears in full strength. Having thus silenced them, our Lord proceeded to show the truth of the doctrine of the resurrection from the books of Moses. God declared to Moses that he was the God of the patriarchs, who had died long before; this shows that they were then in a state of being, capable of enjoying his favour, and proves that the doctrine of the resurrection is clearly taught in the Old Testament as well as in the New. But this doctrine was kept for a more full revelation, after the resurrection of Christ, who was the first-fruits of them that slept. All errors arise from not knowing the Scriptures and the power of God. In this world death takes away one after another, and so ends all earthly hopes, joys, sorrows, and connexions. How wretched are those who look for nothing better beyond the grave!

Verses 34–40

An interpreter of the law asked our Lord a question, to try, not so much his knowledge, as his judgment. The love of God is the first and great commandment, and the sum of all the commands of the first table. Our love of God must be sincere, not in word and tongue only. All our love is too little to bestow upon him, therefore all the powers of the soul must be engaged for him, and carried out toward him. To love our neighbour as ourselves, is the second great commandment. There is a self-love which is corrupt, and the root of the greatest sins, and it must be put off and mortified; but there is a self-love which is the rule of the greatest duty: we must have a due concern for the welfare of our own souls and bodies. And we must love our neighbour as truly and sincerely as we love ourselves; in many cases we must deny ourselves for the good of others. By these two commandments let our hearts be formed as by a mould.

Verses 41–46

When Christ baffled his enemies, he asked what thoughts they had of the promised Messiah? How he could be the Son of David and yet his Lord? He quotes Ps **110**:**1**. If the Christ was to be a mere man, who would not exist till many ages after David's death, how could his forefather call him Lord? The Pharisees could not answer it. Nor can any solve the difficulty except he allows the Messiah to be the Son of God, and David's Lord equally with the Father. He took upon him human nature, and so became God manifested in the flesh; in this sense he is the Son of man and the Son of David. It behoves us above all things seriously to inquire, "What think we of Christ?" Is he altogether glorious in our eyes, and precious to our hearts? May Christ be our joy, our confidence, our all. May we daily be made more like to him, and more devoted to his service.

Chapter 23

Chapter Outline	
Jesus reproves the scribes and Pharisees.	(1–12)
Crimes of the Pharisees.	(13–33)
The guilt of Jerusalem.	(34–39)

Verses 1–12

The scribes and Pharisees explained the law of Moses, and enforced obedience to it. They are charged with hypocrisy in religion. We can only judge according to outward appearance; but God searches the heart. They made phylacteries. These were scrolls of paper or parchment, wherein were written four paragraphs of the law, to be worn on their foreheads and left arms, Ex **13**:**2**–**10**; **13**:**11**–**16**; De **6**:**4**–**9**; **11**:**13**–**21**. They made these phylacteries broad, that they might be thought more zealous for the law than others. God appointed the Jews to make fringes upon their garments, Nu **15**:**38**, to remind them of their being a peculiar people; but the Pharisees made them larger than common, as if they were thereby more religious than others. Pride was the darling, reigning sin of the Pharisees, the sin that most easily beset them, and which our Lord Jesus takes all occasions to speak against. For him that is taught in the word to give respect to him that teaches, is commendable; but for him that teaches, to demand it, to be puffed up with it, is sinful. How much is all this against the spirit of Christianity! The consistent disciple of Christ is pained by being put into chief places. But who that looks around on the visible church, would think this was the spirit required? It is plain that some measure of this antichristian spirit prevails in every religious society, and in every one of our hearts.

Verses 13–33

The scribes and Pharisees were enemies to the gospel of Christ, and therefore to the salvation of the souls of men. It is bad to keep away from Christ ourselves, but worse also to keep others from him. Yet it is no new thing for the show and form of godliness to be made a cloak to the greatest enormities. But dissembled piety will be reckoned double iniquity. They were very busy to turn souls to be of their party. Not for the glory of God and the good of souls, but that they might have the credit and advantage of making converts. Gain being their godliness, by a thousand devices they made religion give way to their worldly interests. They were very strict and precise in smaller matters of the law, but careless and loose in weightier matters. It is not the scrupling a little sin that Christ here reproves; if it be a sin, though but a gnat, it must be strained out; but the doing that, and then swallowing a camel, or, committing a greater sin. While they would seem to be godly, they were neither sober nor righteous. We are really, what we are inwardly. Outward motives may keep the outside clean, while the inside is filthy; but if the heart and spirit be made new, there will be newness of life; here we must begin with ourselves. The righteousness of the scribes and Pharisees was like the ornaments of a grave, or dressing up a dead body, only for show. The deceitfulness of sinners' hearts appears in that they go down the streams of the sins of their own day, while they fancy that they should have opposed the sins of former days. We sometimes think, if we had lived when Christ was upon earth, that we should not have despised and rejected him, as men then did; yet Christ in his Spirit, in his word, in his ministers, is still no better treated. And it is just with God to give those up to their hearts' lusts, who obstinately persist in gratifying them. Christ gives men their true characters.

Verses 34–39

Our Lord declares the miseries the inhabitants of Jerusalem were about to bring upon themselves, but he does not notice the sufferings he was to undergo. A hen gathering her chickens under her wings, is an apt emblem of the Saviour's tender love to those who trust in him, and his faithful care of them. He calls sinners to take refuge under his tender protection, keeps them safe, and nourishes them to eternal life. The present dispersion and unbelief of the Jews, and their future conversion to Christ, were here foretold. Jerusalem and her children had a large share of guilt, and their punishment has been signal. But ere long, deserved vengeance will fall on every church which is Christian in name only. In the mean time the Saviour stands ready to receive all who come to him. There is nothing between sinners and eternal happiness, but their proud and unbelieving unwillingness.

Chapter 24

Chapter Outline	
Christ foretells the destruction of the temple.	(1–3)
The troubles before the destruction of Jerusalem.	(4–28)
Christ foretells other signs and miseries, to the end of the world.	(29–41)
Exhortations to watchfulness.	(42–51)

Verses 1–3

Christ foretells the utter ruin and destruction coming upon the temple. A believing foresight of the defacing of all worldly glory, will help to keep us from admiring it, and overvaluing it. The most beautiful body soon will be food for worms, and the most magnificent building a ruinous heap. See ye not all these things? It will do us good so to see them as to see through them, and see to the end of them. Our Lord having gone with his disciples to the Mount of Olives, he set before them the order of the times concerning the Jews, till the destruction of Jerusalem; and as to men in general till the end of the world.

Verses 4–28

The disciples had asked concerning the times, When these things should be? Christ gave them no answer to that; but they had also asked, What shall be the sign? This question he answers fully. The prophecy first respects events near at hand, the destruction of Jerusalem, the end of the Jewish church and state, the calling of the Gentiles, and the setting up of Christ's kingdom in the world; but it also looks to the general judgment; and toward the close, points more particularly to the latter. What Christ here said to his disciples, tended more to promote caution than to satisfy their curiosity; more to prepare them for the events that should happen, than to give a distinct idea of the events. This is that good understanding of the times which all should covet, thence to infer what Israel ought to do. Our Saviour cautions his disciples to stand on their guard against false teachers. And he foretells wars and great commotions among nations. From the time that the Jews rejected Christ, and he left their house desolate, the sword never departed from them. See what comes of refusing the gospel. Those who will not hear the messengers of peace, shall be made to hear the messengers of war. But where the heart is fixed, trusting in God, it is kept in peace, and is not afraid. It is against the mind of Christ, that his people should have troubled hearts, even in troublous times. When we looked forward to the eternity of misery that is before the obstinate refusers of Christ and his gospel, we may truly say, The greatest earthly judgments are but the beginning of sorrows. It is comforting that some shall endure even to the end. Our Lord foretells the preaching of the gospel in all the world. The end of the world shall not be till the gospel has done its work. Christ foretells the ruin coming upon the people of the Jews; and what he said here, would be of use to his disciples, for their conduct and for their comfort. If God opens a door of escape, we ought to make our escape, otherwise we do not trust God, but tempt him. It becomes Christ's disciples, in times of public trouble, to be much in prayer: that is never out of season, but in a special manner seasonable when we are distressed on every side. Though we must take what God sends, yet we may pray against sufferings; and it is very trying to a good man, to be taken by any work of necessity from the solemn service and worship of God on the sabbath day. But here is one word of comfort, that for the elect's sake these days shall be made shorter than their enemies designed, who would have cut all off, if God, who used these foes to serve his own purpose, had not set bounds to their wrath. Christ foretells the rapid spreading of the gospel in the world. It is plainly seen as the lightning. Christ preached his gospel openly. The Romans were like an eagle, and the ensign of their armies was an eagle. When a people, by their sin, make themselves as loathsome carcasses, nothing can be expected but that God should send enemies to destroy them. It is very applicable to the day of judgment, the coming of our Lord Jesus Christ in that day, **2**Th **2**:**1**. Let us give diligence to make our calling and election sure; then may we know that no enemy or deceiver shall ever prevail against us.

Verses 29–41

Christ foretells his second coming. It is usual for prophets to speak of things as near and just at hand, to express the greatness and certainty of them. Concerning Christ's second coming, it is foretold that there shall be a great change, in order to the making all things new. Then they shall see the Son of man coming in the clouds. At his first coming, he was set for a sign that should be spoken against, but at his second coming, a sign that should be admired. Sooner or later, all sinners will be mourners; but repenting sinners look to Christ, and mourn after a godly sort; and those who sow in those tears shall shortly reap in joy. Impenitent sinners shall see Him whom they have pierced, and, though they laugh now, shall mourn and weep in endless horror and despair. The elect of God are scattered abroad; there are some in all places, and all nations; but when that great gathering day comes, there shall not one of them be missing. Distance of place shall keep none out of heaven. Our Lord declares that the Jews should never cease to be a distinct people, until all things he had been predicting were fulfilled. His prophecy reaches to the day of final judgment; therefore he here, ver. **34**, foretells that Judah shall never cease to exist as a distinct people, so long as this world shall endure. Men of the world scheme and plan for generation upon generation here, but they plan not with reference to the overwhelming, approaching, and most certain event of Christ's second coming, which shall do away every human scheme, and set aside for ever all that God forbids. That will be as surprising a day, as the deluge to the old world. Apply this, first, to temporal judgments, particularly that which was then hastening upon the nation and people of the Jews. Secondly, to the eternal judgment. Christ here shows the state of the old world when the deluge came. They were secure and careless; they knew not, until the flood came; and they believed not. Did we know aright that all earthly things must shortly pass away, we should not set our eyes and hearts so much upon them as we do. The evil day is not the further off for men's putting it far from them. What words can more strongly describe the suddenness of our Saviour's coming! Men will be at their respective businesses, and suddenly the Lord of glory will appear. Women will be in their house employments, but in that moment every other work will be laid aside, and every heart will turn inward and say, It is the Lord! Am I prepared to meet him? Can I stand before him? And what, in fact, is the day of judgment to the whole world, but the day of death to every one?

Verses 42–51

To watch for Christ's coming, is to maintain that temper of mind which we would be willing that our Lord should find us in. We know we have but a little time to live, we cannot know that we have a long time to live; much less do we know the time fixed for the judgment. Our Lord's coming will be happy to those that shall be found ready, but very dreadful to those that are not. If a man, professing to be the servant of Christ, be an unbeliever, covetous, ambitious, or a lover of pleasure, he will be cut off. Those who choose the world for their portion in this life, will have hell for their portion in the other life. May our Lord, when he cometh, pronounce us blessed, and present us to the Father, washed in his blood, purified by his Spirit, and fit to be partakers of the inheritance of the saints in light.

Chapter 25

Chapter Outline	
The parable of the ten virgins.	(1–13)
The parable of the talents.	(14–30)
The judgment.	(31–46)

Verses 1–13

The circumstances of the parable of the ten virgins were taken from the marriage customs among the Jews, and explain the great day of Christ's coming. See the nature of Christianity. As Christians we profess to attend upon Christ, to honour him, also to be waiting for his coming. Sincere Christians are the wise virgins, and hypocrites the foolish ones. Those are the truly wise or foolish that are so in the affairs of their souls. Many have a lamp of profession in their hands, but have not, in their hearts, sound knowledge and settled resolution, which are needed to carry them through the services and trials of the present state. Their hearts are not stored with holy dispositions, by the new-creating Spirit of God. Our light must shine before men in good works; but this is not likely to be long done, unless there is a fixed, active principle in the heart, of faith in Christ, and love to God and our brethren. They all slumbered and slept. The delay represents the space between the real or apparent conversion of these professors, and the coming of Christ, to take them away by death, or to judge the world. But though Christ tarry past our time, he will not tarry past the due time. The wise virgins kept their lamps burning, but they did not keep themselves awake. Too many real Christians grow remiss, and one degree of carelessness makes way for another. Those that allow themselves to slumber, will scarcely keep from sleeping; therefore dread the beginning of spiritual decays. A startling summons was given. Go ye forth to meet Him, is a call to those prepared. The notice of Christ's approach, and the call to meet him, will awaken. Even those best prepared for death have work to do to get actually ready, **2**Pe **3**:**14**. It will be a day of search and inquiry; and it concerns us to think how we shall then be found. Some wanted oil to supply their lamps when going out. Those that take up short of true grace, will certainly find the want of it one time or other. An outward profession may light a man along this world, but the damps of the valley of the shadow of death will put out such a light. Those who care not to live the life, yet would die the death of the righteous. But those that would be saved, must have grace of their own; and those that have most grace, have none to spare. The best need more from Christ. And while the poor alarmed soul addresses itself, upon a sick-bed, to repentance and prayer, in awful confusion, death comes, judgment comes, the work is undone, and the poor sinner is undone for ever. This comes of having oil to buy when we should burn it, grace to get when we should use it. Those, and those only, shall go to heaven hereafter, that are made ready for heaven here. The suddenness of death and of Christ's coming to us then, will not hinder our happiness, if we have been prepared. The door was shut. Many will seek admission into heaven when it is too late. The vain confidence of hypocrites will carry them far in expectations of happiness. The unexpected summons of death may alarm the Christian; but, proceeding without delay to trim his lamp, his graces often shine more bright; while the mere professor's conduct shows that his lamp is going out. Watch therefore, attend to the business of your souls. Be in the fear of the Lord all the day long.

Verses 14–30

Christ keeps no servants to be idle: they have received their all from him, and have nothing they can call their own but sin. Our receiving from Christ is in order to our working for him. The manifestation of the Spirit is given to every man to profit withal. The day of account comes at last. We must all be reckoned with as to what good we have got to our own souls, and have done to others, by the advantages we have enjoyed. It is not meant that the improving of natural powers can entitle a man to Divine grace. It is the real Christian's liberty and privilege to be employed as his Redeemer's servant, in promoting his glory, and the good of his people: the love of Christ constrains him to live no longer to himself, but to Him that died for him, and rose again. Those who think it impossible to please God, and in vain to serve him, will do nothing to purpose in religion. They complain that He requires of them more than they are capable of, and punishes them for what they cannot help. Whatever they may pretend, the fact is, they dislike the character and work of the Lord. The slothful servant is sentenced to be deprived of his talent. This may be applied to the blessings of this life; but rather to the means of grace. Those who know not the day of their visitation, shall have the things that belong to their peace hid from their eyes. His doom is, to be cast into outer darkness. It is a usual way of expressing the miseries of the damned in hell. Here, as in what was said to the faithful servants, our Saviour goes out of the parable into the thing intended by it, and this serves as a key to the whole. Let us not envy sinners, or covet any of their perishing possessions.

Verses 31–46

This is a description of the last judgment. It is as an explanation of the former parables. There is a judgment to come, in which every man shall be sentenced to a state of everlasting happiness, or misery. Christ shall come, not only in the glory of his Father, but in his own glory, as Mediator. The wicked and godly here dwell together, in the same cities, churches, families, and are not always to be known the one from the other; such are the weaknesses of saints, such the hypocrisies of sinners; and death takes both: but in that day they will be parted for ever. Jesus Christ is the great Shepherd; he will shortly distinguish between those that are his, and those that are not. All other distinctions will be done away; but the great one between saints and sinners, holy and unholy, will remain for ever. The happiness the saints shall possess is very great. It is a kingdom; the most valuable possession on earth; yet this is but a faint resemblance of the blessed state of the saints in heaven. It is a kingdom prepared. The Father provided it for them in the greatness of his wisdom and power; the Son purchased it for them; and the blessed Spirit, in preparing them for the kingdom, is preparing it for them. It is prepared for them: it is in all points adapted to the new nature of a sanctified soul. It is prepared from the foundation of the world. This happiness was for the saints, and they for it, from all eternity. They shall come and inherit it. What we inherit is not got by ourselves. It is God that makes heirs of heaven. We are not to suppose that acts of bounty will entitle to eternal happiness. Good works done for God's sake, through Jesus Christ, are here noticed as marking the character of believers made holy by the Spirit of Christ, and as the effects of grace bestowed on those who do them. The wicked in this world were often called to come to Christ for life and rest, but they turned from his calls; and justly are those bid to depart from Christ, that would not come to him. Condemned sinners will in vain offer excuses. The punishment of the wicked will be an everlasting punishment; their state cannot be altered. Thus life and death, good and evil, the blessing and the curse, are set before us, that we may choose our way, and as our way so shall our end be.

Chapter 26

Chapter Outline	
The rulers conspire against Christ.	(1–5)
Christ anointed at Bethany.	(6–13)
Judas bargains to betray Christ.	(14–16)
The Passover.	(17–25)
Christ institutes his holy supper.	(26–30)
He warns his disciples.	(31–35)
His agony in the garden.	(36–46)
He is betrayed.	(47–56)
Christ before Caiaphas.	(57–68)
Peter denies him.	(69–75)

Verses 1–5

Our Lord had often told of his sufferings as at a distance, now he speaks of them as at hand. At the same time the Jewish council consulted how they might put him to death secretly. But it pleased God to defeat their intention. Jesus, the true paschal Lamb, was to be sacrificed for us at that very time, and his death and resurrection rendered public.

Verses 6–13

The pouring ointment upon the head of Christ was a token of the highest respect. Where there is true love in the heart to Jesus Christ, nothing will be thought too good to bestow upon him. The more Christ's servants and their services are cavilled at, the more he manifests his acceptance. This act of faith and love was so remarkable, that it would be reported, as a memorial of Mary's faith and love, to all future ages, and in all places where the gospel should be preached. This prophecy is fulfilled.

Verses 14–16

There were but twelve called apostles, and one of them was like a devil; surely we must never expect any society to be quite pure on this side heaven. The greater profession men make of religion, the greater opportunity they have of doing mischief, if their hearts be not right with God. Observe, that Christ's own disciple, who knew so well his doctrine and manner of his life, and was false to him, could not charge him with any thing criminal, though it would have served to justify his treachery. What did Judas want? Was not he welcome wherever his Master was? Did he not fare as Christ fared? It is not the lack, but the love of money, that is the root of all evil. After he had made that wicked bargain, Judas had time to repent, and to revoke it; but when lesser acts of dishonesty have hardened the conscience men do without hesitation that which is more shameful.

Verses 17–25

Observe, the place for their eating the passover was pointed out by Christ to the disciples. He knows those hidden ones who favour his cause, and will graciously visit all who are willing to receive him. The disciples did as Jesus had appointed. Those who would have Christ's presence in the gospel passover, must do what he says. It well becomes the disciples of Christ always to be jealous over themselves, especially in trying times. We know not how strongly we may be tempted, nor how far God may leave us to ourselves, therefore we have reason not to be high-minded, but to fear. Heart-searching examination and fervent prayer are especially proper before the Lord's supper, that, as Christ our Passover is now sacrificed for us, we may keep this feast, renewing our repentance, our faith in his blood, and surrendering ourselves to his service.

Verses 26–30

This ordinance of the Lord's supper is to us the passover supper, by which we commemorate a much greater deliverance than that of Israel out of Egypt. Take, eat; accept of Christ as he is offered to you; receive the atonement, approve of it, submit to his grace and his government. Meat looked upon, be the dish ever so well garnished, will not nourish; it must be fed upon: so must the doctrine of Christ. This is my body; that is, spiritually, it signifies and represents his body. We partake of the sun, not by having the sun put into our hands, but the beams of it darted down upon us; so we partake of Christ by partaking of his grace, and the blessed fruits of the breaking of his body. The blood of Christ is signified and represented by the wine. He gave thanks, to teach us to look to God in every part of the ordinance. This cup he gave to the disciples with a command, Drink ye all of it. The pardon of sin is that great blessing which is, in the Lord's supper, conferred on all true believers; it is the foundation of all other blessings. He takes leave of such communion; and assures them of a happy meeting again at last; "Until that day when I drink it new with you\rdblquote , may be understood of the joys and glories of the future state, which the saints shall partake with the Lord Jesus. That will be the kingdom of his Father; the wine of consolation will there be always new. While we look at the outward signs of Christ's body broken and his blood shed for the remission of our sins, let us recollect that the feast cost him as much as though he had literally given his flesh to be eaten and his blood for us to drink.

Verses 31–35

Improper self-confidence, like that of Peter, is the first step to a fall. There is a proneness in all of us to be over-confident. But those fall soonest and foulest, who are the most confident in themselves. Those are least safe, who think themselves most secure. Satan is active to lead such astray; they are most off their guard: God leaves them to themselves, to humble them.

Verses 36–46

He who made atonement for the sins of mankind, submitted himself in a garden of suffering, to the will of God, from which man had revolted in a garden of pleasure. Christ took with him into that part of the garden where he suffered his agony, only those who had witnessed his glory in his transfiguration. Those are best prepared to suffer with Christ, who have by faith beheld his glory. The words used denote the most entire dejection, amazement, anguish, and horror of mind; the state of one surrounded with sorrows, overwhelmed with miseries, and almost swallowed up with terror and dismay. He now began to be sorrowful, and never ceased to be so till he said, It is finished. He prayed that, if possible, the cup might pass from him. But he also showed his perfect readiness to bear the load of his sufferings; he was willing to submit to all for our redemption and salvation. According to this example of Christ, we must drink of the bitterest cup which God puts into our hands; though nature struggle, it must submit. It should be more our care to get troubles sanctified, and our hearts satisfied under them, than to get them taken away. It is well for us that our salvation is in the hand of One who neither slumbers nor sleeps. All are tempted, but we should be much afraid of entering into temptation. To be secured from this, we should watch and pray, and continually look unto the Lord to hold us up that we may be safe. Doubtless our Lord had a clear and full view of the sufferings he was to endure, yet he spoke with the greatest calmness till this time. Christ was a Surety, who undertook to be answerable for our sins. Accordingly he was made sin for us, and suffered for our sins, the Just for the unjust; and Scripture ascribes his heaviest sufferings to the hand of God. He had full knowledge of the infinite evil of sin, and of the immense extent of that guilt for which he was to atone; with awful views of the Divine justice and holiness, and the punishment deserved by the sins of men, such as no tongue can express, or mind conceive. At the same time, Christ suffered being tempted; probably horrible thoughts were suggested by Satan that tended to gloom and every dreadful conclusion: these would be the more hard to bear from his perfect holiness. And did the load of imputed guilt so weigh down the soul of Him of whom it is said, He upholdeth all things by the word of his power? into what misery then must those sink whose sins are left upon their own heads! How will those escape who neglect so great salvation?

Verses 47–56

No enemies are so much to be abhorred as those professed disciples that betray Christ with a kiss. God has no need of our services, much less of our sins, to bring about his purposes. Though Christ was crucified through weakness, it was voluntary weakness; he submitted to death. If he had not been willing to suffer, they could not conquer him. It was a great sin for those who had left all to follow Jesus; now to leave him for they knew not what. What folly, for fear of death to flee from Him, whom they knew and acknowledged to be the Fountain of life!

Verses 57–68

Jesus was hurried into Jerusalem. It looks ill, and bodes worse, when those who are willing to be Christ's disciples, are not willing to be known to be so. Here began Peter's denying him: for to follow Christ afar off, is to begin to go back from him. It is more our concern to prepare for the end, whatever it may be, than curiously to ask what the end will be. The event is God's, but the duty is ours. Now the

Scriptures were fulfilled, which said, False witnesses are risen up against me. Christ was accused, that we might not be condemned; and if at any time we suffer thus, let us remember we cannot expect to fare better than our Master. When Christ was made sin for us, he was silent, and left it to his blood to speak. Hitherto Jesus had seldom professed expressly to be the Christ, the Son of God; the tenor of his doctrine spoke it, and his miracles proved it; but now he would not omit to make an open confession of it. It would have looked like declining his sufferings. He thus confessed, as an example and encouragement to his followers, to confess him before men, whatever hazard they ran. Disdain, cruel mocking, and abhorrence, are the sure portion of the disciple as they were of the Master, from such as would buffet and deride the Lord of glory. These things were exactly foretold in the fiftieth chapter of Isaiah. Let us confess Christ's name, and bear the reproach, and he will confess us before his Father's throne.

Verses 69–75

Peter's sin is truly related, for the Scriptures deal faithfully. Bad company leads to sin: those who needlessly thrust themselves into it, may expect to be tempted and insnared, as Peter. They scarcely can come out of such company without guilt or grief, or both. It is a great fault to be shy of Christ; and to dissemble our knowledge of him, when we are called to own him, is, in effect, to deny him. Peter's sin was aggravated; but he fell into the sin by surprise, not as Judas, with design. But conscience should be to us as the crowing of the cock, to put us in mind of the sins we had forgotten. Peter was thus left to fall, to abate his self-confidence, and render him more modest, humble, compassionate, and useful to others. The event has taught believers many things ever since, and if infidels, Pharisees, and hypocrites stumble at it or abuse it, it is at their peril. Little do we know how we should act in very difficult situations, if we were left to ourselves. Let him, therefore, that thinketh he standeth, take heed lest he fall; let us all distrust our own hearts, and rely wholly on the Lord. Peter wept bitterly. Sorrow for sin must not be slight, but great and deep. Peter, who wept so bitterly for denying Christ, never denied him again, but confessed him often in the face of danger. True repentance for any sin will be shown by the contrary grace and duty; that is a sign of our sorrowing not only bitterly, but sincerely.

Chapter 27

Chapter Outline	
Christ delivered to Pilate, The despair of Judas.	(1–10)
Christ before Pilate.	(11–25)
Barabbas loosed, Christ mocked.	(26–30)
Christ led to be crucified.	(31–34)
He is crucified.	(35–44)
The death of Christ.	(45–50)
Events at the crucifixion.	(51–56)
The burial of Christ.	(57–61)
The sepulchre secured.	(62–66)

Verses 1–10

Wicked men see little of the consequences of their crimes when they commit them, but they must answer for them all. In the fullest manner Judas acknowledged to the chief priests that he had sinned, and betrayed an innocent person. This was full testimony to the character of Christ; but the rulers were hardened. Casting down the money, Judas departed, and went and hanged himself, not being able to bear the terror of Divine wrath, and the anguish of despair. There is little doubt but that the death of Judas was before that of our blessed Lord. But was it nothing to them that they had thirsted after this blood, and hired Judas to betray it, and had condemned it to be shed unjustly? Thus do fools make a mock at sin. Thus many make light of Christ crucified. And it is a common instance of the deceitfulness of our hearts, to make light of our own sin by dwelling upon other people's sins. But the judgment of God is according to truth. Many apply this passage of the buying the piece of ground, with the money Judas brought back, to signify the favour intended by the blood of Christ to strangers, and sinners of the Gentiles. It fulfilled a prophecy, Zec **11**:**12**. Judas went far toward repentance, yet it was not to salvation. He confessed, but not to God; he did not go to him, and say, I have sinned, Father, against heaven. Let none be satisfied with such partial convictions as a man may have, and yet remain full of pride, enmity, and rebellion.

Verses 11–25

Having no malice against Jesus, Pilate urged him to clear himself, and laboured to get him discharged. The message from his wife was a warning. God has many ways of giving checks to sinners, in their sinful pursuits, and it is a great mercy to have such checks from Providence, from faithful friends, and from our own consciences. O do not this abominable thing which the Lord hates! is what we may hear said to us, when we are entering into temptation, if we will but regard it. Being overruled by the priests, the people made choice of Barabbas. Multitudes who choose the world, rather than God, for their ruler and portion, thus choose their own delusions. The Jews were so bent upon the death of Christ, that Pilate thought it would be dangerous to refuse. And this struggle shows the power of conscience even on the worst men. Yet all was so ordered to make it evident that Christ suffered for no fault of his own, but for the sins of his people. How vain for Pilate to expect to free himself from the guilt of the innocent blood of a righteous person, whom he was by his office bound to protect! The Jews' curse upon themselves has been awfully answered in the sufferings of their nation. None could bear the sin of others, except Him that had no sin of his own to answer for. And are we not all concerned? Is not Barabbas preferred to Jesus, when sinners reject salvation that they may retain their darling sins, which rob God of his glory, and murder their souls? The blood of Christ is now upon us for good, through mercy, by the Jews' rejection of it. O let us flee to it for refuge!

Verses 26–30

Crucifixion was a death used only among the Romans; it was very terrible and miserable. A cross was laid on the ground, to which the hands and feet were nailed, it was then lifted up and fixed upright, so that the weight of the body hung on the nails, till the sufferer died in agony. Christ thus answered the type of the brazen serpent raised on a pole. Christ underwent all the misery and shame here related, that he might purchase for us everlasting life, and joy, and glory.

Verses 31–34

Christ was led as a Lamb to the slaughter, as a Sacrifice to the altar. Even the mercies of the wicked are really cruel. Taking the cross from him, they compelled one Simon to bear it. Make us ready, O Lord, to bear the cross thou hast appointed us, and daily to take it up with cheerfulness, following thee. Was ever sorrow like unto his sorrow? And when we behold what manner of death he died, let us in that behold with what manner of love he loved us. As if death, so painful a death, were not enough, they added to its bitterness and terror in several ways.

Verses 35–44

It was usual to put shame upon malefactors, by a writing to notify the crime for which they suffered. So they set up one over Christ's head. This they designed for his reproach, but God so overruled it, that even his accusation was to his honour. There were crucified with him at the same time, two robbers. He was, at his death, numbered among the transgressors, that we, at our death, might be numbered among the saints. The taunts and jeers he received are here recorded. The enemies of Christ labour to make others believe that of religion and of the people of God, which they themselves know to be false. The chief priests and scribes, and the elders, upbraid Jesus with being the King of Israel. Many people could like the King of Israel well enough, if he would but come down from the cross; if they could but have his kingdom without the tribulation through which they must enter into it. But if no cross, then no Christ, no crown. Those that would reign with him, must be willing to suffer with him. Thus our Lord Jesus, having undertaken to satisfy the justice of God, did it, by submitting to the punishment of the worst of men. And in every minute particular recorded about the sufferings of Christ, we find some prediction in the Prophets or the Psalms fulfilled.

Verses 45–50

During the three hours which the darkness continued, Jesus was in agony, wrestling with the powers of darkness, and suffering his Father's displeasure against the sin of man, for which he was now making his soul an offering. Never were there three such hours since the day God created man upon the earth, never such a dark and awful scene; it was the turning point of that great affair, man's redemption and salvation. Jesus uttered a complaint from Ps **22**:**1**. Hereby he teaches of what use the word of God is to direct us in prayer, and recommends the use of Scripture expressions in prayer. The believer may have tasted some drops of bitterness, but he can only form a very feeble idea of the greatness of Christ's sufferings. Yet, hence he learns something of the Saviour's love to sinners; hence he gets deeper conviction of the vileness and evil of sin, and of what he owes to Christ, who delivers him from the wrath to come. His enemies wickedly ridiculed his complaint. Many of the reproaches cast upon the word of God and the people of God, arise, as here, from gross mistakes. Christ, just before he expired, spake in his full strength, to show that his life was not forced from him, but was freely delivered into his Father's hands. He had strength to bid defiance to the powers of death: and to show that by the eternal Spirit he offered himself, being the Priest as well as the Sacrifice, he cried with a loud voice. Then he yielded up the ghost. The Son of God upon the cross, did die by the violence of the pain he was put to. His soul was separated from his body, and so his body was left really and truly dead. It was certain that Christ did die, for it was needful that he should die. He had undertaken to make himself an offering for sin, and he did it when he willingly gave up his life.

Verses 51–56

The rending of the veil signified that Christ, by his death, opened a way to God. We have an open way through Christ to the throne of grace, or mercy-seat now, and to the throne of glory hereafter. When we duly consider Christ's death, our hard and rocky hearts should be rent; the heart, and not the garments. That heart is harder than a rock that will not yield, that will not melt, where Jesus Christ is plainly set forth crucified. The graves were opened, and many bodies of saints which slept, arose. To whom they appeared, in what manner, and how they disappeared, we are not told; and we must not desire to be wise above what is written. The dreadful appearances of God in his providence, sometimes work strangely for the conviction and awakening of sinners. This was expressed in the terror that fell upon the centurion and the Roman soldiers. We may reflect with comfort on the abundant testimonies given to the character of Jesus; and, seeking to give no just cause of offence, we may leave it to the Lord to clear our characters, if we live to Him. Let us, with an eye of faith, behold Christ and him crucified, and be affected with that great love wherewith he loved us. But his friends could give no more than a look; they beheld him, but could not help him. Never were the horrid nature and effects of sin so tremendously displayed, as on that day when the beloved Son of the Father hung upon the cross, suffering for sin, the Just for the unjust, that he might bring us to God. Let us yield ourselves willingly to his service.

Verses 57–61

In the burial of Christ was nothing of pomp or solemnity. As Christ had not a house of his own, wherein to lay his head, while he lived, so he had not a grave of his own, wherein to lay his body, when he was dead. Our Lord Jesus, who had no sin of his own, had no grave of his own. The Jews designed that he should have made his grave with the wicked, should have been buried with the thieves with whom he was crucified, but God overruled it, so that he should make it with the rich in his death, Isa **53**:**9**. And although to the eye of man the beholding a funeral may cause terror, yet if we remember how Christ by his burial has changed the nature of the grave to believers, it should make us rejoice. And we are ever to imitate Christ's burial in being continually occupied in the spiritual burial of our sins.

Verses 62–66

On the Jewish sabbath, the chief priests and Pharisees, when they should have been at their devotions, were dealing with Pilate about securing the sepulchre. This was permitted that there might be certain proof of our Lord's resurrection. Pilate told them that they might secure the sepulchre as carefully as they could. They sealed the stone, and set a guard, and were satisfied that all needful care was taken. But to guard the sepulchre against the poor weak disciples was folly, because needless; while to think to guard it against the power of God, was folly, because fruitless, and to no purpose; yet they thought they dealt wisely. But the Lord took the wise in their own craftiness. Thus shall all the rage and the plans of Christ's enemies be made to promote his glory.

Chapter 28

Chapter Outline	
Christ's resurrection.	(1–8)
He appears to the women.	(9, 10)
Confession of the soldiers.	(11–15)
Christ's commission to his disciples.	(16–20)

Verses 1–8

Christ rose the third day after his death; that was the time he had often spoken of. On the first day of the first week God commanded the light to shine out of darkness. On this day did He who is the Light of the world, shine out of the darkness of the grave; and this day is from henceforward often mentioned in the New Testament, as the day which Christians religiously observed in solemn assemblies, to the honour of Christ. Our Lord Jesus could have rolled back the stone by his own power, but he chose to have it done by an angel. The resurrection of Christ, as it is the joy of his friends, so it is the terror and confusion of his enemies. The angel encouraged the women against their fears. Let the sinners in Zion be afraid. Fear not ye, for his resurrection will be your consolation. Our communion with him must be spiritual, by faith in his word. When we are ready to make this world our home, and to say, It is good to be here, then let us remember our Lord Jesus is not here, he is risen; therefore let our hearts rise, and seek the things that are above. He is risen, as he said. Let us never think that strange which the word of Christ has told us to expect; whether the sufferings of this present time, or the glory that is to be revealed. It may have a good effect upon us, by faith to view the place where the Lord lay. Go quickly. It was good to be there, but the servants of God have other work appointed. Public usefulness must be chosen before the pleasure of secret communion with God. Tell the disciples, that they may be comforted under their present sorrows. Christ knows where his disciples dwell, and will visit them. Even to those at a distance from the plenty of the means of grace, he will graciously manifest himself. The fear and the joy together quickened their pace. The disciples of Christ should be forward to make known to each other their experiences of communion with their Lord; and should tell others what God has done for their souls.

Verses 9, 10

God's gracious visits usually meet us in the way of duty; and to those who use what they have for others' benefit, more shall be given. This interview with Christ was unexpected; but Christ was nigh them, and still is nigh us in the word. The salutation speaks the good-will of Christ to man, even since he entered upon his state of exaltation. It is the will of Christ that his people should be a cheerful, joyful people, and his resurrection furnishes abundant matter for joy. Be not afraid. Christ rose from the dead, to silence his people's fears, and there is enough in that to silence them. The disciples had just before shamefully deserted him in his sufferings; but, to show that he could forgive, and to teach us to do so, he calls them brethren. Notwithstanding his majesty and purity, and our meanness and unworthiness, he still condescends to call believers his brethren.

Verses 11–15

What wickedness is it which men will not be brought to by the love of money! Here was large money given to the soldiers for advancing that which they knew to be a lie, yet many grudge a little money for advancing what they know to be the truth. Let us never starve a good cause, when we see bad ones so liberally supported. The priests undertook to secure them from the sword of Pilate, but could not secure these soldiers from the sword of God's justice, which hangs over the heads of those that love and make a lie. Those men promise more than they can perform, who undertake to save a man harmless in doing a wilful sin. But this falsehood disproved itself. Had the soldiers been all asleep, they could not have known what passed. If any had been awake, they would have roused the others and prevented the removal; and certainly if they had been asleep, they never would have dared to confess it; while the Jewish rulers would have been the first to call for their punishment. Again, had there been any truth in the report, the rulers would have prosecuted the apostles with severity for it. The whole shows that the story was entirely false. And we must not charge such things to the weakness of the understanding, but to the wickedness of the heart. God left them to expose their own course. The great argument to prove Christ to be the Son of God, is his resurrection; and none could have more convincing proofs of the truth of that than these soldiers; yet they took bribes to hinder others from believing. The plainest evidence will not affect men, without the work of the Holy Spirit.

Verses 16–20

This evangelist passes over other appearances of Christ, recorded by Luke and John, and hastens to the most solemn; one appointed before his death, and after his resurrection. All that see the Lord Jesus with an eye of faith, will worship him. Yet the faith of the sincere may be very weak and wavering. But Christ gave such convincing proofs of his resurrection, as made their faith to triumph over doubts. He now solemnly commissioned the apostles and his ministers to go forth among all nations. The salvation they were to preach, is a common salvation; whoever will, let him come, and take the benefit; all are welcome to Christ Jesus. Christianity is the religion of a sinner who applies for salvation from deserved wrath and from sin; he applies to the mercy of the Father, through the atonement of the incarnate Son, and by the sanctification of the Holy Spirit, and gives up himself to be the worshipper and servant of God, as the Father, Son, and Holy Ghost, three Persons but one God, in all his ordinances and commandments. Baptism is an outward sign of that inward washing, or sanctification of the Spirit, which seals and evidences the believer's justification. Let us examine ourselves, whether we really possess the inward and spiritual grace of a death unto sin, and a new birth unto righteousness, by which those who were the children of wrath become the children of God. Believers shall have the constant presence of their Lord always; all days, every day. There is no day, no hour of the day, in which our Lord Jesus is not present with his churches and with his ministers; if there were, in that day, that hour, they would be undone. The God of Israel, the Saviour, is sometimes a God that hideth himself, but never a God at a distance. To these precious words Amen is added. Even so, Lord Jesus, be thou with us and all thy people; cause thy face to shine upon us, that thy way may be known upon earth, thy saving health among all nations.

Mark

Mark was a sister's son to Barnabas, Col **4**:**10**; and Ac **12**:**12** shows that he was the son of Mary, a pious woman of Jerusalem, at whose house the apostles and first Christians assembled. From Peter's styling him his son, **1**Pe **5**:**13**, the evangelist is supposed to have been converted by that apostle. Thus Mark was closely united with the followers of our Lord, if not himself one of the number. Mark wrote at Rome; some suppose that Peter dictated to him, though the general testimony is, that the apostle having preached at Rome, Mark, who was the apostle's companion, and had a clear understanding of what Peter delivered, was desired to commit the particulars to writing. And we may remark, that the great humility of Peter is very plain where any thing is said about himself. Scarcely an action or a work of Christ is mentioned, at which this apostle was not present, and the minuteness shows that the facts were related by an eye-witness. This Gospel records more of the miracles than of the discourses of our Lord, and though in many things it relates the same things as the Gospel according to St. Matthew, we may reap advantages from reviewing the same events, placed by each of the evangelists in that point of view which most affected his own mind.

Chapter 1

Chapter Outline	
The office of John the Baptist.	(1–8)
The baptism and temptation of Christ.	(9–13)
Christ preaches and calls disciples.	(14–22)
He casts out an unclean spirit.	(23–28)
He heals many diseased.	(29–39)
He heals a leper.	(40–45)

Verses 1–8

Isaiah and Malachi each spake concerning the beginning of the gospel of Jesus Christ, in the ministry of John. From these prophets we may observe, that Christ, in his gospel, comes among us, bringing with him a treasure of grace, and a sceptre of government. Such is the corruption of the world, that there is great opposition to his progress. When God sent his Son into the world, he took care, and when he sends him into the heart, he takes care, to prepare his way before him. John thinks himself unworthy of the meanest office about Christ. The most eminent saints have always been the most humble. They feel their need of Christ's atoning blood and sanctifying Spirit, more than others. The great promise Christ makes in his gospel to those who have repented, and have had their sins forgiven them, is, they shall be baptized with the Holy Ghost; shall be purified by his graces, and refreshed by his comforts. We use the ordinances, word, and sacraments without profit and comfort, for the most part, because we have not of that Divine light within us; and we have it not because we ask it not; for we have his word that cannot fail, that our heavenly Father will give this light, his Holy Spirit, to those that ask it.

Verses 9–13

Christ's baptism was his first public appearance, after he had long lived unknown. How much hidden worth is there, which in this world is not known! But sooner or later it shall be known, as Christ was. He took upon himself the likeness of sinful flesh; and thus, for our sakes, he sanctified himself, that we also might be sanctified, and be baptized with him, Joh **17**:**19**. See how honourably God owned him, when he submitted to John's baptism. He saw the Spirit descending upon him like a dove. We may see heaven opened to us, when we perceive the Spirit descending and working upon us. God's good work in us, is sure evidence of his good will towards us, and preparations for us. As to Christ's temptation, Mark notices his being in the wilderness and that he was with the wild beasts. It was an instance of his Father's care of him, which encouraged him the more that his Father would provide for him. Special protections are earnests of seasonable supplies. The serpent tempted the first Adam in the garden, the Second Adam in the wilderness; with different success indeed; and ever since he still tempts the children of both, in all places and conditions. Company and conversation have their temptations; and being alone, even in a wilderness, has its own also. No place or state exempts, no business, not lawful labouring, eating, or drinking, not even fasting and praying; often in these duties there are the most assaults, but in them is the sweetest victory. The ministration of the good angels is matter of great comfort in reference to the malignant designs of the evil angels; but much more does it comfort us, to have the indwelling of God the Holy Spirit in our hearts.

Verses 14–22

Jesus began to preach in Galilee, after that John was put in prison. If some be laid aside, others shall be raised up, to carry on the same work. Observe the great truths Christ preached. By repentance we give glory to our Creator whom we have offended; by faith we give glory to our Redeemer who came to save us from our sins. Christ has joined these two together, and let no man think to put them asunder. Christ puts honour upon those who, though mean in this world, are diligent in their business and kind to one another. Industry and unity are good and pleasant, and the Lord Jesus commands a blessing on them. Those whom Christ calls, must leave all to follow him; and by his grace he makes them willing to do so. Not that we must needs go out of the world, but we must sit loose to the world; forsake every thing that is against our duty to Christ, and that cannot be kept without hurt to our souls. Jesus strictly kept the sabbath day, by applying himself unto, and abounding in the sabbath work, in order to which the sabbath rest was appointed. There is much in the doctrine of Christ that is astonishing; and the more we hear it, the more cause we see to admire it.

Verses 23–28

The devil is an unclean spirit, because he has lost all the purity of his nature, because he acts in direct opposition to the Holy Spirit of God, and by his suggestions defiles the spirits of men. There are many in our assemblies who quietly attend under merely formal teachers; but if the Lord come with faithful ministers and holy doctrine, and by his convincing Spirit, they are ready to say, like this man, What have we to do with thee, Jesus of Nazareth! No disorder could enable a man to know Jesus to be the Holy One of God. He desires to have nothing to do with Jesus, for he despairs of being saved by him, and dreads being destroyed by him. See whose language those speak, that say to the Almighty, Depart from us. This unclean spirit hated and dreaded Christ, because he knew him to be a Holy One; for the carnal mind is enmity against God, especially against his holiness. When Christ by his grace delivers souls out of the hands of Satan, it is not without tumult in the soul; for that spiteful enemy will disquiet those whom he cannot destroy. This put all who saw it upon considering, What is this new doctrine? A work as great often is wrought now, yet men treat it with contempt and neglect. If this were not so, the conversion of a notorious wicked man to a sober, righteous, and godly life, by the preaching of a crucified Saviour, would cause many to ask, What doctrine is this?

Verses 29–39

Wherever Christ comes, he comes to do good. He cures, that we may minister to him, and to others who are his, and for his sake. Those kept from public ordinances by sickness or other real hinderances, may expect the Saviour's gracious presence; he will soothe their sorrows, and abate their pains. Observe how numerous the patients were. When others speed well with Christ, it should quicken us in seeking after him. Christ departed into a solitary place. Though he was in no danger of distraction, or of temptation to vain-glory, yet he retired. Those who have the most business in public, and of the best kind, must yet sometimes be alone with God.

Verses 40–45

We have here Christ's cleansing of a leper. It teaches us to apply to the Saviour with great humility, and with full submission to his will, saying, "Lord, if thou wilt," without any doubt of Christ's readiness to help the distressed. See also what to expect from Christ; that according to our faith it shall be to us. The poor leper said, If thou wilt. Christ readily wills favours to those who readily refer themselves to his will. Christ would have nothing done that looked like seeking praise of the people. But no reasons now exist why we should hesitate to spread the praises of Christ.

Chapter 2

Chapter Outline	
Christ heals one sick of the palsy.	(1–12)
Levi's call, and the entertainment given to Jesus.	(13–17)
Why Christ's disciples did not fast.	(18–22)
He justifies his disciples for plucking corn on the sabbath.	(23–28)

Verses 1–12

It was this man's misery that he needed to be so carried, and shows the suffering state of human life; it was kind of those who so carried him, and teaches the compassion that should be in men, toward their fellow-creatures in distress. True faith and strong faith may work in various ways; but it shall be accepted and approved by Jesus Christ. Sin is the cause of all our pains and sicknesses. The way to remove the effect, is to take away the cause. Pardon of sin strikes at the root of all diseases. Christ proved his power to forgive sin, by showing his power to cure the man sick of the palsy. And his curing diseases was a figure of his pardoning sin, for sin is the disease of the soul; when it is pardoned, it is healed. When we see what Christ does in healing souls, we must own that we never saw the like. Most men think themselves whole; they feel no need of a physician, therefore despise or neglect Christ and his gospel. But the convinced, humbled sinner, who despairs of all help, excepting from the Saviour, will show his faith by applying to him without delay.

Verses 13–17

Matthew was not a good character, or else, being a Jew, he would never have been a publican, that is, a tax-gatherer for the Romans. However, Christ called this publican to follow him. With God, through Christ, there is mercy to pardon the greatest sins, and grace to change the greatest sinners, and make them holy. A faithful, fair-dealing publican was rare. And because the Jews had a particular hatred to an office which proved that they were subject to the Romans, they gave these tax-gatherers an ill name. But such as these our blessed Lord did not hesitate to con**verse** with, when he appeared in the likeness of sinful flesh. And it is no new thing for that which is both well done and well designed, to be slandered, and turned to the reproach of the wisest and best of men. Christ would not withdraw, though the Pharisees were offended. If the world had been righteous, there had been no occasion for his coming, either to preach repentance, or to purchase forgiveness. We must not keep company with ungodly men out of love to their vain conversation; but we are to show love to their souls, remembering that our good Physician had the power of healing in himself, and was in no danger of taking the disease; but it is not so with us. In trying to do good to others, let us be careful we do not get harm to ourselves.

Verses 18–22

Strict professors are apt to blame all that do not fully come up to their own views. Christ did not escape slanders; we should be willing to bear them, as well as careful not to deserve them; but should attend to every part of our duty in its proper order and season.

Verses 23–28

The sabbath is a sacred and Divine institution; a privilege and benefit, not a task and drudgery. God never designed it to be a burden to us, therefore we must not make it so to ourselves. The sabbath was instituted for the good of mankind, as living in society, having many wants and troubles, preparing for a state of happiness or misery. Man was not made for the sabbath, as if his keeping it could be of service to God, nor was he commanded to keep it outward observances to his real hurt. Every observance respecting it, is to be interpreted by the rule of mercy.

Chapter 3

Chapter Outline	
The withered hand healed.	(1–5)
The people resort to Christ.	(6–12)
The apostles called.	(13–21)
The blasphemy of the scribes.	(22–30)
Christ's relatives.	(31–35)

Verses 1–5

This man's case was piteous; he had a withered hand, which disabled him from working for his living; and those that are so, are the most proper objects of charity. Let those be helped that cannot help themselves. But stubborn infidels, when they can say nothing against the truth, yet will not yield. We hear what is said amiss, and see what is done amiss; but Christ looks at the root of bitterness in the heart, the blindness and hardness of that, and is grieved. Let hard-hearted sinners tremble to think of the anger with which he will look upon them shortly, when the day of his wrath comes. The great healing day now is the sabbath, and the healing place the house of prayer; but the healing power is of Christ. The gospel command is like that recorded here: though our hands are withered, yet, if we will not stretch them out, it is our own fault that we are not healed. But if we are healed, Christ, his power and grace, must have all the glory.

Verses 6–12

All our sicknesses and calamities spring from the anger of God against our sins. Their removal, or the making them blessings to us, was purchased to us by the blood of Christ. But the plagues and diseases of our souls, of our hearts, are chiefly to be dreaded; and He can heal them also by a word. May more and more press to Christ to be healed of these plagues, and to be delivered from the enemies of their souls.

Verses 13–21

Christ calls whom he will; for his grace is his own. He had called the apostles to separate themselves from the crowd, and they came unto him. He now gave them power to heal sicknesses, and to cast out devils. May the Lord send forth more and more of those who have been with him, and have learned of him to preach his gospel, to be instruments in his blessed work. Those whose hearts are enlarged in the work of God, can easily bear with what is inconvenient to themselves, and will rather lose a meal than an opportunity of doing good. Those who go on with zeal in the work of God, must expect hinderances, both from the hatred of enemies, and mistaken affections of friends, and need to guard against both.

Verses 22–30

It was plain that the doctrine of Christ had a direct tendency to break the devil's power; and it was as plain, that casting of him out of the bodies of people, confirmed that doctrine; therefore Satan could not support such a design. Christ gave an awful warning against speaking such dangerous words. It is true the gospel promises, because Christ has purchased, forgiveness for the greatest sins and sinners; but by this sin, they would oppose the gifts of the Holy Ghost after Christ's ascension. Such is the enmity of the heart, that unconverted men pretend believers are doing Satan's work, when sinners are brought to repentance and newness of life.

Verses 31–35

It is a great comfort to all true Christians, that they are dearer to Christ than mother, brother, or sister as such, merely as relations in the flesh would have been, even had they been holy. Blessed be God, this great and gracious privilege is ours even now; for though Christ's bodily presence cannot be enjoyed by us, his spiritual presence is not denied us.

Chapter 4

Chapter Outline	
The parable of the sower.	(1–20)
Other parables.	(21–34)
Christ stills the tempest.	(35–41)

Verses 1–20

This parable contained instruction so important, that all capable of hearing were bound to attend to it. There are many things we are concerned to know; and if we understand not the plain truths of the gospel, how shall we learn those more difficult! It will help us to value the privileges we enjoy as disciples of Christ, if we seriously consider the deplorable state of all who have not such privileges. In the great field of the church, the word of God is dispensed to all. Of the many that hear the word of the gospel, but few receive it, so as to bring forth fruit. Many are much affected with the word for the present, who yet receive no abiding benefit. The word does not leave abiding impressions upon the minds of men, because their hearts are not duly disposed to receive it. The devil is very busy about careless hearers, as the fowls of the air go about the seed that lies above ground. Many continue in a barren, false profession, and go down to hell. Impressions that are not deep, will not last. Many do not mind heart-work, without which religion is nothing. Others are hindered from profiting by the word of God, by abundance of the world. And those who have but little of the world, may yet be ruined by indulging the body. God expects and requires fruit from those who enjoy the gospel, a temper of mind and Christian graces daily exercised, Christian duties duly performed. Let us look to the Lord, that by his new-creating grace our hearts may become good ground, and that the good seed of the word may produce in our lives those good words and works which are through Jesus Christ, to the praise and glory of God the Father.

Verses 21–34

These declarations were intended to call the attention of the disciples to the word of Christ. By his thus instructing them, they were made able to instruct others; as candles are lighted, not to be covered, but to be placed on a candlestick, that they may give light to a room. This parable of the good seed, shows the manner in which the kingdom of God makes progress in the world. Let but the word of Christ have the place it ought to have in a soul, and it will show itself in a good conversation. It grows gradually: first the blade; then the ear; after that the full corn in the ear. When it is sprung up, it will go forward. The work of grace in the soul is, at first, but the day of small things; yet it has mighty products even now, while it is in its growth; but what will there be when it is perfected in heaven!

Verses 35–41

Christ was asleep in the storm, to try the faith of his disciples, and to stir them up to pray. Their faith appeared weak, and their prayers strong. When our wicked hearts are like the troubled sea which cannot rest, when our passions are unruly, let us think we hear the law of Christ, saying, Be silent, be dumb. When without are fightings, and within are fears, and the spirits are in a tumult, if he say, "Peace, be still," there is a great calm at once. Why are ye so fearful? Though there may be cause for some fear, yet not for such fear as this. Those may suspect their faith, who can have such a thought as that Jesus careth not though his people perish. How imperfect are the best of saints! Faith and fear take their turns while we are in this world; but ere long, fear will be overcome, and faith will be lost in sight.

Chapter 5

Chapter Outline	
The demoniac healed.	(1–20)
A woman healed.	(21–34)
The daughter of Jairus raised.	(35–43)

Verses 1–20

Some openly wilful sinners are like this madman. The commands of the law are as chains and fetters, to restrain sinners from their wicked courses; but they break those bands in sunder; and it is an evidence of the power of the devil in them. A legion of soldiers consisted of six thousand men, or more. What multitudes of fallen spirits there must be, and all enemies to God and man, when here was a legion in one poor wretched creature! Many there are that rise up against us. We are not a match for our spiritual enemies, in our own strength; but in the Lord, and in the power of his might, we shall be able to stand against them, though there are legions of them. When the vilest transgressor is delivered by the power of Jesus from the bondage of Satan, he will gladly sit at the feet of his Deliverer, and hear his word, who delivers the wretched slaves of Satan, and numbers them among his saints and servants. When the people found that their swine were lost, they had a dislike to Christ. Long-suffering and mercy may be seen, even in the corrections by which men lose their property while their lives are saved, and warning given them to seek the salvation of their souls. The man joyfully proclaimed what great things Jesus had done for him. All men marvelled, but few followed him. Many who cannot but wonder at the works of Christ, yet do not, as they ought, wonder after him.

Verses 21–34

A despised gospel will go where it will be better received. One of the rulers of a synagogue earnestly besought Christ for a little daughter, about twelve years old, who was dying. Another cure was wrought by the way. We should do good, not only when in the house, but when we walk by the way, De **6**:**7**. It is common with people not to apply to Christ till they have tried in vain all other helpers, and find them, as certainly they will, physicians of no value. Some run to diversions and gay company; others plunge into business, or even into intemperance; others go about to establish their own righteousness, or torment themselves by vain superstitions. Many perish in these ways; but none will ever find rest to the soul by such devices; while those whom Christ heals of the disease of sin, find in themselves an entire change for the better. As secret acts of sin, so secret acts of faith, are known to the Lord Jesus. The woman told all the truth. It is the will of Christ that his people should be comforted, and he has power to command comfort to troubled spirits. The more simply we depend on Him, and expect great things from him, the more we shall find in ourselves that he is become our salvation. Those who, by faith, are healed of their spiritual diseases, have reason to go in peace.

Verses 35–43

We may suppose Jairus hesitating whether he should ask Christ to go on or not, when told that his daughter was dead. But have we not as much occasion for the grace of God, and the comfort of his Spirit, for the prayers of our ministers and Christian friends, when death is in the house, as when sickness is there? Faith is the only remedy against grief and fear at such a time. Believe the resurrection, then fear not. He raised the dead child to life by a word of power. Such is the gospel call to those who are by nature dead in trespasses and sins. It is by the word of Christ that spiritual life is given. All who saw it, and heard of it, admired the miracle, and Him that wrought it. Though we cannot now expect to have our dead children or relatives restored, we may hope to find comfort under our trials.

Chapter 6

Chapter Outline	
Christ despised in his own country.	(1–6)
The apostles sent forth.	(7–13)
John the Baptist put to death.	(14–29)

The apostles return, Five thousand fed by a miracle.	(30–44)
Christ walks on the sea, He heals those that touch him.	(45–56)

Verses 1–6

Our Lord's countrymen tried to prejudice the minds of people against him. Is not this the carpenter? Our Lord Jesus probably had worked in that business with his father. He thus put honour upon mechanics, and encouraged all persons who eat by the labour of their hands. It becomes the followers of Christ to content themselves with the satisfaction of doing good, although they are denied the praise of it. How much did these Nazarenes lose by obstinate prejudices against Jesus! May Divine grace deliver us from that unbelief, which renders Christ a savour of death, rather than of life to the soul. Let us, like our Master, go and teach cottages and peasants the way of salvation.

Verses 7–13

Though the apostles were conscious to themselves of great weakness, and expected no wordly advantage, yet, in obedience to their Master, and in dependence upon his strength, they went out. They did not amuse people with curious matters, but told them they must repent of their sins, and turn to God. The servants of Christ may hope to turn many from darkness unto God, and to heal souls by the power of the Holy Ghost.

Verses 14–29

Herod feared John while he lived, and feared him still more when he was dead. Herod did many of those things which John in his preaching taught him; but it is not enough to do many things, we must have respect to all the commandments. Herod respected John, till he touched him in his Herodias. Thus many love good preaching, if it keep far away from their beloved sin. But it is better that sinners persecute ministers now for faithfulness, than curse them eternally for unfaithfulness. The ways of God are unsearchable; but we may be sure he never can be at a loss to repay his servants for what they endure or lose for his sake. Death could not come so as to surprise this holy man; and the triumph of the wicked was short.

Verses 30–44

Let not ministers do any thing or teach any thing, but what they are willing should be told to their Lord. Christ notices the frights of some, and the toils of others of his disciples, and provides rest for those that are tired, and refuge for those that are terrified. The people sought the spiritual food of Christ's word, and then he took care that they should not want bodily food. If Christ and his disciples put up with mean things, surely we may. And this miracle shows that Christ came into the world, not only to restore, but to preserve and nourish spiritual life; in him there is enough for all that come. None are sent empty away from Christ but those who come to him full of themselves. Though Christ had bread enough at command, he teaches us not to waste any of God's bounties, remembering how many are in want. We may, some time, need the fragments that we now throw away.

Verses 45–56

The church is often like a ship at sea, tossed with tempests, and not comforted: we may have Christ for us, yet wind and tide against us; but it is a comfort to Christ's disciples in a storm, that their Master is in the heavenly mount, interceding for them. And no difficulties can hinder Christ's appearance for his people, when the set time is come. He silenced their fears, by making himself known to them. Our fears are soon satisfied, if our mistakes are set right, especially our mistakes as to Christ. Let the disciples have their Master with them, and all is well. It is for want of rightly understanding Christ's former works, that we view his present works as if there never were the like before. If Christ's ministers now could cure people's bodily diseases, what multitudes would flock after them! It is sad to think how much more most care about their bodies than about their souls.

Chapter 7

Chapter Outline	
The traditions of the elders.	(1–13)
What defiles the man.	(14–23)
The woman of Canaan's daughter cured.	(24–30)
Christ restores a man to hearing and speech.	(31–37)

Verses 1–13

One great design of Christ's coming was, to set aside the ceremonial law; and to make way for this, he rejects the ceremonies men added to the law of God's making. Those clean hands and that pure heart which Christ bestows on his disciples, and requires of them, are very different from the outward and superstitious forms of Pharisees of every age. Jesus reproves them for rejecting the commandment of God. It is clear that it is the duty of children, if their parents are poor, to relieve them as far as they are able; and if children deserve to die that curse their parents, much more those that starve them. But if a man conformed to the traditions of the Pharisees, they found a device to free him from the claim of this duty.

Verses 14–23

Our wicked thoughts and affections, words and actions, defile us, and these only. As a corrupt fountain sends forth corrupt streams, so does a corrupt heart send forth corrupt reasonings, corrupt appetites and passions, and all the wicked words and actions that come from them. A spiritual understanding of the law of God, and a sense of the evil of sin, will cause a man to seek for the grace of the Holy Spirit, to keep down the evil thoughts and affections that work within.

Verses 24–30

Christ never put any from him that fell at his feet, which a poor trembling soul may do. As she was a good woman, so a good mother. This sent her to Christ. His saying, Let the children first be filled, shows that there was mercy for the Gentiles, and not far off. She spoke, not as making light of the mercy, but magnifying the abundance of miraculous cures among the Jews, in comparison with which a single cure was but as a crumb. Thus, while proud Pharisees are left by the blessed Saviour, he manifests his compassion to poor humbled sinners, who look to him for children's bread. He still goes about to seek and save the lost.

Verses 31–37

Here is a cure of one that was deaf and dumb. Those who brought this poor man to Christ, besought him to observe the case, and put forth his power. Our Lord used more outward actions in the doing of this cure than usual. These were only signs of Christ's power to cure the man, to encourage his faith, and theirs that brought him. Though we find great variety in the cases and manner of relief of those who applied to Christ, yet all obtained the relief they sought. Thus it still is in the great concerns of our souls.

Chapter 8

Chapter Outline	
Four thousand fed by a miracle.	(1–10)
Christ cautions against the Pharisees and Herodians.	(11–21)
A blind man healed.	(22–26)
Peter's testimony to Christ.	(27–33)
Christ must be followed.	(34–38)

Verses 1–10

Our Lord Jesus encouraged the meanest to come to him for life and grace. Christ knows and considers our frames. The bounty of Christ is always ready; to show that, he repeated this miracle. His favours are renewed, as our wants and necessities are. And those need not fear want, who have Christ to live upon by faith, and do so with thanksgiving.

Verses 11–21

Obstinate unbelief will have something to say, though ever so unreasonable. Christ refused to answer their demand. If they will not be convinced, they shall not. Alas! what cause we have to lament for those around us, who destroy themselves and others by their perverse and obstinate unbelief, and enmity to the gospel! When we forget the works of God, and distrust him, we should chide ourselves severely, as Christ here reproves his disciples. How is it that we so often mistake his meaning, disregard his warnings, and distrust his providence?

Verses 22–26

Here is a blind man brought to Christ by his friends. Therein appeared the faith of those that brought him. If those who are spiritually blind, do not pray for themselves, yet their friends and relations should pray for them, that Christ would be pleased to touch them. The cure was wrought gradually, which was not usual in our Lord's miracles. Christ showed in what method those commonly are healed by his grace, who by nature are spiritually blind. At first, their knowledge is confused; but, like the light of the morning, it shines more and more to the perfect day, and then they see all things clearly. Slighting Christ's favours is forfeiting them; and he will make those who do so know the worth of privileges by the want of them.

Verses 27–33

These things are written, that we may believe that Jesus is the Christ, the Son of God. These miracles of our Lord assure us that he was not conquered, but a Conqueror. Now the disciples are convinced that Jesus is the Christ; they may bear to hear of his sufferings, of which Christ here begins to give them notice. He sees that amiss in what we say and do, of which we ourselves are not aware, and knows what manner of spirit we are of, when we ourselves do not. The wisdom of man is folly, when it pretends to limit the Divine counsels. Peter did not rightly understand the nature of Christ's kingdom.

Verses 34–38

Frequent notice is taken of the great flocking there was to Christ for help in various cases. All are concerned to know this, if they expect him to heal their souls. They must not indulge the ease of the body. As the happiness of heaven with Christ, is enough to make up for the loss of life itself for him, so the gain of all the world in sin, will not make up for the ruin of the soul by sin. And there is a day coming, when the cause of Christ will appear as glorious, as some now think it mean and contemptible. May we think of that season, and view every earthly object as we shall do at that great day.

Chapter 9

Chapter Outline	
The transfiguration.	(1–13)
An evil spirit cast out.	(14–29)

The apostles reproved.	(30–40)
Pain to be preferred to sin.	(41–50)

Verses 1–13

Here is a prediction of the near approach Christ's kingdom. A glimpse of that kingdom was given in the transfiguration of Christ. It is good to be away from the world, and alone with Christ: and how good to be with Christ glorified in heaven with all the saints! But when it is well with us, we are apt not to care for others, and in the fulness of our enjoyments, we forget the many wants of our brethren. God owns Jesus, and accepts him as his beloved Son, and is ready to accept us in him. Therefore we must own and accept him as our beloved Saviour, and must give up ourselves to be ruled by him. Christ does not leave the soul, when joys and comforts leave it. Jesus explained to the disciples the prophecy about Elias. This was very suitable to the ill usage of John Baptist.

Verses 14–29

The father of the suffering youth reflected on the want of power in the disciples; but Christ will have him reckon the disappointment to the want of faith. Very much is promised to our believing. If thou canst believe, it is possible that thy hard heart may be softened, thy spiritual diseases may be cured; and, weak as thou art, thou mayest be able to hold out to the end. Those that complain of unbelief, must look up to Christ for grace to help them against it, and his grace will be sufficient for them. Whom Christ cures, he cures effectually. But Satan is unwilling to be driven from those that have been long his slaves, and, when he cannot deceive or destroy the sinner, he will cause him all the terror that he can. The disciples must not think to do their work always with the same ease; some services call for more than ordinary pains.

Verses 30–40

The time of Christ's suffering drew nigh. Had he been delivered into the hands of devils, and they had done this, it had not been so strange; but that men should thus shamefully treat the Son of man, who came to redeem and save them, is wonderful. Still observe that when Christ spake of his death, he always spake of his resurrection, which took the reproach of it from himself, and should have taken the grief of it from his disciples. Many remain ignorant because they are ashamed to inquire. Alas! that while the Saviour teaches so plainly the things which belong to his love and grace, men are so blinded that they understand not his sayings. We shall be called to account about our discourses, and to account for our disputes, especially about being greater than others. Those who are most humble and self-denying, most resemble Christ, and shall be most tenderly owned by him. This Jesus taught them by a sign; whoever shall receive one like this child, receives me. Many have been like the disciples, ready to silence men who have success in preaching to sinners repentance in Christ's name, because they follow not with them. Our Lord blamed the apostles, reminding them that he who wrought miracles in his name would not be likely to hurt his cause. If sinners are brought to repent, to believe in the Saviour, and to live sober, righteous, and godly lives, we then see that the Lord works by the preacher.

Verses 41–50

It is repeatedly said of the wicked, Their worm dieth not, as well as, The fire is never quenched. Doubtless, remorse of conscience and keen self-reflection are this never-dying worm. Surely it is beyond compare better to undergo all possible pain, hardship, and self-denial here, and to be happy for ever hereafter, than to enjoy all kinds of worldly pleasure for a season, and to be miserable for ever. Like the sacrifices, we must be salted with salt; our corrupt affections must be subdued and mortified by the Holy Spirit. Those that have the salt of grace, must show they have a living principle of grace in their hearts, which works out corrupt dispositions in the soul that would offend God, or our own consciences.

Chapter 10

Chapter Outline	
The Pharisees' question concerning divorce.	(1–12)
Christ's love to little children.	(13–16)
Christ's discourse with the rich young man.	(17–22)
The hinderance of riches.	(23–31)
Christ foretells his sufferings.	(32–45)
Bartimeus healed.	(46–52)

Verses 1–12

Wherever Jesus was, the people flocked after him in crowds, and he taught them. Preaching was Christ's constant practice. He here shows that the reason why Moses' law allowed divorce, was such that they ought not to use the permission; it was only for the hardness of their hearts. God himself joined man and wife together; he has fitted them to be comforts and helps for each other. The bond which God has tied, is not to be lightly untied. Let those who are for putting away their wives consider what would become of themselves, if God should deal with them in like manner.

Verses 13–16

Some parents or nurses brought little children to Christ, that he should touch them, in token of his blessing them. It does not appear that they needed bodily cures, nor were they capable of being taught: but those who had the care of them believed that Christ's blessing would do their souls good; therefore they brought them to him. Jesus ordered that they should be brought to him, and that nothing should be said or done to hinder it. Children should be directed to the Saviour as soon as they are able to understand his words. Also, we must receive the kingdom of God as little children; we must stand affected to Christ and his grace, as little children to their parents, nurses, and teachers.

Verses 17–22

This young ruler showed great earnestness. He asked what he should do now, that he might be happy for ever. Most ask for good to be had in this world; any good, Ps **4**:**6**; he asks for good to be done in this world, in order to enjoy the greatest good in the other world. Christ encouraged this address by assisting his faith, and by directing his practice. But here is a sorrowful parting between Jesus and this young man. He asks Christ what he shall do more than he has done, to obtain eternal life; and Christ puts it to him, whether he has indeed that firm belief of, and that high value for eternal life which he seems to have. Is he willing to bear a present cross, in expectation of future crown? The young man was sorry he could not be a follower of Christ upon easier terms; that he could not lay hold on eternal life, and keep hold of his worldly possessions too. He went away grieved. See Mt **6**:**24**, Ye cannot serve God and mammon.

Verses 23–31

Christ took this occasion to speak to his disciples about the difficulty of the salvation of those who have abundance of this world. Those who thus eagerly seek the wealth of the world, will never rightly prize Christ and his grace. Also, as to the greatness of the salvation of those who have but little of this world, and leave it for Christ. The greatest trial of a good man's constancy is, when love to Jesus calls him to give up love to friends and relatives. Even when gainers by Christ, let them still expect to suffer for him, till they reach heaven. Let us learn contentment in a low state, and to watch against the love of riches in a high one. Let us pray to be enabled to part with all, if required, in Christ's service, and to use all we are allowed to keep in his service.

Verses 32–45

Christ's going on with his undertaking for the salvation of mankind, was, is, and will be, the wonder of all his disciples. Worldly honour is a glittering thing, with which the eyes of Christ's own disciples have many times been dazzled. Our care must be, that we may have wisdom and grace to know how to suffer with him; and we may trust him to provide what the degrees of our glory shall be. Christ shows them that dominion was generally abused in the world. If Jesus would gratify all our desires, it would soon appear that we desire fame or authority, and are unwilling to taste of his cup, or to have his baptism; and should often be ruined by having our prayers answered. But he loves us, and will only give his people what is good for them.

Verses 46–52

Bartimeus had heard of Jesus and his miracles, and learning that he was passing by, hoped to recover his eyesight. In coming to Christ for help and healing, we should look to him as the promised Messiah. The gracious calls Christ gives us to come to him, encourage our hope, that if we come to him we shall have what we come for. Those who would come to Jesus, must cast away the garment of their own sufficiency, must free themselves from every weight, and the sin that, like long garments, most easily besets them, Heb **12**:**1**. He begged that his eyes might be opened. It is very desirable to be able to earn our bread; and where God has given men limbs and senses, it is a shame, by foolishness and slothfulness, to make themselves, in effect, blind and lame. His eyes were opened. Thy faith has made thee whole: faith in Christ as the Son of David, and in his pity and power; not thy repeated words, but thy faith; Christ setting thy faith to work. Let sinners be exhorted to imitate blind Bartimeus. Where the gospel is preached, or the written words of truth circulated, Jesus is passing by, and this is the opportunity. It is not enough to come to Christ for spiritual healing, but, when we are healed, we must continue to follow him; that we may honour him, and receive instruction from him. Those who have spiritual eyesight, see that beauty in Christ which will draw them to run after him.

Chapter 11

Chapter Outline	
Christ's triumphant entry into Jerusalem.	(1–11)
The barren fig-tree cursed, The temple cleansed.	(12–18)
Prayer in faith.	(19–26)
The priests and elders questioned concerning John the Baptist.	(27–33)

Verses 1–11

Christ's coming into Jerusalem thus remarkably, shows that he was not afraid of the power and malice of his enemies. This would encourage his disciples who were full of fear. Also, that he was not disquieted at the thoughts of his approaching sufferings. But all marked his humiliation; and these matters teach us not to mind high things, but to condescend to those of low estate. How ill it becomes Christians to take state, when Christ was so far from claiming it! They welcomed his person; Blessed is he that cometh, the "He that should come," so often promised, so long expected; he comes in the name of the Lord. Let him have our best affections; he is a blessed Saviour, and brings blessings to us, and blessed be He that sent him. Praises be to our God, who is in the highest heavens, over all, God blessed for ever.

Verses 12–18

Christ looked to find some fruit, for the time of gathering figs, though it was near, was not yet come; but he found none. He made this fig-tree an example, not to the trees, but to the men of that generation. It was a figure of the doom upon the Jewish church, to which he came seeking fruit, but found none. Christ went to the temple, and began to reform the abuses in its courts, to show that when the Redeemer came to Zion, it was to turn away ungodliness from Jacob. The scribes and the chief priests sought, not how they might make their peace with him, but how they might destroy him. A desperate attempt, which they could not but fear was fighting against God.

Verses 19–26

The disciples could not think why that fig-tree should so soon wither away; but all wither who reject Christ; it represented the state of the Jewish church. We should rest in no religion that does not make us fruitful in good works. Christ taught them from hence to pray in faith. It may be applied to that mighty faith with which all true Christians are endued, and which does wonders in spiritual things. It justifies us, and so removes mountains of guilt, never to rise up in judgment against us. It purifies the heart, and so removes mountains of corruption, and makes them plain before the grace of God. One great errand to the throne of grace is to pray for the pardon of our sins; and care about this ought to be our daily concern.

Verses 27–33

Our Saviour shows how near akin his doctrine and baptism were to those of John; they had the same design and tendency, to bring in the gospel kingdom. These elders did not deserve to be taught; for it was plain that they contended not for truth, but victory: nor did he need to tell them; for the works he did, told them plainly he had authority from God; since no man could do the miracles which he did, unless God were with him.

Chapter 12

Chapter Outline	
The parable of the vineyard and husbandmen.	(1–12)
Question about tribute.	(13–17)
Concerning the resurrection.	(18–27)
The great command of the law.	(28–34)
Christ the Son and yet the Lord of David.	(35–40)
The poor widow commended.	(41–44)

Verses 1–12

Christ showed in parables, that he would lay aside the Jewish church. It is sad to think what base usage God's faithful ministers have met with in all ages, from those who have enjoyed the privileges of the church, but have not brought forth fruit answerable. God at length sent his Son, his Well-beloved; and it might be expected that he whom their Master loved, they also should respect and love; but instead of honouring him because he was the Son and Heir, they therefore hated him. But the exaltation of Christ was the Lord's doing; and it is his doing to exalt him in our hearts, and to set up his throne there; and if this be done, it cannot but be marvellous in our eyes. The Scriptures, and faithful preachers, and the coming of Christ in the flesh, call on us to render due praise to God in our lives. Let sinners beware of a proud, carnal spirit; if they revile or despise the preachers of Christ, they would have done so their Master, had they lived when he was upon earth.

Verses 13–17

The enemies of Christ would be thought desirous to know their duty, when really they hoped that which soever side he took of the question, they might find occasion to accuse him. Nothing is more likely to insnare the followers of Christ, than bringing them to meddle with disputes about worldly politics. Jesus avoided the snare, by referring to the submission they had already made as a nation; and all that heard him, marvelled at the great wisdom of his answer. Many will praise the words of a sermon, who will not be commanded by the doctrines of it.

Verses 18–27

A right knowledge of the Scripture, as the fountain whence all revealed religion now flows, and the foundation on which it is built, is the best preservative against error. Christ put aside the objection of the Sadducees, who were the scoffing infidels of that day, by setting the doctrine of the future state in a true light. The relation between husband and wife, though appointed in the earthly paradise, will not be known in the heavenly one. It is no wonder if we confuse ourselves with foolish errors, when we form our ideas of the world of spirits by the affairs of this world of sense. It is absurd to think that the living God should be the portion and happiness of a man if he is for ever dead; and therefore it is certain that Abraham's soul exists and acts, though now for a time separate from the body. Those that deny the resurrection greatly err, and ought to be told so. Let us seek to pass through this dying world, with a joyful hope of eternal happiness, and of a glorious resurrection.

Verses 28–34

Those who sincerely desire to be taught their duty, Christ will guide in judgment, and teach his way. He tells the scribe that the great commandment, which indeed includes all, is, that of loving God with all our hearts. Wherever this is the ruling principle in the soul, there is a disposition to every other duty. Loving God with all our heart, will engage us to every thing by which he will be pleased. The sacrifices only represented the atonements for men's transgressions of the moral law; they were of no power except as they expressed repentance and faith in the promised Saviour, and as they led to moral obedience. And because we have not thus loved God and man, but the very reverse, therefore we are condemned sinners; we need repentance, and we need mercy. Christ approved what the scribe said, and encouraged him. He stood fair for further advance; for this knowledge of the law leads to conviction of sin, to repentance, to discovery of our need of mercy, and understanding the way of justification by Christ.

Verses 35–40

When we attend to what the Scriptures declare, as to the person and offices of Christ, we shall be led to confess him as our Lord and

God; to obey him as our exalted Redeemer. If the common people hear these things gladly, while the learned and distinguished oppose, the former are happy, and the latter to be pitied. And as sin, disguised with a show of piety, is double iniquity, so its doom will be doubly heavy.

Verses 41–44

Let us not forget that Jesus still sees the treasury. He knows how much, and from what motives, men give to his cause. He looks at the heart, and what our views are, in giving alms; and whether we do it as unto the Lord, or only to be seen of men. It is so rare to find any who would not blame this widow, that we cannot expect to find many who will do like to her; and yet our Saviour commends her, therefore we are sure that she did well and wisely. The feeble efforts of the poor to honour their Saviour, will be commended in that day, when the splendid actions of unbelievers will be exposed to contempt.

Chapter 13

Chapter Outline	
The destruction of the temple foretold.	(1–4)
Christ's prophetic declaration.	(5–13)
Christ's prophecy.	(14–23)
His prophetic declarations.	(24–27)
Watchfulness urged.	(28–37)

Verses 1–4

See how little Christ values outward pomp, where there is not real purity of heart. He looks with pity upon the ruin of precious souls, and weeps over them, but we do not find him look with pity upon the ruin of a fine house. Let us then be reminded how needful it is for us to have a more lasting abode in heaven, and to be prepared for it by the influences of the Holy Spirit, sought in the earnest use of all the means of grace.

Verses 5–13

Our Lord Jesus, in reply to the disciples' question, does not so much satisfy their curiosity as direct their consciences. When many are deceived, we should thereby be awakened to look to ourselves. And the disciples of Christ, if it be not their own fault, may enjoy holy security and peace of mind, when all around is in disorder. But they must take heed that they are not drawn away from Christ and their duty to him, by the sufferings they will meet with for his sake. They shall be hated of all men: trouble enough! Yet the work they were called to should be carried on and prosper. Though they may be crushed and borne down, the gospel cannot be. The salvation promised is more than deliverance from evil, it is everlasting blessedness.

Verses 14–23

The Jews in rebelling against the Romans, and in persecuting the Christians, hastened their own ruin apace. Here we have a prediction of that ruin which came upon them within less than forty years after this. Such destruction and desolation, that the like cannot be found in any history. Promises of power to persevere, and cautions against falling away, well agree with each other. But the more we consider these things, the more we shall see abundant cause to flee without delay for refuge to Christ, and to renounce every earthly object, for the salvation of our souls.

Verses 24–27

The disciples had confounded the destruction of Jerusalem and the end of the world. This mistake Christ set right, and showed that the day of Christ's coming, and the day of judgment, shall be after that tribulation. Here he foretells the final dissolution of the present frame and fabric of the world. Also, the visible appearance of the Lord Jesus coming in the clouds, and the gathering together of all the elect to him.

Verses 28–37

We have the application of this prophetic sermon. As to the destruction of Jerusalem, expect it to come very shortly. As to the end of the world, do not inquire when it will come, for of that day and that hour knoweth no man. Christ, as God, could not be ignorant of anything; but the Divine wisdom which dwelt in our Saviour, communicated itself to his human soul according to the Divine pleasure. As to both, our duty is to watch and pray. Our Lord Jesus, when he ascended on high, left something for all his servants to do. We ought to be always upon our watch, in expectation of his return. This applies to Christ's coming to us at our death, as well as to the general judgment. We know not whether our Master will come in the days of youth, or middle age, or old age; but, as soon as we are born, we begin to die, and therefore we must expect death. Our great care must be, that, whenever our Lord comes, he may not find us secure, indulging in ease and sloth, mindless of our work and duty. He says to all, Watch, that you may be found in peace, without spot, and blameless.

Chapter 14

Chapter Outline	
Christ anointed at Bethany.	(1–11)
The passover, Jesus declares that Judas would betray him.	(12–21)

The Lord's supper instituted.	(22–31)
Christ's agony in the garden.	(32–42)
He is betrayed and taken.	(43–52)
Christ before the high priest.	(53–65)
Peter denies Christ.	(66–72)

Verses 1–11

Did Christ pour out his soul unto death for us, and shall we think any thing too precious for him? Do we give him the precious ointment of our best affections? Let us love him with all the heart, though it is common for zeal and affection to be misunderstood and blamed; and remember that charity to the poor will not excuse any from particular acts of piety to the Lord Jesus. Christ commended this woman's pious attention to the notice of believers in all ages. Those who honour Christ he will honour. Covetousness was Judas' master lust, and that betrayed him to the sin of betraying his Master; the devil suited his temptation to that, and so conquered him. And see what wicked contrivances many have in their sinful pursuits; but what appears to forward their plans, will prove curses in the end.

Verses 12–21

Nothing could be less the result of human foresight than the events here related. But our Lord knows all things about us before they come to pass. If we admit him, he will dwell in our hearts. The Son of man goes, as it is written of him, as a lamb to the slaughter; but woe to that man by whom he is betrayed! God's permitting the sins of men, and bringing glory to himself out of them, does not oblige them to sin; nor will this be any excuse for their guilt, or lessen their punishment.

Verses 22–31

The Lord's supper is food for the soul, therefore a very little of that which is for the body, as much as will serve for a sign, is enough. It was instituted by the example and the practice of our Master, to remain in force till his second coming. It was instituted with blessing and giving of thanks, to be a memorial of Christ's death. Frequent mention is made of his precious blood, as the price of our redemption. How comfortable is this to poor repenting sinners, that the blood of Christ is shed for many! If for many, why not for me? It was a sign of the conveyance of the benefits purchased for us by his death. Apply the doctrine of Christ crucified to yourselves; let it be meat and drink to your souls, strengthening and refreshing your spiritual life. It was to be an earnest and foretaste of the happiness of heaven, and thereby to put us out of taste for the pleasures and delights of sense. Every one that has tasted spiritual delights, straightway desires eternal ones. Though the great Shepherd passed through his sufferings without one false step, yet his followers often have been scattered by the small measure of sufferings allotted to them. How very apt we are to think well of ourselves, and to trust our own hearts! It was ill done of Peter thus to answer his Master, and not with fear and trembling. Lord, give me grace to keep me from denying thee.

Verses 32–42

Christ's sufferings began with the sorest of all, those in his soul. He began to be sorely amazed; words not used in St. Matthew, but very full of meaning. The terrors of God set themselves in array against him, and he allowed him to contemplate them. Never was sorrow like unto his at this time. Now he was made a curse for us; the curses of the law were laid upon him as our Surety. He now tasted death, in all the bitterness of it. This was that fear of which the apostle speaks, the natural fear of pain and death, at which human nature startles. Can we ever entertain favourable, or even slight thoughts of sin, when we see the painful sufferings which sin, though but reckoned to him, brought on the Lord Jesus? Shall that sit light upon our souls, which sat so heavy upon his? Was Christ in such agony for our sins, and shall we never be in agony about them? How should we look upon Him whom we have pierced, and mourn! It becomes us to be exceedingly sorrowful for sin, because He was so, and never to mock at it. Christ, as Man, pleaded, that, if it were possible, his sufferings might pass from him. As Mediator, he submitted to the will of God, saying, Nevertheless, not what I will, but what thou wilt; I bid it welcome. See how the sinful weakness of Christ's disciples returns, and overpowers them. What heavy clogs these bodies of ours are to our souls! But when we see trouble at the door, we should get ready for it. Alas, even believers often look at the Redeemer's sufferings in a drowsy manner, and instead of being ready to die with Christ, they are not even prepared to watch with him one hour.

Verses 43–52

Because Christ appeared not as a temporal prince, but preached repentance, reformation, and a holy life, and directed men's thoughts, and affections, and aims to another world, therefore the Jewish rulers sought to destroy him. Peter wounded one of the band. It is easier to fight for Christ than to die for him. But there is a great difference between faulty disciples and hypocrites. The latter rashly and without thought call Christ Master, and express great affection for him, yet betray him to his enemies. Thus they hasten their own destruction.

Verses 53–65

We have here Christ's condemnation before the great council of the Jews. Peter followed; but the high priest's fire-side was no proper place, nor his servants proper company, for Peter: it was an entrance into temptation. Great diligence was used to procure false witnesses against Jesus, yet their testimony was not equal to the charge of a capital crime, by the utmost stretch of their law. He was asked, Art thou the Son of the Blessed? that is, the Son of God. For the proof of his being the Son of God, he refers to his second coming. In these outrages we have proofs of man's enmity to God, and of God's free and unspeakable love to man.

Verses 66–72

Peter's denying Christ began by keeping at a distance from him. Those that are shy of godliness, are far in the way to deny Christ. Those who think it dangerous to be in company with Christ's disciples, because thence they may be drawn in to suffer for him, will find it much more dangerous to be in company with his enemies, because there they may be drawn in to sin against him. When Christ was admired and flocked after, Peter readily owned him; but will own no relation to him now he is deserted and despised. Yet observe, Peter's repentance was very speedy. Let him that thinketh he standeth take heed lest he fall; and let him that has fallen think of these things, and of his own offences, and return to the Lord with weeping and supplication, seeking forgiveness, and to be raised up by the Holy Spirit.

Chapter 15

Chapter Outline	
Christ before Pilate.	(1–14)
Christ led to be crucified.	(15–21)
The crucifixion.	(22–32)
The death of Christ.	(33–41)
His body buried.	(42–47)

Verses 1–14

They bound Christ. It is good for us often to remember the bonds of the Lord Jesus, as bound with him who was bound for us. By delivering up the King, they, in effect, delivered up the kingdom of God, which was, therefore, as by their own consent, taken from them, and given to another nation. Christ gave Pilate a direct answer, but would not answer the witnesses, because the things they alleged were known to be false, even Pilate himself was convinced they were so. Pilate thought that he might appeal from the priests to the people, and that they would deliver Jesus out of the priests' hands. But they were more and more urged by the priests, and cried, Crucify him! Crucify him! Let us judge of persons and things by their merits, and the standard of God's word, and not by common report. The thought that no one ever was so shamefully treated, as the only perfectly wise, holy, and excellent Person that ever appeared on earth, leads the serious mind to strong views of man's wickedness and enmity to God. Let us more and more abhor the evil dispositions which marked the conduct of these persecutors.

Verses 15–21

Christ met death in its greatest terror. It was the death of the vilest malefactors. Thus the cross and the shame are put together. God having been dishonoured by the sin of man, Christ made satisfaction by submitting to the greatest disgrace human nature could be loaded with. It was a cursed death; thus it was branded by the Jewish law, De **21**:**23**. The Roman soldiers mocked our Lord Jesus as a King; thus in the high priest's hall the servants had mocked him as a Prophet and Saviour. Shall a purple or scarlet robe be matter of pride to a Christian, which was matter of reproach and shame to Christ? He wore the crown of thorns which we deserved, that we might wear the crown of glory which he merited. We were by sin liable to everlasting shame and contempt; to deliver us, our Lord Jesus submitted to shame and contempt. He was led forth with the workers of iniquity, though he did no sin. The sufferings of the meek and holy Redeemer, are ever a source of instruction to the believer, of which, in his best hours, he cannot be weary. Did Jesus thus suffer, and shall I, a vile sinner, fret or repine? Shall I indulge anger, or utter reproaches and threats because of troubles and injuries?

Verses 22–32

The place where our Lord Jesus was crucified, was called the place of a scull; it was the common place of execution; for he was in all respects numbered with the transgressors. Whenever we look unto Christ crucified, we must remember what was written over his head; he is a King, and we must give up ourselves to be his subjects, as Israelites indeed. They crucified two thieves with him, and him in the midst; they thereby intended him great dishonour. But it was foretold that he should be numbered with the transgressors, because he was made sin for us. Even those who passed by railed at him. They told him to come down from the cross, and they would believe; but they did not believe, though he gave them a more convincing sign when he came up from the grave. With what earnestness will the man who firmly believes the truth, as made known by the sufferings of Christ, seek for salvation! With what gratitude will he receive the dawning hope of forgiveness and eternal life, as purchased for him by the sufferings and death of the Son of God! and with what godly sorrow will he mourn over the sins which crucified the Lord of glory!

Verses 33–41

There was a thick darkness over the land, from noon until three in the afternoon. The Jews were doing their utmost to extinguish the Sun of Righteousness. The darkness signified the cloud which the human soul of Christ was under, when he was making it an offering for sin. He did not complain that his disciples forsook him, but that his Father forsook him. In this especially he was made sin for us. When Paul was to be offered as a sacrifice for the service saints, he could joy and rejoice, Php **2**:**17**; but it is another thing to be offered as a sacrifice for the sin of sinners. At the same instant that Jesus died, the veil of the temple was rent from the top to the bottom. This spake terror to the unbelieving Jews, and was a sign of the destruction of their church and nation. It speaks comfort to all believing Christians, for it signified the laying open a new and living way into the holiest by the blood of Jesus. The confidence with which Christ had openly addressed God as his Father, and committed his soul into his hands, seems greatly to have affected the centurion. Right views of Christ crucified will reconcile the believer to the thought of death; he longs to behold, love, and praise, as he ought, that Saviour who was wounded and pierced to save him from the wrath to come.

Verses 42–47

We are here attending the burial of our Lord Jesus. Oh that we may by grace be planted in the likeness of it! Joseph of Arimathea was one who waited for the kingdom of God. Those who hope for a share in its privileges, must own Christ's cause, when it seems to be crushed. This man God raised up for his service. There was a special providence, that Pilate should be so strict in his inquiry, that there might be no pretence to say Jesus was alive. Pilate gave Joseph leave to take down the body, and do what he pleased with it. Some of the women beheld where Jesus was laid, that they might come after the sabbath to anoint the dead body, because they had not time to do it before. Special notice was taken of Christ's sepulchre, because he was to rise again. And he will not forsake those who trust in him, and call upon him. Death, deprived of its sting, will soon end the believer's sorrows, as it ended those of the Saviour.

Chapter 16

Chapter Outline	
Christ's resurrection made known the women.	(1–8)
Christ appears to Mary Magdalene and other disciples.	(9–13)
His commission to the apostles.	(14–18)
Christ's ascension.	(19, 20)

Verses 1–8

Nicodemus brought a large quantity of spices, but these good women did not think that enough. The respect others show to Christ, should not hinder us from showing our respect. And those who are carried by holy zeal, to seek Christ diligently, will find the difficulties in their way speedily vanish. When we put ourselves to trouble and expense, from love to Christ, we shall be accepted, though our endeavours are not successful. The sight of the angel might justly have encouraged them, but they were affrighted. Thus many times that which should be matter of comfort to us, through our own mistake, proves a terror to us. He was crucified, but he is glorified. He is risen, he is not here, not dead, but alive again; hereafter you will see him, but you may here see the place where he was laid. Thus seasonable comforts will be sent to those that lament after the Lord Jesus. Peter is particularly named, Tell Peter; it will be most welcome to him, for he is in sorrow for sin. A sight of Christ will be very welcome to a true penitent, and a true penitent is very welcome to a sight of Christ. The men ran with all the haste they could to the disciples; but disquieting fears often hinder us from doing that service to Christ and to the souls of men, which, if faith and the joy of faith were strong, we might do.

Verses 9–13

Better news cannot be brought to disciples in tears, than to tell them of Christ's resurrection. And we should study to comfort disciples that are mourners, by telling them whatever we have seen of Christ. It was a wise providence that the proofs of Christ's resurrection were given gradually, and admitted cautiously, that the assurance with which the apostles preached this doctrine afterwards might the more satisfy. Yet how slowly do we admit the consolations which the word of God holds forth! Therefore while Christ comforts his people, he often sees it needful to rebuke and correct them for hardness of heart in distrusting his promise, as well as in not obeying his holy precepts.

Verses 14–18

The evidences of the truth of the gospel are so full, that those who receive it not, may justly be upbraided with their unbelief. Our blessed Lord renewed his choice of the eleven as his apostles, and commissioned them to go into all the world, to preach his gospel to every creature. Only he that is a true Christian shall be saved through Christ. Simon Magus professed to believe, and was baptized, yet he was declared to be in the bonds of iniquity: see his history in Ac **8**:**13**–**25**. Doubtless this is a solemn declaration of that true faith which receives Christ in all his characters and offices, and for all the purposes of salvation, and which produces its right effect on the heart and life; not a mere assent, which is a dead faith, and cannot profit. The commission of Christ's ministers extends to every creature throughout the world, and the declarations of the gospel contain not only truths, encouragements, and precepts, but also most awful warnings. Observe what power the apostles should be endued with, for confirming the doctrine they were to preach. These were miracles to confirm the truth of the gospel, and means of spreading the gospel among nations that had not heard it.

Verses 19, 20

After the Lord had spoken he went up into heaven. Sitting is a posture of rest, he had finished his work; and a posture of rule, he took possession of his kingdom. He sat at the right hand of God, which denotes his sovereign dignity and universal power. Whatever God does concerning us, gives to us, or accepts from us, it is by his Son. Now he is glorified with the glory he had before the world. The apostles went forth, and preached every where, far and near. Though the doctrine they preached was spiritual and heavenly, and directly contrary to the spirit and temper of the world; though it met with much opposition, and was wholly destitute of all worldly supports and advantages; yet in a few years the sound went forth unto the ends of the earth. Christ's ministers do not now need to work miracles to prove their message; the Scriptures are proved to be of Divine origin, and this renders those without excuse who reject or neglect them. The effects of the gospel, when faithfully preached, and truly believed, in changing the tempers and characters of mankind, form a constant proof, a miraculous proof, that the gospel is the power of God unto salvation, of all who believe.

Luke

This evangelist is generally supposed to have been a physician, and a companion of the apostle Paul. The style of his writings, and his acquaintance with the Jewish rites and usages, sufficiently show that he was a Jew, while his knowledge of the Greek language and his name, speak his Gentile origin. He is first mentioned Ac **16**:**10**, **11**, as with Paul at Troas, whence he attended him to Jerusalem, and was with him in his voyage, and in his imprisonment at Rome. This Gospel appears to be designed to supersede many defective and unauthentic narratives in circulation, and to give a genuine and inspired account of the life, miracles, and doctrines of our Lord, learned from those who heard and witnessed his discourses and miracles.

Chapter 1

Chapter Outline	
The Preface.	(1–4)

Zacharias and Elisabeth.	(5–25)
Christ's birth announced.	(26–38)
Interview of Mary and Elisabeth.	(39–56)
The birth of John the Baptist.	(57–66)
The song of Zacharias.	(67–80)

Verses 1–4

Luke will not write of things about which Christians may safely differ from one another, and hesitate within themselves; but the things which are, and ought to be surely believed. The doctrine of Christ is what the wisest and best of men have ventured their souls upon with confidence and satisfaction. And the great events whereon our hopes depend, have been recorded by those who were from the beginning eye-witnesses and ministers of the word, and who were perfected in their understanding of them through Divine inspiration.

Verses 5–25

The father and mother of John the Baptist were sinners as all are, and were justified and saved in the same way as others; but they were eminent for piety and integrity. They had no children, and it could not be expected that Elisabeth should have any in her old age. While Zacharias was burning incense in the temple, the whole multitude of the people were praying without. All the prayers we offer up to God, are acceptable and successful only by Christ's intercession in the temple of God above. We cannot expect an interest therein if we do not pray, and pray with our spirits, and are not earnest in prayer. Nor can we expect that the best of our prayers should gain acceptance, and bring an answer of peace, but through the mediation of Christ, who ever lives, making intercession. The prayers Zacharias often made, received an answer of peace. Prayers of faith are filed in heaven, and are not forgotten. Prayers made when we were young and entering into the world, may be answered when we are old and going out of the world. Mercies are doubly sweet that are given in answer to prayer. Zacharias shall have a son in his old age, who shall be instrumental in the conversion of many souls to God, and preparing them to receive the gospel of Christ. He shall go before Him with courage, zeal, holiness, and a mind dead to earthly interests and pleasures. The disobedient and rebellious would be brought back to the wisdom of their righteous forefathers, or rather, brought to attend to the wisdom of that Just One who was coming among them. Zacharias heard all that the angel said; but his unbelief spake. In striking him dumb, God dealt justly with him, because he had objected against God's word. We may admire the patience of God towards us. God dealt kindly with him, for thus he prevented his speaking any more distrustful, unbelieving words. Thus also God confirmed his faith. If by the rebukes we are under for our sin, we are brought to give the more credit to the word of God, we have no reason to complain. Even real believers are apt to dishonour God by unbelief; and their mouths are stopped in silence and confusion, when otherwise they would have been praising God with joy and gratitude. In God's gracious dealings with us we ought to observe his gracious regards to us. He has looked on us with compassion and favour, and therefore has thus dealt with us.

Verses 26–38

We have here an account of the mother of our Lord; though we are not to pray to her, yet we ought to praise God for her. Christ must be born miraculously. The angel's address means only, Hail, thou that art the especially chosen and favoured of the Most High, to attain the honour Jewish mothers have so long desired. This wondrous salutation and appearance troubled Mary. The angel then assured her that she had found favour with God, and would become the mother of a son whose name she should call Jesus, the Son of the Highest, one in a nature and perfection with the Lord God. JESUS! the name that refreshes the fainting spirits of humbled sinners; sweet to speak and sweet to hear, Jesus, a Saviour! We know not his riches and our own poverty, therefore we run not to him; we perceive not that we are lost and perishing, therefore a Saviour is a word of little relish. Were we convinced of the huge mass of guilt that lies upon us, and the wrath that hangs over us for it, ready to fall upon us, it would be our continual thought, Is the Saviour mine? And that we might find him so, we should trample on all that hinders our way to him. Mary's reply to the angel was the language of faith and humble admiration, and she asked no sign for the confirming her faith. Without controversy, great was the mystery of godliness, God manifest in the flesh, **1**Ti **3**:**16**. Christ's human nature must be produced so, as it was fit that should be which was to be taken into union with the Divine nature. And we must, as Mary here, guide our desires by the word of God. In all conflicts, let us remember that with God nothing is impossible; and as we read and hear his promises, let us turn them into prayers, Behold the willing servant of the Lord; let it be unto me according to thy word.

Verses 39–56

It is very good for those who have the work of grace begun in their souls, to communicate one to another. On Mary's arrival, Elisabeth was conscious of the approach of her who was to be the mother of the great Redeemer. At the same time she was filled with the Holy Ghost, and under his influence declared that Mary and her expected child were most blessed and happy, as peculiarly honoured of and dear to the Most High God. Mary, animated by Elisabeth's address, and being also under the influence of the Holy Ghost, broke out into joy, admiration, and gratitude. She knew herself to be a sinner who needed a Saviour, and that she could no otherwise rejoice in God than as interested in his salvation through the promised Messiah. Those who see their need of Christ, and are desirous of righteousness and life in him, he fills with good things, with the best things; and they are abundantly satisfied with the blessings he gives. He will satisfy the desires of the poor in spirit who long for spiritual blessings, while the self-sufficient shall be sent empty away.

Verses 57–66

In these **verse**s we have an account of the birth of John the Baptist, and the great joy among all the relations of the family. He shall be called Johanan, or "Gracious," because he shall bring in the gospel of Christ, wherein God's grace shines most bright. Zacharias recovered his speech. Unbelief closed his mouth, and believing opened it again: he believers, therefore he speaks. When God opens our lips, our mouths must show forth his praise; and better be without speech, than not use it in praising God. It is said, The hand of the Lord was working with John. God has ways of working on children in their infancy, which we cannot account for. We should observe the dealings of God, and wait the event.

Verses 67–80

Zacharias uttered a prophecy concerning the kingdom and salvation of the Messiah. The gospel brings light with it; in it the day dawns. In John the Baptist it began to break, and increased apace to the perfect day. The gospel is discovering; it shows that about which we were utterly in the dark; it is to give light to those that sit in darkness, the light of the knowledge of the glory of God in the face of Jesus Christ. It is reviving; it brings light to those that sit in the shadow of death, as condemned prisoners in the dungeon. It is directing; it is to guide our feet in the way of peace, into that way which will bring us to peace at last, Ro **3**:**17**. John gave proofs of strong faith, vigorous and holy affections, and of being above the fear and love of the world. Thus he ripened for usefulness; but he lived a retired life, till he came forward openly as the forerunner of the Messiah. Let us follow peace with all men, as well as seek peace with God and our own consciences. And if it be the will of God that we live unknown to the world, still let us diligently seek to grow strong in the grace of Jesus Christ.

Chapter 2

Chapter Outline	
The birth of Christ.	(1–7)
It is made known to the shepherds.	(8–20)
Christ presented in the temple.	(21–24)
Simeon prophesies concerning Jesus.	(25–35)
Anna prophesies concerning him.	(36–40)
Christ with the learned men in the temple.	(41–52)

Verses 1–7

The fulness of time was now come, when God would send forth his Son, made of a woman, and made under the law. The circumstances of his birth were very mean. Christ was born at an inn; he came into the world to sojourn here for awhile, as at an inn, and to teach us to do likewise. We are become by sin like an outcast infant, helpless and forlorn; and such a one was Christ. He well knew how unwilling we are to be meanly lodged, clothed, or fed; how we desire to have our children decorated and indulged; how apt the poor are to envy the rich, and how prone the rich to disdain the poor. But when we by faith view the Son of God being made man and lying in a manger, our vanity, ambition, and envy are checked. We cannot, with this object rightly before us, seek great things for ourselves or our children.

Verses 8–20

Angels were heralds of the new-born Saviour, but they were only sent to some poor, humble, pious, industrious shepherds, who were in the business of their calling, keeping watch over their flock. We are not out of the way of Divine visits, when we are employed in an honest calling, and abide with God in it. Let God have the honour of this work; Glory to God in the highest. God's good-will to men, manifested in sending the Messiah, redounds to his praise. Other works of God are for his glory, but the redemption of the world is for his glory in the highest. God's goodwill in sending the Messiah, brought peace into this lower world. Peace is here put for all that good which flows to us from Christ's taking our nature upon him. This is a faithful saying, attested by an innumerable company of angels, and well worthy of all acceptation. That the good-will of God toward men, is glory to God in the highest, and peace on the earth. The shepherds lost no time, but came with haste to the place. They were satisfied, and made known abroad concerning this child, that he was the Saviour, even Christ the Lord. Mary carefully observed and thought upon all these things, which were so suited to enliven her holy affections. We should be more delivered from errors in judgment and practice, did we more fully ponder these things in our hearts. It is still proclaimed in our ears that to us is born a Saviour, Christ the Lord. These should be glad tidings to all.

Verses 21–24

Our Lord Jesus was not born in sin, and did not need that mortification of a corrupt nature, or that renewal unto holiness, which were signified by circumcision. This ordinance was, in his case, a pledge of his future perfect obedience to the whole law, in the midst of sufferings and temptations, even unto death for us. At the end of forty days, Mary went up to the temple to offer the appointed sacrifices for her purification. Joseph also presented the holy child Jesus, because, as a first-born son, he was to be presented to the Lord, and redeemed according to the law. Let us present our children to the Lord who gave them to us, beseeching him to redeem them from sin and death, and make them holy to himself.

Verses 25–35

The same Spirit that provided for the support of Simeon's hope, provided for his joy. Those who would see Christ must go to his temple. Here is a confession of his faith, that this Child in his arms was the Saviour, the salvation itself, the salvation of God's appointing. He bids farewell to this world. How poor does this world look to one that has Christ in his arms, and salvation in his view! See here, how comfortable is the death of a good man; he departs in peace with God, peace with his own conscience, in peace with death. Those that have welcomed Christ, may welcome death. Joseph and Mary marvelled at the things which were spoken of this Child. Simeon shows them likewise, what reason they had to rejoice with trembling. And Jesus, his doctrine, and people, are still spoken against; his truth and holiness are still denied and blasphemed; his preached word is still the touchstone of men's characters. The secret good affections in the minds of some, will be revealed by their embracing Christ; the secret corruptions of others will be revealed by their enmity to Christ. Men will be judged by the thoughts of their hearts concerning Christ. He shall be a suffering Jesus; his mother shall suffer with him, because of the nearness of her relation and affection.

Verses 36–40

There was much evil then in the church, yet God left not himself without witness. Anna always dwelt in, or at least attended at, the temple. She was always in a praying spirit; gave herself to prayer, and in all things she served God. Those to whom Christ is made known, have great reason to thank the Lord. She taught others concerning him. Let the example of the venerable saints, Simeon and Anna, give courage to those whose hoary heads are, like theirs, a crown of glory, being found in the way of righteousness. The lips soon to be silent in the grave, should be showing forth the praises of the Redeemer. In all things it became Christ to be made like unto his brethren, therefore he passed through infancy and childhood as other children, yet without sin, and with manifest proofs of the Divine nature in him. By the Spirit of God all his faculties performed their offices in a manner not seen in any one else. Other children have foolishness bound in their hearts, which appears in what they say or do, but he was filled with wisdom, by the influence of the Holy Ghost; every thing he said and did, was wisely said and wisely done, above his years. Other children show the corruption of their nature; nothing but the grace of God was upon him.

Verses 41–52

It is for the honour of Christ that children should attend on public worship. His parents did not return till they had stayed all the seven days of the feast. It is well to stay to the end of an ordinance, as becomes those who say, It is good to be here. Those that have lost their comforts in Christ, and the evidences of their having a part in him, must bethink themselves where, and when, and how they lost them, and must turn back again. Those that would recover their lost acquaintance with Christ, must go to the place in which he has put his name; there they may hope to meet him. They found him in some part of the temple, where the doctors of the law kept their schools; he was sitting there, hearkening to their instructions, proposing questions, and answering inquiries, with such wisdom, that those who heard were delighted with him. Young persons should seek the knowledge of Divine truth, attend the ministry of the gospel, and ask such questions of their elders and teachers as may tend to increase their knowledge. Those who seek Christ in sorrow, shall find him with the greater joy. Know ye not that I ought to be in my Father's house; at my Father's work; I must be about my Father's business. Herein is an example; for it becomes the children of God, in conformity to Christ, to attend their heavenly Father's business, and make all other concerns give way to it. Though he was the Son of God, yet he was subject to his earthly parents; how then will the foolish and weak sons of men answer it, who are disobedient to their parents? However we may neglect men's sayings, because they are obscure, yet we must not think so of God's sayings. That which at first is dark, may afterwards become plain and easy. The greatest and wisest, those most eminent, may learn of this admirable and Divine Child, that it is the truest greatness of soul to know our own place and office; to deny ourselves amusements and pleasures not consistent with our state and calling.

Chapter 3

Chapter Outline	
John the Baptist's ministry.	(1–14)
John the Baptist testifies concerning Christ.	(15–20)
The baptism of Christ.	(21, 22)
The genealogy of Christ.	(23–38)

Verses 1–14

The scope and design of John's ministry were, to bring the people from their sins, and to their Saviour. He came preaching, not a sect, or party, but a profession; the sign or ceremony was washing with water. By the words here used John preached the necessity of repentance, in order to the remission of sins, and that the baptism of water was an outward sign of that inward cleansing and renewal of heart, which attend, or are the effects of true repentance, as well as a profession of it. Here is the fulfilling of the Scriptures, Isa **40**:**3**, in the ministry of John. When way is made for the gospel into the heart, by taking down high thoughts, and bringing them into obedience to Christ, by levelling the soul, and removing all that hinders us in the way of Christ and his grace, then preparation is made to welcome the salvation of God. Here are general warnings and exhortations which John gave. The guilty, corrupted race of mankind is become a generation of vipers; hateful to God, and hating one another. There is no way of fleeing from the wrath to come, but by repentance; and by the change of our way the change of our mind must be shown. If we are not really holy, both in heart and life, our profession of religion and relation to God and his church, will stand us in no stead at all; the sorer will our destruction be, if we do not bring forth fruits meet for repentance. John the Baptist gave instructions to several sorts of persons. Those that profess and promise repentance, must show it by reformation, according to their places and conditions. The gospel requires mercy, not sacrifice; and its design is, to engage us to do all the good we can, and to be just to all men. And the same principle which leads men to forego unjust gain, leads to restore that which is gained by wrong. John tells the soldiers their duty. Men should be cautioned against the temptations of their employments. These answers declared the present duty of the inquirers, and at once formed a test of their sincerity. As none can or will accept Christ's salvation without true repentance, so the evidence and effects of this repentance are here marked out.

Verses 15–20

John the Baptist disowned being himself the Christ, but confirmed the people in their expectations of the long-promised Messiah. He could only exhort them to repent, and assure them of forgiveness upon repentance; but he could not work repentance in them, nor confer remission on them. Thus highly does it become us to speak of Christ, and thus humbly of ourselves. John can do no more than baptize with water, in token that they ought to purify and cleanse themselves; but Christ can, and will baptize with the Holy Ghost; he can give the Spirit, to cleanse and purify the heart, not only as water washes off the dirt on the outside, but as fire clears out the dross that is within, and melts down the metal, that it may be cast into a new mould. John was an affectionate preacher; he was beseeching; he pressed things home upon his hearers. He was a practical preacher; quickening them to their duty, and directing them in it. He was a popular preacher; he addressed the people, according to their capacity. He was an evangelical preacher. In all his exhortations, he directed people to Christ. When we press duty upon people, we must direct them to Christ, both for righteousness and strength. He was a copious preacher; he shunned not to declare the whole counsel of God. But a full stop was put to John's preaching when he was in the midst of his usefulness. Herod being reproved by him for many evils, shut up John in prison. Those who injure the faithful servants of God, add still greater guilt to their other sins.

Verses 21, 22

Christ did not confess sin, as others did, for he had none to confess; but he prayed, as others did, and kept up communion with his Father. Observe, all the three voices from heaven, by which the Father bare witness to the Son, were pronounced while he was praying, or soon after, Lu **9**:**35**; Joh **12**:**28**. The Holy Ghost descended in a bodily shape like a dove upon him, and there came a voice from heaven, from God the Father, from the excellent glory. Thus was a proof of the Holy Trinity, of the Three Persons in the Godhead, given at the baptism of Christ.

Verses 23–38

Matthew's list of the forefathers of Jesus showed that Christ was the son of Abraham, in whom all the families of the earth are blessed, and heir to the throne of David; but Luke shows that Jesus was the Seed of the woman that should break the serpent's head, and traces the line up to Adam, beginning with Eli, or Heli, the father, not of Joseph, but of Mary. The seeming differences between the two evangelists in these lists of names have been removed by learned men. But our salvation does not depend upon our being able to solve these difficulties, nor is the Divine authority of the Gospels at all weakened by them. The list of names ends thus, "Who was the son of Adam, the son of God;" that is, the offspring of God by creation. Christ was both the son of Adam and the Son of God, that he might be a proper Mediator between God and the sons of Adam, and might bring the sons of Adam to be, through him, the sons of God. All flesh, as descended from the first Adam, is as grass, and withers as the flower of the field; but he who partakes of the Holy Spirit of life from the Second Adam, has that eternal happiness, which by the gospel is preached unto us.

Chapter 4

Chapter Outline	
The temptation of Christ.	(1–13)
Christ in the synagogue of Nazareth.	(14–30)
He casts out an unclean spirit and heals the sick.	(31–44)

Verses 1–13

Christ's being led into the wilderness gave an advantage to the tempter; for there he was alone, none were with him by whose prayers and advice he might be helped in the hour of temptation. He who knew his own strength might give Satan advantage; but we may not, who know our own weakness. Being in all things made like unto his brethren, Jesus would, like the other children of God, live in dependence upon the Divine Providence and promise. The word of God is our sword, and faith in that word is our shield. God has many ways of providing for his people, and therefore is at all times to be depended upon in the way of duty. All Satan's promises are deceitful; and if he is permitted to have any influence in disposing of the kingdoms of the world and the glory of them, he uses them as baits to insnare men to destruction. We should reject at once and with abhorrence, every opportunity of sinful gain or advancement, as a price offered for our souls; we should seek riches, honours, and happiness in the worship and service of God only. Christ will not worship Satan; nor, when he has the kingdoms of the world delivered to him by his Father, will he suffer any remains of the worship of the devil to continue in them. Satan also tempted Jesus to be his own murderer, by unfitting confidence in his Father's protection, such as he had no warrant for. Let not any abuse of Scripture by Satan or by men abate our esteem, or cause us to abandon its use; but let us study it still, seek to know it, and seek our defence from it in all kinds of assaults. Let this word dwell richly in us, for it is our life. Our victorious Redeemer conquered, not for himself only, but for us also. The devil ended all the temptation. Christ let him try all his force, and defeated him. Satan saw it was to no purpose to attack Christ, who had nothing in him for his fiery darts to fasten upon. And if we resist the devil, he will flee from us. Yet he departed but till the season when he was again to be let loose upon Jesus, not as a tempter, to draw him to sin, and so to strike at his head, at which he now aimed and was wholly defeated in; but as a persecutor, to bring Christ to suffer, and so to bruise his heel, which it was told him, he should have to do, and would do, though it would be the breaking of his own head, Ge **3**:**15**. Though Satan depart for a season, we shall never be out of his reach till removed from this present evil world.

Verses 14–30

Christ taught in their synagogues, their places of public worship, where they met to read, expound, and apply the word, to pray and praise. All the gifts and graces of the Spirit were upon him and on him, without measure. By Christ, sinners may be loosed from the bonds of guilt, and by his Spirit and grace from the bondage of corruption. He came by the word of his gospel, to bring light to those that sat in the dark, and by the power of his grace, to give sight to those that were blind. And he preached the acceptable year of the Lord. Let sinners attend to the Saviour's invitation when liberty is thus proclaimed. Christ's name was Wonderful; in nothing was he more so than in the word of his grace, and the power that went along with it. We may well wonder that he should speak such words of grace to such graceless wretches as mankind. Some prejudice often furnishes an objection against the humbling doctrine of the cross; and while it is the word of God that stirs up men's enmity, they will blame the conduct or manner of the speaker. The doctrine of God's sovereignty, his right to do his will, provokes proud men. They will not seek his favour in his own way; and are angry when others have the favours they neglect. Still is Jesus rejected by multitudes who hear the same message from his words. While they crucify him afresh by their sins, may we honour him as the Son of God, the Saviour of men, and seek to show we do so by our obedience.

Verses 31–44

Christ's preaching much affected the people; and a working power went with it to the consciences of men. These miracles showed Christ to be a controller and conqueror of Satan, a healer of diseases. Where Christ gives a new life, in recovery from sickness, it should be a new life, spent more than ever in his service, to his glory. Our business should be to spread abroad Christ's fame in every place, to beseech him in behalf of those diseased in body or mind, and to use our influence in bringing sinners to him, that his hands may be laid upon them for their healing. He cast the devils out of many who were possessed. We were not sent into this world to live to ourselves only, but to glorify God, and to do good in our generation. The people sought him, and came unto him. A desert is no desert, if we are with Christ there. He will continue with us, by his word and Spirit, and extend the same blessings to other nations, till, throughout the earth, the servants and worshippers of Satan are brought to acknowledge him as the Christ, the Son of God, and to find redemption through his blood, even the forgiveness of sins.

Chapter 5

Chapter Outline	
The miraculous draught of fishes, Peter, James, and John called.	(1–11)
A leper cleansed.	(12–16)
A paralytic cured.	(17–26)
Levi called, Christ's answer to the Pharisees.	(27–39)

Verses 1–11

When Christ had done preaching, he told Peter to apply to the business of his calling. Time spent on week days in public exercises of religion, need be but little hinderance in time, and may be great furtherance to us in temper of mind, as to our worldly business. With what cheerfulness may we go about the duties of our calling, when we have been with God, and thus have our worldly employments sanctified to us by the word and prayer! Though they had taken nothing, yet Christ told them to let down their nets again. We must not abruptly quit our callings because we have not the success in them we desire. We are likely to speed well, when we follow the guidance of Christ's word. The draught of fishes was by a miracle. We must all, like Peter, own ourselves to be sinful men, therefore Jesus Christ might justly depart from us. But we must beseech him that he would not depart; for woe unto us if the Saviour depart from sinners! Rather let us entreat him to come and dwell in our hearts by faith, that he may transform and cleanse them. These fishermen forsook all, and followed Jesus, when their calling prospered. When riches increase, and we are tempted to set our hearts upon them, then to quit them for Christ is thankworthy.

Verses 12–16

This man is said to be full of leprosy; he had that distemper in a high degree, which represents our natural pollution by sin; we are full of that leprosy; from the crown of the head to the sole of the foot there is no soundness in us. Strong confidence and deep humility are united in the words of this leper. And if any sinner, from a deep sense of vileness, says, I know the Lord can cleanse, but will he look upon such a one as me? will he apply his own precious blood for my cleansing and healing? Yes, he will. Speak not as doubting, but as humbly referring the matter to Christ. And being saved from the guilt and power of our sins, let us spread abroad Christ's fame, and bring others to hear him and to be healed.

Verses 17–26

How many are there in our assemblies, where the gospel is preached, who do not sit under the word, but sit by! It is to them as a tale that is told them, not as a message that is sent to them. Observe the duties taught and recommended to us by the history of the paralytic. In applying to Christ, we must be very pressing and urgent; that is an evidence of faith, and is very pleasing to Christ, and prevailing with him. Give us, Lord, the same kind of faith with respect to thy ability and willingness to heal our souls. Give us to desire the pardon of sin more than any earthly blessing, or life itself. Enable us to believe thy power to forgive sins; then will our souls cheerfully arise and go where thou pleasest.

Verses 27–39

It was a wonder of Christ's grace, that he would call a publican to be his disciple and follower. It was a wonder of his grace, that the call was made so effectual. It was a wonder of his grace, that he came to call sinners to repentance, and to assure them of pardon. It was a wonder of his grace, that he so patiently bore the contradiction of sinners against himself and his disciples. It was a wonder of his grace, that he fixed the services of his disciples according to their strength and standing. The Lord trains up his people gradually for the trials allotted them; we should copy his example in dealing with the weak in faith, or the tempted believer.

Chapter 6

Chapter Outline	
The disciples pluck corn on the sabbath.	(1–5)
Works of mercy suitable to the sabbath day.	(6–11)
The apostles chosen.	(12–19)
Blessings and woes declared.	(20–26)
Christ exhorts to mercy.	(27–36)
And to justice and sincerity.	(37–49)

Verses 1–5

Christ justifies his disciples in a work of necessity for themselves on the sabbath day, and that was plucking the ears of corn when they were hungry. But we must take heed that we mistake not this liberty for leave to commit sin. Christ will have us to know and remember that it is his day, therefore to be spent in his service, and to his honour.

Verses 6–11

Christ was neither ashamed nor afraid to own the purposes of his grace. He healed the poor man, though he knew that his enemies would take advantage against him for it. Let us not be drawn either from our duty or from our usefulness by any opposition. We may well be amazed, that the sons of men should be so wicked.

Verses 12–19

We often think one half hour a great deal to spend in meditation and secret prayer, but Christ was whole nights engaged in these duties. In serving God, our great care should be not to lose time, but to make the end of one good duty the beginning of another. The twelve apostles are here named; never were men so privileged, yet one of them had a devil, and proved a traitor. Those who have not faithful preaching near them, had better travel far than be without it. It is indeed worth while to go a great way to hear the word of Christ, and to go out of the way of other business for it. They came to be cured by him, and he healed them. There is a fulness of grace in Christ, and healing virtue in him, ready to go out from him, that is enough for all, enough for each. Men regard the diseases of the body as greater evils than those of their souls; but the Scripture teaches us differently.

Verses 20–26

Here begins a discourse of Christ, most of which is also found in Mt **5**; **7**. But some think that this was preached at another time and place. All believers that take the precepts of the gospel to themselves, and live by them, may take the promises of the gospel to themselves, and live upon them. Woes are denounced against prosperous sinners as miserable people, though the world envies them. Those are blessed indeed whom Christ blesses, but those must be dreadfully miserable who fall under his woe and curse! What a vast advantage will the saint have over the sinner in the other world! and what a wide difference will there be in their rewards, how much soever the sinner may prosper, and the saint be afflicted here!

Verses 27–36

These are hard lessons to flesh and blood. But if we are thoroughly grounded in the faith of Christ's love, this will make his commands easy to us. Every one that comes to him for washing in his blood, and knows the greatness of the mercy and the love there is in him, can say, in truth and sincerity, Lord, what wilt thou have me to do? Let us then aim to be merciful, even according to the mercy of our heavenly Father to us.

Verses 37–49

All these sayings Christ often used; it was easy to apply them. We ought to be very careful when we blame others; for we need allowance ourselves. If we are of a giving and a forgiving spirit, we shall ourselves reap the benefit. Though full and exact returns are made in another world, not in this world, yet Providence does what should encourage us in doing good. Those who follow the multitude to do evil, follow in the broad way that leads to destruction. The tree is known by its fruits; may the word of Christ be so grafted in our hearts, that we may be fruitful in every good word and work. And what the mouth commonly speaks, generally agrees with what is most in the heart. Those only make sure work for their souls and eternity, and take the course that will profit in a trying time, who think, speak, and act according to the words of Christ. Those who take pains in religion, found their hope upon Christ, who is the Rock of Ages, and other foundation can no man lay. In death and judgment they are safe, being kept by the power of Christ through faith unto salvation, and they shall never perish.

Chapter 7

Chapter Outline	
The centurion's servant healed.	(1–10)
The widow's son raised.	(11–18)
John the Baptist's inquiry concerning Jesus.	(19–35)
Christ anointed in the house of the Pharisee, The parable of the two debtors.	(36–50)

Verses 1–10

Servants should study to endear themselves to their masters. Masters ought to take particular care of their servants when they are sick. We may still, by faithful and fervent prayer, apply to Christ, and ought to do so when sickness is in our families. The building places for religious worship is a good work, and an instance of love to God and his people. Our Lord Jesus was pleased with the centurion's faith; and he never fails to answer the expectations of that faith which honours his power and love. The cure soon wrought and perfect.

Verses 11–18

When the Lord saw the poor widow following her son to the grave, he had compassion on her. See Christ's power over death itself. The gospel call to all people, to young people particularly, is, Arise from the dead, and Christ shall give you light and life. When Christ put life into him, it appeared by the youth's sitting up. Have we grace from Christ? Let us show it. He began to speak: whenever Christ gives us spiritual life, he opens the lips in prayer and praise. When dead souls are raised to spiritual life, by Divine power going with the gospel, we must glorify God, and look upon it as a gracious visit to his people. Let us seek for such an interest in our compassionate Saviour, that we may look forward with joy to the time when the Redeemer's voice shall call forth all that are in their graves. May we be called to the resurrection of life, not to that of damnation.

Verses 19–35

To his miracles in the kingdom of nature, Christ adds this in the kingdom of grace, To the poor the gospel is preached. It clearly pointed out the spiritual nature of Christ's kingdom, that the messenger he sent before him to prepare his way, did it by preaching repentance and reformation of heart and life. We have here the just blame of those who were not wrought upon by the ministry of John Baptist or of Jesus Christ himself. They made a jest of the methods God took to do them good. This is the ruin of multitudes; they are not serious in the concerns of their souls. Let us study to prove ourselves children of Wisdom, by attending the instructions of God's word, and adoring those mysteries and glad tidings which infidels and Pharisees deride and blaspheme.

Verses 36–50

None can truly perceive how precious Christ is, and the glory of the gospel, except the broken-hearted. But while they feel they cannot enough express self-abhorrence on account of sin, and admiration of his mercy, the self-sufficient will be disgusted, because the gospel encourages such repenting sinners. The Pharisee, instead of rejoicing in the tokens of the woman's repentance, confined his thoughts to her former bad character. But without free forgiveness none of us can escape the wrath to come; this our gracious Saviour has purchased with his blood, that he may freely bestow it on every one that believes in him. Christ, by a parable, forced Simon to acknowledge that the greater sinner this woman had been, the greater love she ought to show to Him when her sins were pardoned. Learn here, that sin is a debt; and all are sinners, are debtors to Almighty God. Some sinners are greater debtors; but whether our debt be more or less, it is more than we are able to pay. God is ready to forgive; and his Son having purchased pardon for those who believe in him, his gospel promises it to them, and his Spirit seals it to repenting sinners, and gives them the comfort. Let us keep far from the proud spirit of the Pharisee, simply depending upon and rejoicing in Christ alone, and so be prepared to obey him more zealously, and more strongly to recommend him unto all around us. The more we express our sorrow for sin, and our love to Christ, the clearer evidence we have of the forgiveness of our sins. What a wonderful change does grace make upon a sinner's heart and life, as well as upon his state before God, by the full remission of all his sins through faith in the Lord Jesus!

Chapter 8

Chapter Outline	
The ministry of Christ.	(1–3)
The parable of the sower.	(4–21)
Christ stilleth the tempest and casteth out devils.	(22–40)
The daughter of Jairus restored to life.	(41–56)

Verses 1–3

We are here told what Christ made the constant business of his life, it was teaching the gospel. Tidings of the kingdom of God are glad tidings, and what Christ came to bring. Certain women attended upon him who ministered to him of their substance. It showed the mean condition to which the Saviour humbled himself, that he needed their kindness, and his great humility, that he accepted it. Though rich, yet for our sakes he became poor.

Verses 4–21

There are many very needful and excellent rules and cautions for hearing the word, in the parable of the sower, and the application of it. Happy are we, and for ever indebted to free grace, if the same thing that is a parable to others, with which they are only amused, is a plain truth to us, by which we are taught and governed. We ought to take heed of the things that will hinder our profiting by the word we hear; to take heed lest we hear carelessly and slightly, lest we entertain prejudices against the word we hear; and to take heed to our spirits after we have heard the word, lest we lose what we have gained. The gifts we have, will be continued to us or not, as we use them for the glory of God, and the good of our brethren. Nor is it enough not to hold the truth in unrighteousness; we should desire to hold forth the word of life, and to shine, giving light to all around. Great encouragement is given to those who prove themselves faithful hearers of the word, by being doers of the work. Christ owns them as his relations.

Verses 22–40

Those that put to sea in a calm, even at Christ's word, must yet prepare for a storm, and for great peril in that storm. There is no relief for souls under a sense of guilt, and fear of wrath, but to go to Christ, and call him Master, and say, I am undone, if thou dost not help me. When our dangers are over, it becomes us to take to ourselves the shame of our own fears, and to give Christ the glory of our deliverance. We may learn much out of this history concerning the world of infernal, malignant spirits, which though not working now exactly in the same way as then, yet all must at all times carefully guard against. And these malignant spirits are very numerous. They have enmity to man and all his comforts. Those under Christ's government are sweetly led with the bands of love; those under the devil's government are furiously driven. Oh what a comfort it is to the believer, that all the powers of darkness are under the control of the Lord Jesus! It is a miracle of mercy, if those whom Satan possesses, are not brought to destruction and eternal ruin. Christ will not stay with those who slight him; perhaps he may no more return to them, while others are waiting for him, and glad to receive him.

Verses 41–56

Let us not complain of a crowd, and a throng, and a hurry, as long as we are in the way of our duty, and doing good; but otherwise every wise man will keep himself out of it as much as he can. And many a poor soul is healed, and helped, and saved by Christ, that is hidden in a crowd, and nobody notices it. This woman came trembling, yet her faith saved her. There may be trembling, where yet there is saving faith. Observe Christ's comfortable words to Jairus, Fear not, believe only, and thy daughter shall be made whole. No less hard was it not to grieve for the loss of an only child, than not to fear the continuance of that grief. But in perfect faith there is no fear; the more we fear, the less we believe. The hand of Christ's grace goes with the calls of his word, to make them effectual. Christ commanded to give her meat. As babes new born, so those newly raised from sin, desire spiritual food, that they may grow thereby.

Chapter 9

Chapter Outline	
The apostles sent forth.	(1–9)
The multitude miraculously fed.	(10–17)
Peter's testimony to Christ, Self-denial enjoined.	(18–27)

The transfiguration.	(28–36)
An evil spirit cast out.	(37–42)
Christ checks the ambition of his disciples.	(43–50)
He reproves their mistaken zeal.	(51–56)
Every thing to be given up for Christ.	(57–62)

Verses 1–9

Christ sent his twelve disciples abroad, who by this time were able to teach others what they had received from the Lord. They must not be anxious to commend themselves to people's esteem by outward appearance. They must go as they were. The Lord Jesus is the fountain of power and authority, to whom all creatures must, in one way or another, be subject; and if he goes with the word of his ministers in power, to deliver sinners from Satan's bondage, they may be sure that he will care for their wants. When truth and love thus go together, and yet the message of God is rejected and despised, it leaves men without excuse, and turns to a testimony against them. Herod's guilty conscience was ready to conclude that John was risen from the dead. He desired to see Jesus; and why did he not go and see him? Probably, because he thought it below him, or because he wished not to have any more reprovers of sin. Delaying it now, his heart was hardened, and when he did see Jesus, he was as much prejudiced against him as others, Lu **23**:**11**.

Verses 10–17

The people followed Jesus, and though they came unseasonably, yet he gave them what they came for. He spake unto them of the kingdom of God. He healed those who had need of healing. And with five loaves of bread and two fishes, Christ fed five thousand men. He will not see those that fear him, and serve him faithfully, want any good thing. When we receive creature-comforts, we must acknowledge that we receive them from God, and that we are unworthy to receive them; that we owe them all, and all the comfort we have in them, to the mediation of Christ, by whom the curse is taken away. The blessing of Christ will make a little go a great way. He fills every hungry soul, abundantly satisfies it with the goodness of his house. Here were fragments taken up: in our Father's house there is bread enough, and to spare. We are not straitened, nor stinted in Christ.

Verses 18–27

It is an unspeakable comfort that our Lord Jesus is God's Anointed; this signifies that he was both appointed to be the Messiah, and qualified for it. Jesus discourses concerning his own sufferings and death. And so far must his disciples be from thinking how to prevent his sufferings, that they must prepare for their own. We often meet with crosses in the way of duty; and though we must not pull them upon our own heads, yet, when they are laid for us, we must take them up, and carry them after Christ. It is well or ill with us, according as it is well or ill with our souls. The body cannot be happy, if the soul be miserable in the other world; but the soul may be happy, though the body is greatly afflicted and oppressed in this world. We must never be ashamed of Christ and his gospel.

Verses 28–36

Christ's transfiguration was a specimen of that glory in which he will come to judge the world; and was an encouragement to his disciples to suffer for him. Prayer is a transfiguring, transforming duty, which makes the face to shine. Our Lord Jesus, even in his transfiguration, was willing to speak concerning his death and sufferings. In our greatest glories on earth, let us remember that in this world we have no continuing city. What need we have to pray to God for quickening grace, to make us lively! Yet that the disciples might be witnesses of this sign from heaven, after awhile they became awake, so that they were able to give a full account of what passed. But those know not what they say, that talk of making tabernacles on earth for glorified saints in heaven.

Verses 37–42

How deplorable the case of this child! He was under the power of an evil spirit. Disease of that nature are more frightful than such as arise merely from natural causes. What mischief Satan does where he gets possession! But happy those that have access to Christ! He can do that for us which his disciples cannot. A word from Christ healed the child; and when our children recover from sickness, it is comfortable to receive them as healed by the hand of Christ.

Verses 43–50

This prediction of Christ's sufferings was plain enough, but the disciples would not understand it, because it agreed not with their notions. A little child is the emblem by which Christ teaches us simplicity and humility. What greater honour can any man attain to in this world, than to be received by men as a messenger of God and Christ; and to have God and Christ own themselves received and welcomed in him! If ever any society of Christians in this world, had reason to silence those not of their own communion, the twelve disciples at this time had; yet Christ warned them not to do the like again. Those may be found faithful followers of Christ, and may be accepted of him, who do not follow with us.

Verses 51–56

The disciples did not consider that the conduct of the Samaritans was rather the effect of national prejudices and bigotry, than of enmity to the word and worship of God; and through they refused to receive Christ and his disciples, they did not ill use or injure them, so that the case was widely different from that of Ahaziah and Elijah. Nor were they aware that the gospel dispensation was to be marked by miracles of mercy. But above all, they were ignorant of the prevailing motives of their own hearts, which were pride and carnal ambition. Of this our Lord warned them. It is easy for us to say, Come, see our zeal for the Lord! and to think we are very faithful in his cause, when we are seeking our own objects, and even doing harm instead of good to others.

Verses 57–62

Here is one that is forward to follow Christ, but seems to have been hasty and rash, and not to have counted the cost. If we mean to follow Christ, we must lay aside the thoughts of great things in the world. Let us not try to join the profession of Christianity, with seeking after worldly advantages. Here is another that seems resolved to follow Christ, but he begs a short delay. To this man Christ first gave the call; he said to him, Follow me. Religion teaches us to be kind and good, to show piety at home, and to requite our parents; but we must not make these an excuse for neglecting our duty to God. Here is another that is willing to follow Christ, but he must have a little time to talk with his friends about it, and to set in order his household affairs, and give directions concerning them. He seemed to have worldly concerns more upon his heart than he ought to have, and he was willing to enter into a temptation leading him from his purpose of following Christ. No one can do any business in a proper manner, if he is attending to other things. Those who begin with the work of God, must resolve to go on, or they will make nothing of it. Looking back, leads to drawing back, and drawing back is to perdition. He only that endures to the end shall be saved.

Chapter 10

Chapter Outline	
Seventy disciples sent forth.	(1–16)
The blessedness of Christ's disciples.	(17–24)
The good Samaritan.	(25–37)
Jesus at the house of Martha and Mary.	(38–42)

Verses 1–16

Christ sent the seventy disciples, two and two, that they might strengthen and encourage one another. The ministry of the gospel calls men to receive Christ as a Prince and a Saviour; and he will surely come in the power of his Spirit to all places whither he sends his faithful servants. But the doom of those who receive the grace of God in vain, will be very fearful Those who despise the faithful ministers of Christ, who think meanly of them, and look scornfully upon them, will be reckoned as despisers of God and Christ.

Verses 17–24

All our victories over Satan, are obtained by power derived from Jesus Christ, and he must have all the praise. But let us beware of spiritual pride, which has been the destruction of many. Our Lord rejoiced at the prospect of the salvation of many souls. It was fit that particular notice should be taken of that hour of joy, there were few such, for He was a man of sorrows: in that hour in which he saw Satan fall, and heard of the good success of his ministers, in that hour he rejoiced. He has ever resisted the proud, and given grace to the humble. The more simply dependent we are on the teaching, help, and blessing of the Son of God, the more we shall know both of the Father and of the Son; the more blessed we shall be in seeing the glory, and hearing the words of the Divine Saviour; and the more useful we shall be made in promoting his cause.

Verses 25–37

If we speak of eternal life, and the way to it, in a careless manner, we take the name of God in vain. No one will ever love God and his neighbour with any measure of pure, spiritual love, who is not made a partaker of converting grace. But the proud heart of man strives hard against these convictions. Christ gave an instance of a poor Jew in distress, relieved by a good Samaritan. This poor man fell among thieves, who left him about to die of his wounds. He was slighted by those who should have been his friends, and was cared for by a stranger, a Samaritan, of the nation which the Jews most despised and detested, and would have no dealings with. It is lamentable to observe how selfishness governs all ranks; how many excuses men will make to avoid trouble or expense in relieving others. But the true Christian has the law of love written in his heart. The Spirit of Christ dwells in him; Christ's image is renewed in his soul. The parable is a beautiful explanation of the law of loving our neighbour as ourselves, without regard to nation, party, or any other distinction. It also sets forth the kindness and love of God our Saviour toward sinful, miserable men. We were like this poor, distressed traveller. Satan, our enemy, has robbed us, and wounded us: such is the mischief sin has done us. The blessed Jesus had compassion on us. The believer considers that Jesus loved him, and gave his life for him, when an enemy and a rebel; and having shown him mercy, he bids him go and do likewise. It is the duty of us all , in our places, and according to our ability, to succour, help, and relieve all that are in distress and necessity.

Verses 38–42

A good sermon is not the worse for being preached in a house; and the visits of our friends should be so managed, as to make them turn to the good of their souls. Sitting at Christ's feet, signifies readiness to receive his word, and submission to the guidance of it. Martha was providing for the entertainment of Christ, and those that came with him. Here were respect to our Lord Jesus and right care of her household affairs. But there was something to be blamed. She was for much serving; plenty, variety, and exactness. Worldly business is a snare to us, when it hinders us from serving God, and getting good to our souls. What needless time is wasted, and expense often laid out, even in entertaining professors of the gospel! Though Martha was on this occasion faulty, yet she was a true believer, and in her general conduct did not neglect the one thing needful. The favour of God is needful to our happiness; the salvation of Christ is needful to our safety. Where this is attended to, all other things will be rightly pursued. Christ declared, Mary hath chosen the good part. For one thing is needful, this one thing that she has done, to give up herself to the guidance of Christ. The things of this life will be taken away from us, at the furthest, when we shall be taken away from them; but nothing shall separate from the love of Christ, and a part in that love. Men and devils cannot take it away from us, and God and Christ will not. Let us mind the one thing needful more diligently.

Chapter 11

Chapter Outline	
The disciples taught to pray.	(1–4)

Christ encourages being earnest in prayer.	(5–13)
Christ casts out a devil, The blasphemy of the Pharisees.	(14–26)
True happiness.	(27, 28)
Christ reproves the Jews.	(29–36)
He reproves the Pharisees.	(37–54)

Verses 1–4

"Lord, teach us to pray," is a good prayer, and a very needful one, for Jesus Christ only can teach us, by his word and Spirit, how to pray. Lord, teach me what it is to pray; Lord, stir up and quicken me to the duty; Lord, direct me what to pray for; teach me what I should say. Christ taught them a prayer, much the same that he had given before in his sermon upon the mount. There are some differences in the words of the Lord's prayer in Matthew and in Luke, but they are of no moment. Let us in our requests, both for others and for ourselves, come to our heavenly Father, confiding in his power and goodness.

Verses 5–13

Christ encourages fervency and constancy in prayer. We must come for what we need, as a man does to his neighbour or friend, who is kind to him. We must come for bread; for that which is needful. If God does not answer our prayers speedily, yet he will in due time, if we continue to pray. Observe what to pray for; we must ask for the Holy Spirit, not only as necessary in order to our praying well, but as all spiritual blessings are included in that one. For by the influences of the Holy Spirit we are brought to know God and ourselves, to repent, believe in, and love Christ, and so are made comfortable in this world, and meet for happiness in the next. All these blessings our heavenly Father is more ready to bestow on every one that asks for them, than an indulgent parent is to give food to a hungry child. And this is the advantage of the prayer of faith, that it quiets and establishes the heart in God.

Verses 14–26

Christ's thus casting out the devils, was really the destroying of their power. The heart of every unconverted sinner is the devil's palace, where he dwells, and where he rules. There is a kind of peace in the heart of an unconverted soul, while the devil, as a strong man armed, keeps it. The sinner is secure, has no doubt concerning the goodness of his state, nor any dread of the judgment to come. But observe the wonderful change made in conversion. The conversion of a soul to God, is Christ's victory over the devil and his power in that soul, restoring the soul to its liberty, and recovering his own interest in it and power over it. All the endowments of mind of body are now employed for Christ. Here is the condition of a hypocrite. The house is swept from common sins, by a forced confession, as Pharaoh's; by a feigned contrition, as Ahab's; or by a partial reformation, as Herod's. The house is swept, but it is not washed; the heart is not made holy. Sweeping takes off only the loose dirt, while the sin that besets the sinner, the beloved sin, is untouched. The house is garnished with common gifts and graces. It is not furnished with any true grace; it is all paint and varnish, not real nor lasting. It was never given up to Christ, nor dwelt in by the Spirit. Let us take heed of resting in that which a man may have, and yet come short of heaven. The wicked spirits enter in without any difficulty; they are welcomed, and they dwell there; there they work, there they rule. From such an awful state let all earnestly pray to be delivered.

Verses 27, 28

While the scribes and Pharisees despised and blasphemed the discourses of our Lord Jesus, this good woman admired them, and the wisdom and power with which he spake. Christ led the woman to a higher consideration. Though it is a great privilege to hear the word of God, yet those only are truly blessed, that is, blessed of the Lord, that hear it, keep it in memory, and keep to it as their way and rule.

Verses 29–36

Christ promised that there should be one sign more given, even the sign of Jonah the prophet; which in Matthew is explained, as meaning the resurrection of Christ; and he warned them to improve this sign. But though Christ himself were the constant preacher in any congregation, and worked miracles daily among them, yet unless his grace humbled their hearts, they would not profit by his word. Let us not desire more evidence and fuller teaching than the Lord is pleased to afford us. We should pray without ceasing that our hearts and understandings may be opened, that we may profit by the light we enjoy. And especially take heed that the light which is in us be not darkness; for if our leading principles be wrong, our judgment and practice must become more so.

Verses 37–54

We should all look to our hearts, that they may be cleansed and new-created; and while we attend to the great things of the law and of the gospel, we must not neglect the smallest matter God has appointed. When any wait to catch something out of our mouths, that they may insnare us, O Lord, give us thy prudence and thy patience, and disappoint their evil purposes. Furnish us with such meekness and patience that we may glory in reproaches, for Christ's sake, and that thy Holy Spirit may rest upon us.

Chapter 12

Chapter Outline	
Christ reproves the interpreters of the law.	(1–12)
A caution against covetousness, The parable of the rich man.	(13–21)
Worldly care reproved.	(22–40)

Watchfulness enforced.	(41–53)
A warning to be reconciled to God.	(54–59)

Verses 1–12

A firm belief of the doctrine of God's universal providence, and the extent of it, would satisfy us when in peril, and encourage us to trust God in the way of duty. Providence takes notice of the meanest creatures, even of the sparrows, and therefore of the smallest interests of the disciples of Christ. Those who confess Christ now, shall be owned by him in the great day, before the angels of God. To deter us from denying Christ, and deserting his truths and ways, we are here assured that those who deny Christ, though they may thus save life itself, and though they may gain a kingdom by it, will be great losers at last; for Christ will not know them, will not own them, nor show them favour. But let no trembling, penitent backslider doubt of obtaining forgiveness. This is far different from the determined enmity that is blasphemy against the Holy Ghost, which shall never be forgiven, because it will never be repented of.

Verses 13–21

Christ's kingdom is spiritual, and not of this world. Christianity does not meddle with politics; it obliges all to do justly, but wordly dominion is not founded in grace. It does not encourage expectations of worldly advantages by religion. The rewards of Christ's disciples are of another nature. Covetousness is a sin we need constantly to be warned against; for happiness and comfort do not depend on the wealth of this world. The things of the world will not satisfy the desires of a soul. Here is a parable, which shows the folly of carnal worldling while they live, and their misery when they die. The character drawn is exactly that of a prudent, worldly man, who has no grateful regard to the providence of God, nor any right thought of the uncertainty of human affairs, the worth of his soul, or the importance of eternity. How many, even among professed Christians, point out similar characters as models for imitation, and proper persons to form connexions with! We mistake if we think that thoughts are hid, and thoughts are free. When he saw a great crop upon his ground, instead of thanking God for it, or rejoicing to be able to do more good, he afflicts himself. What shall I do now? The poorest beggar in the country could not have said a more anxious word. The more men have, the more perplexity they have with it. It was folly for him to think of making no other use of his plenty, than to indulge the flesh and gratify the sensual appetites, without any thought of doing good to others. Carnal worldlings are fools; and the day is coming when God will call them by their own name, and they will call themselves so. The death of such persons is miserable in itself, and terrible to them. Thy soul shall be required. He is loth to part with it; but God shall require it, shall require an account of it, require it as a guilty soul to be punished without delay. It is the folly of most men, to mind and pursue that which is for the body and for time only, more than that for the soul and eternity.

Verses 22–40

Christ largely insisted upon this caution not to give way to disquieting, perplexing cares, Mt **6:25–34**. The arguments here used are for our encouragement to cast our care upon God, which is the right way to get ease. As in our stature, so in our state, it is our wisdom to take it as it is. An eager, anxious pursuit of the things of this world, even necessary things, ill becomes the disciples of Christ. Fears must not prevail; when we frighten ourselves with thoughts of evil to come, and put ourselves upon needless cares how to avoid it. If we value the beauty of holiness, we shall not crave the luxuries of life. Let us then examine whether we belong to this little flock. Christ is our Master, and we are his servants; not only working servants, but waiting servants. We must be as men that wait for their lord, that sit up while he stays out late, to be ready to receive him. In this Christ alluded to his own ascension to heaven, his coming to call his people to him by death, and his return to judge the world. We are uncertain as to the time of his coming to us, we should therefore be always ready. If men thus take care of their houses, let us be thus wise for our souls. Be ye therefore ready also; as ready as the good man of the house would be, if he knew at what hour the thief would come.

Verses 41–53

All are to take to themselves what Christ says in his word, and to inquire concerning it. No one is left so ignorant as not to know many things to be wrong which he does, and many things to be right which he neglects; therefore all are without excuse in their sin. The bringing in the gospel dispensation would occasion desolations. Not that this would be the tendency of Christ's religion, which is pure, peaceable, and loving; but the effect of its being contrary to men's pride and lusts. There was to be a wide publication of the gospel. But before that took place, Christ had a baptism to be baptized with, far different from that of water and the Holy Spirit. He must endure sufferings and death. It agreed not with his plan to preach the gospel more widely, till this baptism was completed. We should be zealous in making known the truth, for though divisions will be stirred up, and a man's own household may be his foes, yet sinners will be converted, and God will be glorified.

Verses 54–59

Christ would have the people to be as wise in the concerns of their souls as they are in outward affairs. Let them hasten to obtain peace with God before it is too late. If any man has found that God has set himself against him concerning his sins, let him apply to him as God in Christ reconciling the world to himself. While we are alive, we are in the way, and now is our time.

Chapter 13

Chapter Outline	
Christ exhorts to repentance from the case of the Galileans and others.	(1–5)
Parable of the barren fig-tree.	(6–9)
The infirm woman strengthened.	(10–17)
The parables of the mustard seed, and leaven.	(18–22)

Exhortation to enter at the strait gate.	(23–30)
Christ's reproof to Herod, and to the people of Jerusalem.	(31–35)

Verses 1–5

Mention was made to Christ of the death of some Galileans. This tragical story is briefly related here, and is not met with in any historians. In Christ's reply he spoke of another event, which, like it, gave an instance of people taken away by sudden death. Towers, that are built for safety, often prove to be men's destruction. He cautioned his hearers not to blame great sufferers, as if they were therefore to be accounted great sinners. As no place or employment can secure from the stroke of death, we should consider the sudden removals of others as warnings to ourselves. On these accounts Christ founded a call to repentance. The same Jesus that bids us repent, for the kingdom of heaven is at hand, bids us repent, for otherwise we shall perish.

Verses 6–9

This parable of the barren fig-tree is intended to enforce the warning given just before: the barren tree, except it brings forth fruit, will be cut down. This parable in the first place refers to the nation and people of the Jews. Yet it is, without doubt, for awakening all that enjoy the means of grace, and the privileges of the visible church. When God has borne long, we may hope that he will bear with us yet a little longer, but we cannot expect that he will bear always.

Verses 10–17

Our Lord Jesus attended upon public worship on the sabbaths. Even bodily infirmities, unless very grievous, should not keep us from public worship on sabbath days. This woman came to Christ to be taught, and to get good to her soul, and then he relieved her bodily infirmity. This cure represents the work of Christ's grace upon the soul. And when crooked souls are made straight, they will show it by glorifying God. Christ knew that this ruler had a real enmity to him and to his gospel, and that he did but cloak it with a pretended zeal for the sabbath day; he really would not have them be healed any day; but if Jesus speaks the word, and puts forth his healing power, sinners are set free. This deliverance is often wrought on the Lord's day; and whatever labour tends to put men in the way of receiving the blessing, agrees with the design of that day.

Verses 18–22

Here is the progress of the gospel foretold in two parables, as in Mt **13**. The kingdom of the Messiah is the kingdom of God. May grace grow in our hearts; may our faith and love grow exceedingly, so as to give undoubted evidence of their reality. May the example of God's saints be blessed to those among whom they live; and may his grace flow from heart to heart, until the little one becomes a thousand.

Verses 23–30

Our Saviour came to guide men's consciences, not to gratify their curiosity. Ask not, How many shall be saved? But, Shall I be one of them? Not, What shall become of such and such? But, What shall I do, and what will become of me? Strive to enter in at the strait gate. This is directed to each of us; it is, Strive ye. All that will be saved, must enter in at the strait gate, must undergo a change of the whole man. Those that would enter in, must strive to enter. Here are awakening considerations, to enforce this exhortation. Oh that we may be all awakened by them! They answer the question, Are there few that shall be saved? But let none despond either as to themselves or others, for there are last who shall be first, and first who shall be last. If we reach heaven, we shall meet many there whom we little thought to meet, and miss many whom we expected to find.

Verses 31–35

Christ, in calling Herod a fox, gave him his true character. The greatest of men were accountable to God, therefore it became him to call this proud king by his own name; but it is not an example for us. I know, said our Lord, that I must die very shortly; when I die, I shall be perfected, I shall have completed my undertaking. It is good for us to look upon the time we have before us as but little, that we may thereby be quickened to do the work of the day in its day. The wickedness of persons and places which more than others profess religion and relation to God, especially displeases and grieves the Lord Jesus. The judgment of the great day will convince unbelievers; but let us learn thankfully to welcome, and to profit by all who come in the name of the Lord, to call us to partake of his great salvation.

Chapter 14

Chapter Outline	
Christ heals a man on the sabbath.	(1–6)
He teaches humility.	(7–14)
Parable of the great supper.	(15–24)
The necessity of consideration and self-denial.	(25–35)

Verses 1–6

This Pharisee, as well as others, seems to have had an ill design in entertaining Jesus at his house. But our Lord would not be hindered from healing a man, though he knew a clamour would be raised at his doing it on the sabbath. It requires care to understand the proper connexion between piety and charity in observing the sabbath, and the distinction between works of real necessity and habits of self-indulgence. Wisdom from above, teaches patient perseverance in well-doing.

Verses 7–14

Even in the common actions of life, Christ marks what we do, not only in our religious assemblies, but at our tables. We see in many cases, that a man's pride will bring him low, and before honour is humility. Our Saviour here teaches, that works of charity are better than works of show. But our Lord did not mean that a proud and unbelieving liberality should be rewarded, but that his precept of doing good to the poor and afflicted should be observed from love to him.

Verses 15–24

In this parable observe the free grace and mercy of God shining in the gospel of Christ, which will be food and a feast for the soul of a man that knows its own wants and miseries. All found some pretence to put off their attendance. This reproves the Jewish nation for their neglect of the offers of Christ's grace. It shows also the backwardness there is to close with the gospel call. The want of gratitude in those who slight gospel offers, and the contempt put upon the God of heaven thereby, justly provoke him. The apostles were to turn to the Gentiles, when the Jews refused the offer; and with them the church was filled. The provision made for precious souls in the gospel of Christ, has not been made in vain; for if some reject, others will thankfully accept the offer. The very poor and low in the world, shall be as welcome to Christ as the rich and great; and many times the gospel has the greatest success among those that labour under worldly disadvantages and bodily infirmities. Christ's house shall at last be filled; it will be so when the number of the elect is completed.

Verses 25–35

Though the disciples of Christ are not all crucified, yet they all bear their cross, and must bear it in the way of duty. Jesus bids them count upon it, and then consider of it. Our Saviour explains this by two similitudes; the former showing that we must consider the expenses of our religion; the latter, that we must consider the perils of it. Sit down and count the cost; consider it will cost the mortifying of sin, even the most beloved lusts. The proudest and most daring sinner cannot stand against God, for who knows the power of his anger? It is our interest to seek peace with him, and we need not send to ask conditions of peace, they are offered to us, and are highly to our advantage. In some way a disciple of Christ will be put to the trial. May we seek to be disciples indeed, and be careful not to grow slack in our profession, or afraid of the cross; that we may be the good salt of the earth, to season those around us with the savour of Christ.

Chapter 15

Chapter Outline	
Parables of the lost sheep, and the piece of silver.	(1–10)
The prodigal son, his wickedness and distress.	(11–16)
His repentance and pardon.	(17–24)
The elder brother offended.	(25–32)

Verses 1–10

The parable of the lost sheep is very applicable to the great work of man's redemption. The lost sheep represents the sinner as departed from God, and exposed to certain ruin if not brought back to him, yet not desirous to return. Christ is earnest in bringing sinners home. In the parable of the lost piece of silver, that which is lost, is one piece, of small value compared with the rest. Yet the woman seeks diligently till she finds it. This represents the various means and methods God makes use of to bring lost souls home to himself, and the Saviour's joy on their return to him. How careful then should we be that our repentance is unto salvation!

Verses 11–16

The parable of the prodigal son shows the nature of repentance, and the Lord's readiness to welcome and bless all who return to him. It fully sets forth the riches of gospel grace; and it has been, and will be, while the world stands, of unspeakable use to poor sinners, to direct and to encourage them in repenting and returning to God. It is bad, and the beginning of worse, when men look upon God's gifts as debts due to them. The great folly of sinners, and that which ruins them, is, being content in their life-time to receive their good things. Our first parents ruined themselves and all their race, by a foolish ambition to be independent, and this is at the bottom of sinners' persisting in their sin. We may all discern some features of our own characters in that of the prodigal son. A sinful state is of departure and distance from God. A sinful state is a spending state: wilful sinners misemploy their thoughts and the powers of their souls, mispend their time and all their opportunities. A sinful state is a wanting state. Sinners want necessaries for their souls; they have neither food nor raiment for them, nor any provision for hereafter. A sinful state is a vile, slavish state. The business of the devil's servants is to make provision for the flesh, to fulfil the lusts thereof, and that is no better than feeding swine. A sinful state is a state constant discontent. The wealth of the world and the pleasures of the senses will not even satisfy our bodies; but what are they to precious souls! A sinful state is a state which cannot look for relief from any creature. In vain do we cry to the world and to the flesh; they have that which will poison a soul, but have nothing to give which will feed and nourish it. A sinful state is a state of death. A sinner is dead in trespasses and sins, destitute of spiritual life. A sinful state is a lost state. Souls that are separated from God, if his mercy prevent not, will soon be lost for ever. The prodigal's wretched state, only faintly shadows forth the awful ruin of man by sin. Yet how few are sensible of their own state and character!

Verses 17–24

Having viewed the prodigal in his abject state of misery, we are next to consider his recovery from it. This begins by his coming to himself. That is a turning point in the sinner's conversion. The Lord opens his eyes, and convinces him of sin; then he views himself and every object, in a different light from what he did before. Thus the convinced sinner perceives that the meanest servant of God is happier than he is. To look unto God as a Father, and our Father, will be of great use in our repentance and return to him. The prodigal arose, nor stopped till he reached his home. Thus the repenting sinner resolutely quits the bondage of Satan and his lusts, and returns to God by prayer, notwithstanding fears and discouragements. The Lord meets him with unexpected tokens of his forgiving love. Again; the reception of the humbled sinner is like that of the prodigal. He is clothed in the robe of the Redeemer's righteousness, made partaker of the Spirit of adoption, prepared by peace of conscience and gospel grace to walk in the ways of holiness, and feasted with Divine consolations. Principles of grace and holiness are wrought in him, to do, as well as to will.

Verses 25–32

In the latter part of this parable we have the character of the Pharisees, though not of them alone. It sets forth the kindness of the Lord, and the proud manner in which his gracious kindness is often received. The Jews, in general, showed the same spirit towards the converted Gentiles; and numbers in every age object to the gospel and its preachers, on the same ground. What must that temper be, which stirs up a man to despise and abhor those for whom the Saviour shed his precious blood, who are objects of the Father's choice, and temples of the Holy Ghost! This springs from pride, self-preference, and ignorance of a man's own heart. The mercy and grace of our God in Christ, shine almost as bright in his tender and gentle bearing with peevish saints, as his receiving prodigal sinners upon their repentance. It is the unspeakable happiness of all the children of God, who keep close to their Father's house, that they are, and shall be ever with him. Happy will it be for those who thankfully accept Christ's invitation.

Chapter 16

Chapter Outline	
The parable of the unjust steward.	(1–12)
Christ reproves the hypocrisy of the covetous Pharisees.	(13–18)
The rich man and Lazarus.	(19–31)

Verses 1–12

Whatever we have, the property of it is God's; we have only the use of it, according to the direction of our great Lord, and for his honour. This steward wasted his lord's goods. And we are all liable to the same charge; we have not made due improvement of what God has trusted us with. The steward cannot deny it; he must make up his accounts, and be gone. This may teach us that death will come, and deprive us of the opportunities we now have. The steward will make friends of his lord's debtors or tenants, by striking off a considerable part of their debt to his lord. The lord referred to in this parable commended not the fraud, but the policy of the steward. In that respect alone is it so noticed. Worldly men, in the choice of their object, are foolish; but in their activity, and perseverance, they are often wiser than believers. The unjust steward is not set before us as an example in cheating his master, or to justify any dishonesty, but to point out the careful ways of worldly men. It would be well if the children of light would learn wisdom from the men of the world, and would as earnestly pursue their better object. The true riches signify spiritual blessings; and if a man spends upon himself, or hoards up what God has trusted to him, as to outward things, what evidence can he have, that he is an heir of God through Christ? The riches of this world are deceitful and uncertain. Let us be convinced that those are truly rich, and very rich, who are rich in faith, and rich toward God, rich in Christ, in the promises; let us then lay up our treasure in heaven, and expect our portion from thence.

Verses 13–18

To this parable our Lord added a solemn warning. Ye cannot serve God and the world, so divided are the two interests. When our Lord spoke thus, the covetous Pharisees treated his instructions with contempt. But he warned them, that what they contended for as the law, was a wresting of its meaning: this our Lord showed in a case respecting divorce. There are many covetous sticklers for the forms of godliness, who are the bitterest enemies to its power, and try to set others against the truth.

Verses 19–31

Here the spiritual things are represented, in a description of the different state of good and bad, in this world and in the other. We are not told that the rich man got his estate by fraud, or oppression; but Christ shows, that a man may have a great deal of the wealth, pomp, and pleasure of this world, yet perish for ever under God's wrath and curse. The sin of this rich man was his providing for himself only. Here is a godly man, and one that will hereafter be happy for ever, in the depth of adversity and distress. It is often the lot of some of the dearest of God's saints and servants to be greatly afflicted in this world. We are not told that the rich man did him any harm, but we do not find that he had any care for him. Here is the different condition of this godly poor man, and this wicked rich man, at and after death. The rich man in hell lifted up his eyes, being in torment. It is not probable that there are discourses between glorified saints and damned sinners, but this dialogue shows the hopeless misery and fruitless desires, to which condemned spirits are brought. There is a day coming, when those who now hate and despise the people of God, would gladly receive kindness from them. But the damned in hell shall not have the least abatement of their torment. Sinners are now called upon to remember; but they do not, they will not, they find ways to avoid it. As wicked people have good things only in this life, and at death are for ever separated from all good, so godly people have evil things only in this life, and at death they are for ever put from them. In this world, blessed be God, there is no gulf between a state of nature and grace, we may pass from sin to God; but if we die in our sins, there is no coming out. The rich man had five brethren, and would have them stopped in their sinful course; their coming to that place of torment, would make his misery the worse, who had helped to show them the way thither. How many would now desire to recall or to undo what they have written or done! Those who would make the rich man's praying to Abraham justify praying to saints departed, go far to seek for proofs, when the mistake of a damned sinner is all they can find for an example. And surely there is no encouragement to follow the example, when all his prayers were made in vain. A messenger from the dead could say no more than what is said in the Scriptures. The same strength of corruption that breaks through the convictions of the written word, would triumph over a witness from the dead. Let us seek to the law and to the testimony, Isa **8**:**19**, **20**, for that is the sure word of prophecy, upon which we may rest, **2**Pe **1**:**19**. Circumstances in every age show that no terrors, or arguments, can give true repentance without the special grace of God renewing the sinner's heart.

Chapter 17

Chapter Outline	
To avoid offences, To pray for increase of faith, Humility taught.	(11–19)
Ten lepers cleansed.	(1–10)

Christ's kingdom.	(20–37)

Verses 1–10

It is no abatement of their guilt by whom an offence comes, nor will it lessen their punishment that offences will come. Faith in God's pardoning mercy, will enable us to get over the greatest difficulties in the way of forgiving our brethren. As with God nothing is impossible, so all things are possible to him that can believe. Our Lord showed his disciples their need of deep humility. The Lord has such a property in every creature, as no man can have in another; he cannot be in debt to them for their services, nor do they deserve any return from him.

Verses 11–19

A sense of our spiritual leprosy should make us very humble whenever we draw near to Christ. It is enough to refer ourselves to the compassions of Christ, for they fail not. We may look for God to meet us with mercy, when we are found in the way of obedience. Only one of those who were healed returned to give thanks. It becomes us, like him, to be very humble in thanksgivings, as well as in prayers. Christ noticed the one who thus distinguished himself, he was a Samaritan. The others only got the outward cure, he alone got the spiritual blessing.

Verses 20–37

The kingdom of God was among the Jews, or rather within some of them. It was a spiritual kingdom, set up in the heart by the power of Divine grace. Observe how it had been with sinners formerly, and in what state the judgments of God, which they had been warned of, found them. Here is shown what a dreadful surprise this destruction will be to the secure and sensual. Thus shall it be in the day when the Son of man is revealed. When Christ came to destroy the Jewish nation by the Roman armies, that nation was found in such a state of false security as is here spoken of. In like manner, when Jesus Christ shall come to judge the world, sinners will be found altogether regardless; for in like manner the sinners of every age go on securely in their evil ways, and remember not their latter end. But wherever the wicked are, who are marked for eternal ruin, they shall be found by the judgments of God.

Chapter 18

Chapter Outline	
The parable of the importunate widow.	(1–8)
The Pharisee and the publican.	(9–14)
Children brought to Christ.	(15–17)
The ruler hindered by his riches.	(18–30)
Christ foreshows his death.	(31–34)
A blind man restored to sight.	(35–43)

Verses 1–8

All God's people are praying people. Here earnest steadiness in prayer for spiritual mercies is taught. The widow's earnestness prevailed even with the unjust judge: she might fear lest it should set him more against her; but our earnest prayer is pleasing to our God. Even to the end there will still be ground for the same complaint of weakness of faith.

Verses 9–14

This parable was to convince some who trusted in themselves that they were righteous, and despised others. God sees with what disposition and design we come to him in holy ordinances. What the Pharisee said, shows that he trusted to himself that he was righteous. We may suppose he was free from gross and scandalous sins. All this was very well and commendable. Miserable is the condition of those who come short of the righteousness of this Pharisee, yet he was not accepted; and why not? He went up to the temple to pray, but was full of himself and his own goodness; the favour and grace of God he did not think worth asking. Let us beware of presenting proud devotions to the Lord, and of despising others. The publican's address to God was full of humility, and of repentance for sin, and desire toward God. His prayer was short, but to the purpose; God be merciful to me a sinner. Blessed be God, that we have this short prayer upon record, as an answered prayer; and that we are sure that he who prayed it, went to his house justified; for so shall we be, if we pray it, as he did, through Jesus Christ. He owned himself a sinner by nature, by practice, guilty before God. He had no dependence but upon the mercy of God; upon that alone he relied. And God's glory is to resist the proud, and give grace to the humble. Justification is of God in Christ; therefore the self-condemned, and not the self-righteous, are justified before God.

Verses 15–17

None are too little, too young, to be brought to Christ, who knows how to show kindness to those not capable of doing service to him. It is the mind of Christ, that little children should be brought to him. The promise is to us, and to our seed; therefore He will bid them welcome to him with us. And we must receive his kingdom as children, not by purchase, and must call it our Father's gift.

Verses 18–30

Many have a great deal in them very commendable, yet perish for lack of some one thing; so this ruler could not bear Christ's terms, which would part between him and his estate. Many who are loth to leave Christ, yet do leave him. After a long struggle between their convictions and their corruptions, their corruptions carry the day. They are very sorry that they cannot serve both; but if one must be quitted, it shall be their God, not their wordly gain. Their boasted obedience will be found mere outside show; the love of the world in some form or other lies at the root. Men are apt to speak too much of what they have left and lost, of what they have done and suffered for Christ, as Peter did. But we should rather be ashamed that there has been any regret or difficulty in doing it.

Verses 31–34

The Spirit of Christ, in the Old Testament prophets, testified beforehand his sufferings, and the glory that should follow, **1**Pe **1**:**11**. The disciples' prejudices were so strong, that they would not understand these things literally. They were so intent upon the prophecies which spake of Christ's glory, that they overlooked those which spake of his sufferings. People run into mistakes, because they read their Bibles by halves, and are only for the smooth things. We are as backward to learn the proper lessons from the sufferings, crucifixion, and resurrection of Christ, as the disciples were to what he told them as to those events; and for the same reason; self-love, and a desire of worldly objects, close our understandings.

Verses 35–43

This poor blind man sat by the wayside, begging. He was not only blind, but poor, the fitter emblem of the world of mankind which Christ came to heal and save. The prayer of faith, guided by Christ's encouraging promises, and grounded on them, shall not be in vain. The grace of Christ ought to be thankfully acknowledged, to the glory of God. It is for the glory of God if we follow Jesus, as those will do whose eyes are opened. We must praise God for his mercies to others, as well as for mercies to ourselves. Would we rightly understand these things, we must come to Christ, like the blind man, earnestly beseeching him to open our eyes, and to show us clearly the excellence of his precepts, and the value of his salvation.

Chapter 19

Chapter Outline	
The conversion of Zaccheus.	(1–10)
The parable of the nobleman and his servants.	(11–27)
Christ enters Jerusalem.	(28–40)
Christ laments over Jerusalem.	(41–48)

Verses 1–10

Those who sincerely desire a sight of Christ, like Zaccheus, will break through opposition, and take pains to see him. Christ invited himself to Zaccheus' house. Wherever Christ comes he opens the heart, and inclines it to receive him. He that has a mind to know Christ, shall be known of him. Those whom Christ calls, must humble themselves, and come down. We may well receive him joyfully, who brings all good with him. Zaccheus gave proofs publicly that he was become a true convert. He does not look to be justified by his works, as the Pharisee; but by his good works he will, through the grace of God, show the sincerity of his faith and repentance. Zaccheus is declared to be a happy man, now he is turned from sin to God. Now that he is saved from his sins, from the guilt of them, from the power of them, all the benefits of salvation are his. Christ is come to his house, and where Christ comes he brings salvation with him. He came into this lost world to seek and to save it. His design was to save, when there was no salvation in any other. He seeks those that sought him not, and asked not for him.

Verses 11–27

This parable is like that of the talents, Mt **25**. Those that are called to Christ, he furnishes with gifts needful for their business; and from those to whom he gives power, he expects service. The manifestation of the Spirit is given to every man to profit withal, **1**Co **12**:**7**. And as every one has received the gift, so let him minister the same, **1**Pe **4**:**10**. The account required, resembles that in the parable of the talents; and the punishment of the avowed enemies of Christ, as well as of false professors, is shown. The principal difference is, that the pound given to each seems to point out the gift of the gospel, which is the same to all who hear it; but the talents, distributed more or less, seem to mean that God gives different capacities and advantages to men, by which this one gift of the gospel may be differently improved.

Verses 28–40

Christ has dominion over all creatures, and may use them as he pleases. He has all men's hearts both under his eye and in his hand. Christ's triumphs, and his disciples' joyful praises, vex proud Pharisees, who are enemies to him and to his kingdom. But Christ, as he despises the contempt of the proud, so he accepts the praises of the humble. Pharisees would silence the praises of Christ, but they cannot; for as God can out of stones raise up children unto Abraham, and turn the stony heart to himself, so he can bring praise out of the mouths of children. And what will be the feelings of men when the Lord returns in glory to judge the world!

Verses 41–48

Who can behold the holy Jesus, looking forward to the miseries that awaited his murderers, weeping over the city where his precious blood was about to be shed, without seeing that the likeness of God in the believer, consists much in good-will and compassion? Surely those cannot be right who take up any doctrines of truth, so as to be hardened towards their fellow-sinners. But let every one remember, that though Jesus wept over Jerusalem, he executed awful vengeance upon it. Though he delights not in the death of a sinner, yet he will surely bring to pass his awful threatenings on those who neglect his salvation. The Son of God did not weep vain and causeless tears, nor for a light matter, nor for himself. He knows the value of souls, the weight of guilt, and how low it will press and sink mankind. May he then come and cleanse our hearts by his Spirit, from all that defiles. May sinners, on every side, become attentive to the words of truth and salvation.

Chapter 20

Chapter Outline	

The priests and scribes question Christ's authority.	(1–8)
The parable of the vineyard and husbandmen.	(9–19)
Of giving tribute.	(20–26)
Concerning the resurrection.	(27–38)
The scribes silenced.	(39–47)

Verses 1–8

Men often pretend to examine the evidences of revelation, and the truth of the gospel, when only seeking excuses for their own unbelief and disobedience. Christ answered these priests and scribes with a plain question about the baptism of John, which the common people could answer. They all knew it was from heaven, nothing in it had an earthly tendency. Those that bury the knowledge they have, are justly denied further knowledge. It was just with Christ to refuse to give account of his authority, to those who knew the baptism of John to be from heaven, yet would not believe in him, nor own their knowledge.

Verses 9–19

Christ spake this parable against those who resolved not to own his authority, though the evidence of it was so full. How many resemble the Jews who murdered the prophets and crucified Christ, in their enmity to God, and aversion to his service, desiring to live according to their lusts, without control! Let all who are favoured with God's word, look to it that they make proper use of their advantages. Awful will be the doom, both of those who reject the Son, and of those who profess to reverence Him, yet render not the fruits in due season. Though they could not but own that for such a sin, such a punishment was just, yet they could not bear to hear of it. It is the folly of sinners, that they persevere in sinful ways, though they dread the destruction at the end of those ways.

Verses 20–26

Those who are most crafty in their designs against Christ and his gospel, cannot hide them. He did not give a direct answer, but reproved them for offering to impose upon him; and they could not fasten upon any thing wherewith to stir up either the governor or the people against him. The wisdom which is from above, will direct all who teach the way of God truly, to avoid the snares laid for them by wicked men; and will teach our duty to God, to our rulers, and to all men, so clearly, that opposers will have no evil to say of us.

Verses 27–38

It is common for those who design to undermine any truth of God, to load it with difficulties. But we wrong ourselves, and wrong the truth of Christ, when we form our notions of the world of spirits by this world of sense. There are more worlds than one; a present visible world, and a future unseen world; and let every one compare this world and that world, and give the preference in his thoughts and cares to that which deserves them. Believers shall obtain the resurrection from the dead, that is the blessed resurrection. What shall be the happy state of the inhabitants of that world, we cannot express or conceive, **1**Co **2**:**9**. Those that are entered into the joy of their Lord, are entirely taken up therewith; when there is perfection of holiness there will be no occasion for preservatives from sin. And when God called himself the God of these patriarchs, he meant that he was a God all-sufficient to them, Ge **17**:**1**, their exceeding great Reward, Ge **15**:**1**. He never did that for them in this world, which answered the full extent of his undertaking; therefore there must be another life, in which he will do that for them, which will completely fulfil the promise.

Verses 39–47

The scribes commended the reply Christ made to the Sadducees about the resurrection, but they were silenced by a question concerning the Messiah. Christ, as God, was David's Lord; but Christ, as man, was David's son. The scribes would receive the severest judgement for defrauding the poor widows, and for their abuse of religion, particularly of prayer, which they used as a pretence for carrying on worldly and wicked plans. Dissembled piety is double sin. Then let us beg of God to keep us from pride, ambition, covetousness, and every evil thing; and to teach us to seek that honour which comes from him alone.

Chapter 21

Chapter Outline	
Christ commends a poor widow.	(1–4)
His prophecy.	(5–28)
Christ exhorts to watchfulness.	(29–38)

Verses 1–4

From the offering of this poor widow, learn that what we rightly give for the relief of the poor, and the support of God's worship, is given unto God; and our Saviour sees with pleasure whatever we have in our hearts to give for the relief of his members, or for his service. Blessed Lord! the poorest of thy servants have two mites, they have a soul and a body; persuade and enable us to offer both unto thee; how happy shall we be in thine accepting of them!

Verses 5–28

With much curiosity those about Christ ask as to the time when the great desolation should be. He answers with clearness and fulness, as far as was necessary to teach them their duty; for all knowledge is desirable as far as it is in order to practice. Though spiritual judgements are the most common in gospel times, yet God makes use of temporal judgments also. Christ tells them what hard things they should suffer for his name's sake, and encourages them to bear up under their trials, and to go on in their work, notwithstanding the opposition they would meet with. God will stand by you, and own you, and assist you. This was remarkably fulfilled after the pouring out of the Spirit, by whom Christ gave his disciples wisdom and utterance. Though we may be losers for Christ, we shall not, we cannot be losers by him, in the end. It is our duty and interest at all times, especially in perilous, trying times, to secure the safety of our own souls. It is by Christian patience we keep possession of our own souls, and keep out all those impressions which would put us out of temper. We may view the prophecy before us much as those Old Testament prophecies, which, together with their great object, embrace, or glance at some nearer object of importance to the church. Having given an idea of the times for about thirty-eight years next to come, Christ shows what all those things would end in, namely, the destruction of Jerusalem, and the utter dispersion of the Jewish nation; which would be a type and figure of Christ's second coming. The scattered Jews around us preach the truth of Christianity; and prove, that though heaven and earth shall pass away, the words of Jesus shall not pass away. They also remind us to pray for those times when neither the real, nor the spiritual Jerusalem, shall any longer be trodden down by the Gentiles, and when both Jews and Gentiles shall be turned to the Lord. When Christ came to destroy the Jews, he came to redeem the Christians that were persecuted and oppressed by them; and then had the churches rest. When he comes to judge the world, he will redeem all that are his from their troubles. So fully did the Divine judgements come upon the Jews, that their city is set as an example before us, to show that sins will not pass unpunished; and that the terrors of the Lord, and his threatenings against impenitent sinners, will all come to pass, even as his word was true, and his wrath great upon Jerusalem.

Verses 29–38

Christ tells his disciples to observe the signs of the times, which they might judge by. He charges them to look upon the ruin of the Jewish nation as near. Yet this race and family of Abraham shall not be rooted out; it shall survive as a nation, and be found as prophesied, when the Son of man shall be revealed. He cautions them against being secure and sensual. This command is given to all Christ's disciples, Take heed to yourselves, that ye be not overpowered by temptations, nor betrayed by your own corruptions. We cannot be safe, if we are carnally secure. Our danger is, lest the day of death and of judgment should come upon us when we are not prepared. Lest, when we are called to meet our Lord, that be the furthest from our thoughts, which ought to be nearest our hearts. For so it will come upon the most of men, who dwell upon the earth, and mind earthly things only, and have no con**verse** with heaven. It will be a terror and a destruction to them. Here see what should be our aim, that we may be accounted worthy to escape all those things; that when the judgements of God are abroad, we may not be in the common calamity, or it may not be that to us which it is to others. Do you ask how you may be found worthy to stand before Christ at that day? Those who never yet sought Christ, let them now go unto him; those who never yet were humbled for their sins, let them now begin; those who have already begun, let them go forward and be kept humbled. Watch therefore, and pray always. Watch against sin; watch in every duty, and make the most of every opportunity to do good. Pray always: those shall be accounted worthy to live a life of praise in the other world, who live a life of prayer in this world. May we begin, employ, and conclude each day attending to Christ's word, obeying his precepts, and following his example, that whenever he comes we may be found watching.

Chapter 22

Chapter Outline	
The treachery of Judas.	(1–6)
The passover.	(7–18)
The Lord's supper instituted.	(19, 20)
Christ admonishes the disciples.	(21–38)
Christ's agony in the garden.	(39–46)
Christ betrayed.	(47–53)
The fall of Peter.	(54–62)
Christ confesses himself to be the Son of God.	(63–71)

Verses 1–6

Christ knew all men, and had wise and holy ends in taking Judas to be a disciple. How he who knew Christ so well, came to betray him, we are here told; Satan entered into Judas. It is hard to say whether more mischief is done to Christ's kingdom, by the power of its open enemies, or by the treachery of its pretended friends; but without the latter, its enemies could not do so much evil as they do.

Verses 7–18

Christ kept the ordinances of the law, particularly that of the passover, to teach us to observe his gospel institutions, and most of all that of the Lord's supper. Those who go upon Christ's word, need not fear disappointment. According to the orders given them, the disciples got all ready for the passover. Jesus bids this passover welcome. He desired it, though he knew his sufferings would follow, because it was in order to his Father's glory and man's redemption. He takes his leave of all passovers, signifying thereby his doing away all the ordinances of the ceremonial law, of which the passover was one of the earliest and chief. That type was laid aside, because now in the kingdom of God the substance was come.

Verses 19, 20

The Lord's supper is a sign or memorial of Christ already come, who by dying delivered us; his death is in special manner set before us in that ordinance, by which we are reminded of it. The breaking of Christ's body as a sacrifice for us, is therein brought to our remembrance by the breaking of bread. Nothing can be more nourishing and satisfying to the soul, than the doctrine of Christ's making atonement for sin, and the assurance of an interest in that atonement. Therefore we do this in rememberance of what He did for us, when he died for us; and for a memorial of what we do, in joining ourselves to him in an everlasting covenant. The shedding of Christ's blood, by which the atonement was made, is represented by the wine in the cup.

Verses 21–38

How unbecoming is the worldly ambition of being the greatest, to the character of a follower of Jesus, who took upon him the form of a servant, and humbled himself to the death of the cross! In the way to eternal happiness, we must expect to be assaulted and sifted by Satan. If he cannot destroy, he will try to disgrace or distress us. Nothing more certainly forebodes a fall, in a professed follower of Christ, than self-confidence, with disregard to warnings, and contempt of danger. Unless we watch and pray always, we may be drawn in the course of the day into those sins which we were in the morning most resolved against. If believers were left to themselves, they would fall; but they are kept by the power of God, and the prayer of Christ. Our Lord gave notice of a very great change of circumstances now approaching. The disciples must not expect that their friends would be kind to them as they had been. Therefore, he that has a purse, let him take it, for he may need it. They must now expect that their enemies would be more fierce than they had been, and they would need weapons. At the time the apostles understood Christ to mean real weapons, but he spake only of the weapons of the spiritual warfare. The sword of the Spirit is the sword with which the disciples of Christ must furnish themselves.

Verses 39–46

Every description which the evangelists give of the state of mind in which our Lord entered upon this conflict, proves the tremendous nature of the assault, and the perfect foreknowledge of its terrors possessed by the meek and lowly Jesus. Here are three things not in the other evangelists. **1**. When Christ was in his agony, there appeared to him an angel from heaven, strengthening him. It was a part of his humiliation that he was thus strengthened by a ministering spirit. **2**. Being in agony, he prayed more earnestly. Prayer, though never out of season, is in a special manner seasonable when we are in an agony. **3**. In this agony his sweat was as it were great drops of blood falling down. This showed the travail of his soul. We should pray also to be enabled to resist unto the shedding of our blood, striving against sin, if ever called to it. When next you dwell in imagination upon the delights of some favourite sin, think of its effects as you behold them here! See its fearful effects in the garden of Gethsemane, and desire, by the help of God, deeply to hate and to forsake that enemy, to ransom sinners from whom the Redeemer prayed, agonized, and bled.

Verses 47–53

Nothing can be a greater affront or grief to the Lord Jesus, than to be betrayed by those who profess to be his followers, and say that they love him. Many instances there are, of Christ's being betrayed by those who, under the form of godliness, fight against the power of it. Jesus here gave an illustrious example of his own rule of doing good to those that hate us, as afterwards he did of praying for those that despitefully use us. Corrupt nature warps our conduct to extremes; we should seek for the Lord's direction before we act in difficult circumstances. Christ was willing to wait for his triumphs till his warfare was accomplished, and we must be so too. But the hour and the power of darkness were short, and such the triumphs of the wicked always will be.

Verses 54–62

Peter's fall was his denying that he knew Christ, and was his disciple; disowning him because of distress and danger. He that has once told a lie, is strongly tempted to persist: the beginning of that sin, like strife, is as the letting forth of water. The Lord turned and looked upon Peter. **1**. It was a convincing look. Jesus turned and looked upon him, as if he should say, Dost thou not know me, Peter? **2**. It was a chiding look. Let us think with what a rebuking countenance Christ may justly look upon us when we have sinned. **3**. It was an expostulating look. Thou who wast the most forward to confess me to be the Son of God, and didst solemnly promise thou wouldest never disown me! **4**. It was a compassionate look. Peter, how art thou fallen and undone if I do not help thee! **5**. It was a directing look, to go and bethink himself. **6**. It was a significant look; it signified the conveying of grace to Peter's heart, to enable him to repent. The grace of God works in and by the word of God, brings that to mind, and sets that home upon the conscience, and so gives the soul the happy turn. Christ looked upon the chief priests, and made no impression upon them as he did on Peter. It was not the mere look from Christ, but the Divine grace with it, that restored Peter.

Verses 63–71

Those that condemned Jesus for a blasphemer, were the vilest blasphemers. He referred them to his second coming, for the full proof of his being the Christ, to their confusion, since they would not admit the proof of it to their conviction. He owns himself to be the Son of God, though he knew he should suffer for it. Upon this they ground his condemnation. Their eyes being blinded, they rush on. Let us meditate on this amazing transaction, and consider Him who endured such contradiction of sinners against himself.

Chapter 23

Chapter Outline	
Christ before Pilate.	(1–5)
Christ before Herod.	(6–12)
Barabbas preferred to Christ.	(13–25)
Christ speaks of the destruction of Jerusalem.	(26–31)
The crucifixion, The repentant malefactor.	(32–43)
The death of Christ.	(44–49)
The burial of Christ.	(50–56)

Verses 1–5

Pilate well understood the difference between armed forces and our Lord's followers. But instead of being softened by Pilate's declaration of his innocence, and considering whether they were not bringing the guilt of innocent blood upon themselves, the Jews were the more angry. The Lord brings his designs to a glorious end, even by means of those who follow the devices of their own hearts. Thus all parties joined, so as to prove the innocence of Jesus, who was the atoning sacrifice for our sins.

Verses 6–12

Herod had heard many things of Jesus in Galilee, and out of curiosity longed to see him. The poorest beggar that asked a miracle for the relief of his necessity, was never denied; but this proud prince, who asked for a miracle only to gratify his curiosity, is refused. He might have seen Christ and his wondrous works in Galilee, and would not, therefore it is justly said, Now he would see them, and shall not. Herod sent Christ again to Pilate: the friendships of wicked men are often formed by union in wickedness. They agree in little, except in enmity to God, and contempt of Christ.

Verses 13–25

The fear of man brings many into this snare, that they will do an unjust thing, against their consciences, rather than get into trouble. Pilate declares Jesus innocent, and has a mind to release him; yet, to please the people, he would punish him as an evil-doer. If no fault be found in him, why chastise him? Pilate yielded at length; he had not courage to go against so strong a stream. He delivered Jesus to their will, to be crucified.

Verses 26–31

We have here the blessed Jesus, the Lamb of God, led as a lamb to the slaughter, to the sacrifice. Though many reproached and reviled him, yet some pitied him. But the death of Christ was his victory and triumph over his enemies: it was our deliverance, the purchase of eternal life for us. Therefore weep not for him, but let us weep for our own sins, and the sins of our children, which caused his death; and weep for fear of the miseries we shall bring upon ourselves, if we slight his love, and reject his grace. If God delivered him up to such sufferings as these, because he was made a sacrifice for sin, what will he do with sinners themselves, who make themselves a dry tree, a corrupt and wicked generation, and good for nothing! The bitter sufferings of our Lord Jesus should make us stand in awe of the justice of God. The best saints, compared with Christ, are dry trees; if he suffer, why may not they expect to suffer? And what then shall the damnation of sinners be! Even the sufferings of Christ preach terror to obstinate transgressors.

Verses 32–43

As soon as Christ was fastened to the cross, he prayed for those who crucified him. The great thing he died to purchase and procure for us, is the forgiveness of sin. This he prays for. Jesus was crucified between two thieves; in them were shown the different effects the cross of Christ would have upon the children of men in the preaching the gospel. One malefactor was hardened to the last. No troubles of themselves will change a wicked heart. The other was softened at the last: he was snatched as a brand out of the burning, and made a monument of Divine mercy. This gives no encouragement to any to put off repentance to their death-beds, or to hope that they shall then find mercy. It is certain that true repentance is never too late; but it is as certain that late repentance is seldom true. None can be sure they shall have time to repent at death, but every man may be sure he cannot have the advantages this penitent thief had. We shall see the case to be singular, if we observe the uncommon effects of God's grace upon this man. He reproved the other for railing on Christ. He owned that he deserved what was done to him. He believed Jesus to have suffered wrongfully. Observe his faith in this prayer. Christ was in the depth of disgrace, suffering as a deceiver, and not delivered by his Father. He made this profession before the wonders were displayed which put honour on Christ's sufferings, and startled the centurion. He believed in a life to come, and desired to be happy in that life; not like the other thief, to be only saved from the cross. Observe his humility in this prayer. All his request is, Lord, remember me; quite referring it to Jesus in what way to remember him. Thus he was humbled in true repentance, and he brought forth all the fruits for repentance his circumstances would admit. Christ upon the cross, is gracious like Christ upon the throne. Though he was in the greatest struggle and agony, yet he had pity for a poor penitent. By this act of grace we are to understand that Jesus Christ died to open the kingdom of heaven to all penitent, obedient believers. It is a single instance in Scripture; it should teach us to despair of none, and that none should despair of themselves; but lest it should be abused, it is contrasted with the awful state of the other thief, who died hardened in unbelief, though a crucified Saviour was so near him. Be sure that in general men die as they live.

Verses 44–49

We have here the death of Christ magnified by the wonders that attended it, and his death explained by the words with which he breathed out his soul. He was willing to offer himself. Let us seek to glorify God by true repentance and conversion; by protesting against those who crucify the Saviour; by a sober, righteous, and godly life; and by employing our talents in the service of Him who died for us and rose again.

Verses 50–56

Many, though they do not make any show in outward profession, yet, like Joseph of Arimathea, will be far more ready to do real service, when there is occasion, than others who make a greater noise. Christ was buried in haste, because the sabbath drew on. Weeping must not hinder sowing. Though they were in tears for the death of their Lord, yet they must prepare to keep holy the sabbath. When the sabbath draws on, there must be preparation. Our worldly affairs must be so ordered, that they may not hinder us from our sabbath work; and our holy affections so stirred up, that they may carry us on in it. In whatever business we engage, or however our hearts may be affected, let us never fail to get ready for, and to keep holy, the day of sacred rest, which is the Lord's day.

Chapter 24

Chapter Outline	
The resurrection of Christ.	(1–12)
He appears to two disciples on the way to Emmaus.	(13–27)

And makes himself known to them.	(28–35)
Christ appears to the other disciples.	(36–49)
His ascension.	(50–53)

Verses 1–12

See the affection and respect the women showed to Christ, after he was dead and buried. Observe their surprise when they found the stone rolled away, and the grave empty. Christians often perplex themselves about that with which they should comfort and encourage themselves. They look rather to find their Master in his grave-clothes, than angels in their shining garments. The angels assure them that he is risen from the dead; is risen by his own power. These angels from heaven bring not any new gospel, but remind the women of Christ's words, and teach them how to apply them. We may wonder that these disciples, who believed Jesus to be the Son of God and the true Messiah, who had been so often told that he must die, and rise again, and then enter into his glory, who had seen him more than once raise the dead, yet should be so backward to believe his raising himself. But all our mistakes in religion spring from ignorance or forgetfulness of the words Christ has spoken. Peter now ran to the sepulchre, who so lately ran from his Master. He was amazed. There are many things puzzling and perplexing to us, which would be plain and profitable, if we rightly understood the words of Christ.

Verses 13–27

This appearance of Jesus to the two disciples going to Emmaus, happened the same day that he rose from the dead. It well becomes the disciples of Christ to talk together of his death and resurrection; thus they may improve one another's knowledge, refresh one another's memory, and stir up each other's devout affections. And where but two together are well employed in work of that kind, he will come to them, and make a third. Those who seek Christ, shall find him: he will manifest himself to those that inquire after him; and give knowledge to those who use the helps for knowledge which they have. No matter how it was, but so it was, they did not know him; he so ordering it, that they might the more freely discourse with him. Christ's disciples are often sad and sorrowful, even when they have reason to rejoice; but through the weakness of their faith, they cannot take the comfort offered to them. Though Christ is entered into his state of exaltation, yet he notices the sorrows of his disciples, and is afflicted in their afflictions. Those are strangers in Jerusalem, that know not of the death and sufferings of Jesus. Those who have the knowledge of Christ crucified, should seek to spread that knowledge. Our Lord Jesus reproved them for the weakness of their faith in the Scriptures of the Old Testament. Did we know more of the Divine counsels as far as they are made known in the Scriptures, we should not be subject to the perplexities we often entangle ourselves in. He shows them that the sufferings of Christ were really the appointed way to his glory; but the cross of Christ was that to which they could not reconcile themselves. Beginning at Moses, the first inspired writer of the Old Testament, Jesus expounded to them the things concerning himself. There are many passages throughout all the Scriptures concerning Christ, which it is of great advantage to put together. We cannot go far in any part, but we meet with something that has reference to Christ, some prophecy, some promise, some prayer, some type or other. A golden thread of gospel grace runs through the whole web of the Old Testament. Christ is the best expositor of Scripture; and even after his resurrection, he led people to know the mystery concerning himself, not by advancing new notions, but by showing how the Scripture was fulfilled, and turning them to the earnest study of it.

Verses 28–35

If we would have Christ dwell with us, we must be earnest with him. Those that have experienced the pleasure and profit of communion with him, cannot but desire more of his company. He took bread, and blessed it, and brake, and gave to them. This he did with his usual authority and affection, with the same manner, perhaps with the same words. He here teaches us to crave a blessing on every meal. See how Christ by his Spirit and grace makes himself known to the souls of his people. He opens the Scriptures to them. He meets them at his table, in the ordinance of the Lord's supper; is known to them in breaking of bread. But the work is completed by the opening of the eyes of their mind; yet it is but short views we have of Christ in this world, but when we enter heaven, we shall see him for ever. They had found the preaching powerful, even when they knew not the preacher. Those Scriptures which speak of Christ, will warm the hearts of his true disciples. That is likely to do most good, which affects us with the love of Jesus in dying for us. It is the duty of those to whom he has shown himself, to let others know what he has done for their souls. It is of great use for the disciples of Christ to compare their experiences, and tell them to each other.

Verses 36–49

Jesus appeared in a miraculous manner, assuring the disciples of his peace, though they had so lately forsaken him, and promising spiritual peace with every blessing. Many troublesome thoughts which disquiet our minds, rise from mistakes concerning Christ. All the troublesome thoughts which rise in our hearts at any time, are known to the Lord Jesus, and are displeasing to him. He spake with them on their unreasonable unbelief. Nothing had passed but what was foretold by the prophets, and necessary for the salvation of sinners. And now all men should be taught the nature and necessity of repentance, in order to the forgiveness of their sins. And these blessings were to be sought for, by faith in the name of Jesus. Christ by his Spirit works on the minds of men. Even good men need to have their understandings opened. But that we may have right thoughts of Christ, there needs no more than to be made to understand the Scriptures.

Verses 50–53

Christ ascended from Bethany, near the Mount of Olives. There was the garden in which his sufferings began; there he was in his agony. Those that would go to heaven, must ascend thither from the house of sufferings and sorrows. The disciples did not see him rise out of the grave; his resurrection could be proved by their seeing him alive afterwards: but they saw him ascend into heaven; they could not otherwise have a proof of his ascension. He lifted up his hands, and blessed them. He did not go away in displeasure, but in love, he left a blessing behind him. As he arose, so he ascended, by his own power. They worshipped him. This fresh display of Christ's glory drew from them fresh acknowledgments. They returned to Jerusalem with great joy. The glory of Christ is the joy of all true believers, even while they are here in this world. While waiting for God's promises, we must go forth to meet them with our praises. And nothing better prepares the mind for receiving the Holy Ghost. Fears are silenced, sorrows sweetened and allayed, and hopes kept up. And this is the ground of a Christian's boldness at the throne of grace; yea, the Father's throne is the throne of grace to us, because it is also the throne of our Mediator, Jesus Christ. Let us rely on his promises, and plead them. Let us attend his ordinances, praise and bless God for his mercies, set our affections on things above, and expect the Redeemer's return to complete our happiness. Amen. Even so, Lord Jesus, come quickly.

John

The apostle and evangelist, John, seems to have been the youngest of the twelve. He was especially favoured with our Lord's regard and confidence, so as to be spoken of as the disciple whom Jesus loved. He was very sincerely attached to his Master. He exercised his ministry at Jerusalem with much success, and outlived the destruction of that city, agreeably to Christ's prediction, ch. **21**:**22**. History relates that after the death of Christ's mother, John resided chiefly at Ephesus. Towards the close of Domitian's reign he was banished to the isle of Patmos, where he wrote his Revelation. On the accession of Nerva, he was set at liberty, and returned to Ephesus, where it is thought he wrote his Gospel and Epistles, about A. D. **97**, and died soon after. The design of this Gospel appears to be to convey to the Christian world, just notions of the real nature, office, and character of that Divine Teacher, who came to instruct and to redeem mankind. For this purpose, John was directed to select for his narrative, those passages of our Saviour's life, which most clearly displayed his Divine power and authority; and those of his discourses, in which he spake most plainly of his own nature, and of the power of his death, as an atonement for the sins of the world. By omitting, or only briefly mentioning, the events recorded by the other evangelists, John gave testimony that their narratives are true, and left room for the doctrinal statements already mentioned, and for particulars omitted in the other Gospels, many of which are exceedingly important.

Chapter 1

Chapter Outline	
The Divinity of Christ.	(1–5)
His Divine and human nature.	(6–14)
John the Baptist's testimony to Christ.	(15–18)
John's public testimony concerning Christ.	(19–28)
Other testimonies of John concerning Christ.	(29–36)
Andrew and another disciple follow Jesus.	(37–42)
Philip and Nathanael called.	(43–51)

Verses 1–5

The plainest reason why the Son of God is called the Word, seems to be, that as our words explain our minds to others, so was the Son of God sent in order to reveal his Father's mind to the world. What the evangelist says of Christ proves that he is God. He asserts, His existence in the beginning; His coexistence with the Father. The Word was with God. All things were made by him, and not as an instrument. Without him was not any thing made that was made, from the highest angel to the meanest worm. This shows how well qualified he was for the work of our redemption and salvation. The light of reason, as well as the life of sense, is derived from him, and depends upon him. This eternal Word, this true Light shines, but the darkness comprehends it not. Let us pray without ceasing, that our eyes may be opened to behold this Light, that we may walk in it; and thus be made wise unto salvation, by faith in Jesus Christ.

Verses 6–14

John the Baptist came to bear witness concerning Jesus. Nothing more fully shows the darkness of men's minds, than that when the Light had appeared, there needed a witness to call attention to it. Christ was the true Light; that great Light which deserves to be called so. By his Spirit and grace he enlightens all that are enlightened to salvation; and those that are not enlightened by him, perish in darkness. Christ was in the world when he took our nature upon him, and dwelt among us. The Son of the Highest was here in this lower world. He was in the world, but not of it. He came to save a lost world, because it was a world of his own making. Yet the world knew him not. When he comes as a Judge, the world shall know him. Many say that they are Christ's own, yet do not receive him, because they will not part with their sins, nor have him to reign over them. All the children of God are born again. This new birth is through the word of God as the means, **1**Pe **1**:**23**, and by the Spirit of God as the Author. By his Divine presence Christ always was in the world. But now that the fulness of time was come, he was, after another manner, God manifested in the flesh. But observe the beams of his Divine glory, which darted through this veil of flesh. Men discover their weaknesses to those most familiar with them, but it was not so with Christ; those most intimate with him saw most of his glory. Although he was in the form of a servant, as to outward circumstances, yet, in respect of graces, his form was like the Son of God His Divine glory appeared in the holiness of his doctrine, and in his miracles. He was full of grace, fully acceptable to his Father, therefore qualified to plead for us; and full of truth, fully aware of the things he was to reveal.

Verses 15–18

As to the order of time and entrance on his work, Christ came after John, but in every other way he was before him. The expression clearly shows that Jesus had existence before he appeared on earth as man. All fulness dwells in him, from which alone fallen sinners have, and shall receive, by faith, all that renders them wise, strong, holy, useful, and happy. Our receivings by Christ are all summed up in this one word, grace; we have received "even grace," a gift so great, so rich, so invaluable; the good will of God towards us, and the good work of God in us. The law of God is holy, just, and good; and we should make the proper use of it. But we cannot derive from it pardon, righteousness, or strength. It teaches us to adorn the doctrine of God our Saviour, but it cannot supply the place of that doctrine. As no mercy comes from God to sinners but through Jesus Christ, no man can come to the Father but by him; no man can know God, except as he is made known in the only begotten and beloved Son.

Verses 19–28

John disowns himself to be the Christ, who was now expected and waited for. He came in the spirit and power of Elias, but he was not the person of Elias. John was not that Prophet whom Moses said the Lord would raise up to them of their brethren, like unto him. He was not such a prophet as they expected, who would rescue them from the Romans. He gave such an account of himself, as might excite and awaken them to hearken to him. He baptized the people with water as a profession of repentance, and as an outward sign of the spiritual blessings to be conferred on them by the Messiah, who was in the midst of them, though they knew him not, and to whom he was unworthy to render the meanest service.

Verses 29–36

John saw Jesus coming to him, and pointed him out as the Lamb of God. The paschal lamb, in the shedding and sprinkling of its blood, the roasting and eating of its flesh, and all the other circumstances of the ordinance, represented the salvation of sinners by faith in Christ. And the lambs sacrificed every morning and evening, can only refer to Christ slain as a sacrifice to redeem us to God by his blood. John came as a preacher of repentance, yet he told his followers that they were to look for the pardon of their sins to Jesus only, and to his death. It agrees with God's glory to pardon all who depend on the atoning sacrifice of Christ. He takes away the sin of the world; purchases pardon for all that repent and believe the gospel. This encourages our faith; if Christ takes away the sin of the world, then why not my sin? He bore sin for us, and so bears it from us. God could have taken away sin, by taking away the sinner, as he took away the sin of the old world; but here is a way of doing away sin, yet sparing the sinner, by making his Son sin, that is, a sin-offering, for us. See Jesus taking away sin, and let that cause hatred of sin, and resolutions against it. Let us not hold that fast, which the Lamb of God came to take away. To confirm his testimony concerning Christ, John declares the appearance at his baptism, in which God himself bore witness to him. He saw and bare record that he is the Son of God. This is the end and object of John's testimony, that Jesus was the promised Messiah. John took every opportunity that offered to lead people to Christ.

Verses 37–42

The strongest and most prevailing argument with an awakened soul to follow Christ, is, that it is he only who takes away sin. Whatever communion there is between our souls and Christ, it is he who begins the discourse. He asked, What seek ye? The question Jesus put to them, we should all put to ourselves when we begin to follow Him, What do we design and desire? In following Christ, do we seek the favour of God and eternal life? He invites them to come without delay. Now is the accepted time, **2**Co **6**:**2**. It is good for us to be where Christ is, wherever it be. We ought to labour for the spiritual welfare of those related to us, and seek to bring them to Him. Those who come to Christ, must come with a fixed resolution to be firm and constant to him, like a stone, solid and stedfast; and it is by his grace that they are so.

Verses 43–51

See the nature of true Christianity, it is following Jesus; devoting ourselves to him, and treading in his steps. Observe the objection Nathanael made. All who desire to profit by the word of God, must beware of prejudices against places, or denominations of men. They should examine for themselves, and they will sometimes find good where they looked for none. Many people are kept from the ways of religion by the unreasonable prejudices they conceive. The best way to remove false notions of religion, is to make trial of it. In Nathanael there was no guile. His profession was not hypocritical. He was not a dissembler, nor dishonest; he was a sound character, a really upright, godly man. Christ knows what men are indeed. Does He know us? Let us desire to know him. Let us seek and pray to be Israelites indeed, in whom is no guile; truly Christians, approved of Christ himself. Some things weak, imperfect, and sinful, are found in all, but hypocrisy belongs not to a believer's character. Jesus witnessed what passed when Nathanael was under the fig-tree. Probably he was then in fervent prayer, seeking direction as to the Hope and Consolation of Israel, where no human eye observed him. This showed him that our Lord knew the secrets of his heart. Through Christ we commune with, and benefit by the holy angels; and things in heaven and things on earth are reconciled and united together.

Chapter 2

Chapter Outline	
The miracle at Cana.	(1–11)
Christ casts the buyers and sellers out of the temple.	(12–22)
Many believe in Christ.	(23–25)

Verses 1–11

It is very desirable when there is a marriage, to have Christ own and bless it. Those that would have Christ with them at their marriage, must invite him by prayer, and he will come. While in this world we sometimes find ourselves in straits, even when we think ourselves in fulness. There was want at a marriage feast. Those who are come to care for the things of the world, must look for trouble, and count upon disappointment. In our addresses to Christ, we must humbly spread our case before him, and then refer ourselves to him to do as he pleases. In Christ's reply to his mother there was no disrespect. He used the same word when speaking to her with affection from the cross; yet it is a standing testimony against the idolatry of after-ages, in giving undue honours to his mother. His hour is come when we know not what to do. Delays of mercy are not denials of prayer. Those that expect Christ's favours, must observe his orders with ready obedience. The way of duty is the way to mercy; and Christ's methods must not be objected against. The beginning of Moses' miracles was turning water into blood, Ex **7**:**20**; the beginning of Christ's miracles was turning water into wine; which may remind us of the difference between the law of Moses and the gospel of Christ. He showed that he improves creature-comforts to all true believers, and make them comforts indeed. And Christ's works are all for use. Has he turned thy water into wine, given thee knowledge and grace? it is to profit withal; therefore draw out now, and use it. It was the best wine. Christ's works commend themselves even to those who know not their Author. What was produced by miracles, always was the best in its kind. Though Christ hereby allows a right use of wine, he does not in the least do away his own caution, which is, that our hearts be not at any time overcharged with surfeiting and drunkenness, Lu **21**:**34**. Though we need not scruple to feast with our friends on proper occasions, yet every social interview should be so conducted, that we might invite the Redeemer to join with us, if he were now on earth; and all levity, luxury, and excess offend him.

Verses 12–22

The first public work in which we find Christ engaged, was driving from the temple the traders whom the covetous priests and rulers encouraged to make a market-place of its courts. Those now make God's house a house of merchandise, whose minds are filled with cares about worldly business when attending religious exercises, or who perform Divine offices for love of gain. Christ, having thus cleansed the temple, gave a sign to those who demanded it, to prove his authority for so doing. He foretells his death by the Jews' malice, Destroy ye this temple; I will permit you to destroy it. He foretells his resurrection by his own power; In three days I will raise it up. Christ took again his own life. Men mistake by understanding that according to the letter, which the Scripture speaks by way of figure. When Jesus was risen from the dead, his disciples remembered he has said this. It helps much in understanding the Divine word, to observe the fulfilling of the Scriptures.

Verses 23–25

Our Lord knew all men, their nature, dispositions, affections, designs, so as we do not know any man, not even ourselves. He knows his crafty enemies, and all their secret projects; his false friends, and their true characters. He knows who are truly his, knows their uprightness, and knows their weaknesses. We know what is done by men; Christ knows what is in them, he tries the heart. Beware of a dead faith, or a formal profession: carnal, empty professors are not to be trusted, and however men impose on others or themselves, they cannot impose on the heart-searching God.

Chapter 3

Chapter Outline	
Christ's discourse with Nicodemus.	(1–21)
The baptism of John of Christ John's testimony.	(22–36)

Verses 1–8

Nicodemus was afraid, or ashamed to be seen with Christ, therefore came in the night. When religion is out of fashion, there are many Nicodemites. But though he came by night, Jesus bid him welcome, and hereby taught us to encourage good beginnings, although weak. And though now he came by night, yet afterward he owned Christ publicly. He did not talk with Christ about state affairs, though he was a ruler, but about the concerns of his own soul and its salvation, and went at once to them. Our Saviour spoke of the necessity and nature of regeneration or the new birth, and at once directed Nicodemus to the source of holiness of the heart. Birth is the beginning of life; to be born again, is to begin to live anew, as those who have lived much amiss, or to little purpose. We must have a new nature, new principles, new affections, new aims. By our first birth we were corrupt, shapen in sin; therefore we must be made new creatures. No stronger expression could have been chosen to signify a great and most remarkable change of state and character. We must be entirely different from what we were before, as that which begins to be at any time, is not, and cannot be the same with that which was before. This new birth is from heaven, ch. **1**:**13**, and its tendency is to heaven. It is a great change made in the heart of a sinner, by the power of the Holy Spirit. It means that something is done in us, and for us, which we cannot do for ourselves. Something is wrong, whereby such a life begins as shall last for ever. We cannot otherwise expect any benefit by Christ; it is necessary to our happiness here and hereafter. What Christ speak, Nicodemus misunderstood, as if there had been no other way of regenerating and new-moulding an immortal soul, than by new-framing the body. But he acknowledged his ignorance, which shows a desire to be better informed. It is then further explained by the Lord Jesus. He shows the Author of this blessed change. It is not wrought by any wisdom or power of our own, but by the power of the blessed Spirit. We are shapen in iniquity, which makes it necessary that our nature be changed. We are not to marvel at this; for, when we consider the holiness of God, the depravity of our nature, and the happiness set before us, we shall not think it strange that so much stress is laid upon this. The regenerating work of the Holy Spirit is compared to water. It is also probable that Christ had reference to the ordinance of baptism. Not that all those, and those only, that are baptized, are saved; but without that new birth which is wrought by the Spirit, and signified by baptism, none shall be subjects of the kingdom of heaven. The same word signifies both the wind and the Spirit. The wind bloweth where it listeth for us; God directs it. The Spirit sends his influences where, and when, on whom, and in what measure and degree, he pleases. Though the causes are hidden, the effects are plain, when the soul is brought to mourn for sin, and to breathe after Christ. Christ's stating of the doctrine and the necessity of regeneration, it should seem, made it not clearer to Nicodemus. Thus the things of the Spirit of God are foolishness to the natural man. Many think that cannot be proved, which they cannot believe. Christ's discourse of gospel truths, ver. #(**11**–**13**), shows the folly of those who make these things strange unto them; and it recommends us to search them out. Jesus Christ is every way able to reveal the will of God to us; for he came down from heaven, and yet is in heaven. We have here a notice of Christ's two distinct natures in one person, so that while he is the Son of man, yet he is in heaven. God is the "HE THAT IS," and heaven is the dwelling-place of his holiness. The knowledge of this must be from above, and can be received by faith alone. Jesus Christ came to save us by healing us, as the children of Israel, stung with fiery serpents, were cured and lived by looking up to the brazen serpent, Nu **21**:**6**–**9**. In this observe the deadly and destructive nature of sin. Ask awakened consciences, ask damned sinners, they will tell you, that how charming soever the allurements of sin may be, at the last it bites like a serpent. See the powerful remedy against this fatal malady. Christ is plainly set forth to us in the gospel. He whom we offended is our Peace, and the way of applying for a cure is by believing. If any so far slight either their disease by sin, or the method of cure by Christ, as not to receive Christ upon his own terms, their ruin is upon their own heads. He has said, Look and be saved, look and live; lift up the eyes of your faith to Christ crucified. And until we have grace to do this, we shall not be cured, but still are wounded with the stings of Satan, and in a dying state. Jesus Christ came to save us by pardoning us, that we might not die by the sentence of the law. Here is gospel, good news indeed. Here is God's love in giving his Son for the world. God so loved the world; so really, so richly. Behold and wonder, that the great God should love such a worthless world! Here, also, is the great gospel duty, to believe in Jesus Christ. God having given him to be our Prophet, Priest, and King, we must give up ourselves to be ruled, and taught, and saved by him. And here is the great gospel benefit, that whoever believes in Christ, shall not perish, but shall have everlasting life. God was in Christ reconciling the world to himself, and so saving it. It could not be saved, but through him; there is no salvation in any other. From all this is shown the happiness of true believers; he that believeth in Christ is not condemned. Though he has been a great sinner, yet he is not dealt with according to what his sins deserve. How great is the sin of unbelievers! God sent One to save us, that was dearest to himself; and shall he not be dearest to us? How great is the misery of unbelievers! they are condemned already; which speaks a certain condemnation; a present condemnation. The wrath of God now fastens upon them; and their own hearts condemn them. There is also a condemnation grounded on their former guilt; they are open to the law for all their sins; because they are not by faith interested in the gospel pardon. Unbelief is a sin against the remedy. It springs from the enmity of the heart of man to God, from love of sin in some form. Read also the doom of those that would not know Christ. Sinful works are works of darkness. The wicked world keep as far from this light as they can, lest their deeds should be reproved. Christ is hated, because sin is loved. If they had not hated saving knowledge, they would not sit down contentedly in condemning ignorance. On the other hand, renewed hearts bid this light welcome. A good man acts truly and sincerely in all he does. He desires to know what the will of God is, and to do it, though against his own worldly interest. A change in his whole character and conduct has taken place. The love of God is shed abroad in his heart by the Holy Ghost, and is become the commanding principle of his actions. So long as he continues under a load of unforgiven guilt, there can be little else than slavish fear of God; but when his doubts are done away, when he sees the righteous ground whereon this forgiveness is built, he rests on it as his own, and is united to God by unfeigned love. Our works are good when the will of God is the rule of them, and the glory of God the end of them; when they are done in his strength, and for his sake; to him, and not to men. Regeneration, or the new birth, is a subject to which the world is very **averse**; it is, however, the grand concern, in comparison with which every thing else is but trifling. What does it signify though we have food to eat in plenty, and variety of raiment to put on, if we are not born again? if after a few mornings and evenings spent in unthinking mirth, carnal pleasure, and riot, we die in our sins, and lie down in sorrow? What does it signify though we are well able to act our parts in life, in every other respect, if at last we hear from the Supreme Judge, "Depart from me, I know you not, ye workers of iniquity?"

Verses 22–36

John was fully satisfied with the place and work assigned him; but Jesus came on a more important work. He also knew that Jesus would increase in honour and influence, for of his government and peace there would be no end, while he himself would be less followed. John knew that Jesus came from heaven as the Son of God, while he was a sinful, mortal man, who could only speak about the more plain subjects of religion. The words of Jesus were the words of God; he had the Spirit, not by measure, as the prophets, but in all fulness. Everlasting life could only be had by faith in Him, and might be thus obtained; whereas all those, who believe not in the Son of God, cannot partake of salvation, but the wrath of God for ever rests upon them.

Chapter 4

Chapter Outline	
Christ's departure into Galilee.	(1–3)
His discourse with the Samaritan woman.	(4–26)
The effects of Christ's conversation with the woman of Samaria.	(27–42)
Christ heals the nobleman's son.	(43–54)

Verses 1–3

Jesus applied himself more to preaching, which was the more excellent, **1**Co **1**:**17**, than to baptism. He would put honour upon his disciples, by employing them to baptize. He teaches us that the benefit of sacraments depends not on the hand that administers them.

Verses 4–26

There was great hatred between the Samaritans and the Jews. Christ's road from Judea to Galilee lay through Samaria. We should not go into places of temptation but when we needs must; and then must not dwell in them, but hasten through them. We have here our Lord Jesus under the common fatigue of travellers. Thus we see that he was truly a man. Toil came in with sin; therefore Christ, having made himself a curse for us, submitted to it. Also, he was a poor man, and went all his journeys on foot. Being wearied, he sat thus on the well; he had no couch to rest upon. He sat thus, as people wearied with travelling sit. Surely, we ought readily to submit to be like the Son of God in such things as these. Christ asked a woman for water. She was surprised because he did not show the anger of his own nation against the Samaritans. Moderate men of all sides are men wondered at. Christ took the occasion to teach her Divine things: he converted this woman, by showing her ignorance and sinfulness, and her need of a Saviour. By this living water is meant the Spirit. Under this comparison the blessing of the Messiah had been promised in the Old Testament. The graces of the Spirit, and his comforts, satisfy the thirsting soul, that knows its own nature and necessity. What Jesus spake figuratively, she took literally. Christ shows that the water of Jacob's well yielded a very short satisfaction. Of whatever waters of comfort we drink, we shall thirst again. But whoever partakes of the Spirit of grace, and the comforts of the gospel, shall never want that which will abundantly satisfy his soul. Carnal hearts look no higher than carnal ends. Give it me, saith she, not that I may have everlasting life, which Christ proposed, but that I come not hither to draw. The carnal mind is very ingenious in shifting off convictions, and keeping them from fastening. But how closely our Lord Jesus brings home the conviction to her conscience! He severely reproved her present state of life. The woman acknowledged Christ to be a prophet. The power of his word in searching the heart, and convincing the conscience of secret things, is a proof of Divine authority. It should cool our contests, to think that the things we are striving about are passing away. The object of worship will continue still the same, God, as a Father; but an end shall be put to all differences about the place of worship. Reason teaches us to consult decency and convenience in the places of our worship; but religion gives no preference to one place above another, in respect of holiness and approval with God. The Jews were certainly in the right. Those who by the Scriptures have obtained some knowledge of God, know whom they worship. The word of salvation was of the Jews. It came to other nations through them. Christ justly preferred the Jewish worship before the Samaritan, yet here he speaks of the former as soon to be done away. God was about to be revealed as the Father of all believers in every nation. The spirit or the soul of man, as influenced by the Holy Spirit, must worship God, and have communion with him. Spiritual affections, as shown in fervent prayers, supplications, and thanksgivings, form the worship of an upright heart, in which God delights and is glorified. The woman was disposed to leave the matter undecided, till the coming of the Messiah. But Christ told her, I that speak to thee, am He. She was an alien and a hostile Samaritan, merely speaking to her was thought to disgrace our Lord Jesus. Yet to this woman did our Lord reveal himself more fully than as yet he had done to any of his disciples. No past sins can bar our acceptance with him, if we humble ourselves before him, believing in him as the Christ, the Saviour of the world.

Verses 27–42

The disciples wondered that Christ talked thus with a Samaritan. Yet they knew it was for some good reason, and for some good end. Thus when particular difficulties occur in the word and providence of God, it is good to satisfy ourselves that all is well that Jesus Christ says and does. Two things affected the woman. The extent of his knowledge. Christ knows all the thoughts, words, and actions, of all the children of men. And the power of his word. He told her secret sins with power. She fastened upon that part of Christ's discourse, many would think she would have been most shy of repeating; but the knowledge of Christ, into which we are led by conviction of sin, is most likely to be sound and saving. They came to him: those who would know Christ, must meet him where he records his name. Our Master has left us an example, that we may learn to do the will of God as he did; with diligence, as those that make a business of it; with delight and pleasure in it. Christ compares his work to harvest-work. The harvest is appointed and looked for before it comes; so was the gospel. Harvest-time is busy time; all must be then at work. Harvest-time is a short time, and harvest-work must be done then, or not at all; so the time of the gospel is a season, which if once past, cannot be recalled. God sometimes uses very weak and unlikely instruments for beginning and carrying on a good work. Our Saviour, by teaching one poor woman, spread knowledge to a whole town. Blessed are those who are not offended at Christ. Those taught of God, are truly desirous to learn more. It adds much to the praise of our love to Christ and his word, if it conquers prejudices. Their faith grew. In the matter of it: they believed him to be the Saviour, not only of the Jews but of the world. In the certainty of it: we know that this is indeed the Christ. And in the ground of it, for we have heard him ourselves.

Verses 43–54

The father was a nobleman, yet the son was sick. Honours and titles are no security from sickness and death. The greatest men must go themselves to God, must become beggars. The nobleman did not stop from his request till he prevailed. But at first he discovered the weakness of his faith in the power of Christ. It is hard to persuade ourselves that distance of time and place, are no hinderance to the knowledge, mercy, and power of our Lord Jesus. Christ gave an answer of peace. Christ's saying that the soul lives, makes it alive. The father went his way, which showed the sincerity of his faith. Being satisfied, he did not hurry home that night, but returned as one easy in his own mind. His servants met him with the news of the child's recovery. Good news will meet those that hope in God's word. Diligent comparing the works of Jesus with his word, will confirm our faith. And the bringing the cure to the family brought salvation to it. Thus an experience of the power of one word of Christ, may settle the authority of Christ in the soul. The whole family believed likewise. The miracle made Jesus dear to them. The knowledge of Christ still spreads through families, and men find health and salvation to their souls.

Chapter 5

Chapter Outline	
The cure at the pool of Bethesda.	(1–9)
The Jews' displeasure.	(10–16)
Christ reproves the Jews.	(17–23)
Christ's discourse.	(24–47)

Verses 1–9

We are all by nature impotent folk in spiritual things, blind, halt, and withered; but full provision is made for our cure, if we attend to it. An angel went down, and troubled the water; and what disease soever it was, this water cured it, but only he that first stepped in had benefit. This teaches us to be careful, that we let not a season slip which may never return. The man had lost the use of his limbs thirty-eight years. Shall we, who perhaps for many years have scarcely known what it has been to be a day sick, complain of one wearisome night, when many others, better than we, have scarcely known what it has been to be a day well? Christ singled this one out from the rest. Those long in affliction, may comfort themselves that God keeps account how long. Observe, this man speaks of the unkindness of those about him, without any peevish reflections. As we should be thankful, so we should be patient. Our Lord Jesus cures him, though he neither asked nor thought of it. Arise, and walk. God's command, Turn and live; Make ye a new heart; no more supposes power in us without the grace of God, his distinguishing grace, than this command supposed such power in the impotent man: it was by the power of Christ, and he must have all the glory. What a joyful surprise to the poor cripple, to find himself of a sudden so easy, so strong, so able to help himself! The proof of spiritual cure, is our rising and walking. Has Christ healed our spiritual diseases, let us go wherever he sends us, and take up whatever he lays upon us; and walk before him.

Verses 10–16

Those eased of the punishment of sin, are in danger of returning to sin, when the terror and restraint are over, unless Divine grace dries up the fountain. The misery believers are made whole from, warns us to sin no more, having felt the smart of sin. This is the voice of every providence, Go, and sin no more. Christ saw it necessary to give this caution; for it is common for people, when sick, to promise much; when newly recovered, to perform only something; but after awhile to forget all. Christ spoke of the wrath to come, which is beyond compare worse than the many hours, nay, weeks and years of pain, some wicked men have to suffer in consequence of their unlawful indulgences. And if such afflictions are severe, how dreadful will be the everlasting punishment of the wicked!

Verses 17–23

The Divine power of the miracle proved Jesus to be the Son of God, and he declared that he worked with, and like unto his Father, as he saw good. These ancient enemies of Christ understood him, and became more violent, charging him not only with sabbath-breaking, but blasphemy, in calling God his own Father, and making himself equal with God. But all things now, and at the final judgment, are committed to the Son, purposely that all men might honour the Son, as they honour the Father; and every one who does not thus honour the Son, whatever he may think or pretend, does not honour the Father who sent him.

Verses 24–29

Our Lord declared his authority and character, as the Messiah. The time was come when the dead should hear his voice, as the Son of God, and live. Our Lord first refers to his raising those who were dead in sin, to newness of life, by the power of the Spirit, and then to his raising the dead in their graves. The office of Judge of all men, can only be exercised by one who has all knowledge, and almighty power. May we believe His testimony; thus our faith and hope will be in God, and we shall not come into condemnation. And may His voice reach the hearts of those dead in sin; that they may do works meet for repentance, and prepare for the solemn day.

Verses 30–38

Our Lord returns to his declaration of the entire agreement between the Father and the Son, and declared himself the Son of God. He had higher testimony than that of John; his works bore witness to all he had said. But the Divine word had no abiding-place in their hearts, as they refused to believe in Him whom the Father had sent, according to his ancient promises. The voice of God, accompanied by the power of the Holy Ghost, thus made effectual to the conversion of sinners, still proclaims that this is the beloved Son, in whom the Father is well pleased. But when the hearts of men are full of pride, ambition, and the love of the world, there is no room for the word of God to abide in them.

Verses 39–44

The Jews considered that eternal life was revealed to them in their Scriptures, and that they had it, because they had the word of God in their hands. Jesus urged them to search those Scriptures with more diligence and attention. "Ye do search the Scriptures," and ye do well to do so. They did indeed search the Scriptures, but it was with a view to their own glory. It is possible for men to be very studious in the letter of the Scriptures, yet to be strangers to its power. Or, "Search the Scriptures," and so it was spoken to them in the nature of an appeal. Ye profess to receive and believe the Scripture, let that be the judge. It is spoken to us as advising or commanding all Christians to search the Scriptures. Not only read them, and hear them, but search them; which denotes diligence in examining and studying them. We must search the Scriptures for heaven as our great end; For in them ye think ye have eternal life. We must search the Scriptures for Christ, as the new and living Way, that leads to this end. To this testimony Christ adds reproofs of their unbelief and wickedness; their neglect of him and his doctrine. Also he reproves their want of the love of God. But there is life with Jesus Christ for poor souls. Many who make a great profession of religion, yet show they want the love of God, by their neglect of Christ and contempt of his commandments. It is the love of God in us, the love that is a living, active principle in the heart, which God will accept. They slighted and undervalued Christ, because they admired and overvalued themselves. How can those believe, who make the praise and applause of men their idol! When Christ and his followers are men wondered at, how can those believe, the utmost of whose ambition is to make a fair show in the flesh!

Verses 45–47

Many trust in some form of doctrines or some parties, who no more enter into the real meaning of those doctrines, or the views of the persons whose names they bear, than the Jews did into those of Moses. Let us search and pray over the Scriptures, as intent on finding eternal life; let us observe how Christ is the great subject of them, and daily apply to him for the life he bestows.

Chapter 6

Chapter Outline	
Five thousand miraculously fed.	(1–14)
Jesus walks on the sea.	(15–21)
He directs to spiritual food.	(22–27)
His discourse with the multitude.	(28–65)
Many of disciples go back.	(66–71)

Verses 1–14

John relates the miracle of feeding the multitude, for its reference to the following discourse. Observe the effect this miracle had upon the people. Even the common Jews expected the Messiah to come into the world, and to be a great Prophet. The Pharisees despised them as not knowing the law; but they knew most of Him who is the end of the law. Yet men may acknowledge Christ as that Prophet, and still turn a deaf ear to him.

Verses 15–21

Here were Christ's disciples in the way of duty, and Christ was praying for them; yet they were in distress. There may be perils and afflictions of this present time, where there is an interest in Christ. Clouds and darkness often surround the children of the light and of the day. They see Jesus walking on the sea. Even the approaches of comfort and deliverance often are so mistaken, as to become the occasions of fear. Nothing is more powerful to convince sinners than that word, "I am Jesus whom thou persecutest;" nothing more powerful to comfort saints than this, "I am Jesus whom thou lovest." If we have received Christ Jesus the Lord, though the night be dark, and the wind high, yet we may comfort ourselves, we shall be at the shore before long.

Verses 22–27

Instead of answering the inquiry how he came there, Jesus blamed their asking. The utmost earnestness should be employed in seeking salvation, in the use of appointed means; yet it is to be sought only as the gift of the Son of man. Him the Father has sealed, proved to be God. He declared the Son of man to be the Son of God with power.

Verses 28–35

Constant exercise of faith in Christ, is the most important and difficult part of the obedience required from us, as sinners seeking salvation. When by his grace we are enabled to live a life of faith in the Son of God, holy tempers follow, and acceptable services may be done. God, even his Father, who gave their fathers that food from heaven to support their natural lives, now gave them the true Bread for the salvation of their souls. Coming to Jesus, and believing on him, signify the same. Christ shows that he is the true Bread; he is to the soul what bread is to the body, nourishes and supports the spiritual life. He is the Bread of God. Bread which the Father gives, which he has made to be the food of our souls. Bread nourishes only by the powers of a living body; but Christ is himself living Bread, and nourishes by his own power. The doctrine of Christ crucified is now as strengthening and comforting to a believer as ever it was. He is the Bread which came down from heaven. It denotes the Divinity of Christ's person and his authority; also, the Divine origin of all the good which flows to us through him. May we with understanding and earnestness say, Lord, evermore give us this Bread.

Verses 36–46

The discovery of their guilt, danger, and remedy, by the teaching of the Holy Spirit, makes men willing and glad to come, and to give up every thing which hinders applying to him for salvation. The Father's will is, that not one of those who were given to the Son, should be rejected or lost by him. No one will come, till Divine grace has subdued, and in part changed his heart; therefore no one who comes will ever be cast out. The gospel finds none willing to be saved in the humbling, holy manner, made known therein; but God draws with his word and the Holy Ghost; and man's duty is to hear and learn; that is to say, to receive the grace offered, and consent to the promise. None had seen the Father but his beloved Son; and the Jews must expect to be taught by his inward power upon their minds, and by his word, and the ministers whom he sent among them.

Verses 47–51

The advantage of the manna was small, it only referred to this life; but the living Bread is so excellent, that the man who feedeth on it shall never die. This bread is Christ's human nature, which he took to present to the Father, as a sacrifice for the sins of the world; to purchase all things pertaining to life and godliness, for sinners of every nation, who repent and believe in him.

Verses 52–59

The flesh and blood of the Son of man, denote the Redeemer in the nature of man; Christ and him crucified, and the redemption wrought out by him, with all the precious benefits of redemption; pardon of sin, acceptance with God, the way to the throne of grace, the promises of the covenant, and eternal life. These are called the flesh and blood of Christ, because they are purchased by the breaking his body, and the shedding of his blood. Also, because they are meat and drink to our souls. Eating this flesh and drinking this blood mean believing in Christ. We partake of Christ and his benefits by faith. The soul that rightly knows its state and wants, finds whatever can calm the conscience, and promote true holiness, in the redeemer, God manifest in the flesh. Meditating upon the cross of Christ gives life to our repentance, love, and gratitude. We live by him, as our bodies live by our food. We live by him, as the members by the head, the branches by the root: because he lives we shall live also.

Verses 60–65

The human nature of Christ had not before been in heaven, but being God and man, that wondrous Person was truly said to have come down from heaven. The Messiah's kingdom was not of this world; and they were to understand by faith, what he had said of a spiritual living upon him, and his fulness. As without the soul of man the flesh is of no value, so without the quickening Spirit of God all forms of religion are dead and worthless. He who made this provision for our souls, alone can teach us these things, and draw us unto Christ, that we may live by faith in him. Let us apply to Christ, thankful that it is declared that every one who is willing to come unto him shall be made welcome.

Verses 66–71

When we admit into our minds hard thoughts of the words and works of Jesus, we enter into temptation, which, if the Lord in mercy prevent not, will end in drawing back. The corrupt and wicked heart of man often makes that an occasion for offence, which is matter of the greatest comfort. Our Lord had, in the foregoing discourse, promised eternal life to his followers; the disciples fastened on that plain saying, and resolved to cleave to him, when others fastened on hard sayings, and forsook him. Christ's doctrine is the word of eternal life, therefore we must live and die by it. If we forsake Christ, we forsake our own mercies. They believed that this Jesus was the Messiah promised to their fathers, the Son of the living God. When we are tempted to backslide or turn away, it is good to remember first principles, and to keep to them. And let us ever remember our Lord's searching question; Shall we go away and forsake our Redeemer? To whom can we go? He alone can give salvation by the forgiveness of sins. And this alone brings confidence, comfort, and joy, and bids fear and despondency flee away. It gains the only solid happiness in this world, and opens a way to the happiness of the next.

Chapter 7

Chapter Outline	
Christ goes to the feast of tabernacles.	(1–13)
His discourse at the feast.	(14–39)
The people dispute concerning Christ.	(40–53)

Verses 1–13

The brethren or kinsmen of Jesus were disgusted, when they found there was no prospect of worldly advantages from him. Ungodly men sometimes undertake to counsel those employed in the work of God; but they only advise what appears likely to promote present advantages. The people differed about his doctrine and miracles, while those who favoured him, dared not openly to avow their sentiments. Those who count the preachers of the gospel to be deceivers, speak out, while many who favour them, fear to get reproach by avowing regard for them.

Verses 14–24

Every faithful minister may humbly adopt Christ's words. His doctrine is not his own finding out, but is from God's word, through the teaching of his Spirit. And amidst the disputes which disturb the world, if any man, of any nation, seeks to do the will of God, he shall know whether the doctrine is of God, or whether men speak of themselves. Only those who hate the truth shall be given up to errors which will be fatal. Surely it was as agreeable to the design of the sabbath to restore health to the afflicted, as to administer an outward rite. Jesus told them to decide on his conduct according to the spiritual import of the Divine law. We must not judge concerning any by their outward appearance, but by their worth, and by the gifts and graces of God's Spirit in them.

Verses 25–30

Christ proclaimed aloud, that they were in error in their thoughts about his origin. He was sent of God, who showed himself true to his promises. This declaration, that they knew not God, with his claim to peculiar knowledge, provoked the hearers; and they sought to take him, but God can tie men's hands, though he does not turn their hearts.

Verses 31–36

The discourses of Jesus convinced many that he was the Messiah; but they had not courage to own it. It is comfort to those who are in the world, but not of it, and therefore are hated by it and weary of it, that they shall not be in it always, that they shall not be in it long. Our days being evil, it is well they are few. The days of life and of grace do not last long; and sinners, when in misery, will be glad of the help they now despise. Men dispute about such sayings, but the event will explain them.

Verses 37–39

On the last day of the feast of tabernacles, the Jews drew water and poured it out before the Lord. It is supposed that Christ alluded to this. If any man desires to be truly and for ever happy, let him apply to Christ, and be ruled by him. This thirst means strong desires after spiritual blessings, which nothing else can satisfy; so the sanctifying and comforting influences of the Holy Spirit, were intended by the waters which Jesus called on them to come to Him and drink. The comfort flows plentifully and constantly as a river; strong as a stream to bear down the opposition of doubts and fears. There is a fulness in Christ, of grace for grace. The Spirit dwelling and working in believers, is as a fountain of living, running water, out of which plentiful streams flow, cooling and cleansing as water. The miraculous gifts of the Holy Spirit we do not expect, but for his more common and more valuable influences we may apply. These streams have flowed from our glorified Redeemer, down to this age, and to the remote corners of the earth. May we be anxious to make them known to others.

Verses 40–53

The malice of Christ's enemies is always against reason, and sometimes the staying of it cannot be accounted for. Never any man spake with that wisdom, and power, and grace, that convincing clearness, and that sweetness, wherewith Christ spake. Alas, that many, who are for a time restrained, and who speak highly of the word of Jesus, speedily lose their convictions, and go on in their sins! People are foolishly swayed by outward motives in matters of eternal moment, are willing even to be damned for fashion's sake. As the wisdom of God often chooses things which men despise, so the folly of men commonly despises those whom God has chosen. The Lord brings forward his weak and timid disciples, and sometimes uses them to defeat the designs of his enemies.

Chapter 8

Chapter Outline	
The Pharisees and the adulteress.	(1–11)
Christ's discourse with the Pharisees.	(12–59)

Verses 1–11

Christ neither found fault with the law, nor excused the prisoner's guilt; nor did he countenance the pretended zeal of the Pharisees. Those are self-condemned who judge others, and yet do the same thing. All who are any way called to blame the faults of others, are especially concerned to look to themselves, and keep themselves pure. In this matter Christ attended to the great work about which he came into the world, that was, to bring sinners to repentance; not to destroy, but to save. He aimed to bring, not only the accused to repentance, by showing her his mercy, but the prosecutors also, by showing them their sins; they thought to insnare him, he sought to convince and convert them. He declined to meddle with the magistrate's office. Many crimes merit far more severe punishment than they meet with; but we should not leave our own work, to take that upon ourselves to which we are not called. When Christ sent her away, it was with this caution, Go, and sin no more. Those who help to save the life of a criminal, should help to save the soul with the same caution. Those are truly happy, whom Christ does not condemn. Christ's favour to us in the forgiveness of past sins should prevail with us, Go then, and sin no more.

Verses 12–16

Christ is the Light of the world. God is light, and Christ is the image of the invisible God. One sun enlightens the whole world; so does one Christ, and there needs no more. What a dark dungeon would the world be without the sun! So would it be without Jesus, by whom light came into the world. Those who follow Christ shall not walk in darkness. They shall not be left without the truths which are necessary to keep them from destroying error, and the directions in the way of duty, necessary to keep them from condemning sin.

Verses 17–20

If we knew Christ better, we should know the Father better. Those become vain in their imaginations concerning God, who will not learn of Christ. Those who know not his glory and grace, know not the Father that sent him. The time of our departure out of the world, depends upon God. Our enemies cannot hasten it any sooner, nor can our friends delay it any longer, than the time appointed of the Father. Every true believer can look up and say with pleasure, My times are in thy hand, and better there than in my own. To all God's purposes there is a time.

Verses 21–29

Those that live in unbelief, are for ever undone, if they die in unbelief. The Jews belonged to this present evil world, but Jesus was of a heavenly and Divine nature, so that his doctrine, kingdom, and blessings, would not suit their taste. But the curse of the law is done away to all that submit to the grace of the gospel. Nothing but the doctrine of Christ's grace will be an argument powerful enough, and none but the Spirit of Christ's grace will be an agent powerful enough, to turn us from sin to God; and that Spirit is given, and that doctrine is given, to work upon those only who believe in Christ. Some say, Who is this Jesus? They allow him to have been a Prophet, an excellent Teacher, and even more than a creature; but cannot acknowledge him as over all, God blessed for evermore. Will not this suffice? Jesus here answers the question. Is this to honour him as the Father? Does this admit his being the Light of the world, and the Life of men, one with the Father? All shall know by their conversion, or in their condemnation, that he always spake and did what pleased the Father, even when he claimed the highest honours to himself.

Verses 30–36

Such power attended our Lord's words, that many were convinced, and professed to believe in him. He encouraged them to attend his teaching, rely on his promises, and obey his commands, notwithstanding all temptations to evil. Thus doing, they would be his disciples truly; and by the teaching of his word and Spirit, they would learn where their hope and strength lay. Christ spoke of spiritual liberty; but carnal hearts feel no other grievances than those that molest the body, and distress their worldly affairs. Talk to them of their liberty and property, tell them of waste committed upon their lands, or damage done to their houses, and they understand you very well; but speak of the bondage of sin, captivity to Satan, and liberty by Christ; tell of wrong done to their precious souls, and the hazard of their eternal welfare, then you bring strange things to their ears. Jesus plainly reminded them, that the man who practised any sin, was, in fact, a slave to that sin, which was the case with most of them. Christ in the gospel offers us freedom, he has power to do this, and those whom Christ makes free are really so. But often we see persons disputing about liberty of every kind, while they are slaves to some sinful lust.

Verses 37–40

Our Lord opposed the proud and vain confidence of these Jews, showing that their descent from Abraham could not profit those of a contrary spirit to him. Where the word of God has no place, no good is to be expected; room is left there for all wickedness. A sick person who turns from his physician, and will take neither remedies nor food, is past hope of recovery. The truth both heals and nourishes the hearts of those who receive it. The truth taught by philosophers has not this power and effect, but only the truth of God. Those who claim the privileges of Abraham, must do Abraham's works; must be strangers and sojourners in this world; keep up the worship of God in their families, and always walk before God.

Verses 41–47

Satan prompts men to excesses by which they murder themselves and others, while what he puts into the mind tends to ruin men's souls. He is the great promoter of falsehood of every kind. He is a liar, all his temptations are carried on by his calling evil good, and good evil, and promising freedom in sin. He is the author of all lies; whom liars resemble and obey, with whom all liars shall have their portion for ever. The special lusts of the devil are spiritual wickedness, the lusts of the mind, and corrupt reasonings, pride and envy, wrath and malice, enmity to good, and enticing others to evil. By the truth, here understand the revealed will of God as to the salvation of men by Jesus Christ, the truth Christ was now preaching, and which the Jews opposed.

Verses 48–53

Observe Christ's disregard of the applause of men. those who are dead to the praises of men can bear their contempt. God will seek the honour of all who do not seek their own. In these **verses** we have the doctrine of the everlasting happiness of believers. We have the character of a believer; he is one that keeps the sayings of the Lord Jesus. And the privilege of a believer; he shall by no means see death for ever. Though now they cannot avoid seeing death, and tasting it also, yet they shall shortly be where it will be no more forever, Ex **14**:**13**.

Verses 54–59

Christ and all that are his, depend upon God for honour. Men may be able to dispute about God, yet may not know him. Such as know not God, and obey not the gospel of Christ, are put together, **2**Th **1**:**8**. All who rightly know anything of Christ, earnestly desire to know more of him. Those who discern the dawn of the light of the Sun of Righteousness, wish to see his rising. "Before Abraham was, I AM." This speaks Abraham a creature, and our Lord the Creator; well, therefore, might he make himself greater than Abraham. I AM, is the name of God, Ex **3**:**14**; it speaks his self-existence; he is the First and the Last, ever the same, Re **1**:**8**. Thus he was not only before Abraham, but before all worlds, Pr **8**:**23**; Joh **1**:**1**. As Mediator, he was the appointed Messiah, long before Abraham; the Lamb slain from the foundation of the world, Re **13**:**8**. The Lord Jesus was made of God Wisdom, Righteousness, Sanctification, and Redemption, to Adam, and Abel, and all that lived and died by faith in him, before Abraham. The Jews were about to stone Jesus for blasphemy, but he withdrew; by his miraculous power he passed through them unhurt. Let us stedfastly profess what we know and believe concerning God; and if heirs of Abraham's faith, we shall rejoice in looking forward to that day when the Saviour shall appear in glory, to the confusion of his enemies, and to complete the salvation of all who believe in him.

Chapter 9

Chapter Outline	
Christ give sight to one born blind.	(1–7)
The account given by the blind man.	(8–12)
The Pharisees question the man that had been blind.	(13–17)
They ask concerning him.	(18–23)
They cast him out.	(24–34)

Christ's words to the man that had been blind.	(35–38)
He reproves the Pharisees.	(39–41)

Verses 1–7

Christ cured many who were blind by disease or accident; here he cured one born blind. Thus he showed his power to help in the most desperate cases, and the work of his grace upon the souls of sinners, which gives sight to those blind by nature. This poor man could not see Christ, but Christ saw him. And if we know or apprehend anything of Christ, it is because we were first known of him. Christ says of uncommon calamities, that they are not always to be looked on as special punishments of sin; sometimes they are for the glory of God, and to manifest his works. Our life is our day, in which it concerns us to do the work of the day. We must be busy, and not waste day-time; it will be time to rest when our day is done, for it is but a day. The approach of death should quicken us to improve all our opportunities of doing and getting good. What good we have an opportunity to do, we should do quickly. And he that will never do a good work till there is nothing to be objected against, will leave many a good work for ever undone, Ec **11**:**4**. Christ magnified his power, in making a blind man to see, doing that which one would think more likely to make a seeing man blind. Human reason cannot judge of the Lord's methods; he uses means and instruments that men despise. Those that would be healed by Christ must be ruled by him. He came back from the pool wondering and wondered at; he came seeing. This represents the benefits in attending on ordinances of Christ's appointment; souls go weak, and come away strengthened; go doubting, and come away satisfied; go mourning, and come away rejoicing; go blind, and come away seeing.

Verses 8–12

Those whose eyes are opened, and whose hearts are cleansed by grace, being known to be the same person, but widely different in character, live as monuments to the Redeemer's glory, and recommend his grace to all who desire the same precious salvation. It is good to observe the way and method of God's works, and they will appear the more wonderful. Apply this spiritually. In the work of grace wrought upon the soul we see the change, but we see not the hand that makes it: the way of the Spirit is like that of the wind, which thou hearest the sound of, but canst not tell whence it comes, nor whither it goes.

Verses 13–17

Christ not only worked miracles on the sabbath, but in such a manner as would give offence to the Jews, for he would not seem to yield to the scribes and Pharisees. Their zeal for mere rites consumed the substantial matters of religion; therefore Christ would not give place to them. Also, works of necessity and mercy are allowed, and the sabbath rest is to be kept, in order to the sabbath work. How many blind eyes have been opened by the preaching of the gospel on the Lord's day! how many impotent souls cured on that day! Much unrighteous and uncharitable judging comes from men's adding their own fancies to God's appointments. How perfect in wisdom and holiness was our Redeemer, when his enemies could find nothing against him, but the oft-refuted charge of breaking the sabbath! May we be enabled, by well-doing, to silence the ignorance of foolish men.

Verses 18–23

The Pharisees vainly hoped to disprove this notable miracle. They expected a Messiah, but could not bear to think that this Jesus should be he, because his precepts were all contrary to their traditions, and because they expected a Messiah in outward pomp and splendour. The fear of man brings a snare, Pr **29**:**25**, and often makes people deny and disown Christ and his truths and ways, and act against their consciences. The unlearned and poor, who are simple-hearted, readily draw proper inferences from the evidences of the light of the gospel; but those whose desires are another way, though ever learning, never come to the knowledge of the truth.

Verses 24–34

As Christ's mercies are most valued by those who have felt the want of them, that have been blind, and now see; so the most powerful and lasting affections to Christ, arise from actual knowledge of him. In the work of grace in the soul, though we cannot tell when, and how, and by what steps the blessed change was wrought, yet we may take the comfort, if we can say, through grace, Whereas I was blind, now I see. I did live a worldly, sensual life, but, thanks be to God, it is now otherwise with me, Eph **5**:**8**. The unbelief of those who enjoy the means of knowledge and conviction, is indeed marvellous. All who have felt the power and grace of the Lord Jesus, wonder at the wilfulness of others who reject him. He argues strongly against them, not only that Jesus was not a sinner, but that he was of God. We may each of us know by this, whether we are of God or not. What do we? What do we for God? What do we for our souls? What do we more than others?

Verses 35–38

Christ owns those who own him and his truth and ways. There is particular notice taken of such a suffer in the cause of Christ, and for the testimony of a good conscience. Our Lord Jesus graciously reveals himself to the man. Now he was made sensible what an unspeakable mercy it was, to be cured of his blindness, that he might see the Son of God. None but God is to be worshipped; so that in worshipping Jesus, he owned him to be God. All who believe in him, will worship him.

Verses 39–41

Christ came into the world to give sight to those who were spiritually blind. Also, that those who see might be made blind; that those who have a high conceit of their own wisdom, might be sealed up in ignorance. The preaching of the cross was thought to be folly by such as by carnal wisdom knew not God. Nothing fortifies men's corrupt hearts against the convictions of the word, more than the high opinion which others have of them; as if all that gained applause with men, must obtain acceptance with God. Christ silenced them. But the sin of the self-conceited and self-confident remains; they reject the gospel of grace, therefore the guilt of their sin remains unpardoned, and the power of their sin remains unbroken.

Chapter 10

Chapter Outline	
The parable of the good shepherd.	(1–5)

Christ the Door.	(6–9)
Christ the good Shepherd.	(10–18)
The Jews' opinion concerning Jesus.	(19–21)
His discourse at the feast of dedication.	(22–30)
The Jews attempt to stone Jesus.	(31–38)
He departs from Jerusalem.	(39–42)

Verses 1–5

Here is a parable or similitude, taken from the customs of the East, in the management of sheep. Men, as creatures depending on their Creator, are called the sheep of his pasture. The church of God in the world is as a sheep-fold, exposed to deceivers and persecutors. The great Shepherd of the sheep knows all that are his, guards them by his providence, guides them by his Spirit and word, and goes before them, as the Eastern shepherds went before their sheep, to set them in the way of his steps. Ministers must serve the sheep in their spiritual concerns. The Spirit of Christ will set before them an open door. The sheep of Christ will observe their Shepherd, and be cautious and shy of strangers, who would draw them from faith in him to fancies about him.

Verses 6–9

Many who hear the word of Christ, do not understand it, because they will not. But we shall find one scripture expounding another, and the blessed Spirit making known the blessed Jesus. Christ is the Door. And what greater security has the church of God than that the Lord Jesus is between it and all its enemies? He is a door open for passage and communication. Here are plain directions how to come into the fold; we must come in by Jesus Christ as the Door. By faith in him as the great Mediator between God and man. Also, we have precious promises to those that observe this direction. Christ has all that care of his church, and every believer, which a good shepherd has of his flock; and he expects the church, and every believer, to wait on him, and to keep in his pasture.

Verses 10–18

Christ is a good Shepherd; many who were not thieves, yet were careless in their duty, and by their neglect the flock was much hurt. Bad principles are the root of bad practices. The Lord Jesus knows whom he has chosen, and is sure of them; they also know whom they have trusted, and are sure of Him. See here the grace of Christ; since none could demand his life of him, he laid it down of himself for our redemption. He offered himself to be the Saviour; Lo, I come. And the necessity of our case calling for it, he offered himself for the Sacrifice. He was both the offerer and the offering, so that his laying down his life was his offering up himself. From hence it is plain, that he died in the place and stead of men; to obtain their being set free from the punishment of sin, to obtain the pardon of their sin; and that his death should obtain that pardon. Our Lord laid not his life down for his doctrine, but for his sheep.

Verses 19–21

Satan ruins many, by putting them out of conceit with the word and ordinances. Men would not be laughed out of their necessary food, yet suffer themselves thus to be laughed out of what is far more necessary. If our zeal and earnestness in the cause of Christ, especially in the blessed work of bringing his sheep into his fold, bring upon us evil names, let us not heed it, but remember our Master was thus reproached before us.

Verses 22–30

All who have any thing to say to Christ, may find him in the temple. Christ would make us to believe; we make ourselves doubt. The Jews understood his meaning, but could not form his words into a full charge against him. He described the gracious disposition and happy state of his sheep; they heard and believed his word, followed him as his faithful disciples, and none of them should perish; for the Son and the Father were one. Thus he was able to defend his sheep against all their enemies, which proves that he claimed Divine power and perfection equally with the Father.

Verses 31–38

Christ's works of power and mercy proclaim him to be over all, God blessed for evermore, that all may know and believe He is in the Father, and the Father in Him. Whom the Father sends, he sanctifies. The holy God will reward, and therefore will employ, none but such as he makes holy. The Father was in the Son, so that by Divine power he wrought his miracles; the Son was so in the Father, that he knew the whole of His mind. This we cannot by searching find out to perfection, but we may know and believe these declarations of Christ.

Verses 39–42

No weapon formed against our Lord Jesus shall prosper. He escaped, not because he was afraid to suffer, but because his hour was not come. And He who knew how to deliver himself, knows how to deliver the godly our of their temptations, and to make a way for them to escape. Persecutors may drive Christ and his gospel our of their own city or country, but they cannot drive him or it out of the world. When we know Christ by faith in our hearts, we find all that the Scripture saith of him is true.

Chapter 11

Chapter Outline	
The sickness of Lazarus.	(1–6)
Christ returns to Judea.	(7–10)

The death of Lazarus.	(11–16)
Christ arrives at Bethany.	(17–32)
He raises Lazarus.	(33–46)
The Pharisees consult against Jesus.	(47–53)
The Jews seek for him.	(54–57)

Verses 1–6

It is no new thing for those whom Christ loves, to be sick; bodily distempers correct the corruption, and try the graces of God's people. He came not to preserve his people from these afflictions, but to save them from their sins, and from the wrath to come; however, it behoves us to apply to Him in behalf of our friends and relatives when sick and afflicted. Let this reconcile us to the darkest dealings of Providence, that they are all for the glory of God: sickness, loss, disappointment, are so; and if God be glorified, we ought to be satisfied. Jesus loved Martha, and her sister, and Lazarus. The families are greatly favoured in which love and peace abound; but those are most happy whom Jesus loves, and by whom he is beloved. Alas, that this should seldom be the case with every person, even in small families. God has gracious intentions, even when he seems to delay. When the work of deliverance, temporal or spiritual, public or personal, is delayed, it does but stay for the right time.

Verses 7–10

Christ never brings his people into any danger but he goes with them in it. We are apt to think ourselves zealous for the Lord, when really we are only zealous for our wealth, credit, ease, and safety; we have therefore need to try our principles. But our day shall be lengthened out, till our work is done, and our testimony finished. A man has comfort and satisfaction while in the way of his duty, as set forth by the word of God, and determined by the providence of God. Christ, wherever he went, walked in the day; and so shall we, if we follow his steps. If a man walks in the way of his heart, and according to the course of this world, if he consults his own carnal reasonings more than the will and glory of God, he falls into temptations and snares. He stumbles, because there is no light in him; for light in us is to our moral actions, that which light about us to our natural actions.

Verses 11–16

Since we are sure to rise again at the last, why should not the believing hope of that resurrection to eternal life, make it as easy for us to put off the body and die, as it is to put off our clothes and go to sleep? A true Christian, when he dies, does but sleep; he rests from the labours of the past day. Nay, herein death is better than sleep, that sleep is only a short rest, but death is the end of earthly cares and toils. The disciples thought that it was now needless for Christ to go to Lazarus, and expose himself and them. Thus we often hope that the good work we are called to do, will be done by some other hand, if there be peril in the doing of it. But when Christ raised Lazarus from the dead, many were brought to believe on him; and there was much done to make perfect the faith of those that believed. Let us go to him; death cannot separate from the love of Christ, nor put us out of the reach of his call. Like Thomas, in difficult times Christians should encourage one another. The dying of the Lord Jesus should make us willing to die whenever God calls us.

Verses 17–32

Here was a house where the fear of God was, and on which his blessing rested; yet it was made a house of mourning. Grace will keep sorrow from the heart, but not from the house. When God, by his grace and providence, is coming towards us in ways of mercy and comfort, we should, like Martha, go forth by faith, hope, and prayer, to meet him. When Martha went to meet Jesus, Mary sat still in the house; this temper formerly had been an advantage to her, when it put her at Christ's feet to hear his word; but in the day of affliction, the same temper disposed her to melancholy. It is our wisdom to watch against the temptations, and to make use of the advantages of our natural tempers. When we know not what in particular to ask or expect, let us refer ourselves to God; let him do as seemeth him good. To enlarge Martha's expectations, our Lord declared himself to be the Resurrection and the Life. In every sense he is the Resurrection; the source, the substance, the first-fruits, the cause of it. The redeemed soul lives after death in happiness; and after the resurrection, both body and soul are kept from all evil for ever. When we have read or heard the word of Christ, about the great things of the other world, we should put it to ourselves, Do we believe this truth? The crosses and comforts of this present time would not make such a deep impression upon us as they do, if we believed the things of eternity as we ought. When Christ our Master comes, he calls for us. He comes in his word and ordinances, and calls us to them, calls us by them, calls us to himself. Those who, in a day of peace, set themselves at Christ's feet to be taught by him, may with comfort, in a day of trouble, cast themselves at his feet, to find favour with him.

Verses 33–46

Christ's tender sympathy with these afflicted friends, appeared by the troubles of his spirit. In all the afflictions of believers he is afflicted. His concern for them was shown by his kind inquiry after the remains of his deceased friend. Being found in fashion as a man, he acts in the way and manner of the sons of men. It was shown by his tears. He was a man of sorrows, and acquainted with grief. Tears of compassion resemble those of Christ. But Christ never approved that sensibility of which many are proud, while they weep at mere tales of distress, but are hardened to real woe. He sets us an example to withdraw from scenes of giddy mirth, that we may comfort the afflicted. And we have not a High Priest who cannot be touched with a feeling of our infirmities. It is a good step toward raising a soul to spiritual life, when the stone is taken away, when prejudices are removed, and got over, and way is made for the word to enter the heart. If we take Christ's word, and rely on his power and faithfulness, we shall see the glory of God, and be happy in the sight. Our Lord Jesus has taught us, by his own example, to call God Father, in prayer, and to draw nigh to him as children to a father, with humble reverence, yet with holy boldness. He openly made this address to God, with uplifted eyes and loud voice, that they might be convinced the Father had sent him as his beloved Son into the world. He could have raised Lazarus by the silent exertion of his power and will, and the unseen working of the Spirit of life; but he did it by a loud call. This was a figure of the gospel call, by which dead souls are brought out of the grave of sin: and of the sound of the archangel's trumpet at the last day, with which all that sleep in the dust shall be awakened, and summoned before the great tribunal. The grave of sin and this world, is no place for those whom Christ has quickened; they must come forth. Lazarus was thoroughly revived, and returned not only to life, but to health. The sinner cannot quicken his own soul, but he is to use the means of grace; the believer cannot sanctify himself, but he is to lay aside every weight and hinderance. We cannot convert our relatives and friends, but we should instruct, warn, and invite them.

Verses 47–53

There can hardly be a more clear discovery of the madness that is in man's heart, and of its desperate enmity against God, than what is here recorded. Words of prophecy in the mouth, are not clear evidence of a principle of grace in the heart. The calamity we seek to escape by sin, we take the most effectual course to bring upon our own heads; as those do who think by opposing Christ's kingdom, to advance their own worldly interest. The fear of the wicked shall come upon them. The conversion of souls is the gathering of them to Christ as their ruler and refuge; and he died to effect this. By dying he purchased them to himself, and the gift of the Holy Ghost for them: his love in dying for believers should unite them closely together.

Verses 54–57

Before our gospel passover we must renew our repentance. Thus by a voluntary purification, and by religious exercises, many, more devout than their neighbours, spent some time before the passover at Jerusalem. When we expect to meet God, we must solemnly prepare. No devices of man can alter the purposes of God: and while hypocrites amuse themselves with forms and disputes, and worldly men pursue their own plans, Jesus still orders all things for his own glory and the salvation of his people.

Chapter 12

Chapter Outline	
Christ anointed by Mary.	(1–11)
He enters Jerusalem.	(12–19)
Greeks apply to see Jesus.	(20–26)
A voice from heaven bears testimony to Christ.	(27–33)
His discourse with the people.	(34–36)
Unbelief of the Jews.	(37–43)
Christ's address to them.	(44–50)

Verses 1–11

Christ had formerly blamed Martha for being troubled with much serving. But she did not leave off serving, as some, who when found fault with for going too far in one way, peevishly run too far another way; she still served, but within hearing of Christ's gracious words. Mary gave a token of love to Christ, who had given real tokens of his love to her and her family. God's Anointed should be our Anointed. Has God poured on him the oil of gladness above his fellows, let us pour on him the ointment of our best affections. In Judas a foul sin is gilded over with a plausible pretence. We must not think that those do no acceptable service, who do it not in our way. The reigning love of money is heart-theft. The grace of Christ puts kind comments on pious words and actions, makes the best of what is amiss, and the most of what is good. Opportunities are to be improved; and those first and most vigorously, which are likely to be the shortest. To consult to hinder the further effect of the miracle, by putting Lazarus to death, is such wickedness, malice, and folly, as cannot be explained, except by the desperate enmity of the human heart against God. They resolved that the man should die whom the Lord had raised to life. The success of the gospel often makes wicked men so angry, that they speak and act as if they hoped to obtain a victory over the Almighty himself.

Verses 12–19

Christ's riding in triumph to Jerusalem is recorded by all the evangelists. Many excellent things, both in the word and providence of God, disciples do not understand at their first acquaintance with the things of God. The right understanding of spiritual nature of Christ's kingdom, prevents our misapplying the Scriptures which speak of it.

Verses 20–26

In attendance upon holy ordinances, particularly the gospel passover, the great desire of our souls should be to see Jesus; to see him as ours, to keep up communion with him, and derive grace from him. The calling of the Gentiles magnified the Redeemer. A corn of wheat yields no increase unless it is cast into the ground. Thus Christ might have possessed his heavenly glory alone, without becoming man. Or, after he had taken man's nature, he might have entered heaven alone, by his own perfect righteousness, without suffering or death; but then no sinner of the human race could have been saved. The salvation of souls hitherto, and henceforward to the end of time, is owing to the dying of this Corn of wheat. Let us search whether Christ be in us the hope of glory; let us beg him to make us indifferent to the trifling concerns of this life, that we may serve the Lord Jesus with a willing mind, and follow his holy example.

Verses 27–33

The sin of our souls was the troubled of Christ's soul, when he undertook to redeem and save us, and to make his soul an offering for our sin. Christ was willing to suffer, yet prayed to be saved from suffering. Prayer against trouble may well agree with patience under it, and submission to the will of God in it. Our Lord Jesus undertook to satisfy God's injured honour, and he did it by humbling himself.

The voice of the Father from heaven, which had declared him to be his beloved Son, at his baptism, and when he was transfigured, was heard proclaiming that He had both glorified his name, and would glorify it. Christ, reconciling the world to God by the merit of his death, broke the power of death, and cast out Satan as a destroyer. Christ, bringing the world to God by the doctrine of his cross, broke the power of sin, and cast out Satan as a deceiver. The soul that was at a distance from Christ, is brought to love him and trust him. Jesus was now going to heaven, and he would draw men's hearts to him thither. There is power in the death of Christ to draw souls to him. We have heard from the gospel that which exalts free grace, and we have heard also that which enjoins duty; we must from the heart embrace both, and not separate them.

Verses 34–36

The people drew false notions from the Scriptures, because they overlooked the prophecies that spoke of Christ's sufferings and death. Our Lord warned them that the light would not long continue with them, and exhorted them to walk in it, before the darkness overtook them. Those who would walk in the light must believe in it, and follow Christ's directions. But those who have not faith, cannot behold what is set forth in Jesus, lifted up on the cross, and must be strangers to its influence as made known by the Holy Spirit; they find a thousand objections to excuse their unbelief.

Verses 37–43

Observe the method of conversion implied here. Sinners are brought to see the reality of Divine things, and to have some knowledge of them. To be converted, and truly turned from sin to Christ, as their Happiness and Portion. God will heal them, will justify and sanctify them; will pardon their sins, which are as bleeding wounds, and mortify their corruptions, which are as lurking diseases. See the power of the world in smothering convictions, from regard to the applause or censure of men. Love of the praise of men, as a by-end in that which is good, will make a man a hypocrite when religion is in fashion, and credit is to be got by it; and love of the praise of men, as a base principle in that which is evil, will make a man an apostate, when religion is in disgrace, and credit is to be lost for it.

Verses 44–50

Our Lord publicly proclaimed, that every one who believed on him, as his true disciple, did not believe on him only, but on the Father who sent him. Beholding in Jesus the glory of the Father, we learn to obey, love, and trust in him. By daily looking to Him, who came a Light into the world, we are more and more freed from the darkness of ignorance, error, sin, and misery; we learn that the command of God our Saviour is everlasting life. But the same word will seal the condemnation of all who despise it, or neglect it.

Chapter 13

Chapter Outline	
Christ washes the disciples' feet.	(1–17)
The treachery of Judas foretold.	(18–30)
Christ commands the disciples to love one another.	(31–38)

Verses 1–17

Our Lord Jesus has a people in the world that are his own; he has purchased them, and paid dear for them, and he has set them apart for himself; they devote themselves to him as a peculiar people. Those whom Christ loves, he loves to the end. Nothing can separate a true believer from the love of Christ. We know not when our hour will come, therefore what we have to do in constant preparation for it, ought never to be undone. What way of access the devil has to men's hearts we cannot tell. But some sins are so exceedingly sinful, and there is so little temptation to them from the world and the flesh, that it is plain they are directly from Satan. Jesus washed his disciples' feet, that he might teach us to think nothing below us, wherein we may promote God's glory, and the good of our brethren. We must address ourselves to duty, and must lay aside every thing that would hinder us in what we have to do. Christ washed his disciples' feet, that he might signify to them the value of spiritual washing, and the cleansing of the soul from the pollutions of sin. Our Lord Jesus does many things of which even his own disciples do not for the present know the meaning, but they shall know afterward. We see in the end what was the kindness from events which seemed most cross. And it is not humility, but unbelief, to put away the offers of the gospel, as if too rich to be made to us, or too good news to be true. All those, and those only, who are spiritually washed by Christ, have a part in Christ. All whom Christ owns and saves, he justifies and sanctifies. Peter more than submits; he begs to be washed by Christ. How earnest he is for the purifying grace of the Lord Jesus, and the full effect of it, even upon his hands and head! Those who truly desire to be sanctified, desire to be sanctified throughout, to have the whole man, with all its parts and powers, made pure. The true believer is thus washed when he receives Christ for his salvation. See then what ought to be the daily care of those who through grace are in a justified state, and that is, to wash their feet; to cleanse themselves from daily guilt, and to watch against everything defiling. This should make us the more cautious. From yesterday's pardon, we should be strengthened against this day's temptation. And when hypocrites are discovered, it should be no surprise or cause of stumbling to us. Observe the lesson Christ here taught. Duties are mutual; we must both accept help from our brethren, and afford help to our brethren. When we see our Master serving, we cannot but see how ill it becomes us to domineer. And the same love which led Christ to ransom and reconcile his disciples when enemies, still influences him.

Verses 18–30

Our Lord had often spoken of his own sufferings and death, without such trouble of spirit as he now discovered when he spake of Judas. The sins of Christians are the grief of Christ. We are not to confine our attention to Judas. The prophecy of his treachery may apply to all who partake of God's mercies, and meet them with ingratitude. See the infidel, who only looks at the Scriptures with a desire to do away their authority and destroy their influence; the hypocrite, who professes to believe the Scriptures, but will not govern himself by them; and the apostate, who turns aside from Christ for a thing of naught. Thus mankind, supported by God's providence, after eating bread with Him, lift up the heel against Him! Judas went out as one weary of Jesus and his apostles. Those whose deeds are evil, love darkness rather than light.

Verses 31–35

Christ had been glorified in many miracles he wrought, yet he speaks of his being glorified now in his sufferings, as if that were more than all his other glories in his humbled state. Satisfaction was thereby made for the wrong done to God by the sin of man. We cannot now follow our Lord to his heavenly happiness, but if we truly believe in him, we shall follow him hereafter; meanwhile we must wait his time, and do his work. Before Christ left the disciples, he would give them a new commandment. They were to love each other for Christ's sake, and according to his example, seeking what might benefit others, and promoting the cause of the gospel, as one body, animated by one soul. But this commandment still appears new to many professors. Men in general notice any of Christ's words rather than these. By this it appears, that if the followers of Christ do not show love one to another, they give cause to suspect their sincerity.

Verses 36–38

What Christ had said concerning brotherly love, Peter overlooked, but spoke of that about which Christ kept them ignorant. It is common to be more eager to know about secret things, which belong to God only, than about things revealed, which belong to us and our children; to be more desirous to have our curiosity gratified, than our consciences directed; to know what is done in heaven, than what we may do to get thither. How soon discourse as to what is plain and edifying is dropped, while a doubtful dispute runs on into endless strife of words! We are apt to take it amiss to be told we cannot do this and the other, whereas, without Christ we can do nothing. Christ knows us better than we know ourselves, and has many ways of discovering those to themselves, whom he loves, and he will hide pride from them. May we endeavour to keep the unity of the Spirit in the bond of peace, to love one another with a pure heart fervently, and to walk humbly with our God.

Chapter 14

Chapter Outline	
Christ comforts his disciples.	(1–11)
He further comforts his disciples.	(12–17)
He still further comforts his disciples.	(18–31)

Verses 1–11

Here are three words, upon any of which stress may be laid. Upon the word troubled. Be not cast down and disquieted. The word heart. Let your heart be kept with full trust in God. The word your. However others are overwhelmed with the sorrows of this present time, be not you so. Christ's disciples, more than others, should keep their minds quiet, when everything else is unquiet. Here is the remedy against this trouble of mind, "Believe." By believing in Christ as the Mediator between God and man, we gain comfort. The happiness of heaven is spoken of as in a father's house. There are many mansions, for there are many sons to be brought to glory. Mansions are lasting dwellings. Christ will be the Finisher of that of which he is the Author or Beginner; if he have prepared the place for us, he will prepare us for it. Christ is the sinner's Way to the Father and to heaven, in his person as God manifest in the flesh, in his atoning sacrifice, and as our Advocate. He is the Truth, as fulfilling all the prophecies of a Saviour; believing which, sinners come by him the Way. He is the Life, by whose life-giving Spirit the dead in sin are quickened. Nor can any man draw nigh God as a Father, who is not quickened by Him as the Life, and taught by Him as the Truth, to come by Him as the Way. By Christ, as the Way, our prayers go to God, and his blessings come to us; this is the Way that leads to rest, the good old Way. He is the Resurrection and the Life. All that saw Christ by faith, saw the Father in Him. In the light of Christ's doctrine, they saw God as the Father of lights; and in Christ's miracles, they saw God as the God of power. The holiness of God shone in the spotless purity of Christ's life. We are to believe the revelation of God to man in Christ; for the works of the Redeemer show forth his own glory, and God in him.

Verses 12–17

Whatever we ask in Christ's name, that shall be for our good, and suitable to our state, he shall give it to us. To ask in Christ's name, is to plead his merit and intercession, and to depend upon that plea. The gift of the Spirit is a fruit of Christ's mediation, bought by his merit, and received by his intercession. The word used here, signifies an advocate, counsellor, monitor, and comforter. He would abide with the disciples to the end of time; his gifts and graces would encourage their hearts. The expressions used here and elsewhere, plainly denote a person, and the office itself includes all the Divine perfections. The gift of the Holy Ghost is bestowed upon the disciples of Christ, and not on the world. This is the favour God bears to his chosen. As the source of holiness and happiness, the Holy Spirit will abide with every believer for ever.

Verses 18–24

Christ promises that he would continue his care of his disciples. I will not leave you orphans, or fatherless, for though I leave you, yet I leave you this comfort, I will come to you. I will come speedily to you at my resurrection. I will come daily to you in my Spirit; in the tokens of his love, and visits of his grace. I will come certainly at the end of time. Those only that see Christ with an eye of faith, shall see him for ever: the world sees him no more till his second coming; but his disciples have communion with him in his absence. These mysteries will be fully known in heaven. It is a further act of grace, that they should know it, and have the comfort of it. Having Christ's commands, we must keep them. And having them in our heads, we must keep them in our hearts and lives. The surest evidence of our love to Christ is, obedience to the laws of Christ. There are spiritual tokens of Christ and his love given to all believers. Where sincere love to Christ is in the heart, there will be obedience. Love will be a commanding, constraining principle; and where love is, duty follows from a principle of gratitude. God will not only love obedient believers, but he will take pleasure in loving them, will rest in love to them. He will be with them as his home. These privileges are confined to those whose faith worketh by love, and whose love to Jesus leads them to keep his commandments. Such are partakers of the Holy Spirit's new-creating grace.

Verses 25–27

Would we know these things for our good, we must pray for, and depend on the teaching of the Holy Ghost; thus the words of Jesus will be brought to our remembrance, and many difficulties be cleared up which are not plain to others. To all the saints, the Spirit of grace is given to be a remembrancer, and to him, by faith and prayer, we should commit the keeping of what we hear and know. Peace is put for all good, and Christ has left us all that is really and truly good, all the promised good; peace of mind from our justification before God. This Christ calls his peace, for he is himself our Peace. The peace of God widely differs from that of Pharisees or hypocrites, as is shown by its humbling and holy effects.

Verses 28–31

Christ raises the expectations of his disciples to something beyond what they thought was their greatest happiness. His time was now short, he therefore spake largely to them. When we come to be sick, and to die, we may not be capable of talking much to those about us; such good counsel as we have to give, let us give while in health. Observe the prospect Christ had of an approaching conflict, not only with men, but with the powers of darkness. Satan has something in us to perplex us with, for we have all sinned; but when he would disturb Christ, he found nothing sinful to help him. The best evidence of our love to the Father is, our doing as he has commanded us. Let us rejoice in the Saviour's victories over Satan the prince of this world. Let us copy the example of his love and obedience.

Chapter 15

Chapter Outline	
Christ the true Vine.	(1–8)
His love to his disciples.	(9–17)
foretold.	(18–25)
The Comforter promised.	(26, 27)

Verses 1–8

Jesus Christ is the Vine, the true Vine. The union of the human and Divine natures, and the fulness of the Spirit that is in him, resemble the root of the vine made fruitful by the moisture from a rich soil. Believers are branches of this Vine. The root is unseen, and our life is hid with Christ; the root bears the tree, diffuses sap to it, and in Christ are all supports and supplies. The branches of the vine are many, yet, meeting in the root, are all but one vine; thus all true Christians, though in place and opinion distant from each other, meet in Christ. Believers, like the branches of the vine, are weak, and unable to stand but as they are borne up. The Father is the Husbandman. Never was any husbandman so wise, so watchful, about his vineyard, as God is about his church, which therefore must prosper. We must be fruitful. From a vine we look for grapes, and from a Christian we look for a Christian temper, disposition, and life. We must honour God, and do good; this is bearing fruit. The unfruitful are taken away. And even fruitful branches need pruning; for the best have notions, passions, and humours, that require to be taken away, which Christ has promised to forward the sanctification of believers, they will be thankful, for them. The word of Christ is spoken to all believers; and there is a cleansing virtue in that word, as it works grace, and works out corruption. And the more fruit we bring forth, the more we abound in what is good, the more our Lord is glorified. In order to fruitfulness, we must abide in Christ, must have union with him by faith. It is the great concern of all Christ's disciples, constantly to keep up dependence upon Christ, and communion with him. True Christians find by experience, that any interruption in the exercise of their faith, causes holy affections to decline, their corruptions to revive, and their comforts to droop. Those who abide not in Christ, though they may flourish for awhile in outward profession, yet come to nothing. The fire is the fittest place for withered branches; they are good for nothing else. Let us seek to live more simply on the fulness of Christ, and to grow more fruitful in every good word and work, so may our joy in Him and in his salvation be full.

Verses 9–17

Those whom God loves as a Father, may despise the hatred of all the world. As the Father loved Christ, who was most worthy, so he loved his disciples, who were unworthy. All that love the Saviour should continue in their love to him, and take all occasions to show it. The joy of the hypocrite is but for a moment, but the joy of those who abide in Christ's love is a continual feast. They are to show their love to him by keeping his commandments. If the same power that first shed abroad the love of Christ's in our hearts, did not keep us in that love, we should not long abide in it. Christ's love to us should direct us to love each other. He speaks as about to give many things in charge, yet names this only; it includes many duties.

Verses 18–25

How little do many persons think, that in opposing the doctrine of Christ as our Prophet, Priest, and King, they prove themselves ignorant of the one living and true God, whom they profess to worship! The name into which Christ's disciples were baptized, is that which they will live and die by. It is a comfort to the greatest sufferers, if they suffer for Christ's name's sake. The world's ignorance is the true cause of its hatred to the disciples of Jesus. The clearer and fuller the discoveries of the grace and truth of Christ, the greater is our sin if we do not love him and believe in him.

Verses 26, 27

The blessed Spirit will maintain the cause of Christ in the world, notwithstanding the opposition it meets with. Believers taught and encouraged by his influences, would bear testimony to Christ and his salvation.

Chapter 16

Chapter Outline	
Persecution foretold.	(1–6)
The promise of the Holy Spirit, and his office.	(7–15)
Christ's departure and return.	(16–22)
Encouragement to prayer.	(23–27)

Christ's discoveries of himself.	(28–33)

Verses 1–6

Our Lord Jesus, by giving his disciples notice of trouble, designed that the terror might not be a surprise to them. It is possible for those who are real enemies to God's service, to pretend zeal for it. This does not lessen the sin of the persecutors; villanies will never be changed by putting the name of God to them. As Jesus in his sufferings, so his followers in theirs, should look to the fulfilling of Scripture. He did not tell them sooner, because he was with them to teach, guide, and comfort them; they needed not then this promise of the Holy Spirit's presence. It will silence us to ask, Whence troubles come? It will satisfy us to ask, Whither go they? for we know they work for good. It is the common fault and folly of melancholy Christians to look only on the dark side of the cloud, and to turn a deaf ear to the voice of joy and gladness. That which filled the disciples' hearts with sorrow, was too great affection for this present life. Nothing more hinders our joy in God, than the love of the world, and the sorrow of the world which comes from it.

Verses 7–15

Christ's departure was necessary to the Comforter's coming. Sending the Spirit was to be the fruit of Christ's death, which was his going away. His bodily presence could be only in one place at one time, but his Spirit is every where, in all places, at all times, wherever two or three are gathered together in his name. See here the office of the Spirit, first to reprove, or to convince. Convincing work is the Spirit's work; he can do it effectually, and none but he. It is the method the Holy Spirit takes, first to convince, and then to comfort. The Spirit shall convince the world, of sin; not merely tell them of it. The Spirit convinces of the fact of sin; of the fault of sin; of the folly of sin; of the filth of sin, that by it we are become hateful to God; of the fountain of sin, the corrupt nature; and lastly, of the fruit of sin, that the end thereof is death. The Holy Spirit proves that all the world is guilty before God. He convinces the world of righteousness; that Jesus of Nazareth was Christ the righteous. Also, of Christ's righteousness, imparted to us for justification and salvation. He will show them where it is to be had, and how they may be accepted as righteous in God's sight. Christ's ascension proves the ransom was accepted, and the righteousness finished, through which believers were to be justified. Of judgment, because the prince of this world is judged. All will be well, when his power is broken, who made all the mischief. As Satan is subdued by Christ, this gives us confidence, for no other power can stand before him. And of the day of judgment. The coming of the Spirit would be of unspeakable advantage to the disciples. The Holy Spirit is our Guide, not only to show us the way, but to go with us by continued aids and influences. To be led into a truth is more than barely to know it; it is not only to have the notion of it in our heads, but the relish, and savour, and power of it in our hearts. He shall teach all truth, and keep back nothing profitable, for he will show things to come. All the gifts and graces of the Spirit, all the preaching, and all the writing of the apostles, under the influence of the Spirit, all the tongues, and miracles, were to glorify Christ. It behoves every one to ask, whether the Holy Spirit has begun a good work in his heart? Without clear discovery of our guilt and danger, we never shall understand the value of Christ's salvation; but when brought to know ourselves aright, we begin to see the value of the Redeemer. We should have fuller views of the Redeemer, and more lively affections to him, if we more prayed for, and depended on the Holy Spirit.

Verses 16–22

It is good to consider how near our seasons of grace are to an end, that we may be quickened to improve them. But the sorrows of the disciples would soon be turned into joy; as those of a mother, at the sight of her infant. The Holy Spirit would be their Comforter, and neither men nor devils, neither sufferings in life nor in death, would ever deprive them of their joy. Believers have joy or sorrow, according to their sight of Christ, and the tokens of his presence. Sorrow is coming on the ungodly, which nothing can lessen; the believer is an heir to joy which no one can take away. Where now is the joy of the murderers of our Lord, and the sorrow of his friends?

Verses 23–27

Asking of the Father shows a sense of spiritual wants, and a desire of spiritual blessings, with conviction that they are to be had from God only. Asking in Christ's name, is acknowledging our unworthiness to receive any favours from God, and shows full dependence upon Christ as the Lord our Righteousness. Our Lord had hitherto spoken in short and weighty sentences, or in parables, the import of which the disciples did not fully understand, but after his resurrection he intended plainly to teach them such things as related to the Father and the way to him, through his intercession. And the frequency with which our Lord enforces offering up petitions in his name, shows that the great end of the mediation of Christ is to impress us with a deep sense of our sinfulness, and of the merit and power of his death, whereby we have access to God. And let us ever remember, that to address the Father in the name of Christ, or to address the Son as God dwelling in human nature, and reconciling the world to himself, are the same, as the Father and Son are one.

Verses 28–33

Here is a plain declaration of Christ's coming from the Father, and his return to him. The Redeemer, in his entrance, was God manifest in the flesh, and in his departure was received up into glory. By this saying the disciples improved in knowledge. Also in faith; "Now are we sure." Alas! they knew not their own weakness. The Divine nature did not desert the human nature, but supported it, and put comfort and value into Christ's sufferings. And while we have God's favourable presence, we are happy, and ought to be easy, though all the world forsake us. Peace in Christ is the only true peace, in him alone believers have it. Through him we have peace with God, and so in him we have peace in our own minds. We ought to be encouraged, because Christ has overcome the world before us. But while we think we stand, let us take heed lest we fall. We know not how we should act if brought into temptation; let us watch and pray without ceasing, that we may not be left to ourselves.

Chapter 17

Chapter Outline	
Christ's prayer for himself.	(1–5)
His prayer for his disciples.	(6–10)
His prayer.	(11–26)

Verses 1–5

Our Lord prayed as a man, and as the Mediator of his people; yet he spoke with majesty and authority, as one with and equal to the Father. Eternal life could not be given to believers, unless Christ, their Surety, both glorified the Father, and was glorified of him. This is the sinner's way to eternal life, and when this knowledge shall be made perfect, holiness and happiness will be fully enjoyed. The holiness and happiness of the redeemed, are especially that glory of Christ, and of his Father, which was the joy set before him, for which he endured the cross and despised the shame, this glory was the end of the sorrow of his soul, and in obtaining it he was fully satisfied. Thus we are taught that our glorifying God is needed as an evidence of our interest in Christ, through whom eternal life is God's free gift.

Verses 6–10

Christ prays for those that are his. Thou gavest them me, as sheep to the shepherd, to be kept; as a patient to the physician, to be cured; as children to a tutor, to be taught: thus he will deliver up his charge. It is a great satisfaction to us, in our reliance upon Christ, that he, all he is and has, and all he said and did, all he is doing and will do, are of God. Christ offered this prayer for his people alone as believers; not for the world at large. Yet no one who desires to come to the Father, and is conscious that he is unworthy to come in his own name, need be discouraged by the Saviour's declaration, for he is both able and willing to save to the uttermost, all that come unto God by him. Earnest convictions and desires, are hopeful tokens of a work already wrought in a man; they begin to evidence that he has been chosen unto salvation, through sanctification of the Spirit and belief of the truth. They are thine; wilt thou not provide for thine own? Wilt thou not secure them? Observe the foundation on which this plea is grounded, All mine are thine, and thine are mine. This speaks the Father and Son to be one. All mine are thine. The Son owns none for his, that are not devoted to the service of the Father.

Verses 11–16

Christ does not pray that they might be rich and great in the world, but that they might be kept from sin, strengthened for their duty, and brought safe to heaven. The prosperity of the soul is the best prosperity. He pleaded with his holy Father, that he would keep them by his power and for his glory, that they might be united in affection and labours, even according to the union of the Father and the Son. He did not pray that his disciples should be removed out of the world, that they might escape the rage of men, for they had a great work to do for the glory of God, and the benefit of mankind. But he prayed that the Father would keep them from the evil, from being corrupted by the world, the remains of sin in their hearts, and from the power and craft of Satan. So that they might pass through the world as through an enemy's country, as he had done. They are not left here to pursue the same objects as the men around them, but to glorify God, and to serve their generation. The Spirit of God in true Christians is opposed to the spirit of the world.

Verses 17–19

Christ next prayed for the disciples, that they might not only be kept from evil, but made good. It is the prayer of Jesus for all that are his, that they may be made holy. Even disciples must pray for sanctifying grace. The means of giving this grace is, "through thy truth, thy word is truth." Sanctify them, set them apart for thyself and thy service. Own them in the office; let thy hand go with them. Jesus entirely devoted himself to his undertaking, and all the parts of it, especially the offering up himself without spot unto God, by the eternal Spirit. The real holiness of all true Christians is the fruit of Christ's death, by which the gift of the Holy Ghost was purchased; he gave himself for his church, to sanctify it. If our views have not this effect on us, they are not Divine truth, or we do not receive them by a living and a working faith, but as mere notions.

Verses 20–23

Our Lord especially prayed, that all believers might be as one body under one head, animated by one soul, by their union with Christ and the Father in him, through the Holy Spirit dwelling in them. The more they dispute about lesser things, the more they throw doubts upon Christianity. Let us endeavour to keep the unity of the Spirit in the bond of peace, praying that all believers may be more and more united in one mind and one judgment. Thus shall we convince the world of the truth and excellence of our religion, and find more sweet communion with God and his saints.

Verses 24–26

Christ, as one with the Father, claimed on behalf of all that had been given to him, and should in due time believe on him, that they should be brought to heaven; and that there the whole company of the redeemed might behold his glory as their beloved Friend and Brother, and therein find happiness. He had declared and would further declare the name or character of God, by his doctrine and his Spirit, that, being one with him, the love of the Father to him might abide with them also. Thus, being joined to Him by one Spirit, they might be filled with all the fulness of God, and enjoy a blessedness of which we can form no right idea in our present state.

Chapter 18

Chapter Outline	
Christ taken in the garden.	(1–12)
Christ before Annas and Caiaphas.	(13–27)
Christ before Pilate.	(28–40)

Verses 1–12

Sin began in the garden of Eden, there the curse was pronounced, there the Redeemer was promised; and in a garden that promised Seed entered into conflict with the old serpent. Christ was buried also in a garden. Let us, when we walk in our gardens, take occasion from thence to mediate on Christ's sufferings in a garden. Our Lord Jesus, knowing all things that should come upon him, went forth and asked, Whom seek ye? When the people would have forced him to a crown, he withdrew, ch. **6:15**, but when they came to force him to a cross, he offered himself; for he came into this world to suffer, and went to the other world to reign. He showed plainly what he could have done; when he struck them down he could have struck them dead, but he would not do so. It must have been the effect of Divine power, that the officers and soldiers let the disciples go away quietly, after the resistance which had been offered. Christ set us an example of meekness in sufferings, and a pattern of submission to God's will in every thing that concerns us. It is but a cup, a small matter. It is a cup that is given us; sufferings are gifts. It is given us by a Father, who has a father's authority, and does us no wrong; a father's affection, and means us no hurt. From the example of our Saviour we should learn how to receive our lighter afflictions, and to ask ourselves whether we ought to oppose our Father's will, or to distrust his love. We were bound with the cords of our iniquities, with the yoke of our transgressions. Christ, being made a sin-offering for us, to free us from those bonds, himself submitted to be bound for us. To his bonds we owe our liberty; thus the Son makes us free.

Verses 13–27

Simon Peter denied his Master. The particulars have been noticed in the remarks on the other Gospels. The beginning of sin is as the letting forth of water. The sin of lying is a fruitful sin; one lie needs another to support it, and that another. If a call to expose ourselves to danger be clear, we may hope God will enable us to honour him; if it be not, we may fear that God will leave us to shame ourselves. They said nothing concerning the miracles of Jesus, by which he had done so much good, and which proved his doctrine. Thus the enemies of Christ, whilst they quarrel with his truth, wilfully shut their eyes against it. He appeals to those who heard him. The doctrine of Christ may safely appeal to all that know it, and those who judge in truth bear witness to it. Our resentment of injuries must never be passionate. He reasoned with the man that did him the injury, and so may we.

Verses 28–32

It was unjust to put one to death who had done so much good, therefore the Jews were willing to save themselves from reproach. Many fear the scandal of an ill thing, more than the sin of it. Christ had said he should be delivered to the Gentiles, and they should put him to death; hereby that saying was fulfilled. He had said that he should be crucified, lifted up. If the Jews had judged him by their law, he had been stoned; crucifying never was used among the Jews. It is determined concerning us, though not discovered to us, what death we shall die: this should free us from disquiet about that matter. Lord, what, when, and how, thou hast appointed.

Verses 33–40

Art thou the King of the Jews? that King of the Jews who has been so long expected? Messiah the Prince; art thou he? Dost thou call thyself so, and wouldest thou be thought so? Christ answered this question with another; not for evasion, but that Pilate might consider what he did. He never took upon him any earthly power, never were any traitorous principles or practices laid to him. Christ gave an account of the nature of his kingdom. Its nature is not worldly; it is a kingdom within men, set up in their hearts and consciences; its riches spiritual, its power spiritual, and it glory within. Its supports are not worldly; its weapons are spiritual; it needed not, nor used, force to maintain and advance it, nor opposed any kingdom but that of sin and Satan. Its object and design are not worldly. When Christ said, I am the Truth, he said, in effect, I am a King. He conquers by the convincing evidence of truth; he rules by the commanding power of truth. The subjects of this kingdom are those that are of the truth. Pilate put a good question, he said, What is truth? When we search the Scriptures, and attend the ministry of the word, it must be with this inquiry, What is truth? and with this prayer, Lead me in thy truth; into all truth. But many put this question, who have not patience to preserve in their search after truth; or not humility enough to receive it. By this solemn declaration of Christ's innocence, it appears, that though the Lord Jesus was treated as the worst of evil-doers, he never deserved such treatment. But it unfolds the design of his death; that he died as a Sacrifice for our sins. Pilate was willing to please all sides; and was governed more by worldly wisdom than by the rules of justice. Sin is a robber, yet is foolishly chosen by many rather than Christ, who would truly enrich us. Let us endeavour to make our accusers ashamed as Christ did; and let us beware of crucifying Christ afresh.

Chapter 19

Chapter Outline	
Christ condemned and crucified.	(1–18)
Christ on the cross.	(19–30)
His side pierced.	(31–37)
The burial of Jesus.	(38–42)

Verses 1–18

Little did Pilate think with what holy regard these sufferings of Christ would, in after-ages, be thought upon and spoken of by the best and greatest of men. Our Lord Jesus came forth, willing to be exposed to their scorn. It is good for every one with faith, to behold Christ Jesus in his sufferings. Behold him, and love him; be still looking unto Jesus. Did their hatred sharpen their endeavours against him? and shall not our love for him quicken our endeavours for him and his kingdom? Pilate seems to have thought that Jesus might be some person above the common order. Even natural conscience makes men afraid of being found fighting against God. As our Lord suffered for the sins both of Jews and Gentiles, it was a special part of the counsel of Divine Wisdom, that the Jews should first purpose his death, and the Gentiles carry that purpose into effect. Had not Christ been thus rejected of men, we had been for ever rejected of God. Now was the Son of man delivered into the hands of wicked and unreasonable men. He was led forth for us, that we might escape. He was nailed to the cross, as a Sacrifice bound to the altar. The Scripture was fulfilled; he did not die at the altar among the sacrifices, but among criminals sacrificed to public justice. And now let us pause, and with faith look upon Jesus. Was ever sorrow like unto his sorrow? See him bleeding, see him dying, see him and love him! love him, and live to him!

Verses 19–30

Here are some remarkable circumstances of Jesus' death, more fully related than before. Pilate would not gratify the chief priests by allowing the writing to be altered; which was doubtless owing to a secret power of God upon his heart, that this statement of our Lord's character and authority might continue. Many things done by the Roman soldiers were fulfilments of the prophecies of the Old Testament. All things therein written shall be fulfilled. Christ tenderly provided for his mother at his death. Sometimes, when God removes one comfort from us, he raises up another for us, where we looked not for it. Christ's example teaches all men to honour their parents in life and death; to provide for their wants, and to promote their comfort by every means in their power. Especially observe the dying word wherewith Jesus breathed out his soul. It is finished; that is, the counsels of the Father concerning his sufferings were now fulfilled. It is finished; all the types and prophecies of the Old Testament, which pointed at the sufferings of the Messiah, were accomplished. It is finished; the ceremonial law is abolished; the substance is now come, and all the shadows are done away. It is finished; an end is made of transgression by bringing in an everlasting righteousness. His sufferings were now finished, both those of his soul, and those of his body. It is finished; the work of man's redemption and salvation is now completed. His life was not taken from him by force, but freely given up.

Verses 31–37

A trial was made whether Jesus was dead. He died in less time than persons crucified commonly did. It showed that he had laid down his life of himself. The spear broke up the very fountains of life; no human body could survive such a wound. But its being so solemnly attested, shows there was something peculiar in it. The blood and water that flowed out, signified those two great benefits which all believers partake of through Christ, justification and sanctification; blood for atonement, water for purification. They both flow from the pierced side of our Redeemer. To Christ crucified we owe merit for our justification, and Spirit and grace for our sanctification. Let this silence the fears of weak Christians, and encourage their hopes; there came both water and blood out of Jesus' pierced side, both to justify and sanctify them. The Scripture was fulfilled, in Pilate's not allowing his legs to be broken, Ps **34**:**20**. There was a type of this in the paschal lamb, Ex **12**:**46**. May we ever look to Him, whom, by our sins, we have ignorantly and heedlessly pierced, nay, sometimes against convictions and mercies; and who shed from his wounded side both water and blood, that we might be justified and sanctified in his name.

Verses 38–42

Joseph of Arimathea was a disciple of Christ in secret. Disciples should openly own themselves; yet some, who in lesser trials have been fearful, in greater have been courageous. When God has work to do, he can find out such as are proper to do it. The embalming was done by Nicodemus, a secret friend to Christ, though not his constant follower. That grace which at first is like a bruised reed, may afterward resemble a strong cedar. Hereby these two rich men showed the value they had for Christ's person and doctrine, and that it was not lessened by the reproach of the cross. We must do our duty as the present day and opportunity are, and leave it to God to fulfil his promises in his own way and his own time. The grave of Jesus was appointed with the wicked, as was the case of those who suffered as criminals; but he was with the rich in his death, as prophesied, Isa **53**:**9**; these two circumstances it was very unlikely should ever be united in the same person. He was buried in a new sepulchre; therefore it could not be said that it was not he, but some other that rose. We also are here taught not to be particular as to the place of our burial. He was buried in the sepulchre next at hand. Here is the Sun of Righteousness set for a while, to rise again in greater glory, and then to set no more.

Chapter 20

Chapter Outline	
The sepulchre found to be empty.	(1–10)
Christ appears to Mary.	(11–18)
He appears to the disciples.	(19–25)
The unbelief of Thomas.	(26–29)
Conclusion.	(30, 31)

Verses 1–10

If Christ gave his life a ransom, and had not taken it again, it would not have appeared that his giving it was accepted as satisfaction. It was a great trial to Mary, that the body was gone. Weak believers often make that the matter of complaint, which is really just ground of hope, and matter of joy. It is well when those more honoured than others with the privileges of disciples, are more active than others in the duty of disciples; more willing to take pains, and run hazards, in a good work. We must do our best, and neither envy those who can do better, nor despise those who do as well as they can, though they come behind. The disciple whom Jesus loved in a special manner, and who therefore in a special manner loved Jesus, was foremost. The love of Christ will make us to abound in every duty more than any thing else. He that was behind was Peter, who had denied Christ. A sense of guilt hinders us in the service of God. As yet the disciples knew not the Scripture; they Christ must rise again from the dead.

Verses 11–18

We are likely to seek and find, when we seek with affection, and seek in tears. But many believers complain of the clouds and darkness they are under, which are methods of grace for humbling their souls, mortifying their sins, and endearing Christ to them. A sight of angels and their smiles, will not suffice, without a sight of Jesus, and God's smiles in him. None know, but those who have tasted it, the sorrows of a deserted soul, which has had comfortable evidences of the love of God in Christ, and hopes of heaven, but has now lost them, and walks in darkness; such a wounded spirit who can bear? Christ, in manifesting himself to those that seek him, often outdoes their expectations. See how Mary's heart was in earnest to find Jesus. Christ's way of making himself known to his people is by his word; his word applied to their souls, speaking to them in particular. It might be read, Is it my Master? See with what pleasure those who love Jesus speak of his authority over them. He forbids her to expect that his bodily presence look further, than the present state of things. Observe the relation to God, from union with Christ. We, partaking of a Divine nature, Christ's Father is our Father; and he, partaking of the human nature, our God is his God. Christ's ascension into heaven, there to plead for us, is likewise an unspeakable comfort. Let them not think this earth is to be their home and rest; their eye and aim, and earnest desires, must be upon another world, and this ever upon their hearts, I ascend, therefore I must seek the things which are above. And let those who know the word of Christ, endeavour that others should get good from their knowledge.

Verses 19–25

This was the first day of the week, and this day is afterwards often mentioned by the sacred writers; for it was evidently set apart as the Christian sabbath, in remembrance of Christ's resurrection. The disciples had shut the doors for fear of the Jews; and when they had no such expectation, Jesus himself came and stood in the midst of them, having miraculously, though silently, opened the doors. It is a comfort to Christ's disciples, when their assemblies can only be held in private, that no doors can shut out Christ's presence. When He manifests his love to believers by the comforts of his Spirit, he assures them that because he lives, they shall live also. A sight of Christ will gladden the heart of a disciple at any time; and the more we see of Jesus, the more we shall rejoice. He said, Receive ye the Holy Ghost, thus showing that their spiritual life, as well as all their ability for their work, would be derived from him, and depended upon him. Every word of Christ which is received in the heart by faith, comes accompanied by this Divine breathing; and without this there is neither light nor life. Nothing is seen, known, discerned, or felt of God, but through this. After this, Christ directed the apostles to declare the only method by which sin would be forgiven. This power did not exist at all in the apostles as a power to give judgment, but only as a power to declare the character of those whom God would accept or reject in the day of judgment. They have clearly laid down the marks whereby a child of God may be discerned and be distinguished from a false professor; and according to what they have declared shall every case be decided in the day of judgment. When we assemble in Christ's name, especially on his holy day, he will meet with us, and speak peace to us. The disciples of Christ should endeavour to build up one another in their most holy faith, both by repeating what they have heard to those that were absent, and by making known what they have experienced. Thomas limited the Holy One of Israel, when he would be convinced by his own method or not at all. He might justly have been left in his unbelief, after rejecting such abundant proofs. The fears and sorrows of the disciples are often lengthened, to punish their negligence.

Verses 26–29

That one day in seven should be religiously observed, was an appointment from the beginning. And that, in the kingdom of the Messiah, the first day of the week should be that solemn day, was pointed out, in that Christ on that day once and again met his disciples in a religious assembly. The religious observance of that day has come down to us through every age of the church. There is not an unbelieving word in our tongues, nor thought in our minds, but it is known to the Lord Jesus; and he was pleased to accommodate himself even to Thomas, rather than leave him in his unbelief. We ought thus to bear with the weak, Ro **15**:**1**, **2**. This warning is given to all. If we are faithless, we are Christless and graceless, hopeless and joyless. Thomas was ashamed of his unbelief, and cried out, My Lord and my God. He spoke with affection, as one that took hold of Christ with all his might; "My Lord and my God." Sound and sincere believers, though slow and weak, shall be graciously accepted of the Lord Jesus. It is the duty of those who read and hear the gospel, to believe, to embrace the doctrine of Christ, and that record concerning him, **1**Jo **5**:**11**.

Verses 30, 31

There were other signs and proofs of our Lord's resurrection, but these were committed to writing, that all might believe that Jesus was the promised Messiah, the Saviour of sinners, and the Son of God; that, by this faith, they might obtain eternal life, by his mercy, truth, and power. May we believe that Jesus is the Christ, and believing may we have life through his name.

Chapter 21

Chapter Outline	
Christ appears to his disciples.	(1–14)
His discourse with Peter.	(15–19)
Christ's declaration concerning John.	(20–24)
The conclusion.	(25)

Verses 1–14

Christ makes himself known to his people, usually in his ordinances; but sometimes by his Spirit he visits them when employed in their business. It is good for the disciples of Christ to be together in common conversation, and common business. The hour for their entering upon action was not come. They would help to maintain themselves, and not be burdensome to any. Christ's time of making himself known to his people, is when they are most at a loss. He knows the temporal wants of his people, and has promised them not only grace sufficient, but food convenient. Divine Providence extends itself to things most minute, and those are happy who acknowledge God in all their ways. Those who are humble, diligent, and patient, though their labours may be crossed, shall be crowned; they sometimes live to see their affairs take a happy turn, after many struggles. And there is nothing lost by observing Christ's orders; it is casting the net on the right side of the ship. Jesus manifests himself to his people by doing that for them which none else can do, and things which they looked not for. He would take care that those who left all for him, should not want any good thing. And latter favours are to bring to mind former favours, that eaten bread may not be forgotten. He whom Jesus loved was the first that said, It is the Lord. John had cleaved most closely to his Master in his sufferings, and knew him soonest. Peter was the most zealous, and reached Christ the first. How variously God dispenses his gifts, and what difference there may be between some believers and others in the way of their honouring Christ, yet they all may be accepted of him! Others continue in the ship, drag the net, and bring the fish to shore, and such persons ought not to be blamed as worldly; for they, in their places, are as truly serving Christ as the others. The Lord Jesus had provision ready for them. We need not be curious in inquiring whence this came; but we may be comforted at Christ's care for his disciples. Although there were so many, and such great fishes, yet they lost none, nor damaged their net. The net of the gospel has enclosed multitudes, yet it is as strong as ever to bring souls to God.

Verses 15–19

Our Lord addressed Peter by his original name, as if he had forfeited that of Peter through his denying him. He now answered, Thou knowest that I love thee; but without professing to love Jesus more than others. We must not be surprised to have our sincerity called into question, when we ourselves have done that which makes it doubtful. Every remembrance of past sins, even pardoned sins, renews the sorrow of a true penitent. Conscious of integrity, Peter solemnly appealed to Christ, as knowing all things, even the secrets of his heart. It is well when our falls and mistakes make us more humble and watchful. The sincerity of our love to God must be brought to the test; and it behoves us to inquire with earnest, preserving prayer to the heart-searching God, to examine and prove us, whether we are able to stand this test. No one can be qualified to feed the sheep and lambs of Christ, who does not love the good Shepherd more than any earthly advantage or object. It is the great concern of every good man, whatever death he dies, to glorify God in it; for what is our chief end but this, to die to the Lord, at the word of the Lord?

Verses 20–24

Sufferings, pains, and death, will appear formidable even to the experienced Christian; but in the hope to glorify God, to leave a sinful world, and to be present with his Lord, he becomes ready to obey the Redeemer's call, and to follow Him through death to glory. It is the will of Christ that his disciples should mind their own duty, and not be curious about future events, either as to themselves or others. Many things we are apt to be anxious about which are nothing to us. Other people's affairs are nothing to us, to intermeddle in; we must quietly work, and mind our own business. Many curious questions are put about the counsels of God, and the state of the unseen world, as to which we may say, What is this to us? And if we attend to the duty of following Christ, we shall find neither heart nor time to meddle with that which does not belong to us. How little are any unwritten traditions to be relied upon! Let the Scripture be its own interpreter, and explain itself; as it is, in a great measure, its own evidence, and proves itself, for it is light. See the easy setting right such mistakes by the word of Christ. Scripture language is the safest channel for Scripture truth; the words which the Holy Ghost teaches, **1**Co **2**:**13**. Those who cannot agree in the same terms of art, and the application of them, may yet agree in the same Scripture terms, and to love one another.

Verse 25

Only a small part of the actions of Jesus had been written. But let us bless God for all that is in the Scriptures, and be thankful that there is so much in so small a space. Enough is recorded to direct our faith, and regulate our practice; more would have been unnecessary. Much of what is written is overlooked, much forgotten, and much made the matter of doubtful disputes. We may, however, look forward to the joy we shall receive in heaven, from a more complete knowledge of all Jesus did and said, as well as of the conduct of his providence and grace in his dealings with each of us. May this be our happiness. These are written that ye might believe that Jesus is the Christ, the Son of God; and that believing ye might have life through his name, ch. **20**:**31**.

Acts

This book unites the Gospels to the Epistles. It contains many particulars concerning the apostles Peter and Paul, and of the Christian church from the ascension of our Saviour to the arrival of St. Paul at Rome, a space of about thirty years. St. Luke was the writer of this book; he was present at many of the events he relates, and attended Paul to Rome. But the narrative does not afford a complete history of the church during the time to which it refers, nor even of St. Paul's life. The object of the book has been considered to be, **1**. To relate in what manner the gifts of the Holy Spirit were communicated on the day of Pentecost, and the miracles performed by the apostles, to confirm the truth of Christianity, as showing that Christ's declarations were really fulfilled. **2**. To prove the claim of the Gentiles to be admitted into the church of Christ. This is shown by much of the contents of the book. A large portion of the Acts is occupied by the discourses or sermons of various persons, the language and manner of which differ, and all of which will be found according to the persons by whom they were delivered, and the occasions on which they were spoken. It seems that most of these discourses are only the substance of what was actually delivered. They relate nevertheless fully to Jesus as the Christ, the anointed Messiah.

Chapter 1

Chapter Outline	
Proofs of Christ's resurrection.	(1–5)
Christ's ascension.	(6–11)
The apostles unite in prayer.	(12–14)
Matthias chosen in the place of Judas.	(15–26)

Verses 1–5

Our Lord told the disciples the work they were to do. The apostles met together at Jerusalem; Christ having ordered them not to depart thence, but to wait for the pouring out of the Holy Spirit. This would be a baptism by the Holy Ghost, giving them power to work miracles, and enlightening and sanctifying their souls. This confirms the Divine promise, and encourages us to depend upon it, that we have heard it from Christ; for in Him all the promises of God are yea and amen.

Verses 6–11

They were earnest in asking about that which their Master never had directed or encouraged them to seek. Our Lord knew that his ascension and the teaching of the Holy Spirit would soon end these expectations, and therefore only gave them a rebuke; but it is a caution to his church in all ages, to take heed of a desire of forbidden knowledge. He had given his disciples instructions for the discharge of their duty, both before his death and since his resurrection, and this knowledge is enough for a Christian. It is enough that He has engaged to give believers strength equal to their trials and services; that under the influence of the Holy Spirit they may, in one way or other, be witnesses for Christ on earth, while in heaven he manages their concerns with perfect wisdom, truth, and love. When we stand gazing and trifling, the thoughts of our Master's second coming should quicken and awaken us: when we stand gazing and trembling, they should comfort and encourage us. May our expectation of it be stedfast and joyful, giving diligence to be found of him blameless.

Verses 12–14

God can find hiding-places for his people. They made supplication. All God's people are praying people. It was now a time of trouble and danger with the disciples of Christ; but if any is afflicted, let him pray; that will silence cares and fears. They had now a great work to do, and before they entered upon it, they were earnest in prayer to God for his presence. They were waiting for the descent of the Spirit, and abounded in prayer. Those are in the best frame to receive spiritual blessings, who are in a praying frame. Christ had promised shortly to send the Holy Ghost; that promise was not to do away prayer, but to quicken and encourage it. A little company united in love, exemplary in their conduct, fervent in prayer, and wisely zealous to promote the cause of Christ, are likely to increase rapidly.

Verses 15–26

The great thing the apostles were to attest to the world, was, Christ's resurrection; for that was the great proof of his being the Messiah, and the foundation of our hope in him. The apostles were ordained, not to wordly dignity and dominion, but to preach Christ, and the power of his resurrection. An appeal was made to God; "Thou, Lord, who knowest the hearts of all men," which we do not; and better than they know their own. It is fit that God should choose his own servants; and so far as he, by the disposals of his providence, or the gifts of his Spirit, shows whom he was chosen, or what he has chosen for us, we ought to fall in with his will. Let us own his hand in the determining everything which befalls us, especially in those by which any trust may be committed to us.

Chapter 2

Chapter Outline	
The descent of the Holy Spirit at the day of Pentecost.	(1–4)
The apostles speak in divers languages.	(5–13)
Peter's address to the Jews.	(14–36)
Three thousand souls converted.	(37–41)
The piety and affection of the disciples.	(42–47)

Verses 1–4

We cannot forget how often, while their Master was with them there were strifes among the disciples which should be the greatest; but now all these strifes were at an end. They had prayed more together of late. Would we have the Spirit poured out upon us from on high, let us be all of one accord. And notwithstanding differences of sentiments and interests, as there were among those disciples, let us agree to love one another; for where brethren dwell together in unity, there the Lord commands his blessing. A rushing mighty wind came with great force. This was to signify the powerful influences and working of the Spirit of God upon the minds of men, and thereby upon the world. Thus the convictions of the Spirit make way for his comforts; and the rough blasts of that blessed wind, prepare the soul for its soft and gentle gales. There was an appearance of something like flaming fire, lighting on every one of them, according to John Baptist's saying concerning Christ; He shall baptize you with the Holy Ghost, and with fire. The Spirit, like fire, melts the heart, burns up the dross, and kindles pious and devout affections in the soul; in which, as in the fire on the altar, the spiritual sacrifices are offered up. They were all filled with the Holy Ghost, more than before. They were filled with the graces of the Spirit, and more than ever under his sanctifying influences; more weaned from this world, and better acquainted with the other. They were more filled with the comforts of the Spirit, rejoiced more than ever in the love of Christ and the hope of heaven: in it all their griefs and fears were swallowed up. They were filled with the gifts of the Holy Ghost; they had miraculous powers for the furtherance of the gospel. They spake, not from previous though or meditation, but as the Spirit gave them utterance.

Verses 5–13

The difference in languages which arose at Babel, has much hindered the spread of knowledge and religion. The instruments whom the Lord first employed in spreading the Christian religion, could have made no progress without this gift, which proved that their authority was from God.

Verses 14–21

Peter's sermon shows that he was thoroughly recovered from his fall, and thoroughly restored to the Divine favour; for he who had denied Christ, now boldly confessed him. His account of the miraculous pouring forth of the Spirit, was designed to awaken the hearers to embrace the faith of Christ, and to join themselves to his church. It was the fulfilling the Scripture, and the fruit of Christ's resurrection and ascension, and proof of both. Though Peter was filled with the Holy Ghost, and spake with tongues as the Spirit gave him utterance, yet he did not think to set aside the Scriptures. Christ's scholars never learn above their Bible; and the Spirit is given, not to do away the Scriptures, but to enable us to understand, approve, and obey them. Assuredly none will escape the condemnation of the great day, except those who call upon the name of the Lord, in and through his Son Jesus Christ, as the Saviour of sinners, and the Judge of all mankind.

Verses 22–36

From this gift of the Holy Ghost, Peter preaches unto them Jesus: and here is the history of Christ. Here is an account of his death and sufferings, which they witnessed but a few weeks before. His death is considered as God's act; and of wonderful grace and wisdom. Thus Divine justice must be satisfied, God and man brought together again, and Christ himself glorified, according to an eternal counsel, which could not be altered. And as the people's act; in them it was an act of awful sin and folly. Christ's resurrection did away the reproach of his death; Peter speaks largely upon this. Christ was God's Holy One, sanctified and set apart to his service in the work of redemption. His death and sufferings should be, not to him only, but to all his, the entrance to a blessed life for evermore. This event had taken place as foretold, and the apostles were witnesses. Nor did the resurrection rest upon this alone; Christ had poured upon his disciples the miraculous gifts and Divine influences, of which they witnessed the effects. Through the Saviour, the ways of life are made known; and we are encouraged to expect God's presence, and his favour for evermore. All this springs from assured belief that Jesus is the Lord, and the anointed Saviour.

Verses 37–41

From the first delivery of that Divine message, it appeared that there was Divine power going with it; and thousands were brought to the obedience of faith. But neither Peter's words, nor the miracle they witnessed, could have produced such effects, had not the Holy Spirit been given. Sinners, when their eyes are opened, cannot but be pricked to the heart for sin, cannot but feel an inward uneasiness. The apostle exhorted them to repent of their sins, and openly to avow their belief in Jesus as the Messiah, by being baptized in his name. Thus professing their faith in Him, they would receive remission of their sins, and partake of the gifts and graces of the Holy Spirit. To separate from wicked people, is the only way to save ourselves from them. Those who repent of their sins, and give up themselves to Jesus Christ, must prove their sincerity by breaking off from the wicked. We must save ourselves from them; which denotes avoiding them with dread and holy fear. By God's grace three thousand persons accepted the gospel invitation. There can be no doubt that the gift of the Holy Ghost, which they all received, and from which no true believer has ever been shut out, was that Spirit of adoption, that converting, guiding, sanctifying grace, which is bestowed upon all the members of the family of our heavenly Father. Repentance and remission of sins are still preached to the chief of sinners, in the Redeemer's name; still the Holy Spirit seals the blessing on the believer's heart; still the encouraging promises are to us and our children; and still the blessings are offered to all that are afar off.

Verses 42–47

In these **verses** we have the history of the truly primitive church, of the first days of it; its state of infancy indeed, but, like that, the state of its greatest innocence. They kept close to holy ordinances, and abounded in piety and devotion; for Christianity, when admitted in the power of it, will dispose the soul to communion with God in all those ways wherein he has appointed us to meet him, and has promised to meet us. The greatness of the event raised them above the world, and the Holy Ghost filled them with such love, as made every one to be to another as to himself, and so made all things common, not by destroying property, but doing away selfishness, and causing charity. And God who moved them to it, knew that they were quickly to be driven from their possessions in Judea. The Lord, from day to day, inclined the hearts of more to embrace the gospel; not merely professors, but such as were actually brought into a state of acceptance with God, being made partakers of regenerating grace. Those whom God has designed for eternal salvation, shall be effectually brought to Christ, till the earth is filled with the knowledge of his glory.

Chapter 3

Chapter Outline	
A lame man healed by Peter and John.	(1–11)
Peter's address to the Jews.	(12–26)

Verses 1–11

The apostles and the first believers attended the temple worship at the hours of prayer. Peter and John seem to have been led by a Divine direction, to work a miracle on a man above forty years old, who had been a cripple from his birth. Peter, in the name of Jesus of Nazareth, bade him rise up and walk. Thus, if we would attempt to good purpose the healing of men's souls, we must go forth in the name and power of Jesus Christ, calling on helpless sinners to arise and walk in the way of holiness, by faith in Him. How sweet the thought to our souls, that in respect to all the crippled faculties of our fallen nature, the name of Jesus Christ of Nazareth can make us whole! With what holy joy and rapture shall we tread the holy courts, when God the Spirit causes us to enter therein by his strength!

Verses 12–18

Observe the difference in the manner of working the miracles. Our Lord always spoke as having Almighty power, never hesitated to receive the greatest honour that was given to him on account of his Divine miracles. But the apostles referred all to their Lord, and refused to receive any honour, except as his undeserving instruments. This shows that Jesus was one with the Father, and co-equal with Him; while the apostles knew that they were weak, sinful men, and dependent for every thing on Jesus, whose power effected the cure. Useful men must be very humble. Not unto us, O Lord, not unto us, but to thy name, give glory. Every crown must be cast at the feet of Christ. The apostle showed the Jews the greatness of their crime, but would not anger or drive them to despair. Assuredly, those who reject, refuse, or deny Christ, do it through ignorance; but this can in no case be an excuse.

Verses 19–21

The absolute necessity of repentance is to be solemnly charged upon the consciences of all who desire that their sins may be blotted out, and that they may share in the refreshment which nothing but a sense of Christ's pardoning love can afford. Blessed are those who have felt this. It was not needful for the Holy Spirit to make known the times and seasons of these dispensations. These subjects are still left obscure. But when sinners are convinced of their sins, they will cry to the Lord for pardon; and to the penitent, converted, and believing, times of refreshment will come from the presence of the Lord. In a state of trial and probation, the glorified Redeemer will be out of sight, because we must live by faith in him.

Verses 22–26

Here is a powerful address to warn the Jews of the dreadful consequences of their unbelief, in the very words of Moses, their favourite prophet, out of pretended zeal for whom they were ready to reject Christianity, and to try to destroy it. Christ came into the world to bring a blessing with him. And he sent his Spirit to be the great blessing. Christ came to bless us, by turning us from our iniquities, and saving us from our sins. We, by nature cleave to sin; the design of Divine grace is to turn us from it, that we may not only forsake, but hate it. Let none think that they can be happy by continuing in sin, when God declares that the blessing is in being turned from all iniquity. Let none think that they understand or believe the gospel, who only seek deliverance from the punishment of sin, but do not expect happiness in being delivered from sin itself. And let none expect to be turned from their sin, except by believing in, and receiving Christ the Son of God, as their wisdom, righteousness, sanctification, and redemption.

Chapter 4

Chapter Outline	
Peter and John imprisoned.	(1–4)
The apostles boldly testify to Christ.	(5–14)

Peter and John refuse to be silenced.	(15–22)
The believers unite in prayer and praise.	(23–31)
The holy charity of the Christians.	(32–37)

Verses 1–4

The apostles preached through Jesus the resurrection from the dead. It includes all the happiness of the future state; this they preached through Jesus Christ, to be had through him only. Miserable is their case, to whom the glory of Christ's kingdom is a grief; for since the glory of that kingdom is everlasting, their grief will be everlasting also. The harmless and useful servants of Christ, like the apostles, have often been troubled for their work of faith and labour of love, when wicked men have escaped. And to this day instances are not wanting, in which reading the Scriptures, social prayer, and religious conversation meet with frowns and checks. But if we obey the precepts of Christ, he will support us.

Verses 5–14

Peter being filled with the Holy Ghost, would have all to understand, that the miracle had been wrought by the name, or power, of Jesus of Nazareth, the Messiah, whom they had crucified; and this confirmed their testimony to his resurrection from the dead, which proved him to be the Messiah. These rulers must either be saved by that Jesus whom they had crucified, or they must perish for ever. The name of Jesus is given to men of every age and nation, as that whereby alone believers are saved from the wrath to come. But when covetousness, pride, or any corrupt passion, rules within, men shut their eyes, and close their hearts, in enmity against the light; considering all as ignorant and unlearned, who desire to know nothing in comparison with Christ crucified. And the followers of Christ should act so that all who con**verse** with them, may take knowledge that they have been with Jesus. That makes them holy, heavenly, spiritual, and cheerful, and raises them above this world.

Verses 15–22

All the care of the rulers is, that the doctrine of Christ spread not among the people, yet they cannot say it is false or dangerous, or of any ill tendency; and they are ashamed to own the true reason; that it testifies against their hypocrisy, wickedness, and tyranny. Those who know how to put a just value upon Christ's promises, know how to put just contempt upon the world's threatenings. The apostles look with concern on perishing souls, and know they cannot escape eternal ruin but by Jesus Christ, therefore they are faithful in warning, and showing the right way. None will enjoy peace of mind, nor act uprightly, till they have learned to guide their conduct by the fixed standard of truth, and not by the shifting opinions and fancies of men. Especially beware of a vain attempt to serve two masters, God and the world; the end will be, you can serve neither fully.

Verses 23–31

Christ's followers do best in company, provided it is their own company. It encourages God's servants, both in doing work, and suffering work, that they serve the God who made all things, and therefore has the disposal of all events; and the Scriptures must be fulfilled. Jesus was anointed to be a Saviour, therefore it was determined he should be a sacrifice, to make atonement for sin. But sin is not the less evil for God's bringing good out of it. In threatening times, our care should not be so much that troubles may be prevented, as that we may go on with cheerfulness and courage in our work and duty. They do not pray, Lord let us go away from our work, now that it is become dangerous, but, Lord, give us thy grace to go on stedfastly in our work, and not to fear the face of man. Those who desire Divine aid and encouragement, may depend upon having them, and they ought to go forth, and go on, in the strength of the Lord God. God gave a sign of acceptance of their prayers. The place was shaken, that their faith might be established and unshaken. God gave them greater degrees of his Spirit; and they were all filled with the Holy Ghost, more than ever; by which they were not only encouraged, but enabled to speak the word of God with boldness. When they find the Lord God help them by his Spirit, they know they shall not be confounded, Isa **17**.

Verses 32–37

The disciples loved one another. This was the blessed fruit of Christ's dying precept to his disciples, and his dying prayer for them. Thus it was then, and it will be so again, when the Spirit shall be poured upon us from on high. The doctrine preached was the resurrection of Christ; a matter of fact, which being duly explained, was a summary of all the duties, privileges, and comforts of Christians. There were evident fruits of Christ's grace in all they said and did. They were dead to this world. This was a great evidence of the grace of God in them. They did not take away others' property, but they were indifferent to it. They did not call it their own; because they had, in affection, forsaken all for Christ, and were expecting to be stripped of all for cleaving to him. No marvel that they were of one heart and soul, when they sat so loose to the wealth of this world. In effect, they had all things common; for there was not any among them who lacked, care was taken for their supply. The money was laid at the apostles' feet. Great care ought to be taken in the distribution of public charity, that it be given to such as have need, such as are not able to procure a maintenance for themselves; those who are reduced to want for well-doing, and for the testimony of a good conscience, ought to be provided for. Here is one in particular mentioned, remarkable for this generous charity; it was Barnabas. As one designed to be a preacher of the gospel, he disentangled himself from the affairs of this life. When such dispositions prevail, and are exercised according to the circumstances of the times, the testimony will have very great power upon others.

Chapter 5

Chapter Outline	
The death of Ananias and Sapphira.	(1–11)
The power which accompanied the preaching of the gospel.	(12–16)

The apostles imprisoned, but set free by an angel.	(17–25)
The apostles testify to Christ before the council.	(26–33)
The advice of Gamaliel, The council let the apostles go.	(34–42)

Verses 1–11

The sin of Ananias and Sapphira was, that they were ambitious of being thought eminent disciples, when they were not true disciples. Hypocrites may deny themselves, may forego their worldly advantage in one instance, with a prospect of finding their account in something else. They were covetous of the wealth of the world, and distrustful of God and his providence. They thought they might serve both God and mammon. They thought to deceive the apostles. The Spirit of God in Peter discerned the principle of unbelief reigning in the heart of Ananias. But whatever Satan might suggest, he could not have filled the heart of Ananias with this wickedness had he not been consenting. The falsehood was an attempt to deceive the Spirit of truth, who so manifestly spoke and acted by the apostles. The crime of Ananias was not his retaining part of the price of the land; he might have kept it all, had he pleased; but his endeavouring to impose upon the apostles with an awful lie, from a desire to make a vain show, joined with covetousness. But if we think to put a cheat upon God, we shall put a fatal cheat upon our own souls. How sad to see those relations who should quicken one another to that which is good, hardening one another in that which is evil! And this punishment was in reality mercy to vast numbers. It would cause strict self-examination, prayer, and dread of hypocrisy, covetousness, and vain-glory, and it should still do so. It would prevent the increase of false professors. Let us learn hence how hateful falsehood is to the God of truth, and not only shun a direct lie, but all advantages from the use of doubtful expressions, and double meaning in our speech.

Verses 12–16

The separation of hypocrites by distinguishing judgments, should make the sincere cleave closer to each other and to the gospel ministry. Whatever tends to the purity and reputation of the church, promotes its enlargement; but that power alone which wrought such miracles by the apostles, can rescue sinners from the power of sin and Satan, and add believers to His worshippers. Christ will work by all his faithful servants; and every one who applies to him shall be healed.

Verses 17–25

There is no prison so dark, so strong, but God can visit his people in it, and, if he pleases, fetch them out. Recoveries from sickness, releases out of trouble, are granted, not that we may enjoy the comforts of life, but that God may be honoured with the services of our life. It is not for the preachers of Christ's gospel to retire into corners, as long as they can have any opportunity of preaching in the great congregation. They must preach to the lowest, whose souls are as precious to Christ as the souls of the greatest. Speak to all, for all are concerned. Speak as those who resolve to stand to it, to live and die by it. Speak all the words of this heavenly, divine life, in comparison with which the present earthly life does not deserve the name. These words of life, which the Holy Ghost puts into your mouth. The words of the gospel are the words of life, words whereby we may be saved. How wretched are those who are vexed at the success of the gospel! They cannot but see that the word and power of the Lord are against them; and they tremble for the consequences, yet they will go on.

Verses 26–33

Many will do an evil thing with daring, yet cannot bear to hear of it afterward, or to have it charged upon them. We cannot expect to be redeemed and healed by Christ, unless we give up ourselves to be ruled by him. Faith takes the Saviour in all his offices, who came, not to save us in our sins, but to save us from our sins. Had Christ been exalted to give dominion to Israel, the chief priests would have welcomed him. But repentance and remission of sins are blessings they neither valued nor saw their need of; therefore they, by no means, admitted his doctrine. Wherever repentance is wrought, remission is granted without fail. None are freed from the guilt and punishment of sin, but those who are freed from the power and dominion of sin; who are turned from it, and turned against it. Christ gives repentance, by his Spirit working with the word, to awaken the conscience, to work sorrow for sin, and an effectual change in the heart and life. The giving of the Holy Ghost, is plain evidence that it is the will of God that Christ should be obeyed. And He will surely destroy those who will not have Him to reign over them.

Verses 34–42

The Lord still has all hearts in his hands, and sometimes directs the prudence of the worldly wise, so as to restrain the persecutors. Common sense tells us to be cautious, while experience and observation show that the success of frauds in matters of religion has been very short. Reproach for Christ is true preferment, as it makes us conformable to his pattern, and serviceable to his interest. They rejoiced in it. If we suffer ill for doing well, provided we suffer it well, and as we should, we ought to rejoice in that grace which enabled us so to do. The apostles did not preach themselves, but Christ. This was the preaching that most offended the priests. But it ought to be the constant business of gospel ministers to preach Christ: Christ, and him crucified; Christ, and him glorified; nothing beside this, but what has reference to it. And whatever is our station or rank in life, we should seek to make Him known, and to glorify his name.

Chapter 6

Chapter Outline	
The appointment of deacons.	(1–7)
Stephen falsely accused of blasphemy.	(8–15)

Verses 1–7

Hitherto the disciples had been of one accord; this often had been noticed to their honour; but now they were multiplied, they began to murmur. The word of God was enough to take up all the thoughts, cares, and time of the apostles. The persons chosen to serve tables must be duly qualified. They must be filled with gifts and graces of the Holy Ghost, necessary to rightly managing this trust; men of truth, and hating covetousness. All who are employed in the service of the church, ought to be commended to the Divine grace by the prayers of the church. They blessed them in the name of the Lord. The word and grace of God are greatly magnified, when those are wrought upon by it, who were least likely.

Verses 8–15

When they could not answer Stephen's arguments as a disputant, they prosecuted him as a criminal, and brought false witnesses against him. And it is next to a miracle of providence, that no greater number of religious persons have been murdered in the world, by the way of perjury and pretence of law, when so many thousands hate them, who make no conscience of false oaths. Wisdom and holiness make a man's face to shine, yet will not secure men from being treated badly. What shall we say of man, a rational being, yet attempting to uphold a religious system by false witness and murder! And this has been done in numberless instances. But the blame rests not so much upon the understanding, as upon the heart of a fallen creature, which is deceitful above all things and desperately wicked. Yet the servant of the Lord, possessing a clear conscience, cheerful hope, and Divine consolations, may smile in the midst of danger and death.

Chapter 7

Chapter Outline	
Stephen's defence.	(1–50)
Stephen reproves the Jews for the death of Christ.	(51–53)
The martyrdom of Stephen.	(54–60)

Verses 1–16

Stephen was charged as a blasphemer of God, and an apostate from the church; therefore he shows that he is a son of Abraham, and values himself on it. The slow steps by which the promise made to Abraham advanced toward performance, plainly show that it had a spiritual meaning, and that the land intended was the heavenly. God owned Joseph in his troubles, and was with him by the power of his Spirit, both on his own mind by giving him comfort, and on those he was concerned with, by giving him favour in their eyes. Stephen reminds the Jews of their mean beginning as a check to priding themselves in the glories of that nation. Likewise of the wickedness of the patriarchs of their tribes, in envying their brother Joseph; and the same spirit was still working in them toward Christ and his ministers. The faith of the patriarchs, in desiring to be buried in the land of Canaan, plainly showed they had regard to the heavenly country. It is well to recur to the first rise of usages, or sentiments, which have been perverted. Would we know the nature and effects of justifying faith, we should study the character of the father of the faithful. His calling shows the power and freeness of Divine grace, and the nature of conversion. Here also we see that outward forms and distinctions are as nothing, compared with separation from the world, and devotedness to God.

Verses 17–29

Let us not be discouraged at the slowness of the fulfilling of God's promises. Suffering times often are growing times with the church. God is preparing for his people's deliverance, when their day is darkest, and their distress deepest. Moses was exceeding fair, "fair toward God;" it is the beauty of holiness which is in God's sight of great price. He was wonderfully preserved in his infancy; for God will take special care of those of whom he designs to make special use. And did he thus protect the child Moses? Much more will he secure the interests of his holy child Jesus, from the enemies who are gathered together against him. They persecuted Stephen for disputing in defence of Christ and his gospel: in opposition to these they set up Moses and his law. They may understand, if they do not wilfully shut their eyes against the light, that God will, by this Jesus, deliver them out of a worse slavery than that of Egypt. Although men prolong their own miseries, yet the Lord will take care of his servants, and effect his own designs of mercy.

Verses 30–41

Men deceive themselves, if they think God cannot do what he sees to be good any where; he can bring his people into a wilderness, and there speak comfortably to them. He appeared to Moses in a flame of fire, yet the bush was not consumed; which represented the state of Israel in Egypt, where, though they were in the fire of affliction, yet they were not consumed. It may also be looked upon as a type of Christ's taking upon him the nature of man, and the union between the Divine and human nature. The death of Abraham, Isaac, and Jacob, cannot break the covenant relation between God and them. Our Saviour by this proves the future state, Mt **22**:**31**. Abraham is dead, yet God is still his God, therefore Abraham is still alive. Now, this is that life and immortality which are brought to light by the gospel. Stephen here shows that Moses was an eminent type of Christ, as he was Israel's deliverer. God has compassion for the troubles of his church, and the groans of his persecuted people; and their deliverance takes rise from his pity. And that deliverance was typical of what Christ did, when, for us men, and for our salvation, he came down from heaven. This Jesus, whom they now refused, as their fathers did Moses, even this same has God advanced to be a Prince and Saviour. It does not at all take from the just honour of Moses to say, that he was but an instrument, and that he is infinitely outshone by Jesus. In asserting that Jesus should change the customs of the ceremonial law. Stephen was so far from blaspheming Moses, that really he honoured him, by showing how the prophecy of Moses was come to pass, which was so clear. God who gave them those customs by his servant Moses, might, no doubt, change the custom by his Son Jesus. But Israel thrust Moses from them, and would have returned to their bondage; so men in general will not obey Jesus, because they love this present evil world, and rejoice in their own works and devices.

Verses 42–50

Stephen upbraids the Jews with the idolatry of their fathers, to which God gave them up as a punishment for their early forsaking him. It was no dishonour, but an honour to God, that the tabernacle gave way to the temple; so it is now, that the earthly temple gives way to the spiritual one; and so it will be when, at last, the spiritual shall give way to the eternal one. The whole world is God's temple, in which he is every where present, and fills it with his glory; what occasion has he then for a temple to manifest himself in? And these things show his eternal power and Godhead. But as heaven is his throne, and the earth his footstool, so none of our services can profit Him who made all things. Next to the human nature of Christ, the broken and spiritual heart is his most valued temple.

Verses 51–53

Stephen was going on, it seems, to show that the temple and the temple service must come to an end, and it would be the glory of both to give way to the worship of the Father in spirit and in truth; but he perceived they would not bear it. Therefore he broke off, and by the Spirit of wisdom, courage, and power, sharply rebuked his persecutors. When plain arguments and truths provoke the opposers of the gospel, they should be shown their guilt and danger. They, like their fathers, were stubborn and wilful. There is that in our sinful hearts, which always resists the Holy Ghost, a flesh that lusts against the Spirit, and wars against his motions; but in the hearts of God's elect, when the fulness of time comes, this resistance is overcome. The gospel was offered now, not by angels, but from the Holy Ghost; yet they did not embrace it, for they were resolved not to comply with God, either in his law or in his gospel. Their guilt stung them to the heart, and they sought relief in murdering their reprover, instead of sorrow and supplication for mercy.

Verses 54–60

Nothing is so comfortable to dying saints, or so encouraging to suffering saints, as to see Jesus at the right hand of God: blessed be God, by faith we may see him there. Stephen offered up two short prayers in his dying moments. Our Lord Jesus is God, to whom we are to seek, and in whom we are to trust and comfort ourselves, living and dying. And if this has been our care while we live, it will be our comfort when we die. Here is a prayer for his persecutors. Though the sin was very great, yet if they would lay it to their hearts, God would not lay it to their charge. Stephen died as much in a hurry as ever any man did, yet, when he died, the words used are, he fell asleep; he applied himself to his dying work with as much composure as if he had been going to sleep. He shall awake again in the morning of the resurrection, to be received into the presence of the Lord, where is fulness of joy, and to share the pleasures that are at his right hand, for evermore.

Chapter 8

Chapter Outline	
Saul persecutes the church.	(1–4)
Philip's success at Samaria. Simon the sorcerer baptized.	(5–13)
The hypocrisy of Simon detected.	(14–25)
Philip and the Ethiopian.	(26–40)

Verses 1–4

Though persecution must not drive us from our work, yet it may send us to work elsewhere. Wherever the established believer is driven, he carries the knowledge of the gospel, and makes known the preciousness of Christ in every place. Where a simple desire of doing good influences the heart, it will be found impossible to shut a man out from all opportunities of usefulness.

Verses 5–13

As far as the gospel prevails, evil spirits are dislodged, particularly unclean spirits. All inclinations to the lusts of the flesh which war against the soul are such. Distempers are here named, the most difficult to be cured by the course of nature, and most expressive of the disease of sin. Pride, ambition, and desire after grandeur have always caused abundance of mischief, both to the world and to the church. The people said of Simon, This man is the great power of God. See how ignorant and thoughtless people mistake. But how strong is the power of Divine grace, by which they were brought to Christ, who is Truth itself! The people not only gave heed to what Philip said, but were fully convinced that it was of God, and not of men, and gave up themselves to be directed thereby. Even bad men, and those whose hearts still go after covetousness, may come before God as his people come, and for a time continue with them. And many wonder at the proofs of Divine truths, who never experience their power. The gospel preached may have a common operation upon a soul, where it never produced inward holiness. All are not savingly converted who profess to believe the gospel.

Verses 14–25

The Holy Ghost was as yet fallen upon none of these coverts, in the extraordinary powers conveyed by the descent of the Spirit upon the day of Pentecost. We may take encouragement from this example, in praying to God to give the renewing graces of the Holy Ghost to all for whose spiritual welfare we are concerned; for that includes all blessings. No man can give the Holy Spirit by the laying on of his hands; but we should use our best endeavours to instruct those for whom we pray. Simon Magus was ambitious to have the honour of an apostle, but cared not at all to have the spirit and disposition of a Christian. He was more desirous to gain honour to himself, than to do good to others. Peter shows him his crime. He esteemed the wealth of this world, as if it would answer for things relating to the other life, and would purchase the pardon of sin, the gift of the Holy Ghost, and eternal life. This was such a condemning error as could by no means consist with a state of grace. Our hearts are what they are in the sight of God, who cannot be deceived. And if they are not right in his sight, our religion is vain, and will stand us in no stead. A proud and covetous heart cannot be right with God. It is possible for a man to continue under the power of sin, yet to put on a form of godliness. When tempted with money to do evil, see what a perishing thing money is, and scorn it. Think not that Christianity is a trade to live by in this world. There is much wickedness in the thought of the heart, its false notions, and corrupt affections, and wicked projects, which must be repented of, or we are undone. But it shall be forgiven, upon our repentance. The doubt here is of the sincerity of Simon's repentance, not of his pardon, if his repentance was sincere. Grant us, Lord, another sort of faith than that which made Simon wonder only, and did not sanctify his heart. May we abhor all thoughts of making religion serve the purposes of pride or ambition. And keep us from that subtle poison of spiritual pride, which seeks glory to itself even from humility. May we seek only the honour which cometh from God.

Verses 26–40

Philip was directed to go to a desert. Sometimes God opens a door of opportunity to his ministers in very unlikely places. We should study to do good to those we come into company with by travelling. We should not be so shy of all strangers as some affect to be. As to those of whom we know nothing else, we know this, that they have souls. It is wisdom for men of business to redeem time for holy duties; to fill up every minute with something which will turn to a good account. In reading the word of God, we should often pause, to inquire of whom and of what the sacred writers spake; but especially our thoughts should be employed about the Redeemer. The Ethiopian was convinced by the teaching of the Holy Spirit, of the exact fulfilment of the Scripture, was made to understand the nature of the Messiah's kingdom and salvation, and desired to be numbered among the disciples of Christ. Those who seek the truth, and employ their time in searching the Scriptures, will be sure to reap advantages. The avowal of the Ethiopian must be understood as expressing simple reliance on Christ for salvation, and unreserved devotion to Him. Let us not be satisfied till we get faith, as the Ethiopian did, by diligent study of the Holy Scriptures, and the teaching of the Spirit of God; let us not be satisfied till we get it fixed as a principle in our hearts. As soon as he was baptized, the Spirit of God took Philip from him, so that he saw him no more; but this tended to confirm his faith. When the inquirer after salvation becomes acquainted with Jesus and his gospel, he will go on his way rejoicing, and will fill up his station in society, and discharge his duties, from other motives, and in another manner than heretofore. Though baptized in the name of the Father, Son, and Holy Ghost, with water, it is not enough without the baptism of the Holy Ghost. Lord, grant this to every one of us; then shall we go on our way rejoicing.

Chapter 9

Chapter Outline	
The conversion of Saul.	(1–9)
Saul converted preaches Christ.	(10–22)
Saul is persecuted at Damascus, and goes to Jerusalem.	(23–31)
Cure of Eneas.	(32–35)
Dorcas raised to life.	(36–43)

Verses 1–9

So ill informed was Saul, that he thought he ought to do all he could against the name of Christ, and that he did God service thereby; he seemed to breathe in this as in his element. Let us not despair of renewing grace for the conversion of the greatest sinners, nor let such despair of the pardoning mercy of God for the greatest sin. It is a signal token of Divine favour, if God, by the inward working of his grace, or the outward events of his providence, stops us from prosecuting or executing sinful purposes. Saul saw that Just One, ch. **22**:**14**; **26**:**13**. How near to us is the unseen world! It is but for God to draw aside the veil, and objects are presented to the view, compared with which, whatever is most admired on earth is mean and contemptible. Saul submitted without reserve, desirous to know what the Lord Jesus would have him to do. Christ's discoveries of himself to poor souls are humbling; they lay them very low, in mean thoughts of themselves. For three days Saul took no food, and it pleased God to leave him for that time without relief. His sins were now set in order before him; he was in the dark concerning his own spiritual state, and wounded in spirit for sin. When a sinner is brought to a proper sense of his own state and conduct, he will cast himself wholly on the mercy of the Saviour, asking what he would have him to do. God will direct the humbled sinner, and though he does not often bring transgressors to joy and peace in believing, without sorrows and distress of conscience, under which the soul is deeply engaged as to eternal things, yet happy are those who sow in tears, for they shall reap in joy.

Verses 10–22

A good work was begun in Saul, when he was brought to Christ's feet with those words, Lord, what wilt thou have me to do? And never did Christ leave any who were brought to that. Behold, the proud Pharisee, the unmerciful oppressor, the daring blasphemer, prayeth! And thus it is even now, and with the proud infidel, or the abandoned sinner. What happy tidings are these to all who understand the nature and power of prayer, of such prayer as the humbled sinner presents for the blessings of free salvation! Now he began to pray after another manner than he had done; before, he said his prayers, now, he prayed them. Regenerating grace sets people on praying; you may as well find a living man without breath, as a living Christian without prayer. Yet even eminent disciples, like Ananias, sometimes stagger at the commands of the Lord. But it is the Lord's glory to surpass our scanty expectations, and show that those are vessels of his mercy whom we are apt to consider as objects of his vengeance. The teaching of the Holy Spirit takes away the scales of ignorance and pride from the understanding; then the sinner becomes a new creature, and endeavours to recommend the anointed Saviour, the Son of God, to his former companions.

Verses 23–31

When we enter into the way of God, we must look for trials; but the Lord knows how to deliver the godly, and will, with the temptation, also make a way to escape. Though Saul's conversion was and is a proof of the truth of Christianity, yet it could not, of itself, convert one soul at enmity with the truth; for nothing can produce true faith, but that power which new-creates the heart. Believers are apt to be too suspicious of those against whom they have prejudices. The world is full of deceit, and it is necessary to be cautious, but we must exercise charity, **1**Co **13**:**5**. The Lord will clear up the characters of true believers; and he will bring them to his people, and often gives them opportunities of bearing testimony to his truth, before those who once witnessed their hatred to it. Christ now appeared to Saul, and ordered him to go quickly out of Jerusalem, for he must be sent to the Gentiles: see ch. **22**:**21**. Christ's witnesses cannot be slain till they have finished their testimony. The persecutions were stayed. The professors of the gospel walked uprightly, and enjoyed much comfort from the Holy Ghost, in the hope and peace of the gospel, and others were won over to them. They lived upon the comfort of the Holy Ghost, not only in the days of trouble and affliction, but in days of rest and prosperity. Those are most likely to walk cheerfully, who walk circumspectly.

Verses 32–35

Christians are saints, or holy people; not only the eminent ones, as Saint Peter and Saint Paul, but every sincere professor of the faith of Christ. Christ chose patients whose diseases were incurable in the course of nature, to show how desperate was the case of fallen mankind. When we were wholly without strength, as this poor man, he sent his word to heal us. Peter does not pretend to heal by any power of his own, but directs Eneas to look up to Christ for help. Let none say, that because it is Christ, who, by the power of his grace, works all our works in us, therefore we have no work, no duty to do; for though Jesus Christ makes thee whole, yet thou must arise, and use the power he gives thee.

Verses 36–43

Many are full of good words, who are empty and barren in good works; but Tabitha was a great doer, no great talker. Christians who have not property to give in charity, may yet be able to do acts of charity, working with their hands, or walking with their feet, for the good of others. Those are certainly best praised whose own works praise them, whether the words of others do so or not. But such are ungrateful indeed, who have kindness shown them, and will not acknowledge it, by showing the kindness that is done them. While we live upon the fulness of Christ for our whole salvation, we should desire to be full of good works, for the honour of his name, and for the benefit of his saints. Such characters as Dorcas are useful where they dwell, as showing the excellency of the word of truth by their lives. How mean then the cares of the numerous females who seek no distinction but outward decoration, and who waste their lives in the trifling pursuits of dress and vanity! Power went along with the word, and Dorcas came to life. Thus in the raising of dead souls to spiritual life, the first sign of life is the opening of the eyes of the mind. Here we see that the Lord can make up every loss; that he overrules every event for the good of those who trust in him, and for the glory of his name.

Chapter 10

Chapter Outline	
Cornelius directed to send for Peter.	(1–8)
Peter's vision.	(9–18)
He goes to Cornelius.	(19–33)
His discourse to Cornelius.	(34–43)
The gifts of the Holy Spirit poured out.	(44–48)

Verses 1–8

Hitherto none had been baptized into the Christian church but Jews, Samaritans, and those converts who had been circumcised and observed the ceremonial law; but now the Gentiles were to be called to partake all the privileges of God's people, without first becoming Jews. Pure and undefiled religion is sometimes found where we least expect it. Wherever the fear of God rules in the heart, it will appear both in works of charity and of piety, neither will excuse from the other. Doubtless Cornelius had true faith in God's word, as far as he understood it, though not as yet clear faith in Christ. This was the work of the Spirit of God, through the mediation of Jesus, even before Cornelius knew him, as is the case with us all when we, who before were dead in sin, are made alive. Through Christ also his prayers and alms were accepted, which otherwise would have been rejected. Without dispute or delay Cornelius was obedient to the heavenly vision. In the affairs of our souls, let us not lose time.

Verses 9–18

The prejudices of Peter against the Gentiles, would have prevented his going to Cornelius, unless the Lord had prepared him for this service. To tell a Jew that God had directed those animals to be reckoned clean which were hitherto deemed unclean, was in effect saying, that the law of Moses was done away. Peter was soon made to know the meaning of it. God knows what services are before us, and how to prepare us; and we know the meaning of what he has taught us, when we find what occasion we have to make use of it.

Verses 19–33

When we see our call clear to any service, we should not be perplexed with doubts and scruples arising from prejudices or former ideas. Cornelius had called together his friends, to partake with him of the heavenly wisdom he expected from Peter. We should not covet to eat our spiritual morsels alone. It ought to be both given and taken as kindness and respect to our kindred and friends, to invite them to join us in religious exercises. Cornelius declared the direction God gave him to send for Peter. We are right in our aims in attending a gospel ministry, when we do it with regard to the Divine appointment requiring us to make use of that ordinance. How seldom ministers are called to speak to such companies, however small, in which it may be said that they are all present in the sight of God, to hear all things that are commanded of God! But these were ready to hear what Peter was commanded of God to say.

Verses 34–43

Acceptance cannot be obtained on any other ground than that of the covenant of mercy, through the atonement of Christ; but wherever true religion is found, God will accept it without regarding names or sects. The fear of God and works of righteousness are the substance of true religion, the effects of special grace. Though these are not the cause of a man's acceptance, yet they show it; and whatever may be wanting in knowledge or faith, will in due time be given by Him who has begun it. They knew in general the word, that is, the gospel, which God sent to the children of Israel. The purport of this word was, that God by it published the good tidings of peace by Jesus Christ. They knew the several matters of fact relating to the gospel. They knew the baptism of repentance which John preached. Let them know that this Jesus Christ, by whom peace is made between God and man, is Lord of all; not only as over all, God blessed for evermore, but as Mediator. All power, both in heaven and in earth, is put into his hand, and all judgment committed to him. God will go with those whom he anoints; he will be with those to whom he has given his Spirit. Peter then declares Christ's resurrection from the dead, and the proofs of it. Faith has reference to a testimony, and the Christian faith is built upon the foundation of the apostles and prophets, on the testimony given by them. See what must be believed concerning him. That we are all accountable to Christ as our Judge; so every one must seek his favour, and to have him as our Friend. And if we believe in him, we shall all be justified by him as our Righteousness. The remission of sins lays a foundation for all other favours and blessings, by taking that out of the way which hinders the bestowing of them. If sin be pardoned, all is well, and shall end well for ever.

Verses 44–48

The Holy Ghost fell upon others after they were baptized, to confirm them in the faith; but upon these Gentiles before they were baptized, to show that God does not confine himself to outward signs. The Holy Ghost fell upon those who were neither circumcised nor baptized; it is the Spirit that quickeneth, the flesh profiteth nothing. They magnified God, and spake of Christ and the benefits of redemption. Whatever gift we are endued with, we ought to honour God with it. The believing Jews who were present, were astonished that the gift of the Holy Ghost was poured out upon the Gentiles also. By mistaken notions of things, we make difficult for ourselves as to the methods of Divine providence and grace. As they were undeniably baptized with the Holy Ghost, Peter concluded they were not to be refused the baptism of water, and the ordinance was administered. The argument is conclusive; can we deny the sign to those who have received the things signified? Those who have some acquaintance with Christ, cannot but desire more. Even those who have received the Holy Ghost, must see their need of daily learning more of the truth.

Chapter 11

Chapter Outline	
Peter's defence.	(1–18)
The success of the gospel at Antioch.	(19–24)
The disciples named Christians, Relief sent to Judea.	(25–30)

Verses 1–18

The imperfect state of human nature strongly appears, when godly persons are displeased even to hear that the word of God has been received, because their own system has not been attended to. And we are too apt to despair of doing good to those who yet, when tried, prove very teachable. It is the bane and damage of the church, to shut out those from it, and from the benefit of the means of grace, who are not in every thing as we are. Peter stated the whole affair. We should at all times bear with the infirmities of our brethren; and instead of taking offence, or answering with warmth, we should explain our motives, and show the nature of our proceedings. That preaching is certainly right, with which the Holy Ghost is given. While men are very zealous for their own regulations, they should take care that they do not withstand God; and those who love the Lord will glorify him, when made sure that he has given repentance to life to any fellow-sinners. Repentance is God's gift; not only his free grace accepts it, but his mighty grace works it in us, grace takes away the heart of stone, and gives us a heart of flesh. The sacrifice of God is a broken spirit.

Verses 19–24

The first preachers of the gospel at Antioch, were dispersed from Jerusalem by persecution; thus what was meant to hurt the church, was made to work for its good. The wrath of man is made to praise God. What should the ministers of Christ preach, but Christ? Christ, and him crucified? Christ, and him glorified? And their preaching was accompanied with the Divine power. The hand of the Lord was with them, to bring that home to the hearts and consciences of men, which they could but speak to the outward ear. They believed; they were convinced of the truth of the gospel. They turned from a careless, carnal way of living, to live a holy, heavenly, spiritual life. They turned from worshipping God in show and ceremony, to worship him in the Spirit and in truth. They turned to the Lord Jesus, and he became all in all with them. This was the work of conversion wrought upon them, and it must be wrought upon every one of us. It was the fruit of their faith; all who sincerely believe, will turn to the Lord, When the Lord Jesus is preached in simplicity, and according to the Scriptures, he will give success; and when sinners are thus brought to the Lord, really good men, who are full of faith and of the Holy Ghost, will admire and rejoice in the grace of God bestowed on them. Barnabas was full of faith; full of the grace of faith, and full of the fruits of the faith that works by love.

Verses 25–30

Hitherto the followers of Christ were called disciples, that is, learners, scholars; but from that time they were called Christians. The proper meaning of this name is, a follower of Christ; it denotes one who, from serious thought, embraces the religion of Christ, believes his promises, and makes it his chief care to shape his life by Christ's precepts and example. Hence it is plain that multitudes take the name of Christian to whom it does not rightly belong. But the name without the reality will only add to our guilt. While the bare profession will bestow neither profit nor delight, the possession of it will give both the promise of the life that now is, and of that which is to come. Grant, Lord, that Christians may forget other names and distinctions, and love one another as the followers of Christ ought to do. True Christians will feel for their brethren under afflictions. Thus will fruit be brought forth to the praise and glory of God. If all mankind were true Christians, how cheerfully would they help one another! The whole earth would be like one large family, every member of which would strive to be dutiful and kind.

Chapter 12

Chapter Outline	
The martyrdom of James, and the imprisonment of Peter.	(1–5)
He is delivered from prison by an angel.	(6–11)
Peter departs, Herod's rage.	(12–19)
The death of Herod.	(20–25)

Verses 1–5

James was one of the sons of Zebedee, whom Christ told that they should drink of the cup that he was to drink of, and be baptized with the baptism that he was to be baptized with, Mt **20**:**23**. Now the words of Christ were made good in him; and if we suffer with Christ, we shall reign with him. Herod imprisoned Peter: the way of persecution, as of other sins, is downhill; when men are in it, they cannot easily stop. Those make themselves an easy prey to Satan, who make it their business to please men. Thus James finished his course. But Peter, being designed for further services, was safe; though he seemed now marked out for a speedy sacrifice. We that live in a cold, prayerless generation, can hardly form an idea of the earnestness of these holy men of old. But if the Lord should bring on the church an awful persecution like this of Herod, the faithful in Christ would learn what soul-felt prayer is.

Verses 6–11

A peaceful conscience, a lively hope, and the consolations of the Holy Spirit, can keep men calm in the full prospect of death; even those very persons who have been most distracted with terrors on that account. God's time to help, is when things are brought to the last extremity. Peter was assured that the Lord would cause this trial to end in the way that should be most for his glory. Those who are delivered out of spiritual imprisonment must follow their Deliverer, like the Israelites when they went out of the house of bondage. They knew not whither they went, but knew whom they followed. When God will work salvation for his people, all difficulties in their way will be overcome, even gates of iron are made to open of their own accord. This deliverance of Peter represents our redemption by Christ, which not only proclaims liberty to the captives, but brings them out of the prison-house. Peter, when he recollected himself, perceived what great things God had done for him. Thus souls delivered out of spiritual bondage, are not at first aware what God has wrought in them; many have the truth of grace, that want evidence of it. But when the Comforter comes, whom the Father will send, sooner or later, he will let them know what a blessed change is wrought.

Verses 12–19

God's providence leaves room for the use of our prudence, though he has undertaken to perform and perfect what he has begun. These Christians continued in prayer for Peter, for they were truly in earnest. Thus men ought always to pray, and not to faint. As long as we are kept waiting for a mercy, we must continue praying for it. But sometimes that which we most earnestly wish for, we are most backward to believe. The Christian law of self-denial and of suffering for Christ, has not done away the natural law of caring for our own safety by lawful means. In times of public danger, all believers have God for their hiding-place; which is so secret, that the world cannot find them. Also, the instruments of persecution are themselves exposed to danger; the wrath of God hangs over all that engage in this hateful work. And the range of persecutors often vents itself on all in its way.

Verses 20–25

Many heathen princes claimed and received Divine honours, but it was far more horrible impiety in Herod, who knew the word and worship of the living God, to accept such idolatrous honours without rebuking the blasphemy. And such men as Herod, when puffed with pride and vanity, are ripening fast for signal vengeance. God is very jealous for his own honour, and will be glorified upon those whom he is not glorified by. See what vile bodies we carry about with us; they have in them the seeds of their own dissolution, by which they will soon be destroyed, whenever God does but speak the word. We may learn wisdom from the people of Tyre and Sidon, for we have offended the Lord with our sins. We depend on him for life, and breath, and all things; it surely then behoves us to humble ourselves before him, that through the appointed Mediator, who is ever ready to befriend us, we may be reconciled to him, lest wrath come upon us to the utmost.

Chapter 13

Chapter Outline	
The mission of Paul and Barnabas.	(1–3)
Elymas the sorcerer.	(4–13)
Paul's discourse at Antioch.	(14–41)
He preaches to the Gentiles, and is persecuted by the Jews.	(42–52)

Verses 1–3

What an assemblage was here! In these names we see that the Lord raises up instruments for his work, from various places and stations in life; and zeal for his glory induces men to give up flattering connexions and prospects to promote his cause. It is by the Spirit of Christ that his ministers are made both able and willing for his service, and taken from other cares that would hinder in it. Christ's ministers are to be employed in Christ's work, and, under the Spirit's guidance, to act for the glory of God the Father. They are separated to take pains, and not to take state. A blessing upon Barnabas and Saul in their present undertaking was sought for, and that they might be filled with the Holy Ghost in their work. Whatever means are used, or rules observed, the Holy Ghost alone can fit ministers for their important work, and call them to it.

Verses 4–13

Satan is in a special manner busy with great men and men in power, to keep them from being religious, for their example will influence many. Saul is here for the first time called Paul, and never after Saul. Saul was his name as he was a Hebrew; Paul was his name as he was a citizen of Rome. Under the direct influence of the Holy Ghost, he gave Elymas his true character, but not in passion. A fulness of deceit and mischief together, make a man indeed a child of the devil. And those who are enemies to the doctrine of Jesus, are enemies to all righteousness; for in it all righteousness is fulfilled. The ways of the Lord Jesus are the only right ways to heaven and happiness. There are many who not only wander from these ways themselves, but set others against these ways. They commonly are so hardened, that they will not cease to do evil. The proconsul was astonished at the force of the doctrine upon his own heart and conscience, and at the power of God by which it was confirmed. The doctrine of Christ astonishes; and the more we know of it, the more reason we shall see to wonder at it. Those who put their hand to the plough and look back, are not fit for the kingdom of God. Those who are not prepared to face opposition, and to endure hardship, are not fitted for the work of the ministry.

Verses 14–31

When we come together to worship God, we must do it, not only by prayer and praise, but by the reading and hearing of the word of God. The bare reading of the Scriptures in public assemblies is not enough; they should be expounded, and the people exhorted out of them. This is helping people in doing that which is necessary to make the word profitable, to apply it to themselves. Every thing is touched upon in this sermon, which might best prevail with Jews to receive and embrace Christ as the promised Messiah. And every view, however short or faint, of the Lord's dealings with his church, reminds us of his mercy and long-suffering, and of man's ingratitude and perverseness. Paul passes from David to the Son of David, and shows that this Jesus is his promised Seed; a Saviour to do that for them, which the judges of old could not do, to save them from their sins, their worst enemies. When the apostles preached Christ as the Saviour, they were so far from concealing his death, that they always preached Christ crucified. Our complete separation from sin, is represented by our being buried with Christ. But he rose again from the dead, and saw no corruption: this was the great truth to be preached.

Verses 32–37

The resurrection of Christ was the great proof of his being the Son of God. It was not possible he should be held by death, because he was the Son of God, and therefore had life in himself, which he could not lay down but with a design to take it again. The sure mercies of David are that everlasting life, of which the resurrection was a sure pledge; and the blessings of redemption in Christ are a certain earnest, even in this world. David was a great blessing to the age wherein he lived. We were not born for ourselves, but there are those living around us, to whom we must study to be serviceable. Yet here is the difference; Christ was to serve all generations. May we look to Him who is declared to be the Son of God by his resurrection from the dead, that by faith in him we may walk with God, and serve our generation according to his will; and when death comes, may we fall asleep in him, with a joyful hope of a blessed resurrection.

Verses 38–41

Let all that hear the gospel of Christ, know these two things: **1**. That through this Man, who died and rose again, is preached unto you the forgiveness of sins. Your sins, though many and great, may be forgiven, and they may be so without any injury to God's honour. **2**. It is by Christ only that those who believe in him, and none else, are justified from all things; from all the guilt and stain of sin, from which they could not be justified by the law of Moses. The great concern of convinced sinners is, to be justified, to be acquitted from all their guilt, and accepted as righteous in God's sight, for if any is left charged upon the sinner, he is undone. By Jesus Christ we obtain a complete justification; for by him a complete atonement was made for sin. We are justified, not only by him as our Judge but by him as the Lord our Righteousness. What the law could not do for us, in that it was weak, the gospel of Christ does. This is the most needful blessing, bringing in every other. The threatenings are warnings; what we are told will come upon impenitent sinners, is designed to awaken us to beware lest it come upon us. It ruins many, that they despise religion. Those that will not wonder and be saved, shall wonder and perish.

Verses 42–52

The Jews opposed the doctrine the apostles preached; and when they could find no objection, they blasphemed Christ and his gospel. Commonly those who begin with contradicting, end with blaspheming. But when adversaries of Christ's cause are daring, its advocates should be the bolder. And while many judge themselves unworthy of eternal life, others, who appear less likely, desire to hear more of the glad tidings of salvation. This is according to what was foretold in the Old Testament. What light, what power, what a treasure does this gospel bring with it! How excellent are its truths, its precepts, its promises! Those came to Christ whom the Father drew, and to whom the Spirit made the gospel call effectual, Ro **8**:**30**. As many as were disposed to eternal life, as many as had concern about their eternal state, and aimed to make sure of eternal life, believed in Christ, in whom God has treasured up that life, and who is the only Way to it; and it was the grace of God that wrought it in them. It is good to see honourable women devout; the less they have to do in the world, the more they should do for their own souls, and the souls of others: but it is sad, when, under colour of devotion to God, they try to show hatred to Christ. And the more we relish the comforts and encouragements we meet with in the power of godliness, and the fuller our hearts are of them, the better prepared we are to face difficulties in the profession of godliness.

Chapter 14

Chapter Outline	
Paul and Barnabas at Iconium.	(1–7)
A cripple healed at Lystra, The people would have sacrificed to Paul and Barnabas.	(8–18)
Paul stoned at Lystra, The churches visited again.	(19–28)

Verses 1–7

The apostles spake so plainly, with such evidence and proof of the Spirit, and with such power; so warmly, and with such concern for the souls of men; that those who heard them could not but say, God was with them of a truth. Yet the success was not to be reckoned to the manner of their preaching, but to the Spirit of God who used that means. Perseverance in doing good, amidst dangers and hardships, is a blessed evidence of grace. Wherever God's servants are driven, they should seek to declare the truth. When they went on in Christ's name and strength, he failed not to give testimony to the word of his grace. He has assured us it is the word of God, and that we may venture our souls upon it. The Gentiles and Jews were at enmity with one another, yet united against Christians. If the church's enemies join to destroy it, shall not its friends unite for its preservation? God has a shelter for his people in a storm; he is, and will be their Hiding-place. In times of persecution, believers may see cause to quit a spot, though they do not quit their Master's work.

Verses 8–18

All things are possible to those that believe. When we have faith, that most precious gift of God, we shall be delivered from the spiritual helplessness in which we were born, and from the dominion of sinful habits since formed; we shall be made able to stand upright and walk cheerfully in the ways of the Lord. When Christ, the Son of God, appeared in the likeness of men, and did many miracles, men were so far from doing sacrifice to him, that they made him a sacrifice to their pride and malice; but Paul and Barnabas, upon their working one miracle, were treated as gods. The same power of the god of this world, which closes the carnal mind against truth, makes errors and mistakes find easy admission. We do not learn that they rent their clothes when the people spake of stoning them; but when they spake of worshipping them; they could not bear it, being more concerned for God's honour than their own. God's truth needs not the services of man's falsehood. The servants of God might easily obtain undue honours if they would wink at men's errors and vices; but they must dread and detest such respect more than any reproach. When the apostles preached to the Jews, who hated idolatry, they had only to preach the grace of God in Christ; but when they had to do with the Gentiles, they must set right their mistakes in natural religion. Compare their conduct and declaration with the false opinions of those who think the worship of a God, under any name, or in any manner, is equally acceptable to the Lord Almighty. The most powerful arguments, the most earnest and affectionate addresses, even with miracles, are scarcely enough to keep men from absurdities and abominations; much less can they, without special grace, turn the hearts of sinners to God and to holiness.

Verses 19–28

See how restless the rage of the Jews was against the gospel of Christ. The people stoned Paul, in a popular tumult. So strong is the bent of the corrupt and carnal heart, that as it is with great difficulty that men are kept back from evil on one side, so it is with great ease they are persuaded to evil on the other side. If Paul would have been Mercury, he might have been worshipped; but if he will be a faithful minister of Christ, he shall be stoned, and thrown out of the city. Thus men who easily submit to strong delusions, hate to receive the truth in the love of it. All who are converted need to be confirmed in the faith; all who are planted need to be rooted. Ministers' work is to establish saints as well as to awaken sinners. The grace of God, and nothing less, effectually establishes the souls of the disciples. It is true, we must count upon much tribulation, but it is encouragement that we shall not be lost and perish in it. The Person to whose power and grace the converts and the newly-established churches are commended, clearly was the Lord Jesus, "on whom they had believed." It was an act of worship. The praise of all the little good we do at any time, must be ascribed to God; for it is He who not only worketh in us both to will and to do, but also worketh with us to make what we do successful. All who love the Lord Jesus, will rejoice to hear that he has opened the door of faith wide, to those who were strangers to him and to his salvation. And let us, like the apostles, abide with those who know and love the Lord.

Chapter 15

Chapter Outline	
The dispute raised by Judaizing teachers.	(1–6)
The council at Jerusalem.	(7–21)
The letter from the council.	(22–35)
Paul and Barnabas separate.	(36–41)

Verses 1–6

Some from Judea taught the Gentile converts at Antioch, that they could not be saved, unless they observed the whole ceremonial law as given by Moses; and thus they sought to destroy Christian liberty. There is a strange proneness in us to think that all do wrong who do not just as we do. Their doctrine was very discouraging. Wise and good men desire to avoid contests and disputes as far as they can; yet when false teachers oppose the main truths of the gospel, or bring in hurtful doctrines, we must not decline to oppose them.

Verses 7–21

We see from the words "purifying their hearts by faith," and the address of St. Peter, that justification by faith, and sanctification by the Holy Ghost, cannot be separated; and that both are the gift of God. We have great cause to bless God that we have heard the gospel. May we have that faith which the great Searcher of hearts approves, and attests by the seal of the Holy Spirit. Then our hearts and consciences will be purified from the guilt of sin, and we shall be freed from the burdens some try to lay upon the disciples of Christ. Paul and Barnabas showed by plain matters of fact, that God owned the preaching of the pure gospel to the Gentiles without the law of Moses; therefore to press that law upon them, was to undo what God had done. The opinion of James was, that the Gentile converts ought not to be troubled about Jewish rites, but that they should abstain from meats offered to idols, so that they might show their hatred of idolatry. Also, that they should be cautioned against fornication, which was not abhorred by the Gentiles as it should be, and even formed a part of some of their rites. They were counselled to abstain from things strangled, and from eating blood; this was forbidden by the law of Moses, and also here, from reverence to the blood of the sacrifices, which being then still offered, it would needlessly grieve the Jewish converts, and further prejudice the unconverted Jews. But as the reason has long ceased, we are left free in this, as in the like matters. Let converts be warned to avoid all appearances of the evils which they formerly practised, or are likely to be tempted to; and caution them to use Christian liberty with moderation and prudence.

Verses 22–35

Being warranted to declare themselves directed by the immediate influence of the Holy Ghost, the apostles and disciples were assured that it seemed good unto God the Holy Spirit, as well as to them, to lay upon the converts no other burden than the things before mentioned, which were necessary, either on their own account, or from present circumstances. It was a comfort to hear that carnal ordinances were no longer imposed on them, which perplexed the conscience, but could not purify or pacify it; and that those who troubled their minds were silenced, so that the peace of the church was restored, and that which threatened division was removed. All this was consolation for which they blessed God. Many others were at Antioch. Where many labour in the word and doctrine, yet there may be opportunity for us: the zeal and usefulness of others should stir us up, not lay us asleep.

Verses 36–41

Here we have a private quarrel between two ministers, no less than Paul and Barnabas, yet made to end well. Barnabas wished his nephew John Mark to go with them. We should suspect ourselves of being partial, and guard against this in putting our relations forward. Paul did not think him worthy of the honour, nor fit for the service, who had departed from them without their knowledge, or without their consent: see ch. **13**:**13**. Neither would yield, therefore there was no remedy but they must part. We see that the best of men are but men, subject to like passions as we are. Perhaps there were faults on both sides, as usual in such contentions. Christ's example alone, is a copy without a blot. Yet we are not to think it strange, if there are differences among wise and good men. It will be so while we are in this imperfect state; we shall never be all of one mind till we come to heaven. But what mischief the remainders of pride and passion which are found even in good men, do in the world, and do in the church! Many who dwelt at Antioch, who had heard but little of the devotedness and piety of Paul and Barnabas, heard of their dispute and separation; and thus it will be with ourselves, if we give way to contention. Believers must be constant in prayer, that they may never be led by the allowance of unholy tempers, to hurt the cause they really desire to serve. Paul speaks with esteem and affection both of Barnabas and Mark, in his epistles, written after this event. May all who profess thy name, O loving Saviour, be thoroughly reconciled by that love derived from thee which is not easily provoked, and which soon forgets and buries injuries.

Chapter 16

Chapter Outline	
Paul takes Timothy to be his assistant.	(1–5)
Paul proceeds to Macedonia, The conversion of Lydia.	(6–15)
An evil spirit cast out, Paul and Silas scourged and imprisoned.	(16–24)
The conversion of the jailer at Philippi.	(25–34)
Paul and Silas released.	(35–40)

Verses 1–5

Well may the church look for much service from youthful ministers who set out in the same spirit as Timothy. But when men will submit in nothing, and oblige in nothing, the first elements of the Christian temper seem to be wanting; and there is great reason to believe that the doctrines and precepts of the gospel will not be successfully taught. The design of the decree being to set aside the ceremonial law, and its carnal ordinances, believers were confirmed in the Christian faith, because it set up a spiritual way of serving God, as suited to the nature both of God and man. Thus the church increased in numbers daily.

Verses 6–15

The removals of ministers, and the dispensing the means of grace by them, are in particular under Divine conduct and direction. We must follow Providence: and whatever we seek to do, if that suffer us not, we ought to submit and believe to be for the best. People greatly need help for their souls, it is their duty to look out for it, and to invite those among them who can help them. And God's calls must be complied with readily. A solemn assembly the worshippers of God must have, if possible, upon the sabbath day. If we have not synagogues, we must be thankful for more private places, and resort to them; not forsaking the assembling together, as our opportunities are. Among the hearers of Paul was a woman, named Lydia. She had an honest calling, which the historian notices to her praise. Yet though she had a calling to mind, she found time to improve advantages for her soul. It will not excuse us from religious duties, to say, We have a trade to mind; for have not we also a God to serve, and souls to look after? Religion does not call us from our business in the world, but directs us in it. Pride, prejudice, and sin shut out the truths of God, till his grace makes way for them into the understanding and affections; and the Lord alone can open the heart to receive and believe his word. We must believe in Jesus Christ; there is no coming to God as a Father, but by the Son as Mediator.

Verses 16–24

Satan, though the father of lies, will declare the most important truths, when he can thereby serve his purposes. But much mischief is done to the real servants of Christ, by unholy and false preachers of the gospel, who are confounded with them by careless observers. Those who do good by drawing men from sin, may expect to be reviled as troublers of the city. While they teach men to fear God, to believe in Christ, to forsake sin, and to live godly lives, they will be accused of teaching bad customs.

Verses 25–34

The consolations of God to his suffering servants are neither few nor small. How much more happy are true Christians than their prosperous enemies! As in the dark, so out of the depths, we may cry unto God. No place, no time is amiss for prayer, if the heart be lifted up to God. No trouble, however grievous, should hinder us from praise. Christianity proves itself to be of God, in that it obliges us to be just to our own lives. Paul cried aloud to make the jailer hear, and to make him heed, saying, Do thyself no harm. All the cautions of the word of God against sin, and all appearances of it, and approaches to it, have this tendency. Man, woman, do not ruin thyself; hurt not thyself, and then none else can hurt thee; do not sin, for nothing but that can hurt thee. Even as to the body, we are cautioned against the sins which do harm to that. Converting grace changes people's language of and to good people and good ministers. How serious the jailer's inquiry! His salvation becomes his great concern; that lies nearest his heart, which before was furthest from his thoughts. It is his own precious soul that he is concerned about. Those who are thoroughly convinced of sin, and truly concerned about their salvation, will give themselves up to Christ. Here is the sum of the whole gospel, the covenant of grace in a few words; Believe in the Lord Jesus Christ, and thou shalt be saved, and thy house. The Lord so blessed the word, that the jailer was at once softened and humbled. He treated them with kindness and compassion, and, professing faith in Christ, was baptized in that name, with his family. The Spirit of grace worked such a strong faith in them, as did away further doubt; and Paul and Silas knew by the Spirit, that a work of God was wrought in them. When sinners are thus converted, they will love and honour those whom they before despised and hated, and will seek to lessen the suffering they before desired to increase. When the fruits of faith begin to appear, terrors will be followed by confidence and joy in God.

Verses 35–40

Paul, though willing to suffer for the cause of Christ, and without any desire to avenge himself, did not choose to depart under the charge of having deserved wrongful punishment, and therefore required to be dismissed in an honourable manner. It was not a mere point of honour that the apostle stood upon, but justice, and not to himself so much as to his cause. And when proper apology is made, Christians should never express personal anger, nor insist too strictly upon personal amends. The Lord will make them more than conquerors in every conflict; instead of being cast down by their sufferings, they will become comforters of their brethren.

Chapter 17

Chapter Outline	

Paul at Thessalonica.	(1–9)
The noble conduct of the Bereans.	(10–15)
Paul at Athens.	(16–21)
He preaches there.	(22–31)
The scornful conduct of the Athenians.	(32–34)

Verses 1–9

The drift and scope of Paul's preaching and arguing, was to prove that Jesus is the Christ. He must needs suffer for us, because he could not otherwise purchase our redemption for us; and he must needs have risen again, because he could not otherwise apply the redemption to us. We are to preach concerning Jesus that he is Christ; therefore we may hope to be saved by him, and are bound to be ruled by him. The unbelieving Jews were angry, because the apostles preached to the Gentiles, that they might be saved. How strange it is, that men should grudge others the privileges they will not themselves accept! Neither rulers nor people need be troubled at the increase of real Christians, even though turbulent spirits should make religion the pretext for evil designs. Of such let us beware, from such let us withdraw, that we may show a desire to act aright in society, while we claim our right to worship God according to our consciences.

Verses 10–15

The Jews in Berea applied seriously to the study of the word preached unto them. They not only heard Paul preach on the sabbath, but daily searched the Scriptures, and compared what they read with the facts related to them. The doctrine of Christ does not fear inquiry; advocates for his cause desire no more than that people will fully and fairly examine whether things are so or not. Those are truly noble, and likely to be more and more so, who make the Scriptures their rule, and consult them accordingly. May all the hearers of the gospel become like those of Berea, receiving the word with readiness of mind, and searching the Scriptures daily, whether the things preached to them are so.

Verses 16–21

Athens was then famed for polite learning, philosophy, and the fine arts; but none are more childish and superstitious, more impious, or more credulous, than some persons, deemed eminent for learning and ability. It was wholly given to idolatry. The zealous advocate for the cause of Christ will be ready to plead for it in all companies, as occasion offers. Most of these learned men took no notice of Paul; but some, whose principles were the most directly contrary to Christianity, made remarks upon him. The apostle ever dwelt upon two points, which are indeed the principal doctrines of Christianity, Christ and a future state; Christ our way, and heaven our end. They looked on this as very different from the knowledge for many ages taught and professed at Athens; they desire to know more of it, but only because it was new and strange. They led him to the place where judges sat who inquired into such matters. They asked about Paul's doctrine, not because it was good, but because it was new. Great talkers are always busy-bodies. They spend their time in nothing else, and a very uncomfortable account they have to give of their time who thus spend it. Time is precious, and we are concerned to employ it well, because eternity depends upon it, but much is wasted in unprofitable conversation.

Verses 22–31

Here we have a sermon to heathens, who worshipped false gods, and were without the true God in the world; and to them the scope of the discourse was different from what the apostle preached to the Jews. In the latter case, his business was to lead his hearers by prophecies and miracles to the knowledge of the Redeemer, and faith in him; in the former, it was to lead them, by the common works of providence, to know the Creator, and worship Him. The apostle spoke of an altar he had seen, with the inscription, "TO THE UNKNOWN GOD." This fact is stated by many writers. After multiplying their idols to the utmost, some at Athens thought there was another god of whom they had no knowledge. And are there not many now called Christians, who are zealous in their devotions, yet the great object of their worship is to them an unknown God? Observe what glorious things Paul here says of that God whom he served, and would have them to serve. The Lord had long borne with idolatry, but the times of this ignorance were now ending, and by his servants he now commanded all men every where to repent of their idolatry. Each sect of the learned men would feel themselves powerfully affected by the apostle's discourse, which tended to show the emptiness or falsity of their doctrines.

Verses 32–34

The apostle was treated with more outward civility at Athens than in some other places; but none more despised his doctrine, or treated it with more indifference. Of all subjects, that which deserves the most attention gains the least. But those who scorn, will have to bear the consequences, and the word will never be useless. Some will be found, who cleave to the Lord, and listen to his faithful servants. Considering the judgement to come, and Christ as our Judge, should urge all to repent of sin, and turn to Him. Whatever matter is used, all discourses must lead to Him, and show his authority; our salvation, and resurrection, come from and by Him.

Chapter 18

Chapter Outline	
Paul at Corinth, with Aquila and Priscilla.	(1–6)
He continues to preach at Corinth.	(7–11)
Paul before Gallio.	(12–17)

He visits Jerusalem.	(18–23)
Apollos teaches at Ephesus and in Achaia.	(24–28)

Verses 1–6

Though Paul was entitled to support from the churches he planted, and from the people to whom he preached, yet he worked at his calling. An honest trade, by which a man may get his bread, is not to be looked upon with contempt by any. It was the custom of the Jews to bring up their children to some trade, though they gave them learning or estates. Paul was careful to prevent prejudices, even the most unreasonable. The love of Christ is the best bond of the saints; and the communings of the saints with each other, sweeten labour, contempt, and even persecution. Most of the Jews persisted in contradicting the gospel of Christ, and blasphemed. They would not believe themselves, and did all they could to keep others from believing. Paul hereupon left them. He did not give over his work; for though Israel be not gathered, Christ and his gospel shall be glorious. The Jews could not complain, for they had the first offer. When some oppose the gospel, we must turn to others. Grief that many persist in unbelief should not prevent gratitude for the conversion of some to Christ.

Verses 7–11

The Lord knows those that are his, yea, and those that shall be his; for it is by his work upon them that they become his. Let us not despair concerning any place, when even in wicked Corinth Christ had much people. He will gather in his chosen flock from the places where they are scattered Thus encouraged, the apostle continued at Corinth, and a numerous and flourishing church grew up.

Verses 12–17

Paul was about to show that he did not teach men to worship God contrary to law; but the judge would not allow the Jews to complain to him of what was not within his office. It was right in Gallio that he left the Jews to themselves in matters relating to their religion, but yet would not let them, under pretence of that, persecute another. But it was wrong to speak slightly of a law and religion which he might have known to be of God, and which he ought to have acquainted himself with. In what way God is to be worshipped, whether Jesus be the Messiah, and whether the gospel be a Divine revelation, are not questions of words and names, they are questions of vast importance. Gallio spoke as if he boasted of his ignorance of the Scriptures, as if the law of God was beneath his notice. Gallio cared for none of these things. If he cared not for the affronts of bad men, it was commendable; but if he concerned not himself for the abuses done to good men, his indifference was carried too far. And those who see and hear of the sufferings of God's people, and have no feeling with them, or care for them, who do not pity and pray for them, are of the same spirit as Gallio, who cared for none of these things.

Verses 18–23

While Paul found he laboured not in vain, he continued labouring. Our times are in God's hand; we purpose, but he disposes; therefore we must make all promises with submission to the will of God; not only if providence permits, but if God does not otherwise direct our motions. A very good refreshment it is to a faithful minister, to have for awhile the society of his brethren. Disciples are compassed about with infirmity; ministers must do what they can to strengthen them, by directing them to Christ, who is their Strength. Let us earnestly seek, in our several places, to promote the cause of Christ, forming plans that appear to us most proper, but relying on the Lord to bring them to pass if he sees good.

Verses 24–28

Apollos taught in the gospel of Christ, as far as John's ministry would carry him, and no further. We cannot but think he had heard of Christ's death and resurrection, but he was not informed as to the mystery of them. Though he had not the miraculous gifts of the Spirit, as the apostles, he made use of the gifts he had. The dispensation of the Spirit, whatever the measure of it may be, is given to every man to profit withal. He was a lively, affectionate preacher; fervent in spirit. He was full of zeal for the glory of God and the salvation of precious souls. Here was a complete man of God, thoroughly furnished for his work. Aquila and Priscilla encouraged his ministry, by attendance upon it. They did not despise Apollos themselves, or undervalue him to others; but considered the disadvantages he had laboured under. And having themselves got knowledge in the truths of the gospel by their long intercourse with Paul, they told what they knew to him. Young scholars may gain a great deal by con**verse** with old Christians. Those who do believe through grace, yet still need help. As long as they are in this world, there are remainders of unbelief, and something lacking in their faith to be perfected, and the work of faith to be fulfilled. If the Jews were convinced that Jesus is Christ, even their own law would teach them to hear him. The business of ministers is to preach Christ. Not only to preach the truth, but to prove and defend it, with meekness, yet with power.

Chapter 19

Chapter Outline	
Paul instructs the disciples of John at Ephesus.	(1–7)
He teaches there.	(8–12)
The Jewish exorcists disgraced. Some Ephesians burn their evil books.	(13–20)
The tumult at Ephesus.	(21–31)
The tumult appeased.	(32–41)

Verses 1–7

Paul, at Ephesus, found some religious persons, who looked to Jesus as the Messiah. They had not been led to expect the miraculous powers of the Holy Ghost, nor were they informed that the gospel was especially the ministration of the Spirit. But they spake as ready to welcome the notice of it. Paul shows them that John never design that those he baptized should rest there, but told them that they should believe on Him who should come after him, that is, on Christ Jesus. They thankfully accepted the discovery, and were baptized in the name of the Lord Jesus. The Holy Ghost came upon them in a surprising, overpowering manner; they spake with tongues, and prophesied, as the apostles and the first Gentile coverts did. Though we do not now expect miraculous powers, yet all who profess to be disciples of Christ, should be called on to examine whether they have received the seal of the Holy Ghost, in his sanctifying influences, to the sincerity of their faith. Many seem not to have heard that there is a Holy Ghost, and many deem all that is spoken concerning his graces and comforts, to be delusion. Of such it may properly be inquired, "Unto what, then, were ye baptized?" for they evidently know not the meaning of that outward sign on which they place great dependence.

Verses 8–12

When arguments and persuasions only harden men in unbelief and blasphemy, we must separate ourselves and others from such unholy company. God was pleased to confirm the teaching of these holy men of old, that if their hearers believed them not, they might believe the works.

Verses 13–20

It was common, especially among the Jews, for persons to profess or to try to cast out evil spirits. If we resist the devil by faith in Christ, he will flee from us; but if we think to resist him by the using of Christ's name, or his works, as a spell or charm, Satan will prevail against us. Where there is true sorrow for sin, there will be free confession of sin to God in every prayer and to man whom we have offended, when the case requires it. Surely if the word of God prevailed among us, many lewd, infidel, and wicked books would be burned by their possessors. Will not these Ephesian converts rise up in judgement against professors, who traffic in such works for the sake of gain, or allow themselves to possess them? If we desire to be in earnest in the great work of salvation, every pursuit and enjoyment must be given up which hinders the effect of the gospel upon the mind, or loosens its hold upon the heart.

Verses 21–31

Persons who came from afar to pay their devotions at the temple of Ephesus, bought little silver shrines, or models of the temple, to carry home with them. See how craftsmen make advantage to themselves of people's superstition, and serve their worldly ends by it. Men are jealous for that by which they get their wealth; and many set themselves against the gospel of Christ, because it calls men from all unlawful crafts, however much wealth is to be gotten by them. There are persons who will stickle for what is most grossly absurd, unreasonable, and false; as this, that those are gods which are made with hands, if it has but worldly interest on its side. The whole city was full of confusion, the common and natural effect of zeal for false religion. Zeal for the honour of Christ, and love to the brethren, encourage zealous believers to venture into danger. Friends will often be raised up among those who are strangers to true religion, but have observed the honest and consistent behaviour of Christians.

Verses 32–41

The Jews came forward in this tumult. Those who are thus careful to distinguish themselves from the servants of Christ now, and are afraid of being taken for them, shall have their doom accordingly in the great day. One, having authority, at length stilled the noise. It is a very good rule at all times, both in private and public affairs, not to be hasty and rash in our motions, but to take time to consider; and always to keep our passions under check. We ought to be quiet, and to do nothing rashly; to do nothing in haste, of which we may repent at leisure. The regular methods of the law ought always to stop popular tumults, and in well-governed nations will do so. Most people stand in awe of men's judgments more than of the judgement of God. How well it were if we would thus quiet our disorderly appetites and passions, by considering the account we must shortly give to the Judge of heaven and earth! And see how the overruling providence of God keeps the public peace, by an unaccountable power over the spirits of men. Thus the world is kept in some order, and men are held back from devouring each other. We can scarcely look around but we see men act like Demetrius and the workmen. It is as safe to contend with wild beasts as with men enraged by party zeal and disappointed covetousness, who think that all arguments are answered, when they have shown that they grow rich by the practices which are opposed. Whatever side in religious disputes, or whatever name this spirit assumes, it is worldly, and should be discountenanced by all who regard truth and piety. And let us not be dismayed; the Lord on high is mightier than the noise of many waters; he can still the rage of the people.

Chapter 20

Chapter Outline	
Paul's journeys.	(1–6)
Eutychus restored to life.	(7–12)
Paul travels towards Jerusalem.	(13–16)
Paul's discourse to the elders of Ephesus.	(17–27)
Their farewell.	(28–38)

Verses 1–6

Tumults or opposition may constrain a Christian to remove from his station or alter his purpose, but his work and his pleasure will be the same, wherever he goes. Paul thought it worth while to bestow five days in going to Troas, though it was but for seven days' stay there; but he knew, and so should we, how to redeem even journeying time, and to make it turn to some good account.

Verses 7–12

Though the disciples read, and meditated, and prayed, and sung apart, and thereby kept up communion with God, yet they came together to worship God, and so kept up their communion with one another. They came together on the first day of the week, the Lord's day. It is to be religiously observed by all disciples of Christ. In the breaking of the bread, not only the breaking of Christ's body for us, to be a sacrifice for our sins, is remembered, but the breaking of Christ's body to us, to be food and a feast for our souls, is signified. In the early times it was the custom to receive the Lord's supper every Lord's day, thus celebrating the memorial of Christ's death. In this assembly Paul preached. The preaching of the gospel ought to go with the sacraments. They were willing to hear, he saw they were so, and continued his speech till midnight. Sleeping when hearing the word, is an evil thing, a sign of low esteem of the word of God. We must do what we can to prevent being sleepy; not put ourselves to sleep, but get our hearts affected with the word we hear, so as to drive sleep far away. Infirmity requires tenderness; but contempt requires severity. It interrupted the apostle's preaching; but was made to confirm his preaching. Eutychus was brought to life again. And as they knew not when they should have Paul's company again, they made the best use of it they could, and reckoned a night's sleep well lost for that purpose. How seldom are hours of repose broken for the purposes of devotion! but how often for mere amusement or sinful revelry! So hard is it for spiritual life to thrive in the heart of man! so naturally do carnal practices flourish there!

Verses 13–16

Paul hastened to Jerusalem, but tried to do good by the way, when going from place to place, as every good man should do. In doing God's work, our own wills and those of our friends must often be crossed; we must not spend time with them when duty calls us another way.

Verses 17–27

The elders knew that Paul was no designing, self-seeking man. Those who would in any office serve the Lord acceptably, and profitably to others, must do it with humility. He was a plain preacher, one that spoke his message so as to be understood. He was a powerful preacher; he preached the gospel as a testimony to them if they received it; but as a testimony against them if they rejected it. He was a profitable preacher; one that aimed to inform their judgments, and reform their hearts and lives. He was a painful preacher, very industrious in his work. He was a faithful preacher; he did not keep back reproofs when necessary, nor keep back the preaching of the cross. He was a truly Christian, evangelical preacher; he did not preach notions or doubtful matters; nor affairs of state or the civil government; but he preached faith and repentance. A better summary of these things, without which there is no salvation, cannot be given: even repentance towards God, and faith towards our Lord Jesus Christ, with their fruits and effects. Without these no sinner can escape, and with these none will come short of eternal life. Let them not think that Paul left Asia for fear of persecution; he was in full expectation of trouble, yet resolved to go on, well assured that it was by Divine direction. Thanks be to God that we know not the things which shall befall us during the year, the week, the day which has begun. It is enough for the child of God to know that his strength shall be equal to his day. He knows not, he would not know, what the day before him shall bring forth. The powerful influences of the Holy Spirit bind the true Christian to his duty. Even when he expects persecution and affliction, the love of Christ constrains him to proceed. None of these things moved Paul from his work; they did not deprive him of his comfort. It is the business of our life to provide for a joyful death. Believing that this was the last time they should see him, he appeals concerning his integrity. He had preached to them the whole counsel of God. As he had preached to them the gospel purely, so he had preached it to them entire; he faithfully did his work, whether men would bear or forbear.

Verses 28–38

If the Holy Ghost has made ministers o**verse**ers of the flock, that is, shepherds, they must be true to their trust. Let them consider their Master's concern for the flock committed to their charge. It is the church He has purchased with his own blood. The blood was his as Man; yet so close is the union between the Divine and human nature, that it is there called the blood of God, for it was the blood of Him who is God. This put such dignity and worth into it, as to ransom believers from all evil, and purchase all good. Paul spake about their souls with affection and concern. They were full of care what would become of them. Paul directs them to look up to God with faith, and commends them to the word of God's grace, not only as the foundation of their hope and the fountain of their joy, but as the rule of their walking. The most advanced Christians are capable of growing, and will find the word of grace help their growth. As those cannot be welcome guests to the holy God who are unsanctified; so heaven would be no heaven to them; but to all who are born again, and on whom the image of God is renewed, it is sure, as almighty power and eternal truth make it so. He recommends himself to them as an example of not caring as to things of the present world; this they would find help forward their comfortable passage through it. It might seem a hard saying, therefore Paul adds to it a saying of their Master's, which he would have them always remember; "It is more blessed to give than to receive:" it seems they were words often used to his disciples. The opinion of the children of this world, is contrary to this; they are afraid of giving, unless in hope of getting. Clear gain, is with them the most blessed thing that can be; but Christ tell us what is more blessed, more excellent. It makes us more like to God, who gives to all, and receives from none; and to the Lord Jesus, who went about doing good. This mind was in Christ Jesus, may it be in us also. It is good for friends, when they part, to part with prayer. Those who exhort and pray for one another, may have many weeping seasons and painful separations, but they will meet before the throne of God, to part no more. It was a comfort to all, that the presence of Christ both went with him and stayed with them.

Chapter 21

Chapter Outline	
Paul's voyage towards Jerusalem.	(1–7)
Paul at Cesarea. The prophecy of Agabus, Paul at Jerusalem.	(8–18)
He is persuaded to join in ceremonial observances.	(19–26)
Being in danger from the Jews, he is rescued by the Romans.	(27–40)

Verses 1–7

Providence must be acknowledged when our affairs go on well. Wherever Paul came, he inquired what disciples were there, and found them out. Foreseeing his troubles, from love to him, and concern for the church, they wrongly thought it would be most for the glory of God that he should continue at liberty; but their earnestness to dissuade him from it, renders his pious resolution the more illustrious. He has taught us by example, as well as by rule, to pray always, to pray without ceasing. Their last farewell was sweetened with prayer.

Verses 8–18

Paul had express warning of his troubles, that when they came, they might be no surprise or terror to him. The general notice given us, that through much tribulation we must enter into the kingdom of God, should be of the same use to us. Their weeping began to weaken and slacken his resolution Has not our Master told us to take up our cross? It was a trouble to him, that they should so earnestly press him to do that in which he could not gratify them without wronging his conscience. When we see trouble coming, it becomes us to say, not only, The will of the Lord must be done, and there is no remedy; but, Let the will of the Lord be done; for his will is his wisdom, and he doeth all according to the counsel of it. When a trouble is come, this must allay our griefs, that the will of the Lord is done; when we see it coming, this must silence our fears, that the will of the Lord shall be done; and we ought to say, Amen, let it be done. It is honourable to be an old disciple of Jesus Christ, to have been enabled by the grace of God to continue long in a course of duty, stedfast in the faith, growing more and more experienced, to a good old age. And with these old disciples one would choose to lodge; for the multitude of their years shall teach wisdom. Many brethren at Jerusalem received Paul gladly. We think, perhaps, that if we had him among us, we should gladly receive him; but we should not, if, having his doctrine, we do not gladly receive that.

Verses 19–26

Paul ascribed all his success to God, and to God they gave the praise. God had honoured him more than any of the apostles, yet they did not envy him; but on the contrary, glorified the Lord. They could not do more to encourage Paul to go on cheerfully in his work. James and the elders of the church at Jerusalem, asked Paul to gratify the believing Jews, by some compliance with the ceremonial law. They thought it was prudent in him to conform thus far. It was great weakness to be so fond of the shadows, when the substance was come. The religion Paul preached, tended not to destroy the law, but to fulfil it. He preached Christ, the end of the law for righteousness, and repentance and faith, in which we are to make great use of the law. The weakness and evil of the human heart strongly appear, when we consider how many, even of the disciples of Christ, had not due regard to the most eminent minister that even lived. Not the excellence of his character, nor the success with which God blessed his labours, could gain their esteem and affection, seeing that he did not render the same respect as themselves to mere ceremonial observances. How watchful should we be against prejudices! The apostles were not free from blame in all they did; and it would be hard to defend Paul from the charge of giving way too much in this matter. It is vain to attempt to court the favour of zealots, or bigots to a party. This compliance of Paul did not answer, for the very thing by which he hoped to pacify the Jews, provoked them, and brought him into trouble. But the all-wise God overruled both their advice and Paul's compliance with it, to serve a better purpose than was intended. It was in vain to think of pleasing men who would be pleased with nothing but the rooting out of Christianity. Integrity and uprightness will be more likely to preserve us than insincere compliances. And it should warn us not to press men to doing what is contrary to their own judgment to oblige us.

Verses 27–40

In the temple, where Paul should have been protected as in a place of safety, he was violently set upon. They falsely charged him with ill doctrine and ill practice against the Mosaic ceremonies. It is no new thing for those who mean honestly and act regularly, to have things laid to their charge which they know not and never thought of. It is common for the wise and good to have that charged against them by malicious people, with which they thought to have obliged them. God often makes those a protection to his people, who have no affection to them, but only have compassion for sufferers, and regard to the public peace. And here see what false, mistaken notions of good people and good ministers, many run away with. But God seasonably interposes for the safety of his servants, from wicked and unreasonable men; and gives them opportunities to speak for themselves, to plead for the Redeemer, and to spread abroad his glorious gospel.

Chapter 22

Chapter Outline	
Paul's account of his conversion.	(1–11)
Paul directed to preach to the Gentiles.	(12–21)
The rage of the Jews Paul pleads that he is a Roman citizen.	(22–30)

Verses 1–11

The apostle addressed the enraged multitude, in the customary style of respect and good-will. Paul relates the history of his early life very particularly; he notices that his conversion was wholly the act of God. Condemned sinners are struck blind by the power of darkness, and it is a lasting blindness, like that of the unbelieving Jews. Convinced sinners are struck blind as Paul was, not by darkness, but by light. They are for a time brought to be at a loss within themselves, but it is in order to their being enlightened. A simple relation of the Lord's dealings with us, in bringing us, from opposing, to profess and promote his gospel, when delivered in a right spirit and manner, will sometimes make more impression that laboured speeches, even though it amounts not to the full proof of the truth, such as was shown in the change wrought in the apostle.

Verses 12–21

The apostle goes on to relate how he was confirmed in the change he had made. The Lord having chosen the sinner, that he should know his will, he is humbled, enlightened, and brought to the knowledge of Christ and his blessed gospel. Christ is here called that Just One; for he is Jesus Christ the righteous. Those whom God has chosen to know his will, must look to Jesus, for by him God has made known his good-will to us. The great gospel privilege, sealed to us by baptism, is the pardon of sins. Be baptized, and wash away thy sins; that is, receive the comfort of the pardon of thy sins in and through Jesus Christ, and lay hold on his righteousness for that purpose; and receive power against sin, for the mortifying of thy corruptions. Be baptized, and rest not in the sign, but make sure of the thing signified, the putting away of the filth of sin. The great gospel duty, to which by our baptism we are bound, is, to seek for the pardon of our sins in Christ's name, and in dependence on him and his righteousness. God appoints his labourers their day and their place, and it is fit they should follow his appointment, though it may cross their own will. Providence contrives better for us than we do for ourselves; we must refer ourselves to God's guidance. If Christ send any one, his Spirit shall go along with him, and give him to see the fruit of his labours. But nothing can reconcile man's heart to the gospel, except the special grace of God.

Verses 22–30

The Jews listened to Paul's account of his conversion, but the mention of his being sent to the Gentiles, was so contrary to all their national prejudices, that they would hear no more. Their frantic conduct astonished the Roman officer, who supposed that Paul must have committed some great crime. Paul pleaded his privilege as a Roman citizen, by which he was exempted from all trials and punishments which might force him to confess himself guilty. The manner of his speaking plainly shows what holy security and serenity of mind he enjoyed. As Paul was a Jew, in low circumstances, the Roman officer questioned how he obtained so valuable a distinction; but the apostle told him he was free born. Let us value that freedom to which all the children of God are born; which no sum of money, however large, can purchase for those who remain unregenerate. This at once put a stop to his trouble. Thus many are kept from evil practices by the fear of man, who would not be held back from them by the fear of God. The apostle asks, simply, Is it lawful? He knew that the God whom he served would support him under all sufferings for his name's sake. But if it were not lawful, the apostle's religion directed him, if possible, to avoid it. He never shrunk from a cross which his Divine Master laid upon his onward road; and he never stept aside out of that road to take one up.

Chapter 23

Chapter Outline	
Paul's defence before the council of the Jews.	(1–5)
Paul's defence. He receives a Divine assurance that he shall go to Rome.	(6–11)
The Jews conspire to kill Paul, Lysias sends him to Cesarea.	(12–24)
Lysias's letter to Felix.	(25–35)

Verses 1–5

See here the character of an honest man. He sets God before him, and lives as in his sight. He makes conscience of what he says and does, and, according to the best of his knowledge, he keeps from whatever is evil, and cleaves to what is good. He is conscientious in all his words and conduct. Those who thus live before God, may, like Paul, have confidence both toward God and man. Though the answer of Paul contained a just rebuke and prediction, he seems to have been too angry at the treatment he received in uttering them. Great men may be told of their faults, and public complaints may be made in a proper manner; but the law of God requires respect for those in authority.

Verses 6–11

The Pharisees were correct in the faith of the Jewish church. The Sadducees were no friends to the Scripture or Divine revelation; they denied a future state; they had neither hope of eternal happiness, nor dread of eternal misery. When called in question for his being a Christian, Paul might truly say he was called in question for the hope of the resurrection of the dead. It was justifiable in him, by this profession of his opinion on that disputed point, to draw off the Pharisees from persecuting him, and to lead them to protect him from this unlawful violence. How easily can God defend his own cause! Though the Jews seemed to be perfectly agreed in their conspiracy against religion, yet they were influenced by very different motives. There is no true friendship among the wicked, and in a moment, and with the utmost ease, God can turn their union into open enmity. Divine consolations stood Paul in the most stead; the chief captain rescued him out of the hands of cruel men, but the event he could not tell. Whoever is against us, we need not fear, if the Lord stand by us. It is the will of Christ, that his servants who are faithful, should be always cheerful. He might think he should never see Rome; but God tells him, even in that he should be gratified, since he desired to go there only for the honour of Christ, and to do good.

Verses 12–24

False religious principles, adopted by carnal men, urge on to such wickedness, as human nature would hardly be supposed capable of. Yet the Lord readily disappoints the best concerted schemes of iniquity. Paul knew that the Divine providence acts by reasonable and prudent means; and that, if he neglected to use the means in his power, he could not expect God's providence to work on his behalf. He who will not help himself according to his means and power, has neither reason nor revelation to assure him that he shall receive help from God. Believing in the Lord, we and ours shall be kept from every evil work, and kept to his kingdom. Heavenly Father, give us by thy Holy Spirit, for Christ's sake, this precious faith.

Verses 25–35

God has instruments for every work. The natural abilities and moral virtues of the heathens often have been employed to protect his persecuted servants. Even the men of the world can discern between the conscientious conduct of upright believers, and the zeal of false professors, though they disregard or understand not their doctrinal principles. All hearts are in God's hand, and those are blessed who put their trust in him, and commit their ways unto him.

Chapter 24

Chapter Outline	
The speech of Tertullus against Paul.	(1–9)
Paul's defence before Felix.	(10–21)
Felix trembles at the reasoning of Paul.	(22–27)

Verses 1–9

See here the unhappiness of great men, and a great unhappiness it is, to have their services praised beyond measure, and never to be faithfully told of their faults; hereby they are hardened and encouraged in evil, like Felix. God's prophets were charged with being troublers of the land, and our Lord Jesus Christ, that he perverted the nation; the very same charges were brought against Paul. The selfish and evil passions of men urge them forward, and the graces and power of speech, too often have been used to mislead and prejudice men against the truth. How different will the characters of Paul and Felix appear at the day of judgement, from what they are represented in the speech of Tertullus! Let not Christians value the applause, or be troubled at the revilings of ungodly men, who represent the vilest of the human race almost as gods, and the excellent of the earth as pestilences and movers of sedition.

Verses 10–21

Paul gives a just account of himself, which clears him from crime, and likewise shows the true reason of the violence against him. Let us never be driven from any good way by its having an ill name. It is very comfortable, in worshipping God, to look to him as the God of our fathers, and to set up no other rule of faith or practice but the Scriptures. This shows there will be a resurrection to a final judgment. Prophets and their doctrines were to be tried by their fruits. Paul's aim was to have a conscience void of offence. His care and endeavour was to abstain from many things, and to abound in the exercises of religion at all times; both towards God. and towards man. If blamed for being more earnest in the things of God than our neighbours, what is our reply? Do we shrink from the accusation? How many in the world would rather be accused of any weakness, nay, even of wickedness, than of an earnest, fervent feeling of love to the Lord Jesus Christ, and of devotedness to his service! Can such think that He will confess them when he comes in his glory, and before the angels of God? If there is any sight pleasing to the God of our salvation, and a sight at which the angels rejoice, it is, to behold a devoted follower of the Lord, here upon earth, acknowledging that he is guilty, if it be a crime, of loving the Lord who died for him, with all his heart, and soul, and mind, and strength. And that he will not in silence see God's word despised, or hear his name profaned; he will rather risk the ridicule and the hatred of the world, than one frown from that gracious Being whose love is better than life.

Verses 22–27

The apostle reasoned concerning the nature and obligations of righteousness, temperance, and of a judgment to come; thus showing the oppressive judge and his profligate mistress, their need of repentance, forgiveness, and of the grace of the gospel. Justice respects our conduct in life, particularly in reference to others; temperance, the state and government of our souls, in reference to God. He who does not exercise himself in these, has neither the form nor the power of godliness, and must be overwhelmed with the Divine wrath in the day of God's appearing. A prospect of the judgment to come, is enough to make the stoutest heart to tremble. Felix trembled, but that was all. Many are startled by the word of God, who are not changed by it. Many fear the consequences of sin, yet continue in the love and practice of sin. In the affairs of our souls, delays are dangerous. Felix put off this matter to a more convenient season, but we do not find that the more convenient season ever came. Behold now is the accepted time; hear the voice of the Lord to-day. He was in haste to turn from hearing the truth. Was any business more urgent than for him to reform his conduct, or more important than the salvation of his soul! Sinners often start up like a man roused from his sleep by a loud noise, but soon sink again into their usual drowsiness. Be not deceived by occasional appearances of religion in ourselves or in others. Above all, let us not trifle with the word of God. Do we expect that as we advance in life our hearts will grow softer, or that the influence of the world will decline? Are we not at this moment in danger of being lost for ever? Now is the day of salvation; tomorrow may be too late.

Chapter 25

Chapter Outline	
Paul before Festus, he appeals to Caesar.	(1–12)
Festus confers with Agrippa respecting Paul.	(13–27)

Verses 1–12

See how restless malice is. Persecutors deem it a peculiar favour to have their malice gratified. Preaching Christ, the end of the law, was no offence against the law. In suffering times the prudence of the Lord's people is tried, as well as their patience; they need wisdom. It becomes those who are innocent, to insist upon their innocence. Paul was willing to abide by the rules of the law, and to let that take its course. If he deserved death, he would accept the punishment. But if none of the things whereof they accused him were true, no man could deliver him unto them, with justice. Paul is neither released nor condemned. It is an instance of the slow steps which Providence takes; by which we are often made ashamed, both of our hopes and of our fears, and are kept waiting on God.

Verses 13–27

Agrippa had the government of Galilee. How many unjust and hasty judgments the Roman maxim, ver. #(**16**), condemn! This heathen, guided only by the light of nature, followed law and custom exactly, yet how many Christians will not follow the rules of truth, justice, and charity, in judging their brethren! The questions about God's worship, the way of salvation, and the truths of the gospel, may appear doubtful and without interest, to worldly men and mere politicians. See how slightly this Roman speaks of Christ, and of the great controversy between the Jews and the Christians. But the day is at hand when Festus and the whole world will see, that all the concerns of the Roman empire were but trifles and of no consequence, compared with this question of Christ's resurrection. Those who have had means of instruction, and have despised them, will be awfully convinced of their sin and folly. Here was a noble assembly brought together to hear the truths of the gospel, though they only meant to gratify their curiosity by attending to the defence of a prisoner. Many, even now, attend at the places of hearing the word of God with "great pomp," and too often with no better motive than curiosity. And though ministers do not now stand as prisoners to make a defence for their lives, yet numbers affect to sit in judgment upon them, desirous to make them offenders for a word, rather than to learn from them the truth and will of God, for the salvation of their souls But the pomp of this appearance was outshone by the real glory of the poor prisoner at the bar. What was the honour of their fine appearance, compared with that of Paul's wisdom, and grace, and holiness; his courage and constancy in suffering for Christ! It is no small mercy to have God clear up our righteousness as the light, and our just dealing as the noon-day; to have nothing certain laid to our charge. And God makes even the enemies of his people to do them right.

Chapter 26

Chapter Outline	
Paul's defence before Agrippa.	(1–11)

His conversion and preaching to the Gentiles.	(12–23)
Festus and Agrippa convinced of Paul's innocence.	(24–32)

Verses 1–11

Christianity teaches us to give a reason of the hope that is in us, and also to give honour to whom honour is due, without flattery or fear of man. Agrippa was well **versed** in the Scriptures of the Old Testament, therefore could the better judge as to the controversy about Jesus being the Messiah. Surely ministers may expect, when they preach the faith of Christ, to be heard patiently. Paul professes that he still kept to all the good in which he was first educated and trained up. See here what his religion was. He was a moralist, a man of virtue, and had not learned the arts of the crafty, covetous Pharisees; he was not chargeable with any open vice and profaneness. He was sound in the faith. He always had a holy regard for the ancient promise made of God unto the fathers, and built his hope upon it. The apostle knew very well that all this would not justify him before God, yet he knew it was for his reputation among the Jews, and an argument that he was not such a man as they represented him to be. Though he counted this but loss, that he might win Christ, yet he mentioned it when it might serve to honour Christ. See here what Paul's religion is; he has not such zeal for the ceremonial law as he had in his youth; the sacrifices and offerings appointed by that, are done away by the great Sacrifice which they typified. Of the ceremonial cleansings he makes no conscience, and thinks the Levitical priesthood is done away in the priesthood of Christ; but, as to the main principles of his religion, he is as zealous as ever. Christ and heaven, are the two great doctrines of the gospel; that God has given to us eternal life, and this life is in his Son. These are the matter of the promise made unto the fathers. The temple service, or continual course of religious duties, day and night, was kept up as the profession of faith in the promise of eternal life, and in expectation of it. The prospect of eternal life should engage us to be diligent and stedfast in all religious exercises. Yet the Sadducees hated Paul for preaching the resurrection; and the other Jews joined them, because he testified that Jesus was risen, and was the promised Redeemer of Israel. Many things are thought to be beyond belief, only because the infinite nature and perfections of Him that has revealed, performed, or promised them, are overlooked. Paul acknowledged, that while he continued a Pharisee, he was a bitter enemy to Christianity. This was his character and manner of life in the beginning of his time; and there was every thing to hinder his being a Christian. Those who have been most strict in their conduct before conversion, will afterwards see abundant reason for humbling themselves, even on account of things which they then thought ought to have been done.

Verses 12–23

Paul was made a Christian by Divine power; by a revelation of Christ both to him and in him; when in the full career of his sin. He was made a minister by Divine authority: the same Jesus who appeared to him in that glorious light, ordered him to preach the gospel to the Gentiles. A world that sits in darkness must be enlightened; those must be brought to know the things that belong to their everlasting peace, who are yet ignorant of them. A world that lies in wickedness must be sanctified and reformed; it is not enough for them to have their eyes opened, they must have their hearts renewed; not enough to be turned from darkness to light, but they must be turned from the power of Satan unto God. All who are turned from sin to God, are not only pardoned, but have a grant of a rich inheritance. The forgiveness of sins makes way for this. None can be happy who are not holy; and to be saints in heaven we must be first saints on earth. We are made holy, and saved by faith in Christ; by which we rely upon Christ as the Lord our Righteousness, and give up ourselves to him as the Lord our Ruler; by this we receive the remission of sins, the gift of the Holy Ghost, and eternal life. The cross of Christ was a stumbling-block to the Jews, and they were in a rage at Paul's preaching the fulfilling of the Old Testament predictions. Christ should be the first that should rise from the dead; the Head or principal One. Also, it was foretold by the prophets, that the Gentiles should be brought to the knowledge of God by the Messiah; and what in this could the Jews justly be displeased at? Thus the true convert can give a reason of his hope, and a good account of the change manifest in him. Yet for going about and calling on men thus to repent and to be converted, vast numbers have been blamed and persecuted.

Verses 24–32

It becomes us, on all occasions, to speak the words of truth and soberness, and then we need not be troubled at the unjust censures of men. Active and laborious followers of the gospel often have been despised as dreamers or madmen, for believing such doctrines and such wonderful facts; and for attesting that the same faith and diligence, and an experience like their own, are necessary to all men, whatever their rank, in order to their salvation. But apostles and prophets, and the Son of God himself, were exposed to this charge; and none need be moved thereby, when Divine grace has made them wise unto salvation. Agrippa saw a great deal of reason for Christianity. His understanding and judgment were for the time convinced, but his heart was not changed. And his conduct and temper were widely different from the humility and spirituality of the gospel. Many are almost persuaded to be religious, who are not quite persuaded; they are under strong convictions of their duty, and of the excellence of the ways of God, yet do not pursue their convictions. Paul urged that it was the concern of every one to become a true Christian; that there is grace enough in Christ for all. He expressed his full conviction of the truth of the gospel, the absolute necessity of faith in Christ in order to salvation. Such salvation from such bondage, the gospel of Christ offers to the Gentiles; to a lost world. Yet it is with much difficulty that any person can be persuaded he needs a work of grace on his heart, like that which was needful for the conversion of the Gentiles. Let us beware of fatal hesitation in our own conduct; and recollect how far the being almost persuaded to be a Christian, is from being altogether such a one as every true believer is.

Chapter 27

Chapter Outline	
Paul's voyage towards Rome.	(1–11)
Paul and his companions endangered by a tempest.	(12–20)
He receives a Divine assurance of safety.	(21–29)

Paul encourages those with him.	(30–38)
They are shipwrecked.	(39–44)

Verses 1–11

It was determined by the counsel of God, before it was determined by the counsel of Festus, that Paul should go to Rome; for God had work for him to do there. The course they steered, and the places they touched at, are here set down. And God here encourages those who suffer for him, to trust in him; for he can put it into the hearts of those to befriend them, from whom they least expect it. Sailors must make the best of the wind: and so must we all in our passage over the ocean of this world. When the winds are contrary, yet we must be getting forward as well as we can. Many who are not driven backward by cross providences, do not get forward by favourable providences. And many real Christians complain as to the concerns of their souls, that they have much ado to keep their ground. Every fair haven is not a safe haven. Many show respect to good ministers, who will not take their advice. But the event will convince sinners of the vanity of their hopes, and the folly of their conduct.

Verses 12–20

Those who launch forth on the ocean of this world, with a fair gale, know not what storms they may meet with; and therefore must not easily take it for granted that they have obtained their purpose. Let us never expect to be quite safe till we enter heaven. They saw neither sun nor stars for many days. Thus melancholy sometimes is the condition of the people of God as to their spiritual matters; they walk in darkness, and have no light. See what the wealth of this world is: though coveted as a blessing, the time may come when it will be a burden; not only too heavy to be carried safely, but heavy enough to sink him that has it. The children of this world can be prodigal of their goods for the saving their lives, yet are sparing of them in works of piety and charity, and in suffering for Christ. Any man will rather make shipwreck of his goods than of his life; but many rather make shipwreck of faith and a good conscience, than of their goods. The means the sailors used did not succeed; but when sinners give up all hope of saving themselves, they are prepared to understand God's word, and to trust in his mercy through Jesus Christ.

Verses 21–29

They did not hearken to the apostle when he warned them of their danger; yet if they acknowledge their folly, and repent of it, he will speak comfort and relief to them when in danger. Most people bring themselves into trouble, because they do not know when they are well off; they come to harm and loss by aiming to mend their condition, often against advice. Observe the solemn profession Paul made of relation to God. No storms or tempests can hinder God's favour to his people, for he is a Help always at hand. It is a comfort to the faithful servants of God when in difficulties, that as long as the Lord has any work for them to do, their lives shall be prolonged. If Paul had thrust himself needlessly into bad company, he might justly have been cast away with them; but God calling him into it, they are preserved with him. They are given thee; there is no greater satisfaction to a good man than to know he is a public blessing. He comforts them with the same comforts wherewith he himself was comforted. God is ever faithful, therefore let all who have an interest in his promises be ever cheerful. As, with God, saying and doing are not two things, believing and enjoying should not be so with us. Hope is an anchor of the soul, sure and stedfast, entering into that within the veil. Let those who are in spiritual darkness hold fast by that, and think not of putting to sea again, but abide by Christ, and wait till the day break, and the shadows flee away.

Verses 30–38

God, who appointed the end, that they should be saved, appointed the means, that they should be saved by the help of these shipmen. Duty is ours, events are God's; we do not trust God, but tempt him, when we say we put ourselves under his protection, if we do not use proper means, such as are within our power, for our safety. But how selfish are men in general, often even ready to seek their own safety by the destruction of others! Happy those who have such a one as Paul in their company, who not only had intercourse with Heaven, but was of an enlivening spirit to those about him. The sorrow of the world works death, while joy in God is life and peace in the greatest distresses and dangers. The comfort of God's promises can only be ours by believing dependence on him, to fulfil his word to us; and the salvation he reveals must be waited for in use of the means he appoints. If God has chosen us to salvation, he has also appointed that we shall obtain it by repentance, faith, prayer, and persevering obedience; it is fatal presumption to expect it in any other way. It is an encouragement to people to commit themselves to Christ as their Saviour, when those who invite them, clearly show that they do so themselves.

Verses 39–44

The ship that had weathered the storm in the open sea, where it had room, is dashed to pieces when it sticks fast. Thus, if the heart fixes in the world in affection, and cleaving to it, it is lost. Satan's temptations beat against it, and it is gone; but as long as it keeps above the world, though tossed with cares and tumults, there is hope for it. They had the shore in view, yet suffered shipwreck in the harbour; thus we are taught never to be secure. Though there is great difficulty in the way of the promised salvation, it shall, without fail, be brought to pass. It will come to pass that whatever the trials and dangers may be, in due time all believers will get safely to heaven. Lord Jesus, thou hast assured us that none of thine shall perish. Thou wilt bring them all safe to the heavenly shore. And what a pleasing landing will that be! Thou wilt present them to thy Father, and give thy Holy Spirit full possession of them for ever.

Chapter 28

Chapter Outline	
Paul kindly received at Melita.	(1–10)
He arrives at Rome.	(11–16)
His conference with the Jews.	(17–22)

Paul preaches to the Jews, and abides at Rome a prisoner.	(23–31)

Verses 1–10

God can make strangers to be friends; friends in distress. Those who are despised for homely manners, are often more friendly than the more polished; and the conduct of heathens, or persons called barbarians, condemns many in civilized nations, professing to be Christians. The people thought that Paul was a murderer, and that the viper was sent by Divine justice, to be the avenger of blood. They knew that there is a God who governs the world, so that things do not come to pass by chance, no, not the smallest event, but all by Divine direction; and that evil pursues sinners; that there are good works which God will reward, and wicked works which he will punish. Also, that murder is a dreadful crime, one which shall not long go unpunished. But they thought all wicked people were punished in this life. Though some are made examples in this world, to prove that there is a God and a Providence, yet many are left unpunished, to prove that there is a judgment to come. They also thought all who were remarkably afflicted in this life were wicked people. Divine revelation sets this matter in a true light. Good men often are greatly afflicted in this life, for the trial and increase of their faith and patience. Observe Paul's deliverance from the danger. And thus in the strength of the grace of Christ, believers shake off the temptations of Satan, with holy resolution. When we despise the censures and reproaches of men, and look upon them with holy contempt, having the testimony of our consciences for us, then, like Paul, we shake off the viper into the fire. It does us no harm, except we are kept by it from our duty. God hereby made Paul remarkable among these people, and so made way for the receiving of the gospel. The Lord raises up friends for his people in every place whither he leads them, and makes them blessings to those in affliction.

Verses 11–16

The common events of travelling are seldom worthy of being told; but the comfort of communion with the saints, and kindness shown by friends, deserve particular mention. The Christians at Rome were so far from being ashamed of Paul, or afraid of owning him, because he was a prisoner, that they were the more careful to show him respect. He had great comfort in this. And if our friends are kind to us, God puts it into their hearts, and we must give him the glory. When we see those even in strange places, who bear Christ's name, fear God, and serve him, we should lift up our hearts to heaven in thanksgiving. How many great men have made their entry into Rome, crowned and in triumph, who really were plagues to the world! But here a good man makes his entry into Rome, chained as a poor captive, who was a greater blessing to the world than any other merely a man. Is not this enough to put us for ever out of conceit with worldly favour? This may encourage God's prisoners, that he can give them favour in the eyes of those that carry them captives. When God does not soon deliver his people out of bondage, yet makes it easy to them, or them easy under it, they have reason to be thankful.

Verses 17–22

It was for the honour of Paul that those who examined his case, acquitted him. In his appeal he sought not to accuse his nation, but only to clear himself. True Christianity settles what is of common concern to all mankind, and is not built upon narrow opinions and private interests. It aims at no worldly benefit or advantage, but all its gains are spiritual and eternal. It is, and always has been, the lot of Christ's holy religion, to be every where spoken against. Look through every town and village where Christ is exalted as the only Saviour of mankind, and where the people are called to follow him in newness of life, and we see those who give themselves up to Christ, still called a sect, a party, and reproached. And this is the treatment they are sure to receive, so long as there shall continue an ungodly man upon earth.

Verses 23–31

Paul persuaded the Jews concerning Jesus. Some were wrought upon by the word, and others hardened; some received the light, and others shut their eyes against it. And the same has always been the effect of the gospel. Paul parted with them, observing that the Holy Ghost had well described their state. Let all that hear the gospel, and do not heed it, tremble at their doom; for who shall heal them, if God does not? The Jews had afterwards much reasoning among themselves. Many have great reasoning, who do not reason aright. They find fault with one another's opinions, yet will not yield to truth. Nor will men's reasoning among themselves convince them, without the grace of God to open their understandings. While we mourn on account of such despisers, we should rejoice that the salvation of God is sent to others, who will receive it; and if we are of that number, we should be thankful to Him who hath made us to differ. The apostle kept to his principle, to know and preach nothing but Christ and him crucified. Christians, when tempted from their main business, should bring themselves back with this question, What does this concern the Lord Jesus? What tendency has it to bring us to him, and to keep us walking in him? The apostle preached not himself, but Christ, and he was not ashamed of the gospel of Christ. Though Paul was placed in a very narrow opportunity for being useful, he was not disturbed in it. Though it was not a wide door that was opened to him, yet no man was suffered to shut it; and to many it was an effectual door, so that there were saints even in Nero's household, Php **4**:**22**. We learn also from Php **1**:**13**, how God overruled Paul's imprisonment for the furtherance of the gospel. And not the residents at Rome only, but all the church of Christ, to the present day, and in the most remote corner of the globe, have abundant reason to bless God, that during the most mature period of his Christian life and experience, he was detained a prisoner. It was from his prison, probably chained hand to hand to the soldier who kept him, that the apostle wrote the epistles to the Ephesians, Philippians, Colossians, and Hebrews; epistles showing, perhaps more than any others, the Christian love with which his heart overflowed, and the Christian experience with which his soul was filled. The believer of the present time may have less of triumph, and less of heavenly joy, than the apostle, but every follower of the same Saviour, is equally sure of safety and peace at the last. Let us seek to live more and more in the love of the Saviour; to labour to glorify Him by every action of our lives; and we shall assuredly, by his strength, be among the number of those who now overcome our enemies; and by his free grace and mercy, be hereafter among the blessed company who shall sit with Him upon his throne, even as He also has overcome, and is sitting on his Father's throne, at God's right hand for evermore.

Romans

The scope or design of the apostle in writing to the Romans appears to have been, to answer the unbelieving, and to teach the believing Jew; to confirm the Christian and to convert the idolatrous Gentile; and to show the Gentile convert as equal with the Jewish, in respect of his religious condition, and his rank in the Divine favour. These several designs are brought into on view, by opposing or arguing with the infidel or unbelieving Jew, in favour of the Christian or believing Gentile. The way of a sinner's acceptance with God, or justification in his sight, merely by grace, through faith in the righteousness of Christ, without distinction of nations, is plainly stated. This doctrine is cleared from the objections raised by Judaizing Christians, who were for making terms of acceptance with God by a mixture of the law and the gospel, and for shutting out the Gentiles from any share in the blessings of salvation brought in by the Messiah. In the conclusion, holiness is further enforced by practical exhortations.

Chapter 1

Chapter Outline	
The apostle's commission.	(1–7)
Prays for the saints at Rome, and expresses his desire to see them.	(8–15)
The gospel way of justification by faith, for Jews and Gentiles.	(16, 17)
The sins of the Gentiles set forth.	(18–32)

Verses 1–7

The doctrine of which the apostle Paul wrote, set forth the fulfilment of the promises by the prophets. It spoke of the Son of God, even Jesus the Saviour, the promised Messiah, who came from David as to his human nature, but was also declared to be the Son of God, by the Divine power which raised him from the dead. The Christian profession does not consist in a notional knowledge or a bare assent, much less in per**verse** disputings, but in obedience. And all those, and those only, are brought to obedience of the faith, who are effectually called of Jesus Christ. Here is, **1**. The privilege of Christians; they are beloved of God, and are members of that body which is beloved. **2**. The duty of Christians; to be holy, hereunto are they called, called to be saints. These the apostle saluted, by wishing them grace to sanctify their souls, and peace to comfort their hearts, as springing from the free mercy of God, the reconciled Father of all believers, and coming to them through the Lord Jesus Christ.

Verses 8–15

We must show love for our friends, not only by praying for them, but by praising God for them. As in our purposes, so in our desires, we must remember to say, If the Lord will, Jas **4**:**15**. Our journeys are made prosperous or otherwise, according to the will of God. We should readily impart to others what God has trusted to us, rejoicing to make others joyful, especially taking pleasure in communing with those who believe the same things with us. If redeemed by the blood, and converted by the grace of the Lord Jesus, we are altogether his; and for his sake we are debtors to all men, to do all the good we can. Such services are our duty.

Verses 16, 17

In these **verse**s the apostle opens the design of the whole epistle, in which he brings forward a charge of sinfulness against all flesh; declares the only method of deliverance from condemnation, by faith in the mercy of God, through Jesus Christ; and then builds upon it purity of heart, grateful obedience, and earnest desires to improve in all those Christian graces and tempers, which nothing but a lively faith in Christ can bring forth. God is a just and holy God, and we are guilty sinners. It is necessary that we have a righteousness to appear in before him: there is such a righteousness brought in by the Messiah, and made known in the gospel; a gracious method of acceptance, notwithstanding the guilt of our sins. It is the righteousness of Christ, who is God, coming from a satisfaction of infinite value. Faith is all in all, both in the beginning and progress of Christian life. It is not from faith to works, as if faith put us into a justified state, and then works kept us in it; but it is all along from faith to faith; it is faith pressing forward, and gaining the victory over unbelief.

Verses 18–25

The apostle begins to show that all mankind need the salvation of the gospel, because none could obtain the favour of God, or escape his wrath by their own works. For no man can plead that he has fulfilled all his obligations to God and to his neighbour; nor can any truly say that he has fully acted up to the light afforded him. The sinfulness of man is described as ungodliness against the laws of the first table, and unrighteousness against those of the second. The cause of that sinfulness is holding the truth in unrighteousness. All, more or less, do what they know to be wrong, and omit what they know to be right, so that the plea of ignorance cannot be allowed from any. Our Creator's invisible power and Godhead are so clearly shown in the works he has made, that even idolaters and wicked Gentiles are left without excuse. They foolishly followed idolatry; and rational creatures changed the worship of the glorious Creator, for that of brutes, reptiles, and senseless images. They wandered from God, till all traces of true religion must have been lost, had not the revelation of the gospel prevented it. For whatever may be pretended, as to the sufficiency of man's reason to discover Divine truth and moral obligation, or to govern the practice aright, facts cannot be denied. And these plainly show that men have dishonoured God by the most absurd idolatries and superstitions; and have degraded themselves by the vilest affections and most abominable deeds.

Verses 26–32

In the horrid depravity of the heathen, the truth of our Lord's words was shown: "Light was come into the world, but men loved darkness rather than light, because their deeds were evil; for he that doeth evil hateth the light." The truth was not to their taste. And we all know how soon a man will contrive, against the strongest evidence, to reason himself out of the belief of what he dislikes. But a man cannot be brought to greater slavery than to be given up to his own lusts. As the Gentiles did not like to keep God in their knowledge, they committed crimes wholly against reason and their own welfare. The nature of man, whether pagan or Christian, is still the same; and the charges of the apostle apply more or less to the state and character of men at all times, till they are brought to full submission to the faith of Christ, and renewed by Divine power. There never yet was a man, who had not reason to lament his strong corruptions, and his secret dislike to the will of God. Therefore this chapter is a call to self-examination, the end of which should be, a deep conviction of sin, and of the necessity of deliverance from a state of condemnation.

Chapter 2

Chapter Outline	

The Jews could not be justified by the law of Moses, any more than the Gentiles by the law of nature.	(1–16)
The sins of the Jews confuted all their vain confidence in their outward privileges.	(17–29)

Verses 1–16

The Jews thought themselves a holy people, entitled to their privileges by right, while they were unthankful, rebellious, and unrighteous. But all who act thus, of every nation, age, and description, must be reminded that the judgment of God will be according to their real character. The case is so plain, that we may appeal to the sinner's own thoughts. In every wilful sin, there is contempt of the goodness of God. And though the branches of man's disobedience are very various, all spring from the same root. But in true repentance, there must be hatred of former sinfulness, from a change wrought in the state of the mind, which disposes it to choose the good and to refuse the evil. It shows also a sense of inward wretchedness. Such is the great change wrought in repentance, it is conversion, and is needed by every human being. The ruin of sinners is their walking after a hard and impenitent heart. Their sinful doings are expressed by the strong words, "treasuring up wrath." In the description of the just man, notice the full demand of the law. It demands that the motives shall be pure, and rejects all actions from earthly ambition or ends. In the description of the unrighteous, contention is held forth as the principle of all evil. The human will is in a state of enmity against God. Even Gentiles, who had not the written law, had that within, which directed them what to do by the light of nature. Conscience is a witness, and first or last will bear witness. As they nature. Conscience is a witness, and first or last will bear witness. As they kept or broke these natural laws and dictates, their consciences either acquitted or condemned them. Nothing speaks more terror to sinners, and more comfort to saints, than that Christ shall be the Judge. Secret services shall be rewarded, secret sins shall be then punished, and brought to light.

Verses 17–24

The apostle directs his discourse to the Jews, and shows of what sins they were guilty, notwithstanding their profession and vain pretensions. A believing, humble, thankful glorying in God, is the root and sum of all religion. But proud, vain-glorious boasting in God, and in the outward profession of his name, is the root and sum of all hypocrisy. Spiritual pride is the most dangerous of all kinds of pride. A great evil of the sins professors is, the dishonour done to God and religion, by their not living according to their profession. Many despise their more ignorant neighbours who rest in a dead form of godliness; yet themselves trust in a form of knowledge, equally void of life and power, while some glory in the gospel, whose unholy lives dishonour God, and cause his name to be blasphemed.

Verses 25–29

No forms, ordinances, or notions can profit, without regenerating grace, which will always lead to seeking an interest in the righteousness of God by faith. For he is no more a Christian now, than he was really a Jew of old, who is only one outwardly: neither is that baptism, which is outward in the flesh: but he is the real Christian, who is inwardly a true believer, with an obedient faith. And the true baptism is that of the heart, by the washing of regeneration and the renewal of the Holy Ghost; bringing a spiritual frame of mind, and a willing following of truth in its holy ways. Let us pray that we may be made real Christians, not outwardly, but inwardly; in the heart and spirit, not in the letter; baptized, not with water only, but with the Holy Ghost; and let our praise be, not of men, but of God.

Chapter 3

Chapter Outline	
Objections answered.	(1–8)
All mankind are sinners.	(9–18)
Both Jews and Gentiles cannot be justified by their own deeds.	(19, 20)
It is owing to the free grace of God, through faith in the righteousness of Christ, yet the law is not done away.	(21–31)

Verses 1–8

The law could not save in or from sins, yet it gave the Jews advantages for obtaining salvation. Their stated ordinances, education in the knowledge of the true God and his service, and many favours shown to the children of Abraham, all were means of grace, and doubtless were made useful to the conversion of many. But especially the Scriptures were committed to them. Enjoyment of God's word and ordinances, is the chief happiness of a people. But God's promises are made only to believers; therefore the unbelief of some, or of many professors, cannot make this faithfulness of no effect. He will fulfil his promises to his people, and bring his threatened vengeance upon unbelievers. God's judging the world, should for ever silence all doubtings and reflections upon his justice. The wickedness and obstinate unbelief of the Jews, proved man's need of the righteousness of God by faith, and also his justice in punishing for sin. Let us do evil, that good may come, is oftener in the heart than in the mouth of sinners; for few thus justify themselves in their wicked ways. The believer knows that duty belongs to him, and events to God; and that he must not commit any sin, or speak one falsehood, upon the hope, or even assurance, that God may thereby glorify himself. If any speak and act thus, their condemnation is just.

Verses 9–18

Here again is shown that all mankind are under the guilt of sin, as a burden; and under the government and dominion of sin, as enslaved to it, to work wickedness. This is made plain by several passages of Scripture from the Old Testament, which describe the corrupt and depraved state of all men, till grace restrain or change them. Great as our advantages are, these texts describe multitudes who call themselves Christians. Their principles and conduct prove that there is no fear of God before their eyes. And where no fear of God is, no good is to be looked for.

Verses 19, 20

It is in vain to seek for justification by the works of the law. All must plead guilty. Guilty before God, is a dreadful word; but no man can be justified by a law which condemns him for breaking it. The corruption in our nature, will for ever stop any justification by our own works.

Verses 21–26

Must guilty man remain under wrath? Is the wound for ever incurable? No; blessed be God, there is another way laid open for us. This is the righteousness of God; righteousness of his ordaining, and providing, and accepting. It is by that faith which has Jesus Christ for its object; an anointed Saviour, so Jesus Christ signifies. Justifying faith respects Christ as a Saviour, in all his three anointed offices, as Prophet, Priest, and King; trusting in him, accepting him, and cleaving to him: in all these, Jews and Gentiles are alike welcome to God through Christ. There is no difference, his righteousness is upon all that believe; not only offered to them, but put upon them as a crown, as a robe. It is free grace, mere mercy; there is nothing in us to deserve such favours. It comes freely unto us, but Christ bought it, and paid the price. And faith has special regard to the blood of Christ, as that which made the atonement. God, in all this, declares his righteousness. It is plain that he hates sin, when nothing less than the blood of Christ would satisfy for it. And it would not agree with his justice to demand the debt, when the Surety has paid it, and he has accepted that payment in full satisfaction.

Verses 27–31

God will have the great work of the justification and salvation of sinners carried on from first to last, so as to shut out boasting. Now, if we were saved by our own works, boasting would not be excluded. But the way of justification by faith for ever shuts out boasting. Yet believers are not left to be lawless; faith is a law, it is a working grace, wherever it is in truth. By faith, not in this matter an act of obedience, or a good work, but forming the relation between Christ and the sinner, which renders it proper that the believer should be pardoned and justified for the sake of the Saviour, and that the unbeliever who is not thus united or related to him, should remain under condemnation. The law is still of use to convince us of what is past, and to direct us for the future. Though we cannot be saved by it as a covenant, yet we own and submit to it, as a rule in the hand of the Mediator.

Chapter 4

Chapter Outline	
The doctrine of justification by faith is shown by the case of Abraham.	(1–12)
He received the promise through the righteousness of faith.	(13–22)
And we are justified in the same way of believing.	(23–25)

Verses 1–12

To meet the views of the Jews, the apostle first refers to the example of Abraham, in whom the Jews gloried as their most renowned forefather. However exalted in various respects, he had nothing to boast in the presence of God, being saved by grace, through faith, even as others. Without noticing the years which passed before his call, and the failures at times in his obedience, and even in his faith, it was expressly stated in Scripture that "he believed God, and it was counted to him for righteousness," Ge **15**:**6**. From this example it is observed, that if any man could work the full measure required by the law, the reward must be reckoned as a debt, which evidently was not the case even of Abraham, seeing faith was reckoned to him for righteousness. When believers are justified by faith, "their faith being counted for righteousness," their faith does not justify them as a part, small or great, of their righteousness; but as the appointed means of uniting them to Him who has chosen as the name whereby he shall be called, "the Lord our Righteousness." Pardoned people are the only blessed people. It clearly appears from the Scripture, that Abraham was justified several years before his circumcision. It is, therefore, plain that this rite was not necessary in order to justification. It was a sign of the original corruption of human nature. And it was such a sign as was also an outward seal, appointed not only to confirm God's promises to him and to his seed, and their obligation to be the Lord's, but likewise to assure him of his being already a real partaker of the righteousness of faith. Thus Abraham was the spiritual forefather of all believers, who walked after the example of his obedient faith. The seal of the Holy Spirit in our sanctification, making us new creatures, is the inward evidence of the righteousness of faith.

Verses 13–22

The promise was made to Abraham long before the law. It points at Christ, and it refers to the promise, Ge **12**:**3**. In Thee shall all families of the earth be blessed. The law worketh wrath, by showing that every transgressor is exposed to the Divine displeasure. As God intended to give men a title to the promised blessings, so he appointed it to be by faith, that it might be wholly of grace, to make it sure to all who were of the like precious faith with Abraham, whether Jews or Gentiles, in all ages. The justification and salvation of sinners, the taking to himself the Gentiles who had not been a people, were a gracious calling of things which are not, as though they were; and this giving a being to things that were not, proves the almighty power of God. The nature and power of Abraham's faith are shown. He believed God's testimony, and looked for the performance of his promise, firmly hoping when the case seemed hopeless. It is weakness of faith, that makes a man lie poring on the difficulties in the way of a promise. Abraham took it not for a point that would admit of argument or debate. Unbelief is at the bottom of all our staggerings at God's promises. The strength of faith appeared in its victory over fears. God honours faith; and great faith honours God. It was imputed to him for righteousness. Faith is a grace that of all others gives glory to God. Faith clearly is the instrument by which we receive the righteousness of God, the redemption which is by Christ; and that which is the instrument whereby we take or receive it, cannot be the thing itself, nor can it be the gift thereby taken and received. Abraham's faith did not justify him by its own merit or value, but as giving him a part in Christ.

Verses 23–25

The history of Abraham, and of his justification, was recorded to teach men of after-ages; those especially to whom the gospel was then made known. It is plain, that we are not justified by the merit of our own works, but by faith in Jesus Christ and his righteousness; which is the truth urged in this and the foregoing chapter, as the great spring and foundation of all comfort. Christ did meritoriously work our justification and salvation by his death and passion, but the power and perfection thereof, with respect to us, depend on his resurrection. By his death he paid our debt, in his resurrection he received our acquittance, Isa **53**:**8**. When he was discharged, we, in Him and together with Him, received the discharge from the guilt and punishment of all our sins. This last **verse** is an abridgement or summary of the whole gospel.

Chapter 5

Chapter Outline	
The happy effects of justification through faith in the righteousness of Christ.	(1–5)
That we are reconciled by his blood.	(6–11)
The fall of Adam brought all mankind into sin and death.	(12–14)
The grace of God, through the righteousness of Christ, has more power to bring salvation, than Adam's sin had to bring misery,	(15–19)
as grace did superabound.	(20, 21)

Verses 1–5

A blessed change takes place in the sinner's state, when he becomes a true believer, whatever he has been. Being justified by faith he has peace with God. The holy, righteous God, cannot be at peace with a sinner, while under the guilt of sin. Justification takes away the guilt, and so makes way for peace. This is through our Lord Jesus Christ; through him as the great Peace-maker, the Mediator between God and man. The saints' happy state is a state of grace. Into this grace we are brought, which teaches that we were not born in this state. We could not have got into it of ourselves, but we are led into it, as pardoned offenders. Therein we stand, a posture that denotes perseverance; we stand firm and safe, upheld by the power of the enemy. And those who have hope for the glory of God hereafter, have enough to rejoice in now. Tribulation worketh patience, not in and of itself, but the powerful grace of God working in and with the tribulation. Patient sufferers have most of the Divine consolations, which abound as afflictions abound. It works needful experience of ourselves. This hope will not disappoint, because it is sealed with the Holy Spirit as a Spirit of love. It is the gracious work of the blessed Spirit to shed abroad the love of God in the hearts of all the saints. A right sense of God's love to us, will make us not ashamed, either of our hope, or of our sufferings for him.

Verses 6–11

Christ died for sinners; not only such as were useless, but such as were guilty and hateful; such that their everlasting destruction would be to the glory of God's justice. Christ died to save us, not in our sins, but from our sins; and we were yet sinners when he died for us. Nay, the carnal mind is not only an enemy to God, but enmity itself, chap. **8**:**7**; Col **1**:**21**. But God designed to deliver from sin, and to work a great change. While the sinful state continues, God loathes the sinner, and the sinner loathes God, Zec **11**:**8**. And that for such as these Christ should die, is a mystery; no other such an instance of love is known, so that it may well be the employment of eternity to adore and wonder at it. Again; what idea had the apostle when he supposed the case of some one dying for a righteous man? And yet he only put it as a thing that might be. Was it not the undergoing this suffering, that the person intended to be benefitted might be released therefrom? But from what are believers in Christ released by his death? Not from bodily death; for that they all do and must endure. The evil, from which the deliverance could be effected only in this astonishing manner, must be more dreadful than natural death. There is no evil, to which the argument can be applied, except that which the apostle actually affirms, sin, and wrath, the punishment of sin, determined by the unerring justice of God. And if, by Divine grace, they were thus brought to repent, and to believe in Christ, and thus were justified by the price of his bloodshedding, and by faith in that atonement, much more through Him who died for them and rose again, would they be kept from falling under the power of sin and Satan, or departing finally from him. The living Lord of all, will complete the purpose of his dying love, by saving all true believers to the uttermost. Having such a pledge of salvation in the love of God through Christ, the apostle declared that believers not only rejoiced in the hope of heaven, and even in their tribulations for Christ's sake, but they gloried in God also, as their unchangeable Friend and all-sufficient Portion, through Christ only.

Verses 12–14

The design of what follows is plain. It is to exalt our views respecting the blessings Christ has procured for us, by comparing them with the evil which followed upon the fall of our first father; and by showing that these blessings not only extend to the removal of these evils, but far beyond. Adam sinning, his nature became guilty and corrupted, and so came to his children. Thus in him all have sinned. And death is by sin; for death is the wages of sin. Then entered all that misery which is the due desert of sin; temporal, spiritual, eternal death. If Adam had not sinned, he had not died; but a sentence of death was passed, as upon a criminal; it passed through all men, as an infectious disease that none escape. In proof of our union with Adam, and our part in his first transgression, observe, that sin prevailed in the world, for many ages before the giving of the law by Moses. And death reigned in that long time, not only over adults who wilfully sinned, but also over multitudes of infants, which shows that they had fallen in Adam under condemnation, and that the sin of Adam extended to all his posterity. He was a figure or type of Him that was to come as Surety of a new covenant, for all who are related to Him.

Verses 15–19

Through one man's offence, all mankind are exposed to eternal condemnation. But the grace and mercy of God, and the free gift of righteousness and salvation, are through Jesus Christ, as man: yet the Lord from heaven has brought the multitude of believers into a more safe and exalted state than that from which they fell in Adam. This free gift did not place them anew in a state of trial, but fixed them in a state of justification, as Adam would have been placed, had he stood. Notwithstanding the differences, there is a striking similarity. As by the offence of one, sin and death prevailed to the condemnation of all men, so by the righteousness of one, grace prevailed to the justification of all related to Christ by faith. Through the grace of God, the gift by grace has abounded to many through Christ; yet multitudes choose to remain under the dominion of sin and death, rather than to apply for the blessings of the reign of grace. But Christ will in nowise cast out any who are willing to come to him.

Verses 20, 21

By Christ and his righteousness, we have more and greater privileges than we lost by the offence of Adam. The moral law showed that many thoughts, tempers, words, and actions, were sinful, thus transgressions were multiplied. Not making sin to abound the more, but discovering the sinfulness of it, even as the letting in a clearer light into a room, discovers the dust and filth which were there before, but were not seen. The sin of Adam, and the effect of corruption in us, are the abounding of that offence which appeared on the entrance of the law. And the terrors of the law make gospel comforts the more sweet. Thus God the Holy Spirit has, by the blessed apostle, delivered to us a most important truth, full of consolation, suited to our need as sinners. Whatever one may have above another, every man is a sinner against God, stands condemned by the law, and needs pardon. A righteousness that is to justify cannot be made up of a mixture of sin and holiness. There can be no title to an eternal reward without a pure and spotless righteousness: let us look for it, even to the righteousness of Christ.

Chapter 6

Chapter Outline	
Believers must die to sin, and live to God.	(1, 2)
This is urged by their Christian baptism and union with Christ.	(3–10)
They are made alive to God.	(11–15)
And are freed from the dominion of sin.	(16–20)
The end of sin is death, and of holiness everlasting life.	(21–23)

Verses 1, 2

The apostle is very full in pressing the necessity of holiness. He does not explain away the free grace of the gospel, but he shows that connexion between justification and holiness are inseparable. Let the thought be abhorred, of continuing in sin that grace may abound. True believers are dead to sin, therefore they ought not to follow it. No man can at the same time be both dead and alive. He is a fool who, desiring to be dead unto sin, thinks he may live in it.

Verses 3–10

Baptism teaches the necessity of dying to sin, and being as it were buried from all ungodly and unholy pursuits, and of rising to walk with God in newness of life. Unholy professors may have had the outward sign of a death unto sin, and a new birth unto righteousness, but they never passed from the family of Satan to that of God. The corrupt nature, called the old man, because derived from our first father Adam, is crucified with Christ, in every true believer, by the grace derived from the cross. It is weakened and in a dying state, though it yet struggles for life, and even for victory. But the whole body of sin, whatever is not according to the holy law of God, must be done away, so that the believer may no more be the slave of sin, but live to God, and find happiness in his service.

Verses 11–15

The strongest motives against sin, and to enforce holiness, are here stated. Being made free from the reign of sin, alive unto God, and having the prospect of eternal life, it becomes believers to be greatly concerned to advance thereto. But, as unholy lusts are not quite rooted out in this life, it must be the care of the Christian to resist their motions, earnestly striving, that, through Divine grace, they may not prevail in this mortal state. Let the thought that this state will soon be at an end, encourage the true Christian, as to the motions of lusts, which so often perplex and distress him. Let us present all our powers to God, as weapons or tools ready for the warfare, and work of righteousness, in his service. There is strength in the covenant of grace for us. Sin shall not have dominion. God's promises to us are more powerful and effectual for mortifying sin, than our promises to God. Sin may struggle in a real believer, and create him a great deal of trouble, but it shall not have dominion; it may vex him, but it shall not rule over him. Shall any take occasion from this encouraging doctrine to allow themselves in the practice of any sin? Far be such abominable thoughts, so contrary to the perfections of God, and the design of his gospel, so opposed to being under grace. What can be a stronger motive against sin than the love of Christ? Shall we sin against so much goodness, and such love?

Verses 16–20

Every man is the servant of the master to whose commands he yields himself; whether it be the sinful dispositions of his heart, in actions which lead to death, or the new and spiritual obedience implanted by regeneration. The apostle rejoiced now they obeyed from the heart the gospel, into which they were delivered as into a mould. As the same metal becomes a new vessel, when melted and recast in another mould, so the believer has become a new creature. And there is great difference in the liberty of mind and spirit, so opposite to the state of slavery, which the true Christian has in the service of his rightful Lord, whom he is enabled to consider as his Father, and himself as his son and heir, by the adoption of grace. The dominion of sin consists in being willingly slaves thereto, not in being harassed by it as a hated power, struggling for victory. Those who now are the servants of God, once were the slaves of sin.

Verses 21–23

The pleasure and profit of sin do not deserve to be called fruit. Sinners are but ploughing iniquity, sowing vanity, and reaping the same. Shame came into the world with sin, and is still the certain effect of it. The end of sin is death. Though the way may seem pleasant and inviting, yet it will be bitterness in the latter end. From this condemnation the believer is set at liberty, when made free from sin. If the fruit is unto holiness, if there is an active principle of true and growing grace, the end will be everlasting life; a very happy end! Though the way is up-hill, though it is narrow, thorny, and beset, yet everlasting life at the end of it is sure. The gift of God is eternal life. And this gift is through Jesus Christ our Lord. Christ purchased it, prepared it, prepares us for it, preserves us to it; he is the All in all in our salvation.

Chapter 7

Chapter Outline	
Believers are united to Christ, that they may bring forth fruit unto God.	(1–6)
The use and excellence of the law.	(7–13)
The spiritual conflicts between corruption and grace in a believer.	(14–25)

Verses 1–6

So long as a man continues under the law as a covenant, and seeks justification by his own obedience, he continues the slave of sin in some form. Nothing but the Spirit of life in Christ Jesus, can make any sinner free from the law of sin and death. Believers are delivered from that power of the law, which condemns for the sins committed by them. And they are delivered from that power of the law which stirs up and provokes the sin that dwells in them. Understand this not of the law as a rule, but as a covenant of works. In profession and privilege, we are under a covenant of grace, and not under a covenant of works; under the gospel of Christ, not under the law of Moses. The difference is spoken of under the similitude or figure of being married to a new husband. The second marriage is to Christ. By death we are freed from obligation to the law as a covenant, as the wife is from her vows to her husband. In our believing powerfully and effectually, we are dead to the law, and have no more to do with it than the dead servant, who is freed from his master, has to do with his master's yoke. The day of our believing, is the day of being united to the Lord Jesus. We enter upon a life of dependence on him, and duty to him. Good works are from union with Christ; as the fruitfulness of the vine is the product of its being united to its roots; there is no fruit to God, till we are united to Christ. The law, and the greatest efforts of one under the law, still in the flesh, under the power of corrupt principles, cannot set the heart right with regard to the love of God, overcome worldly lusts, or give truth and sincerity in the inward parts, or any thing that comes by the special sanctifying influences of the Holy Spirit. Nothing more than a formal obedience to the outward letter of any precept, can be performed by us, without the renewing, new-creating grace of the new covenant.

Verses 7–13

There is no way of coming to that knowledge of sin, which is necessary to repentance, and therefore to peace and pardon, but by trying our hearts and lives by the law. In his own case the apostle would not have known the sinfulness of his thoughts, motives, and actions, but by the law. That perfect standard showed how wrong his heart and life were, proving his sins to be more numerous than he had before thought, but it did not contain any provision of mercy or grace for his relief. He is ignorant of human nature and the perverseness of his own heart, who does not perceive in himself a readiness to fancy there is something desirable in what is out of reach. We may perceive this in our children, though self-love makes us blind to it in ourselves. The more humble and spiritual any Christian is, the more clearly will he perceive that the apostle describes the true believer, from his first convictions of sin to his greatest progress in grace, during this present imperfect state. St. Paul was once a Pharisee, ignorant of the spirituality of the law, having some correctness of character, without knowing his inward depravity. When the commandment came to his conscience by the convictions of the Holy Spirit, and he saw what it demanded, he found his sinful mind rise against it. He felt at the same time the evil of sin, his own sinful state, that he was unable to fulfil the law, and was like a criminal when condemned. But though the evil principle in the human heart produces sinful motions, and the more by taking occasion of the commandment; yet the law is holy, and the commandment holy, just, and good. It is not favourable to sin, which it pursues into the heart, and discovers and reproves in the inward motions thereof. Nothing is so good but a corrupt and vicious nature will pervert it. The same heat that softens wax, hardens clay. Food or medicine when taken wrong, may cause death, though its nature is to nourish or to heal. The law may cause death through man's depravity, but sin is the poison that brings death. Not the law, but sin discovered by the law, was made death to the apostle. The ruinous nature of sin, and the sinfulness of the human heart, are here clearly shown.

Verses 14–17

Compared with the holy rule of conduct in the law of God, the apostle found himself so very far short of perfection, that he seemed to be carnal; like a man who is sold against his will to a hated master, from whom he cannot set himself at liberty. A real Christian unwillingly serves this hated master, yet cannot shake off the galling chain, till his powerful and gracious Friend above, rescues him. The remaining evil of his heart is a real and humbling hinderance to his serving God as angels do and the spirits of just made perfect. This strong language was the result of St. Paul's great advance in holiness, and the depth of his self-abasement and hatred of sin. If we do not understand this language, it is because we are so far beneath him in holiness, knowledge of the spirituality of God's law, and the evil of our own hearts, and hatred of moral evil. And many believers have adopted the apostle's language, showing that it is suitable to their deep feelings of abhorrence of sin, and self-abasement. The apostle enlarges on the conflict he daily maintained with the remainder of his original depravity. He was frequently led into tempers, words, or actions, which he did not approve or allow in his renewed judgement and affections. By distinguishing his real self, his spiritual part, from the self, or flesh, in which sin dwelt, and by observing that the evil actions were done, not by him, but by sin dwelling in him, the apostle did not mean that men are not accountable for their sins, but he teaches the evil of their sins, by showing that they are all done against reason and conscience. Sin dwelling in a man, does not prove its ruling, or having dominion over him. If a man dwells in a city, or in a country, still he may not rule there.

Verses 18–22

The more pure and holy the heart is, it will have the more quick feeling as to the sin that remains in it. The believer sees more of the beauty of holiness and the excellence of the law. His earnest desires to obey, increase as he grows in grace. But the whole good on which his will is fully bent, he does not do; sin ever springing up in him, through remaining corruption, he often does evil, though against the fixed determination of his will. The motions of sin within grieved the apostle. If by the striving of the flesh against the Spirit, was meant that he could not do or perform as the Spirit suggested, so also, by the effectual opposition of the Spirit, he could not do what the flesh prompted him to do. How different this case from that of those who make themselves easy with regard to the inward motions of the flesh prompting them to evil; who, against the light and warning of conscience, go on, even in outward practice, to do evil, and thus, with forethought, go on in the road to perdition! For as the believer is under grace, and his will is for the way of holiness, he sincerely delights in the law of God, and in the holiness which it demands, according to his inward man; that new man in him, which after God is created in true holiness.

Verses 23–25

This passage does not represent the apostle as one that walked after the flesh, but as one that had it greatly at heart, not to walk so. And if there are those who abuse this passage, as they also do the other Scriptures, to their own destruction, yet serious Christians find cause to bless God for having thus provided for their support and comfort. We are not, because of the abuse of such as are blinded by their own lusts, to find fault with the scripture, or any just and well warranted interpretation of it. And no man who is not engaged in this conflict, can clearly understand the meaning of these words, or rightly judge concerning this painful conflict, which led the apostle to bemoan himself as a wretched man, constrained to what he abhorred. He could not deliver himself; and this made him the more fervently thank God for the way of salvation revealed through Jesus Christ, which promised him, in the end, deliverance from this enemy. So then, says he, I myself, with my mind, my prevailing judgement, affections, and purposes, as a regenerate man, by Divine grace, serve and obey the law of God; but with the flesh, the carnal nature, the remains of depravity, I serve the law of sin, which wars against the law of my mind. Not serving it so as to live in it, or to allow it, but as unable to free himself from it, even in his very best state, and needing to look for help and deliverance out of himself. It is evident that he thanks God for Christ, as our deliverer, as our atonement and righteousness in himself, and not because of any holiness wrought in us. He knew of no such salvation, and disowned any such title to it. He was willing to act in all points agreeable to the law, in his mind and conscience, but was hindered by indwelling sin, and never attained the perfection the law requires. What can be deliverance for a man always sinful, but the free grace of God, as offered in Christ Jesus? The power of Divine grace, and of the Holy Spirit, could root out sin from our hearts even in this life, if Divine wisdom had not otherwise thought fit. But it is suffered, that Christians might constantly feel, and understand thoroughly, the wretched state from which Divine grace saves them; might be kept from trusting in themselves; and might ever hold all their consolation and hope, from the rich and free grace of God in Christ.

Chapter 8

Chapter Outline	
The freedom of believers from condemnation.	(1–9)
Their privileges as being the children of God.	(10–17)
Their hopeful prospects under tribulations.	(18–25)
Their assistance from the Spirit in prayer.	(26, 27)
Their interest in the love of God.	(28–31)
Their final triumph, through Christ.	(32–39)

Verses 1–9

Believers may be chastened of the Lord, but will not be condemned with the world. By their union with Christ through faith, they are thus secured. What is the principle of their walk; the flesh or the Spirit, the old or the new nature, corruption or grace? For which of these do we make provision, by which are we governed? The unrenewed will is unable to keep any commandment fully. And the law, besides outward duties, requires inward obedience. God showed abhorrence of sin by the sufferings of his Son in the flesh, that the believer's person might be pardoned and justified. Thus satisfaction was made to Divine justice, and the way of salvation opened for the sinner. By the Spirit the law of love is written upon the heart, and though the righteousness of the law is not fulfilled by us, yet, blessed be God, it is fulfilled in us; there is that in all true believers, which answers the intention of the law. The favour of God, the welfare of the soul, the concerns of eternity, are the things of the Spirit, which those that are after the Spirit do mind. Which way do our thoughts move with most pleasure? Which way go our plans and contrivances? Are we most wise for the world, or for our souls? Those that live in pleasure are dead, **1**Ti **5**:**6**. A sanctified soul is a living soul; and that life is peace. The carnal mind is not only an enemy to God, but enmity itself. The carnal man may, by the power of Divine grace, be made subject to the law of God, but the carnal mind never can; that must be broken and driven out. We may know our real state and character by inquiring whether we have the Spirit of God and Christ, or not, ver. **9**. Ye are not in the flesh, but in the Spirit. Having the Spirit of Christ, means having a turn of mind in some degree like the mind that was in Christ Jesus, and is to be shown by a life and conversation suitable to his precepts and example.

Verses 10–17

If the Spirit be in us, Christ is in us. He dwells in the heart by faith. Grace in the soul is its new nature; the soul is alive to God, and has begun its holy happiness which shall endure for ever. The righteousness of Christ imputed, secures the soul, the better part, from death. From hence we see how much it is our duty to walk, not after the flesh, but after the Spirit. If any habitually live according to corrupt lustings, they will certainly perish in their sins, whatever they profess. And what can a worldly life present, worthy for a moment to be put against this noble prize of our high calling? Let us then, by the Spirit, endeavour more and more to mortify the flesh. Regeneration by the Holy Spirit brings a new and Divine life to the soul, though in a feeble state. And the sons of God have the Spirit to work in them the disposition of children; they have not the spirit of bondage, which the Old Testament church was under, through the darkness of that dispensation. The Spirit of adoption was not then plentifully poured out. Also it refers to that spirit of bondage, under which many saints were at their conversion. Many speak peace to themselves, to whom God does not speak peace. But those who are sanctified, have God's Spirit witnessing with their spirits, in and by his speaking peace to the soul. Though we may now seem to be losers for Christ, we shall not, we cannot, be losers by him in the end.

Verses 18–25

The sufferings of the saints strike no deeper than the things of time, last no longer than the present time, are light afflictions, and but for a moment. How vastly different are the sentence of the word and the sentiment of the world, concerning the sufferings of this present time! Indeed the whole creation seems to wait with earnest expectation for the period when the children of God shall be manifested in the glory prepared for them. There is an impurity, deformity, and infirmity, which has come upon the creature by the fall of man. There is an enmity of one creature to another. And they are used, or abused rather, by men as instruments of sin. Yet this deplorable state of the creation is in hope. God will deliver it from thus being held in bondage to man's depravity. The miseries of the human race, through their own and each other's wickedness, declare that the world is not always to continue as it is. Our having received the first-fruits of the Spirit, quickens our desires, encourages our hopes, and raises our expectations. Sin has been, and is, the guilty cause of all the suffering that exists in the creation of God. It has brought on the woes of earth; it has kindled the flames of hell. As to man, not a tear has been shed, not a groan has been uttered, not a pang has been felt, in body or mind, that has not come from sin. This is not all; sin is to be looked at as it affects the glory of God. Of this how fearfully regardless are the bulk of mankind! Believers have been brought into a state of safety; but their comfort consists rather in hope than in enjoyment. From this hope they cannot be turned by the vain expectation of finding satisfaction in the things of time and sense. We need patience, our way is rough and long; but He that shall come, will come, though he seems to tarry.

Verses 26, 27

Though the infirmities of Christians are many and great, so that they would be overpowered if left to themselves, yet the Holy Spirit supports them. The Spirit, as an enlightening Spirit, teaches us what to pray for; as a sanctifying Spirit, works and stirs up praying graces; as a comforting Spirit, silences our fears, and helps us over all discouragements. The Holy Spirit is the spring of all desires toward God, which are often more than words can utter. The Spirit who searches the hearts, can perceive the mind and will of the spirit, the renewed mind, and advocates his cause. The Spirit makes intercession to God, and the enemy prevails not.

Verses 28–31

That is good for the saints which does their souls good. Every providence tends to the spiritual good of those that love God; in breaking them off from sin, bringing them nearer to God, weaning them from the world, and fitting them for heaven. When the saints act out of character, corrections will be employed to bring them back again. And here is the order of the causes of our salvation, a golden chain, one which cannot be broken. **1**. Whom he did foreknow, he also did predestinate to be conformed to the image of his Son. All that God designed for glory and happiness as the end, he decreed to grace and holiness as the way. The whole human race deserved destruction; but for reasons not perfectly known to us, God determined to recover some by regeneration and the power of his grace. He predestinated, or before decreed, that they should be conformed to the image of his Son. In this life they are in part renewed, and walk in his steps. **2**. Whom he did predestinate, them he also called. It is an effectual call, from self and earth to God, and Christ, and heaven, as our end; from sin and vanity to grace and holiness, as our way. This is the gospel call. The love of God, ruling in the hearts of those who once were enemies to him, proves that they have been called according to his purpose. **3**. Whom he called, them he also justified. None are thus justified but those that are effectually called. Those who stand out against the gospel call, abide under guilt and wrath. **4**. Whom he justified, them he also glorified. The power of corruption being broken in effectual calling, and the guilt of sin removed in justification, nothing can come between that soul and glory. This encourages our faith and hope; for, as for God, his way, his work, is perfect. The apostle speaks as one amazed, and swallowed up in admiration, wondering at the height and depth, and length and breadth, of the love of Christ, which passeth knowledge. The more we know of other things, the less we wonder; but the further we are led into gospel mysteries, the more we are affected by them. While God is for us, and we keep in his love, we may with holy boldness defy all the powers of darkness.

Verses 32–39

All things whatever, in heaven and earth, are not so great a display of God's free love, as the gift of his coequal Son to be the atonement on the cross for the sin of man; and all the rest follows upon union with him, and interest in him. All things, all which can be the causes or means of any real good to the faithful Christian. He that has prepared a crown and a kingdom for us, will give us what we need in the way to it. Men may justify themselves, though the accusations are in full force against them; but if God justifies, that answers all. By Christ we are thus secured. By the merit of his death he paid our debt. Yea, rather that is risen again. This is convincing evidence that Divine justice was satisfied. We have such a Friend at the right hand of God; all power is given to him. He is there, making intercession. Believer! does your soul say within you, Oh that he were mine! and oh that I were his; that I could please him and live to him! Then do not toss your spirit and perplex your thoughts in fruitless, endless doubtings, but as you are convinced of ungodliness, believe on Him who justifies the ungodly. You are condemned, yet Christ is dead and risen. Flee to Him as such. God having manifested his love in giving his own Son for us, can we think that any thing should turn aside or do away that love? Troubles neither cause nor show any abatement of his love. Whatever believers may be separated from, enough remains. None can take Christ from the believer: none can take the believer from Him; and that is enough. All other hazards signify nothing. Alas, poor sinners! though you abound with the possessions of this world, what vain things are they! Can you say of any of them, Who shall separate us? You may be removed from pleasant dwellings, and friends, and estates. You may even live to see and seek your parting. At last you must part, for you must die. Then farewell, all this world accounts most valuable. And what hast thou left, poor soul, who hast not Christ, but that which thou wouldest gladly part with, and canst not; the condemning guilt of all thy sins! But the soul that is in Christ, when other things are pulled away, cleaves to Christ, and these separations pain him not. Yea, when death comes, that breaks all other unions, even that of the soul and body, it carries the believer's soul into the nearest union with its beloved Lord Jesus, and the full enjoyment of him for ever.

Chapter 9

Chapter Outline	
The apostle's concern that his countrymen were strangers to the gospel.	(1–5)
The promises are made good to the spiritual seed of Abraham.	(6–13)
Answers to objections against God's sovereign conduct, in exercising mercy and justice.	(14–24)
This sovereignty is in God's dealing both with Jews and Gentiles.	(25–29)
The falling short of the Jews is owing to their seeking justification, not by faith, but by the works of the law.	(30–33)

Verses 1–5

Being about to discuss the rejection of the Jews and the calling of the Gentiles, and to show that the whole agrees with the sovereign electing love of God, the apostle expresses strongly his affection for his people. He solemnly appeals to Christ; and his conscience, enlightened and directed by the Holy Spirit, bore witness to his sincerity. He would submit to be treated as "accursed," to be disgraced, crucified; and even for a time be in the deepest horror and distress; if he could rescue his nation from the destruction about to come upon them for their obstinate unbelief. To be insensible to the eternal condition of our fellow-creatures, is contrary both to the love required by the law, and the mercy of the gospel. They had long been professed worshippers of Jehovah. The law, and the national covenant which was grounded thereon, belonged to them. The temple worship was typical of salvation by the Messiah, and the means of communion with God. All the promises concerning Christ and his salvation were given to them. He is not only over all, as Mediator, but he is God blessed for ever.

Verses 6–13

The rejection of the Jews by the gospel dispensation, did not break God's promise to the patriarchs. The promises and threatenings shall be fulfilled. Grace does not run in the blood; nor are saving benefits always found with outward church privileges. Not only some of Abraham's seed were chosen, and others not, but God therein wrought according to the counsel of his own will. God foresaw both Esau and Jacob as born in sin, by nature children of wrath even as others. If left to themselves they would have continued in sin through life; but for wise and holy reasons, not made known to us, he purposed to change Jacob's heart, and to leave Esau to his per**verse**ness. This instance of Esau and Jacob throws light upon the Divine conduct to the fallen race of man. The whole Scripture shows the difference between the professed Christian and the real believer. Outward privileges are bestowed on many who are not the children of God. There is, however, full encouragement to diligent use of the means of grace which God has appointed.

Verses 14–24

Whatever God does, must be just. Wherein the holy, happy people of God differ from others, God's grace alone makes them differ. In this preventing, effectual, distinguishing grace, he acts as a benefactor, whose grace is his own. None have deserved it; so that those who are saved, must thank God only; and those who perish, must blame themselves only, Hos **13**:**9**. God is bound no further than he has been pleased to bind himself by his own covenant and promise, which is his revealed will. And this is, that he will receive, and not cast out, those that come to Christ; but the drawing of souls in order to that coming, is an anticipating, distinguishing favour to whom he will. Why does he yet find fault? This is not an objection to be made by the creature against his Creator, by man against God. The truth, as it is in Jesus, abases man as nothing, as less than nothing, and advances God as sovereign Lord of all. Who art thou that art so foolish, so feeble, so unable to judge the Divine counsels? It becomes us to submit to him, not to reply against him. Would not men allow the infinite God the same sovereign right to manage the affairs of the creation, as the potter exercises in disposing of his clay, when of the same lump he makes one vessel to a more honourable, and one to a meaner use? God could do no wrong, however it might appear to men. God will make it appear that he hates sin. Also, he formed vessels filled with mercy. Sanctification is the preparation of the soul for glory. This is God's work. Sinners fit themselves for hell, but it is God who prepares saints for heaven; and all whom God designs for heaven hereafter, he fits for heaven now. Would we know who these vessels of mercy are? Those whom God has called; and these not of the Jews only, but of the Gentiles. Surely there can be no unrighteousness in any of these Divine dispensations. Nor in God's exercising long-suffering, patience, and forbearance towards sinners under increasing guilt, before he brings utter destruction upon them. The fault is in the hardened sinner himself. As to all who love and fear God, however such truths appear beyond their reason to fathom, yet they should keep silence before him. It is the Lord alone who made us to differ; we should adore his pardoning mercy and new-creating grace, and give diligence to make our calling and election sure.

Verses 25–29

The rejecting of the Jews, and the taking in the Gentiles, were foretold in the Old Testament. It tends very much to the clearing of a truth, to observe how the Scripture is fulfilled in it. It is a wonder of Divine power and mercy that there are any saved: for even those left to be a seed, if God had dealt with them according to their sins, had perished with the rest. This great truth this Scripture teaches us. Even among the vast number of professing Christians it is to be feared that only a remnant will be saved.

Verses 30–33

The Gentiles knew not their guilt and misery, therefore were not careful to procure a remedy. Yet they attained to righteousness by faith. Not by becoming proselytes to the Jewish religion, and submitting to the ceremonial law; but by embracing Christ, and believing in him, and submitting to the gospel. The Jews talked much of justification and holiness, and seemed very ambitious to be the favourites of God. They sought, but not in the right way, not in the humbling way, not in the appointed way. Not by faith, not by embracing Christ, depending upon Christ, and submitting to the gospel. They expected justification by observing the precepts and ceremonies of the law of Moses. The unbelieving Jews had a fair offer of righteousness, life, and salvation, made them upon gospel terms, which they did not like, and would not accept. Have we sought to know how we may be justified before God, seeking that blessing in the way here pointed out, by faith in Christ, as the Lord our Righteousness? Then we shall not be ashamed in that awful day, when all refuges of lies shall be swept away, and the Divine wrath shall overflow every hiding-place but that which God hath prepared in his own Son.

Chapter 10

Chapter Outline	
The apostle's earnest desire for the salvation of the Jews.	(1–4)
The difference between the righteousness of the law, and the righteousness of faith.	(5–11)
The Gentiles stand on a level with the Jews, in justification and salvation.	(12–17)
The Jews might know this from Old Testament prophecies.	(18–21)

Verses 1–4

The Jews built on a false foundation, and refused to come to Christ for free salvation by faith, and numbers in every age do the same in various ways. The strictness of the law showed men their need of salvation by grace, through faith. And the ceremonies shadowed forth

Christ as fulfilling the righteousness, and bearing the curse of the law. So that even under the law, all who were justified before God, obtained that blessing by faith, whereby they were made partakers of the perfect righteousness of the promised Redeemer. The law is not destroyed, nor the intention of the Lawgiver disappointed; but full satisfaction being made by the death of Christ for our breach of the law, the end is gained. That is, Christ has fulfilled the whole law, therefore whoever believeth in him, is counted just before God, as much as though he had fulfilled the whole law himself. Sinners never could go on in vain fancies of their own righteousness, if they knew the justice of God as a Governor, or his righteousness as a Saviour.

Verses 5–11

The self-condemned sinner need not perplex himself how this righteousness may be found. When we speak of looking upon Christ, and receiving, and feeding upon him, it is not Christ in heaven, nor Christ in the deep, that we mean; but Christ in the promise, Christ offered in the word. Justification by faith in Christ is a plain doctrine. It is brought before the mind and heart of every one, thus leaving him without excuse for unbelief. If a man confessed faith in Jesus, as the Lord and Saviour of lost sinners, and really believed in his heart that God had raised him from the dead, thus showing that he had accepted the atonement, he should be saved by the righteousness of Christ, imputed to him through faith. But no faith is justifying which is not powerful in sanctifying the heart, and regulating all its affections by the love of Christ. We must devote and give up to God our souls and our bodies: our souls in believing with the heart, and our bodies in confessing with the mouth. The believer shall never have cause to repent his confident trust in the Lord Jesus. Of such faith no sinner shall be ashamed before God; and he ought to glory in it before men.

Verses 12–17

There is not one God to the Jews, more kind, and another to the Gentiles, who is less kind; the Lord is a Father to all men. The promise is the same to all, who call on the name of the Lord Jesus as the Son of God, as God manifest in the flesh. All believers thus call upon the Lord Jesus, and none else will do so humbly or sincerely. But how should any call on the Lord Jesus, the Divine Saviour, who had not heard of him? And what is the life of a Christian but a life of prayer? It shows that we feel our dependence on him, and are ready to give up ourselves to him, and have a believing expectation of our all from him. It was necessary that the gospel should be preached to the Gentiles. Somebody must show them what they are to believe. How welcome the gospel ought to be to those to whom it was preached! The gospel is given, not only to be known and believed, but to be obeyed. It is not a system of notions, but a rule of practice. The beginning, progress, and strength of faith is by hearing. But it is only hearing the word, as the word of God that will strengthen faith.

Verses 18–21

Did not the Jews know that the Gentiles were to be called in? They might have known it from Moses and Isaiah. Isaiah speaks plainly of the grace and favour of God, as going before in the receiving of the Gentiles. Was not this our own case? Did not God begin in love, and make himself known to us when we did not ask after him? The patience of God towards provoking sinners is wonderful. The time of God's patience is called a day, light as day, and fit for work and business; but limited as a day, and there is a night at the end of it. God's patience makes man's disobedience worse, and renders that the more sinful. We may wonder at the mercy of God, that his goodness is not overcome by man's badness; we may wonder at the wickedness of man, that his badness is not overcome by God's goodness. And it is a matter of joy to think that God has sent the message of grace to so many millions, by the wide spread of his gospel.

Chapter 11

Chapter Outline	
The rejection of the Jews is not universal.	(1–10)
God overruled their unbelief for making the Gentiles partakers of gospel privileges.	(11–21)
The Gentiles cautioned against pride and unbelief, The Jews shall be called as a nation, and brought into God`s visible covenant again.	(22–32)
A solemn adoring of the wisdom, goodness, and justice of God.	(33–36)

Verses 1–10

There was a chosen remnant of believing Jews, who had righteousness and life by faith in Jesus Christ. These were kept according to the election of grace. If then this election was of grace, it could not be of works, either performed or foreseen. Every truly good disposition in a fallen creature must be the effect, therefore it cannot be the cause, of the grace of God bestowed on him. Salvation from the first to the last must be either of grace or of debt. These things are so directly contrary to each other that they cannot be blended together. God glorifies his grace by changing the hearts and tempers of the rebellious. How then should they wonder and praise him! The Jewish nation were as in a deep sleep, without knowledge of their danger, or concern about it; having no sense of their need of the Saviour, or of their being upon the borders of eternal ruin. David, having by the Spirit foretold the sufferings of Christ from his own people, the Jews, foretells the dreadful judgments of God upon them for it, Ps **69**. This teaches us how to understand other prayers of David against his enemies; they are prophecies of the judgments of God, not expressions of his own anger. Divine curses will work long; and we have our eyes darkened, if we are bowed down in worldly-mindedness.

Verses 11–21

The gospel is the greatest riches of every place where it is. As therefore the righteous rejection of the unbelieving Jews, was the occasion of so large a multitude of the Gentiles being reconciled to God, and at peace with him; the future receiving of the Jews into the church would be such a change, as would resemble a general resurrection of the dead in sin to a life of righteousness. Abraham was as the root of the church. The Jews continued branches of this tree till, as a nation, they rejected the Messiah; after that, their relation to Abraham and to God was, as it were, cut off. The Gentiles were grafted into this tree in their room; being admitted into the church of God. Multitudes were made heirs of Abraham's faith, holiness and blessedness. It is the natural state of every one of us, to be wild by nature. Conversion is as the grafting in of wild branches into the good olive. The wild olive was often ingrafted into the fruitful one when it began to decay, and this not only brought forth fruit, but caused the decaying olive to revive and flourish. The Gentiles, of free grace, had been grafted in to share advantages. They ought therefore to beware of self-confidence, and every kind of pride or ambition; lest, having only a dead faith, and an empty profession, they should turn from God, and forfeit their privileges. If we stand at all, it is by faith; we are guilty and helpless in ourselves, and are to be humble, watchful, afraid of self-deception, or of being overcome by temptation. Not only are we at first justified by faith, but kept to the end in that justified state by faith only; yet, by a faith which is not alone, but which worketh by love to God and man.

Verses 22–32

Of all judgments, spiritual judgments are the sorest; of these the apostle is here speaking. The restoration of the Jews is, in the course of things, far less improbable than the call of the Gentiles to be the children of Abraham; and though others now possess these privileges, it will not hinder their being admitted again. By rejecting the gospel, and by their indignation at its being preached to the Gentiles, the Jews were become enemies to God; yet they are still to be favoured for the sake of their pious fathers. Though at present they are enemies to the gospel, for their hatred to the Gentiles; yet, when God's time is come, that will no longer exist, and God's love to their fathers will be remembered. True grace seeks not to confine God's favour. Those who find mercy themselves, should endeavour that through their mercy others also may obtain mercy. Not that the Jews will be restored to have their priesthood, and temple, and ceremonies again; an end is put to all these; but they are to be brought to believe in Christ, the true become one sheep-fold with the Gentiles, under Christ the Great Shepherd. The captivities of Israel, their dispersion, and their being shut out from the church, are emblems of the believer's corrections for doing wrong; and the continued care of the Lord towards that people, and the final mercy and blessed restoration intended for them, show the patience and love of God.

Verses 33–36

The apostle Paul knew the mysteries of the kingdom of God as well as ever any man; yet he confesses himself at a loss; and despairing to find the bottom, he humbly sits down at the brink, and adores the depth. Those who know most in this imperfect state, feel their own weakness most. There is not only depth in the Divine counsels, but riches; abundance of that which is precious and valuable. The Divine counsels are complete; they have not only depth and height, but breadth and length, Eph **3**:**18**, and that passing knowledge. There is that vast distance and disproportion between God and man, between the Creator and the creature, which for ever shuts us from knowledge of his ways. What man shall teach God how to govern the world? The apostle adores the sovereignty of the Divine counsels. All things in heaven and earth, especially those which relate to our salvation, that belong to our peace, are all of him by way of creation, through him by way of providence, that they may be to him in their end. Of God, as the Spring and Fountain of all, through Christ, to God, as the end. These include all God's relations to his creatures; if all are of Him, and through Him, all should be to Him, and for Him. Whatever begins, let God's glory be the end: especially let us adore him when we talk of the Divine counsels and actings. The saints in heaven never dispute, but always praise.

Chapter 12

Chapter Outline	
Believers are to dedicate themselves to God.	(1, 2)
To be humble, and faithfully to use their spiritual gifts, in their respective stations.	(3–8)
Exhortations to various duties.	(9–16)
And to peaceable conduct towards all men, with forbearance and benevolence.	(17–21)

Verses 1, 2

The apostle having closed the part of his epistle wherein he argues and proves various doctrines which are practically applied, here urges important duties from gospel principles. He entreated the Romans, as his brethren in Christ, by the mercies of God, to present their bodies as a living sacrifice to Him. This is a powerful appeal. We receive from the Lord every day the fruits of his mercy. Let us render ourselves; all we are, all we have, all we can do: and after all, what return is it for such very rich receivings? It is acceptable to God: a reasonable service, which we are able and ready to give a reason for, and which we understand. Conversion and sanctification are the renewing of the mind; a change, not of the substance, but of the qualities of the soul. The progress of sanctification, dying to sin more and more, and living to righteousness more and more, is the carrying on this renewing work, till it is perfected in glory. The great enemy to this renewal is, conformity to this world. Take heed of forming plans for happiness, as though it lay in the things of this world, which soon pass away. Do not fall in with the customs of those who walk in the lusts of the flesh, and mind earthly things. The work of the Holy Ghost first begins in the understanding, and is carried on to the will, affections, and conversation, till there is a change of the whole man into the likeness of God, in knowledge, righteousness, and true holiness. Thus, to be godly, is to give up ourselves to God.

Verses 3–8

Pride is a sin in us by nature; we need to be cautioned and armed against it. All the saints make up one body in Christ, who is the Head of the body, and the common Centre of their unity. In the spiritual body, some are fitted for and called to one sort of work; others for another sort of work. We are to do all the good we can, one to another, and for the common benefit. If we duly thought about the powers we have, and how far we fail properly to improve them, it would humble us. But as we must not be proud of our talents, so we must take heed lest, under a pretence of humility and self-denial, we are slothful in laying out ourselves for the good of others. We must not say, I am nothing, therefore I will sit still, and do nothing; but, I am nothing in myself, and therefore I will lay out myself to the utmost, in the strength of the grace of Christ. Whatever our gifts or situations may be, let us try to employ ourselves humbly, diligently, cheerfully, and in simplicity; not seeking our own credit or profit, but the good of many, for this world and that which is to come.

Verses 9–16

The professed love of Christians to each other should be sincere, free from deceit, and unmeaning and deceitful compliments. Depending on Divine grace, they must detest and dread all evil, and love and delight in whatever is kind and useful. We must not only do that which is good, but we must cleave to it. All our duty towards one another is summed up in one word, love. This denotes the love of parents to their children; which is more tender and natural than any other; unforced, unconstrained. And love to God and man, with zeal for the gospel, will make the wise Christian diligent in all his wordly business, and in gaining superior skill. God must be served with the spirit, under the influences of the Holy Spirit. He is honoured by our hope and trust in him, especially when we rejoice in that hope.

He is served, not only by working for him, but by sitting still quietly, when he calls us to suffer. Patience for God's sake, is true piety. Those that rejoice in hope, are likely to be patient in tribulation. We should not be cold in the duty of prayer, nor soon weary of it. Not only must there be kindness to friends and brethren, but Christians must not harbour anger against enemies. It is but mock love, which rests in words of kindness, while our brethren need real supplies, and it is in our power to furnish them. Be ready to entertain those who do good: as there is occasion, we must welcome strangers. Bless, and curse not. It means thorough good will; not, bless them when at prayer, and curse them at other times; but bless them always, and curse not at all. True Christian love will make us take part in the sorrows and joys of each other. Labour as much as you can to agree in the same spiritual truths; and when you come short of that, yet agree in affection. Look upon worldly pomp and dignity with holy contempt. Do not mind it; be not in love with it. Be reconciled to the place God in his providence puts you in, whatever it be. Nothing is below us, but sin. We shall never find in our hearts to condescend to others, while we indulge conceit of ourselves; therefore that must be mortified.

Verses 17–21

Since men became enemies to God, they have been very ready to be enemies one to another. And those that embrace religion, must expect to meet with enemies in a world whose smiles seldom agree with Christ's. Recompense to no man evil for evil. That is a brutish recompence, befitting only animals, which are not conscious of any being above them, or of any existence hereafter. And not only do, but study and take care to do, that which is amiable and creditable, and recommends religion to all with whom you con**verse**. Study the things that make for peace; if it be possible, without offending God and wounding conscience. Avenge not yourselves. This is a hard lesson to corrupt nature, therefore a remedy against it is added. Give place unto wrath. When a man's passion is up, and the stream is strong, let it pass off; lest it be made to rage the more against us. The line of our duty is clearly marked out, and if our enemies are not melted by persevering kindness, we are not to seek vengeance; they will be consumed by the fiery wrath of that God to whom vengeance belongeth. The last **verse** suggests what is not easily understood by the world; that in all strife and contention, those that revenge are conquered, and those that forgive are conquerors. Be not overcome of evil. Learn to defeat ill designs against you, either to change them, or to preserve your own peace. He that has this rule over his spirit, is better than the mighty. God's children may be asked whether it is not more sweet unto them than all earthly good, that God so enables them by his Spirit, thus to feel and act.

Chapter 13

Chapter Outline	
The duty of subjection to governors.	(1–7)
Exhortations to mutual love.	(8–10)
To temperance and sobriety.	(11–14)

Verses 1–7

The grace of the gospel teaches us submission and quiet, where pride and the carnal mind only see causes for murmuring and discontent. Whatever the persons in authority over us themselves may be, yet the just power they have, must be submitted to and obeyed. In the general course of human affairs, rulers are not a terror to honest, quiet, and good subjects, but to evil-doers. Such is the power of sin and corruption, that many will be kept back from crimes only by the fear of punishment. Thou hast the benefit of the government, therefore do what thou canst to preserve it, and nothing to disturb it. This directs private persons to behave quietly and peaceably where God has set them, 1Ti **2**:**1**, **2**. Christians must not use any trick or fraud. All smuggling, dealing in contraband goods, withholding or evading duties, is rebellion against the express command of God. Thus honest neighbours are robbed, who will have to pay the more; and the crimes of smugglers, and others who join with them, are abetted. It is painful that some professors of the gospel should countenance such dishonest practices. The lesson here taught it becomes all Christians to learn and practise, that the godly in the land will always be found the quiet and the peaceable in the land, whatever others are.

Verses 8–10

Christians must avoid useless expense, and be careful not to contract any debts they have not the power to discharge. They are also to stand aloof from all venturesome speculations and rash engagements, and whatever may expose them to the danger of not rendering to all their due. Do not keep in any one's debt. Give every one his own. Do not spend that on yourselves, which you owe to others. But many who are very sensible of the trouble, think little of the sin, of being in debt. Love to others includes all the duties of the second table. The last five of the ten commandments are all summed up in this royal law, Thou shalt love thy neighbour as thyself; with the same sincerity that thou lovest thyself, though not in the same measure and degree. He that loves his neighbour as himself, will desire the welfare of his neighbour. On this is built that golden rule, of doing as we would be done by. Love is a living, active principle of obedience to the whole law. Let us not only avoid injuries to the persons, connexions, property, and characters of men; but do no kind or degree of evil to any man, and study to be useful in every station of life.

Verses 11–14

Four things are here taught, as a Christian's directory for his day's work. When to awake; Now; and to awake out of the sleep of carnal security, sloth, and negligence; out of the sleep of spiritual death, and out of the sleep of spiritual deadness. Considering the time; a busy time; a perilous time. Also the salvation nigh at hand. Let us mind our way, and mend our pace, we are nearer our journey's end. Also to make ourselves ready. The night is far spent, the day is at hand; therefore it is time to dress ourselves. Observe what we must put off; clothes worn in the night. Cast off the sinful works of darkness. Observe what we must put on; how we should dress our souls. Put on the armour of light. A Christian must reckon himself undressed, if unarmed. The graces of the Spirit are this armour, to secure the soul from Satan's temptations, and the assaults of this present evil world. Put on Christ; that includes all. Put on righteousness of Christ, for justification. Put on the Spirit and grace of Christ, for sanctification. The Lord Jesus Christ must be put on as Lord to rule you as Jesus to save you; and in both, as Christ anointed and appointed by the Father to this ruling, saving work. And how to walk. When we are up and ready, we are not to sit still, but to appear abroad; let us walk. Christianity teaches us how to walk so as to please God, who ever sees us. Walk honestly as in the day; avoiding the works of darkness. Where there are riot and drunkenness, there usually are chambering and wantonness, and strife and envy. Solomon puts these all together, Pr **23**:**29**–**35**. See what provision to make. Our great care must be to provide for our souls: but must we take no care about our bodies? Yes; but two things are forbidden. Perplexing ourselves with anxious, encumbering care; and indulging ourselves in irregular desires. Natural wants are to be answered, but evil appetites must be checked and denied. To ask meat for our necessities, is our duty, we are taught to pray for daily bread; but to ask meat for our lusts, is provoking God, Ps **78**:**18**.

Chapter 14

Chapter Outline	
The Jewish converts cautioned against judging, and Gentile believers against despising one the other.	(1–13)
And the Gentiles exhorted to take heed of giving offence in their use of indifferent things.	(14–23)

Verses 1–6

Differences of opinion prevailed even among the immediate followers of Christ and their disciples. Nor did St. Paul attempt to end them. Compelled assent to any doctrine, or conformity to outward observances without being convinced, would be hypocritical and of no avail. Attempts for producing absolute oneness of mind among Christians would be useless. Let not Christian fellowship be disturbed with strifes of words. It will be good for us to ask ourselves, when tempted to disdain and blame our brethren; Has not God owned them? and if he has, dare I disown them? Let not the Christian who uses his liberty, despise his weak brother as ignorant and superstitious. Let not the scrupulous believer find fault with his brother, for God accepted him, without regarding the distinctions of meats. We usurp the place of God, when we take upon us thus to judge the thoughts and intentions of others, which are out of our view. The case as to the observance of days was much the same. Those who knew that all these things were done away by Christ's coming, took no notice of the festivals of the Jews. But it is not enough that our consciences consent to what we do; it is necessary that it be certified from the word of God. Take heed of acting against a doubting conscience. We are all apt to make our own views the standard of truth, to deem things certain which to others appear doubtful. Thus Christians often despise or condemn each other, about doubtful matters of no moment. A thankful regard to God, the Author and Giver of all our mercies, sanctifies and sweetens them.

Verses 7–13

Though some are weak, and others are strong, yet all must agree not to live to themselves. No one who has given up his name to Christ, is allowedly a self-seeker; that is against true Christianity. The business of our lives is not to please ourselves, but to please God. That is true Christianity, which makes Christ all in all. Though Christians are of different strength, capacities, and practices in lesser things, yet they are all the Lord's; all are looking and serving, and approving themselves to Christ. He is Lord of those that are living, to rule them; of those that are dead, to revive them, and raise them up. Christians should not judge or despise one another, because both the one and the other must shortly give an account. A believing regard to the judgment of the great day, would silence rash judgings. Let every man search his own heart and life; he that is strict in judging and humbling himself, will not be apt to judge and despise his brother. We must take heed of saying or doing things which may cause others to stumble or to fall. The one signifies a lesser, the other a greater degree of offence; that which may be an occasion of grief or of guilt to our brother.

Verses 14–18

Christ deals gently with those who have true grace, though they are weak in it. Consider the design of Christ's death: also that drawing a soul to sin, threatens the destruction of that soul. Did Christ deny himself for our brethren, so as to die for them, and shall not we deny ourselves for them, so as to keep from any indulgence? We cannot hinder ungoverned tongues from speaking evil; but we must not give them any occasion. We must deny ourselves in many cases what we may lawfully do, when our doing it may hurt our good name. Our good often comes to be evil spoken of, because we use lawful things in an uncharitable and selfish manner. As we value the reputation of the good we profess and practise, let us seek that it may not be evil-spoken of. Righteousness, peace, and joy, are words that mean a great deal. As to God, our great concern is to appear before him justified by Christ's death, sanctified by the Spirit of his grace; for the righteous Lord loveth righteousness. As to our brethren, it is to live in peace, and love, and charity with them; following peace with all men. As to ourselves, it is joy in the Holy Ghost; that spiritual joy wrought by the blessed Spirit in the hearts of believers, which respects God as their reconciled Father, and heaven as their expected home. Regard to Christ in doing our duties, alone can make them acceptable. Those are most pleasing to God that are best pleased with him; and they abound most in peace and joy in the Holy Ghost. They are approved by wise and good men; and the opinion of others is not to be regarded.

Verses 19–23

Many wish for peace, and talk loudly for it, who do not follow the things that make for peace. Meekness, humility, self-denial, and love, make for peace. We cannot edify one another, while quarrelling and contending. Many, for meat and drink, destroy the work of God in themselves; nothing more destroys the soul than pampering and pleasing the flesh, and fulfilling the lusts of it; so others are hurt, by wilful offence given. Lawful things may be done unlawfully, by giving offence to brethren. This takes in all indifferent things, whereby a brother is drawn into sin or trouble; or has his graces, his comforts, or his resolutions weakened. Hast thou faith? It is meant of knowledge and clearness as to our Christian liberty. Enjoy the comfort of it, but do not trouble others by a wrong use of it. Nor may we act against a doubting conscience. How excellent are the blessings of Christ's kingdom, which consists not in outward rites and ceremonies, but in righteousness, peace, and joy in the Holy Ghost! How preferable is the service of God to all other services! and in serving him we are not called to live and die to ourselves, but unto Christ, whose we are, and whom we ought to serve.

Chapter 15

Chapter Outline	
Directions how to behave towards the weak.	(1–7)
All to receive one another as brethren.	(8–13)
The writing and preaching of the apostle.	(14–21)

His purposed journeys.	(22–29)
He requests their prayers.	(30–33)

Verses 1–7

Christian liberty was allowed, not for our pleasure, but for the glory of God, and the good of others. We must please our neighbour, for the good of his soul; not by serving his wicked will, and humouring him in a sinful way; if we thus seek to please men, we are not the servants of Christ. Christ's whole life was a self-denying, self-displeasing life. And he is the most advanced Christian, who is the most conformed to Christ. Considering his spotless purity and holiness, nothing could be more contrary to him, than to be made sin and a curse for us, and to have the reproaches of God fall upon him; the just for the unjust. He bore the guilt of sin, and the curse for it; we are only called to bear a little of the trouble of it. He bore the presumptuous sins of the wicked; we are called only to bear the failings of the weak. And should not we be humble, self-denying, and ready to consider one another, who are members one of another? The Scriptures are written for our use and benefit, as much as for those to whom they were first given. Those are most learned who are most mighty in the Scriptures. That comfort which springs from the word of God, is the surest and sweetest, and the greatest stay to hope. The Spirit as a Comforter, is the earnest of our inheritance. This like-mindedness must be according to the precept of Christ, according to his pattern and example. It is the gift of God; and a precious gift it is, for which we must earnestly seek unto him. Our Divine Master invites his disciples, and encourages them by showing himself as meek and lowly in spirit. The same disposition ought to mark the conduct of his servants, especially of the strong towards the weak. The great end in all our actions must be, that God may be glorified; nothing more forwards this, than the mutual love and kindness of those who profess religion. Those that agree in Christ may well agree among themselves.

Verses 8–13

Christ fulfilled the prophecies and promises relating to the Jews, and the Gentile converts could have no excuse for despising them. The Gentiles, being brought into the church, are companions in patience and tribulation. They should praise God. Calling upon all the nations to praise the Lord, shows that they shall have knowledge of him. We shall never seek to Christ till we trust in him. And the whole plan of redemption is suited to reconcile us to one another, as well as to our gracious God, so that an abiding hope of eternal life, through the sanctifying and comforting power of the Holy Spirit, may be attained. Our own power will never reach this; therefore where this hope is, and is abounding, the blessed Spirit must have all the glory. "All joy and peace;" all sorts of true joy and peace, so as to suppress doubts and fears, through the powerful working of the Holy Spirit.

Verses 14–21

The apostle was persuaded that the Roman Christians were filled with a kind and affectionate spirit, as well as with knowledge. He had written to remind them of their duties and their dangers, because God had appointed him the minister of Christ to the Gentiles. Paul preached to them; but what made them sacrifices to God, was, their sanctification; not his work, but the work of the Holy Ghost: unholy things can never be pleasing to the holy God. The conversion of souls pertains unto God; therefore it is the matter of Paul's glorying, not the things of the flesh. But though a great preacher, he could not make one soul obedient, further than the Spirit of God accompanied his labours. He principally sought the good of those that sat in darkness. Whatever good we do, it is Christ who does it by us.

Verses 22–29

The apostle sought the things of Christ more than his own will, and would not leave his work of planting churches to go to Rome. It concerns all to do that first which is most needful. We must not take it ill if our friends prefer work which is pleasing to God, before visits and compliments, which may please us. It is justly expected from all Christians, that they should promote every good work, especially that blessed work, the conversion of souls. Christian society is a heaven upon earth, an earnest of our gathering together unto Christ at the great day. Yet it is but partial, compared with our communion with Christ; for that only will satisfy the soul. The apostle was going to Jerusalem, as the messenger of charity. God loves a cheerful giver. Every thing that passes between Christians should be a proof and instance of the union they have in Jesus Christ. The Gentiles received the gospel of salvation from the Jews; therefore were bound to minister to them in what was needed for the body. Concerning what he expected from them he speaks doubtfully; but concerning what he expected from God he speaks confidently. We cannot expect too little from man, nor too much from God. And how delightful and advantageous it is to have the gospel with the fulness of its blessings! What wonderful and happy effects does it produce, when attended with the power of the Spirit!

Verses 30–33

Let us learn to value the effectual fervent prayers of the righteous. How careful should we be, lest we forfeit our interest in the love and prayers of God's praying people! If we have experienced the Spirit's love, let us not be wanting in this office of kindness for others. Those that would prevail in prayer, must strive in prayer. Those who beg the prayers of others, must not neglect to pray for themselves. And though Christ knows our state and wants perfectly, he will know them from us. As God must be sought, for restraining the ill-will of our enemies, so also for preserving and increasing the good-will of our friends. All our joy depends upon the will of God. Let us be earnest in prayer with and for each other, that for Christ's sake, and by the love of the Holy Spirit, great blessings may come upon the souls of Christians, and the labours of ministers.

Chapter 16

Chapter Outline	
The apostle recommends Phebe to the church at Rome, and greets several friends there.	(1–16)
Cautions the church against such as made divisions.	(17–20)

Christian salutations.	(21–24)
The epistle concludes with ascribing glory to God.	(25–27)

Verses 1–16

Paul recommends Phebe to the Christians at Rome. It becomes Christians to help one another in their affairs, especially strangers; we know not what help we may need ourselves. Paul asks help for one that had been helpful to many; he that watereth shall be watered also himself. Though the care of all the churches came upon him daily, yet he could remember many persons, and send salutations to each, with particular characters of them, and express concern for them. Lest any should feel themselves hurt, as if Paul had forgotten them, he sends his remembrances to the rest, as brethren and saints, though not named. He adds, in the close, a general salutation to them all, in the name of the churches of Christ.

Verses 17–20

How earnest, how endearing are these exhortations! Whatever differs from the sound doctrine of the Scriptures, opens a door to divisions and offences. If truth be forsaken, unity and peace will not last long. Many call Christ, Master and Lord, who are far from serving him. But they serve their carnal, sensual, worldly interests. They corrupt the head by deceiving the heart; perverting the judgments by winding themselves into the affections. We have great need to keep our hearts with all diligence. It has been the common policy of seducers to set upon those who are softened by convictions. A pliable temper is good when under good guidance, otherwise it may be easily led astray. Be so wise as not to be deceived, yet so simple as not to be deceivers. The blessing the apostle expects from God, is victory over Satan. This includes all designs and devices of Satan against souls, to defile, disturb, and destroy them; all his attempts to keep us from the peace of heaven here, and the possession of heaven hereafter. When Satan seems to prevail, and we are ready to give up all as lost, then will the God of peace interpose in our behalf. Hold out therefore, faith and patience, yet a little while. If the grace of Christ be with us, who can prevail against us?

Verses 21–24

The apostle adds affectionate remembrances from persons with him, known to the Roman Christians. It is a great comfort to see the holiness and usefulness of our kindred. Not many mighty, not many noble are called, but some are. It is lawful for believers to bear civil offices; and it were to be wished that all offices in Christian states, and in the church, were bestowed upon prudent and steady Christians.

Verses 25–27

That which establishes souls, is, the plain preaching of Jesus Christ. Our redemption and salvation by our Lord Jesus Christ, are, without controversy, a great mystery of godliness. And yet, blessed be God, there is as much of this mystery made plain as will bring us to heaven, if we do not wilfully neglect so great salvation. Life and immortality are brought to light by the gospel, and the Sun of Righteousness is risen on the world. The Scriptures of the prophets, what they left in writing, is not only made plain in itself, but by it this mystery is made known to all nations. Christ is salvation to all nations. And the gospel is revealed, not to be talked of and disputed about, but to be submitted to. The obedience of faith is that obedience which is paid to the word of faith, and which comes by the grace of faith. All the glory that passes from fallen man to God, so as to be accepted of him, must go through the Lord Jesus, in whom alone our persons and doings are, or can be, pleasing to God. Of his righteousness we must make mention, even of his only; who, as he is the Mediator of all our prayers, so he is, and will be, to eternity, the Mediator of all our praises. Remembering that we are called to the obedience of faith, and that every degree of wisdom is from the only wise God, we should, by word and deed, render glory to him through Jesus Christ; that so the grace of our Lord Jesus Christ may be with us for ever.

1 Corinthians

The Corinthian church contained some Jews, but more Gentiles, and the apostle had to contend with the superstition of the one, and the sinful conduct of the other. The peace of this church was disturbed by false teachers, who undermined the influence of the apostle. Two parties were the result; one contending earnestly for the Jewish ceremonies, the other indulging in excesses contrary to the gospel, to which they were especially led by the luxury and the sins which prevailed around them. This epistle was written to rebuke some disorderly conduct, of which the apostle had been apprized, and to give advice as to some points whereon his judgment was requested by the Corinthians. Thus the scope was twofold. **1**. To apply suitable remedies to the disorders and abuses which prevailed among them. **2**. To give satisfactory answers on all the points upon which his advice had been desired. The address, and Christian mildness, yet firmness, with which the apostle writes, and goes on from general truths directly to oppose the errors and evil conduct of the Corinthians, is very remarkable. He states the truth and the will of God, as to various matters, with great force of argument and animation of style.

Chapter 1

Chapter Outline	
A salutation and thanksgiving.	(1–9)
Exhortation to brotherly love, and reproof for divisions.	(10–16)
The doctrine of a crucified Saviour, as advancing the glory of God,	(17–25)
and humbling the creature before him.	(26–31)

Verses 1–9

All Christians are by baptism dedicated and devoted to Christ, and are under strict obligations to be holy. But in the true church of God are all who are sanctified in Christ Jesus, called to be saints, and who call upon him as God manifest in the flesh, for all the blessings of salvation; who acknowledge and obey him as their Lord, and as Lord of all; it includes no other persons. Christians are distinguished from the profane and atheists, that they dare not live without prayer; and they are distinguished from Jews and pagans, that they call on the name of Christ. Observe how often in these **verse**s the apostle repeats the words, Our Lord Jesus Christ. He feared not to make too frequent or too honourable mention of him. To all who called upon Christ, the apostle gave his usual salutation, desiring, in their behalf, the pardoning mercy, sanctifying grace, and comforting peace of God, through Jesus Christ. Sinners can have no peace with God, nor any from him, but through Christ. He gives thanks for their conversion to the faith of Christ; that grace was given them by Jesus Christ. They had been enriched by him with all spiritual gifts. He speaks of utterance and knowledge. And where God has given these two gifts, he has given great power for usefulness. These were gifts of the Holy Ghost, by which God bore witness to the apostles. Those that wait for the coming of our Lord Jesus Christ, will be kept by him to the end; and those that are so, will be blameless in the day of Christ, made so by rich and free grace. How glorious are the hopes of such a privilege; to be kept by the power of Christ, from the power of our corruptions and Satan's temptations!

Verses 10–16

In the great things of religion be of one mind; and where there is not unity of sentiment, still let there be union of affection. Agreement in the greater things should extinguish divisions about the lesser. There will be perfect union in heaven, and the nearer we approach it on earth, the nearer we come to perfection. Paul and Apollos both were faithful ministers of Jesus Christ, and helpers of their faith and joy; but those disposed to be contentious, broke into parties. So liable are the best things to be corrupted, and the gospel and its institutions made engines of discord and contention. Satan has always endeavoured to stir up strife among Christians, as one of his chief devices against the gospel. The apostle left it to other ministers to baptize, while he preached the gospel, as a more useful work.

Verses 17–25

Paul had been bred up in Jewish learning; but the plain preaching of a crucified Jesus, was more powerful than all the oratory and philosophy of the heathen world. This is the sum and substance of the gospel. Christ crucified is the foundation of all our hopes, the fountain of all our joys. And by his death we live. The preaching of salvation for lost sinners by the sufferings and death of the Son of God, if explained and faithfully applied, appears foolishness to those in the way to destruction. The sensual, the covetous, the proud, and ambitious, alike see that the gospel opposes their favourite pursuits. But those who receive the gospel, and are enlightened by the Spirit of God, see more of God's wisdom and power in the doctrine of Christ crucified, than in all his other works. God left a great part of the world to follow the dictates of man's boasted reason, and the event has shown that human wisdom is folly, and is unable to find or retain the knowledge of God as the Creator. It pleased him, by the foolishness of preaching, to save them that believe. By the foolishness of preaching; not by what could justly be called foolish preaching. But the thing preached was foolishness to wordly-wise men. The gospel ever was, and ever will be, foolishness to all in the road to destruction. The message of Christ, plainly delivered, ever has been a sure touchstone by which men may learn what road they are travelling. But the despised doctrine of salvation by faith in a crucified Saviour, God in human nature, purchasing the church with his own blood, to save multitudes, even all that believe, from ignorance, delusion, and vice, has been blessed in every age. And the weakest instruments God uses, are stronger in their effects, than the strongest men can use. Not that there is foolishness or weakness in God, but what men consider as such, overcomes all their admired wisdom and strength.

Verses 26–31

God did not choose philosophers, nor orators, nor statesmen, nor men of wealth, and power, and interest in the world, to publish the gospel of grace and peace. He best judges what men and what measures serve the purposes of his glory. Though not many noble are usually called by Divine grace, there have been some such in every age, who have not been ashamed of the gospel of Christ; and persons of every rank stand in need of pardoning grace. Often, a humble Christian, though poor as to this world, has more true knowledge of the gospel, than those who have made the letter of Scripture the study of their lives, but who have studied it rather as the witness of men, than as the word of God. And even young children have gained such knowledge of Divine truth as to silence infidels. The reason is, they are taught of God; the design is, that no flesh should glory in his presence. That distinction, in which alone they might glory, was not of themselves. It was by the sovereign choice and regenerating grace of God, that they were in Jesus Christ by faith. He is made of God to us wisdom, righteousness, sanctification, and redemption; all we need, or can desire. And he is made wisdom to us, that by his word and Spirit, and from his fulness and treasures of wisdom and knowledge, we may receive all that will make us wise unto salvation, and fit for every service to which we are called. We are guilty, liable to just punishment; and he is made righteousness, our great atonement and sacrifice. We are depraved and corrupt, and he is made sanctification, that he may in the end be made complete redemption; may free the soul from the being of sin, and loose the body from the bonds of the grave. And this is, that all flesh, according to the prophecy by Jeremiah, Jer **9**:**23**–**24**, may glory in the special favour, all-sufficient grace, and precious salvation of Jehovah.

Chapter 2

Chapter Outline	
The plain manner in which the apostle preached Christ crucified.	(1–5)
The wisdom contained in this doctrine.	(6–9)
It cannot be duly known but by the Holy Spirit.	(10–16)

Verses 1–5

Christ, in his person, and offices, and sufferings, is the sum and substance of the gospel, and ought to be the great subject of a gospel minister's preaching, but not so as to leave out other parts of God's revealed truth and will. Paul preached the whole counsel of God. Few know the fear and trembling of faithful ministers, from a deep sense of their own weakness They know how insufficient they are, and are fearful for themselves. When nothing but Christ crucified is plainly preached, the success must be entirely from Divine power accompanying the word, and thus men are brought to believe, to the salvation of their souls.

Verses 6–9

Those who receive the doctrine of Christ as Divine, and, having been enlightened by the Holy Spirit, have looked well into it, see not only the plain history of Christ, and him crucified, but the deep and admirable designs of Divine wisdom therein. It is the mystery made manifest to the saints, Col **1**:**26**, though formerly hid from the heathen world; it was only shown in dark types and distant prophecies, but now is revealed and made known by the Spirit of God. Jesus Christ is the Lord of glory; a title much too great for any creature. There are many things which people would not do, if they knew the wisdom of God in the great work of redemption. There are things God hath prepared for those that love him, and wait for him, which sense cannot discover, no teaching can convey to our ears, nor can it yet enter our hearts. We must take them as they stand in the Scriptures, as God hath been pleased to reveal them to us.

Verses 10–16

God has revealed true wisdom to us by his Spirit. Here is a proof of the Divine authority of the Holy Scriptures, **2Pe 1**:**21**. In proof of the Divinity of the Holy Ghost, observe, that he knows all things, and he searches all things, even the deep things of God. No one can know the things of God, but his Holy Spirit, who is one with the Father and the Son, and who makes known Divine mysteries to his church. This is most clear testimony, both to the real Godhead and the distinct person of the Holy Spirit. The apostles were not guided by worldly principles. They had the revelation of these things from the Spirit of God, and the saving impression of them from the same Spirit. These things they declared in plain, simple language, taught by the Holy Spirit, totally different from the affected oratory or enticing words of man's wisdom. The natural man, the wise man of the world, receives not the things of the Spirit of God. The pride of carnal reasoning is really as much opposed to spirituality, as the basest sensuality. The sanctified mind discerns the real beauties of holiness, but the power of discerning and judging about common and natural things is not lost. But the carnal man is a stranger to the principles, and pleasures, and actings of the Divine life. The spiritual man only, is the person to whom God gives the knowledge of his will. How little have any known of the mind of God by natural power! And the apostles were enabled by his Spirit to make known his mind. In the Holy Scriptures, the mind of Christ, and the mind of God in Christ, are fully made known to us. It is the great privilege of Christians, that they have the mind of Christ revealed to them by his Spirit. They experience his sanctifying power in their hearts, and bring forth good fruits in their lives.

Chapter 3

Chapter Outline	
The Corinthians reproved for their contentions.	(1–4)
The true servants of Christ can do nothing without him.	(5–9)
He is the only foundation, and every one should take heed what he builds thereon.	(10–15)
The churches of Christ ought to be kept pure, and to be humble.	(16, 17)
And they should not glory in men, because ministers and all things else are theirs through Christ.	(18–23)

Verses 1–4

The most simple truths of the gospel, as to man's sinfulness and God's mercy, repentance towards God, and faith in our Lord Jesus Christ, stated in the plainest language, suit the people better than deeper mysteries. Men may have much doctrinal knowledge, yet be mere beginners in the life of faith and experience. Contentions and quarrels about religion are sad evidences of carnality. True religion makes men peaceable, not contentious. But it is to be lamented, that many who should walk as Christians, live and act too much like other men. Many professors, and preachers also, show themselves to be yet carnal, by vain-glorious strife, eagerness for dispute, and readiness to despise and speak evil of others.

Verses 5–9

The ministers about whom the Corinthians contended, were only instruments used by God. We should not put ministers into the place of God. He that planteth and he that watereth are one, employed by one Master, trusted with the same revelation, busied in one work, and engaged in one design. They have their different gifts from one and the same Spirit, for the very same purposes; and should carry on the same design heartily. Those who work hardest shall fare best. Those who are most faithful shall have the greatest reward. They work together with God, in promoting the purposes of his glory, and the salvation of precious souls; and He who knows their work, will take care they do not labour in vain. They are employed in his husbandry and building; and He will carefully look over them.

Verses 10–15

The apostle was a wise master-builder; but the grace of God made him such. Spiritual pride is abominable; it is using the greatest favours of God, to feed our own vanity, and make idols of ourselves. But let every man take heed; there may be bad building on a good foundation. Nothing must be laid upon it, but what the foundation will bear, and what is of a piece with it. Let us not dare to join a merely human or a carnal life with a Divine faith, the corruption of sin with the profession of Christianity. Christ is a firm, abiding, and immovable Rock of ages, every way able to bear all the weight that God himself or the sinner can lay upon him; neither is there salvation in any other. Leave out the doctrine of his atonement, and there is no foundation for our hopes. But of those who rest on this foundation, there are two sorts. Some hold nothing but the truth as it is in Jesus, and preach nothing else. Others build on the good foundation what will not abide the test, when the day of trail comes. We may be mistaken in ourselves and others; but there is a day coming that will show our actions in the true light, without covering or disguise. Those who spread true and pure religion in all its branches, and whose work will abide in the great day, shall receive a reward. And how great! how much exceeding their deserts! There are others, whose corrupt opinions and doctrines, or vain inventions and usages in the worship of God, shall be made known, disowned, and rejected, in that day. This is plainly meant of a figurative fire, not of a real one; for what real fire can consume religious rites or doctrines? And it is to try every man's works, those of Paul and Apollos, as well as others. Let us consider the tendency of our undertakings, compare them with God's word, and judge ourselves, that we be not judged of the Lord.

Verses 16, 17

From other parts of the epistle, it appears that the false teachers among the Corinthians taught unholy doctrines. Such teaching tended to corrupt, to pollute, and destroy the building, which should be kept pure and holy for God. Those who spread loose principles, which render the church of God unholy, bring destruction upon themselves. Christ by his Spirit dwells in all true believers. Christians are holy by profession, and should be pure and clean, both in heart and conversation. He is deceived who deems himself the temple of the Holy Ghost, yet is unconcerned about personal holiness, or the peace and purity of the church.

Verses 18–23

To have a high opinion of our own wisdom, is but to flatter ourselves; and self-flattery is the next step to self-deceit. The wisdom that wordly men esteem, is foolishness with God. How justly does he despise, and how easily can he baffle and confound it! The thoughts of the wisest men in the world, have vanity, weakness, and folly in them. All this should teach us to be humble, and make us willing to be taught of God, so as not to be led away, by pretences to human wisdom and skill, from the simple truths revealed by Christ. Mankind are very apt to oppose the design of the mercies of God. Observe the spiritual riches of a true believer; "All are yours," even ministers and ordinances. Nay, the world itself is yours. Saints have as much of it as Infinite Wisdom sees fit for them, and they have it with the Divine blessing. Life is yours, that you may have a season and opportunity to prepare for the life of heaven; and death is yours, that you may go to the possession of it. It is the kind messenger to take you from sin and sorrow, and to guide you to your Father's house. Things present are yours, for your support on the road; things to come are yours, to delight you for ever at your journey's end. If we belong to Christ, and are true to him, all good belongs to us, and is sure to us. Believers are the subjects of his kingdom. He is Lord over us, we must own his dominion, and cheerfully submit to his command. God in Christ, reconciling a sinful world to himself, and pouring the riches of his grace on a reconciled world, is the sum and substance of the gospel.

Chapter 4

Chapter Outline	
The true character of gospel ministers.	(1–6)
Cautions against despising the apostle.	(7–13)
He claims their regard as their spiritual father in Christ, and shows his concern for them.	(14–21)

Verses 1–6

Apostles were no more than servants of Christ, but they were not to be undervalued. They had a great trust, and for that reason, had an honourable office. Paul had a just concern for his own reputation, but he knew that he who chiefly aimed to please men, would not prove himself a faithful servant of Christ. It is a comfort that men are not to be our final judges. And it is not judging well of ourselves, or justifying ourselves, that will prove us safe and happy. Our own judgment is not to be depended upon as to our faithfulness, any more than our own works for our justification. There is a day coming, that will bring men's secret sins into open day, and discover the secrets of their hearts. Then every slandered believer will be justified, and every faithful servant approved and rewarded. The word of God is the best rule by which to judge as to men. Pride commonly is at the bottom of quarrels. Self-conceit contributes to produce undue esteem of our teachers, as well as of ourselves. We shall not be puffed up for one against another, if we remember that all are instruments, employed by God, and endowed by him with various talents.

Verses 7–13

We have no reason to be proud; all we have, or are, or do, that is good, is owing to the free and rich grace of God. A sinner snatched from destruction by sovereign grace alone, must be very absurd and inconsistent, if proud of the free gifts of God. St. Paul sets forth his own circumstances, ver. **9** Allusion is made to the cruel spectacles in the Roman games; where men were forced to cut one another to pieces, to divert the people; and where the victor did not escape with his life, though he should destroy his adversary, but was only kept for another combat, and must be killed at last. The thought that many eyes are upon believers, when struggling with difficulties or temptations, should encourage constancy and patience. "We are weak, but ye are strong." All Christians are not alike exposed. Some suffer greater hardships than others. The apostle enters into particulars of their sufferings. And how glorious the charity and devotion that carried them through all these hardships! They suffered in their persons and characters as the worst and vilest of men; as the very dirt of the world, that was to be swept away: nay, as the offscouring of all things, the dross of all things. And every one who would be faithful in Christ Jesus, must be prepared for poverty and contempt. Whatever the disciples of Christ suffer from men, they must follow the example, and fulfil the will and precepts of their Lord. They must be content, with him and for him, to be despised and abused. It is much better to be rejected, despised, and ill used, as St. Paul was, than to have the good opinion and favour of the world. Though cast off by the world as vile, yet we may be precious to God, gathered up with his own hand, and placed upon his throne.

Verses 14–21

In reproving for sin, we should distinguish between sinners and their sins. Reproofs that kindly and affectionately warn, are likely to reform. Though the apostle spoke with authority as a parent, he would rather beseech them in love. And as ministers are to set an example, others must follow them, as far as they follow Christ in faith and practice. Christians may mistake and differ in their views, but Christ and Christian truth are the same yesterday, to-day, and for ever. Whenever the gospel is effectual, it comes not in word only, but also in power, by the Holy Spirit, quickening dead sinners, delivering persons from the slavery of sin and Satan, renewing them both inwardly and outwardly, and comforting, strengthening, and establishing the saints, which cannot be done by the persuasive language of men, but by the power of God. And it is a happy temper, to have the spirit of love and meekness bear the rule, yet to maintain just authority.

Chapter 5

Chapter Outline	
The apostle blames the Corinthians for connivance at an incestuous person;	(1–8)
and directs their behaviour towards those guilty of scandalous crimes.	(9–13)

Verses 1–8

The apostle notices a flagrant abuse, winked at by the Corinthians. Party spirit, and a false notion of Christian liberty, seem to have saved the offender from censure. Grievous indeed is it that crimes should sometimes be committed by professors of the gospel, of which even heathens would be ashamed. Spiritual pride and false doctrines tend to bring in, and to spread such scandals. How dreadful the effects of sin! The devil reigns where Christ does not. And a man is in his kingdom, and under his power, when not in Christ. The bad example of a man of influence is very mischievous; it spreads far and wide. Corrupt principles and examples, if not corrected, would hurt the whole church. Believers must have new hearts, and lead new lives. Their common conversation and religious deeds must be holy. So far is the sacrifice of Christ our Passover for us, from rendering personal and public holiness unnecessary, that it furnishes powerful reasons and motives for it. Without holiness we can neither live by faith in him, nor join in his ordinances with comfort and profit.

Verses 9–13

Christians are to avoid familiar converse with all who disgrace the Christian name. Such are only fit companions for their brethren in sin, and to such company they should be left, whenever it is possible to do so. Alas, that there are many called Christians, whose conversation is more dangerous than that of heathens!

Chapter 6

Chapter Outline	
Cautions against going to law in heathen courts.	(1–8)
Sins which, if lived and died in, shut out from the kingdom of God.	(9–11)
Our bodies, which are the members of Christ, and temples of the Holy Ghost, must not be defiled.	(12–20)

Verses 1–8

Christians should not contend with one another, for they are brethren. This, if duly attended to, would prevent many law-suits, and end many quarrels and disputes. In matters of great damage to ourselves or families, we may use lawful means to right ourselves, but Christians should be of a forgiving temper. Refer the matters in dispute, rather than go to law about them. They are trifles, and may easily be settled, if you first conquer your own spirits. Bear and forbear, and the men of least skill among you may end your quarrels. It is a shame that little quarrels should grow to such a head among Christians, that they cannot be determined by the brethren. The peace of a man's own mind, and the calm of his neighbourhood, are worth more than victory. Lawsuits could not take place among brethren, unless there were faults among them.

Verses 9–11

The Corinthians are warned against many great evils, of which they had formerly been guilty. There is much force in these inquiries, when we consider that they were addressed to a people puffed up with a fancy of their being above others in wisdom and knowledge. All unrighteousness is sin; all reigning sin, nay, every actual sin, committed with design, and not repented of, shuts out of the kingdom of heaven. Be not deceived. Men are very much inclined to flatter themselves that they may live in sin, yet die in Christ, and go to heaven. But we cannot hope to sow to the flesh, and reap everlasting life. They are reminded what a change the gospel and grace of God had made in them. The blood of Christ, and the washing of regeneration, can take away all guilt. Our justification is owing to the suffering and merit of Christ; our sanctification to the working of the Holy Spirit; but both go together. All who are made righteous in the sight of God, are made holy by the grace of God.

Verses 12–20

Some among the Corinthians seem to have been ready to say, All things are lawful for me. This dangerous conceit St. Paul opposes. There is a liberty wherewith Christ has made us free, in which we must stand fast. But surely a Christian would never put himself into the power of any bodily appetite. The body is for the Lord; is to be an instrument of righteousness to holiness, therefore is never to be made an instrument of sin. It is an honour to the body, that Jesus Christ was raised from the dead; and it will be an honour to our bodies, that they will be raised. The hope of a resurrection to glory, should keep Christians from dishonouring their bodies by fleshly lusts. And if the soul be united to Christ by faith, the whole man is become a member of his spiritual body. Other vices may be conquered in fight; that here cautioned against, only by flight. And vast multitudes are cut off by this vice in its various forms and consequences. Its effects fall not only directly upon the body, but often upon the mind. Our bodies have been redeemed from deserved condemnation and hopeless slavery by the atoning sacrifice of Christ. We are to be clean, as vessels fitted for our Master's use. Being united to Christ as one spirit, and bought with a price of unspeakable value, the believer should consider himself as wholly the Lord's, by the strongest ties. May we make it our business, to the latest day and hour of our lives, to glorify God with our bodies, and with our spirits which are his.

Chapter 7

Chapter Outline	
The apostle answers several questions about marriage.	(1–9)
Married Christians should not seek to part from their unbelieving consorts.	(10–16)
Persons, in any fixed station, should usually abide in that.	(17–24)
It was most desirable, on account of the then perilous days, for people to sit loose to this world.	(25–35)
Great prudence be used in marriage; it should be only in the Lord.	(36–40)

Verses 1–9

The apostle tells the Corinthians that it was good, in that juncture of time, for Christians to keep themselves single. Yet he says that marriage, and the comforts of that state, are settled by Divine wisdom. Though none may break the law of God, yet that perfect rule leaves men at liberty to serve him in the way most suited to their powers and circumstances, of which others often are very unfit judges. All must determine for themselves, seeking counsel from God how they ought to act.

Verses 10–16

Man and wife must not separate for any other cause than what Christ allows. Divorce, at that time, was very common among both Jews and Gentiles, on very slight pretexts. Marriage is a Divine institution; and is an engagement for life, by God's appointment. We are bound, as much as in us lies, to live peaceably with all men, Ro **12**:**18**, therefore to promote the peace and comfort of our nearest relatives, though unbelievers. It should be the labour and study of those who are married, to make each other as easy and happy as possible. Should a Christian desert a husband or wife, when there is opportunity to give the greatest proof of love? Stay, and labour heartily for the conversion of thy relative. In every state and relation the Lord has called us to peace; and every thing should be done to promote harmony, as far as truth and holiness will permit.

Verses 17–24

The rules of Christianity reach every condition; and in every state a man may live so as to be a credit to it. It is the duty of every Christian to be content with his lot, and to conduct himself in his rank and place as becomes a Christian. Our comfort and happiness depend on what we are to Christ, not what we are in the world. No man should think to make his faith or religion, an argument to break through any natural or civil obligations. He should quietly and contentedly abide in the condition in which he is placed by Divine Providence.

Verses 25–35

Considering the distress of those times, the unmarried state was best. Notwithstanding, the apostle does not condemn marriage. How opposite are those to the apostle Paul who forbid many to marry, and entangle them with vows to remain single, whether they ought to do so or not! He exhorts all Christians to holy indifference toward the world. As to relations; they must not set their hearts on the comforts of the state. As to afflictions; they must not indulge the sorrow of the world: even in sorrow the heart may be joyful. As to worldly enjoyments; here is not their rest. As to worldly employment; those that prosper in trade, and increase in wealth, should hold their possessions as though they held them not. As to all worldly concerns; they must keep the world out of their hearts, that they may not abuse it when they have it in their hands. All worldly things are show; nothing solid. All will be quickly gone. Wise concern about worldly interests is a duty; but to be full of care, to have anxious and perplexing care, is a sin. By this maxim the apostle solves the case whether it were advisable to marry. That condition of life is best for every man, which is best for his soul, and keeps him most clear of the cares and snares of the world. Let us reflect on the advantages and snares of our own condition in life; that we may improve the one, and escape as far as possible all injury from the other. And whatever cares press upon the mind, let time still be kept for the things of the Lord.

Verses 36–40

The apostle is thought to give advice here about the disposal of children in marriage. In this view, the general meaning is plain. Children should seek and follow the directions of their parents as to marriage. And parents should consult their children's wishes; and not reckon they have power to do with them, and dictate just as they please, without reason. The whole is closed with advice to widows. Second marriages are not unlawful, so that it is kept in mind, to marry in the Lord. In our choice of relations, and change of conditions, we should always be guided by the fear of God, and the laws of God, and act in dependence on the providence of God. Change of condition ought only to be made after careful consideration, and on probable grounds, that it will be to advantage in our spiritual concerns.

Chapter 8

Chapter Outline	
The danger of having a high conceit of knowledge.	(1–6)
The mischief of offending weak brethren.	(7–13)

Verses 1–6

There is no proof of ignorance more common than conceit of knowledge. Much may be known, when nothing is known to good purpose. And those who think they know any thing, and grow vain thereon, are the least likely to make good use of their knowledge. Satan hurts some as much by tempting them to be proud of mental powers, as others, by alluring to sensuality. Knowledge which puffs up the possessor, and renders him confident, is as dangerous as self-righteous pride, though what he knows may be right. Without holy affections all human knowledge is worthless. The heathens had gods of higher and lower degree; gods many, and lords many; so called, but not such in truth. Christians know better. One God made all, and has power over all. The one God, even the Father, signifies the Godhead as the sole object of all religious worship; and the Lord Jesus Christ denotes the person of Emmanuel, God manifest in the flesh, One with the Father, and with us; the appointed Mediator, and Lord of all; through whom we come to the Father, and through whom the Father sends all blessings to us, by the influence and working of the Holy Spirit. While we refuse all worship to the many who are called gods and lords, and to saints and angels, let us try whether we really come to God by faith in Christ.

Verses 7–13

Eating one kind of food, and abstaining from another, have nothing in them to recommend a person to God. But the apostle cautions against putting a stumbling-block in the way of the weak; lest they be made bold to eat what was offered to the idol, not as common food, but as a sacrifice, and thereby be guilty of idolatry. He who has the Spirit of Christ in him, will love those whom Christ loved so as to die for them. Injuries done to Christians, are done to Christ; but most of all, the entangling them in guilt: wounding their consciences, is wounding him. We should be very tender of doing any thing that may occasion stumbling to others, though it may be innocent in itself. And if we must not endanger other men's souls, how much should we take care not to destroy our own! Let Christians beware of approaching the brink of evil, or the appearance of it, though many do this in public matters, for which perhaps they plead plausibly. Men cannot thus sin against their brethren, without offending Christ, and endangering their own souls.

Chapter 9

Chapter Outline	
The apostle shows his authority, and asserts his right to be maintained.	(1–14)
He waved this part of his Christian liberty, for the good of others.	(15–23)
He did all this, with care and diligence, in view of an unfading crown.	(24–27)

Verses 1–14

It is not new for a minister to meet with unkind returns for good-will to a people, and diligent and successful services among them. To the cavils of some, the apostle answers, so as to set forth himself as an example of self-denial, for the good of others. He had a right to marry as well as other apostles, and to claim what was needful for his wife, and his children if he had any, from the churches, without labouring with his own hands to get it. Those who seek to do our souls good, should have food provided for them. But he renounced his right, rather than hinder his success by claiming it. It is the people's duty to maintain their minister. He may wave his right, as Paul did; but those transgress a precept of Christ, who deny or withhold due support.

Verses 15–23

It is the glory of a minister to deny himself, that he may serve Christ and save souls. But when a minister gives up his right for the sake of the gospel, he does more than his charge and office demands. By preaching the gospel, freely, the apostle showed that he acted from principles of zeal and love, and thus enjoyed much comfort and hope in his soul. And though he looked on the ceremonial law as a yoke taken off by Christ, yet he submitted to it, that he might work upon the Jews, do away their prejudices, prevail with them to hear the gospel, and win them over to Christ. Though he would transgress no laws of Christ, to please any man, yet he would accommodate himself to all men, where he might do it lawfully, to gain some. Doing good was the study and business of his life; and, that he might reach this end, he did not stand on privileges. We must carefully watch against extremes, and against relying on any thing but trust in Christ alone. We must not allow errors or faults, so as to hurt others, or disgrace the gospel.

Verses 24–27

The apostle compares himself to the racers and combatants in the Isthmian games, well known by the Corinthians. But in the Christian race all may run so as to obtain. There is the greatest encouragement, therefore, to persevere with all our strength, in this course. Those who ran in these games were kept to a spare diet. They used themselves to hardships. They practised the exercises. And those who pursue the interests of their souls, must combat hard with fleshly lusts. The body must not be suffered to rule. The apostle presses this advice on the Corinthians. He sets before himself and them the danger of yielding to fleshly desires, pampering the body, and its lusts and appetites. Holy fear of himself was needed to keep an apostle faithful: how much more is it needful for our preservation! Let us learn from hence humility and caution, and to watch against dangers which surround us while in the body.

Chapter 10

Chapter Outline	
The great privileges, and yet terrible overthrow of the Israelites in the wilderness.	(1–5)
Cautions against all idolatrous, and other sinful practices.	(6–14)
The partaking in idolatry cannot exist with having communion with Christ.	(15–22)
All we do to be to the glory of God, and without offence to the consciences of others.	(23–33)

Verses 1–5

To dissuade the Corinthians from communion with idolaters, and security in any sinful course, the apostle sets before them the example of the Jewish nation of old. They were, by a miracle, led through the Red Sea, where the pursuing Egyptians were drowned. It was to them a typical baptism. The manna on which they fed was a type of Christ crucified, the Bread which came down from heaven, which whoso eateth shall live for ever. Christ is the Rock on which the Christian church is built; and of the streams that issue therefrom, all believers drink, and are refreshed. It typified the sacred influences of the Holy Spirit, as given to believers through Christ. But let none presume upon their great privileges, or profession of the truth; these will not secure heavenly happiness.

Verses 6–14

Carnal desires gain strength by indulgence, therefore should be checked in their first rise. Let us fear the sins of Israel, if we would shun their plagues. And it is but just to fear, that such as tempt Christ, will be left by him in the power of the old serpent. Murmuring against God's disposals and commands, greatly provokes him. Nothing in Scripture is written in vain; and it is our wisdom and duty to learn from it. Others have fallen, and so may we. The Christian's security against sin is distrust of himself. God has not promised to keep us from falling, if we do not look to ourselves. To this word of caution, a word of comfort is added. Others have the like burdens, and the like temptations: what they bear up under, and break through, we may also. God is wise as well as faithful, and will make our burdens according to our strength. He knows what we can bear. He will make a way to escape; he will deliver either from the trial itself, or at least the mischief of it. We have full encouragement to flee from sin, and to be faithful to God. We cannot fall by temptation, if we cleave fast to him. Whether the world smiles or frowns, it is an enemy; but believers shall be strengthened to overcome it, with all its terrors and enticements. The fear of the Lord, put into their hearts, will be the great means of safety.

Verses 15–22

Did not the joining in the Lord's supper show a profession of faith in Christ crucified, and of adoring gratitude to him for his salvation ? Christians, by this ordinance, and the faith therein professed, were united as the grains of wheat in one loaf of bread, or as the members in the human body, seeing they were all united to Christ, and had fellowship with him and one another. This is confirmed from the Jewish worship and customs in sacrifice. The apostle applies this to feasting with idolaters. Eating food as part of a heathen sacrifice, was worshipping the idol to whom it was made, and having fellowship or communion with it; just as he who eats the Lord's supper, is accounted to partake in the Christian sacrifice, or as they who ate the Jewish sacrifices partook of what was offered on their altar. It was denying Christianity; for communion with Christ, and communion with devils, could never be had at once. If Christians venture into places, and join in sacrifices to the lust of the flesh, the lust of the eye, and the pride of life, they will provoke God.

Verses 23–33

There were cases wherein Christians might eat what had been offered to idols, without sin. Such as when the flesh was sold in the market as common food, for the priest to whom it had been given. But a Christian must not merely consider what is lawful, but what is expedient, and to edify others. Christianity by no means forbids the common offices of kindness, or allows uncourteous behaviour to any, however they may differ from us in religious sentiments or practices. But this is not to be understood of religious festivals, partaking in idolatrous worship. According to this advice of the apostle, Christians should take care not to use their liberty to the hurt of others, or to their own reproach. In eating and drinking, and in all we do, we should aim at the glory of God, at pleasing and honouring him. This is the great end of all religion, and directs us where express rules are wanting. A holy, peaceable, and benevolent spirit, will disarm the greatest enemies.

Chapter 11

Chapter Outline	
The apostle, after an exhortation to follow him,	(1)
corrects some abuses.	(2–16)
Also contentions, divisions, and disorderly celebrations of the Lord's supper.	(17–22)
He reminds them of the nature and design of its institution.	(23–26)
And directs how to attend upon it in a due manner.	(27–34)

Verse 1

The first **verse** of this chapter seems properly to be the close to the last. The apostle not only preached such doctrine as they ought to believe, but led such a life as they ought to live. Yet Christ being our perfect example, the actions and conduct of men, as related in the Scriptures, should be followed only so far as they are like to his.

Verses 2–16

Here begin particulars respecting the public assemblies, ch. **1**Co **14**. In the abundance of spiritual gifts bestowed on the Corinthians, some abuses had crept in; but as Christ did the will, and sought the honour of God, so the Christian should avow his subjection to Christ, doing his will and seeking his glory. We should, even in our dress and habit, avoid every thing that may dishonour Christ. The woman was made subject to man, because made for his help and comfort. And she should do nothing, in Christian assemblies, which looked like a claim of being equal. She ought to have "power," that is, a veil, on her head, because of the angels. Their presence should keep Christians from all that is wrong while in the worship of God. Nevertheless, the man and the woman were made for one another. They were to be mutual comforts and blessings, not one a slave, and the other a tyrant. God has so settled matters, both in the kingdom of providence and that of grace, that the authority and subjection of each party should be for mutual help and benefit. It was the common usage of the churches, for women to appear in public assemblies, and join in public worship, veiled; and it was right that they should do so. The Christian religion sanctions national customs wherever these are not against the great principles of truth and holiness; affected singularities receive no countenance from any thing in the Bible.

Verses 17–22

The apostle rebukes the disorders in their partaking of the Lord's supper. The ordinances of Christ, if they do not make us better, will be apt to make us worse. If the use of them does not mend, it will harden. Upon coming together, they fell into divisions, schisms. Christians may separate from each other's communion, yet be charitable one towards another; they may continue in the same communion, yet be uncharitable. This last is schism, rather than the former. There is a careless and irregular eating of the Lord's supper, which adds to guilt. Many rich Corinthians seem to have acted very wrong at the Lord's table, or at the love-feasts, which took place at the same time as the supper. The rich despised the poor, and ate and drank up the provisions they brought, before the poor were allowed to partake; thus some wanted, while others had more than enough. What should have been a bond of mutual love and affection, was made an instrument of discord and disunion. We should be careful that nothing in our behaviour at the Lord's table, appears to make light of that sacred institution. The Lord's supper is not now made an occasion for gluttony or revelling, but is it not often made the support of self-righteous pride, or a cloak for hypocrisy? Let us never rest in the outward forms of worship; but look to our hearts.

Verses 23–34

The apostle describes the sacred ordinance, of which he had the knowledge by revelation from Christ. As to the visible signs, these are the bread and wine. What is eaten is called bread, though at the same time it is said to be the body of the Lord, plainly showing that the apostle did not mean that the bread was changed into flesh. St. Matthew tells us, our Lord bid them all drink of the cup, ch. Mt **26**:**27**, as if he would, by this expression, provide against any believer being deprived of the cup. The things signified by these outward signs, are Christ's body and blood, his body broken, his blood shed, together with all the benefits which flow from his death and sacrifice. Our Saviour's actions were, taking the bread and cup, giving thanks, breaking the bread, and giving both the one and the other. The actions of the communicants were, to take the bread and eat, to take the cup and drink, and to do both in remembrance of Christ. But the outward acts are not the whole, or the principal part, of what is to be done at this holy ordinance. Those who partake of it, are to take him as their Lord and Life, yield themselves up to him, and live upon him. Here is an account of the ends of this ordinance. It is to be done in remembrance of Christ, to keep fresh in our minds his dying for us, as well as to remember Christ pleading for us, in virtue of his death, at God's right hand. It is not merely in remembrance of Christ, of what he has done and suffered; but to celebrate his grace in our redemption. We declare his death to be our life, the spring of all our comforts and hopes. And we glory in such a declaration; we show forth his death, and plead it as our accepted sacrifice and ransom. The Lord's supper is not an ordinance to be observed merely for a time, but to be continued. The apostle lays before the Corinthians the danger of receiving it with an unsuitable temper of mind; or keeping up the covenant with sin and death, while professing to renew and confirm the covenant with God. No doubt such incur great guilt, and so render themselves liable to spiritual judgements. But fearful believers should not be discouraged from attending at this holy ordinance. The Holy Spirit never caused this scripture to be written to deter serious Christians from their duty, though the devil has often made this use of it. The apostle was addressing Christians, and warning them to beware of the temporal judgements with which God chastised his offending servants. And in the midst of judgement, God remembers mercy: he many times punishes those whom he loves. It is better to bear trouble in this world, than to be miserable for ever. The apostle points our the duty of those who come to the Lord's table. Self-examination is necessary to right attendance at this holy ordinance. If we would thoroughly search ourselves, to condemn and set right what we find wrong, we should stop Divine judgements. The apostle closes all with a caution against the irregularities of which the Corinthians were guilty at the Lord's table. Let all look to it, that they do not come together to God's worship, so as to provoke him, and bring down vengeance on themselves.

Chapter 12

Chapter Outline	
The variety of use of spiritual gifts are shown.	(1–11)
In the human body every member has its place and use.	(12–26)
This is applied to the church of Christ.	(27–30)
And there is something more excellent than spiritual gifts.	(31)

Verses 1–11

Spiritual gifts were extraordinary powers bestowed in the first ages, to convince unbelievers, and to spread the gospel. Gifts and graces greatly differ. Both were freely given of God. But where grace is given, it is for the salvation of those who have it. Gifts are for the advantage and salvation of others; and there may be great gifts where there is no grace. The extraordinary gifts of the Holy Spirit were chiefly exercised in the public assemblies, where the Corinthians seem to have made displays of them, wanting in the spirit of piety, and of Christian love. While heathens, they had not been influenced by the Spirit of Christ. No man can call Christ Lord, with believing dependence upon him, unless that faith is wrought by the Holy Ghost. No man could believe with his heart, or prove by a miracle, that Jesus was Christ, unless by the Holy Ghost. There are various gifts, and various offices to perform, but all proceed from one God, one Lord, one Spirit; that is, from the Father, Son, and Holy Ghost, the origin of all spiritual blessings. No man has them merely for himself. The more he profits others, the more will they turn to his own account. The gifts mentioned appear to mean exact understanding, and uttering the doctrines of the Christian religion; the knowledge of mysteries, and skill to give advice and counsel. Also the gift of healing the sick, the working of miracles, and to explain Scripture by a peculiar gift of the Spirit, and ability to speak and interpret languages. If we have any knowledge of the truth, or any power to make it known, we must give all the glory of God. The greater the gifts are, the more the possessor is exposed to temptations, and the larger is the measure of grace needed to keep him humble and spiritual; and he will meet with more painful experiences and humbling dispensations. We have little cause to glory in any gifts bestowed on us, or to despise those who have them not. (1Co **12**:**12-26**)

Verses 12–26

Christ and his church form one body, as Head and members. Christians become members of this body by baptism. The outward rite is of Divine institution; it is a sign of the new birth, and is called therefore the washing of regeneration, Tit **3**:**5**. But it is by the Spirit, only by the renewing of the Holy Ghost, that we are made members of Christ's body. And by communion with Christ at the Lord's supper, we are strengthened, not by drinking the wine, but by drinking into one Spirit. Each member has its form, place, and use. The meanest makes a part of the body. There must be a distinction of members in the body. So Christ's members have different powers and different places. We should do the duties of our own place, and not murmur, or quarrel with others. All the members of the body are useful and necessary to each other. Nor is there a member of the body of Christ, but may and ought to be useful to fellow-members. As in the natural body of man, the members should be closely united by the strongest bonds of love; the good of the whole should be the object of all. All Christians are dependent one upon another; each is to expect and receive help from the rest. Let us then have more of the spirit of union in our religion.

Verses 27–31

Contempt, hatred, envy, and strife, are very unnatural in Christians. It is like the members of the same body being without concern for one another, or quarrelling with each other. The proud, contentious spirit that prevailed, as to spiritual gifts, was thus condemned. The offices and gifts, or favours, dispensed by the Holy Spirit, are noticed. Chief ministers; persons enabled to interpret Scripture; those who laboured in word and doctrine; those who had power to heal diseases; such as helped the sick and weak; such as disposed of the money given in charity by the church, and managed the affairs of the church; and such as could speak divers languages. What holds the last and lowest rank in this list, is the power to speak languages; how vain, if a man does so merely to amuse or to exalt himself! See the distribution of these gifts, not to every one alike, ver. #(**29**, **30**). This were to make the church all one, as if the body were all ear, or all eye. The Spirit distributes to every one as he will. We must be content though we are lower and less than others. We must not despise others, if we have greater gifts. How blessed the Christian church, if all the members did their duty! Instead of coveting the highest stations, or the most splendid gifts, let us leave the appointment of his instruments to God, and those in whom he works by his providence. Remember, those will not be approved hereafter who seek the chief places, but those who are most faithful to the trust placed in them, and most diligent in their Master's work.

Chapter 13

Chapter Outline	
The necessity and advantage of the grace of love.	(1–3)
Its excellency represented by its properties and effects;	(4–7)
and by its abiding, and its superiority.	(8–13)

Verses 1–3

The excellent way had in view in the close of the former chapter, is not what is meant by charity in our common use of the word, almsgiving, but love in its fullest meaning; true love to God and man. Without this, the most glorious gifts are of no account to us, of no esteem in the sight of God. A clear head and a deep understanding, are of no value without a benevolent and charitable heart. There may be an open and lavish hand, where there is not a liberal and charitable heart. Doing good to others will do none to us, if it be not done from love to God, and good-will to men. If we give away all we have, while we withhold the heart from God, it will not profit. Nor even the most painful sufferings. How are those deluded who look for acceptance and reward for their good works, which are as scanty and defective as they are corrupt and selfish!

Verses 4–7

Some of the effects of charity are stated, that we may know whether we have this grace; and that if we have not, we may not rest till we have it. This love is a clear proof of regeneration, and is a touchstone of our professed faith in Christ. In this beautiful description of the nature and effects of love, it is meant to show the Corinthians that their conduct had, in many respects, been a contrast to it. Charity is an utter enemy to selfishness; it does not desire or seek its own praise, or honour, or profit, or pleasure. Not that charity destroys all regard to ourselves, or that the charitable man should neglect himself and all his interests. But charity never seeks its own to the hurt of others, or to neglect others. It ever prefers the welfare of others to its private advantage. How good-natured and amiable is Christian charity! How excellent would Christianity appear to the world, if those who profess it were more under this Divine principle, and paid due regard to the command on which its blessed Author laid the chief stress! Let us ask whether this Divine love dwells in our hearts. Has this principle guided us into becoming behaviour to all men? Are we willing to lay aside selfish objects and aims? Here is a call to watchfulness, diligence, and prayer.

Verses 8–13

Charity is much to be preferred to the gifts on which the Corinthians prided themselves. From its longer continuance. It is a grace, lasting as eternity. The present state is a state of childhood, the future that of manhood. Such is the difference between earth and heaven. What narrow views, what confused notions of things, have children when compared with grown men! Thus shall we think of our most valued gifts of this world, when we come to heaven. All things are dark and confused now, compared with what they will be hereafter. They can only be seen as by the reflection in a mirror, or in the description of a riddle; but hereafter our knowledge will be free from all obscurity and error. It is the light of heaven only, that will remove all clouds and darkness that hide the face of God from us. To sum up the excellences of charity, it is preferred not only to gifts, but to other graces, to faith and hope. Faith fixes on the Divine revelation, and assents thereto, relying on the Divine Redeemer. Hope fastens on future happiness, and waits for that; but in heaven, faith will be swallowed up in actual sight, and hope in enjoyment. There is no room to believe and hope, when we see and enjoy. But there, love will be made perfect. There we shall perfectly love God. And there we shall perfectly love one another. Blessed state! how much surpassing the best below! God is love, **1**Jo **4**:**8**, **16**. Where God is to be seen as he is, and face to face, there charity is in its greatest height; there only will it be perfected.

Chapter 14

Chapter Outline	
Prophecy preferred to the gift of tongues.	(1–5)
The unprofitableness of speaking in unknown languages.	(6–14)
Exhortations to worship that can be understood.	(15–25)
Disorders from vain display of gifts;	(26–33)
and from women speaking in the church.	(34–40)

Verses 1–5

Prophesying, that is, explaining Scripture, is compared with speaking with tongues. This drew attention, more than the plain interpretation of Scripture; it gratified pride more, but promoted the purposes of Christian charity less; it would not equally do good to the souls of men. What cannot be understood, never can edify. No advantage can be reaped from the most excellent discourses, if delivered in language such as the hearers cannot speak or understand. Every ability or possession is valuable in proportion to its usefulness. Even fervent, spiritual affection must be governed by the exercise of the understanding, else men will disgrace the truths they profess to promote.

Verses 6–14

Even an apostle could not edify, unless he spoke so as to be understood by his hearers. To speak words that have no meaning to those who hear them, is but speaking into the air. That cannot answer the end of speaking, which has no meaning; in this case, speaker and hearers are barbarians to each other. All religious services should be so performed in Christian assemblies, that all may join in, and profit by them. Language plain and easy to be understood, is the most proper for public worship, and other religious exercises. Every true follower of Christ will rather desire to do good to others, than to get a name for learning or fine speaking.

Verses 15–25

There can be no assent to prayers that are not understood. A truly Christian minister will seek much more to do spiritual good to men's souls, than to get the greatest applause to himself. This is proving himself the servant of Christ. Children are apt to be struck with novelty; but do not act like them. Christians should be like children, void of guile and malice; yet they should not be unskilful as to the word of righteousness, but only as to the arts of mischief. It is a proof that a people are forsaken of God, when he gives them up to the rule of those who teach them to worship in another language. They can never be benefitted by such teaching. Yet thus the preachers did who delivered their instructions in an unknown tongue. Would it not make Christianity ridiculous to a heathen, to hear the ministers pray or preach in a language which neither he nor the assembly understood? But if those who minister, plainly interpret Scripture, or preach the great truths and rules of the gospel, a heathen or unlearned person might become a convert to Christianity. His conscience might be touched, the secrets of his heart might be revealed to him, and so he might be brought to confess his guilt, and to own that God was present in the assembly. Scripture truth, plainly and duly taught, has a wonderful power to awaken the conscience and touch the heart.

Verses 26–33

Religious exercises in public assemblies should have this view; Let all be done to edifying. As to the speaking in an unknown tongue, if another were present who could interpret, two miraculous gifts might be exercised at once, and thereby the church be edified, and the faith of the hearers confirmed at the same time. As to prophesying, two or three only should speak at one meeting, and this one after the other, not all at once. The man who is inspired by the Spirit of God will observe order and decency in delivering his revelations. God never teaches men to neglect their duties, or to act in any way unbecoming their age or station.

Verses 34–40

When the apostle exhorts Christian women to seek information on religious subjects from their husbands at home, it shows that believing families ought to assemble for promoting spiritual knowledge. The Spirit of Christ can never contradict itself; and if their revelations are against those of the apostle, they do not come from the same Spirit. The way to keep peace, truth, and order in the church, is to seek that which is good for it, to bear with that which is not hurtful to its welfare, and to keep up good behaviour, order, and decency.

Chapter 15

Chapter Outline	
The apostle proves the resurrection of Christ from the dead.	(1–11)
Those answered who deny the resurrection of the body.	(12–19)
The resurrection of believers to eternal life.	(20–34)
Objections against it answered.	(35–50)
The mystery of the change that will be made on those living at Christ's second coming.	(51–54)
The believer's triumph over death and the grave, An exhortation to diligence.	(55–58)

Verses 1–11

The word resurrection, usually points out our existence beyond the grave. Of the apostle's doctrine not a trace can be found in all the teaching of philosophers. The doctrine of Christ's death and resurrection, is the foundation of Christianity. Remove this, and all our hopes for eternity sink at once. And it is by holding this truth firm, that Christians stand in the day of trial, and are kept faithful to God. We believe in vain, unless we keep in the faith of the gospel. This truth is confirmed by Old Testament prophecies; and many saw Christ after he was risen. This apostle was highly favoured, but he always had a low opinion of himself, and expressed it. When sinners are, by Divine grace, turned into saints, God causes the remembrance of former sins to make them humble, diligent, and faithful. He ascribes to Divine grace all that was valuable in him. True believers, though not ignorant of what the Lord has done for, in, and by them, yet when they look at their whole conduct and their obligations, they are led to feel that none are so worthless as they are. All true Christians believe that Jesus Christ, and him crucified, and then risen from the dead, is the sun and substance of Christianity. All the apostles agreed in this testimony; by this faith they lived, and in this faith they died.

Verses 12–19

Having shown that Christ was risen, the apostle answers those who said there would be no resurrection. There had been no justification, or salvation, if Christ had not risen. And must not faith in Christ be vain, and of no use, if he is still among the dead? The proof of the resurrection of the body is the resurrection of our Lord. Even those who died in the faith, had perished in their sins, if Christ had not risen. All who believe in Christ, have hope in him, as a Redeemer; hope for redemption and salvation by him; but if there is no resurrection, or future recompence, their hope in him can only be as to this life. And they must be in a worse condition than the rest of mankind, especially at the time, and under the circumstances, in which the apostles wrote; for then Christians were hated and persecuted by all men. But it is not so; they, of all men, enjoy solid comforts amidst all their difficulties and trials, even in the times of the sharpest persecution.

Verses 20–34

All that are by faith united to Christ, are by his resurrection assured of their own. As through the sin of the first Adam, all men became mortal, because all had from him the same sinful nature, so, through the resurrection of Christ, shall all who are made to partake of the Spirit, and the spiritual nature, revive, and live for ever. There will be an order in the resurrection. Christ himself has been the first-fruits; at his coming, his redeemed people will be raised before others; at the last the wicked will rise also. Then will be the end of this present state of things. Would we triumph in that solemn and important season, we must now submit to his rule, accept his salvation, and live to his glory. Then shall we rejoice in the completion of his undertaking, that God may receive the whole glory of our salvation, that we may for ever serve him, and enjoy his favour. What shall those do, who are baptized for the dead, if the dead rise not at all? Perhaps baptism is used here in a figure, for afflictions, sufferings, and martyrdom, as Mt **20**:**22**, **23**. What is, or will become of those who have suffered many and great injuries, and have even lost their lives, for this doctrine of the resurrection, if the dead rise not at all? Whatever the meaning may be, doubtless the apostle's argument was understood by the Corinthians. And it is as plain to us that Christianity would be a foolish profession, if it proposed advantage to themselves by their faithfulness to God; and to have our fruit to holiness, that our end may be everlasting life. But we must not live like beasts, as we do not die like them. It must be ignorance of God that leads any to disbelieve the resurrection and future life. Those who own a God and a providence, and observe how unequal things are in the present life, how frequently the best men fare worst, cannot doubt as to an after-state, where every thing will be set to rights. Let us not be joined with ungodly men; but warn all around us, especially children and young persons, to shun them as a pestilence. Let us awake to righteousness, and not sin.

Verses 35–50

1. How are the dead raised up? that is, by what means? How can they be raised? **2**. As to the bodies which shall rise. Will it be with the like shape, and form, and stature, and members, and qualities? The former objection is that of those who opposed the doctrine, the latter of curious doubters. To the first the answer is, This was to be brought about by Divine power; that power which all may see does somewhat like it, year after year, in the death and revival of the corn. It is foolish to question the Almighty power of God to raise the dead, when we see it every day quickening and reviving things that are dead. To the second inquiry; The grain undergoes a great change; and so will the dead, when they rise and live again. The seed dies, though a part of it springs into new life, though how it is we cannot fully understand. The works of creation and providence daily teach us to be humble, as well as to admire the Creator's wisdom and goodness. There is a great variety among other bodies, as there is among plants. There is a variety of glory among heavenly bodies. The bodies of the dead, when they rise, will be fitted for the heavenly bodies. The bodies of the dead, when they rise, will be fitted for the heavenly state; and there will be a variety of glories among them. Burying the dead, is like committing seed to the earth, that it may spring out of it again. Nothing is more loathsome than a dead body. But believers shall at the resurrection have bodies, made fit to be for ever united with spirits made perfect. To God all things are possible. He is the Author and Source of spiritual life and holiness, unto all his people, by the supply of his Holy Spirit to the soul; and he will also quicken and change the body by his Spirit. The dead in Christ shall not only rise, but shall rise thus gloriously changed. The bodies of the saints, when they rise again, will be changed. They will be then glorious and spiritual bodies, fitted to the heavenly world and state, where they are ever afterwards to dwell. The human body in its present form, and with its wants and weaknesses, cannot enter or enjoy the kingdom of God. Then let us not sow to the flesh, of which we can only reap corruption. And the body follows the state of the soul. He, therefore, who neglects the life of the soul, casts away his present good; he who refuses to live to God, squanders all he has.

Verses 51–58

All the saints should not die, but all would be changed. In the gospel, many truths, before hidden in mystery, are made known. Death never shall appear in the regions to which our Lord will bear his risen saints. Therefore let us seek the full assurance of faith and hope, that in the midst of pain, and in the prospect of death, we may think calmly on the horrors of the tomb; assured that our bodies will there sleep, and in the mean time our souls will be present with the Redeemer. Sin gives death all its hurtful power. The sting of death is sin; but Christ, by dying, has taken out this sting; he has made atonement for sin, he has obtained remission of it. The strength of sin is the law. None can answer its demands, endure its curse, or do away his own transgressions. Hence terror and anguish. And hence death is terrible to the unbelieving and the impenitent. Death may seize a believer, but it cannot hold him in its power. How many springs of joy to the saints, and of thanksgiving to God, are opened by the death and resurrection, the sufferings and conquests of the Redeemer! In **verse** #(**58**), we have an exhortation, that believers should be stedfast, firm in the faith of that gospel which the apostle preached, and they received. Also, to be unmovable in their hope and expectation of this great privilege, of being raised incorruptible and immortal. And to abound in the work of the Lord, always doing the Lord's service, and obeying the Lord's commands. May Christ give us faith, and increase our faith, that we may not only be safe, but joyful and triumphant.

Chapter 16

Chapter Outline	
A collection for the poor at Jerusalem.	(1–9)
Timothy and Apollos commended.	(10–12)
Exhortation to watchfulness in faith and love.	(13–18)
Christian salutations.	(19–24)

Verses 1–9

The good examples of other Christians and churches should rouse us. It is good to lay up in store for good uses. Those who are rich in this world, should be rich in good works, **1**Ti **6**:**17**, **18**. The diligent hand will not make rich, without the Divine blessing, Pr **10**:**4**, **22**. And what more proper to stir us up to charity to the people and children of God, than to look at all we have as his gift? Works of mercy are real fruits of true love to God, and are therefore proper services on his own day. Ministers are doing their proper business, when putting forward, or helping works of charity. The heart of a Christian minister must be towards the people among whom he has laboured long, and with success. All our purposes must be made with submission to the Divine providence, Jas **4**:**15**. Adversaries and opposition do not break the spirits of faithful and successful ministers, but warm their zeal, and inspire them with fresh courage. A faithful minister is more discouraged by the hardness of his hearers' hearts, and the backslidings of professors, than by the enemies' attempts.

Verses 10–12

Timothy came to do the work of the Lord. Therefore to vex his spirit, would be to grieve the Holy Spirit; to despise him, would be to despise Him that sent him. Those who work the work of the Lord, should be treated with tenderness and respect. Faithful ministers will not be jealous of each other. It becomes the ministers of the gospel to show concern for each other's reputation and usefulness.

Verses 13–18

A Christian is always in danger, therefore should ever be on the watch. He should be fixed in the faith of the gospel, and never desert or give it up. By this faith alone he will be able to keep his ground in an hour of temptation. Christians should be careful that charity not only reigns in their hearts, but shines in their lives. There is a great difference between Christian firmness and feverish warmth and transport. The apostle gave particular directions as to some who served the cause of Christ among them. Those who serve the saints, those who desire the honour of the churches, and to remove reproaches from them, are to be thought much of, and loved. They should willingly acknowledge the worth of such, and all who laboured with or helped the apostle.

Verses 19–24

Christianity by no means destroys civility. Religion should promote a courteous and obliging temper towards all. Those give a false idea of religion, and reproach it, who would take encouragement from it to be sour and morose. And Christian salutations are not mere empty compliments; but are real expressions of good-will to others, and commend them to the Divine grace and blessing. Every Christian family should be as a Christian church. Wherever two or three are gathered together in the name of Christ, and he is among them, there is a church. Here is a solemn warning. Many who have Christ's name much in their mouths, have no true love to him in their hearts. None love him in truth, who do not love his laws, and keep his commandments. Many are Christians in name, who do not love Christ Jesus the Lord in sincerity. Such are separated from the people of God, and the favour of God. Those who love not the Lord Jesus Christ, must perish without remedy. Let us not rest in any religious profession where there is not the love of Christ, earnest desires for his salvation, gratitude for his mercies, and obedience to his commandments. The grace of our Lord Jesus Christ has in it all that is good, for time and for eternity. To wish that our friends may have this grace with them, is wishing them the utmost good. And this we should wish all our friends and brethren in Christ. We can wish them nothing greater, and we should wish them nothing less. True Christianity makes us wish those whom we love, the blessings of both worlds; this is meant in wishing the grace of Christ to be with them. The apostle had dealt plainly with the Corinthians, and told them of their faults with just severity; but he parts in love, and with a solemn profession of his love to them for Christ's sake. May our love be with all who are in Christ Jesus. Let us try whether all things appear worthless to us, when compared with Christ and his righteousness. Do we allow ourselves in any known sin, or in the neglect of any known duty? By such inquiries, faithfully made, we may judge of the state of our souls.

2 Corinthians

The second epistle to the Corinthians probably was written about a year after the first. Its contents are closely connected with those of the former epistle. The manner in which the letter St. Paul formerly wrote had been received, is particularly noticed; this was such as to fill his heart with gratitude to God, who enabled him fully to discharge his duty towards them. Many had shown marks of repentance, and amended their conduct, but others still followed their false teachers; and as the apostle delayed his visit, from his unwillingness to treat them with severity, they charged him with levity and change of conduct. Also, with pride, vain-glory, and severity, and they spake of him with contempt. In this epistle we find the same ardent affection towards the disciples at Corinth, as in the former, the same zeal for the honour of the gospel, and the same boldness in giving Christian reproof. The first six chapters are chiefly practical: the rest have more reference to the state of the Corinthian church, but they contain many rules of general application.

Chapter 1

Chapter Outline	
The apostle blesses God for comfort in, and deliverance out of troubles.	(1–11)
He professes his own and his fellow-labourers' integrity.	(12–14)
Gives reasons for his not coming to them.	(15–24)

Verses 1–11

We are encouraged to come boldly to the throne of grace, that we may obtain mercy, and find grace to help in time of need. The Lord is able to give peace to the troubled conscience, and to calm the raging passions of the soul. These blessings are given by him, as the Father of his redeemed family. It is our Saviour who says, Let not your heart be troubled. All comforts come from God, and our sweetest comforts are in him. He speaks peace to souls by granting the free remission of sins; and he comforts them by the enlivening influences of the Holy Spirit, and by the rich mercies of his grace. He is able to bind up the broken-hearted, to heal the most painful wounds, and also to give hope and joy under the heaviest sorrows. The favours God bestows on us, are not only to make us cheerful, but also that we may be useful to others. He sends comforts enough to support such as simply trust in and serve him. If we should be brought so low as to despair even of life, yet we may then trust God, who can bring back even from death. Their hope and trust were not in vain; nor shall any be ashamed who trust in the Lord. Past experiences encourage faith and hope, and lay us under obligation to trust in God for time to come. And it is our duty, not only to help one another with prayer, but in praise and thanksgiving, and thereby to make suitable returns for benefits received. Thus both trials and mercies will end in good to ourselves and others.

Verses 12–14

Though, as a sinner, the apostle could only rejoice and glory in Christ Jesus, yet, as a believer, he might rejoice and glory in being really what he professed. Conscience witnesses concerning the steady course and tenor of the life. Thereby we may judge ourselves, and not by this or by that single act. Our conversation will be well ordered, when we live and act under such a gracious principle in the heart. Having this, we may leave our characters in the Lord's hands, but using proper means to clear them, when the credit of the gospel, or our usefulness, calls for it.

Verses 15–24

The apostle clears himself from the charge of levity and inconstancy, in not coming to Corinth. Good men should be careful to keep the reputation of sincerity and constancy; they should not resolve, but on careful thought; and they will not change unless for weighty reasons. Nothing can render God's promises more certain: his giving them through Christ, assures us they are his promises; as the wonders God wrought in the life, resurrection, and ascension of his Son, confirm faith. The Holy Spirit makes Christians firm in the faith of the gospel: the quickening of the Spirit is an earnest of everlasting life; and the comforts of the Spirit are an earnest of everlasting joy. The apostle desired to spare the blame he feared would be unavoidable, if he had gone to Corinth before he learned what effect his former letter produced. Our strength and ability are owing to faith; and our comfort and joy must flow from faith. The holy tempers and gracious fruits which attend faith, secure from delusion in so important a matter.

Chapter 2

Chapter Outline	
Reasons for the apostle not coming to Corinth.	(1–4)
Directions about restoring the repentant offender.	(5–11)
An account of his labours and success in spreading the gospel of Christ.	(12–17)

Verses 1–4

The apostle desired to have a cheerful meeting with them; and he had written in confidence of their doing what was to their benefit and his comfort; and that therefore they would be glad to remove every cause of disquiet from him. We should always give pain unwillingly, even when duty requires that it must be given.

Verses 5–11

The apostle desires them to receive the person who had done wrong, again into their communion; for he was aware of his fault, and much afflicted under his punishment. Even sorrow for sin should not unfit for other duties, and drive to despair. Not only was there danger last Satan should get advantage, by tempting the penitent to hard thoughts of God and religion, and so drive him to despair; but against the churches and the ministers of Christ, by bringing an evil report upon Christians as unforgiving; thus making divisions, and hindering the success of the ministry. In this, as in other things, wisdom is to be used, that the ministry may not be blamed for indulging sin on the one hand, or for too great severity towards sinners on the other hand. Satan has many plans to deceive, and knows how to make a bad use of our mistakes.

Verses 12–17

A believer's triumphs are all in Christ. To him be the praise and glory of all, while the success of the gospel is a good reason for a Christian's joy and rejoicing. In ancient triumphs, abundance of perfumes and sweet odours were used; so the name and salvation of Jesus, as ointment poured out, was a sweet savour diffused in every place. Unto some, the gospel is a savour of death unto death. They reject it to their ruin. Unto others, the gospel is a savour of life unto life: as it quickened them at first when they were dead in trespasses and sins, so it makes them more lively, and will end in eternal life. Observe the awful impressions this matter made upon the apostle, and should also make upon us. The work is great, and of ourselves we have no strength at all; all our sufficiency is of God. But what we do in religion, unless it is done in sincerity, as in the sight of God, is not of God, does not come from him, and will not reach to him. May we carefully watch ourselves in this matter; and seek the testimony of our consciences, under the teaching of the Holy Spirit, that as of sincerity, so speak we in Christ and of Christ.

Chapter 3

Chapter Outline	
The preference of the gospel to the law given by Moses.	(1–11)
The preaching of the apostle was suitable to the excellency and evidence of the gospel, through the power of the Holy Ghost.	(12–18)

Verses 1–11

Even the appearance of self-praise and courting human applause, is painful to the humble and spiritual mind. Nothing is more delightful to faithful ministers, or more to their praise, than the success of their ministry, as shown in the spirits and lives of those among whom they labour. The law of Christ was written in their hearts, and the love of Christ shed abroad there. Nor was it written in tables of stone, as the law of God given to Moses, but on the fleshy (not fleshly, as fleshliness denotes sensuality) tables of the heart, Eze **36**:**26**. Their hearts were humbled and softened to receive this impression, by the new-creating power of the Holy Spirit. He ascribes all the glory to God. And remember, as our whole dependence is upon the Lord, so the whole glory belongs to him alone. The letter killeth: the letter of the law is the ministration of death; and if we rest only in the letter of the gospel, we shall not be the better for so doing: but the Holy Spirit gives life spiritual, and life eternal. The Old Testament dispensation was the ministration of death, but the New Testament of life. The law made known sin, and the wrath and curse of God; it showed us a God above us, and a God against us; but the gospel makes known grace, and Emmanuel, God with us. Therein the righteousness of God by faith is revealed; and this shows us that the just shall live by his faith; this makes known the grace and mercy of God through Jesus Christ, for obtaining the forgiveness of sins and eternal life. The gospel so much exceeds the law in glory, that it eclipses the glory of the legal dispensation. But even the New Testament will be a killing letter, if shown as a mere system or form, and without dependence on God the Holy Spirit, to give it a quickening power.

Verses 12–18

It is the duty of the ministers of the gospel to use great plainness, or clearness, of speech. The Old Testament believers had only cloudy and passing glimpses of that glorious Saviour, and unbelievers looked no further than to the outward institution. But the great precepts of the gospel, believe, love, obey, are truths stated as clearly as possible. And the whole doctrine of Christ crucified, is made as plain as human language can make it. Those who lived under the law, had a veil upon their hearts. This veil is taken away by the doctrines of the Bible about Christ. When any person is converted to God, then the veil of ignorance is taken away. The condition of those who enjoy and believe the gospel is happy, for the heart is set at liberty to run the ways of God's commandments. They have light, and with open face they behold the glory of the Lord. Christians should prize and improve these privileges. We should not rest contented without knowing the transforming power of the gospel, by the working of the Spirit, bringing us to seek to be like the temper and tendency of the glorious gospel of our Lord and Saviour Jesus Christ, and into union with Him. We behold Christ, as in the glass of his word; and as the reflection from a mirror causes the face to shine, the faces of Christians shine also.

Chapter 4

Chapter Outline	
The apostles laboured with much diligence, sincerity, and faithfulness.	(1–7)
Their sufferings for the gospel were great, yet with rich supports.	(8–12)
Prospects of eternal glory keep believers from fainting under troubles.	(13–18)

Verses 1–7

The best of men would faint, if they did not receive mercy from God. And that mercy which has helped us out, and helped us on, hitherto, we may rely upon to help us even to the end. The apostles had no base and wicked designs, covered with fair and specious pretences. They did not try to make their ministry serve a turn. Sincerity or uprightness will keep the favourable opinion of wise and good men. Christ by his gospel makes a glorious discovery to the minds of men. But the design of the devil is, to keep men in ignorance; and when he cannot keep the light of the gospel of Christ out of the world, he spares no pains to keep men from the gospel, or to set them against it. The rejection of the gospel is here traced to the wilful blindness and wickedness of the human heart. Self was not the matter or the end of the apostles' preaching; they preached Christ as Jesus, the Saviour and Deliverer, who saves to the uttermost all that come to God through him. Ministers are servants to the souls of men; they must avoid becoming servants to the humours or the lusts of men. It is pleasant to behold the sun in the firmament; but it is more pleasant and profitable for the gospel to shine in the heart. As light was the beginning of the first creation; so, in the new creation, the light of the Spirit is his first work upon the soul. The treasure of gospel light and grace is put into earthen vessels. The ministers of the gospel are subject to the same passions and weaknesses as other men. God could have sent angels to make known the glorious doctrine of the gospel, or could have sent the most admired sons of men to teach the nations, but he chose humbler, weaker vessels, that his power might be more glorified in upholding them, and in the blessed change wrought by their ministry.

Verses 8–12

The apostles were great sufferers, yet they met with wonderful support. Believers may be forsaken of their friends, as well as persecuted by enemies; but their God will never leave them nor forsake them. There may be fears within, as well as fightings without; yet we are not destroyed. The apostle speaks of their sufferings as a counterpart of the sufferings of Christ, that people might see the power of Christ's resurrection, and of grace in and from the living Jesus. In comparison with them, other Christians were, even at that time, in prosperous circumstances.

Verses 13–18

The grace of faith is an effectual remedy against fainting in times of trouble. They knew that Christ was raised, and that his resurrection was an earnest and assurance of theirs. The hope of this resurrection will encourage in a suffering day, and set us above the fear of death. Also, their sufferings were for the advantage of the church, and to God's glory. The sufferings of Christ's ministers, as well as their preaching and conversation, are for the good of the church and the glory of God. The prospect of eternal life and happiness was their support and comfort. What sense was ready to pronounce heavy and long, grievous and tedious, faith perceived to be light and short, and but for a moment. The weight of all temporal afflictions was lightness itself, while the glory to come was a substance, weighty, and lasting beyond description. If the apostle could call his heavy and long-continued trials light, and but for a moment, what must our trifling difficulties be! Faith enables to make this right judgment of things. There are unseen things, as well as things that are seen. And there is this vast difference between them; unseen things are eternal, seen things but temporal, or temporary only. Let us then look off from the things which are seen; let us cease to seek for worldly advantages, or to fear present distresses. Let us give diligence to make our future happiness sure.

Chapter 5

Chapter Outline	
The apostle's hope and desire of heavenly glory.	(1–8)
This excited to diligence. The reasons of his being affected with zeal for the Corinthians.	(9–15)
The necessity of regeneration, and of reconciliation with God through Christ.	(16–21)

Verses 1–8

The believer not only is well assured by faith that there is another and a happy life after this is ended, but he has good hope, through grace, of heaven as a dwelling-place, a resting-place, a hiding-place. In our Father's house there are many mansions, whose Builder and Maker is God. The happiness of the future state is what God has prepared for those that love him: everlasting habitations, not like the earthly tabernacles, the poor cottages of clay, in which our souls now dwell; that are mouldering and decaying, whose foundations are in the dust. The body of flesh is a heavy burden, the calamities of life are a heavy load. But believers groan, being burdened with a body of sin, and because of the many corruptions remaining and raging within them. Death will strip us of the clothing of flesh, and all the comforts of life, as well as end all our troubles here below. But believing souls shall be clothed with garments of praise, with robes of righteousness and glory. The present graces and comforts of the Spirit are earnests of everlasting grace and comfort. And though God is with us here, by his Spirit, and in his ordinances, yet we are not with him as we hope to be. Faith is for this world, and sight is for the other world. It is our duty, and it will be our interest, to walk by faith, till we live by sight. This shows clearly the happiness to be enjoyed by the souls of believers when absent from the body, and where Jesus makes known his glorious presence. We are related to the body and to the Lord; each claims a part in us. But how much more powerfully the Lord pleads for having the soul of the believer closely united with himself! Thou art one of the souls I have loved and chosen; one of those given to me. What is death, as an object of fear, compared with being absent from the Lord!

Verses 9–15

The apostle quickens himself and others to acts of duty. Well-grounded hopes of heaven will not encourage sloth and sinful security. Let all consider the judgment to come, which is called, The terror of the Lord. Knowing what terrible vengeance the Lord would execute upon the workers of iniquity, the apostle and his brethren used every argument and persuasion, to lead men to believe in the Lord Jesus, and to act as his disciples. Their zeal and diligence were for the glory of God and the good of the church. Christ's love to us will have a like effect upon us, if duly considered and rightly judged. All were lost and undone, dead and ruined, slaves to sin, having no power to deliver themselves, and must have remained thus miserable for ever, if Christ had not died. We should not make ourselves, but Christ, the end of our living and actions. A Christian's life should be devoted to Christ. Alas, how many show the worthlessness of their professed faith and love, by living to themselves and to the world!

Verses 16–21

The renewed man acts upon new principles, by new rules, with new ends, and in new company. The believer is created anew; his heart is not merely set right, but a new heart is given him. He is the workmanship of God, created in Christ Jesus unto good works. Though the same as a man, he is changed in his character and conduct. These words must and do mean more than an outward reformation. The man who formerly saw no beauty in the Saviour that he should desire him, now loves him above all things. The heart of the unregenerate is filled with enmity against God, and God is justly offended with him. Yet there may be reconciliation. Our offended God has reconciled us to himself by Jesus Christ. By the inspiration of God, the Scriptures were written, which are the word of reconciliation; showing that peace has been made by the cross, and how we may be interested therein. Though God cannot lose by the quarrel, nor gain by the peace, yet he beseeches sinners to lay aside their enmity, and accept the salvation he offers. Christ knew no sin. He was made Sin; not a sinner, but Sin, a Sin-offering, a Sacrifice for sin. The end and design of all this was, that we might be made the righteousness of God in him, might be justified freely by the grace of God through the redemption which is in Christ Jesus. Can any lose, labour, or suffer too much for Him, who gave his beloved Son to be the Sacrifice for their sins, that they might be made the righteousness of God in him?

Chapter 6

Chapter Outline	
The apostle, with others, proved themselves faithful ministers of Christ, by their unblamable life and behaviour.	(1–10)
By affection for them, And by earnest concern, that they might have no fellowship with unbelievers and idolaters.	(11–18)

Verses 1–10

The gospel is a word of grace sounding in our ears. The gospel day is a day of salvation, the means of grace the means of salvation, the offers of the gospel the offers of salvation, and the present time the proper time to accept these offers. The morrow is none of ours: we know not what will be on the morrow, nor where we shall be. We now enjoy a day of grace; then let all be careful not to neglect it. Ministers of the gospel should look upon themselves as God's servants, and act in every thing suitably to that character. The apostle did so, by much patience in afflictions, by acting from good principles, and by due temper and behaviour. Believers, in this world, need the grace of God, to arm them against temptations, so as to bear the good report of men without pride; and so as to bear their reproaches with patience. They have nothing in themselves, but possess all things in Christ. Of such differences is a Christian's life made up, and through such a variety of conditions and reports, is our way to heaven; and we should be careful in all things to approve ourselves to God. The gospel, when faithfully preached, and fully received, betters the condition even of the poorest. They save what before they riotously spent, and diligently employ their time to useful purposes. They save and gain by religion, and thus are made rich, both for the world to come and for this, when compared with their sinful, profligate state, before they received the gospel.

Verses 11–18

It is wrong for believers to join with the wicked and profane. The word unbeliever applies to all destitute of true faith. True pastors will caution their beloved children in the gospel, not to be unequally yoked. The fatal effects of neglecting Scripture precepts as to marriages clearly appear. Instead of a help meet, the union brings a snare. Those whose cross it is to be unequally united, without their wilful fault, may expect consolation under it; but when believers enter into such unions, against the express warnings of God's word, they must expect must distress. The caution also extends to common conversation. We should not join in friendship and acquaintance with wicked men and unbelievers. Though we cannot wholly avoid seeing and hearing, and being with such, yet we should never choose them for friends. We must not defile ourselves by converse with those who defile themselves with sin. Come out from the workers of iniquity, and separate from their vain and sinful pleasures and pursuits; from all conformity to the corruptions of this present evil world. If it be an envied privilege to be the son or daughter of an earthly prince, who can express the dignity and happiness of being sons and daughters of the Almighty?

Chapter 7

Chapter Outline	

An exhortation to holiness, and the whole church entreated to bear affection to the apostle.	(1–4)
He rejoiced in their sorrowing to repentance.	(5–11)
And in the comfort they and Titus had together.	(12–16)

Verses 1–4

The promises of God are strong reasons for us to follow after holiness; we must cleanse ourselves from all filthiness of flesh and spirit. If we hope in God as our Father, we must seek to be holy as he is holy, and perfect as our Father in heaven. His grace, by the influences of his Spirit, alone can purify, but holiness should be the object of our constant prayers. If the ministers of the gospel are thought contemptible, there is danger lest the gospel itself be despised also; and though ministers must flatter none, yet they must be gentle towards all. Ministers may look for esteem and favour, when they can safely appeal to the people, that they have corrupted no man by false doctrines or flattering speeches; that they have defrauded no man; nor sought to promote their own interests so as to hurt any. It was affection to them made the apostle speak so freely to them, and caused him to glory of them, in all places, and upon all occasions.

Verses 5–11

There were fightings without, or continual contentions with, and opposition from Jews and Gentiles; and there were fears within, and great concern for such as had embraced the Christian faith. But God comforts those who are cast down. We should look above and beyond all means and instruments, to God, as the author of all the consolation and good we enjoy. Sorrow according to the will of God, tending to the glory of God, and wrought by the Spirit of God, renders the heart humble, contrite, submissive, disposed to mortify every sin, and to walk in newness of life. And this repentance is connected with saving faith in Christ, and an interest in his atonement. There is a great difference between this sorrow of a godly sort, and the sorrow of the world. The happy fruits of true repentance are mentioned. Where the heart is changed, the life and actions will be changed. It wrought indignation at sin, at themselves, at the tempter and his instruments. It wrought a fear of watchfulness, and a cautious fear of sin. It wrought desire to be reconciled with God. It wrought zeal for duty, and against sin. It wrought revenge against sin and their own folly, by endeavours to make satisfaction for injuries done thereby. Deep humility before God, hatred of all sin, with faith in Christ, a new heart and a new life, make repentance unto salvation. May the Lord bestow it on every one of us.

Verses 12–16

The apostle was not disappointed concerning them, which he signified to Titus; and he could with joy declare the confidence he had in them for the time to come. Here see the duties of a pastor and of his flock; the latter must lighten the troubles of the pastoral office, by respect and obedience; the former make a due return by his care of them, and cherish the flock by testimonies of satisfaction, joy, and tenderness.

Chapter 8

Chapter Outline	
The apostle reminds them of charitable contributions for the poor saints.	(1–6)
Enforces this by their gifts, and by the love and grace of Christ.	(7–9)
By the willingness they had shown to this good work.	(10–15)
He recommends Titus to them.	(16–24)

Verses 1–6

The grace of God must be owned as the root and fountain of all the good in us, or done by us, at any time. It is great grace and favour from God, if we are made useful to others, and forward to any good work. He commends the charity of the Macedonians. So far from needing that Paul should urge them, they prayed him to receive the gift. Whatever we use or lay out for God, it is only giving him what is his own. All we give for charitable uses, will not be accepted of God, nor turn to our advantage, unless we first give ourselves to the Lord. By ascribing all really good works to the grace of God, we not only give the glory to him whose due it is, but also show men where their strength is. Abundant spiritual joy enlarges men's hearts in the work and labour of love. How different this from the conduct of those who will not join in any good work, unless urged into it!

Verses 7–9

Faith is the root; and as without faith it is not possible to please God, Heb **11:6**, so those who abound in faith, will abound in other graces and good works also; and this will work and show itself by love. Great talkers are not always the best doers; but these Corinthians were diligent to do, as well as to know and talk well. To all these good things the apostle desires them to add this grace also, to abound in charity to the poor. The best arguments for Christian duties, are drawn from the grace and love of Christ. Though he was rich, as being God, equal in power and glory with the Father, yet he not only became man for us, but became poor also. At length he emptied himself, as it were, to ransom their souls by his sacrifice on the cross. From what riches, blessed Lord, to what poverty didst thou descend for our sakes! and to what riches hast thou advanced us through thy poverty! It is our happiness to be wholly at thy disposal.

Verses 10–15

Good purposes are like buds and blossoms, pleasant to behold, and give hopes of good fruit; but they are lost, and signify nothing without good deeds. Good beginnings are well; but we lose the benefit, unless there is perseverance. When men purpose that which is good, and endeavour, according to their ability, to perform also, God will not reject them for what it is not in their power to do. But this scripture will not justify those who think good meanings are enough, or that good purposes, and the mere profession of a willing mind, are enough to save. Providence gives to some more of the good things of this world, and to some less, that those who have abundance might supply others who are in want. It is the will of God, that by our mutual supplying one another, there should be some sort of equality; not such a levelling as would destroy property, for in such a case there could be no exercise of charity. All should think themselves concerned to relieve those in want. This is shown from the gathering and giving out the manna in the wilderness, Ex **16**:**18**. Those who have most of this world, have no more than food and raiment; and those who have but little of this world, seldom are quite without them.

Verses 16–24

The apostle commends the brethren sent to collect their charity, that it might be known who they were, and how safely they might be trusted. It is the duty of all Christians to act prudently; to hinder, as far as we can, all unjust suspicions. It is needful, in the first place, to act uprightly in the sight of God, but things honest in the sight of men should also be attended to. A clear character, as well as a pure conscience, is requisite for usefulness. They brought glory to Christ as instruments, and had obtained honour from Christ to be counted faithful, and employed in his service. The good opinion others have of us, should be an argument with us to do well.

Chapter 9

Chapter Outline	
The reason for sending Titus to collect their alms.	(1–5)
The Corinthians to be liberal and cheerful, The apostle thanks God for his unspeakable gift.	(6–15)

Verses 1–5

When we would have others do good, we must act toward them prudently and tenderly, and give them time. Christians should consider what is for the credit of their profession, and endeavour to adorn the doctrine of God their Saviour in all things. The duty of ministering to the saints is so plain, that there would seem no need to exhort Christians to it; yet self-love contends so powerfully against the love of Christ, that it is often necessary to stir up their minds by way of remembrance.

Verses 6–15

Money bestowed in charity, may to the carnal mind seem thrown away, but when given from proper principles, it is seed sown, from which a valuable increase may be expected. It should be given carefully. Works of charity, like other good works, should be done with thought and design. Due thought, as to our circumstances, and those we are about to relieve, will direct our gifts for charitable uses. Help should be given freely, be it more or less; not grudgingly, but cheerfully. While some scatter, and yet increase; others withhold more than is meet, and it tends to poverty. If we had more faith and love, we should waste less on ourselves, and sow more in hope of a plentiful increase. Can a man lose by doing that with which God is pleased? He is able to make all grace abound towards us, and to abound in us; to give a large increase of spiritual and of temporal good things. He can make us to have enough in all things; and to be content with what we have. God gives not only enough for ourselves, but that also wherewith we may supply the wants of others, and this should be as seed to be sown. We must show the reality of our subjection to the gospel, by works of charity. This will be for the credit of our profession, and to the praise and glory of God. Let us endeavour to copy the example of Christ, being unwearied in doing good, and deeming it more blessed to give than to receive. Blessed be God for the unspeakable gift of his grace, whereby he enables and inclines some of his people to bestow upon others, and others to be grateful for it; and blessed be his glorious name to all eternity, for Jesus Christ, that inestimable gift of his love, through whom this and every other good thing, pertaining to life and godliness, are freely given unto us, beyond all expression, measure, or bounds.

Chapter 10

Chapter Outline	
The apostle states his authority with meekness and humility.	(1–6)
Reasons with the Corinthians.	(7–11)
Seeks the glory of God, and to be approved of him.	(12–18)

Verses 1–6

While others thought meanly, and spake scornfully of the apostle, he had low thoughts, and spake humbly of himself. We should be aware of our own infirmities, and think humbly of ourselves, even when men reproach us. The work of the ministry is a spiritual warfare with spiritual enemies, and for spiritual purposes. Outward force is not the method of the gospel, but strong persuasions, by the power of truth and the meekness of wisdom. Conscience is accountable to God only; and people must be persuaded to God and their duty, not driven by force. Thus the weapons of our warfare are very powerful; the evidence of truth is convincing. What opposition is made against the gospel, by the powers of sin and Satan in the hearts of men! But observe the conquest the word of God gains. The appointed means, however feeble they appear to some, will be mighty through God. And the preaching of the cross, by men of faith and prayer, has always been fatal to idolatry, impiety, and wickedness.

Verses 7–11

In outward appearance, Paul was mean and despised in the eyes of some, but this was a false rule to judge by. We must not think that none outward appearance, as if the want of such things proved a man not to be a real Christian, or an able, faithful minister of the lowly Saviour.

Verses 12–18

If we would compare ourselves with others who excel us, this would be a good method to keep us humble. The apostle fixes a good rule for his conduct; namely, not to boast of things without his measure, which was the measure God had distributed to him. There is not a more fruitful source of error, than to judge of persons and opinions by our own prejudices. How common is it for persons to judge of their own religious character, by the opinions and maxims of the world around them! But how different is the rule of God's word! And of all flattery, self-flattery is the worst. Therefore, instead of praising ourselves, we should strive to approve ourselves to God. In a word, let us glory in the Lord our salvation, and in all other things only as evidences of his love, or means of promoting his glory. Instead of praising ourselves, or seeking the praise of men, let us desire that honour which cometh from God only.

Chapter 11

Chapter Outline	
The apostle gives the reasons for speaking in his own commendation.	(1–14)
Shows that he had freely preached the gospel.	(5–15)
Explains what he was going to add in defence of his own character.	(16–21)
He gives an account of his labours, cares, sufferings, dangers, and deliverances.	(22–33)

Verses 1–4

The apostle desired to preserve the Corinthians from being corrupted by the false apostles. There is but one Jesus, one Spirit, and one gospel, to be preached to them, and received by them; and why should any be prejudiced, by the devices of an adversary, against him who first taught them in faith? They should not listen to men, who, without cause, would draw them away from those who were the means of their conversion.

Verses 5–15

It is far better to be plain in speech, yet walking openly and consistently with the gospel, than to be admired by thousands, and be lifted up in pride, so as to disgrace the gospel by evil tempers and unholy lives. The apostle would not give room for any to accuse him of worldly designs in preaching the gospel, that others who opposed him at Corinth, might not in this respect gain advantage against him. Hypocrisy may be looked for, especially when we consider the great power which Satan, who rules in the hearts of the children of disobedience, has upon the minds of many. And as there are temptations to evil conduct, so there is equal danger on the other side. It serves Satan's purposes as well, to set up good works against the atonement of Christ, and salvation by faith and grace. But the end will discover those who are deceitful workers; their work will end in ruin. Satan will allow his ministers to preach either the law or the gospel separately; but the law as established by faith in Christ's righteousness and atonement, and the partaking of his Spirit, is the test of every false system.

Verses 16–21

It is the duty and practice of Christians to humble themselves, in obedience to the command and example of the Lord; yet prudence must direct in what it is needful to do things which we may do lawfully, even the speaking of what God has wrought for us, and in us, and by us. Doubtless here is reference to facts in which the character of the false apostles had been shown. It is astonishing to see how such men bring their followers into bondage, and how they take from them and insult them.

Verses 22–33

The apostle gives an account of his labours and sufferings; not out of pride or vain-glory, but to the honour of God, who enabled him to do and suffer so much for the cause of Christ; and shows wherein he excelled the false apostles, who tried to lessen his character and usefulness. It astonishes us to reflect on this account of his dangers, hardships, and sufferings, and to observe his patience, perseverance, diligence, cheerfulness, and usefulness, in the midst of all these trials. See what little reason we have to love the pomp and plenty of this world, when this blessed apostle felt so much hardship in it. Our utmost diligence and services appear unworthy of notice when compared with his, and our difficulties and trials scarcely can be perceived. It may well lead us to inquire whether or not we really are followers of Christ. Here we may study patience, courage, and firm trust in God. Here we may learn to think less of ourselves; and we should ever strictly keep to truth, as in God's presence; and should refer all to his glory, as the Father of our Lord Jesus Christ, who is blessed for evermore.

Chapter 12

Chapter Outline	
The apostle's revelations.	(1–6)
Which were improved to his spiritual advantage.	(7–10)
The signs of an apostle were in him, His purpose of making them a visit; but he expresses his fear lest he should have to be severe with some.	(11–21)

Verses 1–6

There can be no doubt the apostle speaks of himself. Whether heavenly things were brought down to him, while his body was in a trance, as in the case of ancient prophets; or whether his soul was dislodged from the body for a time, and taken up into heaven, or whether he was taken up, body and soul together, he knew not. We are not capable, nor is it fit we should yet know, the particulars of that glorious place and state. He did not attempt to publish to the world what he had heard there, but he set forth the doctrine of Christ. On that foundation the church is built, and on that we must build our faith and hope. And while this teaches us to enlarge our expectations of the glory that shall be revealed, it should render us contented with the usual methods of learning the truth and will of God.

Verses 7–10

The apostle gives an account of the method God took to keep him humble, and to prevent his being lifted up above measure, on account of the visions and revelations he had. We are not told what this thorn in the flesh was, whether some great trouble, or some great temptation. But God often brings this good out of evil, that the reproaches of our enemies help to hide pride from us. If God loves us, he will keep us from being exalted above measure; and spiritual burdens are ordered to cure spiritual pride. This thorn in the flesh is said to be a messenger of Satan which he sent for evil; but God designed it, and overruled it for good. Prayer is a salve for every sore, a remedy for every malady; and when we are afflicted with thorns in the flesh, we should give ourselves to prayer. If an answer be not given to the first prayer, nor to the second, we are to continue praying. Troubles are sent to teach us to pray; and are continued, to teach us to continue instant in prayer. Though God accepts the prayer of faith, yet he does not always give what is asked for: as he sometimes grants in wrath, so he sometimes denies in love. When God does not take away our troubles and temptations, yet, if he gives grace enough for us, we have no reason to complain. Grace signifies the good-will of God towards us, and that is enough to enlighten and enliven us, sufficient to strengthen and comfort in all afflictions and distresses. His strength is made perfect in our weakness. Thus his grace is manifested and magnified. When we are weak in ourselves, then we are strong in the grace of our Lord Jesus Christ; when we feel that we are weak in ourselves, then we go to Christ, receive strength from him, and enjoy most the supplies of Divine strength and grace.

Verses 11–21

We owe it to good men, to stand up in the defence of their reputation; and we are under special obligations to those from whom we have received benefit, especially spiritual benefit, to own them as instruments in God's hand of good to us. Here is an account of the apostle's behaviour and kind intentions; in which see the character of a faithful minister of the gospel. This was his great aim and design, to do good. Here are noticed several sins commonly found among professors of religion. Falls and misdeeds are humbling to a minister; and God sometimes takes this way to humble those who might be tempted to be lifted up. These vast **verse**s show to what excesses the false teachers had drawn aside their deluded followers. How grievous it is that such evils should be found among professors of the gospel! Yet thus it is, and has been too often, and it was so even in the days of the apostles.

Chapter 13

Chapter Outline	
The apostle threatens obstinate offenders.	(1–6)
He prays for their reformation.	(7–10)
And ends the epistle with a salutation and blessing.	(11–14)

Verses 1–6

Though it is God's gracious method to bear long with sinners, yet he will not bear always; at length he will come, and will not spare those who remain obstinate and impenitent. Christ at his crucifixion, appeared as only a weak and helpless man, but his resurrection and life showed his Divine power. So the apostles, how mean and contemptible soever they appeared to the world, yet, as instruments, they manifested the power of God. Let them prove their tempers, conduct, and experience, as gold is assayed or proved by the touchstone. If they could prove themselves not to be reprobates, not to be rejected of Christ, he trusted they would know that he was not a reprobate, not disowned by Christ. They ought to know if Christ Jesus was in them, by the influences, graces, and indwelling of his Spirit, by his kingdom set up in their hearts. Let us question our own souls; either we are true Christians, or we are deceivers. Unless Christ be in us by his Spirit, and power of his love, our faith is dead, and we are yet disapproved by our Judge.

Verses 7–10

The most desirable thing we can ask of God, for ourselves and our friends, is to be kept from sin, that we and they may not do evil. We have far more need to pray that we may not do evil, than that we may not suffer evil. The apostle not only desired that they might be kept from sin, but also that they might grow in grace, and increase in holiness. We are earnestly to pray to God for those we caution, that they may cease to do evil, and learn to do well; and we should be glad for others to be strong in the grace of Christ, though it may be the means of showing our own weakness. let us also pray that we may be enabled to make a proper use of all our talents.

Verses 11–14

Here are several good exhortations. God is the Author of peace and Lover of concord; he hath loved us, and is willing to be at peace with us. And let it be our constant aim so to walk, that separation from our friends may be only for a time, and that we may meet in that happy world where parting will be unknown. He wishes that they may partake all the benefits which Christ of his free grace and favour has purchased; the Father out of his free love has purposed; and the Holy Ghost applies and bestows.

Galatians

The churches in Galatia were formed partly of converted Jews, and partly of Gentile converts, as was generally the case. St. Paul asserts his apostolic character and the doctrines he taught, that he might confirm the Galatian churches in the faith of Christ, especially with respect to the important point of justification by faith alone. Thus the subject is mainly the same as that which is discussed in the epistle to the Romans, that is, justification by faith alone. In this epistle, however, attention is particularly directed to the point, that men are justified by faith without the works of the law of Moses. Of the importance of the doctrines prominently set forth in this epistle, Luther thus speaks: "We have to fear as the greatest and nearest danger, lest Satan take from us this doctrine of faith, and bring into the church again the doctrine of works and of men's traditions. Wherefore it is very necessary that this doctrine be kept in continual practice and public exercise, both of reading and hearing. If this doctrine be lost, then is also the doctrine of truth, life and salvation, lost and gone."

Chapter 1

Chapter Outline	
The apostle Paul asserts his apostolic character against such as lessened it.	(1–5)
He reproves the Galatians for revolting from the gospel of Christ under the influence of evil teachers.	(6–9)

He proves the Divine authority of his doctrine and mission; and declares what he was before his conversion and calling.	(10–14)
And how he proceeded after it.	(15–24)

Verses 1–5

St. Paul was an apostle of Jesus Christ; he was expressly appointed by him, consequently by God the Father, who is one with him in respect of his Divine nature, and who appointed Christ as Mediator. Grace, includes God's good-will towards us, and his good work upon us; and peace, all that inward comfort, or outward prosperity, which is really needful for us. They come from God the Father, as the Fountain, through Jesus Christ. But observe, first grace, and then peace; there can be no true peace without grace. Christ gave himself for our sins, to make atonement for us: this the justice of God required, and to this he freely submitted. Here is to be observed the infinite greatness of the price bestowed, and then it will appear plainly, that the power of sin is so great, that it could by no means be put away except the Son of God be given for it. He that considers these things well, understands that sin is a thing the most horrible that can be expressed; which ought to move us, and make us afraid indeed. Especially mark well the words, "for our sins." For here our weak nature starts back, and would first be made worthy by her own works. It would bring him that is whole, and not him that has need of a physician. Not only to redeem us from the wrath of God, and the curse of the law; but also to recover us from wicked practices and customs, to which we are naturally enslaved. But it is in vain for those who are not delivered from this present evil world by the sanctification of the Spirit, to expect that they are freed from its condemnation by the blood of Jesus.

Verses 6–9

Those who would establish any other way to heaven than what the gospel of Christ reveals, will find themselves wretchedly mistaken. The apostle presses upon the Galatians a due sense of their guilt in forsaking the gospel way of justification; yet he reproves with tenderness, and represents them as drawn into it by the arts of some that troubled them. In reproving others, we should be faithful, and yet endeavour to restore them in the spirit of meekness. Some would set up the works of the law in the place of Christ's righteousness, and thus they corrupted Christianity. The apostle solemnly denounces, as accursed, every one who attempts to lay so false a foundation. All other gospels than that of the grace of Christ, whether more flattering to self-righteous pride, or more favourable to worldly lusts, are devices of Satan. And while we declare that to reject the moral law as a rule of life, tends to dishonour Christ, and destroy true religion, we must also declare, that all dependence for justification on good works, whether real or supposed, is as fatal to those who persist in it. While we are zealous for good works, let us be careful not to put them in the place of Christ's righteousness, and not to advance any thing which may betray others into so dreadful a delusion.

Verses 10–14

In preaching the gospel, the apostle sought to bring persons to the obedience, not of men, but of God. But Paul would not attempt to alter the doctrine of Christ, either to gain their favour, or to avoid their fury. In so important a matter we must not fear the frowns of men, nor seek their favour, by using words of men's wisdom. Concerning the manner wherein he received the gospel, he had it by revelation from Heaven. He was not led to Christianity, as many are, merely by education.

Verses 15–24

St. Paul was wonderfully brought to the knowledge and faith of Christ. All who are savingly converted, are called by the grace of God; their conversion is wrought by his power and grace working in them. It will but little avail us to have Christ revealed to us, if he is not also revealed in us. He instantly prepared to obey, without hesitating as to his worldly interest, credit, ease, or life itself. And what matter of thanksgiving and joy is it to the churches of Christ, when they hear of such instances to the praise of the glory of his grace, whether they have ever seen them or not! They glorify God for his power and mercy in saving such persons, and for all the service to his people and cause that is done, and may be further expected from them.

Chapter 2

Chapter Outline	
The apostle declares his being owned as an apostle of the Gentiles.	(1–10)
He had publicly opposed Peter for judaizing.	(11–14)
And from thence he enters upon the doctrine of justification by faith in Christ, without the works of the law.	(15–21)

Verses 1–10

Observe the apostle's faithfulness in giving a full account of the doctrine he had preached among the Gentiles, and was still resolved to preach, that of Christianity, free from all mixture of Judaism. This doctrine would be ungrateful to many, yet he was not afraid to own it. His care was, lest the success of his past labours should be lessened, or his future usefulness be hindered. While we simply depend upon God for success to our labours, we should use every proper caution to remove mistakes, and against opposers. There are things which may lawfully be complied with, yet, when they cannot be done without betraying the truth, they ought to be refused. We must not give place to any conduct, whereby the truth of the gospel would be reflected upon. Though Paul conversed with the other apostles, yet he did not receive any addition to his knowledge, or authority, from them. Perceiving the grace given to him, they gave unto him and Barnabas the right hand of fellowship, whereby they acknowledged that he was designed to the honour and office of an apostle as well as themselves. They agreed that these two should go to the heathen, while they continued to preach to the Jews; judging it agreeable to the mind of Christ, so to divide their work. Here we learn that the gospel is not ours, but God's; and that men are but the keepers of it; for this we are to praise God. The apostle showed his charitable disposition, and how ready he was to own the Jewish converts as brethren, though many would scarcely allow the like favour to the converted Gentiles; but mere difference of opinion was no reason to him why he should not help them. Herein is a pattern of Christian charity, which we should extend to all the disciples of Christ.

Verses 11–14

Notwithstanding Peter's character, yet, when Paul saw him acting so as to hurt the truth of the gospel and the peace of the church, he was not afraid to reprove him. When he saw that Peter and the others did not live up to that principle which the gospel taught, and which they professed, namely, That by the death of Christ the partition wall between Jew and Gentile was taken down, and the observance of the law of Moses was no longer in force; as Peter's offence was public, he publicly reproved him. There is a very great difference between the prudence of St. Paul, who bore with, and used for a time, the ceremonies of the law as not sinful, and the timid conduct of St. Peter, who, by withdrawing from the Gentiles, led others to think that these ceremonies were necessary.

Verses 15–19

Paul, having thus shown he was not inferior to any apostle, not to Peter himself, speaks of the great foundation doctrine of the gospel. For what did we believe in Christ? Was it not that we might be justified by the faith of Christ? If so, is it not foolish to go back to the law, and to expect to be justified by the merit of moral works, or sacrifices, or ceremonies? The occasion of this declaration doubtless arose from the ceremonial law; but the argument is quite as strong against all dependence upon the works of the moral law, as respects justification. To give the greater weight to this, it is added, But if, while we seek to be justified by Christ, we ourselves also are found sinners, is Christ the minister of sin? This would be very dishonourable to Christ, and also very hurtful to them. By considering the law itself, he saw that justification was not to be expected by the works of it, and that there was now no further need of the sacrifices and cleansings of it, since they were done away in Christ, by his offering up himself a sacrifice for us. He did not hope or fear any thing from it; any more than a dead man from enemies. But the effect was not a careless, lawless life. It was necessary, that he might live to God, and be devoted to him through the motives and grace of the gospel. It is no new prejudice, though a most unjust one, that the doctrine of justification by faith alone, tends to encourage people in sin. Not so, for to take occasion from free grace, or the doctrine of it, to live in sin, is to try to make Christ the minister of sin, at any thought of which all Christian hearts would shudder.

Verses 20, 21

Here, in his own person, the apostle describes the spiritual or hidden life of a believer. The old man is crucified, Ro **6:6**, but the new man is living; sin is mortified, and grace is quickened. He has the comforts and the triumphs of grace; yet that grace is not from himself, but from another. Believers see themselves living in a state of dependence on Christ. Hence it is, that though he lives in the flesh, yet he does not live after the flesh. Those who have true faith, live by that faith; and faith fastens upon Christ's giving himself for us. He loved me, and gave himself for me. As if the apostle said, The Lord saw me fleeing from him more and more. Such wickedness, error, and ignorance were in my will and understanding, that it was not possible for me to be ransomed by any other means than by such a price. Consider well this price. Here notice the false faith of many. And their profession is accordingly; they have the form of godliness without the power of it. They think they believe the articles of faith aright, but they are deceived. For to believe in Christ crucified, is not only to believe that he was crucified, but also to believe that I am crucified with him. And this is to know Christ crucified. Hence we learn what is the nature of grace. God's grace cannot stand with man's merit. Grace is no grace unless it is freely given every way. The more simply the believer relies on Christ for every thing, the more devotedly does he walk before Him in all his ordinances and commandments. Christ lives and reigns in him, and he lives here on earth by faith in the Son of God, which works by love, causes obedience, and changes into his holy image. Thus he neither abuses the grace of God, nor makes it in vain.

Chapter 3

Chapter Outline	
The Galatians reproved for departing from the great doctrine of justification alone, through faith in Christ.	(1–5)
This doctrine established from the example of Abraham.	(6–9)
From the tenor of the law and the severity of its curse.	(10–14)
From the covenant of promises, which the law could not disannul.	(15–18)
The law was a school master to lead them to Christ.	(19–25)
Under the gospel state true believers are all one in Christ.	(26–29)

Verses 1–5

Several things made the folly of the Galatian Christians worse. They had the doctrine of the cross preached, and the Lord's supper administered among them, in both which Christ crucified, and the nature of his sufferings, had been fully and clearly set forth. Had they been made partakers of the Holy Spirit, by the ministration of the law, or on account of any works done by them in obedience thereto? Was it not by their hearing and embracing the doctrine of faith in Christ alone for justification? Which of these had God owned with tokens of his favour and acceptance? It was not by the first, but the last. And those must be very unwise, who suffer themselves to be turned away from the ministry and doctrine which have been blessed to their spiritual advantage. Alas, that men should turn from the all-important doctrine of Christ crucified, to listen to useless distinctions, mere moral preaching, or wild fancies! The god of this world, by various men and means, has blinded men's eyes, lest they should learn to trust in a crucified Saviour. We may boldly demand where the fruits of the Holy Spirit are most evidently brought forth? whether among those who preach justification by the works of the law, or those who preach the doctrine of faith? Assuredly among the latter.

Verses 6–14

The apostle proves the doctrine he had blamed the Galatians for rejecting; namely, that of justification by faith without the works of the law. This he does from the example of Abraham, whose faith fastened upon the word and promise of God, and upon his believing he was owned and accepted of God as a righteous man. The Scripture is said to foresee, because the Holy Spirit that indited the Scripture did foresee. Through faith in the promise of God he was blessed; and it is only in the same way that others obtain this privilege. Let us then study the object, nature, and effects of Abraham's faith; for who can in any other way escape the curse of the holy law? The curse is against all sinners, therefore against all men; for all have sinned, and are become guilty before God: and if, as transgressors of the law, we are under its curse, it must be vain to look for justification by it. Those only are just or righteous who are freed from death and wrath, and restored into a state of life in the favour of God; and it is only through faith that persons become righteous. Thus we see that justification by faith is no new doctrine, but was taught in the church of God, long before the times of the gospel. It is, in truth, the only way wherein any sinners ever were, or can be justified. Though deliverance is not to be expected from the law, there is a way open to escape the curse, and regain the favour of God, namely, through faith in Christ. Christ redeemed us from the curse of the law; being made sin, or a sin-offering, for us, he was made a curse for us; not separated from God, but laid for a time under the Divine punishment. The heavy sufferings of the Son of God, more loudly warn sinners to flee from the wrath to come, than all the curses of the law; for how can God spare any man who remains under sin, seeing that he spared not his own Son, when our sins were charged upon him? Yet at the same time, Christ, as from the cross, freely invites sinners to take refuge in him.

Verses 15–18

The covenant God made with Abraham, was not done away by the giving the law to Moses. The covenant was made with Abraham and his Seed. It is still in force; Christ abideth for ever in his person, and his spiritual seed, who are his by faith. By this we learn the difference between the promises of the law and those of the gospel. The promises of the law are made to the person of every man; the promises of the gospel are first made to Christ, then by him to those who are by faith ingrafted into Christ. Rightly to divide the word of truth, a great difference must be put between the promise and the law, as to the inward affections, and the whole practice of life. When the promise is mingled with the law, it is made nothing but the law. Let Christ be always before our eyes, as a sure argument for the defence of faith, against dependence on human righteousness.

Verses 19–22

If that promise was enough for salvation, wherefore then serveth the law? The Israelites, though chosen to be God's peculiar people, were sinners as well as others. The law was not intended to discover a way of justification, different from that made known by the promise, but to lead men to see their need of the promise, by showing the sinfulness of sin, and to point to Christ, through whom alone they could be pardoned and justified. The promise was given by God himself; the law was given by the ministry of angels, and the hand of a mediator, even Moses. Hence the law could not be designed to set aside the promise. A mediator, as the very term signifies, is a friend that comes between two parties, and is not to act merely with and for one of them. The great design of the law was, that the promise by faith of Jesus Christ, might be given to those that believe; that, being convinced of their guilt, and the insufficiency of the law to effect a righteousness for them, they might be persuaded to believe on Christ, and so obtain the benefit of the promise. And it is not possible that the holy, just, and good law of God, the standard of duty to all, should be contrary to the gospel of Christ. It tends every way to promote it.

Verses 23–25

The law did not teach a living, saving knowledge; but, by its rites and ceremonies, especially by its sacrifices, it pointed to Christ, that they might be justified by faith. And thus it was, as the word properly signifies, a servant, to lead to Christ, as children are led to school by servants who have the care of them, that they might be more fully taught by Him the true way of justification and salvation, which is only by faith in Christ. And the vastly greater advantage of the gospel state is shown, under which we enjoy a clearer discovery of Divine grace and mercy than the Jews of old. Most men continue shut up as in a dark dungeon, in love with their sins, being blinded and lulled asleep by Satan, through wordly pleasures, interests, and pursuits. But the awakened sinner discovers his dreadful condition. Then he feels that the mercy and grace of God form his only hope. And the terrors of the law are often used by the convincing Spirit, to show the sinner his need of Christ, to bring him to rely on his sufferings and merits, that he may be justified by faith. Then the law, by the teaching of the Holy Spirit, becomes his loved rule of duty, and his standard for daily self-examination. In this use of it he learns to depend more simply on the Saviour.

Verses 26–29

Real Christians enjoy great privileges under the gospel; and are no longer accounted servants, but sons; not now kept at such a distance, and under such restraints as the Jews were. Having accepted Christ Jesus as their Lord and Saviour, and relying on him alone for justification and salvation, they become the sons of God. But no outward forms or profession can secure these blessings; for if any man have not the Spirit of Christ, he is none of his. In baptism we put on Christ; therein we profess to be his disciples. Being baptized into Christ, we are baptized into his death, that as he died and rose again, so we should die unto sin, and walk in newness and holiness of life. The putting on of Christ according to the gospel, consists not in outward imitation, but in a new birth, an entire change. He who makes believers to be heirs, will provide for them. Therefore our care must be to do the duties that belong to us, and all other cares we must cast upon God. And our special care must be for heaven; the things of this life are but trifles. The city of God in heaven, is the portion or child's part. Seek to be sure of that above all things.

Chapter 4

Chapter Outline	
The folly of returning to legal observances for justification.	(1–7)
The happy change made in the Gentile believers.	(8–11)
The apostle reasons against following false teachers.	(12–18)
He expresses his earnest concern for them.	(19, 20)
And then explains the difference between what is to be expected from the law, and from the gospel.	(21–31)

Verses 1–7

The apostle deals plainly with those who urged the law of Moses together with the gospel of Christ, and endeavoured to bring believers under its bondage. They could not fully understand the meaning of the law as given by Moses. And as that was a dispensation of darkness, so of bondage; they were tied to many burdensome rites and observances, by which they were taught and kept subject like a child under tutors and governors. We learn the happier state of Christians under the gospel dispensation. From these **verse**s see the wonders of Divine love and mercy; particularly of God the Father, in sending his Son into the world to redeem and save us; of the Son of God, in submitting so low, and suffering so much for us; and of the Holy Spirit, in condescending to dwell in the hearts of believers, for such gracious purposes. Also, the advantages Christians enjoy under the gospel. Although by nature children of wrath and disobedience, they become by grace children of love, and partake of the nature of the children of God; for he will have all his children resemble him. Among men the eldest son is heir; but all God's children shall have the inheritance of eldest sons. May the temper and conduct of sons ever show our adoption; and may the Holy Spirit witness with our spirits that we are children and heirs of God.

Verses 8–11

The happy change whereby the Galatians were turned from idols to the living God, and through Christ had received the adoption of sons, was the effect of his free and rich grace; they were laid under the greater obligation to keep to the liberty wherewith he had made them free. All our knowledge of God begins on his part; we know him because we are known of him. Though our religion forbids idolatry, yet many practise spiritual idolatry in their hearts. For what a man loves most, and cares most for, that is his god: some have their riches for their god, some their pleasures, and some their lusts. And many ignorantly worship a god of their own making; a god made all of mercy and no justice. For they persuade themselves that there is mercy for them with God, though they repent not, but go on in their sins. It is possible for those who have made great professions of religion, to be afterwards drawn aside from purity and simplicity. And the more mercy God has shown, in bringing any to know the gospel, and the liberties and privileges of it, the greater their sin and folly in suffering themselves to be deprived of them. Hence all who are members of the outward church should learn to fear and to suspect themselves. We must not be content because we have some good things in ourselves. Paul fears lest his labour is in vain, yet he still labours; and thus to do, whatever follows, is true wisdom and the fear of God. This every man must remember in his place and calling.

Verses 12–18

The apostle desires that they would be of one mind with him respecting the law of Moses, as well as united with him in love. In reproving others, we should take care to convince them that our reproofs are from sincere regard to the honour of God and religion and their welfare. The apostle reminds the Galatians of the difficulty under which he laboured when he first came among them. But he notices, that he was a welcome messenger to them. Yet how very uncertain are the favour and respect of men! Let us labour to be accepted of God. You once thought yourselves happy in receiving the gospel; have you now reason to think otherwise? Christians must not forbear speaking the truth, for fear of offending others. The false teachers who drew the Galatians from the truth of the gospel were designing men. They pretended affection, but they were not sincere and upright. An excellent rule is given. It is good to be zealous always in a good thing; not for a time only, or now and then, but always. Happy would it be for the church of Christ, if this zeal was better maintained.

Verses 19, 20

The Galatians were ready to account the apostle their enemy, but he assures them he was their friend; he had the feelings of a parent toward them. He was in doubt as to their state, and was anxious to know the result of their present delusions. Nothing is so sure a proof that a sinner has passed into a state of justification, as Christ being formed in him by the renewal of the Holy Spirit; but this cannot be hoped for, while men depend on the law for acceptance with God.

Verses 21–27

The difference between believers who rested in Christ only, and those who trusted in the law, is explained by the histories of Isaac and Ishmael. These things are an allegory, wherein, beside the literal and historical sense of the words, the Spirit of God points out something further. Hagar and Sarah were apt emblems of the two different dispensations of the covenant. The heavenly Jerusalem, the true church from above, represented by Sarah, is in a state of freedom, and is the mother of all believers, who are born of the Holy Spirit. They were by regeneration and true faith, made a part of the true seed of Abraham, according to the promise made to him.

Verses 28–31

The history thus explained is applied. So then, brethren, we are not children of the bond-woman, but of the free. If the privileges of all believers were so great, according to the new covenant, how absurd for the Gentile converts to be under that law, which could not deliver the unbelieving Jews from bondage or condemnation! We should not have found out this allegory in the history of Sarah and Hagar, if it had not been shown to us, yet we cannot doubt it was intended by the Holy Spirit. It is an explanation of the subject, not an argument in proof of it. The two covenants of works and grace, and legal and evangelical professors, are shadowed forth. Works and fruits brought forth in a man's own strength, are legal. But if arising from faith in Christ, they are evangelical. The first covenant spirit is of bondage unto sin and death. The second covenant spirit is of liberty and freedom; not liberty to sin, but in and unto duty. The first is a spirit of persecution; the second is a spirit of love. Let those professors look to it, who have a violent, harsh, imposing spirit, towards the people of God. Yet as Abraham turned aside to Hagar, so it is possible a believer may turn aside in some things to the covenant of works, when through unbelief and neglect of the promise he acts according to the law, in his own strength; or in a way of violence, not of love, towards the brethren. Yet it is not his way, not his spirit to do so; hence he is never at rest, till he returns to his dependence on Christ again. Let us rest our souls on the Scriptures, and by a gospel hope and cheerful obedience, show that our conversation and treasure are indeed in heaven.

Chapter 5

Chapter Outline	
An earnest exhortation to stand fast in the liberty of the gospel.	(1–12)
To take heed of indulging a sinful temper.	(13–15)

And to walk in the Spirit, and not to fulfil the lusts of the flesh: the works of both are described.	(16–26)

Verses 1–6

Christ will not be the Saviour of any who will not own and rely upon him as their only Saviour. Let us take heed to the warnings and persuasions of the apostle to stedfastness in the doctrine and liberty of the gospel. All true Christians, being taught by the Holy Spirit, wait for eternal life, the reward of righteousness, and the object of their hope, as the gift of God by faith in Christ; and not for the sake of their own works. The Jewish convert might observe the ceremonies or assert his liberty, the Gentile might disregard them or might attend to them, provided he did not depend upon them. No outward privileges or profession will avail to acceptance with God, without sincere faith in our Lord Jesus. True faith is a working grace; it works by love to God, and to our brethren. May we be of the number of those who, through the Spirit, wait for the hope of righteousness by faith. The danger of old was not in things of no consequence in themselves, as many forms and observances now are. But without faith working by love, all else is worthless, and compared with it other things are of small value.

Verses 7–12

The life of a Christian is a race, wherein he must run, and hold on, if he would obtain the prize. It is not enough that we profess Christianity, but we must run well, by living up to that profession. Many who set out fairly in religion, are hindered in their progress, or turn out of the way. It concerns those who begin to turn out of the way, or to tire in it, seriously to inquire what hinders them. The opinion or persuasion, ver. #(**8**), was, no doubt, that of mixing the works of the law with faith in Christ in justification. The apostle leaves them to judge whence it must arise, but sufficiently shows that it could be owing to none but Satan. It is dangerous for Christian churches to encourage those who follow, but especially who spread, destructive errors. And in reproving sin and error, we should always distinguish between the leaders and the led. The Jews were offended, because Christ was preached as the only salvation for sinners. If Paul and others would have admitted that the observance of the law of Moses was to be joined with faith in Christ, as necessary to salvation, then believers might have avoided many of the sufferings they underwent. The first beginnings of such leaven should be opposed. And assuredly those who persist in disturbing the church of Christ must bear their judgment.

Verses 13–15

The gospel is a doctrine according to godliness, **1**Ti **6**:**3**, and is so far from giving the least countenance to sin, that it lays us under the strongest obligation to avoid and subdue it. The apostle urges that all the law is fulfilled in one word, even in this, Thou shalt love thy neighbour as thyself. If Christians, who should help one another, and rejoice one another, quarrel, what can be expected but that the God of love should deny his grace, that the Spirit of love should depart, and the evil spirit, who seeks their destruction, should prevail? Happy would it be, if Christians, instead of biting and devouring one another on account of different opinions, would set themselves against sin in themselves, and in the places where they live.

Verses 16–26

If it be our care to act under the guidance and power of the blessed Spirit, though we may not be freed from the stirrings and oppositions of the corrupt nature which remains in us, it shall not have dominion over us. Believers are engaged in a conflict, in which they earnestly desire that grace may obtain full and speedy victory. And those who desire thus to give themselves up to be led by the Holy Spirit, are not under the law as a covenant of works, nor exposed to its awful curse. Their hatred of sin, and desires after holiness, show that they have a part in the salvation of the gospel. The works of the flesh are many and manifest. And these sins will shut men out of heaven. Yet what numbers, calling themselves Christians, live in these, and say they hope for heaven! The fruits of the Spirit, or of the renewed nature, which we are to do, are named. And as the apostle had chiefly named works of the flesh, not only hurtful to men themselves, but tending to make them so to one another, so here he chiefly notices the fruits of the Spirit, which tend to make Christians agreeable one to another, as well as to make them happy. The fruits of the Spirit plainly show, that such are led by the Spirit. By describing the works of the flesh and fruits of the Spirit, we are told what to avoid and oppose, and what we are to cherish and cultivate; and this is the sincere care and endeavour of all real Christians. Sin does not now reign in their mortal bodies, so that they obey it, Ro **6**:**12**, for they seek to destroy it. Christ never will own those who yield themselves up to be the servants of sin. And it is not enough that we cease to do evil, but we must learn to do well. Our conversation will always be answerable to the principle which guides and governs us, Ro **8**:**5**. We must set ourselves in earnest to mortify the deeds of the body, and to walk in newness of life. Not being desirous of vain-glory, or unduly wishing for the esteem and applause of men, not provoking or envying one another, but seeking to bring forth more abundantly those good fruits, which are, through Jesus Christ, to the praise and glory of God.

Chapter 6

Chapter Outline	
Exhortations to meekness, gentleness, and humility.	(1–5)
To kindness towards all men, especially believers.	(6–11)
The Galatians guarded against the judaizing teachers.	(12–15)
A solemn blessing.	(16–18)

Verses 1–5

We are to bear one another's burdens. So we shall fulfil the law of Christ. This obliges to mutual forbearance and compassion towards each other, agreeably to his example. It becomes us to bear one another's burdens, as fellow-travellers. It is very common for a man to look upon himself as wiser and better than other men, and as fit to dictate to them. Such a one deceives himself; by pretending to what he has not, he puts a cheat upon himself, and sooner or later will find the sad effects. This will never gain esteem, either with God or men. Every one is advised to prove his own work. The better we know our own hearts and ways, the less shall we despise others, and the more be disposed to help them under infirmities and afflictions. How light soever men's sins seem to them when committed, yet they will be found a heavy burden, when they come to reckon with God about them. No man can pay a ransom for his brother; and sin is a burden to the soul. It is a spiritual burden; and the less a man feels it to be such, the more cause has he to suspect himself. Most men are dead in their sins, and therefore have no sight or sense of the spiritual burden of sin. Feeling the weight and burden of our sins, we must seek to be eased thereof by the Saviour, and be warned against every sin.

Verses 6–11

Many excuse themselves from the work of religion, though they may make a show, and profess it. They may impose upon others, yet they deceive themselves if they think to impose upon God, who knows their hearts as well as actions; and as he cannot be deceived, so he will not be mocked. Our present time is seed time; in the other world we shall reap as we sow now. As there are two sorts of sowing, one to the flesh, and the other to the Spirit, so will the reckoning be hereafter. Those who live a carnal, sensual life, must expect no other fruit from such a course than misery and ruin. But those who, under the guidance and influences of the Holy Spirit, live a life of faith in Christ, and abound in Christian graces, shall of the Spirit reap life everlasting. We are all very apt to tire in duty, particularly in doing good. This we should carefully watch and guard against. Only to perseverance in well-doing is the reward promised. Here is an exhortation to all to do good in their places. We should take care to do good in our life-time, and make this the business of our lives. Especially when fresh occasions offer, and as far as our power reaches.

Verses 12–15

Proud, vain, and carnal hearts, are content with just so much religion as will help to keep up a fair show. But the apostle professes his own faith, hope, and joy; and that his principal glory was in the cross of Christ. By which is here meant, his sufferings and death on the cross, the doctrine of salvation by a crucified Redeemer. By Christ, or by the cross of Christ, the world is crucified to the believer, and he to the world. The more we consider the sufferings of the Redeemer from the world, the less likely shall we be to love the world. The apostle was as little affected by its charms, as a beholder would be by any thing which had been graceful in the face of a crucified person, when he beholds it blackened in the agonies of death. He was no more affected by the objects around him, than one who is expiring would be struck with any of the prospects his dying eyes might view from the cross on which he hung. And as to those who have truly believed in Christ Jesus, all things are counted as utterly worthless compared with him. There is a new creation; old things are passed away, and new views and dispositions are brought in under the regenerating influences of God the Holy Spirit. Believers are brought into a new world, and being created in Christ Jesus unto good works, are formed to a life of holiness. It is a change of mind and heart, whereby we are enabled to believe in the Lord Jesus, and to live to God; and where this inward, practical religion is wanting, outward professions, or names, will never stand in any stead.

Verses 16–18

A new creation to the image of Christ, as showing faith in him, is the greatest distinction between one man and another, and a blessing is declared on all who walk according to this rule. The blessings are, peace and mercy. Peace with God and our conscience, and all the comforts of this life, as far as they are needful. And mercy, an interest in the free love and favour of God in Christ, the spring and fountain of all other blessings. The written word of God is the rule we are to go by, both in its doctrines and precepts. May his grace ever be with our spirit, to sanctify, quicken, and cheer us, and may we always be ready to maintain the honour of that which is indeed our life. The apostle had in his body the marks of the Lord Jesus, the scars of wounds from persecuting enemies, for his cleaving to Christ, and the doctrine of the gospel. The apostle calls the Galatians his brethren, therein he shows his humility and his tender affection for them; and he takes his leave with a very serious prayer, that they might enjoy the favour of Christ Jesus, both in its effects and in its evidences. We need desire no more to make us happy than the grace of our Lord Jesus Christ. The apostle does not pray that the law of Moses, or the righteousness of works, but that the grace of Christ, might be with them; that it might be in their hearts and with their spirits, quickening, comforting, and strengthening them: to all which he sets his Amen; signifying his desire that so it might be, and his faith that so it would be.

Ephesians

This epistle was written when St. Paul was a prisoner at Rome. The design appears to be to strengthen the Ephesians in the faith of Christ, and to give exalted views of the love of God, and of the dignity and excellence of Christ, fortifying their minds against the scandal of the cross. He shows that they were saved by grace, and that however wretched they once were, they now had equal privileges with the Jews. He encourages them to persevere in their Christian calling, and urges them to walk in a manner becoming their profession, faithfully discharging the general and common duties of religion, and the special duties of particular relations.

Chapter 1

Chapter Outline	
A salutation, and an account of saving blessings, as prepared in God's eternal election, as purchased by Christ's blood.	(1–8)
And as conveyed in effectual calling: this is applied to the believing Jews, and to the believing Gentiles.	(9–14)
The apostle thanks God for their faith and love, and prays for the continuance of their knowledge and hope, with respect to the heavenly inheritance, and to God's powerful working in them.	(15–23)

Verses 1, 2

All Christians must be saints; if they come not under that character on earth, they will never be saints in glory. Those are not saints, who are not faithful, believing in Christ, and true to the profession they make of relation to their Lord. By grace, understand the free and undeserved love and favour of God, and those graces of the Spirit which come from it; by peace, all other blessings, spiritual and temporal, the fruits of the former. No peace without grace. No peace, nor grace, but from God the Father, and from the Lord Jesus Christ; and the best saints need fresh supplies of the graces of the Spirit, and desire to grow.

Verses 3–8

Spiritual and heavenly blessings are the best blessings; with which we cannot be miserable, and without which we cannot but be so. This was from the choice of them in Christ, before the foundation of the world, that they should be made holy by separation from sin, being set apart to God, and sanctified by the Holy Spirit, in consequence of their election in Christ. All who are chosen to happiness as the end, are chosen to holiness as the means. In love they were predestinated, or fore-ordained, to be adopted as children of God by faith in Christ Jesus, and to be openly admitted to the privileges of that high relation to himself. The reconciled and adopted believer, the pardoned sinner, gives all the praise of his salvation to his gracious Father. His love appointed this method of redemption, spared not his own Son, and brought believers to hear and embrace this salvation. It was rich grace to provide such a surety as his own Son, and freely to deliver him up. This method of grace gives no encouragement to evil, but shows sin in all its hatefulness, and how it deserves vengeance. The believer's actions, as well as his words, declare the praises of Divine mercy.

Verses 9–14

Blessings were made known to believers, by the Lord's showing to them the mystery of his sovereign will, and the method of redemption and salvation. But these must have been for ever hidden from us, if God had not made them known by his written word, preached gospel, and Spirit of truth. Christ united the two differing parties, God and man, in his own person, and satisfied for that wrong which caused the separation. He wrought, by his Spirit, those graces of faith and love, whereby we are made one with God, and among ourselves. He dispenses all his blessings, according to his good pleasure. His Divine teaching led whom he pleased to see the glory of those truths, which others were left to blaspheme. What a gracious promise that is, which secures the gift of the Holy Ghost to those who ask him! The sanctifying and comforting influences of the Holy Spirit seal believers as the children of God, and heirs of heaven. These are the first-fruits of holy happiness. For this we were made, and for this we were redeemed; this is the great design of God in all that he has done for us; let all be ascribed unto the praise of his glory.

Verses 15–23

God has laid up spiritual blessings for us in his Son the Lord Jesus; but requires us to draw them out and fetch them in by prayer. Even the best Christians need to be prayed for: and while we hear of the welfare of Christian friends, we should pray for them. Even true believers greatly want heavenly wisdom. Are not the best of us unwilling to come under God's yoke, though there is no other way to find rest for the soul? Do we not for a little pleasure often part with our peace? And if we dispute less, and prayed more with and for each other, we should daily see more and more what is the hope of our calling, and the riches of the Divine glory in this inheritance. It is desirable to feel the mighty power of Divine grace, beginning and carrying on the work of faith in our souls. But it is difficult to bring a soul to believe fully in Christ, and to venture its all, and the hope of eternal life, upon his righteousness. Nothing less than Almighty power will work this in us. Here is signified that it is Christ the Saviour, who supplies all the necessities of those who trust in him, and gives them all blessings in the richest abundance. And by being partakers of Christ himself, we come to be filled with the fulness of grace and glory in him. How then do those forget themselves who seek for righteousness out of him! This teaches us to come to Christ. And did we know what we are called to, and what we might find in him, surely we should come and be suitors to him. When feeling our weakness and the power of our enemies, we most perceive the greatness of that mighty power which effects the conversion of the believer, and is engaged to perfect his salvation. Surely this will constrain us by love to live to our Redeemer's glory.

Chapter 2

Chapter Outline	
The riches of God's grace towards men, shown from their deplorable state by nature, and the happy change Divine grace makes in them.	(1–10)
The Ephesians called to reflect on their state of heathenism.	(11–13)
And the privileges and blessings of the gospel.	(14–22)

Verses 1–10

Sin is the death of the soul. A man dead in trespasses and sins has no desire for spiritual pleasures. When we look upon a corpse, it gives an awful feeling. A never-dying spirit is now fled, and has left nothing but the ruins of a man. But if we viewed things aright, we should be far more affected by the thought of a dead soul, a lost, fallen spirit. A state of sin is a state of conformity to this world. Wicked men are slaves to Satan. Satan is the author of that proud, carnal disposition which there is in ungodly men; he rules in the hearts of men. From Scripture it is clear, that whether men have been most prone to sensual or to spiritual wickedness, all men, being naturally children of disobedience, are also by nature children of wrath. What reason have sinners, then, to seek earnestly for that grace which will make them, of children of wrath, children of God and heirs of glory! God's eternal love or good-will toward his creatures, is the fountain whence all his mercies flow to us; and that love of God is great love, and that mercy is rich mercy. And every converted sinner is a saved sinner; delivered from sin and wrath. The grace that saves is the free, undeserved goodness and favour of God; and he saves, not by the works of the law, but through faith in Christ Jesus. Grace in the soul is a new life in the soul. A regenerated sinner becomes a living soul; he lives a life of holiness, being born of God: he lives, being delivered from the guilt of sin, by pardoning and justifying grace. Sinners roll themselves in the dust; sanctified souls sit in heavenly places, are raised above this world, by Christ's grace. The goodness of God in converting and saving sinners heretofore, encourages others in after-time, to hope in his grace and mercy. Our faith, our conversion, and our eternal salvation, are not of works, lest any man should boast. These things are not brought to pass by any thing done by us, therefore all boasting is shut out. All is the free gift of God, and the effect of being quickened by his power. It was his purpose, to which he prepared us, by blessing us with the knowledge of his will, and his Holy Spirit producing such a change in us, that we should glorify God by our good conversation, and perseverance in holiness. None can from Scripture abuse this doctrine, or accuse it of any tendency to evil. All who do so, are without excuse.

Verses 11–13

Christ and his covenant are the foundation of all the Christian's hopes. A sad and terrible description is here; but who is able to remove himself out of it? Would that this were not a true description of many baptized in the name of Christ. Who can, without trembling, reflect upon the misery of a person, separated for ever from the people of God, cut off from the body of Christ, fallen from the covenant of promise, having no hope, no Saviour, and without any God but a God of vengeance, to all eternity? To have no part in Christ! What true Christian can hear this without horror? Salvation is far from the wicked; but God is a help at hand to his people; and this is by the sufferings and death of Christ.

Verses 14–18

Jesus Christ made peace by the sacrifice of himself; in every sense Christ was their Peace, the author, centre, and substance of their being at peace with God, and of their union with the Jewish believers in one church. Through the person, sacrifice, and mediation of Christ, sinners are allowed to draw near to God as a Father, and are brought with acceptance into his presence, with their worship and services, under the teaching of the Holy Spirit, as one with the Father and the Son. Christ purchased leave for us to come to God; and the Spirit gives a heart to come, and strength to come, and then grace to serve God acceptably.

Verses 19–22

The church is compared to a city, and every converted sinner is free of it. It is also compared to a house, and every converted sinner is one of the family; a servant, and a child in God's house. The church is also compared to a building, founded on the doctrine of Christ; delivered by the prophets of the Old Testament, and the apostles of the New. God dwells in all believers now; they become the temple of God through the working of the blessed Spirit. Let us then ask if our hopes are fixed on Christ, according to the doctrine of his word? Have we devoted ourselves as holy temples to God through him? Are we habitations of God by the Spirit, are we spiritually-minded, and do we bring forth the fruits of the Spirit? Let us take heed not to grieve the holy Comforter. Let us desire his gracious presence, and his influences upon our hearts. Let us seek to discharge the duties allotted to us, to the glory of God.

Chapter 3

Chapter Outline	
The apostle sets forth his office, and his qualifications for it, and his call to it.	(1–7)
Also the noble purposes answered by it.	(8–12)
He prays for the Ephesians.	(13–19)
And adds a thanksgiving.	(20, 21)

Verses 1–7

For having preached the doctrine of truth, the apostle was a prisoner, but a prisoner of Jesus Christ; the object of special protection and care, while thus suffering for him. All the gracious offers of the gospel, and the joyful tidings it contains, come from the rich grace of God; it is the great means by which the Spirit works grace in the souls of men. The mystery, is that secret, hidden purpose of salvation through Christ. This was not so fully and clearly shown in the ages before Christ, as unto the prophets of the New Testament. This was the great truth made known to the apostle, that God would call the Gentiles to salvation by faith in Christ. An effectual working of Divine power attends the gifts of Divine grace. As God appointed Paul to the office, so he qualified him for it.

Verses 8–12

Those whom God advances to honourable employments, he makes low in their own eyes; and where God gives grace to be humble, there he gives all other needful grace. How highly he speaks of Jesus Christ; the unsearchable riches of Christ! Though many are not enriched with these riches; yet how great a favour to have them preached among us, and to have an offer of them! And if we are not enriched with them it is our own fault. The first creation, when God made all things out of nothing, and the new creation, whereby sinners are made new creatures by converting grace, are of God by Jesus Christ. His riches are as unsearchable and as sure as ever, yet while angels adore the wisdom of God in the redemption of his church, the ignorance of self-wise and carnal men deems the whole to be foolishness.

Verses 13–19

The apostle seems to be more anxious lest the believers should be discouraged and faint upon his tribulations, than for what he himself had to bear. He asks for spiritual blessings, which are the best blessings. Strength from the Spirit of God in the inner man; strength in the soul; the strength of faith, to serve God, and to do our duty. If the law of Christ is written in our hearts, and the love of Christ is shed abroad there, then Christ dwells there. Where his Spirit dwells, there he dwells. We should desire that good affections may be fixed in us. And how desirable to have a fixed sense of the love of God in Christ to our souls! How powerfully the apostle speaks of the love of Christ! The breadth shows its extent to all nations and ranks; the length, that it continues from everlasting to everlasting; the depth, its saving those who are sunk into the depths of sin and misery; the height, its raising them up to heavenly happiness and glory. Those who receive grace for grace from Christ's fulness, may be said to be filled with the fulness of God. Should not this satisfy man? Must he needs fill himself with a thousand trifles, fancying thereby to complete his happiness?

Verses 20, 21

It is proper always to end prayers with praises. Let us expect more, and ask for more, encouraged by what Christ has already done for our souls, being assured that the conversion of sinners, and the comfort of believers, will be to his glory, for ever and ever.

Chapter 4

Chapter Outline	
Exhortations to mutual forbearance and union.	(1–6)
To a due use of spiritual gifts and graces.	(7–16)

To purity and holiness.	(17–24)
And to take heed of the sins practised among the heathen.	(25–32)

Verses 1–6

Nothing is pressed more earnestly in the Scriptures, than to walk as becomes those called to Christ's kingdom and glory. By lowliness, understand humility, which is opposed to pride. By meekness, that excellent disposition of soul, which makes men unwilling to provoke, and not easily to be provoked or offended. We find much in ourselves for which we can hardly forgive ourselves; therefore we must not be surprised if we find in others that which we think it hard to forgive. There is one Christ in whom all believers hope, and one heaven they are all hoping for; therefore they should be of one heart. They had all one faith, as to its object, Author, nature, and power. They all believed the same as to the great truths of religion; they had all been admitted into the church by one baptism, with water, in the name of the Father, and of the Son, and of the Holy Ghost, as the sign of regeneration. In all believers God the Father dwells, as in his holy temple, by his Spirit and special grace.

Verses 7–16

Unto every believer is given some gift of grace, for their mutual help. All is given as seems best to Christ to bestow upon every one. He received for them, that he might give to them, a large measure of gifts and graces; particularly the gift of the Holy Ghost. Not a mere head knowledge, or bare acknowledging Christ to be the Son of God, but such as brings trust and obedience. There is a fulness in Christ, and a measure of that fulness given in the counsel of God to every believer; but we never come to the perfect measure till we come to heaven. God's children are growing, as long as they are in this world; and the Christian's growth tends to the glory of Christ. The more a man finds himself drawn out to improve in his station, and according to his measure, all that he has received, to the spiritual good of others, he may the more certainly believe that he has the grace of sincere love and charity rooted in his heart. (Eph **4**:**17-24**)

Verses 17–24

The apostle charged the Ephesians in the name and by the authority of the Lord Jesus, that having professed the gospel, they should not be as the unconverted Gentiles, who walked in vain fancies and carnal affections. Do not men, on every side, walk in the vanity of their minds? Must not we then urge the distinction between real and nominal Christians? They were void of all saving knowledge; they sat in darkness, and loved it rather than light. They had a dislike and hatred to a life of holiness, which is not only the way of life God requires and approves, and by which we live to him, but which has some likeness to God himself in his purity, righteousness, truth, and goodness. The truth of Christ appears in its beauty and power, when it appears as in Jesus. The corrupt nature is called a man; like the human body, it is of divers parts, supporting and strengthening one another. Sinful desires are deceitful lusts; they promise men happiness, but render them more miserable; and bring them to destruction, if not subdued and mortified. These therefore must be put off, as an old garment, a filthy garment; they must be subdued and mortified. But it is not enough to shake off corrupt principles; we must have gracious ones. By the new man, is meant the new nature, the new creature, directed by a new principle, even regenerating grace, enabling a man to lead a new life of righteousness and holiness. This is created, or brought forth by God's almighty power.

Verses 25–28

Notice the particulars wherewith we should adorn our Christian profession. Take heed of every thing contrary to truth. No longer flatter or deceive others. God's people are children who will not lie, who dare not lie, who hate and abhor lying. Take heed of anger and ungoverned passions. If there is just occasion to express displeasure at what is wrong, and to reprove, see that it be without sin. We give place to the devil, when the first motions of sin are not grievous to our souls; when we consent to them; and when we repeat an evil deed. This teaches that as sin, if yielded unto, lets in the devil upon us, we are to resist it, keeping from all appearance of evil. Idleness makes thieves. Those who will not work, expose themselves to temptations to steal. Men ought to be industrious, that they may do some good, and that they may be kept from temptation. They must labour, not only that they may live honestly, but that they may have to give to the wants of others. What then must we think of those called Christians, who grow rich by fraud, oppression, and deceitful practices! Alms, to be accepted of God, must not be gained by unrighteousness and robbery, but by honesty and industry. God hates robbery for burnt-offerings.

Verses 29–32

Filthy words proceed from corruption in the speaker, and they corrupt the minds and manners of those who hear them: Christians should beware of all such discourse. It is the duty of Christians to seek, by the blessing of God, to bring persons to think seriously, and to encourage and warn believers by their conversation. Be ye kind one to another. This sets forth the principle of love in the heart, and the outward expression of it, in a humble, courteous behaviour. Mark how God's forgiveness causes us to forgive. God forgives us, though we had no cause to sin against him. We must forgive, as he has forgiven us. All lying, and corrupt communications, that stir up evil desires and lusts, grieve the Spirit of God. Corrupt passions of bitterness, wrath, anger, clamour, evil-speaking, and malice, grieve the Holy Spirit. Provoke not the holy, blessed Spirit of God to withdraw his presence and his gracious influences. The body will be redeemed from the power of the grave at the resurrection day. Wherever that blessed Spirit dwells as a Sanctifier, he is the earnest of all the joys and glories of that redemption day; and we should be undone, should God take away his Holy Spirit from us.

Chapter 5

Chapter Outline	
Exhortation to brotherly love.	(1, 2)
Cautions against several sins.	(3–14)
Directions to a contrary behaviour, and to relative duties.	(15–21)

The duties of wives and husbands are enforced by the spiritual relation between Christ and the church.	(22–33)

Verses 1, 2

Because God, for Christ's sake, has forgiven you, therefore be ye followers of God, imitators of God. Resemble him especially in his love and pardoning goodness, as becomes those beloved by their heavenly Father. In Christ's sacrifice his love triumphs, and we are to consider it fully.

Verses 3–14

Filthy lusts must be rooted out. These sins must be dreaded and detested. Here are not only cautions against gross acts of sin, but against what some may make light of. But these things are so far from being profitable. that they pollute and poison the hearers. Our cheerfulness should show itself as becomes Christians, in what may tend to God's glory. A covetous man makes a god of his money; places that hope, confidence, and delight, in worldly good, which should be in God only. Those who allow themselves, either in the lusts of the flesh or the love of the world, belong not to the kingdom of grace, nor shall they come to the kingdom of glory. When the vilest transgressors repent and believe the gospel, they become children of obedience, from whom God's wrath is turned away. Dare we make light of that which brings down the wrath of God? Sinners, like men in the dark, are going they know not whither, and doing they know not what. But the grace of God wrought a mighty change in the souls of many. Walk as children of light, as having knowledge and holiness. These works of darkness are unfruitful, whatever profit they may boast; for they end in the destruction of the impenitent sinner. There are many ways of abetting, or taking part in the sins of others; by commendation, counsel, consent, or concealment. And if we share with others in their sins, we must expect to share in their plagues. If we do not reprove the sins of others, we have fellowship with them. A good man will be ashamed to speak of what many wicked men are not ashamed to do. We must have not only a sight and a knowledge that sin is sin, and in some measure shameful, but see it as a breach of God's holy law. After the example of prophets and apostles, we should call on those asleep and dead in sin, to awake and arise, that Christ may give them light.

Verses 15–21

Another remedy against sin, is care, or caution, it being impossible else to maintain purity of heart and life. Time is a talent given us by God, and it is misspent and lost when not employed according to his design. If we have lost our time heretofore, we must double our diligence for the future. Of that time which thousands on a dying bed would gladly redeem at the price of the whole world, how little do men think, and to what trifles they daily sacrifice it! People are very apt to complain of bad times; it were well if that stirred them more to redeem time. Be not unwise. Ignorance of our duty, and neglect of our souls, show the greatest folly. Drunkenness is a sin that never goes alone, but carries men into other evils; it is a sin very provoking to God. The drunkard holds out to his family and to the world the sad spectacle of a sinner hardened beyond what is common, and hastening to perdition. When afflicted or weary, let us not seek to raise our spirits by strong drink, which is hateful and hurtful, and only ends in making sorrows more felt. But by fervent prayer let us seek to be filled with the Spirit, and to avoid whatever may grieve our gracious Comforter. All God's people have reason to sing for joy. Though we are not always singing, we should be always giving thanks; we should never want disposition for this duty, as we never want matter for it, through the whole course of our lives. Always, even in trials and afflictions, and for all things; being satisfied of their loving intent, and good tendency. God keeps believers from sinning against him, and engages them to submit one to another in all he has commanded, to promote his glory, and to fulfil their duties to each other.

Verses 22–33

The duty of wives is, submission to their husbands in the Lord, which includes honouring and obeying them, from a principle of love to them. The duty of husbands is to love their wives. The love of Christ to the church is an example, which is sincere, pure, and constant, notwithstanding her failures. Christ gave himself for the church, that he might sanctify it in this world, and glorify it in the next, that he might bestow on all his members a principle of holiness, and deliver them from the guilt, the pollution, and the dominion of sin, by those influences of the Holy Spirit, of which baptismal water was the outward sign. The church and believers will not be without spot or wrinkle till they come to glory. But those only who are sanctified now, shall be glorified hereafter. The words of Adam, mentioned by the apostle, are spoken literally of marriage; but they have also a hidden sense in them, relating to the union between Christ and his church. It was a kind of type, as having resemblance. There will be failures and defects on both sides, in the present state of human nature, yet this does not alter the relation. All the duties of marriage are included in unity and love. And while we adore and rejoice in the condescending love of Christ, let husbands and wives learn hence their duties to each other. Thus the worst evils would be prevented, and many painful effects would be avoided.

Chapter 6

Chapter Outline	
The duties of children and parents.	(1–4)
Of servants and masters.	(5–9)
All Christians are to put on spiritual armour against the enemies of their souls.	(10–18)
The apostle desires their prayers, and ends with his apostolic blessing.	(19–24)

Verses 1–4

The great duty of children is, to obey their parents. That obedience includes inward reverence, as well as outward acts, and in every age prosperity has attended those distinguished for obedience to parents. The duty of parents. Be not impatient; use no unreasonable severities. Deal prudently and wisely with children; convince their judgements and work upon their reason. Bring them up well; under proper and compassionate correction; and in the knowledge of the duty God requires. Often is this duty neglected, even among professors of the gospel. Many set their children against religion; but this does not excuse the children's disobedience, though it may be awfully occasion it. God alone can change the heart, yet he gives his blessing to the good lessons and examples of parents, and answers their prayers. But those, whose chief anxiety is that their children should be rich and accomplished, whatever becomes of their souls, must not look for the blessing of God.

Verses 5–9

The duty of servants is summed up in one word, obedience. The servants of old were generally slaves. The apostles were to teach servants and masters their duties, in doing which evils would be lessened, till slavery should be rooted out by the influence of Christianity. Servants are to reverence those over them. They are to be sincere; not pretending obedience when they mean to disobey, but serving faithfully. And they must serve their masters not only when their master's eye is upon them; but must be strict in the discharge of their duty, when he is absent and out of the way. Steady regard to the Lord Jesus Christ will make men faithful and sincere in every station, not grudgingly or by constraint, but from a principle of love to the masters and their concerns. This makes service easy to them, pleasing to their masters, and acceptable to the Lord Christ. God will reward even the meanest drudgery done from a sense of duty, and with a view to glorify him. Here is the duty of masters. Act after the same manner. Be just to servants, as you expect they should be to you; show the like good-will and concern for them, and be careful herein to approve yourselves to God. Be not tyrannical and overbearing. You have a Master to obey, and you and they are but fellow-servants in respect to Christ Jesus. If masters and servants would consider their duties to God, and the account they must shortly give to him, they would be more mindful of their duty to each other, and thus families would be more orderly and happy.

Verses 10–18

Spiritual strength and courage are needed for our spiritual warfare and suffering. Those who would prove themselves to have true grace, must aim at all grace; and put on the whole armour of God, which he prepares and bestows. The Christian armour is made to be worn; and there is no putting off our armour till we have done our warfare, and finished our course. The combat is not against human enemies, nor against our own corrupt nature only; we have to do with an enemy who has a thousand ways of beguiling unstable souls. The devils assault us in the things that belong to our souls, and labour to deface the heavenly image in our hearts. We must resolve by God's grace, not to yield to Satan. Resist him, and he will flee. If we give way, he will get ground. If we distrust either our cause, or our Leader, or our armour, we give him advantage. The different parts of the armour of heavy-armed soldiers, who had to sustain the fiercest assaults of the enemy, are here described. There is none for the back; nothing to defend those who turn back in the Christian warfare. Truth, or sincerity, is the girdle. This girds on all the other pieces of our armour, and is first mentioned. There can be no religion without sincerity. The righteousness of Christ, imputed to us, is a breastplate against the arrows of Divine wrath. The righteousness of Christ implanted in us, fortifies the heart against the attacks of Satan. Resolution must be as greaves, or armour to our legs; and to stand their ground or to march forward in rugged paths, the feet must be shod with the preparation of the gospel of peace. Motives to obedience, amidst trials, must be drawn from a clear knowledge of the gospel. Faith is all in all in an hour of temptation. Faith, as relying on unseen objects, receiving Christ and the benefits of redemption, and so deriving grace from him, is like a shield, a defence every way. The devil is the wicked one. Violent temptations, by which the soul is set on fire of hell, are darts Satan shoots at us. Also, hard thoughts of God, and as to ourselves. Faith applying the word of God and the grace of Christ, quenches the darts of temptation. Salvation must be our helmet. A good hope of salvation, a Scriptural expectation of victory, will purify the soul, and keep it from being defiled by Satan. To the Christian armed for defense in battle, the apostle recommends only one weapon of attack; but it is enough, the sword of the Spirit, which is the word of God. It subdues and mortifies evil desires and blasphemous thoughts as they rise within; and answers unbelief and error as they assault from without. A single text, well understood, and rightly applied, at once destroys a temptation or an objection, and subdues the most formidable adversary. Prayer must fasten all the other parts of our Christian armour. There are other duties of religion, and of our stations in the world, but we must keep up times of prayer. Though set and solemn prayer may not be seasonable when other duties are to be done, yet short pious prayers darted out, always are so. We must use holy thoughts in our ordinary course. A vain heart will be vain in prayer. We must pray with all kinds of prayer, public, private, and secret; social and solitary; solemn and sudden: with all the parts of prayer; confession of sin, petition for mercy, and thanksgiving for favours received. And we must do it by the grace of God the Holy Spirit, in dependence on, and according to, his teaching. We must preserve in particular requests, notwithstanding discouragements. We must pray, not for ourselves only, but for all saints. Our enemies are mighty, and we are without strength, but our Redeemer is almighty, and in the power of his mighty we may overcome. Wherefore we must stir up ourselves. Have not we, when God has called, often neglected to answer? Let us think upon these things, and continue our prayers with patience. (Eph **6:19-24**)

Verses 19–24

The gospel was a mystery till made known by Divine revelation; and it is the work of Christ's ministers to declare it. The best and most eminent ministers need the prayers of believers. Those particularly should be prayed for, who are exposed to great hardships and perils in their work. Peace be to the brethren, and love with faith. By peace, understand all manner of peace; peace with God, peace of conscience, peace among themselves. And the grace of the Spirit, producing faith and love, and every grace. These he desires for those in whom they were already begun. And all grace and blessings come to the saints from God, through Jesus Christ our Lord. Grace, that is, the favour of God; and all good, spiritual and temporal, which is from it, is and shall be with all those who thus love our Lord Jesus Christ in sincerity, and with them only.

Philippians

The Philippians felt a very deep interest for the apostle. The scope of the epistle is to confirm them in the faith, to encourage them to walk as becomes the gospel of Christ, to caution them against judaizing teachers, and to express gratitude for their Christian bounty. This epistle is the only one, among those written by St. Paul, in which no censures are implied or expressed. Full commendation and confidence are in every part, and the Philippians are addressed with a peculiar affection, which every serious reader will perceive.

Chapter 1

Chapter Outline	
The apostle offers up thanksgivings and prayers, for the good work of grace in the Philippians.	(1–7)
He expresses affection, and prays for them.	(8–11)

Fortifies them against being cast down at his sufferings.	(12–20)
He stood prepared for glorifying Christ by life, or death.	(21–26)
Exhortations to zeal, and constancy in professing the gospel.	(27–30)

Verses 1–7

The highest honour of the most eminent ministers is, to be servants of Christ. And those who are not really saints on earth, never will be saints in heaven. Out of Christ, the best saints are sinners, and unable to stand before God. There is no peace without grace. Inward peace springs from a sense of Divine favour. And there is no grace and peace but from God our Father, the fountain and origin of all blessings. At Philippi the apostle was evil entreated, and saw little fruit of his labour; yet he remembers Philippi with joy. We must thank our God for the graces and comforts, gifts and usefulness of others, as we receive the benefit, and God receives the glory. The work of grace will never be perfected till the day of Jesus Christ, the day of his appearance. But we may always be confident God will perform his good work, in every soul wherein he has really begun it by regeneration; though we must not trust in outward appearances, nor in any thing but a new creation to holiness. People are dear to their ministers, when they receive benefit by their ministry. Fellow-sufferers in the cause of God should be dear one to another.

Verses 8–11

Shall not we pity and love those souls whom Christ loves and pities? Those who abound in any grace, need to abound more. Try things which differ; that we may approve the things which are excellent. The truths and laws of Christ are excellent; and they recommend themselves as such to any attentive mind. Sincerity is that in which we should have our conversation in the world, and it is the glory of all our graces. Christians should not be apt to take offence, and should be very careful not to offend God or the brethren. The things which most honour God will most benefit us. Let us not leave it doubtful whether any good fruit is found in us or not. A small measure of Christian love, knowledge, and fruitfulness should not satisfy any.

Verses 12–20

The apostle was a prisoner at Rome; and to take off the offence of the cross, he shows the wisdom and goodness of God in his sufferings. These things made him known, where he would never have otherwise been known; and led some to inquire after the gospel. He suffered from false friends, as well as from enemies. How wretched the temper of those who preached Christ out of envy and contention, and to add affliction to the bonds that oppressed this best of men! The apostle was easy in the midst of all. Since our troubles may tend to the good of many, we ought to rejoice. Whatever turns to our salvation, is by the Spirit of Christ; and prayer is the appointed means of seeking for it. Our earnest expectation and hope should not be to be honoured of men, or to escape the cross, but to be upheld amidst temptation, contempt, and affliction. Let us leave it to Christ, which way he will make us serviceable to his glory, whether by labour or suffering, by diligence or patience, by living to his honour in working for him, or dying to his honour in suffering for him.

Verses 21–26

Death is a great loss to a carnal, worldly man, for he loses all his earthly comforts and all his hopes; but to a true believer it is gain, for it is the end of all his weakness and misery. It delivers him from all the evils of life, and brings him to possess the chief good. The apostle's difficulty was not between living in this world and living in heaven; between these two there is no comparison; but between serving Christ in this world and enjoying him in another. Not between two evil things, but between two good things; living to Christ and being with him. See the power of faith and of Divine grace; it can make us willing to die. In this world we are compassed with sin; but when with Christ, we shall escape sin and temptation, sorrow and death, for ever. But those who have most reason to desire to depart, should be willing to remain in the world as long as God has any work for them to do. And the more unexpected mercies are before they come, the more of God will be seen in them.

Verses 27–30

Those who profess the gospel of Christ, should live as becomes those who believe gospel truths, submit to gospel laws, and depend upon gospel promises. The original word "conversation" denotes the conduct of citizens who seek the credit, safety, peace, and prosperity of their city. There is that in the faith of the gospel, which is worth striving for; there is much opposition, and there is need of striving. A man may sleep and go to hell; but he who would go to heaven, must look about him and be diligent. There may be oneness of heart and affection among Christians, where there is diversity of judgment about many things. Faith is God's gift on the behalf of Christ; the ability and disposition to believe are from God. And if we suffer reproach and loss for Christ, we are to reckon them a gift, and prize them accordingly. Yet salvation must not be ascribed to bodily afflictions, as though afflictions and worldly persecutions deserved it; but from God only is salvation: faith and patience are his gifts.

Chapter 2

Chapter Outline	
Exhortations to a kind, humble spirit and behaviour.	(1–4)
The example of Christ.	(5–11)
Diligence in the affairs of salvation, and to be examples to the world.	(12–18)
The apostle's purpose of visiting Philippi.	(19–30)

Verses 1–4

Here are further exhortations to Christian duties; to like-mindedness and lowly-mindedness, according to the example of the Lord

Jesus. Kindness is the law of Christ's kingdom, the lesson of his school, the livery of his family. Several motives to brotherly love are mentioned. If you expect or experience the benefit of God's compassions to yourselves, be compassionate one to another. It is the joy of ministers to see people like-minded. Christ came to humble us, let there not be among us a spirit of pride. We must be severe upon our own faults, and quick in observing our own defects, but ready to make favourable allowances for others. We must kindly care for others, but not be busy-bodies in other men's matters. Neither inward nor outward peace can be enjoyed, without lowliness of mind.

Verses 5–11

The example of our Lord Jesus Christ is set before us. We must resemble him in his life, if we would have the benefit of his death. Notice the two natures of Christ; his Divine nature, and human nature. Who being in the form of God, partaking the Divine nature, as the eternal and only-begotten Son of God, Joh **1:1**, had not thought it a robbery to be equal with God, and to receive Divine worship from men. His human nature; herein he became like us in all things except sin. Thus low, of his own will, he stooped from the glory he had with the Father before the world was. Christ's two states, of humiliation and exaltation, are noticed. Christ not only took upon him the likeness and fashion, or form of a man, but of one in a low state; not appearing in splendour. His whole life was a life of poverty and suffering. But the lowest step was his dying the death of the cross, the death of a malefactor and a slave; exposed to public hatred and scorn. The exaltation was of Christ's human nature, in union with the Divine. At the name of Jesus, not the mere sound of the word, but the authority of Jesus, all should pay solemn homage. It is to the glory of God the Father, to confess that Jesus Christ is Lord; for it is his will, that all men should honour the Son as they honour the Father, Joh **5:23**. Here we see such motives to self-denying love as nothing else can supply. Do we thus love and obey the Son of God?

Verses 12–18

We must be diligent in the use of all the means which lead to our salvation, persevering therein to the end. With great care, lest, with all our advantages, we should come short. Work out your salvation, for it is God who worketh in you. This encourages us to do our utmost, because our labour shall not be in vain: we must still depend on the grace of God. The working of God's grace in us, is to quicken and engage our endeavours. God's good-will to us, is the cause of his good work in us. Do your duty without murmurings. Do it, and do not find fault with it. Mind your work, and do not quarrel with it. By peaceableness; give no just occasion of offence. The children of God should differ from the sons of men. The more **perverse** others are, the more careful we should be to keep ourselves blameless and harmless. The doctrine and example of consistent believers will enlighten others, and direct their way to Christ and holiness, even as the light-house warns mariners to avoid rocks, and directs their course into the harbour. Let us try thus to shine. The gospel is the word of life, it makes known to us eternal life through Jesus Christ. Running, denotes earnestness and vigour, continual pressing forward; labouring, denotes constancy, and close application. It is the will of God that believers should be much in rejoicing; and those who are so happy as to have good ministers, have great reason to rejoice with them. (Php **2:19-30**)

Verses 19–30

It is best with us, when our duty becomes natural to us. Naturally, that is, sincerely, and not in pretence only, with a willing heart and upright views. We are apt to prefer our own credit, ease, and safety, before truth, holiness, and duty; but Timothy did not so. Paul desired liberty, not that he might take pleasure, but that he might do good. Epaphroditus was willing to go to the Philippians, that he might be comforted with those who had sorrowed for him when he was sick. It seems, his illness was caused by the work of God. The apostle urges them to love him the more on that account. It is doubly pleasant to have our mercies restored by God, after great danger of their removal; and this should make them more valued. What is given in answer to prayer, should be received with great thankfulness and joy.

Chapter 3

Chapter Outline	
The apostle cautions the Philippians against judaizing false teachers, and renounces his own former privileges.	(1–11)
Expresses earnest desire to be found in Christ; also his pressing on toward perfection; and recommends his own example to other believers.	(12–21)

Verses 1–11

Sincere Christians rejoice in Christ Jesus. The prophet calls the false prophets dumb dogs, Isa **56:10**; to which the apostle seems to refer. Dogs, for their malice against faithful professors of the gospel of Christ, barking at them and biting them. They urged human works in opposition to the faith of Christ; but Paul calls them evil-workers. He calls them the concision; as they rent the church of Christ, and cut it to pieces. The work of religion is to no purpose, unless the heart is in it, and we must worship God in the strength and grace of the Divine Spirit. They rejoice in Christ Jesus, not in mere outward enjoyments and performances. Nor can we too earnestly guard against those who oppose or abuse the doctrine of free salvation. If the apostle would have gloried and trusted in the flesh, he had as much cause as any man. But the things which he counted gain while a Pharisee, and had reckoned up, those he counted loss for Christ. The apostle did not persuade them to do any thing but what he himself did; or to venture on any thing but that on which he himself ventured his never-dying soul. He deemed all these things to be but loss, compared with the knowledge of Christ, by faith in his person and salvation. He speaks of all worldly enjoyments and outward privileges which sought a place with Christ in his heart, or could pretend to any merit and desert, and counted them but loss; but it might be said, It is easy to say so; but what would he do when he came to the trial? He had suffered the loss of all for the privileges of a Christian. Nay, he not only counted them loss, but the vilest refuse, offals thrown to dogs; not only less valuable than Christ, but in the highest degree contemptible, when set up as against him. True knowledge of Christ alters and changes men, their judgments and manners, and makes them as if made again anew. The believer prefers Christ, knowing that it is better for us to be without all worldly riches, than without Christ and his word. Let us see what the apostle resolved to cleave to, and that was Christ and heaven. We are undone, without righteousness wherein to appear before God, for we are guilty. There is a righteousness provided for us in Jesus Christ, and it is a complete and perfect righteousness. None can have benefit by it, who trust in themselves. Faith is the appointed means of applying the saving benefit. It is by faith in Christ's blood. We are made conformable to Christ's death, when we die to sin, as he died for sin; and the world is crucified to us, and we to the world, by the cross of Christ. The apostle was willing to do or to suffer any thing, to attain the glorious resurrection of saints. This hope and prospect carried him through all difficulties in his work. He did not hope to attain it through his own merit and righteousness, but through the merit and righteousness of Jesus Christ. (Php **3:12-21**)

Verses 12–21

This simple dependence and earnestness of soul, were not mentioned as if the apostle had gained the prize, or were already made perfect in the Saviour's likeness. He forgot the things which were behind, so as not to be content with past labours or present measures of grace. He reached forth, stretched himself forward towards his point; expressions showing great concern to become more and more like unto Christ. He who runs a race, must never stop short of the end, but press forward as fast as he can; so those who have heaven in their view, must still press forward to it, in holy desires and hopes, and constant endeavours. Eternal life is the gift of God, but it is in Christ Jesus; through his hand it must come to us, as it is procured for us by him. There is no getting to heaven as our home, but by Christ as our Way. True believers, in seeking this assurance, as well as to glorify him, will seek more nearly to resemble his sufferings and death, by dying to sin, and by crucifying the flesh with its affections and lusts. In these things there is a great difference among real Christians, but all know something of them. Believers make Christ all in all, and set their hearts upon another world. If they differ from one another, and are not of the same judgment in lesser matters, yet they must not judge one another; while they all meet now in Christ, and hope to meet shortly in heaven. Let them join in all the great things in which they are agreed, and wait for further light as to lesser things wherein they differ. The enemies of the cross of Christ mind nothing but their sensual appetites. Sin is the sinner's shame, especially when gloried in. The way of those who mind earthly things, may seem pleasant, but death and hell are at the end of it. If we choose their way, we shall share their end. The life of a Christian is in heaven, where his Head and his home are, and where he hopes to be shortly; he sets his affections upon things above; and where his heart is, there will his conversation be. There is glory kept for the bodies of the saints, in which they will appear at the resurrection. Then the body will be made glorious; not only raised again to life, but raised to great advantage. Observe the power by which this change will be wrought. May we be always prepared for the coming of our Judge; looking to have our vile bodies changed by his Almighty power, and applying to him daily to new-create our souls unto holiness; to deliver us from our enemies, and to employ our bodies and souls as instruments of righteousness in his service.

Chapter 4

Chapter Outline	
The apostle exhorts the Philippians to stand fast in the Lord.	(1)
Gives directions to some, and to all in general.	(2–9)
Expresses contentment in every condition of life.	(10–19)
He concludes with prayer to God the Father, and his usual blessing.	(20–23)

Verse 1

The believing hope and prospect of eternal life, should make us steady and constant in our Christian course. There is difference of gifts and graces, yet, being renewed by the same Spirit, we are brethren. To stand fast in the Lord, is to stand fast in his strength, and by his grace.

Verses 2–9

Let believers be of one mind, and ready to help each other. As the apostle had found the benefit of their assistance, he knew how comfortable it would be to his fellow-labourers to have the help of others. Let us seek to give assurance that our names are written in the book of life. Joy in God is of great consequence in the Christian life; and Christians need to be again and again called to it. It more than outweighs all causes for sorrow. Let their enemies perceive how moderate they were as to outward things, and how composedly they suffered loss and hardships. The day of judgment will soon arrive, with full redemption to believers, and destruction to ungodly men. There is a care of diligence which is our duty, and agrees with a wise forecast and due concern; but there is a care of fear and distrust, which is sin and folly, and only perplexes and distracts the mind. As a remedy against perplexing care, constant prayer is recommended. Not only stated times for prayer, but in every thing by prayer. We must join thanksgivings with prayers and supplications; not only seek supplies of good, but own the mercies we have received. God needs not to be told our wants or desires; he knows them better than we do; but he will have us show that we value the mercy, and feel our dependence on him. The peace of God, the comfortable sense of being reconciled to God, and having a part in his favour, and the hope of the heavenly blessedness, are a greater good than can be fully expressed. This peace will keep our hearts and minds through Christ Jesus; it will keep us from sinning under troubles, and from sinking under them; keep us calm and with inward satisfaction. Believers are to get and to keep a good name; a name for good things with God and good men. We should walk in all the ways of virtue, and abide therein; then, whether our praise is of men or not, it will be of God. The apostle is for an example. His doctrine and life agreed together. The way to have the God of peace with us, is to keep close to our duty. All our privileges and salvation arise in the free mercy of God; yet the enjoyment of them depends on our sincere and holy conduct. These are works of God, pertaining to God, and to him only are they to be ascribed, and to no other, neither men, words, nor deeds.

Verses 10–19

It is a good work to succour and help a good minister in trouble. The nature of true Christian sympathy, is not only to feel concern for our friends in their troubles, but to do what we can to help them. The apostle was often in bonds, imprisonments, and necessities; but in all, he learned to be content, to bring his mind to his condition, and make the best of it. Pride, unbelief, vain hankering after something we have not got, and fickle disrelish of present things, make men discontented even under favourable circumstances. Let us pray for patient submission and hope when we are abased; for humility and a heavenly mind when exalted. It is a special grace to have an equal temper of mind always. And in a low state not to lose our comfort in God, nor distrust his providence, nor take any wrong course for our own supply. In a prosperous condition not to be proud, or secure, or worldly. This is a harder lesson than the other; for the temptations of fulness and prosperity are more than those of affliction and want. The apostle had no design to urge them to give more, but to encourage such kindness as will meet a glorious reward hereafter. Through Christ we have grace to do what is good, and through him we must expect the reward; and as we have all things by him, let us do all things for him, and to his glory.

Verses 20–23

The apostle ends with praises to God. We should look upon God, under all our weakness and fears, not as an enemy, but as a Father, disposed to pity us and help us. We must give glory to God as a Father. God's grace and favour, which reconciled souls enjoy, with the whole of the graces in us, which flow from it, are all purchased for us by Christ's merit, and applied by his pleading for us; and therefore are justly called the grace of our Lord Jesus Christ.

Colossians

This epistle was sent because of some difficulties which arose among the Colossians, probably from false teachers, in consequence of which they sent to the apostle. The scope of the epistle is to show, that all hope of man's redemption is founded on Christ, in whom alone are all complete fulness, perfections, and sufficiency. The Colossians are cautioned against the devices of judaizing teachers, and also against the notions of carnal wisdom, and human inventions and traditions, as not consistent with full reliance on Christ. In the first two chapters the apostle tells them what they must believe, and in the two last what they must do; the doctrine of faith, and the precepts of life for salvation.

Chapter 1

Chapter Outline	
The apostle Paul salutes the Colossians, and blesses God for their faith, love, and hope.	(1–8)
Prays for their fruitfulness in spiritual knowledge.	(9–14)
Gives a glorious view of Christ.	(15–23)
And sets out his own character, as the apostle of the Gentiles.	(24–29)

Verses 1–8

All true Christians are brethren one to another. Faithfulness runs through every character and relation of the Christian life. Faith, hope, and love, are the three principal graces in the Christian life, and proper matter for prayer and thanksgiving. The more we fix our hopes on the reward in the other world, the more free shall we be in doing good with our earthly treasure. It was treasured up for them, no enemy could deprive them of it. The gospel is the word of truth, and we may safely venture our souls upon it. And all who hear the word of the gospel, ought to bring forth the fruit of the gospel, obey it, and have their principles and lives formed according to it. Worldly love arises, either from views of interest or from likeness in manners; carnal love, from the appetite for pleasure. To these, something corrupt, selfish, and base always cleaves. But Christian love arises from the Holy Spirit, and is full of holiness. (Col **1:9-14**)

Verses 9–14

The apostle was constant in prayer, that the believers might be filled with the knowledge of God's will, in all wisdom. Good words will not do without good works. He who undertakes to give strength to his people, is a God of power, and of glorious power. The blessed Spirit is the author of this. In praying for spiritual strength, we are not straitened, or confined in the promises, and should not be so in our hopes and desires. The grace of God in the hearts of believers is the power of God; and there is glory in this power. The special use of this strength was for sufferings. There is work to be done, even when we are suffering. Amidst all their trials they gave thanks to the Father of our Lord Jesus, whose special grace fitted them to partake of the inheritance provided for the saints. To bring about this change, those were made willing subjects of Christ, who were slaves of Satan. All who are designed for heaven hereafter, are prepared for heaven now. Those who have the inheritance of sons, have the education of sons, and the disposition of sons. By faith in Christ they enjoyed this redemption, as the purchase of his atoning blood, whereby forgiveness of sins, and all other spiritual blessings were bestowed. Surely then we shall deem it a favour to be delivered from Satan's kingdom and brought into that of Christ, knowing that all trials will soon end, and that every believer will be found among those who come out of great tribulation.

Verses 15–23

Christ in his human nature, is the visible discovery of the invisible God, and he that hath seen Him hath seen the Father. Let us adore these mysteries in humble faith, and behold the glory of the Lord in Christ Jesus. He was born or begotten before all the creation, before any creature was made; which is the Scripture way of representing eternity, and by which the eternity of God is represented to us. All things being created by Him, were created for him; being made by his power, they were made according to his pleasure, and for his praise and glory. He not only created them all at first, but it is by the word of his power that they are upheld. Christ as Mediator is the Head of the body, the church; all grace and strength are from him; and the church is his body. All fulness dwells in him; a fulness of merit and righteousness, of strength and grace for us. God showed his justice in requiring full satisfaction. This mode of redeeming mankind by the death of Christ was most suitable. Here is presented to our view the method of being reconciled. And that, notwithstanding the hatred of sin on God's part, it pleased God to reconcile fallen man to himself. If convinced that we were enemies in our minds by wicked works, and that we are now reconciled to God by the sacrifice and death of Christ in our nature, we shall not attempt to explain away, nor yet think fully to comprehend these mysteries; but we shall see the glory of this plan of redemption, and rejoice in the hope set before us. If this be so, that God's love is so great to us, what shall we do now for God? Be frequent in prayer, and abound in holy duties; and live no more to yourselves, but to Christ. Christ died for us. But wherefore? That we should still live in sin? No; but that we should die to sin, and live henceforth not to ourselves, but to Him.

Verses 24–29

Both the sufferings of the Head and of the members are called the sufferings of Christ, and make up, as it were, one body of sufferings. But He suffered for the redemption of the church; we suffer on other accounts; for we do but slightly taste that cup of afflictions of which Christ first drank deeply. A Christian may be said to fill up that which remains of the sufferings of Christ, when he takes up his cross, and after the pattern of Christ, bears patiently the afflictions God allots to him. Let us be thankful that God has made known to us mysteries hidden from ages and generations, and has showed the riches of his glory among us. As Christ is preached among us, let us seriously inquire, whether he dwells and reigns in us; for this alone can warrant our assured hope of his glory. We must be faithful to death, through all trials, that we may receive the crown of life, and obtain the end of our faith, the salvation of our souls.

Chapter 2

Chapter Outline	
The apostle expresses his love to, and joy in believers.	(1–7)
He cautions against the errors of heathen philosophy; also against Jewish traditions, and rites which had been fulfilled in Christ.	(8–17)
Against worshipping angels; and against legal ordinances.	(18–23)

Verses 1–7

The soul prospers when we have clear knowledge of the truth as it is in Jesus. When we not only believe with the heart, but are ready, when called, to make confession with the mouth. Knowledge and faith make a soul rich. The stronger our faith, and the warmer our love, the more will our comfort be. The treasures of wisdom are hid, not from us, but for us, in Christ. These were hid from proud unbelievers, but displayed in the person and redemption of Christ. See the danger of enticing words; how many are ruined by the false disguises and fair appearances of evil principles and wicked practices! Be aware and afraid of those who would entice to any evil; for they aim to spoil you. All Christians have, in profession at least, received Jesus Christ the Lord, consented to him, and taken him for theirs. We cannot be built up in Christ, or grow in him, unless we are first rooted in him, or founded upon him. Being established in the faith, we must abound therein, and improve in it more and more. God justly withdraws this benefit from those who do not receive it with thanksgiving; and gratitude for his mercies is justly required by God.

Verses 8–17

There is a philosophy which rightly exercises our reasonable faculties; a study of the works of God, which leads us to the knowledge of God, and confirms our faith in him. But there is a philosophy which is vain and deceitful; and while it pleases men's fancies, hinders their faith: such are curious speculations about things above us, or no concern to us. Those who walk in the way of the world, are turned from following Christ. We have in Him the substance of all the shadows of the ceremonial law. All the defects of it are made up in the gospel of Christ, by his complete sacrifice for sin, and by the revelation of the will of God. To be complete, is to be furnished with all things necessary for salvation. By this one word "complete," is shown that we have in Christ whatever is required. "In him," not when we look to Christ, as though he were distant from us, but we are in him, when, by the power of the Spirit, we have faith wrought in our hearts by the Spirit, and we are united to our Head. The circumcision of the heart, the crucifixion of the flesh, the death and burial to sin and to the world, and the resurrection to newness of life, set forth in baptism, and by faith wrought in our hearts, prove that our sins are forgiven, and that we are fully delivered from the curse of the law. Through Christ, we, who were dead in sins, are quickened. Christ's death was the death of our sins; Christ's resurrection is the quickening of our souls. The law of ordinances, which was a yoke to the Jews, and a partition-wall to the Gentiles, the Lord Jesus took out of the way. When the substance was come, the shadows fled. Since every mortal man is, through the hand-writing of the law, guilty of death, how very dreadful is the condition of the ungodly and unholy, who trample under foot that blood of the Son of God, whereby alone this deadly hand-writing can be blotted out! Let not any be troubled about bigoted judgments which related to meats, or the Jewish solemnities. The setting apart a portion of our time for the worship and service of God, is a moral and unchangeable duty, but had no necessary dependence upon the seventh day of the week, the sabbath of the Jews. The first day of the week, or the Lord's day, is the time kept holy by Christians, in remembrance of Christ's resurrection. All the Jewish rites were shadows of gospel blessings.

Verses 18–23

It looked like humility to apply to angels, as if men were conscious of their unworthiness to speak directly to God. But it is not warrantable; it is taking that honour which is due to Christ only, and giving it to a creature. There really was pride in this seeming humility. Those who worship angels, disclaim Christ, who is the only Mediator between God and man. It is an insult to Christ, who is the Head of the church, to use any intercessors but him. When men let go their hold of Christ, they catch at what will stand them in no stead. The body of Christ is a growing body. And true believers cannot live in the fashions of the world. True wisdom is, to keep close to the appointments of the gospel; in entire subjection to Christ, who is the only Head of his church. Self-imposed sufferings and fastings, might have a show of uncommon spirituality and willingness for suffering, but this was not "in any honour" to God. The whole tended, in a wrong manner, to satisfy the carnal mind, by gratifying self-will, self-wisdom, self-righteousness, and contempt of others. The things being such as carry not with them so much as the show of wisdom; or so faint a show that they do the soul no good, and provide not for the satisfying of the flesh. What the Lord has left indifferent, let us regard as such, and leave others to the like freedom; and remembering the passing nature of earthly things, let us seek to glorify God in the use of them.

Chapter 3

Chapter Outline	
The Colossians exhorted to be heavenly-minded;	(1–4)
to mortify all corrupt affections;	(5–11)
to live in mutual love, forbearance, and forgiveness;	(12–17)
and to practise the duties of wives and husbands, children, parents, and servants.	(18–25)

Verses 1–4

As Christians are freed from the ceremonial law, they must walk the more closely with God in gospel obedience. As heaven and earth are contrary one to the other, both cannot be followed together; and affection to the one will weaken and abate affection to the other. Those that are born again are dead to sin, because its dominion is broken, its power gradually subdued by the operation of grace, and it shall at length be extinguished by the perfection of glory. To be dead, then, means this, that those who have the Holy Spirit, mortifying within them the lusts of the flesh, are able to despise earthly things, and to desire those that are heavenly. Christ is, at present, one whom we have not seen; but our comfort is, that our life is safe with him. The streams of this living water flow into the soul by the influences of the Holy Spirit, through faith. Christ lives in the believer by his Spirit, and the believer lives to him in all he does. At the second coming of Christ, there will be a general assembling of all the redeemed; and those whose life is now hid with Christ, shall then appear with him in his glory. Do we look for such happiness, and should we not set our affections upon that world, and live above this?

Verses 5–11

It is our duty to mortify our members which incline to the things of the world. Mortify them, kill them, suppress them, as weeds or vermin which spread and destroy all about them. Continual opposition must be made to all corrupt workings, and no provision made for carnal indulgences. Occasions of sin must be avoided: the lusts of the flesh, and the love of the world; and covetousness, which is idolatry; love of present good, and of outward enjoyments. It is necessary to mortify sins, because if we do not kill them, they will kill us. The gospel changes the higher as well as the lower powers of the soul, and supports the rule of right reason and conscience, over appetite and passion. There is now no difference from country, or conditions and circumstances of life. It is the duty of every one to be holy, because Christ is a Christian's All, his only Lord and Saviour, and all his hope and happiness.

Verses 12–17

We must not only do no hurt to any, but do what good we can to all. Those who are the elect of God, holy and beloved, ought to be lowly and compassionate towards all. While in this world, where there is so much corruption in our hearts, quarrels will sometimes arise. But it is our duty to forgive one another, imitating the forgiveness through which we are saved. Let the peace of God rule in your hearts; it is of his working in all who are his. Thanksgiving to God, helps to make us agreeable to all men. The gospel is the word of Christ. Many have the word, but it dwells in them poorly; it has no power over them. The soul prospers, when we are full of the Scriptures and of the grace of Christ. But when we sing psalms, we must be affected with what we sing. Whatever we are employed about, let us do every thing in the name of the Lord Jesus, and in believing dependence on him. Those who do all in Christ's name, will never want matter of thanksgiving to God, even the Father.

Verses 18–25

The epistles most taken up in displaying the glory of the Divine grace, and magnifying the Lord Jesus, are the most particular in pressing the duties of the Christian life. We must never separate the privileges and duties of the gospel. Submission is the duty of wives. But it is submission, not to a severe lord or stern tyrant, but to her own husband, who is engaged to affectionate duty. And husbands must love their wives with tender and faithful affection. Dutiful children are the most likely to prosper. And parents must be tender, as well as children obedient. Servants are to do their duty, and obey their masters' commands, in all things consistent with duty to God their heavenly Master. They must be both just and diligent; without selfish designs, or hypocrisy and disguise. Those who fear God, will be just and faithful when from under their master's eye, because they know they are under the eye of God. And do all with diligence, not idly and slothfully; cheerfully, not discontented at the providence of God which put them in that relation. And for servants' encouragement, let them know, that in serving their masters according to the command of Christ, they serve Christ, and he will give them a glorious reward at last. But, on the other hand, he who doeth wrong, shall receive for the wrong which he hath done. God will punish the unjust, as well as reward the faithful servant; and the same if masters wrong their servants. For the righteous Judge of the earth will deal justly between master and servant. Both will stand upon a level at his tribunal. How happy would true religion make the world, if it every where prevailed, influenced every state of things, and every relation of life! But the profession of those persons who are regardless of duties, and give just cause for complaint to those they are connected with, deceives themselves, as well as brings reproach on the gospel.

Chapter 4

Chapter Outline	
Masters to do their duty towards servants.	(1)
Persons of all ranks to persevere in prayer, and Christian prudence.	(2–6)
The apostle refers to others for an account of his affairs.	(7–9)
Sends greetings; and concludes with a blessing.	(10–18)

Verse 1

The apostle proceeds with the duty of masters to their servants. Not only justice is required of them, but strict equity and kindness. Let them deal with servants as they expect God should deal with themselves.

Verses 2–6

No duties can be done aright, unless we persevere in fervent prayer, and watch therein with thanksgiving. The people are to pray particularly for their ministers. Believers are exhorted to right conduct towards unbelievers. Be careful in all con**verse** with them, to do them good, and recommend religion by all fit means. Diligence in redeeming time, commends religion to the good opinion of others. Even what is only carelessness may cause a lasting prejudice against the truth. Let all discourse be discreet and seasonable, as becomes Christians. Though it be not always of grace, it must always be with grace. Though our discourse be of that which is common, yet it must be in a Christian manner. Grace is the salt which seasons our discourse, and keeps it from corrupting. It is not enough to answer what is asked, unless we answer aright also.

Verses 7–9

Ministers are servants to Christ, and fellow-servants to one another. They have one Lord, though they have different stations and powers for service. It is a great comfort under the troubles and difficulties of life, to have fellow Christians caring for us. Circumstances of life make no difference in the spiritual relation among sincere Christians; they partake of the same privileges, and are entitled to the same regards. What amazing changes Divine grace makes! Faithless servants become faithful and beloved brethren, and some who had done wrong, become fellow-workers of good.

Verses 10–18

Paul had differed with Barnabas, on the account of this Mark, yet he is not only reconciled, but recommends him to the churches; an example of a truly Christian and forgiving spirit. If men have been guilty of a fault, it must not always be remembered against them. We must forget as well as forgive. The apostle had comfort in the communion of saints and ministers. One is his fellow-servant, another his fellow-prisoner, and all his fellow-workers, working out their own salvation, and endeavouring to promote the salvation of others. The effectual, fervent prayer is the prevailing prayer, and availeth much. The smiles, flatteries, or frowns of the world, the spirit of error, or the working of self-love, leads many to a way of preaching and living which comes far short of fulfilling their ministry. But those who preach the same doctrine as Paul, and follow his example, may expect the Divine favour and blessing.

1 Thessalonians

This epistle is generally considered to have been the first of those written by St. Paul. The occasion seems to have been the good report of the stedfastness of the church at Thessalonica in the faith of the gospel. It is full of affection and confidence, and more consolatory and practical, and less doctrinal, than some of the other epistles.

Chapter 1

Chapter Outline	
The faith, love, and patience of the Thessalonians, are evident tokens of their election which was manifested in the power with which the gospel came to them.	(1–5)
Its powerful and exemplary effects upon their hearts and lives.	(6–10)

Verses 1–5

As all good comes from God, so no good can be hoped for by sinners, but from God in Christ. And the best good may be expected from God, as our Father, for the sake of Christ. We should pray, not only for ourselves, but for others also; remembering them without ceasing. Wherever there is a true faith, it will work; it will affect both the heart and life. Faith works by love; it shows itself in love to God, and love to our neighbour. And wherever there is a well-grounded hope of eternal life, this will appear by the exercise of patience; and it is a sign of sincerity, when in all we do, we seek to approve ourselves to God. By this we may know our election, if we not only speak of the things of God with out lips, but feel their power in our hearts, mortifying our lusts, weaning us from the world, and raising us up to heavenly things. Unless the Spirit of God comes with the word of God, it will be to us a dead letter. Thus they entertained it by the power of the Holy Ghost. They were fully convinced of the truth of it, so as not to be shaken in mind by objections and doubts; and they were willing to leave all for Christ, and to venture their souls and everlasting condition upon the truth of the gospel revelation.

Verses 6–10

When careless, ignorant, and immoral persons are turned from their carnal pursuits and connexions, to believe in and obey the Lord Jesus, to live soberly, righteously, and godly, the matter speaks for itself. The believers under the Old Testament waited for the coming of the Messiah, and believers now wait for his second coming. He is yet to come. And God had raised him from the dead, which is a full assurance unto all men that he will come to judgment. He came to purchase salvation, and will, when he comes again, bring salvation with him, full and final deliverance from that wrath which is yet to come. Let all, without delay, flee from the wrath to come, and seek refuge in Christ and his salvation.

Chapter 2

Chapter Outline	
The apostle reminds the Thessalonians of his preaching and behaviour.	(1–12)
And of their receiving the gospel as the word of God.	(13–16)
His joy on their account.	(17–20)

Verses 1–6

The apostle had no wordly design in his preaching. Suffering in a good cause should sharpen holy resolution. The gospel of Christ at first met with much opposition; and it was preached with contention, with striving in preaching, and against opposition. And as the matter of the apostle's exhortation was true and pure, the manner of his speaking was without guile. The gospel of Christ is designed for mortifying corrupt affections, and that men may be brought under the power of faith. This is the great motive to sincerity, to consider that God not only sees all we do, but knows our thoughts afar off, and searches the heart. And it is from this God who trieth our hearts, that we must receive our reward. The evidences of the apostle's sincerity were, that he avoided flattery and covetousness. He avoided ambition and vain-glory.

Verses 7–12

Mildness and tenderness greatly recommend religion, and are most conformable to God's gracious dealing with sinners, in and by the gospel. This is the way to win people. We should not only be faithful to our calling as Christians, but in our particular callings and relations. Our great gospel privilege is, that God has called us to his kingdom and glory. The great gospel duty is, that we walk worthy of God. We should live as becomes those called with such a high and holy calling. Our great business is to honour, serve, and please God, and to seek to be worthy of him.

Verses 13–16

We should receive the word of God with affections suitable to its holiness, wisdom, truth, and goodness. The words of men are frail and perishing, like themselves, and sometimes false, foolish, and fickle; but God's word is holy, wise, just, and faithful. Let us receive and regard it accordingly. The word wrought in them, to make them examples to others in faith and good works, and in patience under sufferings, and in trials for the sake of the gospel. Murder and persecution are hateful to God, and no zeal for any thing in religion can excuse it. Nothing tends more to any person or people's filling up the measure of their sins, than opposing the gospel, and hindering the salvation of souls. The pure gospel of Christ is abhorred by many, and the faithful preaching of it is hindered in many ways. But those who forbid the preaching it to sinners, to men dead in sin, do not by this please God. Those have cruel hearts, and are enemies to the glory of God, and to the salvation of his people, who deny them the Bible.

Verses 17–20

This world is not a place where we are to be always, or long together. In heaven holy souls shall meet, and never part more. And though the apostle could not come to them yet, and thought he might never be able to come, yet our Lord Jesus Christ will come; nothing shall hinder that. May God give faithful ministers to all who serve him with their spirit in the gospel of his Son, and send them to all who are in darkness

Chapter 3

Chapter Outline	
The apostle sent Timothy to establish and comfort the Thessalonians.	(1–5)
He rejoiced at the good tidings of their faith and love.	(6–10)
And for their increase in grace.	(11–13)

Verses 1–5

The more we find pleasure in the ways of God, the more we shall desire to persevere therein. The apostle's design was to establish and comfort the Thessalonians as to the object of their faith, that Jesus Christ was the Saviour of the world; and as to the recompence of faith, which was more than enough to make up all their losses, and to reward all their labours. But he feared his labours would be in vain. If the devil cannot hinder ministers from labouring in the word and doctrine, he will, if possible, hinder the success of their labours. No one would willingly labour in vain. It is the will and purpose of God, that we enter into his kingdom through many afflictions. And the apostles, far from flattering people with the expectation of worldly prosperity in religion, told them plainly they must count upon trouble in the flesh. Herein they followed the example of their great Master, the Author of our faith. Christians were in danger, and they should be forewarned; they will thus be kept from being improved by any devices of the tempter.

Verses 6–10

Thankfulness to God is very imperfect in the present state; but one great end of the ministry of the word is to help faith forward. That which was the instrument to obtain faith, is also the means of increasing and confirming it, namely, the ordinances of God; and as faith cometh by hearing, so it is confirmed by hearing also.

Verses 11–13

Prayer is religious worship, and all religious worship is due unto God only. Prayer is to be offered to God as our Father. Prayer is not only to be offered in the name of Christ, but offered up to Christ himself, as our Lord and our Saviour. Let us acknowledge God in all our ways, and he will direct our paths. Mutual love is required of all Christians. And love is of God, and is fulfilling the gospel as well as the law. We need the Spirit's influences in order to our growth in grace; and the way to obtain them, is prayer. Holiness is required of all who would go to heaven; and we must act so that we do not contradict the profession we make of holiness. The Lord Jesus will certainly come in his glory; his saints will come with him. Then the excellence as well as the necessity of holiness will appear; and without this no hearts shall be established at that day, nor shall any avoid condemnation.

Chapter 4

Chapter Outline	
Exhortations to purity and holiness.	(1–8)
To brotherly love, peaceable behaviour, and diligence.	(9–12)
Not to sorrow unduly for the death of godly relations and friends, considering the glorious resurrection of their bodies at Christ's second coming.	(13–18)

Verses 1–8

To abide in the faith of the gospel is not enough, we must abound in the work of faith. The rule according to which all ought to walk and act, is the commandments given by the Lord Jesus Christ. Sanctification, in the renewal of their souls under the influences of the Holy Spirit, and attention to appointed duties, constituted the will of God respecting them. In aspiring after this renewal of the soul unto holiness, strict restraint must be put upon the appetites and senses of the body, and on the thoughts and inclinations of the will, which lead to wrong uses of them. The Lord calls none into his family to live unholy lives, but that they may be taught and enabled to walk before him in holiness. Some make light of the precepts of holiness, because they hear them from men; but they are God's commands, and to break them is to despise God.

Verses 9–12

We should notice in others what is good, to their praise, that we may engage them to abound therein more and more. All who are savingly taught of God, are taught to love one another. The teaching of the Spirit exceeds the teachings of men; and men's teaching is vain and useless, unless God teach. Those remarkable for this or any other grace, need to increase therein, as well as to persevere to the end. It is very desirable to have a calm and quiet temper, and to be of a peaceable and quiet behaviour. Satan is busy to trouble us; and we have in our hearts what disposes us to be unquiet; therefore let us study to be quiet. Those who are busy-bodies, meddling in other men's matters, have little quiet in their own minds, and cause great disturbances among their neighbours. They seldom mind the other exhortation, to be diligent in their own calling, to work with their own hands. Christianity does not take us from the work and duty of our particular callings, but teaches us to be diligent therein. People often by slothfulness reduce themselves to great straits, and are liable to many wants; while such as are diligent in their own business, earn their own bread, and have great pleasure in so doing.

Verses 13–18

Here is comfort for the relations and friends of those who die in the Lord. Grief for the death of friends is lawful; we may weep for our own loss, though it may be their gain. Christianity does not forbid, and grace does not do away, our natural affections. Yet we must not be excessive in our sorrows; this is too much like those who have no hope of a better life. Death is an unknown thing, and we know little about the state after death; yet the doctrines of the resurrection and the second coming of Christ, are a remedy against the fear of death, and undue sorrow for the death of our Christian friends; and of these doctrines we have full assurance. It will be some happiness that all the saints shall meet, and remain together for ever; but the principal happiness of heaven is to be with the Lord, to see him, live with him, and enjoy him for ever. We should support one another in times sorrow; not deaden one another's spirits, or weaken one another's hands. And this may be done by the many lessons to be learned from the resurrection of the dead, and the second coming of Christ. What! comfort a man by telling him he is going to appear before the judgment-seat of God! Who can feel comfort from those words? That man alone with whose spirit the Spirit of God bears witness that his sins are blotted out, and the thoughts of whose heart are purified by the Holy Spirit, so that he can love God, and worthily magnify his name. We are not in a safe state unless it is thus with us, or we are desiring to be so.

Chapter 5

Chapter Outline	
The apostle exhorts to be always ready for the coming of Christ to judgment, which will be with suddenness and surprise.	(1–11)
He directs to several particular duties.	(12–22)
And concludes with prayer, greetings, and a blessing.	(23–28)

Verses 1–5

It is needless or useless to ask about the particular time of Christ's coming. Christ did not reveal this to the apostles. There are times and seasons for us to work in, and these are our duty and interest to know and observe; but as to the time when we must give up our account, we know it not, nor is it needful that we should. The coming of Christ will be a great surprise to men. Our Lord himself said so. As the hour of death is the same to each person that the judgment will be to mankind in general, so the same remarks answer for both. Christ's coming will be terrible to the ungodly. Their destruction will overtake them while they dream of happiness, and please themselves with vain amusements. There will be no means to escape the terror or the punishment of that day. This day will be a happy day to the righteous. They are not in darkness; they are the children of the light. It is the happy condition of all true Christians. But how many are speaking peace and safety to themselves, over whose heads utter destruction is hovering! Let us endeavour to awaken ourselves and each other, and guard against our spiritual enemies.

Verses 6–11

Most of mankind do not consider the things of another world at all, because they are asleep; or they do not consider them aright, because they sleep and dream. Our moderation as to all earthly things should be known to all men. Shall Christians, who have the light of the blessed gospel shining in their faces, be careless about their souls, and unmindful of another world? We need the spiritual armour, or the three Christian graces, faith, love, and hope. Faith; if we believe that the eye of God is always upon us, that there is another world to prepare for, we shall see reason to watch and be sober. True and fervent love to God, and the things of God, will keep us watchful and sober. If we have hope of salvation, let us take heed of any thing that would shake our trust in the Lord. We have ground on which to build unshaken hope, when we consider, that salvation is by our Lord Jesus Christ, who died for us, to atone for our sins and to ransom our souls. We should join in prayer and praise one with another. We should set a good example one before another, and this is the best means to answer the end of society. Thus we shall learn how to live to Him, with whom we hope to live for ever.

Verses 12–15

The ministers of the gospel are described by the work of their office, which is to serve and honour the Lord. It is their duty not only to give good counsel, but also to warn the flock of dangers, and reprove for whatever may be amiss. The people should honour and love their ministers, because their business is the welfare of men's souls. And the people should be at peace among themselves, doing all they can to guard against any differences. But love of peace must not make us wink at sin. The fearful and sorrowful spirits, should be encouraged, and a kind word may do much good. We must bear and forbear. We must be long-suffering, and keep down anger, and this to all men. Whatever man do to us, we must do good to others.

Verses 16–22

We are to rejoice in creature-comforts, as if we rejoiced not, and must not expect to live many years, and rejoice in them all; but if we do rejoice in God, we may do that evermore. A truly religious life is a life of constant joy. And we should rejoice more, if we prayed more. Prayer will help forward all lawful business, and every good work. If we pray without ceasing, we shall not want matter for thanksgiving in every thing. We shall see cause to give thanks for sparing and preventing, for common and uncommon, past and present, temporal and spiritual mercies. Not only for prosperous and pleasing, but also for afflicting providences, for chastisements and corrections; for God designs all for our good, though we at present see not how they tend to it. Quench not the Spirit. Christians are said to be baptized with the Holy Ghost and with fire. He worketh as fire, by enlightening, enlivening, and purifying the souls of men. As fire is put out by taking away fuel, and as it is quenched by pouring water, or putting a great deal of earth upon it; so we must be careful not to quench the Holy Spirit, by indulging carnal lusts and affections, minding only earthly things. Believers often hinder their growth in grace, by not giving themselves up to the spiritual affections raised in their hearts by the Holy Spirit. By prophesyings, here understand the preaching of the word, the interpreting and applying the Scriptures. We must not despise preaching, though it is plain, and we are told no more than what we knew before. We must search the Scriptures. And proving all things must be to hold fast that which is good. We should abstain from sin, and whatever looks like sin, leads to it, and borders upon it. He who is not shy of the appearances of sin, who shuns not the occasions of it, and who avoids not the temptations and approaches to it, will not long keep from doing sin.

Verses 23–28

The apostle prays that they might be sanctified more perfectly, for the best are sanctified but in part while in this world; therefore we should pray for, and press toward, complete holiness. And as we must fall, if God did not carry on his good work in the soul, we should pray to God to perfect his work, till we are presented faultless before the throne of his glory. We should pray for one another; and brethren should thus express brotherly love. This epistle was to be read to all the brethren. Not only are the common people allowed to read the Scriptures, but it is their duty, and what they should be persuaded to do. The word of God should not be kept in an unknown tongue, but transplanted, that as all men are concerned to know the Scriptures, so they all may be able to read them. The Scriptures should be read in all public congregations, for the benefit of the unlearned especially. We need no more to make us happy, than to know the grace of our Lord Jesus Christ. He is an ever-flowing and an over-flowing fountain of grace to supply all our wants.

2 Thessalonians

The second epistle to the Thessalonians was written soon after the first. The apostle was told that, from some expressions in his first letter, many expected the second coming of Christ was at hand, and that the day of judgment would arrive in their time. Some of these neglected their worldly duties. St. Paul wrote again to correct their error, which hindered the spread of the gospel. He had written agreeably to the words of the prophets of the Old Testament; and he tells them there were many counsels of the Most High yet to be fulfilled, before that day of the Lord should come, though, because it is sure, he had spoken of it as near. The subject led to a remarkable foretelling, of some of the future events which were to take place in the after-ages of the Christian church, and which show the prophetic spirit the apostle possessed.

Chapter 1

Chapter Outline	
The apostle blesses God for the growing state of the love and patience of the Thessalonians.	(1–4)
And encourages them to persevere under all their sufferings for Christ, considering his coming at the great day of account.	(5–12)

Verses 1–4

Where there is the truth of grace, there will be an increase of it. The path of the just is as the shining light, which shines more and more unto the perfect day. And where there is the increase of grace, God must have all the glory. Where faith grows, love will abound, for faith works by love. It shows faith and patience, such as may be proposed as a pattern for others, when trials from God, and persecutions from men, quicken the exercise of those graces; for the patience and faith of which the apostle gloried, bore them up, and enabled them to endure all their tribulations.

Verses 5–10

Religion, if worth anything, is worth every thing; and those have no religion, or none worth having, or know not how to value it, cannot find their hearts to suffer for it. We cannot by all our sufferings, any more than by our services, merit heaven; but by our patience under sufferings, we are prepared for the promised joy. Nothing more strongly marks a man for eternal ruin, than a spirit of persecution and enmity to the name and people of God. God will trouble those that trouble his people. And there is a rest for the people of God; a rest from sin and sorrow. The certainty of future recompence is proved by the righteousness of God. The thoughts of this should be terrible to wicked men, and support the righteous. Faith, looking to the great day, is enabled partly to understand the book of providence, which appears confused to unbelievers. The Lord Jesus will in that day appear from heaven. He will come in the glory and power of the upper world. His light will be piercing, and his power consuming, to all who in that day shall be found as chaff. This appearance will be terrible to those that know not God, especially to those who rebel against revelation, and obey not the gospel of our Lord Jesus Christ. This is the great crime of multitudes, the gospel is revealed, and they will not believe it; or if they pretend to believe, they will not obey it. Believing the truths of the gospel, is in order to our obeying the precepts of the gospel. Though sinners may be long spared, they will be punished at last. They did sin's work, and must receive sin's wages. Here God punishes sinners by creatures as instruments; but then, it will be destruction from the Almighty; and who knows the power of his anger? It will be a joyful day to some, to the saints, to those who believe and obey the gospel. In that bright and blessed day, Christ Jesus will be glorified and admired by his saints. And Christ will be glorified and admired in them. His grace and power will be shown, when it shall appear what he has purchased for, and wrought in, and bestowed upon those who believe in him. Lord, if the glory put upon thy saints shall be thus admired, how much more shalt thou be admired, as the Bestower of that glory! The glory of thy justice in the damnation of the wicked will be admired, but not as the glory of thy mercy in the salvation of believers. How will this strike the adoring angels with holy admiration, and transport thy admiring saints with eternal rapture! The meanest believer shall enjoy more than the most enlarged heart can imagine while we are here; Christ will be admired in all those that believe, the meanest believer not excepted.

Verses 11, 12

Believing thoughts and expectations of the second coming of Christ should lead us to pray to God more, for ourselves and others. If there is any good in us, it is owing to the good pleasure of his goodness, and therefore it is called grace. There are many purposes of grace and good-will in God toward his people, and the apostle prays that God would complete in them the work of faith with power. This is to their doing every other good work. The power of God not only begins, but carries on the work of faith. And this is the great end and design of the grace of our God and Lord Jesus Christ, which is made known to us, and wrought in us.

Chapter 2

Chapter Outline	
Cautions against the error that the time of Christ's coming was just at hand. There would first be a general apostasy from the faith, and a revealing of the antichristian man of sin.	(1–4)
His destruction, and that of those who obey him.	(5–12)
The security of the Thessalonians from apostacy; an exhortation to stedfastness, and prayer for them.	(13–17)

Verses 1–4

If errors arise among Christians, we should set them right; and good men will be careful to suppress errors which rise from mistaking their words and actions. We have a cunning adversary, who watches to do mischief, and will promote errors, even by the words of Scripture. Whatever uncertainty we are in, or whatever mistakes may arise about the time of Christ's coming, that coming itself is certain. This has been the faith and hope of all Christians, in all ages of the church; it was the faith and hope of the Old Testament saints. All believers shall be gathered together to Christ, to be with him, and to be happy in his presence for ever. We should firmly believe the second coming of Christ; but there was danger lest the Thessalonians, being mistaken as to the time, should question the truth or certainty of the thing itself. False doctrines are like the winds that toss the water to and fro; and they unsettle the minds of men, which are as unstable as water. It is enough for us to know that our Lord will come, and will gather all his saints unto him. A reason why they should not expect the coming of Christ, as at hand, is given. There would be a general falling away first, such as would occasion the rise of antichrist, that man of sin. There have been great disputes who or what is intended by this man of sin and son of perdition. The man of sin not only practises wickedness, but also promotes and commands sin and wickedness in others; and is the son of perdition, because he is devoted to certain destruction, and is the instrument to destroy many others, both in soul and body. As God was in the temple of old, and worshipped there, and is in and with his church now; so the antichrist here mentioned, is a usurper of God's authority in the Christian church, who claims Divine honours.

Verses 5–12

Something hindered or withheld the man of sin. It is supposed to be the power of the Roman empire, which the apostle did not mention more plainly at that time. Corruption of doctrine and worship came in by degrees, and the usurping of power was gradual; thus the mystery of iniquity prevailed. Superstition and idolatry were advanced by pretended devotion, and bigotry and persecution were promoted by pretended zeal for God and his glory. This mystery of iniquity was even then begun; while the apostles were yet living, persons pretended zeal for Christ, but really opposed him. The fall or ruin of the antichristian state is declared. The pure word of God, with the Spirit of God, will discover this mystery of iniquity, and in due time it shall be destroyed by the brightness of Christ's coming. Signs and wonders, visions and miracles, are pretended; but they are false signs to support false doctrines; and lying wonders, or only pretended miracles, to cheat the people; and the diabolical deceits with which the antichristian state has been supported, are notorious. The persons are described, who are his willing subjects. Their sin is this; They did not love the truth, and therefore did not believe it; and they were pleased with false notions. God leaves them to themselves, then sin will follow of course, and spiritual judgments here, and eternal punishments hereafter. These prophecies have, in a great measure, come to pass, and confirm the truth of the Scriptures. This passage exactly agrees with the system of popery, as it prevails in the Romish church, and under the Romish popes. But though the son of perdition has been revealed, though he has opposed and exalted himself above all that is called God, or that is worshipped; and has spoken and acted as if he were a god upon earth, and has proclaimed his insolent pride, and supported his delusions, by lying miracles and all kinds of frauds; still the Lord has not yet fully destroyed him with the brightness of his coming; that and other prophecies remain to be fulfilled before the end shall come.

Verses 13–15

When we hear of the apostacy of many, it is a great comfort and joy, that there is a remnant according to the election of grace, which does and shall persevere; especially we should rejoice, if we have reason to hope that we are of that number. The preservation of the saints, is because God loved them with an everlasting love, from the beginning of the world. The end and the means must not be separated. Faith and holiness must be joined together as well as holiness and happiness. The outward call of God is by the gospel; and this is rendered effectual by the inward working of the Spirit. The belief of the truth brings the sinner to rely on Christ, and so to love and obey him; it is sealed by the Holy Spirit upon his heart. We have no certain proof of any thing having been delivered by the apostles, more than what we find contained in the Holy Scriptures. Let us then stand fast in the doctrines taught by the apostles, and reject all additions, and vain traditions.

Verses 16, 17

We may and should direct our prayers, not only to God the Father, through our Lord Jesus Christ, but also to our Lord Jesus Christ himself. And we should pray in his name unto God, not only as his Father, but as our Father in and through him. The love of God in Christ Jesus, is the spring and fountain of all the good we have or hope for. There is good reason for strong consolations, because the saints have good hope through grace. The free grace and mercy of God are what they hope for, and what their hopes are founded on, and not any worth or merit of their own. The more pleasure we take in the word, and works, and ways of God, the more likely we shall be to persevere therein. But, if we are wavering in faith, and of a doubtful mind, halting and faltering in our duty, no wonder that we are strangers to the joys of religion.

Chapter 3

Chapter Outline	
The apostle expresses confidence in the Thessalonians, and prays for them.	(1–5)

He charges them to withdraw from disorderly walkers, particularly from the lazy and busybodies.	(6–15)
And concludes with a prayer for them, and a greeting.	(16–18)

Verses 1–5

Those who are far apart still may meet together at the throne of grace; and those not able to do or receive any other kindness, may in this way do and receive real and very great kindness. Enemies to the preaching of the gospel, and persecutors of its faithful preachers, are unreasonable and wicked men. Many do not believe the gospel; and no wonder if such are restless and show malice in their endeavours to oppose it. The evil of sin is the greatest evil, but there are other evils we need to be preserved from, and we have encouragement to depend upon the grace of God. When once the promise is made, the performance is sure and certain. The apostle had confidence in them, but that was founded upon his confidence in God; for there is otherwise no confidence in man. He prays for them for spiritual blessings. It is our sin and our misery, that we place our affections upon wrong objects. There is not true love of God, without faith in Jesus Christ. If, by the special grace of God, we have that faith which multitudes have not, we should earnestly pray that we may be enabled, without reserve, to obey his commands, and that we may be enabled, without reserve, to the love of God, and the patience of Christ.

Verses 6–15

Those who have received the gospel, are to live according to the gospel. Such as could work, and would not, were not to be maintained in idleness. Christianity is not to countenance slothfulness, which would consume what is meant to encourage the industrious, and to support the sick and afflicted. Industry in our callings as men, is a duty required by our calling as Christians. But some expected to be maintained in idleness, and indulged a curious and conceited temper. They meddled with the concerns of others, and did much harm. It is a great error and abuse of religion, to make it a cloak for idleness or any other sin. The servant who waits for the coming of his Lord aright, must be working as his Lord has commanded. If we are idle, the devil and a corrupt heart will soon find us somewhat to do. The mind of man is a busy thing; if it is not employed in doing good, it will be doing evil. It is an excellent, but rare union, to be active in our own business, yet quiet as to other people's. If any refused to labour with quietness, they were to note him with censure, and to separate from his company, yet they were to seek his good by loving admonitions. The Lords is with you while you are with him. Hold on your way, and hold on to the end. We must never give over, or tire in our work. It will be time enough to rest when we come to heaven.

Verses 16–18

The apostle prays for the Thessalonians. And let us desire the same blessings for ourselves and our friends. Peace with God. This peace is desired for them always, or in every thing. Peace by all means; in every way; that, as they enjoyed the means of grace, they might use all methods to secure peace. We need nothing more to make us safe and happy, nor can we desire any thing better for ourselves and our friends, than to have God's gracious presence with us and them. No matter where we are, if God be with us; nor who is absent, if God be present. It is through the grace of our Lord Jesus Christ, that we hope to have peace with God, and to enjoy the presence of God. This grace is all in all to make us happy; though we wish ever so much to others, there remains enough for ourselves.

1 Timothy

The design of the epistle appears to be, that Timothy having been left at Ephesus, St. Paul wrote to instruct him in the choice of proper officers in the church, as well as in the exercise of a regular ministry. Also, to caution against the influence of false teachers, who by subtle distinctions and endless disputes, corrupted the purity and simplicity of the gospel. He presses upon him constant regard to the greatest diligence, faithfulness, and zeal. These subjects occupy the first four chapters; the fifth chapter instructs respecting particular classes; in the latter part, controversies and disputes are condemned, the love of money blamed, and the rich exhorted to good works.

Chapter 1

Chapter Outline	
The apostle salutes Timothy.	(1–4)
The design of the law as given by Moses.	(5–11)
Of his own conversion and call to the apostleship.	(12–17)
The obligation to maintain faith and a good conscience.	(18–20)

Verses 1–4

Jesus Christ is a Christian's hope; all our hopes of eternal life are built upon him; and Christ is in us the hope of glory. The apostle seems to have been the means of Timothy's conversion; who served with him in his ministry, as a dutiful son with a loving father. That which raises questions, is not for edifying; that which gives occasion for doubtful disputes, pulls down the church rather than builds it up. Godliness of heart and life can only be kept up and increased, by the exercise of faith in the truths and promises of God, through Jesus Christ.

Verses 5–11

Whatever tends to weaken love to God, or love to the brethren, tends to defeat the end of the commandment. The design of the gospel is answered, when sinners, through repentance towards God and faith in Jesus Christ, are brought to exercise Christian love. And as believers were righteous persons in God's appointed way, the law was not against them. But unless we are made righteous by faith in Christ, really repenting and forsaking sin, we are yet under the curse of the law, even according to the gospel of the blessed God, and are unfit to share the holy happiness of heaven.

Verses 12–17

The apostle knew that he would justly have perished, if the Lord had been extreme to mark what was amiss; and also if his grace and mercy had not been abundant to him when dead in sin, working faith and love to Christ in his heart. This is a faithful saying; these are true and faithful words, which may be depended on, That the Son of God came into the world, willingly and purposely to save sinners. No man, with Paul's example before him, can question the love and power of Christ to save him, if he really desires to trust in him as the Son of God, who once died on the cross, and now reigns upon the throne of glory, to save all that come to God through him. Let us then admire and praise the grace of God our Saviour; and ascribe to the Father, Son, and Holy Ghost, three Persons in the unity of the Godhead, the glory of all done in, by, and for us.

Verses 18–20

The ministry is a warfare against sin and Satan; carried on under the Lord Jesus, who is the Captain of our salvation. The good hopes others have had of us, should stir us up to duty. And let us be upright in our conduct in all things. The design of the highest censures in the primitive church, was, to prevent further sin, and to reclaim the sinner. May all who are tempted to put away a good conscience, and to abuse the gospel, remember that this is the way to make shipwreck of faith also.

Chapter 2

Chapter Outline	
Prayer to be made for all persons, since the grace of the gospel makes no difference of ranks or stations.	(1–7)
How men and women ought to behave, both in their religious and common life.	(8–15)

Verses 1–7

The disciples of Christ must be praying people; all, without distinction of nation, sect, rank, or party. Our duty as Christians, is summed up in two words; godliness, that is, the right worshipping of God; and honesty, that is, good conduct toward all men. These must go together: we are not truly honest, if we are not godly, and do not render to God his due; and we are not truly godly, if not honest. What is acceptable in the sight of God our Saviour, we should abound in. There is one Mediator, and that Mediator gave himself a ransom for all. And this appointment has been made for the benefit of the Jews and the Gentiles of every nation; that all who are willing may come in this way, to the mercy-seat of a pardoning God, to seek reconciliation with him. Sin had made a quarrel between us and God; Jesus Christ is the Mediator who makes peace. He is a ransom that was to be known in due time. In the Old Testament times, his sufferings, and the glory that should follow, were spoken of as things to be revealed in the last times. Those who are saved must come to the knowledge of the truth, for that is God's appointed way to save sinners: if we do not know the truth, we cannot be ruled by it.

Verses 8–15

Under the gospel, prayer is not to be confined to any one particular house of prayer, but men must pray every where. We must pray in our closets, pray in our families, pray at our meals, pray when we are on journeys, and pray in the solemn assemblies, whether more public or private. We must pray in charity; without wrath, or malice, or anger at any person. We must pray in faith, without doubting, and without disputing. Women who profess the Christian religion, must be modest in apparel, not affecting gaudiness, gaiety, or costliness. Good works are the best ornament; these are, in the sight of God, of great price. Modesty and neatness are more to be consulted in garments than elegance and fashion. And it would be well if the professors of serious godliness were wholly free from vanity in dress. They should spend more time and money in relieving the sick and distressed, than in decorating themselves and their children. To do this in a manner unsuitable to their rank in life, and their profession of godliness, is sinful. These are not trifles, but Divine commands. The best ornaments for professors of godliness, are good works. According to St. Paul, women are not allowed to be public teachers in the church; for teaching is an office of authority. But good women may and ought to teach their children at home the principles of true religion. Also, women must not think themselves excused from learning what is necessary to salvation, though they must not usurp authority. As woman was last in the creation, which is one reason for her subjection, so she was first in the transgression. But there is a word of comfort; that those who continue in sobriety, shall be saved in child-bearing, or with child-bearing, by the Messiah, who was born of a woman. And the especial sorrow to which the female sex is subject, should cause men to exercise their authority with much gentleness, tenderness, and affection.

Chapter 3

Chapter Outline	
The qualifications and behaviour of gospel bishops.	(1–7)
And of deacons and their wives.	(8–13)
The reason of writing about these, and other church affairs.	(14–16)

Verses 1–7

If a man desired the pastoral office, and from love to Christ, and the souls of men, was ready to deny himself, and undergo hardships by devoting himself to that service, he sought to be employed in a good work, and his desire should be approved, provided he was qualified for the office. A minister must give as little occasion for blame as can be, lest he bring reproach upon his office. He must be sober, temperate, moderate in all his actions, and in the use of all creature-comforts. Sobriety and watchfulness are put together in Scripture, they assist one the other. The families of ministers ought to be examples of good to all other families. We should take heed of pride; it is a sin that turned angels into devils. He must be of good repute among his neighbours, and under no reproach from his former life. To encourage all faithful ministers, we have Christ's gracious word of promise, Lo, I am with you alway, even unto the end of the world, Mt **28**:**20**. And he will fit his ministers for their work, and carry them through difficulties with comfort, and reward their faithfulness.

Verses 8–13

The deacons were at first appointed to distribute the charity of the church, and to manage its concerns, yet pastors and evangelists were among them. The deacons had a great trust reposed in them. They must be grave, serious, prudent men. It is not fit that public trusts should be lodged in the hands of any, till they are found fit for the business with which they are to be trusted. All who are related to ministers, must take great care to walk as becomes the gospel of Christ.

Verses 14–16

The church is the house of God; he dwells there. The church holds forth the Scripture and the doctrine of Christ, as a pillar holds forth a proclamation. When a church ceases to be the pillar and ground of truth, we may and ought to forsake her; for our regard to truth should be first and greatest. The mystery of godliness is Christ. He is God, who was made flesh, and was manifest in the flesh. God was pleased to manifest himself to man, by his own Son taking the nature of man. Though reproached as a sinner, and put to death as a malefactor, Christ was raised again by the Spirit, and so was justified from all the false charges with which he was loaded. Angels ministered to him, for he is the Lord of angels. The Gentiles welcomed the gospel which the Jews rejected. Let us remember that God was manifest in the flesh, to take away our sins, to redeem us from all iniquity, and to purify unto himself a peculiar people, zealous of good works. These doctrines must be shown forth by the fruits of the Spirit in our lives.

Chapter 4

Chapter Outline	
Of departures from the faith that began already to appear.	(1–5)
Several directions, with motives for due discharge of duties.	(6–16)

Verses 1–5

The Holy Spirit, both in the Old and the New Testament, spoke of a general turning from the faith of Christ, and the pure worship of God. This should come during the Christian dispensation, for those are called the latter days. False teachers forbid as evil what God has allowed, and command as a duty what he has left indifferent. We find exercise for watchfulness and self-denial, in attending to the requirements of God's law, without being tasked to imaginary duties, which reject what he has allowed. But nothing justifies an intemperate or improper use of things; and nothing will be good to us, unless we seek by prayer for the Lord's blessing upon it.

Verses 6–10

Outward acts of self-denial profit little. What will it avail us to mortify the body, if we do not mortify sin? No diligence in mere outward things could be of much use. The gain of godliness lies much in the promise; and the promises to godly people relate partly to the life that now is, but especially to the life which is to come: though we lose for Christ, we shall not lose by him. If Christ be thus the Saviour of all men, then much more will he be the Rewarder of those who seek and serve him; he will provide well for those whom he has made new creatures.

Verses 11–16

Men's youth will not be despised, if they keep from vanities and follies. Those who teach by their doctrine, must teach by their life. Their discourse must be edifying; their conversation must be holy; they must be examples of love to God and all good men, examples of spiritual-mindedness. Ministers must mind these things as their principal work and business. By this means their profiting will appear in all things, as well as to all persons; this is the way to profit in knowledge and grace, and also to profit others. The doctrine of a minister of Christ must be scriptural, clear, evangelical, and practical; well stated, explained, defended, and applied. But these duties leave no leisure for wordly pleasures, trifling visits, or idle conversation, and but little for what is mere amusement, and only ornamental. May every believer be enabled to let his profiting appear unto all men; seeking to experience the power of the gospel in his own soul, and to bring forth its fruits in his life.

Chapter 5

Chapter Outline	
Directions as to the elder and younger men and women.	(1, 2)
And as to poor widows.	(3–8)
Concerning widows.	(9–16)
The respect to be paid to elders. Timothy is to take care in rebuking offenders, in ordaining ministers, and as to his own health.	(17–25)

Verses 1, 2

Respect must be paid to the dignity of years and place. The younger, if faulty, must be rebuked, not as desirous to find fault with them, but as willing to make the best of them. There is need of much meekness and care in reproving those who deserve reproof.

Verses 3–8

Honour widows that are widows indeed, relieve them, and maintain them. It is the duty of children, if their parents are in need, and they are able to relieve them, to do it to the utmost of their power. Widowhood is a desolate state; but let widows trust in the Lord, and continue in prayer. All who live in pleasure, are dead while they live, spiritually dead, dead in trespasses and sins. Alas, what numbers there are of this description among nominal Christians, even to the latest period of life! If any men or women do not maintain their poor relations, they in effect deny the faith. If they spend upon their lusts and pleasures, what should maintain their families, they have denied the faith, and are worse than infidels. If professors of the gospel give way to any corrupt principle or conduct, they are worse than those who do not profess to believe the doctrines of grace.

Verses 9–16

Every one brought into any office in the church, should be free from just censure; and many are proper objects of charity, yet ought not to be employed in public services. Those who would find mercy when they are in distress, must show mercy when they are in prosperity; and those who show most readiness for every good work, are most likely to be faithful in whatever is trusted to them. Those who are idle, very seldom are only idle, they make mischief among neighbours, and sow discord among brethren. All believers are required to relieve those belonging to their families who are destitute, that the church may not be prevented from relieving such as are entirely destitute and friendless.

Verses 17–25

Care must be taken that ministers are maintained. And those who are laborious in this work are worthy of double honour and esteem. It is their just due, as much as the reward of the labourer. The apostle charges Timothy solemnly to guard against partiality. We have great need to watch at all times, that we do not partake of other men's sins. Keep thyself pure, not only from doing the like thyself, but from countenancing it, or any way helping to it in others. The apostle also charges Timothy to take care of his health. As we are not to make our bodies masters, so neither slaves; but to use them so that they may be most helpful to us in the service of God. There are secret, and there are open sins: some men's sins are open before-hand, and going before unto judgment; some they follow after. God will bring to light the hidden things of darkness, and make known the counsels of all hearts. Looking forward to the judgment-day, let us all attend to our proper offices, whether in higher or lower stations, studying that the name and doctrine of God may never be blasphemed on our account.

Chapter 6

Chapter Outline	
The duty of Christians towards believing, as well as other masters.	(1–5)
The advantage of godliness with contentment.	(6–10)
A solemn charge to Timothy to be faithful.	(11–16)
The apostle repeats his warning to the rich, and closes with a blessing.	(17–21)

Verses 1–5

Christians were not to suppose that religious knowledge, or Christian privileges, gave them any right to despise heathen masters, or to disobey lawful commands, or to expose their faults to others. And such as enjoyed the privilege of living with believing masters, were not to withhold due respect and reverence, because they were equal in respect to religious privileges, but were to serve with double diligence and cheerfulness, because of their faith in Christ, and as partakers of his free salvation. We are not to consent to any words as wholesome, except the words of our Lord Jesus Christ; to these we must give unfeigned consent. Commonly those are most proud who know least; for they do not know themselves. Hence come envy, strife, railings, evil-surmisings, disputes that are all subtlety, and of no solidity, between men of corrupt and carnal minds, ignorant of the truth and its sanctifying power, and seeking their worldly advantage. (**1Ti 6:6-10**)

Verses 6–10

Those that make a trade of Christianity to serve their turn for this world, will be disappointed; but those who mind it as their calling, will find it has the promise of the life that now is, as well as of that which is to come. He that is godly, is sure to be happy in another world; and if contented with his condition in this world, he has enough; and all truly godly people are content. When brought into the greatest straits, we cannot be poorer than when we came into this world; a shroud, a coffin, and a grave, are all that the richest man in the world can have from all his wealth. If nature should be content with a little, grace should be content with less. The necessaries of life bound a true Christian's desires, and with these he will endeavour to be content. We see here the evil of covetousness. It is not said, they that are rich, but they will be rich; who place their happiness in wealth, and are eager and determined in the pursuit. Those that are such, give to Satan the opportunity of tempting them, leading them to use dishonest means, and other bad practices, to add to their gains. Also, leading into so many employments, and such a hurry of business, as leave no time or inclination for spiritual religion; leading to connexions that draw into sin and folly. What sins will not men be drawn into by the love of money! People may have money, and yet not love it; but if they love it, this will push them on to all evil. Every sort of wickedness and vice, in one way or another, grows from the love of money. We cannot look around without perceiving many proofs of this, especially in a day of outward prosperity, great expenses, and loose profession.

Verses 11–16

It ill becomes any men, but especially men of God, to set their hearts upon the things of this world; men of God should be taken up with the things of God. There must be a conflict with corruption, and temptations, and the powers of darkness. Eternal life is the crown proposed for our encouragement. We are called to lay hold thereon. To the rich must especially be pointed out their dangers and duties, as to the proper use of wealth. But who can give such a charge, that is not himself above the love of things that wealth can buy? The appearing of Christ is certain, but it is not for us to know the time. Mortal eyes cannot bear the brightness of the Divine glory. None can approach him except as he is made known unto sinners in and by Christ. The Godhead is here adored without distinction of Persons, as all these things are properly spoken, whether of the Father, the Son, or the Holy Ghost. God is revealed to us, only in and through the human nature of Christ, as the only begotten Son of the Father.

Verses 17–21

Being rich in this world is wholly different from being rich towards God. Nothing is more uncertain than worldly wealth. Those who are rich, must see that God gives them their riches; and he only can give to enjoy them richly; for many have riches, but enjoy them poorly, not having a heart to use them. What is the best estate worth, more than as it gives opportunity of doing the more good? Showing faith in Christ by fruits of love, let us lay hold on eternal life, when the self-indulgent, covetous, and ungodly around, lift up their eyes in torment. That learning which opposes the truth of the gospel, is not true science, or real knowledge, or it would approve the gospel, and consent to it. Those who advance reason above faith, are in danger of leaving faith. Grace includes all that is good, and grace is an earnest, a beginning of glory; wherever God gives grace, he will give glory.

2 Timothy

Chapter 1

The first design of this epistle seems to have been, to apprize Timothy of what had occurred during the imprisonment of the apostle, and to request him to come to Rome. But being uncertain whether he should be suffered to live to see him, Paul gives a variety of advices and encouragements, for the faithful discharge of his ministerial duties. As this was a private epistle written to St. Paul's most intimate friend, under the miseries of imprisonment, and in the near prospect of death, it shows the temper and character of the apostle, and contains convincing proofs that he sincerely believed the doctrines he preached.

Chapter 1

Chapter Outline	
Paul expresses great affection for Timothy.	(1–5)
Exhorts him to improve his spiritual gifts.	(6–14)
Tells of many who basely deserted him; but speaks with affection of Onesiphorus.	(15–18)

Verses 1–5

The promise of eternal life to believers in Christ Jesus, is the leading subject of ministers who are employed according to the will of God. The blessings here named, are the best we can ask for our beloved friends, that they may have peace with God the Father and Christ Jesus our Lord. Whatever good we do, God must have the glory. True believers have in every age the same religion as to substance. Their faith is unfeigned; it will stand the trial, and it dwells in them as a living principle. Thus pious women may take encouragement from the success of Lois and Eunice with Timothy, who proved so excellent and useful a minister. Some of the most worthy and valuable ministers the church of Christ has been favoured with, have had to bless God for early religious impressions made upon their minds by the teaching of their mothers or other female relatives.

Verses 6–14

God has not given us the spirit of fear, but the spirit of power, of courage and resolution, to meet difficulties and dangers; the spirit of love to him, which will carry us through opposition. And the spirit of a sound mind, quietness of mind. The Holy Spirit is not the author of a timid or cowardly disposition, or of slavish fears. We are likely to bear afflictions well, when we have strength and power from God to enable us to bear them. As is usual with Paul, when he mentions Christ and his redemption, he enlarges upon them; so full was he of that which is all our salvation, and ought to be all our desire. The call of the gospel is a holy call, making holy. Salvation is of free grace. This is said to be given us before the world began, that is, in the purpose of God from all eternity; in Christ Jesus, for all the gifts that come from God to sinful man, come in and through Christ Jesus alone. And as there is so clear a prospect of eternal happiness by faith in Him, who is the Resurrection and the Life, let us give more diligence in making his salvation sure to our souls. Those who cleave to the gospel, need not be ashamed, the cause will bear them out; but those who oppose it, shall be ashamed. The apostle had trusted his life, his soul, and eternal interests, to the Lord Jesus. No one else could deliver and secure his soul through the trials of life and death. There is a day coming, when our souls will be inquired after. Thou hadst a soul committed to thee; how was it employed? in the service of sin, or in the service of Christ? The hope of the lowest real Christian rests on the same foundation as that of the great apostle. He also has learned the value and the danger of his soul; he also has believed in Christ; and the change wrought in his soul, convinces the believer that the Lord Jesus will keep him to his heavenly kingdom. Paul exhorts Timothy to hold fast the Holy Scriptures, the substance of solid gospel truth in them. It is not enough to assent to the sound words, but we must love them. The Christian doctrine is a trust committed to us; it is of unspeakable value in itself, and will be of unspeakable advantage to us. It is committed to us, to be preserved pure and entire, yet we must not think to keep it by our own strength, but by the power of the Holy Spirit dwelling in us; and it will not be gained by those who trust in their own hearts, and lean to their own understandings. **(2Ti 1:15-18)**

Verses 15–18

The apostle mentions the constancy of Onesiphorus; he oft refreshed him with his letters, and counsels, and comforts, and was not ashamed of him. A good man will seek to do good. The day of death and judgment is an awful day. And if we would have mercy then, we must seek for it now of the Lord. The best we can ask, for ourselves or our friends, is, that the Lord will grant that we and they may find mercy of the Lord, when called to pass out of time into eternity, and to appear before the judgment seat of Christ.

Chapter 2

Chapter Outline	
The apostle exhorts Timothy to persevere with diligence, like a soldier, a combatant, and a husbandman.	(1–7)
Encouraging him by assurances of a happy end of his faithfulness.	(8–13)
Warnings to shun vain babblings and dangerous errors.	(14–21)

Charges to flee youthful lusts, and to minister with zeal against error, but with meekness of spirit.	(22–26)

Verses 1–7

As our trials increase, we need to grow stronger in that which is good; our faith stronger, our resolution stronger, our love to God and Christ stronger. This is opposed to our being strong in our own strength. All Christians, but especially ministers, must be faithful to their Captain, and resolute in his cause. The great care of a Christian must be to please Christ. We are to strive to get the mastery of our lusts and corruptions, but we cannot expect the prize unless we observe the laws. We must take care that we do good in a right manner, that our good may not be spoken evil of. Some who are active, spend their zeal about outward forms and doubtful disputations. But those who strive lawfully shall be crowned at last. If we would partake the fruits, we must labour; if we would gain the prize, we must run the race. We must do the will of God, before we receive the promises, for which reason we have need of patience. Together with our prayers for others, that the Lord would give them understanding in all things, we must exhort and stir them up to consider what they hear or read.

Verses 8–13

Let suffering saints remember, and look to Jesus, the Author and Finisher of their faith, who for the joy that was set before him, endured the cross, despised the shame, and is now set down at the right hand of the throne of God. We must not think it strange if the best men meet with the worst treatment; but this is cheering, that the word of God is not bound. Here we see the real and true cause of the apostle's suffering trouble in, or for, the sake of the gospel. If we are dead to this world, its pleasures, profits, and honours, we shall be for ever with Christ in a better world. He is faithful to his threatenings, and faithful to his promises. This truth makes sure the unbeliever's condemnation, and the believer's salvation.

Verses 14–21

Those disposed to strive, commonly strive about matters of small moment. But strifes of words destroy the things of God. The apostle mentions some who erred. They did not deny the resurrection, but they corrupted that true doctrine. Yet nothing can be so foolish or erroneous, but it will overturn the temporary faith of some professors. This foundation has two writings on it. One speaks our comfort. None can overthrow the faith of any whom God hath chosen. The other speaks our duty. Those who would have the comfort of the privilege, must make conscience of the duty Christ gave himself for us, that he might redeem us from all iniquity, Tit **2**:**14**. The church of Christ is like a dwelling: some furniture is of great value; some of smaller value, and put to meaner uses. Some professors of religion are like vessels of wood and earth. When the vessels of dishonour are cast out to be destroyed, the others will be filled with all the fulness of God. We must see to it that we are holy vessels. Every one in the church whom God approves, will be devoted to his Master's service, and thus fitted for his use.

Verses 22–26

The more we follow that which is good, the faster and the further we shall flee from that which is evil. The keeping up the communion of saints, will take us from fellowship with unfruitful works of darkness. See how often the apostle cautions against disputes in religion; which surely shows that religion consists more in believing and practising what God requires, than in subtle disputes. Those are unapt to teach, who are apt to strive, and are fierce and froward. Teaching, not persecution, is the Scripture method of dealing with those in error. The same God who gives the discovery of the truth, by his grace brings us to acknowledge it, otherwise our hearts would continue to rebel against it. There is no "peradventure," in respect of God's pardoning those who do repent; but we cannot tell that he will give repentance to those who oppose his will. Sinners are taken in a snare, and in the worst snare, because it is the devil's; they are slaves to him. And if any long for deliverance, let them remember they never can escape, except by repentance, which is the gift of God; and we must ask it of him by earnest, persevering prayer.

Chapter 3

Chapter Outline	
The apostle foretells the rise of dangerous enemies to the gospel.	(1–9)
Proposes his own example to Timothy.	(10–13)
And exhorts him to continue in the doctrine he had learned from the Holy Scriptures.	(14–17)

Verses 1–9

Even in gospel times there would be perilous times; on account of persecution from without, still more on account of corruptions within. Men love to gratify their own lusts, more than to please God and do their duty. When every man is eager for what he can get, and anxious to keep what he has, this makes men dangerous to one another. When men do not fear God, they will not regard man. When children are disobedient to their parents, that makes the times perilous. Men are unholy and without the fear of God, because unthankful for the mercies of God. We abuse God's gifts, if we make them the food and fuel of our lusts. Times are perilous also, when parents are without natural affection to children. And when men have no rule over their own spirits, but despise that which is good and to be honoured. God is to be loved above all; but a carnal mind, full of enmity against him, prefers any thing before him, especially carnal pleasure. A form of godliness is very different from the power; from such as are found to be hypocrites, real Christians must withdraw. Such persons have been found within the outward church, in every place, and at all times. There ever have been artful men, who, by pretences and flatteries, creep into the favour and confidence of those who are too easy of belief, ignorant, and fanciful. All must be ever learning to know the Lord; but these follow every new notion, yet never seek the truth as it is in Jesus. Like the Egyptian magicians, these were men of corrupt minds, prejudiced against the truth, and found to be quite without faith. Yet though the spirit of error may be let loose for a time, Satan can deceive the nations and the churches no further, and no longer, than God will permit.

Verses 10–13

The more fully we know the doctrine of Christ, as taught by the apostles, the more closely we shall cleave to it. When we know the afflictions of believers only in part, they tempt us to decline the cause for which they suffer. A form of godliness, a profession of Christian faith without a godly life, often is allowed to pass, while open profession of the truth as it is in Jesus, and resolute attention to the duties of godliness, stir up the scorn and enmity of the world. As good men, by the grace of God, grow better, so bad men, through the craft of Satan, and the power of their own corruptions, grow worse. The way of sin is down-hill; such go on from bad to worse, deceiving and being deceived. Those who deceive others, deceive themselves, as they will find at last, to their cost. The history of the outward church, awfully shows that the apostle spake this as he was moved by the Holy Ghost.

Verses 14–17

Those who would learn the things of God, and be assured of them, must know the Holy Scriptures, for they are the Divine revelation. The age of children is the age to learn; and those who would get true learning, must get it out of the Scriptures. They must not lie by us neglected, seldom or never looked into. The Bible is a sure guide to eternal life. The prophets and apostles did not speak from themselves, but delivered what they received of God, **2**Pe **1**:**21**. It is profitable for all purposes of the Christian life. It is of use to all, for all need to be taught, corrected, and reproved. There is something in the Scriptures suitable for every case. Oh that we may love our Bibles more, and keep closer to them! then shall we find benefit, and at last gain the happiness therein promised by faith in our Lord Jesus Christ, who is the main subject of both Testaments. We best oppose error by promoting a solid knowledge of the word of truth; and the greatest kindness we can do to children, is to make them early to know the Bible.

Chapter 4

Chapter Outline	
The apostle solemnly charges Timothy to be diligent, though many will not bear sound doctrine.	(1–5)
Enforces the charge from his own martyrdom, then at hand.	(6–8)
Desires him to come speedily.	(9–13)
He cautions, and complains of such as had deserted him; and expresses his faith as to his own preservation to the heavenly kingdom.	(14–18)
Friendly greetings and his usual blessing.	(19–22)

Verses 1–5

People will turn away from the truth, they will grow weary of the plain gospel of Christ, they will be greedy of fables, and take pleasure in them. People do so when they will not endure that preaching which is searching, plain, and to the purpose. Those who love souls must be ever watchful, must venture and bear all the painful effects of their faithfulness, and take all opportunities of making known the pure gospel.

Verses 6–8

The blood of the martyrs, though not a sacrifice of atonement, yet was a sacrifice of acknowledgment to the grace of God and his truth. Death to a good man, is his release from the imprisonment of this world, and his departure to the enjoyments of another world. As a Christian, and a minister, Paul had kept the faith, kept the doctrines of the gospel. What comfort will it afford, to be able to speak in this manner toward the end of our days! The crown of believers is a crown of righteousness, purchased by the righteousness of Christ. Believers have it not at present, yet it is sure, for it is laid up for them. The believer, amidst poverty, pain, sickness, and the agonies of death, may rejoice; but if the duties of a man's place and station are neglected, his evidence of interest in Christ will be darkened, and uncertainty and distress may be expected to cloud and harass his last hours.

Verses 9–13

The love of this world, is often the cause of turning back from the truths and ways of Jesus Christ. Paul was guided by Divine inspiration, yet he would have his books. As long as we live, we must still learn. The apostles did not neglect human means, in seeking the necessaries of life, or their own instruction. Let us thank the Divine goodness in having given us so many writings of wise and pious men in all ages; and let us seek that by reading them our profiting may appear to all.

Verses 14–18

There is as much danger from false brethren, as from open enemies. It is dangerous having to do with those who would be enemies to such a man as Paul. The Christians at Rome were forward to meet him, Ac **28**, but when there seemed to be a danger of suffering with him, then all forsook him. God might justly be angry with them, but he prays God to forgive them. The apostle was delivered out of the mouth of the lion, that is, of Nero, or some of his judges. If the Lord stands by us, he will strengthen us in difficulties and dangers, and his presence will more than supply every one's absence.

Verses 19–22

We need no more to make us happy, than to have the Lord Jesus Christ with our spirits; for in him all spiritual blessings are summed up. It is the best prayer we can offer for our friends, that the Lord Jesus Christ may be with their spirits, to sanctify and save them, and at last to receive them to himself. Many who believed as Paul, are now before the throne, giving glory to their Lord: may we be followers of them.

Titus

This epistle chiefly contains directions to Titus concerning the elders of the Church, and the manner in which he should give instruction; and the latter part tells him to urge obedience to magistrates, to enforce good works, avoid foolish questions, and shun heresies. The instructions the apostle gave are all plain and simple. The Christian religion was not formed to answer worldly or selfish views, but it is the wisdom of God and the power of God.

Chapter 1

Chapter Outline	
The apostle salutes Titus.	(1–4)
The qualifications of a faithful pastor.	(5–9)
The evil temper and practices of false teachers.	(10–16)

Verses 1–4

All are the servants of God who are not slaves of sin and Satan. All gospel truth is according to godliness, teaching the fear of God. The intent of the gospel is to raise up hope as well as faith; to take off the mind and heart from the world, and to raise them to heaven and the things above. How excellent then is the gospel, which was the matter of Divine promise so early, and what thanks are due for our privileges! Faith comes by hearing, and hearing by the word of God; and whoso is appointed and called, must preach the word. Grace is the free favour of God, and acceptance with him. Mercy, the fruits of the favour, in the pardon of sin, and freedom from all miseries both here and hereafter. And peace is the effect and fruit of mercy. Peace with God through Christ who is our Peace, and with the creatures and ourselves. Grace is the fountain of all blessings. Mercy, and peace, and all good, spring out of this.

Verses 5–9

The character and qualification of pastors, here called elders and bishops, agree with what the apostle wrote to Timothy. Being such bishops and overseers of the flock, to be examples to them, and God's stewards to take care of the affairs of his household, there is great reason that they should be blameless. What they are not to be, is plainly shown, as well as what they are to be, as servants of Christ, and able ministers of the letter and practice of the gospel. And here are described the spirit and practice becoming such as should be examples of good works.

Verses 10–16

False teachers are described. Faithful ministers must oppose such in good time, that their folly being made manifest, they may go no further They had a base end in what they did; serving a worldly interest under pretence of religion: for the love of money is the root of all evil. Such should be resisted, and put to shame, by sound doctrine from the Scriptures. Shameful actions, the reproach of heathens, should be far from Christians; falsehood and lying, envious craft and cruelty, brutal and sensual practices, and idleness and sloth, are sins condemned even by the light of nature. But Christian meekness is as far from cowardly passing over sin and error, as from anger and impatience. And though there may be national differences of character, yet the heart of man in every age and place is deceitful and desperately wicked. But the sharpest reproofs must aim at the good of the reproved; and soundness in the faith is most desirable and necessary. To those who are defiled and unbelieving, nothing is pure; they abuse, and turn things lawful and good into sin. Many profess to know God, yet in their lives deny and reject him. See the miserable state of hypocrites, such as have a form of godliness, but are without the power; yet let us not be so ready to fix this charge on others, as careful that it does not apply to ourselves.

Chapter 2

Chapter Outline	
The duties which become sound doctrine.	(1–8)
Believing servants must be obedient.	(9, 10)
All is enforced from the holy design of the gospel, which concerns all believers.	(11–15)

Verses 1–8

Old disciples of Christ must behave in every thing agreeably to the Christian doctrine. That the aged men be sober; not thinking that the decays of nature will justify any excess; but seeking comfort from nearer communion with God, not from any undue indulgence. Faith works by, and must be seen in love, of God for himself, and of men for God's sake. Aged persons are apt to be peevish and fretful; therefore need to be on their guard. Though there is not express Scripture for every word, or look, yet there are general rules, according to which all must be ordered. Young women must be sober and discreet; for many expose themselves to fatal temptations by what at first might be only want of discretion. The reason is added, that the word of God may not be blasphemed. Failures in duties greatly reproach Christianity. Young men are apt to be eager and thoughtless, therefore must be earnestly called upon to be sober-minded: there are more young people ruined by pride than by any other sin. Every godly man's endeavour must be to stop the mouths of adversaries. Let thine own conscience answer for thine uprightness. What a glory is it for a Christian, when that mouth which would fain open itself against him, cannot find any evil in him to speak of!

Verses 9, 10

Servants must know and do their duty to their earthly masters, with a reference to their heavenly one. In serving an earthly master according to Christ's will, He is served; such shall be rewarded by him. Not giving disrespectful or provoking language; but to take a check or reproof with silence, not making confident or bold replies. When conscious of a fault, to excuse or justify it, doubles it. Never putting to their own use that which is their master's, nor wasting the goods they are trusted with. Showing all good fidelity to improve a master's goods, and promote his thriving. If ye have not been faithful in that which is another man's, who shall give you that which is your own? Lu **16**:**12**. True religion is an honour to the professors of it; and they should adorn it in all things.

Verses 11–15

The doctrine of grace and salvation by the gospel, is for all ranks and conditions of men. It teaches to forsake sin; to have no more to do with it. An earthly, sensual conversation suits not a heavenly calling. It teaches to make conscience of that which is good. We must look to God in Christ, as the object of our hope and worship. A gospel conversation must be a godly conversation. See our duty in a very few words; denying ungodliness and worldly lusts, living soberly, righteously, and godly, notwithstanding all snares, temptations, corrupt examples, ill usage, and what remains of sin in the believer's heart, with all their hinderances. It teaches to look for the glories of another world. At, and in, the glorious appearing of Christ, the blessed hope of Christians will be complete: To bring us to holiness and happiness was the end of Christ's death. Jesus Christ, that great God and our Saviour, who saves not only as God, much less as Man alone; but as God-man, two natures in one person. He loved us, and gave himself for us; and what can we do less than love and give up ourselves to him! Redemption from sin and sanctification of the nature go together, and make a peculiar people unto God, free from guilt and condemnation, and purified by the Holy Spirit. All Scripture is profitable. Here is what will furnish for all parts of duty, and the right discharge of them. Let us inquire whether our whole dependence is placed upon that grace which saves the lost, pardons the guilty, and sanctifies the unclean. And the further we are removed from boasting of fancied good works, or trusting in them, so that we glory in Christ alone, the more zealous shall we be to abound in real good works.

Chapter 3

Chapter Outline	
Obedience to magistrates, and becoming behaviour towards all, are enforced from what believers were before conversion, and what they are made, through Christ.	(1–7)
Good works to be done, and useless disputes avoided.	(8–11)
Directions and exhortations.	(12–15)

Verses 1–7

Spiritual privileges do not make void or weaken, but confirm civil duties. Mere good words and good meanings are not enough without good works. They were not to be quarrelsome, but to show meekness on all occasions, not toward friends only, but to all men, though with wisdom, Jas **3**:**13**. And let this text teach us how wrong it is for a Christian to be churlish to the worst, weakest, and most abject. The servants of sin have many masters, their lusts hurry them different ways; pride commands one thing, covetousness another. Thus they are hateful, deserving to be hated. It is the misery of sinners, that they hate one another; and it is the duty and happiness of saints to love one another. And we are delivered out of our miserable condition, only by the mercy and free grace of God, the merit and sufferings of Christ, and the working of his Spirit. God the Father is God our Saviour. He is the fountain from which the Holy Spirit flows, to teach, regenerate, and save his fallen creatures; and this blessing comes to mankind through Christ. The spring and rise of it, is the kindness and love of God to man. Love and grace have, through the Spirit, great power to change and turn the heart to God. Works must be in the saved, but are not among the causes of their salvation. A new principle of grace and holiness is wrought, which sways, and governs, and makes the man a new creature. Most pretend they would have heaven at last, yet they care not for holiness now; they would have the end without the beginning. Here is the outward sign and seal thereof in baptism, called therefore the washing of regeneration. The work is inward and spiritual; this is outwardly signified and sealed in this ordinance. Slight not this outward sign and seal; yet rest not in the outward washing, but look to the answer of a good conscience, without which the outward washing will avail nothing. The worker therein is the Spirit of God; it is the renewing of the Holy Ghost. Through him we mortify sin, perform duty, walk in God's ways; all the working of the Divine life in us, and the fruits of righteousness without, are through this blessed and holy Spirit. The Spirit and his saving gifts and graces, come through Christ, as a Saviour, whose undertaking and work are to bring to grace and glory. Justification, in the gospel sense, is the free forgiveness of a sinner; accepting him as righteous through the righteousness of Christ received by faith. God, in justifying a sinner in the way of the gospel, is gracious to him, yet just to himself and his law. As forgiveness is through a perfect righteousness, and satisfaction is made to justice by Christ, it cannot be merited by the sinner himself. Eternal life is set before us in the promise; the Spirit works faith in us, and hope of that life; faith and hope bring it near, and fill with joy in expectation of it.

Verses 8–11

When the grace of God towards mankind has been declared, the necessity of good works is pressed. Those who believe in God, must make it their care to maintain good works, to seek opportunities for doing them, being influenced by love and gratitude. Trifling, foolish questions must be avoided, and subtle distinctions and vain inquiries; nor should people be eager after novelties, but love sound doctrine which tends most to edifying. Though we may now think some sins light and little, if the Lord awaken the conscience, we shall feel even the smallest sin heavy upon our souls.

Verses 12–15

Christianity is not a fruitless profession; and its professors must be filled with the fruits of righteousness, which are by Jesus Christ, to the glory and praise of God. They must be doing good, as well as keeping away from evil. Let "ours" follow some honest labour and employment, to provide for themselves and their families. Christianity obliges all to seek some honest work and calling, and therein to abide with God. The apostle concludes with expressions of kind regard and fervent prayer. Grace be with you all; the love and favour of God, with the fruits and effects thereof, according to need; and the increase and feeling of them more and more in your souls. This is the apostle's wish and prayer, showing his affection to them, and desire for their good, and would be a means of obtaining for them, and bringing down on them, the thing requested. Grace is the chief thing to be wished and prayed for, with respect to ourselves or others; it is "all good."

Philemon

Philemon was an inhabitant of Colosse, a person of some note and wealth, and a convert under the ministry of St. Paul. Onesimus was the slave of Philemon: having run away from his master, he went to Rome, where he was converted to the Christian faith, by the word as set forth by Paul, who kept him till his conduct proved the truth and sincerity of his conversion. He wished to repair the injury he had done to his master, but fearing the punishment his offence deserved might be inflicted, he entreated the apostle to write to Philemon. And St. Paul seems no where to reason more beautifully, or to entreat more forcibly, than in this epistle.

Chapter 1

Chapter Outline	
The apostle's joy and praise for Philemon's steady faith in the Lord Jesus, and love to all the saints.	(1–7)
He recommends Onesimus as one who would make rich amends for the misconduct of which he had been guilty; and on behalf of whom the apostle promises to make up any loss Philemon had sustained.	(8–22)
Salutations and a blessing.	(23–25)

Verses 1–7

Faith in Christ, and love to him, should unite saints more closely than any outward relation can unite the people of the world. Paul in his private prayers was particular in remembering his friends. We must remember Christian friends much and often, as their cases may need, bearing them in our thoughts, and upon our hearts, before our God. Different sentiments and ways in what is not essential, must not make difference of affection, as to the truth. He inquired concerning his friends, as to the truth, growth, and fruitfulness of their graces, their faith in Christ, and love to him, and to all the saints. The good which Philemon did, was matter of joy and comfort to him and others, who therefore desired that he would continue and abound in good fruits, more and more, to God's honour.

Verses 8–14

It does not lower any one to condescend, and sometimes even to beseech, where, in strictness of right, we might command: the apostle argues from love, rather than authority, in behalf of one converted through his means; and this was Onesimus. In allusion to that name, which signifies "profitable," the apostle allows that in time past he had been unprofitable to Philemon, but hastens to mention the change by which he had become profitable. Unholy persons are unprofitable; they answer not the great end of their being. But what happy changes conversion makes! of evil, good; of unprofitable, useful. Religious servants are treasures in a family. Such will make conscience of their time and trusts, and manage all they can for the best. No prospect of usefulness should lead any to neglect their obligations, or to fail in obedience to superiors. One great evidence of true repentance consists in returning to practise the duties which have been neglected. In his unconverted state, Onesimus had withdrawn, to his master's injury; but now he had seen his sin and repented, he was willing and desirous to return to his duty. Little do men know for what purposes the Lord leaves some to change their situations, or engage in undertakings, perhaps from evil motives. Had not the Lord overruled some of our ungodly projects, we may reflect upon cases, in which our destruction must have been sure.

Verses 15–22

When we speak of the nature of any sin or offence against God, the evil of it is not to be lessened; but in a penitent sinner, as God covers it, so must we. Such changed characters often become a blessing to all among whom they reside. Christianity does not do away our duties to others, but directs to the right doing of them. True penitents will be open in owning their faults, as doubtless Onesimus had been to Paul, upon his being awakened and brought to repentance; especially in cases of injury done to others. The communion of saints does not destroy distinction of property. This passage is an instance of that being imputed to one, which is contracted by another; and of one becoming answerable for another, by a voluntary engagement, that he might be freed from the punishment due to his crimes, according to the doctrine that Christ of his own will bore the punishment of our sins, that we might receive the reward of his righteousness. Philemon was Paul's son in the faith, yet he entreated him as a brother. Onesimus was a poor slave, yet Paul besought for him as if seeking some great thing for himself. Christians should do what may give joy to the hearts of one another. From the world they expect trouble; they should find comfort and joy in one another. When any of our mercies are taken away, our trust and hope must be in God. We must diligently use the means, and if no other should be at hand, abound in prayer. Yet, though prayer prevails, it does not merit the things obtained. And if Christians do not meet on earth, still the grace of the Lord Jesus will be with their spirits, and they will soon meet before the throne to join for ever in admiring the riches of redeeming love. The example of Onesimus may encourage the vilest sinners to return to God, but it is shamefully prevented, if any are made bold thereby to persist in evil courses. Are not many taken away in their sins, while others become more hardened? Resist not present convictions, lest they return no more.

Verses 23–25

Never have believers found more enjoyment of God, than when suffering together for him. Grace is the best wish for ourselves and others; with this the apostle begins and ends. All grace is from Christ; he purchased, and he bestows it. What need we more to make us happy, than to have the grace of our Lord Jesus Christ with our spirit? Let us do that now, which we should do at the last breath. Then men are ready to renounce the world, and to prefer the least portion of grace and faith before a kingdom.

Hebrews

This epistle shows Christ as the end, foundation, body, and truth of the figures of the law, which of themselves were no virtue for the soul. The great truth set forth in this epistle is that Jesus of Nazareth is the true God. The unconverted Jews used many arguments to draw their converted brethren from the Christian faith. They represented the law of Moses as superior to the Christian dispensation, and spoke against every thing connected with the Saviour. The apostle, therefore, shows the superiority of Jesus of Nazareth, as the Son of God, and the benefits from his sufferings and death as the sacrifice for sin, so that the Christian religion is much more excellent and perfect than that of Moses. And the principal design seems to be, to bring the converted Hebrews forward in the knowledge of the gospel, and thus to establish them in the Christian faith, and to prevent their turning from it, against which they are earnestly warned. But while it contains many things suitable to the Hebrews of early times, it also contains many which can never cease to interest the church of God; for the knowledge of Jesus Christ is the very marrow and kernel of all the Scriptures. The ceremonial law is full of Christ, and all the gospel is full of Christ; the blessed lines of both Testaments meet in Him; and how they both agree and sweetly unite in Jesus Christ, is the chief object of the epistle to the Hebrews to discover.

Chapter 1

Chapter Outline	
The surpassing dignity of the Son of God in his Divine person, and in his creating and mediatorial work.	(1–3)
And in his superiority to all the holy angels.	(4–14)

Verses 1–3

God spake to his ancient people at sundry times, through successive generations, and in divers manners, as he thought proper; sometimes by personal directions, sometimes by dreams, sometimes by visions, sometimes by Divine influences on the minds of the prophets. The gospel revelation is excellent above the former; in that it is a revelation which God has made by his Son. In beholding the power, wisdom, and goodness of the Lord Jesus Christ, we behold the power, wisdom, and goodness of the Father, Joh **14**:**7**; the fulness of the Godhead dwells, not typically, or in a figure, but really, in him. When, on the fall of man, the world was breaking to pieces under the wrath and curse of God, the Son of God, undertaking the work of redemption, sustained it by his almighty power and goodness. From the glory of the person and office of Christ, we proceed to the glory of his grace. The glory of His person and nature, gave to his sufferings such merit as was a full satisfaction to the honour of God, who suffered an infinite injury and affront by the sins of men. We never can be thankful enough that God has in so many ways, and with such increasing clearness, spoken to us fallen sinners concerning salvation. That he should by himself cleanse us from our sins is a wonder of love beyond our utmost powers of admiration, gratitude, and praise.

Verses 4–14

Many Jews had a superstitious or idolatrous respect for angels, because they had received the law and other tidings of the Divine will by their ministry. They looked upon them as mediators between God and men, and some went so far as to pay them a kind of religious homage or worship. Thus it was necessary that the apostle should insist, not only on Christ's being the Creator of all things, and therefore of angels themselves, but as being the risen and exalted Messiah in human nature, to whom angels, authorities, and powers are made subject. To prove this, several passages are brought from the Old Testament. On comparing what God there says of the angels, with what he says to Christ, the inferiority of the angels to Christ plainly appears. Here is the office of the angels; they are God's ministers or servants, to do his pleasure. But, how much greater things are said of Christ by the Father! And let us own and honour him as God; for if he had not been God, he had never done the Mediator's work, and had never worn the Mediator's crown. It is declared how Christ was qualified for the office of Mediator, and how he was confirmed in it: he has the name Messiah from his being anointed. Only as Man he has his fellows, and as anointed with the Holy Spirit; but he is above all prophets, priests, and kings, that ever were employed in the service of God on earth. Another passage of Scripture, Ps **102**:**25**–**27**, is recited, in which the Almighty power of the Lord Jesus Christ is declared, both in creating the world and in changing it. Christ will fold up this world as a garment, not to be abused any longer, not to be used as it has been. As a sovereign, when his garments of state are folded and put away, is a sovereign still, so our Lord, when he has laid aside the earth and heavens like a vesture, shall be still the same. Let us not then set our hearts upon that which is not what we take it to be, and will not be what it now is. Sin has made a great change in the world for the worse, and Christ will make a great change in it for the better. Let the thoughts of this make us watchful, diligent, and desirous of that better world. The Saviour has done much to make all men his friends, yet he has enemies. But they shall be made his footstool, by humble submission, or by utter destruction. Christ shall go on conquering and to conquer. The most exalted angels are but ministering spirits, mere servants of Christ, to execute his commands. The saints, at present, are heirs, not yet come into possession. The angels minister to them in opposing the malice and power of evil spirits, in protecting and keeping their bodies, instructing and comforting their souls, under Christ and the Holy Ghost. Angels shall gather all the saints together at the last day, when all whose hearts and hopes are set upon perishing treasures and fading glories, will be driven from Christ's presence into everlasting misery.

Chapter 2

Chapter Outline	
The duty of stedfastly adhering to Christ and his gospel.	(1–4)
His sufferings are no objection against his pre-eminence.	(5–9)
The reason of his sufferings, and the fitness of them.	(10–13)
Christ's taking the nature of man, and not his taking the nature of angels, was necessary to his priestly office.	(14–18)

Verses 1–4

Christ being proved to be superior to the angels, this doctrine is applied. Our minds and memories are like a leaky vessel, they do not, without much care, retain what is poured into them. This proceeds from the corruption of our nature, temptations, worldly cares, and pleasures. Sinning against the gospel is neglect of this great salvation; it is a contempt of the saving grace of God in Christ, making light of it, not caring for it, not regarding either the worth of gospel grace, or the want of it, and our undone state without it. The Lord's judgments under the gospel dispensation are chiefly spiritual, but are on that account the more to be dreaded. Here is an appeal to the consciences of sinners. Even partial neglects will not escape rebukes; they often bring darkness on the souls they do not finally ruin. The setting forth the gospel was continued and confirmed by those who heard Christ, by the evangelists and apostles, who were witnesses of what Jesus Christ began both to do and to teach; and by the gifts of the Holy Ghost, qualified for the work to which they were called. And all this according to God's own will. It was the will of God that we should have sure ground for our faith, and a strong foundation for our hope in receiving the gospel. Let us mind this one thing needful, and attend to the Holy Scriptures, written by those who heard the words of our gracious Lord, and were inspired by his Spirit; then we shall be blessed with the good part that cannot be taken away.

Verses 5–9

Neither the state in which the church is at present, nor its more completely restored state, when the prince of this world shall be cast out, and the kingdoms of the earth become the kingdom of Christ, is left to the government of the angels: Christ will take to him his great power, and will reign. And what is the moving cause of all the kindness God shows to men in giving Christ for them and to them? it is the grace of God. As a reward of Christ's humiliation in suffering death, he has unlimited dominion over all things; thus this ancient scripture was fulfilled in him. Thus God has done wonderful things for us in creation and providence, but for these we have made the basest returns.

Verses 10–13

Whatever the proud, carnal, and unbelieving may imagine or object, the spiritual mind will see peculiar glory in the cross of Christ, and be satisfied that it became Him, who in all things displays his own perfections in bringing many sons to glory, to make the Author of their salvation perfect through sufferings. His way to the crown was by the cross, and so must that of his people be. Christ sanctifies; he has purchased and sent the sanctifying Spirit: the Spirit sanctifies as the Spirit of Christ. True believers are sanctified, endowed with holy principles and powers, set apart to high and holy uses and purposes. Christ and believers are all of one heavenly Father, who is God. They are brought into relation with Christ. But the words, his not being ashamed to call them brethren, express the high superiority of Christ to the human nature. This is shown from three texts of Scripture. See Ps **22**:**22**; **18**:**2**; Isa **8**:**18**.

Verses 14–18

The angels fell, and remained without hope or help. Christ never designed to be the Saviour of the fallen angels, therefore he did not take their nature; and the nature of angels could not be an atoning sacrifice for the sin of man. Here is a price paid, enough for all, and suitable to all, for it was in our nature. Here the wonderful love of God appeared, that, when Christ knew what he must suffer in our nature, and how he must die in it, yet he readily took it upon him. And this atonement made way for his people's deliverance from Satan's bondage, and for the pardon of their sins through faith. Let those who dread death, and strive to get the better of their terrors, no longer attempt to outbrave or to stifle them, no longer grow careless or wicked through despair. Let them not expect help from the world, or human devices; but let them seek pardon, peace, grace, and a lively hope of heaven, by faith in Him who died and rose again, that thus they may rise above the fear of death. The remembrance of his own sorrows and temptations, makes Christ mindful of the trials of his people, and ready to help them. He is ready and willing to succour those who are tempted, and seek him. He became man, and was tempted, that he might be every way qualified to succour his people, seeing that he had passed through the same temptations himself, but continued perfectly free from sin. Then let not the afflicted and tempted despond, or give place to Satan, as if temptations made it wrong for them to come to the Lord in prayer. Not soul ever perished under temptation, that cried unto the Lord from real alarm at its danger, with faith and expectation of relief. This is our duty upon our first being surprised by temptations, and would stop their progress, which is our wisdom.

Chapter 3

Chapter Outline	
The superior worth and dignity of Christ above Moses is shown.	(1–6)
The Hebrews are warned of the sin and danger of unbelief.	(7–13)
And of necessity of faith in Christ, and of stedfastly following him.	(14–19)

Verses 1–6

Christ is to be considered as the Apostle of our profession, the Messenger sent by God to men, the great Revealer of that faith which we profess to hold, and of that hope which we profess to have. As Christ, the Messiah, anointed for the office both of Apostle and High Priest. As Jesus, our Saviour, our Healer, the great Physician of souls. Consider him thus. Consider what he is in himself, what he is to us, and what he will be to us hereafter and for ever. Close and serious thoughts of Christ bring us to know more of him. The Jews had a high opinion of the faithfulness of Moses, yet his faithfulness was but a type of Christ's. Christ was the Master of this house, of his church, his people, as well as their Maker. Moses was a faithful servant; Christ, as the eternal Son of God, is rightful Owner and Sovereign Ruler of the Church. There must not only be setting out well in the ways of Christ, but stedfastness and perseverance therein to the end. Every meditation on his person and his salvation, will suggest more wisdom, new motives to love, confidence, and obedience.

Verses 7–13

Days of temptation are often days of provocation. But to provoke God, when he is letting us see that we entirely depend and live upon him, is a provocation indeed. The hardening of the heart is the spring of all other sins. The sins of others, especially of our relations, should be warnings to us. All sin, especially sin committed by God's professing, privileged people, not only provokes God, but it grieves him. God is loth to destroy any in, or for their sin; he waits long to be gracious to them. But sin, long persisted in, will make God's wrath discover itself in destroying the impenitent; there is no resting under the wrath of God. "Take heed:" all who would get safe to heaven must look about them; if once we allow ourselves to distrust God, we may soon desert him. Let those that think they stand, take heed lest they fall. Since to-morrow is not ours, we must make the best improvement of this day. And there are none, even the strongest of the flock, who do not need help of other Christians. Neither are there any so low and despised, but the care of their standing in the faith, and of their safety, belongs to all. Sin has so many ways and colours, that we need more eyes than ours own. Sin appears fair, but is vile; it appears pleasant, but is destructive; it promises much, but performs nothing. The deceitfulness of sin hardens the soul; one sin allowed makes way for another; and every act of sin confirms the habit. Let every one beware of sin.

Verses 14–19

The saints' privilege is, they are made partakers of Christ, that is, of the Spirit, the nature, graces, righteousness, and life of Christ; they are interested in all Christ is, in all he has done, or will do. The same spirit with which Christians set out in the ways of God, they should maintain unto the end. Perseverance in faith is the best evidence of the sincerity of our faith. Hearing the word often is a means of salvation, yet, if not hearkened to, it will expose more to the Divine wrath. The happiness of being partakers of Christ and his complete salvation, and the fear of God's wrath and eternal misery, should stir us up to persevere in the life of obedient faith. Let us beware of trusting to outward privileges or professions, and pray to be numbered with the true believers who enter heaven, when all others fail because of unbelief. As our obedience follows according to the power of our faith, so our sins and want of care are according to the prevailing of unbelief in us.

Chapter 4

Chapter Outline	
Humble, cautious fear is urged, lest any should come short of the promised rest, through unbelief.	(1–10)
Arguments and motives to faith and hope in our approaches to God.	(11–16)

Verses 1–10

The privileges we have under the gospel, are greater than any had under the law of Moses, though the same gospel for substance was preached under both Testaments. There have been in all ages many unprofitable hearers; and unbelief is at the root of all unfruitfulness under the word. Faith in the hearer is the life of the word. But it is a painful consequence of partial neglect, and of a loose and wavering profession, that they often cause men to seem to come short. Let us then give diligence, that we may have a clear entrance into the kingdom of God. As God finished his work, and then rested from it, so he will cause those who believe, to finish their work, and then to enjoy their rest. It is evident, that there is a more spiritual and excellent sabbath remaining for the people of God, than that of the seventh day, or that into which Joshua led the Jews. This rest is, a rest of grace, and comfort, and holiness, in the gospel state. And a rest in glory, where the people of God shall enjoy the end of their faith, and the object of all their desires. The rest, or sabbatism, which is the subject of the apostle's reasoning, and as to which he concludes that it remains to be enjoyed, is undoubtedly the heavenly rest, which remains to the people of God, and is opposed to a state of labour and trouble in this world. It is the rest they shall obtain when the Lord Jesus shall appear from heaven. But those who do not believe, shall never enter into this spiritual rest, either of grace here or glory hereafter. God has always declared man's rest to be in him, and his love to be the only real happiness of the soul; and faith in his promises, through his Son, to be the only way of entering that rest.

Verses 11–16

Observe the end proposed: rest spiritual and eternal; the rest of grace here, and glory hereafter; in Christ on earth, with Christ in heaven. After due and diligent labour, sweet and satisfying rest shall follow; and labour now, will make that rest more pleasant when it comes. Let us labour, and quicken each other to be diligent in duty. The Holy Scriptures are the word of God. When God sets it home by his Spirit, it convinces powerfully, converts powerfully, and comforts powerfully. It makes a soul that has long been proud, to be humble; and a perverse spirit, to be meek and obedient. Sinful habits, that are become as it were natural to the soul, and rooted deeply in it, are separated and cut off by this sword. It will discover to men their thoughts and purposes, the vileness of many, the bad principles they are moved by, the sinful ends they act to. The word will show the sinner all that is in his heart. Let us hold fast the doctrines of Christian faith in our heads, its enlivening principles in our hearts, the open profession of it in our lips, and be subject to it in our lives. Christ executed one part of his priesthood on earth, in dying for us; the other he executes in heaven, pleading the cause, and presenting the offerings of his people. In the sight of Infinite Wisdom, it was needful that the Saviour of men should be one who has the fellow-feeling which no being but a fellow-creature could possibly have; and therefore it was necessary he should actual experience of all the effects of sin that could be separated from its actual guilt. God sent his own Son in the likeness of sinful flesh, Ro **8:3**; but the more holy and pure he was, the more he must have been unwilling in his nature to sin, and must have had deeper impression of its evil; consequently the more must he be concerned to deliver his people from its guilt and power. We should encourage ourselves by the excellence of our High Priest, to come boldly to the throne of grace. Mercy and grace are the things we want; mercy to pardon all our sins, and grace to purify our souls. Besides our daily dependence upon God for present supplies, there are seasons for which we should provide in our prayers; times of temptation, either by adversity or prosperity, and especially our dying time. We are to come with reverence and godly fear, yet not as if dragged to the seat of justice, but as kindly invited to the mercy-seat, where grace reigns. We have boldness to enter into the holiest only by the blood of Jesus; he is our Advocate, and has purchased all our souls want or can desire.

Chapter 5

Chapter Outline	
The office and duty of a high priest abundantly answered in Christ.	(1–10)
The Christian Hebrews reproved for their little progress in the knowledge of the gospel.	(11–14)

Verses 1–10

The High Priest must be a man, a partaker of our nature. This shows that man had sinned. For God would not suffer sinful man to come to him alone. But every one is welcome to God, that comes to him by this High Priest; and as we value acceptance with God, and pardon, we must apply by faith to this our great High Priest Christ Jesus, who can intercede for those that are out of the way of truth, duty, and happiness; one who has tenderness to lead them back from the by-paths of error, sin, and misery. Those only can expect assistance from God, and acceptance with him, and his presence and blessing on them and their services, that are called of God. This is applied to Christ. In the days of his flesh, Christ made himself subject to death: he hungered: he was a tempted, suffering, dying Jesus. Christ set an example, not only to pray, but to be fervent in prayer. How many dry prayers, how few wetted with tears, do we offer up to God! He was strengthened to support the immense weight of suffering laid upon him. There is no real deliverance from death but to be carried through it. He was raised and exalted, and to him was given the power of saving all sinners to the uttermost, who come unto God through him. Christ has left us an example that we should learn humble obedience to the will of God, by all our afflictions. We need affliction, to teach us submission. His obedience in our nature encourages our attempts to obey, and for us to expect support and comfort under all the temptations and sufferings to which we are exposed. Being made perfect for this great work, he is become the Author of eternal salvation to all that obey him. But are we of that number?

Verses 11–14

Dull hearers make the preaching of the gospel difficult, and even those who have some faith may be dull hearers, and slow to believe. Much is looked for from those to whom much is given. To be unskilful, denotes want of experience in the things of the gospel. Christian experience is a spiritual sense, taste, or relish of the goodness, sweetness, and excellence of the truths of the gospel. And no tongue can express the satisfaction which the soul receives, from a sense of Divine goodness, grace, and love to it in Christ.

Chapter 6

Chapter Outline	
The Hebrews are urged to go forward in the doctrine of Christ, and the consequences of apostacy, or turning back, are described.	(1–8)
The apostle expresses satisfaction, as to the most of them.	(9, 10)
And encourages them to persevere in faith and holiness.	(11–20)

Verses 1–8

Every part of the truth and will of God should be set before all who profess the gospel, and be urged on their hearts and consciences. We should not be always speaking about outward things; these have their places and use, but often take up too much attention and time, which might be better employed. The humbled sinner who pleads guilty, and cries for mercy, can have no ground from this passage to be discouraged, whatever his conscience may accuse him of. Nor does it prove that any one who is made a new creature in Christ, ever becomes a final apostate from him. The apostle is not speaking of the falling away of mere professors, never convinced or influenced by the gospel. Such have nothing to fall away from, but an empty name, or hypocritical profession. Neither is he speaking of partial declinings or backslidings. Nor are such sins meant, as Christians fall into through the strength of temptations, or the power of some worldly or fleshly lust. But the falling away here mentioned, is an open and avowed renouncing of Christ, from enmity of heart against him, his cause, and people, by men approving in their minds the deeds of his murderers, and all this after they have received the knowledge of the truth, and tasted some of its comforts. Of these it is said, that it is impossible to renew them again unto repentance. Not because the blood of Christ is not sufficient to obtain pardon for this sin; but this sin, in its very nature, is opposite to repentance and every thing that leads to it. If those who through mistaken views of this passage, as well as of their own case, fear that there is no mercy for them, would attend to the account given of the nature of this sin, that it is a total and a willing renouncing of Christ, and his cause, and joining with his enemies, it would relieve them from wrong fears. We should ourselves beware, and caution others, of every approach near to a gulf so awful as apostacy; yet in doing this we should keep close to the word of God, and be careful not to wound and terrify the weak, or discourage the fallen and penitent. Believers not only taste of the word of God, but they drink it in. And this fruitful field or garden receives the blessing. But the merely nominal Christian, continuing unfruitful under the means of grace, or producing nothing but deceit and selfishness, was near the awful state above described; and everlasting misery was the end reserved for him. Let us watch with humble caution and prayer as to ourselves.

Verses 9, 10

There are things that are never separated from salvation; things that show the person to be in a state of salvation, and which will end in eternal salvation. And the things that accompany salvation, are better things than ever any dissembler or apostate enjoyed. The works of love, done for the glory of Christ, or done to his saints for Christ's sake, from time to time, as God gives occasion, are evident marks of a man's salvation; and more sure tokens of saving grace given, than the enlightenings and tastings spoken of before. No love is to be reckoned as love, but working love; and no works are right works, which flow not from love to Christ.

Verses 11–20

The hope here meant, is a sure looking for good things promised, through those promises, with love, desire, and valuing of them. Hope has its degrees, as faith also. The promise of blessedness God has made to believers, is from God's eternal purpose, settled between the eternal Father, Son, and Spirit. These promises of God may safely be depended upon; for here we have two things which cannot change, the counsel and the oath of God, in which it is not possible for God to lie; it would be contrary to his nature as well as to his will. And as He cannot lie; the destruction of the unbeliever, and the salvation of the believer, are alike certain. Here observe, those to whom God has given full security of happiness, have a title to the promises by inheritance. The consolations of God are strong enough to support his people under their heaviest trials. Here is a refuge for all sinners who flee to the mercy of God, through the redemption of Christ, according to the covenant of grace, laying aside all other confidences. We are in this world as a ship at sea, tossed up and down, and in danger of being cast away. We need an anchor to keep us sure and steady. Gospel hope is our anchor in the storms of this world. It is sure and stedfast, or it could not keep us so. The free grace of God, the merits and mediation of Christ, and the powerful influences of his Spirit, are the grounds of this hope, and so it is a stedfast hope. Christ is the object and ground of the believer's hope. Let us therefore set our affections on things above, and wait patiently for his appearance, when we shall certainly appear with him in glory.

Chapter 7

Chapter Outline	
A comparison between the priesthood of Melchizedec and that of Christ.	(1–3)
The excellence of Christ's priesthood above the Levitical priesthood is shown.	(4–10)
This is applied to Christ.	(11–25)
The faith and hope of the church encouraged from this.	(26–28)

Verses 1–3

Melchizedec met Abraham when returning from the rescue of Lot. His name, "King of Righteousness," doubtless suitable to his character, marked him as a type of the Messiah and his kingdom. The name of his city signified "Peace;" and as king of peace he typified Christ, the Prince of Peace, the great Reconciler of God and man. Nothing is recorded as to the beginning or end of his life; thus he typically resembled the Son of God, whose existence is from everlasting to everlasting, who had no one that was before him, and will have no one come after him, in his priesthood. Every part of Scripture honours the great King of Righteousness and Peace, our glorious High Priest and Saviour; and the more we examine it, the more we shall be convinced, that the testimony of Jesus is the spirit of prophecy.

Verses 4–10

That High Priest who should afterward appear, of whom Melchizedec was a type, must be much superior to the Levitical priests. Observe Abraham's great dignity and happiness; that he had the promises. That man is rich and happy indeed, who has the promises, both of the life that now is, and of that which is to come. This honour have all those who receive the Lord Jesus. Let us go forth in our spiritual conflicts, trusting in his word and strength, ascribing our victories to his grace, and desiring to be met and blessed by him in all our ways.

Verses 11–25

The priesthood and law by which perfection could not come, are done away; a Priest is risen, and a dispensation now set up, by which true believers may be made perfect. That there is such a change is plain. The law which made the Levitical priesthood, showed that the priests were frail, dying creatures, not able to save their own lives, much less could they save the souls of those who came to them. But the High Priest of our profession holds his office by the power of endless life in himself; not only to keep himself alive, but to give spiritual and eternal life to all who rely upon his sacrifice and intercession. The better covenant, of which Jesus was the Surety, is not here contrasted with the covenant of works, by which every transgressor is shut up under the curse. It is distinguished from the Sinai covenant with Israel, and the legal dispensation under which the church so long remained. The better covenant brought the church and every believer into clearer light, more perfect liberty, and more abundant privileges. In the order of Aaron there was a multitude of priests, of high priests one after another; but in the priesthood of Christ there is only one and the same. This is the believer's safety and happiness, that this everlasting High Priest is able to save to the uttermost, in all times, in all cases. Surely then it becomes us to desire a spirituality and holiness, as much beyond those of the Old Testament believers, as our advantages exceed theirs.

Verses 26–28

Observe the description of the personal holiness of Christ. He is free from all habits or principles of sin, not having the least disposition to it in his nature. No sin dwells in him, not the least sinful inclination, though such dwells in the best of Christians. He is harmless, free from all actual transgression; he did no violence, nor was there any deceit in his mouth. He is undefiled. It is hard to keep ourselves pure, so as not to partake the guilt of other men's sins. But none need be dismayed who come to God in the name of his beloved Son. Let them be assured that he will deliver them in the time of trial and suffering, in the time of prosperity, in the hour of death, and in the day of judgment.

Chapter 8

Chapter Outline	
The excellence of Christ's priesthood above that of Aaron is shown.	(1–6)
The great excellence of the new covenant above the former.	(7–13)

Verses 1–6

The substance, or summary, of what had been declared was, that Christians had such a High Priest as they needed. He took upon himself human nature, appeared on earth, and there gave himself as a sacrifice to God for the sins of his people. We must not dare to approach God, or to present any thing to him, but in and through Christ, depending upon his merits and mediation; for we are accepted only in the Beloved. In all obedience and worship, we should keep close to God's word, which is the only and perfect standard. Christ is the substance and end of the law of righteousness. But the covenant here referred to, was that made with Israel as a nation, securing temporal benefits to them. The promises of all spiritual blessings, and of eternal life, revealed in the gospel, and made sure through Christ, are of infinitely greater value. Let us bless God that we have a High Priest that suits our helpless condition.

Verses 7–13

The superior excellence of the priesthood of Christ, above that of Aaron, is shown from that covenant of grace, of which Christ was Mediator. The law not only made all subject to it, liable to be condemned for the guilt of sin, but also was unable to remove that guilt, and clear the conscience from the sense and terror of it. Whereas, by the blood of Christ, a full remission of sins was provided, so that God would remember them no more. God once wrote his laws to his people, now he will write his laws in them; he will give them understanding to know and to believe his laws; he will give them memories to retain them; he will give them hearts to love them, courage to profess them, and power to put them in practice. This is the foundation of the covenant; and when this is laid, duty will be done wisely, sincerely, readily, easily, resolutely, constantly, and with comfort. A plentiful outpouring of the Spirit of God will make the ministration of the gospel so effectual, that there shall be a mighty increase and spreading of Christian knowledge in persons of all sorts. Oh that this promise might be fulfilled in our days, that the hand of God may be with his ministers so that great numbers may believe, and be turned to the Lord! The pardon of sin will always be found to accompany the true knowledge of God. Notice the freeness of this pardon; its fulness; its fixedness. This pardoning mercy is connected with all other spiritual mercies: unpardoned sin hinders mercy, and pulls down judgments; but the pardon of sin prevents judgment, and opens a wide door to all spiritual blessings. Let us search whether we are taught by the Holy Spirit to know Christ, so as uprightly to love, fear, trust, and obey him. All worldly vanities, outward privileges, or mere notions of religion, will soon vanish away, and leave those who trust in them miserable for ever.

Chapter 9

Chapter Outline	

The Jewish tabernacle and its utensils.	(1–5)
Their use and meaning.	(6–10)
These fulfilled in Christ.	(11–22)
The necessity, superior dignity, and power of his priesthood and sacrifice.	(23–28)

Verses 1–5

The apostle shows to the Hebrews the typical reference of their ceremonies to Christ. The tabernacle was a movable temple, shadowing forth the unsettled state of the church upon earth, and the human nature of the Lord Jesus Christ, in whom the fulness of the Godhead dwelt bodily. The typical meaning of these things has been shown in former remarks, and the ordinances and articles of the Mosaic covenant point out Christ as our Light, and as the Bread of life to our souls; and remind us of his Divine Person, his holy priesthood, perfect righteousness, and all-prevailing intercession. Thus was the Lord Jesus Christ, all and in all, from the beginning. And as interpreted by the gospel, these things are a glorious representation of the wisdom of God, and confirm faith in Him who was prefigured by them.

Verses 6–10

The apostle goes on to speak of the Old Testament services. Christ, having undertaken to be our High Priest, could not enter into heaven till he had shed his blood for us; and none of us can enter, either into God's gracious presence here, or his glorious presence hereafter, but by the blood of Jesus. Sins are errors, great errors, both in judgment and practice; and who can understand all his errors? They leave guilt upon the conscience, not to be washed away but by the blood of Christ. We must plead this blood on earth, while he is pleading it for us in heaven. A few believers, under the Divine teaching, saw something of the way of access to God, of communion with him, and of admission into heaven through the promised Redeemer, but the Israelites in general looked no further than the outward forms. These could not take away the defilement or dominion of sin. They could neither discharge the debts, nor resolve the doubts, of him who did the service. Gospel times are, and should be, times of reformation, of clearer light as to all things needful to be known, and of greater love, causing us to bear ill-will to none, but good-will to all. We have greater freedom, both of spirit and speech, in the gospel, and greater obligations to a more holy living.

Verses 11–14

All good things past, present, and to come, were and are founded upon the priestly office of Christ, and come to us from thence. Our High Priest entered into heaven once for all, and has obtained eternal redemption. The Holy Ghost further signified and showed that the Old Testament sacrifices only freed the outward man from ceremonial uncleanness, and fitted him for some outward privileges. What gave such power to the blood of Christ? It was Christ's offering himself without any sinful stain in his nature or life. This cleanses the most guilty conscience from dead, or deadly, works to serve the living God; from sinful works, such as pollute the soul, as dead bodies did the persons of the Jews who touched them; while the grace that seals pardon, new-creates the polluted soul. Nothing more destroys the faith of the gospel, than by any means to weaken the direct power of the blood of Christ. The depth of the mystery of the sacrifice of Christ, we cannot dive into, the height we cannot comprehend. We cannot search out the greatness of it, or the wisdom, the love, the grace that is in it. But in considering the sacrifice of Christ, faith finds life, food, and refreshment.

Verses 15–22

The solemn transactions between God and man, are sometimes called a covenant, here a testament, which is a willing deed of a person, bestowing legacies on such persons as are described, and it only takes effect upon his death. Thus Christ died, not only to obtain the blessings of salvation for us, but to give power to the disposal of them. All, by sin, were become guilty before God, had forfeited every thing that is good; but God, willing to show the greatness of his mercy, proclaimed a covenant of grace. Nothing could be clean to a sinner, not even his religious duties; except as his guilt was done away by the death of a sacrifice, of value sufficient for that end, and unless he continually depended upon it. May we ascribe all real good works to the same all-procuring cause, and offer our spiritual sacrifices as sprinkled with Christ's blood, and so purified from their defilement.

Verses 23–28

It is evident that the sacrifices of Christ are infinitely better than those of the law, which could neither procure pardon for sin, nor impart power against it. Sin would still have been upon us, and have had dominion over us; but Jesus Christ, by one sacrifice, has destroyed the works of the devil, that believers may be made righteous, holy, and happy. As no wisdom, learning, virtue, wealth, or power, can keep one of the human race from death, so nothing can deliver a sinner from being condemned at the day of judgment, except the atoning sacrifice of Christ; nor will one be saved from eternal punishment who despises or neglects this great salvation. The believer knows that his Redeemer liveth, and that he shall see him. Here is the faith and patience of the church, of all sincere believers. Hence is their continual prayer as the fruit and expression of their faith, Even so come, Lord Jesus.

Chapter 10

Chapter Outline	
The insufficiency of sacrifices for taking away sin, The necessity and power of the sacrifice of Christ for that purpose.	(1–18)
An argument for holy boldness in the believer's access to God through Jesus Christ, And for steadfastness in faith, and mutual love and duty.	(19–25)
The danger of apostacy.	(26–31)

The sufferings of believers, and encouragement to maintain their holy profession.	(32–39)

Verses 1–10

The apostle having shown that the tabernacle, and ordinances of the covenant of Sinai, were only emblems and types of the gospel, concludes that the sacrifices the high priests offered continually, could not make the worshippers perfect, with respect to pardon, and the purifying of their consciences. But when "God manifested in the flesh," became the sacrifice, and his death upon the accursed tree the ransom, then the Sufferer being of infinite worth, his free-will sufferings were of infinite value. The atoning sacrifice must be one capable of consenting, and must of his own will place himself in the sinner's stead: Christ did so. The fountain of all that Christ has done for his people, is the sovereign will and grace of God. The righteousness brought in, and the sacrifice once offered by Christ, are of eternal power, and his salvation shall never be done away. They are of power to make all the comers thereunto perfect; they derive from the atoning blood, strength and motives for obedience, and inward comfort.

Verses 11–18

Under the new covenant, or gospel dispensation, full and final pardon is to be had. This makes a vast difference between the new covenant and the old one. Under the old, sacrifices must be often repeated, and after all, only pardon as to this world was to be obtained by them. Under the new, one Sacrifice is enough to procure for all nations and ages, spiritual pardon, or being freed from punishment in the world to come. Well might this be called a new covenant. Let none suppose that human inventions can avail those who put them in the place of the sacrifice of the Son of God. What then remains, but that we seek an interest in this Sacrifice by faith; and the seal of it to our souls, by the sanctification of the Spirit unto obedience? So that by the law being written in our hearts, we may know that we are justified, and that God will no more remember our sins.

Verses 19–25

The apostle having closed the first part of the epistle, the doctrine is applied to practical purposes. As believers had an open way to the presence of God, it became them to use this privilege. The way and means by which Christians enjoy such privileges, is by the blood of Jesus, by the merit of that blood which he offered up as an atoning sacrifice. The agreement of infinite holiness with pardoning mercy, was not clearly understood till the human nature of Christ, the Son of God, was wounded and bruised for our sins. Our way to heaven is by a crucified Saviour; his death is to us the way of life, and to those who believe this, he will be precious. They must draw near to God; it would be contempt of Christ, still to keep at a distance. Their bodies were to be washed with pure water, alluding to the cleansings directed under the law: thus the use of water in baptism, was to remind Christians that their conduct should be pure and holy. While they derived comfort and grace from their reconciled Father to their own souls, they would adorn the doctrine of God their Saviour in all things. Believers are to consider how they can be of service to each other, especially stirring up each other to the more vigorous and abundant exercise of love, and the practice of good works. The communion of saints is a great help and privilege, and a means of stedfastness and perseverance. We should observe the coming of times of trial, and be thereby quickened to greater diligence. There is a trying day coming on all men, the day of our death

Verses 26–31

The exhortations against apostacy and to perseverance, are urged by many strong reasons. The sin here mentioned is a total and final falling away, when men, with a full and fixed will and resolution, despise and reject Christ, the only Saviour; despise and resist the Spirit, the only Sanctifier; and despise and renounce the gospel, the only way of salvation, and the words of eternal life. Of this destruction God gives some notorious sinners, while on earth, a fearful foreboding in their consciences, with despair of being able to endure or to escape it. But what punishment can be sorer than to die without mercy? We answer, to die by mercy, by the mercy and grace which they have despised. How dreadful is the case, when not only the justice of God, but his abused grace and mercy call for vengeance! All this does not in the least mean that any souls who sorrow for sin will be shut out from mercy, or that any will be refused the benefit of Christ's sacrifice, who are willing to accept these blessings. Him that cometh unto Christ, he will in no wise cast out.

Verses 32–39

Many and various afflictions united against the early Christians, and they had a great conflict. The Christian spirit is not a selfish spirit; it puts us upon pitying others, visiting them, helping them, and pleading for them. All things here are but shadows. The happiness of the saints in heaven will last for ever; enemies can never take it away as earthly goods. This will make rich amends for all we may lose and suffer here. The greatest part of the saints' happiness, as yet, is in promise. It is a trial of the patience of Christians, to be content to live after their work is done, and to stay for their reward till God's time to give it is come. He will soon come to them at death, to end all their sufferings, and to give them a crown of life. The Christian's present conflict may be sharp, but will be soon over. God never is pleased with the formal profession and outward duties and services of such as do not persevere; but he beholds them with great displeasure. And those who have been kept faithful in great trails for the time past, have reason to hope for the same grace to help them still to live by faith, till they receive the end of their faith and patience, even the salvation of their souls. Living by faith, and dying in faith, our souls are safe for ever.

Chapter 11

Chapter Outline	
The nature and power of faith described.	(1–3)
It is set forth by instances from Abel to Noah.	(4–7)
By Abraham and his descendants.	(8–19)
By Jacob, Joseph, Moses, the Israelites, and Rahab.	(20–31)
By other Old Testament believers.	(32–38)

The better state of believers under the gospel.	(39, 40)

Verses 1–3

Faith always has been the mark of God's servants, from the beginning of the world. Where the principle is planted by the regenerating Spirit of God, it will cause the truth to be received, concerning justification by the sufferings and merits of Christ. And the same things that are the object of our hope, are the object of our faith. It is a firm persuasion and expectation, that God will perform all he has promised to us in Christ. This persuasion gives the soul to enjoy those things now; it gives them a subsistence or reality in the soul, by the first-fruits and foretastes of them. Faith proves to the mind, the reality of things that cannot be seen by the bodily eye. It is a full approval of all God has revealed, as holy, just, and good. This view of faith is explained by many examples of persons in former times, who obtained a good report, or an honourable character in the word of God. Faith was the principle of their holy obedience, remarkable services, and patient sufferings. The Bible gives the most true and exact account of the origin of all things, and we are to believe it, and not to wrest the Scripture account of the creation, because it does not suit with the differing fancies of men. All that we see of the works of creation, were brought into being by the command of God.

Verses 4–7

Here follow some illustrious examples of faith from the Old Testament. Abel brought a sacrifice of atonement from the firstlings of the flock, acknowledging himself a sinner who deserved to die, and only hoping for mercy through the great Sacrifice. Cain's proud rage and enmity against the accepted worshipper of God, led to the awful effects the same principles have produced in every age; the cruel persecution, and even murder of believers. By faith Abel, being dead, yet speaketh; he left an instructive and speaking example. Enoch was translated, or removed, that he should not see death; God took him into heaven, as Christ will do the saints who shall be alive at his second coming. We cannot come to God, unless we believe that he is what he has revealed himself to be in the Scripture. Those who would find God, must seek him with all their heart. Noah's faith influenced his practice; it moved him to prepare an ark. His faith condemned the unbelief of others; and his obedience condemned their contempt and rebellion. Good examples either convert sinners or condemn them. This shows how believers, being warned of God to flee from the wrath to come, are moved with fear, take refuge in Christ, and become heirs of the righteousness of faith.

Verses 8–19

We are often called to leave worldly connexions, interests, and comforts. If heirs of Abraham's faith, we shall obey and go forth, though not knowing what may befall us; and we shall be found in the way of duty, looking for the performance of God's promises. The trial of Abraham's faith was, that he simply and fully obeyed the call of God. Sarah received the promise as the promise of God; being convinced of that, she truly judged that he both could and would perform it. Many, who have a part in the promises, do not soon receive the things promised. Faith can lay hold of blessings at a great distance; can make them present; can love them and rejoice in them, though strangers; as saints, whose home is heaven; as pilgrims, travelling toward their home. By faith, they overcome the terrors of death, and bid a cheerful farewell to this world, and to all the comforts and crosses of it. And those once truly and savingly called out of a sinful state, have no mind to return into it. All true believers desire the heavenly inheritance; and the stronger faith is, the more fervent those desires will be. Notwithstanding their meanness by nature, their vileness by sin, and the poverty of their outward condition, God is not ashamed to be called the God of all true believers; such is his mercy, such is his love to them. Let them never be ashamed of being called his people, nor of any of those who are truly so, how much soever despised in the world. Above all, let them take care that they are not a shame and reproach to their God. The greatest trial and act of faith upon record is, Abraham's offering up Isaac, Ge **22**:**2**. There, every word shows a trial. It is our duty to reason down our doubts and fears, by looking, as Abraham did, to the Almighty power of God. The best way to enjoy our comforts is, to give them up to God; he will then again give them as shall be the best for us. Let us look how far our faith has caused the like obedience, when we have been called to lesser acts of self-denial, or to make smaller sacrifices to our duty. Have we given up what was called for, fully believing that the Lord would make up all our losses, and even bless us by the most afflicting dispensations?

Verses 20–31

Isaac blessed Jacob and Esau, concerning things to come. Things present are not the best things; no man knoweth love or hatred by having them or wanting them. Jacob lived by faith, and he died by faith, and in faith. Though the grace of faith is of use always through our whole lives, it is especially so when we come to die. Faith has a great work to do at last, to help the believer to die to the Lord, so as to honour him, by patience, hope, and joy. Joseph was tried by temptations to sin, by persecution for keeping his integrity; and he was tried by honours and power in the court of Pharaoh, yet his faith carried him through. It is a great mercy to be free from wicked laws and edicts; but when we are not so, we must use all lawful means for our security. In this faith of Moses' parents there was a mixture of unbelief, but God was pleased to overlook it. Faith gives strength against the sinful, slavish fear of men; it sets God before the soul, shows the vanity of the creature, and that all must give way to the will and power of God. The pleasures of sin are, and will be, but short; they must end either in speedy repentance or in speedy ruin. The pleasures of this world are for the most part the pleasures of sin; they are always so when we cannot enjoy them without deserting God and his people. Suffering is to be chosen rather than sin; there being more evil in the least sin, than there can be in the greatest suffering. God's people are, and always have been, a reproached people. Christ accounts himself reproached in their reproaches; and thus they become greater riches than the treasures of the richest empire in the world. Moses made his choice when ripe for judgment and enjoyment, able to know what he did, and why he did it. It is needful for persons to be seriously religious; to despise the world, when most capable of relishing and enjoying it. Believers may and ought to have respect to the recompence of reward. By faith we may be fully sure of God's providence, and of his gracious and powerful presence with us. Such a sight of God will enable believers to keep on to the end, whatever they may meet in the way. It is not owing to our own righteousness, or best performances, that we are saved from the wrath of God; but to the blood of Christ, and his imputed righteousness. True faith makes sin bitter to the soul, even while it receives the pardon and atonement. All our spiritual privileges on earth, should quicken us in our way to heaven. The Lord will make even Babylon fall before the faith of his people, and when he has some great thing to do for them, he raises up great and strong faith in them. A true believer is desirous, not only to be in covenant with God, but in communion with the people of God; and is willing to fare as they fare. By her works Rahab declared herself to be just. That she was not justified by her works appears plainly; because the work she did was faulty in the manner, and not perfectly good, therefore it could not be answerable to the perfect justice or righteousness of God.

Verses 32–38

After all our searches into the Scriptures, there is more to be learned from them. We should be pleased to think, how great the number of believers was under the Old Testament, and how strong their faith, though the objects of it were not then so fully made known as now. And we should lament that now, in gospel times, when the rule of faith is more clear and perfect, the number of believers should be so small, and their faith so weak. It is the excellence of the grace of faith, that, while it helps men to do great things, like Gideon, it keeps from high and great thoughts of themselves. Faith, like Barak's, has recourse unto God in all dangers and difficulties, and then makes grateful returns to God for all mercies and deliverances. By faith, the servants of God shall overcome even the roaring lion that goeth about seeking whom he may devour. The believer's faith endures to the end, and, in dying, gives him victory over death and all his deadly enemies, like Samson. The grace of God often fixes upon very undeserving and ill-deserving persons, to do great things for them and by them. But the grace of faith, wherever it is, will put men upon acknowledging God in all their ways, as Jephthah. It will make men bold and courageous in a good cause. Few ever met with greater trials, few ever showed more lively faith, than David, and he has left a testimony as to the trials and acts of faith, in the book of Psalms, which has been, and ever will be, of great value to the people of God. Those are likely to grow up to be distinguished for faith, who begin betimes, like Samuel, to exercise it. And faith will enable a man to serve God and his generation, in whatever way he may be employed. The interests and powers of kings and kingdoms, are often opposed to God and his people; but God can easily subdue all that set themselves against him. It is a greater honour and happiness to work righteousness than to work miracles. By faith we have comfort of the promises; and by faith we are prepared to wait for the promises, and in due time to receive them. And though we do not hope to have our dead relatives or friends restored to life in this world, yet faith will support under the loss of them, and direct to the hope of a better resurrection. Shall we be most amazed at the wickedness of human nature, that it is capable of such awful cruelties to fellow-creatures, or at the excellence of Divine grace, that is able to bear up the faithful under such cruelties, and to carry them safely through all? What a difference between God's judgement of a saint, and man's judgment! The world is not worthy of those scorned, persecuted saints, whom their persecutors reckon unworthy to live. They are not worthy of their company, example, counsel, or other benefits. For they know not what a saint is, nor the worth of a saint, nor how to use him; they hate, and drive such away, as they do the offer of Christ and his grace. (Heb **11**:**39**)

Verses 39, 40

The world considers that the righteous are not worthy to live in the world, and God declares the world is not worthy of them. Though the righteous and the worldlings widely differ in their judgment, they agree in this, it is not fit that good men should have their rest in this world. Therefore God receives them out of it. The apostle tells the Hebrews, that God had provided some better things for them, therefore they might be sure that he expected as good things from them. As our advantages, with the better things God has provided for us, are so much beyond theirs, so should our obedience of faith, patience of hope, and labour of love, be greater. And unless we get true faith as these believers had, they will rise up to condemn us at the last day. Let us then pray continually for the increase of our faith, that we may follow these bright examples, and be, with them, at length made perfect in holiness and happiness, and shine like the sun in the kingdom of our Father for evermore.

Chapter 12

Chapter Outline	
An exhortation to be constant and persevere, The example of Christ is set forth, and the gracious design of God in all the sufferings believers endured.	(1–11)
Peace and holiness are recommended, with cautions against despising spiritual blessings.	(12–17)
The New Testament dispensation shown to be much more excellent than the Old.	(18–29)

Verses 1–11

The persevering obedience of faith in Christ, was the race set before the Hebrews, wherein they must either win the crown of glory, or have everlasting misery for their portion; and it is set before us. By the sin that does so easily beset us, understand that sin to which we are most prone, or to which we are most exposed, from habit, age, or circumstances. This is a most important exhortation; for while a man's darling sin, be it what it will, remains unsubdued, it will hinder him from running the Christian race, as it takes from him every motive for running, and gives power to every discouragement. When weary and faint in their minds, let them recollect that the holy Jesus suffered, to save them from eternal misery. By stedfastly looking to Jesus, their thoughts would strengthen holy affections, and keep under their carnal desires. Let us then frequently consider him. What are our little trials to his agonies, or even to our deserts? What are they to the sufferings of many others? There is a proneness in believers to grow weary, and to faint under trials and afflictions; this is from the imperfection of grace and the remains of corruption. Christians should not faint under their trials. Though their enemies and persecutors may be instruments to inflict sufferings, yet they are Divine chastisements; their heavenly Father has his hand in all, and his wise end to answer by all. They must not make light of afflictions, and be without feeling under them, for they are the hand and rod of God, and are his rebukes for sin. They must not despond and sink under trials, nor fret and repine, but bear up with faith and patience. God may let others alone in their sins, but he will correct sin in his own children. In this he acts as becomes a father. Our earthly parents sometimes may chasten us, to gratify their passion, rather than to reform our manners. But the Father of our souls never willingly grieves nor afflicts his children. It is always for our profit. Our whole life here is a state of childhood, and imperfect as to spiritual things; therefore we must submit to the discipline of such a state. When we come to a perfect state, we shall be fully reconciled to all God's chastisement of us now. God's correction is not condemnation; the chastening may be borne with patience, and greatly promote holiness. Let us then learn to consider the afflictions brought on us by the malice of men, as corrections sent by our wise and gracious Father, for our spiritual good.

Verses 12–17

A burden of affliction is apt to make the Christian's hands hang down, and his knees grow feeble, to dispirit him and discourage him; but against this he must strive, that he may better run his spiritual race and course. Faith and patience enable believers to follow peace and holiness, as a man follows his calling constantly, diligently, and with pleasure. Peace with men, of all sects and parties, will be favourable to our pursuit of holiness. But peace and holiness go together; there can be not right peace without holiness. Where persons fail of having the true grace of God, corruption will prevail and break forth; beware lest any unmortified lust in the heart, which seems to be dead, should spring up, to trouble and disturb the whole body. Falling away from Christ is the fruit of preferring the delights of the flesh, to the blessing of God, and the heavenly inheritance, as Esau did. But sinners will not always have such mean thoughts of the Divine blessing and inheritance as they now have. It agrees with the profane man's disposition, to desire the blessing, yet to despise the means whereby the blessing is to be gained. But God will neither sever the means from the blessing, nor join the blessing with the satisfying of man's lusts. God's mercy and blessing were never sought carefully and not obtained.

Verses 18–29

Mount Sinai, on which the Jewish church state was formed, was a mount such as might be touched, though forbidden to be so, a place that could be felt; so the Mosaic dispensation was much in outward and earthly things. The gospel state is kind and condescending, suited to our weak frame. Under the gospel all may come with boldness to God's presence. But the most holy must despair, if judged by the holy law given from Sinai, without a Saviour. The gospel church is called Mount Zion; there believers have clearer views of heaven, and more heavenly tempers of soul. All the children of God are heirs, and every one has the privileges of the first-born. Let a soul be supposed to join that glorious assembly and church above, that is yet unacquainted with God, still carnally-minded, loving this present world and state of things, looking back to it with a lingering eye, full of pride and guile, filled with lusts; such a soul would seem to have mistaken its way, place, state, and company. It would be uneasy to itself and all about it. Christ is the Mediator of this new covenant, between God and man, to bring them together in this covenant; to keep them together; to plead with God for us, and to plead with us for God; and at length to bring God and his people together in heaven. This covenant is made firm by the blood of Christ sprinkled upon our consciences, as the blood of the sacrifice was sprinkled upon the altar and the victim. This blood of Christ speaks in behalf of sinners; it pleads not for vengeance, but for mercy. See then that you refuse not his gracious call and offered salvation. See that you do not refuse Him who speaketh from heaven, with infinite tenderness and love; for how can those escape, who turn from God in unbelief or apostacy, while he so graciously beseeches them to be reconciled, and to receive his everlasting favour! God's dealing with men under the gospel, in a way of grace, assures us, that he will deal with the despisers of the gospel, in a way of judgment. We cannot worship God acceptably, unless we worship him with reverence and godly fear. Only the grace of God enables us to worship God aright. God is the same just and righteous God under the gospel as under the law. The inheritance of believers is secured to them; and all things pertaining to salvation are freely given in answer to prayer. Let us seek for grace, that we may serve God with reverence and godly fear.

Chapter 13

Chapter Outline	
Exhortations to various duties, and to be content with what Providence allots.	(1–6)
To respect the instructions of faithful pastors, with cautions against being carried away by strange doctrines.	(7–15)
Further exhortations to duties, that relate to God, to our neighbour, and to those set over us in the Lord.	(16–21)
This epistle to be seriously considered.	(22–25)

Verses 1–6

The design of Christ in giving himself for us, is, that he may purchase to himself a peculiar people, zealous of good works; and true religion is the strongest bond of friendship. Here are earnest exhortations to several Christian duties, especially contentment. The sin opposed to this grace and duty is covetousness, an over-eager desire for the wealth of this world, with envy of those who have more than ourselves. Having treasures in heaven, we may be content with mean things here. Those who cannot be so, would not be content though God raised their condition. Adam was in paradise, yet not contented; some angels in heaven were not contented; but the apostle Paul, though abased and empty, had learned in every state, in any state, to be content. Christians have reason to be contented with their present lot. This promise contains the sum and substance of all the promises; "I will never, no, never leave thee, no, never forsake thee." In the original there are no less than five negatives put together, to confirm the promise: the true believer shall have the gracious presence of God with him, in life, at death, and for ever. Men can do nothing against God, and God can make all that men do against his people, to turn to their good.

Verses 7–15

The instructions and examples of ministers, who honourably and comfortably closed their testimony, should be particularly remembered by survivors. And though their ministers were some dead, others dying, yet the great Head and High Priest of the church, the Bishop of their souls, ever lives, and is ever the same. Christ is the same in the Old Testament day. as in the gospel day, and will be so to his people for ever, equally merciful, powerful, and all-sufficient. Still he fills the hungry, encourages the trembling, and welcomes repenting sinners: still he rejects the proud and self-righteous, abhors mere profession, and teaches all whom he saves, to love righteousness, and to hate iniquity. Believers should seek to have their hearts established in simple dependence on free grace, by the Holy Spirit, which would comfort their hearts, and render them proof against delusion. Christ is both our Altar and our Sacrifice; he sanctifies the gift. The Lord's supper is the feast of the gospel passover. Having showed that keeping to the Levitical law would, according to its own rules, keep men from the Christian altar, the apostle adds, Let us go forth therefore unto him without the camp; go forth from the ceremonial law, from sin, from the world, and from ourselves. Living by faith in Christ, set apart to God through his blood, let us willingly separate from this evil world. Sin, sinners, nor death, will not suffer us to continue long here; therefore let us go forth now by faith and seek in Christ the rest and peace which this world cannot afford us. Let us bring our sacrifices to this altar, and to this our High Priest, and offer them up by him. The sacrifice of praise to God, we should offer always. In this are worship and prayer, as well as thanksgiving.

Verses 16–21

We must, according to our power, give to the necessities of the souls and bodies of men: God will accept these offerings with pleasure, and will accept and bless the offerers through Christ. The apostle then states what is their duty to living ministers; to obey and submit to them, so far as is agreeable to the mind and will of God, made known in his word. Christians must not think themselves too wise, too good, or too great, to learn. The people must search the Scriptures, and so far as the ministers teach according to that rule, they ought to receive their instructions as the word of God, which works in those that believe. It is the interest of hearers, that the account their ministers give of them may be with joy, and not with grief. Faithful ministers deliver their own souls, but the ruin of a fruitless and faithless people will be upon their own heads. The more earnestly the people pray for their ministers, the more benefit they may expect from their ministry. A good conscience has respect to all God's commands, and all our duty. Those who have this good conscience, yet need the prayers of others. When ministers come to a people who pray for them, they come with greater satisfaction to themselves, and success to the people. We should seek all our mercies by prayer. God is the God of peace, fully reconciled to believers; who has made a way for peace and reconciliation between himself and sinners, and who loves peace on earth, especially in his churches. He is the Author of spiritual peace in the hearts and consciences of his people. How firm a covenant is that which has its foundation in the blood of the Son of God! The perfecting of the saints in every good work, is the great thing desired by them, and for them; and that they may at length be fitted for the employment and happiness of heaven. There is no good thing wrought in us, but it is the work of God. And no good thing is wrought in us by God, but through Christ, for his sake and by his Spirit.

Verses 22–25

So bad are men, and even believers, through the remainders of their corruption, that when the most important, comfortable doctrine is delivered to them for their own good, and that with the most convincing evidence, there is need of earnest entreaty and exhortation that they would bear it, and not fall out with it, neglect it, or reject it. It is good to have the law of holy love and kindness written in the hearts of Christians, one towards another. Religion teaches men true civility and good breeding. It is not ill-tempered or uncourteous. Let the favour of God be toward you, and his grace continually working in you, and with you, bringing forth the fruits of holiness, as the first-fruits of glory.

James

This epistle of James is one of the most instructive writings in the New Testament. Being chiefly directed against particular errors at that time brought in among the Jewish Christians, it does not contain the same full doctrinal statements as the other epistles, but it presents an admirable summary of the practical duties of all believers. The leading truths of Christianity are set forth throughout; and on attentive consideration, it will be found entirely to agree with St. Paul's statements concerning grace and justification, while it abounds with earnest exhortations to the patience of hope and obedience of faith and love, interspersed with warnings, reproofs, and encouragements, according to the characters addressed. The truths laid down are very serious, and necessary to be maintained; and the rules for practice ought to be observed in all times. In Christ there are no dead and sapless branches, faith is not an idle grace; wherever it is, it brings forth fruit in works.

Chapter 1

Chapter Outline	
How to apply to God under troubles, and how to behave in prosperous and in adverse circumstances.	(1–11)
To look upon all evil as proceeding from ourselves, and all good from God.	(12–18)
The duty of watching against a rash temper, and of receiving the word of God with meekness.	(19–21)
And of living according thereto.	(22–25)
The difference between vain pretences and real religion.	(26, 27)

Verses 1–11

Christianity teaches men to be joyful under troubles: such exercises are sent from God's love; and trials in the way of duty will brighten our graces now, and our crown at last. Let us take care, in times of trial, that patience, and not passion, is set to work in us: whatever is said or done, let patience have the saying and doing of it. When the work of patience is complete, it will furnish all that is necessary for our Christian race and warfare. We should not pray so much for the removal of affliction, as for wisdom to make a right use of it. And who does not want wisdom to guide him under trials, both in regulating his own spirit, and in managing his affairs? Here is something in answer to every discouraging turn of the mind, when we go to God under a sense of our own weakness and folly. If, after all, any should say, This may be the case with some, but I fear I shall not succeed, the promise is, To any that asketh, it shall be given. A mind that has single and prevailing regard to its spiritual and eternal interest, and that keeps steady in its purposes for God, will grow wise by afflictions, will continue fervent in devotion, and rise above trials and oppositions. When our faith and spirits rise and fall with second causes, there will be unsteadiness in our words and actions. This may not always expose men to contempt in the world, but such ways cannot please God. No condition of life is such as to hinder rejoicing in God. Those of low degree may rejoice, if they are exalted to be rich in faith and heirs of the kingdom of God; and the rich may rejoice in humbling providences, that lead to a humble and lowly disposition of mind. Worldly wealth is a withering thing. Then, let him that is rich rejoice in the grace of God, which makes and keeps him humble; and in the trials and exercises which teach him to seek happiness in and from God, not from perishing enjoyments.

Verses 12–18

It is not every man who suffers, that is blessed; but he who with patience and constancy goes through all difficulties in the way of duty. Afflictions cannot make us miserable, if it be not our own fault. The tried Christian shall be a crowned one. The crown of life is promised to all who have the love of God reigning in their hearts. Every soul that truly loves God, shall have its trials in this world fully recompensed in that world above, where love is made perfect. The commands of God, and the dealings of his providence, try men's hearts, and show the dispositions which prevail in them. But nothing sinful in the heart or conduct can be ascribed to God. He is not the author of the dross, though his fiery trial exposes it. Those who lay the blame of sin, either upon their constitution, or upon their condition in the world, or pretend they cannot keep from sinning, wrong God as if he were the author of sin. Afflictions, as sent by God, are designed to draw out our graces, but not our corruptions. The origin of evil and temptation is in our own hearts. Stop the beginnings of sin, or all the evils that follow must be wholly charged upon us. God has no pleasure in the death of men, as he has no hand in their sin; but both sin and misery are owing to themselves. As the sun is the same in nature and influences, though the earth and clouds, often coming between, make it seem to us to vary, so God is unchangeable, and our changes and shadows are not from any changes or alterations in him. What the sun is in nature, God is in grace, providence, and glory; and infinitely more. As every good gift is from God, so particularly our being born again, and all its holy, happy consequences come from him. A true Christian becomes as different a person from what he was before the renewing influences of Divine grace, as if he were formed over again. We should devote all our faculties to God's service, that we may be a kind of first-fruits of his creatures.

Verses 19–21

Instead of blaming God under our trials, let us open our ears and hearts to learn what he teaches by them. And if men would govern their tongues, they must govern their passions. The worst thing we can bring to any dispute, is anger. Here is an exhortation to lay apart, and to cast off as a filthy garment, all sinful practices. This must reach to sins of thought and affection, as well as of speech and practice; to every thing corrupt and sinful. We must yield ourselves to the word of God, with humble and teachable minds. Being willing to hear of our faults, taking it not only patiently, but thankfully. It is the design of the word of God to make us wise to salvation; and those who propose any mean or low ends in attending upon it, dishonour the gospel, and disappoint their own souls.

Verses 22–25

If we heard a sermon every day of the week, and an angel from heaven were the preacher, yet, if we rested in hearing only, it would never bring us to heaven. Mere hearers are self-deceivers; and self-deceit will be found the worst deceit at last. If we flatter ourselves, it is our own fault; the truth, as it is in Jesus, flatters no man. Let the word of truth be carefully attended to, and it will set before us the corruption of our nature, the disorders of our hearts and lives; and it will tell us plainly what we are. Our sins are the spots the law discovers: Christ's blood is the laver the gospel shows. But in vain do we hear God's word, and look into the gospel glass, if we go away, and forget our spots, instead of washing them off; and forget our remedy, instead of applying to it. This is the case with those who do not hear the word as they ought. In hearing the word, we look into it for counsel and direction, and when we study it, it turns to our spiritual life. Those who keep in the law and word of God, are, and shall be, blessed in all their ways. His gracious recompence hereafter, would be connected with his present peace and comfort. Every part of Divine revelation has its use, in bringing the sinner to Christ for salvation, and in directing and encouraging him to walk at liberty, by the Spirit of adoption, according to the holy commands of God. And mark the distinctness, it is not for his deeds, that any man is blessed, but in his deed. It is not talking, but walking, that will bring us to heaven. Christ will become more precious to the believer's soul, which by his grace will become more fitted for the inheritance of the saints in light.

Verses 26, 27

When men take more pains to seem religious than really to be so, it is a sign their religion is in vain. The not bridling the tongue, readiness to speak of the faults of others, or to lessen their wisdom and piety, are signs of a vain religion. The man who has a slandering tongue, cannot have a truly humble, gracious heart. False religious may be known by their impurity and uncharitableness. True religion teaches us to do every thing as in the presence of God. An unspotted life must go with unfeigned love and charity. Our true religion is equal to the measure in which these things have place in our hearts and conduct. And let us remember, that nothing avails in Christ Jesus, but faith that worketh by love, purifies the heart, subdues carnal lusts, and obeys God's commands.

Chapter 2

Chapter Outline	
All professions of faith are vain, if not producing love and justice to others.	(1–13)
The necessity of good works to prove the sincerity of faith, which otherwise will be of no more advantage than the faith of devils.	(14–26)

Verses 1–13

Those who profess faith in Christ as the Lord of glory, must not respect persons on account of mere outward circumstances and appearances, in a manner not agreeing with their profession of being disciples of the lowly Jesus. St. James does not here encourage rudeness or disorder: civil respect must be paid; but never such as to influence the proceedings of Christians in disposing of the offices of the church of Christ, or in passing the censures of the church, or in any matter of religion. Questioning ourselves is of great use in every part of the holy life. Let us be more frequent in this, and in every thing take occasion to discourse with our souls. As places of worship cannot be built or maintained without expense, it may be proper that those who contribute thereto should be accommodated accordingly; but were all persons more spiritually-minded, the poor would be treated with more attention that usually is the case in worshipping congregations. A lowly state is most favourable for inward peace and for growth in holiness. God would give to all believers riches and honours of this world, if these would do them good, seeing that he has chosen them to be rich in faith, and made them heirs of his kingdom, which he promised to bestow on all who love him. Consider how often riches lead to vice and mischief, and what great reproaches are thrown upon God and religion, by men of wealth, power, and worldly greatness; and it will make this sin appear very sinful and foolish. The Scripture gives as a law, to love our neighbour as ourselves. This law is a royal law, it comes from the King of kings; and if Christians act unjustly, they are convicted by the law as transgressors. To think that our good deeds will atone for our bad deeds, plainly puts us upon looking for another atonement. According to the covenant of works, one breach of any one command brings a man under condemnation, from which no obedience, past, present, or future, can deliver him. This shows us the happiness of those that are in Christ. We may serve him without slavish fear. God's restraints are not a bondage, but our own corruptions are so. The doom passed upon impenitent sinners at last, will be judgment without mercy. But God deems it his glory and joy, to pardon and bless those who might justly be condemned at his tribunal; and his grace teaches those who partake of his mercy, to copy it in their conduct.

Verses 14–26

Those are wrong who put a mere notional belief of the gospel for the whole of evangelical religion, as many now do. No doubt, true faith alone, whereby men have part in Christ's righteousness, atonement, and grace, saves their souls; but it produces holy fruits, and is shown to be real by its effect on their works; while mere assent to any form of doctrine, or mere historical belief of any facts, wholly differs from this saving faith. A bare profession may gain the good opinion of pious people; and it may procure, in some cases, worldly good things; but what profit will it be, for any to gain the whole world, and to lose their souls? Can this faith save him? All things should be accounted profitable or unprofitable to us, as they tend to forward or hinder the salvation of our souls. This place of Scripture plainly shows that an opinion, or assent to the gospel, without works, is not faith. There is no way to show we really believe in Christ, but by being diligent in good works, from gospel motives, and for gospel purposes. Men may boast to others, and be conceited of that which they really have not. There is not only to be assent in faith, but consent; not only an assent to the truth of the word, but a consent to take Christ. True believing is not an act of the understanding only, but a work of the whole heart. That a justifying faith cannot be without works, is shown from two examples, Abraham and Rahab. Abraham believed God, and it was reckoned unto him for righteousness. Faith, producing such works, advanced him to peculiar favours. We see then, ver. #(**24**), how that by works a man is justified, not by a bare opinion or profession, or believing without obeying; but by having such faith as produces good works. And to have to deny his own reason, affections, and interests, is an action fit to try a believer. Observe here, the wonderful power of faith in changing sinners. Rahab's conduct proved her faith to be living, or having power; it showed that she believed with her heart, not merely by an assent of the understanding. Let us then take heed, for the best works, without faith, are dead; they want root and principle. By faith any thing we do is really good; as done in obedience to God, and aiming at his acceptance: the root is as though it were dead, when there is no fruit. Faith is the root, good works are the fruits; and we must see to it that we have both. This is the grace of God wherein we stand, and we should stand to it. There is no middle state. Every one must either live God's friend, or God's enemy. Living to God, as it is the consequence of faith, which justifies and will save, obliges us to do nothing against him, but every thing for him and to him.

Chapter 3

Chapter Outline	
Cautions against proud behaviour, and the mischief of an unruly tongue.	(1–12)
The excellence of heavenly wisdom, in opposition to that which is worldly.	(13–18)

Verses 1–12

We are taught to dread an unruly tongue, as one of the greatest evils. The affairs of mankind are thrown into confusion by the tongues of men. Every age of the world, and every condition of life, private or public, affords examples of this. Hell has more to do in promoting the fire of the tongue than men generally think; and whenever men's tongues are employed in sinful ways, they are set on fire of hell. No man can tame the tongue without Divine grace and assistance. The apostle does not represent it as impossible, but as extremely difficult. Other sins decay with age, this many times gets worse; we grow more froward and fretful, as natural strength decays, and the days come on in which we have no pleasure. When other sins are tamed and subdued by the infirmities of age, the spirit often grows more tart, nature being drawn down to the dregs, and the words used become more passionate. That man's tongue confutes itself, which at one time pretends to adore the perfections of God, and to refer all things to him; and at another time condemns even good men, if they do not use the same words and expressions. True religion will not admit of contradictions: how many sins would be prevented, if men would always be consistent! Pious and edifying language is the genuine produce of a sanctified heart; and none who understand Christianity, expect to hear curses, lies, boastings, and revilings from a true believer's mouth, any more than they look for the fruit of one tree from another. But facts prove that more professors succeed in bridling their senses and appetites, than in duly restraining their tongues. Then, depending on Divine grace, let us take heed to bless and curse not; and let us aim to be consistent in our words and actions.

Verses 13–18

These **verses** show the difference between men's pretending to be wise, and their being really so. He who thinks well, or he who talks well, is not wise in the sense of the Scripture, if he does not live and act well. True wisdom may be know by the meekness of the spirit and temper. Those who live in malice, envy, and contention, live in confusion; and are liable to be provoked and hurried to any evil work. Such wisdom comes not down from above, but springs up from earthly principles, acts on earthly motives, and is intent on serving earthly purposes. Those who are lifted up with such wisdom, described by the apostle James, is near to the Christian love, described by the apostle Paul; and both are so described that every man may fully prove the reality of his attainments in them. It has no disguise or deceit. It cannot fall in with those managements the world counts wise, which are crafty and guileful; but it is sincere, and open, and steady, and uniform, and consistent with itself. May the purity, peace, gentleness, teachableness, and mercy shown in all our actions, and the fruits of righteousness abounding in our lives, prove that God has bestowed upon us this excellent gift.

Chapter 4

Chapter Outline	
Here are cautions against corrupt affections, and love of this world, which is enmity to God.	(1–10)
Exhortations to undertake no affairs of life, without constant regard to the will and providence of God.	(11–17)

Verses 1–10

Since all wars and fightings come from the corruptions of our own hearts, it is right to mortify those lusts that war in the members. Wordly and fleshly lusts are distempers, which will not allow content or satisfaction. Sinful desires and affections stop prayer, and the working of our desires toward God. And let us beware that we do not abuse or misuse the mercies received, by the disposition of the heart when prayers are granted When men ask of God prosperity, they often ask with wrong aims and intentions. If we thus seek the things of this world, it is just in God to deny them. Unbelieving and cold desires beg denials; and we may be sure that when prayers are rather the language of lusts than of graces, they will return empty. Here is a decided warning to avoid all criminal friendships with this world. Worldly-mindedness is enmity to God. An enemy may be reconciled, but "enmity" never can be reconciled. A man may have a large portion in things of this life, and yet be kept in the love of God; but he who sets his heart upon the world, who will conform to it rather than lose its friendship, is an enemy to God. So that any one who resolves at all events to be upon friendly terms with the world, must be the enemy of God. Did then the Jews, or the loose professors of Christianity, think the Scripture spake in vain against this worldly-mindedness? or does the Holy Spirit who dwells in all Christians, or the new nature which he creates, produce such fruit? Natural corruption shows itself by envying. The spirit of the world teaches us to lay up, or lay out for ourselves, according to our own fancies; God the Holy Spirit teaches us to be willing to do good to all about us, as we are able. The grace of God will correct and cure the spirit by nature in us; and where he gives grace, he gives another spirit than that of the world. The proud resist God: in their understanding they resist the truths of God; in their will they resist the laws of God; in their passions they resist the providence of God; therefore, no wonder that God resists the proud. How wretched the state of those who make God their enemy! God will give more grace to the humble, because they see their need of it, pray for it are thankful for it, and such shall have it. Submit to God, ver. #(**7**). Submit your understanding to the truth of God; submit your wills to the will of his precept, the will of his providence. Submit yourselves to God, for he is ready to do you good. If we yield to temptations, the devil will continually follow us; but if we put on the whole armour of God, and stand out against him, he will leave us. Let sinners then submit to God, and seek his grace and favour; resisting the devil. All sin must be wept over; here, in godly sorrow, or, hereafter, in eternal misery. And the Lord will not refuse to comfort one who really mourns for sin, or to exalt one who humbles himself before him.

Verses 11–17

Our lips must be governed by the law of kindness, as well as truth and justice. Christians are brethren. And to break God's commands, is to speak evil of them, and to judge them, as if they laid too great a restraint upon us. We have the law of God, which is a rule to all; let us not presume to set up our own notions and opinions as a rule to those about us, and let us be careful that we be not condemned of the Lord. "Go to now," is a call to any one to consider his conduct as being wrong. How apt worldly and contriving men are to leave God out of their plans! How vain it is to look for any thing good without God's blessing and guidance! The frailty, shortness, and uncertainty of life, ought to check the vanity and presumptuous confidence of all projects for futurity. We can fix the hour and minute of the sun's rising and setting to-morrow, but we cannot fix the certain time of a vapour being scattered. So short, unreal, and fading is human life, and all the prosperity or enjoyment that attends it; though bliss or woe for ever must be according to our conduct during this fleeting moment. We are always to depend on the will of God. Our times are not in our own hands, but at the disposal of God. Our heads may be filled with cares and contrivances for ourselves, or our families, or our friends; but Providence often throws our plans into confusion. All we design, and all we do, should be with submissive dependence on God. It is foolish, and it is hurtful, to boast of worldly things and aspiring projects; it will bring great disappointment, and will prove destruction in the end. Omissions are sins which will be brought into judgment, as well as commissions. He that does not the good he knows should be done, as well as he who does the evil he knows should not be done, will be condemned. Oh that we were as careful not to omit prayer, and not to neglect to meditate and examine our consciences, as we are not to commit gross outward vices against light!

Chapter 5

Chapter Outline	
The judgments of God denounced against rich unbelievers.	(1–6)
Exhortation to patience and meekness under tribulations.	(7–11)
Cautions against rash swearing Prayer recommended in afflictive and prosperous circumstances, Christians to confess their faults to each other.	(12–18)
The happiness of being the means of the conversion of a sinner.	(19, 20)

Verses 1–6

Public troubles are most grievous to those who live in pleasure, and are secure and sensual, though all ranks suffer deeply at such times. All idolized treasures will soon perish, except as they will rise up in judgment against their possessors. Take heed of defrauding and oppressing; and avoid the very appearance of it. God does not forbid us to use lawful pleasures; but to live in pleasure, especially sinful pleasure, is a provoking sin. Is it no harm for people to unfit themselves for minding the concerns of their souls, by indulging bodily appetites? The just may be condemned and killed; but when such suffer by oppressors, this is marked by God. Above all their other crimes, the Jews had condemned and crucified that Just One who had come among them, even Jesus Christ the righteous.

Verses 7–11

Consider him that waits for a crop of corn; and will not you wait for a crown of glory? If you should be called to wait longer than the husbandman, is not there something more worth waiting for? In every sense the coming of the Lord drew nigh, and all his people's losses, hardships, and sufferings, would be repaid. Men count time long, because they measure it by their own lives; but all time is as nothing to God; it is as a moment. To short-lived creatures a few years seem an age; but Scripture, measuring all things by the existence of God, reckons thousands of years but so many days. God brought about things in Job's case, so as plainly to prove that he is very pitiful and of tender mercy. This did not appear during his troubles, but was seen in the event, and believers now will find a happy end to their trials. Let us serve our God, and bear our trials, as those who believe that the end will crown all. Our eternal happiness is safe if we trust to him: all else is mere vanity, which soon will be done with for ever.

Verses 12–18

The sin of swearing is condemned; but how many make light of common profane swearing! Such swearing expressly throws contempt upon God's name and authority. This sin brings neither gain, nor pleasure, nor reputation, but is showing enmity to God without occasion and without advantage It shows a man to be an enemy to God, however he pretends to call himself by his name, or sometimes joins in acts of worship. But the Lord will not hold him guiltless that taketh his name in vain. In a day of affliction nothing is more seasonable than prayer. The spirit is then most humble, and the heart is broken and tender. It is necessary to exercise faith and hope under afflictions; and prayer is the appointed means for obtaining and increasing these graces. Observe, that the saving of the sick is not ascribed to the anointing with oil, but to prayer. In a time of sickness it is not cold and formal prayer that is effectual, but the prayer of faith. The great thing we should beg of God for ourselves and others in the time of sickness is, the pardon of sin. Let nothing be done to encourage any to delay, under the mistaken fancy that a confession, a prayer, a minister's absolution and exhortation, or the sacrament, will set all right at last, where the duties of a godly life have been disregarded. To acknowledge our faults to each other, will tend greatly to peace and brotherly love. And when a righteous person, a true believer, justified in Christ, and by his grace walking before God in holy obedience, presents an effectual fervent prayer, wrought in his heart by the power of the Holy Spirit, raising holy affections and believing expectations and so leading earnestly to plead the promises of God at his mercy-seat, it avails much. The power of prayer is proved from the history of Elijah. In prayer we must not look to the merit of man, but to the grace of God. It is not enough to say a prayer, but we must pray in prayer. Thoughts must be fixed, desires must be firm and ardent, and graces exercised. This instance of the power of prayer, encourages every Christian to be earnest in prayer. God never says to any of the seed of Jacob, Seek my face in vain. Where there may not be so much of miracle in God's answering our prayers, yet there may be as much of grace.

Verses 19, 20

It is no mark of a wise or holy man, to boast of being free from error, or to refuse to acknowledge an error. And there is some doctrinal mistake at the bottom of every practical mistake. There is no one habitually bad, but upon some bad principle. This is conversion; to turn a sinner from the error of his ways, not merely from one party to another, or from one notion and way of thinking to another. There is no way effectually and finally to hide sin, but forsaking it. Many sins are hindered in the party converted; many also may be so in others whom he may influence. The salvation of one soul is of infinitely greater importance than preserving the lives of multitudes, or promoting the welfare of a whole people. Let us in our several stations keep these things in mind, sparing no pains in God's service, and the event will prove that our labour is not in vain in the Lord. For six thousand years He has been multiplying pardons, and yet his free grace is not tired nor grown weary. Certainly Divine mercy is an ocean that is ever full and ever flowing. May the Lord give us a part in this abundant mercy, through the blood of Christ, and the sanctification of the Spirit.

1 Peter

The same great doctrines, as in St. Paul's epistles, are here applied to same practical purposes. And this epistle is remarkable for the sweetness, gentleness, and humble love, with which it is written. It gives a short, and yet a very clear summary, both of the consolations and the instructions needful for the encouragement and direction of a Christian in his journey to heaven, raising his thoughts and desires to that happiness, and strengthening him against all opposition in the way, both from corruption within, and temptations and afflictions without.

Chapter 1

Chapter Outline	
The apostle blesses God for his special benefits through Christ.	(1–9)
Salvation by Christ foretold in ancient prophecy.	(10–12)
All are exhorted to holy conversation.	(13–16)
Such as is suitable to their principles, privileges, and obligations.	(17–25)

Verses 1–9

This epistle is addressed to believers in general, who are strangers in every city or country where they live, and are scattered through the nations. These are to ascribe their salvation to the electing love of the Father, the redemption of the Son, and the sanctification of the Holy Ghost; and so to give glory to one God in three Persons, into whose name they had been baptized. Hope, in the world's phrase, refers only to an uncertain good, for all worldly hopes are tottering, built upon sand, and the worldling's hopes of heaven are blind and groundless conjectures. But the hope of the sons of the living God is a living hope; not only as to its object, but as to its effect also. It enlivens and comforts in all distresses, enables to meet and get over all difficulties. Mercy is the spring of all this; yea, great mercy and manifold mercy. And this well-grounded hope of salvation, is an active and living principle of obedience in the soul of the believer. The matter of a Christian's joy, is the remembrance of the happiness laid up for him. It is incorruptible, it cannot come to nothing, it is an estate that cannot be spent. Also undefiled; this signifies its purity and perfection. And it fadeth not; is not sometimes more or less pleasant, but ever the same, still like itself. All possessions here are stained with defects and failings; still something is wanting: fair houses have sad cares flying about the gilded and ceiled roofs; soft beds and full tables, are often with sick bodies and uneasy stomachs. All possessions are stained with sin, either in getting or in using them. How ready we are to turn the things we possess into occasions and instruments of sin, and to think there is no liberty or delight in their use, without abusing them! Worldly possessions are uncertain and soon pass away, like the flowers and plants of the field. That must be of the greatest worth, which is laid up in the highest and best place, in heaven. Happy are those whose hearts the Holy Spirit sets on this inheritance. God not only gives his people grace, but preserves them unto glory. Every believer has always something wherein he may greatly rejoice; it should show itself in the countenance and conduct. The Lord does not willingly afflict, yet his wise love often appoints sharp trials, to show his people their hearts, and to do them good at the latter end. Gold does not increase by trial in the fire, it becomes less; but faith is made firm, and multiplied, by troubles and afflictions. Gold must perish at last, and can only purchase perishing things, while the trial of faith will be found to praise, and honour, and glory. Let this reconcile us to present afflictions. Seek then to believe Christ's excellence in himself, and his love to us; this will kindle such a fire in the heart as will make it rise up in a sacrifice of love to him. And the glory of God and our own happiness are so united, that if we sincerely seek the one now, we shall attain the other when the soul shall no more be subject to evil. The certainty of this hope is as if believers had already received it.

Verses 10–12

Jesus Christ was the main subject of the prophets' studies. Their inquiry into the sufferings of Christ and the glories that should follow, would lead to a view of the whole gospel, the sum whereof is, That Christ Jesus was delivered for our offences, and raised again for our justification. God is pleased to answer our necessities rather than our requests. The doctrine of the prophets, and that of the apostles, exactly agree, as coming from the same Spirit of God. The gospel is the ministration of the Spirit; its success depends upon his operation and blessing. Let us then search diligently those Scriptures which contain the doctrines of salvation.

Verses 13–16

As the traveller, the racer, the warrior, and the labourer, gathered in their long and loose garments, that they might be ready in their business, so let Christians do by their minds and affections. Be sober, be watchful against all spiritual dangers and enemies, and be temperate in all behaviour. Be sober-minded in opinion, as well as in practice, and humble in your judgment of yourselves. A strong and perfect trust in the grace of God, is agreeable with best endeavours in our duty. Holiness is the desire and duty of every Christian. It must be in all affairs, in every condition, and towards all people. We must especially watch and pray against the sins to which we are inclined. The written word of God is the surest rule of a Christian's life, and by this rule we are commanded to be holy every way. God makes those holy whom he saves.

Verses 17–25

Holy confidence in God as a Father, and awful fear of him as a Judge, agree together; and to regard God always as a Judge, makes him dear to us as a Father. If believers do evil, God will visit them with corrections. Then, let Christians not doubt God's faithfulness to his promises, nor give way to enslaving dread of his wrath, but let them reverence his holiness. The fearless professor is defenceless, and Satan takes him captive at his will; the desponding professor has no heart to avail himself of his advantages, and is easily brought to surrender. The price paid for man's redemption was the precious blood of Christ. Not only openly wicked, but unprofitable conversation is highly dangerous, though it may plead custom. It is folly to resolve, I will live and die in such a way, because my forefathers did so. God had purposes of special favour toward his people, long before he made manifest such grace unto them. But the clearness of light, the supports of faith, the power of ordinances, are all much greater since Christ came upon earth, than they were before. The comfort is, that being by faith made one with Christ, his present glory is an assurance that where he is we shall be also, Joh **14**:**3**. The soul must be purified, before it can give up its own desires and indulgences. And the word of God planted in the heart by the Holy Ghost, is a means of spiritual life, stirring up to our duty, working a total change in the dispositions and affections of the soul, till it brings to eternal life. In contrast with the excellence of the renewed spiritual man, as born again, observe the vanity of the natural man. In his life, and in his fall, he is like grass, the flower of grass, which soon withers and dies away. We should hear, and thus receive and love, the holy, living word, and rather hazard all than lose it; and we must banish all other things from the place due to it. We should lodge it in our hearts as our only treasures here, and the certain pledge of the treasure of glory laid up for believers in heaven.

Chapter 2

Chapter Outline	
A temper suitable to the Christian character as born again, is recommended.	(1–10)
Holy conversation among the Gentiles directed.	(11, 12)
Subjects exhorted to pay all proper obedience to their civil governors.	(13–17)
Also servants to their masters, and all to be patient, according to the example of the suffering Saviour.	(18–25)

Verses 1–10

Evil-speaking is a sign of malice and guile in the heart; and hinders our profiting by the word of God. A new life needs suitable food. Infants desire milk, and make the best endeavours for it which they are able to do; such must be a Christian's desires after the word of God. Our Lord Jesus Christ is very merciful to us miserable sinners; and he has a fulness of grace. But even the best of God's servants, in this life, have only a taste of the consolations of God. Christ is called a Stone, to teach his servants that he is their protection and security, the foundation on which they are built. He is precious in the excellence of his nature, the dignity of his office, and the glory of his services. All true believers are a holy priesthood; sacred to God, serviceable to others, endowed with heavenly gifts and graces. But the most spiritual sacrifices of the best in prayer and praise are not acceptable, except through Jesus Christ. Christ is the chief Corner-stone, that unites the whole number of believers into one everlasting temple, and bears the weight of the whole fabric. Elected, or chosen, for a foundation that is everlasting. Precious beyond compare, by all that can give worth. To be built on Christ means, to believe in him; but in this many deceive themselves, they consider not what it is, nor the necessity of it, to partake of the salvation he has wrought. Though the frame of the world were falling to pieces, that man who is built on this foundation may hear it without fear. He shall not be confounded. The believing soul makes haste to Christ, but it never finds cause to hasten from him. All true Christians are a chosen generation; they make one family, a people distinct from the world: of another spirit, principle, and practice; which they could never be, if they were not chosen in Christ to be such, and sanctified by his Spirit. Their first state is a state of gross darkness, but they are called out of darkness into a state of joy, pleasure, and prosperity; that they should show forth the praises of the Lord by their profession of his truth, and their good conduct. How vast their obligations to Him who has made them his people, and has shown mercy to them! To be without this mercy is a woful state, though a man have all worldly enjoyments. And there is nothing that so kindly works repentance, as right thoughts of the mercy and love of God. Let us not dare to abuse and affront the free grace of God, if we mean to be saved by it; but let all who would be found among those who obtain mercy, walk as his people.

Verses 11, 12

Even the best of men, the chosen generation, the people of God, need to be exhorted to keep from the worst sins. And fleshly lusts are most destructive to man's soul. It is a sore judgment to be given up to them. There is a day of visitation coming, wherein God may call to repentance by his word and his grace; then many will glorify God, and the holy lives of his people will have promoted the happy change.

Verses 13–17

A Christian conversation must be honest; which it cannot be, if there is not a just and careful discharge of all relative duties: the apostle here treats of these distinctly. Regard to those duties is the will of God, consequently, the Christian's duty, and the way to silence the base slanders of ignorant and foolish men. Christians must endeavour, in all relations, to behave aright, that they do not make their liberty a cloak or covering for any wickedness, or for the neglect of duty; but they must remember that they are servants of God.

Verses 18–25

Servants in those days generally were slaves, and had heathen masters, who often used them cruelly; yet the apostle directs them to be subject to the masters placed over them by Providence, with a fear to dishonour or offend God. And not only to those pleased with reasonable service, but to the severe, and those angry without cause. The sinful misconduct of one relation, does not justify sinful behaviour in the other; the servant is bound to do his duty, though the master may be sinfully froward and per**verse**. But masters should be meek and gentle to their servants and inferiors. What glory or distinction could it be, for professed Christians to be patient when corrected for their faults? But if when they behaved well they were ill treated by proud and passionate heathen masters, yet bore it without peevish complaints, or purposes of revenge, and persevered in their duty, this would be acceptable to God as a distinguishing effect of his grace, and would be rewarded by him. Christ's death was designed not only for an example of patience under sufferings, but he bore our sins; he bore the punishment of them, and thereby satisfied Divine justice. Hereby he takes them away from us. The fruits of Christ's sufferings are the death of sin, and a new holy life of righteousness; for both which we have an example, and powerful motives, and ability to perform also, from the death and resurrection of Christ. And our justification; Christ was bruised and crucified as a sacrifice for our sins, and by his stripes the diseases of our souls are cured. Here is man's sin; he goes astray; it is his own act. His misery; he goes astray from the pasture, from the Shepherd, and from the flock, and so exposes himself to dangers without number. Here is the recovery by conversion; they are now returned as the effect of Divine grace. This return is, from all their errors and wanderings, to Christ. Sinners, before their conversion, are always going astray; their life is a continued error.

Chapter 3

Chapter Outline	
The duties of wives and husbands.	(1–7)
Christians exhorted to agree.	(8–13)
And encouraged to patience under persecutions for righteousness' sake, considering that Christ suffered patiently.	(14–22)

Verses 1–7

The wife must discharge her duty to her own husband, though he obey not the word. We daily see how narrowly evil men watch the ways and lives of professors of religion. Putting on of apparel is not forbidden, but vanity and costliness in ornament. Religious people should take care that all their behaviour answers to their profession. But how few know the right measure and bounds of those two necessaries of life, food and raiment! Unless poverty is our carver, and cuts us short, there is scarcely any one who does not desire something beyond what is good for us. Far more are beholden to the lowliness of their state, than the lowliness of their mind; and many will not be so bounded, but lavish their time and money upon trifles. The apostle directs Christian females to put on something not corruptible, that beautifies the soul, even the graces of God's Holy Spirit. A true Christian's chief care lies in right ordering his own spirit. This will do more to fix the affections, and excite the esteem of a husband, than studied ornaments or fashionable apparel, attended by a froward and quarrelsome temper. Christians ought to do their duty to one another, from a willing mind, and in obedience to the command of God. Wives should be subject to their husbands, not from dread and amazement, but from desire to do well, and please God. The husband's duty to the wife implies giving due respect unto her, and maintaining her authority, protecting her, and placing trust in her. They are heirs together of all the blessings of this life and that which is to come, and should live peaceably one with another. Prayer sweetens their converse. And it is not enough that they pray with the family, but husband and wife together by themselves, and with their children. Those who are acquainted with prayer, find such unspeakable sweetness in it, that they will not be hindered therein. That you may pray much, live holily; and that you may live holily, be much in prayer.

Verses 8–13

Though Christians cannot always be exactly of the same mind, yet they should have compassion one of another, and love as brethren. If any man desires to live comfortably on earth, or to possess eternal life in heaven, he must bridle his tongue from wicked, abusive, or deceitful words. He must forsake and keep far from evil actions, do all the good he can, and seek peace with all men. For God, all-wise and every where present, watches over the righteous, and takes care of them. None could or should harm those who copied the example of Christ, who is perfect goodness, and did good to others as his followers.

Verses 14–22

We sanctify God before others, when our conduct invites and encourages them to glorify and honour him. What was the ground and reason of their hope? We should be able to defend our religion with meekness, in the fear of God. There is no room for any other fears where this great fear is; it disturbs not. The conscience is good, when it does its office well. That person is in a sad condition on whom sin and suffering meet: sin makes suffering extreme, comfortless, and destructive. Surely it is better to suffer for well-doing than for evil-doing, whatever our natural impatience at times may suggest. The example of Christ is an argument for patience under sufferings. In the case of our Lord's suffering, he that knew no sin, suffered instead of those who knew no righteousness. The blessed end and design of our Lord's sufferings were, to reconcile us to God, and to bring us to eternal glory. He was put to death in respect of his human nature, but was quickened and raised by the power of the Holy Spirit. If Christ could not be freed from sufferings, why should Christians think to be so? God takes exact notice of the means and advantages people in all ages have had. As to the old world, Christ sent his Spirit; gave warning by Noah. But though the patience of God waits long, it will cease at last. And the spirits of disobedient sinners, as soon as they are out of their bodies, are committed to the prison of hell, where those that despised Noah's warning now are, and from whence there is no redemption. Noah's salvation in the ark upon the water, which carried him above the floods, set forth the salvation of all true believers. That temporal salvation by the ark was a type of the eternal salvation of believers by baptism of the Holy Spirit. To prevent mistakes, the apostle declares what he means by saving baptism; not the outward ceremony of washing with water, which, in itself, does no more than put away the filth of the flesh, but that baptism, of which the baptismal water formed the sign. Not the outward ordinance, but when a man, by the regeneration of the Spirit, was enabled to repent and profess faith, and purpose a new life, uprightly, and as in the presence of God. Let us beware that we rest not upon outward forms. Let us learn to look on the ordinances of God spiritually, and to inquire after the spiritual effect and working of them on our consciences. We would willingly have all religion reduced to outward things. But many who were baptized, and constantly attended the ordinances, have remained without Christ, died in their sins, and are now past recovery. Rest not then till thou art cleansed by the Spirit of Christ and the blood of Christ. His resurrection from the dead is that whereby we are assured of purifying and peace.

Chapter 4

Chapter Outline	
The consideration of Christ's sufferings is urged for purity and holiness.	(1–6)

And the approaching end of the Jewish state, as a reason for sobriety, watchfulness, and prayer.	(7–11)
Believers encouraged to rejoice and glory in reproaches and sufferings for Christ, and to commit their souls to the care of a faithful God.	(12–19)

Verses 1–6

The strongest and best arguments against sin, are taken from the sufferings of Christ. He died to destroy sin; and though he cheerfully submitted to the worst sufferings, yet he never gave way to the least sin. Temptations could not prevail, were it not for man's own corruption; but true Christians make the will of God, not their own lust or desires, the rule of their lives and actions. And true conversion makes a marvellous change in the heart and life. It alters the mind, judgment, affections, and conversation. When a man is truly converted, it is very grievous to him to think how the time past of his life has been spent. One sin draws on another. Six sins are here mentioned which have dependence one upon another. It is a Christian's duty, not only to keep from gross wickedness, but also from things that lead to sin, or appear evil. The gospel had been preached to those since dead, who by the proud and carnal judgment of wicked men were condemned as evil-doers, some even suffering death. But being quickened to Divine life by the Holy Spirit, they lived to God as his devoted servants. Let not believers care, though the world scorns and reproaches them.

Verses 7–11

The destruction of the Jewish church and nation, foretold by our Saviour, was very near. And the speedy approach of death and judgment concerns all, to which these words naturally lead our minds. Our approaching end, is a powerful argument to make us sober in all worldly matters, and earnest in religion. There are so many things amiss in all, that unless love covers, excuses, and forgives in others, the mistakes and faults for which every one needs the forbearance of others, Satan will prevail to stir up divisions and discords. But we are not to suppose that charity will cover or make amends for the sins of those who exercise it, so as to induce God to forgive them. The nature of a Christian's work, which is high work and hard work, the goodness of the Master, and the excellence of the reward, all require that our endeavours should be serious and earnest. And in all the duties and services of life, we should aim at the glory of God as our chief end. He is a miserable, unsettled wretch, who cleaves to himself, and forgets God; is only perplexed about his credit, and gain, and base ends, which are often broken, and which, when he attains, both he and they must shortly perish together. But he who has given up himself and his all to God, may say confidently that the Lord is his portion; and nothing but glory through Christ Jesus, is solid and lasting; that abideth for ever.

Verses 12–19

By patience and fortitude in suffering, by dependence on the promises of God, and keeping to the word the Holy Spirit hath revealed, the Holy Spirit is glorified; but by the contempt and reproaches cast upon believers, he is evil spoken of, and is blasphemed. One would think such cautions as these were needless to Christians. But their enemies falsely charged them with foul crimes. And even the best of men need to be warned against the worst of sins. There is no comfort in sufferings, when we bring them upon ourselves by our own sin and folly. A time of universal calamity was at hand, as foretold by our Saviour, Mt **24**:**9**, **10**. And if such things befall in this life, how awful will the day of judgment be! It is true that the righteous are scarcely saved; even those who endeavour to walk uprightly in the ways of God. This does not mean that the purpose and performance of God are uncertain, but only the great difficulties and hard encounters in the way; that they go through so many temptations and tribulations, so many fightings without and fears within. Yet all outward difficulties would be as nothing, were it not for lusts and corruptions within. These are the worst clogs and troubles. And if the way of the righteous be so hard, then how hard shall be the end of the ungodly sinner, who walks in sin with delight, and thinks the righteous is a fool for all his pains! The only way to keep the soul well, is, to commit it to God by prayer, and patient perseverance in well-doing. He will overrule all to the final advantage of the believer.

Chapter 5

Chapter Outline	
Elders exhorted and encouraged.	(1–4)
Younger Christians are to submit to their elders, and to yield with humility and patience to God, and to be sober, watchful, and stedfast in faith.	(5–9)
Prayers for their growth and establishment.	(10–14)

Verses 1–4

The apostle Peter does not command, but exhorts. He does not claim power to rule over all pastors and churches. It was the peculiar honour of Peter and a few more, to be witnesses of Christ's sufferings; but it is the privilege of all true Christians to partake of the glory that shall be revealed. These poor, dispersed, suffering Christians, were the flock of God, redeemed to God by the great Shepherd, living in holy love and communion, according to the will of God. They are also dignified with the title of God's heritage or clergy; his peculiar lot, chosen for his own people, to enjoy his special favour, and to do him special service. Christ is the chief Shepherd of the whole flock and heritage of God. And all faithful ministers will receive a crown of unfading glory, infinitely better and more honourable than all the authority, wealth, and pleasure of the world.

Verses 5–9

Humility preserves peace and order in all Christian churches and societies; pride disturbs them. Where God gives grace to be humble, he will give wisdom, faith, and holiness. To be humble, and subject to our reconciled God, will bring greater comfort to the soul than the gratification of pride and ambition. But it is to be in due time; not in thy fancied time, but God's own wisely appointed time. Does he wait, and wilt not thou? What difficulties will not the firm belief of his wisdom, power, and goodness get over! Then be humble under his hand. Cast "all you care;" personal cares, family cares, cares for the present, and cares for the future, for yourselves, for others, for the church, on God. These are burdensome, and often very sinful, when they arise from unbelief and distrust, when they torture and distract the mind, unfit us for duties, and hinder our delight in the service of God. The remedy is, to cast our care upon God, and leave every event to his wise and gracious disposal. Firm belief that the Divine will and counsels are right, calms the spirit of a man. Truly the godly too often forget this, and fret themselves to no purpose. Refer all to God's disposal. The golden mines of all spiritual comfort and good are wholly his, and the Spirit itself. Then, will he not furnish what is fit for us, if we humbly attend on him, and lay the care of providing for us, upon his wisdom and love? The whole design of Satan is to devour and destroy souls. He always is contriving whom he may insnare to eternal ruin. Our duty plainly is, to be sober; to govern both the outward and the inward man by the rules of temperance. To be vigilant; suspicious of constant danger from this spiritual enemy, watchful and diligent to prevent his designs. Be stedfast, or solid, by faith. A man cannot fight upon a quagmire, there is no standing without firm ground to tread upon; this faith alone furnishes. It lifts the soul to the firm advanced ground of the promises, and fixes it there. The consideration of what others suffer, is proper to encourage us to bear our share in any affliction; and in whatever form Satan assaults us, or by whatever means, we may know that our brethren experience the same.

Verses 10–14

In conclusion, the apostle prays to God for them, as the God of all grace. Perfect implies their progress towards perfection. Stablish imports the curing of our natural lightness and inconstancy. Strengthen has respect to the growth of graces, especially where weakest and lowest. Settle signifies to fix upon a sure foundation, and may refer to Him who is the Foundation and Strength of believers. These expressions show that perseverance and progress in grace are first to be sought after by every Christian. The power of these doctrines on the hearts, and the fruits in the lives, showed who are partakers of the grace of God. The cherishing and increase of Christian love, and of affection one to another, is no matter of empty compliment, but the stamp and badge of Jesus Christ on his followers. Others may have a false peace for a time, and wicked men may wish for it to themselves and to one another; but theirs is a vain hope, and will come to nought. All solid peace is founded on Christ, and flows from him.

2 Peter

This epistle clearly is connected with the former epistle of Peter. The apostle having stated the blessings to which God has called Christians, exhorts those who had received these precious gifts, to endeavour to improve in graces and virtues. They are urged to this from the wickedness of false teachers. They are guarded against impostors and scoffers, by disproving their false assertions, ch. **3**:**1–7**, and by showing why the great day of Christ's coming was delayed, with a description of its awful circumstances and consequences; and suitable exhortations to diligence and holiness are given.

Chapter 1

Chapter Outline	
Exhortations to add the exercise of various other graces to faith.	(1–11)
The apostle looks forward to his approaching decease.	(12–15)
And confirms the truth of the gospel, relating to Christ's appearing to judgment.	(16–21)

Verses 1–11

Faith unites the weak believer to Christ, as really as it does the strong one, and purifies the heart of one as truly as of another; and every sincere believer is by his faith justified in the sight of God. Faith worketh godliness, and produces effects which no other grace in the soul can do. In Christ all fulness dwells, and pardon, peace, grace, and knowledge, and new principles, are thus given through the Holy Spirit. The promises to those who are partakers of a Divine nature, will cause us to inquire whether we are really renewed in the spirit of our minds; let us turn all these promises into prayers for the transforming and purifying grace of the Holy Spirit. The believer must add knowledge to his virtue, increasing acquaintance with the whole truth and will of God. We must add temperance to knowledge; moderation about worldly things; and add to temperance, patience, or cheerful submission to the will of God. Tribulation worketh patience, whereby we bear all calamities and crosses with silence and submission. To patience we must add godliness: this includes the holy affections and dispositions found in the true worshipper of God; with tender affection to all fellow Christians, who are children of the same Father, servants of the same Master, members of the same family, travellers to the same country, heirs of the same inheritance. Wherefore let Christians labour to attain assurance of their calling, and of their election, by believing and well-doing; and thus carefully to endeavour, is a firm argument of the grace and mercy of God, upholding them so that they shall not utterly fall. Those who are diligent in the work of religion, shall have a triumphant entrance into that everlasting kingdom where Christ reigns, and they shall reign with him for ever and ever; and it is in the practice of every good work that we are to expect entrance to heaven.

Verses 12–15

We must be established in the belief of the truth, that we may not be shaken by every wind of doctrine; and especially in the truth necessary for us to know in our day, what belongs to our peace, and what is opposed in our time. The body is but a tabernacle, or tent, of the soul. It is a mean and movable dwelling. The nearness of death makes the apostle diligent in the business of life. Nothing can so give composure in the prospect, or in the hour, of death, as to know that we have faithfully and simply followed the Lord Jesus, and sought his glory. Those who fear the Lord, talk of his loving-kindness. This is the way to spread the knowledge of the Lord; and by the written word, they are enabled to do this.

Verses 16–21

The gospel is no weak thing, but comes in power, Ro **1**:**16**. The law sets before us our wretched state by sin, but there it leaves us. It discovers our disease, but does not make known the cure. It is the sight of Jesus crucified, in the gospel, that heals the soul. Try to dissuade the covetous worlding from his greediness, one ounce of gold weighs down all reasons. Offer to stay a furious man from anger by arguments, he has not patience to hear them. Try to detain the licentious, one smile is stronger with him than all reason. But come with the gospel, and urge them with the precious blood of Jesus Christ, shed to save their souls from hell, and to satisfy for their sins, and this is that powerful pleading which makes good men confess that their hearts burn within them, and bad men, even an Agrippa, to say they are almost persuaded to be Christians, Ac **26**:**28**. God is well pleased with Christ, and with us in him. This is the Messiah who was promised, through whom all who believe in him shall be accepted and saved. The truth and reality of the gospel also are foretold by the prophets and penmenof the Old Testament, who spake and wrote under influence, and according to the direction of the Spirit of God. How firm and sure should our faith be, who have such a firm and sure word to rest upon! When the light of the Scripture is darted into the blind mind and dark understanding, by the Holy Spirit of God, it is like the day-break that advances, and diffuses itself through the whole soul, till it makes perfect day. As the Scripture is the revelation of the mind and will of God, every man ought to search it, to understand the sense and meaning. The Christian knows that book to be the word of God, in which he tastes a sweetness, and feels a power, and sees a glory, truly divine. And the prophecies already fulfilled in the person and salvation of Christ, and in the great concerns of the church and the world, form an unanswerable proof of the truth of Christianity. The Holy Ghost inspired holy men to speak and write. He so assisted and directed them in delivering what they had received from him, that they clearly expressed what they made known. So that the Scriptures are to be accounted the words of the Holy Ghost, and all the plainness and simplicity, all the power and all the propriety of the words and expressions, come from God. Mix faith with what you find in the Scriptures, and esteem and reverence the Bible as a book written by holy men, taught by the Holy Ghost.

Chapter 2

Chapter Outline	
Believers are cautioned against false teachers, and the certainty of their punishment shown from examples.	(1–9)
An account of these seducers, as exceedingly wicked.	(10–16)
But as making high pretences to liberty and purity.	(17–22)

Verses 1–9

Though the way of error is a hurtful way, many are always ready to walk therein. Let us take care we give no occasion to the enemy to blaspheme the holy name whereby we are called, or to speak evil of the way of salvation by Jesus Christ, who is the Way, the Truth, and the Life. These seducers used feigned words, they deceived the hearts of their followers. Such are condemned already, and the wrath of God abides upon them. God's usual method of proceeding is shown by examples. Angels were cast down from all their glory and dignity, for their disobedience. If creatures sin, even in heaven, they must suffer in hell. Sin is the work of darkness, and darkness is the wages of sin. See how God dealt with the old world. The number of offenders no more procures favour, than their quality. If the sin be universal, the punishment shall likewise extend to all. If in a fruitful soil the people abound in sin, God can at once turn a fruitful land into barrenness, and a well-watered country into ashes. No plans or politics can keep off judgments from a sinful people. He who keeps fire and water from hurting his people, Isa **43**:**2**, can make either destroy his enemies; they are never safe. When God sends destruction on the ungodly, he commands deliverance for the righteous. In bad company we cannot but get either guilt or grief. Let the sins of others be troubles to us. Yet it is possible for the children of the Lord, living among the most profane, to retain their integrity; there being more power in the grace of Christ, and his dwelling in them, than in the temptations of Satan, or the example of the wicked, with all their terrors or allurements. In our intentions and inclinations to commit sin, we meet with strange hinderances, if we mark them When we intend mischief, God sends many stops to hinder us, as if to say, Take heed what you do. His wisdom and power will surely effect the purposes of his love, and the engagements of his truth; while wicked men often escape suffering here, because they are kept to the day of judgment, to be punished with the devil and his angels.

Verses 10–16

Impure seducers and their abandoned followers, give themselves up to their own fleshly minds. Refusing to bring every thought to the obedience of Christ, they act against God's righteous precepts. They walk after the flesh, they go on in sinful courses, and increase to greater degrees of impurity and wickedness. They also despise those whom God has set in authority over them, and requires them to honour. Outward temporal good things are the wages sinners expect and promise themselves. And none have more cause to tremble, than those who are bold to gratify their sinful lusts, by presuming on the Divine grace and mercy. Many such there have been, and are, who speak lightly of the restraints of God's law, and deem themselves freed from obligations to obey it. Let Christians stand at a distance from such.

Verses 17–22

The word of truth is the water of life, which refreshes the souls that receive it; but deceivers spread and promote error, and are set forth as empty, because there is no truth in them. As clouds hinder the light of the sun, so do these darken counsel by words wherein there is no truth. Seeing that these men increase darkness in this world, it is very just that the mist ofdarkness should be their portion in the next. In the midst of their talk of liberty, these men are the vilest slaves; their own lusts gain a complete victory over them, and they are actually in bondage. When men are entangled, they are easily overcome; therefore Christians should keep close to the word of God, and watch against all who seek to bewilder them. A state of apostacy is worse than a state of ignorance. To bring an evil report upon the good way of God, and a false charge against the way of truth, must expose to the heaviest condemnation. How dreadful is the state here described! Yet though such a case is deplorable, it is not utterly hopeless; the leper may be made clean, and even the dead may be raised. Is thy backsliding a grief to thee? Believe in the Lord Jesus, and thou shalt be saved.

Chapter 3

Chapter Outline	
The design here is to remind of Christ's final coming to judgement.	(1–4)
He will appear unexpectedly, when the present frame of nature will be dissolved by fire.	(5–10)
From thence is inferred the need for holiness, and stedfastness in the faith.	(11–18)

Verses 1–4

The purified minds of Christians are to be stirred up, that they may be active and lively in the work of holiness. There will be scoffers in the last days, under the gospel, men who make light of sin, and mock at salvation by Jesus Christ. One very principal article of our faith refers to what only has a promise to rest upon, and scoffers will attack it till our Lord is come. They will not believe that he will come. Because they see no changes, therefore they fear not God, Ps **55**:**19**. What he never has done, they fancy he never can do, or never will do.

Verses 5–10

Had these scoffers considered the dreadful vengeance with which God swept away a whole world of ungodly men at once, surely they would not have scoffed at his threatening an equally terrible judgment. The heavens and the earth which now are, by the same word, it is declared, will be destroyed by fire. This is as sure to come, as the truth and the power of God can make it. Christians are here taught and established in the truth of the coming of the Lord. Though, in the account of men, there is a vast difference between one day and a thousand years, yet, in the account of God, there is no difference. All things past, present, and future, are ever before him: the delay of a thousand years cannot be so much to him, as putting off any thing for a day or for an hour is to us. If men have no knowledge or belief of the eternal God, they will be very apt to think him such as themselves. How hard is it to form any thoughts of eternity! What men count slackness, is long-suffering, and that to us-ward; it is giving more time to hisown people, to advance in knowledge and holiness, and in the exercise of faith and patience, to abound in good works, doing and suffering what they are called to, that they may bring glory to God. Settle therefore in your hearts that you shall certainly be called to give an account of all things done in the body, whether good or evil. And let a humble and diligent walking before God, and a frequent judging of yourselves, show a firm belief of the future judgment, though many live as if they were never to give any account at all. This day will come, when men are secure, and have no expectation of the day of the Lord. The stately palaces, and all the desirable things wherein wordly-minded men seek and place their happiness, shall be burned up; all sorts of creatures God has made, and all the works of men, must pass through the fire, which shall be a consuming fire to all that sin has brought into the world, though a refining fire to the works of God's hand. What will become of us, if we set our affections on this earth, and make it our portion, seeing all these things shall be burned up? Therefore make sure of happiness beyond this visible world.

Verses 11–18

From the doctrine of Christ's second coming, we are exhorted to purity and godliness. This is the effect of real knowledge. Very exact and universal holiness is enjoined, not resting in any low measure or degree. True Christians look for new heavens and a new earth; freed from the vanity to which things present are subject, and the sin they are polluted with. Those only who are clothed with the righteousness of Christ, and sanctified by the Holy Ghost, shall be admitted to dwell in this holy place. He is faithful, who has promised. Those, whose sins are pardoned, and their peace made with God, are the only safe and happy people; therefore follow after peace, and that with all men; follow after holiness as well as peace. Never expect to be found at that day of God in peace, if you are lazy and idle in this your day, in which we must finish the work given us to do. Only the diligent Christian will be the happy Christian in the day of the Lord. Our Lord will suddenly come to us, or shortly call us to him; and shall he find us idle? Learn to make a right use of the patience of our Lord, who as yet delays his coming. Proud, carnal, and corrupt men, seek to wrest some things into a seeming agreement with their wicked doctrines. But this is no reason why St. Paul's epistles, or any other part of the Scriptures, should be laid aside; for men, left to themselves, pervert every gift of God. Then let us seek to have our minds prepared for receiving things hard to be understood, by putting in practice things which are more easy to be understood. But there must be self-denial and suspicion of ourselves, and submission to the authority of Christ Jesus, before we can heartily receive all the truths of the gospel, therefore we are in great danger of rejecting the truth. And whatever opinions and thoughts of men are not according to the law of God, and warranted by it, the believer disclaims and abhors. Those who are led away by error, fall from their own stedfastness. And that we may avoid being led away, we must seek to grow in all grace, in faith, and virtue, and knowledge. Labour to know Christ more clearly, and more fully; to know him so as to be more like him, and to love him better. This is the knowledge of Christ, which the apostle Paul reached after, and desired to attain; and those who taste this effect of the knowledge of the Lord and Saviour Jesus Christ, will, upon receiving such grace from him, give thanks and praise him, and join in ascribing glory to him now, in the full assurance of doing the same hereafter, for ever.

1 John

This epistle is a discourse upon the principles of Christianity, in doctrine and practice. The design appears to be, to refute and guard against erroneous and unholy tenets, principles, and practices, especially such as would lower the Godhead of Christ, and the reality and power of his sufferings and death, as an atoning sacrifice; and against the assertion that believers being saved by grace, are not required to obey the commandments. This epistle also stirs up all who profess to know God, to have communion with him, and to believe in him, and that they walk in holiness, not in sin, showing that a mere outward profession is nothing, without the evidence of a holy life and conduct. It also helps forward and excites real Christians to communion with God and the Lord Jesus Christ, to constancy in the true faith, and to purity of life.

Chapter 1

Chapter Outline	
The apostle prefaces his epistle to believers in general, with evident testimonies to Christ, for promoting their happiness and joy.	(1–4)
The necessity of a life of holiness, in order to communion with God, is shown.	(5–10)

Verses 1–4

That essential Good, that uncreated Excellence, which had been from the beginning, from eternity, as equal with the Father, and which at length appeared in human nature for the salvation of sinners, was the great subject concerning which the apostle wrote to his brethren. The apostles had seen Him while they witnessed his wisdom and holiness, his miracles, and love and mercy, during some years, till they saw him crucified for sinners, and afterwards risen from the dead. They touched him, so as to have full proof of his resurrection. This Divine Person, the Word of life, the Word of God, appeared in human nature, that he might be the Author and Giver of eternal life to mankind, through the redemption of his blood, and the influence of his new-creating Spirit. The apostles declared what they had seen and heard, that believers might share their comforts and everlasting advantages. They had free access to God the Father. They had a happy experience of the truth in their souls, and showed its excellence in their lives. This communion of believers with the Father and the Son, is begun and kept up by the influences of the Holy Spirit. The benefits Christ bestows, are not like the scanty possessions of the world, causing jealousies in others; but the joy and happiness of communion with God is all-sufficient, so that any number may partake of it; and all who are warranted to say, that truly their fellowship is with the Father, will desire to lead others to partake of the same blessedness.

Verses 5–10

A message from the Lord Jesus, the Word of life, the eternal Word, we should all gladly receive. The great God should be represented to this dark world, as pure and perfect light. As this is the nature of God, his doctrines and precepts must be such. And as his perfect happiness cannot be separated from his perfect holiness, so our happiness will be in proportion to our being made holy. To walk in darkness, is to live and act against religion. God holds no heavenly fellowship or intercourse with unholy souls. There is no truth in their profession; their practice shows its folly and falsehood. The eternal Life, the eternal Son, put on flesh and blood, and died to wash us from our sins in his own blood, and procures for us the sacred influences by which sin is to be subdued more and more, till it is quite done away. While the necessity of a holy walk is insisted upon, as the effect and evidence of the knowledge of God in Christ Jesus, the opposite error of self-righteous pride is guarded against with equal care. All who walk near to God, in holiness and righteousness, are sensible that their best days and duties are mixed with sin. God has given testimony to the sinfulness of the world, by providing a sufficient, effectual Sacrifice for sin, needed in all ages; and the sinfulness of believers themselves is shown, by requiring them continually to confess their sins, and to apply by faith to the blood of that Sacrifice. Let us plead guilty before God, be humble, and willing to know the worst of our case. Let us honestly confess all our sins in their full extent, relying wholly on his mercy and truth through the righteousness of Christ, for a free and full forgiveness, and our deliverance from the power and practice of sin.

Chapter 2

Chapter Outline	
The apostle directs to the atonement of Christ for help against sinful infirmities.	(1, 2)
The effects of saving knowledge in producing obedience, and love to the brethren.	(3–11)
Christians addressed as little children, young men, and fathers.	(12–14)
All are cautioned against the love of this world, and against errors.	(15–23)
They are encouraged to stand fast in faith and holiness.	(24–29)

Verses 1, 2

When have an Advocate with the Father; one who has undertaken, and is fully able, to plead in behalf of every one who applies for pardon and salvation in his name, depending on his pleading for them. He is "Jesus," the Saviour, and "Christ," the Messiah, the Anointed. He alone is "the Righteous One," who received his nature pure from sin, and as our Surety perfectly obeyed the law of God, and so fulfilled all righteousness. All men, in every land, and through successive generations, are invited to come to God through this all-sufficient atonement, and by this new and living way. The gospel, when rightly understood and received, sets the heart against all sin, and stops the allowed practice of it; at the same time it gives blessed relief to the wounded consciences of those who have sinned.

Verses 3–11

What knowledge of Christ can that be, which sees not that he is most worthy of our entire obedience? And a disobedient life shows there is neither religion nor honesty in the professor. The love of God is perfected in him that keeps his commandments. God's grace in him attains its true mark, and produces its sovereign effect as far as may be in this world, and this is man's regeneration; though never absolutely perfect here. Yet this observing Christ's commands, has holiness and excellency which, if universal, would make the earth resemble heaven itself. The command to love one another had been in force from the beginning of the world; but it might be called a new command as given to Christians. It was new in them, as their situation was new in respect of its motives, rules, and obligations. And those who walk in hatred and enmity to believers, remain in a dark state. Christian love teaches us to value our brother's soul, and to dread every thing hurtful to his purity and peace. Where spiritual darkness dwells, in mind, the judgment, and the conscience will be darkened, and will mistake the way to heavenly life. These things demand serious self-examination; and earnest prayer, that God would show us what we are, and whither we are going.

Verses 12–14

As Christians have their peculiar states, so they have peculiar duties; but there are precepts and obedience common to all, particularly mutual love, and contempt of the world. The youngest sincere disciple is pardoned: the communion of saints is attended with the forgiveness of sins. Those of the longest standing in Christ's school need further advice and instruction. Even fathers must be written unto, and preached unto; none are too old to learn. But especially young men in Christ Jesus, though they are arrived at strength of spirit and sound sense, and have successfully resisted first trials and temptations, breaking off bad habits and connexions, and entered in at the strait gate of true conversion. The different descriptions of Christians are again addressed. Children in Christ know that God is their Father; it is wisdom. Those advanced believers, who know Him that was from the beginning, before this world was made, may well be led thereby to give up this world. It will be the glory of young persons to be strong in Christ, and his grace. By the word of God they overcome the wicked one.

Verses 15–17

The things of the world may be desired and possessed for the uses and purposes which God intended, and they are to be used by his grace, and to his glory; but believers must not seek or value them for those purposes to which sin abuses them. The world draws the heart from God; and the more the love of the world prevails, the more the love of God decays. The things of the world are classed according to the three ruling inclinations of depraved nature. **1**. The lust of the flesh, of the body: wrong desires of the heart, the appetite of indulging all things that excite and inflame sensual pleasures. **2**. The lust of the eyes: the eyes are delighted with riches and rich possessions; this is the lust of covetousness. **3**. The pride of life: a vain man craves the grandeur and pomp of a vain-glorious life; this includes thirst after honour and applause. The things of the world quickly fade and die away; desire itself will ere long fail and cease, but holy affection is not like the lust that passes away. The love of God shall never fail. Many vain efforts have been made to evade the force of this passage by limitations, distinctions, or exceptions. Many have tried to show how far we may be carnally-minded, and love the world; but the plain meaning of these **verse**s cannot easily be mistaken. Unless this victory over the world is begun in the heart, a man has no root in himself, but will fall away, or at most remain an unfruitful professor. Yet these vanities are so alluring to the corruption in our hearts, that without constant watching and prayer, we cannot escape the world, or obtain victory over the god and prince of it.

Verses 18–23

Every man is an antichrist, who denies the Person, or any of the offices of Christ; and in denying the Son, he denies the Father also, and has no part in his favour while he rejects his great salvation. Let this prophecy that seducers would rise in the Christian world, keep us from being seduced. The church knows not well who are its true members, and who are not, but thus true Christians were proved, and rendered more watchful and humble. True Christians are anointed ones; their names expresses this: they are anointed with grace, with gifts and spiritual privileges, by the Holy Spirit of grace. The great and most hurtful lies that the father of lies spreads in the world, usually are falsehoods and errors relating to the person of Christ. The unction from the Holy One, alone can keep us from delusions. While we judge favourably of all who trust in Christ as the Divine Saviour, and obey his word, and seek to live in union with them, let us pity and pray for those who deny the Godhead of Christ, or his atonement, and the new-creating work of the Holy Ghost. Let us protest against such antichristian doctrine, and keep from them as much as we may.

Verses 24–29

The truth of Christ, abiding in us, is a means to sever from sin, and unites us to the Son of God, Joh **15**:**3**, **4**. What value should we put upon gospel truth! Thereby the promise of eternal life is made sure. The promise God makes, is suitable to his own greatness, power, and goodness; it is eternal life. The Spirit of truth will not lie; and he teaches all things in the present dispensation, all things necessary to our knowledge of God in Christ, and their glory in the gospel. The apostle repeats the kind words, "little children;" which denotes his affection. He would persuade by love. Gospel privileges oblige to gospel duties; and those anointed by the Lord Jesus abide with him. The new spiritual nature is from the Lord Christ. He that is constant to the practice of religion in trying times, shows that he is born from above, from the Lord Christ. Then, let us beware of holding the truth in unrighteousness, remembering that those only are born of God, who bear his holy image, and walk in his most righteous ways.

Chapter 3

Chapter Outline	
The apostle admires the love of God in making believers his children.	(1, 2)
The purifying influence of the hope of seeing Christ, and the danger of pretending to this, and living in sin.	(3–10)
Love to the brethren is the character of real Christians.	(11–15)
That love described by its actings.	(16–21)
The advantage of faith, love, and obedience.	(22–24)

Verses 1, 2

Little does the world know of the happiness of the real followers of Christ. Little does the world think that these poor, humble, despised ones, are favourites of God, and will dwell in heaven. Let the followers of Christ be content with hard fare here, since they are in a land of strangers, where their Lord was so badly treated before them. The sons of God must walk by faith, and live by hope. They may well wait in faith, hope, and earnest desire, for the revelation of the Lord Jesus. The sons of God will be known, and be made manifest by likeness to their Head. They shall be transformed into the same image, by their view of him.

Verses 3–10

The sons of God know that their Lord is of purer eyes than to allow any thing unholy and impure to dwell with him. It is the hope of hypocrites, not of the sons of God, that makes allowance for gratifying impure desires and lusts. May we be followers of him as his dear children, thus show our sense of his unspeakable mercy, and express that obedient, grateful, humble mind which becomes us. Sin is the rejecting the Divine law. In him, that is, in Christ, was no sin. All the sinless weaknesses that were consequences of the fall, he took; that is, all those infirmities of mind or body which subject man to suffering, and expose him to temptation. But our moral infirmities, our proneness to sin, he had not. He that abides in Christ, continues not in the practice of sin. Renouncing sin is the great proof of spiritual union with, continuance in, and saving knowledge of the Lord Christ. Beware of self-deceit. He that doeth righteousness is righteous, and to be a follower of Christ, shows an interest by faith in his obedience and sufferings. But a man cannot act like the devil, and at the same time be a disciple of Christ Jesus. Let us not serve or indulge what the Son of God came to destroy. To be born of God is to be inwardly renewed by the power of the Spirit of God. Renewing grace is an abiding principle. Religion is not an art, a matter of dexterity and skill, but a new nature. And the regenerate person cannot sin as he did before he was born of God, and as others do who are not born again. There is that light in his mind, which shows him the evil and malignity of sin. There is that bias upon his heart, which disposes him to loathe and hate sin. There is the spiritual principle that opposes sinful acts. And there is repentance for sin, if committed. It goes against him to sin with forethought. The children of God and the children of the devil have their distinct characters. The seed of the serpent are known by neglect of religion, and by their hating real Christians. He only is righteous before God, as a justified believer, who is taught and disposed to righteousness by the Holy Spirit. In this the children of God are manifest, and the children of the devil. May all professors of the gospel lay these truths to heart, and try themselves by them.

Verses 11–15

We should love the Lord Jesus, value his love, and therefore love all our brethren in Christ. This love is the special fruit of our faith, and a certain sign of our being born again. But none who rightly know the heart of man, can wonder at the contempt and enmity of ungodly people against the children of God. We know that we are passed from death to life: we may know it by the evidences of our faith in Christ, of which love to our brethren is one. It is not zeal for a party in the common religion, or affection for those who are of the same name and sentiments with ourselves. The life of grace in the heart of a regenerate person, is the beginning and first principle of a life of glory, whereof they must be destitute who hate their brother in their hearts.

Verses 16–21

Here is the condescension, the miracle, the mystery of Divine love, that God would redeem the church with his own blood. Surely we should love those whom God has loved, and so loved. The Holy Spirit, grieved at selfishness, will leave the selfish heart without comfort, and full of darkness and terror. By what can it be known that a man has a true sense of the love of Christ for perishing sinners, or that the love of God has been planted in his heart by the Holy Spirit, if the love of the world and its good overcomes the feelings of compassion to a perishing brother? Every instance of this selfishness must weaken the evidences of a man's conversion; when habitual and allowed, it must decide against him. If conscience condemn us in known sin, or the neglect of known duty, God does so too. Let conscience therefore be well-informed, be heard, and diligently attended to.

Verses 22–24

When believers had confidence towards God, through the Spirit of adoption, and by faith in the great High Priest, they might ask what they would of their reconciled Father. They would receive it, if good for them. And as good-will to men was proclaimed from heaven, so good-will to men, particularly to the brethren, must be in the hearts of those who go to God and heaven. He who thus follows Christ, dwells in Him as his ark, refuge, and rest, and in the Father through him. This union between Christ and the souls of believers, is by the Spirit he has given them. A man may believe that God is gracious before he knows it; yet when faith has laid hold on the promises, it sets reason to work. This Spirit of God works a change; in all true Christians it changes from the power of Satan to the power of God. Consider, believer, how it changes thy heart. Dost not thou long for peace with God? Wouldst thou not forego all the world for it? No profit, pleasure, or preferment shall hinder thee from following Christ. This salvation is built upon Divine testimony, even the Spirit of God.

Chapter 4

Chapter Outline	
Believers cautioned against giving heed to every one that pretends to the Spirit.	(1–6)
Brotherly love enforced.	(7–21)

Verses 1–6

Christians who are well acquainted with the Scriptures, may, in humble dependence on Divine teaching, discern those who set forth doctrines according to the apostles, and those who contradict them. The sum of revealed religion is in the doctrine concerning Christ, his person and office. The false teachers spake of the world according to its maxims and tastes, so as not to offend carnal men. The world approved them, they made rapid progress, and had many followers such as themselves; the world will love its own, and its own will love it. The true doctrine as to the Saviour's person, as leading men from the world to God, is a mark of the spirit of truth in opposition to the spirit of error. The more pure and holy any doctrine is, the more likely to be of God; nor can we by any other rules try the spirits whether they are of God or not. And what wonder is it, that people of a worldly spirit should cleave to those who are like themselves, and suit their schemes and discourses to their corrupt taste?

Verses 7–13

The Spirit of God is the Spirit of love. He that does not love the image of God in his people, has no saving knowledge of God. For it is God's nature to be kind, and to give happiness. The law of God is love; and all would have been perfectly happy, had all obeyed it. The provision of the gospel, for the forgiveness of sin, and the salvation of sinners, consistently with God's glory and justice, shows that God is love. Mystery and darkness rest upon many things yet. God has so shown himself to be love, that we cannot come short of eternal happiness, unless through unbelief and impenitence, although strict justice would condemn us to hopeless misery, because we break our Creator's laws. None of our words or thoughts can do justice to the free, astonishing love of a holy God towards sinners, who could not profit or harm him, whom he might justly crush in a moment, and whose deserving of his vengeance was shown in the method by which they were saved, though he could by his almighty Word have created other worlds, with more perfect beings, if he had seen fit. Search we the whole universe for love in its most glorious displays? It is to be found in the person and the cross of Christ. Does love exist between God and sinners? Here was the origin, not that we loved God, but that he freely loved us. His love could not be designed to be fruitless upon us, and when its proper end and issue are gained and produced, it may be said to be perfected. So faith is perfected by its works. Thus it will appear that God dwells in us by his new-creating Spirit. A loving Christian is a perfect Christian; set him to any good duty, and he is perfect to it, he is expert at it. Love oils the wheels of his affections, and sets him on that which is helpful to his brethren. A man that goes about a business with ill will, always does it badly. That God dwells in us and we in him, were words too high for mortals to use, had not God put them before us. But how may it be known whether the testimony to this does proceed from the Holy Ghost? Those who are truly persuaded that they are the sons of God, cannot but call him Abba, Father. From love to him, they hate sin, and whatever disagrees with his will, and they have a sound and hearty desire to do his will. Such testimony is the testimony of the Holy Ghost.

Verses 14–21

The Father sent the Son, he willed his coming into this world. The apostle attests this. And whosoever shall confess that Jesus is the Son of God, God dwelleth in him, and he in God. This confession includes faith in the heart as the foundation; makes acknowledgment with the mouth to the glory of God and Christ, and profession in the life and conduct, against the flatteries and frowns of the world. There must be a day of universal judgment. Happy those who shall have holy boldness before the Judge at that day; knowing he is their Friend and Advocate! Happy those who have holy boldness in the prospect of that day, who look and wait for it, and for the Judge's appearance! True love to God assures believers of God's love to them. Love teaches us to suffer for him and with him; therefore we may trust that we shall also be glorified with him, **2Ti 2:12**. We must distinguish between the fear of God and being afraid of him; the fear of God imports high regard and veneration for God. Obedience and good works, done from the principle of love, are not like the servile toil of one who unwillingly labours from dread of a master's anger. They are like that of a dutiful child, who does services to a beloved father, which benefit his brethren, and are done willingly. It is a sign that our love is far from perfect, when our doubts, fears, and apprehensions of God, are many. Let heaven and earth stand amazed at his love. He sent his word to invite sinners to partake of this great salvation. Let them take the comfort of the happy change wrought in them, while they give him the glory. The love of God in Christ, in the hearts of Christians from the Spirit of adoption, is the great proof of conversion. This must be tried by its effects on their temper, and their conduct to their brethren. If a man professes to love God, and yet indulges anger or revenge, or shows a selfish disposition, he gives his profession the lie. But if it is plain that our natural enmity is changed into affection and gratitude, let us bless the name of our God for this seal and earnest of eternal happiness. Then we differ from the false professors, who pretend to love God, whom they have not seen, yet hate their brethren, whom they have seen.

Chapter 5

Chapter Outline	
Brotherly love is the effect of the new birth, which makes obedience to all God's commandments pleasant.	(1–5)
Reference to witnesses agreeing to prove that Jesus, the Son of God, is the true Messiah.	(6–8)
The satisfaction the believer has about Christ, and eternal life through him.	(9–12)
The assurance of God's hearing and answering prayer.	(13–17)
The happy condition of true believers, and a charge to renounce all idolatry.	(18–21)

Verses 1–5

True love for the people of God, may be distinguished from natural kindness or party attachments, by its being united with the love of God, and obedience to his commands. The same Holy Spirit that taught the love, will have taught obedience also; and that man cannot truly love the children of God, who, by habit, commits sin or neglects known duty. As God's commands are holy, just, and good rules of liberty and happiness, so those who are born of God and love him, do not count them grievous, but lament that they cannot serve him more perfectly. Self-denial is required, but true Christians have a principle which carries them above all hinderances. Though the conflict often is sharp, and the regenerate may be cast down, yet he will rise up and renew his combat with resolution. But all, except believers in Christ, are enslaved in some respect or other, to the customs, opinions, or interests of the world. Faith is the cause of victory, the means, the instrument, the spiritual armour by which we overcome. In and by faith we cleave to Christ, in contempt of, and in opposition to the world. Faith sanctifies the heart, and purifies it from those sensual lusts by which the world obtains sway and dominion over souls. It has the indwelling Spirit of grace, which is greater than he who dwells in the world. The real Christian overcomes the world by faith; he sees, in and by the life and conduct of the Lord Jesus on earth, that this world is to be renounced and overcome. He cannot be satisfied with this world, but looks beyond it, and is still tending, striving, and pressing toward heaven. We must all, after Christ's example, overcome the world, or it will overcome us to our ruin.

Verses 6–8

We are inwardly and outwardly defiled; inwardly, by the power and pollution of sin in our nature. For our cleansing there is in and by Christ Jesus, the washing of regeneration and the renewing of the Holy Ghost. Some think that the two sacraments are here meant: baptism with water, as the outward sign of regeneration, and purifying from the pollution of sin by the Holy Spirit; and the Lord's supper, as the outward sign of the shedding Christ's blood, and the receiving him by faith for pardon and justification. Both these ways of cleansing were represented in the old ceremonial sacrifices and cleansings. This water and blood include all that is necessary to our salvation. By the water, our souls are washed and purified for heaven and the habitation of saints in light. By the blood, we are justified, reconciled, and presented righteous to God. By the blood, the curse of the law being satisfied, the purifying Spirit is obtained for the internal cleansing of our natures. The water, as well as the blood, came out of the side of the sacrificed Redeemer. He loved the church, and gave himself for it, that he might sanctify and cleanse it with the washing of water by the word; that he might present it to himself a glorious church, Eph **5:25–27**. This was done in and by the Spirit of God, according to the Saviour's declaration. He is the Spirit of God, and cannot lie. Three had borne witness to these doctrines concerning the person and the salvation of Christ. The Father, repeatedly, by a voice from heaven declared that Jesus was his beloved Son. The Word declared that He and the Father were One, and that whoever had seen him had seen the Father. And the Holy Ghost, who descended from heaven and rested on Christ at his baptism; who had borne witness to Him by all the prophets; and gave testimony to his resurrection and mediatorial office, by the gift of miraculous powers to the apostles. But whether this passage be cited or not, the doctrine of the Trinity in Unity stands equally firm and certain. To the doctrine taught by the apostles, respecting the person and salvation of Christ, there were three testimonies. **1**. The Holy Spirit. We come into the world with a corrupt, carnal disposition, which is enmity to God. This being done away by the regeneration and new-creating of souls by the Holy Spirit, is a testimony to the Saviour. **2**. The water: this sets forth the Saviour's purity and purifying power. The actual and active purity and holiness of his disciples are represented by baptism. **3**. The blood which he shed: and this was our ransom, this testifies for Jesus Christ; it sealed up and finished the sacrifices of the Old Testament. The benefits procured by his blood, prove that he is the Saviour of the world. No wonder if he that rejects this evidence is judged a blasphemer of the Spirit of God. These three witnesses are for one and the same purpose; they agree in one and the same thing.

Verses 9–12

Nothing can be more absurd than the conduct of those who doubt as to the truth of Christianity, while in the common affairs of life they do not hesitate to proceed on human testimony, and would deem any one out of his senses who declined to do so. The real Christian has seen his guilt and misery, and his need of such a Saviour. He has seen the suitableness of such a Saviour to all his spiritual wants and circumstances. He has found and felt the power of the word and doctrine of Christ, humbling, healing, quickening, and comforting his soul. He has a new disposition, and new delights, and is not the man that he formerly was. Yet he finds still a conflict with himself, with sin, with the flesh, the world, and wicked powers. But he finds such strength from faith in Christ, that he can overcome the world, and travel on towards a better. Such assurance has the gospel believer: he has a witness in himself, which puts the matter out of doubt with him, except in hours of darkness or conflict; but he cannot be argued out of his belief in the leading truths of the gospel. Here is what makes the unbeliever's sin so awful; the sin of unbelief. He gives God the lie; because he believes not the record that God gave of his Son. It is in vain for a man to plead that he believes the testimony of God in other things, while he rejects it in this. He that refuses to trust and honour Christ as the Son of God, who disdains to submit to his teaching as Prophet, to rely on his atonement and intercession as High Priest, or to obey him as King, is dead in sin, under condemnation; nor will any outward morality, learning, forms, notions, or confidences avail him.

Verses 13–17

Upon all this evidence, it is but right that we believe on the name of the Son of God. Believers have eternal life in the covenant of the gospel. Then let us thankfully receive the record of Scripture. Always abounding in the work of the Lord, knowing that our labour is not in vain in the Lord. The Lord Christ invites us to come to him in all circumstances, with our supplications and requests, notwithstanding the sin that besets us. Our prayers must always be offered in submission to the will of God. In some things they are speedily answered; in others they are granted in the best manner, though not as requested. We ought to pray for others, as well as for ourselves. There are sins that war against spiritual life in the soul, and the life above. We cannot pray that the sins of the impenitent and unbelieving should, while they are such, be forgiven them; or that mercy, which supposes the forgiveness of sins, should be granted to them, while they wilfully continue such. But we may pray for their repentance, for their being enriched with faith in Christ, and thereupon for all other saving mercies. We should pray for others, as well as for ourselves, beseeching the Lord to pardon and recover the fallen, as well as to relieve the tempted and afflicted. And let us be truly thankful that no sin, of which any one truly repents, is unto death.

Verses 18–21

All mankind are divided into two parties or dominions; that which belongs to God, and that which belongs to the wicked one. True believers belong to God: they are of God, and from him, and to him, and for him; while the rest, by far the greater number, are in the power of the wicked one; they do his works, and support his cause. This general declaration includes all unbelievers, whatever their profession, station, or situation, or by whatever name they may be called. The Son leads believers to the Father, and they are in the love and favour of both; in union with both, by the indwelling and working of the Holy Spirit. Happy are those to whom it is given to know that the Son of God is come, and to have a heart to trust in and rely on him that is true! May this be our privilege; we shall thus be kept from all idols and false doctrines, and from the idolatrous love of worldly objects, and be kept by the power of God, through faith, unto eternal salvation. To this living and true God, be glory and dominion for ever and ever. Amen.

2 John

This epistle is like an abridgement of the first; it touches, in few words, on the same points. The Lady Electa is commended for her virtuous and religious education of her children; is exhorted to abide in the doctrine of Christ, to persevere in the truth, and carefully to avoid the delusions of false teachers. But chiefly the apostle beseeches her to practise the great commandment of Christian love and charity.

Chapter 1

Chapter Outline	
The apostle salutes the elect lady and her children.	(1–3)
Express his joy in their faith and love.	(4–6)
Cautions them against deceivers.	(7–11)
And concludes.	(12, 13)

Verses 1–3

Religion turns compliments into real expressions of respect and love. And old disciple is honourable; an old apostle and leader of disciples is more so. The letter is to a noble Christian matron, and her children; it is well that the gospel should get among such: some noble persons are called. Families are to be encouraged and directed in their love and duties at home. Those who love truth and piety in themselves, should love it in others; and the Christians loved this lady, not for her rank, but for her holiness. And where religion truly dwells, it will abide for ever. From the Divine Persons of the Godhead, the apostle craves grace, Divine favour, and good-will, the spring of all good things. It is grace indeed that any spiritual blessing should be given to sinful mortals. Mercy, free pardon, and forgiveness; for those already rich in grace, need continual forgiveness. Peace, quietness of spirit, and a clear conscience, in assured reconciliation with God, together with all outward prosperity that is really for good: these are desired in truth and love.

Verses 4–6

It is good to be trained to early religion; and children may be beloved for their parents' sake. It gave great joy to the apostle to see children treading in their parents' steps, and likely in their turn to support the gospel. May God bless such families more and more, and raise up many to copy their example. How pleasing the contrast to numbers who spread irreligion, infidelity, and vice, among their children! Our walk is true, our converse right, when according to the word of God. This commandment of mutual Christian love, may be said to be a new one, in respect of its being declared by the Lord Christ; yet, as to the matter, it is old. And this is love to our own souls, that we obey the Divine commands. The foresight of the decay of this love, as well as of other apostacies, or fallings away, might engage the apostle to urge this duty, and this command, frequently and earnestly.

Verses 7–11

The deceiver and his deceit are described: he brings some error concerning the person or office of the Lord Jesus. Such a one is a deceiver and an antichrist; he deludes souls, and undermines the glory and kingdom of the Lord Christ. Let us not think it strange, that there are deceivers and opposers of the Lord Christ's name and dignity now, for there were such, even in the apostles' times. The more deceivers and deceits abound, the more watchful the disciples must be. Sad it is, that splendid attainments in the school of Christ, should ever be lost. The way to gain the full reward is, to abide true to Christ, and constant in religion to the end. Firm cleaving to Christian truth unites us to Christ, and thereby to the Father also; for they are one. Let us equally disregard such as abide not in the doctrine of Christ, and those who transgress his commands. Any who did not profess and preach the doctrine of Christ, respecting him as the Son of God, and salvation by him from guilt and sin, were not to be noticed and countenanced. Yet in obeying this command, we must show kindness and a good spirit to those who differ from us in lesser matters, but hold firmly the all-important doctrines of Christ's person, atonement, and holy salvation.

Verses 12, 13

The apostle refers many things to a personal meeting. Pen and ink were means of strengthening and comforting others; but to see each other is more so. The communion of saints should be maintained by all methods; and should tend to mutual joy. In communion with them we find much of our present joy, and look forward to happiness for ever.

3 John

This epistle is addressed to a converted Gentile. The scope is to commend his stedfastness in the faith, and his hospitality, especially to the ministers of Christ.

Chapter 1

Chapter Outline	
The apostle commends Gaius for piety and hospitality.	(1–8)
Cautions him against siding with Diotrephes, who was a turbulent spirit; but recommends Demetrius as a man of excellent character.	(9–12)
He hopes soon to see Gaius.	(13, 14)

Verses 1–8

Those who are beloved of Christ, will love the brethren for his sake. Soul prosperity is the greatest blessing on this side heaven. Grace and health are rich companions. Grace will employ health. A rich soul may be lodged in a weak body; and grace must then be exercised in submitting to such a dispensation. But we may wish and pray that those who have prosperous souls, may have healthful bodies; that their grace may shine where there is still more room for activity. How many professors there are, about whom the apostle's words must be reversed, and we must earnestly wish and pray that their souls might prosper, as their health and circumstances do! True faith will work by love. A good report is due from those who receive good; they could not but testify to the church, what they found and felt. Good men will rejoice in the soul prosperity of others; and they are glad to hear of the grace and goodness of others. And as it is a joy to good parents, it will be a joy to good ministers, to see their people adorn their profession. Gaius overlooked petty differences among serious Christians, and freely helped all who bore the image, and did the work of Christ. He was upright in what he did, as a faithful servant. Faithful souls can hear their own praises without being puffed up; the commendation of what is good in them, lays them at the foot of the cross of Christ. Christians should consider not only what they must do, but what they may do; and should do even the common actions of life, and of good-will, after a godly sort, serving God therein, and designing his glory. Those who freely make known Christ's gospel, should be helped by others to whom God gives the means. Those who cannot themselves proclaim it, may yet receive, help, and countenance those who do so.

Verses 9–12

Both the heart and mouth must be watched. The temper and spirit of Diotrephes was full of pride and ambition. It is bad not to do good ourselves; but it is worse to hinder those who would do good. Those cautions and counsels are most likely to be accepted, which are seasoned with love. Follow that which is good, for he that doeth good, as delighting therein, is born of God. Evil-workers vainly pretend or boast acquaintance with God. Let us not follow that which is proud, selfish, and of bad design, though the example may be given by persons of rank and power; but let us be followers of God, and walk in love, after the example of our Lord.

Verses 13, 14

Here is the character of Demetrius. A name in the gospel, or a good report in the churches, is better than worldly honour. Few are well spoken of by all; and sometimes it is ill to be so. Happy those whose spirit and conduct commend them before God and men. We must be ready to bear our testimony to them; and it is well when those who commend, can appeal to the consciences of such as know most of those who are commended. A personal conversation together often spares time and trouble, and mistakes which rise from letters; and good Christians may well be glad to see one another. The blessing is, Peace be to you; all happiness attend you. Those may well salute and greet one another on earth, who hope to live together in heaven. By associating with and copying the example of such Christians, we shall have peace within, and live at peace with the brethren; our communications with the Lord's people on earth will be pleasing, and we shall be numbered with them in glory everlasting.

Jude

This epistle is addressed to all believers in the gospel. Its design appears to be to guard believers against the false teachers who had begun to creep into the Christian church, and to scatter dangerous tenets, by attempting to lower all Christianity into a merely nominal belief and outward profession of the gospel. Having thus denied the obligations of personal holiness, they taught their disciples to live in sinful courses, at the same time flattering them with the hope of eternal life. The vile character of these seducers is shown, and their sentence is denounced, and the epistle concludes with warnings, admonitions, and counsels to believers.

Chapter 1

Chapter Outline	
The apostle exhorts to stedfastness in the faith.	(1–4)
The danger of being infected by false professors, and the dreadful punishment which shall be inflicted on them and their followers.	(5–7)
An awful description of these seducers and their deplorable end.	(8–16)
Believers cautioned against being surprised at such deceivers arising among them.	(17–23)
The epistle ends with an encouraging doxology, or words of praise.	(24, 25)

Verses 1–4

Christians are called out of the world, from the evil spirit and temper of it; called above the world, to higher and better things, to heaven, things unseen and eternal; called from sin to Christ, from vanity to seriousness, from uncleanness to holiness; and this according to the Divine purpose and grace. If sanctified and glorified, all the honour and glory must be ascribed to God, and to him alone. As it is God who begins the work of grace in the souls of men, so it is he who carries it on, and perfects it. Let us not trust in ourselves, nor in our stock of grace already received, but in him, and in him alone. The mercy of God is the spring and fountain of all the good we have or hope for; mercy, not only to the miserable, but to the guilty. Next to mercy is peace, which we have from the sense of having obtained mercy. From peace springs love; Christ's love to us, our love to him, and our brotherly love to one another. The apostle prays, not that Christians may be content with a little; but that their souls and societies may be full of these things. None are shut out from gospel offers and invitations, but those who obstinately and wickedly shut themselves out. But the application is to all believers, and only to such. It is to the weak as well as to the strong. Those who have received the doctrine of this common salvation, must contend for it, earnestly, not furiously. Lying for the truth is bad; scolding for it is not better. Those who have received the truth must contend for it, as the apostles did; by suffering with patience and courage for it, not by making others suffer if they will not embrace every notion we call faith, or important. We ought to contend earnestly for the faith, in opposition to those who would corrupt or deprave it; who creep in unawares; who glide in like serpents. And those are the worst of the ungodly, who take encouragement to sin boldly, because the grace of God has abounded, and still abounds so wonderfully, and who are hardened by the extent and fulness of gospel grace, the design of which is to deliver men from sin, and bring them unto God.

Verses 5–7

Outward privileges, profession, and apparent conversion, could not secure those from the vengeance of God, who turned aside in unbelief and disobedience. The destruction of the unbelieving Israelites in the wilderness, shows that none ought to presume on their privileges. They had miracles as their daily bread; yet even they perished in unbelief. A great number of the angels were not pleased with the stations God allotted to them; pride was the main and direct cause or occasion of their fall. The fallen angels are kept to the judgment of the great day; and shall fallen men escape it? Surely not. Consider this in due time. The destruction of Sodom is a loud warning to all, to take heed of, and flee from fleshly lusts that war against the soul, 1Pe **2**:**11**. God is the same holy, just, pure Being now, as then. Stand in awe, therefore, and sin not, Ps **4**:**4**. Let us not rest in anything that does not make the soul subject to the obedience of Christ; for nothing but the renewal of our souls to the Divine image by the Holy Spirit, can keep us from being destroyed among the enemies of God. Consider this instance of the angels, and see that no dignity or worth of the creature is of avail. How then should man tremble, who drinketh iniquity like water! Job **15**:**16**.

Verses 8–16

False teachers are dreamers; they greatly defile and grievously wound the soul. These teachers are of a disturbed mind and a seditious spirit; forgetting that the powers that be, are ordained of God, Ro **13**:**1**. As to the contest about the body of Moses, it appears that Satan wished to make the place of his burial known to the Israelites, in order to tempt them to worship him, but he was prevented, and vented his rage in desperate blasphemy. This should remind all who dispute never to bring railing charges. Also learn hence, that we ought to defend those whom God owns. It is hard, if not impossible, to find any enemies to the Christian religion, who did not, and do not, live in open or secret contradiction to the principles of natural religion. Such are here compared to brute beasts, though they often boast of themselves as the wisest of mankind. They corrupt themselves in the things most open and plain. The fault lies, not in their understandings, but in their depraved wills, and their disordered appetites and affections. It is a great reproach, though unjust to religion, when those who profess it are opposed to it in heart and life. The Lord will remedy this in his time and way; not in men's blind way of plucking up the wheat with the tares. It is sad when men begin in the Spirit, and end in the flesh. Twice dead; they had been once dead in their natural, fallen state; but now they are dead again by the evident proofs of their hypocrisy. Dead trees, why cumber they the ground! Away with them to the fire. Raging waves are a terror to sailing passengers; but when they get into port, the noise and terror are ended. False teachers are to expect the worst punishments in this world and in that to come. They glare like meteors, or falling stars, and then sink into the blackness of darkness for ever. We have no mention of the prophecy of Enoch in any other part or place of Scripture; yet one plain text of Scripture, proves any point we are to believe. We find from this, that Christ's coming to judge was prophesied of, as early as the times before the flood. The Lord cometh: what a glorious time will that be! Notice how often the word "ungodly" is repeated. Many now do not at all refer to the terms godly, or ungodly, unless it be to mock at even the words; but it is not so in the language taught us by the Holy Ghost. Hard speeches of one another, especially if ill-grounded, will certainly come into account at the day of judgment. These evil men and seducers are angry at every thing that happens, and never pleased with their own state and condition. Their will and their fancy, are their only rule and law. Those who please their sinful appetites, are most prone to yield to ungovernable passions. The men of God, from the beginning of the world, have declared the doom denounced on them. Such let us avoid. We are to follow men only as they follow Christ. (Jud **1**:**17-23**)

Verses 17–23

Sensual men separate from Christ, and his church, and join themselves to the devil, the world, and the flesh, by ungodly and sinful practices. That is infinitely worse than to separate from any branch of the visible church on account of opinions, or modes and circumstances of outward government or worship. Sensual men have not the spirit of holiness, which whoever has not, does not belong to Christ. The grace of faith is most holy, as it works by love, purifies the heart, and overcomes the world, by which it is distinguished from a false and dead faith. Our prayers are most likely to prevail, when we pray in the Holy Ghost, under his guidance and influence, according to the rule of his word, with faith, fervency, and earnestness; this is praying in the Holy Ghost. And a believing expectation of eternal life will arm us against the snares of sin: lively faith in this blessed hope will help us to mortify our lusts. We must watch over one another; faithfully, yet prudently reprove each other, and set a good example to all about us. This must be done with compassion, making a difference between the weak and the wilful. Some we must treat with tenderness. Others save with fear; urging the terrors of the Lord. All endeavours must be joined with decided abhorrence of crimes, and care be taken to avoid whatever led to, or was connected with fellowship with them, in works of darkness, keeping far from what is, or appears to be evil.

Verses 24, 25

God is able, and as willing as able, to keep us from falling, and to present us faultless before the presence of his glory. Not as those who never have been faulty, but as those who, but for God's mercy, and a Saviour's sufferings and merits, might most justly have been condemned long ago. All sincere believers were given him of the Father; and of all so given him he has lost none, nor will lose any one. Now, our faults fill us with fears, doubts, and sorrows; but the Redeemer has undertaken for his people, that they shall be presented faultless. Where there is no sin, there will be no sorrow; where there is the perfection of holiness, there will be the perfection of joy. Let us more often look up to Him who is able to keep us from falling, to improve as well as maintain the work he has wrought in us, till we shall be presented blameless before the presence of his glory. Then shall our hearts know a joy beyond what earth can afford; then shall God also rejoice over us, and the joy of our compassionate Saviour be completed. To Him who has so wisely formed the scheme, and will faithfully and perfectly accomplish it, be glory and majesty, dominion and power, both now and for ever. Amen.

Revelation

The Book of the Revelation of St. John consists of two principal divisions. **1**. Relates to "the things which are," that is, the then present state of the church, and contains the epistle of John to the seven churches, and his account of the appearance of the Lord Jesus, and his direction to the apostle to write what he beheld, ch. **1**:**9**–**20**. Also the addresses or epistles to seven churches of Asia. These, doubtless, had reference to the state of the respective churches, as they then existed, but contain excellent precepts and exhortations, commendations and reproofs, promises and threatenings, suitable to instruct the Christian church at all times. **2**. Contains a prophecy of "the things which shall be hereafter," and describes the future state of the church, from the time when the apostle beheld the visions here recorded. It is intended for our spiritual improvement; to warn the careless sinner, point out the way of salvation to the awakened inquirer, build up the weak believer, comfort the afflicted and tempted Christian, and, we may especially add, to strengthen the martyr of Christ, under the cruel persecutions and sufferings inflicted by Satan and his followers.

Chapter 1

Chapter Outline	
The Divine origin, the design, and the importance of this book.	(1–3)
The apostle John salutes the seven churches of Asia.	(4–8)
Declares when, where, and how, the revelation was made to him.	(9–11)
His vision, in which he saw Christ appear.	(12–20)

Verses 1–3

This book is the Revelation of Jesus Christ; the whole Bible is so; for all revelation comes through Christ, and all relates to him. Its principal subject is to discover the purposes of God concerning the affairs of the church, and of the nations as connected therewith, to the end of the world. These events would surely come to pass; and they would begin to come to pass very shortly. Though Christ is himself God, and has light and life in himself, yet, as Mediator between God and man, he receives instructions from the Father. To him we owe the knowledge of what we are to expect from God, and what he expects from us. The subject of this revelation was, the things that must shortly come to pass. On all who read or hear the words of the prophecy, a blessing is pronounced. Those are well employed who search the Bible. It is not enough that we read and hear, but we must keep the things that are written, in our memories, in our minds, in our affections, and in practice, and we shall be blessed in the deed. Even the mysteries and difficulties of this book are united with discoveries of God, suited to impress the mind with awe, and to purify the soul of the reader, though he may not discern the prophetic meaning. No part of Scripture more fully states the gospel, and warns against the evil of sin.

Verses 4–8

There can be no true peace, where there is not true grace; and where grace goeth before, peace will follow. This blessing is in the name of God, of the Holy Trinity, it is an act of adoration. The Father is first named; he is described as the Jehovah who is, and who was, and who is to come, eternal, unchangeable. The Holy Spirit is called the seven spirits, the perfect Spirit of God, in whom there is a diversity of gifts and operations. The Lord Jesus Christ was from eternity, a Witness to all the counsels of God. He is the First-born from the dead, who will by his own power raise up his people. He is the Prince of the kings of the earth; by him their counsels are overruled, and to him they are accountable. Sin leaves a stain of guilt and pollution upon the soul. Nothing can fetch out this stain but the blood of Christ; and Christ shed his own blood to satisfy Divine justice, and purchase pardon and purity for his people. Christ has made believers kings and priests to God and his Father. As such they overcome the world, mortify sin, govern their own spirits, resist Satan, prevail with God in prayer, and shall judge the world. He has made them priests, given them access to God, enabled them to offer spiritual and acceptable sacrifices, and for these favours they are bound to ascribe to him dominion and glory for ever. He will judge the world. Attention is called to that great day when all will see the wisdom and happiness of the friends of Christ, and the madness and misery of his enemies. Let us think frequently upon the second coming of Christ. He shall come, to the terror of those who wound and crucify him by apostacy: he shall come, to the astonishment of the whole world of the ungodly. He is the Beginning and the End; all things are from him and for him; he is the Almighty; the same eternal and unchanged One. And if we would be numbered with his saints in glory everlasting, we must now willing submit to him receive him, and honour him as a saviour, who we believe will come to be our Judge. Alas, that there should be many, who would wish never to die, and that there should not be a day of judgment!

Verses 9–11

It was the apostle's comfort that he did not suffer as an evil-doer, but for the testimony of Jesus, for bearing witness to Christ as the Immanuel, the Saviour; and the Spirit of glory and of God rested upon this persecuted apostle. The day and time when he had this vision was the Lord's day, the Christian sabbath, the first day of the week, observed in remembrance of the resurrection of Christ. Let us who call him "Our Lord," honour him on his own day. The name shows how this sacred day should be observed; the Lord's day should be wholly devoted to the Lord, and none of its hours employed in a sensual, worldly manner, or in amusements. He was in a serious, heavenly, spiritual frame, under the gracious influences of the Spirit of God. Those who would enjoy communion with God on the Lord's day, must seek to draw their thoughts and affections from earthly things. And if believers are kept on the Lord's holy day, from public ordinances and the communion of saints, by necessity and not by choice, they may look for comfort in meditation and secret duties, from the influences of the Spirit; and by hearing the voice and contemplating the glory of their beloved Saviour, from whose gracious words and power no confinement or outward circumstances can separate them. An alarm was given as with the sound of the trumpet, and then the apostle heard the voice of Christ.

Verses 12–20

The churches receive their light from Christ and the gospel, and hold it forth to others. They are golden candlesticks; they should be precious and pure; not only the ministers, but the members of the churches; their light should so shine before men, as to engage others to give glory to God. And the apostle saw as though of the Lord Jesus Christ appeared in the midst of the golden candlesticks. He is with his churches always, to the end of the world, filling them with light, and life, and love. He was clothed with a robe down to the feet, perhaps representing his righteousness and priesthood, as Mediator. This vest was girt with a golden girdle, which may denote how precious are his love and affection for his people. His head and hairs white like wool and as snow, may signify his majesty, purity, and eternity. His eyes as a flame of fire, may represent his knowledge of the secrets of all hearts, and of the most distant events. His feet like fine brass burning in a furnace, may denote the firmness of his appointments, and the excellence of his proceedings. His voice as the sound of many waters, may represent the power of his word, to remove or to destroy. The seven stars were emblems of the ministers of the seven churches to which the apostle was ordered to write, and whom Christ upheld and directed. The sword represented his justice, and his word, piercing to the dividing asunder of soul and spirit, Heb **4**:**12**. His countenance was like the sun, when it shines clearly and powerfully; its strength too bright and dazzling for mortal eyes to behold. The apostle was overpowered with the greatness of the lustre and glory in which Christ appeared. We may well be contented to walk by faith, while here upon earth. The Lord Jesus spake words of comfort; Fear not. Words of instruction; telling who thus appeared. And his Divine nature; the First and the Last. His former sufferings; I was dead: the very same whom his disciples saw upon the cross. His resurrection and life; I have conquered death, and am partaker of endless life. His office and authority; sovereign dominion in and over the invisible world, as the Judge of all, from whose sentence there is no appeal. Let us listen to the voice of Christ, and receive the tokens of his love, for what can he withhold from those for whose sins he has died? May we then obey his word, and give up ourselves wholly to him who directs all things aright.

Chapter 2

Chapter Outline	
Epistles to the churches in Asia, with warnings and encouragements, To the church at Ephesus;	(1–7)
at Smyrna;	(8–11)
at Pergamos;	(12–17)
and at Thyatira.	(18–29)

Verses 1–7

These churches were in such different states as to purity of doctrine and the power of godliness, that the words of Christ to them will always suit the cases of other churches, and professors. Christ knows and observes their state; though in heaven, yet he walks in the midst of his churches on earth, observing what is wrong in them, and what they want. The church of Ephesus is commended for diligence in duty. Christ keeps an account of every hour's work his servants do for him, and their labour shall not be in vain in the Lord. But it is not enough that we are diligent; there must be bearing patience, and there must be waiting patience. And though we must show all meekness to all men, yet we must show just zeal against their sins. The sin Christ charged this church with, is, not the having left and forsaken the object of love, but having lost the fervent degree of it that at first appeared. Christ is displeased with his people, when he sees them grow remiss and cold toward him. Surely this mention in Scripture, of Christians forsaking their first love, reproves those who speak of it with carelessness, and thus try to excuse indifference and sloth in themselves and others; our Saviour considers this indifference as sinful. They must repent: they must be grieved and ashamed for their sinful declining, and humbly confess it in the sight of God. They must endeavour to recover their first zeal, tenderness, and seriousness, and must pray as earnestly, and watch as diligently, as when they first set out in the ways of God. If the presence of Christ's grace and Spirit is slighted, we may expect the presence of his displeasure. Encouraging mention is made of what was good among them. Indifference as to truth and error, good and evil, may be called charity and meekness, but it is not so; and it is displeasing to Christ. The Christian life is a warfare against sin, Satan, the world, and the flesh. We must never yield to our spiritual enemies, and then we shall have a glorious triumph and reward. All who persevere, shall derive from Christ, as the Tree of life, perfection and confirmation in holiness and happiness, not in the earthly paradise, but in the heavenly. This is a figurative expression, taken from the account of the garden of Eden, denoting the pure, satisfactory, and eternal joys of heaven; and the looking forward to them in this world, by faith, communion with Christ, and the consolations of the Holy Spirit. Believers, take your wrestling life here, and expect and look for a quiet life hereafter; but not till then: the word of God never promises quietness and complete freedom from conflict here.

Verses 8–11

Our Lord Jesus is the First, for by him were all things made; he was before all things, with God, and is God himself. He is the Last, for he will be the Judge of all. As this First and Last, who was dead and is alive, is the believer's Brother and Friend, he must be rich in the deepest poverty, honourable amidst the lowest abasement, and happy under the heaviest tribulation, like the church of Smyrna. Many who are rich as to this world, are poor as to the next; and some who are poor outwardly, are inwardly rich; rich in faith, in good works, rich in privileges, rich in gifts, rich in hope. Where there is spiritual plenty, outward poverty may be well borne; and when God's people are made poor as to this life, for the sake of Christ and a good conscience, he makes all up to them in spiritual riches. Christ arms against coming troubles. Fear none of these things; not only forbid slavish fear, but subdue it, furnishing the soul with strength and courage. It should be to try them, not to destroy them. Observe, the sureness of the reward; "I will give thee:" they shall have the reward from Christ's own hand. Also, how suitable it is; "a crown of life:" the life worn out in his service, or laid down in his cause, shall be rewarded with a much better life, which shall be eternal. The second death is unspeakably worse than the first death, both in the agonies of it, and as it is eternal death: it is indeed awful to die, and to be always dying. If a man is kept from the second death and wrath to come, he may patiently endure whatever he meets with in this world.

Verses 12–17

The word of God is a sword, able to slay both sin and sinners. It turns and cuts every way; but the believer need not fear this sword; yet this confidence cannot be supported without steady obedience. As our Lord notices all the advantages and opportunities we have for duty in the places where we dwell, so he notices our temptations and discouragements from the same causes. In a situation of trials, the church of Pergamos had not denied the faith, either by open apostacy, or by giving way so as to avoid the cross. Christ commends their stedfastness, but reproves their sinful failures. A wrong view of gospel doctrine and Christian liberty, was a root of bitterness from which evil practices grew. Repentance is the duty of churches and bodies of men, as well as of particular persons; those who sin together, should repent together. Here is the promise of favour to those that overcome. The influences and comforts of the Spirit of Christ, come down from heaven into the soul, for its support. This is hidden from the rest of the world. The new name is the name of adoption; when the Holy Spirit shows his own work in the believer's soul, this new name and its real import are understood by him.

Verses 18–29

Even when the Lord knows the works of his people to be wrought in love, faith, zeal, and patience; yet if his eyes, which are as a flame of fire, observe them committing or allowing what is evil, he will rebuke, correct, or punish them. Here is praise of the ministry and people of Thyatira, by One who knew the principles from which they acted. They grew wiser and better. All Christians should earnestly desire that their last works may be their best works. Yet this church connived at some wicked seducers. God is known by the judgments he executes; and by this upon seducers, he shows his certain knowledge of the hearts of men, of their principles, designs, frame, and temper. Encouragement is given to those who kept themselves pure and undefiled. It is dangerous to despise the mystery of God, and as dangerous to receive the mysteries of Satan. Let us beware of the depths of Satan, of which those who know the least are the most happy. How tender Christ is of his faithful servants! He lays nothing upon his servants but what is for their good. There is promise of an ample reward to the persevering, victorious believer; also knowledge and wisdom, suitable to their power and dominion. Christ brings day with him into the soul, the light of grace and of glory, in the presence and enjoyment of him their Lord and Saviour. After every victory let us follow up our advantage against the enemy, that we may overcome and keep the works of Christ to the end.

Chapter 3

Chapter Outline	
Epistles to the church at Sardis;	(1–6)
at Philadelphia;	(7–13)
and Laodicea.	(14–22)

Verses 1–6

The Lord Jesus is He that hath the Holy Spirit with all his powers, graces, and operations. Hypocrisy, and lamentable decay in religion, are sins charged upon Sardis, by One who knew that church well, and all her works. Outward things appeared well to men, but there was only the form of godliness, not the power; a name to live, not a principle of life. There was great deadness in their souls, and in their services; numbers were wholly hypocrites, others were in a disordered and lifeless state. Our Lord called upon them to be watchful against their enemies, and to be active and earnest in their duties; and to endeavour, in dependence on the grace of the Holy Spirit, to revive and strengthen the faith and spiritual affections of those yet alive to God, though in a declining state. Whenever we are off our watch, we lose ground. Thy works are hollow and empty; prayers are not filled up with holy desires, alms-deeds not filled up with true charity, sabbaths not filled up with suitable devotion of soul to God. There are not inward affections suitable to outward acts and expressions; when the spirit is wanting, the form cannot long remain. In seeking a revival in our own souls, or the souls of others, it is needful to compare what we profess with the manner in which we go on, that we may be humbled and quickened to hold fast that which remains. Christ enforces his counsel with a dreadful threatening if it should be despised. Yet our blessed Lord does not leave this sinful people without some encouragement. He makes honourable mention of the faithful remnant in Sardis, he makes a gracious promise to them. He that overcometh shall be clothed in white raiment; the purity of grace shall be rewarded with the perfect purity of glory. Christ has his book of life, a register of all who shall inherit eternal life; the book of remembrance of all who live to God, and keep up the life and power of godliness in evil times. Christ will bring forward this book of life, and show the names of the faithful, before God, and all the angels, at the great day.

Verses 7–13

The same Lord Jesus has the key of government and authority in and over the church. He opens a door of opportunity to his churches; he opens a door of utterance to his ministers; he opens a door of entrance, opens the heart. He shuts the door of heaven against the foolish, who sleep away their day of grace; and against the workers of iniquity, how vain and confident soever they may be. The church in Philadelphia is commended; yet with a gentle reproof. Although Christ accepts a little strength, yet believers must not rest satisfied in a little, but strive to grow in grace, to be strong in faith, giving glory to God. Christ can discover this his favour to his people, so that their enemies shall be forced to acknowledge it. This, by the grace of Christ, will soften their enemies, and make them desire to be admitted into communion with his people. Christ promises preserving grace in the most trying times, as the reward of past faithfulness; To him that hath shall be given. Those who keep the gospel in a time of peace, shall be kept by Christ in an hour of temptation; and the same Divine grace that has made them fruitful in times of peace, will make them faithful in times of persecution. Christ promises a glorious reward to the victorious believer. He shall be a monumental pillar in the temple of God; a monument of the free and powerful grace of God; a monument that shall never be defaced or removed. On this pillar shall be written the new name of Christ; by this will appear, under whom the believer fought the good fight, and came off victorious.

Verses 14–22

Laodicea was the last and worst of the seven churches of Asia. Here our Lord Jesus styles himself, "The Amen;" one steady and unchangeable in all his purposes and promises. If religion is worth anything, it is worth every thing. Christ expects men should be in earnest. How many professors of gospel doctrine are neither hot nor cold; except as they are indifferent in needful matters, and hot and fiery in disputes about things of lesser moment! A severe punishment is threatened. They would give a false opinion of Christianity, as if it were an unholy religion; while others would conclude it could afford no real satisfaction, otherwise its professors would not have been heartless in it, or so ready to seek pleasure or happiness from the world. One cause of this indifference and inconsistency in religion is, self-conceit and self-delusion; "Because thou sayest." What a difference between their thoughts of themselves, and the thoughts Christ had of them! How careful should we be not to cheat our owns souls! There are many in hell, who once thought themselves far in the way to heaven. Let us beg of God that we may not be left to flatter and deceive ourselves. Professors grow proud, as they become carnal and formal. Their state was wretched in itself. They were poor; really poor, when they said and thought they were rich. They could not see their state, nor their way, nor their danger, yet they thought they saw it. They had not the garment of justification, nor sanctification: they were exposed to sin and shame; their rags that would defile them. They were naked, without house or harbour, for they were without God, in whom alone the soul of man can find rest and safety. Good counsel was given by Christ to this sinful people. Happy those who take his counsel, for all others must perish in their sins. Christ lets them know where they might have true riches, and how they might have them. Some things must be parted with, but nothing valuable; and it is only to make room for receiving true riches. Part with sin and self-confidence, that you may be filled with his hidden treasure. They must receive from Christ the white raiment he purchased and provided for them; his own imputed righteousness for justification, and the garments of holiness and sanctification. Let them give themselves up to his word and Spirit, and their eyes shall be opened to see their way and their end. Let us examine ourselves by the rule of his word, and pray earnestly for the teaching of his Holy Spirit, to take away our pride, prejudices, and worldly lusts. Sinners ought to take the rebukes of God's word and rod, as tokens of his love to their souls. Christ stood without; knocking, by the dealings of his providence, the warnings and teaching of his word, and the influences of his Spirit. Christ still graciously, by his word and Spirit, comes to the door of the hearts of sinners. Those who open to him shall enjoy his presence. If what he finds would make but a poor feast, what he brings will supply a rich one. He will give fresh supplies of graces and comforts. In the conclusion is a promise to the overcoming believer. Christ himself had temptations and conflicts; he overcame them all, and was more than a conqueror. Those made like to Christ in his trials, shall be made like to him in glory. All is closed with the general demand of attention. And these counsels, while suited to the churches to which they were addressed, are deeply interesting to all men.

Chapter 4

Chapter Outline	
A vision of God, as on his glorious throne, around which were twenty-four elders and four living creatures.	(1–8)
Whose songs, and those of the holy angels, the apostle heard.	(9–11)

Verses 1–8

After the Lord Jesus had instructed the apostle to write to the churches "the things that are," there was another vision. The apostle saw a throne set in heaven, an emblem of the universal dominion of Jehovah. He saw a glorious One upon the throne, not described by human features, so as to be represented by a likeness or image, but only by his surpassing brightness. These seem emblems of the excellence of the Divine nature, and of God's awful justice. The rainbow is a fit emblem of that covenant of promise which God has made with Christ, as the Head of the church, and with all his people in him. The prevailing colour was a pleasant green, showing the reviving and refreshing nature of the new covenant. Four-and-twenty seats around the throne, were filled with four-and-twenty elders, representing, probably, the whole church of God. Their sitting denotes honour, rest, and satisfaction; their sitting about the throne signifies nearness to God, the sight and enjoyment they have of him. They were clothed in white raiment; the imputed righteousness of the saints and their holiness: they had on their heads crowns of gold, signifying the glory they have with him. Lightnings and voices came from the throne; the awful declarations God makes to his church, of his sovereign will and pleasure. Seven lamps of fire were burning before the throne; the gifts, graces, and operations of the Spirit of God in the churches of Christ, dispensed according to the will and pleasure of Him who sits upon the throne. In the gospel church, the laver for purification is the blood of the Lord Jesus Christ, which cleanses from all sin. In this all must be washed, to be admitted into the gracious presence of God on earth, and his glorious presence in heaven. The apostle saw four living creatures, between the throne and the circle of the elders, standing between God and the people. These seem to signify the true ministers of the gospel, because of their place between God and the people. This also is shown by the description given, denoting wisdom, courage, diligence, and discretion, and the affections by which they mount up toward heaven.

Verses 9–11

All true believers wholly ascribe their redemption and conversion, their present privileges and future hopes, to the eternal and most holy God. Thus rise the for-ever harmonious, thankful songs of the redeemed in heaven. Would we on earth do like them, let our praises be constant, not interrupted; united, not divided; thankful, not cold and formal; humble, not self-confident.

Chapter 5

Chapter Outline	
A book sealed with seven seals, which could be opened by none but Christ, who took the book to open it.	(1–7)
Upon which all honour is ascribed to him, as worthy to open it.	(8–14)

Verses 1–7

The apostle saw in the hand of Him that sat upon the throne, a roll of parchments in the form usual in those times, and sealed with seven seals. This represented the secret purposes of God about to be revealed. The designs and methods of Divine Providence, toward the church and the world, are stated, fixed, and made a matter of record. The counsels of God are altogether hidden from the eye and understanding of the creature. The several parts are not unsealed and opened at once, but after each other, till the whole mystery of God's counsel and conduct is finished in the world. The creatures cannot open it, nor read it; the Lord only can do so. Those who see most of God, are most desirous to see more; and those who have seen his glory, desire to know his will. But even good men may be too eager and hasty to look into the mysteries of the Divine conduct. Such desires, if not soon answered, turn to grief and sorrow. If John wept much because he could not look into the book of God's decrees, what reason have many to shed floods of tears for their ignorance of the gospel of Christ of that on which everlasting salvation depends! We need not weep that we cannot foresee future events respecting ourselves in this world; the eager expectation of future prospects, or the foresight of future calamities, would alike unfit us for present duties and conflicts, or render our prosperous days distressing. Yet we may desire to learn, from the promises and prophecies of Scripture, what will be the final event to believers and to the church; and the Incarnate Son has prevailed, that we should learn all that we need to know. Christ stands as Mediator between God and both ministers and people. He is called a Lion, but he appears as a Lamb slain. He appears with the marks of his sufferings, to show that he pleads for us in heaven, in virtue of his satisfaction. He appears as a Lamb, having seven horns and seven eyes; perfect power to execute all the will of God, and perfect wisdom to understand it, and to do it in the most effectual manner. The Father put the book of his eternal counsels into the hand of Christ, and Christ readily and gladly took it into his hand; for he delights to make known the will of his Father; and the Holy Spirit is given by him to reveal the truth and will of God.

Verses 8–14

It is matter of joy to all the world, to see that God deals with men in grace and mercy through the Redeemer. He governs the world, not merely as a Creator, but as our Saviour. The harps were instruments of praise; the vials were full of odours, or incense, which signify the prayers of the saints: prayer and praise should always go together. Christ has redeemed his people from the bondage of sin, guilt, and Satan. He has not only purchased liberty for them, but the highest honour and preferment; he made them kings and priests; kings, to rule over their own spirits, and to overcome the world, and the evil one; and he makes them priests; giving them access to himself, and liberty to offer up spiritual sacrifices. What words can more fully declare that Christ is, and ought to be worshipped, equally with the Father, by all creatures, to all eternity! Happy those who shall adore and praise in heaven, and who shall for ever bless the Lamb, who delivered and set them apart for himself by his blood. How worthy art thou, O God, Father, Son, and Holy Ghost, of our highest praises! All creatures should proclaim thy greatness, and adore thy majesty.

Chapter 6

Chapter Outline	
The opening of the seals, The first, second, third, and fourth.	(1–8)
The fifth.	(9–11)
The sixth.	(12–17)

Verses 1–8

Christ, the Lamb, opens the first seal: observe what appeared. A rider on a white horse. By the going forth of this white horse, a time of peace, or the early progress of the Christian religion, seems to be intended; its going forth in purity, at the time when its heavenly Founder sent his apostles to teach all nations, adding, Lo! I am with you alway, even to the end of the world. The Divine religion goes out crowned, having the Divine favour resting upon it, armed spiritually against its foes, and destined to be victorious in the end. On opening the second seal, a red horse appeared; this signifies desolating judgments. The sword of war and persecution is a dreadful judgment; it takes away peace from the earth, one of the greatest blessings; and men who should love one another, and help one another, are set upon killing one another. Such scenes also followed the pure age of early Christianity, when, neglectful of charity and the bond of peace, the Christian leaders, divided among themselves, appealed to the sword, and entangled themselves in guilt. On opening the third seal, a black horse appeared; a colour denoting mourning and woe, darkness and ignorance. He that sat on it had a yoke in his hand. Attempts were made to put a yoke of superstitious observances on the disciples. As the stream of Christianity flowed further from its pure fountain, it became more and more corrupt. During the progress of this black horse, the necessaries of life should be at excessive prices, and the more costly things should not be hurt. According to prophetic language, these articles signified that food of religious knowledge, by which the souls of men are sustained unto everlasting life; such we are invited to buy, Isa **55**:**1**. But when the dark clouds of ignorance and superstition, denoted by the black horse, spread over the Christian world, the knowledge and practice of true religion became scarce. When a people loathe their spiritual food, God may justly deprive them of their daily bread. The famine of bread is a terrible judgment; but the famine of the word is more so. Upon opening the fourth seal, another horse appeared, of a pale colour. The rider was Death, the king of terrors. The attendants, or followers of this king of terrors, hell, a state of eternal misery to all who die in their sins; and in times of general destruction, multitudes go down unprepared into the pit. The period of the fourth seal is one of great slaughter and devastation, destroying whatever may tend to make life happy, making ravages on the spiritual lives of men. Thus the mystery of iniquity was completed, and its power extended both over the lives and consciences of men. The exact times of these four seals cannot be ascertained, for the changes were gradual. God gave them power, that is, those instruments of his anger, or those judgments: all public calamities are at his command; they only go forth when God sends them, and no further than he permits.

Verses 9–11

The sight the apostle beheld at the opening the fifth seal was very affecting. He saw the souls of the martyrs under the altar; at the foot of the altar in heaven, at the feet of Christ. Persecutors can only kill the body; after that there is no more they can do; the soul lives. God has provided a good place in the better world, for those who are faithful unto death. It is not their own death, but the sacrifice of Christ, that gives them entrance into heaven. The cause in which they suffered, was for the word of God; the best any man can lay down his life for; faith in God's word, and the unshaken confession of that faith. They commit their cause to Him to whom vengeance belongs. The Lord is the comforter of his afflicted servants, and precious is their blood in his sight. As the measure of the sin of persecutors is filling up, so is the number of the persecuted, martyred servants of Christ. When this is fulfilled, God will send tribulation to those who trouble them, and unbroken happiness and rest to those that are troubled.

Verses 12–17

When the sixth seal was opened, there was a great earthquake. The foundations of churches and states would be terribly shaken. Such bold figurative descriptions of great changes abound in the prophecies of Scripture; for these events are emblems, and declare the end of the world and the day of judgment. Dread and terror would seize on all sorts of men. Neither grandeur, riches, valour, nor strength, can support men at that time. They would be glad to be no more seen; yea, to have no longer any being. Though Christ be a Lamb, he can be angry, and the wrath of the Lamb is exceedingly dreadful; for if the Redeemer himself, who appeases the wrath of God, be our enemy, where shall we find a friend to plead for us? As men have their day of opportunity, and their seasons of grace, so God has his day of righteous wrath. It seems that the overthrow of the paganism of the Roman empire is here meant. The idolaters are described as hiding themselves in their dens and secret caves, and vainly seeking to escape ruin. In such a day, when the signs of the times show those who believe in God's word, that the King of kings is approaching, Christians are called to a decided course, and to a bold confession of Christ and his truth before their fellowmen. Whatever they may have to endure, the short contempt of man is to be borne, rather than that shame which is everlasting.

Chapter 7

Chapter Outline	

A pause between two great periods.	(1–3)
The peace, happiness, and safety of the saints, as signified by an angel's sealing 144,000.	(4–8)
A song of praise.	(9–12)
The blessedness and glory of those that suffered martyrdom for Christ.	(13–17)

Verses 1–8

In the figurative language of Scripture, the blowing of the four winds together, means a dreadful and general destruction. But the destruction is delayed. Seals were used to mark for each person his own possessions. This mark is the witness of the Holy Ghost, printed in the hearts of believers. And the Lord would not suffer his people to be afflicted before they were marked, that they might be prepared against all conflicts. And, observe, of those who are thus sealed by the Spirit, the seal must be on the forehead, plainly to be seen alike by friends and foes, but not by the believer himself, except as he looks stedfastly in the glass of God's word. The number of those who were sealed, may be understood to stand for the remnant of people which God reserved. Though the church of God is but a little flock, in comparison with the wicked world, yet it is a society really large, and to be still more enlarged. Here the universal church is figured under the type of Israel.

Verses 9–12

The first fruits of Christ having led the way, the Gentiles converted later follow, and ascribe their salvation to God and the Redeemer, with triumph. In acts of religious worship we come nigh to God, and must come by Christ; the throne of God could not be approached by sinners, were it not for a Mediator. They were clothed with the robes of justification, holiness, and victory; and they had palms in their hands, as conquerors used to appear in their triumphs. Such a glorious appearance will the faithful servants of God make at last, when they have fought the good fight of faith, and finished their course. With a loud voice they gave to God and the Lamb the praise of the great salvation. Those who enjoy eternal happiness must and will bless both the Father and the Son; they will do it publicly, and with fervour. We see what is the work of heaven, and we ought to begin it now, to have our hearts much in it, and to long for that world where our praises, as well as our happiness, will be made perfect.

Verses 13–17

Faithful Christians deserve our notice and respect; we should mark the upright. Those who would gain knowledge, must not be ashamed to seek instruction from any who can give it. The way to heaven is through many tribulations; but tribulation, how great soever, shall not separate us from the love of God. Tribulation makes heaven more welcome and more glorious. It is not the blood of the martyrs, but the blood of the Lamb, that can wash away sin, and make the soul pure and clean in the sight of God; other blood stains, this is the only blood that makes the robes of the saints white and clean. They are happy in their employment; heaven is a state of service, though not of suffering; it is a state of rest, but not of sloth; it is a praising, delightful rest. They have had sorrows, and shed many tears on account of sin and affliction; but God himself, with his own gracious hand, will wipe those tears away. He deals with them as a tender father. This should support the Christian under all his troubles. As all the redeemed owe their happiness wholly to sovereign mercy; so the work and worship of God their Saviour is their element; his presence and favour complete their happiness, nor can they conceive of any other joy. To Him may all his people come; from him they receive every needed grace; and to him let them offer all praise and glory.

Chapter 8

Chapter Outline	
The seventh seal is opened and seven angels appear with seven trumpets, ready to proclaim the purposes of God	(1, 2)
Another angel casts fire on the earth, which produces terrible storms of vengeance.	(3–5)
The seven angels prepare to sound their trumpets.	(6)
Four sound them.	(7–12)
Another angel denounces greater woes to come.	(13)

Verses 1–6

The seventh seal is opened. There was profound silence in heaven for a space; all was quiet in the church, for whenever the church on earth cries through oppression, that cry reaches up to heaven; or it is a silence of expectation. Trumpets were given to the angels, who were to sound them. The Lord Jesus is the High Priest of the church, having a golden censer, and much incense, fulness of merit in his own glorious person. Would that men studied to know the fulness that is in Christ, and endeavoured to be acquainted with his excellency. Would that they were truly persuaded that Christ has such an office as that of Intercessor, which he now performs with deep sympathy. No prayers, thus recommended, was ever denied hearing and acceptance. These prayers, thus accepted in heaven, produced great changes upon earth. The Christian worship and religion, pure and heavenly in its origin and nature, when sent down to earth and conflicting with the passions and worldly projects of sinful men, produced remarkable tumults, here set forth in prophetical language, as our Lord himself declared, Lu **12**:**49**.

Verses 7–13

The first angel sounded the first trumpet, and there followed hail and fire mingled with blood. A storm of heresies, a mixture of dreadful errors falling on the church, or a tempest of destruction. The second angel sounded, and a great mountain, burning with fire, was cast into the sea; and the third part of the sea became blood. By this mountain some understand leaders of the persecutions; others, Rome sacked by the Goths and Vandals, with great slaughter and cruelty. The third angel sounded, and there fell a star from heaven. Some take this to be an eminent governor; others take it to be some person in power who corrupted the churches of Christ. The doctrines of the gospel, the springs of spiritual life, comfort, and vigour, to the souls of men, are corrupted and made bitter by the mixture of dangerous errors, so that the souls of men find ruin where they sought refreshment. The fourth angel sounded, and darkness fell upon the great lights of heaven, that give light to the world, the sun and the moon, and the stars. The guides and governors are placed higher than the people, and are to dispense light, and kind influences to them. Where the gospel comes to a people, and has not proper effects on their hearts and lives, it is followed with dreadful judgments. God gives alarm by the written word, by ministers, by men's own consciences, and by the signs of the times; so that if people are surprised, it is their own fault. The anger of God makes all comforts bitter, and even life itself burdensome. But God, in this world, sets bounds to the most terrible judgments. Corruption of doctrine and worship in the church are great judgments, and also are the usual causes and tokens of other judgments coming on a people. Before the other three trumpets were sounded, there was solemn warning how terrible the calamities would be that should follow. If lesser judgments do not take effect the church and the world must expect greater; and when God comes to punish the world, the inhabitants shall tremble before him. Let sinners take warning to flee from the wrath to come; let believers learn to value and to be thankful for their privileges; and let them patiently continue in well doing.

Chapter 9

Chapter Outline	
The fifth trumpet is followed by a representation of another star as falling from heaven and opening the bottomless pit, out of which come swarms of locusts.	(1–12)
The sixth trumpet is followed by the loosing of four angels bound in the great river Euphrates.	(13–21)

Verses 1–12

Upon sounding the fifth trumpet, a star fell from heaven to the earth. Having ceased to be a minister of Christ, he who is represented by this star becomes the minister of the devil; and lets loose the powers of hell against the churches of Christ. On the opening of the bottomless pit, there arose a great smoke. The devil carries on his designs by blinding the eyes of men, by putting out light and knowledge, and promoting ignorance and error. Out of this smoke there came a swarm of locusts, emblems of the devil's agents, who promote superstition, idolatry, error, and cruelty. The trees and the grass, the true believers, whether young or more advanced, should be untouched. But a secret poison and infection in the soul, should rob many others of purity, and afterwards of peace. The locusts had no power to hurt those who had the seal of God. God's all-powerful, distinguishing grace will keep his people from total and final apostacy. The power is limited to a short season; but it would be very sharp. In such events the faithful share the common calamity, but from the pestilence of error they might and would be safe. We collect from Scripture, that such errors were to try and prove the Christians, **1**Co **11**:**19**. And early writers plainly refer this to the first great host of corrupters who overspread the Christian church.

Verses 13–21

The sixth angel sounded, and here the power of the Turks seems the subject. Their time is limited. They not only slew in war, but brought a poisonous and ruinous religion. The antichristian generation repented not under these dreadful judgments. From this sixth trumpet learn that God can make one enemy of the church a scourge and a plague to another. The idolatry in the remains of the eastern church and elsewhere, and the sins of professed Christians, render this prophecy and its fulfilment more wonderful. And the attentive reader of Scripture and history, may find his faith and hope strengthened by events, which in other respects fill his heart with anguish and his eyes with tears, while he sees that men who escape these plagues, repent not of their evil works, but go on with idolatries, wickedness, and cruelty, till wrath comes upon them to the utmost.

Chapter 10

Chapter Outline	
The Angel of the covenant presents a little open book, which is followed with seven thunders.	(1–4)
At the end of the following prophecies, time should be no more.	(5–7)
A voice directs the apostle to eat the book;	(8–10)
and tells him he must prophesy further.	(11)

Verses 1–7

The apostle saw another representation. The person communicating this discovery probably was our Lord and Saviour Jesus Christ, or it was to show his glory. He veils his glory, which is too great for mortal eyes to behold; and throws a veil upon his dispensations. A rainbow was upon his head; our Lord is always mindful of his covenant. His awful voice was echoed by seven thunders; solemn and terrible ways of discovering the mind of God. We know not the subjects of the seven thunders, nor the reasons for suppressing them. There are great events in history, perhaps relating to the Christian church, which are not noticed in open prophecy. The final salvation of the righteous, and the final success of true religion on earth, are engaged for by the unfailing word of the Lord. Though the time may not be yet, it cannot be far distant. Very soon, as to us, time will be no more; but if we are believers, a happy eternity will follow: we shall from heaven behold and rejoice in the triumphs of Christ, and his cause on earth.

Verses 8–11

Most men feel pleasure in looking into future events, and all good men like to receive a word from God. But when this book of prophecy was thoroughly digested by the apostle, the contents would be bitter; there were things so awful and terrible, such grievous persecutions of the people of God, such desolations in the earth, that the foresight and foreknowledge of them would be painful to his mind. Let us seek to be taught by Christ, and to obey his orders; daily meditating on his word, that it may nourish our souls; and then declaring it according to our several stations. The sweetness of such contemplations will often be mingled with bitterness, while we compare the Scriptures with the state of the world and the church, or even with that of our own hearts.

Chapter 11

Chapter Outline	
The state of the church is represented under the figure of a temple measured.	(1, 2)
Two witnesses prophesy is sackcloth.	(3–6)
They are slain, after which they arise and ascend to heaven.	(7–13)
Under the seventh trumpet, all antichristian powers are to be destroyed and there will be a glorious state of Christ's kingdom upon earth.	(14–19)

Verses 1, 2

This prophetical passage about measuring the temple seems to refer to Ezekiel's vision. The design of this measuring seems to be the preservation of the church in times of public danger; or for its trial, or for its reformation. The worshippers must be measured; whether they make God's glory their end, and his word their rule, in all their acts of worship. Those in the outer court, worship in a false manner, or with dissembling hearts, and will be found among his enemies. God will have a temple and an altar in the world, till the end of time. He looks strictly to his temple. The holy city, the visible church, is trodden under foot; is filled with idolaters, infidels, and hypocrites. But the desolations of the church are limited, and she shall be delivered out of all her troubles.

Verses 3–13

In the time of treading down, God kept his faithful witnesses to attest the truth of his word and worship, and the excellence of his ways, The number of these witnesses is small, yet enough. They prophesy in sackcloth. It shows their afflicted, persecuted state, and deep sorrow for the abominations against which they protested. They are supported during their great and hard work, till it is done. When they had prophesied in sackcloth the greatest part of **1260** years, antichrist, the great instrument of the devil, would war against them, with force and violence for a time. Determined rebels against the light rejoice, as on some happy event, when they can silence, drive to a distance, or destroy the faithful servants of Christ, whose doctrine and conduct torment them. It does not appear that the term is yet expired, and the witnesses are not a present exposed to endure such terrible outward sufferings as in former times; but such things may again happen, and there is abundant cause to prophesy in sackcloth, on account of the state of religion. The depressed state of real Christianity may relate only to the western church. The Spirit of life from God, quickens dead souls, and shall quicken the dead bodies of his people, and his dying interest in the world. The revival of God's work and witnesses, will strike terror into the souls of his enemies. Where there is guilt, there is fear; and a persecuting spirit, though cruel, is a cowardly spirit. It will be no small part of the punishment of persecutors, both in this world, and at the great day, that they see the faithful servants of God honoured and advanced. The Lord's witnesses must not be weary of suffering and service, nor hastily grasp at the reward; but must stay till their Master calls them. The consequence of their being thus exalted was a mighty shock and convulsion in the antichristian empire. Events alone can show the meaning of this. But whenever God's work and witnesses revive, the devil's work and witnesses fall before him. And that the slaying of the witnesses is future, appears to be probable.

Verses 14–19

Before the sounding of the seventh and last trumpet, there is the usual demand of attention. The saints and angels in heaven know the right of our God and Saviour to rule over all the world. But the nations met God's wrath with their own anger. It was a time in which he was beginning to reward his people's faithful services, and sufferings; and their enemies fretted against God, and so increased their guilt, and hastened their destruction. By the opening the temple of God in heaven, may be meant, that there was a more free communication between heaven and earth; prayer and praises more freely and frequently going up, graces and blessings plentifully coming down. But it rather seems to refer to the church of God on earth. In the reign of antichrist, God's law was laid aside, and made void by traditions and decrees; the Scriptures were locked up from the people, but now they are brought to the view of all. This, like the ark, is a token of the presence of God returned to his people, and his favour toward them in Jesus Christ, as the Propitiation for their sins. The great blessing of the Reformation was attended with very awful providences; as by terrible things in righteousness God answered the prayers presented in his holy temple now opened.

Chapter 12

Chapter Outline	
A description of the church of Christ and of Satan, under the figures of a woman and of a great red dragon.	(1–6)
Michael and his angels fight against the devil and his angels, who are defeated.	(7–12)
The dragon persecutes the church.	(13, 14)
His vain endeavours to destroy her, He renews his war against her seed.	(14–17)

Verses 1–6

The church, under the emblem of a woman, the mother of believers, was seen by the apostle in vision, in heaven. She was clothed with the sun, justified, sanctified, and shining by union with Christ, the Sun of Righteousness. The moon was under her feet; she was superior to the reflected and feebler light of the revelation made by Moses. Having on her head a crown of twelve stars; the doctrine of the gospel, preached by the twelve apostles, is a crown of glory to all true believers. As in pain to bring forth a holy family; desirous that the conviction of sinners might end in their conversion. A dragon is a known emblem of Satan, and his chief agents, or those who govern for him on earth, at that time the pagan empire of Rome, the city built upon seven hills. As having ten horns, divided into ten kingdoms. Having seven crowns, representing seven forms of government. As drawing with his tail a third part of the stars in heaven, and casting them down to the earth; persecuting and seducing the ministers and teachers. As watchful to crush the Christian religion; but in spite of the opposition of enemies, the church brought forth a manly issue of true and faithful professors, in whom Christ was truly formed anew; even the mystery of Christ, that Son of God who should rule the nations, and in whose right his members partake the same glory. This blessed offspring was protected of God.

Verses 7–11

The attempts of the dragon proved unsuccessful against the church, and fatal to his own interests. The seat of this war was in heaven; in the church of Christ, the kingdom of heaven on earth. The parties were Christ, the great Angel of the covenant, and his faithful followers; and Satan and his instruments. The strength of the church is in having the Lord Jesus for the Captain of their salvation. Pagan idolatry, which was the worship of devils, was cast out of the empire by the spreading of Christianity. The salvation and strength of the church, are only to be ascribed to the King and Head of the church. The conquered enemy hates the presence of God, yet he is willing to appear there, to accuse the people of God. Let us take heed that we give him no cause to accuse us; and that, when we have sinned, we go before the Lord, condemn ourselves, and commit our cause to Christ as our Advocate. The servants of God overcame Satan by the blood of the Lamb, as the cause. By the word of their testimony: the powerful preaching of the gospel is mighty, through God, to pull down strong holds. By their courage and patience in sufferings: they loved not their lives so well but they could lay them down in Christ's cause. These were the warriors and the weapons by which Christianity overthrew the power of pagan idolatry; and if Christians had continued to fight with these weapons, and such as these, their victories would have been more numerous and glorious, and the effects more lasting. The redeemed overcame by a simple reliance on the blood of Christ, as the only ground of their hopes. In this we must be like them. We must not blend any thing else with this.

Verses 12–17

The church and all her friends might well be called to praise God for deliverance from pagan persecution, though other troubles awaited her. The wilderness is a desolate place, and full of serpents and scorpions, uncomfortable and destitute of provisions; yet a place of safety, as well as where one might be alone. But being thus retired could not protect the woman. The flood of water is explained by many to mean the invasions of barbarians, by which the western empire was overwhelmed; for the heathen encouraged their attacks, in the hope of destroying Christianity. But ungodly men, for their worldly interests, protected the church amidst these tumults, and the overthrow of the empire did not help the cause of idolatry. Or, this may be meant of a flood of error, by which the church of God was in danger of being overwhelmed and carried away. The devil, defeated in his designs upon the church, turns his rage against persons and places. Being faithful to God and Christ, in doctrine, worship, and practice, exposes to the rage of Satan; and will do so till the last enemy shall be destroyed.

Chapter 13

Chapter Outline	
A wild beast rises out of the sea, to whom the dragon gives his power.	(1–10)
Another beast, which has two horns like a lamb, but speaks as a dragon.	(11–15)
It obliges all to worship its image, and receive its mark, as persons devoted to it.	(16–18)

Verses 1–10

The apostle, standing on the shore, saw a savage beast rise out of the sea; a tyrannical, idolatrous, persecuting power, springing up out of the troubles which took place. It was a frightful monster! It appears to mean that worldly, oppressing dominion, which for many ages, even from the times of the Babylonish captivity, had been hostile to the church. The first beast then began to oppress and persecute the righteous for righteousness' sake, but they suffered most under the fourth beast of Daniel, (the Roman empire,) which has afflicted the saints with many cruel persecutions. The source of its power was the dragon. It was set up by the devil, and supported by him. The wounding the head may be the abolishing pagan idolatry; and the healing of the wound, introducing popish idolatry, the same in substance, only in a new dress, but which as effectually answers the devil's design. The world admired its power, policy and success. They paid honour and subjection to the devil and his instruments. It exercised infernal power and policy, requiring men to render that honour to creatures which belongs to God alone. Yet the devil's power and success are limited. Christ has a chosen remnant, redeemed by his blood, recorded in his book, sealed by his Spirit; and though the devil and antichrist may overcome the body, and take away the natural life, they cannot conquer the soul, nor prevail with true believers to forsake their Saviour, and join his enemies. Perseverance in the faith of the gospel and true worship of God, in this great hour of trial and temptation, which would deceive all but the elect, is the character of those registered in the book of life. This powerful motive and encouragement to constancy, is the great design of the whole Revelation.

Verses 11–18

Those who understand the first beast to denote a worldly power, take the second to be also a persecuting and assumed power, which acts under the disguise of religion, and of charity to the souls of men. It is a spiritual dominion, professing to be derived from Christ, and exercised at first in a gentle manner, but soon spake like the dragon. Its speech betrayed it; for it gives forth those false doctrines and cruel decrees, which show it to belong to the dragon, and not to the Lamb. It exercised all the power of the former beast. It pursues the same design, to draw men from worshipping the true God, and to subject the souls of men to the will and control of men. The second beast has carried on its designs, by methods whereby men should be deceived to worship the former beast, in the new shape, or likeness made for it. By lying wonders, pretended miracles. And by severe censures. Also by allowing none to enjoy natural or civil rights, who will not worship that beast which is the image of the pagan beast. It is made a qualification for buying and selling, as well as for places of profit and trust, that they oblige themselves to use all their interest, power, and endeavour, to forward the dominion of the beast, which is meant by receiving his mark. To make an image to the beast, whose deadly wound was healed, would be to give form and power to his worship, or to require obedience to his commands. To worship the image of the beast, implies being subject to those things which stamp the character of the picture, and render it the image of the beast. The number of the beast is given, so as to show the infinite wisdom of God, and to exercise the wisdom of men. The number is the number of a man, computed after the usual manner among men, and it is **666**. What or who is intended by this, remains a mystery. To almost every religious dispute this number has yet been applied, and it may reasonably be doubted whether the meaning has yet been discovered. But he who has wisdom and understanding, will see that all the enemies of God are numbered and marked out for destruction; that the term of their power will soon expire, and that all nations shall submit to our King of righteousness and peace.

Chapter 14

Chapter Outline	
Those faithful to Christ celebrate the praises of God.	(1–5)

Three angels; one proclaiming the everlasting gospel; another, the downfal of Babylon; and a third, the dreadful wrath of God on the worshippers of the beast. The blessedness of those who die in the Lord.	(6–13)
A vision of Christ with a sickle, and of a harvest ripe for cutting down.	(14–16)
The emblem of a vintage fully ripe, trodden in the wine-press of God's wrath.	(17–20)

Verses 1–5

Mount Sion is the gospel church. Christ is with his church, and in the midst of her in all her troubles, therefore she is not consumed. His presence secures perseverance. His people appear honourably. They have the name of God written in their foreheads; they make a bold and open profession of their faith in God and Christ, and this is followed by suitable actings. There were persons in the darkest times, who ventured and laid down their lives for the worship and truth of the gospel of Christ. They kept themselves clean from the wicked abominations of the followers of antichrist. Their hearts were right with God; and they were freely pardoned in Christ; he is glorified in them, and they in him. May it be our prayer, our endeavour, our ambition, to be found in this honourable company. Those who are really sanctified and justified are meant here, for no hypocrite, however plausible, can be accounted to be without fault before God. (Rev **14**:**6-13**)

Verses 6–13

The progress of the Reformation appears to be here set forth. The four proclamations are plain in their meaning; that all Christians may be encouraged, in the time of trial, to be faithful to their Lord. The gospel is the great means whereby men are brought to fear God, and to give glory to him. The preaching of the everlasting gospel shakes the foundations of antichrist in the world, and hastens its downfal. If any persist in being subject to the beast, and in promoting his cause, they must expect to be for ever miserable in soul and body. The believer is to venture or suffer any thing in obeying the commandments of God, and professing the faith of Jesus. May God bestow this patience upon us. Observe the description of those that are and shall be blessed: such as die in the Lord; die in the cause of Christ, in a state of union with Christ; such as are found in Christ when death comes. They rest from all sin, temptation, sorrow, and persecution; for there the wicked cease from troubling, there the weary are at rest. Their works follow them: do not go before as their title, or purchase, but follow them as proofs of their having lived and died in the Lord: the remembrance of them will be pleasant, and the reward far above all their services and sufferings. This is made sure by the testimony of the Spirit, witnessing with their spirits, and the written word.

Verses 14–20

Warnings and judgments not having produced reformation, the sins of the nations are filled up, and they become ripe for judgments, represented by a harvest, an emblem which is used to signify the gathering of the righteous, when ripe for heaven, by the mercy of God. The harvest time is when the corn is ripe; when the believers are ripe for heaven, then the wheat of the earth shall be gathered into Christ's garner. And by a vintage. The enemies of Christ and his church are not destroyed, till by their sin they are ripe for ruin, and then he will spare them no longer. The wine-press is the wrath of God, some terrible calamity, probably the sword, shedding the blood of the wicked. The patience of God towards sinners, is the greatest miracle in the world; but, though lasting, it will not be everlasting; and ripeness in sin is a sure proof of judgment at hand.

Chapter 15

Chapter Outline	
A song of praise is sung by the church.	(1–4)
Seven angels with the seven plagues; and to them one of the living creatures gives seven golden vials full of the wrath of God.	(5–8)

Verses 1–4

Seven angels appeared in heaven; prepared to finish the destruction of antichrist. As the measure of Babylon's sins was filled up, it finds the full measure of Divine wrath. While believers stand in this world, in times of trouble, as upon a sea of glass mingled with fire, they may look forward to their final deliverance, while new mercies call forth new hymns of praise. The more we know of God's wonderful works, the more we shall praise his greatness as the Lord God Almighty, the Creator and Ruler of all worlds; but his title of Emmanuel, the King of saints, will make him dear to us. Who that considers the power of God's wrath, the value of his favour, or the glory of his holiness, would refuse to fear and honour him alone? His praise is above heaven and earth.

Verses 5–8

In the judgments God executes upon antichrist and his followers, he fulfils the prophecies and promises of his word. These angels are prepared for their work, clothed with pure and white linen, their breasts girded with golden girdles, representing the holiness, and righteousness, and excellence of these dealings with men. They are ministers of Divine justice, and do every thing in a pure and holy manner. They were armed with the wrath of God against his enemies. Even the meanest creature, when armed with the anger of God, will be too hard for any man in the world. The angels received the vials from one of the four living creatures, one of the ministers of the true church, as in answer to the prayers of the ministers and people of God. Antichrist could not be destroyed without a great shock to all the world, and even the people of God would be in trouble and confusion while the great work was doing. The greatest deliverances of the church are brought about by awful and astonishing steps of Providence; and the happy state of the true church will not begin till obstinate enemies shall be destroyed, and lukewarm or formal Christians are purified. Then, whatever is against Scripture being purged away, the whole church shall be spiritual, and the whole being brought to purity, unity, and spirituality, shall be firmly established.

Chapter 16

Chapter Outline	

The first vial is poured out on the earth, the second on the sea, the third on the rivers and fountains.	(1–7)
The fourth on the sun, the fifth on the seat of the beast.	(8–11)
The sixth on the great river Euphrates.	(12–16)
And the seventh on the air, when shall follow the destruction of all antichristian enemies.	(17–21)

Verses 1–7

We are to pray that the will of God may be done on earth as it is done in heaven. Here is a succession of terrible judgments of Providence; and there seems to be an allusion to several of the plagues of Egypt. The sins were alike, and so were the punishments. The vials refer to the seven trumpets, which represented the rise of antichrist; and the fall of the enemies of the church shall bear some resemblance to their rise. All things throughout their earth, their air, their sea, their rivers, their cities, all are condemned to ruin, all accursed for the wickedness of that people. No wonder that angels, who witness or execute the Divine vengeance on the obstinate haters of God, of Christ, and of holiness, praise his justice and truth; and adore his awful judgments, when he brings upon cruel persecutors the tortures they made his saints and prophets suffer.

Verses 8–11

The heart of man is so desperately wicked, that the most severe miseries never will bring any to repent, without the special grace of God. Hell itself is filled with blasphemies; and those are ignorant of the history of human nature, of the Bible, and of their own hearts, who do not know that the more men suffer, and the more plainly they see the hand of God in their sufferings, the more furiously they often rage against him. Let sinners now seek repentance from Christ, and the grace of the Holy Spirit, or they will have the anguish and horror of an unhumbled, impenitent, and desperate heart; thus adding to their guilt and misery through all eternity. Darkness is opposed to wisdom and knowledge, and forebodes the confusion and folly of the idolaters and followers of the beast. It is opposed to pleasure and joy, and signifies anguish and vexation of spirit.

Verses 12–16

This probably shows the destruction of the Turkish power, and of idolatry, and that a way will be made for the return of the Jews. Or, take it for Rome, as mystical Babylon, the name of Babylon being put for Rome, which was meant, but was not then to be directly named. When Rome is destroyed, her river and merchandise must suffer with her. And perhaps a way will be opened for the eastern nations to come into the church of Christ. The great dragon will collect all his forces, to make one desperate struggle before all be lost. God warns of this great trial, to engage his people to prepare for it. These will be times of great temptation; therefore Christ, by his apostle, calls on his professed servants to expect his sudden coming, and to watch that they might not be put to shame, as apostates or hypocrites. However Christians differ, as to their views of the times and seasons of events yet to be brought to pass, on this one point all are agreed, Jesus Christ, the Lord of glory, will suddenly come again to judge the world. To those living near to Christ, it is an object of joyful hope and expectation, and delay is not desired by them.

Verses 17–21

The seventh and last angel poured forth his vial, and the downfal of Babylon was finished. The church triumphant in heaven saw it and rejoiced; the church in conflict on earth saw it and became triumphant. God remembered the great and wicked city; though for some time he seemed to have forgotten her idolatry and cruelty. All that was most secure was carried away by the ruin. Men blasphemed: the greatest judgments that can befal men, will not bring to repentance without the grace of God. To be hardened against God, by his righteous judgments, is a certain token of sure and utter destruction.

Chapter 17

Chapter Outline	
One of the angels who had the vials, explains the meaning of the former vision of the antichristian beast that was to reign 1260 years, and then to be destroyed.	(1–6)
And interprets the mystery of the woman, and the beast that had seven heads and ten horns.	(7–18)

Verses 1–6

Rome clearly appears to be meant in this chapter. Pagan Rome subdued and ruled with military power, not by art and flatteries. She left the nations in general to their ancient usages and worship. But it is well known that by crafty and politic management, with all kinds of deceit of unrighteousness, papal Rome has obtained and kept her rule over kings and nations. Here were allurements of worldly honour and riches, pomp and pride, suited to sensual and worldly minds. Prosperity, pomp, and splendour, feed the pride and lusts of the human heart, but are no security against the Divine vengeance. The golden cup represents the allurements, and delusions, by which this mystical Babylon has obtained and kept her influence, and seduced others to join her abominations. She is named, from her infamous practices, a mother of harlots; training them up to idolatry and all sorts of wickedness. She filled herself with the blood of the saints and martyrs of Jesus. She intoxicated herself with it; and it was so pleasant to her, that she never was satisfied. We cannot but wonder at the oceans of Christian blood shed by men called Christians; yet when we consider these prophecies, these awful deeds testify to the truth of the gospel. And let all beware of a splendid, gainful, or fashionable religion. Let us avoid the mysteries of iniquity, and study diligently the great mystery of godliness, that we may learn humility and gratitude from the example of Christ. The more we seek to resemble him, the less we shall be liable to be deceived by antichrist.

Verses 7–14

The beast on which the woman sat was, and is not, and yet is. It was a seat of idolatry and persecution, and is not; not in the ancient form, which was pagan: yet it is; it is truly the seat of idolatry and tyranny, though of another sort and form. It would deceive into stupid and blind submission all the inhabitants of the earth within its influence, except the remnant of the elect. This beast was seven heads, seven mountains, the seven hills on which Rome stands; and seven kings, seven sorts of government. Five were gone by when this prophecy was written; one was then in being; the other was yet to come. This beast, directed by the papacy, makes an eighth governor, and sets up idolatry again. It had ten horns, which are said to be ten kings who had as yet no kingdoms; they should not rise up till the Roman empire was broken; but should for a time be very zealous in her interest. Christ must reign till all enemies be put under his feet. The reason of the victory is, that he is the King of kings, and Lord of lords. He has supreme dominion and power over all things; all the powers of earth and hell are subject to his control. His followers are called to this warfare, are fitted for it, and will be faithful in it.

Verses 15–18

God so ruled the hearts of these kings, by his power over them, and by his providence, that they did those things, without intending it, which he purposed and foretold. They shall see their folly, and how they have been bewitched and enslaved by the harlot, and be made instruments in her destruction. She was that great city which reigned over the kings of the earth, when John had this vision; and every one knows Rome to be that city. Believers will be received to the glory of the Lord, when wicked men will be destroyed in a most awful manner; their joining together in sin, will be turned to hatred and rage, and they will eagerly assist in tormenting each other. But the Lord's portion is his people; his counsel shall stand, and he will do all his pleasure, to his glory, and the happiness of all his servants.

Chapter 18

Chapter Outline	
Another angel from heaven proclaims the fall of mystical Babylon.	(1–3)
A voice from heaven admonishes the people of God, lest they partake of her plagues.	(4–8)
The lamentations over her.	(9–19)
The church called upon to rejoice in her utter ruin.	(20–24)

Verses 1–8

The downfal and destruction of the mystical Babylon are determined in the counsels of God. Another angel comes from heaven. This seems to be Christ himself, coming to destroy his enemies, and to shed abroad the light of his gospel through all nations. The wickedness of this Babylon was very great; she had forsaken the true God, and set up idols, and had drawn all sorts of men into spiritual adultery, and by her wealth and luxury kept them in her interest. The spiritual merchandise, by which multitudes have wickedly lived in wealth, by the sins and follies of mankind, seems principally intended. Fair warning is given to all that expect mercy from God, that they should not only come out of this Babylon, but assist in her destruction. God may have a people even in Babylon. But God's people shall be called out of Babylon, and called effectually, while those that partake with wicked men in their sins, must receive of their plagues. (Rev **18:9-19**)

Verses 9–19

The mourners had shared Babylon's sensual pleasures, and gained by her wealth and trade. The kings of the earth, whom she flattered into idolatry, allowing them to be tyrannical over their subjects, while obedient to her; and the merchants, those who trafficked for her indulgences, pardons, and honours; these mourn. Babylon's friends partook her sinful pleasures and profits, but are not willing to share her plagues. The spirit of antichrist is a worldly spirit, and that sorrow is a mere worldly sorrow; they do not lament for the anger of God, but for the loss of outward comforts. The magnificence and riches of the ungodly will avail them nothing, but will render the vengeance harder to be borne. The spiritual merchandise is here alluded to, when not only slaves, but the souls of men, are mentioned as articles of commerce, to the destroying the souls of millions. Nor has this been peculiar to the Roman antichrist, and only her guilt. But let prosperous traders learn, with all their gains, to get the unsearchable riches of Christ; otherwise; even in this life, they may have to mourn that riches make to themselves wings and fly away, and that all the fruits their souls lusted after, are departed from them. Death, at any rate, will soon end their commerce, and all the riches of the ungodly will be exchanged, not only for the coffin and the worm, but for the fire that cannot be quenched.

Verses 20–24

That which is matter of rejoicing to the servants of God on earth, is matter of rejoicing to the angels in heaven. The apostles, who are honoured and daily worshipped at Rome in an idolatrous manner, will rejoice in her fall. The fall of Babylon was an act of God's justice. And because it was a final ruin, this enemy should never molest them any more; of this they were assured by a sign. Let us take warning from the things which brought others to destruction, and let us set our affections on things above, when we consider the changeable nature of earthly things.

Chapter 19

Chapter Outline	
The church in heaven and that on earth triumph, and praise the Lord for his righteous judgments.	(1–10)
A vision of Christ going forth to destroy the beast and his armies.	(11–21)

Verses 1–10

Praising God for what we have, is praying for what is yet further to be done for us. There is harmony between the angels and the saints in this triumphant song. Christ is the Bridegroom of his ransomed church. This second union will be completed in heaven; but the beginning of the glorious millennium (by which is meant a reign of Christ, or a state of happiness, for a thousand years on earth) may be considered as the celebration of his espousals on earth. Then the church of Christ, being purified from errors, divisions, and corruptions, in doctrine, discipline, worship, and practice, will be made ready to be publicly owned by him as his delight and his beloved. The church appeared; not in the gay, gaudy dress of the mother of harlots, but in fine linen, clean and white. In the robes of Christ's righteousness, imputed for justification, and imparted for sanctification. The promises of the gospel, the true sayings of God, opened, applied, and sealed by the Spirit of God, in holy ordinances, are the marriage-feast. This seems to refer to the abundant grace and consolation Christians will receive in the happy days which are to come. The apostle offered honour to the angel. The angel refused it. He directed the apostle to the true and only object of religious worship; to worship God, and him alone. This plainly condemns the practice of those who worship the elements of bread and wine, and saints, and angels; and of those who do not believe that Christ is truly and by nature God, yet pay him a sort of worship. They stand convicted of idolatry by a messenger from heaven. These are the true sayings of God; of Him who is to be worshipped, as one with the Father and the Holy Spirit.

Verses 11–21

Christ, the glorious Head of the church, is described as on a white horse, the emblem of justice and holiness. He has many crowns, for he is King of kings, and Lord of lords. He is arrayed in a vesture dipped in his own blood, by which he purchased his power as Mediator; and in the blood of his enemies, over whom he always prevails. His name is "The Word of God;" a name none fully knows but himself; only this we know, that this Word was God manifest in the flesh; but his perfections cannot be fully understood by any creature. Angels and saints follow, and are like Christ in their armour of purity and righteousness. The threatenings of the written word he is going to execute on his enemies. The ensigns of his authority are his name; asserting his authority and power, warning the most powerful princes to submit, or they must fall before him. The powers of earth and hell make their utmost effort. These **verses** declare important events, foretold by the prophets. These persons were not excused because they did what their leaders bade them. How vain will be the plea of many sinners at the great day! We followed our guides; we did as we saw others do! God has given a rule to walk by, in his word; neither the example of the most, nor of the chief, must influence us contrary thereto: if we do as the most do, we must go where the most go, even into the burning lake.

Chapter 20

Chapter Outline	
Satan is bound for a thousand years.	(1–3)
The first resurrection; those are blessed that have part therein.	(4–6)
Satan loosed, Gog and Magog.	(7–10)
The last and general resurrection.	(11–15)

Verses 1–3

Here is a vision, showing by a figure the restraints laid on Satan himself. Christ, with Almighty power, will keep the devil from deceiving mankind as he has hitherto done. He never wants power and instruments to break the power of Satan. Christ shuts by his power, and seals by his authority. The church shall have a time of peace and prosperity, but all her trials are not yet over.

Verses 4–6

Here is an account of the reign of the saints, for the same space of time as Satan is bound. Those who suffer with Christ, shall reign with him in his spiritual and heavenly kingdom, in conformity to him in his wisdom, righteousness, and holiness: this is called the first resurrection, with which none but those who serve Christ, and suffer for him, shall be favoured. The happiness of these servants of God is declared. None can be blessed but those that are holy; and all that are holy shall be blessed. We know something thing of what the first death is, and it is very awful; but we know not what this second death is. It must be much more dreadful; it is the death of the soul, eternal separation from God. May we never know what it is: those who have been made partakers of a spiritual resurrection, are saved from the power of the second death. We may expect that a thousand years will follow the destruction of the antichristian, idolatrous, persecuting powers, during which pure Christianity, in doctrine, worship, and holiness, will be made known over all the earth. By the all-powerful working of the Holy Spirit, fallen man will be new-created; and faith and holiness will as certainly prevail, as unbelief and unholiness now do. We may easily perceive what a variety of dreadful pains, diseases, and other calamities would cease, if all men were true and consistent Christians. All the evils of public and private contests would be ended, and happiness of every kind largely increased. Every man would try to lighten suffering, instead of adding to the sorrows around him. It is our duty to pray for the promised glorious days, and to do every thing in our public and private stations which can prepare for them.

Verses 7–10

While this world lasts, Satan's power in it will not be wholly destroyed, though it may be limited and lessened. No sooner is Satan let loose, than he again begins deceiving the nations, and stirring them up to make war with the saints and servants of God. It would be well if the servants and ministers of Christ were as active and persevering in doing good, as his enemies in doing mischief. God will fight this last and decisive battle for his people, that the victory may be complete, and the glory be to himself.

Verses 11–15

After the events just foretold, the end will speedily come; and there is no mention of any thing else, before the appearing of Christ to judge the world. This will be the great day: the Judge, the Lord Jesus Christ, will then put on majesty and terror. The persons to be judged are the dead, small and great; young and old, low and high, poor and rich. None are so mean, but they have some talents to account for; and none so great, as to avoid having to account for them. Not only those alive at the coming of Christ, but all the dead. There is a book of remembrance both for good and bad: and the book of the sinner's conscience, though formerly secret, will then be opened. Every man will recollect all his past actions, though he had long forgotten many of them. Another book shall be opened, the book of the Scriptures, the rule of life; it represents the Lord's knowledge of his people, and his declaring their repentance, faith, and good works; showing the blessings of the new covenant. By their works men shall be justified or condemned; he will try their principles by their practices. Those justified and acquitted by the gospel, shall be justified and acquitted by the Judge, and shall enter into eternal life, having nothing more to fear from death, or hell, or wicked men; for these are all destroyed together. This is the second death; it is the final separation of sinners from God. Let it be our great concern to see whether our Bibles justify or condemn us now; for Christ will judge the secrets of all men according to the gospel. Who shall dwell with devouring flames?

Chapter 21

Chapter Outline	
A new heaven, and new earth: the new Jerusalem where God dwells, and banishes all sorrow from his people.	(1–8)
Its heavenly origin, glory, and secure defence.	(9–21)
Its perfect happiness, as enlightened with the presence of God and the Lamb, and in the free access of multitudes, made holy.	(22–27)

Verses 1–8

The new heaven and the new earth will not be separate from each other; the earth of the saints, their glorified, bodies, will be heavenly. The old world, with all its troubles and tumults, will have passed away. There will be no sea; this aptly represents freedom from conflicting passions, temptations, troubles, changes, and alarms; from whatever can divide or interrupt the communion of saints. This new Jerusalem is the church of God in its new and perfect state, the church triumphant. Its blessedness came wholly from God, and depends on him. The presence of God with his people in heaven, will not be interrupt as it is on earth, he will dwell with them continually. All effects of former trouble shall be done away. They have often been in tears, by reason of sin, of affliction, of the calamities of the church; but no signs, no remembrance of former sorrows shall remain. Christ makes all things new. If we are willing and desirous that the gracious Redeemer should make all things new in order hearts and nature, he will make all things new in respect of our situation, till he has brought us to enjoy complete happiness. See the certainty of the promise. God gives his titles, Alpha and Omega, the Beginning and the End, as a pledge for the full performance. Sensual and sinful pleasures are muddy and poisoned waters; and the best earthly comforts are like the scanty supplies of a cistern; when idolized, they become broken cisterns, and yield only vexation. But the joys which Christ imparts are like waters springing from a fountain, pure, refreshing, abundant, and eternal. The sanctifying consolations of the Holy Spirit prepare for heavenly happiness; they are streams which flow for us in the wilderness. The fearful durst not meet the difficulties of religion, their slavish fear came from their unbelief; but those who were so dastardly as not to dare to take up the cross of Christ, were yet so desperate as to run into abominable wickedness. The agonies and terrors of the first death will lead to the far greater terrors and agonies of eternal death.

Verses 9–21

God has various employments for his holy angels. Sometimes they sound the trumpet of Divine Providence, and warn a careless world; sometimes they discover things of a heavenly nature of the heirs of salvation. Those who would have clear views of heaven, must get as near to heaven as they can, on the mount of meditation and faith. The subject of the vision is the church of God in a perfect, triumphant state, shining in its lustre; glorious in relation to Christ; which shows that the happiness of heaven consists in intercourse with God, and in conformity to him. The change of emblems from a bride to a city, shows that we are only to take general ideas from this description. The wall is for security. Heaven is a safe state; those who are there, are separated and secured from all evils and enemies. This city is vast; here is room for all the people of God. The foundation of the wall; the promise and power of God, and the purchase of Christ, are the strong foundations of the safety and happiness of the church. These foundations are set forth by twelve sorts of precious stones, denoting the variety and excellence of the doctrines of the gospel, or of the graces of the Holy Spirit, or the personal excellences of the Lord Jesus Christ. Heaven has gates; there is a free admission to all that are sanctified; they shall not find themselves shut out. These gates were all of pearls. Christ is the Pearl of great price, and he is our Way to God. The street of the city was pure gold, like transparent glass. The saints in heaven tread gold under foot. The saints are there at rest, yet it is not a state of sleep and idleness; they have communion, not only with God, but with one another. All these glories but faintly represent heaven.

Verses 22–27

Perfect and direct communion with God, will more than supply the place of gospel institutions. And what words can more full express the union and co-equality of the Son with the Father, in the Godhead? What a dismal world would this be, if it were not for the light of the sun! What is there in heaven that supplies its place? The glory of God lightens that city, and the Lamb is the Light thereof. God in Christ will be an everlasting Fountain of knowledge and joy to the saints in heaven. There is no night, therefore no need of shutting the gates; all is at peace and secure. The whole shows us that we should be more and more led to think of heaven as filled with the glory of God, and enlightened by the presence of the Lord Jesus. Nothing sinful or unclean, idolatrous, or false and deceitful, can enter. All the inhabitants are made perfect in holiness. Now the saints feel a sad mixture of corruption, which hinders them in the service of God, and interrupts their communion with him; but, at their entrance into the holy of holies, they are washed in the laver of Christ's blood, and presented to the Father without spot. None are admitted into heaven who work abominations. It is free from hypocrites, such as make lies. As nothing unclean can enter heaven, let us be stirred up by these glimpses of heavenly things, to use all diligence, and to perfect holiness in the fear of God.

Chapter 22

Chapter Outline	
A description of the heavenly state, under the figures of the water and the tree of life, and of the throne of God and the Lamb.	(1–5)
The truth and certain fulfilling of all the prophetic visions, The Holy Spirit, and the bride, the church, invite, and say, Come.	(6–19)
The closing blessing.	(20, 21)

Verses 1–5

All streams of earthly comfort are muddy; but these are clear, and refreshing. They give life, and preserve life, to those who drink of them, and thus they will flow for evermore. These point to the quickening and sanctifying influences of the Holy Spirit, as given to sinners through Christ. The Holy Spirit, proceeding from the Father and the Son, applies this salvation to our souls by his new-creating love and power. The trees of life are fed by the pure waters of the river that comes from the throne of God. The presence of God in heaven, is the health and happiness of the saints. This tree was an emblem of Christ, and of all the blessings of his salvation; and the leaves for the healing of the nations, mean that his favour and presence supply all good to the inhabitants of that blessed world. The devil has no power there; he cannot draw the saints from serving God, nor can he disturb them in the service of God. God and the Lamb are here spoken of as one. Service there shall be not only freedom, but honour and dominion. There will be no night; no affliction or dejection, no pause in service or enjoyment: no diversions or pleasures or man's inventing will there be wanted. How different all this from gross and merely human views of heavenly happiness, even those which refer to pleasures of the mind!

Verses 6–19

The Lord Jesus spake by the angel, solemnly confirming the contents of this book, particularly of this last vision. He is the Lord God faithful and true. Also by his messengers; the holy angels showed them to holy men of God. They are things that must shortly be done; Christ will come quickly, and put all things out of doubt. And by the integrity of that angel who had been the apostle's interpreter. He refused to accept religious worship from John, and reproved him for offering it. This presents another testimony against idolatrous worship of saints and angels. God calls every one to witness to the declarations here made. This book, thus kept open, will have effect upon men; the filthy and unjust will be more so, but it will confirm, strengthen, and further sanctify those who are upright with God. Never let us think that a dead or disobedient faith will save us, for the First and the Last has declared that those alone are blessed who do his commandments. It is a book that shuts out form heaven all wicked and unrighteous persons, particularly those who love and make lies, therefore cannot itself be a lie. There is no middle place or condition. Jesus, who is the Spirit of prophecy, has given his churches this morning-light of prophecy, to assure them of the light of the perfect day approaching. All is confirmed by an open and general invitation to mankind, to come and partake freely of the promises and of the privileges of the gospel. The Spirit, by the sacred word, and by convictions and influence in the sinner's conscience, says, Come to Christ for salvation; and the bride, or the whole church, on earth and in heaven, says, Come and share our happiness. Lest any should hesitate, it is added, Let whosoever will, or, is willing, come and take of the water of life freely. May every one who hears or reads these words, desire at once to accept the gracious invitation. All are condemned who should dare to corrupt or change the word of God, either by adding to it, or taking from it.

Verses 20, 21

After discovering these things to his people on earth, Christ seems to take leave of them, and return to heaven; but he assures them it shall not be long before he comes again. And while we are busy in the duties of our different stations of life; whatever labours may try us, whatever difficulties may surround us, whatever sorrows may press us down, let us with pleasure hear our Lord proclaiming, Behold, I come quickly; I come to put an end to the labour and suffering of my servants. I come, and my reward of grace is with me, to recompense, with royal bounty, every work of faith and labour of love. I come to receive my faithful, persevering people to myself, to dwell for ever in that blissful world. Amen, even so, come, Lord Jesus. A blessing closes the whole. By the grace of Christ we must be kept in joyful expectation of his glory, fitted for it, and preserved to it; and his glorious appearance will be joyful to those who partake of his grace and favour here. Let all add, Amen. Let us earnestly thirst after greater measures of the gracious influences of the blessed Jesus in our souls, and his gracious presence with us, till glory has made perfect his grace toward us. Glory be to the Father, and to the Son, and to the Holy Ghost; as it was in the beginning, is now, and ever shall be, world without end. Amen.

Printed in Dunstable, United Kingdom

68359619R00335